D1558049

Infancy

Infant, Family and Society

Sixth Edition

Alan Fogel
University of Utah

2014
Sloan Publishing
Cornwall-on-Hudson, NY 12520

Library of Congress Cataloging-in-Publication Data

Fogel, Alan.
Infancy : infant, family and society / Alan Fogel, University of Utah. -- Sixth edition.
pages cm
Includes bibliographical references and index.
ISBN 978-1-59738-051-5
1. Infants. 2. Infants--Family relationships. 3. Child development. 4. Parent and infant. 5. Families. I. Title.
HQ774.F63 2014
305.232--dc23
2013049960

Cover photo by Tang Ming Tung, Getty Images
Cover design by K&M Design

Sloan Publishing, LLC
220 Maple Road
Cornwall-on-Hudson, NY 12520

Production Editor: Abbie Dunning
Production Supervisor: Elizabeth Webber
Manufacturing Buyer: Emily Trieste
Marketing Manager: Mya Tice

Printed in the United States of America

10 9 8 7 6 5 4 3 2 1

ISBN-10:   1-59738-051-2
ISBN-13:   978-1-59738-051-5

For all infants and their families.

May each individual find security, peace, fulfillment and self-worth.
May we embrace each other as we embrace complexity and change.
May we find the compassion to care and the courage to forgive.

About the Author

Alan Fogel is a professor of psychology at the University of Utah. Born in Miami, Florida, he earned his B.S. in physics at the University of Miami (1967, Coral Gables, Fla.) and his M.A. in physics at Columbia University (1968, New York, N.Y.) where he was a Faculty Fellow. During his three-year term with the United States Peace Corps in Bogotá, Colombia, Fogel taught physics and worked on developing physics curricula for high schools. Through this experience, Fogel became interested in how people learn, which led to his completion of a Ph.D. in education, in 1976, with a focus on early childhood development, at the University of Chicago.

Dr. Fogel is active as a researcher and author. He has written books on early social and communicative development, *Developing Through Relationships* (University of Chicago Press, 1993) and *Change Processes in Relationships: A Relational–Historical Research Approach* (with A. Garvey, H. Hsu, & D. West-Stroming, Cambridge University Press, 2006). He has co-edited multiple books on research in child development: *Emotion and Early Interaction* (with Tiffany Field, 1982), *Origins of Nurturance: Biological, Cultural, and Developmental Perspectives in Caregiving* (with Gail F. Melson, 1985), and *Dynamics and Indeterminism in Social and Developmental Processes* (with Maria Lyra and Jaan Valsiner, 1997), the *Handbook of Infant Development* (with Gavin Bremner, 2001), and *Human Development in the 21st century: Visionary Policy Ideas from Systems Scientists* (with Barbara J. King and Stuart Shanker, 2008). He has also written an undergraduate text on child development, *Child Development: Individual, Family, and Society* (with Gail F. Melson).

Fogel's scholarly papers on development in infancy, which include studies of emotional, social and communicative development in relation to parents and to peers, and topics of infant development of concern to health care providers and early childhood educators, have been published in *Child Development, Developmental Psychology, Developmental Science, Early Development and Parenting, Infant Behavior and Development, Infancy, Infant and Child Development, International Journal of Behavioral Development, Journal of Developmental Processes,* and *Social Development.* More information, along with free downloads of many of these publications, can be found at: http://www.psych.utah.people/person.php?id=58.

Because of what infants have taught him about being in direct contact with their embodied sensory, movement, and emotional experiences, Fogel has devoted the past 15 years of his life exploring the adult's experience of the body, its senses and feelings. He has been a licensed massage therapist and a Rosen Method Bodywork practitioner since 2004. He is the author of *The Psychophysiology of Self-Awareness: Rediscovering the Lost Art of Body Sense* (2009, W. W. Norton), founding editor of the *Rosen Method International Journal* (www.rosenjournal.org) and currently a certified teacher of Rosen Method Bodywork. He teaches workshops and trainings on Rosen Method and on Embodied Self-Awareness in different national and international locations. For more information see: http://www.alanfogelrosenmethod.abmp.com.

Brief Contents

Contents

Preface

Babies evoke mixed feelings in almost everyone. Common descriptions of babies range from wonderful, cute, delightful, cuddly, soft, and warm on the positive side to noisy, smelly, demanding, and frustrating on the negative side. The way we feel about babies usually depends on how much experience we have had with them, our relationship to the baby, how old we are, what kind of mood we happen to be in, and what we have heard from others about babies.

Everyone has a relationship with infancy, if only because everyone has been a baby. All of us cried, wet our diapers, and felt tiny and dependent on those whom we trusted to provide everything we needed. Because all of us have a different experience as a baby and different experiences with babies, there cannot be a single truth about babies. Babies mean different things to different people.

This book is about what babies mean to me and the experiences I have had with them as a behavioral scientist, friend, uncle, father, and grandfather. This book draws heavily on infancy research that has been conducted in the past 35 years and provides a scientifically based account of infant development. Science has a lot to offer our relationship with infants, but it is not the only source of evidence. The research results reported in this book, combined with your own experience with infants, should lead you closer to an understanding of what babies are for you.

This sixth edition brings some changes to the structure of the book. While most of the chapters covering specific ages during infancy are similar, the opening and closing chapters have major updates. For those who have used the previous editions, you will notice that I have combined Chapters 1 and 2 from the fifth edition into a more streamlined chapter 1 in this edition. Chapters 2 and 3 in this edition are a recombination of material that was in Chapters 3 and 4 of the previous edition. There is an entirely new Chapter 4 in this edition devoted to brain development in order to bring more focus to this highly important and emerging area of infant studies. Finally, Chapter 12 is expanded to include some of the topics that had previously been in so-called "applications" sections.

This book is designed not only to report the facts about infants but also to convey the vitality of infants as developing human beings. One way this is accomplished is by taking a chronological approach to infant development. The goal in each chapter is to construct a multifaceted picture of babies in a particular age period. Similar topics are covered in each chapter, with an eye toward distinguishing the developmental uniqueness of babies at each age. In most chapters, these topics include motor and physical development, perceptual and cognitive development, development of self-awareness, social and language development, family and society. I have also endeavored to include research that describes what infants actually do, think, and feel and on how they behave in everyday contexts.

The chronological approach is not perfect, however. Some topics seem to work better for me, as an author, if I treat them coherently rather than divide them up by age period. When this happens, I cover some topics completely in a single chapter, even if the topic applies across a number of stages. Examples of this are differences in parental treatment of firstborn and laterborn children (Chapter 5), attachment (Chapter 8) and sex differences in treatment of infants and sex-role identity (Chapters 11 and 12). These and other topics can be found with an active use of the table of contents and the index. Students can reread the same topics from an earlier chapter to help clarify how the infant has changed in a particular domain.

Instructors can encourage such integration by asking students in class, in study questions, on homework exercises, and on exams to describe what is similar and different, for example, between the perceptual abilities of 3-month-old (Chapter 6) and 7-month-old infants (Chapter 7). For a shorter course, instructors can skip similar sections in each chapter. Instructors wishing to focus on the infant can skip the "Family and Society" sections. Those desiring a more applied course or a more socially oriented course could skip the "Motor Development" and "Perceptual Development" sections. Another way to shorten the course is to drop whole chapters such as those on prenatal development and childbirth. When I teach from this book, my course focuses primarily on social and emotional development and I also assign supplementary readings of original research studies in addition to the textbook. I also use many of the experiential exercises contained in this book in the classroom.

Pedagogical Features

One way in which infancy is brought to life is in each chapter's "Family and Society" section. In it you will find such topics as the effects of infants on parent and caregiver development, father-mother differences, infant-sibling interactions, maternal employment, and social policies toward infants. Of particular importance is that in many chapters, this section contains a discussion of cultural differ-

ences in infancy and infant care. Students should be reminded that cultures are each unique and that there is no one best way of rearing infants.

Three additional methods are used to focus on infants' real lives. The first is that most chapters have a section entitled "Co-Regulating with Baby." This section contains concrete suggestions for infant care and social interaction with infants. Based on the research reviewed earlier in the chapter, it is written in an informal tone so that students can apply the information if and when they have an opportunity to spend time with babies. A second method is a new feature called "Case Reports." These were adapted from reports written by my former students, as explained on p. 29.

A third method is the use of an "Experiential Exercises" section that appears in most chapters. The "Experiential Exercises" sections contain brief and simple instructions that may help readers to approximate the infant's psychological experience. These exercises were developed by me and my teaching assistants and colleagues over the past 12 years.

Instructions for doing the exercises are given below. Use these instructions for all the chapters. It helps to have someone read the steps while you do the exercises, or you could record them and then follow the recording. They can also be led by the instructor and done in a classroom. The reader should take each step slowly, giving the student time to fully experience. In my classes, I allow students about 10-15 minutes to write down their experiences in a journal. Following that, there is a class discussion in which students are encouraged to share what they did and felt. This is useful to highlight the wide range of individual differences, some of which may come from each person's infancy and early childhood past (see the concept of "participatory memory," Chapter 2).

- Instructors must do the exercises themselves at least several times before teaching them, in order to empathize with the students and to understand the effects

- Students should be as comfortable as possible, nothing should be physically painful

- Students should dress comfortably and may want to remove belts, shoes, or jewelry

- The room should have carpet and variable lighting if possible

- Distractions should be reduced as much as possible to encourage relaxation and engagement

- Accommodations need to be made for pregnant women and other physical limitations

- Students should be told to "take care of yourself" and not follow any instruction that may be difficult or painful

- Each instruction must be spoken clearly and slowly and students must be given plenty of time to feel, sense, and move

- The focus is on somatic and emotional awareness and not on conceptual awareness, thinking, evaluating or judging, i.e., the focus is on cultivating "babymind"

- Instructors should also cultivate their own non-conceptual "babymind" awareness in themselves and in empathy with the students, both in their own embodied practice and while teaching

- Encourage students to focus on their whole body and any feelings, leaving full pauses between each step for them to do this

- Do not talk constantly when leading the exercises: allow for silences

- In the discussion that follows the exercise, avoid judging or evaluating what students say; simply comment about infant experience in general or acknowledge their own experience or just say "thank you"

- There is no wrong way to do these exercises, or to experience them

- Create an atmosphere of relaxation, comfort, and acceptance of each person's point of view

- Students are taking a "risk" to act like a baby and to allow themselves to be vulnerable and the sense of that must be implicit in the instructor's behavior

Instructor Supplements

Infancy, Sixth Edition is accompanied by a **Test Bank** prepared by Professor Denise Bodman, Arizona State University, and a set of **Powerpoint Lecture Slides** prepared by Professor Ilse de Koeyer of the University of Utah. Both are available upon request by contacting the publisher at info@sloanpublishing.com.

This edition is a thorough updating of the research and theory in the field. In revising the book, I did an in-depth search of the current literature since the previous edition (2006). If some topics are covered primarily using older references, it means that no new work has been done in that area. Many older references are retained even when new material is included because the older material continues to contribute to our understanding.

I would like to thank the following consultants for their important and thoughtful written contributions to this book: Dr. Mark Reese (Feldenkrais practitioner and teacher, deceased; Experiential Exercises), Dr. Ilse de Koeyer (Adjunct Assistant Professor, Department of Psychology, University of Utah; Dr. Chris Porter (Professor of Child and Family Development, Brigham Young University), Eileen Rojas (Modern Dancer; Experiential Exercise), Dr. LaDonna Atkins (Associate Professor, Department of Family and Child Studies, University of Central Oklahoma; applications section in Chapter 12 on Infant-Parent Mental Health Consusltants), and Mark E. Ludwig (Associate Professor, California Institute of Integral Studies; section in Chapter 12 on Infant-Parent Mental Health). Finally, I wish to thank Mary Looser and Vito Rontino for their heroic efforts to clean and update the list of references.

Chapter 1

Historical and Contemporary Perspectives on Infant Development

CHAPTER OUTLINE AND OVERVIEW

The Importance of Infancy	*What can be gained from the study of infants? What can be learned by reading this book?*
A Brief History of Babies	*How have responses to and ideas about infants changed historically? What are the historical origins of our current ideas about infants?*
Infants Enter the World of Science	*What is the history of scientific approaches to infants? What is the nature vs. nurture controversy?*
Systems Perspectives on Infant Development	*How are infants connected to the world of people and objects around them? What is the role of the parent-infant relationship in early development?*
Research Methods in Developmental Science	*What are the main scientific approaches to the study of human development? Is science a viable source of information about infants? What is the role of research in changing public policy?*

Have you ever wondered about the details of your own infancy? Did you cry a lot? When did you learn to crawl or to walk? What was the first word you ever said? If you know the answer to any of these questions, it is likely you have asked or were told about it by someone who was an adult when you were a baby. Infancy is mysterious to us. We appear to have no memory of our own infancy; we must rely on the memory of others who were there. And babies themselves cannot tell us what they feel, at least not in words. The mystery of the infant's mind has intrigued parents, philosophers, and theologians for thousands of years.

The twentieth and twenty-first centuries, however, have given us powerful new methods for understanding infancy. Scientific research has helped us understand the limits and possibilities of the infant's ability to sense, move, and feel. We now have solid evidence that some types of environments and forms of care are more conducive than others to the development of healthy and happy babies. Advanced technologies allow us to monitor the brain's development and to observe the stages of prenatal growth. The fields of Infant-Parent Mental Health and Early Childhood Education have developed techniques to improve the lives of many infants and their parents. These approaches have generated strong public interest in babies. Why do we find babies so interesting?

THE IMPORTANCE OF INFANCY

If you read the newspapers or watch television news programs, you will recognize some of these headlines and advertisement leads:

Sixty-year-old women can give birth to their own babies.

Mothers may transmit AIDS to their babies through breast milk.

Day care may have harmful effects on the mother-infant relationship.

"Baby Einstein" and other video media can make babies more intelligent.

If these statements are correct, they have a profound impact on our lives and on society. A sixty-year-old mother may die before the child is an adolescent or become too frail to care for the child. If day care is harmful to infants, we will have to reassess the value of parental work. But are these statements correct? In fact, there is some truth to all of them—but only under certain special conditions. A sixty-year-old can give birth by having a fertilized ovum implanted into her uterus but only if she is in good health and can tolerate taking supplemental hormones. Day care can be harmful in settings where teachers are poorly trained and facilities are inadequate, or when infants are too young to tolerate the demands of a complex social environment; otherwise, it can have some beneficial effects, such as giving children advanced social and cognitive skills peers.

AIDS can be transmitted through breast milk, but this can be prevented by using formula. New research has shown that overuse of language videos and computer games in children under two years of age can actually have a harmful effect! For every hour per day that babies spend watching videos such as "Baby Einstein" and "Brainy Baby," they understand about 6 to 8 words *fewer* at age 2 years than babies who did not watch these videos (Zimmerman, Christakis, & Meltzoff, 2007). In general, video media is not very helpful and may even be harmful for babies under the age of two years.

By the end of this book, you should have a much better idea about how to evaluate claims such as the ones listed above. You will read about these and other issues and learn ways to understand research so you can find the answers for yourself by searching the internet and other sources for current research.

The study of infancy is important for many reasons. A few will be listed here, and you may be able to add some of your own.

Parent, Caregiver, and Clinician Education

Infants require adult guidance, love, and support. For a young couple ready to provide this care, their first baby can be both rewarding and anxiety provoking. What is the best way to feed babies? How much sleep do they need? Can babies be spoiled with too much holding and affection? What does it mean if a baby cries for long periods? Generally speaking, the more parents know about infants and children, the less anxious they will be, and the better the outcomes will be for the child.

Infancy Is a Unique Period in the Life Course

Infancy is a special time in one's life. This is not only because it is the earliest stage of life, but because all of life's stages are unique. Each has its pleasures and problems. For the first few years of life, infants are almost totally dependent on their caregivers for their needs. Most of what happens to them is not within their understanding or control. They cry easily and feel their pain deeply. Infants can spend hours immersed in the pleasure of play and exploration. They are typically not plagued by self-doubt, worries, bills to pay, and the other things that can distract adults from living in the moment. Infants have an ability to take life as it comes, be fully "present" to their experiences, and express their joy or frustration in everyday actions and sensations (Schafer, 2004). For reasons we do not fully understand, nature has required all humans to pass through this period and to experience its total reliance on others, its helpless emotional lows and its carefree emotional highs.

The Experience of the Body and Its Movements and Senses

The consciousness of young infants is almost entirely occupied with bodily sensations, emotions, and sensory experiences. Once children acquire the ability to talk, think, and conceptualize at about 3 years of age, they acquire an intellectual power that distinguishes humans from other animals. On the other hand, the preverbal experience of being a baby in a baby's body is also uniquely human. After infancy, many physical and mental disorders of children and adults can be traced to their having lost touch with their own body, emo-

tions, and senses. Cultural values can often run contrary to the needs of the body, as when work or family stresses cause muscular tension (headaches or backaches, for example) or when cultural ideals of physical beauty lead a person to eat less than her or his own body uniquely requires. We now know that stressful environments—including parental worry and stress, poverty, maltreatment, and a prolonged sense of insecurity—can also distance infants from the direct experience of their bodies, which has long-term consequences for physical and mental health.

Reexperiencing Infant-like States Can Be Healing and Rejuvenating

Some psychotherapeutic techniques recreate within the patient-therapist relationship the innocence and trust found in healthy parent-infant relationships. Some touch therapies use gentle, noninvasive contact to create the type of relaxation and self-awareness that babies experience in their mother's arms. Movement, body awareness, and dance educators often use infant-like movements to help children and adults develop an awareness of their body, reduce stress, and restore a sense of calm. This book includes "Experiential Exercises" based on these practices that will allow you to get a first person perspective on infancy (see next page). Practitioners from all these therapeutic and educational methods assume that there will be a healing effect of recreating—in a safe and protected setting—some of the conditions of being a baby. Reexperiencing some of the traumas of one's own infancy, especially within the supportive contexts of these treatment approaches, can also be therapeutic. Such clinical methods will be discussed in the final chapter.

Improving Health by Early Prevention

Many of the diseases of childhood and adulthood have their origins in the prenatal period and infancy. During prenatal development, for example, the brain is highly vulnerable to disease, malnutrition, parental stress, and toxic substances to which the mother may be exposed. Many disorders can be

Experiential Exercise

Many of the chapters in this book will have a section like this one, called **Experiential Exercises** which are a way for adults to re-experience infancy. Why do we need special exercises to "remember" our infancy? As mentioned in the opening paragraph, most of us have no autobiographical memory of our infancy. **Autobiographical** memories are those in which we can tell a story *about* what happened to us: how, what, where, and when. For most people, our earliest autobiographical memories begin when we are three years or older. This corresponds to the age at which the hippocampus (see Chapter 4), the part of our brain that is responsible for "how, what, where and when" memories does not become sufficiently developed to retain experiences in autobiographical form until at least 3 or 4 years of age.

Our experiences of infancy before the age of 3 years are remembered via what are called **participatory** memories, meaning that they are not *about* a past experience; rather, they are felt as a *being with* or a *reliving* of past experiences. Participatory memories can be formed at any time in life but are the main type of memory during infancy. They are composed of emotions, desires,

and a sense of familiarity, without any specific time or place (Bråten, 1998, 2003; Fogel, 2004; Heshusuis, 1994; Stern, 1985). A participatory memory, for example, is the re-creation of a feeling of what it was like to be cuddled and comforted, rather than a remembrance of a specific situation of being cuddled. An adult's participatory memory of feeling being cuddled as an infant may occur when the adult's body is curled into a fetal posture, that is, by *recreating the body and sensory sensations of an earlier time*.

So, re-evoking infancy experience in these Experiential Exercises requires people to behave a bit like a baby or young child. It is important to do these exercises in a quiet room where you can feel what is happening in your body. Many students feel self-conscious when first doing this. It is, after all, unusual for adults to act like babies! Almost all adults, however, change their minds after actually doing the exercises for a while.

You can also enhance your experiential learning by finding opportunities to interact with infants. You might want to keep a journal of your reactions to each of these exercises and encounters with babies. It is best to write in your journal immediately following

the exercise. Note your physical and emotional reactions.

When adults do these exercises, they say things like, "Being an infant is not as easy as I used to think it was," or "Now I can understand why babies cry when they can't roll over or sit up." As a result of this, students often change their approach from being an observer of infants to being someone who can really share the infant's feelings and experiences. This is a shift from a conceptual stance of *learning about* infants to a participatory stance of *being with* infants.

Finger Painting
(by Alan Fogel)

Finger painting is a wonderful and enjoyable way to begin to re-connect with participatory memories of your early childhood experience. It can be done individually or in groups. Just get the materials at any crafts or toy store, clear a space and time, and start painting. Notice the concrete feelings in yourself, such as emotions or sensations of color, temperature, texture. Notice if any memories come back to you. Are they pleasant or unpleasant? What does this experience tell you about yourself today? About yourself as a child?

prevented by changing maternal behavior during pregnancy, such as by eating properly, avoiding particular drugs and chemicals, and reducing stress. After birth, reducing family stress and enhancing the opportunities for the development of healthy emotional attachments can enhance both physical and mental health and reduce the incidence of psychiatric disorders.

Informed Public Policy

Knowing that many social and medical problems could be prevented by making sure that infants receive proper care and that young parents receive the support necessary to provide the best environment for their children, society can take positive steps toward the achievement of such goals. When such programs for infants and parents receive government funding, politics become involved. Should all families with infants be guaranteed the right to housing, proper nutrition, medical care, and parent education? Currently, these are not guaranteed rights in the United States. They are guaranteed, however, in northern European countries such as Sweden and the Netherlands. Because the quality of day care influences infant development and the parent-child relationship, should there be national standards for day care providers? The United States is one of the few industrialized countries without such standards.

Origins of Individual Differences

Each human being is different. A lot of these differences come from experiences as a child and adult, such as one's school experience, the effects of family and friends, the world of work, and unplanned opportunities and losses that occur during one's life. But do any of the differences between people have their origins in early infancy? If so, which parts of one's uniqueness are most likely connected to what happened as a baby? This is an extremely difficult question to answer because early experiences are rarely preserved in pure form, but rather combine in complex ways with later experiences. Nonetheless, many differences between people during the prenatal and infancy periods can have a lasting impact. In this book, you will discover what is known and what is yet to be discovered about the infantile origins of differences between people.

The importance of studying about infants, as illustrated by each of the topics above, may seem self-evident. The importance of infancy, however, is not always appreciated. An infant born into today's world may experience poverty or wealth, love or abuse, health or disease. More must be done to educate parents and political leaders about the need for protecting infants, who cannot protect themselves.

Was it always this way in the life of infants—this mixture of good and bad? In general, yes. In all periods of the past for which there are archaeolog-ical or historical sources, we can find evidence of both kindness to and neglect of infants. Nevertheless, there is more money, time, and care devoted to infants today than at any other known period of history. Most large supermarkets in Europe, Asia, and North America devote an entire aisle to baby products: diapers, oils, powders, foods, furniture, toys, designer clothing, strollers, packs, books, and magazines. In wealthy countries, it is not unusual for infants to be dressed in expensive high-tech running shoes and athletic clothes before they can even walk! Some babies even have access to computer tablets filled with games and videos.

To give you some insight into these and other contemporary perspectives on infancy, the next section reviews some of the historical trends in the role of the infant in society. Because of limitations of space, the focus will be primarily on the history of Western cultures (European and American). Readers are encouraged to integrate what is known about their non-Western cultural history into this story. I have written a longer history of infancy, including pre-history and other cultures, which can also be consulted (Fogel, 2010).

A BRIEF HISTORY OF BABIES

Early Civilizations

As far back as there are recorded documents, history reveals a mixture of beliefs and practices about infants: love and cruelty, freedom and restriction, tolerance and intolerance (French, 2002). The history and literature of the ancient Greeks and Romans (200 B.C.–A.D. 300) indicates that they advocated a rather harsh upbringing for infants. Shows of affection were avoided, and infants were wrapped tightly in swaddling bands to mold the child's body into one worthy of a citizen. Cold water was used to bathe the child to prevent the child from becoming too soft. Babies hated their baths all the more because nurses would press on the child's skull to make it as round as possible and pull and stretch other body parts to shape them.

Similar beliefs in shaping the physical body of the adult by binding and manipulating the infant can be seen in such non-Western ancient practices as the foot binding of girls in China (which made their feet small but deformed). Head binding among both the ancient Maya of Mexico and among eighteenth-century Europeans was used to give the head an oblong shape (Johnson, 1992).

While it may seem surprising to people today, Roman parents felt this treatment to be an expression of their love. They wanted their children to grow up strong, their bodies nicely proportioned and held in a proper posture. Roman literature, in fact, testifies to a strong devotion between parents and children, especially among the wealthy classes, and attests to the importance of hugging, kissing, and affection after infancy, as the child grew older and began to form his or her own character (Dupont, 1989; Gies & Gies, 1987). Historians of ancient Egypt (2,000–100 B.C.) and Greece (800–200 B.C.) have found evidence of toys and games for children and written documents describing the need to love and protect infants (Greenleaf, 1978).

Fathers' and mothers' devotion to young children, especially among the wealthy, is well documented in Roman literature. One of the most detailed descriptions of parental love at this time comes from Plutarch in the second century B.C. Plutarch shared child care with his wife for all their children. They had one daughter, Timoxena, who died when she was 2 years-old (French, 2001). Because Plutarch was away at the time of his daughter's death, he wrote these words in a letter to his wife.

There is a special savor in our affection for children of that age; the freedom from any crossness or complaint. She herself too had great natural goodness and gentleness of temper: her response to affection and her generosity both gave pleasure and enabled us to perceive the human kindness in her nature… our daughter was the sweetest thing to fondle, to watch, and to hear; and we ought to let the thought of her also dwell

in our minds and lives, for there is much more joy in it than sorrow (Pomeroy, 1999, pp. 59–60).

The recognition of the role of the body in the development of the person is an important aspect of Westerners' Greco-Roman heritage. Both Greeks and Romans believed that exercises for the body led to the development of a strong moral character. Upper-class boys learned athletics and gymnastics, while girls learned music and dance.

It is, however, difficult for people today to reconcile the affection with the cruelty found in ancient cultures. Many early civilizations, such as ancient Rome, practiced **infanticide**, the deliberate killing of unwanted infants. This was partly because Roman laws considered the child as the property of parents, and also made parents responsible for raising healthy and productive heirs (Borstelmann, 1983). It was the duty of the head of the family to decide if a newborn should live or die. This practice eliminated infants who were malformed, but many healthy babies too were left to die because the family was poor or the child unwanted (Dupont, 1989). Infanticide continued in Europe throughout the Middle Ages, and some societies today still practice it (see the section on family planning in Chapter 2).

There is no evidence of infanticide, however, among the ancient Isrealites, whose practices of childrearing are known primarily through the Biblical Old Testament. The biblical period dates from 2000 B.C. to 500 B.C. There are many stories in the Old Testament that reflect the importance of infants and children. Hannah, for example, prayed and made vows to God so that she might conceive and give birth to Samuel. Unlike Rome and Greece, Israelite children were not considered the property of parents, but rather as a gift from God who needed to be protected, loved, and educated.

The Bible also gives detailed—and medically informed—prescriptions regarding women's behavior during menstruation, pregnancy, and childbirth. Direct descriptions of infancy are rare in the Bible, but many stories imply that infants should receive loving care, appropriate blessings for a good and holy life, and that male infants should be circumcised. Parental devotion was evident in stories of the suffering of parents who were asked to sacrifice their infants. When two mothers claimed to be the parent of the same child, Solomon's threat to kill the child revealed the true mother, whose pain was sincere. The Hebrew slave revolt in Egypt, which led to the Exodus and return to the promised land, was precipitated by an Egyptian law to kill Hebrew first-born sons, legalized infanticide meant to limit the Hebrew population. To save Moses, his heartbroken family sent him floating down the Nile, to be adopted with love by Egyptian royal women and actually nursed by his own mother. This story suggests a comparison between the concept of human freedom from slavery in general with the act of saving a single infant from death (Frymer-Kensky, 1995).

The Bible asks parents not only to love but to educate their children. Abraham was told to "instruct" his children (Genesis 18:19). Regarding the important facets of Hebrew culture, parents were asked to "teach them intently to your children... when you sit in your home" (Deuteronomy 6:7). Childrearing involved discipline accompanied by respect for the child, as the following passages illustrate: "Train a child in his own way, and even when he is old, he will not depart from it" (Proverbs 22:6); "Foolishness is bound in the heart of the child but the rod of correction shall drive it from him" (Proverbs 22:15); and "Chasten your son for there is hope, but set not your heart on his destruction" (Proverbs 19:18). While some have interpreted these statements as grounds for justifying corporal punishment, the Old Testament does not specify the type of punishment, but rather makes clear the need for discipline in the context of love. Other Bible stories reveal the undesirable outcomes when discipline is too harsh or nonexistent or when parents fail to educate their children about the stories, rituals, ideals, and history of the culture.

The Middle Ages and the Renaissance

Following the Greeks and Romans, a mix of concern for children coexisted with what people today would consider harshness and deprivation. The early Middle Ages in Europe (A.D. 300–1100) began with the fall of the Roman empire and the gradual spread of Christianity throughout the continent. The largely rural population began to move to cities and towns. At the same time, the political boundaries changed frequently as empires dissolved and local powers asserted themselves. These social changes contributed to an increasingly educated urban population, on the one hand, and to the growth of a class of urban poor who suffered from disease, malnutrition, pollution, and ignorance, on the other. The poor people in the cities lived in much more unhealthy conditions than did the poor in the countryside.

Because of inadequate sanitation and other sources of urban pollution (pollution is not a new problem), infants of the urban poor were more likely to die or to suffer birth defects than those from rural areas. Because cities drew people away from family roots and because disease claimed the lives not only of infants but of mothers in childbirth, many orphaned children walked the streets as beggars, thieves, and prostitutes. As you can see, childhood among the urban poor then was not too much different from what it is today. This is especially true in the large and growing slums found in many of the "megacities" of the twenty-first century (cities with more than 10 million people) such as Lagos (Nigeria), Bombay (India), and Mexico City. This does not mean that poverty inevitably causes problems for parents and children, but it does increase the risk that problems will occur.

The Christian church began to have an impact on the beliefs and practices of European child rearing after around A.D. 400 Christians, following the ancient Hebrew beliefs and practices, advocated parental love and worked to protect children from infanticide, abortion, and maltreatment. Gravestones for infants began to appear at this time, as well as special penances if a parent had done some wrong to a child (Gies & Gies, 1987).

During the late Middle Ages (A.D. 1100–1300), a few written medical texts giving advice on childbirth and early infant care appeared. Trotola, a female physician in twelfth-century Italy, advised rubbing the newborn's palate with honey, protecting the infant from bright lights and loud noises, and stimulating the infant's senses with cloths of various colors and textures and with "songs and gentle voices" (Gies & Gies, 1987). In England during the same period, birth often occurred in a warm chamber with plenty of bathwater, accompanied by the scent of olives, herbs, and roses. It was attended by a female midwife and female friends wishing mother and baby good fortune and joy (Hanawalt, 1993).

Infanticide, however, was still practiced. Although parents had to suffer penances, it was not a crime equivalent to homicide, as it is in most countries today. By the thirteenth century, some cities in Europe had created church-run hospices to adopt orphaned children as an alternative to infanticide. This was partly because of the belief that all life is sacred, and also, according to medieval church doctrine, a child who died unbaptized was barred from heaven for all eternity (Le Goff, 1987). In some countries today, because of urban stress and poverty, infants are left in woods, rivers, and trash bins. Some cities in the United States have begun programs that allow mothers to drop off unwanted infants at local hospitals without fear of prosecution. Social workers then help to find foster homes for these children. Times may have changed, but the problem of unwanted children still remains.

Not until the European Renaissance (1450–1650) do we begin to see the emergence of written philosophies of child rearing in Western cultures. Writers, mostly from the church, condemned the ancient practice of giving children to wet nurses

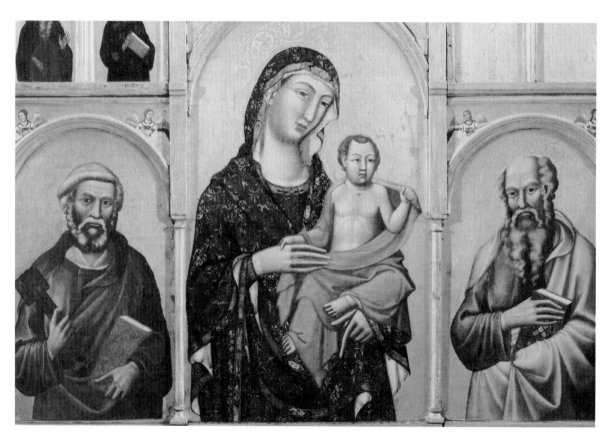

Painting from the late Middle Ages depicting Christ as an infant, but with adult-like features and gestures.
Source: Art Resource

from the poorer classes (a wet nurse was a woman who was paid to nurse the child with her own milk to spare wealthy women the task of nursing the baby themselves) because the child could pick up the habits and diseases of the nurse. The famous Renaissance artist Michelangelo jokingly claimed that his skill in sculpture came from his wet nurse, who was the wife of a stonecutter (Gies & Gies, 1987).

During the Middle Ages, the infant Christ is typically shown in stylized clothing, with adult facial features and mannerisms. One painting depicts Christ as an infant making the Catholic gesture of benediction to a group of people kneeling before him. In Renaissance art (after 1400), by contrast, infants and children began to look and behave differently from adults. Children were sometimes shown playing with toys (Koops, 1996). Not only does the infant Christ begin to look more like a real baby, but we also see the emergence of secular paintings of everyday family life and portraits of individual children. As an aside, Islamic and Jewish traditions forbid the depiction of God in works of art because one of the Ten Commandments prohibits "graven images," and it is rare to see images of people in these traditions because humans were created by God.

The Enlightenment

By the eighteenth century, new ideas about the value of human life, dignity, and freedom had begun to emerge, a shift of consciousness called the Enlightenment. In France, for example, Jean-Jacques Rousseau (1712–1778) argued that childhood was a time of special privilege, that children bring goodness, not original sin, into the world, and that education should be sensitive to the needs and inclinations of the infant and young child. The social movement Rousseau represented, focusing on the natural abilities of the child, was called **romanticism**. Its followers included such great English romantic poets as William Wordsworth (1770–1850), who wrote of childhood in idealized terms.

Behold the Child among his new-born blisses, A six years' darling of pygmy size! See, where 'mid work of his own hand he lies, Fretted by sallies of his mother's kisses, With light upon him from his father's eyes!

(From "Intimations of Immortality from Recollections of Early Childhood," in Williams 1952, 263)

William Blake (1757–1827), another English poet, rejected these simple romantic notions of innocence. In a poem called "The Scoffers," Blake suggested that the scientific achievements of Sir Isaac Newton were far more lasting intellectual milestones than the mocking voice of Rousseau. Charles Dickens was another author who rejected romanticism. Instead of depicting childhood in nineteenth-century England as a time of happy contentment, in *Oliver Twist* and other famous stories he courageously exposed the effects of disease, poverty, child abuse, and child labor for all to see.

All of these writers revealed a new concern for the individual and for the value of children, but they disagreed about what was "natural" compared to what needed to be provided for the child's healthy development. The English philosopher John Locke (1632–1704) accepted the importance of early education for children but believed that children needed more structure than the romantics advocated. Locke thought children needed specific guidance and discipline. Beginning with the assumption that the infant's mind is a *tabula rasa*, a blank slate on which anything could be written, Locke argued that education should provide the skills to make rational choices. The philosophical movement to which he belonged, focusing on education and training, is called **empiricism**.

Both Rousseau and Locke revived the ancient Greek ideals of the body's importance in healthy moral development. Locke wrote that "a sound mind in a sound body is a short but full description of a happy state in this world." Rousseau suggested that children should "run, jump, and shout to their heart's content." Their ideas were carried into educational practice by nineteenth-century educational reformers in Europe and North America, who made sure that school curricula offered art, music, and physical education (Friedrich-Cofer, 1986).

The romantic ideas of freedom and happiness combined with the empiricist ideas of reason and realism to create the philosophical foundations for the revolutions in France and the United States. This period also saw the rise in society of the value of the individual. It had been the custom in the past to give a newborn the same name as an older sibling, or the name of a sibling who had died. Such practices gave way in the eighteenth century to a newfound respect for the individuality of the child. Not only did advice books for parents proliferate, but by 1800 a wide range of inexpensive books were being published exclusively for young children. There was a corresponding recognition of the importance of the nuclear family and the maintenance of a private and sacred family home.

Domesticity became a value for the first time in human history. During the American colonial period, the main value of the family was to raise children according to the family's particular beliefs and values. Many of these families came to the New World specifically to practice their own beliefs, away from the conservatism and religious persecution then pervasive in Europe (Clarke-Stewart, 1998). These values of individuality, autonomy, and self-determination had never before existed in the history of the world, and they changed how adults conceptualized the meaning and value of infancy and childhood.

These ideas also led in the nineteenth century to the growth of social responsibility toward infants and children and the rise of the idea of the child as an integral part of the definition of the family. The so-called "discovery" of the child was due to urban forces in Europe and North America that segregated the family from the workplace, defined the mother's role as major supervisor of the domestic scene, and allowed love or sentiment (rather than family inheritance or economic well-being) to be the bond holding the family together (Hareven, 1985).

Educators in the nineteenth century continued to emphasize the importance of the young child's body in the development of the whole individual. Children who were obese, physically awkward, or handicapped could expect to get guidance from the school. The curriculum included free expression and creativity for the body, such as gymnastics and dance. Team sports and other exercise programs were meant to lay the foundation for the continuation of physical exercise through adulthood. Students were expected to understand the principles of health and hygiene. These programs grew out of the Greco-Roman and Enlightenment emphasis on the importance of the body as well as the mind (Friedrich-Cofer, 1986). Although such programs were gradually dropped from schools, programs of physical activity and healthy lunches are returning now because of a need to reduce the growing epidemics of childhood obesity, diabetes, and sedentary use of electronic devices.

Not only did the child emerge as an individual during this period, but the role of full-time mother and housewife appeared on the historical stage for the very first time. It may be shocking for people in Western cultures in the twenty-first century to realize that the idea of a loving mother taking full-time care of an infant is a very recent cultural invention brought about by the rise of the nuclear family. For most of human history, mothers worked while infants were raised by many different caregivers, such as nurses, siblings, and other relatives.

It should be noted, however, that the development of this segregated nuclear family and its full-time mother was at first confined to the white middle class. Families from other classes and ethnic and racial groups preserved the preindustrial extended family, in which love, work, and education all took place within the home, and child care was shared by all family members. Women worked in the fields and in the home in the company of their babies, just as they had done for most of human history (Hareven, 1982).

One can see a similar pattern of change even in recent history as a result of increasing urbanization of cultures around the world. In Turkey between the 1970s and 2000, to take one example, as mothers became more urban and educated, their concerns shifted from the survival and basic nutrition of the infant toward investing time and energy into the psychological development of children. During the same period, parental insistence on child obedience changed to encourage children to develop more independence and self-reliance. In the United States and other industrialized nations, immigrant families follow the same pattern of change as new generations adopt the mainstream cultural patterns of psychological well-being and individual self-reliance (Greenfield, 2009).

Going against this trend, on the other hand, recent cultural and economic forces have led to the decline of the nuclear family, the reemergence of extended families and communal living, nonparental childcare, and the rise of single-parent families. In the United States, the average divorce rate is 50 percent, and in some states such as California only 25 percent of marriages will last.

Social changes in the nineteenth century led to the growing awareness of the public's responsibility for the welfare and development of infants. Although the first English-language pediatric textbook appeared in 1545, welfare and medical institutions devoted exclusively to children did not open in Europe and the United States until the 1850s, around the same time as the rise of immunization and the pasteurization of milk. Maternal deaths during childbirth declined in this period due to the invention of anesthesia and procedures for sterilizing medical instruments (Greenleaf, 1978).

These medical advances further solidified the family by reducing infant mortality. As each child could be counted on to live a healthy life, families began to consciously reduce the number of children so as to invest more emotional energy in each child. By the middle of the nineteenth century, infancy and childhood had emerged in the public mind as a separate and valuable stage of life (Hareven, 1985). Manufactured baby dolls first appeared in Europe in 1825. In 1840, half of all three-year-olds in Massachusetts were attending infant schools, a practice that later declined because experts began to doubt the wisdom of sending such young children to school (Clarke-Stewart, 1998). The first public playground was developed in Boston in 1885 (a few heaps of sand dumped in a vacant lot), but by 1915, there were well-planned public playgrounds in 430 U.S. cities (Blank & Klig, 1982; Greenleaf, 1978; Zeitz, 1969).

Imagine what it must have been like to raise a baby in North America or Europe before 1850. The pain of childbirth could be helped by home remedies and the advice of a midwife, but there was no protection from serious problems and severe pain. Women could not be sure if they would survive childbirth, and many husbands were left without a wife and mother to raise the new baby. Infants died frequently of causes that were unknown at the time. Daily life with the baby was also much harder than it is today. There were no disposable diapers, no manufactured toys, and no baby foods parents could buy. Parents had to make the infant's clothing, diapers, toys, and food from scratch. A baby gets a lot of diapers dirty in a day, and there were no washers and driers. In fact, cotton fabric did not become widely available until the early nineteenth century (the textile mills of that period contributed to the exploitation of child labor, as depicted in the novels of Charles Dickens, among others). Most clothing before that time was made of wool and was hot and heavy. If you were among the few who were wealthy, you could hire a servant and a wet nurse to care for and feed the baby, although wet-nursing declined rapidly at the end of the nineteenth century because maternal love was deemed better for children. For most families, however, having a baby affected all aspects of their lives. There were no readily available forms of contraception, so most women gave birth regularly every three to five years.

INFANTS ENTER THE WORLD OF SCIENCE

Once infancy was deemed important in the public mind, scientists began to turn their attention toward babies. One of the first scientists to consider the role of infancy was Charles Darwin (1809–1882). Darwin's theory of the evolution of the species views infant and child development as a time when individuals grow and learn the skills needed for survival. In a process Darwin called **natural selection**, individuals who can successfully adapt to the environment will live long enough to reproduce and pass their genes down to the next generation. According to Darwin, the environment does not change the genes but rather influences which genes will survive in future generations to promote the most efficient survival skills (Darwin, 1859).

Darwin's legacy has shaped how we think about infancy. Human infancy bears some resemblance to infant development in all mammals and most especially to the great apes, all of whom share ancient ancestors who evolved to eventually create different animal species. An example of a general cross-species behavior related to survival is the **attachment** bond between parent and infant seen in most mammals, but each species shows this in different ways. Mother cats lick and nuzzle their infants, while mother monkeys groom and cuddle their babies and carry them around. All mammals nurse their young, but the styles of nursing differ between species. In dogs, the mother lies on her side while her puppies nurse. The mother dog does not look at her babies, as in humans, but she may lick them and smell them.

Another thing we have in common with many other species is that the young are biologically more susceptible to the acquisition of new behavior than older individuals. Often there is a limited period of time early in life during which environmental input can make a difference in later behavior. This period of maximum susceptibility is called a **critical period** and is a relatively short (compared to the individual's life span) and clearly demarcated period of time in which learning can occur and during which whatever the animal learns has a permanent and irreversible effect.

In some species of birds, for example, attachment of the infant to an adult occurs only during a period of about two hours, several days after hatching. If a gosling follows its mother around during the critical period, it will develop a preference for the mother over other adults and will stay close to her after the critical period ends and for a long time afterward. This learning of preferences for particular adults is called **imprinting**.

Konrad Lorenz (1965) found imprinting depends not only on genetic codes that program the animal to be available to follow the mother, but on changes that may occur in the environment. Lorenz showed that goslings could become imprinted on a number of different objects including flashlights, electric trains, and even himself. He would walk near the goslings during the critical period, squatting and honking like a mother goose. In his description of these early studies, he wrote, "In the interest of science, I submitted myself literally for hours on end to this ordeal" (Lorenz, 1952, p. 42).

Imprinting can be turned off by environmental events. Ducklings need to hear their own call prior to hatching. In experiments in which duck embryos were made unable to vocalize, they did not recognize the mother's call after hatching and thus could not imprint (Gottlieb, 1991a). Imprinting can also be disrupted by visual events. If, instead of seeing their mothers, quail chicks are exposed to patterned light during the first days after birth, they will not imprint even if they can hear the mother's call (Lickliter & Hellewell, 1992).

Imprinting does not occur in humans and other primate species because the infants are too immature to follow their parents around. Human parents, therefore, play a greater role in the mutual maintenance of proximity. The lasting emotional tie that promotes this proximity is called **attachment**. The critical period for attachment in humans, monkeys and apes is longer and the environmental conditions under which attachment may occur are more complex.

Although Darwin's theory had a major impact on how infancy is conceptualized, he never studied infants directly, except for his own children (see below). The beginning of the twentieth century saw the rise of the direct scientific study of infant development. Earlier debates over romanticism versus empiricism were replaced by discussions about the contributions to development of **nature** (evolution and genes) versus **nurture** (learning and environment).

Nature vs. Nurture

Arnold Lucius Gesell (1880–1961), working out of the nature-romantic tradition, thought that the orderly changes seen in early development were specified by the genes. The genetic timetable for the patterning of development was called **maturation**. Gesell made a career out of the careful measurements of developmental changes in size, motor skill, and behavior in infants and young children. He was the first scientist to use a one-way mirror to observe infants unobtrusively and the first to use film to record their behavior.

Because Gesell believed in genetic maturation, he cared little about individual differences and focused instead on the "average" child. This created anxiety or pride in parents who read his works and discovered that their own children walked or talked later or earlier than the average child. Even today, most parents want their babies to be above average. We now know that babies vary widely in the ages at which they attain developmental milestones, and that most babies—whether slow or fast—develop normally. There is no evidence that early development of walking or talking leads the child to become a star athlete or public speaker.

In the nurture-empiricist tradition, the Russian physiologist Ivan Pavlov (1849–1936) published one of the first demonstrations of learning as a result of systematic environmental manipulation. Pavlov attempted to teach dogs to salivate in the presence of something other than food. He discovered that if a bell was rung every time a hungry dog was presented with food, the dog would later salivate at the sound of the bell without any food present. This process, called **classical conditioning**, or learning by **association**, is illustrated in Figure 1.1.

In the United States, John B. Watson (1878–1958) believed that children could be trained in this

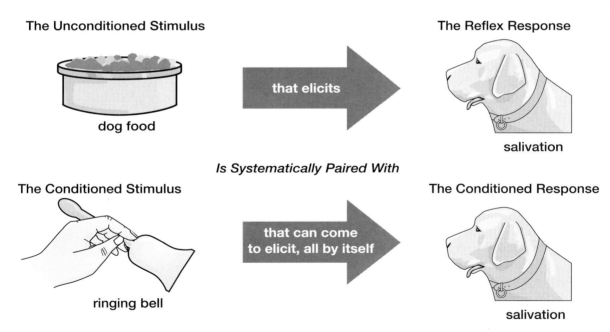

Figure 1.1 Classical conditioning and Pavlov's dog.

Source: J. P. Dworetzky & N. J. Davis, *Human development: A life span approach*, 1989, p. 34. St. Paul, MN: West Publishing. Copyright © by West Publishing Company. Reprinted by permission. All rights reserved.

A North American family and their baby in 1913. Note the children's elegant clothing. Well-educated parents were probably aware of the competing ideas of Watson's behaviorism and Gesell's maturationism.
Photo: Corbis

way to do almost anything, given the right kind of conditioning. He demonstrated this by doing classical conditioning studies in which he taught small children to be afraid of cuddly animals by making loud noises whenever they touched the animals. The fear (unconditioned response) was evoked by the cuddly animals (unconditioned stimulus) that appeared whenever the loud noise (conditioned stimulus) was made. This type of research would be considered unethical today. Nevertheless, Watson's work suggested that all our behavior, even the most basic and innocent, could possibly be controlled by outside forces. Watson left a lasting imprint on North American society. Watson's idea that anyone could succeed regardless of past history or genetic heritage sustained the hopes of many of the newly arrived immigrants.

B. F. Skinner (1904–1990) tried to use classical conditioning for birds. Because classical conditioning theory assumes that all unconditioned responses must be related to unconditioned stimuli, Skinner faced a problem. He could not dis-

cover the unconditioned stimuli for most of the animal's actions: it seemed to emit behavior—like pecking and singing—spontaneously without any obvious external stimulation. Skinner referred to these spontaneously emitted actions as operants. Pigeons, for example, peck (the operant) even when not eating.

Skinner discovered that the rate of emitted operants could be controlled by the consequences of the behavior; that is, by what happened in the environment immediately following the operant's occurrence. In one experiment, a pigeon was placed in a cage with no food tray. On the side of the cage was a colored disk. As the pigeon in the cage emitted the operant of pecking, it pecked at all the parts of the cage at random. When the bird happened to peck the colored disk, a small bit of food was dropped into the cage. Over time, the bird began to narrow down its pecking to the region of the cage containing the disk, and eventually it pecked exclusively at the disk: the animal discovered the contingency between its own pecking, the disk, and the food. The process by which the frequency of an operant is controlled by its consequences is called **operant conditioning**.

Operant conditioning is used routinely in infant studies, especially for studies of perception. In this technique, called a **response-contingent procedure**, infants are conditioned to change their behavior if they can detect certain features of sounds, images, smells, or tastes. Once taught, infants will alter their behavior to hear their favorite sound or to receive their preferred taste.

DeCasper and Fifer (1980) used this technique with an automatic suck recorder, a pacifier that is connected to a pressure transducer (which converts varying degrees of pressure into electrical impulses), which in turn is connected to recording equipment. Each infant in the study was equipped with a set of headphones and a suck recorder. After a two-minute adjustment period, the infant's sucking (the operant) was recorded for five minutes with no sounds coming through the headphones. During this period, the experimenter computed the median duration of the pauses between sucking bouts. If you make a list of the durations of all the pauses observed for the infant, the median is the duration at the midpoint of the list: half the durations are above the median and half below.

In the experimental period, infants sucked as usual, such that half of their pauses were below the median and half above. When the experimenters detected a pause that was longer or shorter than the median interval, they presented the infants with the recorded voice of either their mother (reading a segment of a Dr. Seuss story) or a stranger (reading the same segment). Five of the infants were randomly assigned to a group that could evoke their mother's voice by pausing their sucking for longer than the median pause length and evoke the stranger's voice by pausing for less than the median pause interval. The other five infants had the reverse conditions.

Because the presentation of the adult voices was made contingent upon the duration of the sucking pause, infants quickly learned that by speeding up or slowing down their sucking, they could produce one or the other voice. If the infants had a preference for one or the other voice, they could then systematically shift their pause length to "suck for" that voice. Eight of the ten infants showed a tendency to shift their pause length to produce their own mother's voice.

Consequences that increase the frequency of the preceding operant are called **reinforcers**. A **positive reinforcer** is an action or reward that follows the operant and increases its frequency. In some cases, the frequency of an operant is increased following the removal of an aversive stimulus. Thus, the absence of a consequence that increases the frequency of the operant is called a **negative reinforcer**.

Beyond Nature vs. Nurture: The Origins of Infant Psychology

The problem with theories that rely on either nature OR nurture is that they diminish human experience. One view sees us as completely controlled by our genes or and the other view sees us as completely controlled by our environment. Very few people today think that it is one OR the other, but some combination of both with room in between for free will, personal initiative, emotions, and creativity.

Part of this more integrated view of human development began with Sigmund Freud (1856–1939), who felt that psychological experience is more important in human life than the focus on outward behavior that had been common in both nature and nurture perspectives. He recognized that all infants experienced emotional highs and lows, that infants felt the need for love and possessed powerful desires. Freud's daughter, Anna, devoted most of her life to bringing her father's insights out of the adult psychoanalytic session and into the real lives of parents and children. Anna Freud taught parents to hold and cuddle babies and to be patient while babies discovered and tried to manage their own desires in appropriate ways, leaving room for the infant to have an emotional life (A. Freud, 1965). Unfortunately, the Freuds leaned a bit too far on the side of nurture, faulting parents for their children's developmental problems—in this case, for giving them too little attention and affection and for "selfishly" not understanding the situation from the child's point of view. While parenting is indeed essential, even the most understanding parent sometimes have bad days, and there are many times when infants are in fact incomprehensible and difficult to handle.

Parents simply can't control all the outcomes of their infant's development. In fact, infants actually control their parents' behaviors and feelings toward them. In the mid-twentieth century, it was discovered that parents can be conditioned by their infants almost as much as infants are conditioned by their parents. As infants act naturally to preserve or enhance getting the things they like or avoiding dislikes, their parents learn better ways to fit into their infants' needs (Bijou & Baer, 1965). Suppose, for example, a parent reinforces the child with a response every time the child asks for help and ignores the child whenever the child whines or cries to get help. The child is likely to increase the frequency of verbal requests for help, but in addition, the child will come to expect help whenever he or she asks for help in an appropriate way. On the parent's side, when the child asks for help verbally and without whining, the parent is more likely to provide the assistance. Thus, the increase in the child's verbal requests will condition the parent to increase the frequency with which he or she gives help. Infants also will not learn unless they are interested in something, regardless of parental attempts to change the behavior (Bandura, 1989). Thus, even studies in the nurture-empiricist tradition using conditioning found that parents and infants were influencing each other and what got learned had to do with some desire, interest or motivation intrinsic to each baby.

Bridging Nature and Nurture: Piaget and Constructivism

One of the first theories of human development that explicitly integrated both nature and nurture was that of Jean Piaget (1896–1980), who focused on cognitive development in infants. For Piaget, knowledge is conceived not as a static library of information but as an active process of co-construction between the knower and what is to be known. **Co-construction** means that what one knows depends upon how one acts on the environment and how the environment responds in return to those actions.

Piaget (1952), following Darwin, brought two principles of biological adaptation into his study of the development of intelligent action: assimilation and accommodation. **Assimilation** refers to the process by which individuals use their existing abilities in response to challenges from the environment. It is the application of what one already knows or does to the current situation. **Accommodation** is the alteration of existing abilities to better fit the requirements of the task or situation. Accommodation is more likely to occur if assimilation does not result in an effective adaptation to the environment.

Typically, most actions involve both assimilation and accommodation. Between the ages of six and twelve months, human infants must learn to eat solid foods. This is not an easy task, because the infant's tongue is not yet coordinated enough to keep food in the mouth. While sucking on a breast or a bottle, the baby's tongue moves in and out like a piston. When a baby is first given solid food on a spoon, the baby's response is to move the tongue as if he or she were sucking, which has

Jean Piaget is known for his theorectical contributions and also for his empathetic sensitivity with young children. His many experiments with his own three infants take account of his effects on them and were embedded into the infants' daily activities.

the effect of expelling food from the mouth. Thus, the infant assimilates the tongue and mouth actions of sucking to the eating of solids. Because this simple assimilation leaves the infant hungry, the child must accommodate mouth and tongue movements so they are better adapted to the shape of the spoon and the consistency of the solid foods. The infant's knowledge about food, therefore, is a co-construction between assimilation and accommodation, as each process influences the other to create the resulting action.

Piaget referred to the first two years of life as the **sensorimotor stage** because at that age infants were primarily involved in building knowledge involving their movements and senses. The main feature of sensorimotor intelligence is the growth of infants' understanding of their bodies,

how to use their bodies to solve problems and get what they need, and how their bodies relate to other things in the environment (Piaget & Inhelder, 1969). Piaget divided the sensorimotor stage into six substages. These are described in Table 1.1. Although they will not be discussed in this book, Piaget's discoveries of stages beyond the infancy period are summarized in Table 1.2. The sensorimotor stage was thought to contain the seeds for the post-infancy development of thought, language, social skills, and morality.

Piaget's stages are examples of a sequence of developmental change, which is characterized by the following three features:

Developmental changes are not reversible. **Developmental change** is a reorganization of the entire

TABLE 1.1 Piaget's Substages of Sensorimotor Development

Approximate Age (Months)	Stage	Description
0–2	Reflect schemes	Inborn reflexes such as sucking, looking, and crying establish the infant's first connection to the world.
2–5	Primary circular reactions	Repeated actions (circular) that involve connections within the infant's own body (primary) such as cooing and coordinating arm movements with the mouth to suck on the thumb, initial occurrence of the behavior is discovered by chance.
6–9	Secondary circular reactions	Repeated actions (circular) that involve the connection between the infant and the environment (secondary) such as kicking the crib to make a mobile move or smiling to get another person to smile back. Initial occurrence is discovered by chance.
10–12	Coordination of secondary circular reactions	First sign of goal-directed behavior not motivated by chance occurrences. Combining different circular reactions to achieve goals, such as using one hand to hold an object while the other explores it, or using one object to retrieve or to act on another one.
12–18	Tertiary circular reactions	The use of familiar secondary circular reactions to make new things happen, such as when the child explores how different objects fall from his or her high-chair table, creates new relationships between different objects in play, or uses trial-and-error problem solving.
18–24	Invention of new means through mental combinations	The ability to think before acting by representing actions as mental pictures and symbols. The infant can solve problems without trial and error.

TABLE 1.2   Piaget's Cognitive-Developmental Stages of Child Development

Approximate Age (Months)	Stage	Description
0–2	Sensorimotor	Infants learn through direct experience of the senses and by handling objects and moving them around. They do not understand that things exist outside their own actions.
3–7	Pre-operational	Ability to form mental representations, language, thinking as internalized action but centered on the self's perspective; inability to think logically.
7–11	Concrete operational	Thinking takes the perspective of others and is logical with respect to concrete actions and objects such as the rules of a game; inability to think about abstract things.
12–adult	Formal operational	Thinking about non-concrete, abstract things; ability to solve word problems, form a coherent system of thought relating many ideas, and think about future possibility.

Source: A. Fogel & G. F. Melson, *Child Development*, 1988, p. 39. St. Paul, MN: West. Copyright © by West Publishing Company. Reprinted by permission. All rights reserved.

person such that the earlier patterns of behavior, thought, and feeling cannot be easily recognized or recaptured.

Developmental changes are stable. **Developmental stages** are organized patterns that emerge in development and persist over relatively long periods of months or years.

Developmental changes occur in sequence. Development occurs in an orderly sequence that is similar across infants.

In fact, there are many ways to conceptualize stages of infant development. Each culture, for example, views the stage divisions of an infant's life differently. The Alor people of the Lesser Sundra Islands do not even count the infant's development in days or months, but rather in terms of a series of stages of development. The first stage lasts from birth to the first smile, the second from smiling to sitting up alone or crawling, and the third from this point to the onset of walking. The Chagga of Tanganyika apply different names to infants depending upon their stage of development. A newborn is called mnangu, or "incom-

plete," a mkoku is "one who fills the lap," and a mwana is an infant before the age of three years (Mead & Newton, 1967). These linguistic labels are comparable to the terms newborn, infant, and toddler in English.

Parents and other infant caregivers may use another type of division for the first three years. They may be more concerned about the ages at which infants become capable of independent play with other infants, the age of the beginning of toilet training and the onset of bowel control, or the age at which infants become more relaxed when separated from their parents.

Three basic principles about human infants characterize Piaget's theory:

Individuals play an active role in their own development. The major motivation for developmental change comes from the individual's failure to reach an adaptation to the environment. This experience of failure, when accommodation and assimilation fall short of adaptation, is called **disequilibrium**. Because disequilibrium is defined in relation to what each individual wants to accomplish, it cannot be imposed from the outside: babies seek knowledge about those things that they most want to figure out or accomplish.

Infants develop knowledge by means of their own actions on the environment. The accommodation process literally changes the infant's view of the world, because, by altering his or her own actions, the child comes to "know" new uses for the same objects. Through action, individuals create knowledge. Because knowledge is an active process of creation, Piaget's work this is often referred to as **constructivist theory**, according to which knowledge is built up—constructed—by the child's own action rather than being simply conditioned or imposed on the child from the outside.

Infants will learn better from experiences if those experiences can be assimilated to their current developmental level. The currently available set of skills and knowledge is known as the infant's **schemes**. Schemes can be sensorimotor, that is, involving physical actions such as reaching and chewing. Schemes can also be conceptual, involving ideas, concepts, or thoughts. For accommodation to occur, the infant has to assimilate the existing set of schemes to the environment. For this to happen, the environment should present challenges that are moderate, not overly difficult or beyond the infant's grasp. Thus, the first solid foods have to be soft in consistency (the infant does not have teeth yet) and given on a spoon that is small enough to fit in the infant's mouth. Adults have to hold the spoon at just the right angle and move it in and out of the infant's mouth at the appropriate time.

Piaget's original work on infancy was based on observations of his own three children, Jacqueline, Laurent, and Lucienne, and he is known to have been empathically attuned to young children. His observations are unrivaled in their clarity, accuracy, detail, and theoretical import (see Qualitative Research, below). Piaget's work is clearly distinguished from learning theories and from Darwinian evolutionary theories. Piaget believed that development is not imposed on the infant from the outside, nor is it guided solely by genetically based maturational change. Adaptation suggests a more active, infant-centered perspective in relation to a changing and dynamic environment.

One problem for Piaget's theory is that he failed to take account of the effects of adults on infants. Although he is given credit for helping us understand that infants are active learners, he did not attend to the facilitating and supportive environment that parents often provide and in which infants may exercise their curiosity. For infants to assimilate their eating to spoon feeding, for example, it requires an adult who can choose the right kind of food and spoon, an adult who is actively and constructively engaged with the infant. The role of adults is more explicit in systems theories (discussed in the next section), which offer the possibility for adult-infant co-construction.

Piaget, however, led the growth of research in the 1970s that emphasized infant learning and cognitive development. Parents strove to train their infants to achieve the maximum mental potential at the earliest possible age. This was based on the belief that education (nurture), rather than natural endowment (nature), was the best guarantee of child success (Clarke-Stewart, 1998). Many parents placed their infants into tightly structured study programs to teach them reading, word learning, music, and mathematics before they reached the age of three years. As mentioned at the beginning of this chapter, we now know that too much of this early stimulation actually delays infant learning.

The emphasis on intelligence and mental development led to a steady decline in a balanced view of the whole child as needing education not only for mind but for body, emotions, and social connections. According to one historian, "as the individual child and adolescent with bodies faded from view, many of the humanistic ties which bound scientist, teacher, family, and child faded with them" (Friedrich-Cofer, 1986, p. 133). Children's progress began to be reported in the form of standardized test scores, rather than individualized assessment of mental and physical health. Physical education, music, and art programs that had been created for all children declined or disappeared entirely from schools, replaced by competitive athletics and music programs designed for an elite group of talented students (Cofer, 2008).

This focus on the early structuring of the infant's intellectual growth was followed in the 1980s by an interest in targeting infants who were at risk for developmental difficulties, such as those who were premature, handicapped, or victims of abuse. The focus on risk was associated with a belief in nurture: the idea that all humans could become perfect if given the right kind of child rearing. For healthy and wealthy infants, this meant a quest for developing a "superbaby" and giving children a "head start" (Clarke-Stewart, 1998). It also brought the ideal of a "supermom," who could be employed outside the home and at the same time be a great mother and a wonderful and loving wife, which created a lot of stress for young families. The 1980s also saw a rise in the amount of time fathers spent with their babies.

More recently, however, romantic ideas have returned to scientific studies in psychology and in infant development (Schneider, 1998). Perhaps in reaction to what was seen as an overemphasis on intellectual achievement, since the 1990s we have seen a rise in studies of parent-child relationships, emotional development and attachment, the role of the body and touch, and communication and language. The more rational approaches to infant development continue to grow in such fields as cognitive neuroscience and behavior genetics. On the other hand, some of the trends of the 1970s and 1980s, which focused on babies growing up and getting smart as quickly as possible, were replaced by ideas about having a secure and loving attachment, slowing down and appreciating the beauty of each phase of a baby's life, and the specialness of being a baby.

SYSTEMS PERSPECTIVES ON INFANT DEVELOPMENT

Even though Piaget's work emphasized the integration and co-construction of nature and nuture, the above review makes it clear that most people continue to think of nature and nurture as sepa-

rate and opposing forces: genes *or* environments, cognition *or* emotion, parent *or* child. Life, unfortunately, is not so simple that we can easily put it into neat little categorical boxes. The real story of human development is about the *relationships between these different elements*. Systems theories—such as that of Piaget—share the view that all facets of the child and the environment are important, and that development is a complex process in which outcomes are determined through the active *interaction* of these facets. Systems theories attempt to understand developmental change by considering the *relationships between the components*. It is only recently that systems thinking has begun to have an visible effect on how we think about infants.

A **system** is a relationship between interdependent components, each of which affects the others in reciprocal fashion. The process by which systems components affect each other in a bidirectional and reciprocal way is known as **transaction** (Sameroff & MacKenzie, 2003). In the parent-infant interaction system, for example, the behavior of a parent is likely to depend on the temperament of the infant. Infants who smile more and cry less are likely to have parents who are more relaxed and socially attentive to the infant. This parental social attentiveness, in turn, will affect the infant's continued sociability.

Feedback is a process by which components of a system have an effect on each other's behavior during transactions such as these. If the parent, for example, has had a bad day and is not so relaxed or socially attentive, it is likely that the sociability of the infant will help the parent to calm down. Feedback that maintains a system's characteristics over time despite small deviations is called **deviation-correcting feedback** (or negative feedback).

In other cases, however, the deviation from the normal state of affairs is larger than the system can tolerate and still maintain itself. Suppose, for example, the infant becomes ill and fussy or has a mental or physical handicap. Under normal conditions, the parent would remain cheerful and attentive. If the parent too is under stress, however, the infant's fussiness could lead to an increase in the parent's level of stress, which then leads to the infant's feeling even more distress and crying more, which may lead to parental despair or anger. Feedback that drastically changes a system is called **deviation-amplifying feedback** (or positive feedback).

Deviation-amplifying feedback (like accommodation) generally works to change a system, while deviation-correcting feedback (like assimilation) works to maintain it. Deviation amplification could also change a system for the better. The infant's initial shyness in social situations may, with the support of the parent's attentiveness to the infant's need to feel safe, lead to the enhancement of the infant's social skills with peers and other partners and to the growth of a wider range of shared communication between parent and infant.

This last example shows that systems can have multiple levels. A parent-child relationship system, for example, is embedded within a larger family system. In addition to the feedback between parent and child, a parent's relationship to the infant may also be affected by the parent's marital satisfaction, his or her relationship with other family members, the financial well-being of the family, his or her own job satisfaction, and even society's attitudes about the parenting role. To take this a step further, the family is embedded in a neighborhood with schools, clinics and other services while the neighborhood is contained in a culture and society.

Bio-Ecological Systems Theory

Bio-ecological systems theory is a way to understand the relationships between and within multiple system levels—from person to society—that shape the development of infants into adulthood (Bronfenbrenner, 1979; Bronfenbrenner & Ceci, 1994).

The child. These are the relationships occurring within the individual. These include the relations between genes and their cellular environments, between different body systems such as neurological and cardiovascular, between mind and body, cognition and emotion, assimilation and accommodation, and the coordination of different body parts as in learning to walk or crawl.

Microsystem. The **microsystem** is made up of the relationships between the infant and the environments with which the infant comes in contact. This may include the child and the physical and social environment of the family, or the child in schools, camps, hospitals, play groups, and places of worship. Children are affected by many aspects of their immediate microsystem environment, including social interactions, housing, and nutrition (Melson, 1980).

Mesosystem. The **mesosystem** includes the relationships between the major settings in which children are found, such as the interaction between the family and the day care center. A child who is experiencing many difficulties in day care is likely to force the family to have more interactions with the center's teachers and administrators, and those family-school interactions should, in turn, have an effect on the child's functioning.

Exosystem. The **exosystem** includes other social systems that do not directly contain the developing child but have some effect on him or her. The world of work, neighborhood institutions, the media, the government, the economy, and transportation affect the functioning of the family, school, and other microsystems in which children are found.

Macrosystem. The **macrosystem** contains all of the above subsystems. It includes the beliefs, laws, and values of the culture or subculture and is made up of the written and unwritten principles that regulate everyone's behavior. These principles—whether legal, economic, political, religious, or educational—endow individual life with meaning and regulate the nature and scope of the interactions between the various levels of the total social system. The relationships among these various subsystems are shown in Figure 1.2.

According to bio-ecological systems theory, infants may be influenced by and influence others either by direct transactions or by mediated

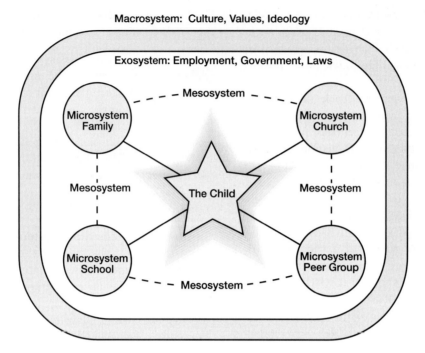

Macrosystem: Culture, Values, Ideology

Exosystem: Employment, Government, Laws

Mesosystem

Microsystem Family

Microsystem Church

Mesosystem

The Child

Mesosystem

Microsystem School

Microsystem Peer Group

Mesosystem

Figure 1.2 Ecological Systems Theory
The child is contained within a nested system of social relationships and institutions. Except in microsystems, children are not direct participants in any of the other social systems that may affect their lives.
Source: Adapted from A. Fogel and G. F. Melson, *Child Development*, 1988, p. 50. St. Paul, MN: West.

transactions. A **direct transaction** occurs as part of a social relationship in which the child is an active participant: the infant-parent, infant-peer, or infant-sibling relationship. A **mediated transaction** occurs when the infant affects or is affected by people with whom the infant may or may not share an active relationship.

An example of a mediated transaction concerns the child's relationship with grandparents. Though children in North American society often spend little time with their grandparents, visiting perhaps only once or twice a year, they nevertheless seem to develop special relationships with them. This can be accounted for by parental mediation. Because the parent's relationship to his or her own parents is so important, this importance is transmitted to the child, who then comes to think of Grandma and Grandpa as special people (Lewis & Feiring, 1978; Lewis, 2005).

With mediated effects, the acts of one individual affect another, who then affects a third

person (see Figure 1.3; Belsky, 1981). This figure includes the effects of one individual (for example, the infant) on the relationship between the parents and, conversely, the effects of the marital relationship on the infant directly and indirectly as it affects each spouse's ability to parent. One other notable aspect of this diagram is that it includes feedback transactions. For example, the marriage may affect a spouse's ability to parent, which may affect the infant, whose subsequent behavior may affect the marital relationship. Each component is capable of affecting every other component in a mutually influential manner.

Dynamic Systems Theory

Some of the pioneers in the study of human development such as Darwin and Piaget were interested in the problem of how new forms arise during development. At different times in evolutionary history, for example, new species emerged

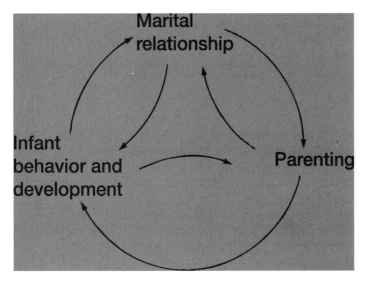

Figure 1.3   Model of Family System Functioning

Source: J. Belsky, Early human experience: A family perspective, 1981, p. 16. *Developmental Psychology, 17*, 3–23. Copyright © by the American Psychological Association. Adapted with permission.

that had never been seen before. Similarly, during the life span of a person, new abilities, emotions, and experiences arise as new developmental stages unfold in time. **Dynamic systems theory** takes account of the process of change in human development by understanding the ways in which the interactions between components of the system can change the very nature of the system itself while at the same time preserving the integrity of the system. According to dynamic systems theory, the generation of novelty, the creation of something new that was not there before, is the primary feature of all living creatures. Everything that is alive has to grow, and as it grows it not only changes but at the same time preserves itself as a unique being (van Geert, 1998). In the most dramatic example, the cocoon, caterpillar, and butterfly are all manifestations of the same individual insect. How does this happen?

Dynamic systems theory takes its current form from the work of the physicist Ilya Prigogine (Prigogine & Stengers, 1984). Most of the matter in the universe slowly expends its energy and then burns out. But Prigogine was interested in phenomena that make their own energy, preserve themselves across time, and become increasingly complex by generating novel forms. This is the process that characterizes all living systems, from single-celled organisms to human beings. The ability of systems to maintain themselves and to

develop new forms is called **self-organization**. The "self" in self-organization means that the maintenance and development of the system arises from the mutual transactions and feedback processes between the components of the system, and the system with the environment, rather than being imposed on the system by some preexisting genetic plan.

Prigogine began his research by studying some nonliving physical systems that had the capacity to create their own energy and become more complex in form. One example is the weather, in which the forms—such as seasons or hurricanes—develop and maintain themselves over time. Despite its dynamic complexity, the weather has patterns that repeat. Every year you can expect it to be cold in the winter and warm in the summer. Every winter is different from every previous winter in particular ways, however, and it is not possible to predict in advance what each new winter will be like.

Many dynamic systems display the following two properties:

1. *They form predictable and stable patterns in their macroscopic behavior.* The seasons in the weather system are one example; the stages of human development are another. All infants go through the same Piagetian six substages in the same sequence during the first three years

of life, just as each year the earth goes through the same four seasons.

2. *They are relatively unpredictable in their microscopic behavior.* One may be able to predict the weather over the coming week or two within a range of possibilities depending upon the season, but the complexity of the weather system always leaves room for something novel to emerge. Similarly, we can describe what ten-month-old infants are likely to do in general, but an individual infant's precise behavior on a given day and how that infant discovers how to walk, for example, cannot be predicted. Something novel happens every day that cannot be anticipated.

This microscopic unpredictability in the context of macroscopic stability is known as **chaos**. Chaos is a mathematical concept that expresses the property of complex systems to have some general structure that repeats over time but never in exactly the same way. The drawing in Figure 1.4 represents chaos. It is the trajectory of a mathematical equation that traces a path in three-dimensional space that is similar on each cycle, but is never exactly the same as any previous cycle. Each person's life course is similar in the transitions between developmental stages, but no two lives are exactly the same. The concept of chaos suggests that dynamic systems display some forms of determinism (predictability) and some forms of **indeterminism** (Fogel, Lyra, & Valsiner, 1997; Prigogine & Stengers, 1984).

Scientists use the following example. Imagine a butterfly is flapping its wings somewhere in South Asia. This movement is just enough to change the flow of a tiny bit of warm air. This tiny change in airflow may happen at just the right moment to

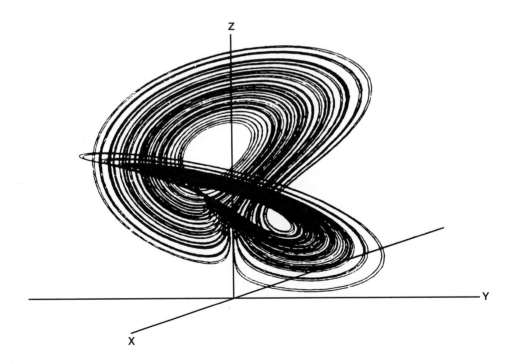

Figure 1.4   A Trajectory of Chaos
A mathematical equation generates a curve that repeats a similar shape in three-dimensional space. Each time the curve repeats the shape, however, it is in a slightly different place from where it has passed through before.
Source: F. Capra, *The web of life*, 1996, p. 135. New York: Anchor Books.

trigger a much larger change in airflow because of deviation-amplifying feedback, which then causes a change in the temperature distribution at higher elevations. At some point and without a specific cause, the conditions are created for a thunderstorm to emerge in the United States. Because of complex feedback processes and emergent novelty, it is impossible to trace the cause of the thunderstorm back to a single source (even the flight path of the butterfly depends in part on wind and weather conditions in that very moment!).

A so-called **butterfly effect** occurs when a very small perturbation creates unpredictable novelty in a system, which then results in macroscopic developmental change in the system. Self-organization, chaos, and the butterfly effect have been used to explain why all snowflakes are similar but no two are exactly alike, the unpredictability of heart rhythms during a heart attack, the development of differences and similarities between living cells, and how even two twins with the same genetic makeup can turn out differently in their personality and behavior (Capra, 1996; Hopkins & Butterworth, 1997).

By the same logic, infant and human development is not fixed to a genetic or maturational timetable (nature), nor is it entirely predictable from adult guidance or infant learning (nurture). While nature and nurture provide the basic components of the system, their relationship produces indeterministic effects: new abilities emerge through the feedback transactions and dynamic fluctuations of self-organization (Fogel & Thelen, 1987; Thelen & Fogel, 1989).

Human development has many examples of butterfly effects; small and unexpected events that can change the course of a life (Fogel, 1990a; Thelen, 1990). A simple word for this is creativity. During conversation, for example, people form their sentences and stories to express something they have in mind. People have to make up their sentences as they speak, and no two sentences are ever exactly alike. In addition, as we hear the responses of others to our words, that feedback sometimes makes us work to clarify our meaning

or even to change it according to the other's perspective. In this sense, communication is creatively self-organized because it emerges in the process of transaction. We can call this type of communication "alive". (Fogel & Garvey, 2007). When babies begin to acquire language, they can create novel sentences never spoken before. Piaget's concept of constructivism also suggests that infants develop via opportunities for playful creativity which allow novelty to enter the system and to enhance growth and development.

RESEARCH METHODS IN DEVELOPMENTAL SCIENCE

As we've seen so far in this chapter, there are many theories of human development, each having a different take on nature or nurture or both together. Each culture, in addition, has its own theory of the formation of individual differences. The ancient Greeks and Romans believed that exposing an infant to a variety of fearful and stressful events early in life would make the child less fearful and more emotionally balanced later. Nineteenth-century Europeans believed just the opposite—that protecting the child from fear-producing experiences was the best way to create an outgoing child (Kagan, Kearsley, & Zelazo, 1978). Which one of these many theories is more correct? How could you decide?

Scientific research on infant development can help us answer this question. Scientists rely on many sources of evidence, they try to separate what is repeatable and stable from what is coincidental, and they attempt to rid observations of bias. Piaget's work is a good example. He made extensive written notes, often on a daily basis, about the behavior of his three infant children. Piaget not only observed natural behavior, but tried out little experiments to test alternate interpretations of what the children could do. At one point, Piaget tried to determine whether his eight-month-old daughter Jacqueline (J.) was capable of imitating mouth movements and sounds. In the following example, Jacqueline seemed to imitate her father's biting movements. Or did she? Piaget was not sure whether Jacqueline only appeared to imitate him because he had started out by imitating movements she could already make.

> J. was moving her lips as she bit on her jaws. I did the same thing, and she stopped and watched me attentively.… J. began to imitate me an hour later.… In order to understand this new development, two circumstances must be noted. Firstly, for some days she had not merely imitated sounds for their own sake but had watched the mouth of the model with great attention. Secondly, as she moved her lips, J. began by making a slight noise with her saliva… and I had imitated this sound at the outset. Her interest in the movements of the mouth was thus clearly due to interest in the production of sound. [Three days later] I resumed the experiment without making any sound and without J. herself having made the movement beforehand. She watched my lips moving and then distinctly imitated me three times, keeping her eyes fixed on my mouth. (Piaget, 1962, pp. 30–31)

Experimental Research Methods

In this example, Piaget used written narrative descriptions that combined observational research with an experiment. An **experiment** is a research study in which one aspect of the situation is manipulated while all other aspects are held constant or controlled. In this case, to discover Jacqueline's ability to imitate mouth movements on her own, Piaget waited for a time when Jacqueline had not made the movement spontaneously for some time, and he did not produce any sound when he made the movements himself. The prior condition (the child makes no similar spontaneous movement and the adult does not imitate the child) and the presentation of the adult model (absence of sound) were controlled. The experimental manipulation is the presence or absence of a movement-only adult model.

In modern versions of Piaget's famous imitation experiment, many other aspects of the situation are controlled: the position in which the child is sitting, the behavior of the adult model, the familiarity of the infant with the adult, and the observation procedures. The following are some standard experimental procedures.

Control groups that do not receive any manipulation are compared to a group of infants who receive the experimental manipulation. Alternatively, different groups can be compared if each receives a different type of manipulation. These are called **contrast groups**. In imitation research, for example, different contrast groups of infants are presented with a different model (tongue protrusion, mouth movement, or a facial expression). If imitation occurs, the frequency of tongue protrusion following the model should be highest in the group that has seen the tongue-protrusion model. This procedure controls for the fact that most babies produce tongue protrusion spontaneously, so that some tongue protrusion would be seen in all the groups.

Random assignment is used to determine which subjects belong to each experimental group. A flip of a coin or some other random process is used to assign subjects to groups. In some cases, it is unethical to use random assignment in a study. For example, suppose we want to compare the effects on language development of differences between mothers in their speech to infants. We obviously cannot randomly assign mothers to infants.

Experiments generally have two important measures, also called variables. The **independent variable** is that which is controlled or manipulated by the experimenter. In the case of imitation studies, the independent variable is the type of model given to the infant. The independent variable is the presumed cause of the phenomenon; that is, different types of models are presumed to cause the infant to imitate different movements. The **dependent variable** is the presumed effect or outcome behavior that is observed in response to the changes in the independent variable. In the case of the imitation study, the dependent variable is the frequency of different actions of the infant, such as the frequency of mouth movements or tongue protrusions. The dependent variable is presumed to be affected by the causal independent variable such that manipulations of the independent variable should lead to systematic changes in the dependent variable.

Observational Research Methods

Many of the important questions in infancy research—such as the effects of prematurity and of variations in parental styles of child care—cannot be studied experimentally. We cannot randomly assign infants to be premature, and we cannot randomly assign particular types of parents to particular types of infants. We use, instead, **observational research** methods that rely on the natural variations within the existing population of infants and families.

The obvious advantage of observational research is that we can study many issues of grave importance to our understanding of early human development that would be unethical or impossible to study experimentally. The problem with observational studies is that the variable on which the groups are assigned (the style of parental child rearing) may also correlate with other factors (such as the mother's social skills and general expressiveness). If this occurs, it is difficult to determine which factor—child rearing, social skills, or expressiveness—is the cause of differences in infant behavior.

Observational studies can be either longitudinal or cross-sectional. In a **longitudinal study**, researchers follow the same group of children as they get older. Longitudinal studies are important for determining how particular early experiences of individuals affect their later development and also for revealing patterns of change over time. Change is measured against the individual's own record of growth. The disadvantage is that the researcher must wait for the child to grow, although this takes less time for infants than for older children because infants grow at a faster rate; few researchers can find the research funding to support such long-term efforts. Another prob-

lem is **attrition**, which occurs when subjects of a longitudinal study drop out of the study before they complete the entire period of observation. Not only does attrition lower the number of subjects in a study, but researchers worry whether the subjects who remain are different from those who drop out, making the study less representative of the larger population.

One of the methods most commonly used today to study developmental change is a **cross-sectional study**, in which the researcher selects a different group of children at each age period of interest. Cross-sectional studies have the advantage of giving us a sense of age change in development without having to wait for the children to grow up. An additional advantage is that researchers who observe children from only two or three different age groups have more time to collect data from a large number of children and thus may find patterns of between-individual variation in behavioral characteristics and age of attainment of developmental milestones. Thus, while cross-sectional studies allow us to make generalizations about groups of infants, they cannot tell us how individual infants develop over time.

Observational research, like experimental research, can be quantitative. **Quantitative research** means that observations are transformed in numerical indices called variables. The variable that is the presumed cause—such as child-rearing styles—is called the predictor variable. The presumed effect—child behavior—is called the outcome variable. There is an analogy between independent variables and predictor variables, and between dependent variables and outcome variables.

Reducing Bias in Research

Regardless of whether one does observational or experimental research, caution must be taken to assure that variables reflect accurate and unbiased measures of the phenomenon. Reliability and validity procedures are ways of attempting to reduce bias in quantitative research. **Reliability** is a measure of the consistency with which an assessment procedure is applied. If one is trying to measure an infant's preference for looking at her mother compared to an unfamiliar woman, observers may be asked to record the duration of time the infant spends looking at each adult. If two people, working independently, are asked to judge the duration of the same event, the measurement of duration is reliable to the extent that the two observers agree with each other.

Validity is the degree to which the procedure accurately measures what it is intended to measure. For example, one might ask if the duration of time the infant spends looking at the mother versus that spent looking at the stranger is a valid measure of the infant's preference for one or the other. A baby may look longer at an unfamiliar face because it is new and the baby is curious about it, not because the baby prefers to look at that face. In this case, the duration of time the infant looks at the stranger would not be a valid measure of preference for the stranger. To test whether the duration of the infant's looking is a valid measure of preference or of curiosity, one would have to compare this measure with other measures of preference and curiosity. An additional measure of preference might be the duration of time the infant smiles at and vocalizes to each adult. An additional measure of curiosity might be the duration of time the infant looks at pictures of novel compared to familiar objects.

Another means of lowering research bias is by assuring that both the subjects and the experimenters are blind to the specific purpose of the research and to the group assignment of the subjects. **Blindness** in quantitative research refers to limiting the access of researchers and participants to knowledge that may bias the outcomes of the study. In a study on the relationship between infant language and mother's speech, for instance, researchers who administer the tests of infant language should not be the same as those who observe the mother's speech, and they should not know anything about the mother's speech score. The mothers should not be aware of the precise measures and relationships being tested, although they might be told that they are participating in a study on infant language development.

Finally, bias in research can be reduced by assuring that the group of infants and parents who participate in a research study is representative of the larger population of infants (**representative research**). A study is representative if its conclusions can be applied to infants who were not direct participants in the study. Most infancy research is done with white, middle-class North American and European infants. It is important to ask whether these findings apply equally to infants from other ethnic groups, cultures, and socioeconomic groups. Research grants from the National Institutes of Health in the United States, which funds both medical and behavioral research on human subjects, cannot be obtained unless the subjects of the study represent both genders and a cross-section of ethnic groups.

Research Ethics and Informed Consent

Research ethics adopted by most institutions in North America require that human subjects give their informed consent to participate in research. **Informed consent** is a voluntary agreement to participate in a research study. Informed consent must be based on accurate information about the purpose, procedures, risks, and benefits of the research study (Keith-Spiegel, 1983). Each researcher must write a proposal describing the details of their research, its risks and benefits, and provide a sample consent form. These documents are reviewed by the institution's **Institutional Research Board (IRB)**, whose mission it is to protect the welfare of humans who participate in research studies.

Special provisions are required by the IRB for research subjects who cannot give consent for themselves, specifically infants and small children. In these cases, one or both parents must sign the consent to participate. Parents are told about the possible risks and benefits of the research, both for themselves and for their infants.

Researchers must pledge to keep the subjects' identity confidential and to limit access to their data only to those persons directly involved with the research. There are several situations, however, in which confidentiality cannot be assured. In the event that the researchers observe behavior constituting child abuse, they are required by law to report it to the appropriate community agency. Also, researchers cannot protect their data if they are subpoenaed in a child-custody dispute. Parents need to be informed about these limits to confidentiality before they agree to participate. Fortunately, these situations rarely occur. In the past thirty-five years of doing infancy research with many hundreds of families, I have never had to violate a subject's confidentiality for these or any other reasons.

Qualitative Research Methods

The previous sections covered quantitative research using experimental and observational methods. In quantitative studies, the phenomenon is measured as a number or category. The number could be an onset time, a duration, a frequency, or a score on a rating scale. Qualitative research, on the other hand, does not use quantity or number. It is characterized by one or both of the following features.

1. *The observers focus on the meaning of the situation for the participants.*
2. *The role of the researcher in the situation is taken explicitly into account.*

To infer the meaning and to take account of the observer, qualitative research needs to examine the research situation in its broader context. The child is observed in relation to the setting, the actors, the sequences of behavior, the history of previous encounters in similar situations, and the presence of the observer. If the researcher is part of the observation as a **participant observer**,

---

Case Report

As you read over the first part of the section of this chapter on qualitative research, you'll notice that all of the research studies were based on observing one or more individual infants and followed their development over time, so-called **developmental case studies**. Qualitative developmental case studies are like biographies of individuals; their life histories as they change over time. Developmental case studies are a particular kind of longitudinal research in which we get to know each "subject" in the study as a unique person who changes as a result of the life events that they encounter.

When I have taught university classes on infant development, I ask students to write a term project that is a developmental case study of their own lives since infancy. The students are asked to come up with a research question. Here are some examples of research questions that students have explored:

Was your attachment with your parents secure or insecure, and how does that affect your current interpersonal relationships with parents and significant others in your life?

What were your eating habits or difficulties as an infant and how does that affect your current relationship to food, diet, weight, or body image?

How did the mental health/illness of your family during infancy affect your current mental health/illness?

If you suffered maltreatment as an infant, how did that experience affect your life?

Are there lasting traces of your infant temperament (e.g., shy vs. outgoing, emotionally sensitive vs. emotionally stable), on your personality today?

Students collect data on their own infancy by interviewing family members who knew them as an infant and as they were growing up. Some students use photos and videos of themselves as infants and children and any memories that they may have of their childhood. Many students interview their current friends, romantic partners, and family members to get data on how other people see them at the current time.

The students then write up this information into a developmental case study of themselves, a kind of autobiography. In this text, when certain topics are discussed (such as infant nutrition, attachment, or temperament) you can find **Case Reports** in the text that might make your understanding of the material more personal. I asked students to sign a consent form allowing me to use their term projects, with the permission of the University of Utah IRB, under the condition that their identity would not be revealed.

he or she has a direct effect on the people being studied and they have an effect on the researcher. If the observer is watching a video or some other recorded data, the researcher's interpretations play a role in deciding what the participant's behaviors mean.

The study done by Piaget on Jacqueline's imitation that was described earlier is an example of qualitative research, because he used a verbal narrative—in his own words—of the whole situation to highlight the broader meaning to Jacqueline of the imitative behavior. Piaget, as the parent, was also a participant observer, taking account of his own role in the outcome. Having recognized the effects of his own behavior on his daughter, he was better able to sort out the possible causes and effects, which led him to design a better experiment.

The earliest known systematic observation and recording of infant behavior, done by educated European and North American parents during the eighteenth and nineteenth centuries, used a similar qualitative approach. Some of these parents kept a daily dairy about their baby's life, a **baby biography**. These diaries satisfied the first characteristic of qualitative research: they were narratives intended to understand the meaning of infant behavior rather than to measure it. The German philosopher Dietrich Tiedemann (1748–1803), for example, recorded the development of motor skills, language, thinking abilities, and social behavior in his infant son. Tiedemann described what we now call the Moro reflex as follows:

> If he was held in arms and then suddenly lowered from a considerable height, he strove to hold himself with his hands, to save himself from falling; and he did not like to be lifted very high. Since he could not possibly have any conception of falling, his fear was unquestionably a purely mechanical sensation, such as older persons feel at a steep and unaccustomed height, something akin to dizziness. (Tiedemann, 1927, p. 216)

Notice that Tiedemann not only described his son's behavior in the manner of observational

research, but also interpreted the meaning of the behavior for the infant when he speculated that the infant's experience was "purely mechanical." Tiedemann may have been an accurate observer of the outward behavior of the baby, but he would not be considered a good qualitative researcher by today's standards. Although we readers can see that his interpretations of the meaning of the child's behavior is based on his own point of view as an adult, Teidemann—unlike Piaget—did not take explicit account of his role in the interpretive process. He was not, in other words, aware of his own biases. Those biases seem to reflect his view that babies of this age are not capable of feeling emotions, which today we know to be inaccurate.

Charles Darwin was also a baby biographer. Darwin was very aware of his role in the interpretive process. When his son, William, was only a few months old, Darwin was a relatively objective observer. But as William became more active and expressive, Darwin added more references to himself and his affections for William. Because Darwin thought these references to himself were unscientific, however, they were deleted in the versions of his diary that he published (Conrad, 1998). Darwin also made explicit mention of his own point of view in a memorial he wrote at the time of the death of his daughter, Anne, when she was 10 years old (Conrad, 2004).

Qualitative researchers today do not think it is unscientific for observers to take account of their own reactions. They suggest that a deeper understanding of the meaning of behavior for the subjects can only come from a deeper self-awareness of the researchers about their own reactions and biases (Moustakas, 1994). Perhaps the only way to get to know another person meaningfully is to share a long-term relationship full of emotions, opinions, and attachments.

Researchers always have some kind of relationship with their subjects. In the quantitative approach, the relationship is one of keeping a distance and remaining objective as an observer. In qualitative research, observers allow themselves to experience some of the feelings of participation that might be present in any interpersonal relationship (Aureli, 1997). Their training and self-awareness, however, allow them to use their own feelings to enhance their understanding of the subject's perspective. On the other hand, quantitative researchers also have biases, which they hope to control by means of reliability and validity measures. Each type of research has its advantages and disadvantages.

The assessment of a student's performance in school, for example, can occur through either a distant or a close teacher-student relationship. In large classes, a quantitative approach is most typically used. Instructors use primarily numerical and presumably objective indices of student performance, based on exams and other graded assignments. In small classes, on the other hand, evaluations are based not only on grades but also on a more in-depth interpersonal relationship between teachers and students. In this situation, the teacher has an opportunity to get to know each student. Experienced teachers are able to develop meaningful interpersonal relationships with their students while maintaining the ability to judge the student's performance and guide her or his learning. Experienced clinicians, such as psychotherapists, also have this skill of being able to evaluate their client's progress while maintaining a strong interpersonal relationship.

The concept of **credibility** in qualitative research is similar to that of validity in quantitative research. A researcher has more credibility if the researcher is highly trained, has spent many hours doing comparable observations, and/or has had a prolonged engagement with the particular subjects of the study (Denzin & Lincoln, 1994). This is true for Piaget, because he was a trained scientist and he obviously had prolonged contact with his own children. In the example of teaching, more experienced teachers tend to be more credible.

Research for the Real World

In this chapter, we learned that that past 200 years has been a period of increased public awareness about the development of infants. In the United States, this has been accompanied by a rise in federal assistance programs to benefit infants and children. Some of these are shown in Table 1.3. It was not always this way. The United States was founded on basic principles of self-reliance and upon the idea that parents had both the responsibility and the right to raise their children without undue intervention from the government. Legally,

TABLE 1.3 Federal Programs in the United States to Assist Infants & Their Families

Program	Purpose
Medicaid (for Low-Income Families)	Covers costs of prenatal care for mothers and postnatal for infants but not their parents.
Supplemental Nutrition for Women, Infants, and Children (WIC, for Low-Income Families)	Provides food vouchers up to 5 years old.
Temporary Assistance to Needy Families (TANF)	Provides some financial support to families of children under 3 years old.
Earned Income Tax Credit	Prrovides tax relief for working but poor families.
State programs of child welfare	Prevents or protects children from abuse and neglect.
Early Head Start	Promotes early child development for poor children under 3 years old.
Parental Leave	In firms of 50 employees or more, parents can take up to 12 weeks off work without penalty but usually without pay.

Source: (Barrett, 2001; Phillips, D., & McCarthy, K. (2005). *The disconnect between research and policy on child care*. New York: Cambridge University Press.

children are viewed as the possessions of their parents, and the government may only interfere with families in extreme circumstances of abuse and neglect. This legal concept, called *parens patriae,* was part of English common law originating in the fifteenth century.

The effects of *parens patriae* can be seen in the history of public welfare in the United States. The first nursery schools, day care centers, and public health programs in the United States were established in the nineteenth century. The state Boards of Charity, begun in 1863, were the first government welfare institutions. They provided protection from abuse for children living in orphanages and working in factories, but not for those living at home with parents. Two White House conferences on children, in 1909 and 1930, led to the creation of the Social Security Acts of the 1930s, which established a retirement pension for older people, a welfare system, aid to dependent children, and financial and rehabilitation services for needy children and their families. Because of the ideals of self-reliance and *parens patriae,* the government confined its protective activities to the most needy segments of society.

In contrast, there are very few government programs to guarantee high quality health care and education for the majority of children under 3 years (Lippit, 2001). Few states have such standards for day care, and there is no national day care policy. In the later twentieth century, national and state legislatures passed laws to provide, as a basic right, parental leave policies so that parents (men and women) with young infants may take up to six weeks of *unpaid* time off from work after their baby is born without fear of losing their jobs.

Although few programs provide direct benefits to families with infants, tax money is used to benefit families in some indirect ways. Corporations receive income tax deductions for providing on-site day care centers. Parents can deduct the cost of child care from their incomes, thereby reducing their overall income tax burden. This, however, is not much of a help to families in which both parents have to work just to get by. They often cannot afford child care of good quality, and the lack of legal standards encourages the proliferation of poor-quality day care.

In many ways, the United States is unique among the developed countries of the world in its reluctance to support infant development as a national policy. Infant health care, proper nutrition, clean and well-managed child care that is affordable, and paid parental leave policies have all been publicly supported by law with tax funds for many years in such countries as France, Sweden, China, and Japan.

In those countries, there is no argument that all infants and children are in the national trust, that they are the most valuable resources a society has, and that all families with infants and children deserve encouragement and government support. In the United States, these issues are controversial because of the fear that government will impinge on the rights of individuals and families. In the United States, it seems that the damage done daily to the mental and physical health of millions of poor and homeless and even some middle-income infants and children is the price we are willing to pay for our frontier-day notions of personal freedom and self-reliance.

In the absence of a set of nationally recognized values in support of infants and children, private-sector advocacy groups that speak out for children's rights have formed at the local, state, and national level. Most of their members are volunteers, and they are supported entirely by private funds. Child and family advocacy has become an important part of the social and political fabric of the United States. Professional advocates—whose salaries are paid by the organizations—work with volunteers, parents, child care professionals, and researchers to make phone calls, prepare position papers, and contact lawmakers. Not all these advocacy groups have similar positions. Some want more funds for day care centers, while others want tax breaks to allow parents to stay home and raise their own children.

While some advocacy groups are founded on religious or cultural values, other groups seek the support of scientific findings that speak directly to the need of infants. Although there are many thousands of research studies on infants, it is rare to find studies of infants in the real world, taking account of the complex interdependent relationships between family income and cultural background, parental work, community resources, the growth of brain and behavior, and childrens' special needs. More research is needed that takes a bioecological systems perspective in which all these factors in the family ecology are taken into account (Phillips & McCartney, 2005; Yoshikawa & Hsueh, 2001). Research on intervention programs becomes especially difficult and costly because there are a vast range of individual, community, religious, and cultural factors that may influence how an intervention program can be implemented with success or failure (see Chapter 12; McCall, 2009).

Advocates and other policy makers in the public and private sectors, however, have different priorities than researchers. These are shown in Table 1.4. This means that researchers must learn to become more "political" about promoting their work for policy makers, and that policy makers need to better appreciate the usefulness of the knowledge gained from scientists. Most scientific professional organizations whose members study infant development, such as the Society for Research in Child Development (www.srcd.org) and the American Psychological Association (www.apa.org), have their own advocates who work with lawmakers to help translate the findings of research into working public policies.

There are advantages and disadvantages when political and economic agendas affect the types of research being done and the types of services provided to communities. Much of the funding for research and intervention on infant development comes from the government and from private foundations, both of which may have political agendas depending on who is in charge. Sometimes politics can promote research in areas that have been neglected, such as the National Institute of Health (www.nih.gov) guidelines for researchers to be inclusive across racial, ethnic and gender categories.

Sometimes political agendas can obscure and direct attention away from pressing needs. The United Nations has been a strong promoter of taking a global perspective on human development, with special emphasis on poor countries that lack clean water, proper infant nutrition, and health care, and may be suffering from the post-traumatic stresses of years of warfare, genocide, and deprivation. The United Nations takes the view that health and welfare of developing infants and children are the best measures of a nation's wealth (Thérien, 2012; http://www.un.org/cyberschoolbus/humanrights/resources/plainchild.asp). The United Nations, however, has relatively little money to implement intervention and research in these areas. Within a wealthy country, taxpayers influence politicians to spend their money on local and national causes. Although some wealthy

TABLE 1.4   Differences Between Policy Makers and Scientists

Policy Makers	Scientists
Serve their constituencies	Seek the "truth"
Act and decide	Understand and explain
Based on relationships between key players	Nonpersonal, unbiased
Based on power and influence	Based on knowledge
Immediate actions	Long-term work
Mistakes are punished	Rewarded for experimenting
Communication is oral	Communication is written and reviewed

Source: Maton, K., & Bishop-Josef, S. (2006). Psychological research, practice, and social policy; Potential pathways of influence. *Professional Psychology: Research & Practice, 37(*2), 140–145; Solarz, A. (2001). Investing in children, families, and communities: Challenges for an interdivisional public policy. *American Journal of Community Psychology, 29*(1), 1.

nations do contribute to alleviating the effects of poverty on a global scale, the gap between rich and poor continues to widen. Private foundations—such as the Bill and Melinda Gates Foundation, dedicated to improving health in poor countries www.gatesfoundation.org)—may arise to fill some of these needs, but in the short term the economics of private enterprise tend to win out over the reality of human suffering.

SUMMARY

The Importance of Infancy

- Prenatal and infant development are frequent topics in the news, on television, and in the movies today.
- The more a parent knows about infants and children, the lower his or her anxiety will be, and the better the outcomes will be for the child.
- Infancy is a unique stage in the life course. This is not only because it is the earliest stage of life, but because all life's stages are unique.
- The preverbal experience of the body is uniquely human. After infancy, many physical and mental disorders of children and adults can be traced to a person's losing touch with his or her own body.
- Because of the vulnerability of infants, many social and medical problems could be prevented by making sure that infants receive proper care and that young parents receive all the support necessary to provide the best environment for their children.
- Many differences between people during the prenatal and infancy periods have a lasting impact on later individual differences.

A Brief History of Babies

- During all periods of recorded history, some infants and children have received love and care while others have been abused or neglected.
- Beginning in the Middle Ages, urbanization brought about changes in the family and in the health and safety of infants.
- In the eighteenth century, the ideas of romanticism and empiricism marked the beginning of philosophical and educational efforts directed toward infants.
- In the nineteenth century, the development of the nuclear family, along with advances in infant medical care, led to the discovery of infancy as an important period in the life course.

The Scientific Perspective on Infancy

- In the nineteenth and twentieth centuries, infants became the subjects of scientific study sparked by the debate over whether nature or nurture has the most influence on behavioral development.
- On the nature side, species evolve by natural selection in which the individuals who are best adapted to their environment can reproduce and pass their genes onto the next generation.
- Critical periods are times in early development when the fetus or infant is particularly susceptible to environmental influence, and on which all later learning and development depend.
- On the nurture side two types of learning processes were studied by scientists in the twentieth century.
- Classical conditioning is learning by association that occurs when unconditioned and conditioned stimuli are paired during training.
- Operant conditioning occurs when the frequency of behavior is controlled by its consequences: reinforcement, punishment, and extinction.
- Freud introduced the idea that infants have an emotional life.
- The Piagetian constructivist approach suggests that infants are intelligent by means of their own explorations in the world. Infant intelligence is of a sensorimotor rather than a verbal-symbolic form.
- Developmental changes are nonreversible and permanent, and they occur in a sequence.
- The division of infancy into stages of development is somewhat arbitrary and depends on the purposes of the culture or group.

Systems Perspectives on Infant Development

- A system is a set of interdependent components, each of which affects the others in reciprocal fashion. The process by which systems components affect each other is known as transaction.
- Bio-ecological systems theory suggests that infant development is related in direct and indirect ways to the family and to society, and vice versa.
- Dynamic systems theory introduces elements of self-organization and indeterminacy into the process of

development. Individual differences are not always predictable as a direct result of particular causes, but rather emerge creatively as part of the complex dynamics of action.

Research Methods in Developmental Science

- Scientists rely on many sources of evidence, try to separate what is repeatable and stable from what is coincidental, and attempt to rid observations of bias.

- An experiment is a research study in which one aspect of the situation is manipulated while all other aspects are held constant or controlled.

- The independent variable is that which is controlled or manipulated by the experimenter. The independent variable is the presumed cause of the phenomenon. The dependent variable is the outcome behavior that is observed in response to the changes in the independent variable.

- Methods that rely on natural variations rather than random assignment to create contrast groups are called observational research methods.

- Longitudinal studies follow the same children at different ages, while cross-sectional studies use different children at different ages.

- In observational studies, the variable that is the presumed cause is called the predictor variable. The pre-sumed effect is called the outcome variable. There is an analogy between independent variables and predictor variables, and between dependent variables and outcome variables.

- Bias is reduced in research by attention to reliability, validity, observer bias, and representativeness.

- Because infants cannot provide informed consent to participate in research, their parents must do so. Researchers need to observe ethical guidelines when using human subjects in research.

- Qualitative research does not use quantity or number. It is characterized by one or both of the following features: (1) the observers focus on the meaning of the situation for the participants; and (2) the role of the researcher in the situation is explicitly taken into account.

- Qualitative researchers' credibility depends upon their skill, experience, and rigor.

- Societies differ in how much of their public funds go to the welfare of children and their families.

- Advocates in a democratic society must participate in the process of changing local, state, and federal programs and policies regarding infant and family development.

- Researchers and policy makers need to better understand their differences to work together for the benefit of children and their families.

Chapter 2

Prenatal Development: From Conception to Childbirth

CHAPTER OUTLINE AND OVERVIEW

Conception and Fertility

What is the process of fertilization? What causes infertility and how can it be treated? What are the most common methods of contraception? How is the birth rate controlled in different countries? Do cultural differences affect choices of contraceptive methods?

Developmental Processes Before Birth

What are the stages of prenatal development? What are the main behavioral, physical, and psychological characteristics of each stage?

The Childbirth Experience

What is the process of labor and delivery? What are the common methods of childbirth?

Although many people think of birth as the beginning of life, it is now known that much of what takes place in the nine-month period before birth has important effects on subsequent development. During prenatal development, all of the major organ systems of the body, including the brain, undergo rapid development. This chapter will cover the normal development of the fetus from conception until the last month of pregnancy, followed by a discussion of childbirth.

CONCEPTION AND FERTILITY

Human development begins with **conception**, the union of a female **ovum** and a male **spermatozoon**. Collectively, spermatozoa and ova are known as **gametes**. During sexual intercourse, many millions of sperm cells enter the vagina. These cells are propelled through the uterus and into the Fallopian tubes, partly by the pumping action of the vaginal and uterine muscles and partly by the swimming movements of the spermatozoa. Only a few hundred sperm cells will reach the Fallopian tubes, and even those will die if they do not encounter an ovum within 24 to 48 hours.

Ova are produced in the ovaries, usually one for each menstrual cycle. Adult females will have about 350 ovulations over approximately 30 years of fertility. The ovum is covered with small hairlike appendages that can be dissolved by an enzyme secreted by the spermatozoa, and the ovum eventually decomposes if it does not encounter a sperm cell. For fertilization to take place, many spermatozoa must bind to the surface of the ovum, after which an opening is made at random for the entrance of a single sperm cell. Once that sperm cell enters the ovum, a chemical reaction occurs to prevent other sperm cells from entering. The fertilized ovum is called a **zygote**.

Within the cell nucleus, the **genotype** or genetic material is in a spiral-shaped molecule called deoxyribonucleic acid (**DNA**). The DNA is segmented into sections, each of which contains a different set of molecular codes. Each of these sections is called a **gene**. The genes are arranged in long strings, much like beads on a necklace, into structures called **chromosomes**. Most chromosomes look like the letter X. The X is made up of two strands of DNA that are joined near their middle, each strand containing many genes (see Figure 2.1).

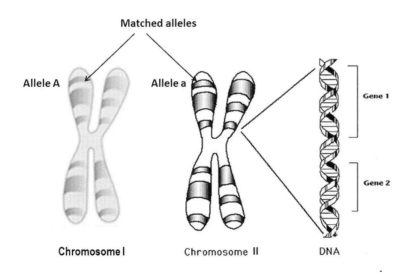

Figure 2.1

Chromosomes are composed of two very long strands of crossed DNA in the shape of an X. Each branch of the chromosomes is divided into segments called genes. Some of the genes that combine to create specific characteristics—such as hair or eye color—are located next to each other into a region of a chromosome. These regions of related genes are called alleles. Chromosomes typically work in pairs. To create a particular hair color, for example, alleles from one chromosome need to connect to their matched partners on the other chromosome, in this case allele A from Chromosome I works together with allele a from Chromosome II.

Except for the gametes which contain only 23 chromosomes, every cell in one's body contains 46 chromosomes, representing about 1 million genes. Chromosomes come in matched pairs, as shown in Figure 2.1 as chromosome I and chromosome II. Half of each pair comes from the individual's mother and the other half comes from the individual's father. Except for the gametes, each cell in a person's body contains exactly the same set of genes and chromosomes. The 46 chromosomes in each cell represent 23 pairs. The 23rd pair contains the genetic code for a male vs. female. Female genotypes contain a matched pair of XX in the 23rd pair, while male genotypes have an X combined with a Y-shaped chromosome (see Figure 2.2).

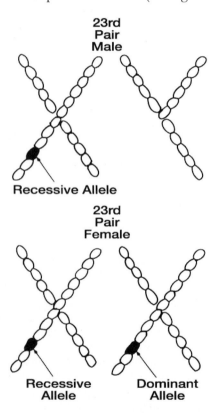

Figure 2.2 Sex-Linked Inheritance

The male Y chromosome is missing dominant alleles that are found on the lower left-hand branch of the female's X chromosome.

Source: A. Fogel & G. F. Melson, *Child development*, 1988, p. 89. St. Paul, MN: West. © West Publishing Company. Reprinted by permission. All rights reserved.

Most of the cells in the body, except for the gametes, grow by **mitosis**, dividing into two identical daughter cells. During mitosis, each chromosome within the cell nucleus makes an exact copy of itself before cell division occurs. The original set of chromosomes and their identical copies do not get mixed up: each set pushes away from the other until they occupy opposite sides of the nucleus. The cell will divide into two new cells only after this physical separation of the two identical sets of chromosomes occurs (McIntosh & Koonce, 1989), thus preserving the identical DNA in each new cell.

Genes rarely act alone in determining a physical or behavioral characteristic, called the **phenotype**. Most phenotypes are derived from **polygenic inheritance**; that is, they arise from the action of a combination of genes. Some of the genes that combine to create specific characteristics—such as skin, hair or eye color—are located next to each other in a region of a chromosome. These regions of related genes are called **alleles**. Chromosomes typically work in pairs. To create a particular hair color, for example, alleles from one chromosome (from the mother) need to connect to their matched partners on the other chromosome (from the father). This is shown in Figure 2.1. With a polygenic characteristic such as skin color, a number of genes from the mother combine with an equal number from the father, and the offspring's skin color is likely to be somewhere between the skin colors of the parents. Children in the same family may exhibit a range of skin colors.

In the past, it was believed that some phenotypic characteristics were inherited by a simple two-allele combination called **dominant-recessive inheritance**. Eye color is one example. The dominant allele (the one related to brown eyes) will always be expressed, even in the presence of a recessive mate (the allele for blue eyes). Thus, a person with brown eyes might actually carry a recessive allele for blue eyes, and two brown-eyed parents could produce a blue-eyed child if the zygote happens to contain two blue recessive alleles and no brown dominant allele. It takes two recessive genes for a trait to appear in the phenotype. The dominant trait appears in the phenotype, however, if only one dominant gene is present, either from the mother or from the father, or if both genes are dominant. Therefore, the dominant characteristic will appear in the phenotype 75 percent of the time.

Because of polygenic inheritance, it is rare for only one or two genes to determine a phenotype in this simple dominant-recessive pattern. Even characteristics that are strongly influenced by a pattern of dominant-recessive inheritance act along with other genes to produce the phenotype. Therefore, eye color, like skin color, comes in many different shades and variations—the typical signature of polygenic inheritance.

Another pattern of inheritance relates to those characteristics that are displayed differentially between the sexes. **Sex-linked inheritance** relates to phenotypes that are tied to genes that appear on the 23rd chromosome (see Figure 2.2). Genetic males have an X and a Y chromosome as their 23rd pair. Not only is the Y chromosome missing one of its arms compared to the X chromosome, but the Y is also considerably smaller than the X. For this reason, one might think that women would have more sex-linked characteristics than men, but this is not the case. For females, the alleles on the X chromosome will express themselves in interaction with their matched alleles on the other X chromosome of the 23rd pair. For males, alleles on the X chromosome of the 23rd pair will express themselves in the absence of an interaction with a matched allele.

Sex-linked inheritance produces primary (genitals) and secondary (facial hair, body shape, etc.) sexual characteristics in males and females. Other sex-linked characteristics are baldness, color blindness, and a disorder of blood clotting processes called hemophilia, all of which occur primarily in males.

In most cases, these latter sex-linked characteristics are caused by a recessive allele on the X chromosome. If the recessive allele is paired with a dominant allele on another X chromosome, that dominant allele will override the influence of the recessive gene. Recall that it takes two recessive genes to produce the characteristic in the phenotype. Females are thus less likely to display the phenotype for baldness because they can inherit both the dominant and recessive allele. A male who inherits a recessive allele for baldness on his X chromosome will not have the corresponding dominant allele on his Y chromosome—there is no site for it to occupy (see Figure 2.2)—and thus is more likely to show baldness in the phenotype. Because the X chromosome in the male's 23rd pair always comes from his mother (Y chromosomes are produced only by males), women are the carriers of these sex-linked characteristics. A male is more likely to have a hairline like his maternal grandfather than like his own father (McClearn, 1970).

Even though every cell in one's body has the same genotype, every individual has a slightly different set of genes, that person's particular genotype. This between-individual genetic variability arises during the creation of the gametes. In the special biological environment of the female ovaries and the male testicles, cells divide by **meiosis** in which the chromosome pairs split and each new cell gets only one half of the pair, leaving each daughter cell—the gamete—with only 23 chromosomes. In a process called **recombination**, just before the chromosome pairs separate, some of the alleles from one member of the pair will change places with another member of the pair. In Figure 2.1, for example, alleles *A* and *a* might change places so that now allele *A* is located on chromosome II and allele *a* moves over to chromosome I.

During ordinary meiosis, many genes will recombine to create a unique set of chromosomes which have a different combination of alleles than the prospective parent in whose ovaries or testes this process is taking place. In addition, every gamete in that parent will have a slightly different arrangement of genes and alleles. When the zygote forms during fertilization, it will combine one of these recombinant gametes from the mother and one from the father into a new cell with 46 chromosomes, 23 pairs. Each zygote will have a completely unique genetic make-up, related to but in some ways different from, each of the parents. This explains how siblings can be genetically different from each other and from the parents. The zygote will divide by mitosis, meaning that all the resulting cells for the rest of that person's life—except for the gametes—will have exactly the same genetic makeup.

The ability to contribute successfully to fertilization or conception is called **fertility**. Male fertility begins at puberty and, for most males, lasts their entire life. Female fertility begins at puberty and lasts until menopause, the cessation of menstrual cycling that occurs when the woman is about 50 years old.

All of a girl's ova are already formed in her ovary during prenatal development, but they remain immature until the girl reaches puberty and begins to menstruate. In other words, any children this girl has will have spent nine months inside their grandmother's body. Near the end of each menstrual period, the time during the menstrual cycle when vaginal bleeding occurs, the pituitary gland secretes a hormone that allows one of the immature ova to ripen. This event leads to the secretion of estrogen, which stimulates the development of a lining in the uterus that will nourish a possible fertilized ovum. About 14 days after the onset of the menstrual period, the ovum is ready to be fertilized as it makes its way from the ovary to the Fallopian tubes. The zygote will journey to the uterus, where it becomes implanted in the newly formed uterine lining. If fertilization does not occur, the uterine lining and ovum are discharged through the vagina during the next menstrual period.

In some cases, more than one ovum ripens. If two ova are fertilized, two different zygotes, called fraternal or **dizygotic (DZ) twins**, develop, each of whom have different DNA. Identical or **monozygotic (MZ) twins** develop when the fertilized zygote divides and splits into two separate zygotes both with the same DNA. Twinning happens in about 1 in 80 pregnancies. About three-fourths of the twins are DZ twins, and the rest are MZ twins. Since they split from the same zygote, MZ twins share identical sets of genetic material, while DZ twins are no more related than any two siblings from the same mother and father. Genetic samples

taken from adult MZ twins, however, sometimes reveal differences in their DNA (see page 44). Triplets occur in 1 out of 6,400 births, while quadruplets happen in 1 out of 512,000 births. Triplets and quadruplets can be either MZ or DZ or some combination.

In recent years, the rate of multiple births has increased due to the growing use of drugs that enhance fertility in females (see Chapter 3 for more details about treatments for infertility). In countries with high rates of usage of fertility drugs, the DZ rate has tripled between 1972 and 1999 while the trizygotic (triplet) rate has increased on average by 10 times. MZ birth rates, however, have remained constant, meaning that the fertility drugs increase the likelihood of multiple ova being released during a fertility cycle (Imaizumi, 2003).

Boys at birth have a set of undifferentiated gametes in their testes, called spermatogonia. The onset of puberty in the male triggers the production of hormones that stimulate the conversion of spermatogonia into fully mature spermatozoa, producing about 2 million sperm cells per day for the rest of the man's life. Male fertility, therefore, is not cyclic like female fertility. During ejaculation, 40 to 500 million sperm cells are expelled through the penis in a liquid medium called seminal fluid or semen. The testes produce the sperm, and the prostate gland and seminal vesicles produce the semen.

Controlling Fertility: Contraception and Family Planning

At the end of 2011 the world had an estimated population of 7 billion people (U.S. Census Bureau, 2009. http://www.census.gov/main/www.popclock.html). This is more than double the number of people alive in 1960 and more than triple the world population in 1927. Although the rate of population growth is slowing, there are likely to be twice as many people alive in 2030 as there are today. Experts do not know how many people the earth can support, especially since global climate changes will bring unpredictable alterations to food production. Most experts are concerned about the quality of life that will result. Although some of the growth is due to the fact that people are healthier and living longer than in the past, much of the population increase is due to high birthrates.

Family planning is the voluntary alteration of normal reproductive patterns using contraception methods. The type of family planning used, if it is used at all, depends on a complex network of social and cultural factors interacting with moral and interpersonal factors within the family. In wealthy countries, family planning is a matter of personal choice for middle- and upper-income families. Family planning becomes a critical issue when the population of a family or a whole country exceeds the ability of the available resources to provide for the health and welfare of the children that are newly born.

Contraception. One of the simplest and least expensive methods of contraception for family planning is called **natural family planning**. The same methods used to chart ovulation for the purpose of enhancing fertility can also tell a couple when to avoid intercourse if they wish not to conceive. If used properly and with the guidance of a physician or family planning counselor, natural family planning can be very successful but it is not foolproof.

A number of more reliable options for contraception are also available. Methods that work prior to fertilization include male or female sterilization, which prevents the production or transport of gametes (used by 15 percent of couples); birth control pills, patches, implants, or injections, which prevent ovulation using hormones (used by 39 percent); condoms and diaphragms, which block the passage of sperm to the vagina (used by 25 percent); and spermicides (foams, sponges, and suppositories), which kill sperm before they can fertilize and are often used in combination with other methods (Forrest & Fordyce, 1993b).

Several other methods are used, but with somewhat higher risk for conception. Breast feeding can suppress ovulation but typically only if the mother exclusively breast feeds, which is usually for no more than 6 months, and if menstruation has not yet resumed. Withdrawal of the penis prior to ejaculation is also used to prevent sperm from entering the vagina, but some sperm may be expelled prior to ejaculation. If the withdrawal method is always used prior to ejaculation, the pregnancy rate is about 4 percent, only slightly higher than the pregnancy rate for condoms (2 percent). If practiced rigorously, withdrawal has a similar rate of effectiveness as using a condom. All these methods work better if couples carefully follow guidelines, but most couples are more lax, increasing the risk of conception from under 4 percent in most cases to as much as 20 to 35 percent (Jones et al., 2009).

Several methods that work after fertilization are also available. The intrauterine device (IUD) prevents the zygote from implanting in the uterine wall. Several "emergency" contraception procedures, also known as "morning after" pills, are available for women who engage in unprotected sexual intercourse. A drug known as RU-486 causes the uterine lining to be expelled, taking the embryo with it; the pill must be followed two days later by an additional drug that causes the uterus to contract and complete the expulsion process. There is also the Preven Kit, approved by the FDA in 1997. It is a series of birth control pills taken for up to 5 days within 72 hours after having unprotected sex. Each of these methods has advantages and disadvantages that depend upon one's religious beliefs, values, convenience, and medical conditions and risks.

On August 24, 2006, the United States Food and Drug Administration ruled that customers over the age of 18 should be able to buy these pills—currently marketed under the name of *Plan B*—without the need for a prescription. Some advocacy groups have worked to ensure access of *Plan B* to rape survivors, military women, and to a variety of pro-choice and family planning organizations. Other groups, based on religious values, seek to reverse the FDA ruling, and some pharmacies have declined to stock the item. In June 2013, the FDA approved the over-the-counter sale of Plan B One-Step with no age restrictions, although older versions of the drug still require a prescription for people under 18. Women and their partners should consult their doctors or family planning clinics for more specific advice and information including risks and side effects (http://women.webmd.com/guide/plan-b).

Cultural perspectives on family planning. Within families in the United States, estimates show that up to 40 percent of all births are unintended, either by being mistimed or unwanted. The rate varies widely, with states in New England at about 35 percent and states such as California, New York, and Florida at around 65 percent (Finer & Henshaw, 2006). In a study of about 6,000 children in the United States, children and mothers from unintended pregnancies fared worse that those whose pregnancies were intended, including maternal depression, lower self-esteem, poor mother-child emotional communication, and in some cases, abuse. Furthermore, unintended births put stress on the whole family such that cognitive, emotional, and economic resources are less available for all children in that family (Barber & East, 2009). Family planning, therefore, may be essential to promote parent and child mental and physical health.

The World Health Organization reports that about one-quarter of pregnancies worldwide are unwanted, and about 50 million of them end in abortion each year. Countries can be divided into two groups based on whether they have low or high population growth rates. In countries with low growth rates, the population increases by about 1 percent each year. The United States falls into this group. In high-growth countries, the population may increase as much as 3 percent per year, doubling every 25 years or so. This high rate of growth increases the chances of pregnancy and birth complications, prematurity, maternal and infant mortality, and a continuation of the cycle of poverty.

Family planning is a controversial issue in the United States. Many people believe that sex education should occur in the home and not in schools, while others oppose publically funded family planning clinics that dispense birth control and also offer consultations related to abortion. Research shows, however, that sex education and public family planning clinics reduce both the number of unwanted children and the number of abortions. This is partly because accurate information about conception and pregnancy can help people make more informed choices, and also because family planning clinics also offer routine women's health care, including prenatal care, that help women maintain reproductive health (Gold et al., 2009, at http://www.guttmacher.org/pubs/NextSteps.pdf).

India, for example, has one-third the area of the United States but three times the population. A significant proportion of the people are illiterate and live in rural areas below the poverty level. They have inadequate food, shelter, and clothing. There is active resistance to family planning, because these families depend for their livelihood on large numbers of children. In the 1970s, India passed a law requiring sterilization for all parents with two or more children who wanted to continue receiving welfare. Although the law was repealed in 1977, sterilization remains the most common form of birth control in India. The voluntary use of other contraception methods (see below) has increased, but not sufficiently to halt the population growth (Kumar, 1994).

China has been more successful in reducing its high birthrate. China has about the same area as the United States, but it has five times as many people. In the past 30 years, however, the Chinese have reduced their birthrate to 1 percent per year by allowing only one child per family (Feeney, 1994). The one-child policy is implemented by granting those who comply more vacation time and more welfare benefits. Elderly women in each village, called "granny police," are charged with counseling and disciplining women who wish to have a second child (Galvin, 1989; Associated Press, 1985).

Estimates are that by 2020, China will have 30 million more males than females, while India and Pakistan face similar male surpluses. Many of these males are now young men, and they are facing a shortage of eligible women to marry. There have also been major social and psychological consequences. There is a reported increase in social violence and homosexuality (Hudson & den Boer, 2004). Only children born under the one-child policy in the two-year period following its implementation in 1979 have been shown to be less trusting, less trustworthy, more risk-averse, less competitive, more pessimistic, and less conscientious individuals compared to children born in the two year period before the policy was implemented (http://esciencenews.com/articles/2013/0110/the.effects.chinas.one.child.policy.its.children).

A change in government policy allows families whose first child is a female to have the opportunity for a second child (Coale & Banister, 1994). A recent change in the One Child Law is a provision that couples who were both without siblings may have two children legally (Rosenberg, 2009; China's One Child Policy, http://geography.about.com/odd/populationgeography/a/onechild.htm). As China's working age population will peak in 2012 and begin to decrease thereafter, there may be more room for families to have more children in the future.

Other Asian countries, such as Taiwan, Japan, and Korea, have also reduced their birthrates to 1 percent per year. In these countries, the change was due not to government policy, but rather to trends toward increased modernization over the past 30 years. With modernization, more people move to the cities where they become better educated and have access to better health care. As a result, the infant mortality rate declines, and more children in the family survive and require financial support. Families therefore voluntarily limit the number of children they choose to have through various contraceptive procedures, including sterilization (Feeney, 1994; Thike, Wai, Oo, & Yi, 1993).

In many African countries, such as the Ivory Coast, where the population is growing at 4 percent per year, women have as many as seven children, and as the infant mortality rate has declined, the population has increased drastically (Remez, 1996). Women use birth control to space births rather than to reduce the number of children. In some African countries, oral contraceptives are believed to be harmful, and in others, religious taboos against touching one's own genitals prevent the use of condoms and diaphragms. Some new birth control devices are proving highly effective, however. One device is a skin implant similar to birth control pills that prevents conception for 5 years and has been well accepted in cultures that use skin scarification as a beauty practice. Injections of birth control hormones work in areas where people have come to associate injections with good health. The use of female, but not male, sterilization is also becoming more accepted (C. Holden, 1988; Jack & Chao, 1992; Were & Karanja, 1994).

On the whole, it seems that culturally adapted interventions work the best, and that education of the people is a necessary ingredient in a successful family planning program. These cultural differences have an impact on the type of sex education offered to young people.

DEVELOPMENTAL PROCESSES BEFORE BIRTH

A Simple Lump of Jelly

Every individual begins life as a zygote that progresses through the initial stages of cell division by mitosis. As a result of mitosis, the number of cells in the developing organism grows rapidly, doubling every few hours. Because mitosis is an exact copying process, each of these cells has the same genetic material. How, then, can the same set of genes create different types of cells in the body? In fact, how does a body form instead of just a huge glob of cells that are all the same?

One of the great mysteries of early development is how, given identical genes in each cell, the different tissues and structures—muscles, blood, sensory receptors, and so on—can develop. The biologist Waddington expressed it thus:

a simple lump of jelly… eventually turns into a recognizable small plant or worm or insect or some other type of organism. Nothing else that one can see puts on a performance which is both so apparently simple and spontaneous and yet, when you think about it, so mysterious. (Waddington, 1966, p. v)

To find some solutions to this mystery, we have to go outside the cell and examine its environment. Research on nonhuman prenatal development has shown that in almost all species of animals, the cells of the zygote form a spherelike cluster (Sameroff, 1984). Because some of the cells are on the surface and some on the interior of the sphere, these different regions are in contact with different environments. The interior cells are next to other cells like themselves, while the exterior cells will have cells like themselves on one side, and be in contact with the cells of the uterine environment on the other side. Each of these environments exposes the cell to different molecules that may be transported into a cell from its neighboring cells. In addition, physical forces on the cell—interior cells have a higher pressure surrounding them—will also affect what happens inside the cell.

In addition to the genome of the cell, the DNA, each cell also has an **epigenome**, a set of biochemical markers that are responsive to the environment and that can activate or silence the actions of particular genes within the DNA of each cell. The epigentic molecules attach to certain regions of the DNA to activate some of the cell's genes and inhibit the action of others. When particular genes are activated, they begin to send specific chemical messages back out to the main cell body, changing the cell's structural characteristics. Although every cell in the body has the genes to become a bone cell, to take one example, only certain cells become bone depending on the epigenetic processes in their local environment. This is the beginning of the process of differentiation of the properties of the interior cells from those of the exterior cells.

Even though MZ twins have identical genotypes, they often turn out to have differences in habits, behaviors, and health issues. As identical twins age, they each get exposed to different environments such as through differences in liv-

ing conditions, diet, exercise, and environmental toxins. It has been found that differences in health and behavior outcomes between MZ twins are associated with differences in their epigenetic markers (Bruder et al., 2008; Curley et al., 2011; van Ijzendoorn et al., 2011).

As cell division proceeds, cells form groups in which distinct molecular processes occur and in which particular groups of genes are active. Boundaries form between the different groups that prevent the processes of one group from leaking into another (Trevarthen, 1973). Thus, the development of the phenotype—the cell's specific characteristic as, for example, neuron or muscle—is the result of a constant and dynamic interaction between the genotype, the epigenome, and the intra- and extracellular environment (Meany, 2010).

The effect of the cell's environment has been shown in a series of experiments on nonhuman embryos. Early in the process of the formation of different regions, cells can be removed from one region and placed in an entirely different one. After a few cell divisions, the transplanted cells resemble the region in which they were placed, not the region that they came from (Spemann, 1938; Ebert & Sussex, 1970). At this stage of development, the cells can literally shift shape and composition to become like the other cells around them. These are the **embryonic stem cells** that may hold the promise of regenerating damaged or diseased tissues when transplanted from embryos into older children and adults who no longer have stem cells in their bodies (Sharon, 2011). *The important point to remember is that even though every cell in the embryo has the same genes, because the epigenome is responsive to the local environment, different genes become active in different types of cells.*

As cells begin to differentiate into distinct regions, physical structures begin to form. The most common type of embryonic structure is the formation of a tube. Figure 2.3 shows how this occurs. In (a), cells on the top of the sheet have been genetically activated to reproduce cells with the ability to stretch. Cells on the bottom of the sheet have been activated with a different set of genes to produce contraction. As cells divide and

(a)

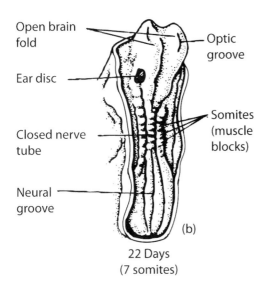

Open brain fold

Optic groove

Ear disc

Closed nerve tube

Somites (muscle blocks)

Neural groove

(b)

22 Days
(7 somites)

Figure 2.3 Creation of a Structure

(a) During the process of cell differentiation, some cells begin to create structures. The early formation of a tube with holes is shown. The cells become less elastic on one side and more elastic on the other, causing the sheet of cells to bend. Differential rigidity around the region of the holes can create spaces between cells. **(b)** In the 22-day-old embryo, such a tube structure will eventually become the spinal cord and spine.

Source: C. Trevarthen, Neurological development and the growth of the psychological functions, 1980. In J. Sants, *Developmental psychology and society*, 46–95. New York: St. Martin's Press. Copyright © by J. Sants. Reprinted by permission of St. Martin's Press, Inc.

are also instances in which certain structures form only to disappear at a later point. The types of developmental changes that occur all during prenatal development are as follows (Meredith, 1975):

Changes in kind. One of the most noticeable prenatal changes is the gradual differentiation of multiple kinds of tissue from the relatively uniform zygote. Certain structures also emerge and disappear. For example, the pronephros, the precursor of the kidney, is only there for 2 weeks, fish-like gill arches are present for three weeks, an external tail appears and disappears between the second and fourth months, and finger pads are seen between the third and fifth months.

Changes in number. Depending upon the particular structure or organ, cell numbers increase and decrease over time. Obviously, the overall number of cells continues to increase.

Changes in position. The relative orientation and position of the organs in the fetus change. When the heart is formed, for example, it lies near what will become the face. Over time it moves lower, more toward the back, and rotates and tilts. Other organs and limbs undertake their own particular paths of migration.

Changes in size. Changes in size vary with the time and location of the organ. Dur-

increased differential stretching and contracting occur, the sheet eventually curls into a tube. Tubes can also be formed when a ball of cells contracts in the center, eventually making a kind of doughnut shape. In all animals, the first tube formed is the gut. In vertebrate animals, one of the early-forming tubular structures is the spinal cord and spine (see Figure 2.3(*b*)). These tubes become organs, veins, cavities, skulls, and other body containers. These shapes are not simply a result of genetic programming, but rather the epigenetic effects of the physical properties of sheets of cells as they fold and bend and collide with each other, thereby affecting which genes become active within the cell (Fleury, 2011).

It is usually assumed that prenatal development is a continuous series of acquisitions along the road to maturity. Prenatal development does show a number of aspects that are continuous, but there ing the second month, the head and neck regions grow faster (cephalocaudal development), there is more growth near the spine than in the front (dorsoventral development), and the growth rate is higher near the shoulders and hips than near the extremities (proximodistal development). As development proceeds, these trends reverse.

Changes in shape. Immediately after fertilization, the organism has an oval shape. Several weeks later, its shape is elongated and is mostly head. There are also changes in the shape of cells and organs.

The problem in thinking in terms of conflicting forces of nature vs. nurture is that, according to research and theory reviewed in this chapter, "genes" and "environments" don't exist in the way that they were conceptualized in the nineteenth and twentieth centuries: they are not separate entities that shape development. They are both always present and always working together. Here are some facts about genetics and environments that you may not know.

Genes are always doing things in our bodies, every second of every day, throughout our lives. They don't just operate prenatally.

The genes we inherit in the sperm and ovum of our parents are not "pure" genetic material: they already carry epigenetic markers that have been created by the environment our parents lived in, before, during, and after conception.

Genes do not directly create outward characteristics like eye color or depression. There are literally hundreds of microbiological steps—each affected by the environment within and outside the body—that must happen to create an eye color or a mood state.

Anything can happen in this chain of bio-environmental steps leading to an outcome that may not have been predicted based on any simple notions of one's genetic make-up or of one's environment.

The discovery of epigenetic factors in development, according to many prominent developmental scientists, has finally put an end to the age-old debate about nature vs. nurture. Epigenetics reveals that development is *always* the product of both genes and environment meeting in the epigenome, which translates environmental factors into genetic activity, which then changes cellular function, which then leads to differences in behavior and body function. Epigenetics illustrates the complex, dynamic system of dialogical relationships between genes and environments that ultimately define the phenotype, our outward characteristics of appearance and behavior (Lewkowicz, 2011; Sameroff, 2010). These are difficult ideas to grasp partly because they go against our strongly held beliefs that there really are differences between nature and nurture, and partly because the science behind these ideas is relatively new.

What Are the Major Phases of Prenatal Development?

The prenatal period is usually divided into three parts: the zygote, the embryo, and the fetus. The period of the zygote begins at the time the ovum is fertilized and lasts about 2 weeks, or until the ovum is implanted in the uterine wall. The period of the **embryo** begins about 2 weeks after fertilization and extends until the end of the second month, at which time the embryo is designated a **fetus**. This designation is applied when the organism begins to resemble a human in its external features, and the bones begin to harden into a more rigid skeletal structure. In this book, the fetal period will be divided into three phases (7 to 16 weeks, 17 to 22 weeks, and 23 to 36 weeks). These divisions correspond to changes in structure and behavior that will be explained below. The period of human gestation lasts about 38 weeks, but this can vary from between 36 and 40 weeks for a full-term infant.

In the first half week, the zygote divides to about 20 cells, and at the end of the week, some differentiation can be noted. At the end of the second week, there is a clearly defined **embryonic disk** that lies between the **amniotic sac** and the **yolk sac**, which have also differentiated out of the original zygote. This organism is now called the **blastocyst** and it implants itself in the lining of the uterus sometime during the third week. The blastocyst, still only 1/125 of an inch long, triggers the secretion of hormones that inhibit menstruation. As the concentration of these hormones, known as **human chorionic gonadotropin (HCG)**, increases, they can be detected in the urine; they are used in laboratory pregnancy tests (see Figure 2.4.

The Period of the Embryo

The blastocyst structure—the embryonic disk, the yolk sac, and the amniotic sac—will differentiate further. The embryonic disk differentiates into three layers. The **endoderm** eventually becomes part of the digestive, urinary, and respiratory systems. The **mesoderm** will become the muscles, bone, circulatory system, and reproductive system. The **ectoderm** will become the central nervous system and brain, the sense organs, and the skin, hair, nails, and teeth.

The yolk sac produces blood cells and becomes part of the liver, spleen, and bone marrow, all of which later produce blood cells. By the end of the embryonic period, the yolk sac has disappeared. The amniotic sac persists throughout gestation. It grows to cover the embryo and contains the amniotic fluid, which provides a cushion for the fetus against sudden movements of the mother's body.

Surrounding all of these developments is a membrane called the **chorion**. The **placenta**, which forms from the outer surface of the chorion, functions as a link between the bloodstreams of mother and embryo, which are not directly connected. The placenta passes nutrients and oxygen from the mother's blood to the fetus's through the umbilical cord and serves to eliminate the fetal

wastes via the mother's bloodstream. The fetus is in the upright position throughout most of the pregnancy, so there is no danger of the cord choking the fetus because of its location, the effect of gravity, and the relative inflexibility of the cord from the pressure of the blood circulating in it (like a hose with the water turned on). The risk of choking increases at birth because the fetus has changed position—head down for delivery—and the head may now come in contact with the cord.

By the third week, one can distinguish the head and primitive circulatory and skeletal systems. By the end of the first month, the heart is beating, and there are cavities for the ears, nose, and mouth (see Figure 2.5). The head is large relative to the rest of the body and has gill arches, and the body has upper limb buds and a small tail. At this point the embryo may be between 3 and 5 millimeters (1/6 inch) long.

Now development is occurring very rapidly. In the next 2 weeks, the beginnings of the eyes, nose, lungs, and liver grow, and bones begin to form. The gill structures are transformed into bones of the inner ear, the neck, and cartilage of the larynx, as well as the eustachian tubes, thyroid and thymus glands, and the trachea. By 6 weeks, the limbs are beginning to differentiate rapidly, and fingers and toes will appear shortly. The tail is still present and may comprise 15 percent of the embryo's total length of 12 millimeters (1/2 inch). The total weight is about 2 grams (1/14 ounce). About half of the weight of an 8-week-old embryo is in its head. It has all of the major organs except genital organs. It has a skeleton, eyebrows, knees, fingers, toes, and buds for teeth. Its rapid growth during this period makes the embryo more vulnerable to environmental risks (see Chapter 3).

The first evidence of prenatal behavior is seen during the embryonic period in the movements of the muscles of the heart. The movements are jerky and spontaneous at first but gradually become more rhythmic as they pump blood cells between the heart, yolk sac, and chorion. The origin of these rhythmic movements is unknown, since they occur before the embryo has developed its nervous system (Hofer, 1981).

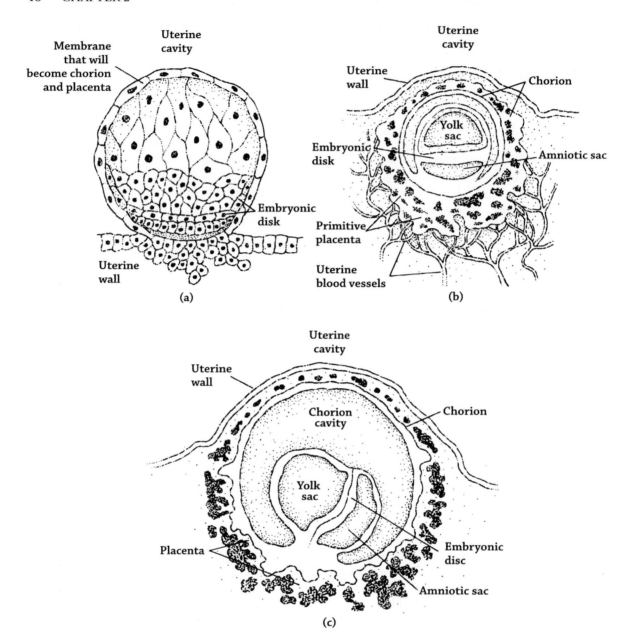

Figure 2.4 Early Stages of Prenatal Development

(a) *Blastocyst stage*: The fertilized egg (zygote) has made its way down the fallopian tube and has undergone repeated cell division and multiplication on the way. It attaches to the uterine lining and begins to grow into the uterine wall in search of nutrients. **(b)**, **(c)** Cell division and differentiation continue at a rapid pace, and specific structures begin to take shape. The developing organism is now a bulge on the uterine wall. **(d)**, **(e)** (*next page*) *Embryo stage*: Gradually, the form of the embryo takes shape. By the end of the first month, the head and the arm and leg buds are visible, a primitive heart has started to pump, and other organs are beginning to develop. At this stage, the human embryo closely resembles the embryos of most other animals.

Source: M. J. Gander & H. W. Gardiner, *Child and adolescent development*, 1981, p. 63. Boston: Little, Brown. Copyright © M. J. Gander & H. W. Gardiner. Reprinted by permission of the publisher.

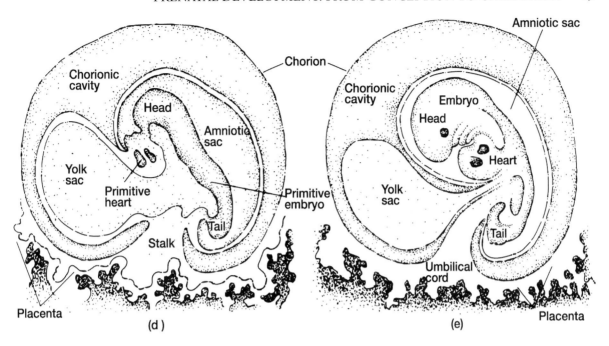

(d)

(e)

By the 32nd day of life (4 ½ weeks), the human embryo has all its major organs and a rudimentary sensory system (see Figure 2.5), but these sense organs are not yet connected to any nerve fibers. The first nerve cells form between 4 and 5 weeks, and the first spontaneous movements of the body occur a week later. By 7 weeks, the embryo is responsive to touch in the mouth region and will turn its head to the side (Trevarthen, 1973).

32 days (5 mm)

The Period of the Fetus I: Seven to Sixteen Weeks (2 to 3 Months)

During the early part of the fetal period, a large number of spontaneous behaviors emerge, including mouth and limb movements. The fetus can be stimulated to act by a number of occurrences. These include maternal muscle contractions, sounds, and changes in maternal glucose and oxygen levels. The *whole body* may shudder or jerk when a sensitive area like the mouth is touched. As the fetus develops during this period, movement responses become more localized to the stimulated area, and specific reflexes emerge. Areas of

Figure 2.5   Sensory Surfaces of a Human Embryo at Four Weeks

Source: Adapted from C. Trevarthen, *Behavioral embryology*. In E. C. Carterette & M. P. Friedman, eds., *Handbook of Perception* (Vol. 3), 1973, p. 93. New York: Academic Press. Adapted by permission of the publisher and editor.

TABLE 2.1   Chronology of Fetal Behavior (First Period)

Age (Weeks)	Behavior
8½	Stroking the mouth region produces flexion of upper torso and neck and extension of arms at the shoulder.
9½	Some spontaneous movements. More of the whole body responds when the mouth is stroked.
10½	Stroking the palms of the hands leads to partial closing of the fingers. Hiccups. Cyclic movements begin.
11½	Other parts of face and arms become sensitive. Head rotation.
12½	Sensitive area spreads to upper chest. Hand-face contact.
13½	Specific reflexes appear: Lip closure, swallowing, Babinski (See Chapter 1), squinting, sucking.
14½	Entire body is sensitive, with more specific reflexes, such as rooting, grasping, finger closing. Body stretching.
15½	Can maintain closure of the fingers (grasp) with muscle tightening, muscle strengthening. Yawning.
16½	Frowning, grimacing.

Sources: D. Hooker, *The prenatal origin of behavior*, 1952. Lawrence: University of Kansas Press; T. R. B. Johnson, R. E. Besinger, & R. L. Thomas, The latest clues to fetal behavior and well-being, 1989. *Contemporary Pediatrics*, 66–84; C. D. Laughlin, Pre- and perinatal brain development and enculturation: A biogenetic structural approach, 1991. *Human Nature*, 2, 171–213; S. S. Robertson, Temporal organization in fetal and newborn movement, 1990. In H. Bloch & B. I. Bertenthal (Eds.), *Sensory-motor organizations and development in infancy and early childhood*. Netherlands: Kluwer Academic; C. Trevarthen, Behavioral embryology, 1973. In E. C. Carterette & M. P. Friedman (Eds.), *Handbook of perception: Vol. 3. Biology of perceptual systems*. New York: Academic Press.

reflex activity spread out to the peripheries of the body, including hands and feet.

The behavior developments during this fetal period are listed in Table 2.1. Fetal behavior can be observed using several different methods. **Ultrasound** is a method in which high-frequency sound waves are bounced off the fetus's body to reveal the outline of the soft tissues. New ultrasound techniques produce 3D (3-dimensional) clear images of the whole body and details. Also available in some hospitals, 4D ultrasound adds the dimension of time to produce brief "movies" of the fetus over time and 4D can be used to study fetal behavior (Avni et al., 2007; Hata et al., 2010). Many 4D ultrasound movies are posted on YouTube and are available for viewing.

The purpose of these early fetal movements is not entirely clear. One experimental technique used with nonhuman embryos involves studying development after a fetal movement has been prevented from occurring, either through severing the nerve connections or by introducing a local anesthetic. Chick embryos that have been prevented

from moving in this way were unable to move later. The muscles and nerves of these chicks developed normally, but their joints had become frozen into bone (Drachman & Coulombre, 1962). In another study with mice, inability to move the tongue embryonically resulted in deformation of the soft palate (Walker & Quarles, 1976). The relatively high incidence of cleft palate in infants of alcoholic mothers may be due to the anesthetic effects of alcohol on fetal mouth movements (Hofer, 1981). Other experiments have shown that movement in the fetus helps to induce the development of nerve endings in the sensory receptors.

About 90 percent of fetuses can be seen in ultrasound pictures to be sucking their right thumb, and 10 percent their left thumb at 15 weeks after conception. A sample of 75 children in England were followed up at age 12 years. All 60 children who sucked their right thumb in utero used their right hand preferentially for most tasks (Hepper et al., 2005). It could be that a genetic influence caused the fetus to suck one or the other thumb, or it could be that the movement experi-

The 6-week-old embryo is less than an inch long. It has a heartbeat, eye patches, a rudimentary brain, and a stomach and liver. At this age there are no connections between the brain and the rest of the body.

Source: Photo originally appeared in *A Child is Born*, by Lennart Nilsson (New York: Random House).

ence of hand preference in utero established the pattern of later handedness.

These early fetal movements may also serve to help the fetus survive as an organism trying to adapt to its environment. As the mother moves about during her normal routine, her movements can shift the position of the fetus, and her activity may change the chemistry and composition of the amniotic fluid and blood supply. Fetal movements may have the effect of reorienting the fetus to the most comfortable position for itself and maximizing its chances of being protected and well nourished (Gandelman, 1992).

This is an example of an epigenetic developmental systems transaction. As fetal tissues and structures form, spontaneous movements are produced. The movements affect the epigenome and alter gene expression to induce further develop-ment in those same tissues and structures, which by feedback strengthens the movement pattern, making it more responsive and predictable.

Aside from behavioral development, physical development is also occurring. The brain forms into two distinct hemispheres beginning around 9 weeks, and by 15 weeks there is an increased ability of the brain to communicate with the sense organs and muscles. Not only can the brain stimulate muscle movement by 15 weeks, but it can also begin to inhibit movement, allowing for the beginnings of motor control (Fifer et al., 2001).

By about 16 weeks, the fetus has become about 3 inches long and weighs about 1/2 ounce. During the period from 12 to 16 weeks, the external genitals form as a result of the interaction of the fetus's epigenome with the environment of the cells. The genetic determination of sex occurs at

Just after three months, the fetus is about 2½ inches long and weighs ½ ounce. Most of the internal organs are formed, and fingers and toes can be seen. At this age, the fetus is capable of reflexive movements such as sucking, swallowing, grasping, and stretching.

Source: Photo originally appeared in *Behold Man*, by Lennart Nilsson (New York: Random House).

conception. Females have two X-shaped chromosomes in the 23rd pair, while males have one X- and one Y-shaped chromosome. All of the ova a woman produces have only X chromosomes. About half of the spermatozoa produced by men contain an X and the other half a Y chromosome in the 23rd place. The genetic sex of the zygote will thus depend on which of the father's spermatozoa actually fertilizes the ovum. For reasons not fully understood, more males are conceived than females, in the ratio of 105 to 100. Over the course of the life span, an increasing number of females survive at every age, so that by age 60, the ratio of males to females is 70 to 100.

Up until the third month after conception, genetic males and genetic females have similar external structures in the genital area. During the second month, the hormone testosterone is secreted in both the male and female fetuses, with higher levels in males. Testosterone affects the epigenome to activate particular genes that induce the development of the internal ducts that will later connect to male genitals. The continued action of testosterone causes the development of the external male genitals at around three months. Female genitals do not require any specific hormone to develop at this stage (Lamb & Bornstein, 1987).

This same fetal testosterone may also begin to make the male fetal brain different from that of the female. In one study, 4 year-old children were shown computer displays of objects moving toward and away from each other. When the children were asked what they thought was happening, those who had the most testosterone when they were fetuses were the least likely to attribute intentions (such as "wants to" or "trying to") to the objects. In other words, the girls—and the boys with the least fetal testosterone—described the objects with social intentions. Because autistic children tend to lack "female" social skills and tend to have more "male" spatial skills, in may be the case that excessive fetal testosterone plays a role in autism (see Chapter 9; Ingudomnukul et al., 2007;

Knickmeyer et al., 2006). Finally, male stereotypical behavior between the ages of 6 and 10 years, *in both boys and girls*, was stronger if there were high levels of testosterone in the amniotic fluid when the children were between 11 and 21 weeks fetal age (Auyeung et al., 2009). Thus, fetal testosterone has a long-lasting masculinizing effect.

These early gender differences in the brain may impact late fetal development. During the third fetal period, male fetuses are more active than females (DiPietro Hodgson, Costigan, & Johnson, 1996). Male fetuses also appear to develop organized states of arousal earlier than females (DiPietro et al., 1996). The findings on activity level suggest that boys are born with more motor experience. Since boys are more active postnatally, this suggests that early gender differences are not due entirely to postnatal environmental and parental influences.

The Period of the Fetus II: Seventeen to Twenty-Two Weeks (4 to 6 Months)

Although the fetus in Period II continues to develop new behavior, in the fetus there is a reduction in the whole body spasms seen in Period I. You might think that the development of the brain would induce more movement, rather than less. Up until this time, the brain stimulated large movements that involved the whole body, including arms and legs. These uninhibited movements originated in the brain stem regions. During Period II between 17 and 22 weeks, the brain is beginning to develop subcortical and cortical cells and neural pathways to inhibit such uncontrolled, spasmlike movements (Fifer et al., 2001). The result is that the movements of the fetus will be more specialized and controlled (see Table 2.2) including specific facial expressions and coordinated hand movements begin to emerge.

This period of prenatal development is characterized by rapid brain development, which will be discussed in more detail in Chapter 4. The brain's weight and volume increase by a factor of four during this period. During Periods I and II, the major process of brain growth is nerve cell division (mitosis), the creation of new nerve cells. After 22 weeks, beginning in Period III new brain cells continue to be formed, but at a much slower rate. Beginning in Period III and following birth, the major process of brain development is an increase in intercell connections and in cell specialization. Thus, during the fetal Periods I and II, when the brain is growing the most rapidly, it is the most susceptible to influences from the environment.

During this period of development, the fetus is changing its physical characteristics. In the fourth month, fine, long hair, **lanugo**, grows over most of the body. Coarser hair appears on the head in the fifth month, and eyebrows and eyelashes grow in the sixth month. During this period, the skin glands secrete a waxy substance, the **vernix caseosa**, that serves to protect the delicate skin. This period is also marked by the formation of fingernails, toenails, and the adult tooth buds.

The inhibition of movement by the brain makes sense from the point of view of physical development. The rapid increase in fetal size means that the fetus has less space in which to move around. At 6 months, the fetus weighs about 900 grams (2 pounds). Most babies born at this age do not survive, and if a baby is less than 600 grams or less than 24 weeks, the chances of survival are exceedingly slim.

The Period of the Fetus III: Twenty-Three to Thirty-Six Weeks (7 to 9 Months)

During this period, fetuses are active about 20 to 30 percent of the time. They move less often than during the first two fetal periods but with more vigor (DiPietro, Hodgson, Costigan, & Johnson, 1996) and this is the time when mothers can first feel the fetus moving. By now, a doctor can detect the fetal heartbeat with a stethoscope. Data from infants born prematurely and also from ultrasound recordings of the fetus inside the womb provide evidence for a large number of new patterns of movement that begin during this period (see Table 2.2). These movement are smoother (less jerky and spasmodic) and more complex than earlier movements, and more responsive to external stimulation (Grant-Buettler et al., 2011).

The fetus in Period III has been observed to cry, grunt, yawn, and show breathing movements. By 28 weeks, the fetus has all the facial, arm, and chest movements of a newborn who is crying, down to a trembling chin (Gingras et al., 2005). Other related research shows that between 26 and 30 weeks, it is likely that the regions of the brain's cortex—the thalamus and its connections—are sufficiently developed for the fetus to feel pain (Fabrizi et al., 2011; Lee at al., 2005; Slater et al., 2006). Because the fetus can make withdrawal and grimacing movements as early at the sixteenth week, it is often assumed that pain can be felt at that time. These grimaces, however, are spontaneous movements that are not linked to any brain activity that could create the sensation of pain.

By the eighth month, the fetus can suck its thumb and open its eyes. Grasping and postural adjustment movements have also been observed. By this time, the fetus can see, hear, feel, and smell

(Morokuma et al., 2008). Thus, by about the seventh month, most fetuses could survive if born, given appropriate intensive care (see Chapter 3).

One of the most remarkable achievements of the late fetal period is the development of clear-cut states of arousal (Hofer, 1981; Johnson et al., 1989). A **state of arousal** is an organized pattern of infant physical and physiological response that is related to the internal level of arousal or activation. States are alternating periods of activation and quiescence. During the fourth and fifth months, periods of activation and quiet in the fetus are irregular, and transitions from quiet to active are sudden and jerky. By the sixth month, a clear and regular alternation between activity and rest occurs about once every 40 minutes, based on data taken from sensors placed on the abdomens of sleeping women (Sterman & Hoppenbrouwers, 1971). This basic rhythm continues unchanged until after birth (S. S. Robertson, 1987).

These simple states of activity and rest during Period II become waking and sleeping states during Period III. Fully developed sleep states appear

TABLE 2.2 Chronology of Fetal Behavior (Second and Third Periods)

Age (Weeks)	Behavior
19	Gag reflex. Early coordinated body movements in response to noxious stimulation (these are different from whole-body spasms of the early part of the first fetal period).
20	Audible crying.
21	As sensitive to touch as a 1-year-old. Beginnings of prenatal learning ability.
24	Hearing structures developed, listens to mother's heartbeat, can blink eyes. Sleep-wake pattern first appears.
25	Moves in rhythm to drumbeats.
26	Lungs can breathe on their own, can regulate body temperature, remembers sounds heard previously, reacts to differences in maternal emotions, can open eyelids, can survive if born prematurely.
32	Brain wave patterns show all primary brain areas functioning. REM sleep and mature sleep-wake pattern. Fetuses sleep about 75 percent of the time. First signs of visual attention.
34	Can habituate, active visual attention.
35	Evidence of visual recognition memory.

Source: J. A. DiPietro, D. M. Hodgson, K. A. Costigan, & T. R. B. Johnson, Fetal neurobehavioral development, 1996. *Child Development*, 67 (5); R. Gandelman, *The psychobiology of behavioral development*, 1992. New York: Oxford University Press; C. D. Laughlin, Pre- and perinatal development and enculturation: A biogenetic structural approach, 1991. *Human Nature*, 2.

in the fetus as early as 24 weeks (DiPietro et al., 1996). From its first appearance, sleep is divided into a period of quiet sleep and a period of active or REM sleep. **REM (rapid eye movement)** sleep is characterized by short, jerky, vertical eye movements, spontaneous body movements, and irregular respiration. The 32-week-old fetus spends about three-quarters of its time in REM sleep. The purpose of REM sleep is not fully understood. One hypothesis (Ruffwarg, Muzio, & Dement, 1966; Vertes, 1986) is that it is a form of self-stimulation similar to earlier body movements.

The last month of gestation is a period during which the fetus gains a considerable amount of weight. From 900 grams at 24 weeks, the fetus typically grows to about 3,500 grams at 36 weeks (about 7 pounds); most of this weight is subcutaneous fat tissues that will provide the newborn with insulation against the cold. Because of this weight gain, the fetus becomes too cramped to move its body. REM sleep may provide a less physically demanding source of movement stimulation to assist the development of the fetal brain and sensory organs.

Another remarkable achievement of the last few months of prenatal development is the emergence of the ability to learn. Using an operant conditioning procedure (see Chapter 1), DeCasper and Sigafoos (1983) found that newborn infants will change their rate of sucking to imitate the sound of a heartbeat. Although these studies do not prove that newborns recognize the specific heartbeat of their mothers, they seem to suggest that a general preference for heartbeat sounds may have been learned before birth. A number of people have speculated that fetuses may become imprinted to the heartbeat sounds of their mothers so that after birth, the sound of heartbeats is comforting to the infants. Indeed, it has been found that a majority of adults hold infants on the left side of the adult's body, closer to the heart (Harris, Spradlin, & Almerigi, 2007; Salk, 1973).

Because the late-term fetus can hear, a number of studies have attempted to see if the fetus can learn songs or speech, or recognize particular voices. Because of the uterine and abdominal walls,

however, fetuses primarily hear lower frequencies of sounds coming from the outside, like the bass notes on the piano (Smith et al., 2003). In one study (Panneton & DeCasper, 1986), researchers asked pregnant women to sing "Mary Had a Little Lamb" frequently during the period 2 weeks prior to their due dates. After birth, the newborns' preference for "Mary Had a Little Lamb" over the song "Love Somebody" was tested using the conditioned sucking procedure (see Chapter 1). The newborns could clearly perceive the difference between the two songs, and in addition, they preferred to listen to the song that they had heard prenatally. DeCasper and Spence (1986) found postnatal preferences for stories read prenatally. Along these same lines, infants preferred hearing their mother's voice, compared to that of a stranger, when the voices were filtered for only the low-frequency components that the fetus might have heard through the insulating uterine wall. When higher-frequency whispered voices were used, newborns showed no preference (Spence & Freeman, 1996).

The studies reviewed so far have tested newborns for preferences related to their experiences before birth. Several studies have tested fetuses before birth and found an ability to learn in utero (James, 2010). One study examined whether fetuses 36 to 39 weeks old could distinguish between a male and a female voice (Lecanuet, Granier-Deferre, Jacquet, Capponi, & Ledru, 1993). Heart rate changes were significantly different when the voice was changed from male to female, or vice versa, and were significantly different from a control group for whom the voice was not changed. Fetal heart rate was also found to habituate to a vibroacoustic sound presented at intervals near the fetal head (Kisilevsky & Hains, 2010; Sandman, Wadhwa, Hetrick, Porto, & Peeke, 1997), and fetal heart rate changes when they hear their own mother speaking compared to the voice of another mother or the voice of the father, both of which were played through a loudspeaker next to the mother's abdomen (Kisilevksy et al., 2003; Kisilevski et al., 2009).

Rat pups that had been exposed prenatally to a mint smell, after birth preferred to suck on mother's teats to which the same smell had been applied (Smotherman & Robinson, 1987). Other work with animal fetuses shows conditioning effects from stimulation due to sound, light, and chemicals (Gandelman, 1992). Human newborns also prefer familiar smells and tastes. They orient more to the odor of their mother's amniotic fluid than to formula milk or to amniotic fluid taken from another woman (Marlier, Schaal, & Soussignan, 1998a; Marlier, Schaal, & Soussignan, 1998b). Mothers who were randomly assigned to drink carrot juice had infants who, at six months, preferred carrot flavor more than infants whose mothers did not drink carrot juice (Menella et al., 2001).

What is the purpose of this learning ability in the fetus? It may be that it has no particular purpose for the fetus, and that its importance is for the development of learning ability that will be required after birth. On the other hand, this research demonstrates that prenatally learned associations become postnatal preferences. Fetuses exposed to prenatal maternal sounds and chemicals are more likely to recognize and prefer those same sounds and sensations after birth, and they are more likely to avoid sounds and smells that they found aversive prenatally. Thus, prenatal learning ability may serve as an early mechanism for mother-infant attachment and for the orientation of infants to the smells, tastes, and sounds of the environment into which they are born (Gandelman, 1992). It may also be that prenatal learning experiences, like prenatal movements, play a role in the development of connections between sensory, motor, and information processing areas of the brain before birth (Laughlin, 1991). These studies also show that the late term fetus can remember stimulation until after birth. At 32 weeks, the fetus can remember a prior sound for about 10 minutes but by 36 weeks, they can remember for as long as 4 weeks (Dirix et al., 2009).

What Is It Like to Be a Late-Term Fetus?

We know that late-term fetuses can recognize and remember different sensory stimulation but do they have psychological experiences of sensation and emotion? To have a psychological, as compared to a physiological, response the individual needs to be able to orient to the sensation, focus on it, and during that period of focused attention, show a recognizable response. From the data on learning reviewed in the previous section, this is very likely to be the case. The ability to self-regulate to pay attention may be firmly established in the final month of gestation, around 33 weeks (Kisilevsky et al., 2004). The onset of fetal crying and other organized states also suggests that they have rudimentary emotion-like experiences connected with distress and arousal. Their psychological world is probably similar to that of the newborn but not as richly textured with the opportunities for learning that occur after birth.

The vestibular system begins to develop after 22 weeks, probably providing an awareness of the orientation of the body with respect to gravity and an awareness of the movement of the whole body, as the mother moves and as the fetus turns inside the mother. In adults, this would be like the sensation of being a passenger in a moving vehicle, as it turns, stops, and starts. Of course, the fetus has no concept of moving and turning. The fetus is just aware of the feeling of being moved. The onset of REM sleep may also be a developmental continuation of an increasing awareness of internal processes. It is likely that the fetus becomes aware of rhythmical and cyclical movements during the late fetal period. Fetuses can probably sense the feelings of waking up and falling asleep. They may also be aware of the rhythms of their mother's heartbeat and breathing and of the sound of her voice.

Using 4D ultrasound, researchers in Japan observed late-term fetal arm movements (Masako-Yamakoshi & Takeshita, 2006). They found that more than half of these arm movements resulted in having the hand contact the mouth. When the hand did contact the mouth, two things were notable. First, there was a tendency to repeat the same movement, almost as if the fetus was consciously intending to do it again. Second, before the actual contact of the hand, the mouth could be observed opening, as if in anticipation of the hand coming closer. The researchers suggest that these observations indicate the beginnings of a bodily self-awareness in the fetal period, a kind of "knowing" how one part of the body relates to another part. This type of self-awareness is clearly observable soon after birth (see Chapter 5).

The fetus's awareness and the possibility that infants retain some participatory memories of this period suggest another question. Does enriched or impoverished experience during the last few months of pregnancy lead to positive or negative developmental pathways? We know that healthy prenatal environments lead to positive development for all periods of prenatal development (Chapter 3). Perhaps a better question is whether specifically enriching the prenatal environment—playing classical music or massaging the fetus, for example—has any lasting effect.

Just because newborns can recognize sounds heard prenatally does not necessarily make them smarter or more talented for having heard them. Fetuses will move their bodies to loud or percussive music, but this does not mean they like it or that it will help them grow. Many books and Internet sites make strong cases for providing this kind of enrichment to the fetus. Beware when reading these materials, and examine the research they present very carefully to be sure about the limitations of their findings. In many cases, the goal is to get you to buy the book, tape, or equipment that is supposed to enhance fetal development.

Having said all that, singing to, talking to, and massaging the fetus can be a healthy and rewarding thing to do for both mother and fetus. These methods give the fetus a sense of familiarity after he or she is born. They are also natural and enjoyable for mother and father and their attachment to the fetus develops. Singing has all the important features of the human voice and language. Lullabies and other songs convey feelings of love and attachment that are essential for the mother to express and certainly cannot hurt the fetus. These things are free of charge, spontaneous, and can be done any time of the day or night, and they make parents feel good.

Do people have memories of their prenatal life, and if so, how would these be experienced by an older child or adult? My interpretation of current research (see also the concept of participatory memory in Chapter 1) is that there is no verifiable evidence for people having specific autobiographical memories for anything in their lives before the age of 3 years.

On the other hand, participatory memories of the prenatal period may exist in the form of preferential orientations for certain kinds of movement, posture, sound, taste, and touch. Examples are the infant's preference for carrot juice at 6 months, if this was consumed by their mothers during pregnancy, and the prevalence of right-handed 12-year-olds who had sucked their right thumb as a fetus.

Here are some suggestions about what you might observe in yourself as possible prenatal participatory memories. We know, for example, that lying in a fetal posture on a comfortable surface can be relaxing and soothing for children and adults. Infants and young children often curl into fetal postures and suck their thumbs, a behavior commonly found in later-term fetuses. Heartbeat-like sounds, such as drumming and other deep rhythms, can be either soothing or arousing in pleasurable ways. Do we like or dislike the kind of food that our mothers ate while they were pregnant with us? Are we more prone to depression or joyfulness because of our mother's experiences and the possible physiological effects on our fetally developed neurotransmitters?

Because emotional and behavioral development continues after birth, and few memories from early life are exact replicas of the early experience, they have been transformed and changed through later experience and interpreted in terms of the remembering person's self-understanding at that time. The impact of the prenatal period on behavioral and psychological development, therefore, is a complex systemic process that has yet to be fully understood.

CHILDBIRTH

This section deals with the infant's transition from prenatal to postnatal life. During the pregnancy period, family members have been anticipating the moment of birth with both hope and concern, while the fetus is making movements that prepare for the next phase of its life. In normal circumstances, the pregnancy period ends with parents already being attached to their infants. The baby is born not only into a world of light and air, but also into a world of love. After reviewing some data on birthrates, the process of birth will be covered. Birth complications that may affect the infant's development will be covered in Chapter 3.

Birthrates

How many babies are born each year? The **birthrate** is the average number of infants born for every 1,000 people. Birthrate data is usually kept by government agencies as part of a country's vital statistics. **Vital statistics** are numerical estimates in a population of events related to birth, death, and the incidence of illnesses and accidents.

The birthrate in the United States is currently 14 per 1,000. The birthrate has been cut almost in half in the United States since 1950. In 1950, women in the United States had an average of three children. This dropped to two children in 1980 and remains about the same today. For the first time, so-called "minority" children in the United States became the majority in 2011, with 50.4 percent of births coming from groups that had been classified as minorities (U.S. Census Bureau, http://www.census.gov, 2013).

The lowest birthrates are in Western Europe and in Eastern Asia (about 7 per 1,000). Some countries, such as Italy and Japan, have an average of only one child per family today. This birthrate is not enough to maintain the present population of those countries, so their work force is increasingly being filled by immigrants. The effect of this is that the racial and cultural balance of these two countries, which traditionally have had a relatively homogenous population, is changing. The highest birthrates in the world are in Eastern, Western, and Middle Africa with some countries having birthrates between 40 and 53 infants per 1,000 people (Population Reference Bureau, http://www.prb.org, 2013).

The Stages of Labor

The birth process itself begins during the last several weeks of pregnancy. The muscles in the uterus begin to contract and expand at irregular intervals, sometimes days or weeks apart. These gentle muscle contractions, called **Braxton-Hicks contractions** or false labor, have two important effects. First, they help to widen (dilate) the cervix to a width of 1 to 2 centimeters. The **cervix** is the membrane at the opening between the uterus and the vagina. Normally closed during pregnancy, the cervix must dilate to a width of about 10 centimeters (5 inches) to enable the fetus to pass from the uterus into the vagina.

Second, the Braxton-Hicks contractions may help to move the fetus closer to the cervix in preparation for birth. In almost all cases, the fetus's head is oriented downward. About 4 percent of all births are **breech presentations** (with the buttocks first), and a small fraction are **transverse presentations** (the fetus is oriented on its side). These presentations are shown in Figure 2.6. Cesarean deliveries are usually recommended when there is a breech or transverse presentation, because the fetus cannot be turned once it has descended into its prebirth position.

Labor begins when contractions start to appear at regular intervals spaced about 10 to 20 minutes apart. Labor is usually divided into three stages (see Figure 2.7). The first stage lasts until the cervix is fully dilated to 10 centimeters and effaced (made thin). Contractions in this stage help to efface and open the cervix. This is the longest stage of labor and may vary in duration from a few minutes to a few days (Guttmacher, 1973). The mean duration of the first stage is about 8 to 14 hours for **primiparous** mothers (mothers giving birth for the first time) and about 6 hours for **multiparous** mothers (Danforth, 1977; Parfitt, 1977). For unknown reasons, the duration of labor has increased in the past 50 years, by about 2.6 hours for first time mothers and 2 hours for second time mothers. Contemporary mothers are also about 4 years older than mothers in the 1960's and older mothers tend to take longer during labor (Laughon, 2012).

During the first stage of labor, the pain of the contractions increases over time. During the early part of the first stage, contractions are regular and moderately intense. Women may be able to walk around, do household chores, watch television, nap, or take a bath. During the late part of the first stage is the time to go to the hos-

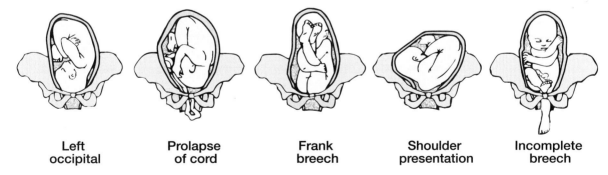

| Left occipital | Prolapse of cord | Frank breech | Shoulder presentation | Incomplete breech |

Figure 2.6   Various Deviations from the Most Optimal Vertex Presentation
The first drawing on the left shows a minor deviation in which the head is first but is turned to the side. The next shows a prolapsed cord. The more extreme presentations are shown in the three drawings on the right.

Source: Adapted from J. F. Rosenblith & J. E. Sims-Knight, *In the beginning: Development in the first two years*, 1985, p. 158. Belmont, CA: Brooks-Cole.

Figure 2.7   Birth Processes: Stage 1 and Part of Stage 2

(a) End of the first stage of labor; the baby's head is moving through the cervix. **(b)** Transition; the baby's head is moving through the birth canal, the vagina. **(c-e)** The second stage of labor; the baby's head is moving through the opening of the vagina. **(c)** It emerges completely. **(d)** The head is then turned so that the rest of the body slides out **(e)**.

Source: A. Fogel & G. F. Melson, *Child development*, 1988, pp. 116–117. St. Paul, MN: West. Copyright © West Publishing Company. Reprinted by permission. All rights reserved.

pital or birthing center. Contractions last 40 to 60 seconds and are spaced at intervals of 3 to 4 minutes. The pain is especially intense in the final phase of the first stage, when the cervix must dilate between 8 and 10 centimeters. This is the time that a woman may elect to begin the use of pain control methods (see next section). Mothers can move around, change positions, or take a warm bath or shower.

In the second stage of labor, the infant passes through the cervix and vagina. For women who choose natural childbirth, the pain of this phase of labor may be accompanied by panic, anger, and confusion (Lesko & Leski, 1984). Some mothers begin to shake or feel nausea. Contractions last 60 to 90 seconds and come once every 2 or 3 minutes. Fortunately, this stage is not as long as the previous stage. As the infant begins to descend

Childbirth can be an exceptionally moving experience for all members of the familiy. In many hospitals, fathers are encouraged to attend the childbirth, providing support for their mates and enhancing their own feelings of participation.
Photo by Emily Waterfield

into the vagina, contractions serve to push the baby out. In natural childbirth, mothers will feel an urge to push. If a local anesthetic is used, mothers feel pressure and will need coaching to determine when to push. The intensity of the pain and feelings of nausea or disorientation are balanced by the sense of relief that the end is near. Some women may begin to feel euphoria.

The final stage of labor is the birth of the placenta, often called the afterbirth. This stage takes less than 1 hour in most cases. By that time, the mother's attention and emotion are occupied with the newborn, and most women do not pay much attention to what is happening in the vaginal area. Contractions continue for several hours as the placenta is expelled and the uterus closes up to prevent bleeding. These contractions are not as intense as during the previous stages, but the woman may continue to experience some pain.

If you ever wondered where the name "labor" comes from, it is because difficult muscular work is involved. Although some fortunate women go through all three stages in a matter of several hours, other mothers may be in labor for 20 or 30 hours, during which time they have little chance to sleep or rest.

Babies are expected to be born 280 days from the first day of the mother's last menstrual period, but only about 4 percent of all births occur on their exact due date. Births occurring within 2 weeks before or after the due date are generally considered to be in the normal range.

The timing of birth is controlled by a protein called corticotropin-releasing hormone (CRH). Women with the highest levels of CRH in their blood during the fourth month of pregnancy were more likely to deliver their infants prematurely. Tests for the concentration of CRH are currently being developed. Given the risks of premature birth (see the section on prematurity in Chapter 3), it may be possible in the future to delay birth by regulating the production of CRH during pregnancy (R. Smith, 1999).

Technologies for Labor and Delivery

Advances in medical technology have led to the development of a variety of tools to assist childbirth. These include **fetal monitoring**, mechanical aids to speed delivery (forceps and vacuum extraction), cesarean section (a surgical rather than vaginal delivery), and drugs to reduce pain and speed labor.

Fetal monitoring is the use of electronic devices to detect and display the fetal signs (heart rate, respiration, blood gases, pH balance) during the delivery and birth process. In invasive fetal monitoring, electrodes are inserted through the vagina and cervix and attached to the fetus. This procedure deprives the mother of opportunity for movement. In a less invasive form, the mother may wear a belt around her abdomen. Invasive fetal monitoring is controversial because it restricts the mother, often requires additional drugs for pain control, and carries a risk of infection for both mother and baby. Experts suggest that fetal monitoring should only be used in high-risk deliveries (Freeman, 1990; Shy et al., 1990). The American College of Obstetrics and Gynecology does not consider fetal monitoring part of standard care for childbirth. Furthermore, research shows that fetal monitoring does not produce healthier infants with fewer complications (*Birth*, 1988). Ultrasound can also be used to determine the position and behavior of the fetus prior to birth.

Forceps are instruments, usually made of metal or plastic, that are shaped to fit around the newborn's head and used to pull the infant through the birth canal. The use of forceps is declining in favor of cesarean section and spontaneous vaginal delivery because they may cause brain and spinal cord injuries if used during early phases of labor (high forceps). The effect of forceps used at the very end of delivery (low forceps) has not been studied. It seems generally safe, although bruises may be left on the head in some cases. With **vacuum extraction**, a cup connected to a suction device is placed on the baby's head. Research shows that the risks of vacuum extraction are lower than with cesarean section or high forceps (Meyer et al., 1987; Nagan et al., 1990). These mechanical methods are used more frequently in the United States than in Europe (Korte & Scaer, 1990).

Vaginal deliveries occurred in about 67 percent of all births in the United States in 2010 and 2011; the remainder—about one-third of all births—were done by cesarean section. In 1960, by comparison, only 4 percent of births were done by cesarean section (http://www.childbirthconnection.org/article.asp?ck=10456). In a **cesarean section**, an incision is made in the mother's abdomen and uterus while she is under a local or general anesthetic. Then the baby and placenta are both removed. Cesarean sections, also called C-sections, were initially used in the case of breech or transverse presentations. C-sections are also recommended in multiple births (twins, triplets, etc.), when the baby's head is too large for the mother's pelvis, when the fetus becomes dangerously entangled in the umbilical cord, and in the case of fetal distress. Some diseases that infect the mother's vagina, such as syphilis, herpes simplex, and AIDS, can be transmitted to the infant during delivery, and a C-section birth helps to prevent the transmission of this infection to the infant. A new drug, nevirapine, can reduce the risk of transmitting AIDS to the newborn. It is inexpensive and can be used in African countries where AIDS has reached epidemic levels.

Fetal distress is a sudden loss of oxygen or a change in the heart rate or respiration of the fetus, usually determined by fetal monitoring. Severe fetal distress can cause serious complications. For example, too much pressure on the fetal head during delivery can cause excess blood pressure and possibly bleeding inside the scalp, called *intraventricular* hemorrhage. Loss of oxygen, which sometimes occurs in long and difficult labors, can lead to fetal brain damage. Using a fetal monitor, a physician can decide if the risk to the infant requires an emergency C-section.

C-sections have saved the lives and health of many mothers and infants. They are not without risk to the mother, however. Because a C-section is a surgical procedure, the mother is at greater risk of infection and postoperative stress. In the past, it was thought that once a woman had a C-section, she could not have vaginal deliveries in the future. This belief is changing as an increasing number of C-section mothers are having vaginal deliveries of later-born children. Because of the risks of C-sections, mothers are encouraged to attempt vaginal delivery on later births if there are no other risk factors (Catling-Paull et al., 2011).

Some people have complained that obstetricians are too quick to perform C-sections in an attempt to avoid lawsuits against them if the baby or mother suffers during a vaginal delivery, or in an effort to make more money by doing surgery compared to a routine delivery. It is difficult to prove these claims, however. Other explanations for the increase in C-sections are better nutrition and therefore larger babies and more accurate fetal monitoring that allows a more sensitive and early detection of fetal distress. More recently, however, a growing number of mothers are choosing to have C-sections rather than vaginal births, perhaps because they can be planned in advance and seem easier for the mother. Excessive fear of childbirth has been shown to account for about 3 percent of C-section births (Sysdsjö et al., 2011).

For most C-sections, there are few lasting negative side effects on mothers or on infants, even in long-term follow-up studies, although it is not associated with any benefits either (Entwisle & Alexander, 1987; Whyte et al., 2004). Fathers may be more involved with C-section infants because the mother receives more medication and takes longer to recover than with a vaginal delivery. Considerably more risks can occur, however, when mothers are scheduled to deliver the baby by C-section earlier than 39 weeks (Tita et al., 2009).

In sum, although C-sections carry some increased risk for the mother due to complications of surgery, if the mother or infant is at actually at risk, the health benefits justify the procedure. On the other hand, if there is no health risk, moth-ers should think twice. While it may seem more convenient and less painful, the fact is that it takes much longer for the mother to recover from major abdominal surgery than from vaginal childbirth. Even under ideal conditions, cesarean section surgery carries greater health risks to the mother and baby, especially before 39 weeks (Clarke & Taffel, 1995, McFarlan, 2004; Tita et al., 2009). Also, there is data indicating that C-section is a modest risk factor for ectopic pregnancy and an important risk factor for placental problems (Hemminki,E., & Meriläinen, J., 1996; McFarlan, 2004).

Drugs and delivery. In either a vaginal or a cesarean delivery, many mothers are given some type of medication to control pain and/or to regulate the course of labor. According to Judeo-Christian tradition, women are supposed to suffer during childbirth as punishment for Eve's sins: "In sorrow thou shall bring forth children" (Genesis 3:16). This belief persisted until 1847, when a Scottish obstetrician, James Young Simpson, gave ether to a delivering mother to ease her pain. In his fight to use pain relievers during childbirth, Simpson had to combat both medical practice and religious values. He argued that the Hebrew word previously translated as "sorrow" should have been translated as "work" or "labor." Furthermore, he cited the "deep sleep" that God imposed on Adam when Eve was "delivered" from one of his ribs. Painless childbirth rapidly became popular and was encouraged by the use of chloroform during two of Queen Victoria's childbirths (Brackbill, 1979).

In most industrialized nations, drugs for **anesthesia** (loss of sensation) and **analgesia** (pain relief) are the methods most used for pain control during labor. Although drugs are medically controlled and have been proved safe for the mother, it is now well established that most general anesthetics administered to the mother cross the placenta during labor and delivery. Unfortunately for the neonate, those organ systems that are the most susceptible to chemical insult (primarily the central nervous system) and those that would be the most effective for drug clearance (the liver and kidneys) are the least well developed. Other organs of the newborn, such as the heart and lungs, are better developed, but these systems have little or nothing to do with helping the system get rid of the drugs.

How long the drugs remain in the newborn's system depends on the type of drug, the time during labor at which it was given, and the dosage given to the mother (Golub, 1996). In general, newborns of women who took analgesia during childbirth were slower to respond to breast feeding, had higher temperatures, and cried more (Ransjö-Arvidson et al., 2001). Some drugs may impair a mother's ability to participate in her delivery by paralyzing muscles normally used to push the baby out, while others may make her drowsy. Many women seem to suffer from gaps in their memories of the childbirth experience. In one study (Affonso, 1977), 86 percent of the women interviewed could not remember some of the events of their childbirth and wanted to know more. They asked the doctor and nurses; they had bad dreams and felt somewhat frustrated. Some mothers asked the same questions over and over. This problem seems to occur when labor is either extremely long or extremely short, in high-risk conditions, or when the level of medication is high.

Epidurals are a local anesthetic administered in the lower (lumbar) spine that block pain sensation in the pelvic area but allow the mother to remain awake and aware. Epidurals have been shown to cause fevers during childbirth in about 15 percent of women. Although there is no measurable effect on the newborn, some doctors may react to the maternal fever by preventive treatment of the newborn for infection (Lieberman et al., 1997). Epidurals also increase the risk for postpartum depression (see Chapter 3). Before electing them, women should discuss the risks and benefits with their doctors or midwives.

On the other hand, for some mothers, anxiety and pain increase dramatically prior to and during labor and delivery (Westbrook, 1978). Research shows that women who choose epidurals, compared to natural childbirth, are more likely to be fearful of childbirth and to take a relatively passive role, preferring to turn over the management

of the birth process to professionals (Heinze & Sleign, 2003). Drugs serve to calm these mothers and reduce their discomfort, making them better able to enjoy the birth of their infant (Shnider, 1981). Prenatal preparation for childbirth is important for the doctor and the parents to understand all the different options available for pain control and to choose the one that is best for mother and infant. In the next section, we turn to different types of childbirth practices, including methods for the behavioral and psychological control of pain.

The Management of Childbirth

Most childbirths in North America and Northern Europe today take place in hospital settings. From a medical perspective, the hospital environment allows a large staff to assist in labor, delivery, and the care of the newborn. Hospitals also provide access to emergency medical care in the event of fetal distress or complications with labor.

At the beginning of the twentieth century, on the other hand, most childbirths took place in the home. Once it became accepted practice to give birth in the hospital, however, the experience of childbirth for women and their families changed. In the home, the mother could be surrounded by familiar sights and sounds and have the support of other family members. In the early days of hospital births, mothers were left in sparsely furnished rooms for labor, and birth took place in a sterile operating chamber. Family members were prohibited from accompanying the mother. The babies were separated from the mothers for several days, bottle feeding was encouraged, and hospitals stays could last up to a week for normal deliveries.

Birthing centers. Today, childbirth in hospitals has become more humane. There is a growing recognition of the need to treat childbirth less like a disease and more like a normal event. Birthing centers are alternatives to standard hospital deliveries. They are based on the idea that most births are natural and nonmedical and should take place in a comfortable, homelike environment. Birthing centers are typically located in hospitals, but they keep medical technology to a minimum and provide comfortable furnishings, quiet, and privacy. Thus, they combine the relative comfort and privacy of a home birth with the availability of medical assistance if it is required.

Parents find birthing centers very rewarding and enriching for their childbirth experience (Eakins, 1986; Waldenström, 1999); such centers are a safe and effective alternative to traditional hospital deliveries for low-risk pregnancies (Rooks et al., 1989). Birthing centers are especially effective for low-income mothers, who benefit from the additional social support and long-term care (Lubic, 1999). Low-income mothers who used a birthing center in New York City tell about the effectiveness of the birthing center in their own words:

> If you have given birth, you have given life, and if you have given life then you can do anything—you can get a job and you can go to school and you can do anything you want as long as you put your mind to it.

> That's the best thing about the birth center concept. It empowers women, and in turn, they empower their families, and families empower the community and it just grows and grows. (Lubic, 1999, p. 21)

In one study of 8,677 childbirths in the United Kingdom, compared to conventional hospital rooms, birthing centers reduced the need for medical interventions and increased maternal satisfaction. Women who gave birth in birthing centers required less analgesia and anesthesia, were more likely to have a vaginal compared to a caesarian birth, had fewer episiotomies (surgical incision on the perineum, the tissue at the posterior base of the vaginal opening that extends toward the anus), and were more likely to initiate breast feeding (Hodnett et al., 2005). Because of a new awareness about the psychological benefits of early mother-infant and father-infant contact, babies are separated from parents only in the case of a medical complication. Otherwise, early and frequent contact is desirable.

Every hospital has different practices, however. Parents who desire the presence of fathers during delivery, rooming in (allowing the newborn to sleep in the mother's room rather than in the hospital nursery), or natural childbirth need to consult their health care providers and inquire about hospital practices. It helps if the parents make their desires known and act assertively to get their personal needs met. Hospitals, like all large institutions, have rules of standard practice, but sometimes these can be tailored to fit the individual and family, if their needs are made known to the hospital staff.

Early discharge. In the case of normal deliveries, hospital stays can last from 1 to 3 days. Some hospitals allow discharge within 3 hours after the birth if the mother receives no analgesia or anesthesia and the infant is in good health. Under these conditions, there is no increased risk associated with early discharge (Mehl, Peterson, Sokolsky, & Whitt, 1976). More recently, early discharge has been allowed on demand in consultation with the physician. In 1998, an act of the U.S. Congress ensured that mothers and infants were not discharged before 48 hours after delivery without the mother's consent (Kanto, 2002).

Women who elect early discharge feel that the home is a better and more supportive environment for comfort, recovery, and early adaptation to their babies. Early-discharge mothers report more social support in the home (availability of relatives and friends) and are more confident in their ability to manage on their own (Lemmer, 1987). On the other hand, early discharge limits the ability of the hospital staff to provide parent education and to detect feeding problems and other abnormalities (Kiely, Drum, & Kessel, 1998). It may also deprive women of some needed rest to recover from the delivery. Women should try to evaluate their preferences and discuss them with staff.

Behavioral Pain Control and Childbirth Preparation

While drugs offer the advantages that they can be administered in controlled doses and are effective, a number of behavioral and psychological alternatives to speed labor and relieve pain are available. Many diverse kinds of pain-relieving methods have been used throughout human history. One common practice, used by the Laotians, the Navaho, and the Cuna of Panama, among others, is the use of music during labor. Among the Comanche and Tewa Indian tribes, heat is applied to the abdomen (M. Mead & Newton, 1967). Other alternative natural pain relief methods for labor may include meditation, massage, acupressure, hypnosis, herbs, and water births (Liebermann, 1992).

Some groups believe that pain and ease of delivery are functions of the mother's body position during labor and delivery. Many cultures encourage women to give birth in a sitting position, usually held from behind by another woman. The Taureg of the Sahara insist that the laboring mother walk up and down small hills to allow the infant to become properly placed to facilitate delivery. Taureg women usually deliver from a kneeling position. In fact, most obstetrics textbooks in the United States at the turn of the century advocated an upright position during labor (M. Mead & Newton, 1967).

For some peoples, prevention is the best cure. The Ainu of Japan believe that maternal exercise will make the fetus small and encourage a shorter labor. This belief is actually supported by recent research (see Chapter 3; Campbell & Mottola, 2001; Clapp et al., 2002) although lower birthweight may be a risk factor in some cases. The Japanese value smaller newborns and are not pleased with multiple births, which they consider too animal-like. In a number of other cultures, including the Hopi of the American Southwest, women are encouraged to exercise during pregnancy (M. Mead & Newton, 1967).

Nonchemical pain control during labor in developed Western countries today is sometimes achieved using the **Lamaze method**. Working in France, Frederick Lamaze developed a system of exercise, breathing, and massage that was based on a theory of pain during labor developed by Grantly Dick-Read in Great Britain (Dick-Read, 1933/1972). According to Dick-Read, women become afraid during childbirth due to the pain that develops when muscles are contracted. He suggested that if women were to employ some commonly known methods of relaxation, their experience of pain would be lessened. Female animals naturally fall into panting and breathing patterns. Using these observations and the work of Dick-Read, Lamaze based his method on the use of rhythmic breathing as a mental distraction from pain and on relaxation methods to prevent it (Karmel, 1959). The Lamaze method has been the most widely used approach to childbirth education in the United States (Leifer, 1999). Dick-Read believed that natural methods, those that had been used over many human generations, were the best choice for many women (Mascucci, 2003).

Mother's reports of higher pain during childbirth has also been associated with negative attitudes toward pregnancy and childbirth (Nettlebladt, Fagerstrom, & Udderberg, 1976) and with a lack of support from the husband. Mothers can perceive when fathers show inadequate involvement in childbirth and this contributes to the mother's feeling of dissatisfaction in the childbirth experience (Mackey, 1995). Parental involvement in childbirth is associated with the father's later involvement in caregiving (Parke, 1995). Women whose husbands were present during the labor and delivery, as well as those whose husbands stayed with them for longer periods, perceived childbirth as less painful (Davenport-Slack & Boylan, 1974; Nettlebladt et al., 1976). It could be, however, that women who were more likely to view childbirth as less painful were those who requested their husband's presence for longer periods during the delivery. In addition, people who choose such approaches are a self-selected group whose positive attitudes about labor and delivery might help them, even under adverse conditions.

There is some debate, though little concrete data, on how childbirth preparation affects women (Wideman & Singer, 1984). Some suggest that the effect is due to education and the ability to anticipate fearful events. Some think it is due to the relaxation techniques and/or the social support provided by the Lamaze approach, while others think the effect is related to positive images about the childbirth experience (Nichols & Humenick, 1988). Here are some examples of imagery techniques that have been used (C. Jones, 1987):

> Imagine that you and your baby are breathing in harmony. Now imagine that you are inside the womb, face-to-face with your unborn child, who is comfortable and secure in a private sea of crystal-clear water. (p. 87)

> Imagine yourself opening. Envision the baby's head against the cervix and the cervix widening to let it pass. At that time, mentally say yes to the contractions as they come and fade away. (p. 145)

Some research has shown, however, that relaxation techniques may be superior to this approach since these images tend to be transitory, whereas breathing and massage can be sustained for longer periods (Markman & Kadushin, 1986). Lamaze-trained mothers, especially if they are accompanied by the father and receive professional support during the delivery, require less pain medication and fewer episiotomies (Copstick, Taylor, Hayes, & Morris, 1986; Hodnett & Osborn, 1989).

Acupuncture and acupressure, massage, hypnosis, relaxation techniques, yoga, warm baths, walking, and music have also been shown to help ease labor pain. Somatic education helps a mother to be more in touch with her body. This reduces anxiety and pain and gives mothers greater confidence in their decisions to use or not to use drugs during delivery. Home-like hospital rooms and relaxation contribute to maternal well-being, lower the need for drugs, and reduce episiotomies. The latter have been shown to lead to longer post-birth recovery times for the mother compared to the stitching of small tears that may occur naturally during vaginal childbirth (Fleming et al., 2003; Hartmann et al., 2005).

Upright postures. During traditional hospital labors and deliveries, women had been confined almost the entire time to a supine position. There is a growing recognition that upright postures may be beneficial to both mother and infant. Anatomically, when a mother is upright, her pelvis widens, access to the birth canal is easier for the fetus, and pushing is more effective because of the assistance of gravity. Upright postures also improve the blood circulation to the mother's abdominal muscles and increase the oxygen supply to the fetus, reduce the need for forceps, lower the rate of episiotomies, and reduce pain (Cottrell & Shannahan, 1987; de Jonge et al., 2004). Some studies find beneficial effects such as fewer birth complications, shortening of labor, less backache pain, and easier pushing (Gardosi, Hutson, & Lynch, 1989; Holland & Smith, 1989; Lupe & Gross, 1986). In a recent meta-analysis of 21 studies with a total of 3,706 women it has been found that the first stage of labor was approximately one hour shorter for women in upright positions compared to those who were lying down (Lawrence, Lewis, Hofmeyr, Dowswell, & Styles, 2009).

Upright postures can be achieved in a number of ways. During labor, some women find it helpful to get up and walk around, stand, or squat. Hospital beds can be tilted so that the mother is sitting. Some hospitals have birthing balls, large inflated exercise balls on which a mother can sit or lean. In other places a birthing bar is used. The bar is suspended about two feet above the bed. It allows the mother to pull herself upright any time during labor. Just changing positions sometimes relieves discomfort.

Midwives and doulas. A **midwife** is a practitioner who has been trained to assist women who are giving birth. Lay midwives receive informal and formal training, while nurse midwives are registered nurses who receive their training as part of their nursing education. Midwives often work alongside doctors and assist the mother as long as the labor is without complications. They are trained to recognize which complications require the attention of a physician. Midwives are usually less costly to parents than physicians, and they also provide both prenatal and postnatal care for the family. Midwives help families understand the various birthing options and the risks and benefits of drugs and surgical procedures, and they work with the family to enhance the healthy development of parents and baby. Midwives assist in the delivery of 80 percent of births worldwide.

Doula is an ancient Greek word meaning "an experienced woman who guides and assists a new mother in her infant-care tasks." A doula works alongside doctors or midwives to provide emotional support during labor and delivery. Doulas are trained to recognize birth as a key life experience that the mother will remember all her life. Doulas serve as advocates and supporters of the parents in preparing for and carrying out their plans for the birth. Doulas attend the birth, provide emotional support and physical comfort measures, and help the mother and her partner communicate with the hospital staff. Randomized clinical trials using low-income first-time mothers found that doula-assisted delivery shortened the labor, reduced the number of forceps and cesarian deliveries, and increased satisfaction with the childbirth experience. Doula-assisted mothers also were more likely to initiate and maintain breast-feeding (Glink, 1998).

Home births.   An alternative to hospital delivery is the modern practice of birth at home. Home births are standard practice in some countries, such as the Netherlands and most of Scandinavia. These births are assisted by professional midwives, and the incidence of infant mortality is lower in these countries than in the United States. On closer examination, though, this effect is due not to home birth itself but to other factors. These countries have a relatively high level of education and a low incidence of poverty. In addition, women who are at risk are not allowed to have home births. These women include very young or very old mothers, unmarried women, low-income women, and those with medical risks (Rosenblith & Sims-Knight, 1985). With a trained professional in attendance, screening for risk, and a nearby hospital in case of emergency, home births in the United States are no more risky than hospital births (R. Cohen, 1981; Hazell, 1975; Howe, 1988; de Jonge, van der Goes, Rav-

elli, Amelink-Verburg, Mol, Nijhuis, Gravenhorst, & Buitendijk, 2009). Currently in the US, only 1 percent of babies are born at home, primarily to mothers older than 35 years who have had other children   (http://www.cdc.gov/nchs/data/data-briefs/db84.htm).

The Leboyer method: Birth without violence.   Frederick Leboyer (1975) suggested that some of the hospital routines used in the 1970s were traumatic for the infant: holding the infant upside down in the cold air, placing the baby on a cold metal scale, putting silver nitrate in his or her eyes, separating the infant from the mother, putting the baby under bright lights, exposing him or her to loud sounds, and prematurely cutting the umbilical cord. With the **Leboyer method**, the delivery room is quiet and dimly lit, and the infant is placed on the mother's warm abdomen right after birth until the umbilical cord stops pulsing. After the cord is cut, the infant is placed in a warm-water bath. Leboyer reports that infants so treated tend to be more relaxed and alert than other infants.

Leboyer's claims that such procedures increase the newborn's alertness have not been verified scientifically. Most studies reporting positive effects were biased by the observer's preference for the method and the lack of a control group (e.g., Rappoport, 1976). One well-controlled study (Nelson et al., 1980) found no difference in alertness between Leboyer and non-Leboyer babies, nor were there any differences in developmental test scores between the two groups at 8 months. Furthermore, half of the Leboyer babies reacted to the warm-water bath following birth with irritated crying. As with upright postures and childbirth preparation classes, it is difficult to establish a conclusive effect for these practices. On the positive side, most of the practices discussed here cannot be shown to have any harmful side effects, and they may be effective for many of the people who use them. LeBoyer's work, however, did have an effect on the formation of birthing centers, which reduce stress on both mother and newborn. The Leboyer method has not been widely used in the U.S. because research has not supported its effectiveness (Maziade, Boudreault, Cote, & Thivierge, 1986).

Regardless of whether a mother chooses a physician, midwife, or doula, it is a good idea to make a birth plan in which the mother, her partner, and her care provider discuss what they would like to happen during labor and delivery. Several Internet sites are also available to help mothers understand their options and to construct a birth plan that suits their needs. It is also important to remember that unexpected events may occur in childbirth. A mother may want a natural childbirth and later may choose drugs for pain control when the pain seems overwhelming. Childbirth is not a competition to see who can do it best, but rather a process that unfolds in a team of family and childbirth assistants who are all attempting to provide the best possible experience for mother and newborn.

What Are Some Cultural Differences in Childbirth and Infant Care Practices?

Not all societies greet the event of birth in the same way. The Cuna of Panama consider birth to be a secret event. In the United States, birth is considered a private affair, with only medical personnel and a few family members in attendance. Some cultures on the extreme end of the privacy dimension consider birth to be defiling and insist that women give birth in a separate area, which often is reserved for such things as childbirth, menstruation, and excrement (M. Mead & Newton, 1967). At the other extreme, the Jahara of South America give birth under a shelter in full view of everyone in the village—even small children. A number of Pacific Island communities also regard the birth of a child as an event of interest to the entire community.

To illustrate the cultural influences on childbirth and child-care practices in the newborn period, a portrait of three traditional cultures from widely different parts of the globe will be presented: Zinancantecan Indians from Mexico, originally of Mayan descent; villagers from the south of Italy; and the Japanese.

No drugs are used during labor among the Zinancantecans. The mother is supported and encouraged by an ever-present midwife. After birth, the newborn is placed naked before a fire. The midwife, who is still in attendance, begins to say prayers asking the gods to look kindly upon this child. A long skirt made of heavy fabric is brought out and put on the infant. Extending beyond the feet, the skirt is worn by both males and females throughout the first year of life. For fear of losing parts of the soul, the newborn is wrapped snugly in several layers of blankets; even the face is covered, except during feedings. This practice is believed to ward off evil spirits and illnesses during the first few months of life (Brazelton, 1977).

On the other side of the Atlantic, birth in a small village in southern Italy usually takes place in a hospital, attended by a midwife. Just after the birth, as in Mexico, the newborn is dressed in clothing and ceremonial linens the family has provided. When the infant is dressed, usually within about 10 minutes of the birth, the midwife goes into the hall, where the mother's entire immediate and extended family has been waiting. They all accompany the midwife back to the mother's room, where everyone takes a turn congratulating, kissing, and fondling both the mother and the baby.

The family then provides a party of pastries and liqueurs to share with one another and with those who attended the birth. During the labor, the mother was never left alone, and she will continue to be supported by rituals like this one. The mother will be visited by many of her friends and relatives for some time after the birth. These visits have the effect of recognizing the contribution the mother has made to the community. This social support system is embodied in the role of the mother-in-law. From a few days before until about 1 month after the birth, she feeds the mother ritual foods of broth, marsala wine, and fresh cheeses. All mothers breast-feed their infants, and the infant usually sleeps in the same bed as the mother or in a nearby cradle (Schreiber, 1977).

Finally, in traditional Japanese society, interdependent relationships between people are viewed as extremely important. Children are valued and loved, and their development is celebrated by a number of community rituals. These rituals start during the fifth month of pregnancy, when the woman begins to wear a special belt (called an *iwata-obi*) around her abdomen under the kimono. This ritual is believed to establish the child's first tie to the community. After birth, the umbilical cord is dried and saved in an ornamental box, reminding the mother and child of their once-close physical bond. From birth until late childhood, children sleep with their parents, because it is believed that sleeping alone breaks the family psychological bonds.

On the day of the birth and on the third and seventh day of the infant's life, elaborate feasts are celebrated among all the relatives. Because these early days are thought to be critical to the infant's survival, the feasts ensure health for the baby. A special naming ceremony is performed on the seventh day, and at 1 month, the baby is taken to the Shinto shrine for blessing. At the age of 100 days, the infant is given a grain of rice as its first token solid food (Kojima, 1986). Although some of these traditional practices are changing due to the urbanization of Japan, the basic commitment to the infant's value remains.

SUMMARY

Conception and Fertility

- Fertilization takes place when one spermatozoon enters the ovum, creating a zygote.

- Female ova are present but immature at birth. Males do not begin to produce spermatozoa until adolescence.

- The choice of family planning/contraceptive methods depends on personal and cultural values. Family planning is most needed in societies where the size of the population outstrips the ability of the economy and resources to provide for everyone's welfare.

- Contraceptive practices vary between individuals. Most people can find a contraceptive

method that suits their needs; however, more research needs to be done to find newer methods.

Developmental Processes Before Birth

- All cells in the body except the gametes have the same set of genes and chromosomes.

- Because the epigenome moderates the effects of the environment on gene expression, development of a cell depends as much on its location and chemical environment as on its genetic composition.

- The period of the embryo begins when the zygote implants in the uterine wall.

- Embryos display rudimentary behavior patterns, such as heartbeats, respiration, and whole-body jerky movements.

- The period of the embryo ends when most of the major internal organs are formed.

- During the period of the fetus, the major developments occur in the brain and nervous system. Later in fetal development, the beginnings of controlled movements, such as facial expressions and grasping take place. After 28 weeks, fetuses have states of arousal and REM sleep, and they can learn.

- Fetal behavior has two purposes: to prepare the child for establishing initial preferences after birth, and to stimulate growth and development of bones, muscles, and the central nervous system.

Childbirth

- The overall birthrate in first-world nations has been declining, but the rate of multiple births has been increasing.

- Labor occurs in three stages: the opening of the cervix, the passage of the infant through the vagina, and the birth of the placenta.

- Both risks and benefits are associated with medical technologies such as fetal monitoring, forceps, and vacuum extraction.

- About 33 percent of births are done by cesarean section. There are some risks to C-sections compared to vaginal deliveries.

- Drugs are used to speed labor and ease pain. Drugs can be safe if used sparingly. Short-term effects are common, but few long-term effects can be demonstrated.

- Conventional hospital childbirth was compared with a number of alternatives, including early discharge, Lamaze childbirth, upright postures, midwives, birthing centers, home births, and the Leboyer technique. If implemented properly, these practices are all effective and safe for those who choose to use them.

- Each society has its own unique way of welcoming newborns into the world. This involves a variety of rituals that ensure the health of the newborn and mother and carry a blessing for a happy life.

Chapter 3

The Fetus and Newborn: Health and Risk

CHAPTER OUTLINE AND OVERVIEW

Prenatal Health and Risk	*What are the factors involved in male and female infertility, and how can it be treated? What are the prenatal causes of birth defects? What can be done to prevent them?*
Pregnancy and the Family	*What are the changes in women's bodies during pregnancy? What are the recommended forms of exercise, diet, social support, prenatal education, and stress regulation that are essential for maternal and infant mental health? What kinds of support do fathers need during pregnancy?*
Childbirth Risk and Health	*What types of problems can occur around the time of birth? What kinds of assessments are used to monitor newborn health and well-being? What is prematurity and how can it be treated?*
Prinatal Mortality	*What are the major causes in newborn death? How can parents who lose a newborn be supported?*

Normal prenatal development and child-birth is covered in Chapter 2. The womb—uterus and placenta—is not, however, an impenetrable shield of nurture and security. The placenta functions as a communication link between mother and fetus. In some cases, the placenta becomes a wonderfully adept censor, keeping potentially harmful substances from crossing into the immature fetal circulatory system. Often, however, it does not. The womb is an environment, albeit a very special and uniquely suitable environment, to which the developing individual must adapt during this phase of life. It is just at the point of the most accelerated development that an organ is most susceptible to potentially harmful environmental influences. This chapter covers complications of fertility, pregnancy, and childbirth.

PRENATAL HEALTH AND RISK

Infertility

During a female's childbearing years, about one in six couples suffers from **infertility**: the inability to conceive successfully after trying for at least one year. Either the male or the female, or both, may be infertile. Female infertility is usually caused by a failure to ovulate (that is, the failure of the immature ova to ripen), or by some process that impedes the journey of the ripened ovum from the ovary to the Fallopian tubes. Failure to ovulate can be caused by factors such as excessive exercise or weight loss, obesity, some sexually transmitted diseases, excessive alcohol use, exposure to toxic chemicals, and hormonal imbalances, many of which are treatable (Ford, MacCormac, & Hiller, 1994; Grodstein, Goldman, & Cramer, 1994). Changes in diet, exercise, and hormonal supplements, called fertility drugs, may be used as treatments. Higher than normal levels of HDL cholesterol have been found to decrease the fertility hormone progesterone, making it likely that in some cases cholesterol medications may also improve fertility (Yates et al., 2011). In cases of

blockage, both drugs and surgery have been tried. Fertility drugs sometimes lead to twinning and multiple births because they stimulate ovulation.

About 1 in 20 men are infertile. Some of these cases are caused by genetic mutations while others may be environmental and social causes such as using marijuana and cigarettes; an industrial chemical (trichloroethylene, TCE) used as a degreasing agent in adhesives, lubricants, paints, and cleaner; wearing excessively tight underwear; taking hot baths or saunas; inability to maintain an erection; and premature ejaculation or failure to ejaculate (Forkert et al., 2003; Howard, 1995; Innocenti et al., 2011). These can be treated with changes in behavior and sex therapies. Male infertility may also be caused by underdeveloped testes, prior injuries, and some childhood diseases. Some of these problems may not be treatable.

The chances of a successful conception can be improved by timing sexual intercourse to the period of the menstrual cycle when ovulation is taking place. Usually, this period lasts about 5 or 6 days before the day of ovulation (Wilcox, Weinberg, & Baird, 1995). Couples can monitor ovulation daily by recording the woman's body temperature, which rises about 1 degree Fahrenheit during ovulation. Ovulation can also be monitored by charting the changes in color, amount, and consistency of the cervical mucus. Kits are now sold in drugstores to monitor changes in hormone levels by testing urine samples.

To enhance fertility, lovemaking and sexual intercourse should be a relaxed experience for the couple. Fertility is also enhanced if both partners are in good physical health, maintain appropriate body weight, eat nutritious diets, exercise regularly, and avoid excessive smoking and drinking. Males should avoid or reduce the use of hot tubs and saunas to prevent elevation of temperature around the testes. Better physical health and fitness (which is correlated with IQ) in males is related to sperm count and sperm concentration regardless of use of alcohol, tobacco and drugs (Arden et al., 2008)

If these natural methods fail and standard drug and surgical treatments for infertility are not successful, couples can choose several more expensive and higher-risk measures. The approach recommended by physicians is artificial insemination, in which sperm from the father or another male donor is transferred directly to the mother's Fallopian tubes (Velde & Cohlen, 1999).

If artificial insemination fails, another approach is **in vitro fertilization (IVF)**, sometimes referred to as *assisted reproductive technology*. In cases where healthy ova ripen but cannot pass to the Fallopian tubes, one of the mother's ova is surgically removed and joined with spermatozoa from the father in a sterile biological medium. After fertilization has taken place and the zygote has made a few cell divisions (it is now called an *embryo*; see below), it is surgically implanted into the mother's uterus.

Generally, in vitro fertilization is very expensive, ranging from $60,000 up to almost $1 million, depending on the problems and the number of unsuccessful cycles (Neumann, Gharib, & Weinstein, 1994). The failure rate for IVF can be as high as 30 percent, although new methods have led to higher success rates (Hyslop et al., 2012). Stress reduction and meditation programs have also been shown to increase fertility for IVF mothers (Domar et al., 2011). Couples who choose these methods have a strong desire for children. One or more such failures can lead to depression and to doubt about themselves and their marriage. Because of the uncertainty of the procedure, many IVF couples delay their psychological preparation for parenthood (McMahon, Tennant, Ungerer, & Saunders, 1999; see the Family and Society section in this chapter). These couples require empathy and support (Osofsky, Rosenthal, & Butterbaugh, 1999).

On the other hand, if the fertilization procedure is successful, long-term pregnancy outcomes for embryos fertilized in vitro are similar to those of natural conceptions (Winston & Handyside, 1993). In the past, there was an increased incidence of multiple births because doctors would implant a number of embryos, hoping that at least one would survive. The number of multiple births has been declining, however, due to technical advances (Thurin et al., 2004). While most IVF babies are as healthy as those normally conceived, there is a slight risk of birth defects such as heart problems, digestive tract problems, and cleft lip and palate (Leslie et al., 1998; Reefhuis et al., 2009). IVF children are also no more likely to suffer from parental acceptance and have similar levels of psychological well-being as those from normal births (MacCallum et al., 2007).

In some cases, many ova are removed from the mother and frozen, in a process called **embryo cryopreservation**. This method is still experimental because the data on long-term pregnancy outcomes are still insufficient (Winston & Handyside, 1993), although it can be useful when other approaches fail (Grover & Permezel, 1994). Reasons for doing this are that it may take many menstrual cycles for success using IVF, so that doing only one surgical removal is less stressful for the mother. If a woman needs radiation treatments for cancer that might damage her ova, or if she is approaching the end of her reproductive years and has not yet conceived, she may wish to have some of her ova removed for fertilization. Another variation on IVF is if sperm function too poorly to break down the lining of the ovum; they can be injected directly into the ovum using **sperm microinjection**, which has shown good success rates.

In other variations of IVF, gametes from a donor may be substituted for those of the parent who cannot produce his or her own. Donors can be family members, friends, or anonymous public donors (Winston & Handyside, 1993). An in vitro zygote from the mother and father can also be implanted into the uterus of another woman, called a **surrogate mother**, who carries the infant until birth and then gives the baby to the parents who contributed the zygote. This practice is more controversial, however, and is used less often.

Societal Factors Related to Infertility Treatments

Advances in technology to treat infertility have raised new social issues about the nature of conception, birth, and parenthood. If the genetic parents contribute the embryo but a surrogate mother carries the baby to birth, whose child is it? Although some states in the United States have laws regulating contracts between the genetic parents and the surrogate, courts have struggled with lawsuits from surrogate mothers who wanted to retain custody of the child (Hansen, 1993). In 1993 Florida passed a statute, the Florida Assisted Reproductive Technology Act, that grants parental rights under two conditions: parents are those who contribute the child's genetic inheritance and those who hold the original written intent to be the child's parents (Maun, Williams, Graber, & Myers, 1994). This law also applies to frozen embryos, which may be used later by the genetic parents or by others.

The underlying premise of this law and others like it is that parenting is a matter of choice rather than destiny. In the freedom-granting politics of the United States, people have come to believe that choosing to have or not to have a child is a right, even if factors such as disease, age, or infertility conspire against it (R. Mead, 1999). As new methods for manipulating reproductive outcomes are invented, each individual and the society as a whole will have to struggle with the morality of such freedoms. Detractors of surrogacy have called it a violation of natural law, a form of prostitution, and an exploitation of poor women. With effective psychological counseling and legal contracts, both parents and surrogates are better protected from misuse of this procedure.

What if parents have fertilized zygotes frozen and then divorce? In one New York case, the mother wanted to use her eggs to get pregnant, but her ex-husband objected. New York courts ruled in the husband's favor, suggesting that parents who undergo this procedure should decide what happens to the zygotes in the event of a separation (Associated Press, May 8, 1998). In Los Angeles, a woman's husband, a 30-year-old man, died suddenly of an allergic reaction. Doctors extracted the sperm from his testicles after death, froze them, and used them to impregnate the wife 15 months later. She had a normal pregnancy and birth (Associated Press, March 28, 1999).

Some women cannot produce healthy ova. A lively business of egg donation has developed during the past few years. Donors are catalogued on the Internet or in private agencies to be matched to infertile couples. One recent newspaper ad read: "Egg donor needed. You must be at least 19 and have a 1400 SAT score." The couple was offering $50,000 for the donation. Such ads appeal to young women with financial needs, because most donors receive considerably less money. Donating eggs is a painful and risky procedure requiring the donor to be injected with large doses of hormones that substantially alter her body chemistry and functioning. The long-term effects on donors' health and fertility are currently unknown. In addition, egg and sperm donation raises the possibility that couples can introduce desired genetic traits into their family line, especially privileged, primarily Caucasian families, who can afford the high cost (R. Mead, 1999). On the other hand, epigenetic processes (see Chapter 2) show that the effects of genes are probabilistic, meaning that the child may not have the same phenotype (body form or intelligence, for example) as the donating parents. Because of these ethical issues, some states in the United States ban donor and surrogacy agreements or ban paid agreements.

We now have the technology to implant postmenopausal women with their own previously frozen embryos or the embryo of a donor couple. Medical evidence shows that women between the ages of 50 and 60 are just as capable of carrying a pregnancy to birth as younger women, although the risks of pregnancy to the mother are somewhat higher (Paulson et al., 2002). In a survey conducted in Australia, only 38 percent of respondents from a representative sample approved of the donation of embryos to postmenopausal women (Bowman & Saunders, 1994). Society will have to ponder the question of what happens to children in middle childhood and adolescence when their parents are of an advanced age and perhaps less capable of the physical demands of parenting (Winston & Handyside, 1993). On the other hand, as postmenopausal parents become more common, they may reveal forms of resilience in older adults that have never been observed.

Fears of fetus farming have also been raised regarding the production of **embryonic stem cells**, embryonic cells that can be transformed into many different types of tissue by implanting them into the bodies of adults whose tissues have been damaged by injury or disease. Stem cell research holds the promise of treating stroke and other brain damage, spinal cord injuries and paralysis, and diseases of the internal organs. Currently, the practice of stem cell research is limited in the United States because new stem cell lines can only be obtained by abortion of embryos. States like California and other countries, however, feel that the promise of stem cell treatments is worth the cost, especially if embryos are obtained by elective abortion and not for payment. Because of the risks of "embryos for sale," however, states and nations need to pass regulatory laws (Baird, 2002).

Some of the social, legal and ethical problems of these technologies might be eliminated if human cloning was available. **Cloning** is a method of creating a zygote by removing the donor mother's DNA from the ova and implanting the DNA from any cell in the body of another person—for example, the intended mother or father. This bypasses the need to use a particular person's ova or sperm. The cloned zygote is genetically identical to the adult DNA donor. Currently, cloning has been successful in a few animal species but is against the law for humans. If the techniques are perfected, cloning may be used simply to grow tissues or organs needed to implant in an ailing adult donor from whom the genetic material was harvested. Or it could be used to create babies with the particular characteristics of the DNA donor. Cloning may solve some problems, but it raises others. Society is only beginning to grasp the ethical issues related to these new technologies (see also the later section on ethical issues in genetic counseling).

Genetically Based Disorders

Because of epigenetic regulation of gene expression, the genotype typically does not completely determine the phenotype. There are, however, genetic factors that are less influenced by the environment and more likely to be expressed in the phenotype. In some cases, genetic factors can cause disorders so severe that the fetus will die and be expelled from the mother's body. This is called spontaneous abortion. It has been estimated that two out of every three conceptions are spontaneously aborted in the early months of pregnancy. In a large majority of these cases, the embryo has genetic or chromosomal abnormalities. In addition, over 80 percent of newborn deaths can be accounted for by neural tube defects (15 percent) and chromosomal and genetic abnormalities (67 percent) (Strobino & Pantel-Silverman, 1987; Tharapel, Bannerman, & Tharapel, 1985; I. D. Young, Clarke, & Rickett, 1986). Thus, spontaneous abortion and mortality of malformed fetuses seem to be natural biological functions to eliminate malformations. In other cases, infants stricken with a serious genetic disorder can live for several years or even longer, depending on available treatments.

Most of the evidence for genetic disorders is derived from genealogical studies in which the path of a disorder can be traced through a family tree. For example, manic-depressive disease occurs in a high incidence in the Old Order Amish community in Lancaster, Pennsylvania. Because the entire population of this Amish community is descended from fewer than one hundred people who settled there before 1750, and because the community kept excellent genealogical, disease, and death records, researchers were able to study the chromosomes of hundreds of afflicted individuals. When this is done, the specific gene that causes the disorder can be detected because it is the only one that is identical in all cases. However, other characteristics also occur along with this gene, making it difficult to say what the gene actually causes. In the general population, some forms of manic-depressive disorder (also called bipolar disorder) may be related to multiple genes, while other forms may not be genetically related. Because of the difficulty of this work, of the 3,000 known genetic disorders, researchers have isolated the genes for only about 30 of them.

Genes cannot be changed, at least with current technology, so treatments must focus on changing the environment and thus changing the epigenome to regulate the expression of the harmful gene. Research shows that the epigenome is responsive not only to therapeutic drugs and other chemicals, diet and lifestyle, and also the behavior of other people, such as the type of maternal behavior toward the infant (Dolinoy, Weidman, & Jirtle, 2007; Szyf, 2007; Plomin & Rutter, 1998; Weaver et al., 2004). A relatively recent innovation, epigenetic therapy, is being used to reverse the formation of cancer cells in adults (Feinberg, 2007).

Consistent sex differences are also used as clues to the genetic origins of certain disorders. Sex-linked inheritance accounts for color blindness and hemophilia in males. Hemophilia is known as the "disease of royalty," because the female descendants of England's Queen Victoria were carriers of the disease, and many of the males in the family inherited it. Hemophilia can be treated today with various medications that aid in blood clotting. Other sex-linked disorders are color blindness and some forms of muscular dystrophy.

Fragile X syndrome, another sex-linked disorder, is caused by an abnormal gene on the bottom end of the X chromosome. It is the most common inherited cause of mental retardation. Males affected with the disorder have autistic-like symptoms (see Chapter 10 on autism) such as hand flapping, self-injurious behavior such as biting the hands, poor eye contact, shyness, repetitive behaviors, and mild to moderate mental retardation. Fragile X males are different from autistic males, however, because the former will begin to interact socially in familiar settings. They may also have deficits in attention and information processing. Girls who are carriers show only mild cognitive deficits. These children tend to have long faces and prominent ears (Burack et al., 1999; Einfeld, 2005; Hagerman, 1996).

Several other single-gene disorders are also related to mental retardation and difficulties with social interaction. **Prader-Willi syndrome** is associated with low muscle tone, obesity, short stature, small hands and feet, and lowered intelligence, especially in short-term memory and mathematical skills. These individuals have poor emotion control such as temper tantrums, self-biting, and mood swings (Bertella et al., 2005; Einfeld, 2005). **Williams syndrome** individuals have short stature, heart defects, and intellectual deficits, especially in spatial abilities. Compared to the other syndromes mentioned here, Williams syndrome individuals are highly social, and in some cases indiscriminately social, seemingly willing and able to talk to anyone about anything (Einfeld, 2005; Gray et al., 2006).

In some cases, a single recessive gene can have multiple effects. **Marfan's syndrome** is one example. This disorder is associated with a weakened heart, mild bone structure deformities, long fingers, and eye lens problems. It is believed that Abraham Lincoln suffered from this disease. **Phenylketonuria (PKU)** is a recessive disorder in which the person cannot properly metabolize phenylalanine, an essential amino acid found in most forms of protein. If detected early, the level of phenylalanine-containing foods in the child's diet can be lowered, thus reducing the chances that mental and nervous deficits will develop (Grosse, 2010). Even with appropriate treatment, however, preschool children with PKU showed less ability for planning and search behaviors, although their memory skills were similar, compared to matched control children who did not have PKU (Welsh, Pennington, Ozonoff, Rouse, & McCabe, 1990). These effects are related to the concentration of phenylalanine in the child's blood, suggesting that additional dietary and drug treatment may provide hope for treatment (Diamond, Prevor, Callender, & Druin, 1997). PKU occurs in 1 in 25,000 births. It can be tested for at birth, and parents can be counseled about their baby's diet (H. L. Levy, Karolkewicz, Houghton, & MacCready, 1970).

Another recessive disorder is **cystic fibrosis**, which affects 1 in 2,500 births. It is the most common genetic disorder among people with a northern European ancestry. The disorder is characterized by the clogging of the lungs with mucus, which leads to infection and death in young adulthood. It can be detected prenatally, and many countries routinely screen newborns for the disease.

Some disorders afflict particular racial or ethnic groups whose members are likely to intermarry, increasing the chances of having a child inherit two recessive genes. Jewish couples in which both members can trace their origins to European ancestry (Ashkenazic Jews) havea 1 in 3,600 chance of producing a baby with **Tay-Sachs disease**, an enzyme deficiency that brings about a steady deterioration of mental and physical abilities. Infants may become blind or deaf, have paralysis, and lose the ability to swallow. Few live past the age of 5 (Silver, 1985).

Black infants have a 1 in 400 chance of inheriting **sickle-cell anemia**, a disorder of the red blood cells in which they tend to clot and block off blood vessels. People afflicted with sickle-cell anemia may become mildly retarded or have heart and kidney problems. Unlike Tay-Sachs disease, sickle-cell anemia can be partially treated, and its victims can live normal lives. The sickle-cell gene is also associated with a positive side effect: those who have the disease as well as those who are merely carriers of the gene are partially immunized against the deadly disease of malaria. People with sickle-cell genes are not good hosts for the malarial parasite, which spends part of its life cycle in the blood. Malarial protection is probably the reason why the sickle-cell gene was maintained in the population.

Huntington's disease is a particularly poignant genetic disorder. It is caused by a dominant gene, so half of the children of a parent with the disease will also acquire it. The problem is that the symptoms do not appear until the age of 35 or 40, well after those children have begun to have children of their own. The symptoms include depression, loss of memory and motor control, and other problems caused by the death of brain cells. It occurs in 1 out of 18,000 births, and there is no treatment. A recently developed test can determine whether an individual carries the gene for Huntington's disease. While such a test may be useful for counseling these individuals about whether or not to have children, it also tells them whether they will acquire the disease themselves. Because many people do not want to learn that they might have an incurable disease, relatively few individuals at risk for this disease come to a clinic for genetic screening (S. D. Taylor, 1994). Another dominant disorder is **familial Alzheimer's disease**, which is also associated with brain deterioration and loss of social and cognitive control.

Other genetic disorders are polygenic. Because these disorders require a combination of factors to occur, their incidence is less than that of the single-gene sex-linked and recessive disorders. Polygenic disorders include cleft lip and cleft palate, spina bifida (exposed spinal cord), some forms of diabetes, and some forms of heart defects. Genetic causes may also be implicated in some forms of schizophrenia, autism, and alcoholism, although less is known about the genetic basis of these conditions. Considerably more research is required to investigate these and other genetic causes.

Chromosomal Disorders

During the process of meiosis, errors can occur as chromosomes split and recombine (see Chapter 2). One gamete may wind up with too many chromosomes, another with too few. A **monosomy** is an abnormality of the 23rd pair, the sex chromosomes. Monosomies occur when one member of the pair is missing. In **Turner's syndrome**, a female has only one X chromosome. This is associated with a lack of complete sex determination, other physical deformities, and mental retardation. Approximately 1 in 2000 infants are born with genitals that are neither male nor female, sometimes called intersexuals. As in all forms of sexual development, the incidence and severity of the genital deformations depend partly on the chromosomes and partly on the prenatal availability of specific sex hormones. Hormonal treatments are increasingly common in these conditions (Robboy & Jaubert, 2007)

A **trisomy** is a chromosome pair that has an extra chromosome accidentally attached to it. Trisomies can occur on the sex chromosomes, resulting, for example, in **Kleinfelter's syndrome**

(XXY) in which the male has female behavioral characteristics and may be mentally retarded, although normal in appearance. The best-known of the trisomies is trisomy 21, in which an extra chromosome is attached to the twenty-first pair. The resulting disorder, which in the past was sometimes called "mongolism" but is now known as **Down's syndrome**, is characterized by short stature, flabbiness, cardiac and glandular abnormalities, small mouth, mental retardation, and folds of skin over the eyes.

It is known that Down's syndrome and other genetic and chromosomal errors are more prevalent in infants born to mothers over 35 years old and for fathers over the age of 40. Errors in the meiosis of sperm cells may account for as much as one-fourth of all Down's cases (Arehart-Treichel, 1979; Zhu et al., 2005). Women are also more at risk for miscarriage when the father of their baby is over the age of 40 (Slama et al., 2005). Because older mothers typically have older male partners, there is no way to determine in a particular couple whether the risk of Down's syndrome is caused by maternal or paternal factors.

For this reason, most parents over the age of 35 are counseled to have amniocentesis (see below) to test for the presence of chromosomal abnormalities during pregnancy. It has been hypothesized that estrogen levels in the mother may explain Down's syndrome. Because estrogen production is highest between the ages of 20 and 35, women older than this may be more likely to have a Down's baby than are women between those ages. Estrogen may enhance the process of meiotic cell division, and its lack may cause incomplete cell division (Crowley, Gulati, Hayden, Lopez, & Dyer, 1979).

Aside from the genetic and chromosomal risks, older couples seem just as capable of bearing children as younger couples. In several studies of first-time mothers over 35 years of age, the rate of complications of pregnancy and birth was no different than for younger first-time mothers (Porreco et al., 2005; Prysak, Lorenz, & Kisly, 1995). Because of this, many women may feel that they can delay childbearing until their early

40s. Research suggests, however, that there is no way to reverse declines in fertility with age, even using IVF and other similar techniques (Wyndham et al., 2012). Prospective mothers should be educated that there are no current methods that can rewind their biological clocks. The same is true for fathers. In addition to Down's syndrome, sperm from older fathers has been linked to lower intelligence in offspring as well as significantly increased incidence of children with autism, schizophrenia, and cancer (Kong et al., 2012; Saha et al., 2009).

Environmental Influence on Prenatal Development

As mentioned at the opening of this chapter, many kinds of hazardous conditions can penetrate the otherwise peaceful world of the fetus. For a pregnant woman and her family, therefore, this section is perhaps the most important in this chapter. It is reasonably easy to avoid many of the things that may cause harm to an unborn baby if you are aware of them. The purpose of this section is not only to report the current research findings on this topic, but also to keep you informed about the ways to achieve a healthy pregnancy.

The study of birth defects is known as **teratology**, from the Greek word *tera*, meaning monster—hardly a pleasant association. Teratology, however, is an extremely valuable area of investigation because it attempts to find the causes of birth defects so that they may be avoided in the future. Up until the 20th century, birth defects were mysterious. They were often attributed to magical, spiritual, or supernatural causes, or else they were read as omens or signs. The ancient Babylonians considered birth defects to be omens because that is how they viewed any "unnatural" occurrence. Many primitive societies today have theories about the causes of birth defects, but these are mostly superstitious beliefs, such as the idea that eating twisted or deformed plants may lead to birth deformities (M. Mead & Newton, 1967).

If the birth defect arises because of some environmental cause rather than a chromosomal or genetic abnormality, then the agent responsible for the defect is known as a **teratogen**. Teratogens come in many different forms, from viruses to chemicals to nuclear radiation, and their existence testifies to the importance of environmental-gene interactions even before birth.

The general public was first made aware of the devastating effects of toxic agents on fetal development through two drugs that were once widely prescribed for pregnant women: thalidomide and DES. Thalidomide was a mild tranquilizer that was available in Europe in the 1950s. Pregnant women took it in the early months of pregnancy to help control nausea and insomnia. It was discovered to be teratogenic after a number of physicians traced the presence of heart defects and deformed or missing limbs to the mother's use of the drug during pregnancy. It was found that the time in fetal development at which the mother had taken the drug determined the particular deformity. If she took it just at the time when the arms were forming, for example, then the arms suffered the most defects.

Another way in which teratogenic agents may operate is illustrated by the case of the drug diethylstilbestrol (DES), a hormone given to pregnant women between 1948 and 1969 to help prevent miscarriage and to enhance reproductive health. Between 500,000 and 2 million women are believed to have taken this drug. In this case, however, the effects did not show up at birth but rather when the offspring of these women had reached adolescence. A rise in the number of cases of vaginal cancer in teenage girls and of sterility and other genital abnormalities in teenage boys was eventually traced back to DES. The good news is that continued follow-up into childbearing years of these girls who had genital problems from their mother's taking of DES showed that none of their daughters had abnormalities (Kaufman & Adam, 2002; Titus-Ernstoff et al., 2006).

The effects of these drugs and the other toxic agents reviewed in this section can be attributed to changes in the epigenome of the fetus. As a result of exposure to a toxin, particular types of epigenetic markers form that shut down the expression of genes that would otherwise be active during normal development. As we saw earlier, all of the female's ova are formed prenatally. Thus, exposure to DES alters the epigenome of the gametes of these females during fetal development, suggesting that some forms of the epigenome can be passed on between generations, much like the inheritance of the genome itself (Whitelaw & Whitelaw, 2006).

As a general rule, the effects of toxic agents on the fetus will depend upon a number of factors. Among them is the point in pregnancy at which the exposure occurs, since two-thirds of all birth defects occur in the first trimester or the first 3 months of pregnancy. The earlier in pregnancy one is exposed to a toxic agent, the greater the risk (see Figure 3.1). On the other hand, the first few days and weeks of embryonic life allow for a minimum of susceptibility.

The effect of the teratogenic agents increases and peaks during the period of the rapid differentiation of the organs and limbs—during the middle of the embryonic period (Chapter 2)—and then declines again. If the exposure occurs during the time when organs are growing at a rapid rate, the result will likely be a structural defect. If it occurs after organ growth is mostly completed, the result will more likely be growth retardation or a behavioral abnormality (Kopp & Parmelee, 1979; Fifer et al., 2001). Cognitive and behavioral impairments will be most likely if the exposure occurs during the peak period of brain development, that is, during fetal periods I and II (see Chapter 2). Other factors include the size of the dosage and the length of exposure, with longer, larger doses creating the greatest risk. A **dose-response relationship** occurs when levels of the drug consumed are directly correlated with the strength of the outcome effect (Bookstein, Sampson, Streissguth, & Barr, 1996; Vorhees & Mollnow, 1987).

As more research has been done, the list of teratogenic agents has increased. Some of these are given in Table 3.1. For some of these agents, the effects are well established in both animal and human studies. Effects that are listed as suspected may have been confirmed in animals but not in humans. One problem with isolating the effects of

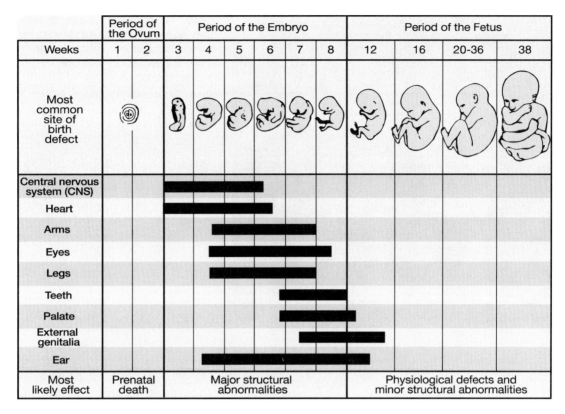

Figure 3.1 Stages of Prenatal Development and Birth Defects

Source: A. Fogel & G. F. Melson, *Child development*, 1988, p. 89. St. Paul, MN: West. Copyright © West Publishing Company. Reprinted by permission. All rights reserved.

particular agents is that more than one factor may occur at the same time. For example, it is difficult to determine the effect of an antinausea drug apart from the infection that caused the severe nausea in the first place (Vorhees & Mollnow, 1987). In this section of the chapter, research on some of the major factors is reviewed in more detail than that shown in Table 3.1.

Substance Abuse. Perhaps the area of teratology that has attracted the most research is the effects of maternal alcohol consumption. **Fetal alcohol syndrome (FAS)**, which was discovered in 1973, is associated with some forms of mental retardation, facial abnormalities such as small narrow heads with widely spaced eyes and an underdeveloped jaw, hyperactivity, growth retardation, cognitive deficits, more premature births and

miscarriages, lower birthweight, and heart defects. FAS occurs at an incidence of 1 to 3 per 1,000 births in the United States (Fifth Special Report to the U.S. Congress on Alcohol and Health, 1984). The heaviest drinkers, those who consume more than five drinks per day on the average, have as much as a 44 percent higher risk of having an FAS child (Kuehn et al., 2012; Landesman-Dwyer, 1981; Molteno et al., 2010; Rosett, 1980).

Infants born to moderate drinkers, those who consume one or two drinks per day, are not likely to have physical deformities. Follow-up studies show that by age 4, however, these children have mild to severe cognitive deficit, learning disabilities and slightly retarded physical growth. This pattern of outcomes has been called *fetal alcohol effects (FAE)* (Abel, Randall, & Riley, 1983). Long-term follow-up studies have shown continuing effects in children in

These five-month-old fraternal twin girls have some of the characteristics of fetal alcohol syndrome: narrow heads, widely spaced eyes, underdeveloped jaws, and growth retardation.

Photo by George Steinmetz

a dose-response relationship as late as 14 years of age, including problems with attention (including Attention Deficit Hyperactivity Disorder, ADHD), speed of information processing, motor coordination, and learning problems (Biederman, 2002; Lee et al., 2004; Roebuck-Spencer et al., 2004; Streissguth et al., 1994). The effects are relatively small for children whose mothers had one drink per day but increase rapidly with higher rates of consumption. Some research shows that occasional *binge drinking* during pregnancy—having multiple alcoholic drinks in one day—may be more harmful than steady low-level consumption. This is because the high and rapid intake of alcohol can damage fetal nerve cells (Jacobson & Jacobson, 2001).

Recent evidence shows that occasional or light drinking (no more than 4 standard drinks per week), has no measurable effects on fetal or infant development (Kelly et al., 2010). Pregnant women, however, are best advised to eliminate all alcohol consumption until after their babies have been born because there may be effects that have not yet been measured (Mullally et al., 2011). On the other hand, if you are currently pregnant and have been a light or occasional drinker since conception, the chances of this having an effect on your baby are relatively small.

Smoking of both tobacco and marijuana during pregnancy has been shown to cause respiratory problems, birth complications, prenatal growth retardation, antisocial behavior, and learning disabilities (such as hyperactivity and impulsivity) in early childhood, although unlike alcohol, smoking does not lower IQ scores or produce cognitive deficits (D'Onofrio et al., 2010; Espy et al., 2011; Fried, 2002; Hurd et al., 2005; Lester & Dreher, 1989; Paradis et al., 2010; Price et al., 2010; Rodriguez & Bohlin, 2005; Wakschlag et al., 2002; Wang et al., 2004). Maternal cigarette smoking has also been associated with a greater risk for infantile excitability, colic and gastrointestinal symptoms, and childhood obesity, asthma and other respiratory disorders, and conduct problems (Gilliland et al., 2001; Law et al., 2003; Maughan et al., 2004; Kries et al., 2002; Søndergaard, et al., 2001). Maternal prenatal cigarette smoking also lowers their sons' sperm count and testes size when these boys reach adolescence and predisposes teens of both sexes to nicotine addiction (Abreu-Villaça et al., 2004; Jensen, 2005; Ramlau-Hansen et al., 2007).

Remarkably, the effect of cigarette smoking on reducing the birthweight of the fetus is the same whether it is the mother or the father who smokes, and if both smoke, the effect is doubled. As in

TABLE 3.1 Common Teratogenic Agents and Their Effects

Agent	Known or Suspected Effects
Drugs	
Alcohol	See text.
Antibiotics	Streptomycin can cause hearing loss; tetracycline can stain teeth and inhibit bone growth. Effects of other drugs have not been fully studied. Acetaminophen appears safe.
Arsenic (in water)	Suspected growth retardation and malformation.
Aspirin	In large amounts, suspected respiratory problems and bleeding at birth for mother and infant.
Barbituates (sedatives)	No long-term effects, but newborns may experience withdrawal and respiratory problems.
Caffeine	No known long-term effects for moderate use, but increased activity, heart rate, and arousal in fetus during periods of maternal consumption.
Chemotherapy	No known effects.
Cocaine	See text.
Diethystilbestrol (DES)	Genetic abnormalities.
Heroin, morphine	Respiratory problems, growth retardation, increased risk for mortality, sleep disturbances; newborns experience withdrawal.
Hydantoins, dilantin, valproic acid (anticonvulsants)	Can cause heart defects, cleft lip and palate, limb reduction, and mental retardation, but some of the effects may be caused by maternal epilepsy.
Lithium (for depression)	Cardiovascular disorders (suspected).
Marijuana	See text.
Methamphetamine (stimulant)	Brain growth retardation and cognitive deficits.
Non-aspirin anti-inflamatories, e.g., ibuprofen	Respiratory problems at birth, miscarriage, male reproductive disorders.
Prozac (and related antidepressants)	No known effects.
Sex hormones (for birth control, fertility, and prevention of miscarriage)	Suspected cardiovascular disorders; no known effects in humans.
Thalidomide	Limb deformities, hearing loss, higher risk of mortality.
Tobacco	See text.
Tranquilizers	No known long-term effects, but newborns may experience withdrawal.
Vitamins	Large doses of vitamin A (used to treat acne) cause defects in heart, head, neck, and brain, and other deformities; large doses of other vitamins are suspected of causing defects.
Diseases (sexually transmitted)	
AIDS	See text.
Chlamydia	Eye infection and risk of pneumonia in newborn.

(continued on next page)

TABLE 3.1   Common Teratogenic Agents and Their Effects (*continued*)

Agent	*Known or suspected effects*
Gonorrhea	Prematurity and eye infection in newborns, higher risk of newborn mortality.
Hepatitus B	Prematurity, low birthweight, higher risk of newborn mortality.
Herpes simplex	Mental retardation, eye damage, higher risk of newborn mortality (can be prevented by cesarean section).
Syphilis	Mental retardation, blindness, deafness, higher risk of mortality.
Diseases (others)	
Anemia (iron deficiency)	Higher risk of stillbirth, newborn mortality, brain damage.
Diabetes	Can cause malformations and higher risk of mortality.
Hypertension	Higher risk of mortality and miscarriage; heart, brain, and spinal cord defects.
Influenza	Cardiovascular and central nervous system defects, spontaneous abortion.
Mumps	Higher risk of spontaneous abortion and stillbirth.
Rh incompatibility	Higher risk of stillbirth, miscarriage, heart defects, and mental retardation.
Rubella	Deafness, cataracts, heart disease, mental retardation, higher risk of spontaneous abortion and stillbirth.
Other viruses	In particular, cytomegalovirus and chicken pox increase the risk of skin and muscle defects, deafness, blindness, mental retardation, and infant mortality.
Environmental hazards	
Lead	Anemia, hemorrhage, increased risk of miscarriage.
Radiation	Small head size, growth retardation, leukemia, cataracts, higher risk of miscarriage and stillbirth.
Methylmercury (in contaminated fish)	Cerebral palsy, neurological disorders.
Pesticides, PCB	Higher risk of stillbirth, low birthweight, mental delays, reproductive abnormalities.
Cleaning agents, solvents	Low birthweight and agression. See text.
Air pollution	Cardiac defects, chromosomal abnormalities, learning deficits, low birth weight (suspected).
Maternal conditions	
Stress	Pregnancy complications, increased risk of Down's syndrome, attentional and motor defects.
Malnutrition	Prematurity, low birthweight, growth retardation, mental retardation.
Age	Down's syndrome (mothers and fathers); autism (fathers).
Depression	Infant depressed behavior and higher stress hormones (cortisol) at birth but no birth defects.

Sources: Alwan et al., 2007; B. A. Buehler et al., 1994 ; D. Bukatko & Daehler, 1995; Chang et al., 2004; R. E. Dahl et al., 1995 ; Ecco, 2012 ; Field et al., 2006 ; R. Gandelman, 1992; M. S. Golub et al., 1998; S. W. Jacobson, et al. 1985; D. Kennedy & Koren, 1998; Kristensen et al., 2010 ; Kulin et al., 1998; B. M. Lester & Dreher, 1998; Li et al., 2011 ; Loomins et al., 2012 ; Lundy et al., 1999; Martinez-Frias et al., 1998; Nakhai-Pour et al., 2011 ; Nehlig & Debry, 1994; Orton et al., 2011; Perera et al., 2005; Räikkönen et al., 2009; Ritz et al., 2002; Rizzo et al., 1997 ; Roy et al., 1998; Schneider et al., 1999; Schuetze & Zeskind et al., 1997; Vorhees & Mollnow, 1987; Vreugdenhil et al., 2002 ; Whyatt et al., 2004.

related studies of older children and adults, passive smoking has effects just as severe as those of direct smoking and causes respiratory problems in those exposed (D. H. Rubin, Krasilnikoff, Leventhal, Weile, & Berget, 1986). Both parents should refrain from smoking during the mother's pregnancy. Programs to prevent smoking in pregnancy have had only limited success, partly because smoking is sustained within the context of a particular culture and nation. Even if a program succeeds in limiting smoking during pregnancy, most parents will begin to smoke again with a year of their child's birth (Cnattingius, 2004; Ershoff, 2004).

With cocaine and intravenous drug use on the rise, there is an increasing incidence of cocaine-addicted pregnant women, as well as women infected with the AIDS virus. Cocaine use by mothers reduces birthweight and creates circulatory, respiratory, and urinary problems. It also increases the risk of Sudden Infant Death Syndrome, attentional difficulties, withdrawal, language delay, and lags in motor development. Although cocaine-exposed infants often fall within the normal range, they have slight deficits in attention and emotional responding compared to nonexposed infants. Also, as with other teratogenic effects related to drug and alcohol abuse, mothers who abuse substances may have other health risks, such as poor diet and poor prenatal care, and these other risks, rather than the drug itself, may be the cause of problems in the newborn. The long-term effects of cocaine on the infant may also be confounded with behavioral factors associated with drug abuse, such as poverty, maternal depression, family disruption, child abuse, and neglect. Alleviation of these contextual factors can in most cases eliminate the effects of the prenatal cocaine exposure (Arendt, Singer, Angelopoulos, Bass-Busdiecker, & Mascia, 1998; Bendersky & Lewis, 1998; Dinehart et al., 2009; Eiden et al., 2009; Espy, Riese, & Francis, 1997; B. A. Lewis et al., 2004; Mayes et al., 1997; Mitra, Ganesh, & Apuzzio, 1994; Morrow et al., 2003; L. T. Singer et al., 2004; Tronick et al., 2005).

One of the problems that occurs with infants born to substance-abusing mothers is that professionals who come in contact with the infant, such as nursing staff, may inadvertently provide less adequate care. This is due to the popular belief by professionals that cocaine and other recreational and illegal drugs have strong and lasting effects on the infant, even though the research evidence suggests that there is considerable controversy about whether such effects actually occur. The lower quality of care by professionals may also be due to stereotypes that stigmatize drug abusers. It is recommended that professionals maintain a neutral and unbiased demeanor toward such infants, who certainly have had no choice in their own fates and may be just as healthy at birth as nonexposed infants (Messinger & Lester, 2008; Meyers & Kaltenbach, 1992).

It is also important to treat both the mother and the infant for the effects of drug withdrawal and to help the family recover from drug abuse. Extra support services are needed to help the family become economically and emotionally stabilized. Comforting an infant who is experiencing withdrawal symptoms is also difficult. It is recommended that the infant be kept quiet in a room with dim lights and low noise levels. Play soft music, hold and rock the baby gently and frequently, speak softly and calmly, and give gentle massages (Pawl, 1992; White, 1992).

Maternal depression. The effects on the fetus of prenatal maternal depression has received particular attention from researchers. The lifetime incidence of depression in women is between 10 percent and 25 percent, and it is estimated that 9 to 14 percent of women show signs of depression during pregnancy. Other estimates show that up to 35 percent of women take psychotropic medication during pregnancy, primarily drugs that are called selective serotonin reuptake inhibitors (SSRIs) including the brand names of Paxil, Prozac, Celexa, and Zoloft, among others. It is difficult to separate the effects of these medications on the fetus compared with the effects of depression alone. In general, there is little evidence that SSRIs cause birth defects. There is some evidence that newborn behavior is somewhat depressed in infants of these women (lower activity level, more sleeping, longer latency to respond to stimulation), and there is some evidence that prenatal maternal depression may lead to children's conduct problems in adolescence. Because chronic depression itself is a risk factor for maternal well-being, maternal care, and infant socioemotional development (see Chapter 6), physicians recommend that mothers continue taking SSRIs during their pregnancies and after as prescribed (Einarson et al., 2001; Field et al., 2006; Gentile, 2011; Hay et al., 2010; Spinelli, 2012; Zeskind & Stephens, 2004).

Maternal anxiety and stress. Compared to depression, maternal stress and anxiety during pregnancy appear to have more toxic effects on prenatal and postnatal development. Fetuses of stressed mothers have a higher activity level than for non-stressed mothers. Infants exposed to prenatal maternal stress cried and fussed more and had difficulties with emotion regulation and social behavior. As children, they are more likely to show symptoms of ADHD and anxiety, lower attention ability, and socioemotional problems. As adolescents, they continue to show problems with ADHD and anxiety and have lower IQ scores compared to children of non-anxious mothers. As adults, these individuals are more susceptible to mental illness, including schizophrenia, depression, and anxiety. When an individual is anxious or feels stressed, there is an increased activation of the hypothalamic-pituitary-adrenal (HPA) axis by which a central nervous system (hypothalamus and pituitary) perception of stress leads to the secretion of the stress hormone cortisol into the blood by the adrenal glands (located above the kidneys) (see Chapter 4). Maternal stress is more harmful to the fetus if it occurs in the first 6 months of pregnancy (Davis & Sandman, 2010).

Elevated cortisol levels are found in anxious mothers. Because cortisol can cross the placenta, it likely affects the development of the fetal brain and HPA axis, making it more susceptible even to mild stresses later in life. It is more difficult to control anxiety, compared to depression, using medication, and the effects of these drugs on the fetus have not been studied. Behavioral stress reduction, including meditation and hypnosis, have been shown to be effective in pregnant women. So has eating chocolate (!), which appears to have a calming effect on some women (DiPietro et al., 2002; Guse et al., 2006; Huizink et al., 2004; O'Connor et al., 2005; Pennell & Whitehouse, 2010; Räikkönen et al., 2004; Rieger et al., 2005; van den Bergh et al., 2004; Wurmser et al., 2006). Recent research is showing specific molecular markers in the epigenome that are affected by prenatal stress, leading to the hope that pharmacological treatments may one day be developed (Essex et al., 2013; Szyf & Bick, 2013)

AIDS. Another area of recent research work is the transmission of acquired immune deficiency syndrome (AIDS) from the pregnant woman to the fetus. AIDS has become a global epidemic, affecting more than 6 million people worldwide. More than 20 million are infected with HIV-1, the virus that causes AIDS. In the United States, AIDS is the leading cause of death among younger men and the fourth leading cause of death among younger women (T. C. Quinn, 1995). The proportion of infants who contract AIDS prenatally varies across studies, but reported percentages range from 15 percent (Europe and North America) to 30 percent (Africa).

AIDS may contribute to low birthweight, although it is difficult to separate its effects from the effects of other risk factors like drug abuse (drug abusers may have contracted the AIDS virus from unclean needles). The biggest risk comes after birth, when infants begin to show signs of the disease. These infants are susceptible to infections that may lead to mental or motor deficits. It is not entirely clear how infants become infected with the AIDS virus. Some may get it prenatally. As with other sexually transmitted diseases (see Table 3.1), there may be a risk of infection by the virus as the infant comes into contact with the mother's body fluids during its passage through the birth canal. In some, but not all, cases, the risk may be reduced by as much as half by cesarean birth (A. Blank, Mofenson, Willoughby, & Yaffe, 1994; Paiva, Hutto, Antunes, & Scott, 1994; Spinillo et al., 1994; Touraine, Sanhadji, & Firouzi,

1994; Towers, Deveikis, Asrat, Nageotte, & Free- man, 1993). A third possible route of transmission is through breast milk after birth (see Chapter 4).

Other toxins. One problem with understanding teratology is that so much of our modern environment is made up of potentially harmful chemicals, pollutants, and radiation (see Table 3.1). Some are harmful to people of all ages, causing cancer and other diseases. In some cases, the fetus may be more susceptible than older children and adults. Another problem in establishing the effects of a teratogenic agent is that these effects are not always seen immediately. Some effects may take 20 or 30 years to develop, if, for example, they affect the functioning of the adult (Karcew, 1994). Teratogens may not always operate through the mother, although there is relatively little evidence at the current time that the father's exposure to drugs and other agents causes birth defects either through the sperm or by contact with the mother during pregnancy (Little & Vainio, 1994).

The findings on the epigenetic transmission of toxic effects to the fetus means that exposure to environmental toxins via maternal behavior during pregnancy has the potential to influence not only the fetus but possibly the fetus' children and grandchildren! Young parents-to-be, therefore, have a responsibility to all their heirs to take care of their physical and mental health during pregnancy and after.

Experts advise that pregnant women should take no drugs unless explicitly advised by a physician. Even a seemingly harmless drug like aspirin, especially when taken late in pregnancy, can cause problems with labor and delivery, although there is no evidence that aspirin causes birth defects (Table 3.1; Kozer et al., 2002). With all prescription drugs, it is wise for the mother to question the physician about the availability of research on the drug's teratogenic effects. Women are counseled to avoid alcohol, cigarettes, X-rays, microwaves, food containing preservatives, colorings and other artificial additives, and contact with people who have viral diseases and other infections. Industrial chemicals called phthalates (found in some nail polish,

perfumes, cosmetic, lotions and plastics) and BPA (found in plastic bottles and food can liners) can affect birth weight and later aggressive behavior (Braun, 2009; Engel, 2010; Spanier, 2011; Zhang et al., 2009). Consult with a physician before taking vitamins or using caffeine (note that many cola drinks contain caffeine). Use sodium bicarbonate (baking soda) as an antacid and natural fiber foods as a laxative. Literature on making pregnancy safe for the baby and mother is available from the March of Dimes Birth Defects Foundation, www. marchofdimes.com.

Can Birth Defects Be Prevented?

The prevention of all forms of birth defects involves two aspects: diagnosis and treatment. If parents suspect that they may be at risk for having children with genetic, chromosomal, or teratogenic disorders, they should consult with their physician. Usually, parents are referred for **genetic counseling**, a service that can help investigate family histories and prescribe certain kinds of diagnostic approaches.

Most chromosomal abnormalities and many genetic disorders can be detected in fetuses as young as 16 weeks by **amniocentesis**. During this procedure, a small amount of amniotic fluid is withdrawn from the mother's uterus through a long hollow needle inserted into the mother's abdomen. The fetal cells present in the fluid can be tested for the presence of more than 100 genetic or chromosomal abnormalities. The sex of the fetus can also be determined.

Usually, amniocentesis is done only in circumstances where some problem is suspected—for example, if the mother or father is over the age of 35 or if there is a history of genetic disorders in the family—because some risk is associated with the procedure. One or 2 out of every 200 women will have a spontaneous abortion after the procedure, and 4 to 6 fetuses may receive minor injuries due to puncture wounds. In addition, the cost of the procedure increases depending upon the number of laboratory tests that are needed to analyze the amniotic fluid. On the positive side, a long-term follow-up study of children aged 7 to 18 whose mothers had amniocentesis, compared to a group of children whose mothers did not undergo the procedure, found no significant differences in the two groups on learning skills and motor and physical development (Baird, Yee, & Sadovnick, 1994).

Another procedure for diagnosing genetic abnormalities is ultrasound. Ultrasound carries less risk than amniocentesis, but it is less able to detect genetic and chromosomal problems: only abnormalities visible on the exterior of the body can be seen and detected using this procedure. Ultrasound has also been used during amniocentesis to help locate the position of the fetus's body before the needle is inserted. Ultrasound can detect the presence of multiple fetuses (Barss, Benacerraf, & Frigoletto, 1985).

One problem with these methods is that they cannot be done until relatively late in the pregnancy, usually at the beginning of the second trimester. By that time, the parents' anxiety levels are likely to be high, and the decision to abort a malformed fetus is more difficult because of the mother's growing emotional attachment to it and because an abortion will require more complex surgical techniques.

In **chorionic villus sampling (CVS)**, a bit of the chorion is sampled. CVS has the advantage of diagnosing a wider range of disorders, and it can be done during the first trimester. It does not require that the physician puncture the amnion, and it is relatively painless because the uterus is entered through the vagina rather than through the abdomen. Ultrasound may be used to guide the sampling procedure. CVS causes only minor discomfort to the mother and has a 100 percent diagnostic success rate. The data on the safety of CVS for the fetus are mixed. Some research reports no increased risk from the use of the procedure (J. E. Green et al., 1988; Smidt-Jensen & Hahnemann, 1988). On the other hand, several studies have found that CVS produces a higher percentage of both spontaneous abortions and limb defects. The incidence of limb deformities may depend on the timing of the test, so more research is needed (Hsieh et al., 1995; Palo et al., 1994). On the other

hand, the actual percentage of problems resulting from these procedures is extremely low—from 0.5 to 2.0 percent of all the tested pregnancies. Families need to weigh the benefits and risks of the procedure against their reasons for seeking genetic counseling (Boss, 1994; Cutillo et al., 1994).

Unfortunately, many types of disorders cannot be detected with any of these diagnostic procedures. In addition, each disorder requires a specific test, and each test can be quite costly. Thus, genetic counseling must be selective and done only with a thorough knowledge of the family history.

In actuality, very few of the causes of birth defects and prenatal disorders are clearly understood, and when defects or disorders are discovered, parents are often upset and confused. Research shows that it is better for parents to consult professional genetic counselors rather than their primary care physicians. Many physicians do not know the field of genetic research and may not understand the options available for parents when a prenatal disorder is detected (Geller et al., 1993; Wright, 1994).

Several disorders, including spina bifida (exposed spine) and anencephaly (exposed brain), can be detected by testing the mother's blood between the fifteenth and eighteenth weeks of pregnancy. The test is for **maternal serum alpha-fetoprotein (MSAFP)**, and it is safe for both mother and fetus. Researchers are developing methods for testing the fertilized zygote before it is implanted. Called **preimplantation genetic diagnosis (PGD)**, the test may provide significant information without spontaneous abortion of an already implanted embryo, which may be an unacceptable risk for some families who would otherwise choose CVS (Verlinsky & Kuliev, 1994). PGD requires procedures similar to those used during in vitro fertilization: the zygote would be removed from the mother for testing and then implanted if it proves healthy.

After such tests are made and a prenatal disorder is discovered, what can be done to treat the problem? Currently, three avenues of treatment are available: the fetus can be treated medically while inside the uterus, the doctor and family can make concrete plans for treatment following the birth, or the family can choose to abort the fetus.

Fetal medicine is one of the fastest-growing fields of medicine. Doctors have had success treating certain disorders by giving specific vitamins to the mother. In other cases, tubes have been inserted into the fetus to draw blood or to drain harmful buildups of fluids from the head or the bladder. Some malformations, such as intestinal openings or blockages and respiratory and neural disorders, can be repaired surgically. Ultrasound can be used to monitor the progress of a disease, the intervention, and the treatment. Fetal medicine can pose risks to both mother and fetus, however, and these need to be carefully evaluated by future research. Among the problems of doing surgery on a fetus are how to move it into the desired position for the intervention, how to make the fetus relax during the procedure, and how to administer anesthetics, all without undue risk to the mother (Collins, 1994; Forestier, Kaplan, & Cox, 1988; Frigoletto, Greene, Benacerraf, Barss, & Saltzman, 1986). A growing number of advanced post-childbirth surgical and drug treatments are becoming available for such disorders as heart defects, facial deformities (cleft palate, for instance), and PKU. Information on genetic counseling is also available from the March of Dimes Birth Defects Foundation.

What Are Some Ethical Issues Raised by Genetic Counseling?

Like in vitro fertilization, genetic counseling and screening for prenatal disorders raise significant ethical questions. If a serious disorder is discovered, few treatments are available, and abortion is often the only option for a family that does not want to bring a child into the world who is likely to be severely handicapped (see the next section). Another side of the picture is the use of prenatal screening to enable parents to choose to carry or abort a child who does not meet their specifications but is otherwise healthy. Already parents can use CVS to determine the embryo's sex and choose to carry to term only a boy or a girl, depending upon their preference.

It is possible that these procedures may produce a higher percentage of wanted compared to unwanted infants. Research in Sweden shows that better parent-child relationships, even over a long-term follow-up lasting 25 years, result from raising children who fit the parents' prenatal sex preference (Stattin & Klackenberg-Larsson, 1991). However, this does not mean that selecting one sex and aborting another will automatically lead to better parent-child relationships.

Consider the following futuristic possibility. Using in vitro fertilization methods, one cell is removed from the developing embryo. In the relatively near future, we will be able to analyze the entire genetic code of this embryo, and we may have some knowledge of how the entire genotype transforms into the phenotype of the whole individual. According to one scientist,

> All of this information could be transferred to a supercomputer, together with information about the environment—including likely nutrition, environmental toxins, sunlight, and so forth. The output will be a color movie in which the embryo develops into a fetus, is born, and then grows into an adult, explicitly depicting body size and shape and hair, skin, and eye color... speech and musical ability; the mother will be able to hear the embryo—as an adult—speak or sing. (Lodish, 1995, p. 1609)

Could medical technology make this happen? That depends upon your whether you believe that the development of the individual is completely determined by the genes, the environment, or their relationship vis the epigenome. Perhaps future computers and molecular research will be so sophisticated that they will be able to anticipate epigenetic-environmental effects, such as the effect of a kind word said by a teacher or a chance meeting that leads to a career choice, and thus generate a lot of possible future adults from a single embryo. Would parents then be permitted to abort an embryo if they did not like any of these simulated adults? Or could parents, with this knowledge, know when and how to expose their children to particular events, thereby controlling the children's entire lives so as to sculpt them into the kind of persons the parents imagine? Would children become mere puppets in the hands of such godlike parents and scientists? Are these ideas any more than fantasy and science fiction? Only the future will tell us.

Elective Abortion

There are many reasons why parents might make the choice to end a pregnancy by means of induced or elective abortion: to prevent birth defects, to protect the life or health of the mother, in cases of rape or incest, because of poverty, and as a means of birth control. The last two reasons—low income and birth control—account for most abortions and in theory are totally preventable with adequate knowledge and access to contraceptive methods.

On an international level, the worldwide trend is toward the liberalization of abortion laws (Henshaw, 1994). Abortion is currently legal in the United States. In their 1973 decision in *Roe v. Wade*, the justices of the U.S. Supreme Court concluded that the decision to terminate a pregnancy is part of a woman's right to privacy guaranteed by the Constitution. The Court's decision divided pregnancy into three equal periods. In the first period (conception to 12 weeks), the decision to abort was up to the mother and her physician. In the second period (13 to 24 weeks), the health and safety of the mother was the main deciding factor. No limitations were placed on the reasons for abortion during these two periods. After 25 weeks, abortions were not permitted, except when the mother's life or health was in extreme danger. In 1992, in *Planned Parenthood v. Casey*, the Court made clear that states may not criminalize abortion prior to 24 weeks nor prevent any woman from exercising her choice to terminate her pregnancy (Kolbert & Miller, 1994). Many states, however, have laws that require women seeking abortion to have counseling, read certain written materials about risks, and/or wait a predetermined period of time, usually 24 hours.

In 2003, the U.S. Congress passed the Partial Birth Abortion Ban Act, which prohibits so-called "partial birth abortions," also known as "intact dilation and extraction." Partial birth abortions are used in the second period and are controversial because of the procedure used. Labor is induced, the cervix dilated, and the fetus pulled out by the feet, leaving the head undelivered. The fetal brain is then extracted before delivering the head. The procedure is used relatively rarely and primarily in cases where the mother's life is in danger. In 2007, the U.S. Supreme court ruled that the Partial Birth Abortion Ban Act does not violate a woman's constitutional right to an abortion guaranteed by *Roe v. Wade*, because the law limits a particular procedure and not abortion per se. Opponents of the ban say that this method is often the only available means to save the mother's life.

A central issue in *Roe v. Wade* was the question of fetal viability. **Viability** refers to the ability of the fetus to survive on its own, without dependence on the mother. Medically speaking, a fetus is viable if after birth it can be sustained on life-support systems in a neonatal intensive care unit (see Chapter 4). Viability begins between 24 and 30 weeks (Grobstein, 1988). These medical findings are consistent with the *Roe* decision.

An entirely different issue is, "When does human life begin?" According to Lewis Thomas of the Memorial Sloan-Kettering Cancer Center in New York City, the question of when human life begins can be resolved "only in the domain of metaphysics. It can be argued by philosophers and theologians, but it lies beyond the reach of science." Taking the opposite view, Charles A. Gardner states:

> There will always be arguments based on spiritual or ethical beliefs to convince an individual of the rightness or wrongness of abortion, but each person should first understand the biology to which those beliefs refer. (Gardner, 1989, pp. 557–559)

With regard to biological development, it is often argued that the zygote at conception is human because it contains all of the necessary genetic instructions to make an individual human being. As we saw earlier in the chapter, however, the zygote can develop only by a complex process of interaction with the prenatal environment. The location and biochemical environment of a cell, not just its genetic code, are what determines the phenotype. There is no preformed person residing in the zygote or even in the embryo; the person is a complex gene-environment interaction that takes a long time and the proper nutrients to grow.

One way to decrease the number of abortions used for family planning is simply to encourage more contraception. In fact, abortion rates have been declining steadily. The rate in 2011 was 19.4 abortions per 1,000 pregnancies in the United States, the lowest since 1974 (http://www.guttmacher.org/pubs/fb_induced_abortion.html). Provision of low cost contraceptive methods seems to be the major factor promoting this change. In one study in which women were given contraception counseling and contraception devices or pills at no cost, the rate of abortions in this cohort of 9,256 women in St. Louis fell to about 5 per 1,000. President Obama's health care law now allows women to get contraception from their health care provider with no co-payment, which is expected to reduce the rate of abortions nationally (Peipert et al., 2012; http://www.kff.org/womenshealth/upload/8379.pdf).

Another alternative to abortion is carrying the infant to term and placing the infant for adoption. However, because many abortions are performed on young women living in poverty who may suffer from drug and alcohol abuse and poor prenatal care, removing abortion rights from these women increases the chances of teratogenic effects, ranging from preterm birth at one extreme and retardation and deformity on the other. The costs to society (who will take care of these children, and who will pay for their care?) and the ultimate quality of life of the children (related to their particular ailments and to the fact that handicapped children in foster care have a high probability of being subjected to child abuse) must be taken into account in formulating public policies on adoption versus abortion. Some have argued that women who seek abortions

are more likely to be mentally ill and therefore not able to make rational choices about terminating their pregnancy. Recent reviews of large-scale research studies shows that women who terminate an unwanted pregnancy are no more likely to be mentally ill than women who carry an unwanted pregnancy to term. Also, there is no evidence that abortion per se has any long-lasting effects on women's mental health (Major et al., 2009).

Another argument used by abortion opponents is that the fetus feels pain prior to 24 weeks. As we saw in the previous chapter, it is anatomically impossible for the fetus to feel pain before about 30 weeks. Anything even closely resembling a human brain does not form until the twentieth week, and brain electrical activity (EEG) resembling that of adults does not begin until between 26 and 30 weeks. This age corresponds with other measures of viability, suggesting that a brain that is capable of feeling pain and behaving intentionally develops only late in fetal life.

Should these scientifically based observations take precedence over moral and ethical considerations? Certainly not. The decision to seek an abortion is a personal one based on social, scientific, medical, and moral considerations and made in consultation with genetic counselors, physicians, family members, or religious counselors.

Risks of Teenage Pregnancies: Education and Contraception for Youth

The majority of infants with birth defects in the United States are born to teenage mothers. The rate of teenage births increased until the 1990s in the United States and has continued to decline gradually since that time for all racial and ethnic groups, reaching its lowest point in 2009 at 39.1 births per 1,000 teens aged 15 to 19. The largest decline was for African American teenagers and for second births for teens who already have one child (National Vital Statistics Report, 2005; Ventura & Hamilton, 2011). Despite the declines, many teens are still giving birth, and the rate of teen pregnancy is almost twice as high for African Americans and Hispanic Americans as that of

Caucasian Americans (Guyer et al., 1998; Ventura & Hamilton, 2011). Teen pregnancy is still a major social problem because teenage mothers require great expense from society to cover their health care and financial support. As for abortion, the reduction in teen birth rate is due primarily to the availability of inexpensive contraception.

Teenage mothers tend to be at risk for all kinds of birth complications. The death rate for infants of teenage mothers by age one year is 3 to 4 times that for infants of older mothers, and the incidence of low-birthweight infants is much higher among infants born to teenagers. Are these problems associated solely with the age of the mother? The evidence suggests that there is nothing inherent in the age of the mother alone that would account for these problems. But teenage mothers seem to be at risk for childbearing because such a large proportion of teenage mothers come from poor socioeconomic conditions, with their attendant problems of poor nutrition, high stress, poor medical care, abuse and neglect, and poor family relationships (Coley & Chase-Lansdale, 1998; Phipps et al., 2002; Scaramella et al., 1998). Teenage mothers are seven times as likely to be poor before pregnancy as older mothers (Alan Guttmacher Institute, 1994). Teen parents, both mothers and fathers, are more likely to have low academic performance, be unpopular among their peers, and be poor (Xie et al., 2001).

Marriage and parenting also place increased stress on teenagers. The demands of child and spouse often conflict with the teen's own needs for development, education, and health, and of mature romantic and marital relationships (Coley & Chase-Lansdale, 1998). Teenage marriages often end in divorce, leaving many teenage mothers with the additional stress of being a single parent. In general, teenage mothers are less likely to be responsive to their young infants than older mothers are, and teenage mother-infant pairs experience less mutual affection and enjoyment compared to infants with older mothers (Barratt & Roach, 1995). Males and females between 30 and 55 years old, both African American and Caucasian American, who married as adolescents earned

less income, completed fewer years of school, held lower-paying jobs, and engaged in more risky sexual behavior than those who married later (Hardy et al., 1998; Meade & Ickovics, 2005; Teti and Lamb, 1989).

Teenage fathers are similar to teenage mothers. They are more likely to be poor and to have come from troubled families. They work and earn more than non-parent peers, but because they obtain less education, their lifetime earning ability is considerably reduced. Because of high rates of divorce among teenage parents, only about 50 percent of teen fathers live with the mother and child sometime after the birth. Cohabitation rates are highest for whites, compared to African Americans and Hispanic Americans. By the time the child is of school age, fewer than 25 percent of teen fathers are still in contact with their children. This low rate of father involvement is related primarily to unstable or hostile relationships between mothers and fathers (Coley & Chase-Lansdale, 1998). To make matters even worse, when the children of teenage parents reach adolescence, they are more prone to delinquency, violence, and arrest than other teens, perpetuating an intergenerational cycle of disadvantage (Pogarsky et al., 2003). Much of this effect on the offspring can be accounted for by father absence during early childhood (Ellis et al., 2003).

Treatments for teenage pregnancy problems are complex. Teen pregnancy prevention programs should begin as early as the eighth grade for high-risk teens and involve the entire community and culture (Young et al., 2004; Coley & Chase-Lansdale, 1998). In general, teenagers are caught in a web of conflicting cultural standards. At home, they may receive the message that sex out of wedlock is prohibited; in school, there is peer pressure to engage in sexual behavior; and in the movies and on television, sexuality and sexual activity are glorified. Many movies and shows present macho and sexist themes in which men repress women. Girls from impoverished homes or those who have suffered physical and sexual abuse may see pregnancy as a way to leave home or establish their own identity. Programs should focus on internal locus of control, academic achievement, making effective life choices, and poverty alleviation (Young et al., 2004).

Once the teen is pregnant, other types of intervention may be used. Better pregnancy outcomes are associated with reduction of psychosocial stress, social support, prenatal care, more parental involvement with the infant, and a sense that these factors would continue through time (Boyce, Schaefer, & Uitti, 1985; Meade & Ickovics, 2005; Zaslow & Eldred, 1997). Intervention programs can provide information about prenatal health and nutrition and postnatal child-rearing methods and also provide teen parents contact with older parents who can serve as mentors, people to whom they can turn to for advice regarding child rearing, staying in school, and other concerns (Rhodes, 1993).

Research in the United States shows that the majority of teenagers do not have basic knowledge of sexuality, conception, and contraception (Ammerman et al., 1992). For this reason, sex education programs in junior and senior high school can significantly reduce the risk of teenage pregnancy and increase the incidence of sexual abstinence among adolescents. Sex education programs have been consistently shown to be more effective than abstinence-only programs in preventing both sexual activity and pregnancy (Barth et al., 1992; Glazer, 1993a; Weed & Jensen, 1993). The fact is that 50 percent of high school students report engaging in sexual activity, and this percentage has not changed significantly between 1990 and 2011. Of those who reported engaging in sexual intercourse, there has been an increase in the percentage reporting condom use, from 46 percent in 1991 to 60 percent in 2011 (www.cdc.gov/healthyyouth/sexualbehaviors) due primarily to effective sex education. This still leaves many young people unprotected, and society needs to respond to this reality in ways that respect and protect these youths, their families, and their children within the bounds of constitutional protections of rights and privacies. In the next section, we examine the effects of pregnancy on the family for women of all ages.

PREGNANCY AND THE FAMILY

New parenthood is a major life transition in adult development. It is a phase of life, not unlike infancy or adolescence, that requires a good deal of adaptation. Like most other important developmental phases, parenthood has its own pleasures and sorrows, rewards and misgivings, and memories both fond and painful. For most people, the first step in becoming a parent is pregnancy. The first issue that new parents must deal with is the physical changes that a woman's body undergoes during that 9-month period.

What Are the Physical Changes Associated with Pregnancy?

As can be seen from our discussion of risk factors during pregnancy, maternal and fetal health is extremely important in maintaining fetal development on a normal course. In this section, the factors and behaviors that promote health during pregnancy will be reviewed, including checkups, diet, and exercise.

What are the first signs of pregnancy? The failure to menstruate is usually considered to be the most reliable indicator, but it is not foolproof. A woman may menstruate for 2 or three months after she has conceived, and failure to menstruate may occur for other reasons, such as age, illness, or emotional upset. Breast changes may also be symptomatic of pregnancy. These may occur in the form of fullness, tingling, or hypersensitivity.

About 80 percent of all pregnancies occur with some nausea, usually in the morning, but this typically passes after 8 weeks. "Morning sickness"— **nausea and vomiting of early pregnancy (NVP)**—is related to biochemical changes in the body, including increased secretion of the hormones prolactin and estradiol. These hormones may provide an adaptive mechanism that functions to provide a reason for the mother to get more sleep and rest or to enhance the development of the placenta and embryo. Infants of women who experienced some form of NVP actually have enhanced cognitive processing at ages 3 and 7 years, most likely the effect of the NVP hormones on infant brain development (Nulman et al, 2009).

During the first 3 months of pregnancy, women are more likely to feel a sense of nausea/disgust around some food and body products, suggesting that NVP may also be adaptive in making mothers more selective of what they eat, thus reducing the possibility of consuming teratogenic agents (Fessler et al., 2005). NVP may be controlled naturally by changes in diet and rest patterns. Other demonstrated sources of relief, at least for some women, include vitamin B6 supplements, ginger, and acupuncture. In extreme cases, some physician-prescribed antihistamines are effective and have no known teratogenic effects (Knight et al., 2001; Niebyl & Goodwin, 2002; Seto, Einarson, & Koren, 1997; Vutyavanich et al., 2001; Werntoft & Dykes, 2001).

Other symptoms of pregnancy are fatigue and frequency of urination. Conclusive diagnosis can only be obtained through laboratory tests, however. Pregnancy test kits are currently available for use at home, but they are not reliable in all cases.

During pregnancy, the uterus grows from about 2 ounces to 2 pounds, and the mother's abdominal muscle fibers grow to about 10 times their original length. Maternal uterine muscles are extremely important for a number of reasons. They will open the cervix at birth to provide a passage for the baby, contract to push the infant out, and continue to contract after birth to restrict the continued flow of blood to the uterus. The latter function is essential to avoid major blood loss. The vaginal muscles also change during pregnancy. The vagina increases in length and capacity, and more blood is supplied to the area. In addition, vaginal secretions increase in quantity and in bacteriological action.

Because of these secretions, sexual intercourse during pregnancy may be more satisfying to some women than it was before. On the other hand, some women report a lowering of libido, especially during late pregnancy (Hamela-Olkowska et al., 2003). In general, sexual intercourse during pregnancy is not harmful. Consultation with one's physician is suggested because each woman is different, and intercourse during late pregnancy may not be advisable in some cases.

Physicians who care for the health of the mother and fetus during pregnancy and who deliver babies are called **obstetrician/gynecologists**. Midwives (see Chapter 2) also provide prenatal care and support. Those who care for the baby immediately after birth and during childhood are called **pediatricians**. Women should be encouraged to discuss all aspects of their pregnancy and delivery with their obstetricians or midwives. To the extent possible, women should select an obstetrician or midwife whose beliefs and practices accord with their own. Most midwives and obstetrician/gynecologists recommend regular prenatal checkups. The frequency of these checkups and what is done depend upon the mother's health status and risk factors.

Proper health care during pregnancy has been shown to prevent many environmentally caused birth defects, reduce the rate of premature births, and reduce prenatal mortality and health risks for both mother and fetus. Due to poverty, fear, or unwanted or teen pregnancy, as many as 20 percent of women in the United States do not receive prenatal care during the first trimester of pregnancy. Government and health care officials are working to reduce this percentage (Fischer & Rozenberg, 1999; Klerman & Goldenberg, 1999).

As pregnancy proceeds, the placenta forms within the uterus and secretes hormones that nurture the fetus and also prepare the mother's body for birth. The placenta is constructed to enhance the exchange of nutrients and other substances between the mother's and the fetus's blood supply (see Figure 3.2). As we saw earlier, the placenta filters some things and allows others to pass through.

In reality, because the fetus has genes from the father as well as the mother, it exists within her as a foreign body. Under most circumstances, such foreign cells would be attacked by a person's immune system. Why does this not happen to the fetus? Apparently, the cells in the uterus near the placenta are responsible for blocking the local production of the immune response system. Studies of how

Artery to mother's system

Vein to mother's system

Mother's blood

Umbilical vein

Umbilical arteries

Placenta (cross section)

Figure 3.2   Changes in Maternal Circulatory System During Pregnancy

A detailed cross-section of the placenta is shown here. Note that the placenta has two portions—the embryo's portion and the mother's—and that they are interwoven. Those parts of the drawing that belong to the embryo are shown in light gray; those of the mother are in a darker gray. The gray umbilical vein and arteries carry the embryo's blood, exchanging nutrients, wastes, and the like with the mother's blood, but the two blood supplies do not come in direct contact.

Source: A. Fogel & G. F. Melson, *Child development*, 1988, p. 108. St. Paul, MN: West. Copyright © West Publishing Company. Reprinted by permission. All rights reserved.

the uterus does this may have applications in cancer research (because cancerous tumors may block the immune system) and in organ transplants, where doctors would like to stop the normal process of rejection (Silberner, 1986).

The placental hormones also induce changes in the breasts as they become ready for lactation. They increase in size as fat is replaced by mammary gland tissue and more blood supply. A clear, yellowish liquid called **colostrum**, high in protein and antibodies, may be secreted by the fourth month of pregnancy. Colostrum is the first food of the breast-fed infant. It is gradually replaced by milk during the first few days after birth (see Chapter 5).

In general, the mother's body adapts itself to work harder. The mother's digestive and eliminative systems (kidneys, intestines, and sweat glands) must begin to take on the requirements of the developing fetus. These extra requirements are often accompanied by discomfort. Typical complaints of pregnant women include leg cramps, varicose veins, temporary changes in skin pigmentation, stretch marks on the abdomen, shortness of breath, lethargy, indigestion, constipation, and moodiness. The quality of sleep also changes. Women wake up more frequently during the night and sleep less deeply (Brunner et al., 1994). The severity of these symptoms depends upon the

woman's body structure, nutritional status, fatigue, and psychological sense of well-being.

All of these facts show how the mother and fetus comprise a unique biological system in which feedback between them accounts for their mutual development. As the fetus changes, the mother's body changes in response, and continued changes in her body and its functioning provide the nourishment and biological support necessary for fetal growth and development. Both mother and fetus act as a system in their exchange of materials with the outside environment. One of the most important aspects of this interchange is the intake of food by the mother.

Nutritional and Exercise Requirements During Pregnancy

The purpose of good prenatal nutrition is to avoid depletion of maternal stores of nutrients, to allow the mother to produce sufficient milk for breast-feeding, and to provide sufficient nutrients for the fetus. Malnutrition during pregnancy does more than simply deplete the mother's nutritional supplies; physical and brain development can be severely hampered in an infant born to a malnourished mother. Because the number of neuronal brain cells does not substantially increase after 20 weeks' gestational age, the early months of pregnancy are a critical period for brain development, and the nutrition that the fetus receives from the mother will determine how many cells are produced.

The recommended diet during pregnancy is shown in Table 3.2. Mothers are advised to eat a diet of balanced foods. A high protein, low carbohydrate diet, recommended in many weight loss programs, is not appropriate because it elevates cortisol levels in both mother and fetus. Balanced maternal diets also promote fetal growth and contribute to the reduction of chronic diseases in adulthood (Herrick et al., 2003; Wu et al., 2004). Pregnant teens require even more careful attention to nutritional needs than adults because their bodies are still growing.

Micronutrients, vitamins and minerals found in foods and in dietary supplements, are also important during pregnancy. Particular micronutrients are essential to a healthy pregnancy. These include folic acid, vitamin B9 (deficiencies limit blood supply to the fetus and cause some birth defects and delivery complications), zinc (lack causes some birth complications, physical, immunological, and neurological growth retardation), iodine (lack contributes to miscarriage, some birth defects, and preterm birth). Other vitamins and minerals are also important (Black, 2001). Taking

vitamin and mineral supplements should be done only in consultation with one's doctor. They may not be necessary with normal diets, and some vitamins may harm the fetus if taken in large quantities. On the other hand, in situations where there is a risk of malnutrition (as in developing countries and in cases of poverty) or for other medical reasons, appropriate supplementation may be useful (Shah & Sachdev, 2004; Vahratian et al., 2004).

For adults in general, omega-3 fatty acids, found in oily fishes, promote neurological development and reduce cardiac and other inflammatory diseases. Research shows that taking these supplements during pregnancy lowers the risk of preterm birth, improves placental blood flow, and reduces the incidence of infant illness during the first 6 months of life. One well-controlled study of 2,109 pregnant women from Massachusetts, however, found a slight *reduction* in fetal growth for women who took the most of these supplements. It is unknown whether this affects later development or whether this slight risk outweighs other possible benefits. Mothers should check with their doctors about the latest information (Imhoff-Kunsch et al., 2010; Oken et al., 2004; Olsen & Secher, 2003; Saldeen & Saldeen, 2004).

The average weight gain for women in pregnancy depends on the size of mother and infant (see Table 3.3). Note that women with higher pre-pregnancy

---

TABLE 3.2 Nutritional Recommendations For a Balanced Diet During Pregnancy

Grain Products (5–12 Servings)
Examples of 1 serving = 1 slice of bread; 30g of cold cereal; 175 mL (3/4 cup) of hot cereal
Examples of 2 servings = 1 bagel, pita or bun; 250 mL (1 cup) of pasta or rice

Vegetables (3–5 servings) and Fruit (2–5 servings)
Examples of 1 serving = 1 medium-size fruit or vegetable; 125 mL (1/2 cup) fresh, frozen or canned vegetables or fruit; 250 mL (1 cup) of salad; 125 mL (1/2 cup) of juice

Milk Products (3–4 servings)
Examples of 1 serving = 250 mL (1 cup) of milk; 50g or 2 slices of cheese; 175 mL (3/4 cup) of yogurt

Protein and Alternatives (2–3 servings, 6–9 ounces per day)
Examples of 1 serving = 50–100 g of meat, poultry or fish; 1–2 eggs; 125–250 mL (1/2–1 cup) of canned beans; 100 g (1/3 cup) of tofu; 30 mL or 2 tablespoons of peanut butter

Other Foods
Taste and enjoyment can also come from other foods and beverages that are not part of the 4 food groups. Some of these foods are higher in fat or calories, so use these foods in moderation.

Source: www.babies.sutterhealth.org/during/preg_nutrition.html

weights should actually gain less during pregnancy. Severe restriction of calories during pregnancy is not recommended and may even be harmful. With the rise in the rate of obesity in industrialized countries, however, overeating creates an increased risk of affecting not only the mother's but the infant's health. Too little weight gain is associated with low-birthweight infants, while excessive weight gain is associated with overly high birthweights and with later childhood obesity (Cogswell, Serdula, Hungerford, & Yip, 1995; Oken et al., 2007; Surkan et al., 2004). In addition to contributing to childhood obesity, maternal obesity during pregnancy is associated with birth complications, gestational diabetes, hypertension, and urinary tract infections in the mother (Kumari, 2001; Sebire et al., 2001). The best means for controlling weight gain without compromising the fetus should be discussed with the mother's doctor.

Mothers can and should continue to exercise during pregnancy and will derive benefits of cardiovascular fitness similar to those they experience when they are not pregnant. Intense exercise is helpful for fetal development but only during the first trimester of pregnancy. After that, too much exercise reduces birthweight, which is a risk factor for later disorders (Campbell & Mottola, 2001; Clapp et al., 2002). Moderate exercise enhances fetal neurodevelopment and contributes to the mother's sense of well-being (Herring et al., 2011). Mothers should check with their physicians to determine the right level of exercise in relation to the condition of their pregnancy, risk factors, and signs for when to stop exercising (Technical Bulletin no. 189, 1994; http://www.webmd.com/baby/guide/exercise-during-pregnancy).

Aside from nutrients, the mother receives information from the social environment, and the feedback processes that govern this exchange may ultimately affect the health and development of the baby. One of the most important sources of interchange for the mother is her relationship with her family and her own psychological adjustment to the state of becoming a parent. Although the effect is most apparent in first-time parents, each new baby brings with it a continuing psychological adaptation within the mother and within each of the other family members.

How Do Mothers Adapt Psychologically to Pregnancy?

In writing about this phase of adult development, Alice Rossi (1968) coined the term "transition to parenthood." According to Rossi, parenthood, and not marriage, is the major transition into adult life. Child psychologist Erik Erikson referred to parenting as "generativity," the giving of one's time and energy to the next generation. The birth of an infant is both a physical and a psychological point of no return. Unlike marriage, birth and parenthood are irreversible processes.

One of the reasons that pregnancy and childbirth are psychologically important is that, to some extent, they constitute a break from one's own childhood. Once people have a child of their own, they lose the "innocence" of being only a child of their parents. The new mother may become more aware of her feelings toward her mother, and what her own mother may have experienced. Meanwhile, the new mother's parents may be encouraged to renew or readjust their feelings about their daughter by attempting to reestablish

Table 3.3   Recommended Weight Gain during Pregnancy

Pre-pregnancy weight	Recommended weight gain
Underweight (BMI less than 18.5)	28 to 40 pounds (about 13 to 18 kilograms)
Normal weight (BMI 18.4 to 24.9)	25 to 35 pounds (about 11 to 16 kilograms)
Overweight (BMI 25 to 29.9)	15 to 25 pounds (about 7 to 11 kilograms)
Obese (BMI of 30 or more)	11 to 20 pounds (about 5 to 9 kilograms)

Source: http://www.mayoclinic.com/health/pregnancy-weight-gain/PR00111

bonds that were strained or broken during adolescence or young adulthood. Later chapters cover the next phases of the transition to parenthood after the baby is born.

Pregnancy is not entirely free of difficulties. The stress of carrying the child and adapting to the physiological changes of one's body, and the psychological conflicts attached to the awareness of inevitable, impending parenthood, contribute to the difficulty of the adaptation (Grimm, 1967). In general, adaptation to pregnancy involves coping with these unexpected emotions and with the physical changes of one's body.

During the later stages of pregnancy, many women in North America become preoccupied with their weight gain. In this culture, a high value is placed on a slender and attractive female body. Even though some women enjoy the sense of being pregnant, most worry about their appearance in some way. Many women feel as though they are losing control over their own bodies; they feel conspicuous or embarrassed at times. In the last months, women may begin to feel awkward and sexually less attractive, and some worry about losing their husbands to more attractive women. Mothers who were ambivalent about their pregnancies and who were concerned about their appearance and behavior, however, eventually adapt to the parenting role (M. Leifer, 1980).

Some women report a decline in cognitive abilities and changes in emotional state during and after pregnancy. Studies show, however, that pregnant women outperform other women on recognition and recall of pregnancy-related words (Christensen et al., 1999). Mothers' brains seem to benefit from pregnancy by significant growth in areas of the brain related to motivation (hypothalamus), emotion (amygdala), sensory processing (parietal cortex) and reasoning and judgment (prefrontal cortex), exactly the areas one might suspect to support caregiving and attachment (Kim et al., 2010). Some of this may be due to epigenetic and genetic mechanisms that support the transition to parenthood. We also now know that fetal brain cells migrate via the umbilical cord and become implanted in the maternal brain. Women with higher fetal cell counts in their brains (based on post-mortem autopsies) also had a lower incidence of Alzheimer's disease (Martone, 2012). So, it may be that the fetus alters brain epigenetics in ways that improve cognitive function.

In the later months of pregnancy, women report an increase in daily hassles and a decrease in events that are uplifting (L. M. Thompson et al., 1997). Research shows that knowledge of pregnancy and childbirth helps a woman adapt successfully to the changes she experiences during pregnancy. Thus, prenatal education programs are particularly helpful for mothers (Rautava et al., 1992). Mindfulness-based stress-reduction programs have also been shown to reduce anxiety and increase positive mood in the later stages of pregnancy (Beddoe et al., 2009; Vieten & Astin, 2008). Other factors that are related to women's successful adaptation to pregnancy include the presence of the father, marital satisfaction, low levels of family stress, social support from family and friends, ability to remain active, and emotional well-being (Dragonas, Petrogiannis, & Adam, 1997; Klinnert et al., 1992; H. Taylor et al., 1997; K. J. Thorpe, Dragonas, & Golding, 1992).

Regarding the protective factor of remaining active, some studies have reported that women adapt better if they continue to work at their jobs during pregnancy, while others have not found this effect. It may be that working is helpful if the mother wants to work and has low family stress (H. Taylor et al., 1997). Mothers who are more conscientious in their prenatal health care appear to be more psychologically involved with their fetus (Fares & Adler, 1998). As one would expect, women's reported feelings of attachment to their fetus increased over the course of pregnancy (Sjögren, 2004).

One study found that women who worried the least about the pregnancies were the most committed to becoming a parent and had the most involved husbands (M. Leifer, 1980). On average, there appears to be a slight decline in reports of marital satisfaction during the first few years of parenthood. Parents who were more likely to

Social support from family and friends is an important factor for women's successful adaptation to pregnancy.
Photo by Emily Waterfield

report that their marriages were satisfying, however, were less likely to experience a decline in feelings of tenderness and less likely to quarrel. Their infants were more securely attached at 12 months (Gloger-Tippelt & Huerkamp, 1998).

What Is the Father's Adaptation to Pregnancy Like?

The firstborn child is a major source of excitement for the entire family. Aside from the mother, the father is the most closely involved with this process, and the evidence suggests that he, too, undergoes some important developmental changes as well as some specific changes in mood and behavior during this period. For the male, pregnancy may be seen as a sign of his masculine potency, but it may also be interpreted as a sign of bondage—an end to his fantasy of a life of adventure

and freedom. Pregnancy can seem, at least initially, either welcoming or threatening.

Many expectant fathers do not see themselves in merely a supportive role. They have a sense that they, like their mates, are experiencing an important development in their lives. Some cultures have traditions, called **couvade**, that encourage expectant fathers to identify with their mates and to act out the female role in a culturally approved manner. Cross-cultural studies have shown that couvade occurs primarily in societies where females are salient and valued in their roles (B. Whiting, 1974).

How is couvade expressed in other societies? Fathers in the Ifugao tribe of the Philippines are not permitted to cut wood during their wives' pregnancy, as a form of identification with the changes in lifestyle associated with being pregnant. In the Easter Islands of the Pacific, the wife leans against the husband during labor and delivery. Among the Lepcha, both parents undergo a ceremonial cleansing in the fifth month of pregnancy (M. Mead & Newton, 1967).

It may be that the high level of involvement of fathers in the childbirth process in Western cultures reflects the increasing recognition of the importance of women's contributions to the family and to society. For a father to take time off from work, spend that time going to prenatal classes, discuss feelings openly, attend the delivery, and actively share in the "woman's" world of childbearing is an open expression of the value and worth of that world. In industrialized countries, fathers connect with the experience of being pregnant via "body-mediated moments." These include touching the mother's belly, feeling fetal movements and listening for the heartbeat, becoming involved in pregnancy testing, ultrasounds, morning sickness, nutrition, and of course, labor and delivery. These methods reduce the father's feelings of being "distant" from the process (Draper, 2002).

Many men do not share these feelings; they see the work of childbearing as less important or too threatening. The temptation to engage in extramarital sex increases during pregnancy, and some men report feeling emotionally distant from their wives during pregnancy and childbirth (Gelles, 1978; K. J. Thorpe et al., 1992). Unfortunately, physical abuse by men of their pregnant partners is not uncommon, affecting about one in six adult women in the United States. Risk of abuse increases with factors such as teenage pregnancy, low social support, low income, unmarried status, unplanned pregnancy, drug and alcohol abuse, and poor prenatal care. Abuse during pregnancy is a significant predictor of continued abuse after the child is born. Domestic violence during pregnancy also lowers a mother's attachment to her fetus and increases negative representations of themselves and the fetus (Gielen et al., 1994; Huth-Bocks et al., 2004; Martin et al., 2004; Parker et al., 1994; D. E. Stewart, 1994; Webster, Sweett, & Stolz, 1994).

Fortunately, most fathers develop a positive psychological attachment to the fetus. Mothers' and fathers' attachment to the fetus was assessed in a sample of 218 women and 147 of their mates. The sample was randomly distributed among income, ethnic, and racial groups, and the pregnancies were developing normally. The parents rated their attachment to the fetus and other feelings, as shown in Table 3.4. Both mothers and fathers were similar in their ratings, although fathers were more likely than mothers to be anticipating the birth, while mothers were somewhat more likely to express overt feelings of love for the fetus (Mercer et al., 1988).

Some of the same factors predict a smooth adaptation to pregnancy for both fathers and mothers; they include knowledge of pregnancy and childbirth, social support, marital satisfaction, low levels of family stress, and emotional well-being. Research shows that no single factor is more important than any other, that a successful transition to fatherhood depends on many different processes, and that men may differ with respect to what helps them the most (Hyssala et al., 1993; Klinnert et al., 1992). Many hospitals offer a variety of prenatal education and childbirth preparation classes. Research shows that similar prenatal education, support and stress reduction techniques that serve mothers, can also help fathers adjust to the transition to parenthood (Yu et al., 2011). These can be very beneficial for maximizing the chances for a healthy and happy pregnancy and childbirth experience for the entire family.

How Do Siblings Adapt to the Pregnancy?

Advice books for parents tend to recommend that the first child be prepared for the arrival of the baby, although there are differences of opinion about how much to say. An early study (Sewall, 1930) found that differences in preparation of the first child during pregnancy did not relate to

TABLE 3.4   Maternal and Paternal Responses to Feelings About the Unborn Baby

Response	Percentage of Women	Percentage of Men
Worry, anxiety, concern	8	4
Pleased, hopeful, positive	14	11
Talks to, loves, attached	18	8
Ambivalent, negative	13	12
Anticipating birth, curious	48	66

Source: R. T. Mercer et al., Further exploration of maternal and paternal fetal attachment, 1988, p. 92. *Research in Nursing and Health, 11*, 83–95.

the severity of the jealousy reactions of the child following the birth of the baby. Other studies (J. Dunn & Kendrick, 1982; Trause et al., 1978) have also found no relationship between prenatal preparation and the later quality of the sibling relationship.

It seems that the first child, typically only 3 or 4 years old, is unlikely to understand the meaning of the mother's attempts at preparation. Even if the child does understand, he or she is unlikely to anticipate the emotional experience that occurs when the new baby arrives. In families in which there is a high level of confrontation between the mother and the first child and in which the mother used prohibition and restraint, the first child was more likely to behave in an interfering or irritating manner toward the new baby (J. Dunn & Kendrick, 1982).

CHILDBIRTH RISK AND HEALTH

Assessing the Infant's Status at Birth

Once a baby is born, a series of assessments may be done to determine whether there are any complications or whether the infant is in need of special attention. Assessments are divided into three basic groups. **Screening assessments** give an indication of the newborn's ability to survive and whether there are any immediate medical needs. **Neurological assessments** test for problems in the newborn's central and peripheral nervous system, such as major brain, spinal cord, or sensory damage.

One of the most widely used newborn screening tests was developed by Virginia Apgar (1953) and is known as the **Apgar score**. The test is relatively easy to do and takes only a few seconds. The rating usually is made at 1 minute and again at 5 minutes after birth. Table 3.5 shows the categories of the Apgar rating and the possible score an infant may receive in each of five areas: respiration, heart rate, muscle tone, color, and reflex irritability. The infant's total score is summed over each of the five areas. A total score of 7 or greater usually indicates that the infant is in no immediate danger, whereas a rating of less than 7 indicates some kind of severe risk to life. If the rating is less than 4, the infant is in critical condition.

The reason for making two ratings is to encourage hospital staff to continue to monitor the newborn over several minutes. Often staff members are distracted by other events and may miss the possible deterioration of the infant's condition. In addition to the Apgar, the infant can be screened on the basis of its physical appearance, color, and the presence of any obvious deformities (Judd, 1985; Olds, London, & Ladewig, 1984; Sardana, 1985). Apgar scores have been found to relate to

TABLE 3.5   The Apgar Rating Scale

Sign	Scale		
	0	1	2
A—appearance (color)	blue, pale	body pink (extremities blue)	completely pink
P—pulse	absent	below 100	over 100
G—grimace (reflex irritability, response to stimulation of sole of foot by a slap)	no response	grimace	cry
A—activity (muscle tone)	limp	slow, flexion of extremities	active motion
R—respiratory effort	absent	slow, irregular	good, strong cry

Source: J. Butterfield and M. Covey (1962). Practical epigram of the Apgar Score. *Journal of the American Medical Association, 181*, 353. Copyright 1962, American Medical Association.

a variety of prenatal and birth complications and infant mortality, especially if the scores decrease between the two testings.

When infants are born preterm, the Dubowitz scale can be used to test the gestational age of the infant at birth. The **gestational age** is the number of weeks since conception (gestation is another word for pregnancy). To check the gestational age, raters use the infant's muscular control, physical size measurements, skin texture and color, amount of lanugo, and the size and development of the ears, breasts, and genitals. The Dubowitz scale can predict the gestational age to within a few days (Dubowitz, Dubowitz, & Goldberg, 1970; Jaroszewicz & Boyd, 1973).

Birth Complications

The infant's early life history is usually divided into three main phases: prenatal, **perinatal** (the period from 1 month before birth to about 1 month after), and **neonatal** (the newborn until the age of 4 to 6 weeks). Perinatal problems usually derive from disorders of delivery, perinatal infections, asphyxia, hypoglycemia (low blood sugar levels), prematurity, and cardiac and respiratory difficulties. Several of these problems appear to be caused by prenatal factors, many of which we discussed earlier in this last chapter. There is considerable evidence that a number of the complications of the perinatal period can be overcome if the infant is exposed to a supportive social and physical environment. Infants who are raised in inadequate social and economic conditions are more likely to develop permanent deficits as a result of a perinatal complication (Kopp & Parmelee, 1979; Sameroff & Chandler, 1975). One of the major birth complications, prematurity, has received a good deal of attention from psychologists, parents, and physicians. Much of this interest has to do with modern improvements in neonatal intensive care that have permitted more premature infants to survive and to mediate the risk of premature birth.

What Is Prematurity?

To classify an infant's status at birth, birthweight and gestational age are used. Table 3.6 lists some of these classifications. As explained earlier in this chapter, lower birthweight can be related to genetic and chromosomal causes but more often results from such factors as smoking and alcohol use and poor maternal health or nutrition. Indeed, cigarette smoking during pregnancy is the largest single preventable cause of low birthweight, accounting for 20 to 30 percent of lowbirthweight cases (Ogunyemi et al., 1998). Exceptional stress and persistent family discord during the pregnancy period have also been associated with low birthweight (Chomitz, Cheung, & Lieberman, 1995; Ramsey, Abell, & Baker, 1986; Reeb et al., 1987; A. Stein et al., 1987). Infertility treatments that

TABLE 3.6 Forms of Prematurity

Classification Factor	Premature Category
Birthweight:	
Less than 1,000 grams (2 lbs. 3 oz.)	Extremely low birthweight (ELBW)
Between 1,000 and 1,500 grams (2 lbs. 3 oz. and 3 lbs. 5 oz.)	Very low birthweight (VLBW)
Between 1,500 and 2,000 grams (3 lbs. 5 oz. and 4 lbs. 6.5 oz.)	Low birthweight (LBW)
More than 2,500 grams (5 lbs. 8 oz.)	Normal birthweight
Gestational age:	
Less than 37 weeks	Premature birth
More than 37 weeks	Full-term birth
Weight less than expected for gestational age	Intrauterine growth retardation
Weight appropriate for gestational age	See weight and term classifications above

produce multiple births and low maternal weight gain also contribute to the incidence of low birthweight (Ogunyemi et al., 1998). A small percentage of infants are low birthweight even if the pregnancy had no known risk factors.

The incidence of low birthweight and infant mortality varies by ethnicity. Low birth weight occurs in about 7 percent of white and Hispanic families, and is almost twice as much for African-Americans (Chomitz et al., 1995; http://www.statehealthfacts.org/comparemaptable.jsp?ind=43&cat=2). There is also a strong correlation between low birthweight and mortality. Mortality rates (see below) are only one-tenth as high as the rates of low birthweight. Typically, low birthweight and mortality increase as the availability of good prenatal health care and nutrition declines.

Problems and Prospects for Premature and Low-Birthweight Babies and Their Families

In 1975, about 40 percent of premature infants developed serious intellectual and neurological deficits in later life. Due to improvements in medical technology and knowledge about the premature infant, this percentage continues to decrease. Infants who would have been severely handicapped a generation ago, had they even survived, have a better prognosis for developing normally. The youngest and smallest babies still run the most risk of complications and death. Babies under 1,000 grams (extremely low birthweight, or ELBW) or of less than 32 weeks' gestational age are currently considered to be at the most risk. Although more of these babies are saved each year, it increases the chances that babies with handicaps will survive from this group (Hack, Klein, & Taylor, 1995). Infants under 1,000 grams (ELBW) show the least improvements in outcomes.

Recent research shows that a large proportion of infants born prematurely, regardless of weight, may have more health, motor, and intellectual problems than full-term infants, both in the short term and in the long term. The short-and long-term consequences of premature birth will now be covered, followed by a review of the research on improvements in neonatal intensive care.

Short-term effects. Because of their early birth and/or low birthweight, prematures are often at a disadvantage in getting a good start on adaptation to the real world. They may suffer more from a lack of oxygen during the birth process (respiratory distress), they are more likely to have jaundice and to suffer physical and mental impairments as a result of the birth process, and many of them will die, depending upon the severity of their complications and birthweight. Two-thirds of premies under 1,000 grams were likely to die in 2000; about 15 perent of those between 1,000 and 1,500 grams died, but less than 5 percent died if they weighed between 1,500 and 2,500 grams (Matthews et al., 2002).

Generalizing about the abilities of premature infants is difficult because they vary widely in weight and gestational age, because prematurity has many different causes, and because the quality of neonatal care is highly variable. In follow-up studies of the effects of prematurity, researchers compare normal infants with premature infants of the same gestational age, rather than comparing infants of the same natal age. For example, a 3-month-old normal infant might be compared with a 4-month-old premature infant, both of whom were conceived at about the same time.

Many premature infants cannot suck from a bottle successfully until they have reached a gestational age of 35 weeks, about the age of a full-term newborn (Brake et al., 1988). Typical patterns of sleep and waking displayed by full-term babies do not begin until 34 weeks' gestational age; until then, premature infants spend considerably more time sleeping than waking (Korner et al., 1988). Thirty-four weeks appears to be the age at which premature infants show a marked increase in their ability to respond appropriately to external stimulation. Before that age, it takes a considerable effort on the part of an adult to keep the baby still and alert in the presence of a new tactile, auditory, or visual stimulus (Als, Duffy, & McAnulty, 1988).

Premature infants often spend weeks in intensive care units. With appropriately gentle medical intervention and sensitive handling, most of these infants will develop normally into adulthood.

Photo by Elizabeth Crews.

Long-term effects. The long-term effects of prematurity independent of other factors cannot be completely determined. This is because many premature infants have other complications, and we cannot assign infants randomly to experimental groups based on prematurity and health status. In addition, many premature and sick infants receive a variety of short-term and long-term interventions—including special attention from their families—that may alleviate their conditions.

Individuals who were born prematurely are shorter and smaller on average than people who were full term at birth. The difference is greatest during the first 2 years of life, during which babies who are small at birth often show some catch-up growth if they receive appropriate care and nutrition (Peña et al., 1987). **Catch-up growth** refers to a more rapid growth rate than for normal infants early in life and a more normal growth rate once the infant reaches a weight that is appropriate for his or her gestational age. For most prematures,

catch-up growth is the most rapid during the first year of life (Peña et al., 1987). Catch-up growth may occur at any point in childhood if the individual suffers a deprivation, accident, or illness and is later restored to normal functioning (Barrett, Radke-Yarrow, & Klein, 1982; Tanner, 1970). Catch-up growth does not mean that the individual will eventually enter the normal range, but rather that he or she will grow faster than normal following the trauma.

The effects of prematurity on intelligence, motor skills, perceptual skills, and emotion are often compounded by heath factors and family factors. These risks—such as respiratory problems, intraventricular hemorrhage (IVH), immature neurological development, low SES, high family stress—when added to prematurity, has a significantly greater impact than prematurity alone (Messinger et al., 1996; Miller et al., 2001; Poehlmann et al., 2011; Saylor et al., 2003; Sostek et al., 1987; Stiefel, Plunket, & Meisels, 1987).

For factors related to the parent-infant relationship, we find in some cases no differences between full-term and very-low-birthweight infants (less than 1,500 grams) in mother- and father-infant attachment at 1 year when the comparison is made at equivalent gestational ages (Easterbrooks, 1989). If parents of premature infants are more active and stimulating during the first year—giving extra holding, vocalizing, and caretaking—these compensatory parenting behaviors contribute directly to what is called **self-righting** in the more healthy premature infants, comparable to catch-up growth (Poehlmann et al., 2011; Weiss et al., 2004). As the more healthy prematures catch up with the full terms, their parents also show more normal levels of behavior toward them (Barratt, Roach, & Leavitt, 1996; Branchfeld, Goldberg, & Sloman, 1980; Crawford, 1982). It may be that these additional parental actions are used to compensate for a less active infant, and they may actually help the infant to recover.

For some parents, however, dealing with a premature infant can have short-term effects and may lead to lasting difficulties in the relationship. Parents experience additional stress, depression, and emotional trauma just by the fact of having their baby in a hospital for a long period of time (Conner & Nelson, 1999; Cronin, Shapiro, Casiro, & Cheang, 1995; Hughes et al., 1994; Nagata et al., 2004; L. T. Singer et al., 1999). In early infancy, prematures become easily overwhelmed with stimulation, smiling less and fussing more, and parents may experience them as unrewarding (Eckerman, Hsu, Molitor, Leung, & Goldstein, 1999). Some parents experience burnout in their role (Barnard, Bee, & Hammond, 1984), and there is a higher than expected percentage of premature infants among children who are later insecurely attached, abused or neglected (R. S. Hunter, Kilstrom, Kraybill, & Loda, 1978). In general, the quality of the home and school environments can have an effect on alleviating long-term effects of prematurity (Dittrichová et al., 1996; Kalmar, 1996; Sansavini et al., 1996). Parents who are better able to accept the facts of the infant's limitations and deal with their own stresses are more likely to have infants with more positive outcomes (Evans et al., 2012).

Many prematures, especially those who were very low birthweight (VLBW), have deficits that last until middle childhood and adolescence and perhaps even longer. These deficits are in such areas as attention, behavior problems and emotional maturity, language skill, memory, intelligence and educational performance, income, social relationships and marriage, perceptual and motor function, self-regulation, serious physical and mental illnesses, and mental retardation (Blackman et al., 1987; Botting et al., 1998; Clark et al., 2008; Grigoroiu-Serbanescu, 1981; Hack et al., 1995; Lefebvre et al., 1988; Luby, 2010; Miller et al., 2001; Moster et al., 2008; Rieck, Arad, & Netzer, 1996; Robson & Cline, 1998; Schmidt et al., 2010; Vicari et al., 2004). In general, researchers have discovered that long-term effects are more severe for infants with the most extreme illnesses, who have lower birthweights, or who grow up in families who suffer the most stress (such as low income and lack of education). More subtle and as yet unmeasured effects of prematurity may last a lifetime.

Remember also that even when there are few differences between premature and full-term infants in later life, it does not mean that life has been normal or easy for the prematures and their families. Their improved status in later life may have been the result of persistent, difficult, and costly interventions on the part of parents and professionals (Lewit et al., 1995). In the next section, early intervention procedures will be covered.

Interventions for Premature Infants

Improvements in neonatal intensive care have saved many lives and improved the health of many premature babies (Battin et al., 1998; Richardson et al., 1998). Better ways have been found to manage the hospital care for these infants, and new methods have been developed to help parents once the infants have come home. Only about 5 percent of newborns require intensive care; most of these are due to low birthweight. Most infants in intensive care will require between 15 and 50 days (Hack et al., 1995).

Medical procedures in the hospital. In a modern neonatal intensive care unit (NICU), an increasing number of procedures are adapted to the special needs of premature infants. The smallest infants need high levels of oxygen, warm temperatures, bedding that does not bruise their thin and delicate skin, and nutrients. In the past, providing these needs produced more complications for the infants, who were exposed to dangerously high levels of noise and light inside incubator boxes, bruised from touch, and scarred from needle pricks. Blindness resulted from too much oxygen and deafness from too much noise.

Research has demonstrated that late-term fetuses, premature infants, and full-term newborns feel pain. Repeated experience of untreated pain has the effect of making infants hypervigilant during social interaction and causing them to exhibit increased tension in response to tactile stimulation. In addition, preemies may suffer from the stress of separation from their mothers and long-term isolation due to hospitalization (Karns, 2000).

Today, premature infants are on open beds in a nursery that has higher concentrations of oxygen in the air. They are warmed with low-intensity lights, and their bedding is extremely soft. Some hospitals use sheepskins or water beds. The babies are touched gently and as little as possible, sound and light are kept at moderate levels, and the oxygen content of the blood is monitored continuously by a probe attached to the skin surface, reducing the need for blood sampling. Pain control is managed by drugs, pacifier sucking or breast feeding when possible, giving sucrose, and providing soothing sounds including playing recordings of the mother's voice (Doheny et al., 2012; Furdon, Pfeil, & Snow, 1998; Holsti et al., 2011; Kawakami, Takai-Kawakami, Kurihara, Shimizu, & Yanaihara, 1996; Korner, 1987; Sell, Hill-Mangan, & Holberg, 1992; Stevens et al., 1999).

Behavioral procedures in the hospital. A variety of approaches have been used either to compensate for missing intrauterine experiences or to try to enhance catch-up growth. One important form of stimulation that a premature lacks is whole-body movement, called **vestibular-proprioceptive stimulation**. Premature infants have received rocking stimulation from adults, in hammocks, from a breathing teddy bear, and from oscillating waterbeds. This rhythmic stimulation has been designed to be similar to the kinds of movements and breathing rhythms that a full-term infant would feel inside the mother during the last weeks of pregnancy. If these natural rhythms are attuned to the needs of individual infants so as not to over-stimulate them, the infants increase weight gain, improve sleeping and other physiological indicators, and can be discharged earlier from the hospital (Gatts, Wallace, Glasscock, McKee, & Cohen, 1994; Ingersoll & Thoman, 1994; Korner, 1987; E. B. Thoman, 1993).

Although prematures, especially the smallest ones, cannot ingest fluids, they can suck readily on a pacifier; this is called **nonnutritive sucking** (NNS). Fetuses of the same gestational age inside the uterus also suck regularly. In several studies, premature infants who were provided with pacifiers on a regular basis required fewer tube feedings, started bottle feeding earlier, slept better, gained more weight, and were discharged earlier from the hospital (G. C. Anderson, Burroughs, & Measel, 1983; T. Field et al., 1982; Woodson, Drinkwin, & Hamilton, 1985). NNS reduces the infant's average heart rate, thus allowing the infant the opportunity to use its energy resources for growth instead of life maintenance (Woodson & Hamilton, 1988).

Another form of behavioral intervention is stroking and handling. It appears that for very-low-birthweight infants (less than 1,500 grams), stroking can actually be detrimental due to the extreme sensitivity of the infant's skin. In studies of this group of infants, talking helped to bring the infants into an attentive state, while talking plus touching caused the infant to withdraw (Eckerman, Oehler, Medvin, & Hannan, 1994; Oehler & Eckerman, 1988; Weiss, 2005).

For babies between 1,500 and 2,500 grams, stroking in the form of back massage, neck rubbing, and movement of arms and legs had remarkable effects. Massage for 15 minutes per day over 10 to 15 days can increase weight 31 to 47 percent compared to prematures who did not receive stroking and also reduce birth complications (Field, 2001; Field et al., 2011). Touch stimulates hormones that regulate the action and development of the brain and body function, including decreases in cortisol and increases in growth hormone and oxytocin. The latter hormone is associated with feelings of well-being and interpersonal attraction. Gentle massage also increases the activity of the parasympathetic (relaxation) nervous system (Dieter et al., 2003; Field, 2001; Field et al., 2011; Schanberg, Bartolome, & Kuhn, 1987). These studies clearly show that the overall amount of stimulation is not important. Rather, some specific forms of stimulation work better than others, and the most effective stimulation will depend on the infant's gestational age and weight. Music in the form of male and female singing voices, for example, leads to earlier discharge, improved respiration, and more weight gain (Cassidy & Standley, 1995; Coleman et al., 1997; Weiss, 2005).

Another approach that emphasizes touch and handling is known as kangaroo care. In **kangaroo care**, the infant, wearing only a diaper, is placed on the parent's chest. The infant's head is turned to the side so the baby's ear is against the parent's heart. Any tubes or wires are taped to the parent's clothing. Preterms who get kangaroo care cry less, sleep for longer periods, gain more weight, have more coordinated breathing and heartbeat patterns, are more attentive and interact better with their parents, have lower cortisol levels, and need less supplemental oxygen. Both mothers and fathers also feel closer to their babies and to each other, experience less stress and less depression, and increase in their confidence that they can take care of the babies at home (G. C. Anderson, 1999; Feldman et al., 2002; Feldman et al., 2003; Gitau et al., 2002; Ludington-Hoe, Ferreira, & Goldsten, 1998; Ludington-Hoe & Swinth, 1996; Messmer et al., 1999; Tallandini & Scalembra, 2006).

Finally, interventions can be made with the parents to educate them about the special needs of the premature infant. Parental visitation to the NICU gives the infant more opportunities for stimulation and aids in the parents' positive perceptions of their infant. Both mothers and fathers benefit from frequent visitations (Levy-Shiff, Sharir, & Mogilner, 1989), and infants who are visited more frequently by parents are released sooner from the hospital (Zeskind & Iacino, 1984). Educational interventions directed at making mothers more aware of their responsibilities and setting more realistic goals are effective in improving the outcomes for their babies (Field et al., 1980; Pridham, 1998; Ravn et al., 2011; van Beek & Samson, 1994; Zeskind & Iacino, 1987).

Even though low-birthweight and premature infants make up only 9 percent of births, they account for 35 percent of the medical costs devoted to infants. Neonatal intensive care is very expensive, at least $100,000 per infant depending on the length of the hospital stay (Rogowski, 1998, 1999). Low-birthweight infants require additional medical treatment during childhood, amounting to an extra $1,200 per year more than normal children. Because many of the families who have low-birthweight children are poor, these costs are borne by government assistance programs such as Medicaid and by increased health insurance premiums for everyone. In addition, prematurity may lead to other long-term costs, such as the prosecution and incarceration of persons who exhibit criminal and delinquent behavior that may result from early brain damage and later deprivation. Thus, it is essential that governments devote funding to study the causes and preventions of prematurity (Lewit et al., 1995).

Prevention costs considerably less. Good prenatal care for low-income women could radically reduce prematurity and birth complications and cost less than $1,000 per child. Simple hospital interventions such as those described here also have long-term benefits to society. The percentage of hospitals using the various techniques mentioned in this section are shown in Table 3.7. Unfortunately, low-income women find it difficult to obtain good prenatal care, Medicaid places limits on the number of allowable prenatal visits, and it takes a long

TABLE 3.7   Uses of Neonatal Stimulation in Hospitals in the United States

Type of stimulation	Percentage of Hospitals in the United States
Doulas during childbirth	30
Maternal massage during childbirth	30
Mother-baby skin-to-skin contact following birth	83
Music in the NICU	72
Rocking in the NICU	85
Kangaroo care in the NICU	98
Nonnutritive sucking in the NICU	96
Breast-feeding in the NICU	98
Infant massage in the NICU	38

Source: Field, T., Hernandez-Reif, M., Feijo, L., & Freedman, J. (2006). Prenatal, perinatal and neonatal stimulation: A survey of neonatal nurseries. *Infant Behavior & Development, 29*(1), 24–31.

time to process claims. Ultimately, the prevention of birth defects will require major changes in our society, including the elimination of poverty and prejudice (Alexander & Korenbrot, 1995).

What Can We Learn about Fetal Psychology from Premature Infants?

Infants born prematurely are the same age as late-term fetuses and have the same behavioral, sensory, and neurological abilities. Because premies have experienced the birth process, and because they had to adapt to life outside the uterus, they may have acquired abilities that the fetus does not possess. On the other hand, the NICU behavioral interventions that are most successful seem to offer clues to the characteristics of the prenatal environment that are most conducive to fetal psychological development.

In Chapter 2, we learned that in the third fetal period, the fetus was responsive to movement, touch, and sound, and that it could suck. Because of the success of interventions involving these modalities with premies, it is reasonable to conclude that fetuses *require* vestibular-proprioceptive, tactile, and auditory stimulation, as well as opportunities for sucking. The prenatal environment is uniquely suited to provide these requirements for growth. Vestibular-proprioceptive stimulation comes from maternal movements. Tactile stimula-

tion is provided in terms of the soft feeling, warm temperature, and constant flow of the amniotic fluid over the fetus's body. Auditory stimulation is provided by the mother's heartbeat and voice. These forms of stimulation are apparently necessary to sustain normal fetal development. They probably are related to feelings of pleasure, comfort, and security.

PERINATAL MORTALITY

Prenatal Mortality

Prenatal mortality, or pregnancy loss, is rather common. *Spontaneous abortion* (the rejection of the zygote or embryo by the mother's body) is believed to occur in 40 to 60 percent of pregnancies (Little, 1988). In many cases, women may not even be aware that they were pregnant. Many spontaneous abortions occur due to genetic and chromosomal abnormalities of the embryo. The term "spontaneous abortion" typically applies to an embryo, while "miscarriage" is used with respect to a fetus. Miscarriage during the fetal period is caused by genetic and chromosomal abnormalities, by some teratogens, by maternal disease such as high blood pressure, and by diseases of the maternal reproductive system. Finally, *stillbirth* is the loss of a full-term infant who dies just before or during delivery. Stillbirth may be caused by some of the same factors as miscarriage and also by poor prenatal care and poverty (Bukowski et al., 2011; Kapoor, Amand, & Kumar, 1994; Katz & Kuller, 1994).

Like prematurity and health risk, infant mortality is greatest in groups who have low incomes and inadequate health care. Most of the causes of perinatal death can be found in poor prenatal care, ill health, or malnutrition of the mother during pregnancy. Current statistics for infant mortality are shown in Table 3.8. Apparently, a trend over time toward decreasing mortality has been going on since records began to be kept in 1750. Balog (1976) traced the changes in mortality over the last 200 years in the United States and found no obvious dips in the rate after major medical advances, such as drugs and sterilization procedures. He concluded that changes in mortality rates reflect trends in general economic growth, a higher standard of living, and better education—in short, social and economic factors. Decline in birthrate is also a factor. In the 1700s, a woman might expect to carry 10 to 15 conceptions to term, which would mean an increased probability of mortality for each infant. The age of the mother, the spacing between pregnancies, and the number of pregnancies all account for a portion of the risk of infant death.

Age and sex are also important factors in determining the probability of infant death. The highest probability of death is when an infant is less than 24 hours old. In fact, if a baby survives beyond the first day, the odds of mortality are extremely low, about 1 per 1,000 or less. With regard to sex, males tend to have a higher death rate all through their life spans. More males are conceived, but more are miscarried or spontaneously aborted.

In the United States, even though mortality has fallen for ethnic groups, African American infants are still twice as likely to die as Caucasian Americans. This difference has existed for at least half a century. What could be the cause? Homicides, birth injuries, and congenital abnormalities are nearly the same in all ethnic groups in the United States, so these are not factors. Hispanic infants are also less likely to die than African American infants. In general, infant mortality comes from a combination of factors including poverty, poor prenatal nutrition and care, teen pregnancy, family stress, obesity, and prematurity.

Research shows that for African American mothers, the stress of racism adds to these other factors to increase infant mortality. Black women describe the lasting effects of their own childhood experiences of racism from teachers and others, and as adults from employers and the community. Poor black women have to make stressful choices about what to eat (e.g., nutritionally poor fast food that is cheap) and where to live (in neighborhoods with high crime rates and poor schools). Because we know that stress impacts fetal development (Chapter 3), the newborns of these mothers are starting life with compromises to their physical functioning (Lu & Lu, 2007).

The most common causes of neonatal mortality among the poor in the United States and in developing nations are respiratory problems and diarrhea. They derive from the immature system's

TABLE 3.8   Rates of Infant Mortality by Country per 1,000 Live Births (2011)

Country	Rate	Country	Rate
Sweden	2.5	United States	6.1
Japan	2.6	Russia	8.1
Denmark	3.4	Mexico	14.0
France	3.6	Brazil	20.0
Italy	3.7	India	50.0
Australia	3.9	Ethiopia	77.0
Canada	5.1	Afghanistan	131.0

Source: Population Reference Bureau: www.prb.org/DataFinder/Topic/Rankings.aspx?ind=5

inability to cope with normal bacterial infections and physical insults and stem largely from deficits—like stress from the mother—acquired prenatally. Studies have shown, for example, that adequate nutritional supplementation during pregnancy can cut the infant death rate by as much as half (Werner, 1979). In the United States, only a very small percentage of infant or maternal deaths can be attributed to ineffective hospital care during and after birth (Escobar et al., 1998).

The prevention and elimination of these problems depend on intervention in the cycle of poverty, racism, and ill health. Community-based clinics providing medical care during pregnancy, simple disease-screening procedures, immunizations, nutrition education, fertility advice, upgrading of parental competence, improved sanitation, and the effective management of diarrhea already are being implemented in many less developed countries. The United Nations has developed and tested a successful health education program called GOBI, which stands for Growth charts, Oral rehydration, Breast-feeding, and Immunization (Werner, 1986). By comparing their own infant's development to standard growth charts, parents can detect growth retardation and conditions such as failure-to-thrive. **Failure-to-thrive** is a condition in which infants fail to respond to the environment and continue to deteriorate even when intervention is available and even when parents do everything possible. Failure-to-thrive has unknown causes, but intervention can help in some cases even though failure-to-thrive children may permanently lag behind others in language, intelligence, and emotional maturity. Oral rehydration—providing fluids—is the primary treatment for infantile diarrhea. Breast-feeding provides adequate and sanitary nourishment as well as natural immunization (see the section on breast-feeding in this chapter). Immunization protects children from many infectious diseases.

How Does the Family Respond to the Death of an Infant?

The loss parents feel when a newborn dies may not be the same feeling as when an older child or some other close relative dies, but pre- and peri-natal death can deeply affect parents (Helmrath & Steinitz, 1978; Puddifoot & Johnson, 1999). If parents are encouraged to mourn the loss and deal successfully with the painful feelings and memories, the bereavement process may lead to more adaptive parenting with later children. Social supports, hospice services, and religious traditions for dealing with death and loss can be extremely comforting for parents. Older children in the family also need support and counseling to understand the loss and their parent's grief (Drotar & Irvin, 1979; A. F. Hartmann, Radin, & McConnell, 1992; Hass & Walter, 2006–2007; Hesse & van Ijzendoorn, 1998; O'Leary, 2007; Speraw, 1994). Non-Western and ancient cultures have developed a variety of healing rituals to help parents resolve their grief and even to attempt to prevent the loss. These practices include ritual purification, special prayers, and herbal medicines. The rituals emphasize the depth of feeling both men and women have for the loss of their child (Kuller & Katz, 1994).

The normal sequence of emotions parents experience after neonatal death is similar to other kinds of grief reactions. Upon hearing the news that their baby has died or will soon die, parents experience shock and denial. They think a mistake has been made and wonder if it can be corrected. The next phase is feelings of sadness and loss mixed with anger. This anger may be directed at others, such as the obstetrician, or it may be directed at themselves in the form of self-blame (Madden, 1994; Wheeler, 1994). Gradually, parents come to accept the death and readjust the reality to their lives. This can often take several years. Having healthy children later on helps this process, but parents continue to fear that something will go wrong with the next child and wonder what their lost child might have been like (Abboud & Liamputtong, 2005).

A number of practitioners have argued that the loss of the newborn should be treated like any other death in the family. Some hospitals simply dispose of the body without allowing the parents any option to view it. In the United Kingdom, hospitals follow the "Sands Guidelines" that follow the parents' needs and wishes about whether or not to view the body, to have an autopsy, and to have a burial or cremation (Schott & Henley, 2007). In all cases, factual and frank discussions with medical personnel, the availability of the autopsy report, and a funeral service may help the parents cope (Dyregrov & Matthiesen, 1987; Hughes et al., 2002; Kotch & Cohen, 1986).

Between life and death, there are some gray areas. Infants may be born viable but suffer from gross deformities or other conditions that would impair later functioning. The issues faced by parents and doctors in these situations are not unlike those faced by the families of persons in comas or with terminal and painful diseases or by those close to the elderly and infirm. **Euthanasia** is the act of causing a painless death or of letting someone die naturally without trying to prolong life with "heroic" medical procedures. As you can imagine, the idea of euthanasia involves some serious and difficult religious, ethical, legal, medical, and personal issues that are not easily resolved. With the advent of sophisticated neonatal intensive care, parents and pediatricians are facing these issues more and more.

Maternal Mortality

Infants are much more likely to die than mothers, although this was not always the case. Improvements in childbirth and prenatal care practices have drastically reduced the maternal death rate. Those countries and ethnicities that have high infant mortality also have high maternal mortality, most typically underdeveloped nations in Africa which can have maternal mortality rates between 500 and 1,100 per 100,000 live births (United Nations Department of Economic and Social Affairs, 1986; https://www.cia.gov/library/publications/the-world-factbook/rankorder/2223rank.html). This may not seem like a lot but in European countries the rate is about 5 per 100,000 births. In the US, the rate is 21 per 100,000. This means that most causes of maternal death—poor prenatal and delivery health care, lack of education, ignorance and superstition, and sanitation—are preventable. The leading causes of maternal death in the United States are pregnancy-induced high blood pressure, hemorrhage (excessive bleeding following childbirth), and respiratory failure (Grimes, 1994).

SUMMARY

Prenatal Health and Risk

- Male infertility is caused by different factors than female infertility. Fertility can often be enhanced by natural methods.
- When natural methods fail, surgery and/or in vitro fertilization may be required. In vitro fertilization is usually safe and effective.
- In vitro fertilization raises social and ethical issues that both parents and society need to consider carefully.
- Some birth defects are caused by genetic or chromosomal abnormalities.
- Many types of environmental factors can influence prenatal development.
- Parents whose fetus is at risk for several defects may choose fetal surgery if available or they may have the option to terminate the pregnancy via elective abortion.
- Elective abortion is a complex issue compounded by health, family, and social factors.

Pregnancy and the Family

- Women's bodies undergo major physical changes during pregnancy.
- Women should exercise regularly and eat a diet suitable for fetal and maternal health.
- Social support, prenatal education, and stress regulation are essential for maternal and infant mental health.
- Fathers also need similar forms of support during pregnancy.

Childbirth Risk and Health

- The newborn has unique physical characteristics, most of which disappear after a few weeks of life. These characteristics are the remnants of prenatal life and the effects of the birth process.
- The art of newborn assessment is rapidly improving. Reliable and valid tests exist for determining the

newborn's risk in terms of survival, neurological problems, gestational age, and behavioral status.

- Perinatal problems account for a large proportion of later deficits.
- Prematurity is the largest single category of birth complication and seems to be caused by a variety of prenatal factors.
- Premature infants are likely to be smaller and sicker and to lag behaviorally, compared to full-term infants.
- The most severe long-term deficits occur primarily for very-low-birthweight infants, under 1,500 grams. Most infants between 1,500 and 2,500 grams tend to recover eventually and lead normal lives, but many will show mild to severe effects of prematurity.
- The type of intervention that improves the long-term outcome for premature infants depends on the infant's gestational age and health. Medical interventions are improving and becoming less invasive. Behavioral procedures are extremely effective in improving health and weight gain at low cost. Parent education is also an effective strategy.

- The research on preterm infants suggests that late-term fetuses require movement, touch, sound, and sucking to continue their development, all forms of stimulation uniquely found in the prenatal environment.

Perinatal Mortality

- Poverty and disease are the biggest causes of infant mortality worldwide.
- Supplemental maternal and infant nutrition, breast-feeding, growth monitoring, rehydration, and immunization can prevent many perinatal deaths.
- Parents who lose an infant can be expected to grieve in the usual manner and thus should be helped through this process by medical personnel and family.
- Euthanasia for newborns is a controversial topic that involves social, psychological, legal, and moral issues.
- Maternal mortality rates are much lower than infant mortality rates.

Chapter 4

The Developing Brain
and Nervous System:
Health and Risk

CHAPTER OUTLINE AND OVERVIEW

Measuring Brain Activity	*What are the current ways to study infant brain activity?*
Basic Structures of the Nervous System	*What are the two types of brain cells and how do they function? What are the main anatomical regions and physiological properties of the brain and nervous system?*
Prenatal and Infant Brain Development: A Critical Period	*Why is the prenatal and first three years of life a critical period for brain development? What parts of the brain and nervous system are developing the most rapidly during this period?*
Optimal and Non-Optimal Brain Development During Infancy	*What are the effects if the environment on brain development? What are the best ways to promote brain development in infancy?*

Brain development in the fetal and infancy periods is becoming one of the new frontiers of infancy research. **Developmental neuroscience** is the study of the developing brain and nervous system as it relates to psychological and behavioral functions such as moving, thinking, and feeling. In this chapter we will review the structure and function of the nervous system, including the brain. This is followed by a review of some of the developmental processes that explain why the fetus and infant are undergoing a critical period for brain development, meaning that the environments to which they are exposed during this period will have a lifetime impact on brain function. Finally, the impact of the environment on the developing brain is discussed, including understanding what types of environment are most conducive to healthy brain developmen. The primary references used in this chapter are recent publications related to the developing brain (Andersen, 2003; Braun, 2011; Fogel, 2013; Freides, 2001; Knowles & Penn, 2012; Porges & Furman, 2011; Posner et al., 2011; Stiles & Jernigan, 2010). Other works will be cited as needed.

MEASURING BRAIN ACTIVITY

The increased interest in the early development of the nervous system is partly due to the rise of new methods for monitoring brain activity that have allowed clinicians to diagnose abnormal brain function at younger ages and have given researchers a new window on the neural processes that underlie normal behavioral development. **EEG** (electroencephalography) can be used to measure brain electrical activity on the surface of the scalp. It can measure brain electrical waves but does not give information about location of activity within the brain. **MEG**, magnetoencephalography, works in a similar way but uses magnetic fields rather than electrical activity. Similar to EEG, it cannot locate particular structures within the brain but it is less distorted by surrounding tissue, which makes it useful for studying fetal brain activity on the surface of the mother's abdomen, through layers of maternal and fetal tissue (**fMEG**). This method

has been used to detect changes in brain activity that reveal learning in the fetal brain (Chapter 3) and it also has potential for the early detection of learning disabilities and brain deficits (Sheridan et al., 2010).

There are also several methods that can track the locations of activated structures deep inside the brain but not all are useful for working with infants. **fMRI** (functional magnetic resonance imaging) uses magnetic fields to detect where in the brain blood is exchanging oxygen, an indicator of which brain regions are active. fMRI is not very useful for studying infants because it requires lying in complete stillness inside of a very noisy tube. Infants must be sleeping or sedated to use this method. A more useful technique for babies is **fNIRS** (functional near infrared spectroscopy) which can also find the spatial location of activation from blood flow changes This method uses infrared light that can pass through skin and other tissue and can be used with infants who can be sitting up or on the lap moving relatively freely. Unlike fMRI which requires special labs and expensive, heavy, stationary equipment, fNIRS probes easily fit over the head and they are portable. Although fNIRS cannot reach the deepest locations in the brain, the results compare well with adult fMRI data. PET (positron emission tomography) requires exposure

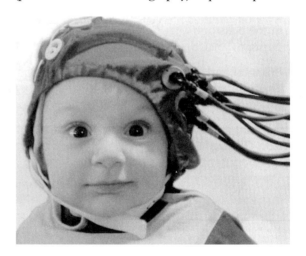

A child with an fNIRS probe.
Photo courtesy of the Language and Literacy Lab, University of Michigan.

to radioisotopes which can be detected in different regions of the brain that are active. Because of the radiation, it is not safe for infants. The main purpose of PET is to trace neurotransmitter activity (Grossman, 2013).

BASIC STRUCTURES OF THE NERVOUS SYSTEM

The Cells of the Nervous System: Neurons and Glia

Neurons are the information storage and transfer cells of the nervous system. *There are about 140 billion neurons in the adult human brain (140,000,000,000).* Neurons process electrical and chemical informa-

tion and transmit that information to other neurons. There are different types of neurons depending on their function in the nervous system, but they all have a similar structure, as shown in Figure 4.1. The cell body of the neurons code and transmit information in the form of electrochemical currents, called **action potentials**. Action potentials travel from the cell body along the **axons** to the axon terminals which can connect to other neurons. The axon transmits the cell's *action*.

The action potentials stimulate the production of neurochemicals at the junction between two neurons, the synapse. The **synapse** connects the axon terminals of the transmitting cell to the dendrites of the receiving cell, as shown in Figure 4.1. **Dendrites** (from the Greek word *dendron*, or tree) are the branching structures that receive

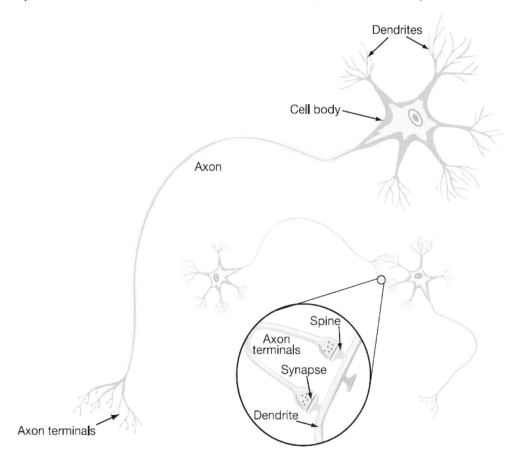

Figure 4.1 Brain Cells
Source: Adapted from Teylor and Chiaia, *A child's brain* (ed. M. Frank). New York: Haworth Press, 1984.

information at the synapse from the axons of other neurons and transmit that information to the body of the connecting cell. Each neuron can connect to as many as 1,000 other neurons (more than 60 trillion interneuron connections!) creating a complicated and dynamic network that is responsible for sensing the environment and regulating thought, emotion, body function and behavior, as well as creating the conscious experience of sensing and feeling the body, the self, and the external world.

There are many types of neurochemicals exchanged between neurons that ultimately alter behavior and feeling states. In general, these chemicals produce either inhibition or arousal of brain function. **Serotonin**, for example, alters mood by creating a state of quiet alertness and feelings of well-being, but too little of it can lead to feelings of depression. Most drugs for treating depression increase serotonin levels. **Dopamine**, another common neurochemical, helps with control of attention and thought, feelings of pleasure and optimism, and regulation of movement. Too much dopamine can create thought disturbances like those found in schizophrenia, and too little leads to disorders of movements such as Parkinson's disease. Other neurochemicals help or hinder voluntary movements, sleep-wake cycles, sexuality and reproduction, the ability to form memories, emotional processing, and stress regulation.

Neurons are found all over the body, not only in the brain and spinal cord. **Afferent neurons** send signals from inside and outside the body to the brain, meaning that they transmit to the brain how things are *affecting* us. Far from the brain, the ends of afferent neurons contain specialized receptors. Receptors are found in the sense organs of the body and translate physical information into neurochemical information that can be sent to the spinal cord and brain for processing. Light, sound, pressure, and temperature, for example, are translated into neurochemical information by receptors in the eyes, ears, and skin. There are also receptors that sense the inner condition of the body including muscle stretch, balance and ori-

entation in space, hunger, thirst, fatigue, itchiness, gut distension, sexual feelings, pleasure, and pain. These neurons related to the inner condition of the body form a crucial part of our sense of self.

The vast majority of neurons are in the spinal cord and brain. Called **processor neurons**, they analyze the stream of afferent information coming from the receptors for the purpose of responding to these signals coming from outside and inside the body. The brain's responses are then sent to efferent neurons which are directly connected to muscles that alter or *effect* internal and external behavior. **Efferent neurons** are found in the gut to regulate digestion, in the heart and blood vessels to regulate circulation, in the lungs and diaphragm for breathing, and in the muscles that regulate movement. For a newborn to get milk from a nipple, for example, many muscles in the head, neck, face, lips, jaw, throat, and gut need to be coordinated to allow for sucking, swallowing, and digesting. Tiny muscles behind the eyes allow the baby to look for the mother, and tiny muscles in the ears can tune hearing to the frequency range of human speech.

The other major group of cells in the nervous system is the **neuroglia**, or more simply **glia**. Like neurons, there are many different types of glia that serve different functions, all of which are especially important during fetal and infant brain development. Some glial cells provide oxygen and nutrients to the neurons via the blood stream, and also remove waste products, among which are neurons that die due to lack of use. Another type of glial cell wraps around the axons to create a layer of insulation called **myelin**, a coating that improves the integrity and speed of conduction of neurochemical information between neurons along the axon. Another type of glial cell, the **radial glia**, provide a kind of scaffold of pathways along which neurons grow and migrate to their proper place within the brain during fetal development. This last type of glia holds neurons in place and is the origin of the term glia, which means "glue." Glia, however, do more than just glue neurons together, as we'll see when we return to the topic of brain development later in this chapter.

Anatomical Structures of the Brain

The human brain can be divided into three basic regions: the brain stem, the limbic system, and the cortex. The **brain stem**, located in back of the head where it joins to the neck, includes the lower brain stem that connects to the spinal cord, the upper brain stem—called the medulla—that connects to the rest of the brain, and the cerebellum, a bulb-like formation between the brain stem and brain (see Figure 4.2). The brain stem contains the roots of the afferent and efferent neurons of the **autonomic nervous system** which is responsible for regulating respiration, heart rate, blood pressure, sucking, swallowing, digestion, and sleep-wake cycles. These autonomic nerves, the ones that control all the internal organs of the body, come directly from the brain stem and travel down the neck and into the chest and abdominal cavities.

The autonomic nervous system has two branches: sympathetic and parasympathetic. The **sympathetic nervous system** prepares the body for action by elevating heart rate, increasing metabolism and respiration rate, creating a state of active alertness and vigilance, and temporarily suppressing digestion. It is responsible for expending the energy reserves in the body. The **parasympathetic nervous system** allows the body to relax, slow down, rest, digest food and information, engage socially with others, learn and grow. It is respon-

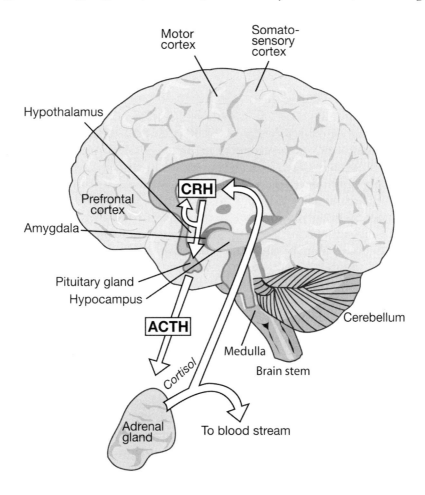

Figure 4.2   Brain Structures that Develop During Infancy

Figure 4.3 The limbic system of the inner brain.

Thalamus

Hippocampus

Amygdala

Hypothalamus

Olfactory bulb

Frontal lobe

sible for building and storing the body's energy resources. Both of these systems are active in early infancy, and babies—as well as adults—need a balance of arousal and rest for healthy development. As we'll see later, too much arousal and stress—in the absence of times for relaxation and recovery—can impair the developing nervous system.

The **limbic system** is located more or less in the very center of the head, between the ears, and includes structures such as the amygdala, the hippocampus, the hypothalamus, and the pituitary gland (see Figures 4.2 and 4.3). This part of the brain is related to processes such as memory, regulation of states like sleeping and waking, breathing, temperature regulation, urinary and bowel control, emotion, and responses to stress vs. relaxation.

A number of structures within the limbic system are important for infant development. The **hippocampus** is a horseshoe-shaped structure (see Figure 4.3) that plays an important role in the formation of memories for events and sequences, known as **autobiographical memory**. Autobiographical memory is the ability to tell a story in words about oneself, and it does not begin until the

third year of life. The **amygdala** is a small bulb at the front end of the hippocampus (see Figure 4.3; amygdala means *almond* in Latin). There are two, a right and a left. The amygdala plays a role in the formation of emotional memories, especially those related to fear and safety, and is functional at birth.

The **hypothalamus** is a small structure in the lower-middle of the limbic system that links the brain to the endocrine (hormonal) system of the body via the pituitary gland and the blood stream. In response to stimulation coming from the body, the hypothalamus begins a cascade of hormones that activate the pituitary gland to release other hormones into the blood stream. The **pituitary** is a hormone-producing endocrine gland. **Hormones** are neurochemicals that circulate in the blood stream. Hormones can affect the regulation of body organs to activate digestion, sexual function, stress regulation and feelings of safety and comfort, milk production in nursing mothers, and cell growth throughout the body. By sending signals to the pituitary to secrete different hormones into the blood stream, the hypothalamus also regulates the brain stem's responses to stress, body temperature, breathing and heart rate, hunger, thirst, and day-night rhythms. The hypothalamus, therefore, is very important in the early development of states of arousal (sleeping and waking), feeding (hunger and satiety), and self-regulation (distress of calming) in the newborn period.

The hypothalamus, pituitary, and amygdala play a major role in the development of responses to stress and trauma, as explained below. When the amygdala senses threat or stress, it sends neurochemicals to the hypothalamus to activate the **HPA Axis,** the system by which the threat/stress is translated into the release of hormones from the hypothalamus (via corticotropin-releasing hormone CRH) to the pituitary, from the pituitary (via adrenocorticotropin-releasing hormone ACTH) to the adrenal glands (located on top of each kidney, near the middle of the back), which results in the secretion of the hormone cortisol into the blood stream (see Figure 4.2).

Cortisol is a blood sugar and, like the sympathetic nervous system, prepares the body for action in response to stress. Cortisol—traveling via the bloodstream—also affects the neurons in the limbic system, where it heightens the formation of memories related to the stressful event and once that event has passed, slows down the production of cortisol via the HPA axis. Hormones also play a role in regulating the autonomic nervous system to help us speed up or to slow down in response to events. The pituitary can also secrete the hormone **oxytocin** into the blood, which gives a feeling of warmth, comfort and safety. Oxytocin is usually secreted when we are in close contact, with loving or supportive touch, to another person.

Let's take breathing as one example of how this system works. The brain stem sends a signal—via the autonomic nervous system—to the lungs and diaphragm muscle to breathe in and out at a regular rhythm. The brain stem can also automatically adjust breathing to the level of physical exertion. The limbic system can override this simple automaticity of the brain stem, making us capable of further modulating that basic rhythm. Because of neural links between the amygdala and brain stem, we typically will hold our breath when feeling afraid, worried or anxious. We also typically relax our bodies and breathe a sigh of relief when we feel safe. The neural connections between the limbic system and brain stem function very rapidly to adjust breathing to the current physical and emotional demands.

The hormones that are released when feeling afraid (cortisol) or safe (oxytocin) further regulate the brain stem and body via the blood stream. Hormones take more time to release and to dissipate, so they provide a longer term regulation of brain stem and body function. The limbic system functions automatically, like the brain stem, but it has more flexibility in regulating the body systems such as breathing in response to changing circumstances. The brain stem and the limbic system are the most functional areas of the brain at birth.

Finally, the **cortex** (from the Latin word meaning the *bark* of a tree, Figure 4.4) is the outer layer of the brain. The cortex is the largest part of the human brain. It completely wraps around and covers the limbic system and forms synaptic connections with the limbic system. The cortex is divided into major anatomical regions called **lobes.** Starting at the back of the brain is the occipital lobe which is where visual information is processed. The temporal lobes, one on each side of the brain and located just behind each ear, contain centers for auditory and speech processing. The temporal lobe also processes our sense of smell.

The parietal lobes sit on top of each side the brain, adjacent to the temporal and occipital lobes and include the sensory and motor cortices. These cortices are connected to the muscles and sense organs of the body via the spinal cord and afferent and efferent motor nerves. Unlike the autonomic nervous system in which the nerves to and from the internal organs come directly from the brain stem, *the sensory and motor nerves come from regions of the spinal cord located near the muscles and sensory receptors.* The nerves for the muscles and sense organs for touch and pressure in the hand and arm come from the upper part of the spinal cord; those for the legs come from the lower parts of the spinal cord.

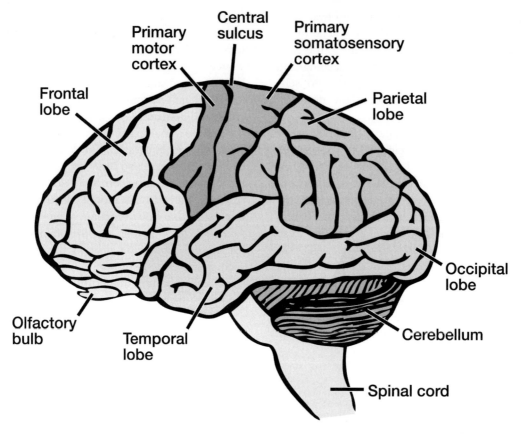

Figure 4.4   The functions of the major lobes of the brain's cortex.

The parietal lobe is also a place where sensory and motor information from different parts of the body are integrated into a cohesive sense of our self in relation to the environment, called the **body schema**. This includes our sense of movement and balance, our ability to locate particular parts of ourselves, to sense our body size and shape, and the awareness that our body has boundaries that separate us from other objects and bodies. The parietal lobes, sometimes in combination with the cerebellum as the base of the brain, allow us to integrate movement into a whole body functional pattern like reaching or walking, sense our body's position in space, to tell the difference between our own movements and those of others, to feel the difference between touching ourselves and being touched by someone else, to distinguish our voice from voices of others, and to know how to navigate safely as we move through the environment. As infants grow in their motor abilities over the first few years of life, this part of the brain is developing.

Another major anatomical area of the brain is the **insula** (or insular cortex, Figure 4.5). This is located underneath the temporal lobes, occupying a space between the temporal lobes and the limbic system. Related to the body schema which gives our sense of self in relation to the environment, the insula creates feelings of **interoception**, allowing us to *feel the inner condition of our bodies*, including the sense of hunger, thirst, itch, hot and cold, aches and soreness, pain, the need to urinate and defecate, and whether we are sick or healthy.

The frontal lobe, also called the **prefrontal cortex** (Figures 4.2 and 4.4) is located roughly above and behind the eyes. This is the most human

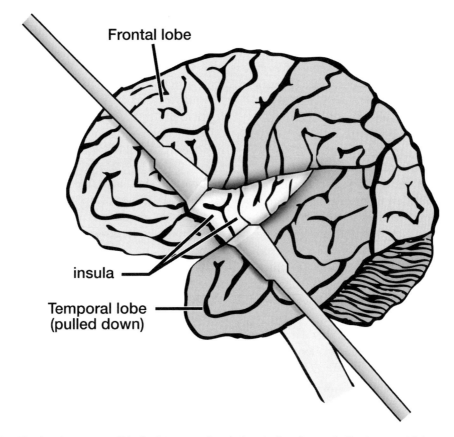

Frontal lobe

insula

Temporal lobe
(pulled down)

Figure 4.5 The insula, responsible for interoception, is located underneath the temporal lobes, occupying a space between the temporal lobes and the limbic system.

part of our brain which assists in reasoning, planning, organizing thoughts and behavior in adaptive ways, regulating emotions and urges, carrying out problem-solving, and making judgments. The prefrontal cortex also plays a role in inhibiting behavior, such as learning to wait for a meal instead of crying at the moment the infant feels hunger. *The prefrontal cortex gives us the possibility of voluntarily (rather than automatically) regulating our body states and patterns of behavior.* Coming back to the example of breathing, the prefrontal cortex allows us to voluntarily hold our breath, such as when we swim underwater, or to voluntarily pace our breathing when we feel afraid.

The prefrontal cortex is composed of two areas, medial (mPFC) and lateral (lPFC). The mPFC connects to emotional processing areas such as the amygdala. hippocampus, and the sen-

sory regions of the parietal lobes. The lPFC is connected to areas related to motor control (sitting still). As early as the first month of life, the mPFC responds to infant-directed and emotional speech, pleasant smells and a few months later to mutual gaze and familiar faces. The mPFC responds to changes in serotonin, the neurotransmitter affecting mood while the lPFC responds to dopamine, which regulates information and attention. The lPFC responds to speech that is not directed to the infant and is not emotional, and to non-human objects. The lPFC plays a role in holding objects in working memory and object permanence (Grossman, 2013; Johnson, 2010).

Finally, the brain is divided into two halves, or hemispheres. The **right hemisphere** controls movements on the left side of the body (the right parietal cortex in particular). The right limbic sensory and prefrontal areas, as well as areas for hearing and vision (recognizing familiar faces), are where the majority of social and emotional activity is processed. These parts of the right hemisphere in particular undergo major developmental changes during the first two years of life when infants are discovering how to recognize the important people in their lives and to regulate their emotions and emotional attachments to those people.

The **left hemisphere** controls movements on the right side of the body (left parietal cortex in particular). The left hemisphere prefrontal, parietal and temporal cortices are more specialized for thinking and language, and develop more rapidly after the first two years of life compared to similar areas on the right hemisphere which develop earlier. In general, the right hemisphere is more holistic and emotional, creating impressions and the perception of larger patterns. The left is more analytic and rational, breaking down impressions and patterns into their component parts. The right hemisphere is more related to novelty and creativity that initially attracts our attention to some event, person or object. After becoming more familiar, the left hemisphere takes over to organize and routinize the activity related to that situation.

PRENATAL AND INFANT BRAIN DEVELOPMENT: A CRITICAL PERIOD

The period from the first weeks after conception through the postnatal age of 3 to 4 years is now understood to be critical for the development of the human brain. What happens to the individual during this approximately 4-year period can determine whether the brain grows in a healthy and developmentally appropriate manner, or whether brain growth is compromised in some way. In this section, we'll review the basic ways in which normal brain development occurs. The next section covers optimal vs. non-optimal brain development, the factors that enhance or hinder brain growth.

Prenatal Development

During the early embryonic period, cells are beginning to divide by mitosis and to differentiate in their structure and function, as explained in Chapter 2. By the end of the third week following conception, the embryonic disc is composed of three different layers of stem cells: the endoderm, the mesoderm, and the ectoderm (see Chapter 2 and Figure 2.4). The stem cells in the ectoderm will become the skin, nails, teeth, sweat glands, sense organs and the nervous system. It is worth noting that the skin, the largest and most sensitive sense organ in the body, grows out of the same layer of stem cells as the brain.

During the first four prenatal months, new neurons and glial cells are created via mitosis in a process called **neurogenesis**. Although neurogenesis continues in small numbers throughout life, *virtually all of one's lifetime supply of neurons are produced during this period*. Neuronal stem cells, also called neuronal progenitor cells, migrate toward specific regions of the newly emerging head of the embryo. This migration is guided by the radial glial cells, which provide the structural cells in the brain that hold the neurons in their place and create a pathway along which neurons grow and migrate.

During the migration process, the neuron's axons extend and send out neurochemicals that will find and create connections to the dendrites of other neurons. The axons lengthen and the cells migrate to form the distinctly different anatomical regions (reviewed in the previous section) of the brain that are also beginning to extend connections to different parts of the body (Andersen, 2003; Mason, 2009; Stiles & Jernigan, 2010). Once neurons reach their final destination in the brain and begin to make connections, they can no longer divide by mitosis (See Figure 4.6).

After the fourth prenatal month, most of the brain's development occurs by making connections between cells and by "pruning," or selective death of unused neurons. Neurogenesis overproduces cells during the first 4 months of prenatal development, after which cells compete to see which are the strongest and most likely to survive. All neurons have an internal "sui-

Figure 4.6 The major phases of brain development, especially the growth and migration of neurons and the development of synapses.
Source: Anderson, 2003.

cide" program, meaning that the cell will die if it is not connected to other cells during development, if it does not get bathed in sufficient neurochemicals, or if it does not receive the appropriate epigenetic signals from the fetal environment to turn off the "suicide" genes. Cell death appears to be a process that corrects errors in the early migration and neurogenesis phase of prenatal development, by weeding out poorly formed or weaker cells. By the time a baby is born, about 50 percent of their prenatal neurons have died (See Figure 4.6; Andersen, 2003; Stiles & Jernigan, 2010).

During the second half of the prenatal period (see Figure 4.6) brain development occurs primarily by **synaptogenesis**, the development of connec-

tions between neurons. The nervous system grows from the brain to the periphery of the body as cells that migrated to become part of the motor cortex, for example, send out axons and connections that eventually meet the nerves connected to the brain stem, spinal cord, and then to the muscles, skin, internal organs, and sense organs (Greenough, Black, & Wallace, 1987). *The initial "wiring up" of the brain to the body is usually completed by the seventh prenatal month*, which is the time when fetuses can begin to feel pain and generate movements under the control of the brain (See Chapter 2; Webb et al., 2001).

In addition to lengthening and making connections during this period of prenatal devel-

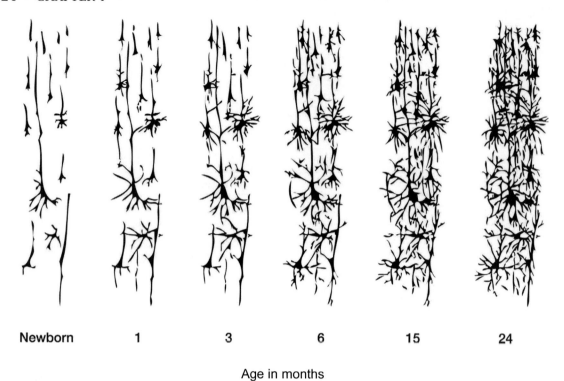

Newborn   1   3   6   15   24

Age in months

Figure 4.7   The development of neural networks via synaptogenesis
Source: Webb et al., 2001.

opment, the axons also become more efficient conductors by developing an insulation-like encasing of glial cells called **myelin**. Myelination improves the speed of electrical conduction along the axon by a factor of about three. Myelination begins in the last few weeks before birth and grows rapidly during the first few postnatal months but continues throughout life (Figure 4.5). Because of the rapid pace of myelination in this time period, one-month-olds process information about three times faster than newborns.

Postnatal Development

The postnatal development of the brain involves processes by which the networks between neurons become more complex, growing more dendrites and axon terminals and making an increasing number of synaptic connections and neurotransmitters (see Figure 4.7; Webb et al., 2001). In the prenatal period, there was an overproduction of neurons via

mitosis, some of which were pruned as weaker cells died. *In the postnatal period, there is an overproduction of synapses which gradually becomes pruned back to the stronger connections.* By 1 year, the child's brain has 150 percent of the number of synapses as the adult's; this number begins to decline in the second year (M. H. Johnson, 2000, 2003).

Figure 4.8 shows that synaptogenesis has an overproduction peak and then a decline that has a similar shape in different areas of the brain. This figure also shows that some brain areas mature earlier than others. Because the shapes of the curves representing the number of synapses are similar, Figure 4.8 seems to suggest that there is steady growth and decline in the number of synapses over time. In actuality, synapses connect and disconnect as the person is engaging with the environment, over time scales of seconds, minutes, or hours. Your synapses are probably doing this right now as you are trying to understand this chapter! The curves in Figure 4.8 relate to the total number

Figure 4.8 Developmental Changes in Synaptic Density of the Human Brain

Source: Adapted from P. Huttenlocher & A. Dabhoklar, Regional differences in synaptogenesis in human cerebral cortex, 1997. *Journal of Comparative Neurology* (4), 387.

of possible connections at any one time. Imagine a telephone network in which the number of calls peaks in the early evening. At any given time, however, millions of calls (connections between phones) are starting or ending. Like a telephone network, it appears that axons are sampling the space around them "looking" for the best connections and "hanging up" on connections that they don't like (Stiles & Jernigan, 2010).

Back to Figure 4.8, note for example, that the auditory cortex develops earlier than the visual cortex. Babies' hearing is better at birth than their vision because they were exposed to sound but not to light stimulation prenatally (see Chapter 5 on newborn sensory development). These sensory systems develop earlier than the prefrontal cortex responsible for the regulation of emotion (waiting patiently for a meal instead of crying, for example). Note also that brain development, espe-

cially in the prefrontal regulatory areas, continues all through life though but at a slower pace than during infancy (Andersen, 2003).

Research also shows that the glial cells that grew prenatally to guide the migration of neurons and their axons continue to function postnatally. As we saw previously, one type of glial cell forms the myelin coating around axons. The radial glial cells help to keep axons healthy with the right balance of neurochemicals, and they may even play an as yet unknown role in inter-neuron communication (Stiles & Jernigan, 2010). We do know that the neurochemical dopamine fosters the branching of dendrites and helps cells to synapse, and glia may play a role in this process.

Neuromotor pathways and brain regions that were developed prenatally and are functional at birth, those that prepare the infant for survival, are called **experience expectant** because the brain appears to be ready and waiting for a specific type of environmental input (such as pain) for which a particular behavioral skill (such as crying) is best adapted. Many areas of the brain, on the other hand, do not have a specialized function at birth. Some cells and synapses have developed prenatally whose only purpose is to become ready to learn about a particular individual's postnatal experiences. These cells and connections are called **experience dependent**. In a "use it or lose it" fashion, as particular sensory and motor patterns are repeated in early development, specific experience-dependent synapses and cells are used more than others. The synapses that are used the most become strengthened, while those that are used the least eventually die (Greenough et al., 1987; Thelen & Smith, 1994).

In reality, all neurons and neural connections are experience dependent in the sense that they develop at some point in time with respect to the kind of environment to which the infant is exposed (M. H. Johnson, 2000). Cells and pathways that at birth are experience expectant were, at some time during prenatal development, made up of neuronal stem cells that were experience dependent. Recall that sucking, which is a well-established experience-expectant pathway at birth, develops out of the tactile and motor experiences of the fetus (Chapter 2) and requires stimulation and repetition during the fetal period for the neural pathways to become strengthened into an experience-expectant behavior at birth. All during development, as we acquire new actions, the neural pathways become more expectant of skill-specific information, which increases the skillfulness of the action.

These changes in cell and synapse development show that the brain's development is highly dependent on the individual's experiences (M. H. Johnson, 2006; Westermann et al., 2007). The brain's construction tailors its development to the experiences of its owner. These neural developmental processes help us to understand how birth defects occur. Alcohol that the mother ingests during pregnancy limits the production of new axons and dendrites (Dow & Reoppelli, 1985), while

lead exposure destroys myelin (Lampert & Schochet, 1968). These conditions limit the number of experience-dependent connections and cause information processing to be slower, making for a less adaptive, less intelligent individual. In the final section of this chapter, we'll discuss how different types of pre- and post-natal environments affect brain development.

Although all the cells of the cortex have formed prenatally, their connections with the limbic and brain stem regions have only begun to develop. The immaturity of the medial prefrontal cortex, to take one example, explains why the infant has some basic emotions like distress, but these emotions are not well regulated. Similarly, the basic reflexes of the newborn (sucking, swallowing, blinking, etc.) are semi-automatic and there is little voluntary control over movement at this age. Infants need adults to help them calm down, to obtain food and other objects, and to stimulate them. For this reason, the way in which adults interact with infants plays a crucial role in how infants develop the connections between the cortex and the other areas. Adults, in other words, have a major influence on infant brain development.

There is a dynamic system of linkages between brain, experience, and behavior. And during the first few months after birth, infants experience stimuli of increasing intensity and complexity, and connections favoring those types of stimuli will be strengthened. By feedback from brain to behavior, the window of sustained attention will widen. As sustained attention allows the infant to inspect and explore specific stimuli, feedback to the brain will correspondingly create connections that make those specific events more easily recognized on subsequent occasions (K. W. Fischer, 1987; Goldman-Rakic, 1987; Hebb, 1949; Thelen & Smith, 1994).

Development of Functional Neural Networks

Although different anatomical structures are typically associated with particular functions, in reality, multiple structures work together as a network of synaptic connections to create organized behavior and body function (Johnson, Grossman, & Kadosh, 2009). There are four basic functional networks of the brain that are important to our understanding of infant development: (1) arousal, attention, and emotion (2) information processing and remembering, (3) regulation and executive function, and (4) self-awareness (Freides, 2001). Each of these functional networks goes through major developmental change during the prenatal and postnatal periods, and these changes correspond with changes in neuronal activity and anatomical structures.

Arousal, attention and emotion. This functional network regulates the sleep-wake cycle as well as cycles related to hunger, thirst, physical arousal during exercise and stress, and sexual-reproductive cycles in adolescents and adults. As we saw during prenatal development (Chapter 2), recognizable sleep-wake states—including REM sleep—do not emerge until the third fetal period, developing out of more primitive activity and rest cycles found in fetal period II. Newborns, as we'll see in a later chapter, can sleep up to 18 hours a day with frequent wakings. The amount of time awake and alert increases with age as does the consistency of sleep periods. By the end of the first year, most but not all babies can sleep through the night. Also during the first year, infants undergo radical changes in feeding patterns as they shift from a liquid diet of milk to eating more solid foods.

The brain areas involved in these functions also shift developmentally. In the third fetal period and the first months of life, sleeping, waking, and feeding are primarily regulated by a network that connects the brain stem, the hypothalamus, and the spinal cord. This is one of the most primitive networks of the brain that is responsible for basic life functions and which does not require any voluntary control. This arousal and attention network expands with age in relation to developmental changes in the infant.

The duration of waking states expands in the postnatal period due to experience-dependent interactions between the infant and environment. The infant's attraction to faces and to colors in the first months of life, for example, leads to activation and synaptogenesis between the primitive brain stem—hypothalamus network with the parietal cortex (sensorimotor function and body schema), and the insular cortex (interoception of feelings of interest and enjoyment). This larger network provides the infant with more internal awareness of what it feels like to stay awake and engage with other people, which then allows the network to sustain increased waking times to "feed" the desire to engage with the environment.

Engaging with the environment, in turn, calls for some kind of orienting response and control of attention to something in the environment like a toy, the mother's face, or food. Infant orienting activates different regions of the parietal cortex that are responsible for linking sensory information (vision from the eyes and occipital lobe, sound from the ears and temporal lobes) to motor movements that create a behavioral orienting response such as turning the head or eyes to see or hear, or opening the mouth to orient to a nipple or spoon (Freides, 2001; Posner et al., 2011). Via positive feedback (see Chapter 1) within the orienting-arousal neural network, changes in states of arousal (longer waking times) are developed by increased skill in orienting, and better orienting is fostered by longer waking states.

Emotions also develop over the first years of life. The emotion of fear, for example, does not fully develop until the end of the first year, as fear of strangers and separation anxiety from the primary caregivers. This is related to the developmental mylenation of the amydala and its connections to other brain networks, which becomes mature at the end of the first year. This is also the time when emotional attachments are forming. Experience dependent brain development that occurs during infant-caregiver interaction in the first year impacts the development of these pathways to the amygdala so that some infants are better able to be soothed by their caregivers than others (secure vs. insecure attachments) (Braun, 2011).

Information processing and remembering. These brain networks for staying awake and paying attention are also connected into a larger network that includes the sensory organs, all the internal organs, and the muscles that move the body. Speech and language processing, for example, are often said to be "located" in the temporal lobes. Studies of the brain, however, show that underlying linguistic ability is a complex network of connections between the temporal lobes, the parietal lobes which integrate sensory-auditory and motor function, and the sensorimotor areas that link directly to the auditory nerve and to the nerves that control the muscles of speech articulation in the mouth, lips, jaw, tongue, and throat (Bouchard et al., 2013; Homae et al., 2011). *This means that what infants and adults learn and remember in some way involves their whole body and not just the brain.* While there is currently a lot of interest in infant brain development, the brain-body network is actually where the development is occurring, not only in the brain.

Information processing, if it is to be efficient, requires learning and memory. Imagine that if every time you sat down to read this book, you had no memory of the previous times you read it. You would not get very far in your studies if this were the case. So, the nervous system evolved a way to encode, or remember, prior experiences to allow us to be more efficient in our actions, to go back to situations that made us feel good, and to avoid the ones that were unpleasant.

There are two basic kinds of memory: procedural-implicit and autobiographical-explicit, both of which will be reviewed in later chapters. **Autobiographical memory** is the ability to relate in words, a story about a sequence of events in the past. This type of memory is not seen until infants are about 3 years-old. This is because the hippocampus, which helps to organize information sequentially (stories have a beginning, middle, and end) does not become functional until that age. The hippocampus is part of the limbic system

located under the interior surface of the temporal lobes.

Before that, infants acquire **procedural memories** which are "ways of doing things." Procedural memories are basically an increased set of synaptic connections between various areas of the cortex with areas of the limbic system and brain stem, linking down to the efferent and afferent nerves going to and from muscles and sense organs in the body, which become myelinated with use and experience doing a particular activity. After a series of initially clumsy attempts to suck on a nipple or eat solid foods, babies' behavior becomes more skilled and efficient. Like riding a bike, once it is learned it is hard to forget it because the ability is "in" the cellular structure of nerves, sense organs, and muscle tissues. We don't have to think about it and, like riding a bike or singing a familiar song, information processing and remembering is a whole body experience, not just in the head.

Regulation and executive function. The growing ability to learn new skills requires a coordinated sequence of movements. For eating this might be attaching to the nipple, sucking, and swallowing; or opening the mouth, waiting for a spoon, closing the mouth, tasting and chewing, then swallowing. For face-to-face interaction, infants need to visually orient to an adult, scan the face looking for where the eyes are directed and the adult's facial expression and voice, organize a response like a smile or coo, and then wait for the adult to do something else.

In the initial phases of learning a new skill, infants and adults use their orienting responses to focus in on each particular part of the task. If, however, we continued to orient to every single component of a task, the task as a whole would take way too long to accomplish. We need, therefore, a mechanism for *inhibition* of the orienting reaction so that we can direct our attention to higher levels of processing that encompass a sequence of actions and sensations. We also need a means to have a *"working" or short-term memory* to remember each of the steps in the sequence, to *compare* our actions between different attempts at the same sequence, between one type of task and another, and between ourselves and another person.

Finally, we need to *regulate our emotions* so that we don't give up on learning something new in the face of complexity, distress, frustration, or fear (Best & Miller, 2010). Most of the neural basis for executive function comes from a network that includes all the prior networks along with their connections to the prefrontal cortex (regulation) and the insula (sense of self), which are the parts of the brain that mature the most slowly. One plateau of prefrontal development (Figure 4.8) occurs around the age of 3 years with the onset of language, autobiographical memory, and new forms of self-control that allow more sustained attention and autobiographical remembering. The second major growth and plateau of prefrontal function begins in adolescence and ends around the age of 25 years (Braun, 2011).

Depending on the person, it takes years to "grow out of," to regulate, the unruly urges and unwise risk-taking of adolescence via increased connections to the prefrontal cortex. Similarly, by age 3 or 4 years, infants have outgrown their earlier impatience, tantrums, and uncontrolled emotions and are better able to express their needs and understand other people. Links between the growing pre-frontal cortex and the amygdala account for the emergence of more independent behavior and self-calming in the absence of direct adult support, an ability that emerges in the second and third years of life (Braun, 2011).

Even though there is a peak in the development of the prefrontal cortex at 3 to 4 years, even newborns have some prefrontal functions available. In early infancy, rudimentary prefrontal circuits help to regulate infant distress, often by soothing or distracting the infant from what was causing the distress. A lot of adult help is needed. Learning to eat solid foods, staying awake for longer periods, and many social and communicative skills that are acquired in the first three years, mostly with the help of adults, foster the development of prefrontal executive function. In some way, adults serve as an "external" prefrontal cortex, filling in the gaps and providing assistance and emotional control when the infant or child can't handle a situation. Interactions with other people around learning skills and dealing with emotions, particularly in attachment relationships, are therefore crucial to early brain development. Similarly, adolescents need a lot of parental guidance in learning to drive safely, managing their emotional urges, monitoring their use of the internet, and dealing with the ups and downs of peer relationship challenges.

Of all the executive functions in infancy, inhibition is perhaps the most important. Compromised inhibitory control in preschoolers is correlated with cognitive, behavioral and emotional problems later in life (Best & Miller, 2010). Interventions for school-age children that foster self-regulation have shown promising results for later school achievement and emotional stability (Shanker, 2013). One of the reasons that inhibition is important is because activation of the amydala, which occurs when people are distressed or fearful, can dampen or shut down prefrontal regulatory functions.

We can't really think clearly or act coherently when we are under stress or threat because the amygdala activates the hypothalamus which then activates the sympathetic nervous system and the secretion of cortisol which prepares the body to meet the stress or challenge. If the situation is overly stressful, emotional and cognitive executive inhibitory function is diminished in favor of immediate response to the stress. Fear also detaches us from our awareness of our own bodies by blocking the pathways to and from the insula and parietal cortex. Prefrontal inhibition of the amygdala, therefore, allows people greater access to their self-awareness and to more adaptive and regulated responses to the environment (Fogel, 2009).

Self-awareness. Most past research on the brain and nervous system has been devoted to how people respond to the environment, how we learn skills such as language and communication, how we regulate our emotional attachments, and how our sensory and motor skills adapt to environmental challenges. More recently, however, neuroscientists have discovered that there are major networks in the nervous system devoted almost entirely to sensing the inner condition of the body and mind (Fogel, 2009; Freides, 2001).

To move across a room, of course we need the motor skills of walking and postural control (it takes babies more than a year to learn how to walk), we need to identify the nature of the surface on which we are walking (flat or inclined, smooth or rough), and we need to have a sense of the objects in the room that we might have to avoid or step around. This is all related to the way the brain and body respond to the challenges of the environment. We also, however, need to know where our own bodies are located with respect to those objects (body schema). We need to feel the differences in our muscles when we walk on different surfaces or when walking uphill or downhill (interoception). In social situations, we need to sense the boundaries between ourselves and other people, where our body leaves off and another's begins, and to feel our own actions as different from those of another person.

All the other basic functions of the nervous system—arousal and attention, information processing and remembering, regulation and executive function—take months and even years to develop during infancy and childhood. Put in more concrete terms, infants develop their motor skills, perceptual abilities, social and language skills, emotional responses, and attachments to other people. As we engage with the world, our nervous system shifts and changes the way it builds networks and connections for all these functions. The same is true for self-awareness.

As we'll see in this book, self-awareness goes through multiple developmental changes during infancy. For most of the first half year, for example, infants cannot distinguish where their body ends and their mother's body begins. The awareness of being a self, separate from others, does not begin until the end of the first year when infants begin to show separation anxiety, suggesting that they begin to perceive their mother or father as a separate person. It takes yet another year for infants to be able to recognize the image in the

mirror as their own, and to begin to use words like *I, me,* and *mine.* Without a sense of self—as in autism and other disorders—people cannot comprehend how they affect others nor feel empathy for another person's feelings.

OPTIMAL AND NON-OPTIMAL BRAIN DEVELOPMENT DURING INFANCY

One way to interpret the discussion in the previous section is that the human brain is not pre-set at birth for all future experiences. On the contrary, what distinguishes humans from most other animals is the degree to which our brain has a talent for learning new skills and patterns. This begins in infancy and can continue through old age. **Neural plasticity** is the ability of the brain and nervous system to seek novelty, learn, and remember by continuing to alter the patterns of connections between neurons.

Brain development continues throughout our lives as we learn new things and adapt to changes in our environment. Brain development during gestation and infancy, however, is unique and never again occurs in the same way during later life. The fetal and infant brain does not simply adapt to the environment. Rather, *the environment becomes permanently incorporated into the very structure of the brain* (Andersen, 2003). This is because the basic structures and connections in the brain are actually forming during this period, and this explains why these early years of development are considered a critical period for brain development (see Chapter 1)

Let's suppose a normal teen or young adult does not get to attend college or high school. There is nothing to prevent that person from going back to school later in life, at least not from a neurological perspective. If they have the time, money, and motivation, it can be done. This is not the case for infants. If infants fail to get exposure to a loving parent or caregiver, they will permanently lack certain abilities to form attachments. If they are not exposed to language in the first three years, they will never become fluent in any language.

Consider an individual who is blind at birth due to an eye defect. The blindness continues for the first few years of life, and then the person later has surgery to correct the eye defect. Even though this person now has visual signals traveling from the eye to the brain, he or she still cannot see the world as the rest of us see it. That's because the regions of the brain required to distinguish objects out of light and shadow develop during the first few years. It is not until 10 months of age that infants can recognize and clearly distinguish one object from another and view it as a separate and permanent entity. There are other instances of infants who are reared in orphanages with little adult attention, or those who are not exposed to appropriate language experience, who will develop severe impairments in social and linguistic function along with brain abnormalities (Nelson, 2007; Paterson et al., 2006).

For most humans with an intact brain, that brain retains a certain amount of plasticity throughout life. Appropriate educational and therapeutic experiences may be able to partially repair the effects of early deprivation. On the other hand, because the brain grows gradually, the infantile patterns of connection are never lost and a person who "recovers" from early deprivation will never be the same as one who never suffered from that experience. The prognosis for treatment and recovery depends upon the severity of the deprivation. The prenatal and infancy period, in other words, builds the foundations on which later development can rest. Later experience can build certain kinds of processes but they will not be as strong or as adaptive as those built upon a more solid foundation (Fox, Levitt, & Nelson, 2010).

Effects of Prenatal and Infant Stress on Brain Development

Stress is probably the single most important factor regulating individual differences in brain development. Its effects can begin before birth and continue throughout life. **Threat** is the sense of being in danger from outside of ourselves (e.g., another person or a collision with an object) or inside (e.g., a physical pain or feeling of anxiety). **Stress** occurs when the body is unable to find a balance between sympathetic and parasympathetic activity. **Trauma** is the condition that results from prolonged sympathetic activation and the resulting depletion of the body's resources and lack of time for recovery. **Shock trauma** is the effect of a relatively brief and sudden event like an accidental injury or a sudden loss. **Developmental trauma** is when exposure to a threatening event occurs over a longer period of time, such as long-term parental neglect or abuse.

The evidence for the negative impact of stress and trauma is consistent across both human and animal studies. Basically, *each baby in the first two years of life comes to assess the world as either a safe or a threatening place*. This assessment is not made as a conscious choice, but rather a nonconscious evaluation by the autonomic nervous system that comes as a result of encountering and coping with difficult experiences in early life. This nonconscious evaluation of safety or threat is called **neuroception**, meaning that the autonomic nervous system (both the sympathetic and parasympathetic branches) makes the decision of how to respond and not the conscious mind (Porges, 2004).

There are three basic patterns of neuroception: immobilization, mobilization, and social engagement (Porges, 2004; Porges & Furman, 2011; see Table 4.1). Mobilization and immobilization are different types of responses to threat. With mobilization, there are two possibilities: fight or flight. These involve a high level of arousal shown in increased heart rate, blood flow, and faster breathing, all activated by the sympathetic nervous system (SNS). Because the body only has a limited amount of metabolic energy resources, this ongoing sympathetic activation is done at the expense of basic body functions such as digestion and immune system support. If we are mobilized too long, it will eventually compromise our physical and mental health.

Engagement with, attention to, and adaptive function with people and objects requires

TABLE 4.1   Three Forms of Neuroconception
(SNS = Sympathetic Nervous System [Arousal]; PNS = Parasympathetic Nervous System [Relaxation]

Social World	Type of Neuroception and the Related Nervous System	Characteristics
Threatening	Immobilization Unmyelinated vagus PNS	Freezing, feigning death, behavioral shutdown, dissociation from the body
Threatening	Mobilization SNS	Fight or flight behavior, increased heart rate, slowed digestion and growth
Safe	Social engagement Balance between myelinated vagus PNS (relaxation) and SNS (arousal)	Relaxation, emotional engagement and regulation, appropriate challenges, growth

Source: Porges, 2004

the ability to relax that is supported by the parasympathetic nervous system (PNS) which tends to decrease heart rate, slow breathing, and lower blood pressure. When we are relaxed and feeling safe, our cardiovascular, digestive and immune systems can work well and keep us healthy. Social and object engagement also require a balance between SNS and PNS activation, which allows us to stay alert and attentive (SNS) and at the same time able to relax and enjoy what we are doing (PSN).

Immobilization due to threat has two possibilities: freeze or faint. If we are not able to respond to stress and threat with mobilization, a more primitive and unmyelinated part of the PNS gets activated. Similar to normal PNS function, the body slows down toward relaxation. Immobilization, however, is an extreme form of PNS activation in which the body not only slows down but also shuts down, leading to a state of feigning death (fainting or sleep-like states), or "deer-in-the-headlights" frozen and unable to move or act. Immobilization is a last-resort survival response of the nervous system that has the effect of tuning out body awareness, pain, and even death.

The PNS vagus nerve connects to most of the internal organs, including the heart and gut organs. When activated, it slows heart rate, acting like a brake on arousal. **Vagal tone**, the availability of a functionally myelinated vagal PNS that can help us relax in the face of stress, is measured by the ability of the heart to adjust its beat-to-beat frequency in the face of stress.

The vagus nerve myelinates slowly over the first 6 months after birth, meaning that fetuses and young infants under six months do not have a vagal brake to modulate the effects on stress. Over the first six months, infants need adult help to develop increased ability to digest food (solid foods are not typically given until 6 months), to calm down when upset, and to have longer periods of social engagement with others. This means, on the one hand, that infants younger than 6 months need more protection from people around them to buffer the effects of stress, and on the other hand, that if this protection is not available, the effects of stress during this period is more likely to have lasting impairments of vagal tone leading to an impairment of the ability to regulate basic body function and manage stress (Porges & Furman, 2011).

Prolonged activation of the SNS and suppression of the PNS also activates the HPA axis (see above) resulting in the secretion of the blood sugar, cortisol. Cortisol gives the body the energetic reserves it needs to respond to stress (fight or flight) and the energy and arousal levels that we also need during normal engagement with the world. On the other hand, if stress is persistent, either prenatally from maternal stress or depression, or postnatally from lack of consistent, loving, and appropriate care and disturbances in social interaction, cortisol is overproduced because the infant's well-being is threatened.

TABLE 4.2 Effects of Stress on the Developing Brain

Stress, via the over-production of cortisol, changes how the brain develops

Amygdala	Hippocampus	Prefrontal Cortex
Increase in CORT receptors in amygdala leads to a bias to detect fear and anxiety, and creates a risk for PTSD and stress-related physical and mental illnesses	Decreased receptors for CORT in the hippocampus leads to decreases in the ability to self-regulate responses to stress, memory problems, overproduction of CORT, adrenal fatigue	Impaired cell growth decreases ability to self-regulate emotions and self-awareness, and impairs ability to form secure attachments

Source: (Eichenbaum & Cohen, 2001; Gunnar & Cheatham, 2003; Schore, 2003).

In small amounts the body needs cortisol, and some cortisol is normally present during the waking day. In large amounts, however, cortisol is toxic to the brain and creates lasting changes that may persist over months and years, as shown in Table 4.2. As shown in the table, when cortisol returns to the brain via the bloodstream, it can alter structures by changing the epigenetic markers that influence cortisol receptors and neurotransmitters in the brain (Andersen, 2003; Braun, 2011; Murgatroyd & Spengler, 2011). The same processes also compromise the immune system leading to higher prevalence of diseases in people who have experienced too much stress (Eichenbaum & Cohen, 2001; Field et al., 2006; Gunnar & Cheatham, 2003; Herschkowitz et al., 1997; Keenan et al., 2003; Schore, 2003).

Because the hippocampus and amygdala are the two areas where memory is formed, cortisol not only changes the neurotransmitters and receptors as well as the connections between the limbic system and the rest of the brain, but cortisol also changes the way early experiences are remembered. Too much stress leads to a tendency to feel fear and threat in the future, even when the future situation is not necessarily fearful to an outside observer. It also leads to **post-traumatic stress syndrome (PTSD)**, a decreasing ability of the individual to cope with the stress (mediated by the right prefrontal cortex) in appropriate ways, creating a person who is more likely to freeze (shut down and become unresponsive in severe cases), fight (tantrums, resistance, negativity), or flee (hide or withdraw) when they feel threatened. We will return to the topic of PTSD in later chapters, especially around the topics of infant attachment and infant mental health.

Prenatal and postnatal stress can occur because of maternal or paternal depression, anxiety, drug addiction, and PTSD, because of stressful life events (divorce and family strife, frequently changing residences, unsafe neighborhoods, crime, warfare and refugee migration, unemployment, natural disasters), poverty, nutritional deficits, and diseases. The risk for future impairment increases with the number of risk factors that occur (Robinson et al., 2011).

What are the consequences of these stress-induced alterations in the structure and neurochemical function of the brain during the prenatal and early infancy periods? Because the brain during this time period is so sensitive to environmental influences, these effects can and do have serious consequences for later functioning. Outcomes can be serious, and in some cases, life-long. Because stress impairs the vagal-parasympathetic system responsible for calming, and dysregulates the HPA axis which changes key areas of the brain related to self-regulation, stress affects both mental and physical health. There are also corresponding epigenetic changes that alter patterns of DNA expression and cell development in future years, particularly affecting these neurological systems of stress regulation and the autonomic nervous system that regulates the health of all the internal organs of the body (Ellison, 2010).

The list of effects of early stressors—mediated by these changes in the brain and nervous system—is long and downright scary. The effects of cortisol on the prefrontal cortex also predispose infants to later problems with executive function and self-control. Toddlers who score low on self-control are more likely to have physical health problems, substance abuse, problems with personal finances, and criminal offenses (Bernier et al., 2010; Moffitt et al., 2011). Prenatally stressed infants are more likely to be born premature or low birth weight, less able to engage in social interaction, have compromised ability to attend, and to control their emotions. Their motor and language development may also be delayed. Adverse effects continue during childhood and adulthood and may include cognitive and memory impairments, learning disabilities, ADHD, depression, anxiety, and poor school performance. There is also a higher risk in later life for chronic diseases including cardiovascular, respiratory, and immune disorders including cancer, and early death. Early stress predisposes teens and adults to unhealthy lifestyles

including substance abuse, aggressiveness and violent behavior, gambling, school failure, gang membership, unemployment, crime, incarceration, and poor parenting of their own children (Davis & Sandman, 2010; diPietro et al., 2007; diPietro, 2010; Enlow et al., 2011; Field, 2011; Field & Diego, 2008; Hay et al., 2010; Ronald et al., 2010; Schetter, 2011; Shonkoff et al., 2011).

Because the brain and nervous system affects the functioning of the entire body, adverse early experiences can have major impacts on both mental and physical health, and on education, work, and social behavior in later life. The evidence, as shown in Figure 4.9 points to alterations in epigenetic markers that may establish lifelong patterns of dysregulation vs. health in stress regulation, biochemistry, neurophysiology, immune function, and metabolism. Because the very biology of the individual is altered by early experience, some have called early brain development a kind of "programming" or "biological memory." While the

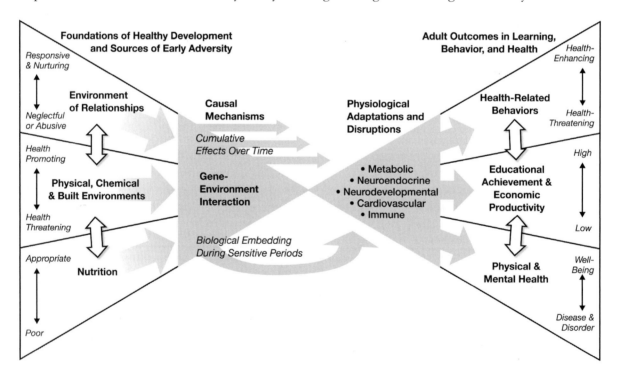

Figure 4.9 Multiple factors that influence the gene-environment interactions that set the stage for brain development.
Source: Anderson, 2003

immature fetus and infant is actually responding to stress in a way that enhances their survival from the stressors in the short-term, because of their immaturity these survival strategies have extremely high long-term costs.

Some type of short-term stress is actually good for infants, children, and adults. Dealing with everyday frustrations, adapting to new experiences, waiting to get our needs met, and exploring an uncertain environment contribute to honing more adaptive responses and to the development of healthy prefrontal and executive function while still being able to regulate the effects of short term stress on the body. Long-term unresolved stress, not mediated by times of restoration and support, however, is toxic to the organism and can cause these more lasting and damaging effects.

How Can We Foster Healthy Brain and Bio-Behavioral Development for Infants?

How can we protect the fetus and infant from the undesirable effects of toxic stress? If the brain and physiology of the body can be so deeply impaired by unfortunate prenatal and infant experiences, can later more healthy, safe and loving environments reverse the damage? How plastic is the brain?

Because the brain during this critical period (the period from the second half of gestation until the third birthday) is so immature and sensitive, whatever happens during that period will remain in the tissues of that person for the rest of their life. The parts of the nervous system and the epigenetic processes that regulate the basic function of body and mind are programmed by these early experiences to expect a certain kind of environment and to survive in that environment. Even if a child has a genetic ability to be relatively resistant to stress, highly adverse environments with high levels of stress will override the genetic protective factors and create epigenetic markers that produce high levels of cortisol and subsequently affect brain development (Ouellet-Morin et al., 2008). If infants develop in very unsafe environments, they will retain the tendencies for hyper- and hypo-

activation of the autonomic nervous system, even when their later environments are safer than those of their early years.

There is some room for hope, however, because each person develops in a different way and responds differently to the environment. While some infants exposed to toxic stress may never recover as adults and suffer from persistent heath and behavior problems, others will find ways to lead healthy and productive lives. It all depends on the severity of the original stress and on the supports and resources that may be available later in life.

Infants who had been raised in poorly managed orphanages and who were severely deprived of social and linguistic input, improved very little even after several years of receiving language enrichment programs. In other cases, however, it appears that the brain can bypass damaged areas and co-opt undamaged and underused areas to serve similar functions, and thus help the person recover more readily from early deprivation. In this way, areas such as the hippocampus which does become damaged due to early stress, may not be repaired but other areas—particular those in the prefrontal cortex that mature later and help with executive function—may be able to at least partially substitute for the cognitive, regulating, organizing and remembering functions of the hippocampus. Thus, if stress that occurs prenatally and during the first year is followed by early intervention programs in preschool and day care during the second year, there is ample room for full or partial recovery (Blair, 2010; Fox, Levitt, & Nelson, 2010).

Consider the following study. For a group of 125 women, fetal cortisol was sampled during amniocentesis. When the children were 17 months, those with high prenatal cortisol had shorter attention spans, fewer language skills, and fewer problem-solving skills but only if their attachment to their mothers was insecure. If they had a secure attachment to mothers, those with high prenatal cortisol showed no effects at 17 months. Thus, secure attachment with mothers completely eliminated the effects of prenatal stress (University of

Case Report
Recovering from Emotional Trauma

The Case Reports in this book are based on undergraduate students' investigations into their own infant development, done in the form of a term project for classes I taught using previous editions of this book. This first case report is about the effects of early trauma, in this particular case, related to a mother's death during the first three years of life. Here are excerpts in the student's own words.

My mother died when I was nine months old and I had a lot of different caregivers during her illness and after her death. My Dad remarried when I was sixteen months-old. My relationship with my stepmother has been very negative but I believe that during the first few years it was mostly positive. I have always suspected that the trauma of losing a mother, having many different caregivers, and trying recreate a mother bond unsuccessfully has affected me significantly. Nevertheless, the impact of losing a parent in my infancy was somewhat cushioned by the fact that I was cared for by patient, nurturing people and a loving father.

I remember as a young child, first feeling fear and later extreme anger with my stepmother. While having many other positive caregivers did help me to feel less fearful of people and become a generally social and happy person, on a much deeper level, it affected my trust in people. I don't think I ever expected them to stay long and I don't think I felt a lot of constant unquestionable love.

I am learning to find peace with these feelings although in the past I have subconsciously backed away from them because of the potential pain that dealing with them could cause. I was more aware of what others were feeling to gauge my own feelings, and I felt great anxiety when it was not positive. This has largely to do with my stepmother who had very erratic and generally negative emotions. When relationships were comforting, I felt extreme peace, happiness and gratitude although I still don't count on these feelings to last. With the slightest hint of negativity or distrust I became extremely agitated and even angry.

I believe that to deal with any trauma in your life, in infancy and childhood, it takes a conscious decision to do it. I now realize the mistakes I made in my life in dealing with people, especially in my confusion and anger. This class helped me to become aware of these patterns and feel more of a sense of peace.

This report is a wonderful example of the research reviewed earlier. Even though her mother's death, changes in caregivers, and conflicts with her stepmother experienced by this student at a young age has had lasting post-traumatic effects on the nervous system—lack of regulatory control (anger, agitation) in the face of stress—this person had a loving and devoted relationship to her father and many other good relationship experiences. All of these were protective factors that led, ultimately, to a more resilient nervous system and opportunities for restoring a more healthy future brain development.

Rochester Medical Center, 2010). Other studies have shown that parental warmth, coupled with early intervention programs for families, can significantly reduce the risk of aggressive behavior in children who had early exposure to toxic stress (O'Neal et al., 2010). Similarly, infants at genetic risk for having lower vagal tone (lower adaptability of the ANS) and who had sensitive parenting during the first year, were no more likely to respond negatively to maternal separation at 12 months than infants who did not have a genetic risk factor. Infants with the risk factor had negative responses to separation only if their mothers were less sensitive to their needs during the first year (Propper et al., 2008). Fathers' unresponsiveness and negative emotions also have similar restorative impacts on the infant's cortisol and vagal reactivity (Mills-Koonce et al., 2011).

In general, the effects of early experience have the potential to be alleviated when certain types of resources are present in the environment in later infancy and early childhood. Parental sensitivity, as shown by these studies, is one factor. Parents, being human themselves, are better able to be sensitive to their infants if the parents themselves have opportunities to develop executive function and self-control, social support, openness to learning, and are not themselves diseased, overstressed, or cognitively impaired. Thus, it is essential for parents to have strong support networks if they are to support their own and their children's resilience in recovery from trauma (Feldman & Vengrober, 2011; Schetter, 2011). On the child's side, in addition to parental support, having the ability to talk about their experiences, dreams, and fears, and having a community of support are all important factors in recovery (Quota et al., 2008; Sagi-Schwartz, 2008). The Case Report in this chapter reveals how these factors worked for one person who was 3-years-old when an ethnic war engulfed the family and the country in which they lived.

Conclusion

As we saw in the chapter on prenatal development, in this case report, and as we shall see later in this book, there are three basic areas of intervention to relieve the effects of early stress and improve the prognosis for healthy brain development: (1) the infant's family and social relationships (reducing family and societal stress), (2) the safety of the built environment (reducing toxic chemicals, using seat belts and car seats, reducing dangers in neighborhoods), and (3) providing adequate nutrition and preventing disorders such as diabetes and obesity. Pediatric and other early childhood care should identify not only physical disease in children but even more importantly, symptoms of family and societal stress (Shonkoff et al., 2011). Unfortunately, not many pediatric doctors and nurses are attuned to the toxic effects of stress on mental and physical health, nor do they know how to respond. We'll return to the topic of remediating the effects of prenatal and infancy stress and stress regulation in the last chapter of this book.

In summary, the first three years of life is a critical period for brain development. When people think of brain development, they are most likely to think about cognitive development and the role of the cortex. Research shows, however, that infancy is not a critical period for cortical and left-brain processes like reading, math, thinking, or musical ability. These abilities develop after the age of 3 years and continue throughout life. *Infancy is a critical period for the development of the limbic system, the insula, and the prefrontal parts of the brain—arousal, attention and emotion; information processing; regulation/executive function; and basic bodily self-awareness—which is fundamentally and crucially dependent upon the quality of sensitive caregiving, love, emotional sharing, and social engagement received and perceived by the infant.* It is considerably more important for infant brain development if parents and other adults to spend quality one-on-one and family time with a baby—playing together, sharing the baby's delight in the world, doing normal caretaking, and providing a sense that the world is safe and secure when the baby feels distressed—than letting the baby play for long periods with expensive toys, or listen to Mozart, or watch baby TV programs, all of which are marketed to parents on the (false) presumption that they help the infant's brain to develop.

SUMMARY

Measuring Brain Activity

- Many of the procedures used to study adult brains are not useful for infants.
- Different types of methods are available to study the electrical, magnetic, and blood flow changes in the infant's brain, although they cannot reach as deeply into the brain as methods used for adults.

Basic Structures of the Nervous System

- The major areas of the brain are the brain stem, limbic system, and cortex.
- The brain stem areas control autonomic functions such as breathing and heart rate.
- The limbic system processes emotions and memories as well as some body functions. Within the limbic system, the important structures during infancy are the hippocampus, amygdale, hypothalamus, and pituitary.

- The prefrontal cortex connects limbic and cortical areas and is responsible for social and emotional regulation. The cortex involves thinking, reasoning, and judging.
- The brain is also divided into two hemispheres, the right more emotional and the left more cognitive and linguistic.

Prenatal and Infant Brain Development: A Critical Period

- The first stage of brain development is the production and migration of neurons and glia during the first 4 prenatal months.
- Most of the development of the brain after that time, both pre- and post-natal, is via making and pruning synaptic connections between neurons.
- Synaptic connections are dependent on the types of experiences and environments to which the infant is exposed.

- Neural networks are developed for (1) arousal, attention and emotion, (2) information processing and remembering, (3) regulation and executive function, and (4) self-awareness.

Optimal and Non-Optimal Brain Development During Infancy

- Stress and trauma can have major impacts on brain function.
- Too much stress in prenatal and infant development can impair emotional and cognitive responses, mental and physical health, and affect lifetime brain function.

Chapter 5

The First Two Months

CHAPTER OUTLINE AND OVERVIEW

Physical and Motor Development	*How is the newborn's behavior organized (sleeping, crying, waking)? In what ways can the newborn act on the environment? How does the brain develop?*
Perceptual Development	*What can newborns see, hear, taste, feel, and smell?*
Cognitive Development	*Can newborns learn? Can they imitate?*
Emotional Development	*What can newborns feel?*
Family and Society	*How do newborns and adults coordinate their behavior and form emotional bond? Are firstborns different from laterborns?*

At birth, the baby must adapt to the physical changes needed to breathe air, to obtain nutrients orally, and to self-regulate body temperature. Birth also introduces a vast array of lights, sounds, touches, tastes, and smells that challenge the newborn's senses. What must the first taste of milk be like, or the first look at a human face? Do these things have any meaning for the newborn infant?

From another perspective, birth is not a major developmental change for the infant. As we saw in Chapters 2 and 3, studies of preterm infants and ultrasound studies of fetuses show that many of the motor and perceptual systems of the newborn are already developed by 36 weeks' gestational age. By this age or before, for instance, the fetus can suck. Furthermore, the amniotic fluid has tastes similar to the mother's milk, since both are flavored by what the mother eats. The mother's voice is already familiar to the infant. Because of prenatal experiences, the newborn is already familiar with movements like breathing and crying, has developed receptors and neural pathways for all the sensory systems, and has a distinct pattern of sleeping and waking states.

The abilities of the newborn infant have been the subject of a great many speculations and investigations by scholars. For thousands of years, philosophers have built theories of the human mind based on what they presumed was acquired by experience and what was already endowed at birth. In the last 150 years, the sciences have taken up the investigation of the newborn's abilities, as psychologists, biologists, physicians, and nurses have tried to answer questions related to their own areas of interest.

The amount of information collected on the newborn in just the past 30 years alone could fill a small library. Studies have been done on such diverse topics as treating newborn diseases, finding the best way to soothe a crying baby, understanding the development of sleeping and waking states, and the ability of the newborn to recognize his or her mother.

Chapter 2 covered the physical features of the newborn and his or her initial adaptations to postnatal life. In this chapter, some of the sensorimotor and psychological abilities of the newborn and how they change over the next 6 or 8 weeks will be examined. This chapter looks at some of the perceptual and cognitive aspects of newborn behavior and at the newborn's initial social interactions with adults. This chapter contains the first Co-Regulating with Baby section, a regular feature of this and the following chapters. This section describes some ways to enjoy the company of newborns and to provide them with developmentally appropriate stimulation. There is also an Experiential Exercises section.

PHYSICAL AND MOTOR DEVELOPMENT

States of Rest and Activity

During the fetal period, distinct periods of rest and activity begin to emerge at about 26 to 28 weeks' gestational age. These primitive patterns of activity and quiescence change cyclically about once every 40 minutes. By 32 weeks, both rest and activity are more complex and are divided into distinct states. A **state** is an organized pattern of physical and physiological responding that is related to the infant's level of activation or arousal. Once infants enter a particular **state** (see Table 5.1), they are likely to remain in that state for as little as 15 minutes or as long as several hours. It is not easy to soothe newborns who are crying, to induce sleep if they are awake, or to arouse them once they are sleeping. This suggests that states are relatively stable behavioral processes that form the base from which all other actions of the newborn must be understood (Wolff, 1993; Zeskind & Marshall, 1991).

At least two sleep states are present at 32 weeks' gestational age: rapid eye movement sleep (called REM sleep or active sleep) and non-REM sleep (called NREM sleep or quiet sleep). By 38 weeks, or full-term gestational age, several other sleep states are present, including periodic sleep (a combination of REM and NREM sleep) and drowsiness (a transitional state between sleep and

TABLE 5.1   Newborn States of Arousal

State Name	Description
Quiet Sleep (NREM)	Respiration is regular, eyes are closed and not moving, and the baby is relatively motionless.
Active Sleep (REM)	Muscles are more tense than in quiet sleep, the eyes may still display REMs, breathing is irregular, and spontaneous startles, sucks, and body movements occur in rhythmic bursts.
Drowsiness	Opening and closing of the eyes, increased activity, more rapid and regular breathing, and occasional smiling.
Quiet alert	Eyes are open and the environment is being scanned; the body is still, and respiration is more rapid than in sleep.
Active alert	Awake with body and limb movements, although infants are less likely to attend to external stimulation and focus their eyes less often than in the quiet alert state.
Crying	Elevated activity and respiration rate, cry vocalization, and facial expression of distress.

waking). These states are described in Table 5.1, along with the waking states of the normal full-term newborn infant. Researchers disagree about the number and type of infant states. Table 5.1 shows 6 levels of state, but some researchers have used as many as 11 different state distinctions (Zeskind & Marshall, 1991).

Sleep States

How much time a newborn spends sleeping and when during the day or night the baby sleeps are issues of great concern to parents. Newborns sleep an average of 16 to 17 hours per day, although this can vary between 11 and 21 hours (Parmelee, Schultz, & Disbrow, 1961). By 2 weeks, the average sleep time is decreased to about 14 to 15 hours, again with large differences between infants (St. James-Roberts & Plewis, 1996). Unlike adult sleep, infant sleep does not occur as one continuous period. Sleep periods range from 2 to 10 hours. For the first few weeks after birth, these periods can occur almost any time during the 24-hour day, to the dismay of sleepless parents. By 3 or 4 months of age, infants regularly sleep more at night than during the day, but night wakings are common throughout infancy and early childhood (Anders, Goodlin-Jones, & Zelenko, 1998).

Some babies show a preference for night sleeping, while others are more likely to wake at night.

Individual infants appear to be highly consistent. Their preference for sleeping through the night or for waking at night remains stable over many years. In a study tracking sleeping over the first three years, about two-thirds of infants fall into a group called "sleepers," waking from sleep about one night per week. The remainder of the group were called "transitional sleepers" who woke every night for the first 6 months, 2 nights per week by 15 months, and only once per week by 3 years. Transitional sleepers were more likely to be boys, more likely to be rated as difficult at 6 months, and/or more likely to have a depressed mother (Weinraub et al., 2012). These individual differences affect the person's later interactions with others. Infants who are awake more at night are perceived as more difficult and show less synchrony in their interactions with mothers (de Graag et al., 2012). Infant sleep difficulty is also associated with lower self-control at 18 months (Bernier et al., 2010). Sleep apparently facilitates brain development and maturation by helping to consolidate day-time learning and memory when the brain is relatively at rest (Tarullo et al., 2011).

There is recent evidence that these individual differences may appear during the late fetal period, affected in unknown ways by maternal patterns of activity during the day/night cycle and by daily fluctuations of maternal and infant hormones. The propensity to sleep through the night,

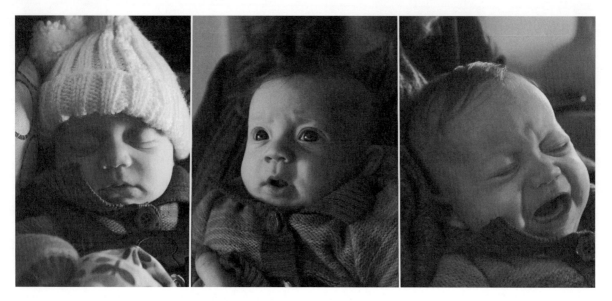

Three newborn states: Sleeping, alert inactivity, and crying.
Photos by Emily Waterfield

then, may be partially acquired prenatally (Cofer et al., 1999; Colombo, Moss, & Horowitz, 1989; Zeskind & Marshall, 1991) but there are no consistent post-birth predictors of a child's sleeping patterns (Adams et al., 2004). Some recent evidence suggests that maternal stress, especially for stay-at-home mothers who are with the infant all day, is related to more infant sleep problems (Sinai & Tikotsky, 2012). Marital instability, which can contribute to maternal stress, is also implicated in infant sleep problems (Mannering et al., 2011).

During childhood, children who prefer being awake during the evening hours have a harder time getting up for school and do less well in school. It helps if parents are aware of whether their child is a morning person (goes to bed early and gets up early) or an evening person and adjust their expectations accordingly (Cofer et al., 1999).

Whether the child goes to bed early or late, some research shows that infants can be trained to sleep through the night during the first month of life. The training procedure is based on reducing stimulation in the late afternoon, when infants naturally tend to become more fussy, and creating the habit of an early bedtime (Godfrey & Kilgore, 1998). The procedure is given in Table 5.2. After using this procedure for 3 to 4 weeks, parents report that their infant is more likely to sleep through the night and to avoid fussing during night wakings. If the time between night feedings is gradually increased, even breast-fed infants can learn to tolerate not getting a night feeding. If the infant does not get fussy until later in the evening, then parents can adjust the times accordingly. On the other hand, it is difficult for parents to follow these routines because of the daily variability of newborn behavior, so there is not a high success rate (St James-Roberts et al., 2001). On the other hand, 30 minutes of gentle massage therapy for infants provided by mothers helped infants to fall asleep earlier and to stay asleep longer (Ferber et al., 2002).

While this procedure may work for some families, training babies to sleep on their own is not necessarily desirable. In some families and some cultures, co-sleeping with parents is the norm. Although no research exists, co-sleeping advocates estimate that worldwide, 80 percent to 90 percent of parents co-sleep with their infants for as long as 1 to 4 years. In North America, co-sleeping goes against the white middle-class cultural norm of raising an independent child and is not recommended by many of the best-known infant care

TABLE 5.2
For families who value independent sleeping, this method can be used to teach young infants to sleep through the night.

1st Month	Place the baby on back or side on a firm mattress. Do not let the baby sleep with breast, bottle, or pacifier in mouth, or while being held.
2nd Month	Reduce the amount of handling and stimulation after 4 p.m., or when evening fussiness begins. Bathe the baby in early evening, 6–7 p.m., follwed by a gental rubdown or massage, and dress the baby for the night. Feed the baby and then put the baby to bed around 7 p.m. Some fussing may persist for 3–5 days. If the baby cries loudly, enter the room every 5–10 minutes and then leave without turning on an overhead light. If feeding is necessary, keep it brief, do not turn on the light, and reduce the amount of stimulation. If this routine is interrupted due to travel or sickness, retraining is necessary.

advice books. On the other hand, a large number of North American and Northern European parents from diverse ethnic and cultural backgrounds report co-sleeping with their babies at least occasionally, and many report long-term co-sleeping arrangements. The practice appears to be more common in non-white ethnic groups in these countries compared to white families (Willinger et al., 2003).

Breast-feeding is cited most frequently as the reason for co-sleeping. Research shows that about 80 percent of breast-feeding infants spend some time in their parents' bed. Co-sleeping increases the rate of breast-feeding each day and also the number of months that the baby is breast-fed. Infant irritability and illness, as well as a parental desire to be close to the baby, are also frequently cited reasons to bed-share (Ball, 2002; McKenna & Volpe, 2007).

Independent sleeping is favored when there is a strong family and cultural value for independence. But does independent sleeping really promote independence later? Parents of preschoolers whose babies either co-slept or did not co-sleep were asked about independence in their children. Non-co-sleeping children were indeed more likely to fall asleep alone, sleep through the night, and be weaned earlier. On the other hand, co-sleepers as infants were more likely to enter quiet sleep states and stay in them longer, and as toddlers were more self-reliant (such as dressing themselves) and were more socially independent, for example, by making friends more easily (Hunsley & Thoman, 2002;

Keller & Goldberg, 2004). In general, however, when children are followed up through the teen years, there seem to be no long-term risks or benefits to co-sleeping (Okami et al., 2002).

Some parents become concerned about a reduction in sexual activity if the baby sleeps in the same bed. In either case, parents can expect to experience some sleep deprivation during the first few months, until the family finds a mutually beneficial way of sleeping. On the other hand, once fathers adapt to co-sleeping, they feel it increases their intimacy with the infant and gets them involved more in the infant's nighttime care (Ball et al., 2000). Whether or not co-sleeping is practiced depends upon the social and cultural attitudes of the parents and their ability to resolve disagreements. Children with the most sleep problems come from homes in which the parents disagree about sleeping arrangements, mothers have a tendency toward depression and sleep problems, and in which there is more marital disharmony (Countermine & Teti, 2010; Germo et al., 2007).

If the average newborn sleeps 17 hours a day, what happens during the rest of the time? On average, about 3 hours are spent in quiet alert, 2 hours in active alert, and 2 to 3 hours in crying. Of course, some babies are awake more than 3 hours and some less. Some babies cry for as much as ten hours per day and others as little as one hour.

Waking States

Waking states are important for the processing of stimulation from the environment—processing that will lead to perceptual and cognitive development. Newborn infants have two basic modes of response to stimulation: orienting and defense. The **orienting response** is a heightened alertness on the part of the individual baby that includes behavioral localization toward the source of the stimulation (a head turn to the source of a sound). A **defensive response** is a behavioral action that involves withdrawal from the source of stimulation. The orienting response involves networks in the sensorimotor and parietal cortex, the visual and auditory areas of the brain, linked into the hypothalamus and brain stem areas that control arousal levels (sleep vs. waking). The defensive response uses the same network but its activation is altered by the amygdala, which senses fear and promotes fight or flight via the autonomic nervous system and the HPA axis (Chapter 4).

Stimulation that is moderate in intensity will elicit orienting responses: soft talking, moderate light levels, and holding and rocking can enhance alertness in the newborn (Arditi et al., 2005). Most adults—whether they are right or left-handed—prefer holding infants on the left side. At first, researchers thought this was because the baby was being held closer to the adult's heart but this hypothesis was never confirmed. More recently, studies have shown that adults are better at perceiving emotions through the left eye and left ear, both of which are connected to the right (more emotional) brain. Thus, left-side holding is likely to enhance emotional communication between parent and infant, not through the heart, but through the senses (Turnbull & Bryson, 2001; Vauclair & Donnot, 2005).

Stimulation that is intense and sharp produces defensive reactions. A sudden change in light level, a loud noise, or a sudden change in body position will produce a blink or a startle response. If the intense stimulus continues, newborns will show a defensive response by turning away, grimacing, or crying. Low-intensity stimulation, such as gentle rocking or whispering, may not produce any reaction in the newborn. When newborns orient to a source of stimulation, they are relatively slow to respond compared with a 2-month-old, whose latency to respond is similar in speed to an adult's (Berg & Berg, 1987; Graham, Anthony, & Zeigler, 1984; Karrer, Monti, & Ackles, 1989). Myelination of the neural pathways involved in orienting account this age difference in speed of processing.

As infants develop, they become able to orient to a wider range of both low- and high-intensity stimulation. It is as though the newborn were looking at the world through a very small window centered on the moderate range of stimulation. Developmental changes expand the size of the window to include both lower and higher intensities of stimulation so that the older infant is more sensitive to subtle cues and less sensitive to intensity.

Crying State

Infants have different kinds of cries that seem to be associated with different kinds of distress. Cries have four phases: expiratory (exhaling; the actual creation of the crying sound), a rest period, an inspiratory period (inhaling), and another rest period. As Table 5.3 shows, the different types of infant cries can be distinguished on the basis of the length of these phases.

One feature of the neonatal pain cry, for example, is an exceptionally long rest phase, which gives the listener the feeling that the baby has stopped breathing. This long silence no doubt accounts for the salience of this cry to an adult. The pain cry also has a long expiration phase, much like the cry evoked when the infant is teased by having a pacifier pulled out of his or her mouth repeatedly. The expiration of the teased cry, however, is not followed by a long rest. These cry patterns repeat themselves over and over to form a crying bout.

Crying also involves a pattern of body movement including facial expressions of distress, movement of the arms and legs, changes in muscle tone and skin color, and alterations in breathing patterns. The intensity of pain or distress changes both the acoustic features of the cry but also the body expressions (J. A. Green, Gustafson, Irwin, Kalinowski, & Wood, 1995; Lock, 2000). The difference between the cries, in responses of the whole body and the cry sounds, suggests that newborn crying

TABLE 5.3   Properties of Neonatal Cries*

Cry Phase	Basic Cry	Angry Cry	Pain Cry	Being-Teased Cry
Expiratory	0.62	0.69	3.83	2.67
Rest	0.08	0.20	3.99	0.07
Inspiratory	0.04	0.05	0.18	0.13
Rest	0.20	0.11	0.16	0.13

All values are time in seconds.

Source: P. H. Wolff, The causes, controls, and organization of behavior in the neonate, 1966. *Psychological Issues 5*, 202–204

is a meaningful "language" that expresses the newborn's internal state (Clarici et al., 2002).

Neonatal crying is symptomatic of a range of "normal" internal states, but it may also reflect a number of abnormal conditions. A series of studies has examined variations in neonatal cry patterns under various conditions of mild to severe abnormalities. Cries were elicited by snapping a rubber band against the sole of the infant's foot. The cry sounds were recorded on a sound spectrograph. In general, infants with more complications required higher levels of stimulation to initiate the cry, took a longer time before they started to cry, had a shorter first cry expiration, cried for a shorter total time, and had cries of a higher pitch than infants with few or no complications. Higher infant arousal also changes the pattern of cry acoustics, all of which have different effects on adult listeners (Boom & Gravenhorst, 1995; J. A. Green, Gustafson, & McGhie, 1998; Wood, 2009).

These studies have several implications. Parents and caregivers can use crying to "read" an infant's internal state, and health professionals can use it to diagnose potential abnormalities. An abnormal cry, however, is not always associated with a serious or permanent underlying abnormality. Such a cry may merely indicate that the infant was born under conditions of stress or that the infant is highly responsive to external stimulation (St James-Roberts et al., 2003). Many birth complications have no lasting effects, and the infant's cries eventually return to normal. Crying, then, just as your grandmother could have told you, is a fairly reliable indicator of a newborn's degree of discomfort, pain, or stress.

Differences Between Infants: Quiet and Colic

Among normally developing newborns with no health complications, there is an increase in the frequency of crying between birth and 2 months of age, particularly during the late afternoon and early evening hours (Anders et al., 1998). After that time, the amount of crying begins a decrease that continues over the first year of life. This developmental phenomenon is similar for infants in many different cultures having different patterns of infant care and response to crying (Barr, 1990). Nevertheless, during this 2-month period of the most intense crying, infants differ with respect to how long they cry during the day. And although there are striking differences between infants in the same culture, there are even bigger differences between cultures.

Hunter-gatherer societies are composed of small bands of humans who sustain themselves by hunting game and gathering wild roots and plants to eat. Although hunter-gatherer societies are believed to have been the only form of human society before the invention of agriculture some 10,000 years ago, relatively few such societies survive today. Research on their child-care practices provides an important comparison for understanding child development in non-Western societies.

In hunter-gatherer societies in Africa, for example, infants cry as frequently as in Western countries. The hunter-gatherer infants, however, sustain their cries for only brief periods and less intensely, while Western babies typically cry for much longer and with more intensity. This difference seems to be due to the fact that in hunter-gatherer societies the infant is in almost constant contact with a caregiver, who carries the infant in a sling or pouch at all times. The infant is never left alone, and the caregiver responds immediately to any fussiness (Barr, 1990; Barr et al., 1991).

Western infants are not tended so closely. They are typically carried only for brief periods and are kept physically separate from the caregiver. Even when parents sensitively respond to the infant cry, the physical separation requires a longer response time than in hunter-gatherer societies. Infants have more time to build the pitch and volume of their cries, and they cry for longer periods until they are tended. In some cases their crying continues even after they are picked up. Research in Germany has shown that when parents are generally slower to respond to infants, the infants cry more (H. Keller et al., 1996; M. Papousek & von Hofacker, 1995). On the other hand, infants who cry more are more likely to be held by their parents during the first months of life (Bonichini et al., 2008).

Of particular concern is a group of infants in Western countries who cry excessively. **Colic** is crying in which: (1) the infant cries at least 3 hours per day, on at least 3 days per week, and for at least 3 successive weeks; (2) the parents judge the crying to be very intense; (3) the infant is otherwise normal; and (4) the infant is relatively unresponsive to soothing and feeding (Barr et al., 1992).

What causes colic? Research has shown that infants with colic, compared to noncolicky infants, are more likely to cry following feeding, to have more distress-related facial expressions, to have more turbulence in the cry sound, and to be rated as more difficult and negative by their parents. This merely reflects the differences in their cries and not the cause of it. No differences have been found, however, between colicky and noncolicky infants in the amount of stomach swelling after feeding, vomiting, hiccuping, or bowel movements (Barr et al., 1992; Lester et al.,1992; Zeskind & Barr, 1997). Thus, digestive problems, as is commonly believed, is not the cause of colic. There are also no overall differences between colicky and

noncolicky infants in the level of sympathetic nervous system arousal, activity level, or in the daily levels of cortisol, a stress hormone (Chapter 4) (Kirjavainen et al., 2001; White et al., 2000).

Some Western parents are attempting to replicate the hunter-gatherer pattern of close physical contact. They advocate what is variously called "natural parenting," "evolutionary parenting" or "attachment parenting," in which they hold infants closely, nurse often, and immediately respond to crying (Kestenberg-Amighi, 2004; Schön & Silvén, 2007). This caregiving approach is based on hunter-gatherer patterns of parenting that arose during human evolution: sensitivitity to emotional and physical needs, breastfeeding on demand, extensive contact and carrying on the caregiver's body, and cosleeping. Touch and holding especially, have been shown to reduce crying, improve vagal tone, enhance immune and digestive function, and reduce stress in infants (Schön & Silvén, 2007). Hunter-gatherer peoples also do not use diapers. Since the baby is constantly in contact with the mother's body, she can feel the baby getting ready to urinate or defecate and will hold the baby away from her over an appropriate location. A "diaper free" movement in Western countries attempts to teach parents the body language and vocalizations—called "elimination communication"—that babies use to express when they are ready to eliminate. The parents then hold the infant over the toilet (www.diaperfreebaby.org).

Comparisons of babies raised with attachment parenting and those in traditional Western infant care show that the attachment parenting infants cried 50 percent less overall. On the other hand, there were no differences between the groups in the amount of unsoothable crying and colic (St. James-Roberts et al., 2006). Even in hunter-gatherer and other societies in which there is almost continual close physical contact with infants, there are individual differences between infants, with some babies crying more than others. Even though the extremely fussy hunter-gatherer infants are less fussy than the extremely fussy Western infants, it suggests that colic, or some form of it, may be universal for some percentage of infants and may even be considered "normal," at least for some infants (Barr, 1998; Barr et al., 1991).

On the other hand, some data suggest that mothers who experienced high levels of stress during pregnancy were three times as likely to have a colicky infant (Søndergaard et al., 2003). Infants with colic sleep less than others, and they have more difficulty establishing a normal day-night rhythm of sleeping and waking (White et al., 2000). Along these lines, colicky infants have more difficulty feeding, including less rhythmic sucking and less ability to adapt to the feeding situation (Miller-Loncar et al., 2004). Finally, in follow-up studies at 3 and 8 years, children who were colicky as infants were more likely to be inattentive, emotionally reactive, and to show heightened sensitivity to touch, food, and other stimulation (Desantis et al., 2004).

These data suggest that colic is not benign, even though all infants end their colicky period around 5 to 6 months of age. Sensory sensitivity and poor emotion regulation brought on by some form of stress could be the cause of colic, but these factors could also be the result of colic, resulting in a more stressed infant nervous system. If we consider the parent-infant relationship as a dynamic system, small factors in early infancy may lead to excessive crying by means of deviation-amplifying feedback. If the infant has some sensitivities to stimulation, if the parents are under stress or uncertain about themselves, it may take only a short time for infant crying to increase to levels that are difficult to regulate (Cuisinier, Janssen, de Graauw, & Hoogduin, 1998; M. Papousek & von Hofacker, 1995). For some infants who cry a great deal during the newborn period, higher levels of crying and fussiness will continue to be characteristic of their behavior during the first year of life and perhaps later (St. James-Roberts, Conroy, & Wilsher, 1998; St. James-Roberts & Plewis, 1998).

Colic also has a negative effect on parents. Both mothers and fathers of excessively fussy babies respond to them less and are less warm with them than parents with normally fussy babies. These very fussy babies also tend to decrease marital satisfaction and marital communication (Räihä et al., 2002; Stifter et al., 2003). Almost 50 percent of mothers of colicky babies report symptoms of moderate to severe depression, with more severe depression associated with lower self-esteem, more parenting stress, and a more difficult infant (Maxted et al., 2005). It seems that the difficulties of responding to the needs of newborns creates temporary depressed moods in mothers, called post-partum blues or post-partum depression. It typically lasts only a few weeks or months and even occurs in adoptive mothers (Foli, 2010).

What can parents do if their infants have colic? Perhaps nothing but wait for it to end in 2 or 3 months. One strategy, however, is to find ways to reduce parental stress, which comes partly from prenatal and family factors and partly from having an unconsolable infant. Some parents may feel that they have to hold their babies all the time, day and night, even if their baby does not calm down. This can be emotionally and physically draining. One study reports parental feelings of frustration, helplessness and ineffectiveness, saying things like, "I was on the edge all the time. It was hideous." (Kaley et al., 2011). This, of course, impairs the ability to respond to cries in the future and may even lead to abusive behavior.

Parents need to get rest and sleep. Once they are certain that the infant is not wet or hungry or sick, it may be important for the parent to leave the infant on its own for short periods. This gives the parents a break and may also promote self-regulatory skills in the infant. In addition, if there is a chance the infant may have sensory sensitivities, steps can be taken to keep noise and lighting levels low, use gentle touch and soft clothing, and keep stimulation to a minimum (Desantis et al., 2004; Lester, 2005). In general, however, there is no single cause of colic and therefore no single treatment that works for every infant and family (Kaley, 2011).

The Effects of Crying on Adults

Even when infants do not have colic, their crying has the effect of alerting adults to potential problems for the infant. Adults orient to the infant cry and then try to figure out the source of that distress. Particular aspects of the cry are more likely to affect how adults perceive the cry. Adults rate cries of high pitch and of long duration as urgent and irritable, while cries of variable pitch are rated as signs of infant sickness (Zeskind, Klein, & Marshall, 1992; Zeifman, 2004). Experimental modifications of infant cry sounds show that adults perceive cries with extremely short pauses as more arousing, aversive, and rough (Zeskind, Wilhite, & Marshall, 1993).

Nonparents appear to be about as responsive to crying as parents (Zeskind, 1980), and generally equal levels of physiological arousal and responsiveness to crying have been found for men and women (Frodi, Lamb, Leavitt, & Donovan, 1978). On the other hand, child abusers have greater physiological arousal and express more annoyance at cries than nonabusers (Frodi & Lamb, 1980).

You might think, therefore, that infants who cry a great deal or who have especially irritating cries are more at risk for insensitive or abusive parental treatment. This seems to be the case only when irritable crying is also associated with abnormal behavioral tendencies typical of infants with mental and motor defects and prematurity (Field, Widmayer, Stringer, & Ignatoff, 1980) or when mothers have a preexisting negative attitude toward their infants that in part contributes to the high levels of infant distress (Crockenberg & Acredolo, 1983; Crockenberg & Smith, 1982). For normally developing infants, crying brings adults closer to them. More irritable infants are held more in the newborn period, and parents spend more time in social play with them at 2 months (Lowinger, 1999).

Infants who are rated by their parents as having a **difficult temperament** in early infancy, based on their irritability and responsiveness to adults, can remain difficult for periods up to several years, although the majority of infants rated as difficult early in life do not remain difficult for more than a few months (Boom & Hoeksma, 1994; C. Lee & Bates, 1985). Difficultness has few consistent effects on normal parent-infant relationships and is not related to measures of maternal warmth or responsiveness (Daniels, Plomin, & Greenhalgh,

1984; Olson, Bates, & Bayles, 1984). Some studies have actually found increased maternal attention directed to infants rated as difficult (Pettit & Bates, 1984).

In summary, most adults find crying to be arousing, and they can reliably perceive differences between types of crying. Adults also respond to crying infants in an attempt to soothe the cry and relieve the source of the discomfort. Because most adults use similar means of trying to relieve infant distress, it is important to examine what research has shown about the effectiveness of these soothing techniques.

What Are the Best Ways to Soothe a Crying Baby?

Many calming techniques have been used historically: sucking, swaddling, rocking, and singing. Do they really work? Under what conditions does one technique work and not another?

Sucking on a pacifier. Whether sucking pacifiers is harmful or beneficial is a question of practical concern to parents. Sucking on a pacifier, or nonnutritive sucking (NNS), occurs in many forms throughout the infancy period. If we count any incidence of NNS—on pacifiers, toys, fingers, thumbs, and adults' fingers—about 60 to 90 percent of all infants will do it. NNS usually stops at the end of the first year of life. It may continue to occur, however, when a child is hungry, tired, or unhappy, until the child reaches 4 to 7 years of age. A small proportion of children suck their thumbs until adolescence or later (see Case Report, this Chapter). In infants, thumb sucking after the age of 4 months appears primarily during sleep (Kessen, Haith, & Salapatek, 1970).

It would appear from these statistics that NNS is not an unusual occurrence in infancy and early childhood. It may even serve some important functions for the infant. Pacification is one reason infants suck. Sucking is an activity that immediately induces a state of calm in the infant, whether it is associated with nutritive intake or not. (You may feel a similar sense of calm while doing the Experiential Exercise in this chapter.) Another reason for NNS is that it feels good. Sucking could also have an inhibitory effect on less pleasant states or behavior.

Regardless of the particular reason, NNS appears to be a spontaneous behavior that has some important benefits to the newborn and the older infant. One study (R. G. Campos, 1989) examined the effects of pacifiers on calming infants at 2 weeks and 2 months of age during routine medical exams. At 2 weeks, the infants received a heel prick to draw blood, and at 2 months, they received an injection. Pacifiers were immediately effective in reducing crying and heart rate acceleration in response to the pain at both ages. NNS also reduces infant blood pressure (Cohen et al., 2002).

Long-term pacifier and thumb sucking may, however, affect the development of the teeth and mouth. Children who sucked pacifiers more than two years, or their thumbs more than three years had upper front teeth that protruded too far over the lower front teeth, so that the teeth did not meet when the jaw was closed. Depending upon the severity, these problems may require orthodontic correction later (Warren & Bishara, 2002).

One study has shown that pacifier use, in boys but not in girls, limited their ability to imitate facial expressions in later childhood which may lower their ability for empathy. The effect was limited to boys and found only for the use of pacifiers. Thumb sucking had no effect on later emotional responsiveness (Niederthal et al., 2012). There may be some way in which pacifiers limit the infant's ability to respond to other's facial expressions but why this might be the case for boys and not girls, and why the same effect was not observed for thumb sucking, has not been investigated.

Swaddling. Swaddling, or wrapping the infant in a blanket, tends to reduce motor movement and spontaneous startles. Swaddling is less effective than the pacifier in reducing pain-elicited distress in 2-week-olds, although it lowers their heart rate (R. G. Campos, 1989). When a pacifier falls out of an infant's mouth, she or he will begin to cry again. Once swaddled, on the other hand, infants remain calm for long periods.

Swaddling is practiced among many traditional cultures such as the Quechua Indians living at high altitude in the Peruvian Andean Mountains. The Quechua swaddle infants in a pouch. The temperature inside the pouch is higher and more stable than in the outside atmosphere, and the humidity is higher. The pouch protects the infant against environmental stress due to cold temperatures and dryness. On the other hand, in the closed environment of the pouch, the infant gets less oxygen and less stimulation than it would without the pouch. Since the Quechua live in unheated surroundings and spend a great deal of time out of doors, the benefits of the pouch seem to outweigh the potential risks (E. Z. Tronick, Thomas, & Daltabuit, 1994).

Massage. Massage is a technique related to swaddling in that the whole body is stimulated and the infant's movements are controlled. Massage has been shown to increase weight gain and responsiveness in preterm infants (see Chapter 3). In normal full-term infants, regular massage for 15 minutes each day has been shown to enhance alertness when awake, deepen sleep, reduce stress, modulate emotions, increase growth rate and weight gain, and lower the amount of crying (Field, 1998; Field et al., 2004). Massage may also have calming effects on adults. Grandparents were assigned either to receive massages for 1 month or to give massages to their grandchildren. Giving massages had more positive effects than receiving them. Those who gave massages had lower depression scores, increased self-esteem, and enhanced health behaviors (Field, 1998). Parents who take relaxation and massage baths with their babies have higher levels of marital satisfaction and self-esteem and lower levels of postpartum depression (Stack, 2000).

Massage is used regularly in a variety of cultures, for example, in India and Guatemala. Touching and massage are known to reduce stress in animals, adults, and infants. Touch stimulation reduces hormones related to stress and increases hormones related to growth (Stack, 2000). Gentle massage has no negative effects, and it can be a rewarding and relaxing experience for both infant and adult, even if not used directly in response to crying. A book on infant massage techniques for caregivers and parents is available (McClure, 1989).

Rocking. The effects of rocking were studied in a group of 36 crying infants who were offered either vertical (on the adult's shoulder) or horizontal (supine) rocking to calm them. In general, rocking in any form helped calm the infants. The best form of rocking to calm a distressed infant turned out to be rocking intermittently (rather than continuously) in the vertical plane. The best form of rocking for putting the infant to sleep was continuous rocking in the horizontal plane (Bryne & Horowitz, 1979).

Sound. Sound, too, has a calming effect on the baby, but apparently not all types of sound work. Intermittent sound increases infant arousal, whereas continuous sound is calming. The calming effect of continuous sound is enhanced when the sound is moderately loud and in the low frequencies of the vocal range (Friedman & Jacobs, 1981; Hazelwood, 1977). Humming and singing lullabies have these features. Singing has been shown to lower stress among pre-term infants (Coleman, Pratt, Stoddard, Gerstmann, & Abel, 1997). High-pitched vocal sounds can be used to alert infants or attract their attention.

The soothing effects of continuous stimulation are not limited to sound: any stimulus that is continuous can work. Sucking, rocking, swaddling, and humming are all forms of continuous stimulation. Using more than one method has a cumulative effect. Individual infants also show a wide range of differences. Some infants are better soothed by one method than another, and some infants appear to be more easily consoled than others, regardless of the particular method used.

Developmental changes also affect what best soothes the baby. While any kind of continuous auditory stimulation soothes in the infant's first 2 months, the mother's voice is more effective by 3 months. Visual stimulation becomes increasingly effective by 3 months, as does stimulation from

objects to touch and hold (Kopp, 1982; Wolff, 1966).

In summary, state is important for the newborn infant for a number of reasons. First, the body needs periods of tranquility and rest to consolidate its resources for growth. Second, the infant's attention to the environment is dependent upon maintaining a stress-free state of quiet alertness. Finally, state regulates the types of interactions newborns have with their adult caregivers. Babies who are fussier require different resources from their parents compared to calmer babies.

Motor Coordinations of the Newborn: Reflexes

Aside from the waking and sleeping states discussed above, newborns possess a variety of semi-automatic patterns of behavior—such as grasping, head turning, and sucking—that actually began to function prenatally, during the final months of fetal development. This kind of semiautomatic behavior is called a **reflex**. Reflexes are triggered only by specific elicitors—such as the presence of fluid in the mouth (sucking) or an object in the palm (grasping)—and they look about the same every time they are triggered. Once triggered, a reflex must run its course without stopping.

Reflexes associated with different parts of the body are listed in Table 5.4. Some of these reflexes reflect primitive forms of orienting behavior, including rooting, sucking, and grasping. Other reflexes are primitive defensive reactions, including the Moro reflex and the reaction to a cloth on the face or the head placed face down. Other reflexes seem to contain the elementary coordinations needed for later adaptive and voluntary movements. These include the stepping, standing, crawling, and swimmer's reflexes. Other reflexes do not seem to have a clear function, such as the Babinski reflex; however, the lack of a Babinski response may indicate neurological disorder.

In spite of the semiautomatic structure of reflexes, there is a wide variability in their display. In the same infant tested on different occasions, a reflex might be present at one time and not later.

TABLE 5.4   Newborn Reflexes

Body Part	Name of Reflex	Description	Baby's Age at Reflex's Disappearance (Months)
Head and Face	Head turning	Place baby face down on a mattress. Baby will turn head to side to free breathing passages.	4
	Rooting	Stroke baby's cheek gently near the mouth. Baby will turn head to the side that is being stroked.	5
	Sucking	Place a nipple-sized object in baby's mouth. Baby will start sucking movements.	6
	Defensive reaction	Cover the baby's nose and mouth with a cloth. Baby will turn head and move arms in an attempt to free breathing passages.	4
Arms	Asymmetrical tonic neck reflex	Turn the baby's head to one side or the other. The baby's arm will extend in the direction in which the head is turned and the other arm will flex upward. This is also called the fencer's reflex.	4
	Moro	Drop the baby's head slightly but abruptly. The baby's arms and legs will spread open and make an embracing movement, as if to grasp hold of something. This is a kind of startle reaction.	6
Hands	Palmer	Lightly touch the baby's palm. The fingers will clamp into a fist.	4
Torso	Swimmer's reflex	While baby is lying on its stomach, gently tap the back along the side and above the waist.	3
	Crawling	Push against the soles of the baby's feet while the baby is lying on the stomach, and rudimentary crawling movements will result.	4
Legs	Standing	Hold the baby gently under the arms while the feet touch a table. As you release support slowly, the baby will begin to show some resistance to the weight by stretching the muscles of the legs.	3
	Stepping	Hold the baby under the arms with the baby's feet touching a table and move the baby forward, keeping contact between table and feet. The baby will take "steps."	3
Foot	Planter	Similar to the Palmer reflex. The toes will curl inward where the instep is lightly touched.	9
	Babinski	Gently stroke the outer side of the bottom of the baby's foot. The toes will curl outward like a fan.	12

Source: A. Fogel & G. F. Melson, *Child development*, 1988, p. 133. St. Paul, MN: West. Copyright © by West Publishing Company. Reprinted by permission. All rights reserved.

Some reflexes become more prominent in the days following birth, having been absent immediately after birth due to birth recovery processes. Some reflexes are easier to elicit in sleep states and others in waking states. The strength and clarity of response also differ between infants. After their cheeks are stroked to elicit rooting, one baby may barely turn his or her head to that side, while another may make a strong head turn, open the mouth, and begin to suck. Other factors that affect the strength and quality of a reflex response are age, time since last feeding, and the number of repeated attempts to evoke the reflex (Kessen et al., 1970; Prechtl, 1977).

Each reflex has its own developmental course starting at different gestational ages. Some reflexes persist throughout life—such as startle and blinking—while others disappear in early infancy. Since the reflexes that disappear do so between 3 and 6 months of age, traditional explanations have assumed that the disappearance is the result of the development of the sensorimotor and prefrontal cortex of the brain which regulates voluntary movement (Molnar, 1978; Peiper, 1963). When adults receive damage to the motor cortex, some of these primitive reflexes reappear (Paulson & Gottlieb, 1968).

This view of the centrality of the brain in regulating reflexes was challenged by several experiments. The stepping reflex is elicited in a newborn when the infant is held upright with the foot gently touching a flat surface. When the foot touches the surface, the newborn will pick up the foot by bending the leg at the knee in a kind of march-step movement. Remarkably, newborns do not pick up both legs at the same time; they alternate steps in the manner of later walking. They are also more likely to take steps when they have the sense that they are moving forward in the environment (created in a lab by having a video of a landscape that gives the impression of moving into it; Barbu-Roth et al., 2009).

It turns out that stepping disappears earlier in infants who have the most rapid weight gain. Researchers studied 4-week-olds who could still step reflexively. To experimentally simulate weight gain, they added weights to the babies' legs in amounts predicted to reflect the possible weight gain of the legs in the next few weeks. These weights practically eliminated stepping. In another experiment, 4-week-olds were tested for stepping while their legs were submerged under water and then again on dry land. The step rate was much higher underwater, again suggesting that weight and gravity, rather than brain development alone, contribute to the disappearance of stepping (Thelen, Bradshaw, & Ward, 1981). The researchers also found that stepping movements could be seen in the form of alternate-leg kicking in any age infant when the infant was lying on his or her back.

In this experiment, the decline in stepping was not due to the effect of weight gain alone. Rather, stepping declines because fat grows faster than muscle after birth. This means that babies' legs simply became too heavy for them to lift on their own! In another study, stepping did not disappear in babies who were given stepping exercises every day. The workout program may have built their tiny muscles to be capable of lifting more than those of the average baby of a particular age. Similar practice also helps babies to sit earlier (N. A. Zelazo, Zelazo, Cohen, & Zelazo, 1993). Neuromotor control may account for increasing skill in stepping and later walking, but not for the disappearance of the reflex in the middle of the first year.

In summary, newborn reflexes are extremely important for orienting the infant to the environment and for protecting the infant from harm. Although we do not know the purpose of all the reflexes, many of them—such as the defensive reaction—have obvious functions. The data also suggest that the actual movements related to reflexes are not simply discharges in the brain, but depend on muscle movement, weight, state, illness and many other factors. Like the spontaneous movements of the fetus (see Chapter 3), reflexes play a role in the active development of the muscles, leading to increased strength and coordination.

You can simulate the newborn's experience of the reflexes by practicing the Experiential Exercises at the end of this chapter. Although adults no longer have the reflexive response to being touched on the palm, our hands still open and close in the same way as newborns' hands. Through practicing different kinds of body awareness exercises, it is possible to rediscover some of the ways in which our bodies have retained characteristics from our newborn period.

Asynchronous Growth

The finding that the newborn stepping reflex disappears when the infant's legs become too heavy is not meant to suggest that 1-month-olds should go on diets, exercise their legs, and do weight training. First of all, giving babies stepping exercises does not make the babies walk any sooner than if they receive no such training (P. R. Zelazo, 1976). Second, there is a good reason why babies of this age need to increase fat rapidly: to keep warm and protect their muscles against shocks. Fat is kept at a minimum prenatally to make birth easier and because most of the fetal energy resources go into brain development. Muscles get stronger later in the first year.

These findings show that infants do not grow "all at once." Different body regions grow faster at different times; this is called **asynchronous growth** and is shown in Figure 5.1. Because physical growth depends on the body's ability to metabolize nutrients to create energy to support the growth, the body invests its growth resources in at most a few domains at a time.

What makes some areas turn on their growth spurt and others turn off? This is difficult to determine, but it may be in part genetically controlled and in part related to opportunities in the environment. Fetal resources are used primarily to develop the brain and perceptual systems. This is due partly to the fact that movement opportunities are limited for a fetus, and muscles do not develop without exercise. Because newborns rely on the care of adults, they do not need strong and able muscles early in life. Chimpanzees, on the contrary, have to be strong enough to cling to their moving and swinging mothers from the day of birth. Their survival depends more on physical strength and speed compared to human newborns.

A comparison of chimpanzee and human newborns' scores on selected items of the Brazelton newborn assessment test confirms this. Chimpanzees score about the same as human newborns on state control, alertness, and attention to social and nonsocial stimuli. Chimpanzees score higher on motor skills in the pull-to-sit task and on irritability (Bard, Platzman, Lester, & Suomi, 1992; Hallock, Worobey, & Self, 1989).

Sucking

One reflex that is of crucial importance to survival is sucking. Sucking is an example of a reflex that begins prenatally and does not disappear.

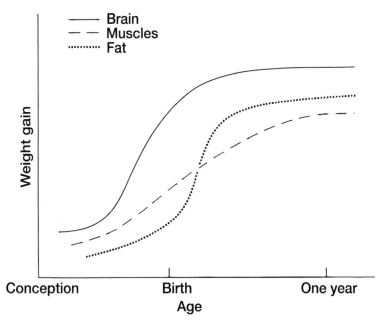

**Figure 5.1
Asynchronous Growth**

This statement is a bit misleading, however, since sucking becomes more voluntary and changes form and mode of expression in later infancy. Nevertheless, because of its importance to survival, almost all infants can suck normally at birth (da Costa et al., 2010). Sucking is accomplished through the combined action of three sets of sucking pads: the lips, the gums, and the fat pads inside the cheeks. It is the gums—not the lips—that form a closed pressure seal around the nipple, while the cheek pads prevent the oral cavity from collapsing from the negative pressure created (Kessen et al., 1970).

As you may notice when practicing the Experiential Exercises in this chapter, sucking is a two-phase process. In the first phase, the lower jaw drops to create negative pressure in the mouth. This method works because the gums form a closed seal around the nipple, but it differs from sucking by an adult, who creates negative pressure by breathing in. In the second phase of sucking, called **milk expression**, the newborn's tongue presses the nipple against the hard palate while moving from the front to the back of the mouth. Finally, the presence of fluid in the mouth triggers the swallowing reflex. Apparently, the newborn sucks and swallows in a single pattern in which the tongue moves in and out while the baby swallows.

The action of the tongue in sucking explains why young infants have trouble eating solids and drinking from a cup: the pushing action of their tongues tends to expel more material from their mouths than they are able to successfully ingest. The ability to separate the expressing and swallowing movements does not occur until late in the first year.

Sucking, like crying, tends to occur in a rhythmic pattern. While the infant is actually sucking, there are usually about two sucks per second. Typically, infants suck in a **burst-pause pattern**: bursts of successive sucks separated by pauses. The bursts usually last from between 5 and 24 sucks. Like the other reflexes, the sucking rate depends primarily on the state of arousal rather than on factors related to hunger. The number of pauses is primarily determined by the milk flow. If the flow is too fast, pauses disappear, reappearing only when the flow is reduced (see Figure 5.2). Pauses do not appear to be associated with fatigue, since infants can suck without pausing for long periods under high milk-flow conditions (Kessen et al., 1970).

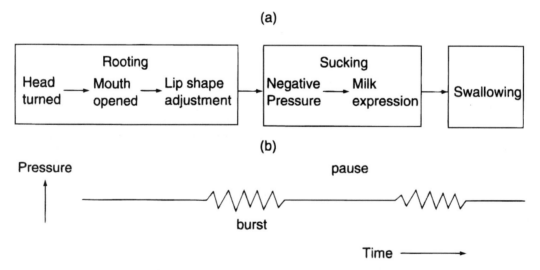

Figure 5.2 Organization of Sucking Behavior
(a) Sequence of acts comprising sucking behavior, from initial orientation to the nipple until swallowing has occurred. **(b)** Changes in sucking pressure with time, showing the characteristic burst-pause pattern.

Earlier in this chapter, it was mentioned that nonnutritive sucking provides a source of pacification for the newborn infant. It would seem natural that infants under 2 months, who cry more than older infants, would use their own hands and fingers as sources of sucking stimulation. In fact, hand-to-mouth behavior is a relatively rare occurrence at this age, but it does happen under some conditions. For example, it occurs in newborns when the arms are flexed and the hands come near the mouth when the baby begins to cry (Hopkins, Janssen, Kardaun, & van der Schoot, 1988), if the infant is given sweetened water when upset (Blass, Fillion, Rochat, Hoffmeyer, & Metzger, 1989; Rochat, Blass, & Hoffmeyer, 1988), or if the infant's hand is held near the mouth by an adult (Fogel, 1985). Apparently, infants do not do this intentionally until about 4 months of age. Before then, the meeting of the hand and the mouth is a happy accident from which the infant can take temporary comfort (Fogel, 1985; Hopkins et al., 1988).

Giving the infant a mildly sweet solution to suck not only increases the frequency of hand-to-mouth contact, but has the additional effect of calming infants who are crying (Barr, Quek, Cousineau, Oberlander, Brian, & Young, 1994; Blass & Ciaramitaro, 1994; Fernandez et al., 2003). Milk is sweet, which may explain the added calming effects of nursing over and above that of nonnutritive sucking. The smell of milk, learned in the first weeks of life, can also contribute to the calming effects of nursing (Delaunay-El Allam et al., 2006).

Case Report
Sucking and Calming

I asked my mother about how she nursed me. She informed me that she would hold me really close to her chest and my little body would curl up around her. I would often tuck my knees into a fetal position and many times she would wrap me in a blanket while being fed. My mother said she would stroke my head as she nursed me. I usually went to sleep while being fed and continued to do so even when in a high chair. My parents have many pictures of me asleep in my food at the dinner table.

I used to suck my finger as a child. My parents remember that I sucked my finger from my early infancy until I began school at age 5. After age five I only did it at home or at night until I reached puberty. My parents insist that my finger sucking did not occur when I was nervous or upset or stressed. Instead, I sucked my fingers when I was relaxed and happy. I would often suck them when I was being held, especially right before I went to sleep. As I sucked my finger I would twirl my hair with the opposite hand. I believe this finger sucking can be attributed to the love, contentment, and deep relaxation I felt while being nursed. The twirling of my hair was just like my mother stroking my head as I went to sleep.

My parents and my boyfriend also pointed out to me that I still stick a finger in my mouth when I am relaxed, especially when watching television. I hadn't noticed it until they pointed it out. I don't suck on it but it rests just inside my lips perhaps serving as a reminder of that past relaxation.

I love being in close contact with people. When I talk with people I like it to be intimate and one-on-one. My boyfriend mentioned that I have a way of really connecting with people when I am having a conversation alone with them. I feel this stems from those very intimate feelings with my mother and that close ventral contact we had. My boyfriend says that he has noticed how I am very comfortable hugging people, even strangers. I love it when he and I cuddle really close together. That contact is very comforting to me and is a way of expressing my love for him.

I love that feeling of curling up. I sleep in the fetal position a lot. I curl up my legs to my chest while working on the computers and sometimes at the dinner table (which drives my mother crazy). My parents, sister, and boyfriend have also noticed something I do that my parents call "nesting". When I am relaxing I will curl up in the corner of the couch with a blanket in a little ball tucking my knees into my chest. My father says it reminds him of a bird's nest that I build around my body with the blanket. I think I acquired this habit from when my mother would wrap me in a blanket and hold me close to her as she nursed me.

I think that in the past few years I have been so stressed and busy and concerned with everything that is going on in my life that I have forgotten about me. I have lost that sense of knowing my body and being inside of myself. I have felt as though I have lost my sense of creativity and happiness. I feel like I have found myself again and I can be more in tune with my creativity and that child-like happiness I once possessed.

If I, as an adult, would take the time to comfort myself when I am troubled rather than burying the feelings deep inside I probably wouldn't feel nearly as stressed out or emotionally burdened. I now know that this is how my body natu-rally relieves stress, so it is a good thing. I was also delighted to find out that many adults still suck their thumbs. A web site, www.thumb-suckingadults.com for adults who still practice non-nutritive sucking revealed just how many adults out there still find comfort from the sucking reflex.

Newborn Hand and Arm Movements

The newborn's arms and hands are among the least controlled parts of the body. By contrast, actions of the face—such as sucking and crying—are highly developed and can be used by the infant to meet specific needs. Newborn hand and arm movements may appear random in real time, but patterns are revealed when these movements are observed carefully in slow motion. In one study on hand and arm movements, newborns were presented with three conditions: a person facing them, a ball moving slowly in front of them, and a control condition with neither a person nor a ball. Results showed a higher frequency of finger movements and flexion of the hand in the social condition compared to the other two conditions. In the object condition, infants were more likely to extend the fingers of their hand (as if to anticipate a grasp), to move the thumb and index finger (as if to grasp), and to extend their arms forward (as if to reach) (Ronnqvist & Hofsten, 1994). In a related study, newborns resisted attempts at manipulation of their arms and were able to visually follow the movements of their arms if they could see them (Meer, Weel, & Lee, 1995). Finally, studies have found that newborns presented with an object in different locations direct more arm and hand movements in the direction of the object (Bloch, 1990).

This research also reveals a surprising amount of coordination in newborn activity that has never before been suspected. It is likely, however, that you could not observe these newborn responses with the naked eye. These studies reveal that the parts of the brain responsible for orienting and for making voluntary movements toward people and objects are already beginning to develop in the first weeks of life. As we will see in the next sections, newborn perception and cognition show similar patterns of adaptability to current conditions and individual experiences.

PERCEPTUAL DEVELOPMENT

The sensory systems of the body—sight, sound, taste, smell, and touch—provide the basic fabric of our psychological experiences. The senses form the ways in which we are connected to the environment. A baby "knows" the mother because she has a characteristic visual shape, auditory pattern in her voice, and quality of touch. She is permeated with fragrance from her body and clothing. Her milk tastes sweet and is flavored by the food she eats. These sensations fill up the baby's psychological experience of other persons and things. There is no overlay of thought or judgment, so common in adults.

Experience that relies on direct perception through the senses, not mediated by thought, is called **ecological perception** (J. J. Gibson, 1966). Ecological perception is available to people of all ages, but its purest form exists during early infancy. The infant is totally attuned to the play of light and color, the melodies of sound, and the pleasure of being touched. In some ways, the infant's psychological world is similar to that which monks and meditators aspire: total awareness in the here-and-now, being fully present in the moment, feeling fully life's sorrows and joys. This kind of experience

Experiential Exercise

Sucking
by Mark Reese,
Feldenkrais Practitioner

Position: Lie on your right side in a fetal position. In other words, curl into a ball with your knees and arms bent, and place your hands not far from your mouth.

1. With your mouth slightly open, gently protrude your lips and tongue and then relax them. As you protrude your lips, allow them to turn slightly inside out. Keep your lips full, soft, and moist. Experiment with slower and faster rhythms. Try protruding your mouth sometimes a little to the left, sometimes to the right (rooting movements), and feel the difference in ease between the two directions due to the pull of gravity.

2. With your lips and tongue slightly protruded, begin to make soft sucking movements with your jaw and mouth. Note that this is very different from the ways you squeeze your lips when you suck through a straw. Try to sense how your head, neck, and the rest of your body become involved in the sucking movement. Rest often, and continue sucking. You will probably find that the longer you suck, the more you will feel how the movement involves your entire body. There is a tendency for the head to move a little forward and tilt slightly back, as if to help the movement of opening the mouth and reaching with it. This gentle movement of the mouth, jaw, and head tends to produce a soothing, wavelike movement down the entire spine, all the way to the pelvis and legs. Rest.

3. In order to help relax your mouth, use your fingers to gently pull your lower lip forward, softly coaxing it to turn inside out. Relax your mouth in order to make your lip more elastic. Rest, and notice the differences in sensation between your upper and lower lips.

4. Repeat the same movements with your upper lip.

5. Return to the sucking movements performed in step 2 and feel the difference. Is it easier? Is your mouth softer and more elastic? Begin to experiment with the length of the sucking bouts, making fewer or greater rhythmical sucking movements before pausing. Rest.

6. If you want to continue the experiment, repeat movements 1 to 5 while lying on your left side and also on your back. Feel how the subtle effects of gravity are different in each position. After birth, the infant must suck differently due to the new needs to coordinate breathing and swallow milk. This is more complex than it might sound. Notice the timing of when you swallow in relation to sucking and how you move your mouth while you swallow. How does sucking influence your breathing just before and just after the swallowing takes place?

Comments

Sucking is one of many movements that we learn to do while still a fetus. Throughout our lifetimes, and especially during our fetal development, our movements help shape the form of our bodies. Just as later in infancy,

weight bearing will alter the curvature of our legs and spine, sucking helps to form our palate. Babies who do not suck normally do not form the high palate that other children have. Also, how infants suck affects the development of their teeth and future patterns of swallowing and speech.

Sucking is the first mouth movement that we master. Later we build on our infant sucking ability as we learn to control thousands of other movements of our mouth and face, including chewing, expressing our emotions, speaking, and singing. Many people experience a deep relaxation of the facial muscles after doing the sucking movements in this lesson. What was your experience?

Somatic Awareness of the Hands
by Alan Fogel

1. Find a comfortable way to sit in your chair. Close your eyes if you feel comfortable doing that.

2. Feel your body touching the chair. Where does(n't) it touch?

3. Become aware of your breathing, that in fact you are breathing. Now observe the movement of your breath flowing gently in and out, connecting your inner space with the surrounding space. Breath is the connection between inside and outside.

4. Notice where in your body you can feel the breath going. Where can you feel the rising and falling patterns of the breath moving through you?

5. Are there any places where you cannot feel the breath? Any places of tension?

6. Notice the parts of your skin that are clothed versus exposed to the air. Notice the differences in sensation. Which feels more comfortable? Adjust your posture if you need to do that.

7. Notice the sounds in the room and how they are affecting you.

8. Now pay attention to your feet. What position are they in? What part of your feet is contacting a surface? Are your feet relaxed? Can you move your feet so they feel more comfortable?

9. Now, notice your hands. Without moving them, notice the position they are in. Does it feel comfortable or uncomfortable? Does this position feel familiar or unfamiliar?

10. Slowly move your hands to a different position. Does it feel comfortable or uncomfortable? Does this position feel familiar or unfamiliar?

11. Separate your hands if you had them together. Slowly begin to curl and uncurl your right hand. Notice how that feels. Notice if you can feel anything in your arms or shoulders as you do this. Gradually reduce the effort. Compare your right side with your left side.

12. Do the same on your left side.

13. Experiment with using your hands to explore your body, clothing, or the chair. Pay attention to the different sensations. Rest.

14. Bring your hands up in front of your face with your eyes closed and let them explore each other through touch.

15. Open your eyes and look at your hands as if you've never seen them before. Relax your hands and close your eyes again.

16. Slowly come back to your breathing, the room, the sounds, the other people in the room, and open your eyes.

Comments

It takes a while for adults to get used to "dropping down" in a "babymind" state of somatic self-awareness. So, it helps to follow all these steps before focusing on the hands. The instructions are meant to bring your attention to very concrete parts of your awareness, and away from your usual patterns of thought.

remains intense during childhood but gradually fades into the background as we devote more of our time to thinking, doing, achieving, and working, and less to simply being fully present to our sensory experience and how that experience connects us directly to the rhythms of the earth and to its inhabitants (Fogel, 2009). Allowing ourselves as adults to be fully immersed in the baby's world can be refreshing and enlightening as we let go of our own everyday thoughts and worries and see the world through the infant's eyes and ears (Schafer, 2004). Practicing the Experiential Exercises and the Co-regulation with Baby sections in this book is a means to reawaken your ecological perception.

The Visual World of the Newborn

The sensory world of the newborn infant is not as sharply focused or as discriminating as that of the adult. Nevertheless, newborns have the ability to see, hear, taste, smell, and feel. There has been a great deal of research on the topic of the newborn's perceptual abilities, especially in the areas of vision and audition. Vision is one of the most powerful of the senses because it is so diverse.

One sees shape, color, distance, texture, and the relative locations of objects in space. Compared to touch, which only takes in information that can be physically contacted by the hand or mouth, vision takes in the entire environment.

The visual world of the newborn, however, is focused primarily on the near environment. When people ask whether newborns can see, they usually are wondering about visual **acuity**. Visual acuity is a measure of the lens's ability to focus images on the retina, as well as the retina's ability to decode the light. A common measure of acuity is the Snellen chart, with the large letter E on the top and successively smaller letters below. An acuity rating of 20/20 is given to a person who can see a particular line on the chart clearly at 20 feet. A person with 20/50 vision is able to see at 20 feet with the same clarity as a person with 20/20 vision can see at 50 feet.

Although estimates vary between studies, a newborn's visual acuity is between 20/300 and 20/800, with an average of about 20/500 (Aslin, 1987). This low level of visual acuity in newborns is not related to an inability of the lens to focus. Rather, it seems to be the result of the immaturity of the dendrites and axons of the neurons in the retina and optic nerve and the relative lack of myelination (L. B. Cohen, DeLoache, & Strauss, 1979; Salapatek & Banks, 1978). By 6 months, as a result of experience-dependent brain development, visual acuity improves to nearly 20/20 in most infants.

This means that the visual world of the newborn is rather blurry, like an out-of-focus photo or film. On the other hand, newborns can see colors (Aslin, 1987). Thus, their visual world is probably filled with fuzzy regions of one color adjoining regions of other colors, each with different levels of brightness, forming an abstract mosaic of light. If you are, like me, sufficiently nearsighted, you will have no trouble replicating the newborn's visual world by simply removing your glasses or contacts. If not, try looking around when your eyes are bleary, when you are very sleepy, or just after waking up.

The eyes do a lot more than just focus their lenses. **Oculomotor skills** are the movements that the eye must make to bring objects into focus, follow moving objects, and adjust for objects at different distances. Newborns' tracking of moving objects is a bit jerky, and they are able to follow only relatively slowly moving objects. More adult-like following begins between 6 and 8 weeks (Aslin, 1981; Kremenitzer, Vaughan, Kurtzberg, & Dowling, 1979).

Scanning occurs as the eye traces a path across a visual stimulus. Since the eye cannot see an entire image all at once, it must make small, rapid movements to move from one point of fixation to the next. One-month-olds tend to scan small, localized regions of a figure, usually around its edges, while by the age of 3 months, infants spend more time scanning finer details of a figure (see Figure 5.3). Adults scan like newborns when they look at large objects from a distance, like a city skyline or a mountain range.

Oculomotor control adjusts the eyes to see objects at different distances. The ability to judge the relative distances between two objects and determine whether objects are close or far is called *depth perception*. We have the sensation of depth because each of our eyes sees a slightly different view of the same object. To see for yourself, try looking at an object nearby with one eye and then the other. The ability to compare the two retinal images, and therefore to see distance, emerges slowly between 3 and 6 months, as the visual pathways become myelinated. Thus, until about 2 to 3 months of age, infants have functional but limited oculomotor skills. However, in spite of these limitations, newborns can use their vision in a variety of ways and may even be able to recognize visual patterns after repeated exposure.

Can newborns see patterns within the complex jumble of lines, depths, and colors that they can see? We know from a number of studies that newborns can detect differences between visual images and seem to prefer some images more than others. Newborns prefer to look at objects with clearly marked edges and outlines. They also prefer circular patterns to straight lines (Fantz, Fagan, & Miranda, 1975). Newborns like to look at the external contours of a figure, especially if the edges are sharp; their gaze tends to follow these lines, and once on a line, they rarely break out to scan other regions of a figure (Haith, 1980; Maurer & Salapatek, 1976).

These pattern preferences in newborns seem to match their relatively poor visual acuity, while allowing them to actively explore objects with their eyes. As we saw in the fetus, active sensory and motor exploration seems to be a form of self-stimulation that is necessary to maintain continued development of the brain and the associated motor skills. In this view, the patterns the newborn prefers are not necessarily meaningful: they merely serve to help the visual system develop by the age of 3 months to a point at which the infant can see the world more clearly and pick out enough details to make meaningful distinctions, such as between a familiar and an unfamiliar person.

This perspective suggests that infants need experience with the perceptual world before they can make sense of it. Starting with some simple preferences for physical features of a stimulus, the infant later comes to attach particular features with other sources of information. Thus, the sounds,

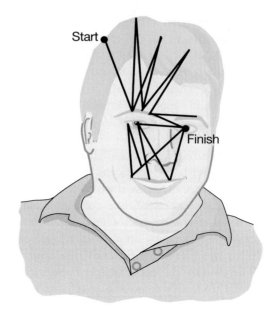

One-month-old

Two-month-old

Figure 5.3 Facial Scanning Patterns
The superimposed lines show where a baby will look at a face. One-month-olds look mostly around the outside, while older babies look at the inner details, espcially at the eyes.

Source: Adapted from A. Fogel & G. F. Melson, *Child development*, 1988, p. 158. St. Paul, MN: West. Copyright © by West Publishing Company. Reprinted by permission. All rights reserved.

smells, and touches that an infant has come to understand as "mother" will only match up with the visual recognition of her at 3 months. The infant constructs perceptions by active engagement and experience.

Although infants have to build up a concept such as "mother" through repeated experiences over many months, they also have preferences at birth that guide them in their search for meaning. Infants are attracted to facelike stimuli and prefer faces over other objects (M. H. Johnson, Dziurawiee, Ellis, & Morton, 1991; Leo & Simion, 2009). Even more remarkable is that infants only 1 day old will change their sucking response to see a picture of their mother's face rather than the face of an unfamiliar female. When the mother is shown wearing a scarf, however, the newborn does not distinguish the mother from a stranger. These findings show that the outline of the face, including the hairline, is an important recognition cue for infants at this age (Pascalis, de Schonen,

Morton, Deruelle, & Fabre-Grenet, 1995; Turati at al., 2006). Perhaps more remarkable is the finding that newborns prefer to look at faces judged by adults to be more attractive. The preference is found regardless of the age, gender, or race of the face (Slater et al., 1998). Newborns also prefer to look at faces in which the other person's gaze is directed toward the infant rather than averted (Farroni et al., 2004).

In summary, research has shown that infants as young as 1 month respond to their mother's face and prefer attractive faces. Due to their relatively poor visual acuity and the slowness of their visual response, newborns' visual relationship to the world is relatively limited; the onset of more mature visual perception does not begin until at least 3 months of age. On the other hand, it is not so bad to begin one's life bathed an the intense sensation of colors and pleasing shapes. To draw or to paint, visual artists must relearn this infant-like way of seeing the world in terms of color and shape, rather than in terms of objects. The infant has other senses in addition, and these are considerably more acute at birth than vision.

Auditory Perception

Auditory perception does not require the same motor components as vision. Thus, developments in the sensitivity of the ears are likely to depend on the maturation of the auditory nerve and the components of the ear's anatomy, which are more mature at birth than those associated with vision. The auditory nerve is almost completely myelinated, and the bones of the middle ear are almost adult size at birth. After birth, most development occurs in the expansion of the auditory canal and the eardrum and the articulation of the auditory cortex in the brain. These processes reach adult levels by about 1 year, which is the same time that infants begin to say their first words (Eilers & Gavin, 1981).

Auditory sensitivity. Sensitivity to sounds involves two basic aspects: loudness and pitch. Loudness is usually measured in decibels (dB). Loud thunder is about 120 dB, 70 dB is a noisy street corner, 60 dB is a normal conversation, and 40 dB is a whisper. Pitch is the frequency of the sound wave and is usually measured in hertz (Hz). One Hz is one cycle per second. A high C on a piano is 3951.07 Hz, and the low C is 65.41 Hz. This range of notes also corresponds to the frequency range of the human voice.

How loud does a sound have to be before a baby can hear it? Sensitivity to sounds is measured by observing a change in heart rate, a blink response, or a head turn; by recording brain waves; or by using a conditioned head turning or conditioned sucking procedure. The softest sounds a newborn baby can hear are in the range of 40 dB to 60 dB (Berg & Berg, 1979), although sounds from 50 dB to 70 dB are necessary to awaken a sleeping infant (Wedenberg, 1956).

In general, the research shows that while most adults can hear sounds as low as 0 dB to 5 dB, the most sensitive newborn cannot hear below about 20 dB (Schulman-Galambos & Galambos, 1979),

although this ability improves over the first year. Babies are more sensitive to sounds in the middle range of the piano's notes, although they tend to prefer higher to lower pitched sounds (Kessen et al., 1970). Finally, babies prefer sounds made up of more than one note containing a wide band of frequencies (Eisenberg, 1976), and they prefer melodic sequences rather than a jumble of unrelated notes (Masataka, 2006; Ruusuvirta et al., 2003).

If we put together all the characteristics of sounds that are most easily heard, and in fact preferred, by newborns, the most common source of such sounds is an adult female voice either talking or singing. Newborns prefer to listen to an adult singing infant-directed songs rather than adult-directed songs (Masataka, 1999). Although newborns are sensitive to a wide range of sounds and will orient to men who raise the pitch of their voice, researchers have speculated that prenatal experience with the sound of the mother's voice may have attuned infants to sounds of that level of loudness and mixture of pitches.

Recognition of mother's voice. We saw in Chapter 2 that newborns preferred to listen to a song or story that their mothers had sung or read aloud 2 weeks prior to birth compared to a song they had not heard, and that newborns seem to prefer heartbeat sounds similar to those they must have heard prenatally. Other research seems to support the view that infants can distinguish the voice of their own mother from the voices of other women. Thus, in addition to recognizing his or her mother visually, as we learned in the last section, a newborn can recognize her voice; as we shall see in the next section, newborns can also recognize their mother's smell. Prenatal and postnatal exposure to the mother thus set the infant on the path to developing a special tie to that particular person. The strong attachments to a particular person that develop later in the first year, therefore, are built upon early perceptual orienting preferences that begin in the last month of prenatal life.

Recognition of speech sounds. How, though, do newborns recognize their mother's voice and distinguish between different songs and stories that they have heard prenatally?

They may detect overall patterns of rhythm and pitch that differentiate one person from another (Rosen & Iverson, 2007; Sansavini, Bertoncini, & Giovanelli, 1997). In addition, infants may be able to hear differences among syllables that give them cues about a speaker's uniqueness.

One-month-olds can distinguish between two very closely related speech sounds: "p" having the sound "puh," and "b" having the sound "buh" (Eimas, Siqueland, Jusczyk, & Vigorito, 1971). By 2 months, babies can recognize not only consonant differences but also vowel differences in sounds (Kuhl, 1981; Swoboda, Kass, Morse, & Leavitt, 1978). They also prefer repeating syllables, perhaps because they are more easily detected (Gervain et al., 2008). Newborns can remember sounds to which they were exposed the day before, and they will change their sucking to hear recordings made in their native language rather than those in a foreign language (Bijeljac-Babic, Bertoncini, & Mehler, 1993; Moon, Lagercrantz, & Kuhl, 2012; Swain, Zelazo, & Clifton, 1993), a preference that no doubt stems from the ability to hear the mother speaking in utero. As explained in Chapter 4, the lateral prefrontal cortex is responsible for these more analytic distinctions in speech sounds, while the medial prefrontal cortex is more emotionally oriented and involved in the recognition of the mother's voice.

It seems that newborns can not only recognize the broad category of speech compared to nonspeech (Vouloumanos et al., 2010) and mother compared to nonmother, but they can also distinguish between some of the finer aspects of speech sounds. This early exposure to sound enhances the development of the auditory components of the brain and auditory nerves and predisposes the infant to similar sounds in the future.

Taste, Smell, and Touch

Newborns appear to be able to distinguish the four basic tastes: sweet, salty, sour, and bitter. We saw earlier how a sweet solution helped to calm a cry-

ing baby. Infants will consume more of a sweeter solution than a less sweet one, although they will stop sucking if the solution gets too sweet (Crook, 1978; Desor, Miller, & Turner, 1973). Sweet fluids seem to relax infants, as shown by the sequence of facial actions in Figure 5.4. At first, babies show a negative expression, followed by relaxation and sucking (Blass, 1997; Rosenstein & Oster, 1988; Steiner, 1973).

In response to sour and bitter tastes, newborns show more consistently negative expressions, especially upper lip raising (as in disgust) and nose wrinkling. They also become more restless and stop sucking (Rosenstein & Oster, 1988; Steiner, 1973). Newborns do not like salty solutions (Crook, 1978).

Some of the same facial expressions as those described above for tastes have been seen in response to smells (Steiner, 1977). Newborns can differentiate between such odors as vinegar, licorice, and alcohol. In response to unpleasant odors, newborns will make faces of disgust. They will turn away from unpleasant odors and turn toward pleasant ones (Lipsitt, Engen, & Kaye, 1963).

Odors may be another way, besides sounds, by which infants recognize their mothers. Infants older than 6 days tend to turn their heads more often to a pad containing their own mother's breast milk than to a pad containing the milk of another woman (MacFarlane, 1975). In a study using similar methodology, breast-fed infants were able to recognize pads containing their own mother's underarm odor compared to pads worn by unfamiliar women, although bottle-fed babies showed no evidence of recognition (Cernoch & Porter, 1985). Breast-fed infants can also distinguish their own mother's perfume from other perfume smells, and they show a clear olfactory preference for breast milk from any woman over other types of smells (Porter, Makin, Davis, & Christensen, 1992; Schleidt & Genzel, 1990). These differences between breast-and bottle-fed infants are probably due to the fact that breast-fed babies spend a longer time in direct contact with their mother's bare skin than bottle-fed babies do.

Interestingly, new mothers—whether their deliveries were vaginal or cesarean— were able

Figure 5.4
Facial Expressions Elicited by the Sweet Solution
Infant negative facial actions are followed by relaxation and sucking.

Source: D. Rosenstein & H. Oster, Differential facial responses to four basic tastes in newborns, 1988, p. 1561. *Child Development, 59*, 1555–1568. Copyright © The Society for Research in Child Development, Inc. Used with permission of the author and publisher.

to recognize their own infant's odors (Porter, Cernoch, & Perry, 1983; Russell, Mendelson, & Peeke, 1983). There seems to be a mutual olfactory (odor) sensitivity between infants and mothers. Thus, infants and mothers have a number of alternative and complementary channels of communication that ensure the beginnings of an emotional bond.

Olfactory and taste responses are probably not mediated by the cortex at this age. Both normal infants and deformed infants born without a cortex were able to detect odors and tastes (Steiner, 1977). This suggests that these perceptions are linked to the limbic and brain stem survival functions related to sucking and feeding.

Finally, newborn infants seem highly sensitive to tactile stimulation. The presence of the newborn reflexes bears witness to this fact because many of them are stimulated by touch. We also saw, in the previous chapter, the benefits of massage and nurturing touch for both preterm and full-term newborns (Weiss et al., 2001). Researchers have found changes in behavior and heart rate when infants are stimulated with touch or with an air puff on various regions of the body (Bell & Costello, 1964; Rose, Schmidt, & Bridget, 1976). Infants' mouths and hands are especially sensitive, and even in the first few weeks of life, they make different kinds of hand and mouth movements when soft or hard objects are placed in their hands or mouths (Rochat, 1987). Newborns are also able to change their hand movements depending upon whether a surface is smooth or textured (Molina & Jouen, 1998). Newborns can visually recognize an object they had previously touched, but not the other way around, attesting to greater tactile compared to visual acuity (Sann & Steri, 2007).

Although it is possible that infants use touch to recognize their mothers, no studies have been done on this topic. Research has shown, however, that infants touch the mother's breast using massage-like hand motions during breast-feeding. These hand movements stop during a sucking pause and resume again during sucking. The purpose of these movements for the baby are not clear, but similar cyclical hand movements have been shown to serve the perception of texture in newborns (Molina & Jouen, 2004). On the other hand, infant massaging plus sucking stimulates the release of the hormone oxytocin from the mother's pituitary gland. Oxytocin facilitates nursing and the feeling of closeness to the infant (Matthiesen et al., 2001).

Newborns also feel pain. In response to normal medical procedures such as injections and circumcision, infants show increased distress and may exhibit disturbances of sleep for the next few days (Emde, Gaensbauer, & Harmon, 1976; Karns, 2000). Newborns during vaginal delivery show more pain-related facial expressions than those born by caesarian section (Delevati & Bergamasco, 1999). Although medical procedures on newborns have traditionally been done without anesthetics, recent findings on pain sensitivity in newborns are leading to the increased use of local anesthetics.

In summary, infants are able to perceive with all their senses, and their sensitivity improves rapidly over the first few weeks and months of life. Certainly, this improvement is due in part to changes in the brain. On the other hand, the changes in the brain depend closely on the kinds of experiences the infant has during this period. There is also evidence that newborns recognize many forms of perception as meaningful: they recognize their mothers, and they cry in response to pain. It is also true that many forms of stimulation have no particular meaning for the infant: a face may be perceived simply as a series of lines, a melody as a sequence of sounds. The process of making sense of sensation is one of the major developmental tasks of infancy and we should not expect infants to come into the world with an understanding of more than a few simple things. In the next section, we take up the issue of the newborn's ability to understand, learn, and feel.

COGNITIVE DEVELOPMENT

The ability to think conceptually, using words or symbols, does not begin until the middle of the second year of life. Newborns and young infants, however, possess a number of ways to process information that are collectively referred to as *cognition*. These processes include learning and memory, orienting and habituation, and imitation.

Can Newborns Learn?

The answer to this question is yes. We have already reported that in late pregnancy, fetuses are capable of learning certain sound patterns, such as songs, and can recognize their mother's voice. This means that fetuses not only learn to distinguish the sounds, but also remember the differences when they hear the sounds weeks later, after they are born, implying that they also have a memory of what they learn. Newborns have important limitations on their learning ability, however. Perhaps a better way to ask the question of whether newborns can learn is to ask under what conditions they are most likely to learn.

Newborns can learn by classical conditioning (see Chapter 1). Researchers used the unconditioned response of rooting and sucking to the unconditioned stimulus (UCS) of a sweet fluid in the mouth. The presentation of the sweet fluid was paired during training with a light stroking of the infant's head (the conditioned stimulus, or CS). After training, the infants rooted and sucked to the stroking stimulus in the absence of the sweet fluid. In addition, when the sweet fluid was removed entirely, the babies rooted and sucked to the stroking, but they also cried, showing that they had learned a connection between the stroking (CS) and the sweet taste (UCS) (Blass, Ganchrow, & Steiner, 1984). Classical conditioning may be possible when the UCS evokes a powerfully rewarding natural response, such as a sweet taste. This may explain the common observation that after a few days of feeding experience, newborns will root and suck at the sight of a nipple, even before they begin to taste the milk. If no milk comes out, they will cry or fuss.

Operant conditioning is much easier to demonstrate in the newborn. Recall that the conditioned sucking procedure (Chapter 1) involves the operant conditioning of infants to alter their sucking rate in the presence of particular sounds or pictures (DeCasper & Fifer, 1980) or syllables (Jusczyk, 1985). Head turning can also be conditioned successfully (H. Papousek, 1967). Once the infants learn the connection between their behavior and the reinforcement, they can signal their preferences with the "correct" sucking rate or head turn direction.

These studies of operant conditioning show that newborns can remember the link between their behavior and its consequence long enough to complete the experiment on that day. Suppose, however, that you trained a week-old infant to suck for the sound of her mother's voice by increasing her sucking rate. Now, if you bring the same baby back to the laboratory on the following day and put her in the experimental setting with no further training, will she remember the training and begin to suck at a faster rate?

This kind of procedure is the basis for most studies on infant memory. Do babies under 2 months of age remember what they learned 24 hours ago? It is very likely that they may remember under certain conditions. Babies of this age seem to remember the sound of their mother's voice and some of her characteristic odors. When a group of mothers was asked to repeat the same word 60 times a day each day to their babies who were between 2 and 4 weeks of age, the infants recognized the word after delays of between 15 and 42 hours (Ungerer, Brody, & Zelazo, 1978). Perhaps the key to establishing a long-term memory in the newborn is a great deal of repetition, rather than a single exposure. In the next chapter, we will review research showing that by 3 months of age, infants can remember things, even from brief exposures, up to 2 weeks later.

If newborns respond to something as if it is familiar, this shows that they can remember it from previous encounters. Newborns are more attracted to familiarity rather than novelty. Unlike older infants, who seem to prefer novelty, newborns prefer the sound of their mother's voice, the smell of their mother's milk, and the sight of their mother's faces (Lock, 2000). They will also choose a familiar face from a set of faces and a familiar sound from a set of sounds (Barrile, Armstrong, & Bower, 1999).

Can Newborns Habituate?

Another form of infant learning and short-term memory is habituation. Like conditioned sucking, habituation is a reliable response that is used as the basis of a number of infant testing procedures. Habituation uses repeated exposure to the same visual or auditory stimulus. Each time the stimulus is repeated is one trial. If a researcher repeatedly shows the same picture to a baby—say, a picture of a face with a sad expression—the baby spends less and less time looking at the picture with each new presentation, acting as though he was getting bored with the same old thing. The gradual decline in looking time over repeated trials of the same stimulus is known as habituation, which results from increasing familiarity with the stimulus.

Researchers select some minimum amount of looking time as the criterion to decide when the baby has become habituated to a stimulus. For example, if the baby's initial looks at a facial expression last about thirty seconds, a reasonable habituation criterion for subsequent trials might be five seconds. Once the baby has reached the criterion looking time, researchers change the picture or sound; in our example, from the face with a sad expression to the same face with a happy expression. If the baby cannot tell the difference between the two expressions, he or she will go on looking at the happy expression for durations shorter than the habituation criterion. However, if the baby can detect a change, the infant will begin to look longer at the happy face than at the last presentation of the sad face. This abrupt increase in looking time after a change in the stimulus is called recovery.

Researchers have found evidence of habituation in newborns' motor and heart rate responses to auditory stimuli (P. R. Zelazo, Brody, & Chaikan, 1984), visual stimuli (Slater, Morison, & Rose, 1984), and tactile stimuli (Kisilevsky & Muir, 1984). In addition, habituation can be shown in premature newborns (Field, Dempsey, Hatch, Ting, & Clifton, 1979).

In summary, studies of learning and habituation in newborns show that some simple forms of learning take place between the late fetal period until about 2 months of age, after which the infant's ability to learn expands. These rudimentary learning abilities may be mediated by the cortex, but they also could be built into the brain stem structures as basic survival mechanisms or into the limbic system if they have emotional relevance (pleasure or distress). These simple learning and memory processes are fundamental to the survival of newborns. The recognition of maternal sounds and smells orients the newborns to their primary resource for survival. Learning how to orient themselves to and approach sources of food (sweet fluids and milk) and how to avoid noxious smells and tastes on future exposures seems so fundamental to survival that a brain stem mediation of such responses is quite plausible. More sophisticated forms of learning and cognition—complex associations, long-term memory, categorization, and inference—must await the further development of the brain's cortical connections and the enhanced acuity of the senses.

Can Newborns Imitate?

Studies have shown that newborns can imitate under certain conditions. Researchers studied 12-to 21-day-old infants' abilities to match tongue protrusion, lip protrusion, mouth opening, hand opening, and hand closing (A. Meltzoff & Moore, 1977). In this study, each infant was shown a series of gestures made by the same adult. If the infant could reliably produce the same gesture following the adult's display of that gesture, compared with following the adult's display of another gesture, imitation could be inferred. The researchers found that infants were much more likely to demonstrate a particular gesture following the modeling of that gesture than at any other time (see Figure 5.5).

A number of replications of this study have been successful in producing correct matching of gestures in very young infants. Another study found

Figure 5.5   Imitations of Facial Expressions in Newborns
Sample photographs from videotape recordings of 2- to 3-week-old infants imitating **(a)** tongue protrusion, **(b)** mouth opening, and **(c)** lip protrusion demonstrated by an adult experimenter.

Source: A. Meltzoff & W. Moore, Imitation of facial and manual gestures by human neonates, 1977, p. 77. *Science*, *198*, 75–78. Copyright © the American Association for the Advancement of Science. Reprinted by permission of the publisher and the author.

correct matching of tongue protrusion and hand-opening models, but it also found that other stimuli could evoke the same responses in the newborns. Moving a ballpoint pen toward and away from the infant's face in the same manner as a tongue might move in and out was also successful in eliciting tongue protrusion in infants. A dangling ring elicited hand opening and closing. It was concluded that the infants were not imitating a particular gesture as much as they were imitating a movement pattern or responding with some oral exploratory behavior (S. W. Jacobson, 1979; S. S. Jones, 1996).

Other work shows that infants do match expressions. During the demonstration of the surprise face, newborns showed more wide eyes and wide mouth opening. During the demonstration of the sad face, they had tight mouths, protruded lips, and furrowed brows. During the happy-face demonstration, infants had more wide-lip expressions. Matching was more likely to occur during the middle trials, suggesting that it is not due to the immediate arousal of the visual display nor is it a reflexive response. These possibilities could be true only if the infants imitated on the first few trials (Field, Woodson, Greenberg, & Cohen, 1982).

Other replications of this work have reported imitation of head movement (A. Meltzoff & Moore, 1989), lip widening and lip pursing with a sample of Nepalese newborns (Reissland, 1988), and tongue protrusion and mouth opening. Infants who imitated more at birth gazed away from their mothers less during social interaction at 3 months, suggesting that early imitation reflects a possible social receptivity (Heimann, 1989).

On the other hand, some teams of researchers have failed to replicate the findings (Koepke, Hamm, Legerstee, & Russell, 1983; B. McKenzie & Over, 1983). Others have argued that although there is a slightly elevated probability of the baby displaying the modeled gesture, in fact, all babies display a wide variety of gestures following the model; furthermore, there are wide individual differences between babies (Anisfeld, 1979).

Thus, although the evidence is in favor of some form of newborn imitation, the response is fleeting and hard to detect. Its occurrence in any form reflects a rather remarkable capacity of the immature human brain and perceptual system to process information and reflect it back to the outside world. Like the simple abilities for learning and habituation, even occasional imitative responses are likely to orient the caregiver in a positive way toward the infant and enhance the probability of an early parent-infant attachment.

For newborns, imitation may be a way of relating to people by establishing a connection of similarity between the baby and another person. Even as adults, we are drawn to people that we perceive as being like us in some way. Imitation is a nonverbal way of establishing this social connection. In one study, not only did newborns imitate the adult's tongue protrusion model, the newborns initiated tongue protrusion as if to get a response back from the adult. The imitation response showed a different pattern of heart rate change compared to the initiation response, suggesting that each type of tongue protrusion felt different to the infants (Nagy & Molnar, 2004).

Six-week-old infants were exposed to an adult who modeled mouth opening and tongue protrusion, which the infants imitated. Then after a delay of 24 hours, the infants saw the same adult once again. Without the adult doing anything, the infants spontaneously produced the imitative response they had learned the day before (A. N. Meltzoff & Moore, 1994). Copying another person as a way of knowing and connecting with them can be seen in later behaviors such as taking another person's point of view, following another person's lead, and letting oneself be influenced by a role model (A. N. Meltzoff & Moore, 1997). It is remarkable that newborns have the rudimentary ability to connect with other people in this way.

Newborn Self-Awareness: The Emergent Self

When a newborn imitates mouth opening or tongue protrusion, it is necessary for them to match a facial expression of their own with that of the adult. This is surprising because newborns have never seen their own face in a mirror, yet somehow, out of all the possible facial expressions, they can pick one of their own that fits with the one they see. This may mean that newborns can feel the movements of their own bodies in relation to the movements of others, an early form of self-awareness (A. N. Meltzoff & Moore, 1997).

Some research suggests that newborns can tell the difference between being touched on their cheeks by another person and touching themselves on the cheek. They are more likely to show the rooting reflex (Table 5.4) when being touched by another person than when touching themselves (Rochat & Hespos, 1997). Newborns also cry more and suck less when they hear the cries of another infant played on a tape recorder compared to when they hear their own cries played on the tape recorder (Dondi, Simion, & Caltran, 1999). Recall from Chapter 2 that late-term fetuses show a similar familiarity with their own movements when they open their mouths as their hand approaches the mouth.

It is possible that these studies merely show that newborns can tell the difference between familiarity and unfamiliarity. On the other hand, the familiarity in these examples comes from their own bodies. It may be that rudimentary self-awareness emerges from the repeated familiarity of living in the same body and experiencing the same sounds and feelings many times. We also know that there are dedicated pathways in the nervous system for self-awareness that are functional at birth. Receptors for **interoception** (the sense of the internal condition of the body)—in the skin for touch, pressure, texture, and temperature, and from the internal organs for bowel fullness, breathing and heart rate—connect into the limbic system, insula, parietal and prefrontal cortices (see Chapter 4) that create possibility of sensing the one's own bodily self.

In addition to the infant's neural and perceptual systems that connect the internal sense of the body with familiar actions, parents tend to respond to the infant's repeating actions in similar ways each time they occur. Thus, the infant's growing awareness of self-familiarity is enhanced by the parent's consistent form of responding (Kaye, 1982). The gentle touch exchanged between parents and newborns during holding, caregiving and feeding can also stimulate interoception and self-awareness. If someone gently touches or holds you, you are more likely to feel, become aware of, and perhaps share whatever had been locked inside of yourself.

This early form of self-awareness that appears during the late fetal period and continues through the first 2 months of life has been called the **emergent self**, the perception of self-sameness over time in behavior, feelings, and states of arousal (Stern, 1985). The emergent self is the sense of familiar experiences of the body and of the familiarity in the way others respond to those experiences.

During the first 2 months, the newborn becomes aware of an occasional sense of self-sameness but it is fleeting. Because newborns spend a lot of time sleeping, eating, or crying, the times that they are in alert states are relatively brief. Imagine being very busy, on the move, unsettled, or seriously ill. People in these situations are so preoccupied that they have little time for feeling themselves. Their sleep and waking patterns may change day to day, and they find it difficult to know when or if they are hungry. Some things, however, emerge as islands of permanence and familiarity: the feeling of falling asleep, a warm bath, a familiar voice, or a predictable routine. One of the remarkable abilities of the newborn is to be able to detect that stability of self-sameness, within the flow of change. It seems, therefore, that the human mind from its earliest beginnings needs to locate the self and its familiar feelings against the background of external stimulation from sight, sound, touch, taste, and smell.

> Right from birth an infant can have some kind of creative experience of being alone with the feelings of the body… exploring the experience of… feeling tensions and contacts of moving, touching their own hands and face, looking at their hands move, listening to the effects of movements within their body and when they move outside things (Trevarthen, 2011, p. 130).

In summary, although newborn cognition is limited to some simple forms of learning, memory, habituation, imitation, and self-awareness, the research reveals that newborns are capable of adapting to their environment to promote their growth and development. Not only can newborns distinguish familiarity from unfamiliarity, they seem to prefer familiar sights, sounds, tastes, and feelings, including those coming from inside themselves. For the first 2 months of life, the infant finds satisfaction in the comforts of home. Newborns do not like to be stressed or challenged, and they do not show much initiative to go out and conquer the world (see the Co-Regulating with Baby section in this chapter). These explorations of the outside world begin to appear in the second and third month (Chapter 6).

EMOTIONAL DEVELOPMENT

Do newborns have the ability to experience emotions? If they can see, hear, taste, smell, learn, and remember, it makes sense to conclude that they also have feelings. In the past, however, many hospital staff assumed that newborns could not feel pain, and medical procedures were administered without anesthetic. Fortunately, newborns are now routinely given anesthesia and we are learning more about what newborns can feel.

The scientific recognition of newborn feelings was the result of an accidental discovery. A group of researchers at Brown University were studying the newborn's ability to learn and also exploring the range of newborn sensitivity to taste and smell (see the earlier sections of this chapter). While investigating newborn taste preferences, Lipsitt (1979b) and Crook (1978) found that the babies sucked in longer bursts, with shorter pauses between bursts, when they were given sweetened water. Within a sucking burst, the interval between sucks is higher for sweetened water than for plain water, and the newborn's heart rate increases while he or she is sucking the sweet water. Thus, the babies were sucking for longer periods and holding the sweet liquid longer in their mouths before swallowing. The researchers concluded that the babies were "savoring" the pleasurable sensation of the sweet taste. In addition, when plain water was given following the sweet water, the babies showed aversive reactions.

All researchers today agree that newborns can feel. The current debate is about the range and depth of the newborn's emotional experience. Newborns, for example, do not feel many of the emotions that are experienced by older infants and children. They do not show signs of anger (which begins about 6 months), nor fear (which begins about 9 months), nor shame (which begins about 18 months).

How do we know what newborns might feel if we can't ask them to describe their inner state? One way is if a facial expression occurs in a situation that would generally elicit a particular emotion in an adult. One example is the newborn's disgust expressions in response to tastes and smells (see Figure 5.4). Crying generally occurs in situations in which one presumes the newborn might feel some distress or pain. In addition to facial expressions, newborns can convey emotion with other parts of their bodies. During distress, for example, there may be reddening of the entire body, kicking and thrashing, contorted arm movements, and stiffening of the body. These whole body responses reflect the activation of the sympathetic nervous system and hormonal secretions that activate changes in behavior and physiology and that are consistent with having emotional feelings.

In addition to disgust and distress, newborns appear to experience the emotions of interest and surprise (Dondi, 1999; Lavelli & Fogel, 2005). These expressions occur during waking states and are keyed to the infant's attention to faces, social interaction, and moving objects. Newborn attention may shift between states of simple attention (simply observing), concentrated attention (when there appears to be an effort made to recognize or to take in the object of attention), and excited attention (when the infant seems momentarily startled but still attentive). These expressions are shown in Figure 6.8 (Chapter 6).

Newborn smiles are more likely to occur during sleep and drowsy states and less frequently when awake (Dondi et al., 2007). Newborn smiling may be related to some kind of simple contentment or relaxation rather than to the feeling of joy that we begin to see more clearly around 2 to 3 months of age. Even during sleep and brief periods of waking however, newborns smile more when they are being touched, suggesting that even at this age, smiling may signal some type of feeling of being connected to another person (Cecchini et al., 2011). In addition, newborns have a wide variety of facial movements that do not fall neatly into one of the usual emotion categories: odd-seeming twists and turns of facial muscles. Only after 2 months of age do these movements begin to coalesce into organized and recognizable patterns of facial expression that are more clearly linked to specific emotions.

The full range of human emotions—like perceptions and cognitions—are experience dependent: they develop over many years in relation to the development of the brain and nervous system. The process of emotional development depends in part on how these incomplete newborn forms of expression are interpreted by adults. Even when adults do not know what the infant wants, feels, or needs, they are quick to attribute meaning to the infant's behavior and respond according to this attribution. In these cases, the adult responds "as if" the baby had a fully developed emotion (Adamson, 1995; Kaye, 1982). Adults observe a contraction of the infant's lip corners, assume the baby is happy, and make happy expressions and sounds to the baby. Or, an infant may cry in such a way as to make the adult think the baby is hungry or tired or angry. After many repetitions of adult interpretive responses to incomplete infant expressions, those expressions begin to consolidate into recognizable patterns.

Although we cannot know for certain what the newborn is feeling, we know that newborns can indeed feel. It seems wise for caregivers to make the assumption that infants of all ages have feelings, since it helps us to understand their needs. The interventions we make that are consonant with our interpretations of infant emotions often seem to have the intended effect. We pick up a crying baby to soothe what we believe to be the child's pain or discomfort as much as to stop the crying, and the subsequent relaxation of the infant confirms our belief about his or her feelings. Let us now look more closely at infant-caregiver interactions.

FAMILY AND SOCIETY

Early Adult-Infant Interaction: The Beginnings of Emotional Ties

As we saw in the last chapter and earlier in this one, adults and infants have sensitivities and responses that make a good mutual fit. Newborn sucking responses are perfectly suited to obtain milk from the breast; the newborn's appearance, sound, and smell are powerful attractors of adult attention and care; and the newborn is primed to recognize the primary caregiver by smell, sound, and possibly by touch.

According to the ideas of evolutionary parenting (Bowlby, 1969), in the early weeks and months of life, we share a common heritage with most other mammals who nurse and show a good deal of solicitude toward their young. Not every order of animals behaves this way. Reptiles give birth to eggs and usually leave the young to fend for themselves after hatching. Bird species do not nurse their young, nor do they give birth to live infants; however, they do show parental caregiving behavior.

After the domestic cat gives birth, the mother lies on her side to expose her nipples. She licks the kittens, which are blind at birth, and the licking helps them orient to her body, nuzzle into her fur, and begin to search for the nipple. After only a few days, each kitten has a preferred nipple and there is rapid improvement in the speed with which a kitten can find its nipple (Rosenblatt, 1972).

The example of the domestic cat illustrates the idea that a complex series of co-actions occurs between mother and infant by which each learns to adjust to the other. Over time, the initial trial-and-error response is reduced, and nursing and other forms of interpersonal interaction become more efficient. In this case the mother, no less than the infant, is subject to the tug of powerful evolutionary forces that ensure the survival of the young. In one study, human mothers of newborns were blindfolded and then guided to touch the hand and cheek of three newborns, their own and two other infants. Two-thirds of the mothers were able to identify their own infant from touching the infant's hands, while half identified their infant from touching the face (Kaitz, Meirov, & Landman, 1993). This study shows that mothers have a nonverbal and nonvisual sensitivity toward their own babies that matches the infants' recognition of their own mothers by auditory, taste, and tactile cues.

Mothers who had higher oxytocin levels, the hormone responsible for feelings of closeness and bonding, spent more time looking at, touching, and interacting affectionately with their newborns (Feldman et al., 2007). On the other hand, interacting with a newborn can increase maternal oxytocin. Mother's oxytocin levels went up during breastfeeding when infants were either touching the breast with their hands or sucking, but not during pauses of newborn activity (Matthiesen et al., 2001).

In general, mutual tactile stimulation increases oxytocin in both parents and infants, and contributes to the subsequent feelings of bonding (Nagasawa et al., 2012). Another study showed that mothers who held their newborns in the first few hours after birth, regardless of whether it was skin-to-skin or with clothes on, enjoyed more responsiveness from their infants at one year than for mothers who left their babies in the crib and did not spend time holding them (Bystrova et al., 2009). Gentle touch of the kind exchanged between parents and infants changes physiology because oxytocin softens and relaxes the body. It also activates parts of the brain responsible for self-awareness (the insula and anterior cingulate cortex), leading both parent and infant to be more attuned to their own, and to each other's, feelings in the moment (Khalsa et al., 2009; Olausson et al., 2002).

When the infant is at risk, early skin-to-skin contact is even more helpful. In the South American nation of Colombia, many families with premature infants do not live close enough to a hospital to have access to NICU. An intervention was developed in which premature infants were given skin-to-skin contact (placed between mother's breasts with only a diaper), 6 hours per day for the first week of life, and then 2 hours per day until the first month. These infants, compared to a group who did not receive this intervention, were more responsive to their mothers' social cues during the first three months. The non-intervention group was able to catch up in later months, but this head start may have been helpful in unknown ways (Bigelow & Power, 2012).

Touch and holding, part of "evolutionary" or "attachment" parenting approaches, are espe-

cially effective in reducing crying, improving vagal tone, enhancing immune and digestive function, and reducing stress in infants (Schön & Silvén, 2007). As we have seen in this section, there is a coregulation between parent and infant that ideally promotes mutual attraction and mutual stress reduction. Parents, however, may need to find additional ways to reduce their own stress because their lives are more complicated than that of the infant. Part of the ability to stay in touch with an infant and reduce stress is the mother's ability to relax, which can be facilitated by practices such as yoga, meditation, dance, movement, and music (http://mindfulmotherhood.org and http://www.mindfulinfantcare.com/Welcome.html).

There is an apparently universal pattern of behavior seen in mothers when presented with their naked newborns immediately after birth. The mothers typically begin to touch the neonates' fingers and toes. This phase usually lasts between 4 and 8 minutes. After this, the mothers move inward, touching the infants' limbs, and end their explorations by an encompassing palm contact with the infant's abdomen, accompanied by massaging movements. The same pattern can be seen in mothers of premature infants (Klaus, Kennell, Plumb, & Zeuhlke, 1970).

It has been shown that fathers, when given the same opportunity to lie next to their newborn children, progress through the same sequence of phases (D. McDonald, 1978; Rodholm & Larsson, 1979). Remarkably, this same pattern of exploration of the newborn has been observed in chimpanzee mothers with their newborn infants (Bard, 1994). The adult response to the first contact with the newborn is similar to adult responses to the cry, the smile, and the facial configuration of the neonate, a part of the species survival characteristics considered by behavior ecology theory.

Although these opportunities for early touch with newborns are clearly important, there is no conclusive evidence linking these first few minutes, days or weeks of early tactile contact with later attachment security or insecurity. In cases of prematurity, adoption, and risk, parents may not have an opportunity for this immediate post-birth physical contact. They can, however, form lasting attachments with their infants in a relatively short period of time when they are finally able to reconnect.

In addition to the physical aspects of communication, there is also a social-psychological component that may form the basis of later interpersonal communication and attachment between adult and infant. Mothers and infants were observed on the day after birth and again at 2 weeks of age during breast-or bottle-feeding while the mother jiggled the infant (Kaye, 1977; Kaye & Wells, 1980). Jiggles were anything the mother did to stimulate sucking, such as shaking the infant or gently moving the nipple in and out of the mouth. Jiggles rarely occurred, but when they did, they tended to occur during pauses in sucking, and mothers claimed they were using the jiggling to get the infant to start sucking again. To test whether the jiggling was effective, the duration of the pauses without jiggles was measured in relation to the duration of the pauses containing a jiggle. When the mother jiggled during a pause, the jiggling actually lengthened the pause. The mother's intervention tended to delay the onset of the next burst of sucks by about 2 seconds. This pattern held true so long as the mother continued to jiggle the infant.

If, however, the mother jiggled momentarily and then stopped, the infant was more likely to begin a burst of sucks than in either the no-jiggle or the continuous-jiggle condition. The pattern that developed—suck-pause, jiggle-stop, suck-pause, jiggle-stop, and so on—is the precursor to later forms of social discourse. The pattern looks very much like a dialogue in which there is an exchange of turns: baby, mother, baby, mother.

This turn-taking situation is still rather one-sided. Although the infant can adjust the timing of the onset of the burst of sucking within a limited range, he or she cannot change the pattern altogether. The mother, on the other hand, is quite capable of changing her behavior to fit the situation. She is able to choose what to do and when to do it. It is almost as if the pauses in sucking serve as "slots" or "spaces" into which the mother can insert her interventions. Although the whole thing has the appearance of turn taking, that seems to

be an illusion created mostly by the mother's ability to adapt to the infant.

As we saw in the section on emotion, newborns require an adult to make them complete, to fill in the missing pieces of their ability, and to give their world psychological coherence. This takes a lot of patience, because newborn expressions and movements are subtle and sometimes confusing.

Bringing coherence to the newborn's awake states is difficult for these reasons and also because the newborn is awake and alert relatively infrequently, and alertness is a rather fragile and easily disrupted state. On the other hand, just as jiggling prolongs sucking pauses, animated adult faces and brightly colored objects prolong periods of alertness (Sander, Stechler, Burns, & Lee, 1979; Wolff, 1987). As a result of repeated attempts to engage, taking advantage of initially brief periods of alertness, the duration of parent-infant face-to-face play and infant attention gradually increases over the first 2 months of life (Lavelli & Fogel, 2002; Thoman, Acebo, Dreyer, Becker, & Freese, 1979). This increase is clearly a product of the dynamically changing parent-infant system along with the experience dependent growth of neural pathways that sustain orienting, attention, emotion and self-awareness.

Newborn Feeding Practices

In the United States, breast-feeding was the general practice until the beginning of the twentieth century. In 1900, only 38 percent of mothers breast-fed, and this percentage declined until only 18 percent were breast-feeding in 1966. The number of women breast-feeding took a major turn upward in the 1970s, so that by 1976, about half of all mothers were breast-feeding at the time of discharge from the hospital. The incidence of breast-feeding in the United States varies with class and education. The rate of breast-feeding in the United States is highest among higher-income, college-educated women who are more than 30 years old and live in the Mountain and Pacific regions of the country. In 2012, about 80 percent of mothers in the United States breastfeed at birth.

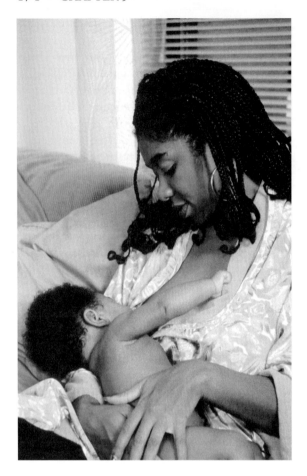

Breast-feeding can be a great source of pleasure for the mother and infant, especially in quiet family times. For some mothers, breast-feeding is inconvenient and difficult. Although breast-feeding is recommended, each family should choose the feeding option that best suits their lifestyle.

Photo by Felicia Martinez/PhotoEdit.

By six months this drops to 47 percent, and by one year to 25 percent of mothers (http://www.cdc.gov/breastfeeding/data/reportcard.htm). This is a significant increase from 61 percent of mothers who initiated breast-feeding at birth in 1996 (American Academy of Pediatrics, 1997).

Most mothers automatically produce milk after birth, even under conditions of maternal malnutrition. In such cases, the milk will be made in less quantity, but it will have the same nutrient quality as that of well-nourished mothers (Kloeblen-Tarver et al., 2002; Rempel & Rempel, 2004). This quality is usually maintained at the expense of the mother's reserve stores of nutrients. In some cases, maternal milk production is slow to start. Formula may safely be introduced to reduce the risk of infant weight loss without impairing the mother's ability to breast feed when her milk comes in (Flaherman & Newman, 2011).

Some women can even breast-feed without having given birth, so that women may be able to nurse their adopted infants. Their success seemed to depend on factors such as the support of the husband and family, preparation by either hand-pumping the breast or nursing another infant at least 1 month in advance, having an infant as young as possible, and nursing a great deal at first. Apparently, sucking stimulation is more effective than hormone treatments in inducing lactation (Hormann, 1977). Breast milk is also available from online human milk banks, though it is expensive and care is needed to select banks in which the milk is screened for disease and infection (http://well.blogs.nytimes.com/2013/02/11/picking-source-of-babys-milk/?ref=ronicarynrabin).

Sucking stimulation can maintain the supply of breast milk even if the infant is feeding only once a day. This kind of minimal breast-feeding is often used by mothers who work outside the home, who are weaning a baby from the breast, or who are using breast-feeding for "comfort" nursing for older infants. It is not necessary to mechanically express milk to maintain the supply during periods of minimal breast-feeding (Michaelson et al., 1988).

The nutritive demands of the lactating mother are far in excess of the demands made during prenatal life because of the accelerated weight gain of the infant just after birth. The milk secreted in just 1 month represents more calories than the net energy cost of pregnancy. The mother can meet this increased nutrient need by eating the equivalent of an additional meal of 500 kilocalories each day.

The composition of human milk not only differs from cow's milk-based infant formulas, but breast milk composition changes over time and according to the infant's nutritional needs (see

Table 5.5). *Colostrum*, the clear, yellowish liquid that is secreted from the breast in the first few days, is relatively high in protein. It also has enzymes that inhibit the growth of bacteria, microorganisms (*Lactobacillus bifidus*) that depress the growth of pathogens, and large "eating" cells (microphages) that enhance the immune system to protect against bacteria and some viruses (American Academy of Pediatrics, 1997; Bocci et al., 1993).

To make cow's milk (used for most commercial infant formulas) be more similar in composition to human milk, it has to be modified. The protein content is lowered, and the milk is treated to make it more easily digested (the whey protein of human milk is easier to digest than that of cow's milk). Vitamins A, D, and C, and sometimes iron are added to fortify the formula as well as fatty acids that are known to stimulate brain develop-

ment. But all the necessary nutrients for brain and body development are the most balanced in breast milk. Formulas can also be tailored to infants with special needs, such as soy formulas for infants with allergies. Formula and breast milk have similar nutrient values, but human milk is more nutritionally matched to infants, changes over time to match the infant's needs, and contains other important substances that promote immunization.

Human milk has a sweet taste. It also takes on some of the flavors found in the maternal diet. Amniotic fluid is also flavored with the mother's foods, suggesting that there is an acculturation toward local foods that begins prenatally (Mennella, 1997). Human milk is also low in sodium, and breast-fed infants have less of a preference for salt than bottle-fed infants (Karns, 2000).

TABLE 5.5 Components of Breast Milk Compared with Formula

Nutrient Factor	Breast Milk	Formula
Fats	Omega 3 fatty acids	Low in Omega 3s
	Automatically adjusts to infant's needs; levels decline as baby gets older	Doesn't adjust to infant's needs
	Rich in cholesterol	No cholesterol
	Nearly completely absorbed	Not completely absorbed
	Contains fat-digesting enzyme, lipase	No lipase
Protein	Soft, easily-digestible whey	Harder-to-digest casein curds
	Lysozyme, an antimicrobial	No lysozyme
	Rich in protein components	Deficient or low in some proteins
	Rich in growth factors	Deficient in growth factors
	Contains sleep-inducing proteins	Does not contain as many sleep-inducing proteins
	Infants aren't allergic to human milk protein	May cause allergies
Immune Boosters	Rich in living white blood cells, millions per feeding	No live white blood cells—or any other cells. Dead food has less immunological benefit.
	Rich in immunoglobulins	Few immunoglobulins and most are the wrong kind
Enzymes and Hormones	Rich in digestive enzymes, such as lipase and amylase	Processing kills digestive enzymes
	Rich in many hormones; thyroid, prolactin, oxytocin, and more than fifteen others	Processing kills hormones, which are not human to begin with
	Varies with mother's diet	Always tastes the same

The Effects of Breast-and Bottle-Feeding on Mother and Infant

Breast-feeding has important health benefits for both the mother and the infant. One advantage of breast-feeding is that it serves as a natural way to help mothers recover from childbirth. The sucking stimulation from the infant triggers the release of several maternal hormones, in particular oxytocin and prolactin. Oxytocin, discussed earlier in this chapter, speeds up contractions during labor. It is essential following the third stage of labor, because continued uterine contractions are necessary to shrink the uterus to normal size and prevent uterine hemorrhage. The oxytocin released by sucking does this naturally. If mothers do not breast-feed, they must be given doses of oxytocin. Oxytocin also stimulates the breast to deliver milk only when sucking occurs and not otherwise. Prolactin stimulates the mammary glands to produce milk.

There is some evidence that breast-feeding has a long-term effect on mothers' health, in particular, the partial prevention of ovarian and breast cancer. Women who breast-fed their first-born infants longer than 1 month had a significantly lower risk of developing breast cancer, at least during the period before the onset of menopause (American Academy of Pediatrics, 1997; Siskind, Schofield, Rice, & Bain, 1989). Breast-feeding also helps women return faster to their pre-pregnancy weight. These two factors—prevention of breast cancer and weight control—were cited as the primary reasons why women chose to breast-feed their babies (Charrol et al., 2004). Breast-feeding also lowers the risk of hip fractures in the postmenopausal period, helps women retain minerals in their bones, and lowers the risk of arthritis, especially if women breast-feed for over 15 months (Karlson et al., 2004). Mothers are more likely to be relaxed during breast vs. bottle feeding, due to oxytocin secretion, an effect which has been shown to apply to both depressed and nondepressed mothers (Field et al., 2010).

There are also health benefits to the infant. Mother's milk contains immunizing agents that protect against a variety of infections, such as respiratory infection, asthma, ear infection, bacterial meningitis, and urinary tract infection. Breast-feeding may also reduce the risk of sudden infant death syndrome (SIDS; see Chapter 6), allergic diseases, and digestive diseases. Recent evidence also shows that breastfeeding significantly reduces the risk of the major epidemics of childhood diabetes and obesity, thus saving lives and reducing health care costs. Finally, there is some evidence that breast-feeding may enhance motor development and state regulation during infancy, and reduce the risk of obesity in later life (American Academy of Pediatrics, 1997, 2005; Connelly & Tracewell, 2012; Feldman & Eidelman, 2002; Hart et al., 2003; Stettler et al., 2005). One study suggests that breast-feeding also enhances cognitive development, but more research is needed to sufficiently justify such claims (Soliday, 2007).

Breast-feeding for more than 6 months significantly reduces the risk of developing childhood cancer, especially lymphomas. Non-breast-fed children are five times more likely to get lymphoma, a form of cancer that is higher in children with immune deficiencies (American Academy of Pediatrics, 1997; Smigel, 1988).

The immunologic effect of human milk derives from the protein called *secretory IgA*, or SIgA. This protein coats the inner lining of the baby's intestines, acting to trap and kill harmful bacteria. SIgA also enters the lungs and breathing passages whenever the infant gurgles and blows milk bubbles and thus may protect against respiratory diseases. If a mother has a bacterial infection, her milk contains higher levels of SIgA, which helps to further protect the infant from catching the mother's infection (Pollitt, Garza, & Leib, 1984).

If breast milk protects the infant against disorders of the immune system, what happens if the mother has an immune system disorder such as AIDS? If a mother is infected with AIDS, HIV is typically present in her breast milk. The chance of an infant's acquiring AIDS from its mother is about 15 percent, but part of this transmission may occur either prenatally or during the birth process. It is difficult to determine which of these routes is most likely to infect the infant.

Medical agencies have come up with conflicting recommendations about whether an AIDS-infected mother should breast-feed. It is thought that SIgA may neutralize the AIDS virus and that the risk of an infant acquiring other diseases because of a lack of breast milk SIgA may be just as high as the risk of getting AIDS from breast milk, especially in poor countries where the incidence of AIDS and other diseases is high. Others believe that the chance of acquiring AIDS from breast milk is not worth the risk of spreading the disease and therefore recommend against breast-feeding. Infected women should consult their physician before making the choice to breast-feed (American Academy of Pediatrics, 1997; D. T. Dunn, Newell, Ades, & Peckham, 1992; Goldfarb, 1993; Kennedy et al., 1990; Peckham, 1993; Porcher, 1992; Van de Perre et al., 1993). Breast-feeding is also not recommended if the mother uses illegal drugs or is receiving chemotherapy for cancer.

Behavioral differences between breast-and bottle-fed infants have been found. A study of 100 healthy, full-term, vaginally delivered newborns found that breast-fed infants are more irritably fussy than bottle-fed infants (DiPietro, Larson, & Porges, 1987). This irritability, however, was associated with a more optimal physiological functioning, such as a slower heart rate, compared to bottle-fed infants. The physiological functioning of breast-fed infants is more energy-efficient, as judged by differences in the patterns of heart rate, breathing, and sleeping of bottle-and breast-fed infants (Zeskind, Marshall, & Goff, 1992).

The higher irritability of breast-fed infants is not due to a less optimal mother-infant interaction. Some research has shown, on the contrary, that breast-fed infants get talked to, smiled at, touched, looked at, and rocked more by their mothers (J. Dunn, 1975; Lavelli & Poli, 1998) during feeding, although no long-term behavioral differences have been found. Nor is the effect due to the fact that breast-fed babies get hungrier than bottle-fed infants (DiPietro et al., 1987). Rather, DiPietro and associates (1987) propose that "the irritability of breast-fed neonates be regarded as the norm of neonatal behavior. Formula may have a depressant effect on behavior" (p. 472). This may be due to the differences in the specific types of proteins and sugars that constitute the two types of milk. If more irritability is the norm, these authors argue that it serves two purposes. First, it enhances physiological functioning by giving the infant experience with varying degrees of arousal. Second, crying may serve to stimulate more mother-infant interaction and provide more opportunities for feeding (Hunziker & Barr, 1986).

Taken together, the benefits of breast-feeding appear to be immunological, physiological, behavioral, and psychological. Because of the growing number of research studies supporting the superiority of breast milk and breast-feeding for both mother and infant, the American Academy of Pediatrics (AAP), the Canadian Paediatric Society, and the American Dietetic Association all strongly encourage breast-feeding (American Academy of Pediatrics, 1997; 2005; Karns, 2000). The AAP recommends:

Exclusive breast-feeding is ideal nutrition and sufficient to support optimal growth and development for approximately the first 6 months after birth. Infants weaned before 12 months of age should not receive cow's milk feedings but should receive iron-fortified infant formula. Gradual introduction of iron-enriched solid foods in the second half of the first year should complement the breast milk diet. It is recommended that breast feeding continue for at least 12 months, and thereafter for as long as mutually desired. (American Academy of Pediatrics, 1997, p. 4)

Although breast-feeding is recommended, personal preferences, illness, family and social support, and cultural norms may influence the choice of feeding method. If formula feeding is chosen, there is no consistent evidence that formula feeding impairs the development of a strong mother-infant attachment (Jansen et al., 2008). The effects of breast feeding are primarily physiological and immunological, which as reviewed above, are extremely important for long-term health outcomes in mother and infant.

Most mothers in the United States either stop breast-feeding altogether before 6 months, or they begin supplementing with formula too early (Li et al., 2003). The major factor for predicting success in breast-feeding is the desire of the mother to do so and the support of her partner. Some fathers have feelings of jealousy, uselessness, and sexual frustration associated with their mate's breast-feeding. Some men may also experience feelings of ambivalence about the breast: Who does it "belong" to? Who and what is it for? Research shows that these feelings can be alleviated somewhat by enhancing the father's participation in the birth experience and by improving father-mother communication on such issues as infant care and sexual fulfillment (Karns, 2000; Teitler, 2001).

An effort is being made in the United States to encourage health-care professionals to promote breast-feeding. Mothers can also receive information and support from local hospitals, clinics, and breast-feeding advocacy groups. These supports are necessary to counteract the effects of cultural beliefs against breast-feeding, embarrassment, lack of self-confidence, and family attitudes (Karns, 2000). Women who breastfeed also need to follow appropriate nutritional guidelines and consume substances such as caffeine and alcohol in moderation (James, 2011; http://ohioline.osu.edu/hyg-fact/5000/pdf/5573.pdf)

What Is the Father's Role with Newborns?

Are fathers important to their newborns? Some studies have found that fathers spend very little time interacting with their newborns; others have found that fathers would like to spend more time with their babies; and still others have shown that when fathers actually do spend time with newborns, they can be just as competent as mothers in administering care and affection. In reality, these studies are not contradictory; they merely represent different aspects of the fathering role. Although we will discuss the father's role and behavior in more detail later, in this chapter we will confine our discussion to studies of fathers and newborns.

Studies of large-scale national samples of parents and infants show that fathers spend between 20 and 35 percent as much time as mothers in direct participation in infant care. Mothers appear to take the primary responsibility, while fathers take the role of helpers and baby-sitters (Lamb, Pleck, Charnov, & Levine, 1987). Men's ability to participate in parenting tasks depends on the amount of social support they receive, particularly from their partners, and the more involved they are, the more involved they become (Leerkes & Burney, 2007).

Father-infant and mother-infant interaction can be enhanced by specific interventions to orient fathers to their newborns. In one program, fathers were given instruction in baby massage and bathing methods when the infants were 4 weeks old. When the infants were 12 weeks old, the fathers who had received the instruction reported more marital satisfaction and less depression, compared to a control group of fathers who were not trained. In addition, 12-week-old infants in the massage and bathing group were more likely to maintain eye contact, smile, and vocalize with their fathers, and the fathers were more likely to be involved with their infants (Samuels, Scholz, & Edmundson, 1992; Scholz & Samuels, 1992). Parents who were given information about newborn responsiveness and behavior when the infant was 2 days old were more likely to interact synchronously with their infants (Wendland-Carro, Piccinini, & Millar, 1999).

Men who adjust better to parenthood have more knowledge about children and better relationships with their wives than men who have trouble adjusting to being fathers. This is in contrast to the factors predicting parental adjustment in women, which include self-esteem, identification with the mothering role, and adaptation to the pregnancy experience (Leerkes & Burney, 2007; Wente & Crockenberg, 1976).

Both fathers and mothers can become attached to their newborns.

The involvement of the father in caregiving affects the mother-infant relationship. Working mothers who left their newborn infants with fathers compared to other infant-care providers reported less anger, depression, and anxiety (Vandell, Hyde, Plant, & Essex, 1997). Families in which the fathers are more involved have wives who show more interest and affection toward the neonate. Of course, this result could be explained the other way around: interested, affectionate mothers may be more adept at encouraging fathers to take part in the care of the infant. Fathers do play an important role, even in the newborn period. They may not do as much as mothers overall, but with some encouragement and training, they are able to become competent caregivers.

Do Firstborns Have Different Interactions with Their Mothers than Laterborns?

Another factor influencing the family system at this period of time is whether the parents have had prior experience with an infant. As a general rule, newborns who are firstborn receive more caregiving interaction (Keller & Zach, 2002). Perhaps because of the novelty of the experience, parents devote more time and energy to the care of the firstborn than to infants born later. One study examined family photo albums and found considerably more photographs of firstborn children than of children born later (Titus, 1976).

Another explanation of the difference is that the mothers of firstborns are less skilled as caregivers. Do they spend more time because they are less efficient at getting the normal caregiving tasks accomplished? Primiparous mothers spend more time in nonfeeding activity during a feeding session. They are more likely to change activity frequently, such as shifting the infant's posture, providing more stimulation, and talking more to the newborn. Their infants spend less time on the nipple and do less sucking when attached than infants born later. These mothers could be spending more time because they are more uncertain about how to handle their infant or because they are more excited by the infant and wish to touch, explore, and talk to the infant. The number of changes of activity decreased over the first 3 days for primiparous mothers, suggesting that it does not take them very long to get down to the business of feeding during the feeding period (E. Thoman, Leiderman, & Olson, 1972).

Another explanation is that first-time mothers are simply more anxious than other mothers. An anxious mood is likely to be caused by lack of security in the child-rearing role, and it may be enhanced by such factors as separation from the infant due to prematurity and illness. Anxiety in first-time mothers at birth is correlated with anxiety at 1 month but not at later follow-up observations (Fleming & Orpen, 1986; Fleming, Ruble, Flett, & Van Wagner, 1990), suggesting that most early insecurities that might influence behavior are reduced after a few months' experience.

In summary, adults and infants seem ready to interact with each other and have feelings and behaviors that mutually complement. Under the right conditions, any adult can interact successfully with a newborn, and with enough exposure to the baby, can develop a lasting attachment. The emotional tie between adults and infants does not seem to depend on a particular experience or a particular starting time. Rather, emotional bonds develop slowly and in a variety of ways. Many senses and behaviors can be involved, and if one pathway is absent (the parents do not have the opportunity for early contact, for example), other pathways are available to enhance the adult-infant communication process.

Co-Regulating With Baby

Co-regulation (see Chapter 2 and Fogel, 1993) refers to periods of communication in which people are continuously adjusting their actions to each other and when both participants have the feeling that something new and creative is occurring. Co-regulation is more than just being responsive and sensitive. It is about being open to the emerging possibilities in a relationship with another person and being sufficiently spontaneous to allow for improvisation and innovation. A co-regulated conversation between adults is one in which ideas and feelings are mutually accepted, in which there is a continuous flow of ideas and feelings, and in which participants have a sense of discovering something new about themselves and each other.

In the Experiential Exercises lessons, it is important to focus your awareness on your body's movements and sensations. Coregulat-

ing with baby is a type of awareness through social communication. As you interact with the baby (or with any person), it is important to pay attention to your own experiences. Usually, if you are feeling unhappy or uncomfortable when communicating, the other person is feeling that also. So as in qualitative research, you can use your own experiences as a guide to help you relate to the baby.

Co-regulating with newborn infants is not easy because they have limited social skills, and the time in which they are awake and alert is relatively brief. With patience, however co-regulating with a newborn can be a wonderful and surprising experience.

A baby's first attempts to gaze at people and objects may be brief. If infants are shown an object while they are alert, they may learn to look for longer periods. For newborns, objects should be brightly

colored with simple shapes, such as a striped ball, a mirror, a shiny bracelet, or a white paper plate with a face painted in thick black lines.

Hold objects about 8 to 10 inches from the baby's face. The infant can best focus his or her vision at this distance. Hold the object steady or move it slowly from side to side. Some newborns show a clear preference for looking at certain objects. Watch to see which ones the baby seems to prefer. Try to vary the distance and speed of the object and see what happens.

An infant may enjoy looking at objects from different points of view and from different positions, such as while being cradled in mother's arms, laying on his or her back, or sitting in an infant seat. A baby's attention may be attracted by objects that make noise or music. A baby's attention is expecially attracted to the high-pitched voices of caregivers.

If the infant becomes overstimulated when watching objects, try showing just one at a time and moving the object more slowly in the baby's visual field. If the baby still apepars to be overstimulated (turning away, crying, sucking a fist, etc.) the game should be put aside until a later time. Use your own feelings as a guide to tell when the infant wants more or has had enough. It is very satisfying when a baby actually engages with you. If you are experiencing feelings of rejection or frustration, it probably is a good indication that you need to change your play or wait until a later time.

Although true eye contact does not begin until about 6 weeks, infants will look in the direction of your eyes and face. You can encourage this by talking gently while holding the baby up near your face. Cutting down on outside sources of stimulation will also help encourage the baby to focus on you. If a baby will not look at your face, cut back on the level of stimultion and give the baby a chance to look at you. Remember that some babies are slow to focus and cannot sustain their attention for long periods. It is important to not take this personally. The baby is not capable of rejecting anyone at this age. Your patience and understanding of the difficult time babies have in attending will eventually be rewarded.

You can follow the baby's direction of gaze with your face until the baby is looking at you, and then give the baby a big smile while saying "Hi!" Newborns like to hear soft whispers and humming sounds. After the baby is looking at you, smiles can sometimes be elicited by quiet, high-pitched voices, gentle tummy strokes, and smiling faces. You will probably be so delighted to be looked at in this way that these responses will seem very natural.

Aside from these activities, babies of this age like to listen to music, to be held and touched, and to be bathed and masssaged. In all these activities, try to create simple routines that the baby can recognize. Observe for signs of over-stimulation and give the baby a chance to rest and relax. Co-regulation may take some trial and error to figure out which is best for you and the infant. When you really connect, it is worth all the effort. Even though newborns have only a limited capacity for attention and interaction, with some gentleness and patience the caregiver can be rewarded with periods of mutually co-regulated attention and enjoyment.

SUMMARY

Physical and Motor Development

- The fetal states of rest and activity develop into sleeping and waking states.

- Newborns sleep about 17 hours per day.

- Responsiveness to the environment is related to orienting and defensive responses. Newborns will orient to stimuli of moderate intensity and complexity.

- Crying is an organized rhythmic activity that has reliable effects on adults. Infants who cry a great deal are not necessarily at risk for problems in parent-infant attachment.

- Colic is a pattern of excessive crying with no known cause. It does not seem to have lasting effects on parents or infants.

- Each method of soothing infants has advantages and disadvantages.

- Reflexes are highly variable within and between infants. Many disappear by about 6 months, while others remain for life. Both brain and motor factors may contribute to the disappearance of reflexes.

- The infant does not grow all at once; different parts of the body grow at different rates and at different times.

- Sucking is a complex activity that can be adapted to the environment.

- Newborn arm and hand movements are directed to objects in different locations and differ between social and physical objects, although detailed videotape analysis is required to observe these patterns.

Perceptual Development

- Newborn visual acuity and visual processing are poor but improve rapidly during the first 3 months.

- Infants can perceive some meaningful visual patterns, but in most cases, they do not attach meanings to their perceptions.
- Hearing, smell, and taste are more acute at birth than vision, perhaps due to prenatal experiences. Infants can recognize their mothers by sound and by smell.

Cognitive Development

- Newborns are susceptible to both operant conditioning and classical conditioning.
- Habituation and conditioning reflect rudimentary memory processes as infants need to compare current with past experiences. Most newborn memories seem to last no more than a few hours, unless the stimulus is repeated often.
- Newborns appear to be able to imitate simple gestures they make themselves. Imitation is irregular and not especially salient to a casual observer.
- Newborns appear to have a rudimentary sense of self, experienced as a feeling of the familiarity of their own bodies, feelings, and behaviors.

Emotional Development

- Newborns have a large repertoire of facial expressions and body movements, some of which are related to emotion expression.
- Newborns can feel distress, contentment, disgust, interest, and surprise.

Family and Society

- Adults and infants seem to have mutually complementary communications that get their interaction started and set the stage for later emotional ties.
- Early physical contact between parents and newborns is satisfying and important.
- Breast milk is superior to other forms of infant feeding. Infants should be breast-fed until twelve months and for as long after as mutually convenient for mother, infant, and family. Solid foods should be supplemented after 6 months.

Chapter 6

Two to Five Months

CHAPTER OUTLINE AND OVERVIEW

Physical and Motor Development	*What are the features of physical growth during this period? What types of motor skills do infants have? How does infant sleep change at this age? What is SIDS? How is it caused? How can it be prevented?*
Perceptual Development	*What perceptual abilities develop during this period? Can infants perceive their own emotions?*
Cognitive Development	*What types of things do infants remember? What type of intelligence do infants have at this age?*
Emotional Development	*What types of emotions can infants at this age feel? What are their capacities for emotion regulation?*
Social Development	*How do adults typically behave with babies of this age? What are some cultural differences in adult-infant interaction? What are the effects of adult behavior on infants? What is the infant's sense of self at this age?*
Family and Society	*What are the developmental tasks of adults in the transition to parenthood? Are there differences in parenting between men and women?*

During the first few months, babies seem to be in a world of their own. They sleep a great deal, they have few means of communication other than crying, and their movements seem self-contained and repetitive. These newborn behavior patterns are organized and highly adaptive for the initial tasks of postnatal survival.

Around the age of 2 months, most babies experience their first major developmental transition since birth. Their motor movements become more purposeful and deliberate, a change from the earlier cyclical and reflexive movements. Their perceptual systems, especially vision, become more acute. Waking time and attention span increase rapidly. Adults first notice these changes at 6 to 8 weeks, when infants become able to establish and maintain eye contact. Around this time, demanding crying wanes and is replaced by other forms of emotional communication, especially smiling in response to other people. These changes lead to more prolonged and satisfying adult-infant social interactions and the beginnings of social play.

As the quality of their attention becomes more focused, infants begin to have memories of past experiences. These memories form the basis of infants' feelings of enjoyment in the company of familiar people and in the ability to anticipate recurring routines, such as meals and baths. This period is truly an exciting time for parents as their baby seems to come alive and to more fully engage with them.

PHYSICAL AND MOTOR DEVELOPMENT

Physical Development

In infancy and early childhood, physical development occurs as a natural accompaniment to psychological development. Physical development is usually measured in terms of height and weight. Additional indices include the circumference of the head, the fat-to-muscle ratio, the emergence of baby teeth, and bone growth. Standard charts for height and weight for boys and girls from birth to 36 months are available from the United States Center for Disease Control web site at (http://www.cdc.gov/growthcharts/).

At birth, most infants are 19 to 21 inches in length and weigh between 7 and 8 pounds. Boys are slightly longer and heavier than girls and remain so, on average, throughout life. The most rapid growth in both height and weight occurs in the first 6 months of life. By this age, height increases by a factor of 1.5, while weight increases by a factor of 2. This is a lot of growth in a short period. Imagine a teenager (the teenage years are the other period of life when rapid growth occurs) whose height increased by half again in 6 months—say, from 5 feet to 7½ feet! Teens grow fast, but not that fast.

Individual differences in birth height and weight are relatively small, since they are limited by the need for the infant's body to fit through the mother's pelvis and vagina during birth. Individual differences become larger with age (the range of heights and weights is wider among 2-year-olds than among 1-year-olds). In addition, as the infants get older, their height becomes a better predictor of their adult height. Infant weight is not a very good predictor of adult weight, because weight is more variable than height and more dependent upon environmental factors. As we saw in Chapter 3, weight gain in premature infants can be influenced not only by diet but also by age-appropriate stimulation.

Also, keep in mind that growth is asynchronous (Chapter 5). Different parts of the body grow at different rates, and growth spurts occur at different times in each body region. Before birth, the head grows faster than the rest of the body, while after birth, the body begins to grow faster. The process by which the head grows earlier than the body is called **cephalocaudal development**. Growth also proceeds outward, first centered on the torso of the body and later on the developing limbs in a process called **proximodistal development**. Because their limbs develop more slowly than the central part of the body, it takes almost a year for babies to begin standing and

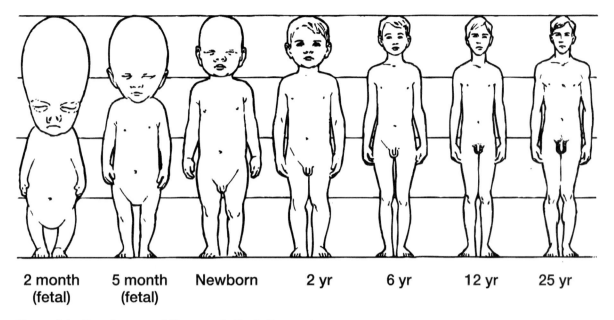

| 2 month (fetal) | 5 month (fetal) | Newborn | 2 yr | 6 yr | 12 yr | 25 yr |

Figure 6.1 Developmental Changes in Body Proportion
The way different proportions of body length accounted for by the head, trunk, and legs at different ages or stages of development. The disproportion is greatest in fetal life. The head decreases from 50 percent of total body length at 2 months postconception to only 25 percent at birth and 12 percent in adulthood.

Source: J. F. Rosenblith & J. E. Sims-Knight, *In the beginning: Development in the first two years*, 1985, p. 296. Belmont, CA: Brooks/Cole. Copyright © Wadsworth, Inc. Reprinted by permission.

walking. These growth processes are illustrated in Figure 6.1.

Motor Development

At the same time that the body is growing physically, the infant is also becoming more skilled at a variety of motor movements. In the realm of motor development, we consider control over posture, locomotion, and the movements of the hands and arms.

Motor development was studied extensively in the early part of the twentieth century (Gesell, 1928; McGraw, 1935; Shirley, 1931). Because of this research, the infant's level of motor development can be assessed today using a variety of standardized testing situations. Some of the commonly used motor developmental assessment tests are listed in Table 6.1. Based on results from using these tests with many infants, both the average age of achievement of a skill and the range of ages

seen in normal infants is usually reported. The age norms for the achievement of body postures and hand and arm control between 2 and 5 months of age are given in Table 6.2 using the standard scores from the Bayley test. Between 2 and 5 months of age, boy and girl infants do not differ, on average, in motor skills or amount of motor activity (Cossette, Malcuit, & Pomerleau, 1991).

These assessment procedures are useful for diagnosing retardation and motor deficits in infants, but they only work well under specific conditions. First, the test norms apply only to infants in a particular cultural and economic group. Second, the test is applicable only if it is administered in precisely the same manner for each infant. The ability to grasp a cube is supposed to be assessed when the infant is supported in a sitting position. What if, instead, you presented the cube while the baby was lying supine? How might such a postural change affect the infant's hand motor skills?

TABLE 6.1 Commonly Used Infant Development Tests

Name of Test	Areas of Competency Assessed
Gesell Scales (Gesell, 1925)	Motor behavior, language behavior, adaptive behavior, and personal-social behavior.
Bayley Scales of Infant Development (Bayley, 1969)	Motor area (gross body coordination) and mental area (adaptability, learning, sensory acuity, and fine motor coordination).
Denver Developmental Screening Test (Frankenburg et al., 1975)	Personal-social behavior, fine motor-adaptive behavior, language behavior, and gross motor coordination.
Einstein Scales of Sensorimotor Development (Escalona & Corman, 1968)	Prehension, object permanence, and space (detour behavior and perspective taking).
Infant Psychological Development Scales (Uzgiris & Hunt, 1975)	Object permanence, development of means, development of imitation, development of causality, development of objects in space, and development of schemes for relating to objects.

Source: A. Fogel & G. F. Melson, *Child development*, 1988, p. 150. St. Paul, MN: West. Copyright © by West Publishing Company. Reprinted by permission. All rights reserved.

TABLE 6.2 Norms for the Development of Motor Behavior Patterns in North America

Test Item	Average Age	Normal Age Range
A. Head and body control		
Holds head erect when upright	7 weeks	3 weeks–4 months
Holds head steady when upright	2.5 months	1 month–5 months
Elevates chest and head in prone position	2.2 months	3 weeks–5 months
Thrusts arms and legs in supine position	1 month	1 week–2 months
Turns from side to back	2 months	3 weeks–5 months
Turns from back to side	2.5 months	2 months–7 months
Sits with support	2.2 months	1 month–5 months
Sits with slight support	3.7 months	2 months–6 months
Sits alone momentarily	5.2 months	4 months–8 months
Pulls self to sitting position	5.7 months	4 months–8 months
B. Hand and arm control		
Holds onto large ring in supine position	1 month	3 weeks–4 months
Grasps 1-inch cube with palm	3.7 months	2 months–7 months
Grasps cube with partial use of thumb	5 months	4 months–8 months
Reaches with one hand	5.5 months	4 months–8 months

Source: Bayley Infant Development Tests, as reported in and adapted from J. F. Rosenblith & J. E. Sims-Knight, *In the beginning: Development in the first two years*, 1985, Tables 8.2 and 8.5. Reprinted by permission of Sage Publications.

Physical exercise and environmental support for motor skills can enhance the infant's ability to achieve motor coordination. As a simple case, consider how an infant seat, a high chair, and an infant walker provide postural support so that babies can execute manual and locomotor movements that they would not be able to do while lying on their backs. Similarly, the positions in which adults hold infants also influence the range of motor skills that the infants can display. In general, the ability of a baby to perform a motor skill depends in part on two factors: the difficulty of the task, and the supports and resources present in the environment in which the task is carried out.

Task difficulty. We saw in the last chapter that infants older than 2 months, when held upright with the feet placed on a surface, cannot execute stepping movements. When the same infant's legs are underwater or when the infant is lying supine, on the other hand, stepping becomes easier. In conditions in which the stepping task is less difficult, in other words, infants can do it (Thelen, Skala, & Kelso, 1987).

Similar effects of task difficulty have been shown for fine motor skills, such as manipulating objects. Between the ages of 2 and 5 months, infants have more difficulty handling objects like balls and cubes than objects that have graspable appendages, such as a cube with holes into which the baby can insert his or her fingers or a ring (which is simply a ball with a hole in the middle). They are also better at grasping small versus larger objects.

At 3 months, grasping movements are relatively primitive. Babies will grasp an object and move it directly to their mouths without even looking at it. Beginning at about 4 months, however, babies will alternate putting the object in their mouths and looking at it, and they can hold the object in one hand while looking at it and finger the object with the other hand (Rochat, 1989). The older baby uses more motor actions and more perceptual systems in exploring the environment (Ruff, Saltarelli, Capozzoli, & Dubiner, 1992). Between 2 and 6 months of age, the movements of the arm and hand become more refined and more adapted to the size and shape of an object (Angulo-Kinzler & Horn, 2001; Bhat & Galloway, 2006; Rochat et al., 2006). Infants also are better able to choose when to use both hands for grasping and holding, or just one hand (Sgandurra et al. 2012), and to isolate only the muscles most needed for the task (such as using just the biceps in the upper arm, rather than using the whole upper body (Bakker et al., 2010; Lee et al., 2008).

Arm and hand movements also differs according to the baby's emotional state (Fogel, 1981; Hannan, 1987; H. Papousek & Papousek, 1977; Trevarthen, 1977). Figure 6.2 shows some of these state-related arm and hand movements. Infants 2 and 3 months of age have also been shown to make index-finger extension movements that look like pointing gestures. Actual pointing gestures do not emerge until about 10 months, when babies learn to use pointing to direct adult's attention. Index-finger extensions, however, are more likely to occur at this age if babies are in an alert and attentive state. Typically, the pointing-like movements are not directed to the object of the infant's attention: pointing is more like an expression of interest and attention than a direct communication about the object at this age (Fogel & Hannan, 1985. Thelen & Fogel, 1989) (see Figure 6.3).

In general, therefore, infants will perform better on easier motor skill tasks. This, of course, is no different at any age. Children can ride a bike with training wheels before they can ride without them. Adults can help infants by making appropriate adjustments when tasks are too difficult.

Supports and resources. As infants develop, they can perform tasks that were once too difficult for them. How do these changes come about? What is the cause of motor development? As explained in the previous chapter, brain development is experience-dependent; that is, the infant has to practice making movements with easy tasks for the brain to develop the connections needed to enhance motor skills (Lobo et al., 2004). Since human infants have a limited ability to move around in the environment or to think about how to make tasks easier, they need social partners to help them. Usually, the

Figure 6.2 State-Dependent Hand and Arm Extensions
The position of hands in different behavioral states of infants: **(a)** alert waking state; **(b)** closed fists in uncomfortable or distressing situations; **(c)** passive waking state; **(d)** transitional states to sleep; **(e)** sleep.
Source: Adapted from H. Papousek, Mothering and the cognitive head start: Psychobiological considerations, 1977, p. 71. In H. R. Schaffer (Ed.), *Studies in mother-infant interaction*, 63–85. Copyright © Academic Press, Inc.

infant's caregiver creates supports and resources by which object manipulation and motor movements are made easier. During simple social play with objects, adults help infants to practice their budding motor skills (Lyra & Ferreira, 1987; Lyra & Rossetti-Ferreira, 1995). At first, when infants are unable to reach, adults will show an object to the baby and demonstrate the object's properties (shaking a rattle or squeezing a soft toy). During this period, adults may also place the object in the infant's hands, allowing the infant to grasp and hold the object or bring the object to the mouth. After infants acquire the ability to reach for objects, adults stop showing and placing and begin to hold the objects steady and within reach of the babies, apparently to give the babies the opportunity to practice reaching. All of these adult-mediated experiences actually contribute to

the development of the ability to reach for objects (Lobo & Galloway, 2008). Once reaching is mastered, mothers begin to challenge the babies with more complex objects and with two objects at one time (Fogel, 1990b; Fogel, Garvey, Hsu, &West-Stroming, 2006).

Another way in which adults provide supports and resources for motor skills is by holding the infants in postures that are most conducive to the execution of those skills. For example, when infants are first learning to sit, they need to balance their bodies with one hand. This detracts from their ability to reach for things with two hands (Rochat, 1989). When adults hold the baby upright, it frees both of the infant's hands. Upright babies are more attentive to the physical environment, while supine babies are more likely to look at their mothers (Fogel, Dedo, & McEwen, 1992; Fogel,

(a)   (b)

Figure 6.3   Development of Pointing
(a) Point at 2 months during face-to-face interaction with mother. Index finger extends while arms are flexed and does not indicate direction of gaze. **(b)** Point at 9 months during free play with mother. Both arm and finger are extended in the direction of the object of interest.

Source: E. Thelen & A. Fogel, Toward an action-based theory of infant development, 1989, p. 53. In J. Lockman & N. Hazen (eds.), *Action in a social context: Perspectives on early development*, 23–63. New York: Plenum Press.

Nwokah, Hsu, Dedo, & Walker, 1993). Similarly, infants in upright rather than supine positions are more likely to reach for objects that are presented within their reach (Savelsbergh & Kamp, 1993).

The effect of adult support for motor development is also seen in some African cultures. One study done in Mali (Bril & Sabatier, 1986) found that mothers put babies through some active workout routines. From birth, the babies were given postural control exercises, including training in sitting and standing. Mothers also stretched the babies' muscles and suspended the babies by their arms and legs (see Figure 6.4). Similar patterns have been found for West African families living in Paris (Rabain-Jamin & Wornham, 1993).

As a result of this practice, many African babies have advanced motor coordination compared to Caucasian babies. In addition, because the babies' limbs are exercised frequently, certain reflexes such as stepping do not disappear after

2 months, as found in North American infants (Super, 1976). On the opposite end of the spectrum are Navaho (from the southwestern United States) infants, who spend many hours strapped tightly onto cradle boards. Their motor development is slower than that of the other groups (Chisholm, 1983).

In summary, differences in task difficulty and in supports and resources for motor development seem to influence the age at which the motor skill is first acquired. Eventually, however, most healthy babies achieve the important motor milestones. These findings show that motor and physical development in the first half year is the result of a systems interaction between infants, adults, and the environment. Generally speaking, the ability of a person to perform a coordinated task is based on three systemic factors: task, environmental supports, and existing abilities. This is shown in Figure 6.5.

Figure 6.4   Postural Manipulations by Adults

Source: B. Bril & C. Sabatier, The cultural context of motor development: Postural manipulations in the daily life of Bambara babies (Mali), 1986, p. 445. *International Journal of Behavior Development, 9,* 439–453

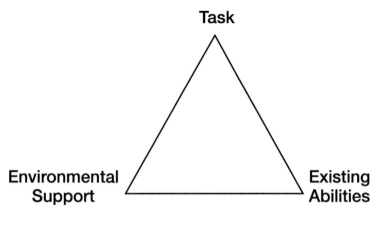

Figure 6.5   Systems Model of Task Difficulty
A task will be easy or difficult for an infant depending upon what the infant is being asked to do (the task), the help and resources the infant receives from others (environmental support), and the skills that the infant brings to the task (existing abilities).

Whether a baby can reach for objects, for example, can be explained according to Figure 6.5 as follows: The task is to reach for an object. The environmental supports are whether the object is within reach or out of reach, whether it is held by an adult or not, and the size and shape of the object. The abilities are whether the infant has learned to reach (after 4 months, usually) and whether the infant can turn, sit upright, or move toward the object. Reaching will be coordinated and successful depending upon how these factors come together.

Sleeping

Infant sleep also changes during this period. By 3 months infants are still sleeping about the same amount as newborns, but they can sleep for longer periods before waking up and are more likely to sleep through the night. About half of their sleep time is in REM sleep. This percentage decreases gradually so that in adults, only 20 percent of sleep is REM sleep.

One concern that arises in this age period is that the most frequent cause of unexpected death in the first year of life is sudden infant death syndrome **(SIDS),** also called *crib death*, which occurs when infants are sleeping. SIDS currently claims the life of 1 infant in every 2,000, which is half of what the SIDS death rate was in 1990, due in part to greater awareness and prevention efforts (see Table 6.3; Karns, 2000).

The vast majority of infant deaths occur during the first few days of life. After the first month, the primary causes of infant death may be labeled "unexpected," since in most industrial societies, fatal infant diseases have all but been eliminated through the use of vaccines and preventive care. Accidents are one of the major causes of unexpected death in the first year of life. These may be traffic accidents or home accidents, such as suffocation, burns, poisoning, and drowning. Although it occurs rarely, the other cause of unexpected death is homicide, such as from maltreatment, infanticide, sexual offenses, kidnapping, and killing accompanied by parental suicide (Hartmann & Molz, 1979).

What causes SIDS?   One of the problems in diagnosing and preventing SIDS is that no single disorder accounts for all the cases. The only thing they have in common is the manner of death. The SIDS diagnosis is applied if parents discover that their baby has died, perhaps at night or during a nap, and there is no apparent cause of death. Some SIDS cases are associated with colds or some mild respiratory infection. In some cases, the infection may be acquired prenatally but it is more likely to have environmental causes. Higher rates of SIDS have been found during outbreaks of influenza (Moreno, Ardanaz, Olivera, Castilla, & de Pedro, 1994). A more consistent link has been found for cigarette smoking in the home, which accounts for 28 percent of SIDS cases (Blackwell et al., 1994; Hilder, 1994; Lindsay, Johnson, Wallace, & Soos,

TABLE 6.3 How To Prevent SIDS

DO:	DON'T:
Place the baby on back (supine) or side when sleeping.	Overheat the baby with excessive clothing or bedding.
Use a firm mattress and bedding materials.	Smoke near the baby.
Remove soft objects and loose bedding materials.	Place the baby on stomach (prone) to sleep.
Breast-feed if possible.	
Obtain adequate prenatal care.	
Use a fan to circulate the air in the baby's room.	

1994; Peduto, Musu, Gatto, & Ghilli, 1994). The effects of smoking may have their origin in pregnancy since smoking, as well as alcohol and drug addiction during pregnancy, increase the risk for SIDS (Friend et al., 2004; Guffanti et al., 2004; Morgan et al., 2002).

Very young infants, as well as older children and adults, often cease breathing for brief periods, a condition known as **apnea.** These pauses in breathing, or apneic pauses, almost always occur during sleep. Since all infants have apneic episodes, these cannot be a direct cause of SIDS. On the other hand, SIDS may be related to some sensorimotor and neurological deficit that prevents the infant from making the correct movements and heart rate changes that will assist in recovery from the apnea (Lipsitt, Sturges, & Burke, 1979). Some of the sensorimotor deficits that may prevent recovery from apnea during the first year may have been caused by loss of oxygen during the perinatal period or by genetic factors associated with low motor control over breathing (Naeye, 1980; Schiffman, Westlake, Santiago, & Edelman, 1980). Slower myelination of the nerves in the brain stem related to the control of breathing has also been found in SIDS infants (Cruz-Sanchez et al., 1997; Morgan et al., 2002).

The inability to cope with relatively mild stresses, such as heat, apnea, or even mild toxicity, may therefore result from some other systemic or neurophysiological weakness. Some victims of SIDS were found to be excessively covered or dressed at the time of death (Stanton, Scott, & Downhan, 1980). Although no one symptom can predict SIDS in all cases, SIDS infants have some of the following: difficulty in waking, shrill crying, few movements during sleep, poor oxygenation of the blood, pneumonia, and repeated hospitalization (Einspieler, Widder, Holzer, & Kenner, 1988; Golding & Peters, 1985).

Can SIDS be prevented? There is currently no foolproof method of preventing SIDS. Some infants may be identified at birth as being at risk. Infants who are from deprived socioeconomic settings, who have suffered oxygen deprivation, who have a high apnea rate, whose mothers smoked, or those who have siblings who died or nearly died of SIDS are all at risk for SIDS.

Since the causes of SIDS are related to respiratory, feeding, temperature regulation and state control problems, some simple procedures are recommended for use with all infants (see Table 6.3). Of these recommendations, perhaps the most important is to avoid a prone (face down) sleeping position. A supine position (on the back) makes it easier for the infant to breathe. Controlled studies have shown a significant reduction—up to 50 percent—in the SIDS death rate when parents place their infants in the supine position (Goldman, 1994; Helweg-Larsen, Lundemose, & Bille, 1994; Wigfield, Gilbert, & Fleming, 1994). Research also shows that having a fan in the bedroom to keep the air moving and re-circulate exhaled carbon dioxide can reduce the death rate by as much as 72 percent. Of course parents need to take usual safety precautions when using a fan (Coleman-Phox et al., 2008).

A parent can also use a home apnea monitor, which emits an alarm if the infant stops breathing during sleep. This system has both advantages and disadvantages for use in the home. Monitor use can cause extreme anxiety for the first month and lead to a restricted social life for the parents. Once they get over their initial anxiety, however, parents feel that home monitoring is beneficial; it causes few marital problems, and few parents resent the extra burden involved. Also, new research shows that monitoring for only 24 hours can determine if the infant is at risk for SIDS (l'Hoir et al., 1994; Rebuffat, Groswasser, Kelmanson, Sottiaux, & Kahn, 1994).

How can the SIDS victim's parents and family be helped? Bereavement over SIDS victims shows a similar pattern over time as that for neonatal death: negativism, anger, shock, disbelief, and guilt (see Chapter 4). Following the death of the infant, wives may become more dependent on their husbands for support. This, combined with the possibility that a husband may secretly resent or blame his wife for the death, may cause marital discord (Gruen, 1987). Siblings in the family may also be affected, both because of a sense of loss and because parental preoccupation may detract from the parents' relationship with the older children. Siblings may also suffer from grief reactions similar to those of the parents (McConkie-Rosell & Iafolla, 1993; M. Powell, 1991). In some cases, even professionals, such as nursing staff, who come in contact with the family may also be affected by the death (McCalin & Mandell, 1994).

Parents may contact one of several national groups that have been organized by parents of SIDS victims, such as the American SIDS Institute (www.sids.org) or the National SIDS/Infant Death Resource Center (www.sidscenter.org). These groups are dedicated to medical research, providing support for survivors and public education and informing the parents of their right to an autopsy. Parents should also treat the death as meaningful and rely on the same religious and spiritual rituals that would help them in the event of death for any family member (Fabrena & Nutini, 1994).

PERCEPTUAL DEVELOPMENT

Perceptual development, similar to motor development, is also influenced by the kinds of experiences the child encounters. Lack of exposure to sensory information can impede the experience-dependent articulation of brain pathways for sensory acuity and information processing. The period from 2 to 5 months includes a major shift in perceptual development. During the first 2 months, infants can see, hear, smell, taste, and feel. Newborns have clear preferences for certain types of perceptual experiences, such as looking at sharp and bold outlines of figures or listening to high-pitched voices. In some cases, infants under 2 months can recognize particular patterns that seem to have a meaning to them—looming objects, their mothers' voices and smells—but pattern detection is the exception rather than the rule. Between 2 and 4 months, infants begin to recognize and prefer meaningful patterned stimuli (a smiling face, for example) regardless of its level of intensity, complexity, or sharpness.

Visual Pattern Perception

The visual world comes to us in the form of line, shape, brightness and color. Adults do not perceive these simple features, however; they perceive whole objects. Newborn infants perceive the lines and colors but do not detect the whole object. Adults perceive like a newborn when they are trying to draw or paint an object and they need to break it down into its basic elements. Consider the following figure: 母. Does this mean anything to you? To a Chinese or Japanese speaker, this figure means "mother." To the rest of the world, it is just an interesting shape made by intersecting lines. Before 2 months, many of the things babies see may seem as if they are looking at Chinese without knowing the language.

The ability to perceive whole patterns, rather than lines and shapes, increases dramatically at about 3 months. To discover this, researchers show infants a picture of a figure— usually two-dimensional—during a familiarization period. Then, using habituation procedures (Chapter 5), the familiar figure is replaced with either an unfamiliar one or same figure rotated into different orientations or seen from different angles. Generally, by

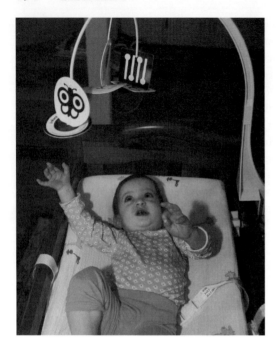

Visual perception develops by seeing the same object from a number of different perspectives. Colorful mobiles with varied shapes are particularly interesting. Research using mobiles has found that babies of this age can tell the difference between a familiar mobile and the same one with only a single piece removed.

Photo: Emily Waterfield

3 months, infants will dishabituate when a totally novel figure is introduced, but not when a different view of the familiar figure is shown (Bornstein, Krinsky, & Benasich, 1986). This means they see the different images as if they were different views of the same figure. If they were just seeing lines, the different orientations of the same figure would appear to the babies to be different figures.

Another procedure is to observe scanning movements made by infants looking at pictures of simple figures, such as circles and squares, drawn with dashed or dotted lines. Infants older than 3 months will scan these figures as if they were drawn with a solid line. If one of the dashed-line elements is drawn at an orientation that does not follow the outline of the figure, infants will scan this element more than the other elements that appear to them to be part of a pattern (Van Giffen & Haith, 1984). This means they expect visual patterns to form into a meaningful whole.

By 3 months, infants are able to visually differentiate familiar from unfamiliar faces from a variety of live and photographed faces of mothers compared to unfamiliar women (Kurzweil, 1988). They also prefer faces from their own ethnic-racial group over faces from a different group

(Bar-Haim et al., 2006; Hayden et al., 2012; Kelly et al., 2005). Infants of this age prefer looking at faces over nonface stimuli that have been carefully constructed to have exactly the same complexity, brightness, and black-and-white contrasts (Dannemiller & Stephens, 1988) (see Figure 6.6). Remarkably, both 3-month-olds and 6-month-olds prefer to look longer at faces that adults have judged as attractive than at faces adults judged as less attractive (Langlois et al., 1987).

Why should infants prefer faces over other types of visual stimuli? Faces have clear outlines and moderate complexity. They are composed of closed circular shapes that babies like to look at. Babies seem to prefer shapes that are symmetrical (shapes in which one side is the mirror image of the other). Faces have vertical symmetry, and 3-month-olds prefer vertical symmetry to horizontal symmetry (Bornstein & Krinsky, 1985).

Is it a fortunate coincidence that faces happen to have just those elements that make them attractive to babies? Or is the visual system designed in such a way that its first preferences direct it toward social objects? It could be that both things are true. We share similar visual systems with other vertebrate species, and most vertebrates have symmetri-

(a)   (b)

(c)   (d)

Figure 6.6   Stimuli Used in Face Preference Survey

Source: J. L. Dannemiller & B. R. Stephens, A critical test of infant patterns preference models, 1988, p. 212. *Child Development, 59*, 210–216. Copyright © The Society for Research in Child Development, Inc.

cal faces. Perhaps both faces and visual systems evolved together in relation to each other. In either case, exposure to faces in the first 3 or 4 months of life changes the patterning of the visual system of the brain, leading to all later abilities to process information from faces, including the identity and emotions of other people (Slater et al., 2010).

Preference for the face continues to develop throughout the first year of life (Maurer, 1985). Three-month-olds can perceive some facial expressions. They are best at recognizing a smile, particularly if it is a wide, open-mouth smile and if their mothers encourage attention to faces (Kuchuk, Vibbert, & Bornstein, 1986). Not until 6 months, however, do infants become competent at recognizing a variety of specific facial expressions and emotions.

Visual Perception of Moving Objects

One problem with the research presented so far is that most of the test stimuli are drawings or photographs—in other words, static two-dimen-sional representations. You might think that babies would be more familiar with moving three-dimensional objects and faces and thus might recognize differences between moving objects better than stationary ones. This seems to be true. Infants at this age look longer at dynamic faces and moving patterns than at static ones (C. A. Samuels, 1985). By 3 or 4 months, infants perceive moving objects as whole units. By 5 months, infants will reach for small moving objects that appear to be in front of larger stationary objects, but do not reach for small moving objects that are behind the larger object (Van de Walle & Spelke, 1996).

By using movement cues, 4-month-old infants are also aware that objects are solid and that they take up their own space. In one study, a platform resembling a drawbridge was rotated back until it hit the top of an object projected on a screen; then the platform stopped. In another condition, the platform kept rotating as if it were passing directly through the solid object. Babies looked longer at the second event, suggesting that they were puzzled by this spatial impossibility (Baillar-

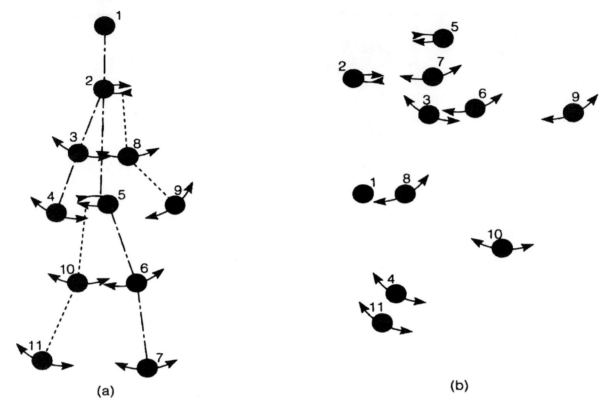

Figure 6.7   Motion Perception Stimuli
Panel **(a)** shows a display of eleven point-lights moving as if attached to the head and major joints of a person walking. The arrows drawn through the points represent the perceived motions of the display. Panel **(b)** depicts the scrambled walker display, which is identical to (a) except that the relative locations of the point-lights are scrambled. Correspondingly numbered points in the two displays undergo identical motions.

Source: B. I. Bertenthal, D. R. Proffitt, & J. E. Cutting, Infant sensitivity to figural coherence in biomechanical motions, 1984, p. 217. *Journal of Experimental Child Psychology, 37*, 213–230.

geon, 1987). In some studies, a moving object is made to disappear behind a small barrier and then re-emerge on the other side. Infants of this age will continue to track the presumed path of the object and "expect" to see it emerge on the other side of the barrier (Bremner et al., 2007; von Hofsten et al., 2007). It appears that infants become increasingly skilled at detecting moving objects and their trajectories over the first 6 months, and this depends upon their ongoing experience with objects (Johnson et al., 2003).

Finally, infants appear to detect complex patterns of motion. Using a "point-light display" technique (Figure 6.7), the movements of a human body walking can be represented by a series of moving lights on the joints. A computer can then invert this light display or move the lights to create displays that would not be biologically possible (joints in incorrect locations and body parts moving in opposite ways). Between 3 and 5 months, infants prefer to look at normal walkers or runners over inverted or biologically impossible ones (Bertenthal, Proffitt, Kramer, & Spetner, 1987; Fox & McDaniels, 1982).

As with the infant's preference for faces, it appears that the perceptual system early in life is disposed to detect real-world information. Infants are able to see whole objects and not just patterns. They are better at detecting relevant information (such as whether the object can be reached and grasped or whether the object is familiar) if they are able to see the object from multiple perspectives and in motion. This is also true of faces: infants take less time to recognize familiar faces from unfamiliar ones when the faces are shown as a video rather than a still photo, or if the faces are smiling, making them seem more real even if not in motion (Otsuka et al., 2009; Turati et al., 2011).

Some have suggested that the perception "this is a whole object" is derived from detecting the object's invariant properties as seen from different perspectives (Ruff, 1978; 1985). **Invariance** refers to those aspects of an object that remain the same regardless of how the object is viewed. For example, a ball always has a round shape no matter how you look at it. A cube has sides of equal length and three visible sides that meet in right-angle corners regardless of which side of the object you are looking at or from what direction. Adults immediately detect the invariances of most simple objects without much thought. It is not clear whether babies do the same or have to puzzle over whether two views of something are indeed the same thing. We also do not know how infants detect invariance (do they compare angles, distances, overall shapes, or what?); but there is no doubt that infants like to seek out invariant properties of objects at a very early age. In other words, the infant is *able* to perceive meaningful wholes because human infants are predisposed to finding the similarities and differences between things; no one has to tell a baby to do this.

Auditory Perception

We saw in the last chapter that infant auditory perception is rather good during the first 2 months of life. Infants recognize and prefer their mothers' voices at birth, for example. By 4 months, infants prefer human speech to nonspeech sounds (Fernald, 1985). Infants appear to be able to detect different emotions expressed in the voice earlier than they can see differences between facial expressions. Five-month-old infants listen longer to positive compared to negative vocalizations, and

they smile more to voices expressing approval and frown more to voices expressing disapproval (Fernald, 1993). They can also detect human sounds like coughing or yawning as distinct from environmental sounds like water running, and the human sounds are processed in the speech-related areas of the temporal lobes, just as in adult conversations (Blasi et al, 2011).

Because the babies cannot understand the content of the speech, they must detect the emotional information—via the medial prefrontal cortex—from the auditory cues alone: pitch, timing, and intensity. The ability to detect emotion from speech improves if the infant can also see the adult's face making an expression that is related to the positivity or negativity of the sounds (Walker-Andrews & Lennon, 1991).

Infants at four months like music. When exposed to consonant (as opposed to dissonant) music, they look more in the direction of the sound and become less motorically active, apparently because they are listening more intently (Zentner & Kagan, 1998). Infants of this age show more sustained attention to maternal singing compared to motherese (maternal speech directed to infants), and they can remember songs for at least a week without hearing them in between (Nakata & Trehub, 2004; Trainor et al., 2004). Infants like play songs ("Eensy Weensy Spider") and lullabies ("Rock-a-Bye, Baby") better if they are sung directly to them in a loving tone of voice, compared to prerecorded songs (Trainor, 1996; Trainor, Clark, Huntley, & Adams, 1997), suggesting that the song is less important to the infants than the way it is sung to them. Infants also direct more attention to their own bodies when being sung lullabies and more attention to the singer when being sung play songs (Rock, Trainor, & Addison, 1999). Perhaps these traditional melodies were developed over many centuries simply by watching how infants respond to the sounds.

As reviewed in the Chapter 4, all of these emotional qualities of speech sounds are supported by developments in the medial prefrontal cortex (MPFC). The lateral prefrontal cortex (LPFC) underlies the ability to perceive the non-emotional aspects of speech. Speed of auditory processing, for example, improves in the first 6 months. At birth, infants can recognize sounds and locate sound sources, but only if the sound is repeated many times or is heard for at least 20 seconds. By 3 to 4 months, sounds can be recognized after shorter exposures, and infants can localize the source of briefly heard sound at wider angles from the midline of the body than they could at birth (Jusczyk, Kennedy, & Jusczyk, 1995; Morrongiello, Fenwick, & Chance, 1990). This means that infants at this age appear to process sounds at about the same speed as adults.

They are also able to recognize the differences of sequences of sounds presented in different orders and by 6 months, they able to detect longer sequences and pick out specific parts of sequences, like a particular word in a sentence (Lewkowicz, 2008; Seidl & Cristiá, 2008). This LPFC speech analysis function no doubt underlies the MPFC abilities to recognize the emotional differences between musical melodies.

Cross-Modal Perception

Infants of this age have **cross-modal perception**, the ability to integrate information coming from at least two sensory modalities. After about 4 months, infants expect sights and sounds to "go together." Infants prefer, for example, to hear a film soundtrack where the visual object's movements and the sound are synchronized, rather than a soundtrack that has been altered (Bahrick, 1988), and they prefer to look at moving faces in which the lips are moving in synchrony with the vocalizations (Patterson & Werker, 1999). Babies prefer to look at visual objects that make a noise compared to silent objects (Lawson & Ruff, 1984). Sound localization is improved by 3 months if the infant has visual cues about the sound source, compared to a sound heard in the dark or made from behind a screen (Morrongiello & Rocca, 1987).

These studies show that by the time infants reach the age of 3 or 4 months, their world is not disjointed. Objects are perceived as coherent wholes. Infants expect the different properties of the same objects to go together, and they will respond by looking away more if things are presented to them in a disjointed form. As we will see later in this chapter, this ability extends beyond object perception to include social communication. When communication patterns are experimentally altered, infants of this age notice the difference and may even become upset.

COGNITIVE DEVELOPMENT

Cognition involves the processing of perceived information. Cognition includes learning and memory and the ability to mentally compare different situations to evaluate their similarities and differences. In actuality, because perception involves memory (the comparison of past and present in the detection of the familiar and of invariant properties of objects and sounds), it is often difficult to separate one from the other. A number of important developmental changes take place in these areas between the ages of 2 to 5 months.

Habituation

From the ages of 2 to 5 months, infants improve in their speed of information processing, due in part to rapid changes in myelination and the experience-dependent formation of synapses, and in part to an increasing ability to focus attention on familiar types of tasks. While a newborn could take as long as 5 or 10 minutes to habituate to a repeating stimulus, by 3 months of age, infants typically habituate within 1½ to 2 minutes. By 6 months, this time drops to half a minute (Bornstein, 1985). Like all cognitive and perceptual tasks, the speed of information processing also depends on the complexity and difficulty of the stimulus and on the infant's alertness at the time of testing.

There are individual differences in the speed of habituation. Infants who are fast habituators at 3 months are more likely to be fast habituators at 6 months (Colombo, Mitchell, O'Brien, & Horowitz, 1987). Infants who are faster habituators tend to have parents who stimulate their ability to focus visual attention (Bornstein & Benasich, 1986). Slower habituators are more likely to have perinatal risk factors: illness, malnutrition, and poor state control (Bornstein, 1985). Faster habituators are more efficient in their information processing (Frick, Colombo & Saxon, 1999). Thus, speed of habituation may be used as an early index of cognitive differences. Although these individual differences seem to be fairly good predictors over a period of 4 or 5 months, they are not likely to predict long-term differences in cognitive development.

Long-Term Memory

We saw in the last chapter that infants have short-term memories lasting several hours or days right from birth. By 3 months, infants can remember situations for up to 2 weeks, as was shown using a contingent learning procedure (Sullivan, Rovee-Collier, & Tynes, 1979). Babies were placed supine in cribs with brightly colored mobiles suspended overhead. Experimenters decided beforehand that they would move the mobile if the baby kicked with either the right or the left foot (but not with both feet). The mobile was moved more the harder the infant kicked, thus increasing the speed of conditioning. On the initial training day, the babies were given about 15 to 20 minutes of training. Then the babies were brought back to the same laboratory a few days later and placed in cribs without any further training. Infants who were tested less than 2 weeks after training managed to repeat the same leg movements they learned during training, although the longer the delay between training and testing, the longer it took the infants to remember to kick in a particular way. After a delay of longer than 2 weeks, infants behaved as if they had never seen the mobile.

If infants are retrained at intervals shorter than 2 weeks, the memory can be reactivated for an indefinite period (Rovee-Collier, Enright, Lucas, Fagan, & Gekoski, 1981). In another study, infants were given a reminder by showing them a mobile 24 hours before 2 weeks had elapsed since their original training. If the mobile was moving, the infants remembered their earlier training when tested the next day, but if the mobile was stationary, the infants could not remember their initial training (Hayne & Rovee-Collier, 1995). On the other hand, giving the infants a reminder by showing them a cloth of the same color that had draped the crib during training was just as effective as the moving mobile in helping them to remember the earlier procedure as much as 4 weeks after training (Hayne & Findlay, 1995). These studies suggest that infants can remember for an indefinite period, so long as they continue to receive nonverbal reminders of the early situation (Rovee-Collier & Barr, 2000).

Infant memory, however, is very specific to the situation in which the initial learning occurs. When babies are retested in different cribs, in the same cribs with different colored bumpers, or with different mobiles, they are less likely to remember the event (Butler & Rovee-Collier, 1989). When infants are retested with different odors in the room or with different music playing, they are also more likely to forget the training (J. Fagen et al., 1997; G. B. Rubin, Fagen, & Carroll, 1998). These findings suggest that familiar, routine environments may be important for infant memory at this age, as they begin to develop a sense of permanence and stability of the world and what to expect from it. The findings also show that infants pick up visual, auditory, and odor cues that become part of the memory for them.

On the other hand, lack of stability in the environment may have negative consequences for cognitive development. Crying and the negative emotion associated with it seem to create a kind of amnesia for experiences associated with the crying (J. W. Fagen, Ohr, Singer, & Klein, 1989). Using a similar mobile-kicking contingent procedure, during training the experimenters substituted a mobile with only 2 components for one with 10 components. Some of the infants cried as a result of this change; others did not. The infants who cried were not able to reactivate the kicking technique to the 10-component mobile even 1 week later. The infants who did not cry when the mobile was changed could easily reactivate the kicking.

Apparently, the emotion associated with a learning situation becomes part of the memory, as do the specific sights, sounds, and smells of the surrounding environment in which the training takes place. This suggests that infants remember whole situations, rather than specific events. These memories can last indefinitely with periodic reminders, but over time, novel aspects of a repeating situation may become integrated into the memory. These findings suggest that infants of this age have a sense of **self-history,** the experience that the past can be connected to the present by means of recreating one's own actions in similar situations.

These findings call for reevaluation of the common observation that people do not remember their experiences as infants, a phenomenon known as **infantile amnesia** (see Chapter 11). To remember specific infantile experiences, one would have to be in almost exactly the same situation and the same emotional state as during the original experience. Since older children and adults are unlikely to ever be in exactly the same kinds of situations as when they were infants (primarily because their perceptual, cognitive, emotional, and physical abilities have all changed), they are unlikely to be able to retrieve early memories *for specific events* (Hayne & Rovee-Collier, 1995).

On the other hand, people may in fact have memories of early infancy, but because it is difficult to replicate the exact context, they may be unable to locate the memories in a specific time and place (Rovee-Collier & Barr, 2000). In one study, children who were 2½ years old were retested in a procedure that had required them to reach for objects in the dark when they were 6 months of age. Compared to infants who did not have the experience at 6 months of reaching in the dark, the children who had the experience were better at the task at 2½ years, even though it is unlikely that these children remembered the actual experience of doing this when they were 6 months old (Perris, Myers, & Clifton, 1990). In a similar study,

2½ year-olds who had experienced a "still-face" experiment (when the adult stops interacting and just stares at the baby; see below) when they were 5 months old looked less at a photo of the person who had done the still-face compared to two other photos. Other 2½-year-olds who did not participate in the experiment at 5 months showed no preference between these faces (Bornstein et al., 2004).

These studies of infant memory provide support for the idea of *participatory memories,* the ability to reexperience a feeling, an odor, a body posture, or a pattern of movement without remembering a specific time or place when it first occurred. Even though the specific time and place cannot be remembered, these memories seem to come from a very early period in one's life. When older individuals have memories in which a sense of familiarity is coupled with amnesia for how, when, and where the memory was acquired, such memories may "feel" baby-like. You may feel something similar while doing the Experiential Exercises.

Piagetian Perspectives on Cognitive Development

The findings on the holistic and integrative way in which infants remember provide support the theories of Jean Piaget (refer to Chapter 1). Piaget viewed infant actions as adaptations to the environment that involve the whole infant; motor, cognitive, and emotional aspects are interconnected. During the newborn period, which Piaget called Sensorimotor Stage I, the majority of the infant's actions are in the form of semi-automatic reflexes. The infant uses reflexes (such as rooting, sucking, and grasping) to adapt to the environment, but reflexes are not rigid and mechanical. We saw in the last chapter that even reflexes can be accommodated to a particular situation, as in sucking on different-shaped nipples or displaying stepping movements only when lying supine.

During the period from about 1 to about 5 months, which Piaget called Sensorimotor Stage II, infants begin to act more purposefully. They are able to recognize the connections between their behavior and events in the environment, as we saw in the research related to making mobiles move when kicking. We know from some studies that even newborns can recognize the connections between their behavior and the environment. For example, infants can be trained using conditioned sucking techniques to suck in a particular way to hear their own mother's voice. However, it takes a long time to train newborns to do this and the training is not always successful.

By 2 to 3 months, the ability to recognize simple connections between behavior and its effect is very well established and can be seen in almost everything the baby does. Piaget noticed this in each of his own three children—Laurent, Lucienne, and Jacqueline. As they discovered the relationship between their behavior and its effects, they would repeat the same behavior many times and often with great delight. Observations 6.1 and 6.2, taken directly from Piaget's observation notes, describe how Laurent at 2 months and 21 days of age repeatedly bends his head back to look at his crib. At about the same age, Lucienne repeatedly coughs for the "fun" of it.

Piaget called these repetitive movements *circular reactions*. During Sensorimotor Stage II, the circular reactions described in the box are called **primary circular reactions**. Primary circular reactions are repetitive movements in which the infant focuses on his or her own actions. In some cases, the actions involve other objects (like kick-ing to get a mobile to move), and in other cases, they involve the infant's own body. The infants at this stage do not appear to be interested in the object for its own sake.

According to Piaget, *the meaning of a particular object or person to the infant is the action and experience the child brings to it*. For example, a rattle means "grasp-able, seeable, suckable." During this stage of sensorimotor development, the rattle is not yet "an *object* to be grasped, seen, or sucked," for that kind of conceptualization of the rattle as object would require that the infant understand the object as if observing it from outside the self, which does not begin until 9 months of age. In Stage II, the "object" is "known" simply by the actions that can be performed on it. Infant actions are not intended to explore the object's properties, but rather to experience their own behavior and its effects. This suggests that infants during this period are developing a sense of **self-agency**, the feeling that they are a causal agent that can successfully affect their own bodies and the environment.

Later in Stage II, infants begin to combine different primary circular reaction schemes into more unified behavior patterns. An example of this is the development of visually guided reaching at about 4 months. Piaget viewed this as the integration of vision, arm, and hand actions: the baby somehow makes the connection between seen objects and his or her own actions. These observations are consistent with the finding that babies of this age have the ability for cross-modal

---

Observations

Stage II Behavior (Piaget, 1952, pp. 70, 79)

Observation 6.1

At 0;2(21), in the morning, Laurent spontaneously bends his head backward and surveys the end of the bassinet from this position. Then he smiles, returns to his normal position and then begins again. …

Observation 6.2

In certain special cases the tendency to repeat, by circular reactions, sounds discovered by pure chance, may be observed. Thus at 0;2(12) Lucienne, after coughing, recommences several times for fun and smiles. Laurent puffs out his breath, producing an indefinite sound. At 0;2(26) he reproduces the peals of his voice which ordinarily accompany his laughter, but without laughing and out of pure phonetic interest. At 0;2(15) Lucienne uses her voice in similar circumstances.

perception, and that their memories are integrated wholes of sights, sounds, smells, and movements. This suggests that infants have a sense of **self-coherence**, the feeling that they and the objects around them are integrated wholes that have distinct boundaries.

One aspect of self-agency and self-coherence at this age is the experience of contingency (see Chapter 5). Two-month-olds are capable of discovering contingencies, and one study has shown that the babies enjoy it. In a study done by Watson (1973), the movements of a mobile were linked to infants' head presses on an automatic pillow. If the infants discovered that the mobile would move with respect to their head presses, they usually smiled and cooed. In contrast, if the pillow was "capricious" and inconsistently rewarded head presses, infants became frustrated and distressed. Other research shows that infants are more likely to display these emotions when people behave contingently than when objects behave contingently (Legerstee, 1997).

Once a contingency is discovered, infants come to expect or anticipate a similar pattern in the future. Infants of this age prefer to interact with strangers who have been trained to respond with the same kinds of contingencies as the infant's mother (A. E. Bigelow, 1998). Related research has shown that if infants are exposed to a visual series of repeating events, they can anticipate the likely next event in the sequence (Canfield & Haith, 1991; S. W. Jacobson et al., 1992; Wentworth & Haith, 1992).

These findings have implications for the kinds of experiences adults should provide for infants during Piaget's Stage II. If babies realize that their environment is controllable—that their own actions will produce predictable responses in the people and objects around them—they will show increasing positive involvement with the world. If the environment is capricious, infants will become distressed, angry, and withdrawn or simply uninterested (Watson, 1973). It is important, therefore, for adults to adapt their behavior to be responsive to infants so the infants will gain a sense of efficacy that will lead to further exploration. In early

infancy, exploration, cognition, and motor behavior are all part of the same underlying developmental process.

The primary circular reactions create powerful motivations for babies to become engaged in the environment. They especially enjoy when adults create highly ritualized and repetitive situations as in feeding, playing, bathing, and diapering. A limitation of babies of this age is that they do not enjoy deviations from the routines, which makes it difficult for them to adapt quickly to new caregivers. Even though Piaget integrated motor, perceptual, cognitive, and emotional aspects of the infant, he failed to recognize the role of adults in supporting infant development. Even before infants can reach for and manipulate objects, adults bring objects into view, manipulate the objects in appropriate ways (like shaking a rattle and turning a ball around), and place them into the babies' hands (see the earlier discussion of supports and resources for motor development in this chapter). We return to these interactive systems processes in the section on social development.

EMOTIONAL DEVELOPMENT

The studies of contingency learning clearly show that the infant's emotions are affected by changes in the contingency of the environment. In this section, we take a closer look at emotional development in terms of three related topics: emotion expression, emotion experience, and emotion regulation. The development of emotional expression involves the study of the behavioral manifestations of emotional experience, the inner world of feelings. Self-control over emotions is called **emotion regulation**.

These three areas of emotional development—expression, experience, and self-regulation—will concern us throughout this book. Many other areas of interest also fall under the general heading of emotional development. These include people's verbal expression of their emotions, their ability to conceptualize their emotions, and their ability to perceive another person's emotions. These abilities mostly apply to the older infant and young child, and the later chapters of this book will touch on them.

Emotional Expression and Experience

Distress, anger, and wariness. Infants were once thought to have all the basic emotional expressions at birth (Peiper, 1963), but these are reflexive movements that disappear after several weeks. A 1-month-old infant has only a relatively small number of functional expressions, and these are primarily related to the emotion of distress. The expression involves frowning (knitted brows with the mouth turned down at the corners). It usually is accompanied by crying, generally with the eyes closed. Younger infants often exhibit a trembling of the lips during crying, as well as a reddening of the face if the cry is intense enough. Chapter 5 described the different auditory characteristics of the types of crying seen in young infants. Adults have a difficult time categorizing the distress expressions of infants under 4 months into recognizable adult emotions, which suggests that infants do not have a fully differentiated set of adult-like emotions (Matias & Cohn, 1993; Oster, Hegley, & Nagel, 1992).

The duration of distress significantly decreases during the first 3 months. In spite of this, adults rate the cries of 6-month-olds as more intense than the cries of younger infants, primarily because the older infants' cries, while shorter in duration, are louder and more energetic (Leger, Thompson, Merritt, & Benz, 1996). After 3 months, infants develop a brief negative-sounding vocalization, usually called *fussing* as distinguished from crying, that accompanies a distress facial expression. Fussing babies usually vocalize for a brief period, then become silent or coo for a while, and then return to fussing (Hopkins & von Wulfften Palthe, 1987). Even though crying lessens in almost all infants over the course of the first year, infants who cried more during the first 3 months, such as those with colic, are likely to cry more on average for the rest of the first year of life (McGlaughlin & Grayson, 1999).

By 4 months, infants may still exhibit intense distress cries, but now they often cry with their eyes open and looking at their parent in particular, an expression that has been interpreted as anger. In fact, the longer infants look, the longer they cry, suggesting that the attention may play a feedback role to increase or lessen the anger (Axia, Bonichini, & Benini, 1999; Moscardino & Axia, 2006; M. D. Lewis, Lamey, & Douglas, 1999). Crying may also be accompanied by directed actions such as kicking, pulling, or pushing, and it may involve few or no tears.

Fear, another expression related to distress, does not appear until later in the first year, but infants at 4 months can show "wary" or hesitant expressions. Infants of this age are capable of turning their heads or looking away from an unpleasant or confusing situation. Their wary or ambivalent expressions consist of an increased rate of gazing away from and looking back at the situation, combined with a reduction of expressions of positive affect (Bronson, 1972; Sroufe, 1979).

Attention and enjoyment. During waking states, infants of 1 month may exhibit a range of expression between alertness and drowsiness. When infants are alert, their eyes are wide and bright, and their brows and mouth may alternate between movement and stillness. Infants of this age have difficulty switching their attention from one thing to another and may stare motionless for long periods. They often fade into brief periods of "dulling." Their eyes, although open and fixed, take on a glazed or dull quality. Smiles usually are not seen during alert states until about 6 to 8 weeks of age.

Around the age of 2 months, a significant change can be seen in infants' facial expressions. They are more complex and animated and better coordinated with events in the environment around them (Sroufe, 1995). When smiling, infants learn cognitive tasks more slowly than when showing an attentive expression without smiling. This shows that smiling corresponds to a non-analytical emotional experience (Rose, Futterweit, & Jankowski, 1999). Attention also changes. Infants look for longer periods and they can more easily

Figure 6.8   Interest and Enjoyment Expressions

(a) Simple attention: Visual fixation in a quiet alert state.

(b) Concentrated attention: Visual fixation with effortful movements of brow and mouth.

(c) Excited attention: Visual fixation with active motor movement of arms, legs, and/or mouth.

(d) Astonished attention: Fascinated and motionless visual fixation.

(e) Smile: Relaxed visual fixation with smiling.

(f) Cooing: Visual fixation, with mouth making the shape of a vocalization, either with or without actual vocalizing.

Source: Manuela Lavelli, University of Verona, Italy.

shift their gaze from one thing to another, apparently due to experience-dependent brain development in the part of the limbic system, prefrontal, and motor cortex that regulates attention and movement (Robertson et al., 2001).

After 2 months, babies also develop new facial expressions of attention and enjoyment, shown in Figure 6.8. In the first two months of life, infants show primarily simple and concentrated attention. After 2 months, more complex attention expressions, as well as smiling and cooing expressions, appear (Lavelli & Fogel, 2005). These developments in the expression of attention suggest that the infant is also developing different attention-related emotional experiences such as concentration, excitement, and astonishment.

Smiling during face-to-face interaction also develops between 2 and 5 months. Beginning at 3 months, smiling occurs in clusters during social interactions. Infants smile four or five times in rapid succession, followed by a relative pause of 20 or 30 seconds, after which a new bout of smiles begins (Fogel, 1982a). By this age, infants show multiple types of smiles that communicate different types of positive emotional experience. A smile involving the raising of the cheeks and some wrinkling around the eyes (called a Duchenne smile) is observed in the context of mother-infant face-to-face play when the infant is held upright and is able to see the mother smiling and talking (see Figure 6.9). A smile that involves an extremely wide-open mouth and dropping of the jaw (play smile) is observed when infants are held closer to the mother, kissed, or tickled (Messinger, Fogel, & Dickson, 1998). Duchenne smiles appear to be related to visually and cognitively pleasurable events (peek-a-boo games, for example), while play smiles are related more to tactile and physically arousing events (like tickling games).

In the period between 2 and 5 months, all types of smiles may occur interchangeably during social play, suggesting that the infant is beginning to experience a complex range of positive feelings (Fogel et al., 2000, 2006; Mendez et al., 2009; Messinger, Fogel, & Dickson, 2001). In addition, about 15 percent of smiling is followed immediately by looking

Figure 6.9   Duchenne and Non-Duchenne Smiles
An infant's non-Duchenne smile (on the left) followed approximately 2 seconds later by a Duchenne smile (on the right) in which the cheeks are raised more prominently.
Source: Daniel S. Messinger, University of Miami.

away from the social partner, which some researchers have interpreted as an early manifestation of "coyness." (Reddy, 2000). Infants are more likely to display coy smiles in the presence of strangers and when they can see themselves in a mirror, compared to interactions with familiar people without a mirror. Although the experience of infants at this age appears to show some awareness of being seen by others, it is not until 18 months that infants show signs of true embarrassment when they see themselves in a mirror. These studies do, however, reveal some kind of emerging sense that babies are aware of the attention of others and it makes the infant temporarily avert their gaze from the other person (Colonessi et al., 2013).

After 2 months of age, infants also begin to express positive emotions through vocalizations. During the first 2 months of life, infants' vocalizations are of three sorts: cry, discomfort, and "vegetative" (Stark, Rose, & McLagen, 1975). The cry is used to express acute distress, whereas discomfort sounds are associated with distress that is not as severe; they are more like fussing or complaining than crying. The infant's vegetative repertoire includes a series of biological noises, such as the cough, burp, sneeze, hiccup, suck, snort, grunt, and sigh. These sounds are all so basic to the biological necessities of the infant organism that there is very little individual variation across infants, nor do they change much in sound characteristics over time.

Somewhere between 5 and 8 weeks, most infants begin to "coo." As distinguished from the other sounds already in the infant's repertoire, cooing is primarily an expression of comfort. If all the infant's sounds are analyzed with sophisticated sound recording and frequency amplitude-resolving equipment, all the auditory properties of cooing can be found in the more primitive forms of sound making. According to Stark (1978), these findings suggest that infants are beginning to take the sounds they made reflexively and recombine them in the form of exploratory vocal activity. Recalling Lucienne's coughing for fun, we see that infants begin to use their voicing in repetitive ways reminiscent of other circular reactions.

Two kinds of infant non-distress vocalizations appear after 2 months: speech-like and non-speech-like. Speech-like sounds are produced in the front of the mouth and have a more resonant quality. Non-speech-like sounds are produced in the back of the mouth, lack projection, and have a more nasal quality. Speech-like sounds—of which cooing is one—increase between 2 and 5 months, while non-speech-like sounds decline (Hsu, Fogel, & Cooper, 2000). Mothers also respond differentially to these two types of vocalization, and the speech-like vocalizations often occur when the baby is smiling, suggesting that speech-like sounds are expressions of positive emotion (Hsu & Fogel, 2001; Hsu, Fogel, & Messenger, 2001)

Emotion is closely related to the social communication system. So, different communicative tasks—different types of play (social-visual versus social-tactile), for example—will require different forms of facial communication and will be accompanied by different types of internal feelings (J. J. Campos, Campos, & Barrett, 1989; Fogel et al., 1992). Just as the infant's cognition is integrated across different perceptual modalities, infants have organized patterns of expressive movements that are integrated across the face, vocalization and body movement that occur in specific types of communicative situations (Hsu & Fogel, 2003; Lavelli & Fogel, 2005; Weinberg & Tronick, 1994; Yale, Messinger, Cobo-Lewis, Oller, & Eilers, 1999). Examples of organized patterns of emotion are positive engagement (positive facial expressions and vocalizations, looking at adult or objects, mouthing parts of own body); attentive engagement (facial expressions of attention, looking at adult or objects, mouthing objects); passive withdrawal (facial expressions of sadness, fussy vocalizations); and active protest (facial expressions of anger, fussy and cry vocalizations, pickup requests, and escape movements). These organized patterns are flexible, dynamic, and tied into the communication system. These patterns also show that infants have some control over the type of social and emotional processes in which they participate; that is, they are developing emotion regulation skills.

Development of Emotion Regulation

Emotion regulation, the ability to control one's internal state and outward expression, gradually emerges over the first years of life. During the first 4 months, increases in emotion regulation are shown by several transitions: a decrease in the overall amount of crying, an ability to easily shift gaze from one thing to another, and the mastery of continuous and repeated bouts of smiling.

If emotion regulation works well, it allows the individual to control the intense or overwhelming aspects of a situation without losing touch with it. A baby may look away momentarily from a positive interaction with an adult to cope with the high level of arousal. Emotion regulation is shown not merely by looking away, but by the overall pattern of looking away and then back in a repeated fashion.

A second important emotion regulation skill that develops in the infant's third month is the smile itself. Studies on the relationship between heart rate changes and the occurrence of smiling have shown that smiles occur neither when the heart rate is increasing nor when it is at its peak, but rather when the heart rate is on the decline (Sroufe & Waters, 1976). Smiling is a relaxation response, and it seems to be a way of reducing arousal without looking away from the situation. On the other hand, after particularly intense smiles, 5-month-olds may need to look away from the situation, an indication that with intense positive emotion, multiple emotion regulation strategies may be required (Stifter & Moyer, 1991).

While infants are developing new ways to maintain attention during periods of emotional arousal, they also are widening the range of arousal levels they can tolerate. At the upper end of arousal, the 1-month-old is able to tolerate stimulation only if it is gentle and slowly changing, whereas the 3-month-old can handle a wider variety of stimulation with more abrupt changes, such as a highly animated, talking adult.

Another contribution to emotion regulation is the baby's developing sensorimotor skills. During this period, the ability of infants to regulate their own distress improves as they can reach for objects and hold them without dropping them (Kopp, 1989). In relation to hand-to-mouth activity, discussed in the last chapter, infants can calm themselves down after 4 months, when they can reliably get the hand to the mouth and keep it there while engaged in other activities (Thelen & Fogel, 1989; Toda & Fogel, 1989). During experimental perturbations of the mothers' behavior (see the Experimental Disturbances of Play Frames sec-

---

Experiential Exercise

Mutual Gazing
by Alan Fogel

This exercise is about the parental role and the infant experience during face- to-face interaction and during movements of the infant toward and away from the parent using either gaze. The class is divided up into pairs who do not know each other very well. Once a partner is chosen, pairs sit on the floor or in chairs facing each other.

1. Explain that now students will play the role of either the parent or the child, after which the roles will be changed. Speaking to the parents: your responsibility is to witness the child with a steady gaze. "Parents" should continue to feel their own emotions and arousal, but it is important to keep those feelings inside and just observe them. Their job is to be there for the child. As adults, they should be able to control their emotions. Speaking to the children: you can do anything you want while sitting there. You can feel free to look at your parent or look away as much as you need or want to. Allow about 2 minutes.

2. Repeat the same process with the same roles, only this time the adult, instead of being attentive, acts distracted by something in the room.

3. Repeat the same process with the same roles, only this time the adult, instead of being attentive, acts intrusive, trying to get the "baby's" attention.

4. Then change roles, repeating the instructions to the parents and then to the children.

5. Sit in pairs and discuss the experience with each other.

tion below), 6-month-olds, but not 3-month-olds, were able to retain their composure by putting their hands in their mouths or focusing their visual attention on what their hands were doing (usually exploring their clothing or the infant seat) (Toda & Fogel, 1993).

Researchers are gradually beginning to recognize that young infants use their whole bodies in emotion expressions and emotion regulations. Emotion regulation derives from the use of some nonemotional action pattern (like reaching for objects) to help the baby calm down when upset (J. J. Campos, Campos, & Barrett, 1989; Kopp, 1989). On the other hand, reaching for objects and other sensorimotor skills brings the infant into contact with situations never before encountered. The ability to reach generates new pleasures and also new sources of frustration. In this sense, emotion and emotion regulation are not mere responses to the situation, but also represent the baby's goals in the situation (J. J. Campos, Campos, & Barrett, 1989).

A final contribution to emotion regulation is the infant's adult partner. Often caregivers can provide just the right support that, when combined with the infant's own abilities, results in a spontaneous relaxation. Not surprisingly, when a baby cries the parent is likely to pick up, hold, rock, touch, feed, talk to, and/or sing to the baby. Parents who did this more frequently and consistently in response to crying at 2 months had babies who cried for a shorter period at 6 months (Jahromi & Stifter, 2007). There is a correspondence between the amount of parental soothing behavior and infant crying duration, with less of both at 6 compared to 2 months (Jahromi, Putnam, & Stifter, 2004).

A small percentage of infants fall into the category of having a regulatory disorder. These infants have disturbances of sleep, feeding, state control, sensory and perceptual processing, and self-calming. In some cases, these infants may be later diagnosed with autism or other developmental disorders (see Chapter 12). In one study (DeGangi et al., 1996) regulatory disordered infants given a 12-week intervention during the first 6 months were compared between 7 months and 3 years with regulatory disordered infants who did not receive treatment. The treatment consisted of training parents to be more responsive to their infant's needs, following the infant's lead, and learning what the infant may want (Greenspan & Weider, 1997). Although all of the regulatory disordered children still had regulatory difficulties at the age of 3 years, the untreated children showed more emotional and social problems, such as depression and aggression.

Emotion regulation, therefore, is the result of both infant and adult contributions and the unfolding of the parent-infant relationship around regulatory issues. We now turn to a review of the adult-infant relationship.

SOCIAL DEVELOPMENT

Infants of this age show the widest range of emotion expressions primarily in the company of adults. By the age of 2 months, infants make distinctly different actions toward adults compared to other animate stimuli. For example, infants are more likely to smile, vocalize, and make relaxed arm movements with responsive adults than with peers (Fogel, 1979), inanimate faces (Field, 1979a), or animate or inanimate toys (Ellsworth, Muir, & Hains, 1993; Legerstee, 1991, 1992; Legerstee, Pomerleau, Malcuit, & Feider, 1987). In this section, we first examine the effects of infants on adult behavior and some cultural differences in adult behavior. Then, we discuss how adult behavior affects infants.

The Effect of Infants on Adult Behavior

Exaggeration. With young infants, adults tend to exaggerate particular aspects of their speech and body movement. Facial expressions are made larger than usual, as in mock surprise and mock sadness. Adults shake and nod their heads in deliberate movements. When speaking, adults raise the pitch of their voices and have wider variations in pitch than when speaking to other adults. This has been found in a large number of different cultures (Fernald & Kuhl, 1987; Fernald & Simon,

1984; J. L. Jacobson, Boersma, Fields, & Olson, 1983; M. Papousek, Papousek, & Bornstein, 1985; Stern, Spieker, Barnett, & MacKain, 1983). Even in languages in which the pitch of a syllable conveys linguistic meaning—tonal languages such as Mandarin Chinese—researchers have found overall increases of pitch when adults talk to babies compared to other adults (Grieser & Kuhl, 1988).

Slowing down and simplification. A second aspect of adult behavior with young infants is the tendency to slow down and simplify behavior. Each action, such as a head nod or a facial expression, is held for a longer period with an infant than with another adult. In addition, when talking to infants, adults leave longer pauses between their individual actions (Fernald & Simon, 1984; M. Papousek et al., 1985). Adults prolong particular syllables and speak more slowly overall, giving their speech a melodic or singsong quality (M. Papousek & Papousek, 1981). Similarly, adults reduce the complexity of their behavior and their speech when talking to infants, using single words instead of sentences or simple actions, such as a single head nod and a wide smile. They also pause and wait for the infant to catch up (Kokkinaki, 2008).

Rhythm and repetition. Adults also use highly repetitive and rhythmic activities. They may say the same word or phrase many times with minor variations or make a series of exaggerated head nods punctuated with a clap or a vocalization. Different rhythms are used depending upon the purpose of the behavior (soothing versus attention getting) and the baby's responsiveness to the adult (Fogel, 1977; H. Papousek & Papousek, 1987). In addition to the coordination of behavioral rhythms, described in this section, there are also physiological rhythmic coordinations, including the matching of heart rhythms between parent and infant, with parallel increase and decreases in heart rate depending upon the level of interactive arousal (Feldman et al., 2011).

Parental speech to infants contains characteristic melodies that are related to ordinary tasks of parent-infant communication. For example, adults use different melodic contours to prohibit, elicit

attention, encourage infant participation, encourage imitation, approve, and soothe. Furthermore, these melodies are similar in many different languages, including tonal languages such as Chinese (M. Papousek, 1994; M. Papousek, Papousek, & Symmes, 1991).

When applied to speech, exaggeration, slowing down, rhythm, and melody make up a package that investigators have called **infant-directed (ID)** speech or more commonly, **motherese**. Infant-directed speech has a higher pitch and more exaggerated contrasts between high-and low-pitched sounds and is more melodic than speech directed toward adults. Not only does it appear to occur in many different languages, but motherese also appears in monkeys (Maestripieri & Whitham, 2007). This is most likely because these speech characteristics fit the kinds of listening preferences of infants after the age of 4 months, and they are more likely to pay attention to adults who use ID speech (Colombo, Frick, Ryther, Coldren, & Mitchell, 1995; Cooper, Abraham, Berman, & Staska, 1997; 1994; Schachner & Hannon, 2011).

The features of motherese even appear in deaf mothers using signed languages. One study found that a mother's signs to an infant, compared to signing to another adult, are significantly slower in tempo, are repeated more frequently, and use exaggerated movements related to each sign (Masataka, 1992). Mothers of deaf infants exaggerate their nonverbal and facial behaviors when with their infants, although they also exaggerate their directiveness and control over the infants and they touch their babies more than with hearing infants (Koester, 1994; Koester et al., 2000). Researchers have identified a nonverbal form of motherese, dubbed "motionese." When interacting with or demonstrating objects to young infants compared to interacting with an adult, adults' movements are higher in enthusiasm, range of motion, repetitiveness, and simplicity (Brand et al., 2002; Brand et al., 2007).

Similar patterns of motherese appear in lullabies. When lullaby melodies from different areas of the world were played without words to adults who were unfamiliar with those particular lullabies,

TABLE 6.4   Summarized Descriptions of Probable Causes of Maternal Laughter

1. *Onset of infant behavior or facial expression.* Child produces a change in bodily posture, movement, or facial expression (smiling, banging a toy, or tilting the head).

2. *Onset of infant vocalization.* Child produces a sound, string of sounds, words, or phrase, excluding those related to bodily functions such as a sneeze or cough.

3. *Onset of infant laughter.* Child laughs aloud with a long or short laugh and accompanying active smile facial expression.

4. *Premastery.* Child strives to achieve a goal, such as standing up, holding a large object, or holding two objects at a time, but does not succeed.

5. *Social games.* A game is a playful social interaction in which a behavior is repeated more than twice. Games are characterized by repetition, nonliterality, mutual involvement, and usually turn alternation. At an early age, mutual involvement may be only attentiveness, and turn alternation may be minimal. There is almost always a lack of negative affect.

6. *Maternal interaction.* The mother engages in any playful social activity, such as shaking a toy near the infant or tickling him or her, that is not repeated more than twice.

7. *Other.* Includes mastery achievement such as walking for the first time, no apparent cause, reaction to a continued infant state such as sleeping, and mother laughing at her own joke or comment.

Source: E. Nwokah & A. Fogel, 1993.

the adults could differentiate them from songs not meant to be sung to infants (Trehub, Unyk, & Trainor, 1993). There are only a few cultures, such as the Quiche Maya in Guatemala, where motherese has not been observed in adult speech (Pye, 1986). Maternal singing tends to be adapted to the infant's states of attention and involvement in the interaction (Delavenne et al., 2013).

Unlike other rhythmic vocalizations, maternal laughter occurs at times when mothers are particularly enjoying their babies and thus may reflect a deep sense of appreciation for specific aspects of infant behavior. As Table 6.4 shows, mothers especially enjoy it when the infant discovers something new or masters a skill, smiles or laughs, or plays a game with her, or when the mother perceives her own behavior as funny or enjoyable (Nwokah & Fogel, 1993).

Matching and attunement. A large share of adult behavior is aimed at matching or imitating the infant's behavior. Although infants can imitate adults, adults imitate babies much more. This imitation may involve matching infant vocal sounds, pitches, rhythms, facial expressions, body movements, and so on (Malatesta & Haviland, 1982;

Moran, Krupka, Tutton, & Symons, 1987; H. Papousek & Papousek, 1987). A concept related to matching is **attunement** (Stern, 1985), in which the adult's behavior is similar to the infant's but not an exact copy. For example, the infant may shake his or her arm up and down in a rhythmical motion. The parent may respond in a different modality, such as vocalizing "yea-yea-yea-yea" in exactly the same rhythm as the baby's arm movements.

Turn taking. Adults also engage in turn-taking behavior with babies. In the early months, infants do not yet have a concept of turn taking. Adults fill in the natural pauses of the infant's actions with their own actions, creating the appearance of turn taking (Brazelton, Koslowski, & Main, 1974; J. Cohn & Tronick, 1988; Fogel, 1977). This adult-controlled pattern of turn taking has been called **protoconversation** (M. C. Bateson, 1975; Trevarthen, 1977). During this early period, adults often overlap their vocalizations and actions with those of the infant, creating a sense of shared emotion, as when adults vocalize at the same time the baby is cooing (G. P. Ginsburg & Kilbourne, 1988; Stern, Jaffe, Beebe, & Bennett, 1975).

Between 4 and 6 months, infants begin to shift to a more interactive mode of behavior: they learn to wait until the adult pauses before beginning their own actions. Infants appear to take the initiative more often by looking in the mother's direction and waiting until she responds before smiling or vocalizing (J. Cohn & Tronick, 1988; Kaye & Fogel, 1980). By about 5 months, then, infants are beginning to become true social partners, rather than merely appreciative audiences for the display of motherese.

These developmental changes in infants coupled with the special features of infant-directed adult behavior, create regularly recurring communication routines called **frames** (Fogel, 1993). Some of the frames that emerge during this period are social games like face-to-face play, tickle and other tactile games, peekaboo, and frames for playing with toy objects. There are also frames for caregiving, such as bedtime, bathing, and feeding routines. Frames are the natural result of everyday communication (see the Co-Regulating with Baby section for more details). While some frames are similar between families (see the section on cultural differences below), parents and infants often develop frames that are unique to their relationship and give it a special meaning and sense of familiarity for the participants.

Maternal touch. Touch is one of the most important, and least understood, modalities of communication with infants. In Chapter 3, we saw that touch can help the recovery of preterm infants. In Chapter 5, we saw how crying and state regulation in the first two months can be soothed and regulated via parental touch. Mothers touch infants as much as 75 percent of the time. There are many different types of touch. Infants influence the way in which parents touch them and these forms of touch change with age. During the first 2 months, parents use more nurturing touch such as stroking and patting. As infants begin to engage more socially, around 2 to 3 months, mothers are more likely to use static touch (just holding the baby or holding an arm or foot), playful touch, and tickling. As the infant begins to use smiling and cooing to communicate, the overall amount of touch declines after 4 months, most of which occurs in the form of static-holing-supportive touch (Jean, Stack, & Fogel, 2009).

The effects of individual differences between infants on adults. Just as infants prefer to listen to adults making infant-directed speech, adults prefer infant vocalizations that are relaxed and resonant and have greater pitch contours. These types of sounds are considered more speech-like (K. Bloom, D'Odorico, & Beaumont, 1993; K. Bloom & Lo, 1990).

Adults are drawn to facial features that have baby-like characteristics, such as large eyes, a round face, thin eyebrows, and a small nose bridge (Zebrowitz & Montepare, 1992). Individual differences in infant facial attractiveness affect maternal behavior. In a study of newborns and 3-month-olds, mothers were more affectionate and playful if their infants were judged by adult raters to be attractive. Mothers with less attractive infants were more attentive to other people besides the infant and were more likely to spend time in care-taking routines rather than affectionate behavior. These differences were not as strong at 3 months as they were at birth. In a related study, mothers of 6-month-olds expected less attractive infants to be more developmentally advanced (Langlois, Ritter, Casey, & Sawin, 1995; Ritter, Casey, & Langlois, 1991). Mothers of infants with cleft lip and cleft palate are less sensitive and more directive with their infants compared to mothers of normal infants (Koomen & Hoeksma, 1992). Research also shows that women during childbearing years with higher levels of female hormones such as estrogen and progesterone, are more likely to perceive babies as cute than postmenopausal women or men (Sprengelmeyer et al., 2009).

Gender differences between infants also affect adult behavior, at least in middle-class white North American and Northern European families. When talking to girls, both mothers and fathers are more likely to comment on the present situation and the infant's current state. Comments about absent or future events are more common when parents talk with boys. Parents use first names more when talking to boys compared to girls (Pecheux, Labrell, & Pistorio, 1993). Mothers of male infants stimulate them more in general, while mothers of girls are more likely to stroke and caress their infants (Grant, 1994). Apparently gender-typical socialization can begin very early in life.

Even at birth, babies differ from each other in emotional responsivity and social behavior. Some babies have highly expressive facial and body movements, and others are relatively poker-faced or inexpressive. Such differences can be found throughout the first year of life (Stifter, Fox, & Porges, 1989). These differences in infant temperament are discussed in more detail in Chapter 7.

Some research has shown that the infants who are less expressive are actually more aroused by stimulation than the more expressive infants. The low-expressive infants tend to have higher overall heart rates, higher cortisol (see Chapter 4; a hormone related to stress and arousal), and higher muscle tension (Field, 1987; N. A. Fox & Davidson, 1988; Kagan, Reznick, & Snidman, 1987). These children have been referred to as inhibited, because they are physiologically predisposed to be highly responsive to stimulation but tend to withdraw from stimulation rather than express signs of engagement or enjoyment. Very similar patterns of individual differences have been observed in infant monkeys (Suomi, 1987). Parents' brains tend to release dopamine, leadings to feelings of pleasure-reward when they see their infant smiling (Stratheam et al., 2008), so more expressive babies are likely to have happier parents.

It is clear that babies make some contribution to how others respond to them. A baby who is easily aroused is likely to withdraw from social interaction rather quickly. Adults often overreact to this withdrawal by trying even more aggressively to get the baby's attention, which in turn causes the baby to withdraw even more (Field, 1987; Gianino & Tronick, 1988). Under most circumstances, adults are highly attuned to the baby's responses. Most adults, regardless of age or parenting experience, are able to correctly identify an infant's state just by hearing the sounds the baby makes in each state

(M. Papousek, 1989). On the other hand, if infants are persistently difficult to handle, mothers rate their own self-efficacy as parents lower than mothers whose infants are not so difficult (Teti & Gelfand, 1991). When communicating with infants, it is important for adults to be aware of their own emotions and the effects of those emotions on their behavior, as described in the Co-regulating with Baby section of this chapter.

In summary, adult behavior is consistently different toward boys and girls, toward attractive and unattractive infants regardless of gender, and toward infants differing in expressiveness. These findings are not surprising if one thinks about Western culture, which encourages independence, values different attributes in boys and girls, and promotes an abstract ideal of beauty in its products and practices (just look at the infants in any advertisement for baby products or, for that matter, at any adult models used in commercial advertisements). Perhaps the surprising point is that these cultural ideals begin to be instilled as early as the first months of life. In the next section, we turn to the topic of cultural differences.

Cultural Differences in Adult Behavior Toward Infants

We have already mentioned that some aspects of motherese may be universally seen in all cultures. In general, because babies are similar around the world, we can expect them to elicit similar sorts of behavior from adults. On the other hand, there are some notable cultural differences in adult-infant communication.

We have already seen how some African mothers interact with their babies using postural manipulation and motor exercise. In a study of infant development in Nigeria, Elauma infants were compared to a group of infants in Oxford, England (Whiten & Milner, 1986). The Elauma are hunter-gatherers. At 3 months of age, Elauma infants spend almost all their time, whether awake or asleep, in physical contact with an adult or within three feet of the adult. When the Elauma infants cry, they are responded to more often and more quickly than are the English babies, and the response from the adult is more likely to be physical than verbal. The Elauma infant is more a part of the mother's everyday life. She carries the baby around with her, and babies often ride on the mothers' backs or sit in their laps while the mothers go about their daily chores. The babies sleep next to their mothers.

The pattern of close physical contact and rapid response to crying (called attachment parenting; see Chapter 5) is common among hunting and gathering cultures worldwide (Konner, 1977). Hunter-gatherer groups move camps several times a year. They are egalitarian with respect to age and gender differences and have little political hierarchy. Another study compared German mother-infant interaction with that of the Nso, a hunter-gatherer group. Once infants began smiling and cooing, the German mother used more distal communication and less touch and physical closeness. The Nso mothers continued to rely on proximal and tactile communication even after smiling began, and were less likely to respond to vocal cues (Kärtner et al., 2010; Keller et al., 2008).

In one study, a hunter-gatherer group (the Aka) was compared with a neighboring agricultural group (the Ngandu) in Central Africa. The Ngandu are sedentary farmers with strong chiefs and clear inequalities in age and gender roles. In the Aka, men and women contribute equally to infant care and other tasks. Roles are divided along traditional lines in the Ngandu. The Ngandu have more infant-care devices, the infants wear more clothing, and are more likely to be physically separate from their mothers compared to the Aka. The Ngandu mothers are more likely to let their infants fuss or cry. Like mothers in the urban cultures, they tend to use more distal play and object play with their babies (Hewlett, Lamb, Shannon, Leyendecker, & Schölmerich, 1998). This study shows that differences in infant care are not due simply to urban versus rural factors, or Western versus non-Western, but rather to differences in lifestyle. The more egalitarian society, used to equality and sharing of resources, seems to promote closer and more lasting contact with the infant.

Japanese mothers also react in different ways to their babies than North American mothers. Japanese mothers spend less time in physical contact with their babies than American mothers when the babies are awake, although Japanese babies sleep with their mothers at night. American mothers hold, rock, bounce, touch, and kiss their babies considerably more than Japanese mothers, and when interacting with babies, American mothers hold their faces closer to the babies (Caudill & Weinstein, 1969; Fogel, Toda, & Kawai, 1988; Otaki, Durrett, Richards, Nyquist, & Pennebaker, 1986; Shand & Kosawa, 1985).

TABLE 6.5 Examples of Baby Talk Used by Japanese Mothers

English Equivalent	Adult Speech	Baby Talk	Explanation
Are you hungry?	Onaka suita?	Onaka shuita	Phonological change
Let's play	Asobimashee	Achobimachoo	Phonological change
Please	Doozo	Doojo	Phonological change
Eye	Me	Meme	Duplication
It hurts	Itai	Itai-tai	Duplication
Get up	Okiru	Okki	Shortening
Hiccup	Shakkuri	Hikku hikku	Mimic sound of action
Lamp	Denki	Denki-san	Use of honorific
Dirty	Katanai	Batchii	Entirely new word

Source: S. Today, A. Fogel, & M. Kawai, Maternal speech to three-month-old infants in the United States and Japan, 1990, p. 287. *Journal of Child Language, 17*, 279–294.

TABLE 6.6   Hindu Beliefs About the Stages of Infancy and Childhood

Stage	Mode of Relationship	Ritual Performed at the End of the Stage
Garbha (fetus)	Symbolic	Jatakama: Birthing ritual
Ksheerda (infancy)	Dyad intimacy (0–1 month)	Namakarana: Naming ceremony; the child meets the father and siblings for the first time
	Dyad in family (1–4 months)	Nishakarmana: First outing, first look at the sun and moon
	Dyad in world (4–8 months)	Annaprasana: Introduction to solid foods, weaning from the breast
Ksheerannada		Chudakarana: First ritual cutting of (early childhood) hair

Source: P. Sharan, One view of the cultural context for the study of childrearing in India, 1988, p. 8. *Newsletter of the International Society for the Study of Behavioral Development, 13*, 1–8.

When they verbalize to babies, Japanese and American mothers are quite different. Over the course of an entire day, Japanese mothers tend to use more negative vocalizations, such as prohibitions and expressions of negative feelings. When actually engaged in a playful interaction with their babies, Japanese mothers use more nonsense sounds and more baby talk, as shown in Table 6.5 while American mothers use more complete sentences and more recognizable adult words. When an American mother might use vocalizations to get her baby's attention, a Japanese mother either uses vocal noises or makes noise with her hands, like clapping and finger snapping (Bornstein, Tal, et al., 1992; Fogel, Toda, & Kawai, 1988; Toda, Fogel, & Kawai, 1990). American mothers are more likely to label objects, while Japanese mothers are more likely to talk about how to incorporate objects into social play (Fernald & Morikawa, 1993).

Navajo mothers rarely talk to infants, although they are responsive to babies' cries and touch the babies a great deal. Traditional Navajo keep babies more physically distant from their mothers with the use of cradle boards (Callaghan, 1981; J. S. Chisholm, 1983). Similar patterns of behavior have been observed among the Maya Indians of Mexico (Brazelton, 1977).

In the Japanese and Native American cultures, adults believe, as did the seventeenth-century European romantics, that infants are precious and innocent beings who are close to God, and that they should generally be kept quiet and not influenced by adults until they begin to make some of their own initiatives, around the age of 6 months. This "hands-off" respect for the infant's autonomy and individuality is not found in the West. Influenced by John Locke's seventeenth-century idea of empiricism, we try to affect sleeping, feeding, and interactive social behavior from an early age. We want our babies to be scheduled, to smile at us, and not to cry (Fogel, Stevenson, & Messinger, 1992). American and European adults especially like to encourage independence through didactic (teaching) behaviors leading to infant socialization (Bornstein, Tamis-LeMonda, et al., 1992).

The East Asian (Indian) philosophy of child rearing is summed up in the elaborate rituals performed for infants in Hindu culture in India (see Table 6.6). Indian families tend to keep the babies quiet and introduce them very gradually to the world. This introduction does not begin in earnest until 6 to 9 months, when early childhood is considered to begin. Indian mothers talk to and touch their babies more than the Japanese do. Indian mothers are more likely to create closeness with the infant by overlapping vocalizations (rather than turn-taking), and more physical closeness, compared to North American infants (Gratier,

2003). Infant massage is commonly practiced in India, and even the mothers receive regular massage from their female relatives.

Some of the recent interest in somatic awareness and touch therapies in North America and Europe (see Chapter 12) been adapted from ancient Indian somatic practices such as Yoga, Buddhist meditation, and massage. Chinese and Japanese somatic awareness methods such as tai chi, judo, kendo, and zen also have their origins in ancient Indian culture.

The Effects of Adult Behaviors on Infants

We do not know to what extent parents' use of motherese and related verbal and nonverbal baby-directed communication actually contributes to infant social and emotional development. A large number of studies have documented correlations between mother behavior during social interaction and infant behavior at the same age and also at later ages. Unfortunately, it is impossible to determine whether these correlations result from the effects of the parents on the infants or from differences between infants that may affect the way the parents behave.

Some research, however, asks mothers to modify their normal behavior with their infants so that the effect of such changes on the infants can be assessed. These studies reveal that beginning at 2 months of age, babies seem highly sensitive to how others interact with them.

The effect of adult contingent responsiveness. Contingency refers to the responsiveness of the adult to the infant's behaviors. A contingent response is an appropriate one that immediately follows some infant action, like a maternal smile following an infant's smile. When responses are contingent, infants tend to smile, coo, and look more at the adults. When responses are noncontingent, infants are more likely to fuss, cry, or look away (Bigelow & Rochat, 2006; Legerstee & Varghese, 2001; Striano et al., 2005; Yale et al., 2003). Infants also look and smile more when adults are producing

the kinds of exaggerated behavior described earlier, such as motherese (Cooper, Abram, Berman, & Staska, 1997).

Experimental disturbances of play frames. The infant's reaction to contingent responsiveness can also be assessed by experimentally perturbing interaction sequences during normal play frames. In one type of study, infants and mothers play face-to-face games with each other, but instead of actually being face-to-face, they are each viewing a videotaped image of the other. Under these conditions, the infants respond normally. The researchers then show the infant a videotape of the mother playing with the infant that was made on an earlier occasion. In this condition, the mother's behavior is more or less the same, but she is no longer responding contingently to the infant. When this occurs, infants decrease the amount of smiling and gazing at the television monitor compared to when they were interacting "live" (Hains & Muir, 1996; L. Murray & Trevarthen, 1985; Nadel, Carchon, Kervella, Marcelli, & Plantey-Reserbat, 1999).

In another type of study, peekaboo games are played with infants, some in the normal way and other times in a disorganized way, such as by saying "peekaboo" before covering the face or not uncovering the face at the expected time. Once again, infants smile and gaze more when the frame is organized in the expected way compared to the disorganized play (Fogel et al., 2006; Rochat, Querido, & Striano, 1999).

In another type of study procedure used with babies between 2 and 5 months, the mother is asked to play with and talk to her baby as she might do at home. After several minutes of positively toned play, the experimenter asks the mother to perturb her behavior by ceasing to talk and holding her face in a neutral, nonexpressive pose. This is called the **still-face** procedure.

What do babies do when confronted with this unexpectedly unresponsive mother? Some babies continue to smile and look at the mother for a few seconds; then they stop smiling and look away from the mother for increasingly longer periods of time. If the distorted mother behavior goes on for more than a few minutes, the baby becomes increasingly distressed and withdrawn. When mothers are asked to resume their normal interactions, most of the infants begin to cry if they have not cried already, perhaps with the intent to communicate the prior distress (J. F. Cohn & Tronick, 1983; Toda & Fogel, 1989; Tronick, Als, Adamson, Weise, & Brazelton, 1978). The same effects are observed in different cultures (Kisilevsky et al., 1998) and with both mothers and fathers (Braungart-Rieker, Garwood, Powers, & Notaro, 1998; Kisilevsky et al., 1998).

At the age of 3 to 4 months, infants are more distressed at the still face than at separation from the mother (Field, Vega-Lahr, Scafidi, & Goldstein, 1986). Babies get equally upset if the still face is posed by the live mother or an image of the mother over closed-circuit television, but there is no change in the infants' behavior if the television mother continues to be expressive while the sound is turned off (Gusella, Muir, & Tronick, 1988). Apparently, it is the sight of the unresponsive mother, rather than the absence of the mother, that is upsetting to the babies (Striano, 2004). In addition, the still-face suppresses the parasympathetic (relaxation) nervous system (the vagus nerve pathway) and increases the level of cortisol, both signs of a physiological stress response (see Chapter 4; Haley & Stansbury, 2003; Moore & Calkins, 2004).

In another variant of the procedure, mothers are allowed to touch their infants while maintaining the still face. In this case, the effect of the still face on the infant is significantly less noticeable. When being touched during the still face, infants continue to smile and gaze at both the mothers' hands and face. This effect is helped by the fact that the mother's touch during the still-face activates the parasympathetic nervous system (and also possibly oxytocin, a relaxation hormone) and the infant uses more self-soothing forms of touch—stroking, hand-to-mouth, etc.—as well (Jean & Stack, 2009; Moszkowski, Stack, & Chiarella, 2009; Stack & Arnold, 1998; Stack & LePage, 1996; Stack & Muir, 1992). Therefore, touching can compensate for the sight of an unresponsive mother. Touching

that is affectionate and soothing can help infants regulate emotions even under normal circumstances (Hertenstein, 2002; Moreno et al., 2006). If both of the infant's parents are present and the parent with whom the infant is interacting is asked to perform a still-face, the infant turns to the other parent and begins to interact normally (Fivaz-Depeursinge & Corboz-Warnery, 1999).

Finally, if mothers are more sensitive and contingently responsive during the normal play episodes, infants recover more quickly following the still-face episode and these infants show less physiological activation of the sympathetic and cortisol systems (Bigelow & Walden, 2009; Conradt & Ablow, 2010; Haley & Stansbury, 2003; Kogan & Carter, 1996; Lowe et al, 2012; Moore & Calkins, 2004; Moore et al., 2009). It could also be the case, however, that infants who have poor physiological regulation are less responsive to maternal contingencies and more highly reactive to interactive disturbances, because physiological reactivity in the newborn period predicts the infant's responsiveness to the mother at 3 months (Feldman, 2006).

These studies reveal that infants are certainly sensitive to changes in contingency and breaks in communication frames. In addition, infants also seem to be able to recover from such breaks by simple interventions such as having access to touch or to another adult. More serious effects on the infants are seen when parental unresponsiveness goes on for a long period of time and there is no one else to whom the infant can turn.

The effects of maternal depression and other mental illness on infants. Even though the still-face is a very brief intervention, it produces both behavioral and physiological effects. These effects are relatively short term as the infant calms down following the experiment. One might expect that long-lasting maternal nonresponsiveness, such as with maternal depression, may have serious consequences for infant brain and psychological development.

Like all adults, mothers can suffer from mental illness. About 10 to 20 percent of mothers are clinically depressed during the infant's first year of life. Maternal depression has a strong effect on infants, since its main symptom is a lack of emotionality. Depressed people are not merely sad; rather, they are characterized by a flat emotional tone and preoccupation with themselves. A depressed mother's sleep and appetite may change, she may resort to substance abuse, she may not be able to concentrate or lose interest in the normal tasks of childcare, and she may feel worthless and inadequate as a mother (Ostler, 2009). These factors make depressed mothers less responsive as parents, which can be a major problem (Josefsson et al., 2001). This also means that most of the research on post-partum mental illness is focused on depression. Other forms of mental illness will be discussed later in this section.

In developing countries with more poverty, stress, malnutrition and lack of equal rights for women, the rate of maternal depression and the risks for infants are considerably higher. Maternal depression rates in developing countries can be as high as 50 percent and lead to higher risk for mothers including disease, domestic violence, and social stigma. Infants of depressed mothers in developing countries are more likely to be underweight and stunted, developmentally delayed or disabled, and will have life-long risk of poor educational and job performance, and poor health (Surkan et al., 2011; Wachs et al., 2009).

Depressed mothers worldwide, when interacting with infants under 6 months of age, do not use the exaggerated and positive actions typical of normal mothers, including a lack of animated talking and singing (Beebe et al., 2007; de l'Etoile & Leider, 2011; Kaplan, Bachorowski, & Zarlengo-Strouse, 1999); they are less affectionate and show more negative forms of touch, such as poking and pulling (Fleming, Ruble, Flett, & Saul, 1988; Malphurs, Raag, Field, Pickens, & Pelaez-Nogueras, 1996); they are not often contingently responsive to their babies (Donovan, Leavitt, & Walsh, 1998; Zlochower & Cohn, 1996); they rate their infant's behavior more negatively than non-depressed mothers (Field, Morrow, & Adelstein, 1993; Field, Grizzle, Scafidi, & Schanberg, 1996; C. R. Fox & Gelfand, 1994); they tend to hold their babies on the right (less emotional) side (see Chapter 5;

Weatherill et al., 2004); or they alternate between disengagement and intrusiveness (J. F. Cohn, Matias, Tronick, Lyons-Ruth, & Connell, 1986).

Depressed mothers have trouble tracking the activities of their infants and may fail to protect them from potential dangers by letting the babies fall off their laps, for example, or letting them get into electrical equipment. Compared to nondepressed mothers, depressed mothers report having more parenting stress, more daily hassles, less marital satisfaction, and less social support (C. R. Fox & Gelfand, 1994; Gelfand, Teti, & Fox, 1992; Simons, Lorenz, Wu, & Conger, 1993).

Infants of depressed mothers are more likely to be fussy, to show more negative facial expressions, to have low levels of physical activity, and to be withdrawn. They orient less to their mothers and gaze less at them compared to infants of nondepressed mothers, and they are less able to discriminate between familiar and unfamiliar objects, and between one or another facial expression. These infants are more agitated during still face experiments, showing more reactive forms of withdrawal. Infants of depressed mothers also have higher levels of circulating cortisol as well as asymmetries in brain activity indicative of a withdrawn mood state. These patterns can be seen even when these infants interact with nondepressed adults (Bornstein et al., 2011; Bornstein et al., 2012; J. F. Cohn et al., 1986; J. F. Cohn, Campbell, Matias, & Hopkins, 1990; Dawson et al., 1999; Field et al., 1988; Field, Healy, & LeBlanc, 1989; S. Hart, Field, Letourneau, & Del Valle, 1998; N. A. Jones et al., 1997; Moszkowski et al., 2009; Pickens & Field, 1995; Skothiem et al., 2013).

There is some controversy, however, about the long-term consequences of maternal mental illness for the infant. Most of the studies showing infant depression when interacting with nondepressed adults have used adults who are unfamiliar to the infant, which could account for the less than positive behavior of the infants. When infants of depressed mothers are observed interacting with their nondepressed fathers or with familiar nursery school teachers, these infants do not show signs of depression. In fact, these infants seem to "perk

Case Report
Maternal Depression

Prior to taking this class, I had never spent much time talking to my mom about my infancy or early childhood. It was when I told her about this project and began to interview her that the question came to me. I asked her if there was anything that stood out to her when she thought back to early memories of me that might be interesting for me to investigate. Her expression immediately became solemn and she told me that she had felt guilty about one aspect of my infancy for a long time. I had extreme colic for the first six months of my life and she felt poorly about how she had coped with it. Apparently my older sister (her first born) had colic too, and she had done everything in her power to keep her from crying. She soothed her, rocked her, distracted her, talked to her, fed her and any other idea that came across she tried. When I was born with colic she just didn't feel she had the capacity to do the same for me. On top of this, she became pregnant when I was just six months-old. The odd thing was that as soon as she found out she was pregnant, my colic went away but she was now preoccupied with the idea of having another baby so soon. My younger sister was born when I was just 15 months old, giving my mom three children under the age of five to take care of. To this day she still feels like I was never given the amount of time and attention I deserved.

At the beginning of each exercise my general response is mistrust, "a clenched stomach" and a "hot face". I initially feel removed from the exercise, which I think is a way of protecting myself when I feel a little vulnerable and insecure. As a child I don't think I had the capacity to mentally remove myself from a situation the way I do now, so instead I would physically remove myself by hiding. I truly am the result of a neglected childhood, but I am working in my adulthood to create secure attachments and an open heart.

I have a really hard time asking for help and an even harder time receiving help. In conducting an interview with my boyfriend, he said that when I feel sad, hurt, or in some way unloved, I get mad before I express what I'm really feeling underneath that. He also says that when I get moody he knows that it's best to give me space for at least an hour. Then, when we come back together he knows I'll be more level-headed.

My first memory of feeling this way from about four years old, wanting to be held by my mom but feeling like it would be a burden to ask her. This continued on through elementary and up until my adulthood. I'm pretty sure it started in infancy, possibly due to the fact that my mom was pregnant and very preoccupied with my older sister when I was only six months old. In some ways this can be considered a good thing. I have been a very independent person for a long time. In other ways, I think it can be detrimental when I really do need help but am unable to ask and receive it. Another characteristic that may have originated in infancy is the way that I suppress my anger. In a way it is an effect of not being able to ask for help. When my needs aren't met, it's hard for me to ask for them to be met (because I feel like they aren't going to be), then I just become angry in an unexpressed subtle way. I had a major temper as a child because of this. I would hold it in, hold it in, hold it in, and then explode!

My strongest memory from my early childhood is of me standing with my arms extended upward toward my mom. In this memory, I am crying heavily and begging my mom to hold me. She is on the phone not looking down. This was a reoccurring theme for me as a child. I would almost always end up on the floor crying myself to sleep. I do believe that this really did happen because I have confirmed it with my mom. She said that she had learned from some friends that if you don't respond to your child when they're crying and whining that eventually they will stop asking for things that way. In my opinion, this can be very traumatizing for a child at such a young age. Children are only beginning to regulate their negative emotions at 12 to 18 months, but clearly unable to stop themselves from crying when feeling upset, unsettled or needy.

All of this research and reading has really affected my understanding of myself today by helping me to, first of all, become aware of some of my patterns of responding and behaviors. In addition, the research has helped me to understand where these responses may have originated from, my infancy. However, in my interviews my family did say that after my colic I became a very bubbly and sweet hearted toddler. I was always dancing and playing with bugs. I loved my little sister and was very energetic. Maybe the relationship I had with my dad and the relationship I had with my grandparents when they came around helped me to cope with the neglect I got from my overwhelmed mother.

up" and be ready to engage and learn with others (Kaplan et al., 2004; Kaplan et al., 2010; Pelaez-Nogueras et al., 1994). A large-scale demographic study of 262 families found no significant effects of maternal mental illness on infant behavior at 4 and 12 months (Seifer, Sameroff, Anagnostopolou, & Elias, 1992). Effects on infants are more likely to show up if their mothers remain depressed over many years and if the infants have few opportunities to interact regularly with nondepressed adults. These effects include alterations of brain development (enlarged amygdala and heightened fear; higher levels of cortisol), and increased risk for childhood depression (Lupien et al., 2011).

It is important to note that fathers are just as likely to be depressed or show other mental illness as mothers (Paulson & Sharnail, 2010), which can also affect infants in similar ways as maternal mental illness. Fathers, however, are less likely to be the primary caregiver in most families, so that maternal mental illness is typically the more significant risk.

Maternal stress and anxiety is another factor that contributes to poor mother-infant communication. Between 9 and 30 percent of mothers suffer from serious post-birth anxiety, usually brought on by the stress of pregnancy and parenthood. Anxious mothers show excessive worry over childcare, health, and work. They are irritable, carry a lot of muscle tension, and can be restless. Extreme forms of anxiety include panic attacks and hyperventilation (Ostler, 2009).

We saw in Chapter 3 that stress-anxiety during pregnancy can affect the fetus. Mothers who are stressed after birth often over-, rather than under-arouse their babies (Kaitz et al., 2011). These mothers can be hypervigilant for signs of worry, but they do not recognize infant cues to slow down or to change behavior (Beebe et al., 2011). When the infant looks away, rather than waiting patiently for the infant to self-regulate and look back, these mothers "go after" the infant, trying desperately to get the infant's attention because the mother takes the infant's self-regulatory behavior as a sign of rejection. Her behavior creates stress and physiological arousal for the baby, who begins the neuroception patterns of flight or freeze (see Chapter 4). This in turn makes the mother more anxious and more insistent, creating a mutually escalating spiral of "chase-and-dodge," resulting in neurophysiological and emotional dysregulation (Beebe, 2004). Left untreated, these dyads go on to develop an insecure attachment relationship (see Chapter 8).

Other forms of maternal mental illness occur less frequently and the effects on infants have not been studied in sufficient detail. These include obsessive compulsive disorder, eating disorders, bipolar disorder and psychosis. These are serious conditions that can be dangerous for mother, infant, and family. Extreme neglect, violence and abuse, and even death can result from these conditions. Early detection and treatment is necessary to protect everyone in the family (Almeida et al., 2009). These mothers should be under some form of psychological or psychiatric treatment. Infants of mothers who are in treatment, including psychotherapy and/or medication, are significantly less likely to be affected by the mother's mental illness (Weikum et al., 2012).

A number of intervention programs have become available (Almeida et al, 2009; McKay et al., 2009). One type of program teaches mothers to focus on childcare tasks, to pay attention to the needs of their infants, and to use touch in addition to facial and vocal behavior (Leitch, 1999; Pelaez-Nogueras, Field, Hossain, & Pickens, 1996). In one such program, the therapist makes a videotape of the mother and infant interacting. While watching the video with the mother, the therapist can point out times when the baby withdraws and teach the mother to regulate her own behavior while helping the baby (Beebe, 2004). Another type of intervention program focuses on increasing positive moods in the mothers and infants. This can be accomplished either by giving infants and/or their mothers daily massages or by using music therapy (Field, 1998; Field, Grizzle, Scafidi, F., & Schanberg, 1996). Sensitive touch, apparently, can partially alleviate the effects of negative mood for mothers and for infants during periods of maternal unavailability.

In summary, during play frames, parents modify their behavior in a way that infants can most readily appreciate, and infants' smiling and gazing encourage the parents to continue. During everyday communication, the mutual influence is co-regulated and dynamic. The effects of one partner on the other can only be determined by looking at individual differences between infants (such as infants who are difficult) or between parents (such as maternal depression) or during experimental perturbations of adult behavior. During the process of interacting with people and objects, infants of this age are beginning to develop a new sense of themselves, called the ecological self.

Self-Awareness: The Sense of an Ecological Self

We know that infants of this age perceive objects and people as coherent wholes. They perceive familiar patterns of interaction—frames—as coherent wholes, and they get upset when those patterns are altered. We also learned that infants of this age practice a form of self-exploration, the primary circular reactions by which they feel themselves move and act. Given these abilities, can young infants perceive themselves as a coherent entity?

The traditional test of self-recognition is done by secretly putting a spot of red makeup (rouge) on the infant's forehead and placing the infant in front of a mirror. Touching the red spot while looking in the mirror is taken as evidence that the infant recognizes his or her own image in the mirror. Infants do not pass this "rouge test" of mirror self-recognition until 18 months (see Chapter 10).

Many infancy researchers now believe that infants between 2 and 5 months can also recognize themselves as separate and whole individuals, but not by their image in a mirror. We also saw, in Chapter 4, that one of the essential functions of the infant's brain is to feel and sense the inner condition and the boundaries of the body. Infants under 6 months of age do have some type of self-awareness: what is called an ecological self. This conclusion is based on some of the research already reviewed in this chapter on infant perception, cognition, emotion, and social behavior. The ecological self has four basic features (Kaye, 1982; Neisser, 1991; Stern, 1985):

1. *Self-agency* is the sense that one is capable of generating one's own actions and expecting that these self-generated actions will have consequences, such as the sense that it gets dark when the eyes are closed or the arm moves when one wants it to move.

2. *Self-coherence* is the sense of being a whole physical entity with boundaries and limitations, such as sensing the difference between touching someone or something and being touched by someone.

3. *Self-affectivity* is the sense of having inner emotional feelings that routinely go together with specific experiences, such as feeling happy when one's mother approaches and sad when she leaves.

4. *Self-history* is the sense of enduring, of having a past, of going on even through changes, as when one acts and feels in similar ways with familiar people or in familiar situations.

Each of these four aspects of the ecological self is experienced *in relation to* something else. One senses self-coherence, for example, by feeling where one's own body ends and where the environment begins. An ecology is a system of relationships, as in the ecosystem of plants and animals. Plants and animals cannot live without each other. They exchange oxygen and carbon dioxide. Animals eat plants and plants depend upon animals (worms and insects) to decompose their remains to create soils in which the plants can grow. So, while plants and animals are mutually interdependent, they each have their boundaries and can be identified one from the other.

Infants (and adults) can see some part of their own bodies—their nose, at a minimum—at all times in their field of vision. You can check this by closing one eye and looking straight ahead: you will see your nose in your peripheral vision. This means

For a baby of this age, the act of touching the toes is not automatic. It takes a while for the baby to focus on the task of discovering (self-agency) where to find the toes with the hands (self-coherence), to remember how to do it each time (self-history), and the discovery is usually accompanied by enjoyment at the achievement (self-affectivity).

Photo by Emily Waterfield

that at the same time you are seeing things in the environment, you are also seeing part of yourself. Thus, your perception of the environment is also a perception of yourself in relation to the environment (Fogel, 1993; J. J. Gibson, 1966). This is why this early sense of self is called the ecological self, the self which is sensed as being situated in relation to the environment. **Self-agency** is the sense of the relationship of one's action and its effect on the environment. **Self-affectivity** is the sense of one's emotions as experienced in the company of another feeling person. **Self-history** is a sense of the relationship with one's past (Fogel, 2000; Trevarthen & Aitken, 2001).

Cross-modal perception, the relationship between the different senses, is one source of the ecological self. By 3½ months, infants begin to watch their hands moving in front of them. Because they can also feel their arms and hands making these movements, it is likely that this cross-modal experience gives the infants a sense of self-recognition through self-coherence. Babies recognize their hands as their own because the hands are the same ones the babies have been feeling for months (Neisser, 1991; Stern, 1995). In a similar way, infants can recognize their own sounds because their different forms of vocalization (contented or distressed) will be cross-modally associated with different internal feelings (Gustafson, Green, & Kalinowski, 1995).

Young infants also explore their own bodies, feeling the relationship between the touching hand and the part of their bodies that is being touched. In the first few hours of life, newborns touch their own head in an ordered sequence beginning with the mouth, then moving to the face, head, ear, nose, and eyes. This process occurs only when the infant is awake (Kravitz et al., 1978, as reported in Butterworth, 1990). As described in Chapters 3 and 5, just prior to hand-to-mouth contact, late-term fetuses and newborns will open their mouth in anticipation. Once infants can reach, around the fourth month, they self-explore by touching different parts of the body, beginning with the fingers and ending months later with the toes (Kravitz et al., 1978, as reported in Butterworth, 1990).

Experiential Exercise

The Ecological Self
by Ilse de Koeyer

As humans, we can see part of our bodies in our field of vision at all times. You can try this by closing one eye and looking straight ahead: you will see your own nose. Thus, whenever you perceive your environment, you perceive yourself— parts of your body, its boundaries, and the quality and aliveness of your own movements. Perceiving the environment is co-perceiving yourself. The ecological self is the sense of self as situated in the environment. Starting at least around 2 months and probably from birth, young babies already have a sense of themselves in this way. This sense of self is still present in adults, but much more in the background of experience. You can explore your ecological sense of self during everyday activities.

1. Self-agency: the sense that your own actions will have consequences (closing your eyes and it gets dark; moving your arm when it wants to move). You may notice this most when your movements are blocked or thwarted.

2. Self-coherence: the sense of being a whole physical entity with boundaries and limitations (sensing the difference between touching and being touched; moving your hands and seeing them move at the exact same time). An example of this in adulthood is when you move something and at the very same time something falls behind you. You may wonder "Was that me?"

3. Self-affectivity: the sense of having emotional feelings that routinely go together with certain experiences (seeing mom and feeling happy; feeling sad when she leaves). Do you get a warm feeling when you see a loved one, or some other feeling? Do you have a sense of security when you get home, or some other feeling?

4. Self-history: the sense of the relationship with your past, the sense of familiarity with certain people or situations you find yourself in. This characteristic is part of the 3 others. For example, your body knows exactly how to sit down on a chair or how to get into the car. Or you may feel a sense of familiarity when you come home or see a loved one.

The ecological self extends to the use of tools or other objects. For example, when you use a pair of scissors, they become an extension of yourself. A good example is driving. As you move around in your car, it is as if it becomes part of you. You may notice a lack of agency, for instance, when you try to start your car and it doesn't respond. Also, you may find that your sense of your ecological self feels different when you walk, ride on your bike, or drive. In all of these situations, your body moves around in different ways, and this may make you see and notice different aspects of the environment. Experiment with moving around in different ways (fast, slow, careful, large or small movements, etc.) and experience the differences in how you perceive yourself in the world.

In one experiment, 3- to 5-month-old infants were shown videotaped images of their own legs. The video cameras were suspended above the infants to photograph the legs. The infants could see the video image of their legs, but they could not see their own legs directly. The infants were wearing striped leg-length socks to make their legs visually salient. Using this method, the researchers could manipulate the video image to show the infant's legs either as the infant would see them normally or in mirror image, with the right leg on the left side and vice versa. Infants gazed longer and kicked more to the reversed mirror image of their legs, suggesting that they could recognize the normal configuration of their own bodies and were curious about the unusual-looking reversed legs. The increased kicking also suggests that the infants were trying to figure out if the video legs were indeed their own (Rochat & Morgan, 1995). Similar experiments have been done using infant arm movements (Schmuckler, 1996).

Finally, babies of this age were shown videos of themselves played back to them live or delayed. The babies could tell the difference between these two situations, suggesting that they are used to the feeling of self-contingency (Reddy et al., 2007). Infants at 5 months apparently sense that their own behavior has an effect on the parent: following a period in which they have been vocalizing during face-to-face play, the infant will become silent during maternal still-face (Goldstein et al., 2009).

Another unique experiment was done with conjoined twins who were born connected at their lower abdomens, facing each other. A week before they were surgically separated at 4 months, researchers noticed that the twins sometimes sucked on their own hands and sometimes on their sister's hands.

When twin A (Alice) was sucking on her own fingers, one of us placed one hand on her head and the other hand on the arm that she was sucking. We gently pulled the sucking arm away from her mouth and registered (in our own hands) whether her arm put up resistance to being moved from her mouth and/or whether her head strained forward to go after the retreating hand. In this situation, Alice's arm registered the interruption of sucking, but she did not give evidence of straining forward with her head. The same procedure was followed when Alice was sucking on her sister Betty's fingers rather than her own. When Betty's hand was gently pulled from Alice's mouth, Alice's arms showed no resistance, but Alice's head did strain forward. Alice seemed, in this case, to have no confusion as to whose fingers belonged to whom and which motor plan would best reestablish sucking. (Stern, 1985, pp. 78–79).

This suggests that the ecological self is experienced in relation not only to the physical environment but also to the social environment. As one interacts with another person, it is possible to feel the part of the interaction that comes from the self in comparison to that part contributed by the other. This is illustrated in Figure 6.10. Even

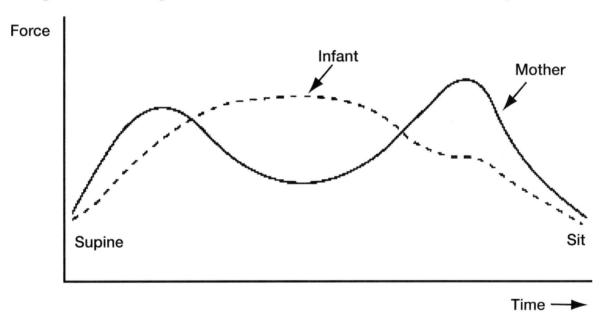

Figure 6.10 Self and Other Experiences During Co-Regulation
The diagram shows the amount of effort exerted by mother and infant when the infant is pulled by the mother from a supine to a sitting position. The dashed curve shows the infant's effort, while the solid curve shows how the mother exerts more or less force depending upon the co-regulated dialogue. Infants feel themselves when they are exerting more force than the mother, and they feel their mothers when the mother's force is more dominant.

Source: A. Fogel, *Developing through relationships*, 1993, p. 18. Chicago: University of Chicago Press. Reprinted with permission from the University of Chicago Press.

during a continuous movement, such as when the mother takes the infant's arms and pulls the infant into a sitting position, there is a co-regulated dialogue in which the effort of the mother and baby changes but remains in balance. Sometimes the baby pulls a bit harder than the mother, feeling himself or herself as an agent in the co-regulation. Sometimes the baby does not have the strength to pull so the mother pulls harder, allowing the infant to feel the mother's side of the co-regulated dialogue. The baby can feel his or her effort as less than, more than, or the same as the mother's.

As with the example of seeing the nose in the visual field, the experience of the ecological self is always an experience of a self in relation to the environment (Fogel, 1993). This kind of participatory co-regulated relationship with another person also gives the infant information about the other person in relation to the self, a sense of **intersubjectivity** (Bråten, 1998; Trevarthen, 1998; Trevarthen & Aitken, 2001). Interestingly, when babies of this age hear their own name spoken, it activates an area of the prefrontal cortex adjacent to the area that responds to eye-to-eye contact with another person (Grossmann et al., 2010).

In summary, the ecological self is a sense of one's body in the environment and the ability to recognize one's own movements. This sense of self comes from the infant's experiences relating to other people, the environment, and their own bodies. You can better appreciate the infant's and your own ecological self by doing the Experiential Exercises at the end of each chapter (see Case Report, this Chapter). Participating in active communication with an infant, as suggested by the Co-Regulating with Baby section, is a way to sense your own compared to the infant's contribution to the dialogue. Infants of this age do not have a cognitive concept of themselves or of their mothers as whole people with different feelings, ideas, and motivations. The emergence of self-concepts begins during the third year of life (see Chapter 11). Thus, when doing the exercises, try to focus your attention on the movements and sensations of your body. To the extent that you can do this

in a *participatory* way—without thought, judgment, evaluation, or conceptualization—you will be connecting with your ecological self, that part of yourself that began when you were between 2 and 5 months old. In the next section, we turn to a discussion of the social and cultural factors affecting the way parents behave.

FAMILY AND SOCIETY

Family systems theory suggests that each member of the family is part of a feedback system with every other family member. In addition, when families have three or more members, the relationship between two of them can affect the third and vice versa. From this perspective, we might predict that the birth of a baby would bring major changes for a family. If it is a first birth, the married couple must adjust to becoming a three-person system. In a three-person family, a new baby creates disequilibrium and necessitates an adjustment by each of the other family members. In addition, developmental changes occur in all members of a family, including the adults and older siblings. In this section, we consider how adults develop through the transition to parenthood that occurs after the birth of the baby.

Developmental Tasks of Early Parenthood

After a child is born, parents must learn to cope with a variety of new conditions, including a total alteration of lifestyle, lack of sleep, and the adjustment of the marital relationship to include new family members. In general, new parents must address four types of problems (Sollie & Miller, 1980).

First, there are the energy demands associated with infant care, such as loss of sleep and extra work, resulting in fatigue. Mothers, if they are the primary caregivers, must continue with the ordinary household tasks while trying to keep up with the baby. Fathers in the United States spend about half the time that mothers do in caregiving, and there are no differences across Caucasian, Hispanic, and African American groups (Hossain, Field, Pickens, Malphurs, & Del Valle, 1997) and no differences across groups differing in income level (Roopnarine et al., 2005). This suggests that there are few ethnic differences in the amount of father involvement, contrary to cultural stereotypes.

Women who are employed before the birth of the child must decide whether or not to continue working after the child is born. Theoretically, men should make the same decision, but in the vast majority of cases, it is the woman who decides whether or not to return to work. In general, women who are most concerned about the potential conflicts between family and work are the most likely to remain home with the infant. The type of work done by the mother outside the home does not predict whether she will stay home or go back to work (Symons & McLeod, 1994). On the other hand, if the mother chooses to work, some work environments are more consistent with the maintenance of positive parenting. In particular, parenting is enhanced if the mother works in an environment that is challenging, includes a complex variety of different people, and is stimulating (Greenberger, O'Neil, & Nagel, 1994; see Chapter 7 for a complete discussion of maternal employment).

Second, new parenthood places stress on the marital relationship. Problems may include less time spent together and perhaps jealousy of the baby for taking time away from the marriage. It may take many months for sexual relationships to become mutually gratifying and still more time before the couple is free to go out alone. Parents generally perceive a decline in marital satisfaction over the first year of the infant's life (Gloger-Tippelt & Huerkamp, 1998), especially if their infant is particularly fussy or has colic (Meijer et al., 2007). Interpersonal conflicts increase over the first year, and parents report less marital cohesion, less partner support, and less ability to cope. In general, couples with more conflicts felt less mutual support and

found it more difficult to cope. These findings suggest that, while not a crisis that ends marriages, the first year of parenthood may be a difficult adjustment period for some couples (Frosch, Mangelsdorf, & McHale, 1998; Levy-Shiff, Dimitrovsky, Shulman, & Har-Even, 1998; Wicki, 1999). Marital conflict and aggression affect infant interactive and physiological behavior, including vagal tone and sleep problems (Graham et al., 2010; Mannering et al., 2011; Parade & Leerkes, 2011).

Third, parents begin to feel the responsibility of caring for and rearing a child. No matter how psychologically prepared one is before the birth, the reality of the child's presence makes clear the lifelong commitment of parenthood. Parents may have doubts about whether they can manage this responsibility and be good parents for their child.

Finally, parents must cope with the additional costs of raising a child, in the form of food, clothing, and education. Just going to see a movie may cost double what it did before the child was born, after the cost of a baby-sitter is included. Whatever income a working mother might earn will be lessened by the cost of the child's daytime care. In addition, parents worry about day-to-day problems, such as infant health and sickness, crying, nutrition, and how to resolve conflicts (McKim, 1987; Wilkie & Ames, 1986).

Predictors of Success in the Transition to Parenthood

In general, the degree to which parents will adopt the parenting role depends on both developmental factors in the life of the adult and concurrent factors inside and outside the family system. Adult developmental factors include the adults' relationships with their own parents, their prior experience with child care, their self-esteem and belief in their own self-efficacy as a parent, and their readiness to have children. Concurrent factors include the marital relationship, other family members, the amount of social support available to the parents, and nonfamily factors, such as income and job satisfaction.

One of the key issues in the transition to parenthood is the effect of the infant on the marriage. Having a baby does not seem to alter existing marital relationships. Couples who have the most conflicts prenatally also have the most postnatally (Cowan & Cowan, 1981). The equality versus inequality of role relationships before childbirth tends to predict the amount of marital satisfaction after birth. In general, couples who are more likely to share responsibilities report higher marital satisfaction and fewer adjustment problems after childbirth than more traditional couples (Cowan & Cowan, 1981; Solmeyer & Feinberg, 2011; Wicki, 1999). Other factors found to increase marital satisfaction following childbirth are a positive and warm relationship with one's own parents (Belsky & Isabella, 1985) and a postbirth experience that is *not* more difficult than anticipated (Belsky, Ward, & Rovine, 1986).

Marital quality itself is strongly associated with both men's and women's involvement in the parenting role. For mothers, a high level of marital satisfaction is related to warmth and sensitivity toward infants, and the amount of father involvement in the marriage plays a major role in the long-term ability of mothers to cope with child rearing. For fathers, marital satisfaction is associated with more positive attitudes toward the parenting role and with more time spent with the infant (S. S. Feldman & Nash, 1986; Vandell, Hyde, Plant, & Essex, 1997). Generally speaking, parents who feel less secure in their interpersonal relationships are more likely to show signs of sympathetic nervous system stress reactivity, which subsequently makes them less sensitive to their infants (Groh & Roisman, 2009; Joosen et al., 2013).

Personality factors also affect adaptation to parenthood. Men who have had a good relationship with their own fathers and who have some personality traits traditionally associated with femininity (affiliation, warmth, nurturance) make better parents. Fathers who are more invested in their careers and who are in midlife are less likely to show warmth toward infants, although they are more involved in the practical and financial aspects of child care, beause they make more money than younger fathers (S. S. Feldman & Nash, 1986; Levy-Shiff, 1994; R. D. Parke & Tinsley, 1987).

Although much has been studied about the physiological changes of women after childbirth, it is only recently that scientists have discovered that men also change their physiology in ways—much like mothers—that specifically prepare them to enter the parental role. Fathers who spend at least 3 hours per day in a parenting role had lower testosterone levels than fathers who spent less time with their infants or men of the same age who were not parents (Gettler et al., 2011). Lower testosterone may sensitize men to infant sounds, sights, and smells, making them more available to their children and less likely to engage in more typical male pursuits. Men with two or more children are also less likely to die from a heart attack in later life. The causes are not known, but high testosterone is often linked to heart disease (Eisenberg et al., 2011).

Interestingly, a very different set of personality factors is associated with parenting for women. Women who have higher self-esteem and a less egocentric orientation, that is, away from their own needs and toward the needs of others, show more nurturance toward their children. Unlike men, women who have children later in life show higher caregiving responsibility and more satisfaction with parenthood. Older primiparous (first-time) mothers are more confident of their skills and may interact more successfully with their babies than younger primiparous mothers (S. S. Feldman & Nash, 1986; Heinicke & Guthrie, 1992; R. D. Parke & Tinsley, 1987).

Although men's involvement in infant care depends primarily on social factors, such as marriage, job, and the social acceptability of parenting, women are more likely to be involved parents without such social supports. On the other hand, women's parenting suffers most when their self-esteem is low or when they experience depressed moods (Belsky, 1984; S. S. Feldman & Nash, 1986; Jessee et al., 2010). In an earlier section of this chapter, we discussed the serious nature of maternal depression for infants.

Co-Regulating With Baby

Between 2 and 5 months, infants are only beginning to become aware of themselves. They do this primarily by engaging in primary circular reactions, repeated explorations of their own bodies and the effects of their bodies on the environment. As part of that environment, you can help babies to discover themselves by encouraging circular reactions and playing co-regulated games involving repetition with variations. In the first month or two, you can gently talk to the baby each time you feed, diaper, or bathe him or her. The infant will come to recognize a particular voice in a particular place; this will contribute to a sense of familiarity and encourage positive feelings associated with recognition.

Gently move the baby's arms and legs up, down, in, and out, playing an "exercise" game. Gently touch the baby's cheeks and other skin surfaces, or blow softly and repeatedly on the arms and abdomen. Remember that at this age, the baby has a limited range of arousal tolerance and cannot handle too much stimulation. You have to be sensitive to cues for termination: head turning, avoidance reactions, crying, and spitting up are common responses to overstimulation. Do not be discouraged if this happens; use what you learned from this experience to adjust your behavior the next time you play. When you feel the play is going right, it is probably because it is also going right for the baby too.

I have already mentioned appropriate kinds of face-to-face play as the baby approaches 2 to 3 months. Remember to imitate, to exaggerate your expressions, to use themes and variations, and to make your responses contingent upon the baby's. You also can buy or design toys that are contingent: mobiles and other objects that dangle and can be swiped at. You can place a rattle in the infant's hand so that he or she can have the experience of "making" noise; or let the baby band a pot with a spoon. Do not try to force the infant into a play situation; just be available to support the infant when he or she wants to get involved.

In general, your job is to encourage the baby to move, see, feel, and hear in a way that is safe and that leads to growing discovery of the self-other relationship. This happens best in mutually satisfying, co-regulated communication frames that are appropriate for this age. Toys are less important now than they will be later, because it is very hard to construct a toy that can co-regulate with the baby.

Do not forget that all babies are different. Whereas one infant seems to be abler to take as much play as you care to offer, another may be slow to warm up and require a much more relaxes and gentle pace. Being aware of your own feelings in relation to the baby is the key to success. You may become impatient, for example, with a baby who is slower to respond to you. Try to examine the source of that impatience in your own life and self-history. Perhaps the impatience is a participatory memory from your own early life, or perhaps it is due to a current stressful situation. You may not be able to rid yourself of impatient feelings, but you can make an effort not to let those feelings interfere with entering into a creative co-regulation with this particular baby. If you can allow yourself to do that, the mutual enjoyment will certainly play a role in helping you to relax, which will be beneficial for both yourself and the baby.

SUMMARY

Physical and Motor Development

• The most rapid period of physical growth in human life occurs between birth and 6 months.

• Some developmental disorders may be detected from standardized tests of infant motor skill.

• Motor performance depends on the level of brain development, on the complexity of the task, and on the types of supports and resources available in the environment, especially from adults.

• SIDS does not have a known cause but is believed to be linked to sensorimotor difficulties of respiration.

• Several preventive steps can be taken with infants at risk for SIDS, but none is foolproof.

• Parents who lose a baby to SIDS need special counseling and understanding from relatives and their community.

Perceptual Development

• Acuity and speed of information processing improve in all perceptual modalities between 2 and 5 months.

• Infants can detect color differences and a wide variety of visual patterns. They can perceive the solidity of objects and can recognize them from different points of view and using different sense modalities.

• Infants have a strong preference for looking at faces and at moving objects and are better able to perceive differences between objects if the objects are moving.

• Infants show a preference for infant-directed speech and songs.

• Cross-modal perception is the ability to perceive that different sense modalities give complementary information on the same object.

Cognitive Development

• The time taken for habituation decreases, and the infant's attention span increases.

• Infants have participatory memories for up to 2 weeks, but reminders make the memories longer. Memory is dependent upon emotional and contextual cues present at the time of the learning.

• Infantile amnesia may be due to the fact that infant memory is so closely related to the situation in which the infant was first exposed to the stimulus. Since the exact situation rarely recurs later, people seem to forget what happened to them as infants. People do, however, have participatory memories of feelings and sensations from infancy, even though they cannot locate the exact time, place, or situation.

• The main form of adaptation is primary circular reactions, in which the infants are exploring the effects of their own body movements and vocalizations.

Emotional Development

• A distinction can be made between emotion expression, emotion experience, and emotional regulation.

• The infant's emotional expression becomes more complex and varied. Infants can use their whole bodies for emotional expression.

• Negative emotions decrease over time, while positive emotions increase.

• Improvements in emotional regulation occur, but new challenges create new sources of frustration for babies.

Social Development

• Adults display characteristic patterns of behavior with infants that include motherese-type vocalizations and actions.

• Some aspects of motherese are universal, but cultures differ in the amount and type of verbal versus nonverbal behavior that is directed toward infants.

• Research shows that adults are affected by their infants' behavior, and infants are affected by adult behavior, making the origins of individual differences hard to determine in most cases.

• Infants are at risk when mothers have emotional disorders such as depression.

• Infants can perceive an ecological self, the sense that they have agency, coherence, location in the environment, and feelings that belong to them.

Family and Society

• Parents must adapt to a number of new challenges during the transition to parenthood.

• Different factors predict the success of adaptation to parenthood for men and women.

Chapter 7

Six to Nine Months

CHAPTER OUTLINE AND OVERVIEW

Physical and Motor Development   *What are the infant's motor skills at this age? Do infants have a preferred hand? How do motor skills develop? What are the nutritional requirements of infants? How should solid foods be introduced? When can infants feed themselves?*

Perceptual Development   *Can infants perceive object properties at this age? Can they appreciate pictures in books and on television?*

Cognitive Development   *What kinds of concepts do infants of this age have? Do they know that objects exist when out of sight?*

Emotional Development   *What are the negative emotions at this age? What are the positive emotions? Can infants recognize the facial expressions of other people? Do infants have lasting temperamental characteristics?*

Social and Language Development   *What are the typical frames of parent-infant communication at this age? In what ways is infant babbling related to speech? Can infants recognize speech sounds? What are some cultural differences in communication? What is the infant's sense of self at this age?*

Family and Society   *What are the effects of maternal employment on infants and families? Are males and females equally responsive toward infants?*

Between the ages of 6 and 9 months, infants grow more adventurous. This development is physical, in that babies can creep or crawl, at least for short distances, on their own. It is also psychological, in that infants begin to take initiatives and to call attention to themselves. Infants of this age develop a serious interest in the object world, and they come to understand that objects are whole entities with an existence separate from their own.

PHYSICAL AND MOTOR DEVELOPMENT

By the age of 5 months, infants can sit supported, and they can reach and grasp objects. Between 6 and 9 months, improvements in posture lead to independent sitting and to supported standing. Muscle strength improvements allow babies to roll over and to move their bodies by creeping or by crawling (see Experiential Exercises, this chapter).

By 9 months, infants can take a few steps while holding on to furniture or an adult hand. Their grasp becomes more precise, so that by 9 months, infants can pick up small objects such as peas or carrot slices using just the tips of the thumb and index finger. Some of these developments are listed in Table 7.1.

Hand Movements and Hand Preference

One of the distinguishing features of the human brain is that the left and right hemispheres serve different functions (see Chapter 4). Because brain hemisphere specialization is linked to **handedness**, or the preference for the use of one hand over another, the emergence in infancy of a preferred hand is thought to be related to milestones in the development of the brain. If there is a hand-use preference in early infancy, it might suggest that the left and the right cortices of the infant's brain are already functioning differently.

TABLE 7.1   Norms for the Development of Motor Behavior Patterns in North America

Test Item	Average Age	Normal Age Range
A. Head and body control		
Holds head erect when upright	7 weeks	3 weeks–4 months
Holds head steady when upright	2.5 months	1 month–5 months
Elevates chest and head in prone position	2.2 months	3 weeks–5 months
Thrusts arms and legs in supine position	1 month	1 week–2 months
Turns from side to back	2 months	3 weeks–5 months
Turns from back to side	2.5 months	2 months–7 months
Sits with support	2.2 months	1 month–5 months
Sits with slight support	3.7 months	2 months–6 months
Sits alone momentarily	5.2 months	4 months–8 months
Pulls self to sitting position	5.7 months	4 months–8 months
B. Hand and arm control		
Holds onto large ring in supine position	1 month	3 weeks–4 months
Grasps 1-inch cube with palm	3.7 months	2 months–7 months
Grasps cube with partial use of thumb	5 months	4 months–8 months
Reaches with one hand	5.5 months	4 months–8 months

Source: Bayley Infant Development Tests, as reported in and adapted from J. F. Rosenblith & J. E. Sims-Knight, *In the beginning: Development in the first two years*, 1985, Tables 8.2 and 8.5. Reprinted by permission of Sage Publications.

At first glance, there seems to be good evidence for left-right differences. About 50 to 70 percent of infants begin to exhibit a hand preference at about 2 months of age, around the time when visually guided reaching begins. Like adults, more of these infants who have a preference reach with their right, rather than with their left hands. Furthermore, this hand preference is relatively stable in babies over the first year of life (McDonnell, Anderson, & Abraham, 1983; Young, Segalowitz, Misek, Alp, & Boulet, 1983).

On closer examination, however, these left-right differences are not the same as those found in adults. Almost all adults have a hand preference and of these, about 90 percent of adults in all cultures are right handed. In infants under one year, however, only about 30 to 50 percent show a preference for the right hand in reaching, while 10 to 30 percent have a left-hand preference. The remaining infants show no hand preference. In adults, hand preference is correlated with the hand preference of one's parents, but this is not true for infants (McCormick & Maurer, 1988). Thus, it seems that infants do have a right-side bias, but it is not nearly as strong nor as stable as adults'. More permanent adult-like hand preferences in infants do not emerge until the second year of life, suggesting that hemispheric specialization is not fully developed until late in infancy and perhaps even later.

Why should we prefer to use one hand more than the other? Actually, handedness does not mean that we use one hand and not the other; it means that each of our hands may be doing different things. When a baby explores an object, the hand that is doing the grasping and manipulating is no less important than the hand that is holding the object steady. Perhaps handedness evolved to allow each hand to perform a different but complementary function (Fagard & Jacquet, 1989)? In fact, when babies use both hands to explore an object, their preferred hand is doing most of the exploring while their other hand is doing the holding. Even when babies do not have a stable hand preference during the first two years, they tend to chose a preferred hand by two years of age (Nelson et al., 2013).

There are many ways a baby can use the non-dominant hand. Postural control while sitting is important for the development of skilled reaching. Before infants can sit upright steadily, they reach for objects with two hands at the same time. After they can sit steadily, they are able to reach with a single hand, allowing them to use their other hand for balance. Infants of this age also seem to know how far they can reach for an object based on how stable they are in a sitting posture. They reach out farther when they feel more stable and do not reach when they feel unstable (Rochat & Goubet, 1995; Rochat, Goubet, & Senders, 1999; Rochat & Senders, 1990).

Although single-handed reaches are difficult for babies without the postural counterbalance provided by the other hand and arm, infants can be so motivated to grasp an object that they overactivate their lower trunk muscles (sometimes with a lot of grunting and straining!) to keep themselves upright to get an object (Harbourne et al., 2013). Two-handed reaches after the infant can sit without strain and effort are more sophisticated. Because of the effective postural control, infants can reach for larger objects (like a big ball) and they can cross the midline of the body to retrieve objects off to one side (van Hof et al., 2002).

Infants during this age period also develop the eye-hand coordination necessary to catch moving objects. As their motor skill improves, they are better able to perceive which kinds of moving objects they might be able to catch. By 7 months of age, if a ball is rolling very fast toward the infant, for example, the infant is less likely to attempt to catch it than if the ball is rolling more slowly. This suggests that infants' perception of moving objects in time develops along with their visual skill at tracking the objects and their manual skill at catching them (van Hof et al., 2008). Similarly, by eight or nine months, infants are learning to adjust the shape of their grasping hand according to the size and hardness of an object, prior to actually picking up the object (Barrett et al., 2008; Corbetta & Snapp-Childs, 2009). Also by nine months, infants are more likely to distinguish between an object and a realistic photograph of the same object, by

Experiential Exercise

Rolling Over
by Eileen Rojas, Modern Dancer

1. Lying on your back, place an object right above your head. Pick it up with your hand and, lying down, move your arm backward and place your object there.

2. Close your eyes and concentrate on your breathing.

3. Direct your internal focus to your abdominal area. Imagine the walls of your abdomen filling up with air like a balloon. You can put a hand on your belly to feel it go up and down with each breath. Feel the air reach all the way to your lower back and pelvis. Feel your back widen into the floor with each breath. Continue.

4. As you do this, think about how babies' movements are initiated from their core (abs, pelvis, stomach). Movements in the arms and legs result sequentially from core movements and a connection between the head and tail.

5. As you continue to breathe deeply, flex your abdominal muscles and then release them. What does it feel like to flex just your abs? Repeat. Do you feel any reactions in other parts of your body? Do you feel a connection between your head and tail because of your abdominal muscles? Rest.

6. Now, as you lie on your back, still breathing, turn your head toward your right shoulder. Direct your gaze above your shoulder to the object you placed there earlier. Stare at your object for a moment. Babies often stare at the things they want, although they cannot reach them. Rest (30 sec.)

2. Again, shift your head to the right and look up at your item of desire, still breathing. This time as you stare at your item, engage your abdominal muscles. Flex and release them as you did earlier. See if this affects any other part of your body. Rest.

3. Try to imagine a little baby lying on his back looking at something so hard that it takes his head further and further reaching towards his toy making his back arch. Arch back.

4. Once again, shift your head to the right and look up at your object again. Let your focus reach further and further, so far that you can't help but arch your back and start turning to your side. You may feel your hands or your feet trying to assist you, but try to use just your abdominal/core muscles and your head and tail connection to get you to a balanced position on your side. Remember babies' arm and leg muscles are not as strong or developed as their core. Try to refrain as much as possible from using your arms to help you get to your side. What may help you get over?

5. Try to balance on your side as if your body were a seesaw and you want it to remain in the middle without either side touching the ground. Once you figure out how to balance there, release your abdominals and see if you fall forward or backward.

6. Try this a few times, continuing to breathe, reaching for the object, and using the core.

7. This time as you balance on your side, experiment with what

may turn you on your belly. You might have gotten there already but this time try to feel the weight of the pelvis. Try to feel how gravity and momentum may affect you, and continue being aware of your core.

8. Once on your belly, rest, breathe, and take an inventory of your body. Take a look at your object.

9. You may notice that one of your arms is under the weight of your chest. Don't just move your arm. Remember, babies aren't that strong. Try to engage your abdominals as you lift your head to create a space under your chest to move your arm through. Again, imagine that arching image and the stretch between the head and the tail that can help lift your torso just enough to swipe your arm through.

10. You made it, you rolled over. Now look and see where that object is. Can you reach it? If you can, grab it. If you can't reach it, how does that make you feel?

Beginning to Crawl
by Mark Reese, Feldenkrais Practitioner

Position and Suggestions: Stand on your hands and knees. You may want to use extra padding under your knees if the pressure on the floor is too uncomfortable. Rest a while on your back after each variation before going on to the next one.

1. In slow motion begin to lift your right knee a millimeter (one-eighth inch) or two away from the floor and return it to the floor. Do not lift your foot, only the knee. Notice how your pel-

vis shifts over the left leg and then returns to the middle when your right knee returns to the floor. Each time you lift your knee, notice how the weight distribution changes on the two hands. Now, gently lift and lower your left knee just a small amount and return it to the floor. Notice how you shift your weight onto your right knee, and alter the weight on your hands in order to lift your knee. Do everything in slow motion and pause between movements so you can discover the nuances. Alternate lifting one knee and then the other. Which knee is easier to lift? Rest on your back.

2. Bring your knees and feet together to touch each other. Again, lift one knee and then the other just a small amount. Notice how easy it is to lift the knees when the legs are together. Your base of support is now more narrow, so that you are less stable but more movable. Rest on your back.

3. Move your knees very far apart. Again, alternate lifting one knee and then the other, and notice how much more difficult it is. Your base of support is now wider, so that you are more stable, but it is harder to move. Rest on your back.

4. Now experiment with different distances between your knees in order to find the optimum position. Where is the best balance between stability and instability? Rest on your back.

5. Repeat movements 1 to 4 with your hands. Discover how you need to shift your weight and determine the best distance for your hands to be apart. Rest on your back.

6. Now lift your right hand and foot just a small amount, and at the same time see if you can lift and lower them simultaneously. Discover how you need to balance and shift your weight. Always pause after each movement. Now lift and lower your left hand and left foot. Alternate between lifting the right hand and foot and then the left hand and foot. Which side is easier to lift? Rest on your back.

7. Lift and lower your right hand together with your left knee. How do you need to shift your weight? Now do the other diagonal, lifting and lowering your left hand together with your right knee. Try to lift the knee and hand at exactly the same time. Which diagonal is easier to lift? Which is easier, lifting diagonals or lifting the hand and foot on the same side? Rest on your back.

8. Lift both hands off the floor and move in the direction of sitting on your heels. As you shift your weight back, begin to lift one hand before the other and see which hand you lift first. Rest on your back.

9. Rock back and forward on your hands and knees. Find a comfortable rhythm. Can you find a rhythm that feels connected to the movement of crawling? Do you feel like you are preparing yourself to advance forward? Look around. Does anything in the environment draw your attention?

10. Now begin to crawl forward several steps and then back. Notice the order you use in lifting the hands and knees. If you move the hand and knee on the same side, this is called homolateral crawling. If you move your hand on one side as you move your knee on the other side, this is called the contralateral crawling. As you crawl, experiment with both homolateral and contralateral crawling. Does it change from one to the other when you change direction to crawl either backward or forward? Is it easier to go backward or forward? Many babies go backward first. Can you feel why this is so? If you are confused, maybe you are not yet ready to crawl.

11. Return to the movements in step 1. Is it easier than it was at the beginning? After resting on your back, get up on your feet and walk. Has revisiting crawling improved the fluency of your walking?

making grasping motions toward the former and rubbing motions toward the latter (Ziemer, 2012).

Crawling

Being able to extend one arm independently of the other is also believed to be important for the development of crawling. Observations of infants reveal that there are different types of crawling (see Table 7.2). As long as babies are still reaching with two hands at the same time (showing no hand preference), they either creep or rock. They begin to crawl as soon as they can reach with one hand, probably because crawling requires the extension of one hand and leg and then the other (Goldfield, 1989). The Experiential Exercises in this chapter may help you to understand in your own body how this could be challenging for a baby.

Not all infants go through the sequence of types of crawling shown in Table 7.2. Some infants creep before they crawl, while others skip the creeping phase and go directly to crawling. Infants

TABLE 7.2 Operational Definitions of Locomotor Stages

Pivot	Arms alternatively flex and extend, one after the other, causing the trunk to pivot on the abdomen. Symmetrical leg extension is followed by forward flexion of one knee, in adduction. Head lifts.
Low creep	Both arms are flexed symmetrically or extended symmetrically, or one is flexed while the other is extended. Legs flex, one at a time. Face is lifted, but chest and abdomen contact supporting surface.
High creep	Both arms are extended, and both legs are flexed symmetrically. Knees are forward under trunk in adduction, lifting abdomen and chest from supporting surface. Head is well up from floor, and eyes look ahead.
Rocking	Arms extend symmetrically, and both legs are flexed symmetrically. Knees are forward under trunk, lifting abdomen and chest from supporting surface. Infant rocks back and forth, remaining in one location.
Crawling	Both arms extend downward from shoulder, then extend forward, alternately. Legs flex forward alternately. Arms and leg on opposite sides of the body move simultaneously.

Note: These definitions were modified from Gesell and Ames (1940).

Source: E. C. Goldfield, Transition from rocking to crawling: Postural constraints on infant movement, 1989, p. 916. *Developmental Psychology 25*, 913–919. Reprinted by permission.

who creep before they crawl, however, are better at crawling than those who do not creep. When they crawl, the creepers move faster and their movements are larger and more efficient, although the non-creepers become proficient crawlers after a couple of weeks (Adolph, Vereijken, & Denny, 1998). There is no evidence, therefore, of any permanent effects of the delay in crawling proficiency for the non-creepers. On the contrary, infants are creative in combining all of the types of movements related to crawling, each in their own unique way. Apparently, infants use whatever means are available to achieve their goals, rather than staying with the most advanced form of movement all the time (Goldfield, 1993).

How Motor Skills Develop

The research on crawling shows that even though infants can get up on their hands and knees in a crawling posture, they still cannot crawl because they lack one of crawling's necessary skill components: alternate extension of the arms and legs. When doing the Experiential Exercises in this chapter, you can see how difficult it is to achieve this skill. A similar analysis could be applied to the development of walking. In the age period covered in this chapter, 6 to 9 months, infants can stand and take a few steps, but they cannot yet walk. Why not? Nine-month-old infants seem to possess the prerequisites of walking. They can pull themselves into a standing position, take steps while holding onto something, and alternate their leg movements. What they lack, however, is the ability to control balance.

This was discovered in research using a "moving-room" technique (see Figure 7.1). A baby stands in a miniature room, the floor of which is stationary but whose walls and ceiling are moved either toward or away from the baby. Infants under 1 year will fall in the direction in which the wall appears to be moving. Infants older than 1 year may sway but are less likely to lose their balance (Bertenthal & Bai, 1989). The moving room recreates the visual experience of moving without asking the baby to take steps at the same time. It is this visual experience of the room seeming to flow past the eyes that appears to cause babies to lose their balance.

This research suggests that perception of one's own movement in space is a key ingredient in controlling the posture necessary for locomotor development. Creeping or crawling experience enhances the infants' self-awareness in relation to objects in space: their ability to understand the differences between close and distant objects, and their ability to remember novel events (Clearfield, 2004; Herbert et al., 2007).

Balance and posture also influence other motor developmental processes. The difference between a creep and a crawl (Table 7.2 and the Experiential Exercises section of this chapter), for example, is the ability to balance on the hands and knees while moving forward. Once balance is acquired in the crawl, infants' movements become more efficient and uniform (Adolph, Vereijken, Denny, Gill, & Lucero, 1995). Infants who had experience with creeping or crawling were observed in the moving room apparatus and compared with infants who had not yet begun to locomote themselves. Those infants who had already begun self-produced locomotion were better able to make postural adjustments to the moving room, showing that the balance needed for walking may come from earlier experiences of balance while trying to crawl (Higgins, Campos, & Kermoian, 1996).

Infants can execute walking movements, for example, if they are supported in their posture— by an infant walker or an adult—and allowed to move their legs cyclically (Thelen & Ulrich, 1991). The onset of walking is later in infants with fewer opportunities to exercise these movements.

Infants in northern climates who are born in summer and fall will walk on their own an average of 3 weeks later than infants born in winter and spring. The reason for this is that babies born in winter and spring are more likely to be practicing walking skills in the summer or fall, and the warmer temperatures give them more opportunity for movement without the constriction of a lot of clothing (Benson, 1993).

In general, infant motor development is facilitated by giving babies opportunities to move and explore on their own, with or without equipment. In one study, infants were ranked according to how much they used equipment such as a jolly jumper, walker, exersaucer, playpen, or swing. Those infants who used such equipment more had higher scores on motor development assessments at 8 months of age (Abbott & Bartlett, 2001). Infants who crept, crawled, or used one of these devices also had better control over balance in the moving room apparatus, even before they could walk on their own (Uchiyama et al., 2008). It is recommended that moderate use of these devices may not be detrimental so long as infants are also exposed to free play experience on the floor with adults.

Figure 7.1 Schematic Drawing of Moving-Room Apparatus
Depicted inside the room is a child falling backward as a function of the room moving toward the child. This compensatory response would occur if the child perceived the optical flow produced by the room movement as specifying a forward sway rather than a movement of the walls.

Source: Adapted from B. I. Bertenthal & D. L. Bai, Infants' sensitivity to optical flow for controlling posture, 1989, p. 39. *Developmental Psychology, 25*, 936–945.

INFANT NUTRITION: LEARNING TO EAT SOLID FOODS

Another aspect of motor development is the ability to eat solid foods. Just as reaching requires developments in object perception and sitting, eating solid foods comes at an age when multiple changes are occurring. For example, the fetal supplies of iron stored in the infant's body begin to decline around 6 months, the time when the infant's body is beginning to need a supplementation of nutrients (mother's milk has little iron). This change coincides with the time when the baby teeth begin to emerge from the gums, the ability to make fine motor movements with the hands to grasp and pick up objects, and the decline of the extrusion reflex of the tongue, which serves to express milk (Chapter 5) but also pushes out most things that are placed in the mouth. In other words, the baby begins to develop the ability to handle solid food, chew it, and swallow it. Is this more than a chance coincidence? We will probably never really know, but it all works out nicely for the baby, who develops the skill to consume solid foods just at the time when he or she needs them.

When Should Solid Foods be Introduced?

The American Academy of Pediatrics maintains that infants do not need supplementary foods besides milk until 6 months (American Academy of Pediatrics, 2003). Aside from those mentioned in the previous paragraph, by 6 months, the baby has certain abilities that will help in processing solid foods. These include enzymes to digest carbohydrates, chewing and swallowing skills, and the ability to express satiety by head shaking (R. A. Stewart, 1981). Data indicate no relationship between the early introduction of solid foods or the amount of food the baby eats and whether the baby will sleep through the night. Thus, no clear benefits can be gained from the early introduction of solid foods (Chubet, 1988; Grunwaldt, Bates, & Guthrie, 1960).

Can the Early Introduction of Solid Foods Do Any Harm?

Some hazards are associated with the early introduction of solid foods. The best source of nutrition for infants under 6 months is milk—preferably human. Any solid food is inferior nutritionally, so proportionately more is required to satisfy nutritional needs. This will lead to less consumption of milk and to a tendency to distend or overtax the stomach, resulting in short term gastrointestinal upset and, in the long term, possible obesity. Early feeding of solids also has been associated with the development of food allergies, kidney malfunction, iron deficiency, and an increased likelihood of developing strong food dislikes (Committee on Nutrition, 1998; Guthrie, 1979; Pipes, 1985; C. H. Robinson, 1978; Weir & Feldman, 1975).

How Should Solids Be Introduced?

By the age of 5 months, the digestive systems of most babies develop the enzymes to digest most proteins, and saliva production increases to lubricate swallowing. Drooling begins about this time, because the production of saliva exceeds the baby's ability to keep it under control. Furthermore, chewing, swallowing, and teeth pushing up under the gums all make it easier to handle the demands of eating solids (Guthrie, 1979; Pipes, 1985; Sheppard & Mysak, 1984).

The first teeth typically do not erupt through the gums until about 8 months, although individual infants may vary from the average dates of tooth eruption by as much as 6 months before or after (Lunt & Law, 1974; R. McDonald & Avery, 1983). In response to teething, some babies become fussy, while others do not seem to notice, although most babies like to bite semisoft objects as their teeth are coming in. Infants under a year may be given cookies to chew on, and babies older than 1 year may be given large carrot sticks.

Weaning is the process by which children reduce their intake of milk and become accustomed to the foods eaten by adults. General guidelines on how to introduce solid foods are available from a number of sources. Because of the possibility of food allergies, most experts recommend introducing one food at a time—for at least a week or two—before trying another. New foods should be offered in small amounts at first, and caregivers should never force infants to take a food they do not like.

Even in the first six months, infants develop taste preferences. They prefer formulas that they are used to, even if those formulas are rated as bland or even bitter by adults (Mennella et al., 2004). Thus, solid food should be seasoned lightly or not at all. Salts and sugars are not harmful in small quantities, but there is no need for them, and infants will develop sometimes life-long preferences for what they are used to eating. Parental eating habits and weight can be transmitted to infants via the foods they are given (Guthrie, 1979; Nguyen, 2012; C. H. Robinson, 1978).

This is shown in research on the precursors to childhood obesity. Generally, mothers who are heavier are more likely to offer food to help infants to calm down, and this includes milk as well as solid foods. The infants of these mothers are more likely to become over-weight as they get older (Anzman-Frasca, 2013). To avoid these patterns, it is better to offer other forms of soothing (such as hugging, rocking, and giving distractions) than food. Children are much more likely to follow the food advice and preferences of parents and teachers than other sources (including cartoons), so if you want your baby to develop healthy eating habits, your own eating habits will need to be as healthy (Nguyen, 2012).

Of course, eating healthy foods does more than prevent obesity. Diets that are high in micro-nutrients such as vitamins, minerals, and omega-3 fatty acids can promote healthy cognitive and emotional development (Nyaradi et al., 2013). Some commercially available baby foods contain added sugars and salts, but one can buy foods without these substances, and organic baby foods with no additives are also available. Since infants and young children typically eat some between-meal snacks, it is important to provide both meals and snacks that are high in nutrition and low in calories (Skinner et al., 2004).

Solid foods are usually introduced to babies in the following order: cereals (one at a time), strained fruit or juice (except orange), vegetables, proteins (meat and cheese), egg yolk (not until 8 months), and egg white (not until 10 to 12 months) (Guthrie 1979; C. H. Robinson, 1978). This order is related to a number of developmental factors, such as production of digestive enzymes, the consistency of the food and the ability to chew, and the possibility of an allergic reaction (gluten in grains and egg whites are some of the biggest troublemakers in this regard). Since cow's milk should not be used for the first year, dry cereals should be mixed with breast milk or formula. Rice cereals are the most easily tolerated in the first year, and rice or soy milk formulas can also be found (Karns, 2000). It is estimated that between 15 and 25 percent of parents do not follow these guidelines, risking food refusal and allergies (Briefel et al., 2004).

Infants can eat a vegetarian diet with certain precautions (Karns, 2000). Vegetarian diets are high in bulk, and infants need denser foods such as nuts, olives, dates, and avocados. Macrobiotic diets present the greatest risk, but infants who eat milk and/or eggs have normal growth patterns. Infants need to ingest dietary fat for a number of reasons: it is a source of energy; it is a carrier of fat-soluble vitamins such as A, D, E, and K; and infants need certain essential fatty acids.

Up until 1 year, food should be mashed or chopped until it is fine enough not to cause choking. Foods most likely to cause choking are hot dogs, grapes, raw vegetables, popcorn, nuts, and hard candy (Karns, 2000). Finger foods are good for 6-month-olds, and by 9 to 12 months, infants can begin to feed themselves with a spoon. Until about 18 months, spilling and messing food is quite common. Why should babies not explore food just as they do everything else? A good recommendation is for the feeder to come armed with a towel, a sponge, and a sense of humor.

If infants persist in spilling food as part of a game or to get the caregiver's attention, caregivers can remove the food temporarily, while firmly stating that food is for eating. It is usually not necessary to coax infants to eat: they will eventually eat to satisfy their hunger. Thus, intake in any one meal is not so important. Caregivers may wish to insist on proper mealtime behavior (considering the limits of the infant's motor abilities and allowing for a little bit of fun), but insisting that the infant eat particular foods and particular amounts of foods is generally not recommended. Babies may avoid food because of its taste, size, shape or because they are not hungry.

At the end of the first year, babies who are teething like to chew on carrots or dry toast but tend to mangle these foods more than consume them. Babies often go on food jags, refusing to eat more than one or two different kinds of foods. They can be erratic in their appetites and seem to have strong ideas about when and what to eat (Pipes, 1985). Picky eaters have been reported at all infant ages, for both sexes, all ethnicities, and all ranges of household incomes. Parents may need to introduce a new food up to 15 times before a picky eater may be willing to taste it (Carruth et al., 2004).

How to eat is also a big concern for most babies. They may eat something only if it is presented in a ritualized way—cut or arranged a certain way or served on a certain dish. There is not too much the caregiver can do except live with these idiosyncra-

sies, accepting them with good humor and the recognition that preferences are part of being human. Some people like their hamburgers with catsup and others like mustard; some people like grits with their breakfast and others eat bagels. Generally, infants have preferences for foods that have familiar tastes and smells, are prepared (cooked, cut, and arranged) in familiar ways, and those foods which are part of their home environment. Parents and caregivers need to be mindful of these familiarity preferences to make novel foods more acceptable (Aldridge et al., 2009).

For a baby, a meal is more than food intake: it is an occasion for play, learning, and socializing. Mealtimes are an important part of the infant's social, cognitive, and emotional development, not just a refueling for physical growth. Parents should try not to rush meals and should cut down on stimulation, such as the television, that might compete with the social aspects of feeding the baby.

As shown in the example later in this chapter in the observation box (Observation 7.3) related to communication, mealtimes contain complex sequences of co-regulated social interaction. Issues of control arise often. The baby wants to hold the spoon, for example, but is doing more banging than eating (babies are not very efficient spoon users until 9 or 10 months of age (Kochukhova & Gredebäck, 2010). The mother takes the

Self-feeding requires more coordination than most infants can manage. Parents need to give infants foods that are easily handled.
Photo by Emily Wakefield

spoon and begins to feed the baby, who starts to protest and refuses to eat. Mother eventually returns the spoon to the baby. The best solution is to allow the baby as much time as needed to complete the meal. When this is not possible, caregivers do need to model more appropriate eating habits, but without undue domination. In eating, as in other aspects of development, infants will never learn independent behavior unless they are allowed to develop their own sense of control and achievement in this realm. Patience and praise are the best teaching tools.

PERCEPTUAL DEVELOPMENT

New Developments in the Recognition of Objects and Depth

In the last chapter, we saw that by 4 months, infants are able to recognize objects even though they may look different when seen from different orientations. By 4 months, infants perceive objects as being solid and will become puzzled if one solid object appears to pass through another. Infants of this age can also perceive differences in distances between objects and will reach preferentially to objects they perceive as nearer to them. For infants under 6 months, however, object recognition and depth perception are easier if the objects are moving and if real objects, rather than pictures of objects, are presented.

After 6 months, however, infants can infer object properties and depth merely from visual cues alone (Craton, 1996; Soska & Johnson, 2013; Wilcox & Baillargeon, 1998). Another way to say this is that by 6 months, infants can "see" three dimensions when they are shown objects in two dimensions, as in a drawing or a photograph. Suppose two pictures of different sizes but of the same object, such as a car, are placed next to each other. Adults looking at the pictures with one eye (monocular vision) would assume that the smaller car is farther away. Looking with two eyes, adults can easily see that two cars are at the same distance but of different sizes. These perceptual conclu-

sions must be based only on the relative sizes of the pictures and not on the movements of one car away from the other or the movements of the perceiver in a three-dimensional space.

By about 7 months of age, infants with a patch over one eye will reach toward the larger of two identical pictures of a face, apparently perceiving it as closer (Yonas, Pettersen, & Granrud, 1982). If a small and a large checkerboard are used, the infants do not reach more frequently for the larger one, since checkerboards have no standard size. If the infants are allowed to reach while looking with both eyes, they do not show a preference for the larger object, either the car or the checkerboard. Thus, by 7 months, infants use visual cues, such as size, to judge depth.

Also by 7 months, infants can use other visual cues to judge depth. If one object partially blocks the view of another, the blocked object is perceived as farther away (Granrud & Yonas, 1984). Relative shading in a drawing depicting a bump or a depression causes 7-month-olds, but not 5-month-olds, to reach for the object shaded like a bump (Granrud, Yonas, & Opland, 1985). Both 5-and 7-month-olds reach for actual bumps. Finally, by 7 months, when objects are presented in a perspective drawing, infants use the perspective information to reach for the object that is apparently nearer to them (Arterberry, Yonas, & Bensen, 1989). Infants' ability to recognize objects in two dimensions leads to increased interest in picture books and television at this age.

During this period, infants learn to perceive object properties through touch as well as through vision. Perception of the properties of an object using touch is called **haptic perception**. Through haptic perception, infants soon after birth can distinguish different properties of objects primarily by using their mouths. In the early months, the mouth is perhaps the most sensitive haptic organ. Between 4 and 6 months, infants begin examining objects by active exploration combining hand, mouth, and vision (Morange-Majoux, Cougnot, & Bloch, 1997; Oakes & Tellinghuisen, 1994; Ruff, 1986). After 6 months, infants develop specialized hand movements to detect information about

TABLE 7.3   Haptic Perception-Action Correspondences for Infants

Object Property	Haptic Action
Size, volume	Enclosing external contours
Hardness	Applying pressure
Exact shape	Following the contour with fingers
Temperature	Static palm or finger contact
Texture	Side-to-side movements of palms or fingers

specific object properties such as size, texture, and shape (Bourgeois et al., 2005; Bushnell & Boudreau, 1993). To perceive an object's relative size, for example, infants will enclose their hands around the outside of the object. Other perception-action correspondences are shown in Table 7.3. Through both haptics and vision, therefore, infants become increasingly sophisticated in their knowledge of object properties.

Other Perceptual Developments

By 3 months of age, infants like to look at faces. As discussed in the last chapter, 5 month-olds can distinguish familiar from unfamiliar faces, and faces of the same vs. other ethnicities. By 6 to 9 months, infants still prefer to look at faces compared to objects (Gliga et al., 2009), and they can recognize ethnic differences even from black & white photos (Anzures et al., 2011).

Recognizing differences between unfamiliar faces, however, does not begin until after 9 months of age. Infants between 6 and 9 months can recognize the faces of different unfamiliar people they have seen before but only if they have spent some time studying the faces of those people (Quinn & Tanaka, 2009). At this age period, infants are more likely to recognize and remember what a person does rather than what their face looks like (Bahrick & Newell, 2008). In addition, because most infants of this age spend most of their time interacting with a female (their mother or caregiver) compared to males, they are more likely to distinguish unfamiliar female faces compared to unfamiliar male faces (Rennels & Davis, 2008).

Infants in this age period can recognize differences between simple melodies. Six-month-olds can discriminate between six-note melodies differing by only one note (Trehub, Bull, & Thorpe, 1984), and they can discriminate between melodies in which the pauses between notes are varied (Thorpe & Trehub, 1989). By this age, therefore, babies can recognize some nursery rhymes and simple melodies heard in songs. By this age, infants prefer low-pitched melodies for lullabies (low and soft) and high-pitched melodies for play songs (up and bouncy), although they cannot tell the differences between happy and sad songs until they are at least 9 months-old (Flom et al., 2008; Tsang & Conrad, 2010).

Also by this age, babies show continuing evidence of cross-modal perception. Thus, infants are sensitive to distortions in the sound track of a film showing a rattle shaking at a particular rhythm. If the sound is faster or slower than the rattle's movements, the babies notice the difference (Bahrick, 1987). As the visual and auditory display becomes more complicated, however, infants preferentially process the sound but not the vision, reflecting the fact that even at 6 months, auditory perception is more advanced than visual perception (Lewkowicz, 1988, 1996). This auditory dominance is also true for adults, as when light displays flashed to accompany music seem to move at the same beat as the music. If the visual displays are flashed in a regular manner that makes their rhythm salient, however, infants and adults will pay more attention to the visual compared to the auditory display (Lewkowicz, 1994). These findings are important because they show that cross-modal perception is becoming more controlled for infants: under certain conditions, they can distinguish between the separate attributes of each modality.

Infants older than 6 months can also use cross-modal perception to infer information about object properties. Infants of this age who are familiarized with an object only by touch can recognize the object by sight alone (Ruff & Kohler, 1978), and infants will alternatively look at and touch objects and put them into their mouths while exploring them (Ruff, 1984). Furthermore, if babies hear a sound in the dark, they will reach for an object in the direction of the sound. Infants can also distinguish whether the object is within or out of their reach based on hearing its sound in the dark (Clifton, Perris, & Bullinger, 1991; Perris & Clifton, 1988). Infants were given sweet and tart foods in cups of different colors. On subsequent color-choice trials, the infants consistently picked the color that had been paired with the sweet food (Reardon & Bushnell, 1988). Finally, infants will choose the appropriate facial expression to match the sounds of an aggressive compared to a non-aggressive dog (Flom et al., 2009).

In summary, these studies of perception show that by the middle of the first year of life, infants can use subtle cues to infer regularities in their perceptual world. They can now learn from pictures in books and on television. They can pick up relationships between different senses to pay attention to aspects of their environment that most interest them, such as the color of the baby food jar that contains their favorite flavor.

These perceptual abilities lead to clear preferences, as we will see later in the chapter. Babies begin to take the initiative in expressing their desires for particular pictures, objects, and tastes. As infants learn to perceive finer distinctions in the world, they also learn about themselves, about whether they like or dislike these distinctions. In this way, the parts of the brain related to perceptual and motor development are also linked to the parts of the brain that are responsible for how these perceptions and movements feel inside the infant's body and thus to an expansion of self-awareness (see Chapter 4).

COGNITIVE DEVELOPMENT

Memory

As we've seen for perceptual and motor development, during the period from 6 to 9 months, the infant's brain continues to grow and change. Brain development also supports changes in memory and cognition. Studies using kicking to make mobiles move have shown that infant memory during this period is similar to memory at 3 months. However, while 3-month-olds can remember how to produce mobile movements for up to 14 days, 7-month-olds can remember for as long as 21 days without a reminder (Hill, Borovsky, & Rovee-Collier, 1988).

In the previous chapter, we saw how 3-month-olds required the exact duplication of the original learning situation to remember something. By 7 months, their memories are somewhat less context dependent, meaning that infants can remember a salient event that has been learned in several different but related situations. Infants of this age have more control over reactivating their own memories and do not have to rely entirely on contextual cues (Amabile & Rovee-Collier, 1991; Bhatt, Rovee-Collier, & Weiner, 1994). Infants also can remember longer sequences of events, like longer melodies or longer sequences of flashing colored lights on electronic toys (Bahrick et al., 2002; Ross-Sheehy et al., 2003).

One thing that limits infant memory events is that they remember too much with too many small details about a particular situation. Another way of saying this is that infants have not yet learned strategies for sorting through what is important in their experiences (Rovee-Collier & Cuevas, 2009). Infants see the trees and not the forest.

During this age period, however, infants are beginning to figure out what is more important to learn and remember. Recall that younger infants can hear the sound contrasts from all languages, but beginning in the period between 6 and 9 months (see section on Speech Perception, below), they are becoming specialists in the languages heard in the home, selectively narrowing their ability to discern and remember. This is similar to the overproduction and later pruning of synapses in the brain (see Chapter 4): infants are first generalists and then they become more selectively attuned to the distinctions they need to survive in their local environment. Whatever the reason, infants in this age period are taking a more active and selective role in the processing of information.

Increasing Use of Concepts to Organize and Process Information

This increasingly active and selective information processing means that infants in this age period are able to group different stimuli into higher-order conceptual categories. Using a habituation procedure, infants dishabituated to an unfamiliar face but not to the same face in a different pose. This shows that the babies had organized all the different poses they saw into a higher-order concept of a particular face. Seven-month-olds, but not 5-month-olds, were able to do this (L. B. Cohen & Strauss, 1979). In a similar type of study, 7-month-old infants were habituated to different faces having the same facial expression (a smile). They dishabituated to a different face with a non-smile expression but not to a different face with a smile expression (R. F. Caron, Caron, & Myers, 1982).

In an interesting variant of this procedure, infants were familiarized with somewhat distorted versions of a prototype figure (Younger & Gotlieb, 1988). A **prototype** figure is one that is the clearest example of the form being represented. If infants are actively organizing the images of the distorted figures into a category, then they should prefer to look at a related prototype compared to an unrelated prototype, in a test trial in which both are available to look at. Infants who were familiarized with the "plus sign" distortions preferred the "plus sign" prototype at ages 3, 5, and 7 months. Only 7-month-olds could recognize the prototype from the distorted versions.

Because of their growing ability to perceive objects as whole entities, infants of this age are beginning to relate objects together into higher-order classifications. Seven-month-olds, for example, can distinguish horses from some other four-legged mammals such as cats, zebras, and giraffes (Eimas & Quinn, 1994). Infants develop motor categorizations for objects, grouping them into things shakable, drinkable, squeezable, and so on (Baldwin, Markman, & Melartin, 1993; Bushnell & Boudreau, 1993; Catherwood, 1993). By 9 months, infants can distinguish these object properties visually as well as haptically (Coldren & Colombo, 1994). Infants of this age are better at creating categories for objects if they have had prior experiences with objects in those categories, and especially if they have been allowed to manually explore these objects (Bornstein & Mash, 2010; Mash & Bornstein, 2012; Perone et al., 2008)

Infants of this age are able to judge whether objects are too big to fit into containers, when shown objects and containers of various sizes, and especially if they can see the objects moving into the container (Aguiar & Baillargeon, 1998; Smitsman et al., 2009). They understand that moving objects should follow along their prior path of movement and that larger objects can support smaller objects (Baillargeon & De Vos, 1991; Baillargeon, Needham, & De Vos, 1992; Sitskoorn & Smitsman, 1995). Infants will respond differentially when the same object is placed above as opposed to below another object, showing that they have a category for these kinds of spatial relationships (Quinn, Cummins, Kase, Martin, & Weissman, 1996).

Infants of this age may even have a concept of number or quantity of objects. Infants were habituated to a puppet jumping in the air either two or three times. They dishabituated when the number of jumps changed, from two to three or from three to two (Wynn, 1998). Piaget discovered that his children had a sense of quantity at 11 months of age when he tried to get them to imitate sounds (Piaget, 1952, p. 241). If Piaget said "papa," Laurent replied with "papa." If Piaget said "pa," so did Laurent. By adding more "pa" syllables, Piaget discovered that Laurent had trouble with more than three. Saying "papapapapa" only got a "papapapa" in return.

Other research found that 10-to 12-month-olds could easily discriminate visual arrays that differed only in number, particularly for one versus two objects, one versus three objects, and two versus three objects. They had a harder time with four versus three objects, and no luck at all discriminating four from five objects (M. Strauss & Curtis, 1981; Wood & Spelke, 2005). Infants of this age can also notice the difference in size between two different quantities of objects, but only if the larger group is at least 4 times as large as the smaller group (Cordes & Brannon, 2009). Studies like these show that infants of this age have a concept of quantity—more versus less—but they do not prove that infants of this age know numbers and can do math problems. That ability begins in the third year (Brannon et al., 2006; Mix, Levine, & Huttenlocher, 1997; Xu et al., 2005). All of the infant's rudimentary categorical abilities will develop rapidly after 9 months (see Chapter 8).

Piaget's Third Sensorimotor Stage: Secondary Circular Reactions

The infant's growing abilities to perceive and conceptualize the properties of objects were also noticed by Piaget. Beginning at about 4 months and continuing until about 8 or 9 months, infants pass through Piaget's third stage of sensorimotor development: the stage of **secondary circular reactions**. This stage is a natural extension of the preceding one. Instead of only repeating actions that they discover by chance on their own bodies (the primary circular reaction), infants soon begin to repeat actions that, by chance, produce some effect on the objects and people in the environment. The idea of *chance*—the fortuitous discovery of some interesting result—is what distinguishes this stage from the ones that follow. Once the chance discovery is made, however, infants make deliberate, intentional attempts to repeat that action.

In a primary circular reaction, babies repeat a movement of their own bodies but do not make the connection between that movement and its effect. The movement creates a good feeling (a sound or a sight), but the babies seem focused on the efforts of their own bodies. In secondary circular reactions, babies are focused more on the objects in the environment. They not only repeat actions that produce effects on objects; they also vary the actions to explore changes in the effect. Piaget (1952) suggested that infants are trying to "make interesting sights last."

Babies between 6 and 9 months will drop objects off the edge of their high chairs, perhaps listening for different sounds or looking at different movements when the objects hit the floor. They shake objects in different ways to notice the effect or repeatedly dump things (such as their food) out of containers.

Infants in this period tend to apply the movements they use for particular objects as a way of representing or referring to the object (see Observation 7.1). When Piaget shakes his son's rattles, Laurent at 4 1/2 months is too busily engaged in playing with the toy he is holding to actually strike his rattle. He seems to indicate the potential action by making a striking movement in the air. Instead of saying verbally, "Those are my rattles," Laurent expresses himself through a motor movement that has the exact form of his previous interactions with that object.

Inferring the Intentions of Other People

By 7 months, Laurent knew that he would be fed shortly after he heard his mother's bed creak. Earlier in his life, he would cry with hunger as soon as he woke up. Now he cries in relation to certain environmental events that have come to have a meaning for him. Like the act of "pretend" striking, the cry is a motor way of saying, "That's the sound of my food!"

Repeated occurrences in the environment take on meaning for the baby (see Observation 7.2), and infants are learning that the actions of people are different from those of inanimate objects. As infants are becoming more intentional and goal directed, they are also beginning to perceive the intentional behavior of other people. Six-month-olds watched a person repeatedly grasping one of two possible objects. After multiple times choosing the preferred object, the person suddenly

Observations

Stage III Behavior (Piaget, 1952, pp. 187, 195)

Observation 7.1

Laurent: at 0;4(21) has an object in his hands when, in order to distract him, I shake the hanging rattles which he is in the habit of striking. He then looks at the rattles without relinquising his toy and outlines with his right hand the movement of "striking."

Observation 7.2

At 0;7(10): Laurent cries in the morning as soon as he hears his mother's bed creak. Until then, although awake, he did not show his hunger. But, at the slightest creak, he moans and thus demands his bottle.

chose the other object. Infants tended to look longer at this unexpected choice of the non-preferred objects, implying that they perceived the person to have a preference to choose the first object. In some cases, however, the non-preferred object was hidden from the person's view (either by a large screen or when the person had her back to the non-preferred object). In this case, when the person chose the non-preferred object (following multiple grasps for the preferred one), the infants did NOT look longer.

This suggests that the infants believed the person had no way to choose one object from another because the infants believed that the person could not see the second object. In other words, infants can infer when a person has an intention to compare and to choose one object over another (Luo & Johnson, 2009). Other similar studies have shown that by 6 months, infants believe that other people's action is goal-directed rather than random (Marsh et al., 2010; Woodward, 1999). This ability to follow the goal-directed actions of others seems to be a factor in helping infants to construct their own goal-directed actions (Daum et al., 2009; Mahajan & Woodward, 2009) and they are more likely to imitate goal-directed rather than non-goal-directed actions on objects (Hamlin et al., 2008).

Also, during this age period, infants can distinguish between good and bad intentions toward other people. Eight month-olds prefer to watch characters behave positively toward "nice" or prosocial others, and also prefer characters who act

negatively toward "naughty" or antisocial others. The infants themselves, when given a choice, will behave positively or negatively toward others, depending on the others' behavior (Hamlin et al., 2011). Infants of this age also prefer to watch two adults talking face-to-face, rather than back-to-back (Augusti et al., 2010). These studies show that infants in this age period are developing rather sophisticated cognitive understandings about people, action, and communication.

How is it possible for infants to infer intentions (a cognitive construct) by simply watching the actions of others? The part of the nervous system that controls motor movements like reaching and grasping includes the nerves in the arm and hand and their links to the motor and parietal cortices (Chapter 4). All motor actions are inherently organized, especially in the parietal cortex, toward achieving some kind of goal. It is probably not an accident that the parietal cortex is also one of the few locations in the brain for so-called "mirror neurons. **Mirror neurons** are neurons that fire when we watch someone else perform a motor action, a goal-directed movement, leading the observer's nervous system to have similar intentions and emotions as the person being observed. Thus, watching someone else behave intentionally creates in the viewer a similar intention as held by the actor. Mirror neurons also play a role in empathy because emotional expressions are motor movement patterns, which can then affect the viewer in the same way as the actor (Gallese et al., 2009).

Out of Sight, Out of Mind?

Given what we know about the memory of infants under 9 months, it seems quite likely that they should be able to remember objects when they can no longer see them. In one study, infants aged 7 to 8 months saw an object sitting on one of two red placemats that were 8.5 inches (21.5 centimeters) apart. Next, two purple screens big enough to hide the object were slid in front of the placemats (see Figure 7.2). A hand then reached behind the screen and reappeared holding the object in either a possible situation or an impossible situa-

tion (Figure 7.2). Infants looked longer at the hand following the impossible situation compared to the possible one, showing that they remembered the object's location and were surprised when the object appeared from behind the screen opposite that behind which they had seen it placed (Baillargeon & Graber, 1988). In a similar study with infants of the same age, this time with their parents present in the room, the infants not only looked longer at the impossible situation; they also looked more at their parents as if to share their puzzlement (Walden et al., 2007).

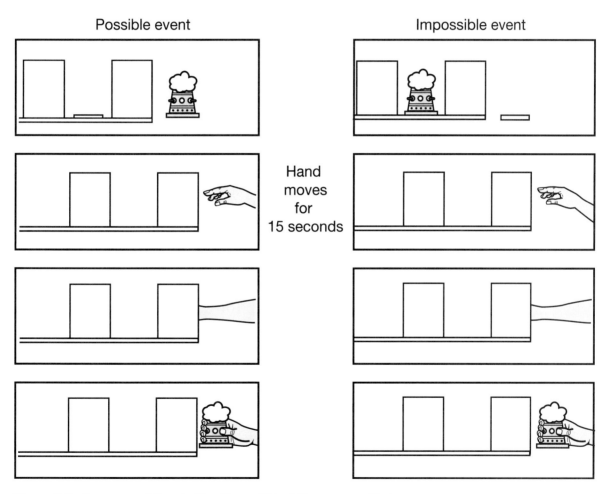

Possible event   Hand moves for 15 seconds   **Impossible event**

Figure 7.2   Sequence of Events Used in an Object-Permanence Task

Source: Adapted from R. Baillargeon & M. Graber, Evidence of location memory in 8-month-old infants in a nonsearch AB task, 1988, p. 505. *Developmental Psychology, 24,* 502–511. Copyright © American Psychological Association. Reprinted with permission.

This type of research has been repeated for different kinds of visual events in which objects appear and disappear in possible and impossible ways. Infants between 3 and 7 months come to understand that objects seen in the light will still be in the same place when the lights are turned off (Clifton et al., 1991; Clifton et al., 1994). In one study, infants were shown an object falling and making a noise on impact, after which they were allowed to reach for the fallen object. Next, the lights were turned off. When the infants heard the sound of the impact, they reached for the object in the dark at the same location (Goubet & Clifton, 1998; McCall & Clifton, 1999). Generally speaking, if infants have prior exposure to the situation in which the object is to be located, or if they can still hear or partially see the hidden object, their memory abilities at this age allow them to search for the object in the correct location (Bojczyk & Corbetta, 2004; Marcovitch et al., 2002; Moore & Meltzoff, 2008).

In summary, infants of this age are becoming aware of objects and people and whole entities. They can appreciate that objects have features and boundaries, that they occupy unique locations in space, and that they do not disappear when out of sight. The same is also true for infant's conceptions of people. People, however, are understood by infants as having intentions. The ability to perceive another's intentions corresponds with the infant's awareness of their own intentions, their ability to have an effect on the environment. We will return to this topic in the section below on the sense of self at this age. Another characteristic of people is that they experience and display emotions, a topic to which we shall turn next.

EMOTIONAL DEVELOPMENT

The Development of Negative Emotions

Until the beginning of Piaget's Stage III (around 5 months), babies have basically one response to a negative experience: they cry. With the onset of secondary circular reactions, infants become more "aware" that they can cause things to happen in the environment. This sense of themselves as a causal agent—part of the ecological self—accounts in part for the reduction in the amount of crying that occurs between 3 and 5 months. When infants cannot succeed at being an effective causal agent—when they cannot get a toy they want, for example—a new source of negative experience enters their lives: *anger*.

Anger in infants is a direct result of their having their intentions disrupted. Although both anger and distress are accompanied by crying, the facial expression during anger is different from that of distress, as is the baby's underlying feeling (Izard, 1981; Sroufe, 1979). In one study, infants' reactions to inoculations were observed at 2, 4, and 7 months. At 2 and 4 months, infants reacted with physical distress, a direct response to pain. Distress is expressed by crying with tightly shut eyes. By 7 months, the babies responded with more angry expressions, crying with open, vigilant eyes (Izard, 1981; Izard, Hembree, & Huebner, 1987).

It is almost as if the quality of the gaze signals that the infant is angry at the person being watched. If you have an opportunity to experience this with a baby (see the Co-Regulating with Baby section of this chapter), you can feel what it is like when an upset baby looks at you in this particular way. Anger can be expressed in many different ways as infants get older, such as by kicking, biting, sulking, yelling, pouting, or temper tantrums (Barrett & Campos, 1987; Campos & Barrett, 1984).

Separation from the mother is another situation that causes negative emotions. Before the age of 6 months, infants cry with distress, particularly if their mothers leave, act depressed, or perform a still face in the middle of a feeding or play session. The distress arises from the cessation of the pleasurable interaction. After 6 months, infants respond to parental separation with some anger, especially if the parent happens to be a part of the infant's activity—such as during play or feeding—when he or she leaves (Izard, 1981). Expressions of anger are also seen in 7-month-olds when a teething biscuit is removed from their mouths or when their arms are restrained (Stenberg, Campos, & Emde, 1983).

Another negatively toned emotion seen at this age is **wariness**. Infants may become quiet and stare at a stranger or a strange situation, knit their brows, become momentarily sober, and look away (Bronson, 1972). Because wariness allows the infant to observe what is happening, it is a considerably more adaptive reaction to strange situations than is the withdrawal of infantile fussing and crying of previous ages (Emde, Gaensbauer, & Harmon, 1976; Malatesta et al., 1986).

Aside from these general trends, there are also individual differences. Infants of this age were taught to pull a string attached to their wrist to activate a slide projection of an infant's face accompanied by the *Sesame Street* theme song. After they learned this procedure, the experimenters stopped turning on the slide projector and music when the infant pulled the string. Most of the infants reacted to this contingency failure with anger, although some showed expressions of sadness. When the contingency was renewed, the infants who expressed anger immediately became interested again in the task, while those who showed sadness reacted to the renewal of the contingency with less enjoyment (Lewis et al., 1992). This shows that anger is an adaptive and useful response for some babies, who perceive the renewal of the contingency as under their control. The babies who were saddened, however, may perceive themselves as helpless to change the course of events.

At this age, then, the helpless fussing of earlier ages gives way to demanding crying, anger, and wariness. Each of these forms of negative emotional expression is considerably more adaptive from the infant's point of view, and these developments reflect some significant advances in the infant's ability to cope with negative situations. Wariness, for example, allows for even more prolonged inspection of the potentially worrisome stimulus rather than a simple rejection of it. We might say that the end result of this increasing sophistication in the realm of negative responding is to bring the infant back into a positive engagement with the environment.

The Development of Positive Emotions

The positive emotions also become more complex during this age period. In one study, mothers and infants were observed playing peekaboo and tickle games. Different types of smiles had different emotional meanings depending upon whether the infant was attending to the mother or not (Fogel, Nelson-Goens, Hsu, & Shapiro, 2000; Fogel, Hsu, Shapiro, Nelson-Goens, & Secrist, 2006). Simple smiling (lip corner retraction without cheek raising; see Chapter 6) accompanied by gazing at the mother during peekaboo represents an *enjoyment of recognition* or perhaps an *enjoyment of readiness to engage in play*. The feeling may be similar to an adult's experience of being delighted to be with a familiar person and to engage in enjoyable things together. Simple smiles occurring without gazing at mother after a previous tickle are often accompanied by gasping for air and sighing. The feeling associated with these smiles may be an *enjoyment of relief* or perhaps an *enjoyment of relaxation*, similar to pauses between laughter episodes in playful conversations of children and adults.

Duchenne smiles (lip corner retraction with cheek raising) occur with gazing at the mother primarily when she uncovers her face during peekaboo. These smiles may reflect an *enjoyment of agency*, sensing oneself as an active rather than passive participant in the game (Holt, Fogel, & Wood, 1998; Stern, 1985). This may mean that the pleasure of peekaboo is in the experience of active visual searching for when and how the mother will reappear after hiding. Duchenne smiles without gazing at the mother occur most frequently during a tickle, often as infants turn their whole bodies away as if trying to hide or to protect themselves. These Duchenne smiles may reflect an *enjoyment of hiding* or perhaps an *enjoyment of escape*, as during hiding and chasing games in older infants and children.

Beginning around 8 or 9 months of age, infants begin to show *anticipatory smiles*, meaning that after smiling when looking at an object, the infant will spontaneously turn to smile at a nearby adult (Venezia et al., 2004), as if to share the emotion with the adult. These are different from *reactive smiles*, which are responses to making eye contact with an adult. Babies who were more likely to smile at their caregivers during a still-face procedure at 6 months (see Chapter 6) are more likely to show anticipatory smiles at 8 months, and these same babies were rated as higher on social competence at 30 months (Parlade et al., 2009). This suggests that there may be a long-term predisposition in some infants to more positive social emotions.

These findings reveal that infants of this age are showing the beginnings of adult-like emotional experiences. When co-regulating with an infant of this age, one gets the impression that babies are aware of their feelings and of some of the effects of those feelings on others. Taken together with the gazing at the adult that occurs in anger expressions, there is a growing ability in infants of this age to communicate with others about emotions (see the Co-Regulating with Baby section in this chapter).

The first laughs could be seen in the previous stage, primarily as a result of tickling and other vigorous stimulation. By the age of 6 months, babies will laugh at your jokes. They will laugh when you play tug with them, when they see you suck on their pacifiers or bottles, and when they try to pull the bottles out of your mouth (Fogel, Nwokah, & Karns, 1993; Nwokah et al., 1993; Sroufe, 1979).

Babies also laugh at very abrupt and highly arousing stimuli. They may laugh at things that once made them cry, such as a loud noise or a loss of balance. The laugh will sometimes follow a very serious or wary expression, almost as if the babies were trying to make up their minds about whether to get upset or enjoy the situation. In one study, 8-month-old babies watched while someone wearing a scary mask approached them. When the mask was worn by a stranger, the babies cried. When it was worn by their mothers, the babies laughed (Sroufe & Wunsch, 1977).

Emotion Regulation

This experiment suggests that by this age, the infant is beginning to use cognition to *decide what to feel*, a process known as **appraisal**. Appraisal is one aspect of emotion regulation, the ability to control the form and timing of one's emotional expression and feeling state. By the second half of the first year of life, infants are beginning to be able to control what they feel. When they get upset, they do not cry as long. They are also better able to wait for a meal or to get something they want before crying.

Infants develop different strategies to regulate their emotions although not all of them are successful. In one study of the still-face experiment, for example, when the mothers were performing the still-face, infants were seen to distract themselves by looking elsewhere, soothe themselves by sucking on their hands or touching their face or body, or by high intensity kicking or banging. The infants who used the first two strategies—distraction or self-soothing—showed less crying after the mother resumed her normal interactive behavior. Those who used the kicking and banging strategies actually cried more in the return-to-normal phase of the experiment (Ekas et al., 2013).

Distraction and self-soothing both have calming effects. During the second half of the first year, infants are more likely to use distraction because it involves a higher level of attention regulation and prefrontal cortical control that is becoming more available to infants during this age period. Self-soothing, on the other hand, declines over the first year. Kicking and banging actually increase the level of arousal of the infant's autonomic nervous system, most likely increases cortisol, and does not serve the function of calming. Use of this strategy actually increases with age, most likely because of the infant's growing awareness their behavior can affect others. Kicking and banging, therefore, may be a way of getting the caregiver's attention and using the caregiver for emotion regulation (Ekas et al., 2013). This type of behavior has its developmental peak around the second birthday in the form of temper tantrums. When infants in the second and third years learn to use language to express their feelings and ask for what they need, this high intensity (kicking and banging) form of emotion regulation tends to decrease.

In another related study, mothers were asked to briefly restrain their infant's arm by holding it to the infant's side for 90 seconds. Infants who showed a more rapid orienting response to the arm restraint were more likely to cry, turn away from the mother, and try to escape. This shows that some infants are more easily aroused and less able to remain calm or to use self-soothing or distraction strategies when stressed (Porter & Jones, 2011). These more reactive infants are even more likely to express resistance and anger to arm restraint once they learn to crawl, perhaps because they have more experience with behavior related to moving (Roben et al., 2012). It is likely that these infants who seem more reactive are actually more expressive about their feelings to caregivers. At six months, infants who were more reactive to arm restraint were more likely have responsive caregivers (Stone & Porter, 2012) and they were more likely to become socially extraverted as preschoolers (He et al., 2013).

There are also gender differences in emotion regulation. Six-month-old boys and girls were observed during face-to-face play, followed by maternal still-face (see Chapter 6). During the still-face condition, boys were more likely than girls to show expressions of anger, to fuss, to gesture to be picked up, or to try to get out of the infant seat. Boys also were more likely to try to get the mother's attention by smiling and vocalizing to her. Girls, on the other hand, spent more time gazing at objects and showing expressions of interest. The boys also had a more positive interaction with the mother during the normal face-to-face period (Weinberg, Tronick, Cohn, & Olson, 1999).

You might think these findings are counterintuitive. Under the assumption that girls may be more social, shouldn't girls be more positive with their mothers and more upset during the still face because of an apparent break in the mother-infant communication? This study, however, does not reveal that boys are more social than girls but, rather, that boys are less able to regulate their emotions under stressful conditions. The girls were able to manage their emotions during the still face by becoming more observant of the objects in the environment (using distraction). The more positive interaction between mothers and sons during the normal condition may reflect a necessity to quickly re-engage a co-regulated communication because boys are more upset when there are breakdowns in communication (Weinberg et al., 1999).

This interpretation is supported by a study of disciplinary strategies used by parents during this age period. Male infants were more likely than females to cry and fuss when hearing their mother's harsher tones of voice directed at them. As a consequence, mothers tended to use less harsh and more affectionate disciplinary language with their boy, compared to their girl babies (Ahl et al., 2013).

In summary, the findings on emotion regulation show that infants of both genders are highly tuned into their emotional communication with others. They are able to experience subtle differences of emotion as a function of how their attention is directed and whether the communication is co-regulated or disrupted. The result is that in older children and adults, males and females, emotions are related to their early experiences in interpersonal communication.

Recognition of Emotional Expressions

Research shows that infants' ability to recognize and discriminate among different emotional expressions increases between 6 and 9 months. Babies seem more capable of recognizing smiles than other expressions (Bornstein & Arterberry, 2003). Infants were familiarized with pictures of faces with smiles of different intensities. Later, they dishabituated to non-smile expressions but not to smiles differing in intensity (Ludemann, 1991; Ludemann & Nelson, 1988). Their ability at this age to distinguish between other expressions, such as fear and anger, is relatively poor (Nelson, 1987). Curiously, 7-month-old infants whose mothers are high in their display of positive emotions are more likely to respond to negative facial expressions, perhaps because of their relative novelty (de Haan et al., 2004).

On the other hand, as we saw in the last chapter, infants recognize emotion in the voice earlier than emotion in the face. When facial expressions of emotions are combined with voices expressing those emotions, 7-month-olds improve considerably in their ability to distinguish between emotions (Caron, Caron, & McLean, 1988; Phillips et al., 1990; Soken & Pick, 1992). When faces are presented dynamically, that is, by videorecordings rather than still pictures, 7-month-old infants' ability to distinguish different types of expression also improves (Soken & Pick, 1999). Infants also more readily recognize emotional differences if the facial expression is paired with a matching (compared to a mismatched) intonation pattern, as when an angry expression is matched with an angry versus happy tone of voice (Grossman et al., 2006).

There is a higher level of infant brain activation in response to angry compared to fearful faces and voices, perhaps because the angry voices activate the amygdala and alert the infants to a sense of threat (Hoehl et al., 2009). Infants are also less likely to be able to regulate their emotion and attention following exposure to fearful faces because of the activation of the threat response (Peltola et al., 2008). Infants' responses to emotional tones of voice occur in the right temporal cortex, the same area used by adults to identify emotion in voice and music (Grossman et al., 2010).

Except for a happy expression, to which infants will respond with a smile, there is little evidence that infants of this age view facial expressions alone as meaningful emotion signals (Nelson, 1987). The ability to extract meaning from viewing another person's face is extremely slow to develop, but we will see the beginnings of this skill in the next stage (see Chapter 8). It is not clear why infants have a concept for smiles earlier than they do concepts for other facial expressions. It makes sense, however, that the infant would be particularly attuned to facial expressions related to happiness, which probably increase the infant's sense of connection to the other person.

Infants of this age prefer to look at faces judged by adults to be attractive, regardless of the race or gender of the faces they are looking at (Langlois et al., 1991). Apparently, attractiveness, like recognition of particular people, can be inferred from more global features of the face that do not involve specific expressions (Rubenstein, Kalakanis, & Langlois, 1999). Infants can also distinguish between the faces of children and adults (Bahrick, Netto, & Hernandez-Reif, 1998). In summary, infants of this age have a rudimentary ability to perceive information from the face, and this ability will continue to improve in the coming months.

Infant Temperament

Another question related to infant emotional development is whether there are lasting patterns of emotional responding and emotion regulation in infants. We know that at any age different infants exhibit differing amounts of difficulty, fussiness, or happiness. The question is whether these differences persist over time. Is the same infant who is difficult at 3 months also difficult at 6 or 12 months? **Temperament** is a persistent pattern of emotion and emotion regulation in the infant's relationship to people and things in the environment.

Researchers have identified a number of expressive and responsive dimensions along which infants vary. One list of temperamental dimensions is given in Table 7.4. On each dimension, some children are especially high or especially low, and such extreme cases have been referred to as "easy" or as "difficult" (see Table 7.4; Thomas & Chess, 1977). Considerably shorter lists of temperamental dimensions have been developed by other groups of researchers and are shown in Tables 7.5 and 7.6.

In addition to proposing different definitions of temperament, each research team has a slightly different view of the origins of stable temperaments. According to Thomas and Chess, temperament is a style of approach to the environment and

TABLE 7.4   Temperamental Characteristics Crucial in Classifying Children as Easy or Difficult

Temperamental Quality	Two months	Two Years
Activity Level	Does not move when being dressed or during sleep.	Enjoys quiet play with puzzles. Can listen to records for hours.
	Moves often in sleep. Wriggles when diaper is changed.	*Climbs furniture. Explores. Gets in and out of bed while being put to sleep.*
Rhythmicity	Has been on 4-hour feeding schedule since birth. Regular bowel movement.	Eats a big lunch every day. Always has a snack before bedtime.
	Awakes at different time each morning. Size of feeding varies.	*Nap time changes from day to day. Toilet training is difficult because bowel movement is unpredictable.*
Approach/ Withdrawal	Smiles and licks washcloth. Has always liked bottle.	Slept well the first time he stayed overnight at grandparents' house.
	Rejected cereal the first time. Cries when strangers appear.	*Avoids strange children in the playground. Whimpers first time at beach. Will not get into water.*
Adaptability	Was passive during first bath, now enjoys bathing. Smiles at nurse.	Obeys quickly. Stayed contentedly with grandparents for a week.
	Still startled by sudden, sharp noises. Resists diapering.	*Cries and screams each time hair is cut. Disobeys persistently.*
Intensity of Reaction	Does not cry when diapers are wet. Whimpers instead of crying when hungry.	When another child hit her, she looked surprised, did not hit back.
	Cries when diapers are wet. Rejects food vigorously when satisfied.	*Yells if he feels excitement or delight. Cries loudly if a toy is taken away.*
Quality of Mood	Smacks lips when first tasting new food. Smiles at parents.	Plays with sister; laughs and giggles. Smiles when he succeeds in putting shoes on.
	Fusses after nursing. Cries when carriage is rocked.	*Cries and squirms when given a haircut. Cries when mother leaves.*

* Temperamental ratings and behaviors for difficult children are in italic type; those for easy children are in regular type.

Source: From Thomas, Chess, & Birch, 1970. In A. Fogel & G. F. Melson, *Child development*, 1988, p. 209. St. Paul, MN: West. Copyright © by West Publishing Company: All rights reserved.

may be affected by the situation. For Plomin (Buss & Plomin, 1984; Plomin & Saudino, 1994), temperament is stable because it is an inherited personality trait that appears early in life. While some traits are acquired, the three dimensions shown in Table 7.5 are believed to have some inherited basis (Goldsmith et al., 1987; Goldsmith, Buss, & Lemery, 1997; Goldsmith et al., 1999).

Research done using twin studies has found that some aspects of temperament are partly inherited (Emde & Hewitt, 2001; Friedman et al., 2011). Inhibition to the unfamiliar (see Table 7.6),

as observed in the laboratory, and infant negative emotions, as rated by parents, both have some genetic influence (Emde et al., 1992). Negativity and inhibition both appear early in life and are persistent characteristics in 5 to 10 percent of all infants up until at least the ages of 5 to 7 years. In addition, similar proportions of persistently inhibited children are found in different countries and even in infant monkeys, which further suggests some genetic contribution (Garcia-Coll, Kagan, & Reznick, 1984; Kagan, 1997; Kagan & Reznick, 1984; Kagan et al., 1988; Kagan et al., 1994; Lewis,

TABLE 7.5 Dimensions of Infant Temperament (Buss and Plomin, 1984)

Temperamental Quality	Description
Emotionality	Emotional infants have strong fear, anger, or distress responses, as shown by high ANS activity. Emotional infants may also respond more to minimal aversive events and may be less easy to calm or to appease. Emotional infants tend to "specialize" in one emotion, showing, for example, strong anger but not strong fear or distress.
Activity	Active infants tend to be busy or energetic. They move around a lot and prefer more active forms of play.
Sociability	Sociable infants tend to spend more time in the company of others. This concept refers more to frequent initiation of contact with a wide range of individuals than to intimate contact with attachment figures. Sociable infants prefer being with people rather than alone and seem genuinely pleased by social contact.

Source: Information from A. H. Buss & R. Plomin, Temperament: Early developing personality traits, 1984. Hillsdale, NJ: Erlbaum. Used with permission.

TABLE 7.6 Temperamental Dimensions of Reactivity (Rothbart & Derryberry, 1981) and Inhibition (Kagan, 1987)

Reactivity	Includes brain activation, ANS processes, and hormonal processes. High reactivity includes both a rapid response and a high-intensity response, and it may also include a slow recovery from the response.
Inhibition	Inhibited children are restrained, watchful, and gentle. They tend to experience uncertainty about how to respond or how to think about a situation. Inhibition can also be characterized by particular brain, ANS, and hormonal processes.

1993; Mullen, Snidman, & Kagan, 1993; Reznick et al., 1986; Shwalb, Shwalb, & Shoji, 1994; Worobey & Lewis, 1989). Activity level has also been found to have genetic links (Saudino, 2012).

One long-term study found that infants who were the most inhibited at 4 months were more likely to be subdued in unfamiliar situations, to have a dour mood, to report more anxiety, and to have an overactive sympathetic nervous system response when they were teenagers (see Chapter 4) (Kagan et al., 2007). Another study found that adults who were inhibited as infants showed a higher activation in the amygdala (the part of the limbic system responsive to fear) when viewing pictures of unfamiliar faces than adults who were not inhibited as infants. This fear of new faces reflects the persistence of social anxiety in inhibited individuals (Schwartz et al., 2003).

According to both Rothbart (Rothbart & Derryberry, 1981; Rothbart, Derryberry, & Posner, 1994) and Kagan (1987), temperament is rooted in biological processes but not necessarily inherited. For these researchers, behavioral characteristics called temperamental must be associated with specific central nervous system (CNS) and autonomic nervous system (ANS: sympathetic-arousal and parasympathetic-relaxation) activity (Costa & Figueiredo, 2011; S. D. Calkins, Fox, & Marshall, 1996; Kagan, Reznick & Snidman, 1987; Rothbart, 1986). In one study, infant testosterone levels at 3 to 4 months of age were related to negative affect irritability in males. The male tendency during child and adulthood toward less ability to regulate emotions, including distress and proneness to anger, may be a result of higher levels of testosterone (Alexander & Saenz, 2011).

In this view, temperament involves both mind and body, emotional state and physiology. Infants and children who have difficulties with attention and emotion regulation—those rated as highly reactive, emotional, inattentive, or inhibited—have different patterns of activity in the prefrontal cortex compared to well-regulated infants (Hane et al., 2008; Rothbart, Sheese, & Posner, 2007). The prefrontal cortex is that part of the brain associated with self-regulation (Chapter 4).

In the case of inhibition, the prefrontal cortex is less able to regulate the activation of the amygdala (sense of threat and fear, see Chapter 4) which then leads to higher activation of the sympathetic nervous system. For example, inhibition (see Table 7.6) is related to brain-wave and heart-rate patterns as well as to stress responses such as heart-rate acceleration, cortisol secretion, and sympathetic nervous system activation, which are present at an early age for some inhibited infants and may persist for many years (S. Calkins & Fox, 1994; N. A. Fox, 1989; M. Gunnar, 1994; M. Gunnar, Mangelsdorf, Larson, & Hertsgaard, 1989; Healy, 1989; Huffman et al., 1998; M. Lewis & Ramsay, 1995; C. A. Nelson, 1994).

Inhibited infants and adults may also show higher levels of activation in the insula and other areas related to self-awareness of interoception (see Chapter 4), meaning that they are more sensitive to changes in their own physiological state. Because they can more readily sense the internal feelings of stress (such as increased heart rate and faster breathing) they are more likely to have a fear response to their own inner state, increasing their sense of anxiety or worry and further accelerating the activation of the sympathetic nervous system and cortisol secretion (Kagan et al., 2007).

Some research has shown that infant temperament, and its associated physiological features, are correlated with parental personality. Infants who are more inhibited or negative, for example, are more likely to have parents who are introverted, shy, depressed or anxious (Henrichs et al., 2009; Kochanska et al., 2004; Murray et al., 2008; Pauli-Pott et al., 2004; Rickman & Davidson, 1994). Also, persistent infant inhibition and high levels of negativity and anxiety are related to lower scores on maternal adaptation to pregnancy, maternal sensitivity to the infant after birth, and maternal self-esteem (Blair et al., 2008;

Crockenberg & Leerkes, 2004; Fish, Stifter, & Belsky, 1991; Gartstein & Bateman, 2008; Martin, Noyes, Wisenbaker, & Huttunen, 1999; Mount et al., 2010). Mothers who rate infant cries as more aversive are more likely to rate their infants as difficult (Pedersen & Moran, 1996). These findings, while they suggest that parents play a role in the development of infant temperament, do not necessarily rule out a partial genetic explanation for inhibition, because parents and infants could both share similar genetic make-ups.

Another finding that may call the genetic explanation into question is that children do not necessarily exhibit continuity of temperament. Inhibited children may, with appropriately sensitive child rearing, eventually lose their extreme sensitivity. Normal children may become more inhibited in extremely stressful environments. While extreme fussiness at birth predicts later emotionality in full-term infants (Worobey & Blajda, 1989), fussiness at birth is not related to later behavior in premature infants (Riese, 1987). Irritability is reduced and moderated by secure attachment relationships (Stupica et al., 2011). The stress of premature birth may have made it impossible to assess the infant's temperament at the time of birth. If there is a biological predisposition toward inhibition or other temperamental factors, such as emotionality, it does not operate in the absence of environmental influences (Kagan, 1987; Wachs, 1988).

While some temperamental characteristics in infancy, such as inhibition (see above) predict long-term personality characteristics or behavior disorders, not all of the person's behavior is related to early temperament. Temperament may have short-term influences on cognitive information processing, as when an inhibited infant is unlikely to approach a novel stimulus, but there is less evidence that temperament contributes to longer-term cognitive deficit or enhancement (J. E. Bates, 1987; Kagan, 1987; M. D. Lewis, 1993).

One reason may be that parents adjust their short-term behavior to the child's reactivity. If parents respond cautiously to inhibited children or work to desensitize them, and if they reduce the intensity of stimulation for highly active children, the parental behavior may attenuate the long-term effects of the early temperamental characteristic (Gandour, 1989; Kagan, 1987; Kagan, Snidman, & Arcus, 1998; S. Park, Belsky, Putnam, & Crnic, 1997; Penela et al., 2012; Stright et al., 2008).

Chinese children who are more inhibited are actually more likely to be cooperative, liked by peers, and do well in school. In China, where being modest and cooperative is a social value, inhibition leads to better success in school settings and gives these children a social advantage over those who are more outgoing (Chen et al., 2009). On the other hand, early family stress, controlling or insensate parenting, and marital conflict may prolong and accentuate a child's inhibition and negative emotionality (Blandon et al., 2010; Burney & Leerkes, 2010; Crockenberg et al., 2007; Lipscomb et al., 2011; Sullivan et al., 2008; Volbrecht & Goldsmith, 2010)

Aside from parental factors, factors in the infant may contribute to the stability of temperament. Inhibited children who showed more positive emotion and longer periods of sustained attention were less likely to be inhibited at age 3 than inhibited children who tended to be more negative (S. Park et al., 1997; Pérez-Edgar et al., 2010). It seems that both parental and child factors can interact to influence the stability of temperament over time.

Temperament assessed at the end of the infancy period, between 2 and 4 years of age, tends to show long-term stability (Lemery, Goldsmith, Klinnert, & Mrazek, 1999). Two-year-olds who were rated as more difficult had more attention problems and aggressive behavior at 12 years (Guerin, Gottfried, & Thomas, 1997). Three-year-olds who were rated low on self-control had more adjustment problems and interpersonal conflicts as adults (Newman, Caspi, Moffitt, & Silva, 1997). Children at 4 to 6 years who were rated as more inhibited were more likely at 23 years to continue to be inhibited, show more of a delay in finding a stable partnership and finding a full-time job. In this same study, 4 to 6 year-olds who were rated as more aggressive were more likely at 23 years to be

underachievers and have higher delinquency rates (Asendorpf et al., 2008).

In summary, temperamental characteristics such as inhibition and negativity clearly exist in infants and may persist over many years. Less clear is the origin of these temperamental characteristics. The evidence suggests that they have multiple and complex causes related to inheritance, physiology, environment, and parent-child relationships. Temperament is apparently best explained by some type of systems theory. In the next section, we turn to the problem of how temperament is measured.

The Measurement of Temperament

One of the problems in studying temperament is that it must be observed over a long period of time. Temperament is by definition those aspects of infants that are consistent over some period of time. A child who is sociable on a particular day is not necessarily temperamentally sociable unless there is a consistent pattern of such behavior over a weeks or months. For this reason, the study of temperament is more difficult than other areas of research because the investigator has to identify what stays the same when other things are changing. Because infants change in so many ways, it is difficult to capture their essence (J. E. Bates, 1987; J. E. Bates, Wachs, & Emde, 1994; Kagan, 1987; Wachs & Bates, 2000).

Another problem is that of language. Even though we might have some strong intuition about the consistent temperament of a baby we know, it is hard to describe that consistency in words. Once a word such as "inhibited" is chosen, it cannot describe exactly what the temperamental quality is, and the word itself often distorts what is unique about the baby (Kagan, 1987). To call a baby "inhibited" does not do justice to the fact that the child may play, walk, and talk like most other children. Under certain circumstances, however, such as in the presence of an unfamiliar person, this child may be especially shy.

Given the difficulties in identifying a common-sense concept of temperament, it should come as no surprise that researchers have found temperament to be a difficult construct to measure in a reliable and valid manner. Some have attempted to observe children's responses to particular situations over a long period, such as their reactions to distress and separation, or to examine their overall activity level. More typically, parents are asked to rate their children's temperaments under the assumption that the parents have the most complete, long-term experiences with the children and can better assess any stable characteristics (J. E. Bates, 1987).

On the other hand, what is probably the best source of information about the child's temperament is not always reliable. When mothers and fathers are asked to rate the same child, their reports agree only about half the time (J. E. Bates & Bayles, 1984). Similarly, there is only a moderate amount of agreement between mothers and outside observers (J. E. Bates, 1980), although there is more overall agreement about the difficulty of an infant than about any other dimension of temperament.

Some evidence also suggests that parental temperament rating is related to other measures of the infant's behavior. Infants who were rated as "difficult" had cries that were independently rated as more irritating and had longer pauses between cry sounds, giving their cries a greater sense of urgency (Huffman et al., 1994). Mothers' ratings of infant temperamental fussiness correlated with direct observations of crying behavior at 3 months (Crockenberg & Acredolo, 1983). Infant fear and pleasure responses as measured in a laboratory setting correlated with similar dimensions of parent-rated infant temperament (H. H. Goldsmith & Campos, 1990). The correlation between parental reports and actual behavior is improved if infants are selected only from the extreme ends of the behavioral scale. Infants who were either extremely inhibited or extremely uninhibited in a laboratory situation had parents who also rated them in this manner (Garcia-Coll et al., 1984). These findings suggest that there is some correspondence between parental reports and actual behavior.

Why then, would adults differ on how they rate the child? It could be that each parent and each observer have different experiences with the child

and thus have different "databases" from which to draw conclusions. Also, the child may actually behave differently across situations and in the company of different observers. It could also be that the questions asked on rating forms (ranging from general questions about the overall difficulty of the child to specific questions about the child's reaction to strangers) are not sufficiently sensitive to capture the individuality of the child.

Another possibility is that the parental reports reflect the parents' personalities more than the child's (Matheny, Wilson, & Thoben, 1987; Miebert, 1991; Vaughn, Bradley, Joffe, Seifer, & Barglow, 1987) or reveal something about the current psychological state of the parents. Mothers who were multiparous and extroverted were more likely to rate their infants as easy than other mothers (J. E. Bates, Freeland, & Lounsbury, 1979). Other studies found that mothers from low-income groups who were African American, had a history of mental illness, or scored high on tests of anxiety rated their infants' temperament as more difficult than mothers who did not fall into any of these groups (Sameroff, Seifer, & Elias, 1982; Vaughn, Taraldson, Crichton, & Egeland, 1981).

Another way to test the validity of temperament measures is to study their consistency over repeated testings. On the whole, parental reports and observational measures are only moderately stable over the infancy period. In other words, children who are rated as "fearful," "inhibited," or "sociable" at 1 year are not necessarily rated the same way at 3 years (J. E. Bates, 1987; Seifer, Sameroff, Barrett, & Krafchuk, 1994). This could be because the infants themselves changed or the parents changed in the way they perceived the infants.

In summary, parents' ratings of infant temperament have some usefulness, but they must be interpreted with caution. Some ratings reflect the parents' own personalities or current levels of stress and may be inconsistent over time. It is not surprising that parents' interpretations of their infant's temperament are colored by their own experiences. No less is true of adults' interpretations of the behavior and personality of

Case Report
The Ups and Downs of Being Uninhibited

This report illustrates the stability of temperament from infancy to adulthood. In this case, the individual has always been outgoing, rather than inhibited or shy. Inhibition, as discussed in this chapter, is difficult for those people who are easily overwhelmed. Being uninhibited may seem like a better way to be in the world, but as you'll see from reading this report, it is not always easy.

I have grown up to be a rather honest and confident person. My mother is the same way. I have always been encouraged to explore and to ask questions. My mother has been sensitive to my needs since I was a baby, but she never let me walk all over her. My mother also encouraged me to observe everything and to converse with others. I tend to let people know what I am feeling in the moment, and I like to express my opinions and ideas. When I walk into a room or down the street, or when I meet people, I observe what I see by noticing

details and remembering small things.

In my interview with my mother, she recalled that as an infant I would lie in the crib and stare at the mobile above me for hours. I loved to look at things and concentrate. Even before I could speak fluently, my parents would check books out of the library along with the audio recordings and encourage me to look and listen. My heightened sense of awareness was reinforced by the secure attachment I had with my mother. She spent hours with me playing and encouraging me to speak and be aware of how I was feeling. I did not like to go to strangers, but I did not freak out when I was left with a baby sitter that I knew. My mother said that I was a very friendly baby who was always laughing.

In interviewing my boyfriend of four years, I discovered parallels in what he observes and what my family recalls from my infancy. He observes my capacity to vocalize my needs

and wants in the moment. He says that I am less inhibited than most people to express my moods, which range from extremely excited to being sad. He observes my ability to look at things in wonder and amazement, almost as if it was my first time to see them. Yet, he often accuses me at times of always having something to say about everything!

Having a secure attachment to my primary caregiver, I believe that my ability to maintain very long and lasting relationships, to show affection toward many, and to be aware of how I feel, how others feel, and to be aware of all around me, stem from my infancy. I also have the horrible habit of asking "why." This I have done since I was a tiny infant. This causes me to look at people in the eye until I feel they have given me a complete answer. According to my sister, I had this attribute when I was small and ended up in "time out" often.

other adults. The best research strategy is to use a combination of parental reports, direct observations, and physiological measures (such as cortisol and sympathetic nervous system activity) made at repeated intervals in the child's life.

SOCIAL AND LANGUAGE DEVELOPMENT

Social-Object Frames

Because of the newly developed motor, perceptual, and cognitive abilities for acting upon

objects, a good deal of parent-infant communication at this age is focused on objects. In the previous developmental period, much of the parent-infant communication involved mutual gazing and frames for face-to-face play in the absence of objects. While infants smiled and cooed, their parents made exaggerated facial expressions and vocalizations. These types of frames are very satisfying to both participants. As infants become increasingly interested in objects, between 4 and 6 months of age, and the earlier face-to-face frames give way to social-object play frames, parents sometimes feel a sense of disappointment. For the infant's part, the developmental task is to integrate interest in objects with the desire to remain socially and emotionally connected to the parents.

In the first part of this developmental period, infants are primarily focused on the objects themselves. It is up to the parents to provide frames for mutual communication about objects. Typically, this is done by holding objects within the infant's reach, making objects attractive to infants, helping the infants steady the object to explore it, and sometimes just sitting nearby and commenting while the infant manipulates or sucks on a toy (Fogel et al., 2006). The types of actions performed by parents at this age are shown in Table 7.7.

When using the actions shown in Table 7.7, parents employ strategies with toys similar to those they used earlier with their own faces, taking advantage of simple changes in rhythm, timing, and exaggeration to help infants attend to particular objects or to particular properties of objects. Parents will animate a toy dog, for example, by making it jump and matching the intensity of the jumping to the changes in the infant's delight (Stern, 1985). When trying to get the infant's attention to a jar of vitamins, a mother shook it rhythmically, saying, "shakey, sha...key, SHA... KEY!," increasing the volume and changing the timing of pauses between syllables (Zukow-Goldring, 1997).

The infant's ability to coordinate his or her attention to people and to objects is enhanced if parents regularly create frames in which these kinds of object-directed actions occur. The more attentive and animated the parents are with respect to the infant's attention to objects, the more likely it is that the infant will learn to co-regulate attention with others (Brighi, 1997). If the parent animates the object's movements while saying the name of the object, the infant is more likely to remember the sound that goes with the object (Gogate et al., 2013; Matatyaho & Gogate, 2008). This is important, because infants who are more attentive to what adults do and say are more likely to learn language and come to share, by 3 or 4 years of age, the mental perspectives of other people (Moore, Angelopoulos, & Bennett, 1997; Morales, Mundy, & Rojas, 1998; Striano & Rochat, 1999).

By the end of this developmental period, infants begin to be more aware of the adult and of the triadic relationship between the object, the self, and the adult. As discussed earlier, by around 8 months, infants become aware that other people have intentions, that they are agents. This change is also seen in the infant's growing ability to appreciate and to make "jokes," clowning with adults. Prior to 8 months, the infant might bang a ball on the table. If the parent discourages the activity, the infant may stop momentarily and begin again or else ignore the parent. By about 8 months, the infant may bang the ball on the table, look at the parent, and grin mischievously (Lock, 2000; Reddy, 2000).

At 6 months, infants appear to be in a receptive mode, ready to participate in the frames created by the parents. By 8 months, infants are beginning to take initiatives in social frames. In one experiment, mothers were asked to see if infants would take the

TABLE 7.7   Attention-Directing Strategies of Parents

Act-ons	Moving the infant through some activity, such as pulling the infant up and saying "up."
Shows	Moving an object across the infant's line of sight, or moving the object toward and away from the infant.
Demonstrations	Using a particular action on an object, such as how to comb a doll's hair or how to shake a rattle.
Points	Using a gesture to direct the infant's attention to a particular feature of an object or to a specific location in space, such as *over there*.

Source: Adapted from P. Zukow-Goldring. A social ecological realist approach to the emergence of the lexicon: Educating attention to amodal invariants in gesture and speech, 1997. In C. Dent-Read & P. Zukow-Goldring (eds.), *Evolving explanations of development: Ecological approaches to organism-environment systems*, pp. 199–250. Washington, D.C.: American Psychological Association.

initiative in asking for help. During ordinary play with objects, mothers were asked either to hold a toy out of the infant's reach, stop demonstrating a toy, or delay giving help even if the child seemed to need immediate assistance. One-third of the 6-month-olds and two-thirds of the 9-month-olds showed evidence of asking the mother for help by gazing at her, making a demanding vocalization, or making a gesture (such as pulling on her arm) that indicated a help request (Mosier & Rogoff, 1994). By 8 months, infants "ask" to be picked up by making sad facial expressions or raising their hands above their heads, especially if adults indicate a willingness to pick them up (Service, Lock, & Chandler, 1989). Finally, the frequency with which infants make demands of mothers increases markedly once the infants begin to walk (Biringen et al., 1995).

Another aspect of initiative taking is that infants during this period are becoming more selective with respect to adults than during the previous period. By 8 or 9 months, infants will smile and laugh more toward familiar and trusted adults than toward unfamiliar ones. They may show some wariness in response to unfamiliar persons, but this has not yet blossomed into the more severe fearful reactions to strangers seen in some infants after the age of 10 months.

Babbling: A Prerequisite for Later Vocal Communication

From the beginning of life, infants communicate vocally with the cry. In the period between 2 and 5 months, cooing or speech-like vocalization emerges. These are primarily vowel-like sounds such as "oooo" and "aaaah." At birth and up until 4 to 6 months, the infant's tongue fills most of the oral cavity, and it can only execute some primitive thrusting movements designed to help in sucking and swallowing (see Chapter 5). The young infant's epiglottis, a small fold of tissue behind the tongue, is in contact with the soft palate at the back of the roof of the mouth. This configuration covers the air tube from the lungs (the larynx) and helps prevent choking and inhaling of food par-

ticles. Beginning at 4 months, the oral cavity and vocal tract widen and lengthen, and the epiglottis begins to move away from the soft palate. The net effect is to allow air to be taken in and pushed out through the infant's mouth more readily, with the epiglottis moving up and down to stop the flow of air (Kent, 1981).

Before the age of 4 months, infants cannot breathe well through their mouths. This is why it is important to keep the very young baby's nasal passages clear of mucus. After 4 months, oral breathing allows the infant a much greater latitude for making new types of sounds. After 6 months, infants begin to explore sound production by using their ability to vary the direction of air flow, the pitch of the sound, and its loudness by abruptly stopping the air flow with the epiglottis (Zlatin, 1973). We can compare the oral and laryngeal manipulation of airflow to the manual manipulation of objects. The result is **babbling**, a string of vowel and consonant sounds. In babbling, sometimes the syllables are repeated (da-da-da-da) and sometimes alternated (da-do-da-do). It may sound almost as though the babies are talking to themselves as they roll off these syllables to accompany their eating or playing.

Many parents report that babbling sounds like speech. Although infants of this age are not imitating the words of speech, there is evidence that babbling has the intonation contours (the rising and falling pitches) of sentences (Nakazima, 1972). Indeed, in a study done in French-, Chinese-, and Arabic-speaking homes, the intonation contours of babbling match quite well the intonation contours of the speech spoken in the infant's home (DeBoysson-Bardies, Sagant, & Durand, 1984).

In one experimental study, some mothers were asked to respond contingently to infant babbling by smiling or talking or touching the baby for a 10-minute period. Another group of mothers were asked not to respond to the babbling also for 10 minutes. Following this, the infant's babbling was studied for the following 10 minutes. Infants whose mothers were contingent produced more "mature" babbles that had more recognizable syllables, strong contrasts between consonants and vowels, and a more fully voiced sound (Goldstein et al., 2003). This suggests that babbling may be speech-like because it occurs during parent-infant contingent vocal interaction.

The relationship of babbling to future speech is further supported by research showing that right-handed reaching and rhythmical banging with the hands increases in frequency at the same age infants begin to babble (Locke, 1993). The right hand is controlled by the left brain, and the left brain is known to be the primary location of speech processing. This means that the infant's vocalizations at this age come increasingly under the control of the left brain, setting the stage for linking vocalization and cognition necessary for the development of speech. Another study carefully tracked the way babies opened their mouths when smiling compared to babbling. When babbling, there was a slightly wider mouth opening on the right side; when smiling, the mouth opened more on the left side (Holowka & Petitto, 2002). This study confirms that the right brain is more emotional while the left brain more linguistic, a difference that begins in the second half-year of life and contributes to the development of left-right hemisphere differentiation in the brain.

Another link between babbling and future speech is that babbling typically occurs along with rhythmic arm and hand movements. Babies of this age are more likely to move their hands and arms, rather than their legs, while babbling, and specifically there is a preference to move the right arm. This work suggests that pre-speech babbling is linked "linguistically" to a kind of pre-gesture rhythmic movement of the hands (Iverson & Fagan, 2004).

Early observations suggested that even deaf babies babble in ways similar to hearing babies up until about 9 months of age (Lenneberg, 1969). More recent research suggests that this is not the case, as shown in a careful descriptive analysis of babbling in deaf infants (Oller & Eilers, 1988). First of all, the onset of babbling in deaf infants is substantially delayed, in some cases occurring between 6 and 18 months later than in hearing infants. Second, deaf infants produce consider-

ably fewer well-formed consonant-vowel syllables. Although this study does not show that hearing infants copy the speech sounds of adults at this age, it does show that the ability to hear oneself vocalize contributes to the development of vocalization.

Why do babies babble? One idea, following Piaget, is they like hearing themselves make these sounds and in the process, they are exploring new ways to make sound: a kind of vocal play. Infants also use babbling to practice making smooth vocal transitions from one sound to another. If babies learn one syllable, "da" for example, they will tend to repeat it as "da-da-da." Later, they might learn another syllable, "do." They cannot immediately make the sequence "da-do-da-do." Instead, they may put the "do" at the beginning or ending of the "da" sequence, such as "do-da-da-da" or "da-da-da-do." Eventually, with literally hundreds or thousands of repetitions, they can master saying "da-do-da-do." It turns out that baby songbirds go through a similar learning process when adding new sounds to their vocal repertoire, suggesting a common neural mechanism for learning vocal communication across species (Lipkind et al., 2013)

Language and Speech Perception

The development of auditory perception seems to parallel the development of sound production in hearing infants. Before the age of 6 months, infants are universal language perceivers. They can distinguish important sound contrasts from many different languages. Infants between 6 and 9 months are beginning to organize the sounds they hear, especially speech sounds, into conceptual categories. Recall that in research on visual perception, after being familiarized with a set of somewhat distorted figures, infants preferred to look at the prototype figure that best fit the series of distorted figures seen before. A similar study done with distorted versions of speech syllable prototypes yielded very similar results (Grieser & Kuhl, 1989). The auditory stimuli were syllables in which the vowel sound was subtly altered in pitch using a computer simulation.

This means that infants of this age hear the variations of the sound as the "same" as the prototype sound. Since the prototype sounds for babies are those most commonly heard in their linguistic environment, it means that as they get older, infants will be less likely to hear a wide diversity of sounds and more likely to hear sounds that "sound like" those occurring in the native language (Kuhl, 1998).

A developmental study (Werker & Tees, 1984) looked at infants between 4 and 6 months and between 10 and 12 months from three different language groups: English, Salish (a Native Canadian language), and Hindi. Babies from each group were tested with syllable contrasts from each language. Syllables were chosen in such a way that a native speaker could hear the differences between them, but a non-native speaker could not. An example of this is the contrast in English between /ra/ and /la/. Japanese speakers cannot distinguish perceptually between these two syllables and often get them mixed up when they speak English. English speakers have a similarly difficult time distinguishing between the Japanese syllables /ki/ and /kii/, as in *kite* (come) and *kiite* (listen). In the second syllable, the /ii/ sound (pronounced like the "e" in "be") is held just slightly longer than the /i/ sound in the first syllable; otherwise, the two sounds are identical.

The results of the study showed that the younger infants could distinguish the syllable contrasts from all the languages, but the older infants could only distinguish between the contrasts of the language heard in the home. A later study replicated these findings using computer-simulated sound contrasts similar to those found in English and in Hindi (Werker & Lalonde, 1988). Thus, between the ages of 6 and 9 months, infants lose a perceptual sensitivity that they had at an earlier age. On the other hand, as discussed earlier, infants gain in the ability to form and remember concepts.

The loss of perceptual sensitivity may be related to the selective processes of brain development discussed in Chapter 4. At first, synapses are overproduced, and later some (those that are responsive to the sounds heard in the environment) are selected and strengthened, while synapses for sounds that are not frequently heard disappear. In the auditory cortex, the overproduction occurs during the first 6 months; by 10 months, the number of synapses has started to drop (Goldman-Rakic, 1987).

Infants of this age can distinguish between a wide variety of speech sounds in their native language but are less sensitive than adults (Aslin, 1987). Their ability to distinguish between sounds improves when the test sounds are embedded in a series of familiar speech sounds (Karzon, 1985) or in sentences in which adults are speaking motherese (Fernald, 1985).

Infants can apparently distinguish between the intonation patterns of different languages. Some infants from monolingual English-speaking homes and some from bilingual English-and-Spanish-speaking homes were familiarized with a video display of a woman reciting a passage in either English or Spanish. In the test condition, infants dishabituated to the woman reciting a passage in the language they had not heard during familiarization but not to a different passage read in the language with which they had been familiarized (Bahrick & Pickens, 1988). In American English, the majority of two-syllable words are stressed on the initial syllable (strong-weak pattern of stress). By 9 months, American infants preferred to listen to words having a strong-weak stress pattern, compared to a weak-strong stress pattern. Six-month-olds showed no such preference (Jusczyk, Cutler, & Redanz, 1993). Infants of this age also prefer the regional accents of their native language compared to accents of the same language from a different region (Butler et al., 2011).

Overall, these results show that by the second half of the first year of life, even though infants would not be considered to be speaking or understanding language, they are beginning to recognize and produce some of the characteristics of their native language as a system of sounds. Babbling infants may sound to adults as if they are trying to talk, but it is more appropriate to view them as exploring how to make familiar sounds, those

TABLE 7.8 Descriptions of Conventional Games

Gonna get you: Mother repeatedly tickles, grabs, jostles, or provides other tactual/kinesthetic stimulation to the infant. Often includes a repeated vocalizaton such as "I'm gonna get you" or "Ahhhhh-boom!" that terminates just as physical contact is made. (Active participation by an infant could include fleeing when approached or attempting to "get" the mother.)

Pat-a-cake: Primary components are the mother's saying "pat-a-cake" and clapping or banging performed by either the mother or the infant. (Active participation by the infant would include beginning to clap only after the mother said "pat-a-cake" or patting the mother's hands.)

Horsie: Primary component is the mother's bouncing the infant, who is sitting on her knees or foot. The mother's verbalizations include "Want to play horsie?" or "Ride the horsie." (Active participation by the infant involves initiating the game or trying to prolong it by continuing to bounce after the mother has stopped.)

Peekaboo: One member of the dyad is hidden and reappears. Hiding is typically accompanied by the mother's calling to the child (if the mother is hidden) or by her asking "Where's [child's name]?" (if the child is hidden). Reappearance is typically accompanied by verbalizataions such as "Peekaboo," "Peepeye," or "There he/she is!" (Mother may control all the hiding and uncovering, or the infant may actively perform some of these activities.

Ball: Involves the infant's repeatedly receiving and losing the ball. (Mother may hold up both ends of the game by tossing the ball to the infant and then taking it away, or the infant may actively participate by presenting or returning the ball to the mother.)

Vocal game: Minimal requirement is that the mother be attempting to elicit a word or vocalization from the infant. In expanded form, these interactions are verbal or vocal-verbal "conversations."

Build tower–knock down: One member of the dyad builds a tower of blocks, and the other knocks the tower over. The sequence may be repeated many times. (Active participation by the infant is typically limited to knocking the tower down.)

Give and take: Involves a repeated giving and receiving of objects. Receiving by the mother is often accompanied by a carefully articulated "Thank you." Typically, the infant gives and the mother receives, although the mother often returns the object to the infant.

Point and name: One member of the dyad (usually the infant) repeatedly points to objects, each time waiting for a vocalization by the other (usually the mother, in the form of naming the object), before pointing to the next object. Pointing is sometimes accompanied by a questioning vocalization or by the query, "What's this?"

Miscellaneous: Any traditional infant game that occurs very infrequently at a particular age. Included are the game "Overboard," in which the mother repeatedly turns the infant upside down and says "Little girl overboard," and the game "So Big," in which the mother says, "How big are you?" and the infant stretches his or her arms out while the mother says, "So big." Also included are sequences with a toy telephone in which the receiver is put to the infant's ear and the mother says "Hello," and interactions in which one or both members of the pair wave or say, "Bye-bye."

Source: G. E. Gustafson, J. A. Green, & M. J. West, The infant's changing role in mother-infant games: The growth of social skills, 1979, p. 304, *Infant Behavior and Development, 2*, 301–308. Reprinted by permission of Ablex Publishing Company.

heard in the home environment, rather than as trying to communicate with sounds. Nevertheless, this is a remarkable ability. The intonation patterns of language are complex and rich.

It seems as if babies first learn the music and later they learn the words. This music—the intonation pattern—is learned in the context of parent-infant frames, including social games. And, speaking of music, infants older than 9 months are better at discriminating differences between the rhythmic structure of songs from their own culture (the ones they hear frequently) compared to songs from another culture (Hannon & Trehub, 2005; Soley & Hannon, 2012). By this age, it

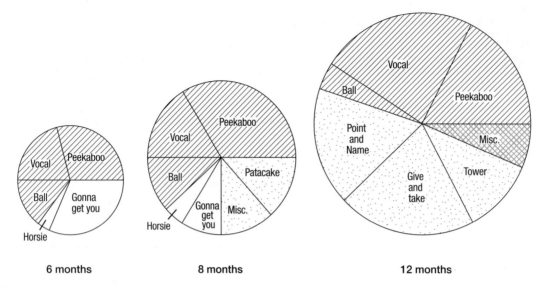

6 months　　　　**8 months**　　　　**12 months**

Figure 7.3　Relative Frequency of Parent-Infant Games
Dotted areas represent games in which the infant's role is explicitly active; blank areas represent games in which the infant's role is typically passive. Hatched areas represent games played at all ages. Cross-hatched areas represent both active and passive games.

Source: G. E. Gustafson, J. A. Green, & M. J. West, The infant's changing role in mother-infant games: The growth of social skills, 1979, p. 304, *Infant Behavior and Development, 2*, 301–308. Reprinted by permission of Ablex Publishing Company.

appears, we are tapping our feet more to familiar compared to unfamiliar music.

Infants also appear to prefer patterns of non-verbal communication, gesture and body language, that are directed to them rather than non-verbal communication more typically used with adults. Infant directed non-verbal communication (sometimes called "motionese" in relation to infant directed speech, discussed in Chapter 6, called "motherese") includes being in close proximity to the infant, exaggeration and greater range of motion of gestures, more turn-taking and gazing at the infant, and more repetition (Brand & Shallcross, 2008). The more an adult uses repetition and exaggeration, the more attention the infant pays to the adult (Koterba & Iverson, 2009).

Also, during this age period of 6 to 9 months, infants shift their facial attention to the mouth, rather than to the eyes of an adult who is speaking to them, as if they need to use the non-verbal mouth shapes to help hear the sound (Lewkowicz & Hansen-Tift, 2012), while deaf infants focus their attention on the adult's hands that are making sign language gestures (Palmer et al., 2012).

Finally, all this increased infant attention to the sounds and gestures of their native language actually contributes to their language development. Beginning at six months, infants can remember the sounds associated with some familiar objects in their environment (Bergelson & Swingley, 2012). They can correctly identify pictures of "mommy" and "daddy" according to these sounds, and they do not associate these sounds with pictures of other adults. Similarly, they can identify some body parts like hands and feet (Tincoff & Jusczyk, 2012). Infants of this age are better able to match words and pictures if the sounds are made in infant directed rather than in adult speech (Singh et al., 2009).

In summary, it appears that the brain and body of the infant are becoming increasingly attuned to the sounds and communication patterns of the languages spoken in the home. As they lose their ability to be universal language perceivers, they gain in their ability to follow, understand, and

(a) North America

(a) Africa

(b) North America

(b) Africa

Figure 7.4 Infant-Carrying Practices
In warm climates, infants spend more time in skin-to-skin contact with adults. Infants in cold climates must wear protective clothing, making them more difficult to carry for long periods.
Source: A. Fogel & G. F. Melson, *Child development*, 1988, p. 187. St. Paul, MN: West. Copyright © West Publishing Company. Reprinted by permission. All rights reserved.

learn the basics of speech, gesture and intonation patterns as part of ongoing everyday interactions. When babies begin to say their first words, usually some time after 10 months of age, they have already internalized a great deal about language and communication.

Parent-Infant Interpersonal Communication

By 8 months, the infant is much more likely to take the initiative in play situations rather than simply respond to the caregiver (Gustafson, Green, & West, 1979; Kaye & Fogel, 1980). Social play is more frequent and more spirited, with laughter and squealing in the sound track. In addition to the social-object frames discussed earlier, a large variety of new social frames emerges in the parent-infant relationship at this age.

Table 7.8 describes the typical playful frames found in parent-infant play during the second half-year of life. Figure 7.3 shows the relative frequency of each game at 6, 8, and 12 months of age. As infants get older, they learn to play an increasing number of new social games, such as "point and name" and "give and take" at 12 months. In playing those games that are played at every age—such as ball, vocal games, and peekaboo—infants take an increasingly active role as they get older. Games like "gonna get you" and "horsie," in which the 6-month-old played a relatively passive role, occur only rarely at 12 months (Gustafson et al., 1979; Rome-Flanders et al., 1995).

Note that these games are typical of white middle-class North American populations and do not necessarily represent what parents and infants do in other cultures. Furthermore, even in this particular population, games were observed in only about 10 percent of all social interaction episodes. The rest of the time is taken up with frames for caregiving (such as feeding, calming, bathing, and bedtime rituals) and for infant solitary play with objects, which increases at this age.

Cultural Differences in Parent-Infant Relationships

There are wide differences between cultures in the amount of time mothers spend with babies, in parental beliefs about infant care, and in the types of activities they perform when with the babies. Climate is one factor that accounts for cultural differences in child-rearing patterns. In warm countries, infants tend to be carried by their caregivers, to remain in close physical contact throughout most of the day and night, and to be breast-fed longer than infants reared in cold climates. Infants in cold climates are more likely to be separated from their mothers at an earlier age. They sleep in cradles, are carried in strollers and buggies, and are kept at a distance from the parents through the use of infant seats and playpens (Agiobu-Kemmer, 1986; Keller et al., 2004; Whiten & Milner, 1986; J. Whiting, 1981).

These differences are believed to be due to the need to wrap babies in cold climates against the cold (see Figure 7.4). Because both the adult and infant must wear many layers of protective clothing, parent-infant skin contact is very difficult. Over many centuries, child-rearing practices have evolved to adapt to this fundamental ecological constraint (J. Whiting, 1981).

There are also cultural differences in parental beliefs about emotion regulation and parent-infant communication about emotions that emerge in the second half year (Bornstein et al., 2008; Harkness et al., 2007). In North America, for example, parents are most frequently concerned about providing sufficient stimulation for the baby's brain and overall development. This means that parents want infants to learn how to handle a variety of toys, books, and adults without getting upset. At the same time, North American parents want their infants to know they are loved by giving explicit reassurances. One mother said of her infant:

Right now, at his age, I try to hold him as much as I can, and I have Michael hold him as much as he can, and I have Tony give him kisses because I feel that even at this age we're instilling love in him, and he knows we love him, and I don't want him to ever think that he's not loved. (Harkness et al., 2007, p. 20)

Korean mothers are like the North Americans in their interest in providing books, reading, music and other stimulation to foster the infant's development. The Koreans do not expose the infant to a variety of people outside the immediate family. The baby is seen as vulnerable, in need of protection, and that it is up to the parents to follow the baby's lead and adapt. According to one Korean mother:

Being a mom is a very happy event but at the same time I feel a heavy responsibility… I think I have to be flexible. If I push him too much then it will be too stressful for the baby and for me too. So I have to learn and study about parenting. And I need to plan ahead. (Harkness et al., 2007, p. 31)

Another Korean mother said, "I am willing to hold him whenever he wants to be held even though it might be physically hard on me" (p. 31), a theme of parental co-dependence on the infant that does not appear salient in North American and Northern European cultures.

Mothers from Italy, a more southern culture in a warmer climate, had similar feelings about expressing love and feeling emotional closeness with the baby as the North American mothers but the Italians were not as focused on cognitive stimulation and brain development. Instead, Italian mothers made attempts to expose the infant to social and family groups, and they judged their infants not on

Observations

Early Communicative Interactions Rely on Adult Interpretations (Lock, 1980)

Observation 7.3

Mary: age 7(10): A spoonful of food has just been placed in Mary's mouth when the telephone rings. Mother takes Mary's left hand and wraps it round the spoon handle, which is sticking from Mary's mouth.

Mother: "You take it while Mummy answers the phone."

Mary: pulls the spoon from her mouth and while eating waves it about. While still holding the spoon, she pushes her hand around in her dinner and then starts licking her hand. While she is doing this mother returns.

Mother: "There's a clever girl, are you feeding yourself? Here, let's wipe you, you're ever so mucky."

She takes the spoon from Mary to wipe her.

Mary cries and struggles, then reaches out toward the spoon.

Mother: "All right, here you are. Let me show you."

She gives Mary the spoon and then guiding her hand, places it into the dish and then to Mary's mouth.

Mother: "Oh, aren't we clever! Aren't we clever!"

Observation 7.4

Mary: age 7(27): Mary is in her chair, having finished her afternoon meal.

Mother comes through the door with a packet of biscuits in her hand. The door is behind Mary and out of her view. As mother comes in, Mary coos and smiles, turning around to see her mother.

Mother: "Yes, you heard me coming, didn't you?"

She enters Mary's field of view, and Mary reaches out towards her mother's hand; her whole body straining in the chair.

Mother: "Yes, they're your favourites, aren't they?"

---

whether they felt love or had enough stimulation but rather on whether they liked the company of other people, whether they were socially alive and engaged (*vivacitâ*).

Research on Latin American cultures reveals similar patterns. Franco, Fogel, Messinger, & Frazier (1996) did a study of mother-infant physical contact during play between 26 Hispanic American and 26 Anglo-American mothers and their 9-month-old infants. Although the overall amount of touching and physical contact did not differ between groups, Hispanic mothers touched, kissed, hugged, and held their infants physically closer than Anglo mothers. On questionnaires, the Hispanic mothers reported placing a higher value on touch and affection than Anglo mothers. These cultural differences were the same in all income levels in the sample.

As a general rule, the cultures of southern Europe and Central and South America have close patterns of touching, physical contact, kissing, and hugging even between adults. It seems that these behaviors are seen as expressions of close social ties between people at all ages. Puerto Rican mothers, for example, are more likely than Anglo mothers to physically direct the child's body and behavior during play and feeding situations. The Anglo mothers are more likely to use praise and suggestions, focusing on verbal means of communication (Harwood et al., 1999).

In more technical and industrial societies, mother-infant play is embedded in a matrix of communication and warmth. In these societies—including, for example, Japan, Korea, Europe, and North America, and urban families everywhere—the parent will begin to *interpret the infant's intentions*. Assuming that the parent has made a correct interpretation, the next step is usually to *help the infant carry out the intended act*. In addition, parents often *create new intentions* that were not there in the first place. Instead of simply helping infants get objects they see, parents may hold out an object to get the baby interested or make sounds or movements to try to get the baby to imitate them (Adamson, 1995; Kaye, 1982; Lock, 1980; Rogoff, 1990).

The situation is much like the study of music or language, for example, in which teachers require that their pupils learn simple exercises. The student has little notion of the purpose of learning scales, arpeggios, the parts of speech, or conjugations. Nevertheless, the instructor understands the relationship of the exercises to the final skilled performance. Some examples of these kinds of instructional interactions involving a 7-month-old baby are given in Observations 7.3 and 7.4.

By contrast, in nontechnical agricultural and hunter-gatherer communities, adults are more directive and ritualistic in their interactions with infants (Bornstein et al., 2008; Whiten & Milner, 1986). Among the Gusii, an agricultural community in Kenya, when mothers taught children to do a task, they used a lot of repetition, provided direct demonstration of the whole task (they did not break it into simpler components), and pulled on the infants' hands to encourage participation. The mothers used very little vocalization and little praise or reinforcement (Dixon, LeVine, Richman, & Brazelton, 1984). Chomorro mothers, from a fishing community on the Pacific island of Guam, were highly directive when interacting with infants; they talked quickly, dominated the interactions, were highly repetitive, and abruptly shifted activities in a manner more suited to their own pace than to the infants' (Carlile & Holstrum, 1989).

It is not necessarily the case that one style of play and teaching is better than another. Each style has evolved to fit the needs of the particular culture. Problems may arise, however, when cultures are forced to interact. Cultural-minority families from traditional backgrounds are often at a disadvantage when they enter urban environments. Their styles of interaction are not well suited to the urban lifestyle and the demands of school-based learning. Hispanic Americans, as a minority culture in the United States, often feel self-conscious about their cultural styles of raising infants. They report feeling self-conscious in the company of their Anglo-American neighbors and think of themselves as "too affectionate" with their infants (Franco et al., 1996). These patterns of cultural tension reveal how difficult it is for some parents to maintain the traditional values and practices of their minority culture. In support of this observation, research shows that as Latin American families acculturate to North American society—learning English, becoming educated in North American schools, and adopting Northern cultural values— they are less likely to preserve the language and cultural values of the home country (Cabrera et al., 2006). The research reviewed in this section shows that cultural differences are integrated into the development of brain, body, and mind during infancy, well before the child enters school.

Self-Awareness: The Sense of a Differentiated Ecological Self

In the previous stage, infants developed a sense of an ecological self. Between 3 and 5 months, infants can perceive a sense of their own agency in relation to others, their own emotions, a sense of coherence across sensory systems, and a sense of their own history. This sense of self comes from self-exploration through primary circular reactions, repeated actions of the infant's own body. Infants between 3 and 5 months old may feel as if there is a coherence between moving their hand to touch their own face and the sensation felt in the face. They know that this feels different from other kinds of contact with their face, say, from their blanket or another person's touch.

Infants of that age, however, do not know that there is a self and another person who are different centers of subjective experience. All they know is that some touches feel different from others, and that there is a special significance to touches that are accompanied by a sense of their own movements (that is, self-touches). Babies between 3 and 5 months cannot put labels on these different kinds of touches. They have a sense of agency, but only for these simple actions on their own body. They do not know they can affect the world beyond their body. They experience the world receptively and unquestioningly.

A 3-month-old baby is aware of the environment in the same way that a fish is aware of water.

A fish "knows" that to propel its body it must exert a certain force, and that the force is different at different times (we, as outside observers, would be able to observe that these different times are changes in the speed and direction of the water currents). The fish, however, does not know water as a separate entity, different from itself. The fish has an ecological self. It knows what to do and how to move, has a memory of past experiences, and can adapt to changes, but it cannot separate itself from the ecology.

Between 6 and 9 months, we see the first evidence that babies are becoming aware of a world "out there" in relation to the self. They are still part of the ecology of relationships with things and people (indeed, so are all of us), but now they are starting to see that the ecology has local regions, each of which has different properties and each of which has an existence in relation to the self. As they begin to differentiate objects as whole entities having an existence even when out of sight, they also begin to see themselves as being different from but related to those objects.

Infants of this age call attention to themselves in a number of ways that did not exist in the previous stage. These features make up a sense of a **differentiated ecological self**.

1. *Asking for help.* If their needs are not met, infants are beginning to find ways to let others know. Asking for help suggests that the infant believes the source of help comes from outside their own bodies.

2. *Taking the initiative.* Infants will start games, like covering their face as if to ask to play peekaboo. It is as if they are "waking up" to the fact that they are not completely helpless. If they do or do not like something, they can actually do something to make it happen or to change what is already happening.

3. *Clowning and showing off.* Infants begin to do things to get an emotional reaction from others. They act clever or silly, violate social rules to get a laugh from others, make odd facial expressions, put their pajamas on their head, and blow "raspberries" (Reddy, 2000). This

suggests that the infant has a sense of other people as different from the self, at least insofar as being an audience.

4. *Demanding.* The quality of crying changes as infants become angry at others and persist in their demands until something changes.

5. *Hiding and escaping.* Infants like to play peekaboo, tickle, and chase games that involve a temporary separation from the other followed by a reunion. This suggests that they have a growing ability to differentiate themselves from other people and objects, and that they have a sense of permanence (a person or an object can reappear after hiding).

Infants' emotions are becoming more complex, and they are beginning to take events into their own hands. Infants of this age, however, do not yet have a sense of subjectivity. They have feelings—getting angry or happy—but cannot yet stand apart from those feelings. They do not have a sense of an "I" that feels, and, consequently, they do not have a sense that other people are separate subjects with their own feelings. Other people are still being treated partially as extensions of the infant's own needs—as an audience for the infant's jokes or as a satisfier of the infant's demands—and are not seen in their own right as separate individuals.

The differentiated ecological self is more advanced than the fish in water. The infant now senses that the "water" is different but believes that the water is there only for the self. Can you think of times that you were demanding without regard for another person's feelings? Or when you needed an audience for confirmation, without thinking about the emotional state of your partner? If so, you were behaving like a 9-month-old!

The sense of a **subjective self** begins after the age of 10 months (see Chapter 8), When infants begin to point at objects in the company of others, as if to say they have a sense of having a perspective on the world that truly differs from that of other people. This means that by 10 months, infants begin to have a sense of being a subject, an "I" who can perceive or feel and who can share those feelings with other people. The subjective self seems to have an understanding that other people can feel similar or different types of emotions as the self. Between 6 and 9 months, the infant's positive and negative emotions become more complex, and each has some interpersonal significance. Anger is typically directed toward another person. It highlights the concerns of the self that may have been violated. The enjoyment of escape during tickle and chase games is a feeling of trying to get away from someone else. So, while infants of this age are not yet aware of others as separate subjects, they are beginning to experience others as a meaningful part of their own emotional life.

As you are doing the Experiential Exercises and/or the Co-Regulating with Baby exercises, try to see if you can experience the differentiated ecological self. What do you experience about yourself in relation to the environment? Is it ecological, differentiated ecological, or subjective? How do you know?

FAMILY AND SOCIETY

In the section on social development, we looked at styles of parent-infant interaction in the family and how it is influenced by the cultural context. In general, factors in the social and environmental ecology outside the family such as culture have an indirect influence on infant development. In this section, we examine maternal employment as one ecological factor that affects the family. Even though infants may never enter the workplace, work will have a mediated effect on them through their parents. Also in this section, we look at the relative roles of fathers and siblings.

Maternal Employment: Its Effects on Infants and Parents

The number of working mothers with children under the age of 6 years in the United States has been steadily increasing for the past 50 years. In 2011, 68 percent of women with children under the age of six years were in the work force (up from 64 percent in 2001). About one-third of these

women work part-time, the rest full-time (http://www.prb.org/Publications/Articles/2012/us-working-mothers-with-children.aspx). Mothers earn more than fathers in about 40 percent of United States households, up from 11 percent in 1960. This change is due to increased employment opportunity for women and also because a higher proportion of women compared to men now graduate from institutions of higher education. More women than men receive bachelors, masters, and doctoral degrees in the US (www.census.gov).

This chapter covers the impact of the maternal work role on the American family and especially how it has affected both parents and infants. It should be noted that our discussion focuses on paid work, either inside or outside the home. Mothers do a substantial amount of unpaid work—child care, cooking, cleaning, gardening, and chauffeuring—which is estimated to be worth about $27,000 per woman per year. Much of this work goes unrecognized (Eyer, 1996).

First of all, how does maternal employment affect the mother's relationship with her infant and the infant's development? In general, infant-mother attachment is not seriously altered by maternal employment (Easterbrooks & Goldberg, 1985; Youngblut, Loveland-Cherry, & Horan, 1993). On the other hand, if attachment is going to be affected, it is most likely to decline between employed mothers and their infant sons rather than their daughters (Chase-Lansdale & Owen, 1987).

Why are boys more affected? It may be that boys are perceived as more independent and as requiring less parental nurture and attention than girls, who are seen as more vulnerable (Parke & Sawin, 1980). Thus, when mothers are under extra stress and time pressures from their jobs, they may spend less time with their sons than with their daughters. Other research suggests that there is a correlation between a son's insecure attachment and a mother's perceived level of stress. Mothers who felt more stressed by their jobs and the demands of family life had less securely attached sons (Benn, 1986). The effects of stress are compounded for low-income mothers, for whom not

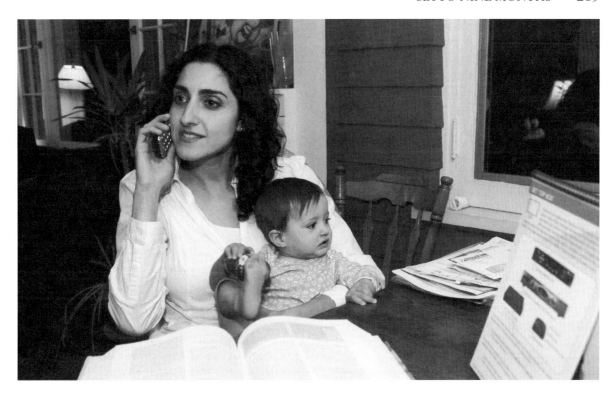

A working mother must learn to balance multiple demands of work and family, even if she does not take her baby to work with her.
Photo: Emily Waterfield

just employment but also the stresses of living in poverty may affect attachment in both sons and daughters (Barglow, 1987a). We also saw, earlier in this chapter, that male infants are more easily distressed and less emotionally regulated than females. So, the absence of regularly available maternal support may affect boys more than girls.

The impact of maternal work on infant-mother attachment is mediated by the mother's adjustment to the work role. Better psychological adjustment will lead to more sensitive infant care. Thus, researchers have asked what factors promote maternal adjustment to employment. A number of studies find that the important variable is the mother's desire to work, not the mere fact of working. Mothers who are doing what they prefer—either working or staying at home with their children—tend to be well adjusted. On the other hand, there are adverse effects on adjustment if the mother does not want to work but has to for

economic reasons, or if the mother would like to return to work but feels she should stay home with her children (Alvarez, 1985; DeMeis, Hock, & McBride, 1986; Pistrang, 1984; Stifter, Coulehan, & Fish, 1993). In addition, if mothers perceive that their children are suffering because of their absence from the home, they are more likely to feel stress and conflict between work and family roles (Lee et al., 2003).

On the other hand, staying home with the baby is also stressful for some mothers. Research has shown that problems with coping, dissatisfaction with life, depression, and loneliness are significantly higher in young mothers who do not work outside the home than in those who do, and that there are higher levels of functioning in families in which the mothers are employed (Sogaard, Kritz-Silverstein, & Wingard, 1994; Vandell & Ramanan, 1992). Studies suggest that there is no overall difference for mothers or infants between full-time work vs. unemployment: each one presents its own challenges for the infant and family, although there are important advantages for poor families when mothers are working (Brooks-Gunn et al., 2010; Coley & Lombardi, 2013). Part-time employment, however, seems to have clear benefits for both mothers and families. Mothers employed part-time—compared to full-time or unemployed—have fewer depressive symptoms, better physical health, less conflict between work and family, more positive parenting and more involvement in school or daycare settings (Buehler & O'Brien, 2011).

Whether mothers work by choice or because of necessity, they typically end the day fatigued because of a phenomenon called **role overload**. Role overload occurs when the demands of a role are more than an individual can easily cope with, or when the same person is required to perform too many roles. After a full day at work, many women come home to traditional conceptions of the roles of both wife and mother. Women often continue to do most of the infant care and most of the housework, compared to men, even if they are working as many hours outside the home as the men (L. C. Jones & Hermann, 1992; Scarr, 1984). Role overload is inevitable for single parents.

Role overload and its consequences for the mother increase if the child has a difficult temperament at age 1 year or a hostile aggressive temperament at age 3. In this case, mothers are more likely to perceive themselves as less competent in both the parenting and work roles, and are more likely to feel depressed (Hyde et al., 2004). A mother who is already under pressure from both home and work, therefore, is likely to reach a breaking point if she feels she cannot handle her own child.

When women work, however, there are more pressures on fathers, and they too can experience a form of role overload. When women remain at home, fathers can choose when and how to become involved with their infants. These fathers show more positive emotion toward their infants and are more attuned to the infants' needs, especially if the infants are boys (Manlove & Vernon-Feagans, 2002). In contrast, fathers whose wives work experience more tension and frustration with being called upon to take more child-care responsibility. During the first year, such fathers show more negative behavior with their infants. After the first year, however, they are just as sensitive to their infants as the husbands of mothers who do not work outside the home (Grych & Clark, 1999). These are general patterns, however, so each family may be different in the balance of mother and father roles.

Parental Leave Policies

Unfortunately, the amount of work a person does outside the home is only partially defined by the individual. Much has to do with cultural and economic demands placed on workers by society and by employers. Most work situations in the United States take little account of a person's obligations to family. An inflexible daily work schedule leaves little time or opportunity for parents to be involved in the day-to-day life of the family. Corporations often have a policy of moving their employees from city to city as part of a training and advancement program.

This is especially the case for women. Even when mothers are paid, they earn only 71 cents for every dollar earned by a man in the same position. They are often relegated to low-paying jobs such as secretary (98 percent are women), child-care providers (98 percent), nurses (93 percent), and bank tellers (91 percent). Even highly educated women face job and salary discrimination, especially if they get pregnant or are raising a child (Eyer, 1996). These sources of discrimination in the ecological system make working especially burdensome for women and increase their level of guilt.

Some alternatives exist, but they are not widespread. More flexible work schedules (flextime) began to be instituted in Europe in the early 1960s. Workers can have time off to take a child to the doctor, watch their child participate in sports, or do whatever they desire. After a child is born, Swedish workers, for example, are legally entitled to maternity and paternity leaves. Some Swedish employers allow husbands and wives to share the same jobs.

That way both can work and spend time at home. Swedish women earn about 90 percent the wages men do for similar jobs, and 86 percent of women with young children are in the work force (Eyer, 1996).

The opportunity to take infant care leave of some type, without suffering loss of income or profession, is mandated by law in at least 75 nations, including all the industrial societies in the world. In 1993, the U.S. Congress enacted the Family and Medical Leave Act of 1993 (FMLA, Public Law 103–3), which established a family leave policy. This law provides unpaid leave from employment for up to 12 weeks without loss of rank or position in the workplace in businesses with more than 50 employees. The leave applies to both mothers and fathers as well as to non-pregnancy-related illnesses. Unfortunately, 95 percent of businesses are exempt from the FMLA because they have fewer than 50 employees. In addition, most parents cannot afford to take unpaid leaves (Eyer, 1996). During the economic downturn in the past 4 years, small businesses that may have elected to provide some paid leave are less likely to provide it now.

Research shows that mothers who take shorter leaves are more likely to feel stress and symptoms of depression, show negative emotions toward their infants and spouses, and have less interest in their infants. Fathers who took shorter leaves and worked for employers who did not have a positive reaction to the employee's fatherhood were less involved with their infants and had less communication with their spouse about the infant (R. Clark et al., 1997; Feldman et al., 2004). This means that even with the FMLA, too few parents are able to take advantage of parental leave, with negative consequences for themselves and their children.

Better pay and benefits for part-time work could also be helpful for young parents. Many employers provide medical insurance, unemployment compensation, and other benefits only to full-time employees. A parent who would like to spend more time at home is caught between the demands of the family and the very real needs to be covered by those benefits. Employer-sponsored day care (see Chapter 8), is also helping working parents.

The Affordable Care Act of 2009 (HR 3962) allows people who are not eligible for employer health benefits to apply for medical insurance at reasonable cost, making it possible for parents to work part time and also have health care insurance for their families. Since insurance under this law is only available after January 2014, no one knows how it will impact parental leave practices. With little opportunity to take time off from work, for example, young mothers cannot breast-feed for as long as recommended by the American Academy of Pediatrics. Mothers may choose drug-assisted childbirth or C-sections, even if they would have preferred a natural birth, to get themselves back on their feet sooner and back to work (Galtry & Callister, 2005). Compared to other industrialized countries, the United States is not a nation that fully supports children and families.

Some advocacy groups in the United States are working to promote the adoption of European-style parental leave policies at the state and national level (Gornick & Meyers, 2003; Secret & Sprang, 2001). In addition, some progressive private companies have realized that supporting working mothers is one way to preserve talent and loyalty. They have taken the lead responding to their female workers' child-rearing needs by providing flexible schedules and leaves, part-time employment with full benefits, and paid personal time beyond the 12 weeks of paid leave mandated by FLMA. These are companies such as Bayer, Chrysler, Ford, Johnson & Johnson, Microsoft, and Verizon. A complete list of the 100 best companies for working mothers compiled by *Working Mother* magazine is available at http://www.workingmother.com/best-company-list/146788.

Age and Sex Differences in Nurturance toward Infants

As the results of research on maternal employment suggest, infant care is thought to be part of women's work. Implicit in this belief is that nurturance is part of the female biological heritage, and that women should be able to do this under any circumstances and without support. In actuality, these beliefs are simply not true. Research has shown that the interest and ability to care for babies is present in both males and females early in life and will continue in both genders if fostered by the social environment. In the following sections, we review age and sex differences in responses to infants.

Preschool Age

Are there differences between boys and girls in their responses toward infants? One study that used a single female infant placed in a playpen in a nursery school found that girls approached the baby more than did boys. Once the children were near the baby, however, both boys and girls spoke to, reached out for, and touched the baby equally (Berman, Monda, & Merscough, 1977). Another study used both male and female infants in a waiting-room situation. Preschool children were asked to wait in a laboratory room with a baby and mother for 10 minutes. In this rather unusual situation, many children did not approach the baby. When they did, boys and girls approached in equal numbers, and there were no differences in the types of interaction attempted by male and female children. They usually sat down on the floor, handed the baby toys, or showed the baby his image in a mirror (Melson & Fogel, 1982).

These children almost never talked to the baby. If they wanted to find something out or make a comment, they would talk to the baby's mother about the baby. In addition, there was a same-sex effect for these unfamiliar infant-preschooler pairs similar to that found for sibling pairs (Dunn & Kendrick, 1982). At the ages of 2 and 3 years, boys were more likely to approach male babies, and girls were more likely to approach female babies (Melson & Fogel, 1982).

One interesting twist in this study was that by the time children were 4 to 5 years old, there were still no overall sex differences in the amount of time males and females interacted with the baby. However, both the males and the females pre-ferred to interact with female babies. Perhaps the older boys no longer identify with the babies. By the time the boys were 5 years old, being a boy and being a baby were no longer compatible.

If adults encourage children to become involved with unfamiliar infants, both boys and girls increase their amount of interaction with the babies, and both boys and girls ask the adults questions about the babies (Fogel, Melson, Toda, & Mistry, 1987). Interviews with children in kindergarten and second grade reveal equal interest and equal knowledge about infant care on the part of boys and girls (Melson, Fogel, & Toda, 1986). In general, the research suggests that few sex differences are found among children in their attitudes, knowledge about, and behavior toward infants if they are exposed to infants with adult guidance (Melson & Fogel, 1988). For most children, this exposure occurs in the context of the family, with baby brothers or sisters.

Siblings

Similar types of sex differences have been observed among siblings; that is, same-sex dyads tend to be more positive in their interactions than mixed-sex dyads (Dunn & Kendrick, 1982; Lamb, 1978b). On the other hand, when preschool-age children talk to their infant brothers and sisters, both boys and girls modify their speech to make it sound more like motherese (Dunn & Kendrick, 1982).

The children's speech includes simple utterances, repetition, and high pitch, as in the following example taken from a 4-year-old talking to her younger brother: "Harry! Harry! Have my camera! Have my camera! Naughty boy. You... aah! Aah! No!" (Dunn & Kendrick, 1982, p. 124). In some cases, the preschoolers used repetition twice as often as their mothers when talking to babies. About 25 percent of the preschool-age children were observed to use endearing terms toward the baby and to ask soliciting questions (Are you hungry? Are you getting frustrated?). On the other hand, the majority of the preschoolers rarely asked questions of the baby, whereas question asking is a major form of adult speech to infants (Dunn & Kendrick, 1982).

Later Childhood

Among children aged 8 to 14 years, girls interact more with babies and ignore them less than do boys. Interestingly, however, there are no sex differences in blood pressure, skin conductance, and heart rate: both boys and girls are equally aroused or unaroused by the sight of an infant. Girls, it would seem, make the choice to interact, whereas boys do not (Frodi & Lamb, 1978). A similar study of African American children also found that girls are more likely to look at the babies than boys (Berman, Goodman, Sloan, & Fernandez, 1978).

These differences in male versus female interest in babies continue through high school (Feldman & Nash, 1979a) but they seem to vanish for college students and for young adults (Feldman and Nash, 1978, 1979a; Frodi, Lamb, Leavitt, & Donovan, 1978). Some studies with adults have compared the responses of parents to babies with those of nonparents. The most responsive group is usually new mothers. Men's child-rearing status does not affect their responsiveness to babies (Feldman & Nash, 1978; Sagi, 1981). Mothers tend to be more accurate in their identification of the type of cry (pain, distress, and so on) than fathers, but both mothers and fathers can distinguish their own infant's cry from cries of unfamiliar infants (Wiesenfeld, Malatesta, & DeLoach, 1981).

Parenthood: Mothers versus Fathers

In most comparisons of fathers' and mothers' styles of interaction with infants, fathers are found to be more physical and active with infants than mothers. Fathers are reported to be less contingently responsive with infants and have a style of play and interaction that is more directive and characterized by abrupt changes of activity. By contrast, mothers' games are quieter and more likely to depend on the pace set by the infant. Mothers also engage in proportionately more caregiving than fathers (Lamb et al., 1982; Parke & Sawin, 1980; Pedersen, Suwalsky, Cain, & Zaslow, 1987; Ricks, 1985; Sagi, 1981). These differences are considered important for infants. While contingent responsiveness fosters infants' understanding of the connections between their own actions and those of others, the more directive and unexpected style of father-infant play may lead infants to develop adaptive responses to challenges as they strive to keep up with the father's expectations.

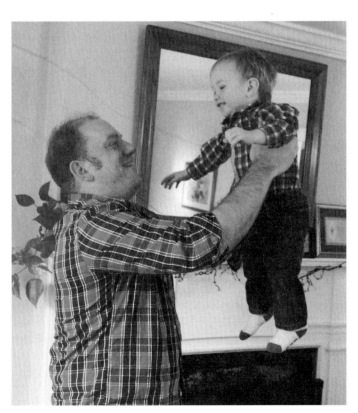

Fathers and mothers play different types of games with their babies. Both paternal and maternal styles of play are important to infant development.
Photo: Emily Waterfield

We observed mother-infant and father-infant play in 60 middle-class families (K. L. Dickson, Walker, & Fogel, 1997). Unlike previous studies done as much as 15 or 20 years earlier, our observations of North American, primarily Caucasian fathers in the 1990s found virtually no differences in play style or contingent responsiveness with their 1-year-old infants. It is quite likely that cultural changes have made middle-class fathers more involved and sensitive parents. In another study, mothers and fathers in England were videotaped interacting with their infants with an observer present and later without the observer present. There were fewer mother-father differences when the observer was absent. This suggests that fathers may be somewhat more self-conscious when observed and therefore may appear to be less sensitive (C. Lewis et al., 1996).

There are large cultural differences in the amount of father involvement. In most Asian countries, mothers are expected to play a more traditional role and devote most of their time to the infant while the father works outside the home. In one study done in Taiwan, for example, mothers held, smiled, talked to, and played with infants more than fathers, but both parents displayed similar amounts of soothing and affection toward their infants (Sun & Roopnarine, 1996).

Anthropologists studied primate species that differed in the amount of father involvement. Orangutans and chimps are species in which mothers do virtually all the infant care. Siamangs and gorillas have about as much father care as humans. Owl monkeys and titi monkeys are species in which the fathers do more of the care than mothers. There was a direct correspondence between the amount of infant care and the average life span. Generally speaking, doing more child care is correlated with living longer. Females outlive males in those species where there is more female care, and vice versa (Allman, Rosin, Kumar, & Hasenstaub, 1998). Although this study does not prove that individuals who do more child care will live longer, it certainly suggests that there may be important health benefits, for both men and women, to being involved in child care. Other related research shows that people who give up their own time to help or care for others, at any age, are more likely to live longer and be healthier. Giving, more than receiving, has health benefits (Post, Neimark, & Moss, 2007).

Grandparents

The next phase of caring for infants, following parenting, is becoming a grandparent. Investigators studied the responsiveness to babies of 30 parents of adolescents, 28 parents whose grown children had left home, and 26 grandparents of infants. As you might have guessed, grandparents were more responsive to babies than the other two groups. Grandmothers were more responsive than grandfathers, but grandfathers were more responsive than men at other ages, who tended to be less responsive to babies than their wives (Feldman & Nash, 1979b).

There are very few empirical studies of grandparents and grandchildren and only a handful on grandparent-infant relationships. With the decline of the extended family living under one roof, developmentalists have not taken much interest in grandparents as a source of influence on infants. In many cases, grandparents do not live near their children, and the once-a-year contact with the family is hardly enough to make much of an impression on an infant.

The degree to which grandparents become involved in infant care varies considerably. In some families, grandparents have daily contact with the infants and participate in caregiving as well as play. In others, there may be little or no contact. One reason for this difference may be that adults can become grandparents as young as 30 years of age or as old as 90. Younger grandparents are still employed and have little time for infant care and very old grandparents may not have the strength or health to be involved (Bales, 2002; Kornhaber & Woodward, 1981; Tinsley & Parke, 1984). Some grandparents also report little interest in being involved with their grandchildren, regardless of how close they live or how much free time they have (Mueller et al., 2002).

In all cultures, grandparents and infants share a special relationship.
Photos: Left: Wikipedia Commons. Right: Emily Waterfield

A few studies have been done on grandmother-infant attachment (see Chapter 8) at 1 year. The subjects were white, primarily middle-class families in which the grandmother lived nearby and had relatively frequent contact with the infant. This research shows that mothers and grandmothers are nearly interchangeable as attachment figures: infants approach both in times of stress. The more time a grandmother spends with the baby, the more secure the attachment relationship (Myers, Jarvis, & Creasey, 1987; Schaffer & Emerson, 1964).

Spending time with the infant also means spending time with their own daughters or daughters-in-law. This allows for more communication about differences of opinion and belief about child rearing, which improves the mother-grandmother relationship and also the grandmother-infant attachment. In the 1990s, mothers and grandmothers were generally in agreement over beliefs. Mothers, however, were more accepting on the whole than grandmothers of table messiness and nudity indoors, more relaxed about when to begin toilet training, and less rigid in differentiating sex roles in child play. This sample did not, however, differ in their basic beliefs about moral domains;

the disagreements were more about personal and social behaviors (Honig & Deters, 1996).

Some studies have shown that grandmothers in African American families are considerably more involved with their infant grandchildren than in Caucasian American families. The grandparents tend to live close by their grown children and devote much of their free time to their children's infants (Cherlin & Furstenberg, 1986; Pearson, Hunter, Ensminger, & Kellam, 1990; Wilson, 1986). Compared to Caucasian parents, African American parents of infants have more frequent contact with kin—including grandmothers—and respect the advice of relatives, showing concern for what the relative thinks is important (Wilson, 1986).

This strong network of ties between relatives was carried to the Americas from traditional African societies. Research has shown that the extended family system is important in the reduction of family stress, especially for low-income, teenage, and single mothers. Typically, the grandmothers are warmer and more patient with the infants than are the infants' teenage mothers. In addition to providing a buffer against the effects of mothers who have too many of their own problems to cope with their babies, the grandmothers serve as valuable sources of advice and instruction about parenthood for their own daughters. With the support of their mothers, many of these adolescent and at-risk parents are able to continue in their education and eventually become economically self-supporting and caring parents (Colletta & Lee, 1983; Furstenberg, Brooks-Gunn, & Morgan, 1987; Spieker & Bensley, 1994; Stevens, 1984; Wakschlag, Chase-Lansdale, & Brooks-Gunn, 1996).

These studies suggest that involvement between infants and grandparents is dependent on ecological systems factors, including ethnicity, culture, life history factors, and patterns of residence (Mueller & Elder, 2003). These factors also determine the amount of mutual reliance and mutual trust between family members, both of which affect the quality of the social network of kinship in which

the child develops. Social support networks are discussed more thoroughly in Chapter 10.

In summary, it seems that the biggest differences in male versus female responsiveness to infants appear in middle childhood and adolescence. Preschool boys, men of child-rearing age, and grandfathers are about equally responsive to babies as their female counterparts. These studies suggest that sex differences in interest in babies may be related to society's expectations of how males and females should behave rather than to some underlying biological predisposition favoring females. Males' interest in babies corresponds to the times in the life cycle when men are exposed to babies and are expected to take an interest in them. Women are more likely to be expected to be interested in babies all through their lives.

Co-Regulating With Baby

At the beginning of this stage, babies are just beginning to reach out and grasp things with some success. Over these 4 to 5 months, babies get better at grasping and holding only objects, and they get better at locomotion. Any kind of play in which objects are handed to or taken from the baby is most appealing in this stage. As the baby gets good at moving around, you can play a kind of "catch and fetch" game by rolling a ball across the floor and letting the baby retrieve it. Babies have their own version of this game. They love to push toys off tables or throw them down, and they expect the caregiver to rush to pick them up, put them back, and wait for the next round of pushing and throwing. You can guess who gets tired of this game first. Play these games, but be aware of your

own limits of patience. Change the game and the setting before you get upset with the baby.

You can create inviting laces into which infants can crawl, like cardboard boxes and "houses" of couch pillows. Place objects on the floor away from the infant to encourage crawling to them. You will need to prepare the house, because now the baby can get into cupboards and closets. Make sure dangerous substances are in locked cabinets. It helps to provide one lower-level cabinet the baby can get into, filled with things the baby can take out and put back. The more comfortable you feel about the house being safe for the baby, the more likely you will be to let the baby explore.

Toward the end of this period, babies really get the idea of listening

to words. Their favorite words are often names—their own names, of course, and names like "Mommy" and "Daddy." Try to punctuate all your games with words. Babies quickly learn to associate tonal patterns with behavioral sequences. When the infant responds with delight, you will know that you have gotten the rhythm right. Give yourself an opportunity to make mistakes, and forgive yourself when you do.

This is the stage in which the baby perfects the art of anticipation. Games that have a set pattern and a "punch line" the baby can look forward to are perfect. A good example is singing "Pop Goes the Weasel." Chase games, like "I'm gonna get you," tickle games, and the classic peekaboo, are just right for babies of this age group. Watch for different types of smiles (*with cheek raises and/or wide open mouth) and see if you can tell what each of them means for the baby.

Although the baby does not understand the words of the sentences you say, he or she can use differences in tonal patterns as a way of sensing the significance of your words. Games that ask questions of the baby begin to work in this stage. Questions have a pattern of rising intonation near the end of the sentence that a baby can recognize as being different from other kinds of statements. This rising pitch creates a sense of anticipation. Of course, you have to answer the questions yourself, but your answer gives the baby a sense of completeness and therefore delight. Examples are "How big is the baby?" and "Where is the baby?" (a variant on peekaboo).

Babies of this age know when things are about to happen. They watch out the window as their parents leave for work, and they look for them when they hear the door opening or footsteps sounding in the hall. Babies also learn the sounds and sights of siblings and friends and usually get excited when they see or hear them approach. These behaviors give the baby's family members the clear sense that the baby recognizes and appreciates them. Notice how your feelings change when the infant seems to learn these routines. It is important to exercise babies' bodies as well as their minds. Helping babies stand, holding their arms to let them "walk," and picking them up are good ways to do this. Babies of this age like vigorous games, such as being tickled or tossed up in the air and swung around. Gentleness and care are important, because babies' bodies are somewhat weak, and it is easy to dislocate an arm if you are not careful. Seek a level of excitement at which both you and the baby are having fun.

Babies of this age develop their own motor games. They will rock themselves, bounce on their legs, bang on things, and crawl and climb around the house to the extent of their ability. In general, these motor games and rhythmical movements are essential for normal motor and mental developmental However, the caregiver must be on the alert for potentially dangerous situations. Make sure the things babies like to hold onto to pull themselves up are secure, as well as that there are no dangerous objects—too heavy, too sharp, too small—in their normal path of movement. The baby's delight at finding his or her way around will more than compensate you for these efforts.

SUMMARY

Physical and Motor Development

- During this period, infants learn to locomote by crawling; they can sit alone and pull themselves up to standing. Grasping and reaching are well coordinated.

- Infants have a preferred hand, but their hand preference may change during the first year of life. Hand preference leads to the development of different uses for each hand that are necessary for the acquisition of unimanual reaching and crawling.

- Walking develops after infants gain postural control.

- The age at which solid foods are started coincides with changes in the infant's physical and motor development that make eating solids possible.

- Foods should be introduced one at a time to allow babies to express possible allergies.

- Younger babies need food that is ground or mashed.

- Eating is a social experience, and parents should allow plenty of time for meals.

Perceptual Development

- Infants can now perceive objects from visual cues alone, allowing them to process information in pictures and on television.

- Haptic perception is also used to perceive object properties through action.

- Infants can recognize melodies and relate sound patterns to visual patterns.

Cognitive Development

- Infant memory improves in duration, and infants can process information faster than in the previous stage.

- Infants now try to form concepts out of their perceptual experiences. Concept formation appears to be organized around prototypes.

- Using secondary circular reactions, infants discover relationships between their actions and the environment, and they vary their actions to observe the effects.

- Infants of this age can remember object locations, so long as they do not have to act on the objects.

Emotional Development

- Anger and wariness are two new negative emotions seen during this period.

- Laughter emerges as a new positive emotion, and other positive emotions develop at this age.

- Infants can recognize positive facial expression better than negative expression; however, they do not seem to attribute meaning to those expressions.

- Infants have stable temperamental characteristics, although the origins of these patterns are not understood.

- Measuring temperament is difficult because it requires understanding how the infant changes or remains the same over long periods of time.

Social and Language Development

- Infants can communicate nonverbally through action; however, they do not fully understand the meaning of their own behavior. Adults are required to interpret the infant's meaning, which ultimately contributes to the infant's understanding of communication.

- Infant social play becomes oriented toward objects, and parents can play a role in directing the infant's attention to objects and their properties.

- Parent-infant games are elaborated during this period. There are cultural differences in the amount of play versus caregiving that are related in part to ecological factors.

- infants develop a differentiated ecological self. They do things to call attention to themselves and thus make the first distinctions between self and other.

- Babbling mimics the intonation patterns of speech and develops in conjunction with auditory perception of speech sounds. However, infants are not using babbling to express themselves in a meaningful, linguistic manner.

- In specializing in their perception of the language spoken in the home, infants lose their sensitivity to sound contrasts that are not made in that language.

Family and Society

- Typically, maternal employment does not affect the attachment between mothers and infants. The important factor is whether the mother desires to return to work, in which case her adjustment is more successful.

- Parental leave policy helps the family's initial adjustment to a new baby, but few parents can take advantage of it.

- At all ages, boys and girls are equally responsive to and knowledgeable about babies. Differences arise in social situations in which individuals are encouraged toward or away from nurturing roles.

- Preschool-age siblings are capable of adapting their speech and behavior to the needs of the baby.

- Fathers often have a more directing and challenging style than mothers, but in most cases, their behavior with infants is similar.

Chapter 8

Ten to Twelve Months

CHAPTER OUTLINE AND OVERVIEW

Physical and Motor Development	*How do infants learn to walk? What are the developments of the infant's ability to explore? What are the main threats to health and safety? What kinds of immunizations are recommended for infants?*
Perceptual and Cognitive Development	*What kinds of concepts do infants have at this age? Are infants aware of objects when the objects are out of sight?*
Emotional Development	*What new emotions can infants feel at this age? How do infants use adults to regulate their emotions?*
Social and Language Development	*What words and gestures do infants use at this age? How do infants interact with peers at this age? What is the sense of self at this age? How do attachments develop and what are some individual differences in attachment?*
Family and Society	*Can infants form attachments to people other than the mother? Can infants become attached to adoptive parents?*

The period from 10 to 12 months brings several of the most important achievements of the infancy period. First of all, infants develop strong and permanent attachments to their primary caregivers, typically the members of the immediate family. They prefer to stay close to these people, they do not like separations, and they may become afraid of strangers under certain circumstances. The infant's sense of security or insecurity in those attachment ties has lasting implications for mental health and the success of interpersonal relationships. Second, infants develop a subjective sense of self. They learn ways to communicate their perceptions and feelings to others and at the same time learn that others have a view of the world different from their own. It takes a lifetime, of course, to learn how to communicate our ideas to others and to appreciate how other people feel and think. At this stage, however, infants have begun this journey toward intersubjectivity.

PHYSICAL AND MOTOR DEVELOPMENT

Physical and Locomotor Development

By the age of 1 year, infant growth rates have leveled off (see the growth charts at the Center for Disease Control: http://www.cdc.gov/growthcharts/clinical_charts.htm). Most year-old boys are between 28¼ inches (71.75 cm) and 32 inches (81.25 cm) in length, and girls are between 27½ inches (69.85 cm) and 31¼ inches (79.38 cm). Both boys and girls will continue to grow at a rate of about 4 to 5 inches (10 to 13 cm) per year for the next several years. At 1 year, boys weigh between 18½ and 26½ pounds (8.4 to 12.0 kg), while girls weigh between 17¼ and 24¾ pounds (7.8 to 11.2 kg). By the 12th month, most babies are eating a variety of solid foods, including table foods that are cut up for them. Most infants are holding their own spoons and can drink from a cup with both hands. By this time, almost all infants will have experienced teething pains and will have several teeth to help them chew their food.

With respect to motor developments, 11 months is the average age at which infants can stand alone (the range is 9 to 16 months), and at 11¾ months, the average baby can walk alone (the range is 9 to 17 months). By 1 year, most infants can sit down from a standing position, and most can climb up and down stairs by crawling.

Infants between 3 and 15 months were observed every 3 weeks in a laboratory going up and down a moderate slope (Adolph, 1997). The methods used to go up and down depended upon whether the infant was a belly crawler (also called a creeper; see Chapter 7), a hands-and-knees crawler, or a walker (see Figure 8.1). Most of the infants adapted their locomotion by checking out the slope in relation to their abilities. The more experience they had with the slope, the more conservative they became in their method and the less need there was to rescue the infant from a possible fall. With experience, infants began to make "smart" locomotor decisions that required less adult guidance, and parents reported a similar progression at home.

Infants used four different strategies, depending upon their ability. There was the quick glance followed by a plunge, typically when infants felt the surface was safe enough to proceed. If the glance suggested some difficulty, the infants took a long look while swaying their bodies, then proceeded with their typical method of locomotion. If that did not work, infants took more time to look, and they also touched the slope to check the slant. This was sometimes followed by their typical means of locomotion and sometimes by an alternative means. If these techniques did not work, as a last resort, infants would hold onto the landing and try out different means of locomotion before proceeding. At this point, if they perceived the slope as too risky they would await a rescue from the adult. If not, they typically chose a sliding method.

Infant behavior on slopes can also be affected by adults. When adults encourage infants to come down slopes that are too risky for their ability,

Figure 8.1 Possible locomotor methods for going up and down hills for belly crawlers, hands-and-knees crawlers, and walkers.
(a) 3 uphill, **(b)** downhill

Source: Adapted from K. E. Adolph, Learning in the development of infant locomotion, 1997, p. 51. *Monographs of the Society for Research in Child Development, 62*(3).

walkers but not crawlers are more likely to make the attempt, perhaps because they trust their locomotion skills more. Discouraging infants from attempting slopes they are able to navigate is less successful: only about half the infants, whether or not they could walk, hesitate to descend (Adolph et al., 2008). It is probably not news that babies of this age are more likely to respond to "yes" than to "no" when they are moving around.

The first months of independent walking initiate what some refer to as the toddler period of infant development. The label "toddler" seems to derive from the characteristic gait of the child who has not fully mastered the skill of walking. The earliest forms of childhood bipedalism have

a distinct resemblance to a duck out for a jog—a sight that never fails to produce humorous delight in most caregivers.

What accounts for this precarious-looking form of locomotion? When adults walk, both legs are moving at the same time: while one is moving forward, the other moves backward relative to the body. This kind of movement is called symmetrical gait. In the gait of toddlers, many steps are symmetrical, but many are also asymmetrical. This happens because the toddlers often plant one foot and then seem to fall forward onto the other foot in a robot-like walk. Toddlers still have trouble balancing and they need to walk this way to keep from falling.

Thus, while adult walkers are smoothly making every step symmetrical, toddlers have much more variable steps. Smoothness of gait reaches nearly adult levels about 6 months after the infant begins walking, regardless of the age at which the infant started taking steps (J. E. Clark, Truly, & Phillips, 1993; J. E. Clark, Whitall, & Phillips, 1988). If infants are given support by an adult, their variability lessens, and they seem to be better-coordinated walkers. This suggests that balance, not the timing, of the limb movements is the limiting factor (Bril & Breniere, 1993; Clark, Whitall, & Phillips, 1988). Balance improves gradually over time with increases in muscle strength and experience walking (Roncesvalles et al., 2001). This occurs because toddlers attempt to take longer strides from time-to-time, seemingly to test out and enhance their ability to balance (Badaly & Adolph, 2008). While learning to walk, infants also sway more when sitting, again seeming to "play" with feeling their control over balance (Chen et al., 2007).

Locomotion has benefits other than the ability to move from place to place. After beginning to walk, 10-month-old infants increase their frequency and duration of social contacts. This occurs whether the walking is supported or unsupported. It appears that an upright infant is more likely to be able to look, vocalize, and smile at adults (Gustafson, 1984). Independent walking confers even more social abilities on infants including more time interacting with toys and mothers, and more vocalizations and gestures, including pointing at objects (Clearfield, 2011).

Even more surprising is that locomotor experience enhances cognitive development. As we will see in the next section, one of the tests typically used to assess cognitive knowledge in infancy is the ability to search for hidden objects. Infants with more locomotor experience, who are apparently more accustomed to moving around in the environment, are the most likely to persist in searches for hidden objects. The locomotor experience could be either crawling or assisted walking (Bai & Bertenthal, 1992; Bertenthal, Campos, & Barrett, 1984; Kermoian & Campos, 1988). The development of walking also facilitates the search for hidden objects by blind infants, even though blind infants walk later than sighted infants (Bigelow, 1992). Being able to move oneself through the environment is essential for understanding spatial arrangements and the locations of things in that space. This may occur because walking changes how infants relate to objects. While crawling, they prefer objects that are nearby. When walking, infants move across the room to get objects, they carry objects, and approach adults with objects (Karasik et al., 2011).

The motor skill of reaching continues to improve during this period. Between 6 and 8 months, infants discover that they can lean forward to get objects just outside their reach. By 10 months, infants understand the limits of how far they can reach both by leaning forward and by extending their arms. By 12 months, infants are able to use mechanical and social aids to get things out of their reach, such as using a long object to get another or asking an adult for help (McKenzie et al., 1993). Banging objects also becomes more precise, with infants using more vertical trajectories of their arms with shorter strokes to deliver a more precise hit on their target (Kahrs et al., 2013).

Fine motor development also is intimately linked to cognitive and perceptual development. In one research study (Ruff, 1984), infants at 6, 9, and 12 months were observed while playing with objects that differed in weight, shape, or texture. Infants were handed one object to explore and then given another differing only in one property (for example, two cubes of the same size and weight, one with a bumpy texture and the other with a smooth texture). Between 6 and 12 months, mouthing the objects decreased, while fingering increased. The 12-month-olds also used more actions that were specific to the properties of the object. If only the object's texture was changed, babies increased the amount of time they looked at and fingered the object. If only the shape was changed, looking at and fingering the object increased, but so did rotating the object and transferring it between both hands. Although infants do not finger or look at heavier objects differently than lighter objects, they do use a stronger grip for the heavier ones (Molina & Jouen, 2003).

Related research has shown that by 12 months, infants use touching, listening, watching, and mouthing as alternative sources of information gathering. This involves more than intersensory coordination; it is the coordination of different types of motor skills in the service of directed exploration of objects (Bushnell, 1982; Gottfried, Rose, & Bridger, 1977).

This research shows that by 12 months, infants are using specific actions that are adapted to the type of object they are holding. Motor skill improvements and improvements in the ability to relate information cross-modally (such as between vision and touch) are essential in fostering cognitive development because they put infants into direct contact with more aspects of their world.

During this stage of development, the baby begins to crawl and toddle around the house, which can lead to potentially dangerous situations. Beginning at this age and continuing into early childhood, infants need to be protected from some of the obvious dangers in their environment.

What Are the Main Threats to Infant Safety?

Each year, about 3,500 children under the age of 4 years die in the United States from unintentional injuries. This accounts for about 35 percent of all deaths in this age group, making injuries the leading cause of death (Karns, 2001). Many more injuries occur that do not result in death. For every death, there are 1,120 emergency room visits and an unknown number of untreated injuries or injuries treated at home. Infant mortality due to unintentional injuries can be categorized as follows: motor vehicle collisions (32 percent), fire (19 percent), drowning (18 percent), choking (7 percent), falls (3 percent), poisoning (2 percent), and other causes (19 percent) (Lewit & Baker, 1995). In this section, we discuss each of these different causes of injury.

Collisions and falls: Automobile accidents are the leading cause of injury and death among infants. In the United States, about 1,100 children under 4 years of age die every year in such accidents, and 7,000 infants per year suffer injuries. The tragedy is that most of these could be prevented by the use of well-designed car seats and seat belts, because most injuries occur when infants are riding in the front seat of a car on someone's lap. Even though every state has a safety restraint law for infants, less than half of all infants are safely strapped in. Safety restraints are highly effective, and the number of deaths per year has been dropping under the new safety belt laws (D. Davis, 1985; National Safety Council, 1987).

Buy an infant car seat that is easy to install correctly. The seat should be in the center of the back seat. Be firm with the baby and do not let him or her out of the seat even if the child fusses. Do not let the child eat lollipops or hold sharp or pointed objects while the car is moving, and do not put loose items like groceries in the back seat (Chubet, 1988).

At home, falls and collisions can be prevented by taking simple precautions. Never leave a baby unattended on a table or a bed, block off access to stairs, and keep the baby's high chair away from a table or wall that could be used as leverage to push the chair over. Even though babies at this age have developed a wariness of the deep side of a visual cliff (see the "Emotional Development" section earlier in this chapter), most infants do not have sufficient control over their locomotor skills at this age to prevent a fall.

All infants suffer minor tumbles and shocks as they try to expand their motor skills. These are generally not serious unless there is some suspicion of a broken bone or a severe head injury. A number of excellent books are available for parents and other caregivers on the diagnosis of medical problems in infants and children. Be sure to read about the signs of concussion and know what to do if you see one. Severe head injury trauma can occur even from short falls onto hard surfaces (Prange et al., 2003).

Infants can also fall from cribs, high chairs, walkers, windows, and grocery carts. Cribs should be checked for sturdiness and should have a mattress that can be lowered as the baby grows. The posts or slats should be no more than 2 3/8 inches apart to prevent infants from getting their heads stuck. Be sure that mobiles are securely fastened and will not fall if the baby grabs them. Do not use plastic bags to cover the mattress, and do not allow any strings within reach of the baby. Do not tie pacifiers to strings, as the baby can easily become entangled or choke (Chubet, 1988).

High chairs should not have sharp edges, springs that can catch the baby's skin, or straps in which the baby can become entangled. The seat should not be so slippery that it causes the baby to slide down. It should be extremely easy to remove the tray without hurting the baby. Walkers are safe if the wheelbase is wider than the seat and grip area and if they are not used near stairs or near furniture with sharp edges. Always strap infants into grocery carts, and never allow children to stand in a cart. For high chairs, walkers, jumpers, grocery carts, and changing tables, the most important rule is that *under no circumstances are you to leave the baby unattended.* If the phone rings, either ignore it or take the baby with you to answer it.

Finally, if you live in a building with more than one story, do not trust screens to keep an active toddler from falling out a window. Windows can be blocked so that they can open only enough for ventilation but not wide enough for a baby to fit through. Safety gates are recommended near stairs or to block off rooms that hold dangers for the baby. Buy gates that will not pinch a baby and that are easy for adults to open and close (otherwise they will stay open).

Poisoning: Modern households are filled with lethal poisons, and most of them are kept within easy reach of an inquisitive infant. The cabinets under the kitchen and bathroom sinks are the most likely repositories of poisonous substances in the house: soaps, detergents, cleaning fluids, cosmetics, insecticides, and other toxic substances. It is wise to keep all such substances completely out of the infant's reach, because parental discipline is often not effective at this age in totally keeping the infant away from these dangers. Cabinets should be locked or childproofed or the toxic substances moved well out of the infant's reach. Even if most things have childproof caps, the caps and outer surfaces of the containers may contain enough toxin to make the infants ill if they should put them in their mouths. Child-care providers and parents should learn some of the common poisons and their antidotes. A poison antidote chart is available from most hospitals and pediatricians and should be posted in the kitchen or bathroom, where it can be readily consulted in an emergency.

Other potential sources of poisonous material include the leaves and flowers of houseplants and lead and lead-based paints. Never allow babies to be in rooms where there are paint flakes and plaster dust. Like plaster dust, baby powders can be toxic and are so fine that they can easily clog immature lung passages. Breathing can also be obstructed by plastic bags, and uninflated or broken balloon pieces are especially dangerous (although inflated balloons are not). Exposure to lead can lead to behavior problems, mental retardation, learning disabilities, and language impairment (Kaiser et al., 2008).

Finally, infants—like fetuses—are affected by passive smoking; for infants, the danger lies in inhaling the smoke from burning cigarettes or the exhalations of smokers. Infants exposed to passive smoking had more sympathetic (stress and arousal) and less parasympathetic (calming and relaxing) nervous system arousal and higher heart rates compared to infants not exposed to smoke (Schuetze & Eiden, 2006).

Swallowing small objects: If a small object becomes lodged in an infant's throat, it can disrupt breathing or cause choking. As with poisons, any object that can easily fit into an infant's mouth should be removed from the child's reach. The most common cause of suffocation at this age is latex balloons. Mylar and paper balloons are better, but all balloons can explode, which may cause pieces to become lodged in the baby's throat. Beads, coins, uncooked grains, paper clips, and so on are candidates for chokers. Be sure the button eyes of stuffed toys are sewn on securely and that rattles (with beads inside) are not cracked. As the infant learns to stand while holding onto furniture, small objects on the tops of tables and desks are vulnerable to the infant's reach. Make sure they are on high shelves or in childproofed drawers. Foods that are cut too small can also be dangerous for babies who cannot yet chew effectively. Hot dogs, peanuts, and other hard foods are not recommended. Parents may want to be trained in the Heimlich maneuver and other methods for helping a choking infant.

Burns and drowning: Infants suffer more from home fires and smoke inhalation than do older children and adults. They are less mature and have more sensitive skin and lungs. They are also less able to escape on their own. Many burns also occur from overly hot bathwater, stove tops, splashing grease, and radiators. Be sure the child knows the meaning of the word "hot." Keep the infant away from sources of heat, and always test the bathwater before putting the baby in.

Baths also present the danger of the child's slipping and/or drowning. Be sure to use nonslip pads in the bottom of the sink or tub. You can also buy a molded sponge in which the baby can sit. Keep infants away from pools, and keep toilet seats down. Never leave a baby unattended near or in water. Parental attention is imperative at all times when a baby is near water; bathtub seats and molded sponges are no substitute for an adult's vigilance.

Other dangers: Sharp and pointed objects are another common source of danger. Pencils, pens, and screwdrivers should never be given to infants of this age. If they want to scribble, let them use a nontoxic crayon (not a felt-tipped marker). Heavy objects, especially those infants can pull down on top of themselves, are also potential dangers. Keep the baby away from ropes or cords (such as venetian blind pulls), and avoid clothing that ties around the neck. The best way to prevent many dangers is to crawl around and look at the house from the point of view of someone who is 2 feet tall, curious, and clumsy. Sun exposure can damage infant skin more readily than for adults. Infants should have sunblock, appropriate clothing, and a hat when out of doors for more than a few minutes at a time.

Finally, toys are potentially dangerous. They should have no small parts, such as buttons, that are detachable, and small objects, such as marbles should not be used. Toys should have no sharp edges, small holes, or openings that can cut, trap, or pinch fingers or tongues. Toys should be sturdy. Plastic is always better than glass, which can break or shatter. Toys should not contain any strings, elastic bands, or ropes longer than 10 or 12 inches. Stuffed toys should not be so soft that the baby can suffocate, and they should be easy to wash.

Emergency Procedures

Even with the best attempts at prevention, infants will sometimes face life-threatening accidents or injuries. It is recommended that parents and caregivers be familiar with the basics of first aid and cardiopulmonary resuscitation (CPR). A number of excellent infant health books and web sites are available, and first aid classes can be found through local health organizations. CPR is useful in cases of shock or drowning to help the infant resume breathing and provide heart massage. Simple but specific techniques should be learned to control bleeding, treat burns, stop choking, stop electrical shock, and treat poisoning (Chubet, 1988).

What Are Some Important Health Considerations?

Most of the serious diseases of infancy and early childhood have been eliminated due to immunization procedures. Babies should be given a series of inoculations during the first 2 years of life. These are shown in Table 8.1. It is generally recommended that children not receive immunizations later than scheduled so as to avoid unnecessary exposure.

Most of the common diseases of infancy involve gastrointestinal or respiratory problems. Symptoms of the former include vomiting, stomach pains, diarrhea, and constipation. Signs of the

TABLE 8.1 Recommended Immunization Schedule (Birth—6 years) (2001)

Vaccine	Age for Administration
Hepatitis B (HiB)	Birth–3 months (first); 1–4 months (second); 6–18 months (third)
Diptheria Tetanus Pertussus (DTP)	2 months (first); 4 months (second); 6 months (third); 15–18 months (fourth); 4–6 years (fifth)
Heamophilius influenza Type b (Hib)	2 months (first); 4 months (second) 6 months (third); 12–15 months (fourth)
Inactivated Polio (IPV)	2 months (first); 4 months (second); 6–18 months (third); 4–6 years (fourth)
Pneumococcal Conjugate (PCV)	2 months (first); 4 months (second); 6 months (third)
Measles, Mumps, Rubella (MMR)	12–15 months (first); 4–6 years (second)
Varicella	12–18 months
Hepatitis A	24 months (in selected areas)

Source: Centers for Disease Control and Prevention (2001). Recommended childhood immunization schedule—United States, 2001. *Morbibity and Mortality Weekly Report, 50*(1), 10.

latter are a runny nose, sore throat, coughing or wheezing, and trouble breathing. A fever is also a sign of illness. Consult medical care manuals. They generally give advice about which conditions can be treated at home and which require a doctor's attention.

Although some illnesses are caused by viral or bacterial infections, repeated occurrences of particular symptoms should be taken as warning signs. The infant may be exposed to infectious or unsanitary conditions, or the illness may be a symptom of an allergic reaction. In the latter case, the physician should work with the family to isolate the possible source of the allergy.

Another related health factor is the quality of infant sleep. By 10 months, most infants are sleeping through the night with only occasional night wakings. Infants who are more likely to wake up at night and to remain awake longer have higher levels of stress during the daytime, as measured both by cortisol levels and behavior patterns. Aside from higher cortisol, infants of this age who have sleep problems are more likely to still be co-sleeping with the parents and/or breast feeding, more likely to be distressed at separation from the parents, and more likely to cry during the day (DeLeon & Karraker, 2007; Lucas-Thompson et al., 2009). Most of these sleep problems are temporary—resulting from the developmental onset of fear-based emotions in the period (see below)—and they probably have the most effects on parents who have to wake up to help the infant return to sleep. All children and adults who experience daytime stress are more likely to have sleep problems. When that stress continues or fails to be regulated, there may be long-term consequences for regulatory ability later in childhood (Bernier, 2013).

PERCEPTUAL AND COGNITIVE DEVELOPMENT

Conceptualizing Relationships between Objects and Events

By the age of 7 months, infants are just beginning to understand that objects exist as whole entities and they are starting to categorize objects on the basis of their similarity to a prototype. By 10 months, infants are beginning to discover the relationships between objects, between people and objects, and between people. This can be seen, for example, in the development of **relational play.** Relational play is action that demonstrates a knowledge of the relationships between two objects, for example, putting lids on pots, cups on saucers, or spoons in cups (Fenson, Kagan, Kearsley, & Zelazo, 1976). The more perceptually distinct the two objects, the more likely it is that babies will combine them correctly (Bates, Carlson-Luden, & Bretherton, 1980). For example, if a box and its lid are different colors, infants will be more likely to see how they go together. Also, if the adult places the lid of the box on a table positioned near the top of the box, rather than near the bottom, babies are more likely to put the lid on the box in an appropriate manner. Year-old infants can tell the difference between a visual display of a block that enters an opening of a box and one that rests precariously on the rim of the opening (Sitskoorn & Smitsman, 1997). These studies suggest that infants understand how different objects may be related to each other. A block is supposed to go inside the opening rather than rest on the rim.

Infants of this age are also able to perceive the relationship between a tool and its use. Infants first saw a toy sitting on the far end of a long piece of cloth. The near end of the cloth was pulled by an experimenter, moving the toy closer to the experimenter. Next they saw the toy sitting next to the cloth. In one instance the cloth was pulled and the toy did not move closer (as expected) and in another instance the cloth was pulled and the toy moved closer (an impossible event). The infants were surprised when seeing the impossible event, suggesting that they understood the relationship between the cloth tool and the object being retrieved (Schlesinger & Langer, 1999; Sommerville & Woodward, 2005; Sommerville et al., 2008). In another variant of this procedure, infants watched one puppet (the giver) give a flower to another puppet (the receiver). When the two puppets' positions were reversed, the infants still expected the original giver puppet to continue being the giver regardless of physical location (Schöppner et al., 2006).

Forming relationships between objects can also be seen in studies in which infants were placed in front of a tray containing different groups of identical objects, for example, four identical human figures, four balls of the same color, and four identical toy cars. Six-month-olds pick up the objects in random sequence, even though they can visually distinguish the different types of objects in a standard habituation procedure. By 12 months, infants will pick up three or four identical objects in a row before going on to pick up other objects. About 40 percent of 12-month olds will take those identical objects and place them in a new pile by themselves (Starkey, 1981). By 10 months, infants are able to classify pictures of animals (dogs versus cats), male versus female faces, and plants versus kitchen utensils (Furrer & Younger, 2005; G. Levy & Haaf, 1994; Mandler & McDonough, 1998; B. A. Younger & Fearing, 1999). The ability of infants of this age to categorize objects is related to their familiarity with those objects (McDonough & Mandler, 1998; Oakes, Coppage, & Dingel, 1997).

Infants of this age are also able to perceive the relationship between a prior event and a subsequent event, that is, between a cause and an effect. Infants can understand that when one toy car hits another toy car, the second one should move as a result of the collision (L. B. Cohen & Oakes, 1993). They also understand the relationships between faces and voices, that a male voice belongs with a male face and a female voice belongs with a female face, or that a toy when squeezed should make a sound (Perone & Oakes, 2006; Poulin-Dubois et al., 1994). They prefer to view human bodies that are drawn in the correct proportions rather than bodies that are distorted, suggesting that they see the body as a whole composed of specifically related parts (Zeiber, 2010). Finally, they can infer the weight of an object by observing how much that object compresses a cotton wool pad on which the object is sitting (Hauf et al., 2012).

The Emergence of Infant Intentional Action

In the studies just reviewed, infants are acting as if their object play has particular goals, such as combining objects in a meaningful way. This delib-

---

Observations

Stage IV Behavior (Piaget, 1954, p. 219)

Observation 8.1

At 0;8(8) Jacqueline tries to grasp her celluloid duck but I also grasp it at the same time she does. Then she firmly holds the toy in her right hand and pushes my hand away with her left.

Observation 8.2

At 0;8(17) after taking the first spoonful of medicine, she pushes away her mother's hand which extends to her a second one.

---

erate combination of different actions into a unified pattern of behavior suggests that infants are intending to act in this way. This is different from what occurred in earlier periods, when infants first discovered actions by chance and then repeated those actions as primary or secondary circular reactions. This intentional and deliberate form of action is what Piaget (1952) called the *coordination of secondary circular reactions*. In Observations 8.1 and 8.2, Jacqueline's pushing away of her parent's hand shows how the infant can combine different actions with each hand to achieve a goal.

Notice that to perform these deliberate actions, the infant must relate two simpler secondary circular reactions, such as holding the toy in one hand and pushing the adult away with the other. Infants are also relating two actions when they search for hidden objects. To find an object that they see being hidden behind a barrier or a cover, infants have to move the barrier with one hand and grasp the uncovered object with the other hand. We saw in the last chapter that younger infants remember the hidden object's location, although they do not reach for the object once it is out of sight. Piaget found that by 10 months, infants will readily search for the hidden object and seem delighted to find it under the cover.

Now suppose you have two identical handkerchief-sized pieces of colored cloth on a table at which you are sitting opposite the infant. You engage the infant with an attractive toy, such as a set of colored keys, and then you hide the keys under one of the pieces of cloth. Infants 10 months and older, but not younger, will lift the cloth to retrieve the keys. Now suppose you take the keys back from the baby and hide them under the other piece of cloth. Infants younger than about 15 months typically will look under the first piece of cloth and will not persist in looking under the second piece of cloth to find the object even though it was hidden in their plain view! This is easy to demonstrate with a year-old infant, if you want to convince yourself that babies could actually make such an obvious error.

This mistaken search for the missing object is called the **A-not-B error** by infancy researchers. The infants who find the object at location A, the first location, cannot find the object at location B, the second location. This error has aroused the curiosity of many infant researchers. Why does it happen? It seems as if infants lose the intention to find the object after more than one hiding.

According to Piaget, the infants act as if part of their definition of the object includes its location. In other words, infants do not yet conceive of a whole independent object as you and I might. Rather, infants define the object as the "keys-under-the-cloth," or the "ball-under-the-chair." This sort of thing also happens to adults. Most of us have had the experience of meeting someone briefly, say, at a party, and then failing to recognize the same person in another location, such as at the grocery store. If we encountered that person at another party at the same place, we would have no trouble recognizing the individual.

Following Piaget's elegant first experiments and his contextual explanation, there have been a number of seemingly contradictory results. First

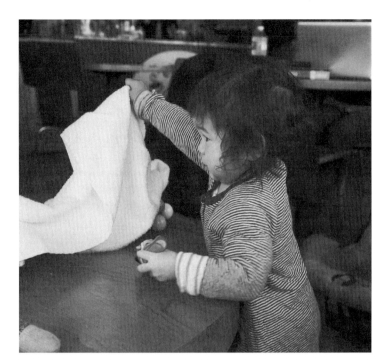

When an object is hidden, young infants often act as if it does not exist anymore.
Photo by Emily Waterfield

of all, it should be noted that by 9 months, infants are almost 100 percent correct in reaching for hidden objects at the A location (Wellman, Cross, & Bartsch, 1986). Second, if objects are displaced at several different locations without being hidden or if objects are hidden under transparent covers, so long as the infants are first familiarized with the covers and objects, they are almost 100 percent correct in reaching for the object in either location, A or B (Butterworth, 1977; Yates & Bremner, 1988). The only case in which this is not true is if the object or the infant is moved along complex paths with many twists and turns (B. Landau & Spelke, 1988). This suggests that following the path of a moving object in space is not limiting the infant's ability to search where the objects are hidden at location B.

Memory of the hidden object cannot be a problem for 9-month-olds, as shown by the studies of Baillargeon (discussed in Chapter 7), in which 8-month-old infants remembered an object's location so long as they did not have to act on it. It appears, then, that infants of this age already have a concept of objects as existing when out of sight, and they do not appear to associate objects with particular locations, because they will directly search for the object in multiple locations so long as they can see the object.

The A-not-B error is made most frequently when the object is out of sight, but even then, infants succeed under certain conditions:

- If there is no delay between the hiding and the opportunity to search for the object, they can find it. Errors are increased if infants are restrained for at least 3 seconds after the object is hidden at location B (Diamond, 1988; Diamond & Doar, 1989).

- If the infants are shown the object being hidden in the A location multiple times, they are more likely to search in the B location (Marcovitch & Zelazo, 1999).

- If the infants are allowed to lean their bodies in the direction of the hidden object, they can sometimes find it even after a delay by following the direction of their lean (Diamond & Doar, 1989).

- If the objects are hidden under covers that are perceptually very different, it is easier for the infants than if the objects are hidden under identical covers (Bremner, 1978).

- It also helps if the infants are familiar with the objects or if the objects are interesting to them (Munakata, 1997). They will search more readily for their hidden mothers than for an unfamiliar person or a large object (Bigelow, MacDonald, & MacDonald, 1995).

The A-not-B error is not a serious deficit for infants, and they overcome it within a few months or if the objects are presented in ways that facilitate their search, as described above. The importance of the A-not-B error lies in questions it raises for understanding human development. Development offers many examples in which the emergence of a new skill (like searching for hidden objects) is accompanied by a curious but not serious deficit (like being unable to search in more than one hiding place). When we discuss language development in Chapter 9, we will encounter another example, called *overgeneralization,* which occurs when children begin to make grammatical errors after they have seemingly acquired the correct rule. Developmental researchers would like to better understand why these patterns occur.

Imitation

Imitation is another skill that requires making a conceptual relationship between two actions, in this case, between another person's actions and one's own. The imitations of newborns occur only for acts that they can already do. Observing an adult doing the same types of acts increases the probability of the newborn's selecting a similar act. However, newborn imitation is slow and does not happen for all infants. Six-month-olds can imitate actions that they have not done before, but only if you give them many demonstrations and allow them plenty of time to process the information (Kaye & Marcus, 1978). Between 10 and 12 months, infants become more proficient at imitating actions that they see for the first time or have not done before.

Typically, babies are better at imitating actions that are close to what they can already do. Nine-month-old infants can imitate simple actions on objects such as opening a box, shaking a toy rattle, and pushing a button. In addition, when the same babies were shown the objects 24 hours later, they reproduced the actions that had been modeled previously (A. Meltzoff, 1988). Imitation that occurs following a delay from the time the action is observed is called **deferred imitation.** Deferred imitation also shows that infants can remember the relationships they learn, at least for a short time. If infants are allowed to imitate the action immediately, they can remember and imitate after longer delays compared to infants who were only allowed to watch and not imitate the action (Lukowski et al., 2005).

Individual Differences in Cognition and Attention

The basic trends in cognitive development discussed in this chapter have been found to occur at about the same ages in different cultures around the world (Agiobu-Kemmer, 1986). On the other hand, within any group there are individual differences in the age of attainment of cognitive milestones and in the quality of cognitive abilities.

One important component of cognition is the ability to attend to objects for a long enough time to remember their locations, watch their paths of movement, or learn about their properties during exploratory play. Individual differences in the duration of sustained attention to objects have been found at the age of 1 year (Power, Chapieski, & McGrath, 1985). Infants who can sustain attention for longer periods engage in higher levels of exploratory play (Caruso, 1993; L. Fenson, Sapper, & Minner, 1974) and score higher on developmental tests of mental and motor abilities (Kopp & Vaughn, 1982; Ruff, Lawson, Parrinello, & Weissberg, 1990).

What factors account for individual differences in attention? To some extent, these differences may be related to differential development of the brain and may be partly constitutional (Rothbart & Posner, 1985). On the other hand, differences in the caregiving environment have been shown to influence the quality of infant attention.

When mothers are trained to enhance their object-related behaviors during social play with infants—by demonstrating object properties, pointing to and naming objects, and asking infants questions about the object—the complexity of the infants' exploratory play is enhanced (Belsky, Goode, & Most, 1980; Tamis-LeMonda et al., 1992; Tomasello, 1995). Actually, this effect works best for infants who have short attention spans. Their duration of attention increases following an intervention in which adults work to point out object properties and refocus the infants after a loss of attention, while the duration of attention for high-attending infants does not change following the intervention (Lawson, Parrinello, & Ruff, 1992; Parrinello & Ruff, 1988).

These studies suggest that adults can play important roles in the cognitive development of infants, particularly if their actions are designed to enhance the infants' attention to objects and their properties. At this age, adults do not need to teach or reinforce but rather to support the infants' own initiatives and help the infants to regulate their limited attention spans. A similar pattern of parental support also enhances word and language learning. These results also suggest that adult behavior needs to be adapted to the individual infant. Babies who are less active and poor attenders may need a more involved adult to help organize their play. Babies who are more active and attentive may have different needs for adults, perhaps to be an appreciative audience to whom the infants can show off their self-directed achievements.

In summary, infants of this age are making the discovery that objects and events are related to each other. They can combine objects according to their function (lids on pots), their category (trucks vs. cars), or how they need to be combined to achieve a goal (using a fork to get food). As we shall see, this ability to form mental relationships between things is related to important develop-ments in emotion, communication, and the sense of self.

EMOTIONAL DEVELOPMENT

As the sections on cognitive and motor development suggest, the infant's life is becoming increasingly integrated into patterns of intentions and relationships. Motor skills create the tools with which the infant can operate on the environment to achieve goals, and goals increasingly structure the way in which the infant behaves. During the previous age period, infants became upset when someone caused them pain or when some expected event did not happen. Between the ages of 10 and 12 months, infants become upset when their goals are blocked and are pleased when they achieve an intended goal. They also develop new emotions regarding their relationships with other people: fear, sadness and affection.

The Development of Anger

Anger is the emotion most frequently elicited in infants when their goals have been disrupted. An angry expression has distinct characteristics. The mouth is open with a square shape that is angled downward toward the back of the mouth. The brows are lowered, and the eyes are opened and intense (see Figure 8.2). In the expression of distress, the mouth is similar, but the eyes are usually closed or partially closed (Figure 8.2). Anger typically involves a bracing of the jaw.

When the infant is crying and making the anger expression at the same time, the state of emotion is more intense. When anger expressions were observed without crying, EEG recordings from the infants' scalps showed heightened activity in the left frontal region. When the infants were angry and crying, there was more activity in the right frontal region. The right frontal area is believed to be associated with more intense states of negative emotions. These results suggest that low levels of anger, without crying, are probably more cognitively-based (left brain) and maintain the infant's orientation toward the environment (N. A. Fox & Davidson, 1988).

The emotion of anger began in the previous stage as a more vigilant and intense form of distress. Between 10 and 12 months, anger becomes more purposeful and directed. Infants do such things as stomp their feet, hit away objects or interfering hands, or slap and kick (Sroufe, 1979). These expressions have the quality of outbursts, and they coincide with the development of goal-directed behavior seen in other realms of infant functioning during this period.

The Development of Wariness and Fear

Around the age of 6 months, infants develop a wary look, which may involve a raised brow furrowing above the nose and a relatively relaxed mouth. Wariness is related to the emotion of fear, since both involve an inhibition of action and may reflect a tendency for the individual to withdraw from the situation. The expression of fear includes the raised and furrowed brow of wariness while the mouth corners are retracted straight back (Figure 8.2).

True fear expressions are rare in infancy, but they first appear around the age of 10 months (Camras et al., 2007; Demos, 1982). Fear expressions may appear briefly and then change to anger or sadness (see Figure 8.2). Fear is more likely to be expressed by behavioral inhibition in the absence of a facial expression. Infants may stop their movements or actively avoid approaching the source of the fear. Infants feel fear when unexpected or threatening events occur. Below are some of the situations that may arouse fear in year-old infants.

Heights. Fear of heights has been assessed using the **visual cliff** situation. A piece of hard, clear plastic is extended over a box with a shallow side and a deep side. Beginning at 9 months of age, infants show fear in approaching the deep side of the cliff (E. J. Gibson & Walk, 1960; A. Schwartz, Campos, & Baisel, 1973).

Unpredictable objects and movements. Infants will show fear responses to any objects—either people or inanimate moving objects—that loom unexpectedly in front of them (Bronson, 1972; Cicchetti & Mans, 1976). Surprising events, like a jack-in-the-box popping up, may also cause fear (Ricciuti & Poresky, 1972). Unpredictable, noisy mechanical toys can cause fear. However, in one study, infants were given control over the movements of such toys. When the infants were in control, the toys were significantly less fearsome (Gunnar, Leighton, & Peleaux, 1984).

Acquired fears. Infants may become fearful of an otherwise benign situation because it reminds them of something they found stressful, fearful, or painful in the past. These fears can be said to arise from a conditioned association. They are different from fears of such things as snakes, spiders, heights, or looming objects, which may be universal. Infants do appear to have an untrained fear of snakes, especially if they are shown in a film compared to a still photo (DeLoach & LoBue, 2009). Acquired fears are learned. Examples are fear of particular people, of doctor's offices, or of certain kinds of sounds, such as a dog's bark (Bronson, 1972; see Observation 8.3).

Strangers. Fear of strangers takes two forms. One is an acquired fear of particular people or people wearing a particular kind of clothing or hairstyle. The other is a general wariness of the unfamiliar that appears in most infants in every culture beginning about 8 months of age. Infants show *less fear* if the stranger approaches them slowly and keeps an appropriate distance (Kaltenbach, Weinraub, & Fullard, 1980; Ricard & Decarie, 1993); if their mothers are present when the stranger approaches (Eckerman & Whatley, 1975; Ricciuti, 1974); if they are with familiar caregivers, such as baby-sitters or child-care providers (N. A. Fox, 1977; Ricciuti, 1974); if the stranger is a little person or a child (Bigelow, MacLean, Wood, & Smith, 1990; Brooks & Lewis, 1976); if the stranger does not tower over them (Weinraub

(a) Enjoyment   (b) Sadness

(c) Distress   (d) Anger   (e) Fear

Figure 8.2   Infant Expressions

Source: C. Izard, *The maximally discriminative facial movement coding system*, 1983 (January), p. 97. Instructional Resources Center, University of Delaware, Newark, DE, pp. 93, 95–98.

Observations

Stage IV Behavior (Piaget, 1952, p. 249)

Observation 8.3

At 1;1(10) she [Jacqueline] has a slight scratch which is disinfected with alcohol. She cries, chiefly from fear. Subsequently, as soon as she again sees the bottle of alcohol she recommences to cry, knowing what is in store for her. Two days later, same reaction, as soon as she sees the bottle and even before it is opened.

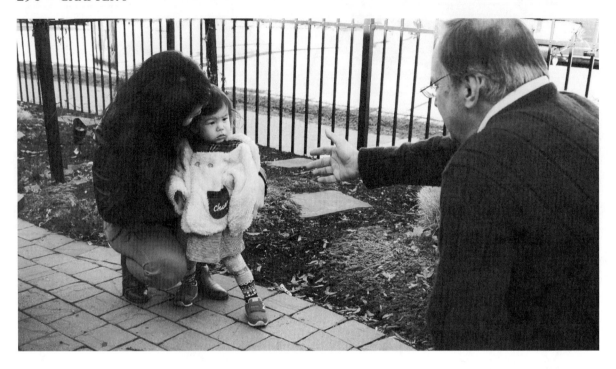

Infants of this age are naturally wary of new situations. They find great comfort in the company of familiar caregivers.
Photo by Emily Waterfield.

& Putney, 1978); if the stranger is sensitive to the infants' signals and allows the approach to be regulated by the infants (Mangelsdorf, 1992); and if the infants are in an unfamiliar setting, such as a laboratory, compared to a home (Brookhart & Hock, 1976; Skarin, 1977).

You might expect a baby to be less fearful at home than in a strange place, but this is not the case. In strange places, infants seem to expect to see unusual or unfamiliar things. When the stranger intrudes on the familiar and predictable setting of the home, however, the infant gets disturbed. In fact, mothers take their babies many places, such as doctors' offices and grocery stores, and the babies are rarely upset by the many unfamiliar people they meet in those situations. A number of studies have shown that babies can engage in positive and rewarding social interaction soon after meeting a new person. If the stranger proves acceptable to the baby, the baby often will spend more time playing with this interesting visitor than with his or her own mother (Klein & Durfee, 1976; Ross & Goldman, 1977b).

If you want to make friends with a baby of this age, the rules are much the same as with anyone else: go slowly, be sensitive to signs of withdrawal or wariness, let the baby get to know you on his or her own terms, and make sure the baby is properly chaperoned by his or her mother or caregiver before you make any serious proposals. Finally, do not forget that year-old babies develop acquired fears. If the baby screams in terror at the mere sight of you, it could be that you remind the baby of a negative encounter. Even though it is hard to keep from feeling downright insulted, it is probably not your fault. It may take some extra sensitivity on your part to help the baby learn to like you for yourself.

The Development of Sadness

The emotion of sadness has a different expression than anger and fear. During sadness, the brows are raised at the center and drop at the sides, and the mouth corners are drawn back and down (see Figure 8.2). As we reported for anger, sadness without crying is less intense, showing left-frontal brain activity. With crying, sadness is accompanied by right-brain activation. In the earlier months, sadness accompanies disappointment when an expected event fails to happen, for example, when the baby expects to receive a treat or a hug and does not get it. By 9 or 10 months, sadness accompanies a feeling of loss. Because infants can now connect their memory of absent objects with some concrete action on the objects, the infants may become sad if an object disappears and they cannot find it after a search.

In some cases, but not all, sadness accompanies separation from caregivers. This emotion is sometimes called *separation distress*. Research has shown, however, that if mothers leave their babies behind in the company of the regular caregiver (the grandmother, baby-sitter, father, and so on), there is little or no separation distress (Ricciuti, 1974; Stayton, Ainsworth, & Main, 1973; Suwalsky & Klein, 1980). Infants respond more positively to separation from their mothers if they are left with any other person, particularly a familiar one; if they are left with toys of any kind; if they can see or hear their mothers in an adjoining room (Corter, 1977); and if they are left with their own pacifiers (Halonen & Passman, 1978; Hong & Townes, 1976). The mothers saying "bye-bye" or making some other parting gestures before they left had no effect on 1-year-olds (Corter, 1977). These parting gestures do seem to help older infants, however. In general, the longer parents take to say good-bye, the harder it is for the babies to initially adjust to the new situation (Field, Gewirtz, et al., 1984; Weinraub & Lewis, 1977). Babies who go to a new preschool or day care center, or who must be hospitalized, show less distress if accompanied by peer friends or by siblings (Field, Vega-Lahr, & Jagadish, 1984; Heinicke & Westheimer, 1966; J. Robertson & Robertson, 1971).

There are cultural differences in infant response to separation, as shown by a study of brief (30-second) mother-infant separations in Japan (Hoshi & Chen, 1998). About half of the Japanese infants showed distress, even at this brief separation, perhaps because of the close contact between Japanese mothers and their infants and because separation is relatively rare. In addition, about one-third of the mothers apologized to the infant during the reunion. Their apologies were done in an intonation pattern that matched the infant's crying, such as saying *Hai, hai, gomen nei, gomen nei, oh, oh* (yes, yes, oh, I'm so sorry, so sorry, well, well). The mothers seemed to endorse the infant's feelings as if to join in their misery and seek their forgiveness, a pattern of emotional sharing commonly seen in Japanese adults. Whether Western mothers do the same is unknown but such behavior has never been reported in the thousands of studies on separation in Western countries.

If infants are separated from parents for long periods and are not provided with adequate substitute caregivers, more serious depression and withdrawal can result, including both behavior and physiological changes (Reite, Kaemingk, & Boccia, 1989; Tizard & Tizard, 1971). These effects can be ameliorated to some extent once the infants are restored to stable adult care, either with their biological parents or with adoptive parents (Reite et al., 1989; Suomi & Harlow, 1972; Tizard & Tizard, 1971). The effect on infants of substitute care by nonparental caregivers is an important topic to which we will return.

The Development of Enjoyment and Affection

In the earlier months, infants showed positive responses to their caregivers. The smile of recognition appears at 2 months, and laughter of enjoyment during social play appears at 5 months. At 10 months, the infant has a deeper and more lasting type of positive feeling that has been called affection (Sroufe, 1979). Affection has a characteristic expression that is similar to a simple smile in the mouth region accompanied by a widening of the eyes (see Figure 8.2). Such smiles occur at the approach of familiar caregivers and are accompanied by right-brain activation. Infants' smiles at strangers usually lack the wide-eye component; such smiles activate the left side of the brain (N. A. Fox & Davidson, 1988).

After a brief separation, infants often feel genuinely happy to see the caregiver. This is a positive emotion that goes beyond the particular situation and expresses a lasting bond. Infants express these feelings not only to caregivers but also to favorite toys and to siblings. Infants of this age smile more in the presence of people, especially familiar people, and their favorite objects (S. S. Jones, Collins, & Hong, 1991). As we saw in the last chapter, smiling is related partly to emotion and partly to communication with others. Smiling is a reflection of a socially shared emotion.

Differential responsiveness to people on reunion is probably one of the earliest and most reliable ways of telling who the most important people in a baby's life are (Stayton, Ainsworth, & Main, 1973). In a stressful situation, if both the mother and another caregiver are present, infants will approach the mother (Klein & Durfee, 1976). Even when infants spend more hours of the day in the company of caregivers, as on an Israeli kibbutz, they show more positive responses when reunited with their mothers after a brief separation than when reunited with their **metapelets,** or caregivers (N. A. Fox, 1977). These findings suggest that babies have a growing awareness of the specialness of certain people and respond to them in ways that communicate the depth of their feelings.

The Development of Mixed Emotions

Before leaving the topic of emotions, it is necessary to touch on the subject of mixed emotional expressions. In one study, a stranger presented dolls and teddy bears to infants of this age. The babies alternatively reached out toward the objects and pulled their arms back (Ricciuti & Poresky, 1972). Lest we think this sort of ambivalence was merely an artifact of testing infants in an unfamiliar laboratory setting, we should note that another study found evidence for mixed emotions by naturalistic observation in the infants' homes. This study found that pure expressions of joy, anger, distress, excitement, or fear occur only about half the time. The other half of the time the infant's face expresses more than one emotion (Demos, 1982).

Enjoyment, for example, often is expressed with elements of excitement or surprise, as when a smile is combined with a "jaw-drop," producing a wide-open, smiling mouth. This is called a *play smile* (see Chapter 7). Play smiles in 12-month-olds occur during games involving some physical activity or touch combined with an element of excitement. These are games like tickle, chase, and tossing the baby in the air. Play smiles are more likely to occur in physical games and thus appear more during father-infant play than in mother-infant play (L. Dickson, Fogel, & Messinger, 1997). Smiles have also been observed to occur with nose wrinkles, blinks, blows, and waves; each combination reflects a slight variation in the meaning of the enjoyment. Try each one out and see if you can figure out what it might mean.

In an effort to regulate emotion, distress will sometimes be combined with biting or stiffening the lip, showing that the baby is trying to control the crying. One-year-old babies often alternate between distress and enjoyment, showing that they are able to maintain interest in a toy or in social interaction even though they may be tired or frustrated. One-year-olds will sometimes look directly at the caregiver when crying, or they may pull at the caregiver, gesture to be picked up, or point to the offending object or event (Gustafson & Green, 1991). Relaxed touching and holding by the caregiver can provide encouragement for the infant's efforts to gain control over frustration, teaching the baby the capacity to persist (Hertenstein & Campos, 2001). The baby can learn that feeling distressed and frustrated does not necessarily mean the end of the game—that these "negative" affects are both tolerable and manageable (Demos, 1982).

Another example of a mixed emotion appearing at this age is jealousy. Year-old infants were observed while their mothers and a strange adult female played with a picture book or a child-sized doll. Infants showed more protest and negative

This baby is experiencing a mixed emotion. If you cover the eyes and look only at the mouth, what would you say the baby feels? Now cover the mouth, looking only at the eyes, and guess the baby's feelings. Putting the two parts together gives a mixed emotion.
Photo by Mary Kate Denny, PhotoEdit

vocalization and their play was more inhibited in the mother-with-doll condition (Hart, Field, Letourneau, & Del Valle, 1998). These responses were interpreted as jealousy because the infant was not upset about the mother with a book, nor about the stranger's behavior. Jealousy is an example of wanting to approach the mother but avoiding her at the same time.

Because of the emergence of mixed emotions, new forms of parent-child play develop as a way to help infants understand and cope with emotional changes. Teasing games are especially important in this regard. A tease takes something that has a serious emotional tone and alters it into a more positive tone. Between 9 and 12 months, infants learn the art of teasing and also become able to appreciate the teases of others (see Observations 8.4, 8.5, and 8.6). The contradictory messages in these games provide important opportunities for infants to learn how to regulate their emotions, how to affect other people, and also how to have fun (Nakano, 1995; Reddy, 1991; Reddy, 2000). Teasing is relatively more frequent in father-infant than in mother-infant play (Labrell, 1994).

In summary, these findings show that infants are becoming emotionally complex. Not only are they aware of the relationships between objects and between events, they are also aware of the relationships between their different feelings. They may not always be able to resolve these relationships but at a minimum, their emotional life is becoming more diverse. In the "Social Development" section in this chapter, we shall see that infants are also becoming more aware of interpersonal relationships. Indeed, findings show that jealousy and teasing are clearly emotions that take account of different kinds of interpersonal relationships.

Individual Differences in Emotion Regulation

As we saw in the previous section, infants of this age are learning emotion regulation to maintain some self-control in the face of highly arousing (either exciting or distressing) situations. At this age, infants show differences in how they use people or objects to regulate emotions.

Observations

Teasing Games (Nakano, 1995; Reddy, 1991)

Observation 8.4

Rebecca (8.5 months) "accidentally" discovers her impact on others of going in front of the television in her walker while someone is watching. After that, each time the television is turned on, Rebecca scoots, stands in front of it and giggles. Mother makes getting Rebecca away from the television into a game by playing "I'm gonna get you," while grabbing her away.

Observation 8.5

Stephanie (7 months) developed a shrill shriek that she used when she was not getting enough attention. In the supermarket, her mother heard the shriek, turned toward Stephanie quickly and with alarm, to find Stephanie sitting in her stroller grinning at her mother.

Observation 8.6

Mother claps her hands rhythmically to get her 10-month-old's attention. When the infant looks at her hands, the mother says, "my hands are stuck together and I can't pull them apart." She shrieks with an exasperated tone and asks the baby for help getting her hands apart. At the moment when the baby reaches out to help, the mother startles the baby by pulling her hands apart, saying "Bang!" at the same time. The mother answers the baby's surprised look with a smile and laugh and then the baby smiles joyfully.

Heart-rate measures have shown that even when infants do not cry during maternal separation, they do get aroused. We may observe an extended glance at the door, perhaps a sad expression, and then a concerted effort to become involved with the toys. It is almost as if the babies were using the toys to prevent feeling sad and lonely. Conversely, other infants who may ignore their mother when she returns from a separation also show elevated heart rates. These babies are coping with their ambivalent feelings about their mother in relation to the feeling of loss they must have experienced when she was out of the room (Sroufe, 1979).

Some infants are temperamentally more fearful and withdrawn, and they are more likely to become fearful or sad in stressful situations, such as during separations and in the presence of strangers or unusual situations (Blackford & Walden, 1998; Bohlin & Hagekull, 1993; K. A. Buss & Goldsmith, 1998; J. J. Campos et al., 1975; Connell, 1985; Kagan, 1989; R. A. Thompson, Connell, & Bridges, 1988). These differences in emotionality are associated with individual differences in brain asymmetry. That is, infants who become easily distressed to the point of crying by a maternal separation have more marked differences between left- and right-brain activity in the frontal area (N. A. Fox & Davidson, 1987). These findings show that the infant's ability to remain attentive to the situation, rather than to withdraw, may be in part responsible for higher levels of regulation of fear (Kochanska et al., 1998; M. D. Lewis et al., 1997).

This suggests that there is a relationship between cognition (attention) and emotion regulation. Findings reported earlier in this chapter, that sustained attention to tasks is related to exploratory play, are also relevant here. Some infants are more focused, attentive, and not easily upset, while others seem more emotional and require more support from adults in challenging situations. We do not know about the long-term consequences of these differences. Most likely, they are simply normal temperamental differences that need to be taken into account when co-regulating with a baby.

Developments in the Infant's Ability to Perceive Emotion and Intention Expressed by Other People

By 6 or 7 months, infants are capable of perceiving a few simple facial expressions. By 9 or 10 months, however, infants can distinguish more expressions, and they are beginning to use the emotional information displayed by others in a meaningful manner. These developments in the perception of emotions in other people are one of the ways in which the infant is becoming increasingly aware of relationships. Even more important, infants at this age are beginning to get the idea that other people have emotions that differ from their own. This is shown by some of the following processes.

Affective sharing occurs when infants wish to communicate their feelings to another person or to confirm their feelings with another person. An example would be when a baby discovers an interesting relationship (such as how a lid goes onto a pot), smiles, and then looks to the caregiver. In this case, the infant is expecting a smile in return, as a way of confirming his or her own feeling of accomplishment.

Social referencing occurs when infants face an uncertain situation. In this case, they look to another person's emotional expressions to help them decide what to do in this situation. When infants are presented with a noisy, unpredictable toy, they may look around to see how adults are responding to the toy. Positive responses from the adults may encourage the infants to approach the toy. Try the social referencing Experiential Exercise of this chapter.

Underlying both affective sharing and social referencing is the development of the ability to delay an immediate emotional reaction to a situation and to evaluate how one is going to feel about the situation. **Appraisal** is the ability to use cognitive comparisons of alternate interpretations to regulate one's emotions. The appraisal at this age, however, differs from the appraisal seen during the period between 6 and 9 months. In that earlier

Experiential Exercise

Social Referencing
by Ilse de Koeyer

Spread out across the room toys (different shapes, colors, things that can make sound) and "scary" objects or things that can break (such as, remote controls, scissors, medicine bottles).

Start to walk around the room, in any direction your feet are taking you. You can move in circles, squares, or lines, however you wish. Now, find yourself a partner. See if you can do that without using words. Also find yourselves a place to sit down on the floor.

Sit opposite from each other on the floor. One of you will play the baby, the other will be an adult. Please divide roles now. We will change roles later.

If you are in the role of baby, imagine that you are here for the first time and you are full of wonderment. You could imagine you were in a strange country. You feel like you want to explore and learn more, but you also want to make sure that it is safe to do that. To find out, you will look at your "guide," your "parent."

After observing your "parent's" reaction, look back at the object you were looking at before. How do you feel about it now? Do you still want to explore it? Would you like to approach it? Avoid it? Would you like to move further away from it?

If you are in the role of parent, you may also imagine that you are in this strange country. You, as the adult, may not know this particular situation, either. But based on your previous experiences, you may have a better sense of this place and the objects in it. During the exercise, your child will be looking at you to figure out how to feel about a particular object he or she is looking at. You need to show them how you feel, as clearly as possible, in a nonverbal way. Improvise your reaction, so the children won't know beforehand which emotion you will be showing.

Maybe you would like him or her to explore and play with the object. You may very much enjoy watching your child, and feel happy being in this room, with him or her. You could show that by giving him or her a big smile or nodding your head. Maybe you think this thing is dangerous and you are concerned about your child. Maybe you feel annoyed because you've told your toddler 100 times NOT to play with it… now she wants to grab it again. Whatever feeling you choose, go into that feeling 100 percent and express it to your child in a nonverbal way, with your face and body.

Do this multiple times, with different objects.

Then change roles and do the same thing.

Discuss together in pairs.

period, infants are often observed to show a slight delay in their emotional reactions, as if deciding what to feel in a particular situation. After 10 months, however, the infant has the ability to look to *another person* to decide what to feel.

Between 9 and 12 months of age, affective sharing is the most common response in social situations, and it tends almost always to involve positive emotions (Hornick & Gunnar, 1988; Klinnert, 1984; Walden & Ogan, 1988). When infants in this age range are given novel toys or shown a rabbit in a cage, for example, they tend to focus mostly on the objects and look at the caregiver for confirmation, primarily the display of a positive expression by the caregiver (Hagekull, Stenberg, & Bohlin, 1993).

Between 10 and 12 months, infants begin to use social referencing systematically, although social referencing does not occur as frequently as affective sharing in naturalistic situations (Hornick & Gunnar, 1988; C. A. Nelson, 1985). By 10 months, if mothers display a negative expression, some infants will avoid crossing a visual cliff, avoid playing with toys or avoid approaching a rabbit in a cage, and they will show more aversive responses to strangers to whom the mothers show negative expressions. Opposite patterns of behavior can be seen if the mothers display positive expressions in these situations, although negative expressions seem to have a more powerful effect on regulating infant behavior at this age (Feiring, Lewis, & Starr, 1984; M. R. Gunnar & Stone, 1984; Hornick, Risenhoover, & Gunnar, 1987; Sorce, Emde, Campos, & Klinnert, 1985; Zarbatany & Lamb, 1985). Infants will reference almost any available adult and show equal responsiveness to mothers, fathers, and strangers; and they can use both adult facial expression and adult voices in the absence of facial expressions (Dickstein & Parke, 1988; Klinnert et al., 1986; Mumme, Fernald, & Herrera, 1996; Vaish & Striano, 2004).

Female infants are more likely to regulate their distance from fearful objects as a result of maternal referencing than are males (Blackford & Walden, 1998; W. D. Rosen, Adamson, & Bakeman, 1992). These findings are consistent with the gender differences reported in the previous chapter, in which females were observed to be more effective at regulating their emotions during a still-face condition than males. By 10 months, when emotional regulation becomes more social for both boys and girls, girls begin to use other people more effectively to regulate themselves than boys. A study of 9-month-olds in Sweden found that mother-daughter dyads spent more time in close proximity than did mother-son dyads, once again suggesting that girls begin to use their mothers as emotional guides more than boys at this age (Lindahl & Heimann, 1997).

In addition to this directed referencing in uncertain situations, infants are influenced by adults' emotions and attention. During a play period, mothers were instructed to use facial and vocal expressions of either joy or sadness. In the joy condition, infants expressed more joy and looked more at their mothers while engaging in higher-level play behavior. In the sadness condition, infants expressed more negative emotions, looked less at their mothers, and played less (Barna & Legerstee, 2005; Stenberg & Hagekull, 1997; Termine & Izard, 1988).

In summary, these studies show that by the second half of the first year of life, emotion is no longer a private experience. Perhaps without intending to do so, infants nevertheless begin to alter their own emotions according to what others are expressing. It would not be correct to infer that infants understand the feelings of others at this age or even that infants can differentiate their own feelings from those of others. These developments begin almost a year later. They are simply aware that feelings can be shared and that they "have" feelings. Coupled with new perceptual and cognitive skills, infants probably discover that particular types of facial expression are related to actions that either enhance or interrupt their own activities. Thus, by the end of the first year, those facial expressions of adults have become part of the means by which infants regulate their own actions. From the adult's perspective, the infants are becoming more socially responsive and are entering into more meaningful social communications.

SOCIAL AND LANGUAGE DEVELOPMENT

In this section, we cover new developments in the infant's communication with adults, including the beginnings of spoken language. Following that, we discuss caregiver-infant attachment. Finally, we will look at the beginnings of infant-peer relationships.

Perceiving and Joining with Other's Intentions: The Emergence of Coordinated Joint Attention

The development in emotional communication at this age—affective sharing, and social referencing—is reflected in a new pattern in parent-infant communication. During this period, infants seem to become less obsessive in their attention to objects and more likely to observe how adults use objects and to follow the adult's line of gaze or pointing to detect something about what the adult is looking at. This aspect of coordinated joint attention is called **joint visual attention** (Butterworth, 2000; Corkum & Moore, 1995). This requires some increased prefrontal regulatory ability, to suppress attention to themselves and begin to observe, track, and join with other people (Henderson et al., 2002; van Hecke et al., 2012).

Infants are especially likely to follow the gaze of people, or of robotic objects that behave in some intentional way (S. Johnson, Slaughter, & Carey, 1998; Yoon & Johnson, 2009) and for that reason, they are more likely to follow the direction of an adult's head turning when the adult has open rather than closed eyes (Brooks & Meltzoff, 2005). By 10, but not 9 months, when watching two people communicate, infants can tell the difference between mutual compared to averted gaze (Beier & Spelke, 2012). This means that gaze following is genuinely a way to coordinate and communicate with another mind, not simply a mechanical act of following a moving object.

The infant appears to realize, for the first time, that other people have intentions. This inspires the infant to act in a way that helps to coordinate intentions between self and other (Lock, 2000).

This ability is called **intersubjectivity** (Trevarthen & Hubley, 1978) or **coordinated joint attention** (Adamson, 1995). Infants will use social referencing to adults who are looking at the infants over adults who are looking away from the infants, suggesting that infants are aware of the adult as another person who has the intention to communicate with the infants or not to communicate (Stenberg, 2003; Striano & Rochat, 2000). Infants of this age will look more at adults whose actions seem intentionally directed toward an object compared to adults whose actions appear unrelated to that object (Falck-Ytter et al., 2006; Johnson et al., 2007). They will also imitate adult movements and gestures in situations where the adult's actions on objects are clearly intentional (Zmyj et al., 2009). Infants of this age will look more at an adult who appears to know what to do with an object (an expert) compared to an adult who does not appear to know how the object works (non-expert) (Stenberg, 2013), and they prefer to watch people who are collaborating together compared to people who are not working toward the same goal (Henderson et al., 2013).

Those infants at 12 months who are more likely to pay attention to the intentions of other people, follow their gaze, are also more likely to understand others' perspectives (theory of mind, Chapter 11) at 4 years of age (van Hecke et al., 2012; Wellman et al., 2008). Conversely, lack of coordinated joint attention may be a precursor to later manifestations of infantile autism (Chapter 12, Hoehl et al., 2009). Similarly, infants at 12 months who respond to the distress of others are more likely to show prosocial behavior in the second year of life (Roth-Hanania et al., 2011). Affective sharing (especially, smiling at an object and then turning to smile at an adult) at one year predicts social competence in the third year (Parlade et al., 2009).

The Emergence of Intentional Gestures

Developmentally, infants first become involved in frames for coordinated joint attention between 9 and 10 months. Next, they begin to produce

At 1-2 months
Spontaneous pointing.

At 6 months
Pointing used to
explore objects.

At 9 months
Pointing intentionally
used as a gesture.

Figure 8.3 Developmental Changes in Infant Pointing

Source: A. Fogel & G. F. Melson, *Child development*, 1988, p. 175. St. Paul, MN: West. Copyright © by West Publishing Company. Reprinted by permission. All rights reserved.

simple gestures, like pointing and requesting, at around 10 months. Finally, at 11 months, infants begin to follow the direction of the adult's gaze or pointing gesture. These developments are followed during the next few months (see Chapter 9) by increasing gesture and word use. In fact, the more coordinated joint attention shared by mother and infant during this age period, the more rapidly infants will develop skills for complex play involving linguistic and gestural communication in the second year (Bigelow et al., 2004; Brooks & Meltzoff, 2005; Carpenter, Nagell, & Tomasello, 1998).

At 3 to 5 months, pointing is a spontaneous display of attention or interest (Fogel & Hannan, 1985); after 5 months, pointing is used instrumentally to touch or tap objects while exploring (Bates, O'Connell, & Shore, 1987; Fogel & Thelen, 1987), but it is not until about 10 months that infants use pointing in intentionally communicative ways (see Figure 8.3). We can say that infants use pointing and

other gestures to intentionally communicate if they look between the adult and the object alternately—coordinated joint attention—and if they keep trying to communicate when the initial attempt does not succeed (Bates et al., 1987; Lock, 1980; see Figure 8.4). Infants will point to interesting objects the adult is not looking at (as if wanting to direct the adult's attention there) and they will point to objects the adult shows interest in (as if wanting to share that interest) again suggesting that points at this age are part of intentional communication (Liszkowski et al., 2007; Tomasello et al., 2007)

In addition to pointing during this age period, infants begin to use gestures such as showing, offering, giving, and requesting (Camaioni, 2000). Before 10 months, infants hand objects to their mothers in the course of exploratory play with the objects. When this happens, the infants never take their eyes off the object. They look at the object as their mothers take it and then hand it back.

Figure 8.4   Gestural Communication at One Year

Source: A. Lock, *The guided reinvention of language*, 1980, p. 98. London: Academic Press.

If mothers playfully keep the object, the infants become frustrated. Beginning at 10 months, infants alternate their gaze between mother and object during the offering, especially if the infant initiates the object exchange. When the mother requests an object, the infant does not look at her during the offer. Finally, and importantly, when infants initiate offers and alternate gaze, they are likely to smile or laugh when the offer is completed. Although communicative offering continues to be part of the infant's repertoire, the smile and laugh during offering lasts only a few weeks. It suggests that infants are pleased with the discovery of a new communicative ability and that positive emotion may help to consolidate the developmental achievement (D. S. Messinger & Fogel, 1998; Reinecke & Fogel, 1994).

Adults can use the infant's ability for joint visual attention to direct his or her attention to an object ("Look, there's a doggie"), a person ("Where's Daddy?"), a picture in a book, or even a particular feature of an object ("Where's Mommy's nose?"), thus creating a host of new opportunities for learn-ing and communication (Zukow-Goldring, 1997). Infants actually have better word comprehension if the words are paired with a simultaneous gesture (Caselli et al., 2012; Rader & Zukow-Goldring, 2012). The infant's attention to the adult's gestures means that the infant wants to be included in what the adult is doing. If the adult turns away to talk to another person, the infant may try to engage also with the other person (Nadel & Tremblay-Leveau, 1999), or they may shows signs of jealousy, as discussed earlier.

Adults typically respond to infant gestures by interpreting what the infant wants. This includes coordinating their activities using objects with those of the infant, such as playing an object manipulation game by building with blocks or feeding a baby doll. In addition, caregivers are using words more deliberately as part of their actions on objects. An example would be describing in words what the baby is doing, requesting objects, offering objects, and saying, "Here's the baby's bottle" (Bakeman & Adamson, 1984; Hodapp, Goldfield, & Boyatzis, 1984; F. T. Hunter, McCarthy, Mac-

TABLE 8.2   The First Seven "Words" in One Child's Vocabulary

Utterance	Age (Months)	Meaning
eh	8	Said to people, distant objects, and toys.
Dididi	9	Disapproval (loud) or comfort (soft).
Mama	10	Refers to food; also means tastes good, and hungry.
Nnene	10	Scolding.
tt!	10	Used to call squirrels.
Piti	10	Always used with a gesture and always whispered; meaning that's interesting.
Duh	10	Used with same gesture as for piti; seems to be a comment on ongoing action.

Source: W. Leopold, *Speech development of a bilingual child*, 1949. Chicago: Northwestern University Press, 1949. Copyright © Northwestern University Press. Also in A. Fogel & G. Melson, *Child development*, 1988, p. 177. St. Paul, MN: West. Copyright © West Publishing Company. Reprinted by permission. All rights reserved.

Turk, & Vietze, 1987). In the next sections, we will discuss the infant's use of words and the infant's understanding of the parent's words.

Speech Production by Infants: First Words

Between 9 and 12 months, in the context of frames for coordinated joint attention, infants begin to make a variety of sounds that attentive caregivers recognize as words or wordlike utterances (Camaioni, Aureli, Bellagamba, & Fogel, 1999). As in the development of babbling, these new sounds are made possible by further anatomical developments of the vocal tract. The sounds are used repeatedly in similar situations and not in other situations. Table 8.2 lists the first seven "words" in one child's vocabulary, recorded in one of the early studies of language development. Some research suggests that the child's first words of this sort have sound patterns similar to the favorite sounds the child makes when babbling. Since the babbling sounds are also similar to those heard in the linguistic environment of the home (see Chapter 7), these early words will begin to sound intelligible to adults (DeBoysson-Bardies, 1990).

Researchers disagree over whether these sounds are true words or true names for things, since they are arbitrary and idiosyncratic, rather than conventional. Instead, they seem like accom-paniments to action, like saying "brrroom" when moving a toy car or grunting when exerting physical effort (Bates et al., 1987; McCune, 1989).

The meaning of such sounds, as well as of many of the infant's gestures, still depends on the interpretive activity of the caregiver who recognizes a relationship between the sound or gesture and the situation in which the child uses it (Adamson, Bakeman, Smith, & Walters, 1987; Lock, 1980). Observations 8.7, 8.8, and 8.9 provide some examples of caregiver interpretations of infant acts, both verbal and nonverbal, at this age.

This combination of communication and emotion that we saw with gestures has also been discovered in relation to the use of first words. When infants actually utter a word, they tend to have a neutral facial expression. Immediately following the word, their expression changes, typically to a positive expression (Bloom & Beckwith, 1989). Once the infants begin to use the words more regularly, they no longer smile after saying them. The smiling is related to the infant's achievement of making their very first words.

Developments in Infant Perception of Adult Speech

Before the age of about 10 months, infants are capable of perceiving differences in intonation patterns, which allows them to recognize differences

Observations

Coordinated Joint Engagement (Trevarthen & Hubley, 1978, p. 200)

Observation 8.7

At 40 weeks, Tracey's mother became an acknowledged participant in actions. Tracey repeatedly looked up at her mother's face when receiving an object, pausing as if to acknowledge receipt. She also looked up to her mother at breaks in her play, giving an indication of willingness to share experiences as she had never done before.

Observations

Communicative Behavior (Lock, 1980)

Observation 8.8

Mary; age 12(20): (1) Mary turns around in her chair and tries to pick up an apple from behind her. (2) She fails and turns back to her mother, who has been watching her, and cries. (3) Mother: "What do you want?" (4) Mary gesturally reaches toward the apple. Mother then gives it to her.

Observation 8.9

Mary; age 11(5): Mary is sitting in her high chair with mother next to her. She has finished eating. Some of her toys are on the table in front of her. Mother picks up a squeaky duck and shows it to Mary.

Mother: "Who's this?" (squeak, squeak) "Who is it? Is it the duck? What does the duck say?"
Mary: "ugh."
Mother: "He doesn't say 'ugh.' He says 'quack, quack, quack, quack' ... 'quack, quack, quack, quack' Ooh, and *who's* this? It's the doggie, isn't it? And what does the doggie say? What does the doggie say? Mary? Oh, he doesn't yawn? What does the doggie say? 'Woof, woof, woof, woof, woof,' 'Woof, woof, woof, woof, woof.' Don't you want the doggie? Oh, you say it, 'woof, woof, woof, woof, woof.'" Mary say it. 'Woof, woof, woof, woof, woof.' And who's this? Who's this? It's Teddy, isn't it? And Teddy says 'aah.' It's Teddy, isn't it? Aah, love Teddy. Ah, is it Teddy? Aah."
Mary picks up the dog.
Mother: "Oh, is that your doggie? What does the doggie say? What does the doggie say? What does the doggie say? 'Woof, woof, woof, woof, woof.' 'Woof, woof, woof, woof, woof.' Doesn't he?"

between melodies and passages of speech. They are getting better at recognizing the same words spoken by people who use different "accents" or dialects of the same language, and they can use the intonation patterns to infer beginnings and endings of words, even within songs (Lebedeva & Kuhl, 2010; Johnson & Seidl, 2009; Schmale et al., 2010)

In speaking to year-old children, adults continue to raise the overall pitch and to exaggerate the intonation contours of sentences. In one study, adults were recorded while talking to 1-year-olds and to other adults about attention getting, approval, prohibition, comfort, and play. Then the tapes were synthetically modified to remove all speech content while preserving the intonation. These modified tapes were played to other adults who were asked to judge the content of the speech. The judges were significantly likely to be more correct about the original content of the speech (e.g., whether the speech was about approval or prohibition) when they heard the modified speech to babies rather than the modified speech to adults (Fernald, 1989). This means that there are more cues to speech content in intonation patterns when adults are speaking to babies than in speech to other adults.

In related work, speech to year-old infants was sampled in France, Italy, Germany, Japan, Britain, and the United States. In all cases, the speech had similar exaggerated intonation contours, although the American mothers did the most exaggeration (Fernald et al., 1989). Thus, the capacity to recognize meaningfully different speech intonation patterns is well established by the age of 1 year (Ferland & Mendelson, 1989; Trehub, Thorpe, & Morrongiello, 1987). Futhermore, mothers who speak more clearly by emphasizing sound contrasts within and between words have infants who are better able to perceive differences in intonation patterns (Liu et al., 2003).

There is some evidence that adults actually make their speech more exaggerated and simpler for year-old infants than they did earlier in the first year. When the baby was 3 months old, the parents mostly were content to comment on the baby's condition or state or make some general inferences about their relationship to the baby (see Chapter 6). By the time the baby is 8 months old, parents tend to use more commanding and directive language in relation to specific aspects of their baby's behavior. Compared with parents' speech to 4-month-olds, their speech to 8-month-olds is more related to what the child is doing; it is somewhat simpler in structure, almost as if the parents are simplifying their sentences because they think the infant is capable of understanding now (Sherrod et al., 1978).

By the end of the first year, parents begin to make specific verbal responses in commenting about infant activity, such as saying, "Put the toy over here," which enhances the infant's ability to make connections between action and speech. Parents not only name objects, but they name small details of the objects, such as color, texture, response properties, and the infant's familiarity with the object. They also make the object more real, such as making a toy cow moo or a stuffed dog bark. In some cultures, infants are treated to pop quizzes: "What does the cow say?" The mother corrects the baby's pronunciations and gives little compliments when things are done correctly. She instructs the child on how to play with a toy or how to behave, and she uses polite expressions, such as "please" and "thank you" (West & Rheingold, 1978).

Parents often do not correct infants, and they seem to enjoy the verbal mistakes infants make. The Marquesas Islanders enjoy their infants'

incomplete development. They try to get the babies to perform their incomplete movements or to make verbal mistakes. These are humorous and enjoyable moments for the family (Martini & Kirkpatrick, 1981).

In addition to becoming perceptually attuned to the speech spoken in the home, infants are beginning to grasp the meanings of some words and gestures. For example, around 9 months, infants will make the appropriate action when parents say things like "play pat-a-cake" or "wave bye-bye to Daddy." Soon parents begin spelling out words like "bottle" or "candy" when speaking to each other in the baby's presence, so as not to get the baby interested at that moment (Bates, O'Connell, & Shore, 1987).

How does a baby of this age know that different words might refer to distinct objects? One reason is their developing skills at category learning, discussed earlier. If infants take a greater role in coordinating joint attention—such as by looking frequently between the adult speaker and the object—they learn words more easily (Gogate et al., 2006). Infants who show great attention to the intentions of adults at this age have more advanced language skills in the second year (Baldwin & Moses, 2001; Newman et al., 2006). Another reason infants learn that objects and words are connected is the way adults alter their speech patterns, intonation, questions, and gestures in the presence of different objects. Because infants are now more aware of the adult's perspective, and if the adults use different sounds and gestures for different objects, then the infant picks up on this (Dewar & Xu, 2007; Gogate et al., 2001; Pruden et al., 2006).

Infant-Peer Relationships

At the beginning of the first year of life, infants make different responses to peers than to their parents. At 3 months of age, infants are more likely to look at a peer for long periods and to make abrupt, jerky movements of the body while watching the peer. Their behavior toward their mothers is much smoother, with more smiling and vocalizing (Fogel, 1979).

(a) Paula, in center of the picture, and Esther toe-holding together. **(b)** Ann, at right; and Joe play footsie.

Source: Selby & Bradley, 2003

From 6 to 12 months, peer play is more likely in the absence of objects (Eckerman & Whatley, 1977; J. L. Jacobson, 1981; Vandell, Wilson, & Buchanan, 1980). When babies get together, they explore each other with mutual touches, smile and gesture at each other, and imitate each other. By the age of 1 year, peer play in the absence of objects begins to take on the quality of a dialogue, with mutual exchanges of tickling, touching, and laughing at each other (Ross & Goldman, 1977a). In one study of 9-month-old infants playing together, the infants imitated each other by touching their own feet with their own hands, which was then followed by the infants touching their feet together (see photos). These tactile games were embedded in a long sequence of mutual gaze, vocalization, self and other touching (Selby & Bradley, 2003).

By 12 months, toys are becoming more important to the maintenance of the social interaction (J. L. Jacobson, 1981; Vandell et al., 1980). Games with toys have the same reciprocal quality as purely social games. There is mutual giving and taking of objects, offering and receiving, rolling and throwing balls back and forth, and so on. By this age, taking turns is such an essential part of peer play that interactions usually are disrupted if one child fails to take his or her turn (Ross & Goldman, 1977a). In comparison, infants at 12 months express a wider range of emotions in their interactions with their mothers and take more turns with them, perhaps due to the mothers' attempts to create dialogues through active structuring of the interaction (Adamson & Bakeman, 1985; Vandell & Wilson, 1987).

Self-Awareness: The Sense of a Subjective Self

Our review of affective sharing and social referencing shows that infants have a sense of themselves, as people who can feel and whose feelings can be appraised not only by others but also by the self. The fact that infants begin to gesture and use words suggests that they make a deliberate attempt to share what is on their mind with others. In addition, infants of this age will pay more attention to adults making sounds and words that they can make themselves (DePaolis et al., 2011). When infants are making their own vocalizations while exploring a novel object, they are more likely to remember how an adult names the object than if they are silent when exploring (Goldstein et al., 2010). Finally, if 12-month-old infants are given experience wearing a blindfold, they are more likely to infer that a blindfolded adult cannot be intentional toward an object to which the adult's head is turned (Meltzoff & Brooks, 2008). These studies all suggest that infants are incorporating their own self experience into how they respond to others.

When infants of this age show off, they act as if they are saying, "Look at me." The infants are not, however, actually saying "look at me." Babies of this age do not use the word "I," nor do they have a language to describe themselves or a concept of "self." These will take almost another year to develop. Intentional communicative actions like showing off, pointing and requesting, and social referencing are fundamentally different from the fish-in-water sense of the ecological self or from the self-centered use of others in the differentiated ecological self. The form of self-awareness that emerges at the end of the second year is called the **subjective self** (Stern, 1985).

How can an infant have a sense of "I" but no word or concept for it? Imagine looking into someone's eyes in a way that says "I love you" or "I'm afraid of you." You do not need any words to express this. It is clear, however, that there is an "I" that feels love or fear, and also that this "I" comes into awareness in the act of trying to communicate nonverbally, in a participatory way, with

another person. Teenagers will sometimes show off and act silly when around members of the opposite sex. Perhaps all people do this when they are falling in love! These behaviors call attention to the self in a way that says "look at me" without actually saying it. In many cases, the person who is doing the showing off is not even conceptually aware of it. Their behavior is a participatory form of self-consciousness in communication.

The development of attachment (see next section) during this age period is another way in which infants reveal the sense of a subjective self. They begin to look at other people in a participatory way that says "I love you" or "I'm afraid." The infant's showing off at this age means "look at me," and also "I know you will look at me because we love each other." They communicate their sense of affection, fear, or loneliness by making deliberate attempts at approaching or avoiding, by signaling their desire to be with particular people, and by asking for comfort and assistance. Because the subjective self is participatory, babies do not think about whether or not to do these things, they just engage in the actions and experience the consequences.

Why is it a developmental achievement to acquire an "I"? Imagine the experience of an intense emotion, such as losing one's temper at someone. During the experience there is no sense of "I" or "you." There is just the anger that is directed outward. This is the experience of the differentiated ecological self. Later, however, a person can say, "I completely lost myself," or "I didn't know what I was doing." At the time such statements are made, one is subjectively aware of oneself as *having had an experience of anger*. One is also conceptually aware of the differences between self and other, so that, hopefully, apologies and restitutions can be made.

Now imagine teenagers or adults who are strong enough to really inflict harm on others or the self but who do not have a sense of a subjective or conceptual self. These people would be a danger to themselves and to other people, and a number of psychopathological conditions stem from not progressing emotionally beyond the differentiated ecological sense of self. Some of these disturbances of the mature sense of self, such as autism, have their origins during this early period of infancy.

According to psychoanalytic theories, for example, when the infant's intentional communicative actions are not recognized by the family system to help the infant appreciate what acts lead to what consequences, then the inner experience will not be felt as the infant's own (Sander, 1962). The capricious and confusing messages given by their parents may fail to create a sense of "I" for the infant. If these conditions persist until they become teenagers, these children suffer from **dissociation**, or the inability to connect themselves with their experiences. They hurt themselves and others as if there were no self to feel the hurt.

People can also lose their sense of "I" when they become depressed or alienated. In these conditions, one feels helpless to change circumstances, as if the "I" is not an effective, intentional being. Infants who experience their world as excessively controlling or intrusive develop a similar inability to develop subjectivity. So, the sense of a subjective self is crucial to mental health. We need to know who we are in relation to other people, what we need and how to ask appropriately for it, and how to communicate about those things with other people.

At this age, babies begin to develop some of the human frailties of the self that plague us all: vulnerability to loss and separation from loved ones, irrational fears, and insatiable curiosity. There are some limits to this. Babies of this age do not suffer from self-doubt or pride. These peculiarly human vulnerabilities need at least another year before they begin to flower.

The wonderful news is that the vast majority of infants at this age develop a healthy sense of a subjective self with at least one person and that this sense of self arises naturally and spontaneously during frames for coordinated joint attention. Infants simply need to be able to express themselves though gestures, to have someone respond appropriately, and to take pleasure in creating playful and satisfying communicative routines. It is not necessary to teach babies about themselves. You only have to be aware of the signs of their budding self-awareness and to be available when infants need your assistance, when they look to you for guidance, and when they want you to share in their discoveries.

The Development of Attachment

It is not a coincidence that the developments in cognition, emotion, and communication occur in the same age period as we begin to see the emergence of clear and lasting attachments to parents and other significant figures in the child's life. These abilities set the stage for the child to see others as intentional beings who are important for the continued development of the child's goals, for the resolution of emotionally difficult situations, and for the expression and receipt of affection.

Attachment refers to a lasting emotional tie between people such that the individual strives to maintain closeness to the object of attachment and acts to ensure that the relationship continues. The process by which infants develop lasting, affectionate emotional ties to adults over the first few years of life has been the subject of a great deal of scientific research. Before reviewing the findings of these studies, let us first look at some of the theoretical perspectives on how attachment develops.

Psychoanalytic theory suggests that attachment is the expectation that needs can be met and that distress will not continue for long without some relief. After the baby is 2 or 3 months old, parents begin to notice that the baby's cry is a little less urgent when the baby is hungry or tired. At this time, psychoanalytic theory prescribes that the parents should wait a short time before responding to the baby. If the baby calms down, the parents have allowed the baby to meet this small crisis with his or her own resources. Not only do these minor frustrations lead the baby toward self-control, but they also make the baby aware of the person who is responsible for satisfying the oral needs. This awareness gradually expands into a dependency on that particular person and later into affection, attachment, and trust.

An attachment relationship is one in which each partner seeks to maintain physical and emotional closeness to the other.
Photo by Emily Waterfield

Learning theory has focused not on the feelings or concepts of the infant, but on the behaviors observed when caregivers and infants are together. Caregivers seek positive reinforcements from their infants. For example, when parents pick up a baby, they expect the baby to become calm or to smile. When parents feed the baby, they expect the baby to coo and gurgle. When these positive reinforcements occur, the frequency of the same parental actions is increased on future occasions, which in turn reinforces the calming down, smiling, cooing, and gurgling of the baby. Learning theory, therefore, predicts that attachment behaviors develop by a complex process of mutual reinforcements (Cairns, 1979; Gewirtz, 1972).

Behavior ecology theory suggests that adults have inherited some kinds of caregiving responses that are triggered in the presence of infants and young children and that infants are innately drawn to particular aspects of the caregiver. In a classic study of the maternal-infant feedback system in infant monkeys (Harlow & Harlow, 1965), the babies were provided one "mother" made of wire mesh with a milk bottle attached and another "mother" of the same size made of wire covered with a soft cloth. The monkeys took food from the wire mother but spent almost all of the rest of the time with the softer mother substitute. In fearful situations, the monkeys clung to the soft mother and, when they got older, were even seen to carry the cloth mother around as a security object.

For monkeys, contrary to the predictions of psychoanalytic theory, physical contact with the mother is more important than food in the formation of attachments. Contrary to the predictions of learning theory, infant monkeys became attached to the soft object (an innate preference) and not to the object that gave positive reinforcement—the food-giving wire mother.

Studies of human infants (Schaffer & Emerson, 1964) have shown that they are most attached to the people who play and interact with them. Some babies who live in extended families with many siblings and who have mothers who concentrated primarily on caretaking tasks such as feeding and diapering are less attached to the mother than to any aunt, uncle, or older sibling who spend the most time playing with the baby. This suggests that attachment in humans is based more on social interaction and communication than on feeding or physical contact as predicted by psychoanalytic theory.

John Bowlby (1969) suggested that mutual responsiveness and attraction between adults and infants resulted not because of mutual reinforcements but because the physical appearance and behavior of both the adult and the infant innately attract the other. Table 8.3 shows the stages in the development of attachment as proposed by Bowlby.

The newborn and small infant's physical appearance, called *babyishness,* elicits protective responses from adults. Babies also have a host of behaviors, such as crying, sucking, smiling, looking at the caregiver preferentially, following the adult around, and becoming distressed when the adult leaves, that have the net effect of orienting the caregiver to the infant and increasing the time that the infant spends in proximity to the caregiver. Because of the universality of this mutual attraction and its importance for survival, attachment can be thought of neurologically as experience expectant (see Chapter 4) because neurological processes exist at birth that require the presence of an adult (Barnett, Butler, & Vondra, 1999; Schore, 2003). The way attachment forms over the first years of life—whether it is secure or insecure, and to whom—is experience dependent affecting both brain and behavior (Schore, 2003).

Bowlby suggests that as the infant develops cognitively, attachment shifts from relying on innate responses to any adult to identifying and recognizing a particular adult and seeking that adult in an intentional, goal-oriented manner. This facet of attachment is neurologically experience dependent because the child's developmental history plays a role in the nature of his or her attachment to the parent (Barnett et al., 1999). The baby establishes a goal of maintaining proximity to the parent and uses information about the parent's present and past movements as well as his or her own locomotor skills and current needs to keep the parent within view or to seek contact when needed.

By 8 or 9 months of age, because of the developments in goal-oriented action and emotion reviewed earlier in this chapter, infants begin to develop some of the same kinds of emotional feelings of closeness to the parents that the parents had felt for the infant since before the birth. We know this because infants of this age begin to display affectionate responses to the parents. During reunions after brief separations, 1-year-olds feel genuinely happy to see the parent and may approach briefly for a hug or kiss (Sroufe, 1979). Infants will follow the parent and may be distressed at separation.

Bowlby's theory has been refined and expanded by others. Mary Ainsworth, who studied attachment in Uganda and North America (Ainsworth, 1979), suggests that there is a distinction between the attachment **system** (the network of feelings

and cognitions related to the object of attachment) and **attachment behavior** (the overt signals such as crying and following that bring the parent and child into close proximity). She points out that each child's attachment system would be expressed through behavior in a unique way. For example, if a baby does not get upset when his or her mother leaves, it does not indicate a lack of attachment. Rather, it may indicate the infant's relative feelings of security to carry on temporarily without the mother present.

Ainsworth believed that virtually all infants are attached to their parents but differ in the sense of security they feel in relation to the adult. The ease with which a distressed infant feels comforted by a caregiver is called the *quality of attachment* and has four basic patterns: securely attached, insecurely attached–resistant, insecurely attached–avoidant, and disorganized-disoriented (Ainsworth, Bell, & Stayton, 1971, Ainsworth et al., 1978; Main & Solomon, 1986).

Attachment quality is assessed in the Ainsworth Strange Situation Test (ASST), in which infants are observed with their caregivers in an unfamiliar playroom (Ainsworth & Bell, 1970). The test consists of eight episodes:

1. Parent and infant are brought to the observation room by the observer.

2. Parent and infant play together for several minutes.

3. Parent and infant play with an unfamiliar adult.

4. The mother leaves the baby with the stranger for 3 minutes.

5. The stranger leaves, and the mother returns.

6. The mother leaves the baby alone.

7. The stranger returns without the mother.

8. The stranger leaves, and the mother is reunited with her baby.

The ASST and the four types of attachment quality by which infants can be classified have been shown to be highly reliable and valid. Test-retest reliability has been found in middle-class North

American samples (Waters, 1983). This means that a baby who is classified as securely attached at one age will typically remain so at later ages—but not always.

An infant who demonstrates **secure attachment** will seek comfort from the caregiver during the reunion (episode 8) and, once comforted, will return to independent play. Securely attached infants show interest in objects and in the stranger and will get acquainted with the unfamiliar setting by making brief forays, always returning to the adult's side, and using the caregiver as a *secure base* from which to explore. Such infants will feel comfortable and secure in most situations.

There are three types of insecure attachments. Infants who demonstrate **insecure-resistant attachment** have a more difficult time feeling comfortable in a strange situation. They will vacillate between mother and an interesting object, but once near the object, they will not explore as freely as will the securely attached infants. The resistant infant is more wary of strangers and tends to get more upset when the mother leaves the room. During the reunion, such infants show ambivalent responses to the mother, first approaching her and then pushing her away. Insecure-resistant infants (also called insecure-ambivalent) tend to be temperamentally vulnerable to stress, have limited coping skills other than the mother, have mothers who are inconsistently available, and have limited skills at independent exploratory behavior (Cassidy, 1994; Cassidy & Berlin, 1994; Leerkes & Wong, 2012).

Infants who display **insecure-avoidant attachment** tend not to be upset when left with an unfamiliar person or in a strange setting. During the reunion episode, they may avoid approaching caregivers for comfort and may actively resist any attempts to be comforted by turning away and squirming to get down if picked up. Insecurely attached–avoidant infants may seem neutral in their emotions regarding the mother. However, this apparent calm may be superficial. These infants show a pattern of physiological arousal indicative of masked anger and they can be observed self-soothing rather than relying on the mother (Cassidy, 1994; Leerkes & Wong, 2012; Spangler & Grossman, 1993).

The first three types of attachment, both secure and insecure, are considered to be within the normal range of functioning. You can begin to get a sense of your own attachment style by doing the Experiential Exercise in this chapter. You can also use the criteria for each of the three attachment styles above as a guide to think about the attachment patterns in your current relationships with parents or romantic partners.

Disorders of Attachment

In some cases, attachment patterns are so severely disturbed that they will typically require the intervention of a Parent-Infant Mental Health specialist (see Chapter 12) because the problems are too difficult for the family to handle alone. One type of disturbed attachment can be assessed in the ASST at the final reunion with the parent. Infants who exhibit **disorganized-disoriented attachment** display contradictory behavior during the ASST. The infant may give a broad smile and then abruptly turn away from the mother. Or, the infant may approach the mother by crawling backward toward her with gaze averted from her. Other infants may have frozen postures during reunion, sitting and staring at a wall or sucking their thumbs, a sign of a dissociative response. Although this pattern of attachment occurs considerably less often than the first three, it is very disturbing to watch these infants.

Almost all infants who show this type of attachment come from families with a history of child abuse, maltreatment, maternal psychopathology, infant malnutrition, and/or alcoholism. It is likely that these parental behaviors are the result of the stress experienced by the parent (such as a dysfunctional or abusive spousal relationship) in relation to the parent's past history of stress and trauma (such as a history of being abused or maltreated) (Bernier & Meins, 2008). Characteristics of parents whose infants display disorganized-disoriented attachment include giving contradictory signals to the infant, being frightening to the

---

Experiential Exercise

Attachment Styles
(by Alan Fogel)

This exercise is about the parental role and the infant experience related to approaching and avoiding. It is similar to the "Mutual Gazing" exercise in Chapter 6 except that the emphasis here is on seeking or avoiding proximity. The goal is to experience, through the exercise, your own attachment style—secure, resistant, avoidant, or disorganized. The class is divided up into pairs who do not know each other very well. With pair members facing each other, half of the group will stand along one wall of the room and the other half of the group along the opposite wall.

As in the gazing exercise, students will play the role of either the parent or the child, after which the roles will be changed. Speaking to the parents: your responsibility is to witness the child with a steady gaze. "Parents" should continue to feel their own emotions and arousal but it is important to keep those feelings inside and just observe them. Their job is to be there for the child. As adults, they should be able to control their emotions.

Speaking to the children: Come about half way across the room and stop, looking at your parent. Take a few moments to feel this. Now close the space between you and your parent again by half and feel the difference. Finally, approach the parent no closer than arm's length and without touching. Parents and children should feel the differences in the different distances. Finally, children return to the opposite side of the room.

Again, speaking to the children: Now, you can move anywhere you want in the room, either close to or far away from your parent. You can do anything you like (explore, play with the other children, stay by yourself). Let youself "go" and do what you really feel like doing (no touching others!) but remember where you parent is located. You can feel free to look at your parent or look away as much as you need or want to. Allow about 2 minutes.

Repeat the same process with the same roles, only this time the adult, instead of being attentive, acts *distracted* by something in the room.

Repeat the same process with the same roles, only this time the adult, instead of being attentive, acts *intrusive*, trying to get the "baby's" attention.

Then change roles, repeating the instructions to the parents and then to the children.

Sit in pairs and discuss the experience with each other.

---

infants, being frightened by the infant, intrusive or abusive behavior toward the infant, seductive or sexual behavior toward the infant, or acting emotionally distant from the infant (Carlson et al., 1989; Forbes et al., 2007; Madigan et al., 2006; Main & Solomon, 1985; O'Conner, Sigman, & Brill, 1987; Pipp-Siegel, Seigel, & Dean, 1999; Valenzuela, 1990).

Because parental behavior in this type of attachment relationship is so disturbed, it is not surprising that infants develop severe and disturbed reactions. These infants tend to show hostile, aggressive, and other maladaptive behaviors when they enter preschool and they are at risk for developing psychopathology when they get older (Forbes et al., 2007; van Ijzendoorn et al., 1992; Lyons-Ruth, Alpern, & Repacholi, 1993).

Two other types of attachment disturbance are assessed outside the ASST, typically by a mental health specialist to whom the child is referred.

Reactive attachment disorder (RAD) is a standard psychiatric diagnosis (DSM-IV 313.89). It begins before age 5 and is marked by one of two types of patterns. (1) *Inhibitions*. The child is excessively inhibited, hypervigilant, or ambivalent and contradictory. The child may, for example, respond to caregivers with frozen vigilance, mixed approach-avoidance, and resistance to comforting. This type of RAD is similar to disorganized-disoriented attachment. (2) *Disinhibitions*. The child shows indiscriminate sociability with inability to form appropriate selective attachments. The child may, for example, be overly familiar with strangers, show seductive or manipulative or other inappropriate behavior, or lack the ability to become attached to any particular attachment figure.

This disorder is always associated with disturbances in parental care, such as failures to meet the child's physical or emotional needs, abuse and neglect, and changes in caregivers—such as going from one foster home to another—so that no stable attachment can form. Children with RAD can be disturbing to be with. They can be unpredictable and they don't respond to social overtures. They can appear to "look right through you," as if they do not have an awareness of other people's emotions. As they get older, they can become violent with caregivers, animals, or other children. They are prone to lying and stealing and may show sexually inappropriate behavior. Treatment is difficult and there are relatively few centers that are equipped to handle RAD cases (see www.radkid.org for more information).

Separation anxiety disorder (DSM-IV 309.21) is one of a number of psychiatric anxiety disorders. It is much more severe than the typical separation anxiety felt by most infants. A child diagnosed with this disorder refuses to be separated from the parent, even to go to bed, and has excessive distress when not at home with parents. The behavior must be intense, last at least 1 month, and be inappropriate for the child's age to meet the criteria for diagnosis. It is more prevalent in children who can voice their concerns verbally. This disorder is more likely if the child is temperamentally inhibited or if one parent or close relative has panic disorder or another form of severe anxiety.

Separation anxiety disorder must be diagnosed by a mental health specialist but even some normally functioning infants become anxious at separation. Whether the child is diagnosed with this disorder or not, parents and caregivers can ease the anxiety over separation using some of the simple strategies shown in Table 8.3.

Brain development in infancy is especially experience dependent upon relationships with caregivers. Because infants are relatively helpless to get their needs met, according to Bowlby's theory, they require another person on which to rely for basic soothing, protection, and love. The infant brain is primarily a social—rather than a cognitive—organ, designed to seek out faces and voices at birth in experience expectant ways, and also designed to develop feelings and behaviors that orient them toward safety and security in an experience dependent fashion.

Disturbances of attachment lead to experience dependent pathologies in infant brain development, particularly in the right limbic and pre-frontal areas responsible for emotion regulation and feelings of safety. Inconsistent or frightening parenting creates patterns of neuroception of mobilization (fight or flight) or immobilization (freezing). The result is that the hypothalamus generates stress hormones through the HPA axis that lead to an overproduction of cortisol, which then leads to changes in receptors for stress and fear in the right hippocampus and amygdala, which then become hypersensitive to fearfulness. Finally, the prefrontal cortex becomes damaged so that normal pathways of emotion regulation (such as seeking assistance and care from other people) are not available (see Chapter 4; Schore, 2003; Vrtička & Vuilleumier, 2012).

Maladaptive strategies for emotion regulation, such as those described in the behavior patterns of disorganized and RAD infants, become predominant. There is also an impairment of self-awareness and a failure to develop **subjective self-awareness** (discussed earlier). Because the pathologies of attachment are not only behavioral, but also physiologically based in neuron-hormonal cellular structures and pathways, they take a long time and special efforts to treat. Early intervention is much more successful at dealing with attachment problems (see Chapter 12) than waiting until later in life.

Antecedents of Attachment

What are the possible causes of secure and insecure attachments at 1 year of age? There are three possible explanations: variations in the parent's ability to create a warm and sensitive relationship with her baby during the first year, temperamental factors in the child that no parental response can change, and issues that arise in the relationship between parent and infant that cannot be attributed directly to either one of them.

TABLE 8.3   Ways to Help an Infant With Separation Anxiety

Have baby-sitters come before the child develops stranger anxiety. If you leave your baby with a sitter for short periods when they respond well to any caring person, they'll become accustomed to being with different people.

Schedule separations after naps or feedings. Babies are more susceptible to separation anxiety when they're tired or hungry.

Have a consistent primary caregiver. If you hire a caregiver, try to keep him or her on the job from the baby's infancy into toddlerhood.

Practice separation for brief periods and short distances, increasing as the child can tolerate it. Praise the child for managing well. If your baby initiates separation by going into another (babyproofed) room, wait a few minutes before going after him; this will enhance his sense of independence.

Make new surroundings familiar. Let your child become comfortable with new surroundings with you present. The first time you leave a child with a relative, for example, shouldn't be the first time you and the child have visited that relative's house. Allow your child to bring a favorite object of hers or yours.

Develop a "goodbye" ritual. Rituals are reassuring and can be as simple as a special wave through the window or a special kiss.

Have a calm, positive attitude. Babies and toddlers are sensitive to your moods and will pick up any tension in your voice, face, touch, or gestures. And don't give in to the child's tears, which are a ploy to get you to stay. If you keep running back when your baby fusses at being without you, that just reinforces the anxious behavior.

Tell your child when you go that you are leaving and that you will return. Then go. Don't stall or repeat goodbyes; that will just make your child more anxious and clingy. Tell the child where you're going and when you'll be back in terms he can understand. Conversely, don't sneak away without saying goodbye; that will undermine the child's sense that she can rely on you.

Because Bowlby's theory focuses on the mother-infant relationship as the source of attachment, Ainsworth and others have predicted that sensitive maternal behavior toward the infant will be one of the main causes of secure attachment. Many studies have shown that the more responsive the mother is to the infant's needs at 3 months, such as during face-to-face play or in responding relatively soon to the infant's cries, the more likely the baby is to be securely attached at 1 year (Ainsworth, Bell, & Stayton, 1971; Belsky, Rovine, & Taylor, 1984; Blehar, Lieberman, & Ainsworth, 1977; Carmen et al., 1993; De Wolff & van Ijzendoorn, 1997; Grossman et al., 1985; Pedersen & Moran, 1996; Posada et al., 2004; Tomlinson et al., 2005). Related research has revealed similar maternal factors during the first year that are associated with attachment at 12 months. For example, there is a relationship between secure attachment and maternal tender style, including a moderate tempo of speech, expressions of quiet pleasure, few directives, no impatience, even attentiveness,

prompt soothing, and general responsiveness to all types of infant behavior. Reciprocal and mutually rewarding social interactions are also associated with secure attachment. Infants and mothers who show coordinated joint attention are more likely to be securely attached. These links between maternal sensitivity and infant attachment appear to be similar across different cultural and ethnic groups (Bakermans-Kranenburg et al., 2004; Bigelow et al., 2010; Grossman et al., 1985; Isabella, 1993; 1998; Isabella & Belsky, 1989; Isabella & Belsky, 1991; Leerkes, 2011; Schölmerich et al., 1995; Schölmerich et al., 1997; Vereijken, Riksen-Walraven, & Kondo-Ikemura, 1997).

Behavior ecology theory does not expect all mothers to be equally sensitive. According to this theory, the parent's investment in time and effort toward the child must be balanced by an investment in the parent's own survival. In cases where the mother is under stress, living in poverty, or depressed, or has limited physical or emotional resources, behavior ecology theory predicts that the infant will adapt by displaying more demanding and dependent behavior. The insecure patterns of attachment, therefore, are just as adaptive from the perspective of survival as the secure attachment pattern (Thompson, 1995). This means that the "causes" of security or insecurity are not "in" the mother's handling of the infant but rather "in" the relationship between the mother and her ecological context: her family of origin, her relationship with her husband, economic status, job, neighborhood, and other factors (Belsky, 1995; Hrdy, 1999; Thompson, 1995). This perspective takes the blame away from the mother and leads one to examine the larger systems in which the mother lives.

This systems perspective is supported by a number of findings. First of all, factors in the mother's family affect attachment. Mothers who perceive themselves as having little control over their children's behavior and who suffer from depressed moods are more likely to have insecurely attached infants. These maternal behaviors are the result of family history factors (Donovan & Leavitt, 1989; Isabella, 1998; Izard et al., 1991; Smith & Pederson, 1988; Teti et al., 1995). The disturbed behavior of mothers of disorganized-disoriented infants can also be explained by trauma, harsh punishment, and/or sexual abuse in the mother's early history (Bernier & Meins, 2008; Lyons-Ruth, Bronfman, & Parsons, 1999). Mothers who are more insecure in their own attachment relationships with their parents and partners are less likely to be sensitive to the infants' distress (Ablow et al., 2013; Flykt et al., 2010). Finally, the mother's ability to be insightful about her infant's state of mind, her "reflective function," predicts attachment security vs. insecurity on the one hand, and is predicted by the mother's own attachment to her parents and early history of trauma (Bernier & Dozier, 2003; Fonagy & Target, 2005; Meins et al., 2012).

In such cases, one can clearly see a pattern of intergenerational transmission of psychopathology. The parents' attachment to their own parents can be assessed using the Adult Attachment Interview. The parents' rating of security or insecurity with regard to their own parents is moderately associated with their child's attachment to them as assessed in the ASST at 12 months (Steele, Steele, & Fonagy, 1996).

Contributing to the systems perspective, infant behavior can also affect the mother's behavior and hence attachment. Infant temperament as well as colic and feeding problems may mediate the mother's responsiveness. Mothers who have extremely fussy or difficult babies are rated as less sensitive, most likely because they have learned that their interventions are not always effective (Mills-Koonce et al., 2007). Lack of security of attachment may therefore reflect primarily an inborn inability on the part of the baby to regulate distress and a heightened feeling of anxiety or wariness and only secondarily an effect of the mother's behavior (Chatoor et al., 1998; Goldsmith & Alansky, 1987; Hart & Behrens, 2013; Isabella, 1993; Lamb et al., 1984; Mills-Koonce, Propper, & Barnett, 2012; Rosen & Rothbaum, 1993).

Some studies suggest that infant temperament is a direct predictor of attachment (Seifer et al., 1996). For example, temperamental fearfulness is related to resistant behavior in the strange situation (Thompson, Connell, & Bridges, 1988). Children who at 3 months were less sociable and preferred playing with toys to playing with people were more likely to be scored as avoidant at 12 months, and vice-versa, infants who were more likely to attend to their mothers and who were better co-regulated with them at 3 months were more likely to be secure at 12 months (Beebe et al., Lewis & Feiring, 1989; Völker, 2007). Infant negative emotionality is also associated with insecure attachment (Seifer et al., 2004; Vaughn et al., 1992). Some scholars have suggested that whether the child is secure or insecure is related primarily to maternal sensitivity, while different types of insecurity may be more related to the infant's temperament (Susman-Stillman et al., 1996). On the other hand, infants rated as secure are more likely to show affective sharing and to enjoy being touched, and less likely to be difficult (Pedersen & Moran, 1996).

It is unlikely, however, that either the mother or the infant is the sole determiner of attachment quality. A 3-month-old may cry more because the mother is not responsive to his or her needs, thus setting up a negative cycle of infant fussiness countered by maternal insensitivity that leads to a lack of security of attachment at 1 year (Belsky, Rovine, & Taylor, 1984; van Ijzendoorn & Baker-mans-Kranenburg, 2004). In an even more complex pattern of findings, highly active and intense young infants became securely attached so long as their mothers did not try to pick them up and cuddle them often. On the other hand, active and intense infants became avoidant in the strange situation if they had mothers who insisted on a great deal of physical contact (Bohlin et al., 1989). Insecure attachments at 12 months were predicted by newborn fussiness, but only for those mothers who were not responsive to the infant's cries at 3 months and who had few opportunities for social support outside the home (Crockenberg, 1981).

Attachment is fundamentally about the co-regulation of proximity: how partners negotiate their closeness and sense of comfort and safety (or lack of it) with the other person. Recent evidence suggests that co-regulation in the first year—the ability of parents and infants to co-create mutual engagement (rather than one responding to the other in a way that is not reciprocated)—predicts attachment security at one year (Beebe et al., 2010; Evans & Porter, 2009)

In addition, parents who are at risk for failures of attachment—teenage mothers, adoptive mothers, or single parents—can often inspire babies toward secure attachments. It is only when these parental risk factors are compounded by a lack of support networks, poverty, or a history of psychiatric disorders that insecure attachments develop (Allen et al., 1984; Belsky, 1995; Brooks-Gunn & Furstenberg, 1986; Huth-Bocks et al., 2004; Jacobson & Frye, 1991; Sameroff & Seifer, 1983; Singer et al., 1985; Zeanah et al., 2005).

During the first year of the infant's life, mothers who were at risk for attachment problems (due to low income, poor social support, and anxiety or depression) were allowed to participate in a program that provided social support, education for infant care, and psychotherapy. Compared to control families of the same group who did not receive the intervention, there was a higher percentage of securely attached infants in the intervention groups (Boom, 1994; Lieberman, Weston, & Pawl, 1991).

These findings suggest that neither parent nor infant is solely responsible for the attachment outcome. Bowlby's concept of attachment suggests that it does not evolve from one or another person's sole influence, but rather has more to do with the way the parent and infant have developed their relationship to maintain proximity in times of stress (Sroufe, 1995). This idea is supported by evidence showing that infants can form different types of attachments in different relationships. Mothers and fathers form unique attachments to infants and make unique contributions to their development (see below), and infants also can form independent attachment relationships with professional caregivers (Cox et al., 1992; Easterbrooks & Goldberg, 1984; Goossens & van Ijzendoorn, 1990; Oppenheim, Sagi, & Lamb, 1988; Schaffer & Emerson, 1964; Volling & Belsky, 1992).

Each relationship has a unique character and develops through its own life history, in much the same way that each person has a unique temperament and developmental course (Fogel, 1993). The types of attachment security represent ways parents and infants have developed to communicate about their feelings and needs in a stressful situation. As in any interpersonal relationship (think of your own relationships with friends or romantic partners, for example), some couples can easily communicate their feelings and support each other in times of stress. Other couples tend to become anxious and hesitant under stress (insecure resistant/ambivalent), while still others resolve the problem by avoiding difficult topics of discussion (insecure avoidant).

Cultural Differences in Attachment

According to the systems theory of attachment, culture should also contribute to differences in attachment, independent of maternal and infant behavior. Cross-cultural research has generally found this to be the case. While all cultures that have been studied have about the same percentage of secure infants (Posada et al., 1995; Tomlinson et al., 2005), they differ according to the types of insecurity found. In general, avoidant classifications are more frequent in North America and northern Europe, while resistant classifications are more frequent in Japan, Indonesia, and Israel (Grossman et al., 1985; Miyake, Chen, & Campos, 1985; Sagi et al., 1985; Thompson, 1995; Van Ijzendoorn & Kroonenberg, 1988; Zevalkink, Riksen-Walraven, & van Lieshout, 1999).

A number of explanations have been offered for these differences. The Strange Situation Test may be too stressful for Japanese infants, who are rarely separated from their mothers or exposed to strangers during their first years of life (Takahashi, 1986). The higher percentage of resistant infants in the Japanese sample may be the result of the infants' becoming overly stressed during the testing situation and thus resisting attempts by the mother at comforting. We saw earlier that Japanese infants became rather upset at even a 30-second separation, and the separation period in the ASST is longer and repeated frequently. A similar pattern of closeness and rapid response to infant distress may be observed in Indonesia (Zevalkink et al., 1999).

The resistant attachments in Israeli infants come primarily from infants who are reared in a communal setting called a kibbutz. These infants spend most of their time with peers and caregivers and see their parents relatively infrequently (Sagi et al., 1994). These infants may prefer to be comforted by people other than their parents, especially in the context of the ASST. In partial confirmation of this hypothesis, the parent's security on the Adult Attachment Interview was less strongly related to the infant's security of attachment in Israeli kibbutz samples in which the infant slept at home with the parents than in kibbutz samples in which infants co-slept communally with other infants. The home sleeping samples were more similar to those found in North America and northern Europe (Aveizer et al., 1999; Sagi et al., 1997).

On the other hand, it is thought that the higher percentages of avoidant infants in North America and northern Europe may be due to higher demands for infant independence in those countries. As infants are encouraged to play independently and to occupy themselves at a distance from the mothers, they may be less likely to approach the mother for comfort.

A related issue concerns the security of attachment of infants who from an early age spend

Case Report
Attachment Styles

This report contains two cases showing the complexity of attachment relationships. The first case illustrates how secure attachments can form and remain stable during one's life, assuming the ongoing presence of love and support from the caregivers. The second case is one of disorganized attachment.

Case 1. I am interested in how my mother and I developed such a deep attachment. I have always been very close to my

mother and grandmother. They have been my greatest sources of support and encouragement. Even as I moved away, there was an attachment that did not wane. They are who I seek when I need to be consoled.

During the experiential exercises, I noticed that my body often made rocking movements which seemed to soothe my tension. I also recalled a time during this semester when I was sitting in a reclining chair

watching television and my boyfriend began to laugh at me. I then realized I had curled up in a fetal position and I was rocking myself. I had been so lost in myself, I had not noticed. Even though he was laughing, I kept doing it because it felt comforting.

I asked my mother if she had any significant stories about my infancy. She told one I had heard before, about the time I was six months-old and she was rocking me late one night. I raised my head, made eye contact, and said "Mama." I did not speak again for another couple of months. My grandmother recalled how she would rock me to console me or to put me to sleep. She would also rock me "just to love me."

I began to realize that it was not just the rocking that was significant, as it was the combination of touch, security, eye contact, and generosity of love that has helped me develop such a deep and personal relationship with these two women. I still hold my Mom's hand when we go on walks, just because it feels good. One of the insights I take from this class is the importance of expressing love to insure the success of all infants. The ability to safely open up and receive and reciprocate love affects a person's physical, emotional, mental and spiritual health.

This second example is a case of disorganized attachment related to maternal depression.

Case 2. This is a personal exploration of discovering my attachment to my mother. In essence my aim is to provide relief for a female adult who suffered from disorganized attachment due to maternal depression through exploration, understanding, and

catharsis. This semester, I discovered two main themes of my experience. One is an overwhelming feeling of loneliness and secondly symptoms of dissociation and evidence for disorganized attachment to my mother.

Entries in my personal journal reveal that my mother failed to recognize me as an individual with my own inner life. I was around the age of 19. "Sometimes I look at people and wonder if I am real. They look like objects to me. I begin to feel like an object myself. No existence, hollow. Do I touch them to see if their skin is warm? I just stare and feel sick. I hear things. They talk. I continue to blankly stare. I say nothing." Sometimes the hurt I felt by my mom was inescapable. Her physical body was there, but her soul was gone. To leave the situation without physically running away, I would stare endlessly at objects or whatever my line of eyesight had in store. This blank stare separated me from engaging with my mother and also allowed for imitation of my mother's identity.

I watched video footage of me crawling and interacting with the world as a baby. There wasn't as much distress in my face as I thought there would have been. In one instance, when I took my first steps, I reached for my mother's leg for protection.

I think that part of the hidden problem is that on the outside so much of my life looked normal. When I watched these films with my parents, my dad started to get nostalgic and he left the room. Later he came back, and was talking with my mother. For the first time he acknowledged that he wasn't around much when they were first married.

During this semester, as I was thinking about my infancy, my psychologist one day commented that I have a newfound verbal skill to express my feelings. It was as though a veil had been lifted from my hearing, once I was able to let out all the horrible verbal messages my mother told me as a child. I think in some ways I decided, unconsciously of course, to shut down: To not listen and stare blankly into space.

Disorganized attachment is often characterized by conflicting feelings toward the parent, both approach and avoidance. Avoidance can sometimes take the extreme forms described here, including various forms of dissociation such as staring, going blank, losing track of time, being detached. These are self-protective strategies to avoid feeling the pain resulting from the lack of emotional connection.

a good deal of time in day care. Although the results are mixed, with many studies finding no differences in attachment between day care and home care infants, some studies find that day care infants are more avoidant than home care infants (see Chapter 9 for a fuller discussion). This is consistent with the pattern of more avoidant infants in countries that encourage independence at an early age.

These findings may also reflect a potential limitation of the ASST. It may be too stressful for Japanese infants, for example, who are not used to such separations from their mothers. On the contrary, infants who are used to daily separations from mother may not be disturbed by the series of separations and strangers in the ASST, and they may appear avoidant when their mothers return. At a minimum, the findings on cross-cultural differences reflect the need to interpret the results of the ASST with some sensitivity to the cultural and contextual factors of the infant and family.

Does Attachment Security in Infancy Predict Later Behavior?

One of the successes of the ASST is its ability to predict child behavior many years into the future. Securely attached children at 1 year, for example, were found during later infancy and early childhood to be more sociable with peers (Fagot, 1997; McCartney et al., 2004; McElwain et al., 2011; Park & Waters, 1989; Slade, 1987b; Wood et al., 2004) and unfamiliar adults (Main & Weston, 1981; Thompson & Lamb, 1982), to be more aware of their emotions (Steele et al., 1999), and to be more securely attached to their mothers at 6 years of age (Main & Cassidy, 1988; Teti et al., 1991). Securely attached infants are also more likely to be better problem solvers in preschool and kindergarten, to be more persistent and enthusiastic, to be more socially competent and less lonely, and to have fewer behavioral problems (Bates, Maslin, & Frankel, 1985; Berlin, Cassidy, & Belsky, 1995; Block & Block, 1980; Erickson, Sroufe, & Egeland, 1985; Meins, 1998; Sroufe, 1983; Wartner et al., 1994).

Children who were maltreated in infancy and were scored as having a disorganized attachment at 1 year continue to be disorganized during early childhood (Barnett, Ganiban, & Cicchetti, 1999). Disorganized children are more likely to display evidence of child externalizing behavior problems (disobedience, fighting, withdrawal) and adolescent psychopathology, in particular **dissociation** (mental confusion, lack of **subjective self-awareness**, out-of-body experiences, accident proneness, and self-harm or suicide proneness) (Carlson, 1998; Fearon et al., 2010; Lyons-Ruth, Easterbrooks, & Cibelli, 1997). Clearly, disorganized attachment in infancy is a serious developmental problem and should be cause for concern and possible intervention at an early age.

Because insecure attachment activates the HPA axis to overproduce cortisol, it may create long-term physiological imbalances in the body and brain. Insecure attachments may predispose some people to forms of mental illness, particularly depression (Beatson & Taryan, 2003), and it may contribute to the early pubertal maturity of teen girls leading to a higher risk of early sexual intercourse, teen pregnancy, and sexually transmitted diseases (Belsky et al., 2010). Avoidant attachments are associated with conditions related to pain (such as frequent headaches) while resistant attachment are related to chronic fatigue, stroke, heart attack, or high blood pressure (Lachlan et al., 2010).

We are still left with the question of how early attachment patterns are maintained over time and are translated into a variety of behavioral competencies or dysfunctions. Bowlby (1969; 1980) proposed that attachment has long-term effects because of an **internal working model.** An internal working model is a sense of self and of other people that allows one to anticipate future behavior, react to new situations in a competent manner, and appraise the likelihood of success for action. For example, based on past experiences with the mother, the infant constructs a model of her as the person from whom particular types of support are likely to be received. As the infant's internal working model becomes solidified through experiences with the mother, actual behavioral monitoring of the mother becomes less necessary, and the infant is able to tolerate separations and react favorably to reunions.

Thus, the internal working model is relatively stable and is updated gradually. The model is determined in part by interactive experiences but eventually comes to affect interactions. Thus, a baby who has been disappointed by the mother many times in the past is not likely to accept changes in the mother's behavior if at a later time she desires more closeness to the baby (see Case Report, this chapter; Bretherton, 1985). The notion of an internal working model is related to a number of cognitive and emotional theories that postulate the existence of a generalized representation of the individual's history of interpersonal experiences between self and other (Bretherton, 1987; Stern, 1985). It is also supported by the neurophysiological differences between secure and insecure infants, reviewed earlier.

These ideas may have potential for explaining some of the long-term correlations of child behavior with earlier attachment classification, especially if we consider that caregivers also have internal working models of themselves and their infants. The long-term stability of interaction patterns between mothers and infants may be maintained by stable internal working models in both mother and infant, which may enhance or inhibit interpersonal closeness over a long period of time (Main, Kaplan, & Cassidy, 1985).

Of interest in this regard is a study on adolescents who were evaluated in the ASST with their mothers when they were 12 months old. No relationship was found between their 1-year attachment classification and their behavior and emotional adjustment during adolescence. On the other hand, their behavior was related to their views on the supportiveness and emotional availability of their parents, information obtained from the Adult Attachment Interview when the adolescents were 10 years old (Beijersbergen et al., 2012; Sameroff & Emde, 1989; Sroufe, 1989;

Zimmermann et al., 1995). Insecure infants showed antisocial conduct at 5 years only if their parents used coercion and power assertion in their disciplinary style, or if there was coercion and conflict between the parents (Davies et al., 2013; Kochanska et al., 2009). Finally, more behavior problems emerged in later childhood for children who had insecure attachments to both parents. Having at least one secure attachment seems to protect children from poor outcomes (Kochanska & Kim, 2013).

In summary, parent-child attachment has been the subject of a great deal of research. Although there are different theoretical interpretations of the findings, one thing is clear. The early development of the parent-infant relationship is crucial for the continuing social and emotional development of the infant. On the other hand, attachment can change as relationships improve or worsen, and infants can derive benefits from a secure attachment to any person. The results speak not only to the negative effects of inconsistent, unavailable, and abusive parents, but also to the resilience of relationships and their ability to change for the better under optimal conditions of social and cultural support.

FAMILY AND SOCIETY

Because this chapter introduces attachment and its development, in this section we will discuss attachments to other family members besides the traditional attachment figure—the infant's mother.

Are Infants More Attached to Mothers or to Fathers?

On the whole, there are few differences between attachment to mother and to father (Bridges & Connell, 1991; N. A. Fox, Kimmerly, & Schafer, 1991). In a sample of 41 maritally intact families in the United States, 78 percent of the infants had the same type of attachment security with both parents (Rosen & Burke, 1999). The remaining

22 percent of the sample was more attached to one than the other (not necessarily the mothers). In general, the more time the father spends with the infant, the more extroverted the father, and the greater the father's marital and work satisfaction, the more likely it is the father and infant will share a secure attachment and mutual communication (Belsky, 1996; Cox, Owen, Henderson, & Margand, 1992; Pedersen, Suwalsky, Cain, & Zaslow, 1987; Volling & Belsky, 1992).

Failure to become securely attached to one person does not preclude becoming securely attached to another (See the first case in this chapter's Case Report). In a small percentage of families, however, infants will be insecurely attached to both parents (Lamb, 1978b; Main & Weston, 1981) and such children are more likely to have behavioral difficulties in later childhood (Kochanska & Kim, 2013). If an infant becomes securely attached to either the mother or the father, the baby will be significantly less wary of strangers than an infant who is not securely attached to either parent (Main and Weston, 1981).

When parents are present in a childcare setting, distressed two-year-olds are more likely to approach their parents than their caregiver, regardless of their attachment quality to the parents. On the other hand, toddlers in the day care setting calm down more readily if they have a secure attachment to the parent to whom they approach, whether it is the mother or the father (Umemura et al., 2013).

Attachment between Adoptive Parents and Their Infants

The transition to parenthood for adoptive parents is rather different than for biological parents. Adoptive parents are already in a special category because typically many of them cannot have children of their own. They may have a history of infertility and may have made many attempts to treat it (see Chapter 3). They are also people with a very great desire to have children. If adoptive parents are not infertile, then they probably have a strong desire to rear children who would otherwise be disadvantaged.

Thus, it is not surprising that adoptive parents enter parenthood with much higher expectations for success than biological parents. Adoptive parents also experience more stress, at least initially. The "delivery" of their infants is often sudden and may follow a period of several years of waiting. They are thrust into the parenting role without the prior stage of pregnancy during which most new parents adjust to that role. Also, they may worry about how their own parents will feel about having a grandchild who is not their kin. Adoptive couples want to be seen as "real" parents by family, friends, and the workplace (Levy-Shiff, Goldschmidt, & Har-Even, 1991; Shahmoon-Shanok, 1999).

Research during the infancy period shows that there are few differences between adoptive and nonadoptive families in the outcomes of parent-child attachment and marital relationships despite the differences in the transition to parenthood (Humphrey & Kirkwood, 1982; Levy-Shiff et al., 1991; Singer et al., 1985). Even when adoptive infants come from at-risk groups, attachment can be facilitated with simple interventions that prepare the parents for the task at hand (Juffer et al., 1997). There is about the same percentage of secure infants (about 70 percent) in nonadoptive samples as in domestic adoptions within the same racial group, transracial adoptions, and adoptions of infants from other countries (Juffer & van Ijzendoorn, 2005; Juffer & Rosenboom, 1997; Marcovitch et al., 1997).

This pattern also holds for infants adopted from Romanian orphanages, in which infants are known to have suffered deprivations of care. On the other hand, the longer time spent in the orphanage has a negative effect on adoptive parent-infant attachment (See Chapter 12 about the effects of long-term deprivation; K. Chisholm, 1998; Marcovitch et al., 1997). Infants adopted from orphanages often suffer from PTSD (see Chapter 4) and have higher levels of cortisol (stress hormone) and lower levels of oxytocin (affiliation hormone) even after several years living with adoptive parents compared to infants reared by their biological parents (Fries et al., 2005).

Even foster parenting, in which the infants' stay is not permanent, secure attachments can form between parent and infant. This is especially true if the foster placements occur earlier than 24 months, if the foster parent has a strong commitment to the child, and if foster parents allow themselves to experience delight with the child. With delight, there are measurable increases in foster parent oxytocin levels and brain activation indicating emotional connection with the infant (Bernard & Dozier, 2011; Bick et al., 2013; Smyke et al., 2010)

One reason for the overall success of adoptive parent-child attachment may be that adoptive parents are older or have higher incomes and take a more mature approach to the adjustments required to help the infant adapt (Palacios & Sánchez-Sandoval, 2006). Adoptive parents are more likely to name their children after family members (parents and other relatives) than are nonadoptive parents, perhaps as a way to integrate the child into the family (J. L. Johnson, McAndrew, & Harris, 1991). This success may also reflect the resilience of infants and the plasticity of the infant brain, leading to the ability to respond to loving care when it is provided.

Just because there may be a secure attachment does not guarantee that the adoptive child-parent relationship will be without problems. Research on adults who were adoptees shows that they are more likely to rate their parents as more critical and less fair minded than nonadoptees (Silverman, Dickens, Eals, & Fine, 1993). Is it possible that differences between adopted and nonadopted children may not emerge until later in childhood and adulthood? It may also be that the reports of adult adoptees may be influenced by a feeling of loss about not being raised by their birth parents rather than by the quality of the adoptive parent-child relationship. This is compounded when adoptive children come from different racial or ethnic groups, or even from different countries than their adoptive parents.

The results suggest that adoption is a viable alternative for infertile parents and can provide a nurturing environment for infants who have been given up by their own parents. On the other hand, adoptive parent-child relationships are always going to be different from those in nonadoptive families. If the child has had significant trauma prior to adoption, there is the risk of an attachment disorder (see section on Attachment, this chapter). With the rise of international adoptions, there is also the potential for the child's sense of loss of the home culture and language. In cases of potential risk, parents may want to consult an infant mental health specialist (see Chapter 10; Rochat & Richter, 2007). Adoption can be a reflection of the human capacity for multiple and unique forms of love that transcend biological ties and there a growing number of services for adoptive families to smooth the transition (see http://www.nlm.nih.gov/medlineplus/adoption.html).

Co-Regulating with Baby

The year-old infant is awake and aware. There is not too much you can do that the baby will not notice. This will give you the sense that the baby has become more of an equal participant in play and love. The year-old infant is cocky and assured, generally quite happy, and easily delighted by small surprises, like finding a hidden object or the mother's face behind a blanket. The ability to do things for themselves—things they have done with help in the past or that have been done for them—is a great source of amusement for babies. Letting babies hide things, such as their own face or their mother's during peekaboo games, is one example. Self-feeding is another, as is letting babies get their own diapers, hold the pins (if they are closed), or wash themselves in the bath. Needless to say, all these babyish attempts at self-care are as much a delight to the caregivers as to the infants.

Do not let the first birthday pass without an appropriate celebration. Babies can really join in the festive spirit, although they have no idea what it is all about and have no conception of themselves as objects of all the attention. At age 1, babies are just going along with everyone else's fun. They will imitate when their parents try to blow out the candles, they will clap along with everyone else, and they will have a great time pulling off the wrapping paper. Do not be too surprised if the wrapping gets more attention than the gift. For the baby, each is just an interesting object to explore. The ideas of gifts, giving, gratitude, and politeness are still a long way down the developmental path.

There are a number of games you can play with the baby. Hiding is a popular one; be sure to try all the variations of hiding objects and people, as well as letting the baby do some of the hiding. Babies of this age like to be picked up, thrown, and swung around (carefully and gently, of course). They like to have cross-modal experiences. Make a book with different colors, shapes and textures; let them smell and touch flowers or soaps of different colors. Sounds and sights can be combined with nursery rhymes

acted out with the hands and face (for example, "Eensy Weensy Spider"). Add some bouncing on the knee or tickling to complete the experience. Dancing with the baby to music combines all these experiences with physical closeness. This closeness can also be achieved by taking the baby into the bath with you if you have the opportunity.

Babies like to play with their own images in mirrors, although they do not yet recognize the images as themselves. Do not leave a baby alone with a breakable mirror. Read books with the baby and name pictures in them. Ask the baby if he or she can recognize the pictures from the words you say.

There are many other things to do with babies of this age: consult child care books and your own imagination. The main thing to keep in mind is that play is a form of learning—one that affects the whole child. A knee-bouncing nursery rhyme has cognitive, perceptual, linguistic, motor, and social elements. It is also important

to encourage the baby's efforts by showing your enthusiasm for accomplishments, as well as by encouraging the effort involved in the attempts. Most important of all, plan to give the baby at least some "quality" time during the day. This is a time when you are not distracted by other chores or worries and can devote your full attention to the baby; it may be during play, bathing, or feeding. The baby needs to bask in the warm light of total attention, love, and approval for at least some part of the day to develop a healthy sense of a subjective self that is connected in meaningful ways to other people. The baby also needs to learn how to control his or her needs, how to wait when you are busy, how to defer gratification, and other socialization tasks. You will find these easier to teach the baby if you provide enough pure and simple indulgence at other times. I will have more to say about socialization and discipline in later chapters. At age 1, the main message is, Enjoy!

SUMMARY

Physical and Motor Development

- During this period, infants begin to walk. Balance is the limiting factor in the stability and regularity of their steps.
- The onset of independent locomotion enhances both cognitive and social development.
- Infants' exploratory actions are more coordinated and adapted to the properties of objects.
- Caregivers need to be aware of the common sources of danger and accidents for infants.
- Caregivers should learn emergency treatment techniques to handle a variety of potential hazards.
- Health care and immunization is essential for normal development.

Perceptual and Cognitive Development

- Infants can perceive and act on relationships between objects, such as between cups and saucers, between causes and effects, between objects and their hiding places, and between the actions of others and their own actions.
- Infants act in deliberate and intentional ways, persisting until a goal is achieved.
- Although infants can find hidden objects in some circumstances, they are still puzzled by complicated paths of movement and multiple hiding places.

- Infants can now imitate actions that they have never performed before and can reproduce acts even after a 24-hour delay.
- Individual differences in cognition result from an interaction between infant temperament and attentional skills and adult intervention.

Emotional Development

- New forms of expression of anger, fear, sadness, and joy all develop at this age.
- Infants can now express mixed emotions and ambivalence.
- Affective sharing and social referencing both enhance infants' ability to use information about other people's emotional expressions, although infants do not yet understand that others have emotions.
- Teasing games are opportunities for infants to experience mixed emotions and develop their skills at emotion regulation.

Social and Language Development

- Infants and parents develop frames for coordinated joint attention and joint visual attention.
- Intentional communication begins at this age, more with gestures than with words. Most gestures are related to infants' interactions with objects.
- At this age, genuine turn-taking exchanges with peers begin. Infant-peer relationships evolve around different themes from those that define infant-adult relationships.
- Specific attachments develop. The quality of attachment can be assessed using the Ainsworth Strange Situation Test (ASST).
- The ASST has both advantages and disadvantages. The results for a particular infant may reflect the infant as much as the infant-caregiver relationship and the ecological system.
- Disorders of attachment are both behavioral and neurophysiological.

Family and Society

- Infants are able to form attachments equally with mothers and fathers, although the type of attachment with each parent varies across families and depends on time spent and quality of interaction.
- Most adoptive infants and their parents can form close and lasting attachments but there are some conditions that make adoption more risky for parents and children.

Chapter 9

Twelve to Eighteen Months

CHAPTER OUTLINE AND OVERVIEW

Physical and Motor Development *What kinds of motor skills can infants perform at this age?*

Cognitive Development *What are the developments in conceptualization and categorization?*

Emotional Development *How does the infant use speech and gesture to express emotions?*

Social and Language Development *What are the properties of early language production and comprehension? How does the infant relate to peers and parents?*

Family and Society *How do peers interact at this age? What are the effects of non-parental care on infants?*

Babies of this age are full of energy. They start getting into everything, or so it seems. With their almost constant activity and newfound mobility leading them into forbidden or dangerous areas, babies of this age require much more supervision than was necessary in earlier stages. This chapter will trace the beginnings of spoken language. Language acquisition began at earlier ages in the form of nonverbal social exchanges between the infant and the parent or caregiver. Between the ages of 9 and 12 months, some infants develop a rudimentary vocabulary. In this chapter, we will see how these prelinguistic interactions lead naturally into linguistic communication. This chapter will also cover the concurrent emotional and social developments in the first half of the second year of life.

PHYSICAL AND MOTOR DEVELOPMENT

Walking Becomes More Skilled

As we saw in the last chapter, balance is the limiting factor in the emergence of stable walking. A complete sense of balance takes a long time to develop. Walking tends to smooth out and have less of an unstable toddler look about 6 months after the infant begins to walk (J. E. Clark, Whitall, & Phillips, 1988). Around this time, infants begin to show the ability to stand on one foot with help and to walk up and down stairs with help. These skills emerge at about 16 months for the average baby (a range of 12 to 23 months) (Rosenblith & Sims-Knight, 1985). By this age a baby's steps are longer, narrower (more under the hips), straighter, and more consistent (Adolph et al., 2003). You can experience the differences between your own and an infant's walk with the Experiential Exercise in this chapter.

Balance is still an issue in more challenging tasks. Infants can use handrails, and are more likely to use a handrail in situations in which they perceive that the handrail is positioned in a way that it can actually help them to balance (Berger & Adolph, 2003; Berger, Adolph & Kavookjian, 2010). Babies still use crawling for going up and down stairs or over steeper drop-offs (Kretch & Adolph, 2013). When experimenters put a pack of 15 percent of the infant's weight on the front or the back of a 14-month-old baby, the baby had more difficulty maintaining balance (Garciaguirre et al., 2007). On the other hand, when infants are carrying objects in their hands as they walk, their balance is better than if they are not carrying something (Karasik et al., 2012). These studies show that infants of this age are not only improving their motor skills but also that they are learning how and when to employ particular skills that are best suited to navigate the current situation (Berger, Adolph & Kavookjian, 2010; Berger, Friedman, & Polis, 2011).

Infants of this age period begin to adjust their behavior to the type of surface on which they walk. When jogging, for example, people run more slowly and step more carefully on a rocky surface than on a smooth one. They do not wait until they step onto the rocks to slow down. Instead, they use perceptual information about the surface to adjust their steps before they get to the rocks. Do walking infants have the same kind of link between their perception and action?

Several studies suggest that infants can perceive how different types of surface affect their locomotor actions. Infants prefer to walk on matte rather than shiny surfaces. If the matte surface looks like it is moving in waves (the researchers used a water bed), infants shift to crawling (Gibson et al., 1987). They also prefer to walk on rigid compared to deformable surfaces (Toselli et al., 2001). We saw in the last chapter how infants adjusted their locomotor behavior when encountering a sloping surface. Fourteen-month-old infants are able to regulate their locomotor behavior depending upon the steepness of the slope. If they perceive the slope as too steep for walking down, they sit and slide down (Adolph, Gibson, & Eppler, 1990). These studies show that an awareness of the surface on which one is acting is an essential ingredient of advanced motor skills.

Experiential Exercise

Kinesthetic empathy (by Alan Fogel, using concepts from Dance Movement Therapy (Tortora, 2004)).

Part I:

This exercise focuses on the movement of walking. In this part, the leader talks about how psychological states may be communicated in posture and movement. Begin with a few stretches of upper arms with deep breaths. The leader then demonstrates each of the following movement dimensions and students are asked to stand and do their own versions.

Body inter-relationships: (1) move only one part of body, keeping other parts still, such as upper or lower, arms only, one leg, etc. (2) Coordinate different parts with each other such as right arm and left leg shake, (3) Have the left leg shake and the right arm rotate, etc.

Use of space: Taking up a lot of space with arms and legs extended vs. contracted and small.

Sequencing: Try different walking sequences such as extending arm and leg on same side of body vs. opposite side.

Shape: Rounded, straight, snake-like.

These patterns are combined when making any ordinary movement and can communicate to others about one's psychological state using *kinesthetic empathy*, the ability to feel another's experience simply by watching their movements. The leader demonstrates some common states (e.g., sadness, haste, anger) with his or her body by walking in front of the class while the students guess the feeling being demonstrated. Attempts should be made to focus on body movement and not on facial expression. Then, the students are asked to try this for themselves using some of the following prompts. The leader gives only the first word (e.g., "proud") and the students try it and describe what they did.

Proud: Chest out, shoulders back and down, head high, regular steps.

Dejected: Chest caved in, shoulders hunched, head down, slow and small steps.

Determination: Straight arms and legs, head forward of body, forceful steps.

I'm cool: Shoulders and hips relaxed and swaying, head loose.

Vigilant: Closed posture, small rapid steps, rapid shifts of head direction.

Toddler: Hip rotations, heavy legs, little knee bend, no leg swing (A video of a toddler walking can be used to illustrate this and students can then try it out). It helps to switch between adult and toddler walking to compare the differences.

Talk about what each of these felt like, especially trying to walk like a toddler. What is the difference between adult and toddler walking, especially in the balancing and leg swing?

Part II:

In this part, the class divides itself up into triads. There are three roles: witness, walker, and follower. The walker walks around in their more or less normal way and the follower tries to match the walk while the witness observes. This is done silently. Everyone is asked to notice their own experience. The roles change until everyone has played each role with each of the partners. Using kinesthetic empathy, students discuss the experience of following and being followed in their triads sharing with each other about what it was like to "be" the other person and using the concepts from Part I. A general discussion can focus on how parents use these skills with their babies, and how this method can be used in treating infants and young children with difficulties. Also, it can lead into a discussion of how babies take on the walk or movement patterns of their parents: this is more than copying but involves feeling a connection and empathy.

Coordinated Actions with the Hands

Explorations of objects with the hands also are related to the infant's perception of the surface on which the objects are placed. During explorations of different types of toys, year-old infants were placed at either a foam or a hard table. At the foam table, infants did more mouthing and held the object with both hands. At the hard table, infants used each hand differently (one for support and the other for object manipulation, or each hand held a different object), and they used the table to explore the objects by scooting and banging (Palmer, 1989).

As infants progress in their ability to adapt their skills to the properties of objects and surfaces, they are more able to use objects as means toward goals rather than as goals in themselves. Thus, at the beginning of the second year, we see the emergence of deliberate tool usage in infants. A practical tool infants in many cultures need to use is the spoon. One research team has charted the development of spoon use in the second year of life in detail (Connolly & Dalgleish, 1989). Their work has produced a fascinating story about the developmental unfolding of a skill. They classified different types of spoon grips, different heights at which the spoon was lifted between bowl and mouth, different paths the spoon takes between the bowl and the mouth, and different uses of the opposite hand.

In the first stage, infants take the spoon in and out of their mouths or in and out of their dishes, but these two repetitive cycles are not connected. No food actually makes it from the dish to the mouth. In the second stage, there emerges the outlines of the complete action sequence, but babies are not paying attention to how much food gets onto the spoon. Often the only taste the babies get is the food that manages to cling to the convex surface of the spoon. The movements from the dish to the mouth are jerky, and the spoon is not held in a grip that permits it to contain the food. During these two stages, caregivers need to help feed infants.

By the third stage, the action sequence of moving the spoon from the dish to the mouth now incorporates the function of moving the food. Although still not very efficient, at least the babies are getting somewhere. In this stage, not only is the action sequence functional, but it is correcting itself for errors. Thus, the babies will keep dipping the spoon into the dish until they are satisfied that it is holding enough food. They will also hold the dish steady. Similarly, the infants will continue to put the spoon into their mouths until it is clean. Infants at this stage can also alternate which hand holds the spoon and the type of grip (McCarty, Clifton, & Collard, 1999).

This study shows that spoon use can be a complicated motor challenge for a baby. These developments take 6 to 8 months from the onset of spoon use. The use of other grip tools that are directed toward the self—hair brushes for example—develops in similar ways. Grip tools that are directed toward objects—like a hammer—take longer to learn (McCarty et al., 2001). In general, infants of this age are learning to make more subtle adjustments to their motor skill, and they are relying more on visual guidance Successful tool use involves not only making all the right moves at the right time, but also the ability to adjust the movement to correct errors that occur in the process (Carrico & Berthier, 2008).

COGNITIVE DEVELOPMENT

The period between 12 and 18 months encompasses Piaget's Stage V of sensorimotor development. As Observations 9.1 and 9.2 show, infants in Piaget's Stage V are not merely using familiar means to achieve their goals: they are creatively inventing new ways of doing things. This is the stage that Piaget called **tertiary circular reactions**, the beginnings of active experimentation and the search for novelty. In the previous stages, infants were most comfortable in familiar settings and were most likely to use the means they had discovered—largely by chance—to handle situa-

Observations

Stage V Behavior (Piaget, 1952, pp. 269, 285)

Observation 9.1

At 0;10(11) Laurent grasps in succession a celluloid swan, a box, etc., stretches out his arm and lets them fall. He distinctly varies the position of the fall. Sometimes he stretches out his arm vertically, sometimes he holds it obliquely, in front of or behind his eyes, etc. When the object falls in a new position (for example on his pillow), he lets it fall two or three more times in the same place, as though to study the spatial relation; then he modifies the situation.

Observation 9.2

At 0;10(27) seated on her bed Lucienne tries to grasp a distant toy when, having by chance moved the folded sheet she saw the object sway slightly. She at once grasped the sheet, noticed the object shake again and pulled the whole thing toward her.

tions that arose. In Stage V, children become able to adapt to brand-new situations, both by using tried and true methods and by seeking out and discovering new methods of acting upon the environment. Stage V is sometimes called the stage of trial-and-error behavior, because infants attempt new combinations of action schemes until they find the one that will solve the problem.

A characteristic behavior of infants at this age is experimenting to discover new ways of doing things. Infants are increasingly aware of themselves as a persistent part of the series of actions in the experiment. Infants discover that a distant object can be retrieved by pulling the blanket on which the object sits, or they find new ways to open containers. They try to figure out which objects best fit into particular containers. Unlike the previous stage, in which infants tried out new means to reach a single goal, babies in this stage seem to have multiple goals, and they examine the techniques available to determine which are best suited to the particular goal they have in mind at the moment and which are better suited to other goals.

In the previous stage, the infant was able to find a hidden object if the adult showed the baby where the object was being hidden. The baby often was fooled, however, if the adult moved the object in plain view to a new location. The Stage V infant is no longer so easily tricked. So long as the object can be seen moving from one place to another, the baby can follow the path of the object and find its hiding place, even after a long series of moves or after a 24-hour delay (Moore & Meltzoff, 2004). This accomplishment implies that the infant has an increased awareness of space and an increased cognitive ability to comprehend and remember cause and effect sequences of events over longer periods of time (Gredebäck et al., 2009).

In the area of imitation, the infant is able to model acts that are completely different from those seen before. This flexibility allows the toddler to become a very good copycat. The baby will try to imitate complicated actions done by an older sibling or a peer without having much understanding of the reason for those actions. These are the origins of role play and dramatic play, both of which will take on increased significance after 18 months, when the infant will begin to understand what it means to play a role and get vicarious experience by so doing. Babies between 12 and 18 months are simply having fun copying.

Imitation has been used as a way to study infants' understanding of the world and their memory skills. As we saw in the last chapter, before the age of 1 year, infants are beginning to understand that other people have intentions. In one study, 14- to 18-month-olds watched adults operate simple tools, such as one in which a party favor appears after pressing a lever. Sometimes the adult said "There!" (intentional action) after pressing the level and other times "Whoops!" (accidental action). Infants were twice as likely to imitate the adult if the action was intentional, showing that they use intention to make sense of adult behavior.

They are not, in other words, simply reproducing a mechanical action but acting for a purpose, the same purpose observed in the adults around them (Bellagamba & Tomasello, 1999; Carpenter, Ahktar, & Tomasello, 1998; Carpenter, Call & Tomasello, 2005; Sodian et al., 2007; Southgate & Csibra, 2009). In other studies, 12-month-olds were more interested in a toy the experimenter reached for inside of a transparent box than in the box, also showing that the infants seemed to understand the purpose of the adult's reaching (Woodward & Sommerville, 2000).

Imitation has also been used to demonstrate how infants of this age remember. During the first year, memory is nonverbal. Infants under 1 year can remember how to kick to make a mobile move, remembering the task in action. Can infants older than a year remember a task they observed but did not actually perform? Researchers have found that infants as young as 13 months can do this, but the infants' "descriptions" of what they saw are given by means of imitation.

To take one example, an infant of this age period is shown a teddy bear, a blanket, and a book, and the experimenter enacts a scene of putting the teddy bear to bed. A week later, given the same materials, children of this age can reenact the sequence of pretend events without seeing the adult (Bauer, 1996; Chen, Sanchez, & Campbell, 1997; Hanna & Meltzoff, 1993; A. Meltzoff, 1988). Infants will remember for longer if they are given multiple demonstrations and if they can imitate the demonstration immediately. In addition, children of this age will spontaneously use words as they are reenacting the original event, commenting on their own actions in a way that suggests that verbal memories are beginning to form around the nonverbal memories (Bauer, 1996). In the next developmental period, infants begin to have verbal-conceptual memories.

Finally, infants develop more advanced categorization skills during this period. Recall that in the first year, infants could understand the relationships of particular examples to a simple category, such as faces, birds, or geometric figures of a certain prototypical shape. A simple categorization task is to recognize different sizes and shapes of birds as belonging to the category "bird." A higher-order task is to be able to group birds, fish, lions, cats, and dogs into an "animal" category. Experiments have shown that by 15 months, infants can correctly form higher-order categories for familiar objects. They can classify animals together, for example, but they will not include cars with the animals (Oakes, Plumert, Lansink, & Merryman, 1996; Roberts & Cuff, 1989).

EMOTIONAL DEVELOPMENT

In this stage, the infant gains a new sense of self-awareness and control over emotional expressions. In the previous stage, infants were able to use the adults around them to regulate their own level of arousal. Social referencing enabled the infant to determine the appropriate way to react to a situation simply by watching a nearby adult. Infants also approached an adult caregiver when they needed comfort, and they used the caregiver as a secure base from which to explore the environment. After 12 months infants still seek help from adults in regulating their emotions, but now we can see the beginnings of an attempt to control their own positive and negative emotions.

Positive Emotion

In the previous stages, infants might smile at their caregivers or laugh at a "joke," but these emotions were direct responses to the environmental events that provoked the emotion. Now infants can remain happy over a long period without the continuation of the stimulating event. This prolonged feeling of enjoyment has been called *elation* (Sroufe, 1979). Infants also play an active role in creating situations in which happiness is produced and maintained. During the previous age period, babies would show off to provoke repeated laughs from the caregiver. During the period between 12 and 18 months, babies will self-consciously exaggerate facial expressions, making funny faces or sticking out their tongues for an especially receptive audience (Demos, 1982). This exaggeration of actual routines in play can also be seen during co-regulated communication frames. By 18 or 20 months, babies and mothers play emotion games in which the children slap their mothers lightly, for example, the mothers pretend to cry, and then the children comfort them (Bretherton, Fritz, Zahn-Waxler, & Ridgeway, 1986).

Finally, infants show delight in their own achievements (Sroufe, 1979). Because they are becoming aware of their own abilities to act on the environment, to create new means, and to experiment, they appreciate the sense of accomplishment that mastery over a new task brings. The babies' obvious delight when they take their first steps or find a toy they have been searching for is an example of this new sense of self-appreciation.

Babies continue to show their affection for the special people in their lives. These expressions may change from physical contact to expressions from a distance, such as a smile and a wave. In one study of infants' behavior upon reunion with their mothers after a brief separation, 11-month-olds approached their mothers and sought physical contact immediately. Fourteen-month-olds, in contrast, were less likely to approach the mothers upon their return and more likely to use some form of signaling from a distance: crying, whining, or raising their arms as if to ask to be picked up. By 19 months, the babies rarely even used this form of signaling. When their mothers returned, the babies were content merely to look at them before resuming their play (Serifica, 1978).

Negative Emotion

In the previous stages, situations of stress tended to evoke fear or distress from the infant almost immediately. During an episode of separation from the mother, for example, infants were likely to cry or approach another friendly adult for comfort. After 12 months, infants visibly fight back tears and use other self-comforting behaviors such as stroking and hugging themselves and redirecting their attention to a toy (Bridges, Grolnick, & Connell, 1997; Parritz, 1996; Sroufe, 1979). Because babies at this

age are not so overwhelmed with the distress, they search more for their mothers (Serifica, 1978). When their mothers are out of the room, infants often alternate between pouting and frowning (Sroufe, 1979) or biting their lower lips to control distress (Demos, 1982). As previously mentioned, the baby who so successfully fought back tears during separation almost certainly will burst into tears upon the mother's return. Studies done in the United States and in the Gusii agricultural society in Kenya have both shown a relative reduction in approaches to the mother and fewer bids for attention and support (Reed & Leiderman, 1981).

As infants get older, parents are more willing to expose them to potentially stressful events. Parents are less likely to intervene when the infant has an everyday problem—such as an argument with a sibling, waking up at night, a nonserious fall, or needing attention. Parents are also more likely to leave the infant with a baby-sitter or in child care, and they are more likely to take trips without the infant. This is partly because infants are beginning to cope with these events (Hildebrandt, Lake, & Parry, 1994).

There are individual differences in the infant's ability to cope. Infants who are temperamentally inhibited and who have insecure attachments are more likely to show distress at even minor stresses (Nachmias et al., 1996). Infant emotion regulation is also related to the parent. Mothers who are more intrusive or who are more disengaged and insensitive to their infant's negative emotions, have infants who are more likely to be angry and irritable (Feldman, Dollberg & Nadam, 2011; Gudmundson & Leerkes, 2012).

When the mother takes a short (2- or 3-day) trip, leaving the infant in the company of the father or another caregiver, infants of this age experience relatively few sleep or behavior problems and can maintain their typical level of positive smiling and verbal interaction with adults. For longer separations, such as when the mother is in the hospital for a prolonged period, infants are likely to show more severe disturbances in their routines and less positive engagement, both while the mother is away and for some weeks after she returns. Infants with more difficult and withdrawn temperaments take these longer separations harder than others (Field, 1994). These findings suggest that infants of this age can cope with a wide range of stresses, but they need adult support and encouragement. After the parents return, they should also expect to spend extra time reestablishing the infants' routines and providing emotional reassurance.

SOCIAL AND LANGUAGE DEVELOPMENT

Because this stage is important in the development of language, and because we already have hinted at the importance of spoken language for human behavior and development, this section will introduce some of the basic concepts of language development used in the next three chapters.

What Are the Basic Properties of Languages?

Hundreds of languages, as well as countless dialects, are spoken around the world today. Some other languages, such as American Sign Language, are not spoken at all. All human languages—no matter where or how they are used (spoken, signed, or written)—share important properties that distinguish them from other kinds of communication systems, such as those found among other animals or those used for specific purposes, such as computer languages.

Human language has three basic properties (Brown, 1973). The first, **semanticity**, is the capacity of a language to carry meaning for both speaker and listener. Human adults are geared to find meaning in words and in all forms of social behavior. It is not unusual for an adult to try to interpret a gesture or a phrase made by someone else, whether that person intended it as meaningful or not. It is only at the end of the first and the beginning of the second year that infants begin to use words and gestures in meaningful ways.

Productivity refers to the ability of a speaker to express many different meanings with a relatively small number of words simply by rearranging them into novel combinations following the rules of grammar. Infants during the one-word stage of this age period cannot be productive in their language use, but when they begin to combine words into sentences, after 18 months, language becomes more productive.

Displacement is the property of language that enables speakers to describe distant or absent objects and communicate abstract notions such as peace and justice, and it allows speakers to discuss the past, present, and future. Displacement is based on the fact that words bear an arbitrary relationship to the things they represent. The English word "cat" does not look or sound like a cat, but English speakers can understand what it means. Infants of this age are beginning to use words that have an arbitrary relationship to the objects they represent.

Aside from these three properties, language has a characteristic structure and function that sets it apart from other systems of communication. The structure of language, called grammar or **syntax**, refers to the fact that out of all possible combinations of word order, only a small number are meaningful to the native speaker. The function of language everywhere is to communicate. The study of a language's social and communicative function is called **pragmatics**. Pragmatics is more concerned with why people say something than with how they say it.

What Are the Theories of Language Acquisition?

Learning theory. Developmental psychologists and developmental psycholinguists of this century first viewed language development in behavioral terms. Like any other behavior, speech can be conditioned and imitated (Bandura, 1977; Bijou & Baer, 1965). Nevertheless, learning theory cannot fully account for the fact that sentences have a very similar structure all over the world (subject, verb, and object—though not necessarily in that order). Imitation and reinforcement may help explain the learning of specific words and phrases but not the presence of linguistic universals of syntax. Another problem with the learning theory perspective is that it cannot explain why language is acquired at the particular time in the infant's life that it is. Why does it happen right at the end of the first year and coincident with Piaget's Stages IV and V? If learning were the only mechanism available, we might expect to see a much wider range of ages for language acquisition than we now see.

Behavior ecology theory. Theories based more on biological factors arose to try to explain these two problems with learning theory. As for the observation that all language has essentially the same structure, Noam Chomsky (1975) reasoned that each infant is born with a rudimentary notion of syntactic structure—an innate universal grammar. According to Chomsky, this is the only way to explain how infants, especially after 18 months, can take sounds and organize them into meaningful sentences. Careful scrutiny of children's one-word productions and the incipient word order found in early two-and three-word utterances led to an attempt to write down grammatical rules for infant speech (McNeill, 1970).

The problem, as we shall see, is that infant speech does not easily fit into these simple rules: there are too many exceptions. Martin Braine (1976) has concluded that rather than expressing some underlying universal grammar, the child's "first productive structures are formulae of limited scope for realizing specific kinds of meanings" (p. 4). Language acquisition, according to Braine, is better understood from the point of view of pragmatics—what the child is trying to say and why— rather than from a syntactic, or structural, perspective.

Functional theory. As a response to the deficiencies in both learning and biological theories, pragmatic or functional theories of language acquisition have attempted to study language development in its natural context: the parent-infant interaction. In contrast to purely psychological, or individual-oriented, theories, the functional approach attempts to study language development in relation to the social system in which it naturally occurs. The key

milestones of the functional theory of language acquisition are not individual achievements (such as babbling, single-word utterances, and multiword sentences) but achievements of the parent-infant dyad, such as taking turns, paying **coordinated joint attention** to an external object (both parent and infant direct their attention to the same thing), and sharing meaning of particular gestures, words, and phrases (Camaioni, 2001).

Coordinated Joint Attention as a Frame for Language Development

In the previous chapter, we saw how parents and infants create frames for coordinated joint attention. From a functionalist perspective, these frames are essential prerequisities for the emergence of language. Once a joint focus of attention is created, it is relatively easy for infants to begin to associate objects and events with words. Studies show that infants are more likely to acquire the correct object word if they are looking at the object being named (P. J. Dunham, Dunham, & Curwin, 1993; Woodward & Hoyne, 1999). In addition, infants who are more skilled in establishing joint attention acquire language at an earlier age than children who are less able to jointly attend (Mundy & Gomes, 1998).

During frames for coordinated joint attention, the adult's level of language use, the specific instruction regarding objects and their uses and names, has a great impact on the child's language development (Broerse & Elias, 1994; McCune, 1995; Tamis-LeMonda & Bornstein, 1990; Tamis-LeMonda et al., 1996). Infants learn words better if their parents use infant-directed speech (more pronounced intonation patterns) when naming objects (Estes & Hurley, 2013) and if the objects and words are familiar and shown repeatedly, as in reading the same picture books many times (Fennell, 2012; Simcock & DeLoache, 2008; Thieseen & Yee, 2010). Because of this parental guidance, infants use significantly more words and gestures and their play is more symbolic and relational when with mothers compared to with peers (Turkheimer, Bakeman, & Adamson, 1989; Zukow, 1986). A similar finding has been reported

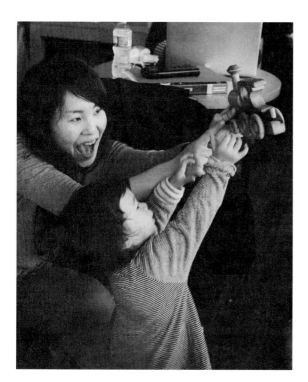

Once coordinated joint attention is established, infants can acquire gestures and words more easily.
Photo: Emily Waterfield

comparing parent-infant and older sibling-infant interactions (Teti, Bond, & Gibbs, 1988).

Adults can use combinations of pointing, showing, and words to direct infant's attention to objects and also to highlight specific features of the objects (Deák et al., 2008). The more mothers do this, the more advanced the child's language skills (Baldwin, 1995; Zukow, 1990; Zukow-Goldring, 1996). Some mothers are more likely to emphasize single words in their speech. They do this either by saying only one word in an utterance ("dog"), by repeating the same word in a subsequent utterance ("That's a dog; look at the dog"), or by changing a word in a repeating sentence frame ("That's a cat; that's a dog"). Mothers who were more likely to do this had children who, as their language skills improved, were more likely to speak clearly and not run their words together (Pine, Lieven, & Rowland, 1997). The child's participation in frames for shared book reading at 14 months predicted language skills 4 months later (Laakso, Poikkeus, & Lyytinen, 1999), and infants who were better at joining in frames for joint attention at 15 months were more socially competent at 30 months (van

Hecke et al., 2007). These studies all show that participation in frames for coordinated joint attention significantly enhances language acquisition, providing support for the functionalist theory.

The adult's role in creating frames for coordinated joint attention is also matched by the infant's ability to participate in these frames and pay attention to objects and words. Earlier than 12 months, when adults point at an object, infants are more likely to look at the adult's hand than at the object. Around 15 months this changes, and infants are more likely to pay attention to an object or a feature of an object when adults point (Desrochers, Morissette, & Ricard, 1995; Vaish & Woodward, 2010). At the beginning of the second year, infants begin to take the initiative in creating joint frames of reference (Aureli & Presaghi, 2010). They develop the ability to follow their mothers' line of vision (Butterworth & Cochran, 1980; Scaife & Bruner, 1975); they begin to use pointing to direct their mothers' interest to something they want and will repeat the gesture if it seems the mother is not paying attention (Leung & Rheingold, 1981; Liszkowski et al., 2008); and they begin to imitate their parent's words more consistently (Masur & Rodemaker, 1999).

The ability to search for new means to reach goals imparts this persistence to the infant's communicative attempts. If infants do not get what they want by pointing or reaching for it, they are likely to look at their mothers, pull on them, point or reach for something, and look back at their mothers until they get what is needed (Blake,

McConnell, Horton, & Benson, 1992; Liszkowski et al., 2008; Lock, 1980; Mayes, Carter, & Stubbe, 1993). If the mother is asked not to respond to the infant's requests or pretends not to understand the infant, the infant will repeat the request using more exaggerated movements, like leaning or whining, or will change the form of the request such as by replacing a gesture with a word or vice versa (Marcos & Chanu, 1992). These studies suggest that a good deal of language acquisition is infant-initiated. The infant has something to say or wants to know a word and approaches the adult for assistance (L. Bloom, Margulis, Tinker, & Fujita, 1996). These observations are consistent with Piaget's descriptions of an active and persistent infant during this stage.

In the last chapter, we saw the emergence of simple intentional gestures, such as pointing and offering. The child persists until a desired result is obtained but tends to repeat the same gesture. After 12 months, infants begin to use gestures in combinations to communicate more complex meanings (Lock, 1980), as shown in Observation 9.3. In this example, the child first cries intentionally, and then, after the mother arrives, the child points.

Intersubjectivity, the ability to act cooperatively and to incorporate others as meaningful agents in one's actions, also expands at this age. During the previous age period, infants became aware of how their communicative actions affected others. Between 12 and 18 months, infants become more aware of the relationship between self and other. **Metacommunicative events** are communicative acts that refer to the communication in the relationship itself, in contrast to ordinary communicative events, which refer to the world outside the relationship, such as gesturing toward or talking about objects and other people. When infants persist in trying to get an adult's attention or assistance, they are using metacommunication by referring—implicitly or explicitly—to a failure of communication within the relationship.

We have studied metacommunication in infants during this age period during mother-infant play with a pair of toy telephones (Fogel & Branco, 1997; Reinecke & Fogel, 1994). When infants are less than 1 year old, they treat the telephone as a physical object, something to push and bang. When mothers try to get the infants to pretend that the toy phone is a real phone, that is, to pretend to talk to someone, the infants resist. The infants' metacommunication consists of pushing the phone away if the mother tries to hold it to their ear, making disgusted facial expressions, shaking their heads, and grabbing the phone away from the mother.

Metacommunication changes as the relationship changes. One infant who could pretend play with a toy phone put it to her ear and said, "Dada?" The mother, talking on the other phone, said, "No, it's Grandma." The infant responded with "Dada," and this exchange continued for five rounds, with mutual smiling. In the last round, however, the baby's tone of voice became more serious. The mother interpreted this as a metacommunication and said, "Should we put the phone away?" The baby held the phone and without looking at the mother said (in an emphatic robotlike tone), "Da-da-da-da-da." The mother took the phone away

---

Observations

Communicative Behavior (Lock, 1980)

Observation 9.3

Paul; age 13 months (27 days): Paul is playing with his football, which becomes stuck among chair legs. He tries to free it but is unable to. He starts crying while on his hands and knees, then moves to a sitting position and continues wailing. Mother comes in.

Mother: "What's the matter? What's the matter?"

Paul continues crying but also points in the direction of the chair.

Mother: "Oh, have you got it stuck again? I think you do it on purpose some times," and she gives him the ball.

Paul continues crying but less and less vigorously, until he stops.

saying, "OK," showing that she understood the infant's metacommunication meant not wanting to pretend talk to grandma. After the phone was taken away, the baby continued, "Da-da, da-da, da-da," almost squealing the sounds and smiling at the mother. This type of behavior is different from clowning, seen during the previous age period, because the infant seems to be commenting on the mother-infant relationship rather than simply being a participant.

The Emergence of Conventional Gestures and Words

During the previous age period, infants used a variety of gestures and words. Their gestures were simple acts of directing another person's attention, such as pointing and requesting. Prior to 1 year, infant words are most likely to mimic sounds that accompany an action, like saying "vrooom" when playing with a toy car. After 1 year, gestures and words become conventional. **Conventional actions** are those that represent an action or object using some type of ritualized manner of expression (Acredolo & Goodwyn, 1985; Camaioni et al., 2003; Camaioni, 2001; McCune-Nicolich, 1981). For example, a child who wants her hair combed will hold a comb and pretend to comb her hair. Pretending to drink from a cup might signal the need

for a drink. Waving "bye-bye" is another conventional gesture. Such gestures may refer to the past or the future and to objects that are out of sight. Thus, they have the character of words that are used to name objects and events. At this age, gestures are easier to learn for infants than words (Goodwyn & Acredolo, 1993). The developmental sequence of conventional gestures is given in Table 9.1.

Some time between 10 and 16 months, most infants begin to use words to communicate some intention. One manifestation of this developmental change is the onset of naming. Naming is the intentional use of a gesture or a word to refer to a specific object or event. Carlotta, one of the infants whose speech development has been reported in the literature (E. Bates, Camaioni, & Volterra, 1975; E. Bates, O'Connell, & Shore, 1987), used the sound "bam" when knocking over a tower of blocks. Several weeks later, Carlotta was sitting silently among her toys. She stopped, looked up, and said "bam," and then she turned and started to bang on her toy piano. What has changed here? The word "bam" has been removed from its original context as an accompaniment to action and is now being said in advance of the action to stand symbolically for the action that is about to occur. Another example of naming is given in Observation 9.4.

Around the same time, Carlotta began to do other naming procedures. When asked during the

TABLE 9.1 Developmental Order of Emergence of Conventional Gestures

Gesture	Average Age (in months) of first appearance
Waving	8.4
Clapping	8.9
Dancing to music	10.2
Giving	11.9
Hugging	12.7
Shaking head no	13.3
Lip smacking	15.3
Blowing kisses	15.6
Nodding head yes	15.9
Fingers to lips (shhh)	16.8
Shrugging shoulders	16.9

Source: Crais, Douglas, & Campbell (2004)

Observations

Communicative Behavior (Lock, 1980)

Observation 9.4

Peter, age 13 months (13 days):
  (a) Mother is putting Peter's slippers on. Peter reaches upwards, laughs and shrieks "Lieee."

Mother: "Yes, it's the light"
Peter: "Dieee."
Mother: "That's right, light, light."
  (b) I am talking to Mother. Peter comes up to me and touches my wrist.
Peter: "Dik do."
Andy: "Yes, it's a tick tock."

I continue talking to mother, the above occurring without intruding into our conversation.

---

reading of a book, "How does the doggie go?" Carlotta consistently replied, "Woowoo." She also said "woowoo" when she saw a dog in real life or heard a dog barking. At the same age, she was rapidly developing names for toys, foods, and clothing. Parents are also likely to reply to a child's gesture with some kind of word, additionally enhancing the emergence of language through gestures (Goldin-Meadow et al., 2007).

Babies of this age can be taught conventional gestures—sign language—to understand and express their feelings prior to having acquired the words. There are a number of websites and books that give parents helpful advice about what kinds of signs work best with babies and how to teach a baby to understand and use the signs (www.mybabycantalk.com, www.babysignlanguage.com. Fingers to the mouth, for example, might mean "hungry" or "eat." Tilting the head to the side and resting it on a hand might mean "sleepy" or "tired."

Parents report that infants can learn the signs easily and appear to enjoy using them. These gestures facilitate communication between children and adults, giving the child an opportunity to express something important and giving the adult the sense that the child has an inner life that is not yet ready to be described in words. Here is an example:

River (14 months) was not a timid baby. He wanted to walk, run, and climb long before he could easily coordinate these actions. When learning to walk up or down stairs, River would often be distracted by other things going on or toys he was holding. To keep him from hurting himself, his Dad told River to 'focus.' When his Dad would see River climbing stairs or doing other physically challenging tasks, he would say, 'River, focus!!' while pointing to his own forehead with his index finger. River picked up this unintentional sign, and began to point to his own forehead, reminding himself to focus when walking down stairs or along narrow walkways (Vallotton, 2011, p. 127).

In this example, River was able to not only understand the meaning of his father's gestural sign, he was able to use it for his own self-regulation. Parents who have learned how to foster infant signing report that they have gained a new respect for their infants' abilities to communicate, reason, and feel (Vallotton, 2011). Infant signing also improves relationships between children and nonparental childcare providers (Vallotton, 2009).

Infants' early words tend to be used like conventional gestures in the sense that they are like the conventionally used adult word and that they are used consistently in similar situations. Table 9.2 shows the top 20 words or vocal sounds used by children speaking three different languages (English, Mandarin Chinese, and Cantonese Chinese). The numbers in parentheses show what percentage of children used that word or sound. You can see that although there are language-based differences, there is also a great deal of similarity. This suggests that these early utterances reflect everyday events and actions (Tardif et al., 2008).

TABLE 9.2   Top 20 Words or Vocal Sounds Used by Children in Three Languages

United States (n = 264)	Hong Kong (n = 367)	Beijing (n = 336)
Daddy (54)	**Daddy (54)**	**Mommy (87)**
Mommy (50)	*Aah (60)*	**Daddy (85)**
BaaBaa (33)	**Mommy (57)**	*Grandma–(Paternal) (40)*
Bye (25)	*YumYum (36)*	*Grandpa–(Paternal) (17)*
Hi (24)	*Sister–Older (21)*	**Hello?/Wei? (14)**
UhOh (20	**UhOh (Aiyou) (20)**	*Hit (12)*
Grr (16)	*Hit (18)*	Uncle–Paternal (11)
Bottle (13)	Hello?/Wei? (13)	Grab/Grasp (9)
YumYum (13)	Milk (13)	*Auntie–Maternal (8)*
Dog (12)	Naughty (8)	**Bye (8)**
No (12)	*Brother–Older (7)*	**UhOh (Aiyou) (7)**
WoofWoof (11)	*Grandma–Maternal (6)*	*Ya/Wow (7)*
Vroom (11)	*Grandma–Paternal (6)*	*Sister–Older (7)*
Kitty (10	**Bye (5)**	**WoofWoof (7)**
Ball (10)	Bread (5)	*Brother–Older (6)*
Baby (7)	*Auntie–Maternal (4)*	Hug/Hold (6)
Duck (6)	*Ball (4)*	Light (4)
Cat (5)	*Grandpa–(Paternal) (4)*	*Grandma–Maternal (3)*
Ouch (5)	Car (3)	Egg (3)
Banana (3)	**WoofWoof (2)**	*Vroom (3)*

Note: All words weere translated into English equivalents where possible. Boldface indicates the word is common across all three languages. Italics indicates commonality across two languages.

Source: Tardif et al., 2008.

The first conventional words children acquire are for objects (*car*, *shoes*, *teddy*, *cup*), for social interaction (*hello*, *no*, *yes*, *bye-bye*), and for some simple concepts (*gone*, *more*, *there*). Infants of this age acquire only about one to three words per month (Adamson, 1995; Camaioni, 2001). Once they begin to use words, infants seem to prefer objects and events for which they already have a word or name (Schafer, Plunkett, & Harris, 1999). During picture-book reading, for example, infants will spend more time on pictures for which they already know a name.

These first words lack an important property that is discovered by infants only after 18 months: words are symbols. Symbols, as we will see in the next chapter, stand for or represent something else. A word is not the real thing; it is an arbitrary pattern of sound that represents that thing. Between 12 and 18 months, infants seem to use the words and gestures as if they are part of the real thing, and they use those words only when the real thing is present or nearby. Infants of this age are aware of *semanticity* but not of *displacement*.

When children first acquire a word or first make one up, a considerable period of time passes before they use that word in the same way adults use it. Infants make many errors in the application of words. In one type of error, called **overextension**, the child uses the word for instances not included in the adult's definition. For example, a child might use the word "car" for a wide range of vehicles, including motorcycles, bicycles, trucks, and planes. Does this mean the child does not really understand the true meaning of the word "car"? Or does it mean that the child has a faulty concept of cars and believes that all vehicles are cars?

Children's overextending while naming an object reflects their active attempt to try to categorize objects. By naming all vehicles "cars," children "elaborate for themselves the similarities among things" (K. Nelson, Rescorla, Gruendel, & Benedict, 1978, p. 964). Bowerman (1978) reported that her daughter Eva first used the word "moon" to describe seeing a real crescent moon and then extended the word's use to such things as grapefruit sections, lemon slices, and steer horns—anything she saw with a crescent shape. In such cases, the child does not appear to be saying that "a car is a plane" or "a lemon slice is a moon." Instead, the child may be saying that "a car is like a plane" or "a lemon slice is like a moon," much as an older child might say, "It looks like a car," or "Look, it's crescent shaped."

Generally, adults have three choices when infants overextend their word use. They can accept the child's own version of the word; they can say that the child is not correct; or they can provide the correct label for the object. However, even when the adult says something like "That's not a cookie" in response to the child's overextension of the word "cookie" to refer to a hamburger, the child may not understand or hear the negation. Failure to understand the word "not" may lead the child to interpret the adult's response to mean "It's okay to call that a cookie. Mommy said it, too" (Gruendel, 1977). When the adult stops referring to the object with the child's overextension and uses only the adult word for it, the child soon picks up the correct name.

Relationship of Production to Comprehension

The same child who used the word "car" to describe many different vehicles was able to readily point out the correct vehicle when asked a question like "Where's the truck?" In another case, a child could correctly point out strawberries when asked but insisted on calling them "apple." Research has shown that 13-month-olds can understand about 50 words, but they cannot speak 50 words until they are about 19 months of age. Thus, infants can comprehend a word considerably earlier than they can produce it.

The earliest instances of word comprehension have been found at the age of 10 months for objects that are both salient and very familiar. At that age, however, it takes great effort to teach infants to understand a word, and they may rely more on the adult's pattern of intonation and gesture in identifying the correct object. By 17

months, however, infants can acquire word meanings easily—sometimes after a single exposure—and it may be from overheard conversation and not necessarily speech directed to the infant (Floor & Akhtar, 2006; Masur, 1993; Woodward, Markman, & Fitzsimmons, 1994).

Not all children have such noticeable lags between comprehension and production; in fact, some children can understand far more than they produce, while for others production is much more closely related to comprehension. How can this be? Some children who produce little but understand a great deal may suffer from a speech or hearing disorder, but this accounts for only a small percentage. Some children may be overly cautious about speaking out until they are certain that they understand how to use the word, which may be related to a temperamental propensity to shyness (E. Bates, et al., 1989). Lags in production may also be related to the amount of explicit naming done by caregivers (Vibbert & Bornstein, 1989). Currently, there is no complete explanation of what accounts for these individual differences.

On the other hand, those children who have high linguistic comprehension show high levels of gestural production. Thus, even though they hesitate to communicate with words, they have articulated a rich array of symbolic gestures (E. Bates et al., 1987). This can be seen clearly in deaf children, who develop a large number of gestural signs that signify objects and actions at ages similar to when hearing children develop linguistic names (Petitto, 1985; Reilly, McIntire, & Bellugi, 1985). Thus, virtually all children at this age try to make themselves understood in one way or another.

The lag between comprehension and production suggests that children in the second year know more than their verbal behavior would indicate, and that their efforts to speak are not crude groupings reflecting incomplete understanding but active efforts to make sense out of a complex world of objects and people. The young child's speech, therefore, may be an important part of the process of cognitive and conceptual development.

Self-Awareness: Further Elaborations of the Subjective Self

During the period from 9 to 12 months, the subjective self emerges. At this age, the infant has a sense of being a subject who can feel and experience and who is different from other subjects. The subjective self is shown by such behaviors as showing off, intentional communication, and social referencing. These same behaviors continue during the period between 12 and 18 months, and other similar behaviors are added. In the realm of showing off, for example, infants at this age will exaggerate their facial expressions and other social actions as if they are exploring their own subjectivity in relation to another person. As we saw in the section and language development, 12-to 18-month-olds will not only gesture or use a word, they will persist when their attempts are not understood. They lean toward the adult, whine, use additional gestures, or pull on the adult's arm.

In the realm of social referencing, infants of this age still rely on adults, but they also discover that they have some emotion regulation skills of their own. They attempt to control their own distress by biting their lip or hugging themselves. When with another person, babies will look toward that person for confirmation of an achievement, but they will also smile, jump, or wave their arms to recognize the achievement for themselves. Finally, infants of this age will metacommunicate, showing that they have a concept of themselves as a participant in a relationship that persists over time.

One gets the sense that the subjective self in this age period is becoming more elaborated, that the infant is filling in the blanks of self-experience and trying out the possibilities and limitations of it. It is interesting that all of this self-exploration and self-knowing goes on for at least 9 months before the infant acquires the word "I," which begins during the next developmental period. In the period between 12 and 18 months, the infant is still a lived self rather than a conceived self.

Infants begin to imitate complex sequences of adult action, almost as if trying the activity on for size. They may, for example, pick up a toy telephone and try to talk "like Mommy," imitating the mother's actual telephone conversation. Or they may want to type on the computer or stir the pot. Without any understanding of what the computer is used for, and without an "I" that wants to take control, what could these actions possibly mean for the baby? Most likely, by copying these actions, the infants are coming to feel themselves as purposeful, feeling subjects.

This kind of behavior happens in older children and adults. Imagine listening to a song on the radio. You do not understand all the words, you do not want to be a rock star, you just like the way the song sounds and want to try singing it yourself. Maybe you can reproduce some of the words of the song. If not, you either hum or make up some of the words. It is all playful and enjoyable. You do not think about it as "I am singing this song," but you nevertheless feel yourself singing it and it feels good, or silly, or funny, or whatever. You are aware that you are doing the singing; it is not the performer that you heard singing, but you don't think about this. You just feel it.

These examples reveal why infants of this age seem to be having so much fun. It is as if they are always experimenting with new things and feeling themselves doing it. On the other hand, they have not yet gotten to the point where they have formed a sense of self that has possessions, goals, or plans. So, while they are full of energy and love to feel themselves, they are not burdened by expectations for success or failure, they are not troubled by meeting a particular schedule, and they do not feel ashamed of themselves if they make a mistake. They do not even have a concept of a mistake. If we adults could reserve part of each week for this kind of carefree joyfulness, we would probably be a lot happier with ourselves.

FAMILY AND SOCIETY

How Do Infants Communicate with Peers at This Age?

Peer relationships are one way to observe the growing link between language and social development.

Toddler friendships are genuine and important. Sharing and contingent responses are just beginning at this age.
Photo by Emily Waterfield.

Peers increasingly attempt to show contingent responses to one another (Mueller & Lucas, 1975), for example, in sharing behavior, which begins in this stage (Rheingold, Hay, & West, 1976). In response to a verbal request or a visual regard on the part of one infant, a peer will show or give an object to the infant who requests it. Although this does not happen all the time, peers tend increasingly to focus their attention jointly on the same object of interest (Eckerman, Whatley, & Kutz, 1975). In general, however, joint attention occurs much less at this age during peer play compared to adult play (Turkheimer, 1989). At this age, about 77 percent of peer play is parallel play, that is, peers play alongside each other but independently (Howes & Matheson, 1992).

Between peers, toys have a different role from the one they have between adults and infants. With adults, toys can be objects of a request or an offer, or the subject of naming and labeling routines. Toys are just part of a more complex interaction involving many levels of meaning. On the other hand, with peers, toys become the major focus of attention and serve as vehicles for the initiation and maintenance of social interactions. If someone else in the room is touching or manipulating a toy, the infant is likely to approach that person and make contact with the toy. Intentional communication—unlike a single-minded interest in the toy itself—requires that the infant not only touch the toy but also look at the other person and verbalize to that person about the object. Babies 11 to 13 months of age are likely to smile, vocalize, and gesture to an adult just before and just after making contact with a toy the adult is touching, but this happens less often between peers (Eckerman, Whatley, & McGehee, 1979; Turkheimer et al., 1989). In one study of infants during this age period, a novel toy was introduced into play between adults and infants and then between infant peers (Marcos & Verba, 1990). In the infant-adult interaction, the infant pointed to the toy and looked at the mother, requesting the toy's name and wanting to use it. When the same toy was introduced between two peers, they just looked at each other and laughed.

Does the Mother's Presence Affect the Way an Infant Plays with Peers?

Because of the infant's newfound awareness of persons as potential communicators, we might expect the parent's presence to affect peer interaction. Infants still approach peers for different reasons than they approach parents. In general, given the simultaneous presence of both mother and peer, a child is more likely to initiate play with a peer (Vandell, 1979). With their mothers, children are more likely to seek physical contact and show negative emotions like distress and anger.

To answer the question posed at the beginning of this section, however, we need to compare the infant's behavior toward peers when the mother is present with that when she is absent. In a familiar setting—a parent co-op nursery school—10- and 14-month-olds were found to be more social and less negative to peers when their mothers were out of the room (Field, 1979). More conflict, toy snatching, and crying occurred when the mothers were present, even when the infants were playing with peers. These behaviors may serve as signals to the mother of the infant's relative discontent about something.

What Other Situational Constraints Affect Peer Relationships?

The mother's presence during a peer interaction is referred to as a **situational constraint**—an aspect of the environment that affects the nature of the peer relationship. Other situational constraints include the infant's familiarity with the peer and each infant's level of peer experience. Familiarity has been shown to affect how 1-year-olds play together. When children are asked to identify which other children are their friends, friends are more likely to interact together than nonfriends, even under controlled laboratory situations in which friend and nonfriend pairs are formed artificially and allowed to play by themselves for a short period of time (Becker, 1977; Young & Lewis, 1979). Friends are more likely than nonfriends to touch and lean on each other, more likely to initiate interactions with each other, and more likely to show positive affect with each other (M. Lewis, Young, Brooks, & Michalson, 1975).

Apparently, then, friendship can be shown to exist as early as 12 months of age. Although it is not clear from these studies whether infants at this age have the same kind of attachment to their friends as older children and adults do, infants are more comfortable and expressive in the company of familiars.

The amount of experience an infant has had with peers is not as strong a situational constraint as peer familiarity. Some evidence suggests that experienced toddlers are more active in peer encounters than relatively inexperienced toddlers, and that the experienced toddlers are more likely to show more complex social behaviors such as mutual imitation and cooperative play (Mueller & Brenner, 1977; Vandell, 1979). Nevertheless, infants seem to need little prior exposure to other infants to act competently in their company, and infants seem to understand the ins and outs of peer play very quickly.

The Effects of Nonparental Child Care on Infants and Parents

One of the most significant contributions to our understanding of the effects of nonparental care of infants has been the National Institute of Child Health and Human Development (NICHD) study of early child care. Child care in this case means care given by any person other than the child's mother. A total of 1,364 children took part in the study, which began in 1991. The composition of this nationwide sample was 76 percent Caucasian Americans, 13 percent African Americans, 6 percent Hispanic Americans, and the remainder were other minorities. The study sample came from a wide range of income and education levels, using a wide variety of types of child care, including center child care, child care homes, and in-home care from relatives or nannies. The researchers assessed multiple variables, including the child's experience in child care, quality of child care, family income, parental psychological adjustment, quality of the mother-child interaction, and the home environment.

The statistics from this representative sample show the importance of child care for infants and their families in the United States. The children in this sample received an average of 33 hours of nonmaternal care per week. Hispanic infants used nonmaternal care the least, while black infants used it the most. Most of the infants were placed into some type of care prior to 4 months of age. When they first entered care, half of the infants were with the father or grandparent, 20 percent were in child care homes, and only 8 percent

TABLE 9.3 Primary Child Care Arrangements Used by Working Mothers with Children Under the Age of Three Years

	Percentage
Parent Care	27
Relative Care	27
Center-based Care	22
Family Child Care	17
Nanny/Baby Sitter	7

Source: Capizzano et al., 2000

were in a child care center. Mothers with higher incomes and those who had an economic need to work were most likely to place their children in child care. After the first year, there are an increasing number of children in center care (see Table 9.3). The findings from this and other child care research will be reported in the remainder of this section.

After 23 years of research, we can now conclude with more certainty that the effects of child care on children still depend on the quality of that care. We know that high-quality child care is correlated with successful outcomes for children. Children in high-quality care receive better caregiving from staff, are more securely attached to their caregivers, and are more competent with their peers and with adults than are children in low-quality care. Children and teens that had been in high-quality care score better on school readiness and on cognitive and linguistic abilities, have fewer behavior problems, and are more securely attached to both their mothers and their care providers (Alvbers et al., 2010; Burchinal, Bryant, Lee, & Ramey, 1996; Dearing et al., 2009; de Schipper et al., 2006; Howes, 1997; Howes, Galinsky, & Kontos, 1998; Howes, Phillips, & Whitebook, 1992; Love et al., 2003; NICHD Early Child Care Research Network, 1997a; 1998a; 2002; 2003; Vandell et al., 2010). High quality child care is especially important to reduce later behavior problems in low-income African American boys (Vptruba-Drzal et al., 2010) and for children whose mothers have low levels of education (Côté et al., 2013).

We also know what is necessary to create high-quality care (NICHD Early Child Care Research Network, 1996; see Table 9.4) and this is vitally important. Children who have overcontrolling and intrusive caregivers in their childcare placements have higher levels of cortisol (a stress hormone) leading to more anxiety in girls and more angry and aggressive behavior in boys (Gunnar et al., 2010). Infants who are in multiple different nonparental care environments during the same day or week are also more at risk for behavior problems, regardless of quality of care (Morrissey, 2009). Children who are temperamentally anxious or withdrawn seem to do better in home care compared to center-based care environments (Coplan, Findlay & Schneider, 2010).

In addition to the quality of child care, research also shows that the quality of the family environment is one of the most important predictors of outcomes for children who attend child care. In one large-scale study in Sweden, children who were in high-quality child care under the age of 1 year performed better in school at 8 and 13 years of age than other children (Andersson, 1992). Part of this result may be accounted for by the fact that children who entered child care early in this study had two professional parents. It is well known that parents with higher levels of education and income have children who achieve better in school. A similar study in Israel found that the social competence and communicative skill of children in preschool were more related to parental positive interaction with the children than to early child care experience (N. K. Rosenthal, 1991). If mothers were depressed and/or not contingently responsive to the children, their children in child care had lower scores on social and cognitive tests and had more

TABLE 9.4 Accepted Standards of High-Quality Child Care*

Group size	Caregiver-child ratio between 1:4 and 1:10 over 3 years of age; between 1:4 and 1:8 over 2 and under 3 years; between 1:3 and 1:6 over 1 and under 2 years; and 1:3 under 1 year.
Caregivers	Trained in specialized, formal teacher-training programs that emphasize early childhood education and experienced in working in child care settings. Caregivers should be nurturant, supportive, and responsive to children's cues; they should talk to, hug, and smile at children and enjoy their company. Also, they should be willing to firmly and appropriately enforce guidelines for behaviors that affect the rights and safety of others, as well as have respect for parents' points of view and concerns.
Staffing	Low staff turnover, staff support, and low burnout; only one or two caregivers should be responsible for the same child.
Curriculum	Planned in advance, emphasis on development. Age-appropriate and safe toys, flexible program with special events and outside trips. Curriculum adapted to needs of the individual child. Opportunities for diverse activities and movement.
Parents	Should be informed daily about child's day and any special problems or special achievements; should be encouraged to visit at any time and to participate if desired.
Faculty	Clean, bright, safe, lots of room for toddlers to move about. Nap times and quiet areas, access to a fenced outside play area. Emergency essentials available. Food safe and nutritious.

* Applicable to child care centers and family child care.
Source: K. Magid & C. A. McKelvey, *High risk: Children without a conscience*, 1987, p. 170. New York: Bantam; S. Provence, Infant day care: Relationships between theory and practice, 1982, p. 34, in E. F. Zigler & E. W. Gordon (Eds.), *Day care: Scientific and social policy issues*, 33–35. Boston: Auburn House; S. Scarr, *Mother care/other care*, 1984, p. 212. New York: Basic Books; K. S. Weintraub & L. N. Furman, Child care: Quality, regulation, and research, 1987, p. 333. *Social Policy Report: Society for Research in Child Development*, 2, 317–342.

behavior and attachment problems (NICHD Early Child Care Research Network, 1998a,b).

Most researchers agree that high quality child care *after the age of 12 months* is not harmful and is often beneficial to the child. Compared to home-reared infants, child care infants are more cognitively and socially advanced and are more likely to show compliance to rules (Clarke-Stewart, 1984; Schuetze, Lewis, & DiMartino, 1999; Volling & Feagans, 1995). *Infants older than 12 months* are able to adjust to repeated separations from their mothers during ordinary child care attendance. The separation reactions of infants on their first day of child care are considerably greater than after 1 or 2 weeks, including higher levels of cortisol in the first hour after the parent leaves (Ahnert et al., 2004; Field, 1991). Infants, even those who are insecurely attached to their mothers, are able to use caregivers and teachers as attachment figures and secure bases (Howes & Smith, 1995). Insecurely attached infants, however, have higher cortisol responses following separation and may therefore need more help adapting to the transition to child care (Ahnert et al., 2004).

In contrast to these findings, a number of research studies have reported that the proportion of infants with insecure attachments increases if the infants have been in child care for at least 4 months beginning *before the first birthday* and for more than 20 hours per week; that is, children whose mothers are employed more than half time (Barglow, 1987a; Belsky & Rovine, 1988; Caldera & Hart, 2004; P. Schwartz, 1983; Vaughn, Grove, & Egeland, 1980). In samples of infants in the United States whose mothers do not work outside the home, the proportion of secure attachments is about 65 to 75 percent. In these samples of early child care infants, the proportion of secure attachments across all studies is 57 percent (Belsky & Rovine, 1988). The difference in security between early child care and home care infants is small but statistically significant.

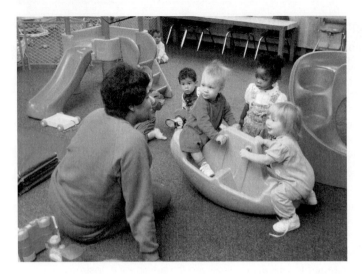

The effects of nonparental child care on infants depend on the conditions of the child care setting, the infant's age, and the parent-infant relationship. Only a small percentage of infants in the United States are able to attend a high-quality child care facility.
Photo by Elizabeth Crews

What accounts for those infants who develop insecure attachments? The infants most at risk for insecure attachments tend to be boys who are rated as difficult and/or fussy, who are insecure-avoidant, and who have mothers who have strong career orientations, work full time, and express less anxiety about being separated from their infants. Generally speaking, the quality of the mother-infant relationship is a stronger predictor of insecure attachments than the child care situation. Insensitive mothering coupled with low-quality child care accounts for most of the reported insecurity of attachment (Barglow, 1987a; Belsky & Braungart, 1991; Belsky & Rovine, 1988; Chase-Lansdale & Owen, 1987; NICHD Early Child Care Research Network, 1997b). If the quality of care is high and mothers are sensitive, there appear to be few adverse effects of the early child care experience on infant-mother attachment, either at 1 year or later (Burchinal, Bryant, Lee, & Ramey, 1992; Lamb, Sternberg, & Prodromidis, 1992; NICHD Early Child Care Research Network, 1997b; Roggman, Langlois, Hubbs-Tait, & Rieser-Danner, 1994).

In cases where the mother is insensitive, a high-quality child care experience can be beneficial. Research shows that the security of the early child care infant's attachment to mother does not predict social and emotional competence in preschool; rather, the security of attachment to the substitute caregiver and/or the quality of the early care setting is the best predictor of social and emotional competence in preschool (Howes, 1988; Howes & Stewart, 1987; Oppenheim, Sagi, & Lamb, 1988; Phillips, McCartney, & Scarr, 1987; Schindler, Moely, & Frank, 1987; Vaughn, Deane, & Waters, 1985). These relationships were found for infants in the United States in child care centers or family child care homes and on Israeli kibbutzim in which the child's primary attachment is with the metapelet. As we saw in the last chapter, for infants primarily reared at home, it is the child's attachment to the mother that is the best predictor of preschool social behavior (Egeland & Hiester, 1995).

Under the age of 1 year, therefore, infants appear to be more sensitive to the effects of child care quality and to the availability of nonparental attachment figures within the child care setting. These factors are less important for infants older than 1 year, who have already formed a strong attachment to one or both parents. In addition to attachment issues, more hours spent in child care under the age of 1 year is related to lower school readiness scores at age 5, while hours in child care after the age of 1 year are related to higher school readiness at age 5 (NICHD Early Child Care Research Network, 2004).

Does this mean that one should not place children under the age of 1 year in child care for more than a few hours a week, and that mothers or fathers should plan to stay home with infants for at least 1 year? Some observers make a strong case for this position on the following grounds: First, this early experience outside the home somewhat reduces the importance of the parental role. Second, and more important, it may not be possible in the United States today to guarantee high-quality child care for more than a handful of children. If this is true, one may be justified in supporting home care for infants under a year (Barglow, 1987b; Belsky & Rovine, 1988; Magid & McKelvey, 1987). In addition, some mothers want to stay at home with their children if they can afford it financially.

On the other hand, some parents may not be disturbed by a change in their parental role. The findings do not mean that parents are unimportant, only that they have a different type of relationship and provide different sorts of needs for their children than parents who choose to stay at home. In many countries, such as Israel, China, and the former Soviet Union, extensive out-of-home child care is an accepted part of the culture. Advocates of child care in the United States argue that if child care were made more of a national priority, we could guarantee high-quality care for all infants. In the meantime, these advocates provide guidelines for parents to use in evaluating the quality of care to assure a good setting for their infants (Howes, 1988; Phillips, McCartney, & Scarr, 1987; Scarr, 1984).

Child Care Policy and Practice

In 1987, Congress began to draft new federal child care legislation in collaboration with a number of child advocacy groups, including the Children's Defense Fund, the Society for Research in Child Development, the American Psychological Association, the American Academy of Pediatrics, and the American Federation of Teachers. Called the ABC bill (Act for Better Child-care), it was designed to provide child care for low-to-moderate income families and to provide incentives for states to improve the quality of care in centers and in family child care. The ABC bill was finally enacted in late 1990.

The ABC bill, however, met the needs of only a small percentage of children and families. Although we are one of the world's wealthiest nations, we are subsidizing child care for less than 10 percent of our children under 6 years, compared to 100 percent in Sweden, 90 percent in France, and 50 percent in Israel and Hungary. More than half of young children in the United States are in second-rate child care situations, with substandard facilities, poor staff training, and high staff turnover, despite the overwhelming evidence showing the importance of high-quality child care. Three million children in the United States under the age of 14 years are in programs guided by no national standards that reflect current knowledge obtained by research in child development. Licensed child care facilities currently account for only 25 percent of out-of-home care for children. The rest of the children are in nonlicensed, family-run child care homes.

Although more employers are providing child care at work, these employers still represent less than .1 percent of the nation's employers. Only 2 percent of the 1.2 million companies with more than 10 employees have child care on site (Sancier & Mapp, 1992). The private sector is not stepping in and picking up the responsibility. The generally poor care available to many children and the even worse care available to children from low-income and minority groups (Kontos, Howes, Shinn, & Galinsky, 1997; Shonkoff, 2010; Slaughter, 1980; Weintraub & Furman, 1987) testify to the large gap between children's needs and the willingness of our leaders to provide adequately for them.

Slaughter (1980) gives several reasons for the lack of effective child care policies. The first is the myth that the modern family can be independent and self-sufficient. Despitegrowing evidence to the contrary, people tend to think they are the masters of their own destiny. Hence, there is a strong resistance to the idea of social policy and social legislation (Bennett, 1987). Although a parent may believe that child care services should be found close to or in the home, the reality is that many parents leave their children in situations that are often inadequate and unregulated by state and federal laws.

A second reason given by Slaughter is the fragmentation of social services that exists for families, especially for high-risk families with low incomes. Support services are scattered among many different agencies, making it difficult for parents to obtain necessary services and nearly impossible for the government to exert reasonably efficient regulatory controls. Efforts to unify and streamline these services typically meet with strong political opposition, because many of them fall under the authority of different branches and departments of government (Weintraub & Furman, 1987).

Cultural differences in child care have received relatively little attention. In some societies, non-maternal care is the norm rather than the exception. In these cultures, the mother is not believed to be the sole contributor to the child's development. For most of the research on child care reported earlier in this chapter, outcome measures reflected the child's independent competence and ability, such as social and intellectual competence. In other societies, children are not expected to become autonomous but rather to focus on group sharing and cooperation. In such cultures, outcome measures should relate to group orientations rather than to individuals. The cultural diversity of child care philosophies, both for type of care and desired outcomes, have not been sufficiently studied (Friedman, Randolph, & Kochanoff, 2000; Leach, 1997; M. K. Rosenthal, 1999).

In summary, while a great deal of research and practice has been done with respect to child care, we have a long way to go in the United States. More work needs to be done to study how to improve child care quality, how to address cultural differences, and how to implement these findings into workable public policies.

Co-Regulating With Baby

In some ways, babies of this age seem quite fearless—walking into the street, putting screwdrivers into electrical outlets, sticking fingers into their eyes, and perching precariously at the top of a flight of stairs. Caregivers need to limit the child's access to certain dangerous or precarious areas of objects. This is best accomplished by establishing physical barriers, such as a baby fence across the entrance to basement stairs, or by offering the baby some alternatives for exploration. Although babies of this age understand the meaning of "no" and even come to use it on their own, overuse of negative language by parents ultimately may dilute its effectiveness. Of course, parents do not have to walk around saying "no" all the time. Other common and important prohibitive words include "yucky," "hot," or "that's Mommy's."

The major attractions of the baby's world at this age are adults and containers. Babies want to try out everything the adult does. This may mean trying to talk on the telephone, eat from Dad's plate, sit in Mom's chair at the table instead of the usual highchair, "smoke" Dad's pipe, or "read" the newspaper. While this behavior may seem cute at first, it often gets in the way of household routines and stretches the limits of health and safety. Adults can offer alternatives, like toy telephones, feeding the baby first before the adults eat, or just spending time with the baby and allowing the child to play at being grown up.

At this age, babies love to pull things out of and put things into containers. Unfortunately, this could mean kitchen cabinets, fishbowls, detergent boxes, ears, mouths, and eyes. Some parents try to arrange the house so the baby has his or her own drawer stocked with an array of harmless kitchen gadgets and plastic cups and dishes. The situation is not as easy to handle when the baby decides to tear the pages out of an older brother's favorite book. Toddlers' natural urges to test the limits of their environment are not intentionally negative or malicious in any way. Nevertheless, babies must come to understand the effects their actions have on people around them. The older siblings' angry responses and the adult's prohibitions are part of that process. So are the tears and tantrums that often result.

Babies do not restrict their exploratory activities to inanimate objects. Parts of others' bodies are also fair game. Babies will recklessly pull off your glasses, twist your nose, pull your hair, pull on your necklace, pat you, and even hit you. Toward the end of this developmental period, at 15 to 18 months, babies will do some of these things just to get your attention. Showing off, which I have already discussed, and putting on performances for admiring audiences are also part of trying to attract the attention and laughter of others.

To some extent, babies need to know that you recognize and appreciate them, and that you are willing and able to share a laugh with them. It is also important to impose and enforce reasonable limits on what you consider to be overexuberance. This may be particularly true with attention getting begins to look downright mischievous, as in hitting, throwing food, or pulling and tugging.

Social games are still important to the baby, such as peekaboo or give and take. Babies of this age like to sit on an adult's lap and identify mutual body parts, like touching their own nose and then the adult's. Looking at pictures and books, talking on the telephone with the baby, playing with puppets, and action rhymes like "Pop Goes the Weasel" and "This Little Piggy" are all favorites. Babies love it when you act as a tour guide to the world of the adult. This could involve holding their hands and walking places where they could not go on their own, like up and down stairs or outside. You can pick them up and let them see things that are not visually accessible from their normal viewing height, let them be "helper" and carry a pot or utensil, or let them listen to your watch licking (or sounding its alarm, if you have an electronic watch).

Although babies are starting to test the limits of their world, they have not yet fully discovered their own unique individuality, something that occurs in the next stage of development. For these reasons, many parents think that 12 to 18 months is the "best" age for a baby. The next stage, however, brings with it the mastery of the symbol, a genuine turning point in the child's development: the transition from action to thought.

SUMMARY

Physical and Motor Development

- At this age, infants can adjust their locomotor movements to the characteristics of the surface. They will not cross a wavy surface or downward-sloping surface while standing. They perform different actions on objects when the table is hard than when it is soft.

- Spoon use becomes more efficient during this period, including corrections for the amount of food on the spoon and entering the mouth.

Cognitive Development

- Infants are experimenting to find new ways to cause similar effects, such as trying alternate strategies to reach goals through trial-and-error exploration.

- Infants can now conceive of higher-order categories, such as "animals" and "vehicles."

Emotional Development

- Infants are getting better at making good feelings last and controlling negative feelings.

- Infants know how to tease adults by varying the patterns of normal routines or stopping just short of misbehavior and laughing.

Social and Language Development

- Languages have properties that distinguish them from other forms of communication.

- Functional theories of language are discussed at length, and most of the recent research is on how infants use language to communicate.

- At this age, infants develop both linguistic and gestural referential communication, naming, gestural combinations, and the ability to coordinate their communications with those of the adult.

- Infants typically comprehend more than they can produce, although the gap between comprehension and production is much larger for some infants than for others.

- Particular forms of adult response seem more conducive to infant language development than others.

- Infants are able to metacommunicate; that is, to communicate about their relationships with others and change the way in which the communication occurs.

- Linguistic communication is more likely in certain situations, and gestural communication is more likely in others.

Family and Society

- Peer interaction is more focused on direct actions on objects, while adult-infant interac-

tion has more referential communication about objects.

- Peers are more likely to get along better when one of the parents is not around.

- Child care has different effects on infants and families, depending on the age of the child upon entering child care, the parent's feelings about child care and returning to work, and the quality of care.

- There is a growing gap between the need for child care in the United States and public support for it.

- The role of the researcher in forming public policy has been limited by the belief that families should be self-sufficient and by the fact that child care services are fragmented.

- Cultural differences have not been adequately considered in research on and planning social policy for child care.

Chapter 10

Eighteen to Twenty-Four Months

CHAPTER OUTLINE AND OVERVIEW

Motor and Cognitive Development	*Can babies of this age use a toilet and sleep through the night? What do symbolic thought and pretend play contribute to the child's thinking? What are the effects of TV and other media at this age?*
Emotional Development	*How do symbolic thought and the sense of self affect the infant's emotions? How do children of this age cope with stress? How do they deal with separations from parents?*
Social and Language Development	*What are the patterns of parent-infant communication at this age? What is the best way to discipline infants? How do children begin to combine words? What are some individual differences in language development? How can adults facilitate language development? How do infants interact with peers? What are the advances in the conception of self at this age? What is infantile autism?*
Family and Society	*What occurs during peer play at this age?*

351

This age period sees a major change in the realm of cognition. Babies are now beginning to think; they are able to plan things out before acting, thus eliminating much of the trial-and-error quality seen in the last stage. The ability to think without having to act is at the root of our capacity to plan, dream, and solve complex problems. Infants of this age are beginning to establish a sense of themselves as individuals with intentions, rights, and possessions, an "I." With this sense of a possessive "I" come the emotions of defiance and negativism, which bring the 2-year-old into direct conflict with caregivers, siblings, and peers. Self-awareness often can bring self-doubt and feelings of shame, as well as feelings of pride. Infants need to discover how to handle the new experience of personal autonomy and yet still maintain close and affectionate ties with the people around them. We will see how language develops rapidly during this period, as infants begin to express more complex ideas in sentences rather than single words, and peer relationships become more complex and more verbal.

MOTOR AND COGNITIVE DEVELOPMENT

Motor Advances

Infants' locomotion is so stable that they now prefer to be independent walkers and may resist holding an adult's hand. They easily make the transition from walking to running, so by this age, most infants can run reasonably well (Forrester, Phillips, & Clark, 1993). More experience with self-propelled locomotion also increases the infant's awareness of and memory for spatial locations (Clearfield, 2004). It is not until the third year, however, that infants living in cultures where there are homes with stairs can negotiate them on their own.

During this period, fine motor skills are improving. Infants are now able to solve puzzles in which different shaped pieces are fit into slots of the same shapes (Street et al., 2011) and build precari-

ous towers out of blocks (Chen et al., 2010). Most 18-month-olds can feed themselves, and most prefer to manage their own food. Self-dressing is well under way by 18 months, and many infants will be able to put on their own coats, shoes, and socks by the time they are 2 years old.

During this period, toddlers are increasingly aware of themselves and their own activity in relation to others (see section on self-awareness, this chapter). Their actions with objects are more precise and effective when the actions are self-directed (using a spoon, for example) rather than directed elsewhere (banging with a hammer). When imitating and learning from adults, infants are more likely to watch adults' hands if the adult is doing a task that the infants can at least partly perform on their own. In negotiating slopes, infants are less likely to follow an encouraging adult if they perceive the slope to be too dangerous for themselves, and less likely to follow a discouraging adult if the infant feels the slope is safe for them (Claxton, McCarty & Keen, 2009; Schmitow & Kochukhova, 2013; Tamis-LeMonda et al., 2008).

One of the big advances that is likely to occur at this age, at least from a parent's perspective, is toilet learning. Based on findings from some African countries in which toilet learning begins in the first month of life (see Chapter 6), it is likely that infants have the potential to regulate their bowels and bladders well before they are trained in most Western countries. So why should people in Western cultures wait so long? The reason is that in these African societies, there is almost constant physical contact between the mother and infant, enabling mothers to detect the signs of impending elimination. In societies where physical contact is at a minimum, infants must signal their intentions across a distance. Typically, this means using words. So the trick in Western societies is to help the child associate the need to eliminate with a verbal communication about being taken to the toilet. Toilet learning in industrialized cultures is most likely to begin between 18 months and 3 years, although it may take up to a year to complete (see, however, discussion of the "diaperfree" movement: www.diaperfreebaby.org, plus web sites that offer advice on toilet learning such as: http://www.zeroto-three.org/child-development/early-development/all-about-potty-training.html).

Another aspect of physical development that concerns parents is the child's sleep patterns. Most infants of this age are still napping during the afternoon, and they can sleep through most of the night. It is not uncommon, however, for infants between the ages of 1 and 3 years to wake occasionally at night. The style in which parents handled the situation, such as how much the baby was encouraged to "cry it out," does not affect whether the baby wakes at night nor does sleep deprivation by keeping the baby awake during the day. Some infants—like adults—are night owls, probably from birth or even prenatally, and this pattern tends to persist for many years (Cofer et al., 1999; see also the discussion of sleeping in Chapter 5). Other research suggests that children with lower proportions of night time sleep have deficits in prefrontal executive function, especially impulse control (Bernier et al., 2010). Although no documented method exists for changing sleep patterns, there are some strategies that help parents and children (see http://www.zerotothree.org/child-development/sleep/). These methods, however, do not guarantee that the child will remain asleep throughout the night.

Cognitive Development: Symbolic Play

Piaget has referred to the sixth and final stage of sensorimotor development as the *invention of new means through mental combinations*. In the previous stage, the infant could experiment with new ways of making things happen. However, all this trial and error happened in the sphere of real action. The child had to actually do all the alternatives to get to the goal.

All this changes in Stage VI, because children no longer have to physically carry out the actions: they can think about the possible paths to a goal, eliminate the most improbable ones, and only then act. According to Piaget (1952), the child's first thoughts are internalized action sequences. Babies now can find objects after any number of visible or invisible displacements; they can go around a detour to get at something.

At the heart of all forms of human thought is the **symbol**, a representation of a thing or event that is conventionally shared among the members of a community. A road sign is a symbol of what lies ahead, such as a curve or a steep hill or an intersection. A word is a symbol for the object it

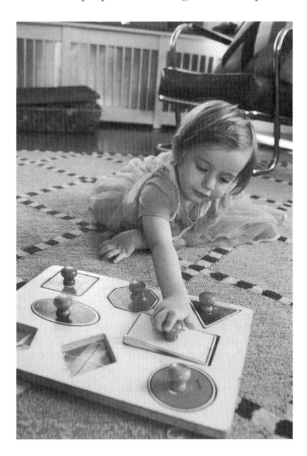

Exploring objects that are challenging to understand leads to a sense of mastery and personal competence. Exploratory play also contributes to cognitive development. At this age, play becomes more symbolic and includes pretending.

Photo by Emily Waterfield

represents. A plastic bowl can be used for eating, or it can be used symbolically when a child pretends that the bowl is a hat or a boat. By 18 or 20 months, infants understand that the symbolic object (the bowl) is not the same thing as the thing it represents (the hat or the boat), or that a pretend snack is not the same as a real snack (Lilliard & Witherington, 2004; Younger & Johnson, 2004).

Symbols appear only gradually in children's repertoires. At first, children represent objects by performing some gestural action related to the objects and physically similar to the represented objects, like moving one's open hand through the air to represent an airplane or a bird. Later, symbols become arbitrary, in the sense that the form of the symbol bears no physical resemblance to the thing it represents. The word "airplane," for example, neither looks nor sounds like an airplane. Words as verbal symbols are arbitrary in this sense, but they are also a form of **conventional communication**: how and when they are used in communication is not arbitrary but bound by the rules of meaning and grammar of the linguistic community. See the descriptions of verbal symbol usage that Piaget made of his own children in Observations 10.1 and 10.2.

In Stage VI, the symbol becomes detached from its original context of meaning and becomes something that, like objects, can be manipulated and explored. Several researchers have developed systems for classifying different levels of symbolic play (see Tables 10.1 and 10.2). Although there is no clear-cut age at which infants begin to display a particular level of play, by 18 months most babies are entering some of the early stages of pretend play. By the age of 2 years, most children can execute complex sequences of play requiring multiple symbols and advance planning, such as pretending to cook a whole meal using blocks and pegs to substitute for food and utensils (Belsky & Most, 1981; Ungerer et al., 1981).

Sequential Actions on Toys and Other Objects

Even during the first year of life, infants begin to organize the information they see and hear into meaningful groups of items or events. At first, this is done at the level of simple categories: faces, birds, cars, and the like. Next, infants group items into higher-level categories, such as animals and vehicles. By 18 months, another important principle of categorization emerges: categorization by sequential order, or by cause and effect. Infants at this age remember items and events better if they are organized into a sequence. For example, in a bath sequence with a teddy bear, the bear's shirt is removed, the bear is put into the tub, the bear is washed, and then it is dried. Infants can remember exact sequences up to 2 weeks later whether they are familiar sequences, such as the bath, or unfamiliar, such as events related to a train ride. Some evidence suggests that even when events are not related naturally, infants will remember them by the sequence in which the events were observed (Bauer & Dow, 1994; Bauer & Leventon, 2013).

When concepts and memories are organized in terms of how the events are related to each other in time, this kind of conceptual organization is

Observations

Stage VI Behavior (Piaget, 1962, pp. 121, 124)

Observation 10.1

At 0;6(30) Jacqueline said cry, cry to her dog and herself imitated the sound of crying. On the following day she made her bear, a duck, etc. cry. At 1;7(1) she made her hat cry.

Observation 10.2

At 1;8(30) Jacqueline stroked her mother's hair, saying pussy, pussy. At 1;9(0) she saw a shell and said cup. The next day, seeing the same shell she said glass, then cup, then hat and finally boat in the water.

TABLE 10.1 Level of Symbolic Play

1. Presymbolic acts, such as combing one's own hair

2. Self-symbolic acts, such as pretending to be sleeping

3. Object-centered symbolic games, such as feeding a doll

4. Object-combination symbolic games, such as taking a baby doll and a teddy bear for a walk.

5. Planned symbolic games, such as saying "let's cook dinner," before actually doing it.

Source: L. M. Nicolich, Beyond sensorimotor intelligence: Assessment of symbolic maturity through analysis of pretend play, 1977. *Merrill-Palmer Quarterly, 23*, 89–100.

TABLE 10.2 Levels of Exploratory and Pretend Play

1. *Mouthing*: Indiscriminate mouthing of materials.

2. *Simple manipulation*: Visually guided manipulation (excluding indiscriminate banging and shaking) at least 5 seconds in duration that cannot be coded in any other category (e.g., turn over an object, touch and look at an object).

3. *Functional*: Visually guided manipulation that is particularly appropriate for a certain object and involves the intentional extraction of some unique piece of information (e.g., turn dial on toy phone, squeeze piece of foam rubber, flip antenna of Buzy Bee toy, spin wheels on cart, roll cart on wheels).

4. *Relational*: Bringing together and integrating two or more materials in an inappropriate manner, that is, in a manner not initially intended by the manufacturer (e.g., set cradle on phone, touch spoon to stick).

5. *Functional-relational*: Bringing together and integrating two objects in an appropriate manner, that is, in a manner intended by the manufacturer (e.g., set cup on saucer, place peg in hole of pegboard, mount spool on shaft of cart).

6. *Enactive naming*: Approximate pretense activity but without confirming evidence of actual pretense behavior (e.g., touch cup to lip without making drinking sounds, tilting head back, or tipping cup; raise phone receiver in proximity of ear without making talking sounds; touch brush to doll's hair without making combing motions).

7. *Pretend self*: Pretense behavior directed toward self in which pretense is apparent (e.g., raise cup to lip; tip cup, make drinking sounds, or tilt head; stroke own hair with miniature brush; raise phone receiver to ear and vocalize).

8. *Pretend other*: Pretense behavior directed away from child toward other (e.g., feed doll with spoon, bottle, or cup; brush doll's hair; push car on floor and make car noise).

9. *Substitution*: Using a "meaningless" object in a creative or imaginative manner (e.g., drink from seashell; feed baby with stick as "bottle") or using an object in a pretense, act in a way that differs from how it has previously been used by the child (e.g., use hairbrush to brush teeth after already using it as a hairbrush on self or other).

10. *Sequence pretend*: Repetition of a single pretense act with minor variation (e.g., drink from bottle, give doll drink; pour into cup, pour into plate) or linking together different pretense schemes (e.g., stir in cup, then drink; put doll in cradle, then kiss good night).

11. *Sequence pretend substitution*: Same as sequence pretend except using an object substitution within sequence (e.g., put doll in cradle, cover with green felt piece as "blanket"; feed self with spoon, then with stick).

12. *Double substitution*: Pretense play in which two materials are transformed, within a single act, into something they are not in reality (e.g., treat peg as doll and a piece of green felt as a blanket and cover peg with felt and say "night-night"; treat stick as person and seashell as cup and give stick a drink).

Source: J. Belsky & K. Most, From exploration to play: A cross-sectional study of infant free play behavior, 1981, p. 635. *Developmental Psychology, 17*, 630–639. Copyright © 1981 by the American Psychological Association. Reprinted with permission.

called a **script** (K. Nelson, 1978). Scripts become increasingly important as ways of representing complex aspects of reality, such as remembering to get dressed, eat, get in the car, get out of the car, walk inside the day care center, take off one's coat, and go to one's assigned area. All of the separate events required to get from bed to the day care center would be difficult to remember if they were not organized into expectable sequences of events. Thus, although 2-year-olds cannot memorize long lists of new words or concepts, they can execute complex sequences of related actions.

Children's toy preferences at this age reflect their growing cognitive sophistication. Between 18 and 24 months, for example, children love pegboards in which they can fit objects of different shapes in the corresponding holes (matching symbols mentally; Örnkloo & van Hofsten, 2007). The more practice that children have with this and other symbolically challenging toys, they better they become and the more they can use their memory to find the correct match (Hayne, Barr, & Herbert, 2003).

Containers are another favorite toy for children this age. Children love to put things into containers, and they also enjoy nesting-cup toys, in which smaller cups are placed inside successively larger cups (sequential categorization). By the age of 18 months, infants understand the concept of containment, as shown by the following experiment. Infants were shown videotapes of sand being poured into cups and tubes. In some cases, the sand poured right through the container and came out the other side (violation condition). In other cases, the sand did not go through the container but filled it up to the rim (nonviolation condition). Only infants older than 18 months looked longer at the violation condition, suggesting that they found this sequence of events unusual (A. J. Caron, Caron, & Antell, 1988).

On the other hand, when actually presented with a set of nesting cups, children of this age period have trouble stacking them without errors. The infants might combine one or two cups correctly. Then they take a small cup and place it at the large end of their stack. Typically, infants under 24 months of age try to force the cup to fit, perhaps because they see that it might fit if the bottom cup were not in the way. At this point, most infants of this age will actually take the cups apart and start all over again or else just give up; they do not attempt alternative solutions, such as simply moving the cup to the other end of the stack (DeLoache, Sugarman, & Brown, 1985).

These studies show that even though infants recognize what is necessary for containment, they have trouble organizing their actions when a series of containers is present, which is why such toys are challenging at this age. This is similar to the A-not-B error in Stage IV, in which infants understand that objects exist when out of sight but persist in searching for them where they were last seen. If they fail, they give up the search. It is not until about 2 ½ years that infants are able to understand that two objects could have multiple relationships with each other: a cup that will not fit when placed on top of another might fit when placed under it. When younger infants place one cup on top of another, they fail to realize that the order of placement of the same two cups could be reversed.

Smart Toys, TV, and the Internet: Do They Make Babies Smarter?

Increasingly, parents who can afford it are buying so-called "smart toys." These are typically high-tech gadgets such as robots, digital images that move on a screen, buttons that "speak" or play music when pressed. There is also a line of "Baby Einstein" products from the Disney Corporation that include DVDs and CDs with lullabies and images, hand signs, and baby "movies." Television stations also broadcast shows aimed at children under the age of three years. Smartphones and tablets offer an increasing number of baby apps that make sounds, rattle, shake, change colors and deliver age-appropriate games.

After 18 months, infants begin to be more interested in television and smart toys (Barr & Hayne, 1999; Valkenburg & Vroone, 2004). Even so, surveys show that by *3 months* of age, about 40 percent of children in the United States are exposed to regular viewings of TV, DVDs, or videos. Children younger than a year are exposed to an average of 1 hour per day and by 2 years to an average of 1.5 hours per day. About 75 percent of parents report that their children under age 2 watch TV, and 1 in 5 of these children watch at least 2 hours per day (Cardinal & Lumeng, 2007). Parents' reasons for using these media are entertainment, baby-sitting, and education (Zimmerman et al., 2007).

But do smart toys and videos really make a baby smarter? Or perhaps a better question is: do they make a baby smarter than low-tech toys like pegboards, nesting cups, and blocks? Many parents and child advocates are strongly against using smart toys. They claim that smart toys and TV put infants in a passive role instead of actively exploring their world. The critics think smart toys will create television addicts and sedentary children. In North America, excessive television watching by children takes up time that could be used for movement activities and social interaction.

One study shows that smart toys are neither beneficial nor harmful (Plowman, 2004). If we think of infants as engaging with the world at their own level, then it makes little difference what kind of toy is available so long as it is interesting to the children. This also means that parents can encourage cognitive and brain development with inexpensive low-tech toys just as easily as with expensive ones.

TV, DVD, and video viewing, under some conditions, may have harmful effects on cognition and brain development for children under the age of 3 years, just the opposite of the marketing pitches about these products. Children who watch more hours of TV, DVD or video at ages 1 and 3 are more likely to have problems with aggression by age 4, and attention and hyperactivity at age 7, regardless of gender, health, prenatal exposure to tobacco or alcohol, maternal depression, or ethnicity (Christakis et al., 2004; Ostrov, Gentile, & Crick, 2006). Watching TV and baby DVDs and videos under the age of three significantly affects communication and language. For every hour of TV watched per day, 2-year-olds know 6 to 8 fewer

vocabulary words at age 2 years (Okuma & Tanimura, 2009; Zimmerman et al., 2007).

These studies suggest that TV before the age of 3 years can actually make infants less smart rather than smarter. It is not clear why. It could be that they put the infant in a passive role. We know from research cited above and in previous chapters that infants learn best by acting and not by simply observing. Before the age of 2 years, in Piaget's stages I to V, the mental life of infants is in doing rather than in simply observing and thinking.

One reason for the language impairment could be that the videos, while visually interesting, show scenes that cannot be easily verbalized. In the language development section below, note that infants learn words better in the company of a live adult who refers to concrete objects in an action context (shared goals and coordinated joint attention) that has direct meaning for the infant (Do you want some juice?). Also, infants imitate actions from live adults who can give contingent feedback, compared to televised adults who are not contingent (Barr, Muentener, & Garcia, 2007; Nielsen, Simcock, & Jenkins, 2008; Schmitt & Anderson, 2002).

Even background TV can have harmful effects. A study was done on children at 1, 2 and 3 years as they played with a variety of toys. During half of the hour-long play period, there was a TV on in the background. During the time the TV was on, children glanced only briefly at the TV. Even so, when the TV was on, the duration of sustained engagement with and attention to the toys was lower. So, even if it appears the child pays little attention to the TV, it nevertheless disrupts their concentration. In general, distraction via background noise, including background music, has a disruptive effect on toddler attention (Barr et al., 2010; Schmidt et al., 2008; Wyss et al., 2013).

Children under the age of 3 should not be left alone in front of the TV or smart toy for long periods. If parents choose to let their child watch with them, it may be an enjoyable learning experience but exposure times should be low, probably 15 to 30 minutes per day or less. Most child development experts advocate that parents should carefully monitor children's smart toy and TV viewing at any age and limit the amount of time children are allowed to watch. Indeed, toddlers are more likely to pay careful attention to TV when their parents interact with them while watching (Fender et al., 2010; Fiddler, Zack, & Barr, 2010). An adult co-viewing with a child creates a social-linguistic interaction around the media which may reduce or eliminate the adverse effects of solo viewing on vocabulary development (Mendelsohn et al., 2010). Similarly, especially for children older than 3 years, and even for adults, developing a social-emotional connection with the TV character facilitates learning (Richert, Robb, & Smith, 2011).

These media can indeed be engaging for toddlers and they are not going away. Some scholars are arguing that under the right conditions, such as with parental guidance and age-appropriate content, infant media could have beneficial effects on brain and cognitive development (Courage & Howe, 2010; Linebarger & Vaala, 2010). Studies showing impaired brain development from too much TV and media have not been replicated (Courage & Setliff, 2009; Wartella, Richert, & Robb, 2010), perhaps because media developers have become more aware of toddler's needs and limitations. Some research suggests that attention problems may only occur at very high levels of watching. Also, the association between higher levels of TV watching and hyperactivity may also occur because parents of hyperactive children may put them in front of the TV more often, as a way to calm them down (Foster & Watckins, 2010; Wartella, Richert, & Robb, 2010).

For children under 3 years of age, the bottom line is that care must be taken to ensure that the child is learning and developing, not zoning out and not becoming irritable. Older children, on the other hand, can get more out of well-designed smart toys, TV, and the Internet because of their more advanced cognitive and social skills. One study found that children who watched more of *Sesame Street* at age 5 had higher scores in high school on English, math, and science, spent more time reading books outside of school, perceived themselves as more competent, and were less

aggressive than children who watched less (Huston et al., 2001).

Because of the ready availability of these devices, and adults' own absorption with them, there is a growing tendency in Western countries to replace active engagement in the environment with vicarious electronic media; playing video games about outdoor adventures, for example, rather than just playing outside. Outdoor play and other nature experiences have been shown to lower depression, improve attention and concentration, and increase self-discipline, yet children in the United States spend an average of only 30 minutes of unstructured outdoor time per week (Thigpen, 2007; Zaradic & Pergams, 2007). Young parents have to make choices, both for themselves and their infants, about how best to spend their time together.

EMOTIONAL DEVELOPMENT

The more complex event memories and concepts and the ability to think symbolically account for some of the changes in emotional development during this period of infancy. The infants' emotional expressions continue to become more complex and more closely related to communicative situations. They are less likely to show full-face expressions typical of earlier ages (see Figure 8.2). Now, their facial expressions can be more subtle, involving fewer facial muscles, to reveal more complex feelings and a greater ability to regulate emotions. Supporting this view, 18-month-olds who showed more full-face expressions were more likely to be rated as having a difficult temperament (Izard & Abe, 2004).

During the second year, the infants' predominant emotional expressions are smiling and laughter (Malatesta et al., 1989). Prior to this period, smiles occur when infants accomplish a task such as the successful completion of an offering or a request gesture (Messinger & Fogel, 1997). After 18 months, infants are more likely to smile when both they and their mothers establish joint activity and attention, and when they experience periods of affective sharing, rather than just at their own achievements (S. S. Jones, Raag, & Collins, 1990; Mundy, Kasari, & Sigman, 1992). Infants of this age are also increasingly likely to initiate positive emotions in their communications with the parent, acting like a more emotionally autonomous individual (Grolnick, Cosgrove, & Bridges, 1996).

Our studies on infant laughter have revealed significant changes between the first and second year of life (Nwokah, Hsu, Dobrowolska, & Fogel, 1994). During the first year, most infant laughter occurs while the mother is smiling or laughing. In the second year, infant laughter takes on a specific meaning within the mother-infant communication system. A solitary infant laugh might mean "this is fun," an infant laugh following the mother's laugh might mean "if you think this is funny, so do I," and infant laughter while the mother is not displaying positive emotion, especially during teasing situations, might mean "I enjoy it when you look shocked so long as you are not really angry." Laughter also serves as an attention-getting device. A laugh can reestablish visual attention or direct the mother's attention back to the infant, who may laugh at his or her own antics.

We also found that mother-infant dyads developed their own styles of laughing together. For example, a mother would frame an opportunity for infant laughter by providing all the facial features of a laugh, such as a wide open mouth, and wait until the infant provided the actual laugh before she laughed in unison. Or, mother and infant might stare silently, smiling at each other, and then burst out laughing almost simultaneously.

How Does Symbolic Thought Affect the Child's Emotional Experiences?

The ability to form mental images and create symbols increases the range of the infant's emotional experiences. In the previous stage, fear, for example, could be triggered by a concrete event that might remind the infant of a related and unpleasant past event. Seeing someone in a white coat might remind the infant of a doctor and cause the infant to become frightened and cry.

After 18 months, fear can be evoked by a symbolic mental image, such as a monster or the thought of being sucked down the drain of a sink. Starting at this age, children develop fears of the dark and of things that might lurk behind doors, refrigerators, and other unseen places (Sroufe, 1979). Dreams, which at this age begin to take on representational forms that can be remembered and talked about, also can be a source of fears, although nightmares do not appear until after the second birthday (Piaget, 1962; also see Chapter 11). Piaget reported observing instances of dreaming in one child as young as 21 months; she called out the names of several of her friends in the middle of the night, and on one occasion said, in her sleep, "Kitty's hiding."

Symbolic skills also increase the probability that infants will talk about their emotions. Indeed, by 20 months, about one-third of all children will talk about one or more of the following states: sleep/fatigue ("tired"), pain ("ouch"), distress ("sad"), disgust ("yuck"), affection ("love Mommy"), and value ("good," "bad") (Bretherton et al., 1986; Ridgeway, Waters, & Kuczaj, 1985). By the age of 24 months, infants engage in conversations about their feelings, talk about the causes of their feelings, and play games with siblings in which they pretend to have certain kinds of feelings (J. Dunn, Bretherton, & Munn, 1987). These types of conversations are illustrated in Observations 10.3 and 10.4. Aside from the connection between emotions and symbols, this kind of talk also shows that the child is becoming increasingly aware of internal experience. The verbal expression of that internal experience is one of the major characteristics of the existential self that emerges at this age, compared to the subjective self during the previous age period (see section on self-awareness, below).

Self-Conscious Emotions

At this age, as we will see in the section on self-awareness in this chapter, children can recognize themselves in a mirror. The primary emotion that they experience when they first recognize them-

Observations

Communicative Behavior Between Siblings
(J. Dunn, Bretheron, & Munn, 1987)

Observation 10.3

Family M., child 24 months: Baby sibling is crying after child knocked him (accidentally). Mother comes into room.
  Child: Poor Thomas.
  Mother: What?
  Child: I banged his head.
  Mother: You banged it?
  Child: Yes.
  Mother: Are you going to kiss it?
  Child: Yes
  Mother: Kiss his head.

Observation 10.4

Family Th., child 24 months: Older sibling has been showing a child a book with pictures of monsters. Child leaves sibling and goes to Mother.
  Child: Mummy, Mummy. (whines)
  Mother: What's wrong?
  Child: Frighten.
  Mother: The book?
  Child: Yes.
  Mother: It's not frightening you!
  Child: Yes!
  Mother: It did, did it?
  Child: Yes.

selves is embarrassment. In one study, infants' reactions to the mirror were compared with infants' reactions to an unfamiliar adult. To the adult, the predominant expression was wariness, defined as an attentive look, a sober facial expression, and a cessation of ongoing action or vocalization, followed by a gaze aversion. To the mirror, infants were embarrassed, as shown by a turning to the nearest adult with a smiling facial expression, followed by a gaze aversion and movement to touch the hair, hands, or face in a self-conscious manner (M. Lewis et al., 1989).

Embarrassment, or *shame*, is fundamentally different from the other emotions that infants had experienced up to this point in their lives. Shame is a **self-conscious emotion**, that is, it requires an awareness of a self that can be seen by another. Shame is always felt in the eyes of someone else. To feel shame, one has to realize that others are different from the self, and that the self is *exposed*, separate, and likely to be evaluated by others (M. Lewis, 1995). Other self-conscious emotions are guilt, jealousy, and pride (K. C. Barrett & Nelson-Goens, 1997). Self-conscious emotions begin to emerge around the child's second birthday.

Pride occurs when infants see themselves as effective and competent individuals in the eyes of another person, able to achieve and to have an impact on others. In previous stages, children expressed enjoyment at being a cause, at being contingent, and at having an effect on others. In this stage, the feeling of pride is the result of meeting their own standards, as well as the awareness of having accomplished a personal goal in the eyes of another person.

Children observed an experimenter rolling a ball to knock down a bowling pin, and later the children were asked to do it themselves. Children smiled when the pin fell in both conditions, but they only looked at the experimenter when they had done the task themselves. This look seems to be one indication of a sense of pride. Similarly, children of this age period are more likely to show pride reactions when achieving goals they determine for themselves rather than those set for them by their mothers (Stipek, 1995). Some behavioral characteristics of pride and shame are shown in Table 10.3.

Both pride and shame are developed in the context of communicating about success or failure in meeting socially accepted standards, rules, and achievements (K. C. Barrett & Nelson-Goens, 1997). Children at this age become aware of standards, such as completing an entire puzzle or finishing one's food. Rules include cleaning up after playing with toys or not touching electrical outlets. Achievements occur when children reach a level

TABLE 10.3 Characteristics of Pride and Shame

	Pride	Shame
Situation	Success at achieving standard	Failure to achieve standard
Behavior	Approach others, show/tell, stand erect, smile broadly	Increase distance from others, reduce exposure, hide face
Social	Self as dominant, achiever	Self as submissive, small
Self	Maintenance of good feelings about self	Maintentance of others' respect
Other	"Everyone thinks I am good"	"Everyone is looking at me"
Vocalization	Wide, full voice	Narrow, thin voice
Physiology	High heart rate, flushed face	Low heart rate, blushing

Sources: K. C. Barrett, A functionalist approach to shame and guilt, 1995, p. 42. In J. P. Tangney & K. W. Fischer (Eds.), *Self-conscious emotions: The psychology of shame, guilt, embarassment, and pride*, 25–63. New York: Guilford Press; M. Lewis, S. M. Alessandri, & M. W. Sullivan, Differences in shame and pride as a function of children's gender and task difficulty, 1992, p. 633. *Child Development, 63*, 630–638; M. F. Mascolo & K. W. Fisher, Developmental transformations in appraisals for pride, shame, and guilt, 1995, p. 100. In J. P. Tangney & K. W. Fischer (Eds.), *Self-conscious emotions: The psychology of shame, guilt, embarassment, and pride*, 62–113. New York: Guilford Press.

of new mastery after putting in some effort, such as putting on their own shirt.

The parent's responses to these everyday events play a role in the development of the toddler's emotions. Children whose parents respond most positively to the child's achievements and to when the child follows everyday social rules are more likely to show guilt reactions when a doll they are playing with during an experimental situation breaks. This doll had been designed by the experimenter to come apart easily. When it appears they have broken the doll, these children are more likely to point out the problem to the experimenter and try to repair the doll. Children whose parents were more negative in response to children's failure during everyday social situations were more likely to pretend that the doll did not break and to avoid mentioning the problem to the experimenter (K. C. Barrett & Nelson-Goens, 1997).

It is possible that the parents of these children react more positively because they can see the child is very sensitive to failure. It is also possible that when parents are highly supportive and positive, children develop high standards for themselves. Most likely, there is a co-regulation between parents and children, such that their styles of emotional communication become more similar over time, with each influencing the other

(K. C. Barrett & Nelson-Goens, 1997; Dunsmore & Halberstadt, 1997).

In the realm of *anger*, a growing sense of independence and a feeling that the self is separate from others and "possesses" things and feelings, leads to *defiance, negativism,* and *aggression* (Sroufe, 1979). These feelings, which arise out of earlier feelings of anger provoked by frustration or the immediate situation, are due more to the *mental idea* that the self is and should be independent. We will discuss more about the emotion of defiance in a later section on discipline and compliance.

How Do Infants of This Age Cope with Stress?

At this age, children come to rely on their teddy bears and favorite blankets to comfort themselves in stressful situations and when their parents are not around. Children can become attached to these objects in the sense that they desire constant proximity with the objects and show signs of anxiety and distress when separated from the objects. Studies compared the behavior of children who were attached to a blanket with others who were not (Passman, 1977; Passman & Weisberg, 1975). The children, who ranged in age from 20 to 40 months, were observed individually in a novel

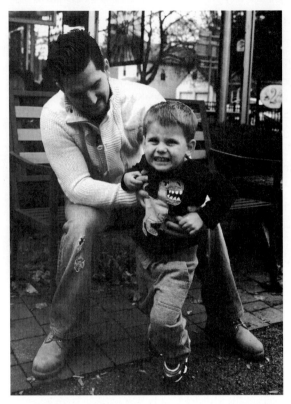

Defiance is one way infants come to know themselves in relation to other people.

Photo by Emily Waterfield

play situation with either their mother, their blanket, a favorite toy, or no available objects. Children of this age who are attached to an object, so long as they are with that object, show similarly high levels of exploratory play and low levels of distress as when their mother is present. It seems that a blanket can be an effective substitute for the parent, at least for brief periods. There are a number of reasons why this might be true. Blankets are soft and cuddly, and they carry plenty of familiar smells that may remind the child of the comforts of home and impart an increased sense of security.

Children's reliance on blankets as sources of comfort comes at a time when they are becoming aware of their physical and psychological separateness from the caregiver. Although this sense of self as an independent individual does not fully take hold until the third year of life, when the conceptual self emerges (see Chapter 11), the development of the existential self (see below) at the end of the second year can be thought of as an important transitional phase in the growth of independence. The blanket and other such attachment objects, therefore, have been called **transitional objects** (Winnicott, 1971), because they seem to serve as an intermediate bridge between a child's total reliance and dependence on the mother and the development of individuation.

In countries where there is relatively more physical contact between infants and caregivers, a transitional attachment is less likely to develop (Super, 1981). In a study of Italian children, only 4.9 percent of rural children had transitional object attachments, whereas 31.1 percent of urban children in Rome had them (Gaddini, 1970). Korean infants used transitional objects less than a matched sample of United States infants, and there was less sucking on fingers and pacifiers among the relatively more indulged (compared with North American) Japanese infants (Caudill & Weinstein, 1969; Hong & Townes, 1976). Only 38 percent of Japanese infants had an object attachment compared to 62 percent of United States infants. While the U.S. infants used their objects when distressed or when sleeping, the Japanese infants were more likely to use the object only at bedtime (Hobara, 2003).

There are individual differences in infants' reactions to stressful or frustrating situations. In one study, infants were exposed to a variety of frustrating situations—for instance, a desirable object was placed in a Plexiglas container so the child could not get it, or food was placed nearby but the child could not eat it, or the child was asked to sit for 5 minutes in a highchair. Some children screamed loudly when frustrated, while others showed little or no distress. Those who were more distressed were more likely to act out by hitting, kicking, or banging. These more distressed children were less able to use self-comforting strategies, such as finding something to distract themselves, seeking the mother, or making a constructive attempt to get the toy or the food (S. D. Calkins & Johnson, 1998; Raver, 1996).

The mothers of the more distressed children were also more likely to do things to help the children, rather than letting the children solve the problem themselves. This may be because the mothers know the children will have negative reactions and want to avoid the distress. Or it may be because the mothers never let the children do things on their own, so the children never acquire their own coping skills (S. D. Calkins et al., 1998; S. D. Calkins & Johnson, 1998). On the other hand, if mothers have a history of talking to their infants about their feelings, thereby giving children more of a sense of their own emotional state, the children are better regulated (Taumoepeau & Ruffman, 2006). These findings suggest that the parent plays a crucial role in the development of emotion-regulation skills.

Some evidence suggests that infants of this age who are less able to regulate their negative emotions may have deficits in neurological development that began at an earlier age. Children whose mothers smoked prenatally, for example, are more disruptive and less able to self-calm than other infants (Wakschlag et al., 2006). Infants who were less able to establish joint attention with their parents in the first year are more likely to show emotion-regulation difficulties by the end of the second year.

Generally speaking, children of this age adopt the emotion-regulation styles found in their families (Dunsmore & Halberstadt, 1997). In one study of 2-year-olds in a preschool setting, children tended to seek comfort and assistance from caregivers who reported a family history similar to that of the children's mothers. If the mothers had a positive relationship with their own parents in the past and present, their children sought out caregivers who also had a positive relationship with their own parents. Similarly, if the children's parents were conflicted or ambivalent about their own parents, so were the caregivers that the children approached (Shulman, Becker, & Sroufe, 1999).

This finding is rather surprising. One might expect that children whose mothers were more conflicted would turn to more secure adults when given the opportunity. On the other hand, even adults typically choose partners who have similar family histories and attachment styles. Somehow there is an attraction to the same negative or positive behaviors that were displayed by their parents (P. A. Frazier et al., 1996). This work supports the idea that children and adults develop internal working models with expectations for particular kinds of attachment styles and continue to replicate those styles, even when it is not in their best interests. Breaking out of the cycle of difficult interpersonal relationships often requires individual, couple, or family psychotherapy.

These findings show the importance of the parent-infant relationship and the active role of adults in emotion regulation at this age. A transitional object is useful but cannot replace an adult. Children of this age are better able to cope on their own with distress and frustration when an adult is nearby. They typically have limited ability to do this, such as finding alternative objects to play with when the one they want cannot be obtained, as shown in the study just reviewed and in other related research (Grolnick, Bridges, & Connell, 1996). Children of this age do not have the ability to comfort themselves verbally, which appears during the next age period. Even at this age, when children are beginning to acquire language, most of their emotion regulation is accomplished nonverbally.

What Happens to Children During Separations from Their Primary Caregivers?

By the end of the second year, because of cognitive advances related to understanding scripts and sequences, infants begin to take their own initiatives in separating from the parents. Infants of this age, observed with their parents in a public park, were not afraid to wander some distance from the parents. Although males left the parents' side more often than females, there were no significant sex differences in how far the children went or how much total time they spent at a distance (Ley & Koepke, 1982).

The situation is different, however, when the parents initiate a separation. This could happen for many reasons. The parents may want to go out in the evening, or they may need to travel away from the child for several days. This is often the age when mothers go into the hospital to have a second child. Other separation occasions include a parent's business trips and even brief hospitalizations for a child who is ill or needs an operation.

Research suggests that separation episodes are more tolerable to the infant if the parent prepares the child for them beforehand. In one study (Weinraub & Lewis, 1977), children were least upset during the separation if the mother explained that she would be leaving and gave the child instructions on what to do in her absence. This was especially true for children who were more developmentally advanced and could better understand the mother's instructions. It also seemed to help the child during the separation if the mother spent more time at a distance, and less time in close physical contact with the infant, in the 3 minutes just prior to the departure.

In a related study (Lollis, 1990), mothers were instructed to be extremely brief in separating from their infants. They were told to say only, "I'm going to leave for a little while. You stay here and play until I come back." These departures took only about 20 seconds. Another group of mothers were asked to take leave of the infants quickly, but no instructions were given about what the mothers should say. These uninstructed mothers took a bit longer but prepared the infants for the separation more thoroughly. The infants who were prepared more thoroughly fared better during the separation. Infants are more predisposed to separate

from parents if they are dropped off at a familiar day care setting or preschool, due primarily to the presence of peers already in the setting (Gunnar, Senior, & Hartup, 1984).

The best way for parents to prepare their 2-year-olds for a brief separation is to avoid close contact just before they leave, give the children some concrete suggestions about what they might do while the parents are gone, and try to tailor speech to the comprehension level of the infants. Even given this advice, and knowing that children of this age do quite well in brief separations, parents still find it difficult to leave their babies alone in a strange place with a new baby-sitter or to go out on their own for the first time. This phenomenon is called **parental separation anxiety**, which afflicts many working parents those who leave their children behind in day care (Hock & DeMeis, 1990; Jarvis & Creasey, 1991).

One additional finding should provide at least a small measure of comfort to parents or prospective parents. Researchers discovered that the infant's immediate response to the parent's departure was not correlated with anything the parent said or did. Only after this initial response, when the infant finally calmed down, did the baby's behavior begin to reflect the efforts of the parent's work at preparation (Weinraub & Lewis, 1977). Indeed, it seems common for babies of this age to protest loudly during the actual departure of the parent. As soon as it is clear that these protests are ineffective, the 2-year-old generally is capable of quieting down and even enjoying the situation.

SOCIAL AND LANGUAGE DEVELOPMENT

The period between 18 and 24 months is marked by a number of important changes in language, due in part to the child's more conceptual, sequential, and symbolic forms of cognition. First, there is a dramatic increase in the size of children's vocabulary, and second, children begin to put words into a sequence of a multiword sentence, the beginnings of syntax (grammar).

The Vocabulary Spurt

Between 12 and 18 months, new words are acquired slowly, a few per week. Sometime around 18 months, there is typically a rapid increase in vocabulary in which children begin to acquire five or more words per week. This growth of vocabulary consists primarily of object names. It is as if children discover that objects have names and become obsessed with naming things and asking for the names of things, in what has been called the *naming insight* (McShane, 1980). They may repeatedly ask "What-da?" to request object names and point to many different objects, wanting to hear the name (Camaioni, 2000).

Word learning is facilitated if the child can direct attention to the object being named by the adult (Fernald, Perfors, & Marchman, 2006). The need for attention regulation in language development is supported by research that shows activation in the prefrontal cortex, as well as the more typical language areas of the temporal cortex, during this period of language learning (Redkay et al., 2008). In addition, problems with attention regulation and word understanding can inhibit language development over time (Fernald & Marchman, 2012).

By 18 months, children have an active vocabulary of about 90 words, but by 24 months this has expanded to 320 words. A typical 6-year-old knows 14,000 words, and a high school graduate knows about 60,000. People learn nine or ten words per day between the ages of 2 and 18 years (Adamson, 1995). This means that most language is actually acquired after the infancy period.

Although nouns predominate in all languages that have been studied (Bornstein et al., 2004), children in this age period also acquire some verbs (*play, kiss*), adjectives (*hot, yucky*), and adverbs (*up, more*). They can use words to make comments on objects (*gone, dirty*) and on their own actions and feelings (*uh-oh, tired*) (E. Bates, O'Connell, & Shore, 1987). When children use a verb or an adjective, it suggests that they are referring not simply to the word itself, but to several words or things. Saying "gone," for example, implies that some object is no longer present; "hot" refers to an object that is at a high temperature.

When children under 18 months say "shoe," they may be referring to the shoe in the form of simply naming. After 18 months, they may point to the shoe and say "dirty" or "Mommy." This type of behavior could be interpreted as "the shoe is dirty" or "this is Mommy's shoe." It seems, therefore, that just before the acquisition of multiword speech, infants begin to use single words in more complex ways that suggest a subject and a predicate (E. Bates et al., 1987; Greenfield & Smith, 1976; Lock, 1980).

Multiword Speech

The main advance in language at this age is the emergence of the sentence. Correlational studies show that sentences emerge at about the same age (on the average, about 20 months) when children begin to pursue objects after multiple hidings, use tools in deliberate ways, and engage in symbolic play. This is also the age at which they can combine symbolic objects and gestures in novel ways, classify objects by sorting, and solve complex problems mentally without trial-and-error behavior (E. Bates et al., 1987; McCune-Nicolich, 1981; Piaget, 1962). Again, we can see how cognitive abilities guide language learning.

The onset of sentences with a series of words parallels the emergence of the use of a series of related gestures, or a combination of words and gestures, to communicate meaning (Acredolo & Goodwyn, 1988; Lock, 1980; Mayer & Musatti, 1992; McCune-Nicolich, 1981). An example would be pulling on the mother's skirt, lifting the arms up, looking distressed, and perhaps saying, "Mommy up." Prior to using two-word sentences, the child may combine a gesture and a word to achieve a similar meaning. Thus, seeing a sleeping bird, the child might point at the bird and say "nap." A month later, the child can say "bird nap" to mean the same thing: "the bird is taking a nap" (Iverson & Goldin-Meadow, 2005). Because gestures convey meanings in ways that are similar to words, a larger of the gestural vocabulary at 18 months predicts a larger verbal vocabulary at 42 months. A larger repertoire of word-gesture combinations at 18 months predicts sentence complexity at 42 months (Rowe & Goldin-Meadow, 2009). Gestures, however, convey and express meaning in different ways than words because they involve actions of the whole body and they can be seen rather than heard (Suanda & Namy, 2013).

In this phase, children discover they can create new meanings simply by changing *the order in which several words are spoken together*. When gestures and words first are used in intentional communication, they are a direct extension of some sensorimotor act of the child. These **idiosyncratic communication** gestures only gradually develop into **conventional communication** signs. We see a parallel

development in the realm of grammar or syntax: the first two-word combinations are idiosyncratic usages that only later become conventionalized in the form of adult syntax (see Table 10.4).

The child's first multiword utterances are not as sophisticated as adult grammar. Apparently, children first use word order to express meanings with a fairly limited set of speech patterns. These speech patterns are better thought of as **formulas** than as sentences: children seem to use a particular kind of word sequencing in which they can "fill in the blanks" to vary the meaning of the phrase. Table 10.5 gives these early formulas, along with their meanings and some examples.

Formulas similar to those found in Table 10.5 have been reported for children from six different language groups. For example, "more milk" is

TABLE 10.4   Development of Conventionalized Semantics and Syntax

Age	Semantics	Syntax
9–12 months	Sensorimotor gestures	
12–18 months	Idiosyncratic words (symbols)	
19–24 months	Conventional words (signs)	
Over 24 months		Idiosyncratic word order
		Conventional word order

Experiential Exercise

Words and Feelings
By Alan Fogel

This exercise is in the context of the amazing developmental transition around 18 months, when infants begin to use symbolic language and thought, hearing words and understanding that they each have a particular meaning, speaking words for the first time and being understood (or not, and being frustrated), and having thoughts inside their head for the first time. Yet these words still ring with feelings and continue to do so throughout childhood.

Begin with a relaxation. Lie on the floor—relax—notice breathing, heartbeat, skin, muscle tension. Notice your thoughts coming and going, words in your head.

Part I
Leader reads a list of words like the following, slowly with pauses between them and with appropriate feeling and intonation.

Notice changes in your feelings and emotions as each word is read. Let the words wash over you. Let the sounds vibrate and resonate. Notice your feelings.

Sun: Dog; Apple; Good; Down; Snow; Yes; Play; Mother; Anger (or Grrrr!); Cat; Father; Fun; Wind; Pain (or Ouch!); Water; Friend; Love; Want; Bird; Fear (or Scared); Warm; Juice; No!; River; Baby; Happy; Me; Rain; Wind; Water; Snow; Moon; No!!; Cat; Dog; Bird; Apple; Juice; Drink; Shame; Joy; Fun; Up; Down; No!!!; Rain; Mountain; Good; Relax

Part II
Leader reads a short children's story, one with many emotion words.

TABLE 10.5 Early Two-Word Combinations

Function	Formula	Example
Drawing attention to something	*see* + X *here* + X	see car here milk
Object's properties	*big/little* + X *hot* + X *old* + X	big house hot pipe old cookie
Possession	X + Y	doggy hold pig tail Kendall birthday
Plurality	*number* + X	two book
Recurrence	*more* + X *other* + X	more raisins other hand
Disappearance	*all gone* + X *all done* + X	all gone airplane all done juice
Negation	*no* + X *not* + X	no water no eat
Actor-action relations		sits doll sleeps baby Kendall break Mommy hit Kendall
Location	X + preposition	rock outside milk in there milk in cup
Request	*want* + X	want dessert want get down

Source: M. D. S. Braine, Children's first word combinations, 1976, p. 57. *Monographs of the Society for Research in Child Development, 164,* 56–57

found in Germany as "mehr Milch," in Russia as "yesche moloka," and in Finland as "lisaa kakkua" (Slobin, 1970). Similar patterns can be seen in the first word combinations of deaf children acquiring sign language. One study found combinations of hand signs that could be interpreted as "Daddy work" (Daddy is at work) and "Barry train" (referring to a brother's train) in a language-learning deaf child (Dale, 1976).

The speech examples in Table 10.5 are sometimes called **telegraphic speech**, because they tend to leave out small words such as prepositions and word endings such as *-ing*, *-s* sounds, and *-ed*, which add additional refinements to the meaning of words and sentences. Usually, simpler endings such as *-ing*, the plural *-s*, and the possessive *-'s* are

acquired first, followed by the more difficult use of the verb "to be" with all its tenses, auxiliaries, and contractions (deVilliers & deVilliers, 1973). The additional discovery of combining words increases what a child of this age can say, but it is not until the third year that children become able to speak in fluent sentences (Adamson, 1995).

Individual Differences: Two Types of Speech Style

While these syntactic refinements are taking place, children continue to develop a vocabulary. This entails increasing the number of conventional words they know how to use and refining the meanings of the words that have been overextended or used incorrectly in the past. Young children show two distinct styles of vocabulary acquisition: **referential speech** and **expressive speech**. Differences between referential and expressive word use are summed up in Table 10.6.

Some examples of expressive language are "I don't want it," "Don't do it," "I'll get it," and "I don't know where it is." These phrases have the characteristics of being spoken as a single word, because the individual words are poorly articulated. There is no evidence that the use of either of these styles of language acquisition relates to later behavior in any way. Indeed, most children use them both in different contexts; for example, in referential versus interpersonal situations (Camaioni, 2000; K. Nelson, 1981). Some studies have shown that as children get older, they tend to favor one style over another—a more social-oriented versus object-oriented approach—although the evidence is based almost entirely on a few case studies.

Children's use of one or the other style may reflect the speech spoken to them. If a caregiver responds to questions by clearly labeling objects, the child may focus more on individual words. If the caregiver uses social control language like "D'ya wanna go out" or "I dunno where it is," the child is likely to hear these as whole phrases rather than as a series of single words.

Relationship Between Language Development and the Social Environment

It is extremely rare for adults to correct children's language errors directly. What do adults actually say and do that might be conducive to the development of speech? One major trend is an increasing reliance on verbal suggestions and commands, as compared to nonverbal gestures, in the last half of the second year. When this happens, mothers tend to emphasize two basic verbal forms: requests and comments. Requests may include asking for information through "what" and "where" questions ("What's this?" "Where's the doggie?"). Mothers also request that the children speak about something ("Talk to Daddy on the telephone"; "Tell me what you saw in the park"). Comments are responses to the children's utterances or attempts to initiate a conversation ("Yes, that's an apple"; "The duck is swimming"; "This is the same car we saw the other day") (Stella-Prorok, 1983).

Similar patterns were found in a study of picture book reading (Ninio, 1983). Mothers referred to pictures using simple labeling, "what" questions ("What's that?" "What does the doggie say?"), and "where" questions ("Where's the kitty?") that elicited pointing by the children. Mothers also imitated their infants' utterances. Imitation was most likely to occur when the child made an error of pronun-

TABLE 10.6 Two Styles of Word Use in Infancy

Attribute	Referential Speech	Expressive Speech
Word Type	Object names	Social routines
Part of Speech	Nouns	Pronouns
Syntax	Single Words	Phrases
Size of Vocabulary	Large	Small
Content	Substantive	Relational
Production	Original	Imitative
Articulation	Clear	Mumbled
Situational	Referential	Interpersonal
Context	As in reading books	As in free social play

Source: K. Nelson, Individual differences in language development: Implications for development and language, 1981, p. 182. *Developmental Psychology, 17*, 170–187. Adapted with permission of Katherine Nelson.

ciation. Rather than correct the child's speech, the mother simply repeated the correct pronunciation (Bohannon & Stanowicz, 1988).

Research that measures the total amount of maternal speech provides only indirect evidence that these methods actually promote speech development, although generally mothers who talk more to their infants have infants who are more advanced linguistically (Sigman et al., 1988; Tomasello, Mannle, & Kruger, 1986). More to the point, if mothers time their verbal inputs to instances when the infants are looking at them or at an object, the infants develop higher language production scores compared to situations in which the mothers first attract the children's attention to an object and then comment on it (M. Harris, Jones, & Grant, 1985; Tomasello & Farrar, 1986; Whitehurst et al., 1988). It also helps if mothers verbally direct their infants' attention to an object before saying something about it (Flom & Pick, 2003). Clear speech to the child also helps. Children of this age seem to notice the differences between well-pronounced and mispronounced words, and between grammatical and nongrammatical speech, and will pay more attention to the former (Kedar, Casasola, & Lust, 2006; Soderstrom & Morgan, 2007; Swingley, 2007).

In general, the child develops greater linguistic competence when the adult uses speech that is more responsive to the child's focus of interest and uses the child's interest to achieve a joint focus of attention before talking (Aureli, 1994; Baldwin, 1993; Hoff-Ginsberg, 1986; M. Papousek, Papousek, & Bornstein, 1985; Yu & Smith, 2012). To the extent that maternal speech around the world shares some of the characteristics mentioned above, then it is likely to be the particular style of speaking to the child, rather than simply the amount of child-directed speech, that is the important factor.

The use of requests and comments as the primary mode of maternal speech may also be understood from the results of a study on infant imitation of adult actions during the period from 18 to 24 months (Hay, Murray, Cecire, & Nash, 1985). Infants were shown how to use a party hat as a horn or a shoe and how to use a string of beads as a telephone or a comb. The infants showed a much greater tendency to imitate adults' novel actions using these objects if the adults explained in words what they were doing ("I think you need a new shoe. Here's a pretty new shoe!"). Thus, verbal requests for action, when embedded in an action sequence, are more likely to be acted on by the child, providing more opportunities for language to be coupled with action. These studies show that children play a role in what words they choose to try out, opting for words that appear to be connected to intentional adult action. They also suggest that adults adapt their speech style to that of the children.

Guided Participation between Infants and Adults

Up until the 1960s, the parent-infant relationship was viewed as a one-way process: parental behavior affects infant behavior. This was due to the general acceptance of learning theories based on operant and classical conditioning, which view the parent as the primary socializer. In these theories, parents got all the credit for child-rearing success and all the blame for child-rearing failure. A large body of research since then has confirmed the systemic, transactional nature of the parent-infant interaction. This change in theoretical orientation toward the parent-infant relationship contributed in part to a revival in the 1970s and 1980s of the nearly forgotten work of Lev Semanovich Vygotsky (1896–1934), a Soviet educator who worked with parents and founded a number of schools.

Vygotsky suggested that all individuals are defined by the social group, and that their knowledge is an active social construction. Vygotsky found that adults do not directly socialize the child into the culture but rather follow the child's own motivations to learn. By careful observation of what the infant wants to understand, adults can introduce forms of guidance that allow the infant to realize his or her goals. Vygotsky referred to this process as the **zone of proximal development**; that is, the time during which the proximal (next) achievement in skill is about to occur but has not occurred yet (see Figure 10.1; Wertsch & Tulviste, 1992). We saw how this occurs in language development. When parents give the name of an object after their infants gaze and point to the object, the infants are more likely to learn the word. Adults who tailor their guidance to fit the child's needs for support and information in the zone of proximal development will have the most lasting impact on learning.

More broadly, with the concept of **guided participation** (Rogoff, 1990), children set the agenda for what they want to do and how much they want to be involved. The more skilled partner collaborates in the child's goals by giving the child responsibility for certain actions that are part of the larger task but within the range of the child's competence. In this first phase, the parental role is to establish coordinated joint attention beginning from the child's initiatives. The adult must also constrain the child's participation for the sake of the child's or others' safety or rights. Eventually, the adult transfers responsibility for larger segments of the task to the child, in relation to

the growth of the child's competence as assessed by the adult (Bodle, Zhou, Shore, & Dixon, 1996; Bruner, 1983; Heckhausen, 1988; Kaye, 1982; Lock, 1980; Raver, 1996; Rogoff, 1990). These points are summarized in Table 10.7.

There are cultural differences in styles of guided participation. In one study (Rogoff, Mistry, Goncu, & Mosier, 1993), mothers from the United States were compared with Maya Indian mothers from Guatemala on how they helped their 20-month-old children use a set of nesting dolls. The U.S. mothers acted more like peers, wanting to take turns in combining dolls and commenting on the process. These mothers took seriously their role as teacher. The Maya mothers retained more of an adult-child status differential. They assumed the children would eventually acquire the ability to do the task. They monitored the children's progress and gave verbal instructions, but they did not get very involved in the task.

One United States mother tried to play games with the dolls, then offered them to the child for "his turn." She gave instructions ("Put the lid on") and then cheered when the child did this ("Yeah!

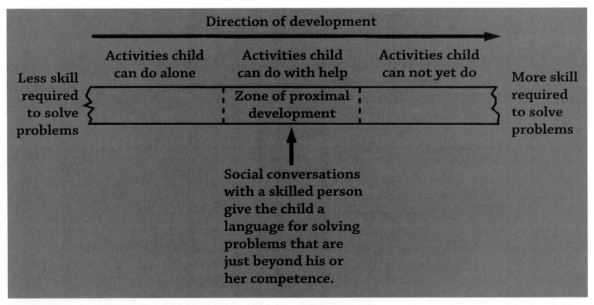

Figure 10.1 Vygotsky's Concept of the Zone of Proximal Development

TABLE 10.7   Components of Guided Participation Between Adults and Young Children

Child sets the agenda according to interest and skill level

Adult adjusts level of child's participation according to child's skill

Adult constrains child's participation for the safety and rights of others

Adult transfers responsibility to child according to on-going assessment of child's abilities

Source: Adapted from B. Rogoff, *Apprenticship in thinking: Cognitive development in social context*, 1990. New York: Oxford University Press.

You're so smaaart!"). This mother tried to change the agenda when she judged that the baby's attention waned. She commented on all the child's actions and made requests for actions throughout the task.

A typical Maya mother demonstrated how the dolls come apart and go back together, using a few words to encourage the child to look. The baby wanted to handle the doll, but soon after, the mother took it back and again demonstrated how to do it. She pointed out the features of the task verbally as she performed the action. After that, she let the infant try for some time on his own, while she watched but did not intervene. When he ran into trouble, the mother would say something to help ("Do this one first"). When the child made

a successful move, the mother would simply say "Okay" or "I see" in a quiet tone.

Both of these cases illustrate the general principles of guided participation listed in Table 10.7, but they differ markedly from each other. Similar differences in levels of involvement have been observed between American and North African mothers with infants of this age (Guillain et al., 1998). American mothers were more actively involved than those in North Africa, but both practiced guided participation.

The important idea is that when adults become collaborators or participants in what children spontaneously seem interested in doing, children can achieve higher levels of language play and cognitive development compared to when adults do not become involved. (O'Connell & Bretherton,

Picture-book reading is a particularly good setting for guided participation in language development.
Photo: Emily Waterfield

1984; Slade, 1987a; Zukow, 1980). Particular types of adult involvement, however, are more effective in promoting higher cognitive levels in the development of symbolic play.

The establishment of coordinated joint attention with children of this age is less likely to occur if mothers are depressed or have a low sense of self-efficacy (D. F. Goldsmith & Rogoff, 1997; Teti, O'Connell, & Reiner, 1996). Parents who understand the relationship between play and development and who engage the child in higher levels of symbolic play are more likely to encourage the child's participation at a higher level of performance (Bornstein et al., 1999; Damast, Tamis-LeMonda, & Bornstein, 1996). Children develop higher levels of symbolic play when their mothers give more options that stimulate the child's creativity. If a child tries to put a doll into a toy cup, an options-limiting maternal response might be, "No, dolls don't go like that. We play with dolls in the dollhouse." An options-promoting reply might be, "Is the doll going swimming in the cup? Maybe she would like to have some lemonade in the dollhouse when she's done?"

Remarkably, the same process of guided participation that helps human infants acquire language also occurs when baby chimpanzees and baby bonobos are taught to use signs in the company of human adults. Chimpanzees and bonobos, along with gorillas, are great apes and our closest primate relatives. Compared to animals who are raised by their own mothers, chimpanzees and bonobos who are raised with human adults acquire signs in ways similar to that in which human infants acquire verbal and gestural language, at least up until the age of 2 years (Savage-Rumbaugh et al., 1993; Tomasello, Savage-Rumbaugh, & Kruger, 1993). There is no evidence that nonhumans can acquire grammar, outside of a few simple formulas.

Aside from cultural differences in guided participation and development, there are also individual differences. More explicit instructions (compared to sharing and mutuality) are given to children who are temperamentally difficult or who show attachment problems; such instructions are also more likely to be used by fathers than by mothers (Fagot & Kavanagh, 1993; Marcos, 1995). Sharing and mutuality also vary depending upon the task or situation.

In particular, instances of parent-infant pretend play evoke relatively more sharing than instances in which the child is trying to or is expected to learn something (Nishida & Lillard, 2007). Pretending can be used just for fun as parent and child together create pretend scenarios, such as going for a ride in the car (using the couch as the car), playing house (using a cardboard box as the house), or reversing roles (the mother becomes the child and vice versa). Pretending can also be used to metacommunicate about more serious conflicts or disagreements. Mothers may engage in pretend play to give the child something to do, to redirect an otherwise undesirable activity, or to make light of a negative emotion (Farver & Howes, 1993; Haight, Masiello, Dickson, Huckeby, & Black, 1994; Haight & Miller, 1992). Pretend play is more likely to be used for guidance, such as teaching proper conduct, in Taiwanese than in North American families. The North American families were more likely to use pretend play for fun and fantasy games (Haight, Wang, Fung, Williams, & Mintz, 1999).

The Development of Discipline and Compliance

As it turns out, these basic principles of guided participation and collaboration in infants' activities are the foundation for effective discipline of children at this age. These principles include adjusting one's actions to the child's agenda and providing clarity about adult guidelines and standards (T. Gordon, 1988; Rocissano, Slade, & Lynch, 1987). Research suggests that in Western cultures the most effective forms of parental discipline combine empathy and firmness. Caregivers should be sensitive to the reasons for the child's behavior and to the natural negative reactions children are likely to have when restrictions are imposed.

The most successful discipliners make firm demands and are appropriately expressive of their own angry or distressed reactions to the child's behavior rather than using power as a means of controlling the child. These kinds of parents, whose style is called **authoritative parenting** (Baumrind, 1973), have children who show purposive, independent behavior, are cooperative with adults, show friendliness to peers, and are more likely to imitate their mothers; they are also more likely to become upset when they have violated standards of conduct (Kochanska, Forman, & Coy, 1999; Spinrad et al., 2007).

First, it is important to get the child's attention; second, it helps if the child is already starting to do what is wanted. In other words, parents can make their children look more compliant than they actually are by timing their requests for compliance to coincide with a behavior of the child that was most likely to lead to the desired response (Deák et al., 2008). If a baby is playing, for example, and you want to do something else, such as go out, give her a bath, or feed her dinner, one approach is to sit down on the floor next to the baby and start playing along with her. The parent might become part of the baby's play for only a few minutes to maneuver the game to a logical conclusion. For example, the parent might pick up the ball the baby is playing with, roll it back and forth with the baby a few times, tap it playfully on her stomach and nose, and then pick up the baby with a tickle and carry her to the dinner table or bathtub. In this way a parent can skillfully change the baby's goals without causing a confrontation.

The importance of these recommendations was confirmed in a study by G. W. Holden (1983). Unobtrusive observations were made of 24 middle-class mothers and their 2-year-old infants in the supermarket. What were mothers' strategies in dealing with undesired behavior, such as asking for food, reaching for things, standing in the cart, and ignoring the mothers' requests? One group of mothers used *contingent responses*; that is, they scolded or reprimanded the infant after the transgression had occurred. The other group of mothers used *preventive responses*, such as talking to the child while shopping and giving the child something to eat. The children of the mothers who used preventive measures showed fewer instances of undesired behavior. Preventive measures fall under the heading of **parental proactive behavior**, including any action that has the goal of a positive outcome for the child. Table 10.8 lists some examples of proactive behavior used by adults.

Finally, it is worth noting that even though infants of this age want to try things out for themselves and often resist parental requests that directly interfere with their own actions, the infants also have a strong desire to be part of the social group and to join in with whatever adults might be doing. Infants are attracted to objects that adults are handling and want to do the same, and they seem to think that most household tasks the adult is doing are fun and want to join in (Hay, Murray,

TABLE 10.8   Examples of Parental Proactive Behavior

Type	Short Term	Long Term
Direct	Occupy with activities. Divert attention. Engage child in game. Prepare verbally for upcoming situations. Set limits in advance. Monitor child's action when danger is present.	Take child on an outing. Train child to be wary of dangers. Organize peer groups. Select a day care center.
Indirect	Place child in car seat. Dress child appropriately for weather. Use night light. Serve appropriate foods.	Buy a home in a neighborhood conducive to child's development. Build a fence to keep child from danger. Keep poisons locked up. Purchase safe toys and furniture.

Source: G. W. Holden, How parents create a social environment via proactive behavior, 1985, p. 130. In T. Garling & J. Valsiner (Eds.), *Children within environments: Towards a psychology of accident prevention*, 116–142. New York: Plenum Press

Cecire, & Nash, 1985; Rheingold, Cook, & Kolowitz, 1987). Rather than ignoring or complaining about the children being nuisances for interfering, adults can encourage the children's collaboration by giving them small tasks. This requires the adults to slow down and think about how best to include the children's efforts (Rogoff, 1990).

These adult forms of guidance, however, only work at this age because infants are developing more self-control. In one study, an experimenter placed an attractive toy on the table while talking with a child. The experimenter then told the child that she (the experimenter) had to go out of the room to get something and asked the child to please wait and not to touch the toy. By age 2 years, children could wait on average for a full minute before being tempted to touch the toy, a long time for a 2-year-old (Vaughn, Kopp, & Krakow, 1984). Compliance is more easily assured if infants are shown how their behavior affects others. For this to happen, verbal skills are necessary, and indeed, compliance with requests is correlated with verbal development and with parents using simple language that the child can understand (Hakman & Sullivan, 2009; Kaler & Kopp, 1990; Schneider-Rosen & Wenz-Gross, 1990; Vaughn, Kopp, & Krakow, 1984).

Some parents, however, use more **authoritarian** styles including coercive and controlling techniques. One research study examined 69 families with their firstborn sons when they were 15 and 21 months old. Some of the families at each age were identified as "troubled." The parents in these families used control as the primary disciplinary method and were unlikely to use guided participation and authoritative parenting; the children in these families showed the most defiance and the most negative emotion. The more troubled families included men who showed more negative attitudes and were less social and less friendly than men in nontroubled families. Both mothers and fathers in such families, however, were more likely to use control techniques in place of guidance and authoritative approaches (Belsky, Woodworth, & Crnic, 1996). In general, fathers play a greater role in discipline and play as children become verbal, and fathers who

are rated as more sensitive and involved with their children have children who are more socially competent and less defiant in both Caucasian American and African American families with toddlers (M. M. Black & Krishnakumar, 1998; Kelley, Smith, Green, Berndt, & Rogers, 1998). Teenage mothers tend to be more coercive and tend to infer more anger and defiance in the emotion expressions of infants (Strassberg & Treboux, 2000). A vicious cycle can develop so that harsh parenting creates defiance and negativity, which in turn sparks harsh parenting (Scaramella & Leve, 2004).

One form of coercive parental behavior is **corporal punishment**, such as spanking, defined as using physical force that causes pain to the child but not injury. One investigation on corporal punishment summarized the results of 88 different studies with a total of 36,309 children. Children who had experienced corporal punishment in the early years were more likely to show poor self-control, have a poor relationship with their parents throughout childhood, show more behavioral problems and aggression, more depression, show more criminal or antisocial behavior as teens, and abuse their own children or spouse in adulthood (Berlin et al., 2009; Gershoff, 2002; Maguire-Jack et al., 2012). On the other hand, parents who resort to coercive and corporal punishment methods are themselves troubled, having a history of depression, low self-efficacy, and higher levels of stress. It could be that these factors also account for some of the observed outcomes of coercive parenting (MacKenzie et al., 2012; Pelaez et al., 2008; Pierce et al., 2010).

These results, although powerful, do not say that all children who experience corporal punishment will using this style of discipline with their own children. Some parents and psychologists suggest that occasional spanking may be used in serious offenses, such as running out into the street, especially if the spanking is later accompanied by authoritative style explanations, recognition of the child's feelings, and expressions of love. There are also cultural differences. In Caucasian American families, children who were spanked were at 5 times greater risk for later behavior problems

Case Report:
Discipline

In this case report, a person who had received harsh and coercive parenting from her mother is beginning to learn that she has the capability to relate to others in a more loving and open way.

In terms of parenting styles, the authoritarian parent is demanding, but unresponsive to the child, tends to use punitive and harsh punishment, physical enforcement, reprimands, and prohibitive interventions. An authoritative parent is sensitive to the child's needs, does not use punitive discipline, and reasons with the child in a loving and affectionate manner.

My mother told me that when I was born, she wanted the perfect child. Being the first born, everyone gave me everything! I was always with my mom and I didn't really like being with my dad since he was never around. I started to talk at seven months and my mother would yell at me if I said a word wrong. She said that the last thing she wanted was a girl that couldn't talk right. If I started to cry then she would yell at me some more, then turn around, and leave me alone. Every time I cried I would be yelled at, this was because my mother did not want your "typical" little girl that cries about everything and that talks as if she has her nose plugged. I grew up always knowing that crying was bad and that if I did cry my mother was never going to comfort me.

She also mentioned that she has noticed that I was not allowed to cry, to talk wrong, to play with dolls, or to want to just hang on to her. Her attitude towards me has made me unforgiving, cold, and many times, I seem to have no consideration for the feelings of others. She taught me that in this world it is all about "me, me, me." I am currently learning to move away from this idea but it's really hard. I hate the way she is and I realize that every day I am more like her. The attachment I have with her is not really strong. I love her because she's my mother but other than that, nope. I don't understand her, I don't agree with her on anything.

Since then, my father has been my best friend. He would cry, laugh, goof around, and he did so many others things that I always wanted to do but could never do them because of my mother. Now I say that I am securely attached to my father who has taught me to see things in a new way. I am learning to cry, I am learning to show others that I care and that it is OK to do so. I am learning to accept myself and to love myself. It has been great to learn all of these things.

but for African American and Hispanic American families, spanking had no relationship to child outcome (Slade & Wissow, 2004; Stacks et al., 2009). In the latter two ethnic groups, spanking is viewed as a normal parental behavior and is rarely done impulsively or in anger. In general, parents are encouraged to focus on praise for good behavior, proactive parenting, respect for the child's own point of view, and use of milder sanctions, such as time out, when possible.

Another thing to consider is that toddler defiance is not necessarily a bad thing. It is often a way for children to express their feelings, to assert their budding self-awareness, and to experiment with taking initiative and taking charge. Toddlers are more likely to show negative behavior if their parents do not respond to their bids for help or attention (Ekas et al., 2011). These are all important developmental achievements (Dix et al., 2007). On the other hand, only about 12 percent of toddlers show frequent or severe oppositional and defiant behavior. This kind of defiance that is aggressive or violent is typically a sign of an emerging vicious cycle of parental coercion and increased child aggression (Baillargeon et al., 2011; Brook et al., 2001; Calkins, 2002).

Self-Awareness: The Sense of an Existential Self

From early in the first year, infants can differentiate their own feelings and movements from those of others, and they can distinguish their own acts relative to the environment. This is called the

ecological self (see Chapter 6). Beginning at 9 months, infants have a sense of their own subjectivity, the **subjective self**, but they do not yet have a concept of "I."

With the advent of script-based conceptual memory, infants are now able to categorize and remember sequences of events that are most familiar to them. Among such sequences are the actions performed and the feelings experienced by the children themselves. Because of script-based memory, the infant at 18 months is beginning to put all of these self-experiences together into a whole picture of himself or herself as someone who can be recognized and distinguished from other people.

One method that has been developed to study this change in self-awareness is to observe infants' reactions to their own mirror images (M. Lewis & Brooks-Gunn, 1979). Initially, infants are put in front of the mirror for a few minutes. Even young infants will show interest in the mirror image, touching the mirror or parts of themselves, smiling and showing other emotions. After this period of free play with the mirror, the experimenter removes the infants and pretends to wipe their faces with a cloth. In actuality, the experimenter dabs a bit of red rouge on the infants' noses with-

out the babies realizing it. Then, the babies are returned to the mirror. If the infants recognize that the mirror image is of themselves, they will touch their own noses, but not the mirror image nose. By 24 months, the majority of children will touch their own noses after seeing the red spot. Table 10.9 describes the steps in the infant's development of self-recognition. The sense of self that accompanies this ability for self-recognition in a mirror is called the **existential self**.

Beginning at 18 months, the infants can say things like "I cry" or "I tired," indicating that not only does the child have the subjective sense of one who gets tired, but he or she can also combine that with a pronoun indicating a person who has or *possesses* that feeling. The growth of the prefrontal cortex, associated with self-monitoring and self-regulation, along with increased maturation in the parietal cortext (related to body schema awareness, Chapter 4) underlie these developments (Frith & Frith, 2001; Lewis & Carmody, 2008).

Children's earliest linguistic references to the self are with the personal pronoun *I* rather than words like *me*, *mine*,or *my*. When using *I*, children express their intended actions ("I do it," "I hold it"), make requests or proposals ("I wanna play with that one"), or state a proposition ("I have the crayon"). They rarely use the word *you* (Imbens-Bailey & Pan, 1998). Typically, use of personal pronouns—especially those indicating *possession* (Mine!)—begins around the same time or a little bit after mirror self-recognition (Courage, Edison, & Howe, 2004; Lewis & Ramsay, 2004).

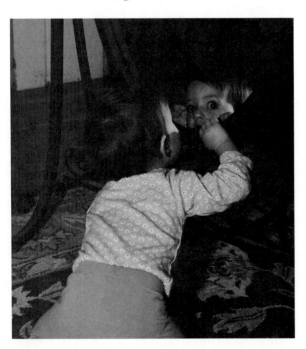

By eighteen months, most babies can recognize their own image in a mirror.
Photo by Emily Waterfield

TABLE 10.9 Stages in the Development of the Existential Self, the Ability to Recognize the Physical Features of the Self

Behaviors	Approximage Age in Months	Interpretation
Emergence of Self as Subject, as Active, Independent, Causal Agent		
I. Interest in mirror image; regards, approaches, touches, smiles, vocalizes. Does not differentially respond to self versus Other in mirror, videotape, or pictorial representation.	5–8	No evidence that self is perceived as a causal agent, independent of others. No featural differentiation between self and other.
II. Understands nature of reflective surface; contingency play, imitation, rhythmic movements, bounding, waving; can locate objects in space, attached to body. Differentiates between contingent and noncontingent videotape representations of self.	9–12	Active agent in space emerges, awareness of cause-effect relationship between own body movements and moving visual image.
III. Uses mirror to locate people/objects in space. Reaches toward person, not image, and reaches toward object not attached to body. Distinguishes between self-movement and movement of others on videotape.	12–15	Self-other differentiation with regard to agency. Appreciates self as an active, independent agent separate from others, who can also cause his or her own movements in space.
Emergence of Self as an Object of One's Knowledge		
IV. In mirror and videotape, demonstrates mark-directed behavior. Sees image and touches rouge on nose. Points to self. Distinguishes between self and other in pictorial representation and videotape.	15–18	Featural recognition of self; internal schema for own face that can be compared to external visual image.
V. Verbal labeling: infant can state name, attach appropriate personal pronoun to own image in mirror. Can distinguish self from same-gender infant in pictures and can label self.	18–24	Appreciation that one has unique featural attributes that can be verbally labeled as the self.

Source: S. Harter, Developmental perspectives on the self-system, 1983, p. 283. In E. M. Hetherington (Ed.), *Handbook of child psychology: Socialization, personality, and social development* (Vol. 4), pp. 265–290. New York: Wiley. Reprinted by permission of John Wiley & Sons, Inc.

In this study (Pipp, Fischer, & Jennings, 1987), infants were given the standard rouge test on themselves and also on their mothers. A number of different self and other recognition tasks were given to the children as well (see Table 10.10). (As an aside, these tasks are great fun to do with babies of this age and would work as exercises for co-regulating with baby.) In addition to these recognition tasks, infants were asked to perform actions either on a doll, on themselves, or on their mothers. An example would be pretend feeding the doll or self or pretend feeding the mother.

The results show that before 18 months, infants are able to correctly recognize their mothers and respond correctly to questions about mother at earlier ages than those at which they can recognize and respond to questions about themselves. This is consistent with studies of concept development done in the first year: infants are able to recognize the common features of objects and

TABLE 10.10   Self- and Other Physical Feature Recognition Tasks

Infant Version	Mother Version
Infant touches own nose with rouge after seeing self in mirror.	Infant touches mother's nose with rouge after seeing mother in mirror.
"Where's [child's name]?"	"Where's Mommy?"
"Who's that?" (said while pointing to child).	"Who's that?" (said while pointing to mother).
"Whose shoe is that?" (said while pointing to child's shoe).	"Whose shoe is that?" (said while pointing to mother's shoe).
"Are you a boy or a girl?"	"Is Mommy a boy or a girl?"

Source: S. Pipp, K. W. Fischer, & S. Jennings., Acquisition of self- and mother knowledge in infancy, 1986, p. 90. *Developmental Psychology, 23,* 86–96.

Experiential Exercise

Mirror Self-Recognition
by Alan Fogel

The purpose of this exercise is to evoke the experience of seeing oneself in a mirror for the very first time, and thus to re-create some of the feelings of a toddler finding the "existential self" during the "rouge" test: the sense of otherness or foreignness of the mirror image, sense of shame or pride, etc. Because we adults all have extensive experience with mirrors, the exercise relies on using a mirror to observe one's own face in unusual ways and with more scrutiny than is typical for most people.

Students should bring to class a small hand-held mirror. Students sit comfortably with a mirror and something on which to write. Notes are made following each step of the exercise. A brief relaxation exercise may be done before starting.

1. Please look at your face in the mirror. Take as much time as you need. Look especially at parts of your face that you don't typically notice or see. As you study your face, remain aware of your sensations and emotions. Possible emotions may be curiosity, disgust, embarrassment, a sense of unfamiliarity, or enjoyment. Also remain aware of your body sensations as you do this. Notice the parts of your face that you like and the parts that you do not like. Write down your experience and then close your eyes and rest. (2 to 3 minutes)

2. Sometimes each eye has its own point of view. With your eyes closed notice whether there are differences in how each eye feels. Open your eyes and this time, cover one of your eyes with a piece of folded paper. Again, examine your face and notice your feelings and sensations. Ask yourself: Who is this person? Do I know this person? Do I like this person? Write down your experience, and then close your eyes and rest. (2 to 3 minutes)

3. With your eyes closed, consider the possibility that the other eye may see yourself differently than the one you just looked through. Cover your other eye. Repeat the looking with the same questions as for the first eye. Take a minute to compare the views of yourself with each eye. Write, rest. (2 to 3 minutes)

4. It has been said that the eyes are the windows to the soul. This time look directly into one of your eyes and examine it and your feelings about that eye. Finally, look directly into the other eye and repeat what you just did. Compare your views of each eye. Write down your experience, and then close your eyes and rest. (2 to 3 minutes).

---

group them into categories. Before 18 months, on the other hand, infants are more successful at performing actions on themselves or the doll than on the mother. After 18 months, infants were equally adept at describing self and mother.

Other research finds that children's awareness of their bodies with regard to the environment also changes at this age. Children aged 15, 18, and 21 months were asked to do things like put on clothing that was too small, pass through openings that were too narrow, or pick up a mat on which they were sitting or standing. The older children were better at judging their own size and weight and did not try to do the tasks that did not fit their body size (Brownell, Zerwas, & Ramani, 2007; Moore et al., 2007). Children who had passed the mirror self-recognition test were better at adjusting their own body to the demands of a motor coordination task (Moore et al., 2007).

In the previous age period, infants preferred to imitate intentional rather than mechanical actions of adults. After 18 months, infants are also beginning to reason about other people's desires. In one study, 14- and 18-month-old infants watched while adults ate either crackers or broccoli. For some babies at each age, the adult said "Mmm," making a happy expression, when eating the crackers, and "Eeew," making a disgusted expression, when eating the broccoli. For other infants, the adult acted as if she liked the broccoli but not the crackers. The adult then asked the infants to offer her one or the other type of food. Fourteen-month-olds offered the adult only crackers, assuming that the adult would like what the child liked, regardless of the adult's expressed preferences. The 18-month-olds, on the other hand, offered whichever food the adult seemed to prefer. This means the older infants were beginning to be aware of the psychological desires of the adult and respond appropriately (Repacholi & Gopnik, 1997). These older babies realized that their own preferences were not necessarily the same as the adult's, a major advance in distinguishing between the internal experiences of self and other.

Infants of this age have a growing sense of the other and the self-with-other. With familiar partners, children of this age will point to things that have they have shared in the past with that partner, indicating a growing sense of "we" in which partners have a shared history (Liebal et al., 2010). Infants of this age will show more sharing and helping behavior if they perceive the adult to be in need of help (Brownell et al., 2009; 2013; Dunfield et al., 2011).

Infants differ in their level of self and other understanding, however. Some infants are better at the task of self and other recognition. These infants notice more details and can respond with more complex answers to the questions in Table 10.10. These more self-and other-aware infants are more securely attached to their mothers and fathers, show more concern for other's distress, can coordinate mirror image imitation, and are more competent in peer play (Asendorpf & Baudonniere, 1993; Asendorpf, Warkentin, & Baudonniere, 1996; Pipp, Easterbrooks, & Brown, 1993; Pipp, Easterbrooks, & Harmon, 1992; Zahn-Waxler, Radke-Yarrow, Wagner, & Chapman, 1992). These studies suggest that positive social relationships are likely to enhance one's understanding of oneself and one's relationships to others.

Other research shows that children who reacted with greater distress to inoculations and who had higher levels of the stress hormone cortisol (see Chapter 5) during the first year of life were more likely to be able to recognize themselves in the mirror at 18 months than infants with who reacted with less distress during the first year. This finding suggests that infants who are more sensitive to their internal experiences are more likely to be aware of themselves at this age (M. Lewis & Ramsey, 1997). Interestingly, insecurely attached children, who are also more likely to have higher cortisol responses, use different language to describe themselves compared to securely attached children. The insecure children at this age are more likely to talk about their own negative, as compared to positive, feelings (Lemche et al., 2007).

Babies of this age become aware that they are being watched. This must be a rather startling discovery for a baby, as the following example may illustrate. Think of some ways that you express yourself privately, ways you have not shown to anyone or even talked about with anyone, like singing in the shower, writing poetry, or drawing pictures. You are probably perfectly happy doing these things alone and you can feel yourself, your mind and body, as you do them. This is your subjective self coming out. Now imagine that someone overhears you, or finds your poems and reads them, or sees your drawings. Your privacy has been invaded and you would most likely be embarrassed. This is the voice of your existential self waking up to the fact that you can be exposed when you least expect it.

On the positive side, this brings an increased awareness of other people and of membership in a community. The developmental challenge for infants of this age, then, is to open up to the pleasures (pride, mastery, sharing) and pains (shame, defiance, having to comply) of being an active member of a community. This is not easy to do, and in fact, it is a lifelong issue that only *begins* at 18 months.

Infantile Autism: A Disturbance of Self and Relationships

As we discussed above, some children are slower to develop an existential self than others, but they still fall into the range of typical development. A small group of children, however, fail to develop an existential self: children who are diagnosed with **autism spectrum disorder (ASD)**. ASD is a range of related developmental disorders with symptoms that may include impaired ability to interact socially, speech and language deficits, sensory sensitivities, and unusual movements of the body. About two to four times as many males as females are diagnosed with autism spectrum disorders (ASD). This range of disorders related to autism has increased in its incidence in the past ten years. In the 1990s, ASD occurred in about 1 in 1,000 individuals (Ozonoff and South, 2001) while in 2010 it was estimated to occur in about 1 in 110. This increase is not due solely to better diagnoses but rather to possible genetic and environmental causes (Baird et al., 2006; Lord & Bishop, 2010; Newschaffer et al., 2007; Rutter, 2005) which are not fully understood.

Heredity is one known cause. The rate of autism in infant siblings is much higher than in the general population, 1 in 20 compared to 1 in 110, and male siblings are three times as likely to be affected as females (Ozonoff et al., 2011). Another potential cause of autism is the advanced age of the father. With parenting occurring at older ages and the possibility of genetic mutations

in sperm cells with increased age (Chapter 3), this is one possible explanation for the rise in autism diagnosis. Autism is also associated with low birth weight (although not all low birth weight infants will become autistic), deficiency of maternal folic acid at the time of conception, the pregnant mother's exposure to pesticides and air pollution, and her obesity (Glicksman, 2012).

Autistic children have a difficult time establishing coordinated joint attention with others, and therefore they are not able to enter into early forms of intersubjectivity by which typically developing infants acquire an understanding about relationships, self, and others. Autistic children typically do not use social referencing or affective sharing, do not respond appropriately to the desires or distress of others, are less distressed at separation from mothers, are less likely to imitate others, do not pretend, and are unlikely to initiate social interaction. When they talk, it is typically in monologues, and they have a difficult time letting others contribute to the conversation. They are more likely to focus on the physical-perceptual features of faces and speech rather than the social-emotional aspects, suggesting a preference for lateral, as opposed to medial prefrontal processing (Chapter 4; Järvinen-Paley et al., 2008; Klin & Jones, 2008)

By the time typically developing infants are 18 months old, they have established a sense of an existential self and other. It is quite likely that many autistic children never develop this ability. Children diagnosed with autism do not show embarrassment in front of a mirror or when getting a photo taken, and they do not seem to have a sense of guilt, suggesting that they cannot see themselves in the eyes of others. Autistic children are less likely to use personal pronouns or to refer to themselves in conversations (Carpenter, Tomasello, & Striano, 2005; Charman et al., 1997; Hobson, 1993; Hobson & Mayer, 2005; Hobson et al., 2006; Ozonoff & South, 2001; Sigman & Kasari, 1995; Sigman & Ruskin, 1999; Trevarthen, Aitken, Papoudi, & Robarts, 1998).

On the other hand, autistic children can develop secure attachments with their mothers (Ozonoff & South, 2001), although autistic children are more likely than nonautistic to show disorganized patterns of attachment even with parents rated as sensitive (van Ijsendoorn et al., 2007). They can use pointing and requesting gestures to ask for what they want, even though they may have a difficult time in establishing coordinated joint attention (Camaioni, Perucchini, Muratori, & Milone, 1997). They can also be more advanced in some perceptual and object-related skills. They can imitate object-related tasks better than typically developing children but have a difficult time imitating facial expressions, vocalizations, and social movements.

Compared to children who are either hearing impaired, language impaired, or mentally retarded, or who have no disorders, 3- to 6-year-old autistic children are less likely to be able to perform motor imitation—such as imitating stirring a cup with a spoon, talking on a toy telephone, giving a drink to a toy animal, touching their nose, or raising an arm. Autistic children's play is less likely to be symbolic and more likely to be aggressive or self-stimulatory, and they are less likely to approach peers to initiate social play. Finally, autistic children are more likely to use toys in ways different from their appropriate functions, such as banging a toy telephone rather than pretending to talk (Heimann, Ullstadius, Dahlgren, & Gillberg, 1992; Sigman & Ruskin, 1999; W. L. Stone, Lemanek, Fishel, Fernandez, & Altemeier, 1990). On the other hand, they can acquire pretend play when adults use guided participation strategies.

One of the more unusual features of a small number of autistic children is that they may be exceptional in one specific area. Some autistic children can solve remarkably complicated mathematical calculations in their heads much faster than someone with a calculator can do it. Some are gifted artists but draw only one subject, such as public buildings and monuments. Some have specialized knowledge in an odd area such as plumbing fixtures or animal classifications. It is important to remember, however, that autism covers a wide spectrum of symptoms, and only a few autistic individuals will have these abilities.

Intense interests such as these have been found in about one-third of normally developing children. Examples of such interests include trains, vehicles, dinosaurs, dressing up, blenders, tea sets, tools, puzzles, balls, fictional characters, and airplanes. In some unusual cases, children may be intensely interested in bodies and injuries, United States presidents, pouring liquids, and brooms. While these interests are normal, they have a striking similarity to autism symptoms in two respects: the age of onset is 18 months, and they are shown predominantly by boys (DeLoache, Simcock & Macari, 2007). This suggests that autistic children may pick up on a normal developmental process but carry it to an extreme of preoccupation and expertise.

Autism is very difficult to treat. In the most severe cases, individuals may remain institutionalized all their life. Others with high-functioning autistism, or Asperger syndrome, have been able to hold jobs and create a life for themselves. One autistic adult, Temple Grandin, has become a well-known agricultural engineer and has written her autobiography as well as a book about the feelings and experiences of animals based on her experiences as an autistic person (Grandin, 2005; Grandin & Scariano, 1986). Another autistic adult, Donna Williams, has also written a series of books about her life (Williams, 1999), which was marked with abuse and neglect in addition to autism. The prognosis for many autistic children, however, is that they will change little and acquire only minimal social skills (limited receptiveness to others, socialization to rules) and self-care (Harty, 1990; Lelorde, Barthelemy, Martineau, & Bruneau, 1991).

Is Early Diagnosis of Autism Possible?

Autism is believed to have its origins in early infancy and possibly prenatal development. It is known to be associated with some genetic and chromosomal abnormalities and may result from brain and other physiological problems that emerge during early development. These include abnormalities in the face and language processing areas of the brain, limbic system, the auditory region of the brain stem, and myelin pathologies. Children with autism have impairments in the limbic areas of the brain—the amygdala—responsible for regulating fear, suggesting that some of their behavior may be withdrawal from an environment perceived as threatening. Some evidence suggests that the genes responsible for regulating the growth rate of the brain may be impaired, resulting in too rapid brain cell growth, followed by insufficient pruning of unused cells and lower rates of connectivity and synaptogenesis (Courchesne, 2004; Dawson et al., 2004; Herault, Martineau, Petit, & Perrot, 1994; Kemper & Bauman, 1993; Lewis & Elman, 2008; Singh, Warren, Odell, Warren, & Cole, 1993; Trevarthen et al., 1998; Webb et al., 2011; Wolff et al., 2011; Wong & Wong, 1991).

Even though autism originates in early infancy, it typically is not diagnosed until children are between 4 and 5 years of age. One reason for this is that the symptoms change with age and may overlap with other problems, such as hearing and speech disorders. If autism could be diagnosed earlier, preventive and more successful treatments might be possible. Recently, some breakthroughs in the early diagnosis of autism have occurred.

One methodology used by the researchers looking for early signs of autism is *retrospective*. This involves comparing autistic children, diagnosed at age 4 or 5 years, with nonautistic children. The researchers search for older records of these children's development before the age at which they were diagnosed. Past medical records, parent interviews and reports, home videos of children's first-year birthday parties, and various other records have all been searched for data, although these data sources are not always reliable.

An alternative approach is to do *prospective random sample* research on a large population of infants, assess them on a few chosen criteria, and then determine whether they later develop autism. This approach requires very large samples (to find 10 autistic children, the study would need at least 1000 infants). A final, and more promising, approach is to gather data *prospectively on high risk infant siblings* of children who had been conclusively diagnosed with autism. The infant siblings of children diagnosed with autism form a high risk group—who have a much higher probability of autism than the general

population—and a comparison group of infants with older siblings who have never been diagnosed with autism form a low risk group.

Prospective random sampling and retrospective data show that by the age of 18 months, there are clear signs of difference between typically developing and autistic children. One study discovered four behaviors that, if they occurred together in the same 1-year-old child, led to a correct classification of these children as later diagnosed with autism. These behaviors were lack of pointing, of showing objects, of looking at others, and of orienting to their name. Another study found that children with two or more of the following symptoms at 18 months were most likely to be diagnosed as autistic at 30 months: lack of pretend play, lack of pointing, lack of interest in social relationships, absence of social play, and inability to establish joint attention with the caregiver. Specialists recommend that an 18-month-old who shows this combination of symptoms be referred to a specialist in autistic assessment for possible diagnosis and treatment (Adrien et al., 1993; Baron-Cohen, Allen, & Gillberg, 1992; Baron-Cohen et al., 1996; Osterling & Dawson, 1994; Rogers & DiLalla, 1990). There is now a website for parents that gives simple screening checklists and other materials, which is intended to help parents decide whether their child should be referred for diagnosis: www.autismspeaks.org/what-autism/diagnosis/screen-your-child.

If autism could be diagnosed before 18 months, there is hope that early interventions could be more effective than ones occurring after 3 or 4 years of age. This is because the brain grows rapidly in the first two years in an experience-dependent manner. One retrospective study has discovered abnormal movement patterns between 4 and 6 months of age that are presumed to distinguish autistic from typically developing infants (Teitelbaum et al., 1998). The authors studied the home videos of 17 infants who had been diagnosed with autism when they were 3 years old and compared them with home videos of typically developing 4- to 6-month-old infants. When rolling over, for example, typically developing infants turn their pelvis to one side, followed by the trunk, and then the head. Later they lead with the head, followed by the trunk and pelvis. Three of the babies later diagnosed with autism turned over by lying on their sides and, while lifting their heads and legs at the same time, flopped their body in a single movement either onto their backs or onto their stomachs. Some of the autistic infants fell from sitting positions easily, showing no compensatory actions, so that they appeared to topple like a cut tree. When learning to crawl, some of the autistic infants had a hard time adjusting their base of support, leaned on their elbows instead of their hands, and had a difficult time distributing their weight evenly because of asymmetries between right and left sides.

This finding was recently confirmed with a prospective high risk sample. Compared to low risk siblings, those at high risk were slower to develop sitting and standing postures and initiated fewer postural changes (such as from lying down to sitting) than the low risk infants (Nickel et al., 2013). It is well known that autistic children and adults have motor asymmetries and sometimes walk unsteadily. They often have an aversion to touch, eye contact, and other forms of sensory stimulation. Autistic children's difficulty in imitating another person is believed to be due to neuromotor deficits, the failure to clearly link perception and action (Ozonoff & South, 2001). Both Donna Williams and Temple Grandin describe the difficulties they have with being touched, for example, and the lengthy process by which they discovered means to safely touch and be touched. It is plausible, therefore, that early appearing movement and sensory deficits may play some role in autism.

Another prospective study of children who were later diagnosed with autism has found shorter durations of eye gaze to a face, and a decline in the amount of time looking at faces between 2 and 6 months compared to children who did not have autism (Jones & Klin, 2013). The researchers used a computerized eye-tracking device and sophisticated statistical analysis, so it is unlikely that someone just watching the baby would be able to tell if their looking patterns were abnormal. Because many of the signs of autism reflect difficulties in social communication, however, this finding is potentially significant.

Other prospective study using high-risk infant siblings shows deficits in joint attention and referential communication (such as pointing), both gestural and vocal, in infants as young as 8 months, with these patterns becoming more pronounced by 12 months (Ibañez, Grantz & Messinger, 2013; Ozonoff et al., 2010). A retrospective study of home videos revealed that infants later diagnosed with ASD, compared to those later diagnosed with mental retardation, looked at others and oriented to the names of other people less, they used fewer gestures, and engaged more in repetitive motor activity (Osterling, Dawson & Munson, 2002). At 9 months, high risk infant siblings produced fewer speech-like vocalizations and more non-speech vocalizations (grunts, gurgles, etc.) and fewer consonant-vowel sounds typical of babbling in the second half of the first year (Paul et al., 2011).

Treatments for Autism in the First Two Years of Life

Most treatment approaches for young infants who are at risk for autism focus on improving the child's ability to engage with another person and to develop coordinated joint attention. There is a growing amount of research on the effectiveness of these interventions. In one study, autistic infants, ages 21 to 33 months, were randomly assigned to two family interventions. One of the interventions had a component that encouraged the children to imitate and be imitated, create joint attention with others, and promote affective sharing, which in fact increased these behaviors compared to the control group (Landa at al., 2011). Another similar intervention to improve joint attention in parents and high risk infants proved effective, compared to controls, in enhancing joint attention and functional play (Kasari et al., 2010). The Early Start Denver Model, which focuses on promoting social coordination and emotion sharing has been shown to be effective in toddlers between 18 and 30 months, not only improving social skills but lowering the possibility for later autism diagnosis (Dawson et al., 2010).

The results related to early sensorimotor deficits may lead to new ways of treating infants for movement and sensory disorders that might possibly affect the development of the brain and improve the chances for later cognitive and emotional development. Many professionals feel that treatments begun early enough may have a more lasting effect than treatments begun after 4 or 5 years of age.

FAMILY AND SOCIETY

Peer Interactions

The last aspect of social development to be discussed in this chapter is the change in the child's relationship to peers at this age. When given a choice of whom to play with, infants almost always choose a peer—familiar or unfamiliar—over their mothers. They spend more time with the peer and make fewer bids for their mother's attention when a peer is present (Rubenstein, Howes, & Pedersen, 1982). A similar pattern can be seen in a day care setting: 2-year-olds spend more time with one another than with teachers (Finkelstein, Dent, Gallacher, & Ramey, 1978).

When the tables are turned and the adult is with an adult peer while the child is not, the child increases the number of bids for attention and close contact. In fact, the child is more demanding of the mother's attention when she is with a friend than when the mother and child are home alone (Rubenstein et al., 1982). This finding should come as no surprise to any parent who has tried to carry on a conversation with a friend while the baby is around. It is probably best not to ignore the child's need for attention and wish to be included. At the same time, children have to understand that they cannot necessarily be a part of everything that the parent does.

We saw in previous chapters that toddler-peer play is different in quality from toddler-parent play. Studies of 19-month-olds show that this trend continues with age. Toddlers are more likely to play with, imitate, offer toys to, and talk to peers than to their mothers, although they touch peers and mothers about the same amount of time (Rubenstein & Howes, 1976). When they play with their mothers, toddlers are more likely to have longer periods of sustained attention to single objects (N. L. Cohen & Tomlinson-Keasey, 1980).

Sometime between 18 and 24 months, peer play begins to take on a more gamelike quality. Children take simple turns involving complementary roles, such as offering and accepting, throwing and catching, or simple verbal exchange ("You're a sissy"; "No, I'm not"). Words are used in such games, but not at the same level of elaboration as in adult-infant games. At this age also, there are few instances of actual cooperation and collaboration on a task, as may be found during adult-infant interaction, although cooperation with peers becomes more pronounced after 24 months (Brownell, 1986; Brownell, Ramani, & Zerwas, 2006; Eckerman, Davis, & Didow, 1989; Howes & Matheson, 1992; Warneken & Tomasello, 2007).

Children of this age are just beginning to form lasting relationships with peers. A **relationship** is a continuing pattern of communication between two or more people in which past encounters provide a historical background for future encounters. It is not until the end of the second year of life that children can form lasting relationships—friendships—with other children. "Compatible friends" direct mostly positive behaviors toward each other and refrain from conflicts. Enemies, or "fighting friends" tend to engage in conflicts most of the time they get together. Other children tend not to interact with each other (ignoring), either positively or negatively. It could be said that even these ignoring pairs have a relationship, because the same children tend to ignore each other day after day (Ross et al., 1992).

Finally, the types of toys used in peer play influence the types of interactions between the children. Eighteen-month-old infants were observed playing in pairs in four different play settings: a typical play setting, one with no play materials, one with only small portable toys, and one with only large nonportable play equipment (DeStefano & Mueller, 1982). The researchers found more sophisticated social interaction and a greater expression of positive emotion in the setting with the large play equipment (ladders, slides, and boxes). With the small portable toys, more conflict and more negative emotion was expressed. This is understandable, because children tend to fight over the possession of small toys. With only large toys, children tend to treat the environment as a space to be shared and enjoyed together.

Surprisingly, the children were most creative in the no-toy situation: they actually invented their own toys! The radiator became a "base," they took off articles of clothing to be used as play objects, and they even used each other as if they were toys. When playing with infants, adults tend to introduce toys and other play materials to keep the pace of play up or keep the toddlers out of their way. Perhaps peer interaction provides time for the child to be more inventive and develop independent initiatives.

When conflicts over small toys do arise, children younger than 24 months are more likely to share than older children, who are more likely to use force or coercive language to regain their toys from a peer. The use of force is not the most common approach to toy conflicts, although it is used when other measures fail to succeed. This may be because the older children have a more consolidated sense of self that includes possessions (see Chapter 11), and also because the younger child would prefer to avoid serious conflicts (Caplan, Vespo, Pedersen, & Hay, 1991; Hay, Caplan, Castle, & Stimson, 1991; Hay et al., 2011). Although it is relatively rare at this age, a third child may come over to intervene in the toy conflict between two other children (Ross et al., 1992).

Co-Regulating With Baby

The most striking and remarkable aspect of this stage of development is the emergence of the child's sense of an existential self. For the first time, the baby no longer seems so much like a baby: the child begins to behave in more adult-like ways. Whole new realms of interpersonal communication are possible for those interested in taking advantage of them.

One of the most notable signs of the child's new grasp on personhood is the interesting use of negation. At first, this happens with an insistent "no!" Later, with improved language, it becomes something like "I won't do it," or "I don't want to." Babies often say no just for the purpose of exploring its effect on others; at other times, they do so because they have a legitimate complaint or disagreement that needs attention.

This behavior signals a new recognition of personal boundaries and limitations. The difficulty during the "no" stage comes when caregivers and children are at odds on an issue or when the children insist on making up their own minds and then cannot handle the responsibility they seem to want to have for themselves.

It helps to give the children experience in making choices they can handle; for example, deciding what kind of juice they would like or what color socks they would like to wear. If the children know they can make responsible decisions about some things, it may be easier to discourage them from insisting on making other decisions that the caregiver knows they should not make. This is the essence of proactive parenting.

As in other aaspects of dealing with children, a sense of humor is a good ally. You can sometimes make "no" into a game by repeating it back in an obviously playful tone of voice, as well as by suggesting obviously silly alternatives to the child's unreasonable request or to the caregiver's snubbed demand. In this way, the toddler may discover that refusing to do something does not always have to end up in a fight with Mon or Dad.

It is not always possible to be so flexible, as when a child refuses to hold your hand when crossing the street. However even this can be made into a kind of game ritual. Once you establish a pattern of doing things like crossing streets, changing diapers, putting the child to bed, or reading a story, a child likes to stick to the initial routines faithfully. At this age, some of these frames have a ritualistic quality because the child like to do them the same way each time. Although rituals can become downright boring and tedious for a caregiver, it is important to realize that they are necessary ways of maintaining order, safety, and health in a generally peaceful manner. You may not understand why a sandwich cut in quarters tastes better than one cut in half, but if that is what it takes to get a meal down, then why not cut it that way? Good-natured co-regulation in areas like this is an effective way to build trust so the child will understand you when you need to insist on compliance in more serious situations.

One area in which children show self-assertion is getting dressed. It is very difficult to know how much children need or want you to do for them and how much they can or want to do for themselves. Although babies of this age are just about able to put on their socks and shoes, for example, they still have some trouble getting socks over that inconvenient bend at the ankle or trying to figure out which shoe goes on which foot. Your effort to co-regulate can be courteous as well as respectful by helping get things started and then letting the child finish. Some examples are putting on a sock partway, giving the child an oversized sock to put on, or handing the child the proper shoe. Other situations include providing a step stool to reach the sink, turning on the faucet partway, pulling out the child's chair just enough for the child to climb up to the table on his or her own, and pushing the chair in once the child is settled.

Language helps all these problems immensely. Children are less likely to have a tantrum or cry when they are able to express their problems with words. Caregivers can help this along by modeling words, related to inner feelings, such as mad, tired, scared, happy, sad, or hurt.

Language also leads to new and interesting games and conversations with the child. Naming is a compelling game at this age. Reading books becomes more fun. Also at this age, children discover the fun of playing outdoors, where there are many new things to name and explore. Car rides are usually a big treat, because children gradually come to recognize general categories of objects ("The cow like the cow in the book"). They also recognize specific things like the kind of gasoline station where their mother always stops. Every time they pass that type of gasoline station, children can recognize it, and they will happily search until they see another one. These kinds of discoveries almost always are accompanied by feelings of great pride on the children's part, and they want everyone to appreciate the accomplishment.

As already mentioned, pretending and tool using are important at this age. In the realm of object exploration, children are discovering how to make towers and trains, as well as how to destroy them in a flash. The following are traditional pastimes, guaranteed to delight any child of 1½ years; riding a tricycle or scooter; playing catch by rolling the ball; pushing and pulling large objects such as wagons or chairs; climbing on the sofa, chairs, and playground equipment; and playing a real game of hide-and-seek.

The second birthday is rather different from the first. Because of the ability to form mental representations, babies about to be 2 years old are able to look forward to their second birthdays, think about presents, get excited about the occasion, and ask whether they will have cake. Although they still do not fully understand the concept of a birthday, they are aware that they are part of a special event that is somehow centered upon them. In the next chapter, I will follow the development of that important sense of self-awareness as it unfolds in the third year of life.

SUMMARY

Motor and Cognitive Development

- Infants combine words in flexible formulas that allow different meanings to be constructed but are not as rigid as grammar.
- Motor advances include self-feeding, toilet training, and stable sleep patterns.
- The ability to think about actions without actually performing them develops. Infants can solve some problems mentally, without trial and error.
- Symbolic play develops by the combination of different types of symbols into complex event sequences. Infants still do not understand all the connections between their own actions on objects.
- Script-based memories allow for categorization of events according to the sequences in which they typically occur.
- Media such as DVDs, TV, computers, tablets and smartphones may have some benefits for children but can also detract from normal development. It is better for children of this age if adults supervise and play along with them.

Emotional Development

- Fears originate in mental and symbolic images, and some dreaming begins. Infants develop new emotions, such as defiance, embarrassment, and pride.
- Transitional objects serve to comfort infants when adults are unavailable.
- Smiling and laughter develop as important forms of communication about positive emotion.
- Pride and shame develop as emotions related to the existential self.
- Separations are easier for children if parents explain what will happen and when they will return, if the environment is one in which the infants feel comfortable, and if the infants have experience with separations.

Social and Language Development

- A vocabulary spurt begins at this age, corresponding with the insight that things have names.
- Symbolic play and tool use correlate with the onset of multiword speech and the vocabulary spurt at around 20 months.
- Individual differences in style and amount of speech emerge at this age.
- A linguistic environment conducive to infant language development is one in which adults are responsive to the infant's speech initiative by commenting and asking questions.
- Apes appear to have language abilities similar to those of human infants, and with human adult guidance, they can acquire signed languages.
- Guided participation is a general principle that applies to language, play, and discipline interactions.
- Discipline can be achieved by guided participation and by proactively regulating the environment.
- An existential sense of self emerges when children can recognize themselves in the mirror and when they begin to use the word "I."
- Infantile autism, a pathology of self and relationships, can be diagnosed as early as 18 months, which may lead to the development of new treatments.

Family and Society

- Peers begin to play more reciprocal games. They also begin to form lasting relationships.

Chapter 11

Twenty-Four to Thirty-Six Months

CHAPTER OUTLINE AND OVERVIEW

Motor and Cognitive Development	*How does the child's thinking affect action? What are some uses of and individual differences in pretend play? How does memory develop at this age? What new forms of self-and other-awareness emerge at this age? How does gender play a role in self-concept?*
Emotional Development	*What are the different forms of positive emotion at this age? How do children talk about their emotions? Can children at this age understand the emotions of other people?*
Social and Language Development	*In what way are verbs acquired? How does grammar develop? What are the conversational skills at this age? What changes occur in parent-infant relationships?*
Family and Society	*What happens between children of this age and their peers and siblings? Are there interfamily differences in sibling interaction?*

This chapter is intended as a bridge between infancy and the preschool years. Although there is no clear demarcation between these two periods, a number of factors suggest that the infancy period is not completely over until late in the third year of life. At this time, infants can genuinely engage in linguistic and cooperative interactions with their peers, siblings, and parents. The 3-year-old has a command of family relationships that the 2-year-old does not. By the age of 3 years, the child can nurture a younger sibling and take independent stands against older siblings. Productive grammatical speech does not emerge until the end of the third year, although even this speech is still fairly simple in structure. Children of this age also develop a self-concept, for example, an awareness of themselves as boys or girls.

MOTOR AND COGNITIVE DEVELOPMENT

Motor Development

From a motor perspective, the third year is an exciting developmental period. Table 11.1 lists some of the motor achievements that occur in the third year. Age norms are not available for all these items, so they are listed according to whether they develop early or late in the third year. It is important to remember that there are wide individual differences in the age these skills are acquired, so some children will not be doing all of these things by the end of the third year.

Most infants have developed their adult hand preference by the age of 3 years, although for some infants a stable preference does not finally emerge until the age of 5 years (Hardyck & Petrinovich, 1977; Ramsay, 1980). There is no evidence that left-handed children (about 12 percent of the population) have cognitive and motor deficits, and it is unjustified on typical developmental grounds to try to encourage children to switch their hand preference (Tan, 1985).

Whether right-or left-handed, by age 3, children are drawing squiggles and making simple shapes on paper. Research shows that these early drawings are not usually mirrors of the child's emotional life but reflect the motor limitations of the arm and the hand (Freeman, 1980). Once children begin to draw shapes, they prefer simple ones, such as circles and rectangles. Eventually, these shapes are combined into more complex pictures (Goodnow, 1977). The development of one child's ability to copy a square is shown in Figure 11.1. Note that even Matthew's first drawings using spiral forms, there is a crude representation of a square. During the period when Matthew was using the spiral forms shown here, he was also representing human figures with spirals. After he was able to draw the square at 2 years, 9 months, and 13 days, his drawings of human figures began to look more realistic and include facial details. This research shows that children in the third year develop the ability to draw simple visual units (like circles and squares) from which they construct more complex images (Stiles, 1995). Children of this age can also identify, when asked, what they have drawn and can remember the "content" of their drawing for up to 6 months (Gross & Hayne, 1999). It takes at least another year for children to draw symbolic objects such as letters, words, and graphic symbols like smiley faces (T. C. Callaghan, 1999).

The drawings shown in Figure 11.1 were done when the child was asked to copy a particular figure. Not all the drawings that children produce during this period are meant to represent something in the world, and it is not always appropriate for adults to interpret the drawings as being real or representational. Rather, the child may be using the materials to explore the medium: to discover what kinds of shapes, lines, and colors can be made with this brush or that crayon.

Another aspect of motor development is physical play. During the first 2 years, physical play consists primarily of explorations of the body's abilities, primary and secondary circular reactions, and the child's efforts to acquire new motor skills such as sitting, standing, and walking. During the second and third years, children develop what is called **exercise play**. Exercise play is playful locomotor movement that is physically vigorous, such

TABLE 11.1 Motor Achievements During the Third Year of Life

	Small Motor	*Large Motor*
First half of third year	Uses large crayons and pencils. Uses hand gestures and sign language.	Rides large-wheel toys. Walks up and down stairs with both feet on each step. Jumps with two-foot takeoff. Throws a ball 4 to 5 feet. Walks sideways and backward. Runs. Engages in free-ranging movement out of doors.
Second half of third year	Uses building toys with many possible shapes (blocks, Legos, etc.). Uses paints and clay. Hammers.	Walks up and down stairs by alternating each foot. Walks a line, heel-to-toe. Hops 2 or 3 times. Walks a short balance beam. Throws a ball 10 feet. Engages in rough-and-tumble play. Finds route in unfamiliar places.

Figure 11.1 Squares Produced by Matthew When Asked to Copy the Square Model
Source: J. Stiles. The early use and development of graphic formulas: Two case study reports of graphic formula production by 2- to 3-year-old children, 1995, p. 132. *International Journal of Behavioral Development, 18*(1), 127–149. Reprinted by permission of the International Society for the Study of Behavioral Development.

as running, chasing, and climbing; it may or may not be social. It accounts for about 7 to 14 percent of behavior in day-care settings for 3-year-old children (Pellegrini & Smith, 1998). Boys tend to engage in exercise play more than girls, and boys of this age have a higher overall activity level than girls (Campbell & Eaton, 1999; Pellegrini & Smith, 1998).

Exercise play appears to have the same sorts of benefits for young children as for adults. It increases fitness, endurance, strength, and skill. There is some evidence that physical play in young children reduces fat and increases the ability of the body to regulate temperature (Thigpen, 2007). Some have suggested that exercise play enhances cognitive ability, but research has not been able to clearly distinguish the effects of exercise play from the effects of just having playground breaks during the more demanding cognitive tasks in day care and preschool. In any case, it is clear that both boys and girls need exercise play for the healthy development of both body and mind (Pellegrini & Smith, 1998).

By the end of the third year, most children have learned how to use the toilet. There are no differences in age of toilet learning depending upon whether a child attended child care outside the home, but girls tend to be trained earlier (on average, at about 35 months) compared to boys (at 39 months) (Schum et al., 2001). Children first acquire words for the potty, to show that they need to go. Flushing the toilet and washing hands are skills learned next. The final level of learning, which may take one or more years, is using a regular toilet, wiping efficiently, and staying dry all night (Schum et al., 2002).

The Emergence of Thinking Grounded in Action

During the third year, children increase their ability to perform complicated sequences of action, as demonstrated by the following investigation (Bullock & Lutkenhaus, 1988). Researchers gave children three tasks. The first was to build a house from blocks in a particular fashion modeled by the experimenter. The next was to clean a blackboard, and the last was to dress a doll so that it would not be cold. After age 2, but not before, the children were able to perform all the actions in the sequence given by the experimenter (the constructed house, the cleaned blackboard, and the dressed doll).

When the younger children made an error in putting the blocks together to build the house, they simply stopped or went on to another activity. The older children were able to correct the error and persist until the task was completed to a reasonable approximation of the standard. This ability to combine a series of actions together in a flexible way and to persist until a standard or conventional goal is reached is a major cognitive achievement. This achievement is reflected in a variety of areas, including object play, pretend play, social play, peer play, self-control, and language (Bauer, Schwade, Wewerka, & Delaney, 1999; Brownell, 1988; Jennings, 2004). Self-control is seen in the ability to wait as requested by an adult (Vaughn et al., 1986). In the realm of language, for example, children at this age are beginning to use grammatical syntax in which a number of words are combined according to conventional usage into a flexible sequence.

What causes these changes to occur? Since attention span also increases around the same age, you might think that an increase in some kind of cognitive capacity allows the infant to process a longer series of actions. Some researchers believe, on the contrary, that longer attention is the result of more skilled action sequences that require the child to spend more time following through with the details of completing a task (Ruff & Lawson, 1990).

In related studies, it has been found that the more children comprehend of television programs, such as *Sesame Street*, the longer they will watch, and that television watching increases markedly at 30 months, about the same time these other changes are happening (Anderson & Lorch, 1983). This kind of more focused attention to television is different from what was observed during the previous age period.

Self-produced action does appear to affect cognition. In one study, 3-year-olds were taken into a children's area in a natural history museum (Hazen, 1982). Some of the children were allowed to explore the area on their own, while others were led through it by an adult. Those who went on their own had a more accurate spatial cognition of the layout of the area than those who were led. This study shows that self-produced action involves active cognitive processing, and that by their action, children are increasing their knowledge of the environment.

Language Aids both Thought and Action

If attention increases as a result of more articulated sequential action, that still leaves open the question of what accounts for the development of children's ability to execute these more complex action sequences? In the last chapter, we reviewed research showing that younger infants appear more skilled in pretend play and language when in the company of adults compared to peers. The adult guidance and the adult language seem to regulate the infant's actions, providing a kind of external support system for engaging in longer sequences of action and language, sequences that the infant cannot maintain alone or with a peer. After 30 months, it seems, infants have begun to internalize these social-linguistic sequential processes as thought, carrying them over into their activities in the absence of adults.

How do we know this? Beginning at 30 months, children begin to use language to regulate their behavior. For example, in one study, children were given a peg-and-hammer toy and told to hammer the pegs into the board in a particular order according to the color of the peg. If the children were allowed to say out loud the given order while hammering, they were more accurate than if told not to speak (Balamore & Wozniak, 1984).

At around 30 months, children begin, literally, to talk to themselves. **Private speech** is the use of language to regulate one's own behavior without the intention of a social communication. Private speech is different from the child's speech play seen in the first year (such as saying "mmmmm" while eating) because private speech uses both conventional words and conventional syntax. Private speech is a way in which children incorporate previous experiences with social-linguistic regulation into their individual self-regulation.

Research has shown that private speech occurs in the following situations: the child talks about an intended action ("I put that there"), describes ongoing action ("Banging it"), makes a statement to an inanimate object ("Get out of my way, chair!"), or asks a question and then answers it ("Why are you crying, dolly? Because I'm sad"). In all cases, these words are said without looking at anyone else or seeking social confirmation (Berk, 1986; Furrow, 1984). In this way, babies turn social dialogue into private monologue and language into thought, and the result is the self-regulation of action (Vygotsky, 1978).

The Development of Pretending and the World of Make-Believe

Pretend play, introduced in the last chapter, is a kind of private speech that allows children to construct their own version of reality. At the beginning of the third year, children develop more complex forms of pretending. The child begins to reconstruct whole scenes and experiences in play:

At 2;1(9) Jacqueline put her doll's head through the balcony railing with its face turned toward the street and began to tell it what she saw: "You see the lake and the trees. You see a carriage, a horse," etc. The same day she seated her doll on the sofa and told it what she herself had seen in the garden. (Piaget, 1962, p. 127)

In the previous example, the child tried to faithfully reproduce reality. In the following example, the child makes some attempt to change or correct reality to make it more to her own liking. These games are the beginning of **imaginative pretend play**, in which the child is able to invent whole new situations in make-believe:

At 2;4(8) Jacqueline, not being allowed to play with the water being used for washing, took an empty cup, went and stood by the forbidden tub and went through the actions, saying: "I'm pouring out the water." (Piaget, 1962, p. 131)

The final type of pretend play that occurs during the third year of life is what Piaget called **liquidating pretend play**. This usually happens after the child experiences something unpleasant or threatening. Later, the child will try to relive the difficult situation in play as a way of coping with it. By removing it from its original unpleasantness, the child is better able to understand and assimilate what went on:

At 2;7(2) Jacqueline had fallen down and cut her lip. She consoled herself by projecting it all on to "Cousin Andree," who took the form of a doll: "Oh! It's Cousin Andree. They're washing her because she fell down and hurt her lip. She made a little hole in it. She cried."

At 2;7(15) a friend of her mother went for a walk with them. Jacqueline, who did not care for the presence of the third person, expressed frankly what she felt: "She's naughty … she can't talk … I don't like people to laugh." Then, as soon as the walk was over, Jacqueline accepted her, put her beside her in the bath, then in her bed, talked to her, and went for the walk again with her (all in imagination). (Piaget, 1962, p. 133)

These kinds of games allow the self to emerge victorious in the face of failure or to save face in the case of embarrassment. Children of this age also develop **pretend role play**, in which they act out the roles of mother, father, or other important figures in their lives, typically in the company of adults or peers.

During this same period in which children are developing their pretending skills, they can also understand when adults refer to pretend situations. In one study, adults pretended that a cup contained tea. The adults also did things like "pouring" or "spilling" the tea. After 28 months (2

years, 4 months), children can participate in these pretend episodes. They will "drink" from the cup and help "clean up" the "spilled" tea. The children also use language that makes clear they understand the situation is make-believe and not real (P. L. Harris & Kavanaugh, 1993; Rokoczy, Tomasello, & Striano, 2004).

Pretending is also manifested as dreaming, which children of this age can talk about for the first time. Dreams often concern experiences the child has had, physical changes such as toileting, and strong emotions.

At 2;2(23) X. woke up crying: "Poupette has come back." Poupette was a little girl she had met the day before and who had obviously worried her by uninceremoniously taking possession of all her toys. At 2;8(11) X. woke with a loud scream: "It was all dark, and I saw a lady over there (pointing to her bed). That's why I screamed." Then she explained that it was a horrid lady who stood with her legs apart and played with her feces. (Piaget, 1962, p. 177)

These dreams are classic nightmares, or dreams about fears that are still so frightening that the dream is unable to resolve them or make them better. In one case the child fears her toys will be stolen, and in another she fears her own feces. The latter is a common problem in 2-and 3-year-old children who are becoming aware that their own bodies can manufacture these products. Children of this age are both fascinated by their feces and repelled and confused by them at the same time (Erikson, 1950). Some children feel possessive about these products and may refuse toilet learning for fear of losing part of themselves. Other children may show more curiosity and playfulness about their stools and urine than most parents are able to tolerate, and still others do not seem to be at all concerned with these matters.

Another common dream in very young children is the "transposition of an organic stimulus" (Piaget, 1962). A good example is when children dream about a watering can at just the moment when they feel like (or are in the process of) urinating. Dreams other than nightmares may fulfill a wish, or they may take a painful event and finish it off with a happy ending. According to Freud (1900/1953), dreams are the "guardians" of sleep. Without dreams to transform and soothe our minds, we might keep waking up with painful or troublesome thoughts.

Because of these new abilities, children no longer have to be content with what actually happens. They can make up a better outcome as they play with dolls, siblings, and peers. We all do this when we imagine becoming famous, getting out of our difficulties and achieving success, or taking revenge on someone who has wronged us. The only problem for 3-year-olds is that they are never sure about the limits of this newfound ability to make up a more congenial world. If they could make things up so easily, why is everything not just pretend? Children may think they can make their parents disappear by wishing it. A boy might believe that he will change into a girl if he talks in a high voice for a long time. If the real can be imaginary, then the imaginary could be real. Children fear their own imaginary monsters, get shaken awake by nightmares, and worry that they will lose themselves when their feces get sucked down the toilet drain. These fears are very real for children of this age, and they often do not have a sufficient command of language to fully express themselves.

Memory Development

Autobiographical Memory. By age 2, infants are beginning to organize their memories according to sequences of events. When words are added to these sequences, they become stories or narratives about a past experience. The ability to create a verbal narrative of past experiences is called **autobiographical memory**. Autobiographical memory (sometimes called explicit or verbal memory) serves to create a sense of one's life events ("I was left alone…"), past times ("…when I was four years old…"), and places ("…at the preschool"). Autobiographical memory is constructed in conversations with others beginning in the third year of life.

The ability to form autobiographical memories is based on the maturation of the **hippocampus** (Chapter 4), that part of the limbic system that is responsible for the organization of sequences of events in memory. The hippocampus does not develop as quickly as other parts of the limbic system, and is not fully mature until 3 to 4 years of age. This helps to explain why such memories do not begin to form until this age.

Children whose autobiographical memory is more detailed have mothers who, during conversations, are more likely to elaborate on children's recall by filling in the details of the past event and asking questions of children to clarify their stories about themselves (Fivush, 1994; Haden et al., 2001; Harley & Reese, 1999; Wang, 2006). Children with more advanced verbal skills are better at autobiographical remembering (Simcock & Hayne, 2003) and children who use more mental state words like "thinking," "knowing," and "remembering" are better at producing autobiographical details (Cherney, 2003). This suggests that hippocampal maturation is experience dependent.

There is a link between autobiographical memory beginning around the age of 2 or 3 years, and the age after which adults can remember their early childhood. Typically, adults can recall only one or two specific incidents from early childhood, and not usually before the age of two or three years. Adults can have more detailed autobiographical memories of events and situations beginning from when they were five or six years old. This phenomenon is known as **infantile amnesia**, the inability to recall an autobiographical narrative before the age of 2 or 3 years. Since the infant's brain does not encode experiences in a narrative sequential manner until this age, it makes sense that no such memories remain of one's life at earlier ages.

So, if adults are unable to autobiographically remember their infancy, what about young children and teens? Because they are closer in years to their infancy experience, perhaps they remember better than adults? Like adults, the ability of children to verbally narrate a situation from infancy depends on whether or not they had verbal skills at the time of the event they are trying to remember. Researchers studied children who had a traumatic injury that brought them to the hospital emergency room some time during their first two years of life (C. Peterson, 1999; C. Peterson & Bell, 1996; C. Peterson & Rideout, 1998). If the injury occurred around the age of 2 years, children could recall the situation verbally up to two years later. One such child had burned his hand on a lawnmower exhaust when he was just under 2 years old. A year and a half later, he could state that he burned his hand, who was there, why it happened, and that he saw a doctor.

A similar finding comes from a controlled study in which 2 to 3 year-olds were exposed to a distinctive magic show and then interviewed about the event one day later. The researchers met with the children 6 years later and about one-third of the children were able to verbally recall the event even though there were no photos or videos made of the event. (Jack, Simcock, & Hayne, 2012). So, it appears that having the ability to form autobiographical memories after two years aids in autobiographical remembering up to 6 years later.

In another study, children between 6 and 19 years and their parents were interviewed about the child's earliest memory. The youngest children (6 to 9 years) were able to remember events that occurred when they were 2 to 3 years-old (but no earlier) but the older children (10 to 19 years) could only remember events beginning when they were 4 years-old. These remembered events were all confirmed by parents. For some reason, it is more difficult to autobiographically remember events before 4 years of age, after the age of 10 years. This is most likely because the hippocampus is still in the process of maturation until 4 years of age (Peterson, Grant & Boland, 2005).

What if the event occurs before the age of two years, before there is the ability for autobiographical remembering? At 16 months, a child fell and cut his forehead. His emergency room visit was traumatic for him, since he had to be tightly wrapped in a blanket to keep him from moving during the stitching. For the next few months, he showed sleep disturbances and fear of strangers, did not want to leave the house, and became hysterical when blankets were put on him. He was interviewed by the researchers when he was 22 months old. At that time he still did not have verbal skills sufficient to describe the situation, but when he heard the word "hospital," he pointed to the place on his forehead where he had received the stitches. He was shown several pictures, one of which was of his doctor. He picked up the doctor's picture and showed it to his father, saying, "Doc, doc." When interviewed 18 months after the accident (at 34 months of age), he still had no verbal memory of it, but his parents said he still refused to be wrapped in a smock when getting his hair cut.

These studies make clear that verbal-language skills at the time of the incident contribute to children's autobiographical memories of early infancy (Kolling et al., 2010; Solter, 2008). These studies also show that if an incident, especially a traumatic one, occurs earlier than age 2, some kind of memory remains but it is not in the form of an autobiographical narrative.

While the concept of infantile amnesia suggests that we do not have memories of infancy before the age of two years, the research on this topic is limited to autobiographical memory. So, what does happen to all of our experiences in the first two years of life? Do we really forget them? Memories of early infancy, if they exist, are likely to be very different from autobiographical memories. Like the example of the child who did not like to be wrapped in a blanket or a smock, memories of early infancy are more likely to be non-verbal forms of memory involving sensations, emotions, and movements. The child may not consciously "know" why he is afraid of being wrapped up in a blanket because he is unable to verbally articulate and understand why, but the memory persists in body movement and felt experience. There are two types of memory that are not autobiographical: procedural and participatory.

Procedural Memory. Procedural memories, in contrast to the narrative-sequential autobiographical memories that are organized in the hippocampus, are primarily non-verbal. Rather than stories about the self, procedural memories (sometimes called motor, perceptual, or implicit memories) are the remembering of "ways of doing and sensing things" (Kolers & Roediger, 1984). Many of the memories that we retain from the infancy period are procedural, those which underlie our ability to act in the world on the basis of what we have learned in the past. Procedural memories are typically not encoded verbally but rather in patterns of action, sensation, and feeling.

When particular patterns of movement, posture, and/or emotions occur repeatedly in particular situations, they are more likely to be remembered procedurally by the areas of the sensory, motor, and parietal cortices that were involved in the initial learning. This is the way adults remember how to ride a bike, drive a car, play a musical instrument, and many other daily activities. This is most likely the way in which we "remember" patterns of infantile attachment and temperament that persist into adulthood: our ways of doing things with others (Lyons-Ruth, 2000). Most likely, we looked at our parents' faces many thousands of times during infancy. Some part of that experience must remain even though we can't "see" those faces in our minds.

Movement patterns learned in infancy, such as kicking, reaching, crawling, and rolling over, underlie all later complex movements of older children and adults. Patterns of emotional responses in infancy form the basis for many later adult emotional predispositions (Fogel, 2003; Shore, 1994; Stern, 1985; Thelen & Smith, 1994). Because these memories are just part of everyday behavior, we don't have the experience of "remembering." We just do the activity without being aware that it is based on many prior experiences with people and the world.

Participatory Memory. There is a third kind of memory that is neither autobiographical nor procedural. **Participatory memories**, are not "about" a past experience; rather, they are felt as a being with or a reliving of past experiences. They are composed of a felt experience of emotions and sensations, often without a narrative context nor without any specific time or place (Bråten, 1998, 2003; Fogel, 2013; Heshusius, 1994; Stern,

1985). On the other hand, they become alive and real in one's awareness, unlike procedural memories which are often unconscious.

An example of a participatory memory is a child who had witnessed her mother being blown up by a bomb when she was 12 months old. During play therapy at 4½ years, the child thrashed about on the floor, made loud explosion-like noises, and scattered the toys around the room, all in relation to a doll that represented the "mother" (Gaensbauer, 2004). The evidence for participatory memories of infancy is indirect and comes mostly from therapeutic and other emotionally salient situations. While autobiographical memories are primarily mental, participatory memories often involve the whole body.

Research on adults who experienced traumas as adults (such as assault, emotional trauma, war, or an automobile accident) also shows that their memories of the trauma are often not autobiographical but rather are re-lived in the body. Adults often do not have an autobiographical memory of the traumatic event. They may re-experience pain, shake, or break out in a cold sweat and experience a feeling of intense fear (Smyth & Pennebaker, 1999; Terr, 1994). One of the features of trauma is that events unfold too quickly for the hippocampus to process their sequential order, leading to a failure to form autobiographical memory. In an automobile accident or a physical assault, for example, rapid neuroception via the amygdala, sympathetic nervous system, and HPA axis (Chapter 4) is the primary neural process. Fear is the primary emotion. Conscious, autobiographical memory formation via the hippocampus is bypassed.

Traumatic participatory memories will continue to persist longer if the conditions that created the memories—or similar conditions—persist and continue to be reenacted. This might be the case with war veterans with PTSD who respond to loud noises and honking horns as if they were still in a war zone (Hudson & Sheffield, 1998). This is because the amygdala alters its cellular structure with trauma, leaving the person vulnerable to perceive fear—re-enacting the prior trauma—even in relatively benign situations (see Chapter 4).

People with adult amnesia due to brain injury are more likely to have participatory memories than autobiographical memories. They may look and act like "themselves," using their body-based participatory memories even though they do not remember autobiographically who they are when asked questions about themselves (Baddeley, 1994; Hirst, 1994). Interestingly, many cases of adult amnesia are related to damage to the hippocampus (see above and Chapter 4).

More research is needed, however, to better understand why some participatory memories of infancy and early childhood remain and others do not. Because these memories are sensory-emotional, they often cannot be confirmed factually. There is controversy over whether such memories can be falsely implanted in a child by therapists and investigators who seek to verify that child abuse, to take one example, may have occurred (Theirry & Spence, 2002). The existence of participatory memories from infancy is controversial.

Nevertheless, there is some evidence to suggest that, in addition to procedural memories, participatory memory may be another way to remember our infancy experiences.

Understanding Other People and Their Emotions

As we saw in the previous chapter, the development of self-understanding and self-concept develops in parallel with the development of understanding others. Children of this age are developing categories for other people, describing others' emotions, and understanding that other people have emotions and states of mind. These findings raise the question of whether infants of this age have a **theory of mind**, an understanding that other people have psychological states, and that those states may be different from their own.

In addition to labeling their own emotions, 2-year-olds can talk about the emotions of other

---

Case Report
Participatory Memories

Students in my classes sometimes reported participatory memories that occurred when doing the experiential exercises in this book. Participatory memories cannot be evoked just by thinking about them. Thinking about the past is the way that we access autobiographical memories. Participatory memories are more likely to arise when we repeat a similar pattern of movement, sensation and feeling that occurred in the original experience. The experiential exercises put people into baby-like postures and movements. If you choose to do some of these exercises, pay attention to the possibility for having participatory memories. They are often brief moments of alive experience, and they have a déjà-vu quality, as when a feeling takes you over without explanation.

Case 1: When doing the experiential exercise on sucking [Chapter 5], I had a very strong participatory memory. My entire body was engaged in the sucking motion. I completely forgot where I was and my attention was fully focused on the sucking. While I was sucking, I felt a deep sense of contentment. I re-experienced familiar feelings of being happy, loved, and warm.

Case 2: After looking at my face in different ways during the mirror exercise [Chapter 10], the face of my mom all of a sudden came into my mind. I didn't get it then but I do now. I spent three years looking straight into my mother's eyes when I was

a baby and I noticed over Thanksgiving holiday that her eyes look just like mine! Every time I look at my eyes, I am reminded of her and I feel safe, I feel at home!

Notice that these memories are sudden and unexpected, unlike autobiographical memories which are more controlled and thoughtful. These memories are not about a specific time, place, or sequence—unlike autobiographical memories—but rather a more general impression. Unlike procedural memories which are more or less automatic and unconscious, the memories reported here are emotional and alive in the moment, taking the person into a different state of awareness and feelings and out of ordinary daily life.

TABLE 11.2 Statements of Emotion Made by Two-Year-Olds

Positive	I give a hug. Baby be happy.
	I laugh at funny man.
	I not cry now. I happy.
	Mommy exercise. Mommy having a good time.
Negative	Me fall down. Me cry.
	It's dark. I'm scared.
	No cry, Mama. It will be all right.
	I feel bad. My tummy hurts.
	Mommy, you went away. I was sad.
	He's sad. He'll be happy when his daddy comes home.
	I'm mad at you, Daddy. I'm going away, good-bye.
	If you go on vacation again, I'll cry.

Source: I. Bretherton, J. Fritz, C. Zahn-Waxler, & D. Ridgeway, Learning to talk about emotions: A functionalist perspective, 1988. *Child Development, 57*, 529–548.

people (Bretherton et al., 1986; Hoffman, 1975; Radke-Yarrow & Zahn-Waxler, 1984). Types of emotion talk about self and others are shown in Table 11.2. Children of this age appear to have a sense of empathy toward others. Two-year-olds are visibly affected by the emotions of others. In an experimental situation, children observed an experimenter having either an angry or a pleasant conversation with their mother. In the angry situation, the children expressed concern for their mother, sought her reassurance, and tried to comfort her (Cummings, Pellegrini, Notarius, & Cummings, 1989). Children of this age also show "concerned attention" toward others who are in distress, combined with helpful initiatives toward the other person and attempts to elicit help from bystanders (R. A. Thompson, 1998).

In general, girls show more caring and concern for the distress of others than boys. In play sessions with peers, boys show slightly more anger than girls, but the differences are not strong (Malatesta-Magai et al., 1994). Children of mothers with severe depression show more caring behavior than children of nondepressed mothers, perhaps because the children have had to prematurely attend to the emotional states of others to get attention in return (Radke-Yarrow, Zahn-Waxler, Richardson, Susman, & Martinez, 1994). It is not uncommon for children of this age to blame themselves for their mother's depressed feelings (thinking that their mother's feeling is the result of something the child did) (R. A. Thompson, 1998). Observations with peers suggests that children show more empathy with a peer's distress if it was the child himself or herself who caused the distress (Demetriou & Hay, 2004).

In one experiment, children of this age were given a doll that would break as soon as they began to play with it. Most of the children reacted to the planned mishap with frustration, shame, anger, or sadness, and they attempted to correct the problem by putting the doll back together. On the other hand, children of depressed mothers were more likely to suppress their frustrations by showing more solicitude toward their depressed parent. It seems that children of depressed mothers may become disconnected from their own feelings in an attempt to protect their parent from undue emotional arousal (Cole, Barrett, & Zahn-Waxler, 1992).

On the other hand, children who score high on tests of understanding others' emotions are more likely to come from families in which there was more coordinated joint attention and greater ability to infer the intentions of others during the second year. In the third year, theory of mind skills are higher when there is more frequent talk about feelings and the causes of feelings (a reflection of parents' sensitivity and openness to the child's inner states), an opportunity to observe parents talking with siblings about their feelings and behavior, encouragement to cooperate with their siblings during coordinated play, and a secure attachment with the mother (Aschersleben, Hofer & Jovanovic, 2008; Doan & Wang, 2010; J. Dunn, 1998; Ereky-Stevens, 2008; Garner, 2003; Kristen et al., 2011; Laranjo et al., 2010; McElwain & Volling, 2004; Nelson, Adamson & Bakeman, 2008; Roth & Assor, 2010; Ruffman, Slade & Crowe, 2002; Watson, Painter, & Bornstein, 2001). It seems that emotional understanding of others not related to guilt is facilitated in families in which emotional discourse occurs between all the members.

Some research suggests that children who are temperamentally inhibited or overly uninhibited (poor effortful control, see below) are less likely to show understanding of others' feelings (Carlson, Mandell, & Williams, 2004; Chasiotis et al., 2006; Hughes & Ensor, 2007). Children who are either inhibited or overly active may be less susceptible to observing the nuances of family emotional dialogues. They may require a more directive style of parental teaching to understand others' emotions (Zahn-Waxler & Robinson, 1995). Children who are raised in bilingual families score higher on theory of mind tasks, most likely because they have learned to slow down and listen more carefully to others, a skill that contributes to the development of self-regulation (Kovács, 2009).

These findings suggest that children's concept of self and emotional states of self are associated with their relationships to other people. Children of this age are aware of multiple forms of self-other relationships (P. J. Miller et al., 1992). They can talk about sharing activity with others ("We went down by the pool"), distinguish themselves as part of a relationship ("No one was holding my hand"; "You were far away"), and **metacommunicate** about their interpersonal relationships with others ("I hate Leslie"; "He wanted to play with me"). This suggests that the emotional self-awareness forms as part of a network of interpersonal relationships such that individuality is always defined in terms of one's connections, relations, similarities, and differences (Fogel, 1993).

Other findings also support this view that children can understand some aspects of others' mental states. Three-year-olds—both boys and girls—can modify their speech in the form of motherese when talking to a baby (J. Dunn & Kendrick, 1981). Children as young as 3 years are able to describe the kinds of things you might do to take care of a baby (Melson, Fogel, & Toda, 1986). When asked to show a picture to another person, 3-year-olds turned the picture around to face that person (Lempers, Flavell, & Flavell, 1977). Children of this age were more likely to gesture toward a "lost" object when they knew that the parent was unaware of the object's location than when the parent was aware of the location (O'Neill, 1996; Tomasello, Call, & Gluckman, 1997), suggesting that children of this age not only recognize but understand the intentions of other people. They are less likely to be responsive to another person's approval or disapproval if that person is not looking at them (Rapacholi, Meltzoff & Olsen, 2008).

These studies show that children have an understanding of some of the needs of other people that go beyond other's emotions and may include their mental state, but they do not demonstrate conclusively that 3-year-olds have a theory of mind. A child can copy the parent's speech to a baby brother or sister or just describe what others do for a baby without really understanding what it is like to be a baby. The use of emotion language could perhaps refer to facial expressions and actions of other people that the children have come to label in a particular way without realizing that others have feelings like themselves. Two year-olds will spontaneously help others in need, even without the prompting of an adult, but they will not help adults who are perceived as having an intention to harm someone (Hepach, Vaish & Tomasello, 2011; Svetlova, Nichols & Brownell, 2010; Vaish, Carpenter & Tomasello, 2010; Warneken & Tomasello, 2013).

You do not have to presume that the child understands that other people have minds or feelings, and some scholars suggest that genuine empathy for others does not begin to develop until 4 or 5 years of age (Selman, 1980). Adults, for example, can operate computers just by following instructions without having any notion at all of what makes computers work. Similarly, 2-year-olds who are exposed to robot toys that respond to them and talk to them will enter into conversations with the robots, apparently without thinking about how the robots work or what the robots might be feeling (P. J. Dunham, Dunham, Tran, & Akhtar, 1991).

On the other hand, evidence in favor of a rudimentary theory of mind comes from studies on the development of the ability to deceive others. Three-year-old children were left alone in a room with what they were told was a surprise toy. They were asked not to peek while the experimenter left the room. Observed from behind a one-way mirror, almost all of the children peeked, but when the experimenter returned and asked, "Did you peek?" only 38 percent of those who peeked admitted that they had done so. The ones who confessed showed little change in facial expression. The ones who actually peeked but said they had not peeked showed an increase in smiling, while those who peeked but refused to answer the question showed an increase in nervous self-touching (Lewis, Stanger, & Sullivan, 1989).

Do these differences in facial expression suggest that children may be aware of what adults are thinking; that is, do the children assume that the adult believes they peeked and therefore try to change the adult's beliefs? In a related study (Chandler, Fritz, & Hala, 1989; Hala, Chandler, & Fritz, 1991), children were asked to hide a treasure from an experimenter. They could do this in a number of ways: by covering up the trail to the treasure, by creating false leads about where the treasure was hidden if the experimenter asked for help, and by lying. Children as young as 2½ years used all three strategies, suggesting that they were acting to create a false belief in the adult. To create a false belief, you have to have a theory of mind; that is, you have to assume that others are capable of holding some beliefs. According to the authors, the children "not only slyly lied and disingenuously misled, but they did so with what often amounted to disarming delight in leading others astray" (Chandler et al., 1989, p. 1275).

Nevertheless, even though a case can be made that children of this age have a theory of mind,

it is likely to be a rather simple theory, something like: "Adults will believe what I want them to believe, and they can't really tell that I'm trying to deceive them." In other words, children of this age probably believe that adults are in some ways extensions of themselves and entirely in tune with their wishes.

According to P. L. Harris (1989), children need the following abilities to have a genuine theory of mind: self-awareness, the capacity for pretending, and the ability to distinguish reality from pretending. We know that by the beginning of the third year, most children have both self-awareness and the ability to pretend. These factors are necessary because, as Harris suggests, a theory of mind requires one to imagine that others have feelings like one's own. Because we have no direct confirmation of another's feelings, we have to imagine what someone might feel under certain circumstances.

What 3-year-olds lack, however, is the ability to separate pretend from reality (R. P. Hobson, 1991; Woolley & Cox, 2007). Until children can do this, they will see others as mere extensions of their own desires. How do we know children of this age cannot always separate reality from fantasy? One study found that when adults entered into a child's pretend game, the child became confused about the difference. A mother pretended to hold up an umbrella and suggested to her 30-month-old son that he hold out his hand to feel the rain. He did this and then very soberly looked at the palms of his hands to see if they were wet (DeLoache & Plaetzer, 1985). Another child, while playing at cooking, turned to a peer and said, "This is pretend, right?" (Slade, 1986). Another was pretending to be a monster by making growling noises. She became afraid of the noises she herself made and began to cry (DiLalla & Watson, 1988).

Of course, children in the third year can sometimes make the fantasy-reality distinction, but it would be more accurate to say that they are never really sure which is which. A greater feeling of certainty does not emerge until the age of 4 years, and therefore, it is not until this age that children solidify a theory of mind, an appreciation of the feelings and desires of others as independent from their own, and a similar universal pattern occurs across languages and cultures (Barrett et al., 2013; P. L. Harris, 1989, 1998). In language, children before the fourth year do not produce words representing conditional or temporary states, such as *could* and *would* as opposed to *can* and *will* (Kuczaj & Maratsos, 1983). By the age of 4 years, a child might say to a younger sibling, "You don't get it. It's just pretend. I could have fooled you!" On the other hand, at the beginning of the third year, it is fair to say that children begin to catch glimmers of the differences between self and other as part of their ongoing social interactions.

Self-and Other-Awareness: The Emergence of the Conceptual Self

The use of symbolic language to talk about the self and others, as well as the emergence of private speech and autobiographical memory, ushers in a new phase of self-awareness during the third year of life: the conceptual self, or a self-concept. The **conceptual self** is the ability to have a self-concept that includes an awareness of an autobiographical history, the ability to distinguish one's own mind from those of others, and to identify one's membership in conceptual categories, such as "I am a boy," and "I am a brother." Thus, by the end of the second year, you might hear a child say, "I'm not a baby anymore!"

Perhaps the most salient aspect of the conceptual self is identification with being either a boy or a girl; noticing sex differences in behavior and appearance, and show early signs of interest in nudity and sexuality. Although there are cultural differences in the frequency of sexual behavior, normally developing children (not sexually abused) of both genders become interested in watching other people undress and in seeing their genitals. They begin to hug non-family members, they like to walk around naked and expose their genitals, they try to touch other children's genitals, and they stimulate their own genitals with their hands (Larsson & Svedin, 2002). This interest in sexuality is a normal form of curiosity about their own and

other's bodies and part of the development of **gender identity**: the sense of affiliation as being either male or female.

Not all children identify with members of their biological gender. In some cases, this is because the child has a birth defect in which the genitals do not completely form, or in which they have characteristics of both males and females, or internal characteristics of one gender and external characteristics of the other gender (called **intersex**, but an older term is hermaphroditism). Some of these cases are caused by genetic and chromosomal abnormalities (see Chapter 3; Berenbaum & Bailey, 2003; Zucker, 1999). Another potential cause is too high or too low levels of maternal testosterone during the period of prenatal development when the genitals are forming (see Chapter 2). Even when the genitals are normal, some individuals may develop an identity with the "opposite" gender, in some cases for a few years and in other cases for a lifetime (as in homosexuality, transsexuality, bisexuality, and transvestitism (Fausto-Sterling, 2012; Hines et al., 2002; Reiner & Gearhart, 2004).

As a result of curiosity about one's own gender identity, children of this age develop **gender labeling**, when the child can identify self or other verbally as male or female. This begins at about 18 months (G. Levy, 2000; Poulin-Dubois, Serbin, & Derbyshire, 1998). Up until the age of 3 years, however, children do not understand that these labels reflect enduring characteristics of people. Two-year-olds will say correctly that they are a boy or a girl and will even engage in gender-stereotyped toy play, but they do not understand that a boy will always grow up to be a man. Children believe that gender might be changed by changing one's appearance or dress, which might explain why they are fairly rigid in their adoption of gender-role stereotypes ("Ladies can't wear pants"; "Boys don't play with dolls"). Children may actively discourage each other from playing with opposite gender–typed toys or even with members of the opposite sex (Gelman, Collman, & Maccoby, 1986). They will also look longer at gender inappropriate behavior (such as a man putting on lipstick), suggesting that they already have a sense of what males and females are likely to do ordinarily (Serbin, Poulin-Dubois, & Eichstedt, 2002).

Cognitive and linguistic factors play some role, because children who are more linguistically and cognitively advanced are also more stereotypic in their gender-role concepts. Two-to-three-year-old children who are more advanced in gender labeling (those who give the correct gender response to the question, "Who are you?") and who score higher on verbal intelligence tests are also more explicit about gender-role behaviors. That is, they will classify tasks and tools as male (car repair, shovels) or as female (cooking, irons). These children will also more readily adopt same-sex playmates in peer groups. Generally speaking, children who are more gender stereotypical at age 3 will continue to be so throughout childhood (Golombak et al, 2008; Halim et al., 2013). Some studies have found that boys begin gender labeling and gender stereotyping somewhat earlier than girls, but other research finds the opposite pattern. Regardless, girls are more likely to play with opposite-sex toys than are boys (Bauer, 1993; Fagot, Leinbach, & Hagan, 1990; McGuire, 1988; Zosuls et al., 2009).

One area that has been studied a great deal is parental influence over the child's choice of toys and gender role choices—specifically, parental reactions to traditional masculine toys (trucks, hammers, guns) and feminine toys (dolls, kitchen utensils) for their boys and girls. This is a difficult area in which to do research because reactions to a child's behavior regarding gender roles are highly culture specific. Interpreting this research is complicated because different studies use different measures (observations, questionnaires, parental reports) and because most of the research is done in middle-class Caucasian American families. However, with these qualifications, the following conclusions can be reached.

Few parents explicitly instruct their children in the gender-appropriate choice or use of toys. Gender-role stereotypes are communicated to children by the parents' emotional reactions to the children's choice of toys. First of all, when children are between 18 and 24 months, parents have more emotional reactions, both positive and negative and not necessarily gender stereotyped, to any kind of gender-related toy. Children who begin gender labeling early have parents who evince more emotional reactions to gender-typed toys during this early period (Fagot & Leinbach, 1989).

During the second year, as the children's toy choices, clothing and hair styles become more gender typed, and they tend to imitate other children of the same gender. The same pattern is true in ethnic minority children in the United States. Some parents begin to discourage gender-inappropriate toys, clothing, and actions and encourage gender-appropriate selections, again through emotional reactions rather than instruction (Caldera, Huston, & O'Brien, 1989; Fagot & Leinbach, 1989; Grace et al., 2008; Halim et al., 2013). As in gender labeling, girls are more likely to play with "boy" toys than the other way around. A similar pattern of relative toy "equality" in girls and toy stereotyping in boys has been found in rhesus monkeys, suggesting that genetic differences may play some role in gender-role activity (Hassett et al., 2008).

Parents also contribute to gender-role identity by discouraging aggression and encouraging prosocial behavior in girls and by encouraging responsibility in boys. In addition, most parents dress and cut their children's hair in gender-appropriate ways to avoid other people's incorrect identification of the children's gender, although children also play a role in these choices (McGuire, 1988; Power & Parke, 1986). In addition, parents talk in general about gender and gender roles, and it is nearly impossible to talk about someone, even a pet animal, without mentioning personal pronouns such as "he" and "she" (Gelman, Taylor, & Nguyen, 2004).

Sex differences in emotional communication occur outside the context of which toys are used. Girls talk more spontaneously and earlier in development about their emotions compared to boys (Cervantes & Callanan, 1998; Farver & Wimbarti, 1995). Research suggests that this may also be due partly to differences in parent-child emotional communication. Parents are more likely to respond to their daughters with a similar emotion, creating a shared emotional state (Robinson, Little, & Biringen, 1993). In talking about emotions with daughters, parents are more likely to provide a way to resolve their emotions with another person. With sons, parents more typically encourage the child to resolve the situation on their own and to stand up for themselves. With anger, for example, parents encourage daughters to make up with their friend who took a toy by approaching or playing with the friend. Parents are more likely to encourage sons to retaliate (Fivush, 1994).

Few studies have found differences between mothers and fathers in the encouragement of gender-appropriate behavior. Mothers and fathers typically agree on the kinds of gender roles they want for their children (Fagot & Hagan, 1991; Fagot & Leinbach, 1989). In one study, the types of speech, length of utterances, and number of questions and directives were the same for mothers and fathers when each interacted individually with the infant (Golinkoff and Ames, 1979). A study of verbal and nonverbal behavior of mothers and fathers found no parental sex differences in responsiveness to the infant, use of stimulation, affection, or effectiveness (A. Clarke-Stewart, 1978).

Even though mothers and fathers are using similar behavior toward the children, the early onset of gender labeling and the frequency of gender-typed toy play in children are predicted by personality characteristics of the father rather than of the mother. Early labelers, both boys and girls, have fathers who have more traditional gender-role orientations and who engage in more traditionally masculine tasks (car washing, lawn mowing, carpentry) than feminine tasks (laundry, cooking, dishwashing) at home. In homes where mothers work outside the home or where fathers are absent (single-parent mother-headed homes), children tend to have less traditional gender-role stereotypes (Fagot & Leinbach, 1989; Fagot, Leinbach, & O'Boyle, 1992; McGuire, 1988; Stevenson & Black, 1988).

On the other hand, that both male and female adult's attitudes affect children's gender-role choices. In an experimental study, 3 year-olds were exposed for two weeks to a preschool classroom that was either high in gender differentiation (physical separation and different bulletin boards for boys vs girls, singling out boys or girls when requesting something) or neutral. After this relatively brief period of 2 weeks, the children in the high gender salience classroom had more gender stereotypes, less positive ratings of and decreased play with opposite sex peers (Hilliard & Liben, 2010).

More than likely, gender differences emerging at this age are the result of the stabilizing of earlier patterns of parental beliefs and practices and psychobiological differences in the child and their responses to the parents (Fausto-Sterling, Coll, & Lamarre, 2011). It is certainly true that gender-role development in the third year is a topic of interest for both parents and children, and that children are using information available in the environment, as well as their own feeling and thinking about self-concept, to form ideas about gender roles.

Gender role development at this age is part of a more general awareness of one's own body schema. In one study, children were shown a doll or another person while stickers were put on certain body parts (starting with the nose). By 30 months, most children could place stickers on their own bodies at the same location as seen in the doll or person (Brownell et al., 2010). This is more advanced than the existential self, which requires recognizing the self in a mirror. Children with a conceptual self are also beginning to become familiar with the specific features of their own bodies, learning names for these features (nose, arm, leg) and sensing how their bodies are different from those of other people.

Having a self-concept also changes the way children think and remember. After the age of 2 years, events that are self-related draw the child's attention and are more likely to be remembered than other-related events (Ross, Anderson & Campbell, 2011). The same holds true for adults: we are more likely to remember what we say in a conversation compared to what other people say. Much of this is connected to the verbal use of the words "my" and "mine," and an awareness of the self as having possessions. When this first

TABLE 11.3   Stages of Development of Self- and Other-Awareness

Stage	Self-awareness	Other awareness
Emergent Self (late fetal to 2 months)	A sense of familiarity, occasional feelings of self-sameness over time.	Preference for familiar sounds, touches, sights of other people.
Ecological Self (2 to 6 months)	A sense of connection in one's own body's movements, sensations, and emotions; feeling of being the agent of one's own actions.	Feeling one's part in co-regulatory activities but without a sense of the other as a separate person.
Differentiated Ecological Self (6 to 9 Months)	Emergence of a distinct personality, taking initiative; emergence of anger and a growing sense of personal boundaries.	Aware of other people but only as extensions of one's own needs and desires: asking for help, showing off, demanding.
Subjective Self (9 to 18 Months)	Intentional communication, coordinated joint attention (pointing and requesting), showing off and expecting a response, emergence of fear and a sense of vulnerability.	Aware of other people as instruments of one's needs, but having different intentions and a different point of view (but there is no sense of the other as having emotions), sense of loss during separations, affective sharing and social referencing.
Existential Self (18 to 24 Months)	Self-recognition in a mirror, use of personal pronouns, sense of ownership and having possessions; self-conscious emotions of pride, shame and defiance (tantrums).	Aware of other people as having emotions and being able to see the infant, beginning of empathy but others are believed to have similar emotions and perspectives as the infant.
Conceptual Self (2 to 5 years)	A self-concept that includes an awareness of an autobiographical history, the ability to distinguish one's own mind from those of others (theory of mind), and to identify one's membership in conceptual categories, such as "I am a boy," and "I am a brother."	Aware of others as different people, with different emotions, intentions and perspectives; beginnings of a moral self (conscience) as being part of a larger community.

happens, at the end of the second year, children make aggressive claims towards their possessions (Mine!) and show temper tantrums reflecting a sense of personal entitlement (see Chapter 10).

During the third year, via conversations about self and other emotions and possessions and a growing self-concept and theory of mind, there is an expansion of the child's consciousness that encompasses a view of the self in relation to others as someone who can reflect upon and share the meanings and stories of self and other people. Children develop from a sense of personal entitlement at the end of the second year to learning concepts of sharing, justice, and equity: a budding moral sensibility in the third year (Rochat, 2010).

Much of this advance takes place in the realm of autobiographical narratives in which, via conversation, the child is able to enter into a world of shared meaning with others in a way that includes a personal history, an unfolding future, and a world of fiction and imagination about different times, places, and ways of being (Nelson, 2010). This expanded *consciousness* sets the stage for a *conscience*, that is, for acting according to the rules of the social world and developing a set of moral standards (Kochanska et al., 2010), all of which begins to develop more rapidly after the third year.

The ability to have a moral conscience in which we pay attention to others and regulate our emotions in the service of the interpersonal harmony of family and community is an amazing human achievement. This is the culmination of a three-year journey of growing self- and other-awareness that begins in the late fetal period (see Table 11.3). The third year is itself just another beginning of a life-long journey of moral behavior. As we grow up and mature, we continue to develop a broader sense of self and other, how we fit into the world, our own personal identity and our rights and obligations to others. There is no end point on this journey but rather a continuing process of inquiry, emotion, passion, and engagement. We cannot avoid mistakes and the resulting hurt and pain. The best we can hope for is that we learn from those mistakes and grow towards a greater sense of compassion and life wisdom.

EMOTIONAL DEVELOPMENT

Positive Emotion

During the third year of life, toddlers become more active and child-like when participating in social relationships with others. One way this occurs is by an increasingly sophisticated repertory of emotional forms of communication. The research I have done with my colleagues shows this pattern with respect to the development of laughter in the third year (Nwokah, Davies, Islam, Hsu, & Fogel, 1993). Recall that infants can produce different types of smiles (Duchenne, or cheek-raise, smiles, and play, or jaw-drop, smiles). We found that these different types of smiles are associated with specific types of social communicative situations during the first year of life. Duchenne smiles are more likely with peekaboo games, for example, and play smiles with tickling games. A similar pattern occurs with laughter. Three-year-old children have different types of laughs—called comment, chuckle, rhythmical, and squeal—and each laugh is associated with a specific type of communicative situation (Nwokah et al., 1993).

A *comment laugh* is brief and sounds like an exclamation; typically, it follows a funny action on the part of the mother. Here is an example of a communicative situation for a comment laugh:

Mother and Betsy are playing with a toy picnic set. Betsy starts to open a bag of plastic potato chips. Mother makes a pretend, sad face and says quietly and wistfully, "Are you gonna share the chips with me?" Betsy replies, "Yeah." Mother opens her mouth, smiles, and says, "Okay," as she throws her head back and laughs. Betsy watches, smiles, and gives a short comment laugh while turning to peek into the chip bag.

A *chuckle laugh* is soft with a low tone and reflects mild amusement. Chuckles occur in situations involving more excitement than the situations that evoke comment laughs. The following is an example from our data:

Betsy is standing and puts a toy doll's feeding bottle into her own mouth. Mother says, "Yukk!" and attempts to grab the bottle from Betsy's mouth. Betsy quickly pulls backward and sits down so mother misses. As Betsy sits down she emits a chuckle laugh with a wide grin, but keeps the bottle in her mouth, continuing to look at mother.

A *rhythmical laugh* is the longest type of laughter; it consists of a series of regularly spaced syllables (ha-ha-ha). Rhythmical laughs occur in a wide variety of highly arousing situations, usually when both partners are laughing:

Mother has a Daffy Duck puppet on her hand. Betsy is lying on her back on the floor and mother makes the puppet talk. Betsy says, "Shut up, Daffy Duck!" Mother then tickles Betsy's leg with the puppet. Betsy makes a rhythmical laugh as she tries to roll away, her eyes half closed and her mouth wide open.

Finally, a *squeal laugh* is a long, high, shrill sound. The following example illustrates its occurrence:

Betsy is holding a puppet while lying on her stomach. Mother, while smiling, moves her hand slowly to the puppet to get hold of it. Betsy gives a squeal laugh as mother touches the puppet. Betsy's head is raised with a wide open mouth smile.

As this research shows, children use laughter and other facial expressions and body movements, along with words, to express their positive feelings. These findings also show an increasing awareness of the emotions of self and other.

Theory of mind development in this age period also impacts positive emotions. After age 2 years, toddlers are more likely to "get" the meaning of simple jokes. They can tell the difference between jokes (putting a shoe on a hand instead of a foot) compared to mishaps (writing with the wrong end of a pen). In addition, they are able to look at the adult's face and voice to infer whether the adult thinks the situation is funny or not (Hoicka & Gattis, 2008).

Negative Emotions: Anger, Shame, and Sadness

By the third year, children are becoming increasingly skilled at regulating their emotion expression depending upon the situation. Children of this age are more likely to show negative emotions when with their parents, and more likely to show sadness when they have their parent's attention (Buss & Kiel, 2004). Children are also more likely to show their bad feelings with their parents if they have a history of successfully talking about and sharing those feelings with that parent (Spinrad et al., 2004).

Recall from Chapter 4 that the prefrontal cortex reaches a peak of synaptogenesis in the third year, meaning that there is more impulse control at this age than earlier. This is shown in an increase of **effortful control**, the ability of children to make a voluntary effort to calm themselves, to sustain their attention by delaying their responses, to slow down motor activity, suppress impulses and anger, and lower their voice (Eisenberg et al., 2005; Kochanska et al., 2000).

Effortful control grows steadily during the third and fourth years of life and reflects a coordination of regulation in the HPA axis, the parasympathetic (self-calming) nervous system, and the relationship of regulatory areas of the pre-

frontal cortex with emotional areas of the sensorimotor cortex and the amygdala (Cole et al., 2011; Thompson, Lewis, & Calkins, 2008). Specifically, amygdala reactions of fearfulness and anxiety are lowered and regulated by the ventromedial portion of the prefrontal cortex (Goldsmith, Hill & Davidson, 2008). Because of the association with the HPA axis and the amygdala (the perception of threat and stress increases cortisol secretion), environmental and family stress is an important contributor to the development of externalizing problems and lower levels of effortful control (Kolak & Vernon-Feagans, 2008).

The lack of effortful control—the inability to release from and resolve negative emotions—is related to a wide variety of environmental factors (stress, chaotic homes and neighborhoods), family factors (insensitive, rejecting, overprotective, or coercive parenting), temperamental factors (inhibition, externalizing problems, anxiety, and a tendency towards depressed moods) and cognitive factors (poor language skill, poor ability to recognize attributes of the self) (Buss, 2011; Cole, Luby & Sullivan, 2008; Eisenberg et al., 2005; Hutt, Buss & Kiel, 2013; Izard et al., 2008; Jennings et al., 2008; Kochanska et al., 2000; Roben et al., 2013; Spinrad et al., 2007; van der Bruggen et al., 2010).

One form of anger is physical aggression, such as hitting, kicking, and biting; otherwise known as temper tantrums. The rate of normal physical aggression is higher between the ages of 24 and 36 months than at any other time in the life course. Children with higher rates of temper tantrums during this period are more likely to remain aggressive and to develop externalizing behaviors in later childhood reflecting a lack of effortful control (Giesbrecht et al., 2010). Boys show more aggression and anger, a pattern that begins in the third year and continues through adulthood (Alink et al., 2006; Chaplin & Aldao, 2012; Persson, 2005). These differences may be the result of the sex differences in parental emotion regulatory processes such as those discussed above in which boys are socialized to stand up for themselves (Lindsey &

Mize, 2001). They could also be related to gender differences in temperamental emotion regulation discussed in previous chapters, that is, testosterone predisposes male infants to be more irritable than females. Probably both processes contribute to this gender difference.

Another form of emotion dysregulation is that children are beginning to show longer-lasting negative mood states. The first signs of depression appear at this age. Depressed 3-year-olds are sadder, grouchier, more whiney, have poorer appetites, more sleep problems, and more trouble concentrating than non-depressed peers. Depressed children express the feeling that nothing is "fun" (Luby et al., 2003). These symptoms are similar to those of depressed older children and adults. It is one of the downsides of having a conceptual self and autobiographical memory: children can begin to identity with their own negative feelings and realize that they have a long-lasting negative mood state.

Talking about Emotions

Children of this age can talk about their feelings and label emotional and physiological states accurately (Denham, 1986; M. Lewis & Michalson, 1983), they can talk about future and past emotions, and they can discuss the causes and consequences of emotions (Bretherton, Fritz, Zahn-Waxler, & Ridgeway, 1986; Reissland & Harris, 1991). By 28 months, most children have extensive emotion vocabularies for positive emotions (*happy, fun, good time, funny, like, love, feel better, proud*) and negative ones (*sad, scared, mad, yucky, messy, feel bad*). This development is cross-cultural: children from different cultural groups acquire emotion words around this age. Also common across different cultural groups is that children talk about their own and other people's emotions first, and then, about 6 months to 1 year later, begin to talk about their own and others' thoughts (*know, think*) (Tardif & Wellman, 2000).

In summary, emotion becomes increasingly social as it is subject to labeling and explicit regula-

tion by others. The ways adults respond to happy expressions versus temper tantrums ultimately affect the child's own emotional understanding. In general, research suggests that adults should accept children's emotions as genuine expressions of feeling, while working toward changing the manner in which the emotion is expressed or talked about ("I can see that you're angry, but I don't permit throwing things in the house"). The general principles for dealing with emotions are the same as those discussed in the previous chapter for guided participation: accept the child's initiative (even if this is negative) and then find ways to encourage the child into culturally and socially acceptable forms of expression (Demos, 1982; Lewis & Michalson, 1983; Rogoff, 1990). As children understand more about their own and other's emotions, this kind of conversation enhances the development of the conceptual self.

SOCIAL AND LANGUAGE DEVELOPMENT

As reviewed in the last chapter, there is a vocabulary spurt that occurs near the end of the second year. Sometime during the third year, or later for some children, there is a spurt in the **mean length of utterance (MLU)**. The MLU is the average number of morphemes in each utterance spoken by the child. A *morpheme* is a meaningful unit of language; it is usually a word, but it can also be a word ending, such as *-ed, -s,* or *-ing*. The word "walking," for example, has two morphemes: *walk | ing*. Increases in MLU for three children are shown in Figure 11.2. Notice the wide range of individual variation. Eve has an increase in MLU before Adam and Sarah have even begun to use more than one or two morphemes in an utterance (R. Brown, 1973).

These utterances are becoming less formulaic (see Chapter 10) and more like a flexible and productive standard grammar for the language spoken in the home (Bates, O'Connell, & Shore, 1987). Speaking in a sentence requires at least two basic components: a subject and a verb. In a grammatical sentence, the components must agree with one another in number (and gender in gender-based languages, such as Spanish and French). Sentences do not truly emerge until children begin to use verbs in a systematic manner—near the end of the second year of life.

In most cases, children acquire verbs more slowly than nouns. The time between when the first noun is acquired (about 10 months) and the first verb is acquired (about 20 months of age) is about the same as the time between birth and the first nouns are acquired. While English is a noun-based language, other languages such as Korean and Mandarin Chinese are more likely to organize their sentences around verbs. In these languages, verbs occur at the ends of sentences and can occur alone. Verbs, therefore, are more salient to both children and adults using these languages. Children acquiring these languages have more verbs in their early vocabularies than those speaking English, but in all languages, nouns predominate over verbs during the second and third years (Tardif, 1996; Tardif, Gelman, & Xu, 1999).

Nouns and verbs are fundamentally different. Nouns represent the descriptions of things or objects. Nouns refer to concrete things the child can see, touch, or feel. Verbs, in contrast, tell us about the relationship between things—between the subject and the object, for example. The ability to understand relationships between things and to express these in words begins late in the second year (S. S. Jones, Smith, & Landau, 1991; Waxman & Senghas, 1992).

Because verbs are relational, they can express nontangible things. When you say "The ball rolls across the floor," the verb represents a transient action—one that relates the ball and the floor. The words *ball* and *floor*, in contrast, make fewer intellectual demands on the listener; these objects are there for all to see whenever they wish to but the action is transitory. Verbs can also represent abstract properties that are difficult for a young child to appreciate, for example, *to think* and *to feel*.

When children first start to express action words, they often combine the action and its result

in the same word. The word *up* can be used for a variety of situations, such as being lifted, being put down, asking to be picked up or to climb on someone's lap, climbing up or down stairs, or even requesting out-of-reach objects (Clark, 1978). *Off*, *on*, *out*, and *open* can be used in similarly generic ways. The next step in the development of action expression is the use of simple verbs, such as *do* and *make*. The initial meaning of these words is not always clear to the listener, because the child uses them in many different ways. Thus, it is important to see the child speaking in the context of the ongoing activity (Table 11.4). A final way children express actions is by using an object word to talk about the action (E. V. Clark, 1978). Some examples include "The man is keying the door" (opening the door with a key); "I'm souping" (eating soup); or "Pillow me!" (throw a pillow at me).

Children of this age also make errors in the use of verbs similar to the overextension of nouns discussed in the previous chapter. Some examples are given in Table 11.5. Such errors usually happen after the children understand the similarity in meaning between verbs that they accidentally substitute for each other (Bowerman, 1978). *Put* and *give*, for example, are both words that a person uses to make an object move from one place to another. The substitution "errors" shown in Table 11.5 require that the child understand the basic relationship between *put* and *give*, since children rarely substitute words that have no semantic relationship to each other.

If you think about the order of events in an action sequence (rolling a ball from me back to you), some words represent the source of the action (*from*, *out*, *off*, *away*), some represent the path of the action (*back*, *up*, *down*, *across*, *through*), and some represent the goal or end point of the action (*to*, *in*, *at*, *there*). Children acquire these words developmentally in the same order: source-path-goal (Stockman & Vaughn-Cooke, 1992). Source words are acquired at the end of the first year ("Get this *out* her mouth [said taking a thermometer out of a doll's mouth]"; "Go *away* [telling a cat to leave the play area]"). Path words are acquired in the

Figure 11.2   Average Length of Utterance in Morphemes at Different Ages for Three Children

Source: From Brown, Cazden, & Bellugi-Klima, The child's grammar from I to III, 1969, p. 29. In J. P. Hill (Ed.), *Minnesota Symposium on Child Psychology* (Vol. 2) Copyright © The University of Minnesota Press. Reprinted by permission. Also in A. Fogel & G. F. Melson, *Child development*, 1988, p. 286. St. Paul, MN: West. Copyright © by West Publishing Company. Reprinted by permission. All rights reserved.

middle of the second year ("He climb *up* a tree [looking at a picture of a boy in a tree]"; "Make the man go *around* [placing a toy figure on a merry-go-round]"). Finally, goal words are acquired at the end of the second year ("All of 'em go *to* here [putting items in a purse]"; "I blow *at* Coty [aiming soap bubbles at Coty]").

These results show that language development in the third year is influenced by the temporal relations between elements in a sequence (Naigles & Kako, 1993; Stockman & Vaughn-Cooke, 1992). Children are better able to acquire

new nouns when they occur in sentences with a familiar verb. If there are a number of foods on the table and the adult says, "rutabaga," the child may have difficulty picking out the right object and may not pay attention to the word. If the adult says, "Daddy is *eating* the rutabaga," it gives the child a clue about the object to which the word *rutabaga* refers (Goodman, McDonough, & Brown, 1998). Once children get the verb, they can easily combine it with different objects (eating rutabaga, eating broccoli, eating soup, etc.) and it helps their learning if the talk about eat-

TABLE 11.4   Uses of Do, Go, and Make in the Third Year*

Verb	Utterance	Context
Do	I do it again.	Said as knocks over blocks.
	You ...do ...doing that.	Said as watches O build blocks into a tower.
	You do do it. OK?	Asking O to unroll some computer tape, after trying unsuccessfully to do it himself.
	You do that!	Indicating which toy O should take out of a box.
	Uh oh. I did.	Said as he turned off the tape recorder by pushing a knob.
	The clown do!	Asking O to make the toy clown do what clowns do.
Make	Make name!	Telling O to write his name.
	I make a little doggie.	Said as cut a dog shape out of Play-Doh.
	Make a dog.	Telling O what to draw next.
	Make it go in there.	Asking O to get a crayon back into its box.
	Make that.	Said as pointed to the hand moving on a clock; seemed to be request for O to move the hand down.
Go	It go there.	Talking about a block lying on the floor.
	Red went Boom.	Talking about a red block that fell on the floor.
	They go in the car.	Talking about two storybook characters.
	'N turn go up.	Said as turned a puzzle piece the right way up.
	'N go like that.	Said as dropped puzzle pieces on the floor.

*Examples cited come from the first month of recordings from S, a child taped at weekly intervals for 1 year from age 2 years. The utterances cited occurred without any immediately preceding use of the particular general purpose verb by either the observer (O) or the parents.
Source: E. Clark, Strategies for communicating, 1978, p. 957. *Child Development, 49*, 953–959. Copyright © The Society for Research in Child Development. Reprinted by permission of the Publisher and the author.

TABLE 11.5   Verb Substitution Errors

A. *Put* substituted for *give*.

E (2–2):   I go *put* it to Christy. (Starting off with a rubber band, then gives it to C.)

E (2–4):   Can I go *put* it to her? (Then takes juice and gives it to C.)

E (2–4):   M: It's all gone. (Re: C's juice.) E: Then *put* her some more.

E (2–4):   How come you're *putting* me that kind of juice? (As M prepares to give unfamiliar juice to E.)

E (2–4):   Were *putting* our things to you. (To D after M has told children that it's time to give him their Father's Day presents.

B. *Give* substituted for *put*.

E (2–7):   *Give* some ice in here, Mommy. *Put* some ice in here, Mommy. (Pointing to ice crusher.)

E (2–9):   *Give* those crayons right here (Indicated to M spot on table near where she is sitting.)

E (2–10):   I'm gonna *give* your glasses right here. (M: Huh?) I'm gonna *put* your glasses right here.

E (2–10):   Don't *give* those next to me. (As C dumps things on couch near E's seat.)

*C = Christy, E = Eva, M = Mother, D = Daddy.
Source: M. Bowerman, Systematizing semantic knowledge: Changes over time in the child's optimization of word meaning, 1978, pp. 984–985. *Child Development, 49*, 977–987. Copyright © The Society for Research in Child Development. Reprinted by permission of the publisher and the author.

ing is happening with respect to fewer people (just mommy and daddy, for example) (Macguire et al., 2008; Naigles, Hoff & Vear, 2009; Newman, 2011). This may help explain the vocabulary spurt that began during the previous age period. As children begin to acquire verbs it also helps them to learn even more nouns.

Adding the Proper Endings

Children still have more to learn about verbs in the preschool years, in particular about verb meaning and tense. One interesting phenomenon is that just after children acquire the past tense of regular verbs (such as *looked* for *look* or *helped* for *help*), they apply the *-ed* rule to all verbs, including irregular verbs. So, instead of saying *went*, the child says *goed*. Instead of saying *made*, the child says *maked*. This pattern of grammatical error is called **overregularization**. Overregularization errors are relatively rare, happening only 2.5 percent of the time the child intends to use an irregular past tense. They occur from the age of 2 years up through the elementary school years. These errors probably reflect minor memory slips and are not symptomatic of poor language development (Marcus, Pinker, Ullman, & Hollander, 1992). In fact, they actually reflect progress in learning the underlying grammatical rules.

The way children acquire plurals is very similar to the way they acquire verb tenses. Children first acquire some irregular forms such as *men* and *children* almost without realizing that they are plurals of *man* and *child*. Once they acquire the general rule of adding an *s*, they apply that rule to anything, even the words they previously had acquired in the irregular plural forms: *mans* and *childs* (Berko, 1958).

Another type of meaningful word ending is negation. Although younger infants express negation by saying *no* or *not*, children of this age use contractions, such as *can't* and *don't* (H. H. Clark & Clark, 1977). Although the ability to put the proper endings on words is slow to be acquired, apparently by the age of 2 years children can understand the difference between words with different end-

ings, another instance in which comprehension precedes production (Gerken, Landau, & Remez, 1990).

When Do Children Begin to Ask Questions?

After children master the subject-verb-object composition of sentences, they usually move quickly beyond simple declarative sentences to form questions. Questions usually begin with *wh*-words, and a definite developmental sequence in the order of acquisition of these words has been found (see Table 11.6). The ages listed in Table 11.6 are approximations, and we can expect individual differences in the age of acquisition.

The reason for this developmental sequence is that the *wh* questions differ in their complexity. *What*, *where*, and *who* all ask for single-word responses that usually are simply extracted from a situation: "What did Bobby make?" "A tower." *Why*, *how*, and *when* require a more extended response giving a reason, process, or time.

The initial use of questions by 2-year-olds also reflects a rudimentary ability to use the questions in a fully expressive manner. Most of the questions addressed by children of this age are not dependent upon the previous topic of discussion. Thus, children often use questions to start a conversation rather than to continue one. The only exceptions to this rule are *why* questions (L. Bloom, Merkin, & Wootten, 1982). Although some parents get annoyed with the constant "why"s of their young children, the ability to ask *why* reflects a growing linguistic sophistication that foreshadows a more complex use of verbs and other *wh*-questions over the next few years.

Children definitely want information when they ask a question. They are not just trying to get the adult's attention (Chouinard, 2007). They will typically stop asking questions when they get an answer that satisfies the intention of their question or that gives a fuller explanation of what an object can do rather than just giving the name of the object. Children of this age are more likely to ask follow-up questions if an adult responds. If the adult does

TABLE 11.6 Order of Acquisition of *wh-* Questions

Age (Months)	Question
26	Where and What
28	Who
33	How
35	Why
36	Which, Whose, and When (occured rarely at this age)

Source: L. Bloom, S. Merkin, & J. Wootten, Wh-questions: Linguistic factors that contribute to the sequence of acquisition, 1982, p. 1089. *Child Development, 53*, 1084–1092.

not respond to their question, toddlers will likely re-ask their question or provide their own explanation, showing that they are really listening to what the adult has to say, or does not say (Frasier, Gelman & Wellman, 2009; Kemler Nelson & O'Neil, 2005; Kemler Nelson, Egan, & Holt, 2004).

Children's question asking tells us that they have become aware of the importance of language for communication. When children ask *why* questions, they are not only requesting information but are saying, "I know you know the answer," "I know I can use language to get a response or an explanation from you," and possibly even "I have the right, duty, and privilege to ask you this question." These unstated forms of linguistic awareness, or awareness about the function of language and of the implicit relationship between speakers, are known as **metalinguistic knowledge** (Kaye, 1982; P. J. Dunham & Dunham, 1996; Y. Levy, 1999). Metalinguistic means "above" or "outside of" language itself.

In What Ways Is the Two-Year-Old's Language Limited?

In spite of the major accomplishments in the linguistic realm taking place during the third year of life, children still have a great deal more to learn about language. They still make errors in pronunciation, fail to comprehend certain words and sentences, and have only rudimentary conversational skills.

Young children acquiring English have an endearing tendency to confuse *r* and *l* and to make them both sound like *w*. Audio frequency analysis of children who said *gwass* for both *glass* and *grass* can detect differences between the child's pronunciation of the two words, however, even though the human ear could not. This means that children are in fact attempting the correct pronunciation (Kornfeld, 1971). This is also confirmed in a study of children who confused *r* with *w*. They all said *wake* to refer to the garden tool used to gather leaves. About two-thirds of the group was able to tell the difference between an adult's pronunciation of *wake* and *rake*. Finally, children will become annoyed when adults try to mimic their mispronunciations (Locke, 1979; W. R. Miller, 1964).

Some researchers have collected recorded samples of children's private speech with a microphone hidden in their cribs. During these monologues, children have been heard to practice their pronunciation. One child practiced the *r* in *story* as follows: "Stoly/Stoly here/want a stoly/Dave, stoly/story, story/story's de hat/story's de big hat/store's a hat" (R. H. Weir, 1966).

This is further evidence that comprehension continues to be ahead of production. Even though children can hear the difference, and even though they apparently are attempting to pronounce the words correctly, they are still unable to do this perfectly. This error tends to persist in the speech of some children until school age, whereas other children never have problems with the *r-l* distinction. All children, however, need a good deal of time to get the correct pronunciations of most of the words they use routinely.

Some children, however, continue to have difficulty with pronunciation even during preschool. Such children show more delay in learning other features of language, such as MLU, grammar, and vocabulary (Carson et al., 2003). They are also more likely to have difficulty learning to read (McBride-Chang & Kail, 2002). Continuing pronunciation difficulties into the fourth and fifth year, therefore, may be a reason to have a child assessed for possible language and/or hearing intervention.

Finally, children of this age have trouble comprehending unusual grammatical sequences. If you were told that the robin is being kissed by the blue jay, how would you answer the questions "Who did the kissing?" and "Who was the kisser?" You are probably wishing all your test questions were this easy. However, 2-year-olds have trouble getting the right answer. Half the time they said the robin was the kisser, and half the time they said the blue jay (Bever, 1970). They all got the right answer when they were told "The bluejay kisses the robin" or "It's the robin that the bluejay kisses." The first sentence—the one that confused the children—is a passive construction. Evidently, whenever the children hear a noun followed by a verb, they assume the noun represents the actor. Not until children are in elementary school can they easily understand sentences such as "Donald Duck was liked by Goofy" (Maratsos, Kuczaj, Fox, & Chalkley, 1979).

How Well Can a Two-Year-Old Carry on a Conversation?

The mother and child in Table 11.7 were reading a picture-book together. In the same study from which this conversation was taken, mothers and children also played with a set of toy teacups and plates, as well as with a doll family with a table, chairs, a dog, and a car, among other things (Kaye, 1982). The children were videotaped at 26 months and again at 30 months doing these things with their mothers.

What is the difference between this conversation and one you might hear between two adults? When adults talk to each other, the conversation is likely to continue because both partners are used to taking initiatives and starting new thoughts. In Table 11.7, the parent was more likely to get a response from the child if she asked the child a question or created a situation that required a response from the child. Thus, the parent needs to keep prompting the child to continue the conversation. At this age, the child does not have a mature ability to carry on dialogue, even though the child may have mastered the words and phrases of the language. As an apprentice conversationalist, the child can respond to the adult, who makes the child look more capable than he or she really is (Kaye, 1982; C. E. Snow, 1977).

Research has shown that by age 2, social class differences in linguistically based parent-child communication emerge. One study in the United States found that middle-income dyads spend twice as much time in mutual play as lower-income dyads. Mothers in lower-income groups spend more time reading to themselves, and their children are observed more often in independent play (Farran & Haskins, 1980). Even within middle-income groups, there seem to be individual differences. Parents with professional backgrounds—especially

TABLE 11.7   A Conversation

Mother	Child (30 Months)
1. (Points to picture) What is that one?	2. Kitty cat.
3. Well what is it?	4. Kitty cat.
5. Well, I know there's a kitty.	6. Huh?
7. What's he riding in?	8. Airplane.
9. Right.	10. (turns page)

Source: K.Kaye, *The mental and social life of babies*, 1982, p. 100. Chicago: University of Chicago Press. Copyright © The Society for Research in Child Development, Inc. Reprinted by permission of the publisher and the author.

teachers—are more likely to read to and interact with their children than parents with blue-or white-collar jobs (Feiring & Lewis, 1981). In observations of parents reading picture-books to their children, Ninio (1980) found that middle-income Israeli mothers asked more questions, talked more during the reading session, and modeled more new words than the low-income mothers. In general, middle-income children have more advanced language development and larger vocabularies than lower-income children (Hoff, 2003).

Discipline and Compliance in the Third Year

During the third year of life, children widen the scope of their activities and language, not all of which fits into their parents' ideas about appropriate behavior. Parents need to provide continued discipline to orient the child toward acceptable and competent patterns of action. Parents introduce a wide variety of controls over toddler behavior. Children are told to do things ("Tie your shoe") and not to do things ("Don't yell"), and they are asked to control their future actions ("Be good while I'm gone"). Parents ask children to perform actions requiring a high level of competence ("Take care of your brother"; "Put the crayons away"; "Say thank you"; "Don't write on the wall"; "Go play in the other room"). Children can either comply or resist. Resistance can be passive or it can involve direct defiance, with the child exploring all the different ways of using the word *no* (Kuczynski & Kochanska, 1995).

The findings on parental discipline and child compliance at this age are similar to those reported in the previous chapter. Research shows that authoritative patterns of parental discipline (combining firmness, respect for the child, and warmth; see Chapter 10) are associated with cooperative and compliant children. On the other hand, oppositional children have parents who attempt to control the child's behavior. Oppositional children receive fewer demands for performing competent behavior and fewer requests to control their future actions.

It is not clear whether this style of parenting causes oppositional children, or whether the parents adapt their style to a less compliant child by making fewer demands on the child. Most likely, this is a relational pattern that emerges during the history of their prior communications. In any case, the parent and child enter into a cycle in which the parents avoid confronting the child, and the child is deprived of opportunities to become more competent. In other cases, a negative cycle of mutual conflict and parental nagging results (Kuczynski & Kochanska, 1995; Laible, Panfile & Makariev, 2008).

It is difficult to break these cycles, and they may persist for one or more years (Aber, Belsky, Slade, & Crnic, 1999). Intervention from a third party, another adult family member or a family therapist, may be needed if they persist and lead to breakdowns in parent-child communication. Intervention is helpful because these negative cycles often lead to behavior problems of the child, including attention difficulties and aggression with peers and in child-care and school settings (Aken et al., 2008; Lipscomb et al., 2011; Lorber & Egeland, 2011).

The good news is that during the third year, the frequency of defiance and refusals to cooperate gradually diminishes. It is replaced by children's use of negotiation strategies. Instead of simply saying "no" or "I don't want to," when asked to clean up their toys, to take one example, by 30 months or so children may begin to say things like "Let me play a little longer and then I'll clean up," "You clean some and I'll clean some," or "Don't leave and I'll clean up" (Klimes-Dougan & Kopp, 1999). This type of child behavior is more likely to occur if parents are less confrontational during conflicts and more likely to hear the child's perspective and negotiate (Laible & Thompson, 2002).

FAMILY AND SOCIETY

Peer Interactions

By the third year of life, children are capable of engaging in social interaction and of adapt-

---

Experiential Exercises

Observing Children using Naturalistic Qualitative Methods
by Alan Fogel

Naturalistic observation is the practice of studying real-world situations as they unfold naturally. Following the principles of qualitative research (see Chapter 1), this form of observation is non-manipulative, unobtrusive and non-controlling. It is open to whatever emerges and as such must be lacking in predetermined constraints on outcomes. In contrast, experimental research attempts to control conditions through manipulating, changing, or holding constant external influences and in which a very limited set of outcome variables are mea-sured. Naturalistic observation is a "discovery-oriented" approach. It focuses on capturing process, documenting variations, and exploring important individual differences in experiences and outcomes. Thus, an important part of qualitative methods includes the investigator's personal experiences and insights. It is important to understand and acknowledge your own history and influence in the existing system during your direct participation (Patton, 1990).

Arrange to observe at a day care center, nursery school or home where there are children aged 2 to 4 years. At some locations you can choose to observe only or participate with the children. In either case plan on spending 2 to 3 hours in observation.

During your observation or following your participation at one of the sites, record field notes about your observations. Emphasize your experience as a participant and as an observer (even if you are not in direct contact with the children). Report any insights that you may have about personal experiences or memories that are elicited through your observations. This is a very free format, so be open to any thoughts, feelings, or ideas that come up for you. This is an opportunity to reflect on your own experience and think critically about its direct relevance to you personally and to the research we have reviewed on early childhood development.

---

ing to the messages and demands of the listener (Wellman & Lempers, 1977). Between 22 and 30 months, infants increase their rates of verbalizations to peers, watch each other more, and increase their overall rates of social interaction (Mueller et al., 1977). Children also show a greater tendency to engage in mutual social play, and a decreasing amount of parallel play is seen near the end of the third year (Bakeman & Brownlee, 1980).

The kinds of interactions taking place, as well as the content of the interactions, are also undergoing important changes. Children gradually incorporate their symbolic play into peer interactions. No longer content to construct elaborate pretend sequences on their own, preschool children work together to elaborate a pretend game. At first, children simply copy or echo their partners in their peer exchanges. Later, they provide complementary responses, and finally, they elaborate and embellish the other's responses (Camaioni, Baumgartner, & Perucchini, 1991; Garvey, 1974).

Table 11.8 shows some of the social processes that account for this development in the ability of peers to achieve and maintain coordinated action (Eckerman & Didow, 1989). One important change is that peers begin to imitate each other, first nonverbally and later verbally. Based on both naturalistic observations and observations in which adults acted like peers and imitated children, research shows that the experience of being imitated is a powerful motivator of social behavior. Being imitated by someone gives one immediate and recognizable feedback of one's effect on the other person and inspires one to imitate him or her in return (Eckerman, 1993; Eckerman & Stein, 1990). Some examples of imitation that are specific to peer relationships in the third year are given in Table 11.9.

A second component of increasing peer coordination, also shown in Table 11.9, is the emergence of complementary roles and alternative responses. In this case, the child makes a different but appropriate response to the partner's over-

TABLE 11.8 Development of Emerging Skills in Achieving Coordinated Action

Age Period	Behavior Skills	Characteristic Interaction
Younger than 16 months	Assume and maintain complementary role in familiar, ritualized games.	Sustained ritualized games, little coordinated action in other contexts.
16–18 months	Imitation of nonverbal acts as general strategy for coordinated action in nonritualized contexts; repeated imitation across turns of action.	Widespread imitation of other's acts, resulting in imitation games and games with both imitative and complementary roles.
28–32 months	Verbalizations coordinated to another's actions begin to occur with appreciable frequency; increasingly accompany nonverbal forms of coordinated action with verbal regulations, descriptions, and imitations. Increasingly respond to another's overtures with alternative overtures composed of words and nonverbal actions or words alone.	Words coordinated to partner's actions increasingly occur in context of games structured largely by nonverbal imitation; words begin to serve as turns in games. Games intermixed with periods of negotiation of topic for interactions
Older than 32 months	Use of overtures thematically related to ongoing activities to vary or elaborate on the ongoing coordinated action.	Games less repetitive across turns; coordinated action sustained for longer periods of time, with changes in topic occurring during the bout.

Source: C. O. Eckerman & S. M. Didow, Toddler's social coordinations: Changing responses to another's invitation to play, 1989, p. 803. *Developmental Psychology, 25*, pp. 794–804

TABLE 11.9 Types of Imitative and Complementary Actions Seen in Peer Interactions During the Third Year

Type of Act	Example
Imitative	Exchanging an object; playing catch, peekaboo; hitting each other; both running, copying sounds, laughing, screaming; faking laugh or cry; clapping; sticking out tongues; singing; jumping.
Complementary	Finding a hidden peer; playing leader and follower; giving/following directives ("Go jump"; "Come here"); answering question.

Source: C. O. Eckerman, C. C. Davis, & S. M. Didow, Toddler's emerging ways of achieving social coordination with a peer, 1989, p. 448. *Child Development, 60*, pp. 440–453; L. Kuczynski, C. Zahn-Waxler, & M. Radke-Yarrow, Development and content of imitation in the second and third years of life: A socialization perspective, 1987, p. 280. *Developmental Psychology, 23*, pp. 276–282.

ture. This might even occur as a slight variation in the context of imitation: one child might throw a ball and the other a beanbag. A third developmental change is the growing use of language as part of a coordinated interaction. Instead of overt actions, the child begins to use words as directives, requests, or comments and responses.

Imitation, therefore, seems to serve as a social bridge between the simple kinds of uncoordinated peer play seen in the second year and the complex coordinated interactions seen later in the third year. One of the social functions of imitation is that it increases a feeling of closeness between two people (Nadel & Fontaine, 1989; Uzgiris, 1983). Thus, we might expect similar feelings of interpersonal closeness to emerge between 2-year-old peers.

Peers use both language and nonverbal action for metacommunication about their relationship.

Children can engage in pretend fighting by meta-communicating (such as smiling or saying "This is pretend"). Or a child can deflect a real attack by making it into a game with a teasing expression. Often children play in a very intense way and pretend to scream as if in pain. If one child accidentally gets hurt, a change in that child's intonation or posture can metacommunicate to the other children the more serious nature of the scream (Fogel & Branco, 1997). When conflicts over toys develops, children are sensitive to who actually owns the toy, with owners most likely to end up with the toy, suggesting that the development of moral self and other awareness contributes to the resolution of peer conflicts (Ross, 2013).

Do Two-Year-Olds Behave the Same No Matter Whom They Are With?

The answer to this question is no. Children of this age can adapt their behavior to the characteristics of the other child and the type of relationship they have with that child. One dimension of relationship difference is friendship. Research shows that there is a difference in social interaction between children who call themselves friends and those who do not (Ross & Lossis, 1987). In one study, children were left in an unfamiliar room either with a familiar peer, with an unfamiliar peer, or by themselves. The children with the familiar peer were the most comfortable, and the children left alone were the most upset (Ispa, 1981).

In another study, children were asked to rank all their nursery school playmates according to how much they liked being with each person. The children were paired off and taken to an unfamiliar place, where they played together. Half the pairs were made up of children who rated each other as preferred playmates, and half were made up of children who did not rate each other as preferred. At the end of 10 minutes of play in the new setting, an experimenter took one of the children off to play a special game, leaving the other in the room alone. Children whose friends left them behind were more likely to be disturbed during the separation than children left behind by non-

friends. Thus, there is some indication that peer friendships show an attachment-like quality—that children are fond of their friends and like to be with them (Melson & Cohen, 1981).

Beginning at this age, children's play groups form a **dominance hierarchy;** a pattern of social relationships in which the members of a group are ranked according to their relative power or lack of power over others. A child who is with a more dominant peer will do more observing and take a less assertive and active role in exploring the environment. The same child with a subordinate peer will take more of a leadership role and have more initiative in the play (P. H. Hawley & Little, 1999). Finally, adults affect peer relationships. In a child care setting, peers are more likely to engage with each other if they are not immediately near an adult caregiver. It seems that when an adult in close by, children of this age will prefer to interact with the adult (Legendre & Munchenbach, 2011).

Do Family Factors Affect Peer Relationships?

Family factors do affect peer relationships. One study found that children without siblings were more sociable with unfamiliar peers than were firstborns with siblings, and firstborns were more sociable than children born later. This could be because the children born later had the most nonpeers to play with or because they expected from peers the same kinds of aggressive rivalry they received from their siblings, making them more wary of peers (M. E. Snow, Jacklin, & Maccoby, 1981). The child's relationship to the parents also matters. Children who are more securely attached to their mothers and who demonstrate better self-control in frustrating situations also are more likely to show competence in peer encounters (Calkins, Gill, Johnson, & Smith, 1999; Matas, Arend, & Sroufe, 1978). Children who have an insecure-avoidant relationship with their mothers are more likely to show hostile-aggressive behavior with their peers, while children with an insecure-resistant attachment show less self-assertion and are less able to concentrate on pretending and exploring (McElwain et al., 2003).

Do Sociocultural Factors Affect Peer Relationships?

Sociocultural factors also affect peer relationships. For example, Israeli children who were brought up in kibbutzim (farm cooperatives) showed more cooperative play with one another than Israeli children reared in an urban environment (Shapira & Madsen, 1969). The more a society is family oriented rather than peer-group oriented, the less the children will be encouraged to play in peer groups. This has been found in Mexico (Madsen & Shapira, 1970) and Switzerland (Boehm, 1977).

In smaller, agrarian societies, such as some African tribal societies, children have relatively few age-mates living in the same village. Children in these settings tend to play in mixed-age groups rather than peer groups (Konner, 1975). Mixed-age groupings are rare in modern, urbanized settings. They typically occur between siblings in the same family. Even preschools tend to be age segregated in Western countries. Although there is little research on the topic, we might suspect that some of the same benefits that exist in sibling relationships—such as the ability to lead and follow, to imitate and serve as a role model, to learn and teach—would exist in mixed-age groupings of children outside the family. For example, when socially isolated preschool children were asked to interact with children younger than themselves, the older child became more sociable over time (Furman, Rahe, and Hartup, 1979).

Societies differ in the amount adults supervise peer groups. In urban settings, young children are always under the watchful eyes of a caregiver, for obvious ecological reasons. In rural societies and smaller societies, children are relatively less supervised, even at a young age. The Foré people of New Guinea allow infants total freedom of movement as soon as they can walk (Sorenson, 1979). In the Marquesas Islands, starting at 2 years of age, children spend most of the day in unsupervised peer groups ranging in size from three to six children. They are allowed to play near the sea, in boathouses, on bridges, and near streams (Martini & Kirkpatrick, 1981). Neither Sorensen nor Martini and Kirkpatrick ever observed children becoming lost or injured, but how the children avoided accidents is not clear. These examples suggest that 2-year-olds are indeed autonomous individuals, as well as that the social and physical ecology of the setting determines the manner in which that autonomy is expressed.

Societies differ in how much structure they provide for peer relationships. In Japan, young children wear uniforms, and their activities are coordinated by an adult.
Photo by Alan Oddie/PhotoEdit.

Types of Sibling Interactions

In earlier chapters, we discussed the infant's relationship with an older sibling. In this section, the infant will be discussed from the perspective of being both the older and the younger sibling. We will cover types of interactions between siblings and interfamily differences in sibling interactions. All sibling pairs share both positive and negative interactions. Furthermore, no matter what the interaction is, the children get something specific from their siblings that they do not receive in other relationships.

If the 2-year-old is a younger sibling, he or she will spend a lot of time paying attention to the older sibling and following him or her around. Younger siblings have been observed to imitate older siblings more often than they are imitated by older siblings; younger siblings are more likely to follow older siblings' directions and suggestions, and they are more compliant in taking designated roles in games. Furthermore, infants with older siblings are more likely to imitate other people in general, suggesting that they have come to see themselves in the role of follower rather than a leader (Abramovitch, Corter, Pepler, & Stanhope, 1986; Barr & Hayne, 2003; Stoneman, Brody, & MacKinnon, 1984).

In one study, 23-month-old children were observed both with and without their older siblings (H. R. Samuels, 1980). When they were with the siblings, the toddlers went farther from their mothers, left their mothers sooner, stayed away longer, and showed more independent exploratory behavior than did toddlers whose siblings were not present. The increased boldness seems to be due almost entirely to their following the older siblings around and imitating their behavior. In this way, younger children have the advantage of an older guide as they begin to explore the environment. This study does not suggest that the older sibling intentionally chooses to lead the way and teach the younger one, only that the younger one will follow what the older one does. Parents often remark that the laterborns seems to do things at a younger age than the firstborn;

such imitative behavior may partially explain this observation.

On the other hand, older siblings are more likely to give directives, to orient the attention of the younger children, to command and prohibit, to support, and to tease. Older siblings address infants in a form of motherese, except they rarely ask questions of the babies (J. Dunn & Kendrick, 1982; C. P. Jones & Adamson, 1987; R. A. Stewart, 1983). Older siblings who had experienced more discussion of internal states and emotions with their mothers were more likely to be sensitive to the emotional states of their younger siblings and the younger siblings in turn were more likely to be comforted by and learn from their older brothers or sisters, perhaps because the older siblings were more advanced in empathy and theory of mind (Howe & Rinaldi, 2004; Klein, Feldman, & Zarur, 2002). Observations 11.1 and 11.2 show representative directives of 2- to 3-year-old siblings to their baby sisters.

After the birth of a new baby, older children tend to seek help more, seek proximity to their mothers more, and cry more. Research shows that the older child has good reason for behaving this way. The mother's behavior to the older child changes somewhat when the new baby is around: confrontation increases and positive involvement with the firstborn decreases. Even when the mother is not occupied with the baby, she tends to spend less time with the older child (Kendrick & Dunn, 1980; R. A. Stewart, Mobley, Van Tuyl, & Salvador, 1987). The increase in confrontations between mother and firstborn is due primarily to an increase in "deliberate naughtiness" on the part of the older child. It seems that the older child's feelings of being displaced are met by the mother's increased workload as she cares for two young children instead of only one (Kendrick & Dunn, 1980).

On the other hand, 2-year-olds are becoming more sensitive to the dynamics of the family environment. They are really very skilled at knowing just how to annoy the younger sibling (teasing, making disparaging remarks, showing a toy spider to a sibling who does not like spiders), on the one hand, and enlisting the support of the mother dur-

---

Observations

Speech to Younger Siblings by Three-Year-Olds

Observation 11.1 (England)

The younger sister, Robin, has just picked up a piece of candy from the floor and is licking it. The older brother, Duncan, tells Robin that the dog, Scottie, will eat it. When Robin doesn't listen, Duncan pushes her gently through the door.

Duncan: "No, don't you eat it. Scottie will eat it. Scottie will eat it. No, not you. Scottie will eat it. Not you. Scottie. Not you. Shall we go in door? Right, come on. Come on. In door, Robin. In door." (J. Dunn & Kendrick, 1982, p. 126).

Observation 11.2 (Mexico)

Older sister Victoria and younger sister Lucha play in their courtyard with a small rabbit. Lucha is having some trouble keeping the rabbit in one place and is trying to do so by holding its ears.

Victoria: "Mira tu no sabes!" (Look, you don't know how!) Victoria then demonstrates how to hold the rabbit correctly (Zukow, 1990, p. 30).

---

ing sibling conflicts (J. Dunn & Munn, 1985), on the other. Tattling occurs between siblings of this age in the majority of families. Sometimes children tattle to get the mother on their side during a conflict. Other times, tattling is used just to inform the parent about the sibling's misbehavior. Children tattle primarily about physical aggression and about property damage and disputes (den Bak & Ross, 1996). Ongoing jealousy leads to continuing sibling conflict (Kolak & Volling, 2011).

The older siblings also become adept at making eloquent justifications to the mother for their disputes with the sibling. For example, after taking a toy away from a younger brother, the older child might say to mother, "He took it first!" or "But I needed that" (J. Dunn & Munn, 1987). They also become able to steer the direction of a mother-baby interaction toward their own needs or concerns (J. Dunn & Shatz, 1989).

Although older siblings do not shy away from causing conflict with the younger ones, when the conflict is between the mother and the younger sibling, the 2-year-old sibling might be the first to come to the rescue of the baby. Some of the strategies used by the older child to diffuse the conflict between mother and younger sibling include repeating the sibling's action that the mother did not like (drawing the mother's attention away from the younger one), giving the younger child a similar object to the one the mother had just taken away, prohibiting or scolding the mother for her punishment of the sibling, and comforting the sibling.

Although some conflict is inevitable in family relationships, sibling relationships have many positive aspects. In conversations between siblings when the mother is present, for example, infants are able to join in the talk between mother and older sibling at a much higher level than when they are with the mother alone. This is because the older child does not always have the ability to reply as a full conversational partner (see Table 11.7), which leaves room for the young sibling to enter into the conversation (Barton & Tomasello, 1991).

There is also evidence that siblings have a special relationship that is different from the parent-child relationship. In particular, siblings like to talk more about their emotions with each other than with parents. Older siblings verbally label the younger sibling's emotional reactions ("You don't like that, do you? I don't want it!"). Siblings like to share jokes about "yucky" bugs or gender categories ("You like Barbie dolls!"). They also express feelings of liking and disliking ("I'm really proud of you [accompanied by kissing]!" "Ginny, you drive me mad!") (J. R. Brown & Dunn, 1992; N. Howe, 1991). There is also evidence that siblings form attachments to each other and would rather be together than with an unfamiliar peer (Kier & Lewis, 1993). These experiences lead to a shared history of being together in mutual support that may last a lifetime (Kramer, 2010).

In some societies, it is common for older siblings, even those as young as 3 years, to have some responsibilities for taking care of babies (with adult supervision). Sibling caretakers for infants typically are found in societies that are relatively less complex and more traditional (Whiting & Whiting, 1975). If the division of labor in the family is such that the mother cannot stay at home to take care of the infant, siblings are likely to take over this function. In non-technological societies, all family members are called upon to do extra work. The children have more chores around the house than children in technological societies, and infant care is one of these tasks.

In Taira, a village in Okinawa, preschool girls patted, bounced, and talked to infants to calm them. If this did not work, the girls returned them to mothers or grandmothers. Girls in Taira never bathed or fed infants, nor did they put them to bed. In Tarong, on the island of Luzon in the Philippines, child "nurses" were trained at age 3 to entertain, rock, and hold the baby, but adults continued to supervise them.

Among the Gusii living in Nyansongo, Kenya, child nurses were somewhat older (5 to 8 years), and they were given more responsibility. They were assigned the total care of an infant beginning when the infant was around 2 months of age. They fed, bathed, and cared for the infants while the mothers worked in nearby fields (Whiting & Whiting, 1975). In the Marquesas Islands, 2-year-olds are important as companions, instructors, and comforters of their infant siblings. The adults hold these children in high esteem and often ask them to show off the baby. Children are relied upon to calm an infant if an adult fails (Martini & Kirkpatrick, 1981).

In summary, these studies reveal that siblings are important to each other's development. Younger siblings benefit from the guidance and protection of a role model, and they also acquire self-protective social skills and learn how to resolve conflicts. Older siblings benefit from being tutors and caregivers by focusing their attention on the needs of others. When they are scolded for annoying the younger child, the older children understand the nature of codes of conduct and some complex social and emotional regulatory skills.

Interfamily Differences in the Types of Sibling Interactions

Why do some siblings fight more than others? What should parents do to help their children get along better with each other? A number of family and child factors have been associated with a higher incidence of both mother-older child and older child-younger child confrontations.

Each sibling's relationship with the mother. Research shows that each sibling's attachment to the mother affects the quality of the sibling relationship. When the mother is present with the children, securely attached 2-year-old younger siblings are

Older children can be important as models and teachers for their younger siblings. The younger child seems to enjoy the company of the older, even if the younger one does not always understand what is going on.
Photo by Emily Waterfield

less likely to be aggressive to the mother or to the older sibling when the mother plays exclusively with the older sibling. Older siblings who are securely attached are more likely to respond to the needs and distress of the younger sibling in the mother's absence; older siblings who are not securely attached are less likely to do so (Teti & Ablard, 1989). A similar result has been found for twins (Vandell, Owen, Wilson, & Henderson, 1988). It is typical for both children in the same family to have similar attachment classifications (Ward, Vaughn, & Robb, 1988).

The older sibling's prior relationships outside the family. Higher-quality sibling relationships are associated with the older sibling's relationships with peers outside the family. Children who are more positive with their siblings show more positive peer play, fewer peer conflicts, more extended pretend play with peers, and more lasting peer friendships (Kramer & Gottman, 1992). Children with more knowledge of emotion and role-taking skills are more positive with their younger siblings (Garner, Jones, & Palmer, 1994).

Both sibling interaction and social competence with peers are related to the child's security of attachment, so you might think that the relationship between positive peer play and positive sibling interaction is simply the result of a more secure attachment to the mother. The research shows that while the parent-child relationship is important for developing the child's ability to care for the younger sibling, the child's experience with peers makes its own independent contribution (Kramer & Gottman, 1992). With peers, children are exposed to some basic rules of respect and responsibility for others—the beginnings of moral understanding—that carry over into relationships at home, especially if the child's socially responsive behavior is supported by the parents.

Sex and age differences between siblings. Another factor that may play a role in the incidence of positive versus negative sibling relationships is the sex composition of the sibling pair. Although there is a great deal of variability across families, same-sex pairs tend to have fewer instances of aggression

than mixed-sex pairs, and parents are more likely to treat children in same-sex pairs equally than children in mixed-sex pairs (Corter, Abramovitch, & Pepler, 1983; R. A. Stewart et al., 1987). Firstborn females are somewhat more prosocial, whereas firstborn males are somewhat more aggressive; however, these differences do not appear across all studies. Finally, the number of years between siblings does not seem to have any measurable effect on the amount of prosocial or aggressive behavior exchanged between them (Abramovitch, Corter, & Landau, 1979).

Temperamental differences between siblings. Because the findings on age and sex differences between the siblings do not strongly predict the level of conflict between the siblings, some researchers have suggested that temperamental factors might be more important. Indeed, research shows that temperament is a better predictor. If one of the siblings is rated as having a generally negative mood and as being temperamentally nonadaptable, the siblings are less likely to engage in joint play. A mismatch in the temperament of the siblings is related to higher levels of conflict (Munn & Dunn, 1989).

One interpretation of these results is that the temperamental characteristics of the children affect the way that they relate to each other. Another interpretation is possible, however. One of the issues related to the measurement of infant temperament is that a parental rating of infant temperament is generally used (see Chapter 6). This introduces a possible bias in the parent's perception of the child, independent of the child's actual behavior.

The alternative interpretation related to differences in temperament between siblings is that these differences are created in part by the parents, who attempt to differentiate between siblings by viewing them as different individuals in a process called **sibling de-identification**. In this regard, research has shown that parents tend to rate the first two children in the family as having different temperaments, while temperaments for later-born children are rated more alike (F. S. Schachter & Stone, 1985). In a longitudinal study in which observers studied mother-infant interaction for the first two children in the family when each was 24 months old, the researchers found that mothers expressed similar levels of affection and verbal responsiveness to both children but the amount of parental control of the children differed. Control was measured by the amount of direct interventions in the child's actions in the form of commands, rejections, and disciplinary actions (J. Dunn, Plomin, & Daniels, 1986).

In summary, many factors are likely to play a role in how well siblings get along with each other. From a family systems perspective, it is difficult to say with certainty that a single factor taken in isolation is the cause of sibling aggression. Temperament, although strongly related to sibling conflict, could be multiply determined by parent-child and child-child interactions over the course of the first years of life. Is the child really difficult, or has the child come to be labeled as difficult? Or is difficult temperament a stance one takes in the face of a sibling who is constantly rejecting or ignoring? It may be some time before we can sort out the answers to these questions.

Parent intervention in sibling disputes. Parents can choose whether or not to intervene in sibling disputes. The effects of their actions depend upon the age of the siblings. When the older child is under 3, parental non-involvement in sibling disputes tends to predispose the siblings to continued conflict. Parents of children of this age tend to intervene primarily in the most serious fights. Before the intervention, children are most likely to use aggression and coercion in disputes. Immediately following the intervention, children are more likely to use negotiation strategies to resolve their conflicts, suggesting that parents can indeed play a role in helping children to negotiate. On the other hand, non-involvement is a more effective strategy for older siblings who are less close and less involved with each other if the parent intervenes in their disputes in any way. This means that over time, siblings develop new ways to negotiate their disputes on their own. Self-interested justifications decrease and cooperative discourse increases (J. Dunn, Kreps, & Brown, 1996; Kramer, Perozynski, & Chung, 1999; Perlman & Ross, 1997).

At least in middle-class Caucasian North American families, when parents intervene, it is typically as third-party mediators. Parents tend to favor younger siblings in such disputes and to discipline the older sibling. When fathers disciplined the older sibling primarily and mothers disciplined both siblings equally, these families were rated as more harmonious, both in the marital relationship and in the sibling relationships. If both parents pick on the older sibling, that child is more likely to show behavior problems in preschool (Volling & Elins, 1998). Better developmental outcomes are likely, therefore, when parents expect the older sibling to be the more responsible person and when the younger sibling is sometimes disciplined by at least one parent. This not only helps the older sibling become more responsible, but also helps prevent his or her feeling that the parents favor the younger sibling.

When parents intervene, they are not likely to get involved in children's claims of ownership ("It's mine") or possession ("I had it first"). Parents in general are more interested in getting children to share their activities rather than fight over who owns something, and they act to prevent property damage. Parents want children to resolve their differences, to play together harmoniously, and to end the dispute as quickly as possible (Ross, 1996). In summary, parental involvement in sibling disputes decreases over age as children develop, primarily from their parents, new ways to negotiate peaceful settlements. There are, however, between-family differences in these patterns.

Co-Regulating With Baby

In the second year of life, children discover the power of assertiveness over their parents. In the third year, they can become more verbally and physically aggressive, although this begins to be replaced by more verbal negotiation strategies by the end of the third year. Aggressive behaviors are natural developments of the child's growing self-awareness and the child's exploration of the limits of the self's power and ability. It helps to remain calm in such situations, to ensure that the wronged child is properly attended, and not to overreact. Biting, however, needs to be dealt with firmly because of the risks to the health of the bitten child.

Parents may worry when they see their children manually exploring their genitals for the first time. A parent may want to distract the child by offering a toy, but reprimanding is not recommended. Self-exploration is a natural part of development, as is a child's curiosity about the sex organs of others, the origins of babies, and so on. It helps to keep your answers to sex-related questions simple, direct, and honest. The child does not treat these questions with any more prurient interest that questions about the moon, the grass, or the picture- book, so why should you?

Children need to be introduced to a wide range of experiences and places, but only gradually and at a pace that seems most comfortable to them. As children are developing self-help skills, it is easy to let them take greater responsibility for some of these tasks. Examples are picking out and putting on clothes, wiping themselves, washing and drying their own hands, and so on.

One of the most striking contradictions of this age is that the children's growing appreciation of reality and their own place in it is mixed with a growing fantasy life and a whole new crop of very unrealistic (at least to the adult) fears that dome up in dreams and while awake. Remember that such fears are very real to children. The fears may arise because the children begin to notice things they never noticed before and realize there are things they do not understand.

Because a child's fears seem silly and inconsequential to an adult, there is a tendency to laugh at them or to tease the child about them. This does not help the child, who probably needs reassurance more than anything else. Two-year-olds are beginning to have worries just like anyone else. They may have nightmares, bite their nails. Stutter, or show other signs of behavior disruption. Parents are justified in feeling concerned, but it is important to try to understand the source of children's worries and help them to solve the problems.

Children are also becoming more active participants in the adult world. They may want to help out around the house, pre=school, or day care center. Even though this may mean letting work done more slowly with some extra mess, it pays to encourage these pudding designs of helpfulness, at least one in a while. It is a good idea to talk about the next thing that is going to happen while you are engaged in a task. This helps the child understand that one thing leads to another. Telling the child about expectable fugue events may also help alleviate their fears. Taking about a visit to the doctor, a new baby-sitter, or some other potentially disturbing situation can be a very effective means of avoiding trouble before it begins. Teaching good habits, such as staying clean, picking up toys, and putting away clothing, can be started at this time, and the child's own initiatives are not to be ignored. You will have to play the role of a negotiator, reminder, and coach for many years to come, so do not be discouraged if the child does not understand how to do these things right away.

In the realm of play, 2-year-old children enjoy such activities as working with clay and finger painting. These activities are wonderful ways to let children creatively express their newfound fine motor schools. Children of this age also like sand and water, which go best with pails and shovels. Cars and pegboards are also of great interest. Be sure the toys you get are safe—nontoxic, not sharp or jagged, and with no parts that can be swallowed.

At this age, children get involved in many exciting things, and they want to have their own say about most things. The problem is that they have trouble striking a balance between alternatives and extremeness. It is typical for 2-year-olds to play too long and get overtired. It is hard for children to relax at bedtime; they may need a story, a talk with parents, or just some time to themselves before they can settle down. It is common to see movement from one extreme to another at this age, for example, staying dry all day and then suddenly wetting, or screaming for dinner and then turning it down when it finally appears. These swings can be frustrating for parents, but they are necessary steps on the path to autonomous self-regulation.

SUMMARY

Motor and Cognitive Development

- Motor skills become more complex and adaptive during the third year, including running, jumping, constructing with blocks, and making art.

- Motor skills become integrated with language and cognition, as language regulates the execution of a motor skill and self-produced movement enhances cognition.

- Children are now able to execute complex sequences of action, work toward an adult standard, and correct their own errors.

- Language becomes internalized as private speech, such that prior forms of social regulation now become self-regulatory.

- Make-believe and pretend become complex and creative.

- A sense of conceptual self emerges, including age and gender self-labeling.

- The acquisition of gender-role stereotypes is a complex developmental process involving cognitive understanding of gender and family role relationships.

- Descriptions of emotional states of the self and others become elaborate.

- Three-year-olds can act by taking the behavior of others into account, but they do not yet behave as if they have a clear theory of the other's mind.

- Children of this age lack the ability to differentiate reality from make-believe in most cases.

Emotional Development

- New developments emerge in both positive and negative emotion expression.

- There are individual differences in children's willingness to express negative feelings or to show aggression.

Social and Language Development

- Grammar emerges with the use of verbs and the ability to add the appropriate endings to words for tense and number.

- Complex question asking emerges.

- Limitations of language include pronunciation problems, inability to appreciate complex grammar, and lack of skill in maintaining conversations.

- Toddlers who are more compliant have parents with more authoritative child-rearing styles.

- Peer interaction shows evidence of coordinated actions, imitative and complementary turn taking, and the emergence of friendships.

Family and Society

- Older and younger siblings derive different benefits from their mutual interactions. Younger siblings benefit from the guidance and protection of the older sibling and develop self-protection skills. Older siblings pay attention to the needs of others and develop skills in a leadership role.

- Interfamily differences in sibling conflict may depend on the children's prior relationships and attachments to parents and to their peers, on the sex similarity of the pair, on the temperament of the children, and on sibling deidentification by the parents.

Chapter 12

The Effects of the Infancy Period on the Formation of Individual Differences

CHAPTER OUTLINE AND OVERVIEW

Development as a Complex Dynamic Process	*How can we understand the long-term effects of prenatal and infancy experiences? Is it possible to overcome early risk factors? Is infancy an important period of the life course even if we do not have an autobiographical memory of that time?*
The Effects of Infant and Parental Factors	*Does any particular factor have more influence over later outcomes than another? Are infant factors more important than parental contributions, or vice-versa?*
The Effffects of Risk and Disadvantage	*What are the types of risk factors in infancy? What are the long-term effects of these risks?*
The Effects of Intervention and Education Programs	*How can risk be alleviated? What types of programs work best for infants and parents at risk?*

Is what happens to a person during infancy important or critical for later development? Do traumatic experiences in infancy, such as poverty, maltreatment, or maternal depression, affect later cognitive or social functioning? Can we predict whether a child will be bright, average, or dull from scores on assessment tests done in early infancy? Can later developmental dysfunctions be diagnosed from early infant testing? Are there intervention programs that improve the outcomes for infants at risk? What is the importance of infancy in the human life cycle?

DEVELOPMENT AS A COMPLEX DYNAMIC PROCESS

Before getting into the research about these questions, it might help to put them in a broader perspective. How, for example, should we interpret strong evidence predicting later outcomes from something that occurred during infancy? We might be fortunate to find an early marker for some later disorder or an early sign of intelligence or social adjustment so that we could tailor educational and intervention programs to their needs. Medical research operates on this principle. Once a link between a gene or a virus and some disease is found, researchers can then seek out treatments that deal with the root cause of the disease. As we shall see in this chapter, human development, however, cannot be improved with just a simple fix.

No single early factor—such as the prenatal environment, parental sensitivity, or infant temperament—predicts later outcomes 100 percent of the time. Most of the factors related to early human development are influential for later outcomes, but only some of the time, and only for some people and not others. The answers to the questions raised in the first paragraph, therefore, are not simple. Early development is a complex process, and we need to take the time to understand that complexity if we are to do justice to the important issues facing infants, families, and society.

We don't have an autobiographical memory of our infancy, so perhaps we might feel it is dis-connected to the rest of our lives. The phases of an individual's life, however, are never completely unconnected; there is always some influence of the earlier phases on later ones. The most salient example of apparent developmental disconnection is the life cycle of moths and butterflies. Here we have stages of development that are so radically different—larva, cocoon, and adult—that it seems almost certain that the experiences of the larva, for example, could not impact on the adult. And yet there are such influences. The olfactory (smell) experiences of the larva have been shown to influence the food choices of the adult (Klopfer, 1988).

In humans, developmental processes of the infant are embedded in family systems, and families are embedded in the multiple and interconnecting systems of the larger society and culture, all of which may affect developmental outcomes (refer to the bio-ecological and dynamic systems theories in Chapter 1). Perhaps a more realistic way to ask the questions in the first paragraph is: *Under what circumstances, in what combinations, and for which types of individuals do early factors impact later outcomes?* If a child exhibits a desirable tendency early in life, we would like to find ways to preserve it, and if he or she suffers an unfortunate circumstance early, we would wish to bring the individual back to a closer approximation of typical development and behavior.

When complex developmental systems are perturbed by some risk factor, the response of the whole system is not necessarily a change for the worse. Often, in fact, the system achieves a kind of dynamic balancing act in which it returns to a stable mode of functioning (see Chapter 1; Fogel, 1993; Fogel & Thelen, 1987; Sroufe et al., 2005; Thelen & Smith, 1994). A good example is the development of some premature infants. Due to the compensatory actions of the parents to provide extra support and stimulation for their infant at risk, the developmental course of the infant may approach that of full-term infants, and the family system may return to a stable mode of functioning following an earlier period of stress and uncertainty (see section on perinatal factors, below). Availability of resources (home, family, nutrition,

What makes children different from each other? The formation of individual differences is a complicated field of study about which we understand very little. These children are all supposed to be doing the same thing, but each has interpreted it differently.

Photo by Emily Waterfield

support, etc.) opens development up to a wider range of possibilities (see section on intervention programs, below). In the research reviewed in this chapter, we will see examples in which the effects of early predispositions and risk factors can be attenuated or even eliminated as causal factors for later development (Sroufe, Coffino & Carlson, 2010).

Alternatively, system dynamics may progressively move a child and family off the typical developmental course. An example of a continuing spiral of negative effects that amplify each other is the cycle of persistent poverty, ill health, infant disadvantage, and maladaptive parental behavior (see section on poverty, below). The more the continued trauma depletes the system of resources, the more likely that the child will develop some type of developmental difficulty (Brauth, Hall, & Dooling, 1991; Klopfer, 1988; Sroufe et al., 2005). Lack of resources constrains development and forces individuals into the limitations of their heredity and their early experiences.

In addition, individuals vary in how they are affected by their experiences (Wachs, 2000). Suffering abuse as an infant, to take one example, does not guarantee that individuals will go on to abuse their own infants. Only a small proportion of abused children become child abusers (see section on maltreatment, below). The IQ range of children who were prenatally exposed to alcohol can range from retarded to having normal intelligence. There is a range of severe to mild retardation even in the case of major genetic disorders, such as fragile X syndrome (Chapter 3, and section on perinatal factors, below). There is a wide range of outcomes, therefore, even when individuals have some things in common at an earlier point in time.

In summary, there are two basic principles for developmental change. One is that *development is a complex multifactor process*. The other is that *no two individuals respond in the same way to the same factor*. Variability and the opportunity to capitalize on chance outcomes is inherent to the developmental process (Fogel, 1993; Thelen & Smith, 1994; Wachs, 2000). In the following sections of this chapter, we review some of the findings on the relationship between early infancy factors and later developmental outcomes.

THE EFFECTS OF INFANT AND PARENTAL FACTORS

Perinatal Factors

The long-term effects of heredity on later behavior were discussed in Chapters 2 and 3. The data suggest that the effects of one's heredity are non-deterministic. That is, not everyone with the same types of genes or chromosomes will inherit the phenotypic characteristic typically associated with those genes or chromosomes. Even among those who show common phenotypic features, there will be a great deal of variation between individuals (Wachs, 2000). Some genetic structures have a higher probability of being expressed in the phenotype, and these structures are typically associated with severe disorders. The genetic contributions to behavior, cognition, emotion, and personality have a much lower probability of being expressed universally in the phenotype because many genes are involved and because they require a specific set of environmental contingencies—they are sensitive to an epigenetic process—to be expressed (Plomin & Rutter, 1998).

In general, the total number of perinatal risk factors has an additive effect, decreasing the ability to cope with the typical stresses of the first months of life and increasing the probability that the infant may fall behind in developmental progress (Bradley et al., 1994; Dobrovka-Krol et al., 2010; Feldman & Eidelman, 2009; Rutter, 1987; Sroufe, Coffino & Carlson, 2010; Yumoto, Jacobson & Jacobson, 2008).

In addition, the more severe the perinatal disorder, the more likely that there will be long-term effects. Infants who have very low birthweight (VLBW, less than 1,500 grams), for example, are more passive, less attentive, and less securely attached to their mothers than full terms of the same gestational age. Some VLBW infants have

continuing motor, social, cognitive, and attentional deficits at preschool and school age (Bracewell & Marlow, 2002; Kanazawa, Shimizu, Kamada, Tanabe, & Itoigawa, 1997; Landry, 1995; Mangelsdorf et al., 1996; Tessier, Nadeau, Boivin, & Tremblay, 1997).

Other extreme factors, such as auditory neurological deficits measured at birth (A. D. Murray, 1988) and other forms of severe brain damage at birth have also been found to be related to later cognitive and sensory impairment (A. Stewart, 1983). Early visual impairment is associated with slower development in all domains during the preschool period (Hatton, Bailey, Burchinal, & Ferrell, 1997). Finally, particular types of early-onset teratogens, especially those that occur during the periods of rapid growth of the limbs, organs, and brain, are generally continuous with later disorders Fetal alcohol syndrome predicts later learning disabilities, and excessive maternal cigarette smoking predicts violence in adulthood, especially for males (Brennan, Grekin, & Mednick, 1999; Karr-Morse & Wiley, 1997; B. A. Lewis et al., 2004; Metosky & Vondra, 1995). Nevertheless, it is important to remember that even in the worst cases of risk, there is variability in outcome between individuals (Wachs, 2000). Down's syndrome infants, for example, are better at daily living skills and communication if they come from cohesive families with sensitive parents (Hauser-Cram et al., 1999).

Given an appropriately responsive environment, the more mild perinatal complications may not create any lasting deficits (Sameroff & Chandler, 1975), suggesting that the environment can provide a **buffering** against difficulties of early adjustment. Infants have a **self-righting** ability; if mothers are not under stress and are predisposed to providing competent care, the infant at risk evokes more maternal attention and solicitude than typically developing infants (Eizirik, Bohlin, & Hagekull, 1994; Landry et al., 1996; Liaw & Brooks-Gunn, 1993; Wijnroks, 1998). This increased solicitude may be a factor in alleviating the early deficits over the first year or two of life, even for some infants who have severe deficits such as VLBW or teratogen-exposed infants

(Knickmeyer et al., 2005; Landry, Smith, & Swank, 2006).

In a multiracial, multiclass sample of 670 infants born on the Hawaiian island of Kauai, all groups of children—regardless of race, social class, or age of mother—had about the same proportion of perinatal complications. In this sample, 13 percent suffered moderate complications, and 3 percent had severe complications. In this sample, however, income rather than perinatal risk predicted how well the infant recovered from the complication. Children born into lower-income families were less likely to recover fully by age 2. By age 10, the effects of perinatal problems had all but disappeared for all the groups, but children from lower-income groups had lower scores on intelligence tests and were doing worse in school than children from middle-income groups (Werner, Bierman, & French, 1971). This research shows that between-individual variability is multidetermined in part by perinatal factors and in part by later environmental factors. If there are adequate economic resources, if the parents are not under psychosocial stress, and if the perinatal complications are not too severe, the effects may not persist over the long term.

Motor Development

Can you make your baby more advanced in motors skills by extra practice and workouts? There does not seem to be any continuity between early motor practice, physical stature and weight, and later developmental outcomes (Gorman & Pollitt, 1993; Largo, 1993). In infants at risk, however, physical and motor stimulation can have an important remedial effect leading to catch-up growth. This is especially the case if infants have moderate to severe disorders of self-regulation, such as poor motor coordination, difficulties with state regulation (such as sleeping or feeding problems), sensory deficits (such as blindness or deafness), or impaired emotion regulation (difficulty self-calming or regulating arousal), or pervasive sensorimotor problems such as autism. Unless these conditions are treated with some type of interven-

tion program, they are likely to remain stable and continuous into the preschool years and later (Aylward, 2004; Degangi et al., 2000; Mayberry, Lock, & Kazmi, 2002).

The general conclusion that extra motor stimulation in the first two or three years of life does not contribute to lasting individual differences unless the infant is at risk, however, does not apply for older children. In the preschool and later years, practice with a motor skill does have a definite effect on later ability, as when children are taught sports, art, dance, gymnastics, and music. Training and guidance during this period does in fact lead to later excellence in those areas and may be a critical period for their development (Sternberg & Davidson, 1985; Wallach, 1985). It is more difficult to achieve high levels of expertise in athletics and the arts unless training begins before adolescence.

Culture

Cultures differ, broadly speaking, according to whether they focus on individual development and achievement or on the family and the group. We saw, for example, that in some cultures older children are expected to provide child care for their younger siblings. In these collectivistic cultures, children are socialized from an early age to respect authority, to give their time to support the family, and to avoid standing apart from the group. Many Asian, African, Latin/Hispanic, Native American, and other indigenous cultures are collectivistic (Keller et al., 2004; Super & Harkness, 2010). In ways such as this, culture can have a great deal of impact on social and emotional processes such as sharing, empathy, and self-disclosure. Culture can also affect gender-specific behavior, depending upon cultural attitudes toward traditional or nontraditional sex-role orientations. Culture influences styles of touching infants. Many collectivistic and indigenous cultures allow for considerably more touching than North American and Northern European cultures. These styles of touching lead to differences in how infants learn to regulate emotions—individually or with others (Stack, 2010). Compared to Anglo mothers, who use more distal touch, Hispanic mothers used more close body holding and affectionate touch (Franco et al., 1996).

Even though culture has a major impact on later outcomes, there is also a great deal of variability within cultures (Killen & Wainryb, 2000). Not all people raised in the North American culture of individuality are self-seeking and achievement oriented. Similarly, many people from collectivistic cultures are focused on getting ahead at the expense of others. This suggests that sensitivity to the differences between ethnic and cultural minorities in a nation is likely to facilitate child development (Johnson et al., 2003). Even though someone belongs to a particular ethnic or national group, it does not mean that they or their families are like everyone else in that group. Especially in immigrant families, the culture of the family is constantly changing as old traditions and new ways of interacting are being modified to fit the current circumstances. Parents and caregivers need to be sensitive to these issues of change and adaptation, avoid stereotyping, and seek resources to facilitate ongoing adaptation (Maschinot, 2008).

Gender

Gender differences during infancy have been related to a number of outcome factors. For example, males seem to be more vulnerable to the effects of environmental stress. When they grow up in homes that are overcrowded, noisy, or confusing, males show deficits in their cognitive development, while females growing up in similar environments do not. Boys, especially if they are exposed to harsh or depressed mothers, are more likely to show externalizing problems as they get older (aggression, defiance, irritability, mood swings, whining, jealousy) (Miner & Clarke-Stewart, 2008).

Environmental opportunities to explore large areas in the home are more beneficial for the long-term cognitive development of males than females. Females, but not males, who are provided with a great deal of stimulus variety (different colors, shapes, and textures in the home) show higher levels of cognitive development (Rutter, 1979; Wachs & Gruen, 1982). One also has to remember

that there are individual differences among boys and among girls such that the general pattern does not hold for everyone.

Intellectual Development

Environmental-specificity effects have been found in studies of factors in early infancy that promote cognitive and intellectual development. For example, early exposure in the first year to an enriched home environment with a variety of inanimate objects and to contingently responsive inanimate objects leads to greater skill in problem solving and exploratory play in the second year (Molfese, DiLalla, & Bunce, 1997; Saltaris et al., 2004). The provision of age-appropriate play materials during the first two years, and linguistic interaction with children, strongly predicts a child's Stanford-Binet IQ score at 4 1/2 years (Bradley & Caldwell, 1976), as well as school readiness and literacy (Forget-Dubois et al., 2009; Rodriguez & Tamis-LeMonda, 2011; van Doorninck, Caldwell, Wright, & Frankenburg, 1981).

The development of spatial relations and perspective taking can best be predicted by avoidance of noise, confusion, and environmental overcrowding during the first two years. In contrast, exploratory play skills in the second and third year are best enhanced by caregivers providing objects that respond when the child moves them—such as mobiles and rattles—and a variety of objects in the first year. These factors, plus a well-organized environment and the use of age-appropriate play materials, are the best predictors of a child's ability to invent new means and plan effective strategies (Wachs, 1982; Widmayer et al., 1990).

In a habituation task, for example, some infants habituate rather quickly and require less looking time overall to process the visual stimulus. These efficient information-processing strategies in early infancy are correlated with higher childhood standardized cognitive and language development test scores. Infants who at 4 months continued to fixate on an unchanging stimulus had lower intelligence test scores in middle childhood (Dougherty & Haith, 1997; Marchman & Fernald,

2008; Rose & Feldman, 1997; Tamis-LeMonda & Bornstein, 1989). Efficient information processing and remembering, especially when combined with a maternal style focusing on directing the infant's attention to tasks, leads to more advanced cognitive and language outcomes (Kavšek, 2004; Lewis, Alessandri, & Sullivan, 1992; McCall & Carriger, 1993; Rose, Feldman, & Jankowski, 2009; Tamis-LeMonda & Bornstein, 1989, 1993).

Verbal interaction with the child in the early years of life, not surprisingly, is one of the strongest and most distinctive predictors of later language competence in toddlers and preschoolers (Hart & Risley, 1992; Huttenlocher, Haight, Bryk, Seltzer, & Lyons, 1991; Sokolov, 1993; Wachs et al., 1993). Interventions for children at risk for poor language acquisition have been successful by training parents to talk with and read to infants. Children who stutter are helped when parents talk more slowly, giving the children time to take their turn in the conversation at their own pace (Ramig, 1993; Swan, 1993; Winslow & Guitar, 1994). These effects compound over time, so that children who talk early and competently also read earlier and are more advanced conceptually; thus, they have a head start on the literacy skills required for schooling (Crain-Thoreson & Dale, 1992; P. J. Dunham & Dunham, 1995).

In summary, the child's environment and information-processing abilities during infancy play some role in the prediction of later intelligence. These factors interact, however, and no one factor can account for all the variability. In addition, children who suffer from poor information processing during the first six months will vary in their outcomes, some scoring lower and some scoring higher on IQ tests during later childhood. It is possible to enhance cognitive development for some children by talking with and reading to them. There is no evidence, however, that extra cognitive stimulation during infancy can create a genius.

Temperament

Our review of **temperament** in Chapter 7 showed that there is limited evidence for conti-nuity in infant temperament. Only when children fall into extreme groups on irritability, emotionality, reactivity, or inhibition can long-term stability be observed. We also found that stability in infant temperamental characteristics is more likely to be seen in the short term—six months to a year—rather than over several years. At older ages, stability can be seen for several years or more, but transformation and change are the rule just as often as stability (Caspi & Silva, 1995; Hagekull & Bohlin, 2003; Pedlow, Sanson, Prior, & Oberklaid, 1993).

Nevertheless, some children, under certain conditions, will show long-term continuity of temperament. This can occur when the parents have a temperamental pattern similar to that of the infant, and especially when both parent and infant show temperamental anxiety, inhibition or shyness, which suggests that when parent and child share an attribute, their mutual interaction enhances the possibility that their genetically based inhibition will continue to be manifested in the phenotype (P. Cohen, Kasen, Brook, & Hartmark, 1998; Murray et al., 2008; Schmitz et al., 1999). Part of this effect is genetically linked, and part of it is environmental. When temperamentally anxious children are raised by non-inhibited adoptive mothers, they are less likely to show anxiety (Brooker et al., 2011). Similarly, children who have a measured genetic risk for anxiety behave more like non-risk infants when raised by sensitive mothers who compensate for their tendency to withdraw (Leve et al., 2010; Propper et al., 2008).

Parental Contributions

Maternal employment and child care.   With respect to maternal employment or child care, long-term effects are mediated by other factors, such as maternal sensitivity and number of hours working per week (Brooks-Gunn, Han, & Waldfogel, 2002; Chin-Quee & Scarr, 1994). One of the major risks related to maternal employment is for the mother herself, especially if she has an economic need to work but would prefer to stay at home, or if she is highly career motivated and suffers from role overload (Stifter, Coulehan, & Fish, 1993). In some but not all cases, these mothers may have some difficulty establishing a secure relationship with their infants. The risks in child care lie primarily in the quality of care available and the age at which the child attends (see Chapter 9). The risks are highest for infants under one year who do not have supportive family environments and who are in poor-quality care. These children may fare worse than their peers in preschool and kindergarten. It is important to remember, once again, that the severity and duration of these effects vary greatly across infants. Some infants who are reared in low-quality child care show no deficits, while others do.

Attachment. Research on attachment (see Chapter 8) has found a relationship between parental sensitivity in the first year and later security of attachment, and between security of attachment at age 1 year and later social and intellectual competence in preschool. Attachment measured at one year moderately predicts attachment security in childhood and for some people, into adulthood and even into the next generation (Fraley, 2002; Gloger-Tippelt et al., 2002; Hagekull & Bohlin, 2004). Mothers who remember being accepted by their own mothers when they were children were more likely to be sensitive to their own infants (Kretchmar & Jacobvitz, 2002). The effects of even secure infant attachment can be mediated by other life events during childhood, such as parental divorce (Beckwith, Cohen, & Hamilton, 1999). There is only a moderate predictability between attachment security in infancy and ability to resolve conflicts and shared emotions in romantic relationships in early adulthood (Sroufe et al., 2005). Children with disorganized attachments are more likely to show behavior problems at all later school ages and more likely to develop psychopathologies in childhood and adolescence (separation anxiety disorder, oppositional disorder, depression, phobias, and dissociation). In all these cases, however, there is variability in the severity of the outcomes across individuals (Carlson, 1998; Madigan et al., 2004; Sroufe et al., 2005; Weinfield, Whaley, & Egeland, 2004). While most attachments remain stable, some infants will change their attachment security, becoming either more or less secure over time.

Caregiving and disciplinary styles. Parents who use more guided participation and authoritative parenting styles (Chapter 10) with their children—and who show more contingent responsiveness, mother-infant synchrony, and parenting involvement during the first two years—are more likely to have children with more advanced language and cognitive skills, independence, emotion regulation, cooperativeness, and social competence (Bradley & Caldwell, 1995; Feldman, Greenbaum, & Yurmiya, 1999; Wachs, 1993). Lack of maternal responsiveness during infancy also predicts disruptive behavior problems (aggression, defiance, antisocial behavior) during early and middle childhood and the effect is consistent across cultural groups (Bor et al., 2003; Ispa et al., 2004). Maternal depression during early infancy predicts infant cognitive development at 18 months and preschool language, cooperation with peers, and behavior problems (Leadbeater, Bishop, & Raver, 1996; Murray, Fiori-Cowley, Hooper, & Cooper, 1996; NICHD Early Child Care Research Network, 1999).

It is important to remember that all of the findings related to parent effects on children are based on correlations, which have two implications; first, the parent's style could be shaped by the child's behavior, at least in part; second, the correlations are typically positive but small, meaning that while a general association exists between caregiving and child behavior, there is wide variability between families. Simply put, while many children who experience maternal insensitivity during infancy will have behavior problems, learning, or attachment difficulties, there are others who do not have such difficulties. The important question is not whether sensitive parenting matters. It does matter. Warm, effective and loving parents are a necessary and irreplaceable part of infant development. Even so, the complexity of interactive and family processes as well as child factors influence how long and how much parental behavior influences child development.

THE EFFECTS OF RISK AND DISADVANTAGE

Poverty

About 20 to 25 percent of children in the United States live in poor families compared to 5 to 10 percent in most other developed nations (Hernandez, 1997; McLoyd, 1998). On a worldwide scale, there are 2.2 billion children in the world of which 1 billion, almost half, are living in poverty. Most of these children have little or no access to adequate health care, shelter, clean water, or education. The United Nations estimates that 30,000 children in the world die *every day* from the consequences of poverty. The conditions of poverty, acting through generational developmental cycles, perpetuate the suffering and widen the gap between rich and poor (Shonkoff, 2010; Yoshikawa, Aber & Beardslee, 2012).

Poverty is a case where consistency of negative outcomes can be maintained over long periods in the absence of other mediating factors. Children and parents from poor families suffer more from depression, poor peer relationships, social withdrawal, and low self-esteem (Bronfenbrenner, 1986; Duncan, Ziol-Guest, & Kalil, 2010; Middlemiss, 2003; Mistry et al., 2004; Pike et al., 2006). Poor children are more likely to have physical ailments, school problems, aggressiveness, depression, low self-esteem, deviant behavior, and language and cognitive deficits. Stress, poor nutrition and health interact with behavior to create increasingly negative patterns. These factors feed off each other, leading to increasingly dismal cycles of loss, stress, and despair. When these factors are then compounded with racial and social-class prejudice, the risk to mental health is enormous (McLoyd, 1998).

On the other hand, some poor children can thrive depending upon circumstances. Children who come from homes that focus on promoting child development, that value education, and that provide support, closeness, and protection from the stresses of poverty do better than children not provided with these buffers (Davis & Mantler, 2004; Ispa et al., 2004; Mackner, Black, & Starr, 2003).

Stable and consistent educational environments encourage successful cognitive and emotional development for poor children (Crosnoe et al., 2010; Lugo-Gil & Tamis-LeMonda, 2008). Even in the case of poverty, therefore, some children show resilience that allows them to transcend their circumstances. On the other hand, children who are psychobiologically more vulnerable and sensitive to the environment (inhibited, high cortisol, anxious) are more likely to suffer from the effects of poverty (Blair et al., 2011; Obradović et al., 2010).

Stress

Another major risk factor in early development is severe stress on the infant and the family. Stress may be due to economic deprivation, disease, hospitalizations and other extended separations, family changes due to relocation or parental or sibling death, extreme conditions of social unrest, such as those created by war, persecution, natural disaster, or famine, and migration or flight as refugees. The research is complicated, detailed in some areas and not in others, and often dependent on personal recollections. Nevertheless, after extensive review of this literature, it can be concluded that a single stressful incident in early infancy has negligible long-term effects. However, multiple or long-term stresses create cyclical patterns of increasing risk and deprivation and are more likely to be associated with long-term emotional or behavioral disorders in later childhood (Rutter, 1979; Wachs, 2000).

Research on the neurophysiological processes related to stress, such as elevated levels of cortisol from overactivation of the HPA axis (Chapter 4), shows that ongoing parental stress in early infancy is correlated with elevated cortisol in their 4½-year-olds (Essex et al., 2002). Relationship stress and insecure attachment can also overactivate the HPA axis, leading to long-term susceptibility to even minor stress and a predisposition to depression (Beatson & Taryan, 2003).

Even with multiple or long-term stressors, however, some children show remarkable resilience and adaptability (Wachs, 2000). In some cases, an early stressor can prepare an individual to adapt to a similar stressor later in development, as when children who are repeatedly separated from parents in child care become less susceptible to the effects of routine separation from parents. On the other hand, some stressors can make people hypersensitive to repeated exposures, as in the example of the 3-year-old boy who did not like to be wrapped up in a cloth when getting a hair-cut because doctors had wrapped him in a blanket while stitching up an injury he had received when he was a baby (see Chapter 11). There is a great deal of variability in how a stressor will affect someone and how long the effect will be felt. Once again, there are no simple answers.

Parental Psychopathology

Do parental anxiety disorder, depression, and other forms of mental illness affect the chances that the child will develop some form of mental illness or other deficit in later years? In general, there is only a small correlation, or none at all, between mater-nal psychopathology and later child outcome. The chances of the child being affected are increased if there is a familial genetic predisposition, on the severity of the parent's mental illness, if the child is temperamentally inhibited or aggressive, if there are a series of environmental and familial stress-ors, and if the attachment relationship is insecure. On the other hand, the chances are reduced if there is a sensitive non-pathological parent avail-able, if the child has good self-regulatory control, and if the child perceives the environment to be secure and supportive (Hay et al., 2001; Henriks-son & McNeil, 2004; Mezulis, Hyde, & Clark, 2004; Muris, 2006; Spence et al., 2002).

Child Abuse and Neglect

Abuse typically refers to cases in which a child sustains a nonaccidental injury from a parent or other caregiver. *Neglect* is a pattern of ignoring the basic developmental needs of the child for physi-cal and psychological support and nourishment and which are typically the responsibility of the caregiver to provide (Strauss & Kantor, 2005).

Both are considered forms of child maltreatment. Approximately 5 to 6 million cases of suspected child maltreatment are reported annually to Child Protective Service agencies in the United Staets. Although not all of these cases are confirmed, the number of children abused may actually be higher because not all cases are reported. It is estimated that 3 to 5 children die every day as a result of abuse, with children under one year accounting for almost half of the deaths, and 18,000 children per year receive permanent disabilities from abuse. Abuse occurs equally in all ethnic and income groups and for both boys and girls, but girls are 4 times more likely to be sexually abused. At least 20 percent of American women and 5 to 15 percent of men are likely to have been sexually abused as children (Lambie, 2005).

Parental factors play an important role in child abuse. Abusive parents show fewer positive emo-tions, interact with their babies less, are more likely to use coercion and corporal punishment with their infants, and talk less to their babies than are nonabusive parents (Boddy & Skuse, 1994; Straus, 1994; Valentino et al., 2011). Abusive parents are less adept at verbal skills in general, score lower in abstract reasoning, and show a reduced capacity for planning and control over impulses. Abusing fathers, in particular, are lower in parental warmth and interpersonal relationships, and they are more introverted than nonabusing fathers (Hyman & Mitchell, 1977; Wu et al., 2004). Child abusers have been found to be hypersensitive to their infants. Instead of adaptively tuning out a loud or pierc-ing cry, the abusers are likely to become annoyed and aroused by the crying (Frodi & Lamb, 1980). Abusers are less able to correctly identify emotion signals, and in some cases, they interpret negative emotion as positive (Kropp & Haynes, 1987).

At 2 years, maltreated children show more anger, frustration, and opposition, as well as a rela-tive slowdown in developmental progress over the first year. They are more likely to have deficits in cognition, memory, attention, impulse control, and emotion regulation (Éthier, Lemelin, & Lacharité, 2004; Hart & Rubia, 2012). As explained in Chap-ter 8, there is a higher proportion of disorganized attachment in maltreated children (Carlson, Cicchetti, Barnett, & Braunwald, 1989; Lamb, Gaensbauer, Malkin, & Schultz, 1985; Main & Solomon, 1986). Other negative effects of maltreatment on infants include a lack of concern for the distress of peers and an often inappropriate response to distress, such as physical aggression (Main & George, 1985). Maltreated infants have shorter MLU (mean length of utterance), less speech related to their own emotional states, and less speech that is relevant to the ongoing topic of conversation (Coster, Gersten, Beeghly, & Cicchetti, 1989).

These effects may all have a common source in disturbances of the neurohormonal systems responsible for the emotion regulation, responsiveness to fear and stress, and **post traumatic stress disorder** or PTSD (see Chapter 4). Maltreated infants and children have dysregulated **HPA axis** and **cortisol** levels, higher **sympathetic nervous system** activation, are more likely to show symptoms of PTSD such as perceiving danger even when it is not present, and inability to cope with normal life stresses (Bugental, Martorell, & Barraza, 2003; Cicchetti, Rogosch, Gunnar & Toth, 2010; Cicchetti et al., 2010; Pollak et al., 2005; Shea et al., 2004).

Because of the complexity of factors and individual differences in children, not all parents who were abused as children will go on to abuse their own children and not all children who had been abused will show negative outcomes. There is a higher probability of long-term effects of early maltreatment if the abused child continues to experience violence and aggression, poverty and stress, school problems, problems maintaining intimate relationships, low impulse control, depression or mental illness, panic and anxiety disorders, low self-esteem, or is a teen parent (Berlin, Appleyard & Dodge, 2011; Bugental & Happaney, 2004; Coleman & Widom, 2004; Dixon et al., 2005; Evans, Hawton, & Rodham, 2005; Goodwin, Fergusson, & Horwood, 2005; Hildyard & Wolfe, 2002). Higher welfare benefits and more social support reduce the likelihood of abuse (Berger, 2004; Huebner, 2002; Lyons, Henly, & Schuerman, 2005). Community and neighborhood support systems for par-

ents, especially those that provide human services for families as a whole rather than for single individuals, can be effective in the prevention of child maltreatment (Berger, 2004; Huebner, 2002; Lyons, Henly, & Schuerman, 2005).

Deprivation of Normal Parental Care

Total deprivation of parental care, such as in the studies by Harry Harlow of monkeys who were raised without parents (see Chapter 1) is rare in humans. The closest analogies are infants reared in institutional settings such as orphanages. Orphanages are almost nonexistent in North America and Western Europe, where it is the practice to place abandoned children in foster or adoptive care. Institutionalization is more common in Eastern Europe, Russia, and China, and many international adoptions to the United States are from these countries.

The worst cases of institutional deprivation—lack of adequate nutrition, stimulation, and affection—have come from Romania, where children, as well as everyone else in that country, suffered for many years under a repressive dictator. After he was murdered by a mob in 1989, the country was opened to outsiders, and many of the children were placed into adoptive care. A team of researchers has been studying these Romanian children and their developmental outcomes. Many of these children suffered from language and cognitive delays, brain abnormalities especially in the limbic and prefrontal areas that develop most rapidly in infancy and are responsible for basic functions and self-regulation (see Chapter 4), social and emotional problems, attention deficits and hyperactivity (Nelson, 2007).

On the other hand, some children's deficits were more severe than others. The more severe cases were institutionalized for longer than 6 months. The effects on these children of psychological deprivation were small head circumference, increased conduct and externalizing problems in childhood and adolescence, deficits in memory, attention, and facial emotion processing, higher cortisol levels, smaller stature, and earlier puberty (Moulson et al., 2009; Moulson et al., 2010; Pollack et al., 2010; Rutter et al., 2010). If the children were placed in an adoptive or foster family, their risk for these outcomes decreased and their attachment quality increased, except for a small minority who appeared to have sustained some type of brain damage that was resistant to the experience-dependent development possible in the adoptive family environment (Moulson et al., 2009; Moulson et al., 2010; Rutter et al., 2004; Rutter et al., 2007; Smyke et al., 2010; Wilson, 2003).

Another group of orphanages in St. Petersburg, Russia provided adequate medical and nutritional care, sanitation, toys, and professional services but there were no affectionate interactions with caregivers, who just did business-like tasks. There were 9 to 12 caregivers per week, with children exposed to as many as 60 to 100 different caregivers in the first two years. Interventions were implemented in these institutions that focused on providing warm, affectionate, and sensitive care, reducing the number of caregivers to which the infants were exposed, and creating a "family hour" in which caregivers and infants could spend quality time in the absence of caregiving tasks. This intervention improved all the deprivation-related outcomes, including more normal levels of head circumference and physical growth, and more effective socioemotional behavior and coping abilities. These findings, taken together, suggest that the socioemotional deprivation is the crucial factor in sustaining poor outcomes (The St. Petersburg-USA Orphanage Research Team, 2008).

Infants with Special Needs

Infants with special needs may have suffered from a birth defect that affects the brain or body, or they may have acquired a disability following birth. This population of infants is referred to in many ways: special needs, developmentally challenged, developmentally disabled, handicapped, or developmentally delayed. These infants place demands upon their caregivers that typically developing infants do not, including extra visits to doctors and hospitals, special difficulties (such as soiling and wetting), special housing or equipment needs, financial difficulties, special care arrangements, special clothing, and special transportation (Rapoport, Rapoport, & Strelitz, 1977). Research suggests that premature infants and infants with special needs, Down's syndrome, and other illnesses are overrepresented in the maltreated population (Bugental & Happaney, 2004; Sidebotham & Heron, 2003; Wu et al., 2004). Because of the stress on the parents, siblings receive lower amounts of parental time and emotional energy. As a result, siblings may have trouble with peer relationships, become restless and disobedient, display temper tantrums, or live in a state of emotional misery (Heiman, 2002). In general, the more serious disabilities requiring more care and adaptive equipment result in the biggest impacts on parental and family life (Kelly & Booth, 2002).

If there are no neurological problems, however, there are few or no differences between special needs and normally developing infants and their families (Clements & Barnett, 2002; Tessier et al., 2002). The developmental prognosis is better for infants with special needs whose social interactions with their mothers are more like those of typically developing infants (Meadow-Orlans & Spencer, 1996). In general, most families who are provided with adequate social, economic, and psychological support come to an effective resolution of the issues of caring for a special needs infant, although it may take a long time. Most (75 percent) parents of special needs infants report the growth of feelings of love, joy, and acceptance over time (Heiman, 2002; Mintzer, Als, Tronick, & Brazelton, 1985; Shonkoff, Hauser-Cram, Krauss, & Upshur, 1992).

THE EFFECTS OF INTERVENTION AND EDUCATION PROGRAMS

Infant-Parent Mental Health[1]

Infant-Parent Mental Health (IPMH) is a current, multi-disciplinary mental health specialization

---

[1]Written by Mark Ludwig, LCSW, Associate Professor, Department of Somatic Psychology, California Institute of Integral Studies, San Francisco, CA.

focusing on the relational context for the total development of young children. The IPMH paradigm is based on an essential commitment to trans-disciplinary integration and to the treatment of developmental, relational, and emotional distress from a whole-child-in-relationship perspective. Mounting research evidence over the past 3 decades (Fogel, 1993; Stern, 1985; Tronick, 2007) has thrust the developmental and relational experience of infants into the foreground of clinical inquiry and mental health practice. Extensive professional and public interest in the significance of these early experiences for later child, adolescent, adult, couples, and family functioning has spurred greater efforts to unravel the complexities of early psychophysical, neurological, and emotional development (Fonagy et al., 2004; Perry, 2005; Schore, 2003; Siegel, 2001). This research points toward the overarching and predominant developmental importance of the quality of the early caregiver-infant relationship.

Basic concepts of IPMH. The core of IPMH is a dynamic systems model of human development (see Chapter 1). Due to our relatively long gestation (compared to other mammals) and 'pre-mature" birth (human newborns are completely incapable of taking care of themselves) infants and children require a prolonged period of needs management by caregivers. The child's needs system is therefore functionally dependent on an intimate relationship with a caregiver and from the wider context of co-existing family, social, and cultural systems. We might think, for example, about the children's growing ability to participate in their own feeding by gesturing to communicate hunger, setting the pace of the feeding, and moving toward self-feeding. On the other hand, across the whole early feeding process, there is an interdependent need to rely on the caregiver to provide the nutritional elements and respond appropriately to the child's signals. These interactions are seen as developing the implicit relational and self systems that will guide healthy social-emotional choices in the unfolding development of the person.

As children develop via co-regulatory processes, their self-regulatory capacities grow to sup-plant this early interdependence. As this happens, caregivers help less with tasks the children can perform themselves but continue to stand by in an attuned fashion to provide containment, support, and perspective. IPMH practitioners understand that humans "swim in a human sea," in a lifelong matrix of essential and sustaining mutual "holdings." A variety of research reviewed in this book indicates that the adult's capacity for forming and maintaining mature relationships is predicated on and predicted by the nature of the successes and shortcomings of early childhood relational experience (Fonagy et al., 2004; Sroufe et al., 2010).

In addition to dynamic systems thinking and interpersonal neurobiology research, attachment (Bowlby's theory, see Chapter 8) and psychotherapeutic approaches are frequently integrated to help deepen our understanding of the complex developmental impact of early child-parent interaction in IPMH. From Bowlby, the study of interactional behavior patterns and of the process by which children develop **internal working models** (see Chapter 8) of themselves, their caregivers and the world have created a rich and sustaining framework for clinical intervention.

Donald Winnicott, the English pediatrician and psychoanalyst, was among the first to emphasize the dyadic focus of this approach with his assertion that "there is no baby without a mother" (Winnicott, 1971). Complementary perspectives were described by Margaret Mahler and Louis Sander (Mahler et al., 1975; Sander, 1962) who proposed developmental stages during the first three years that involved changes in the infant-caregiver system (see Table 12.1). Renee Spitz extensively researched the massive developmental failures visited on institutionalized children who were not provided with regular intimate interaction with a stable caregiver (Spitz, 1965, see topic of deprivation in Chapter 12). Finally, Selma Fraiberg, a psychoanalytically-oriented clinical social worker, opened the door to the problem of transgenerational transmission of developmental psychopathology when she introduced the notion of "ghosts in the nursery" (Fraiberg, Adelson, & Shapiro, 1975). The "ghosts' in question were the

TABLE 12.1   Louis Sander's Stages of the Development of Mother-Infant Reciprocity

Approximate Age (Months)	Description
0–3	The parent is concerned with helping the infant cope with the biological function and the establishment of regular patterns of sleeping, feeding, arousal and quieting. The infant begins to show differential responsiveness to the caregiver.
4–6	The beginnings of mutual play and reciprocal interactions can be seen. The parent and infant learn to anticipate signals from each other to coordinate feeding, playing, and caretaking activities.
7–9	The infant begins to take the initiative in social exchanges and shows preferences for certain kinds of social activities over others. The infant experiences feelings of success or frustration in meeting goals.
10–13	The infant makes directed demands on the mother and tries to test her availability. The parent is used as a secure base for exploration.
14–20	Infants take their own initiatives in a wider variety of settings. Infants learn to achieve success and pleasure autonomously (apart from the mother).

Source: Adapted from L. W. Sander. Issues in early mother-child interaction, 1962. *Journal of the American Academy of Child Psychiatry, 1*, 141–166.

unconscious maternal thoughts and feelings about herself, her baby, and herself as a baby with her own caregivers; thoughts that had an impact on how she raised her own children.

More recently, the study of interpersonal neurobiology (Schore, 2012) has contributed a great deal to the discussion of how caregiver's experience-dependent neural templates function as mental models of the children in their care. This transgenerational transmission has created urgency around providing prenatal and early parenting education to counter the potential negative impact of seemingly innocuous interaction patterns in the early life of children.

The human genome revolution of the past decades is having an enormous impact on IPMH theory and practice. Epigenetics, the study of gene-environment interaction (Chapter 2), has become an important focus in the field. As secure parent-child interaction is the single most stress-reducing and safety-inducing dynamic of early childhood, interest has been focused on the effects of suboptimal interactions on epigentically-induced psychopathology and physical illness (Steele et al., 2010, Parade et al., 2012). As we saw in Chapter 4, parts of the brain (amygdala, prefrontal cortex, and hippocampus) and its neurotransmitters are altered in function as a result of stress. Some of these changes are related to how genes within the nerve cells are turned on or off in response to stress, resulting in the changes in brain function described in Chapter 4 (decrease in self-regulatory ability and heightened proneness to anxiety and attachment disorders).

Clinical practice in IPMH. In IPMH practice, the caregiver-child relationship is the "client" rather than the parent or the child individually. The unique constitutional elements of each member of the dyad as well as the particular qualities of the way in which they interact are relevant in this matter. Because it is often the case that parents who have unconscious "ghosts" were themselves maltreated, intervention with such parents can break the cycle of intergenerational transmission of pathology. Working with traumatized parents in relation to their infants has been called a search for "angels in the nursery," allowing such parents to tap into their own strengths and desires to be a better parent to provide the child with a sense of being understood, feeling accepted, and creating a sense of security (Lieberman et al., 2005). Angels in the nursery are adults in the parent's early childhood experience who did not cause the child stress but instead may have provided a sense of love and safety. Here is one example of an adult remembering her childhood during a psychotherapy session. Note how the description is very sensory and feeling-based, like a participatory memory, suggesting the importance of pre-verbal experience.

> My aunt… she was just always a very gentle, very loving… she'd brush my hair very gently and never pulled my hair, like my mom did. My mom was always in a hurry to get the hair brushed… get it over and done with, and my aunt would just take her time, and be so gentle…. She was like a warm blanket, she was just wonderful (Lieberman et al., 2005, p. 509).

A good example of effective relationship-based IPMH practice is portrayed in the PBS *Frontline* documentary focused on Toronto's "Wait, watch and wonder" approach, "When the Bough Breaks." Three middle class families struggle with problems between parents and infants—sleeping and eating issues in this case—which they initially think are "in" their children. As the story unfolds, they and the viewers come to understand how the caregivers' attitudes and behaviors are an essential part of the story (view this online at www.frontline.org).The following section of this chapter, on the work of IPMH consultants, provides another example.

A collaborative model. In the past, parents—and particularly mothers—were often blamed for "causing" the infant's problems. IPMH has a refreshing new take on this situation, using strength-based and collaborative models of caregiver facilitation. Caregiver curiosity regarding children and their internal world is actively supported. As a field that accepts the fact of transgenerational transmission of relational patterns, there has been a healthy reduction in caregiver scapegoating. A revolutionary form of clinician supervision has also grown up in the IPMH field, an approach which extends this empathic model to the sometimes rough world of clinical supervision. In **reflective supervision**

the clinician-supervisor dyad mirrors the clinician-caregiver and caregiver-child dyad in continuing the ethos of sustaining relationships based on mutual reflection and collaboration (Heffron, 2010). IPMH is ultimately a preventative approach, responding to difficulties in the infant-parent relationship before they become major problems. Interventions are designed to make contact with the dyad in multiple ways such as those shown in Table 12.2 (Weatherston, 2000).

Assessment and diagnosis. A growing number of assessment tools can be used by IPMH consultants to look at the qualities of the infant-parent relationship such as temperament, dyadic "fit," rhythms, gaze coordination, and mutual arousal profiles (Barnard, 1985; Zeanah et al., 2005; Slade, 2005). Three decades ago there was a paucity of diagnostic classifications for disturbances of childhood and no relationship-based diagnostic systems of any kind. The DC: 0-3R (2005) is a diagnostic manual specifically for disorders of children under the age of 3 years. In addition to having categories for problems with separation, sleeping, feeding, anxiety, depression, and PTSD, the DC: 0-3R also developed an innovative diagnostic axis for different types of parent-infant relationships that may be problematic. Categories in the relationship dimension include disruptions in parental behavior serious enough to cause symptoms in the child, such as parents who are under-involved or over-involved, having infants who are anxious or tense in response, or parents who are abusive or neglectful (DC: 0-3R, 2005).

More recently, attachment researchers have been investigating and developing assessment tools in the crucial area of caregiver reflective capacity (Steele & Steele, 2008) and "maternal mind-mindedness" (Meins et al., 2013). Reflective function is the capacity to reflect on one's own mental experience, those of others, and the mutual influencing dynamics. These studies attempt to understand the complex developmental components that come into play within caregivers as they attempt to perceive, interpret and respond to the robust and subtle expressions and cues regarding the child's

TABLE 12.2   Intervention Practices in Infant-Parent Mental Health

Explicate and encourage normal developmental processes

Educate the caregiver about being responsive to the child's needs

Stabilize and support the caregiver-child "fit"

Elucidate with the caregiver the unique qualities of this baby

Help support the caregiver's tracking, cueing and response processes

Support mutual attunement and make experiences shareable

Support the ability of the caregiver to self-reflect on own actions

Point out mutually reinforcing negative interaction patterns

Help parents to find pleasure in their relationship with the infant

Attend to the parent's own history of trauma and unresolved loss from childhood

Target punitive parenting practices and dysregulating caregiver and child behaviors within a context of cultural sensitivity

Support contingent communication and face-to-face exchanges, especially those featuring mutually pleasurable transactions

Support the "something new" that can emerge in open dyadic interaction

internal state. A scale of reflective functioning has been developed (Fonagy et al., 1998) and is in use as a guide to parenting education and intervention (Steele et al., 2010)

Focus on multiply sressed dyads. While IPMH treatment models are effective with a range of populations including "normal" families, the focus of treatment has typically been on multiply stressed infants and caregivers: premies, foster care, Child Protective Service cases, early Head Start referrals, drug- and alcohol-exposed infants. Two programs with a national scope are particularly relevant here. *A Home Within* is a pro bono network of therapists and supervisors committed to guaranteeing long-term support for foster care children (Heineman & Ehrensaft, 2006). The *Circle of Security* (Marvin et al., 2002) model is an attachment-based, 20-week intervention that uses video clips of caregiver-child interactions shown in small caregiver-therapist groups. The focus is on education in attachment dynamics and supporting the healthy interaction patterns of each dyad. The original treatment methods were developed with families referred through the Spokane, Washington Early Head Start program.

Video based interventions. Frame-by-frame video microanalysis is an important technology for studying infant-caregiver interactions (see Chapter 1). Now, video based interventions are also increasingly common in IPMH programs (Downing, 2005, Downing et al., 2008). Watching interactions together with the therapist provides the caregiver with an opportunity to jointly consider caregiving decisions and to reflect on internal states of self and child without the pressure of live interactions. In particular, video seems to facilitate caregivers' attunement to child's experience and helps them understand any limits in their capacity to mentalize the child's inner states. The *Circle of Security* model of intervention (Marvin et al., 2002) uses attachment concepts and video viewing of their child in the "Strange Situation" assessment process to help parents appreciate their child's actual inner state and understand the child's over-adapted "mis-cueing."

Home visits. Since the generative work of Selma Freiberg in the 1960's, home visits have been a staple of infant-caregiver work. IPMH-trained post-natal visiting nurses and mental health professionals have a uniquely potent point of contact (Lester and Sparrow, 2011). By and large, parents of young children, regardless of their opportunities and circumstances, are very invested in being good parents. Because the IPMH model is primarily a model of prevention, these early contacts provide important opportunities for support, education, referral, and information (van Doesum et al., 2008).

Careers with Infants: Infant-Parent Mental Health Consultants[2]

Elayna screams when other children get near her. At 17 months of age, she is very irritable, often throwing intense tantrums, especially when she is tired. Elayna has been attending an infant and child care center for about five months. The staff at the facility have become increasingly concerned about Elayna's behavior.

Elayna's mother is 21, single, and was 19 when Elayna was born. Recently, overwhelmed with the stress of working to support herself and her child, she moved back in with her family to gain needed support for herself and her infant daughter. Not long after she moved back home, Elayna's mother and grandmother both expressed concerns for Elayna to the center staff. They described how the staff at the previous center Elayna attended would often call her mother, asking her to pick Elayna up because her incessant crying would keep the other infants awake.

After visiting with Elayna's family, the staff at the center decided to make an appointment with an infant-parent mental health (IPMH) consultant (see previous section on IPMH). The staff hoped this consultation would assist with developing strategies to help them and Elayna's family provide a more healthful environment for Elayna and the other children at the center.

IPMH consultants can develop programs to help prevent future problems such as school failure, child abuse, sickness, and teen/adult mental illness. IPMH is an interdisciplinary field that is rapidly growing as a result of research identifying behavioral and mental health problems in infants

and toddlers. As defined by the national professional advocacy organization, *Zero to Three*, IPMH includes "the young child's capacity to experience, regulate, and express emotions, form close and secure relationships, and explore the environment and learn. All of these capacities will be best accomplished within the context of the care giving environment that includes family, community, and cultural expectations for young children" (Zeanah et al., 2005, p. 4).

As described in the previous section, the field of IPMH focuses on relationship-based interaction, with the understanding that relationships are central to healthy development and that an infant is best understood within the context of the important adults in his or her life. Infants learn about the world through relationships with their parents, family members, and care providers. Infants who feel secure and loved have better social and emotional skills. Research reviewed in this book has shown that early experiences impact a child's brain development, physical health, and life-long mental health (see, for example, Gunnar & Barr, 1998). Even an infant can display stress as evidenced by problems with attachment, behavior, or digestion. Today, infants and toddlers face significant time away from their families, often and unfortunately placed in inconsistent and/or poor quality child care. Societal problems such as substance abuse, poverty, and maltreatment also contribute to IPMH problems.

Based on recent research indicating IPMH consultations can improve aspects of child care programs, Elayna's child care staff requests a referral, stating that Elayna is a child with challenging behaviors (Alkon, Ramler, and MacLennan, 2003). Carolyn Morris, a local IPMH consultant, agrees to the engagement. Carolyn observes Elayna in her child care classroom, talks with her teachers, mother, and her grandmother. As an IPMH specialist, Carolyn's goal is to develop an understanding of each family's challenges by occupying the role of keen observer and listener. Carolyn's role as an IPMH consultant is not to impose her own agenda, but instead to listen to the experiences and desires of the family and care providers. For

---

[2]Written by Dr. LaDonna Atkins, Associate Professor, Department of Family and Child Studies, University of Central Oklahoma)

Carolyn, developing a sense of trust and respect for cultural and individual uniqueness is essential. Carolyn will gather information, reflect, and may suggest further assessments or strategies for improvement. Carolyn may work with the family on her own or as part of a team. When the fact gathering is complete, Carolyn will create a plan for the family and center while still continuing to observe, discuss and support the family as they care for Elayna's individual circumstances.

In Elayna's case, Carolyn recommended positive play activities to strengthen the bond between Elayna, her caregivers, and her family. Carolyn suggested the staff follow Elayna's lead but also encourage Elayna to engage in parallel type play so she can slowly get used to other children. Carolyn also encouraged the staff to evaluate their environment. She suggested that the environment have several private spaces where Elayna could be off by herself. Carolyn encouraged Elayna's family to establish a predictable schedule. She also talked to the family about reading Elayna's cues so they could learn to use distraction techniques such as singing or reading a book before Elayna's tantrums started. Carolyn also made the decision to conduct additional observations of Elayna's attachment and her use of communication skills. She understands that her suggestions are only the first steps and eventually more assessments and/or therapeutic strategies may be recommended.

Child care centers offer a unique setting for mental health consultants. Child care in America today serves a significant number of children. The opportunity and need for educating caregiving staff and families is unlimited. IPMH specialists may also be found working in hospitals, home visitation programs, and community agencies. The increasing interest in IPMH has led many states and communities to adopt plans for varying levels of services for the under-three age group.

A growing need for more education in the infant and family field has spawned new training programs, and endorsement and certification programs are being implemented around the world. The first of the IPMH academic programs was the Infant Parent Mental Health Training Program at the University of Michigan. The Fielding Graduate University in Santa Barbara, CA, now has a psychology doctoral program with an IPMH specialization. Other professional training opportunities in IPMH are: *Zero to Three*: a national program supporting early intervention; Interdisciplinary Council on Developmental and Learning Disorders, Maryland; The Infant-Parent Institute, Champaign, IL; Infant-Parent Training Institute at the Jewish Family and Child Services, Boston, MA; Napa Infant-Parent Mental Health Fellowship Program, Napa, CA; the Mills College Master's program in IPMH in Oakland, CA, and the Erikson Institute, Chicago, IL. For more information, see www.zerotothree.org and The World Association for Infant Mental Health, at waimh.org.

Being an IPMH consultant is one of many careers in which it is possible to work with infants. Other careers are listed in Table 12.3. Careers vary considerably in the amount of training required (such as medical schools, nursing schools, business schools, massage schools, psychology, or social work programs) and in the salaries of workers. More information about each career is available by searching the internet.

Other Types of Education and Intervention Programs for Infants and Families

In addition to IPMH programs, there are a wide variety of structured intervention and education programs designed to meet the needs of parents and infants. These include health care, education, counseling services, internet-based services, films, books, social services, housing, welfare, and recreational facilities. They offer services ranging from childbirth education to well-baby care, to parent training programs, to early childhood education for disadvantaged toddlers. Parents who receive more of these kinds of supports are less likely to be punitive in their child rearing, more likely to play and be affectionate with their infants, respond more quickly to the babies' cries, have more secure attachments, are more nurturing, have more positive attitudes about child rearing, and abuse their infants less (Berlin, O'Neal, & Brooks-Gunn, 1998;

Caughy, DiPietro, & Strobino, 1994; Greenspan & Wieder, 1997; Lyons-Ruth, Connell, Grunebaum, & Botein, 1990; D. R. Powell, 2001; Roggman et al., 2004; Scarr & Eisenberg, 1993; Spitz, 1992; Wasik, Ramey, Bryant, & Sparling, 1990). Young fathers, who typically would be less likely to join a group outside the home, find that Internet support groups—such as www.fathersnetwork.org and www.fathers.net—enhance parenting self-efficacy and satisfaction (Hudson et al., 2003).

Interventions for parents at risk for maltreatment, especially those that involve the parent in an active way to solve problems rather than simply teaching them to follow rules, seem the most successful (Bugental & Schwartz, 2009). A program designed to decrease parental frightening behavior and enhance sensitivity (the ABC program) has been effective in reducing the proportion of disorganized attachments in the infants of maltreating parents (Bernard et al., 2012). Another program focused on reducing parental stress and providing strategies for parental anger and emotion regulation (Parent-child Intervention Therapy) was helpful in reducing abuse and increasing parental sensitivity (Thomas & Zimmer-Gembeck, 2011).

Malnutrition can have severe short-and long-term effects on reducing infant energy, emotional responsiveness, attention, and play (Lozoff et al., 1998; M. A. McDonald, Sigman, Espinosa, & Neumann, 1994; Pollitt et al., 1996; Wachs, 2000). Interventions involving nutritional supplementation are generally successful if they are accompanied by parent-child behavior interventions to enhance maternal sensitivity (Pollitt et al., 1996; Valenzuela, 1997). In a study done in Colombia, malnutrition was treated in one group with only food supplementation for the entire family and in another group with food supplementation plus parent education during home visits. The children in the group that received supplementation plus parent education were taller and heavier at the age of 6 years, and there were fewer cases of mental retardation than in the food-only group (Super, Herrera, & Mora, 1990).

Interventions designed for premature infants have also shown signs of success. The most successful interventions combine long-term pediatric care with parent education and family support. These programs enhance children's cognitive and behavioral development and also increase the competence and enthusiasm of the parents (Achenbach, Phares, Howell, Rauh, & Nurcombe, 1990; Brooks-Gunn, Klebanov, Liaw, & Spiker, 1993; Spiker, Ferguson, & Brooks-Gunn, 1993).

Intervention programs for parents of special needs infants work best if they provide emotional support and the supportive network of a system of other parents with similar problems. Such programs, which teach parents how to respond to and anticipate the needs of their individual children have a significant success rate. Mothers in such intervention programs enjoy and respond more to their special needs infants (Calhoun, Rose, Hanft, & Sturkey, 1991; Gavidia-Payne & Stoneman, 1997; Glidden, 2002; Kellyi & Booth, 2002).

In addition, local and state governments provide support services for children with special needs through child care and school systems, as well as through hospital programs. Federal funds are available through such programs as Developmental Disabilities, Early Periodic Screening Diagnosis and Treatment, Head Start, Education of the Handicapped (PL 94–142), Title XX Social Services, and the National Institute for Mental Health. Most of these programs make funds available through community and state education and welfare agencies (McPherson, 1983). Another federal law (PL 99–457) provides for family-centered, rather than child-centered, services. This law encourages the states to implement comprehensive, multidisciplinary, and interagency services for early intervention with families and children who have special needs. The program focuses on identifying family strengths, goals, and needs while developing an intervention plan to meet those needs (Rounds, 1991).

In general, some programs work some of the time for some groups. Overall, however, intervention programs provide an important source of enrichment and encouragement for parents who are under social and economic stress. In this perspective, short-term relief from stress may be as valuable as any long-term developmental benefit. Virtually all researchers and practitioners agree that early intervention is important and should continue for many years into the future (Shonkoff, 2010). The best chance for success are multisite, multimethod intervention programs which have been shown to decrease reliance on welfare, reduce parental substance abuse, and lower the incidence of criminal acts when the infants become adolescents (Honig, 2004; A. J. Reynolds, 1998). The most successful programs are those that provide high-quality educational child care for the infant coupled with home-and center-based support services for the parents and families. Neither parent education alone nor child care alone is as effective as the two are in combination (M. M. Black & Krishnakumar, 1998; D. R. Powell, 2000; C. T. Ramey & Ramey, 1998; Yoshikawa, 1999).

Perhaps one of the best-known early intervention programs that follow this multi-method model is **Head Start,** a federally funded national preschool (3 to 6 years) education program with goals similar to the projects mentioned above. In 2012, there were over one million children under the age of 5 years enrolled at an annual cost of only $7,600 per child. Some Head Start programs include family service centers (to provide job training and education for parents), transition to elementary school programs (to provide training for elementary school teachers who will teach the Head Start graduates), comprehensive child developmental centers (to provide training in prenatal nutrition and parent skills), and family childcare projects (to allow single parents to work full time while supporting the child and family). Head Start children, compared with those who attended other day care or had no support, do better in preschool and elementary school, have fewer teen pregnancies, have a higher high school graduation rate, are more likely to be employed, and are less likely to have been arrested (Berrueta-Clement et al., 1984; Ludwig & Phillips, 2007; S. L. Ramey, 1999).

Complementary and Alternative Approaches to Treatment

Finally, there are intervention and education programs for infants and parents that can be called "alternative" because they use approaches that have not been part of mainstream psychological, behavioral, educational, and social services interventions. The approaches focus on supporting the infant and parent by using directly perceived sensory, motor, and emotional engagement. The Feldenkrais Method (www.feldenkrais.com) contains thousands of "Awareness through Movement" lessons based on the movements performed by babies as they first learn to roll, sit, crawl, walk, and explore their bodies in the environment. Adult and child students are asked to make small, slow movements, reduce their efforts, and sense how even simple movements are connected with every part of the body. This book contains some Awareness through Movement lessons, those written by Feldenkrais practitioner Mark Reese (Reese, 1985) and found in the Experiential Exercises sections of Chapters 5 and 7. Feldenkrais practitioners also use a hands-on technique called functional integration. In this work, students lie on a padded table as a practitioner gently touches and moves them, often in babylike ways, to promote deep relaxation, kinesthetic awareness, and openness to learning new ways to move. This approach has been used for children with muscular problems, cerebral palsy, Down's syndrome, autism, and other movement- and sensory-related developmental problems (www.anatbanielmethod.com, childspacemethod.com).

Bodymind centering (BMC) is a method of body and movement awareness based on the normal stages of infant sensorimotor development (Hartley, 1995). Bodymind centering was created by a dance teacher and physical therapist, Bonnie Bainbridge Cohen, during the 1960s and 1970s. Cohen discovered that she could help many of her clients by taking them step by step through the sensorimotor stages of prenatal and infant development. BMC has been used in the treatment of parent-infant relationships at risk (Frank, 2001;

Clockwise from upper left: BMC with infants; Feldenkrais Functional Integration; Dance movement therapy; Body Mind Centering, Bonnie Bainbridge Cohen.

Sources: http://www.somaticstudies.com/index.html; www.anatbanielmethod.com; www.adta.org/resources/media.cfm; www.bodymindcentering.com

www.somaticstudies.com/ruellafrank.html) and working directly with infants who experience sensorimotor difficulties (Brook, 2001b; http://body-mindsomanautics.com/). An Experiential Exercise based on BMC can be found in Chapter 2.

Related to BMC is Dance Movement Psychotherapy, in which infants and children can be engaged using expressive dance-like movements to foster a more integrated sense of self in relation to other people. It has been successful for infants and children with autism, communication delays, sensory integration difficulties, hyperactivity, and trauma (Tortora, 2006; www.suzitortora.

org). Infants and children learn to sequence their movements in space and time to connect with others and achieve personal goals. One of the key concepts of this work is kinesthetic empathy, the ability to feel another person's feelings by moving like that other person. Dance movement psychotherapists use kinesthetic empathy with their clients, and children learn this by engaging with the therapist. You can better understand this approach by doing the Experiential Exercises in Chapters 7 and 9.

Finally, infant massage and other touch therapies for infants were discussed in Chapter 5. Massage has been shown to increase weight gain and responsiveness in preterm infants and to modulate emotions, increase growth rate and weight gain, and reduce crying in full-terms (Field, 1998; Field et al., 2004). Adults who give massages had lower depression scores, higher levels of marital satisfaction, increased self-esteem, and enhanced health behaviors (Field, 1998; Stack, 2000). There are many resources for learning about infant massage (www.infantmassageusa.org; www.liddlekidz.com).

CONCLUSIONS

The research reviewed in this chapter shows that many factors in early infancy have significant effects on outcomes in childhood and adulthood. The prenatal and perinatal environment, genetics, parental sensitivity, culture, gender, risk factors (poverty, stress), and temperament, among many other things, play a role in the formation of the individual through time. Throughout this chapter, two major principles have been discussed: that no one of these factors can work in isolation (development is multifactorial and complex), and that no two individuals are affected in the same way by any one factor or any set of factors acting in combination. Multifactor processes and between-individual variability have been found for virtually every research study in which more than one factor is measured on the same group of infants (Wachs, 2000).

Development is a continuously unfolding process of change. Little by little, many influences, actions, feelings, and thoughts transform us as we live from day to day. Day-to-day change is subtle, sometimes regressing rather than going forward, like babies who first crawl backward when they are really trying to move ahead. This inability to predict and control human development is not a bad thing. An individual whose developmental fate is determined by a predictable set of causes and effects could not be open to the opportunity for discovery, exploration, risk taking, and personal growth. Creativity, surprise, and the excitement of the unknown keep pulling us

forward as much as our genes and environments push us from behind.

One should distrust any claims that a single factor from early infancy has lasting outcomes for all infants exposed to it. Even though we cannot know or understand how any particular factors contribute to healthy development, we do know that babies—indeed, people of all ages—should be afforded healthy, safe, enriched, and loving opportunities. We do not need research to convince us that every human being is entitled to good prenatal care, a warm and loving home, quality education, and economic security. It is just the right thing to do. Research clearly shows that people are more likely to become healthy, happy, productive, and intelligent if they have these things. Because of the complexity of human development, we can only say that, in general, intelligence, social skills, and emotional control are promoted in healthy, safe, and loving environments. We can only say that, in general, these abilities are more likely to be deficient in impoverished and insensitive rearing conditions. We can say with certainty that *infancy is important* and that each person will get something different from their early years, both potentials and limitations.

Events that occur during infancy do have some impact on later life, even if we cannot trace that impact to a specific event for a specific person. Whether or not we can consciously (autobiographically) remember our infancy, we contain patterns of movement, thought, and feeling from infancy that persist in our minds and bodies and contribute to the person we are today. And what about you and your own early life experiences? As you encounter infants and young children in personal and professional roles, and as you enter into the infant's world through the research and exercises in this book, you will have to piece together the general principles from your own personal experiences. It will be up to you to bridge the gap between the abstract and the specific. In doing so, you will be rewarded with a deepening understanding of human life and human development, with all its richness and surprises.

SUMMARY

Development as a Complex Dynamic Process

- Development is a complex process involving multiple factors.
- No two individuals respond in the same way to the same factor. Variability and the opportunity to capitalize on chance outcomes is inherent to the developmental process.

Effects of Infant and Parental Factors

- If there are adequate economic resources, if the parents are not under psychosocial stress, and if the perinatal complications are not too severe, the effects do not persist over the long term.
- Extra motor stimulation in the first two or three years of life does not contribute to lasting individual differences unless the infant is at risk.
- Even though culture has a major impact on later outcomes, there is also a great deal of variability within cultures. Parents and caregivers need to be sensitive to issues of cultural change and adaptation, avoid stereotyping, and seek resources to facilitate cross-cultural understanding.
- Gender differences during infancy have been related to a number of outcome factors. One has to remember that there are individual differences among boys and among girls such that the general pattern does not hold for everyone.
- The child's environment and information-processing abilities during in¬fancy play some role in the prediction of later intelligence. These factors interact, how¬ever, and no one factor can account for all the variability. It is possible to enhance cognitive development for some children by talking with and reading to them. There is no evidence, however, that extra cognitive stimulation during infancy can create a genius.
- There is limited evidence for conti¬nuity in infant temperament. Only when children fall into extreme groups on irritability, emotionality, reactivity, or inhibition can long-term stabil¬ity be observed.
- All of the findings related to parent effects on children are based on correlations, which have two implications; first, the parent's style could be shaped by the child's behavior, at least in part; second, the corre¬lations are typically positive but small, meaning that while a general association exists between caregiving and child behavior, there is wide variability between families.

Effects of Risk and Disadvantage

- Poverty is a case where consistency of negative outcomes can be maintained over long periods in the absence of other mediating factors. On the other hand, some poor children who come from homes that focus on promoting child development, that value education, and that provide support, closeness, and protection from the stresses of poverty do better than children not provided with these buffers.
- A single stressful incident in early infancy has negligible long-term effects. However, multiple or long-term stresses create cyclical patterns of increasing risk and deprivation and are more likely to be associated with long-term emotional or behavioral disorders in later childhood.
- In general, there is only a small correlation, or none at all, between maternal psychopathology and later child outcome. The chances of the child being affected are increased if there is a familial genetic predisposition, if the parent's mental illness is severe, if the child is temperamentally inhibited or aggressive, if there are a series of environmental and familial stress¬ors, and if the attachment relationship is insecure.
- Not all parents who were abused as children will go on to abuse their own children and not all children who had been abused will show negative outcomes. There is a higher probability of long-term effects of early maltreatment if the abused child continues to experience vio-

lence and aggression, poverty and stress, school problems, problems maintaining intimate relationships, low impulse control, depression or mental illness, panic and anxiety disorders, low self-esteem, or is a teen parent.

- Socioemotional deprivation has more long-term effects than physical deprivation.

- If there are no neurological problems, however, there are few or no differences between special needs and normally developing infants and their families.

Effects of Intervention and Education Programs

- Infant-Parent Mental Health (IPMH) is a current, multi-disciplinary Mental Health specialization focusing on the relational context for the total development of young children based on an essential commitment to trans-disciplinary integration and to the treatment of developmental, relational, and emotional distress from a whole-child-in-relationship perspective.

- Being an IPMH consultant is one of many careers in which it is possible to work with infants. Other careers are listed in Table 12.3. Careers vary considerably in the amount of training required (such as medical schools, nursing schools, business schools, massage schools, psychology, or social work programs) and in the salaries of workers.

- In general, some programs work some of the time for some groups of infants. Overall, however, intervention programs provide an important source of enrichment and encouragement for parents who are under social and economic stress.

- Short-term relief from stress may be as valuable as any long-term developmental benefit.

- Virtually all researchers and practitioners agree that early intervention is important and should continue for many years into the future.

Glossary

A

Accommodation A change in individual functioning and skill in order to meet new environmental demands.

Action potentials Electrochemical currents that transmit information in neurons. These currents travel from the cell body along the axons to the axon terminals.

Acuity The ability of a perceptual system to resolve incoming information into sharp focus.

Affective sharing Occurs when the child seeks confirmation from others for his or her own felt emotion.

Afferent neurons send signals from inside and outside the body to the brain, meaning that they transmit to the brain how things are *affecting* us.

Allele A gene whose action depends upon at least one other gene, its allelic counterpart, to produce the phenotype. Usually, alleles are at the same location on each chromosome of a pair.

Amniocentesis Sampling a small amount of amniotic fluid for the purpose of determining the genetic and chromosomal make-up of the fetus.

Amniotic sac A membrane that encloses the embryo and fetus and contains amniotic fluid in which the fetus floats, providing a natural cushion.

Amygdala A small bulb at the front end of the hippocampus (amygdala means almond in Latin). There are two, a right and a left. The amygdala plays a role in the formation of emotional memories, especially those around fear and safety, and is functional at birth

Anal stage A period that begins some time in the second year of life when the primary sensitive zone becomes the anal region of the body.

Analgesia Pain-relieving drugs.

Anesthesia Drugs used to mask the sensation of pain.

A-not-B error An error in finding hidden objects that occurs when an object is hidden first in one place (A) and then in another place (B). The child finds the object at A but not at B.

Apgar score A screening test used to rate the infant's current health status and likelihood of crisis, rated at 1 and 5 minutes after birth.

Apnea Short cessation of respiratory movements.

Appraisal The ability to evaluate a situation and its circumstances before making an emotional response.

Appraisal The process by which an individual uses cognitive judgments to regulate emotional experiences.

Assimilation The adaptive utilization of those aspects of the environment that are within the limits of our skills and biological processing capacities.

Association The psychological linkage between a stimulus and a response that occurs in the environment at about the same time.

Asynchronous growth Refers to the fact that growth occurs in different regions of the body at different times and different rates.

Attachment The maintenance of close proximity between infant and caregiver as part of an enduring relationship.

Attachment behavior The overt set of signals, such as smiling, crying, and following that bring parent and infant into close proximity.

Attachment system The network of feelings and cognitions related to the object of attachment.

Attrition The loss of subjects over time in longitudinal research studies.

Attunement Cross-modal matching of infant behavior by an adult or vice versa.

Authoritarian parenting uses coercive and controlling techniques.

Authoritative parenting A style of parenting that combines warmth and firmness.

Autonomic nervous system is responsible for regulating internal organs including respiration, heart rate, blood pressure, sucking, swallowing, digestion, and sleep-wake cycles.

Autism spectrum disorder (ASD). ASD is a range of related developmental disorders with symptoms that may include impaired ability to interact socially, speech and language deficits, sensory sensitivities, and unusual movements of the body.

Autobiographical memory The ability to remember experiences as events and sequences expressed verbally as a story about oneself.

Axon A nerve fiber that conducts electrical activity away from the cell body of the neuron.

B

Babbling Vocal behavior that includes reduplication (repetition) of consonant-vowel syllables.

Baby biography A detailed written observation of the day-to-day changes in the behavior of a single infant; one of the first forms of scientific observations of infant behavior.

Behavior genetics The study of between-individual variability in phenotypes as a result of variability in environments or in genotypes.

Behavioral assessments Tests used to measure the newborn's behavioral status, including reflexes, orientation to external stimuli, and state control.

Birthrate The average number of infants born for every 1,000 women of childbearing age.

Bio-ecological systems theory A way to understand the relationships between and within multiple system levels – from person to society—that shape the development of infants into adulthood.

Blastocyst A fertilized ovum during the first 2 weeks of prenatal development, before implantation in the uterus.

Blindness The provision of limited information about the goals and conditions of a research study in order to prevent bias from subjects or observers.

Bodymind centering A somatic awareness technique in which verbal directions and touch are used to guide people step by step through the reexperiencing of the sensorimotor stages of prenatal and infant development.

Bonding The feelings of attachment the caregiver derives from close contact with the baby.

Brain stem A structure located at the lower back of the head that includes the lower brain stem that connects to the spinal cord, the upper brain stem or medulla, and is connected to the cerebellum. This part of the brain contains areas responsible for autonomic activities, such as respiration, heart rate, body temperature, sucking, and other reflexes.

Braxton-Hicks contractions Contractions that serve to move the fetus into its prebirth position; also called false labor.

Breech presentation A presentation in which the fetus is aligned buttocks first against the cervix.

Buffering The ability of the environment to maintain infant development on a typical course in spite of deviations caused by early infant risk factors.

Burst-pause pattern The pattern of sucking behavior in which the baby sucks for a few minutes, stops, and resumes sucking.

Butterfly effect The idea that small effects can have major consequences as they are amplified in a dynamic system, with the implication that it is impossible to trace the system backward in time to isolate single causes for later changes in the system.

C

Catch-up growth The higher rate of physical development seen in some cases of early deprivation or birth complications, compared to the normal growth rate.

Cephalocaudal development Growth that proceeds from the top of the body to the bottom.

Cervix The opening between the uterus and the vagina.

Cesarean section Delivery of the fetus through an incision in the mother's abdomen and uterus.

Chaos A mathematical concept that expresses the property of complex systems of having some general structure that repeats over time but never in exactly the same way.

Chorion The inner lining of the placenta separating it from the amniotic sac.

Chorionic villus sampling (CVS) A test for birth defects in which a small amount of the chorion is sampled. It can be done earlier in pregnancy than amniocentesis.

Chromosome An arrangement of about 20,000 genes, aligned in a long string. Each cell in the body contains 46 chromosomes, except for the gametes, which contain 23 chromosomes.

Classical conditioning Learning by association; the linking together of a stimulus and a response occurring at the same time.

Clinical infant The view of infant experience that emerges from the re-experiencing by children and adults of infant-like movements, sensations, and states of being.

Cloning A method of creating a zygote by removing the donor mother's DNA from the ova and implanting the DNA from any cell in the body of another person.

Co-construction The process by which what one knows depends upon how one acts on the environment and how the environment responds to those actions.

Colic A complaint of excessive crying (at least 3 hours per day, for a least 3 days per week, for at least 3 weeks) in an otherwise normal infant.

Colostrum A clear, yellowish, high-protein liquid secreted by the breasts beginning in the fourth month of pregnancy and continuing until several days after birth.

Compensation The provision of additional environmental support for infants who suffer from early deficits.

Conception The fertilization of an ovum.

Conceptual memories Memories of specific categories for type of event ("I was left alone"), time ("when I was five years old"), and place ("at the preschool"); recall about an event that is communicated in the form of a verbal narrative or story.

Conceptual self The ability of people to have a self-concept that includes autobiographical memory, the ability to distinguish one's own mind from those of others, and to identify one's membership in conceptual categories, such as "I am a boy," "I am a brother," and "I am not a baby."

Constructivist theory A theory in which knowledge is built up by the child's own action rather than being imposed on the child from the outside.

Continuity The preservation of individual characteristics across ages.

Contrast group A group used in experimental studies that receives a different manipulation or intervention from the experimental group.

Control group A group used in experimental studies that does not experience the intervention or manipulation received by the experimental group; allows a test of the effects of the manipulation compared with no manipulation.

Conventional actions Actions that represent another action or an object using some type of ritualized manner of expression, such as waving or saying "bye-bye."

Conventional communication A communicative act, such as a word, that is used by all members of the same speaking community.

Coordinated joint attention The process by which people co-regulate intentions with other people by attending to the same things at the same time (also called *intersubjectivity*).

Core self The experience of being an active agent that does things in the world, has feelings, and has a history of prior experiences.

Corporal punishment Using physical force for the purpose of discipline that causes pain to the child but not injury.

Cortex The outer layer of the brain, and the largest part of the human brain, that covers the limbic system and connects with it. The cortex is responsible for perception, movement, cognition, and most important, the voluntary regulation of behavior and emotion.

Cortisol, like the sympathetic nervous system, prepares the body for action in response to stress. It increases blood sugar needed for action and, via the blood, feeds back into the limbic system, where it heightens the formation of memories related to the stressful event. On the other hand, prolonged activation of cortisol due to ongoing stress suppresses the immune system and physical growth.

Couvade A father's attempt to experience the mother's feelings during pregnancy and delivery, seen in the form of culturally accepted rituals.

Credibility A form of validity in qualitative research based on the skill, experience, and rigor of the observer.

Critical period A relatively short, well-defined period in the life cycle when the individual is particularly receptive to certain kinds of environmental stimulation; if that stimulation is not received, the individual is not likely to profit from later exposure to similar stimuli, and other normal developmental processes may be disrupted.

Cross-modal perception Integration of information across more than one perceptual modality.

Cross-sectional study A research study in which age differences are studied using different infants at each age.

Cystic fibrosis A genetic disorder that causes clogging of the lungs with mucus.

D

Dance Movement Psychotherapy A somatic awareness practice in which infants and children can be engaged using expressive dance-like movements to foster a more integrated sense of self in relation to other people.

Defensive response Avoidance or aversive response to noxious or potentially threatening stimuli.

Deferred imitation Imitation that occurs following a delay from the time the action is seen modeled.

Dendrites The branching structures on the neuron that receive information at the synapse from other neurons and transmit it to the cell body.

Dependent variable Measurable outcome behavior observed in response to changes in an independent variable; the presumed effect of a causal independent variable in an experimental study.

Determinism The view that all natural phenomena are the result of some specifiable set of causes.

Developmental case studies Research that follows individuals as they change over time. Data is not averaged across people to show the uniqueness of each person's pattern of change, like a biography of a person's life.

Developmental change Change that is nonreversible, not temporary, and not haphazard.

Developmental neuroscience is the study of the developing brain and nervous system as it relates to psychological and behavioral functions such as moving, thinking, and feeling.

Developmental stage A stable and persistent pattern of behavior, thought, and feeling that continues over a long period of time (months or years).

Deviation-amplifying feedback Feedback that drastically changes a system as a result of a small deviation.

Deviation-correcting feedback Feedback that maintains a system's characteristics over time in spite of small deviations.

Differentiated ecological self The awareness that the ecology has localized entities, such as self and other or self and object, shown by the different ways in which infants call attention to themselves, such as asking for help, taking the initiative, clowning and showing off, demanding, and hiding and escaping.

Difficult temperament A parental judgment regarding the relative non-responsiveness of the infant to parental interventions.

Direct transaction A transaction that occurs as part of a social relationship in which the child is an active participant: the infant-parent, infant-peer, or infant-sibling relationship.

Disequilibrium The infant's experience during failures at adaptation; the motivational force that leads the infant to adapt by means of assimilation and accommodation.

Disorganized-disoriented attachment The infant shows confused behavior in the Strange Situation Test, such as approaching the mother and then suddenly withdrawing.

Displacement The property of language to express concrete and abstract ideas and describe objects that are not physically in the speaker's presence.

Dissociation The inability to connect with one's own body or with one's own emotional experiences. May include the following symptoms: mental confusion, lack of subjective self-awareness, out-of-body experiences, accident proneness, and self-harm or suicide proneness

Dizygotic twins Twins formed when two ova are fertilized at the same time.

DNA (Deoxyribonucleic acid) A molecule that contains a biochemical code for the production of body tissues. Genes are sections of DNA that control the development of specific characteristics and functions of the individual.

Dominance hierachy A pattern of social relationships in which the members of a group are ranked according to their relative power or lack of power over others.

Dominant-recessive inheritance A two-gene inheritance pattern in which the recessive gene appears in the phenotype only if no dominant gene is present.

Dopamine A neurochemical that helps with control of attention and thought, feelings of pleasure and optimism, and regulation of movement.

Dorsoventral development Growth that begins at the spine and moves toward the front of the body.

Dose-response relationship A relationship between a drug's dosage and its effects in which increasing dosages lead to stronger effects.

Down's syndrome A chromosomal disorder that causes short stature, cardiac abnormalities, flabbiness, small mouth, and mental retardation.

Dramatists Children who classify objects based on a script or story in which the objects are embedded.

Dynamic systems theory An account of the process of change in human development by understanding the ways in which the different components of the system relate to each other and in the process, change the very nature of the system itself while at the same time preserving the integrity of the system.

E

Ecological perception The kind of experience that relies on direct perception through the senses, not mediated by thought or judgment.

Ecological self The ability to experience the body and its senses, feelings, and movements in relation to the environment.

Ecological self The ability to recognize the body and its senses, feelings, and movements.

Ectoderm One of the cell layers in the embryonic disk that will become the central nervous system, brain, sense organs, skin, hair, nails, and teeth (see also endoderm and mesoderm).

EEG (electroencephalography) is used to measure brain electrical activity on the surface of the scalp. It gives information about brain electrical waves but does not give info about location of activity within the brain.

Efferent neurons are directly connected from the central nervous system to muscles that alter or *effect* internal and external behavior.

Effortful control The ability of toddlers to make a voluntary effort to calm themselves and sustain their attention by delaying their responses, slowing down motor activity, suppressing impulses, and lowering their voice.

Ego The sum total of the person's regulatory functions, which includes coping, information processing, and emotions; the ego mediates between the person's needs and the demands of the environment.

Embryo The period of prenatal development beginning in the second week after conception and extending until the third month of pregnancy.

Embryo cryopreservation Freezing fertilized embryos for later implantation into the uterus.

Embryonic disk A layer of cells in the blastocyst that will eventually become the embryo's body.

Embryonic stem cells Embryonic cells that can be transformed into many different types of tissue by implanting them into the bodies of adults whose tissues have been damaged by injury or disease.

Emergent self The perception of sameness over time in behavior, feelings, and states of arousal; the sense of familiarity of the body that persists even when objects and people come and go.

Emotion regulation The ability to control the form and timing of one's emotional expression and feeling state.

Empiricism An eighteenth-century philosophical idea that knowledge is derived from direct observation and that human problems can be solved with logical reasoning.

Endoderm A layer of cells in the embryonic disk that will become the digestive, respiratory, and urinary systems (see also ectoderm and mesoderm).

Environmental specificity Continuities between the environment and the individual's development are found only for specific facets of the individual with specific features of the environment. Specific individuals are better able to profit from some environments than from others.

Epidurals are a local anesthetic administered in the lower (lumbar) spine that blocks pain sensation in the pelvic area but allows the mother to remain awake and aware.

Epigenome A set of biochemical markers that are responsive to the environment and that turn on or turn off the actions of particular genes within each cell.

Euthanasia Letting an individual die naturally without medical intervention, except to relieve pain.

Event-related potentials The detection and computation of electrical current on the surface of the scalp to map regions of brain activity.

Exercise play Playful locomotor movement that is physically vigorous, such as running, chasing, and climbing.

Existential self The ability to recognize one's own features as different from someone else's. It involves an awareness of the self as someone who can be recognized and can be distinguished as a whole person from other people.

Exosystem Includes systems that do not contain the developing child but that do affect the child's well-being, such as the parent's work, the government, and the economy.

Experience dependent Brain regions and pathways that are not fully formed and must await environmental input for their development.

Experience expectant Brain regions and pathways that are more or less fully developed at birth, allowing the infant to adapt to particular types of environmental stimuli related to basic survival.

Experiment A research strategy in which some factors are manipulated by the experimenter, while others are controlled or held constant across groups.

Expressive speech Speech that is socially oriented and uses more, but less well articulated, words per utterance.

F

Failure-to-thrive The slow deterioration of an infant's condition and lack of responsiveness to intervention; seen in cases of malnutrition and disease.

Familial Alzheimer's disease A genetic disorder that causes deterioration of the central nervous system, leading to lack of mental and motor control.

Family planning The voluntary alteration of normal reproductive patterns using contraception methods.

Feedback A process by which components of a system have an effect on their own behavior during their transactions with other components.

Feldenkrais method A system of somatic awareness and movement education that reawakens, develops, and organizes capacities for kinesthetic (sensorimotor) learning.

Fertility The ability to achieve fertilization and become pregnant.

Fetal alcohol syndrome (FAS) A teratogenic disorder caused by excessive alcohol consumption by a pregnant mother. Effects include physical malformations and attentional disorders.

Fetal distress A sudden loss of oxygen to the fetal brain caused by respiratory or heart problems or a restriction of the blood supply through the umbilical cord.

Fetal monitoring The use of electronic equipment to detect fetal heart rate, breathing, and other physiological signs during the birth process.

Fetus The period from the third month of prenatal life until delivery of the newborn.

Flextime A policy allowing flexible work schedules for working parents.

fMRI (functional magnetic resonance imaging) uses magnetic fields to detect where in the brain blood is exchanging oxygen, an indicator of which brain regions are active. fMRI is not very useful for studying infants who must be sleeping or sedated to use this method.

fNIRS (functional near infrared spectroscopy) can find the spatial location of activation from blood flow changes, like fMRI. This method uses infrared light that can pass through skin and other tissue and can be used with infants who can be sitting up or on the lap moving relatively freely. fNIRS probes easily fit over the head and they are portable.

Fontanels Spaces between the bones of the newborn's skull, which can be felt as soft spots on the scalp.

Forceps An instrument that clamps around the infant's head to pull it through the birth canal.

Formal support systems Community programs that are specifically designed to serve the needs of parents and infants; usually funded by the government.

Formulas Flexible word orders that make up the first sentences of infants; not the same as mature grammar.

Fragile X syndrome A sex-linked genetic disorder that is the most common inherited cause of mental retardation.

Free association A method of recovering unconscious memories by having clients lie down and encouraging

them to relax in an environment safe enough to say anything without fear of retribution or judgment.

Gametes Spermatozoa or ova: reproductive cells having 23 chromosomes each.

Gender identity The affiliation with being either male or female based on a curiosity about children's own and other's bodies.

Gender labeling The ability to identify self or other verbally as male or female.

Gene A section of the DNA molecule that comprises the smallest unit of the codes for inherited characteristics.

Generativity The life stage in Erik Erikson's clinical theory in which people focus on the nurture and support of others, typically shown in parental behavior.

Genetic counseling Assessing the parents' likelihood of producing a child with genetic or chromosomal abnormalities.

Genotype The set of chemical messages within the DNA that direct the formation of protein within a cell nucleus; an individual's genetic inheritance.

Gestational age The age of the infant starting from the date of conception.

Glial cells (or glia) Brain cells that support the development and function of the neurons. Some glial cells provide oxygen and nutrients to the neurons via the blood stream, and also remove waste products; Another type of glial cell wraps around the axons to create a layer of insulation called **myelin**; Another type of glial cell, the **radial glia**, provide a kind of scaffold of pathways along which neurons grow and migrate to their proper place within the brain during fetal development.

Guided participation Collaboration of a responsive adult on a task the infant is already doing, allowing the infant to take small, culturally appropriate roles.

Gynecologist A physician who specializes in women's reproductive health (see also obstetrician).

H

Habituation The gradual decrease in looking or listening time across repeated presentations of the same visual or auditory stimulus.

Handedness The preferential use of one hand over the other; also refers to the use of each hand to do different things.

Haptic perception The perception of the properties of an object using touch.

HCG (human chorionic gonadotropin) A hormone whose presence signals the onset of pregnancy.

Head Start A federally funded program for enriched early childhood education and parent education for disadvantaged families.

Heritability The proportion of individual variability in a group that can be explained as owing primarily to individual differences in genetic make-up.

Hippocampus A horseshoe-shaped structure in the limbic system that plays an important role in the formation of memories for events and sequences, what is known as autobiographical memory.

Historical processes Developmental processes that are not simple accumulations of past events but are uniquely emergent creations that can never be exactly repeated.

Homeostasis The maintenance of biological functions within normal levels; for example, the regulation of body temperature.

Hormones are neurochemicals that circulate in the blood stream. Hormones can affect the regulation of body organs to activate digestion, sexual function, stress regulation and feelings of safety and comfort, milk production in nursing mothers, and cell growth throughout the body.

HPA Axis The system by which the neuroception of stress is translated into the release of hormones from the hypothalamus to the pituitary (via corticotropin-releasing hormone, CRH), from the pituitary to the adrenal gland (via adrenocorticotropic hormone, ACTH), which results in the secretion of the hormone cortisol into the blood stream

Huntington's disease A genetic disorder that causes progressive brain damage and death.

Hypothalamus is a small structure in the middle of the limbic system that links the brain to the endocrine (hormones) systems of the body via the pituitary gland. It regulates stress, body temperature, hunger, thirst, and day-night rhythms.

I

Id The uninhibited expression of the individual's basic needs; during infancy, these needs are centered primarily around the oral and anal zones.

Idiosyncratic communication A form of communication that the individual makes up. It requires a familiar adult to interpret its meaning.

Imaginative pretend play Play in which the child invents make-believe situations.

Imprinting A process in which the young of some animal species become attached to an object or person by means of a brief exposure to that object or person.

In vitro fertilization Fertilization achieved in a laboratory, outside the mother's body, by surgically removing ova and uniting them with spermatozoa.

Independent variable The variable controlled or manipulated by the experimenter; the presumed cause of the effects measured by the dependent variables in experimental research.

Indeterminism The idea that not all natural phenomena can be predicted from known laws or principles.

Infant psychiatry The application of clinical psychology to work with infants and their families.

Infant-directed (ID) speech A style of speech that includes exaggerated pitch, loudness, marked rhythms, and clear melodies (see also *motherese*).

Infanticide The deliberate killing of newborn infants as a means to limit family size.

Infantile amnesia The lack of adult autobiographical memory of one's life before the age of two or three years.

Infant-Parent Mental Health (IPMH) An emerging multidisciplinary specialization focusing on the relational context of the total development of young children with a deep commitment to transdisciplinary integration and to the treatment of developmental, relational, and emotional distress from a whole-child-in-relationship perspective.

Infants with special needs Infants who suffer from prenatal and postnatal deficits, deformities, and developmental delays that create additional challenges for them and their families.

Infertility Failure to achieve fertilization.

Informal support system A family's social network of relatives, friends, and community resources.

Informed consent The voluntary consent by human research subjects, based on a complete description of the procedures, risks, and benefits of the research; a fundamental ethical principle of human research.

Insecure-avoidant attachment The infant does not approach the mother during the reunion episode of the Strange Situation Test and makes active efforts to get away if the mother tries to comfort the infant.

Insecure-resistant attachment An ambivalent pattern of responding in the Strange Situation Test such that the infant cannot feel comfortable with either the mother or the toys. Not as extreme or as abrupt as the disorganized-disoriented pattern.

Institutional Research Board (IRB) A committee of research professionals who work at a particular institution, such as a University, who reviews and approves research proposals that involve the use of human subjects. IRBs must follow federal guidelines for the protection of human subjects.

Insula a brain region that creates feelings of **interoception**, allowing us to *feel the inner condition of our bodies*, including the sense of hunger, thirst, itch, hot and cold, aches and soreness, pain, the need to urinate and defecate, and whether we are sick or healthy.

Internal working model A set of mental representations and expectations one has about attachment figures.

Interoception Feeling the inner condition of our bodies, including the sense of hunger, thirst, itch, hot and cold, aches and soreness, pain, the need to urinate and defecate, and whether we are sick or healthy.

Intersex A birth defect in which the genitals do not completely form or in which infants have characteristics of both males and females or internal characteristics of one gender and external characteristics of the other gender

Intersubjectivity The experience of another person in relation to the actions of the self. During participatory co-regulated dialogue, the infant can feel how her or his agency affects the other person and how the other's agency affects the infant's own.

Invariance Detection of what is similar about an object in spite of variations in the conditions under which it is perceived; the basis of recognizing the same object from different perspectives.

Joint visual attention The ability of partners to follow the direction of the other's gaze or pointing gesture.

K

Kangaroo care A method of communication with premature infants in which the infant, wearing only a diaper, is placed on the parent's chest. The infant's head is turned to the side so that the baby's ear is against the parent's heart.

Karyotype An arrangement of chromosome pairs for easy examination; made by photographing a micrograph of a set of chromosomes and then cutting the photograph and placing the chromosome pairs in order.

Kinesthetic empathy The ability to feel another person's feelings by moving like that other person, based on dance movement psychotherapy.

Kleinfelter's syndrome A chromosomal disorder that causes female-like males and mental retardation.

L

Labor Muscle contractions leading to the birth of the fetus and placenta.

Lamaze method Pain relief during labor that uses breathing and relaxation techniques.

Lanugo Fine hair that grows over most of the fetus's body, beginning in the fourth month.

Leboyer method An approach to delivery in which the newborn is kept warm in a water bath and subjected to low levels of sound and light.

Left hemisphere The left half of the brain that controls movements on the right side of the body. It is specialized for thinking and language and develops more rapidly after the first two years of life.

Limbic system A brain area that is located more or less in the very center of the head, between the ears, and includes structures such as the amygdala, the hippocampus, the hypothalamus, and the pituitary gland. This part of the brain is related to processes; such as attention, states like sleeping and waking, urinary and bowel control, emotion and responses to stress and trauma, and memory.

Liquidating pretend play Play in which the child's make-believe situation alters reality to better suit the child's desires.

Longitudinal study A research study that follows developmental changes in the same individual over time.

M

Macrosystem The system of beliefs, values, and rules of the society and culture.

Marfan's syndrome A genetic disorder associated with a weakened heart, mild bone structure deformities, long fingers, and eye lens problems.

Mastery motivation The desire to become competent at a particular goal.

Maternal serum alpha-fetoprotein (MSAFP) A prenatal test for spina bifida (exposed spine) and anencephaly (exposed brain) using the mother's blood; performed between the 15th and 18th week of pregnancy.

Maturation Developmental change that is controlled by hereditary timing mechanisms.

Mean length of utterance (MLU) The average number of morphemes across all the utterances of a child.

Meconium The contents of the newborn's intestines; a greenish-black substance containing digested amniotic fluid and particles of hair and skin.

Mediated transaction A transaction that occurs when the infant affects or is affected by people with whom the infant does not share an active relationship.

MEG, magnetoencephalography, works similar to an EEG but uses magnetic fields rather than electrical activity.

Similar to EEG, it cannot locate particular structures within the brain but it is less distorted by surrounding tissue, which makes it useful for studying fetal brain activity on the surface of the mother's abdomen, through layers of maternal and fetal tissue (fMEG)

Meiosis The process of cell division that produces gametes, resulting in only half the usual number of chromosomes.

Mesoderm A layer of cells in the embryonic disk that leads to the development of muscles, bones, and the circulatory and reproductive systems (see also ectoderm and endoderm).

Mesosystem The system of relationships between the settings in which children live, such as between the home and the school setting.

Metacommunicative events Communicative acts that refer to the relationship between partners rather than to the world outside the relationship.

Metalinguistic knowledge An understanding of the uses and functions of language, independent of knowledge of semantics and syntax.

Metapelet A substitute caregiver on an Israeli kibbutz.

Micronutrients Vitamins and minerals found in foods and in dietary supplements.

Microsystem The system of interpersonal relationships between the child and other people.

Midwife A professional trained to assist women during childbirth.

Milk expression The second phase of sucking, in which the infant presses the nipple against the roof of the mouth with the tongue to force milk out.

Mirror neurons are neurons that fire when we watch someone else perform a motor action, a goal-directed movement, leading the observer's nervous system to have similar intentions and emotions as the person being observed.

Mitosis The cell-division process by which each chromosome makes a copy of itself before cell division takes place.

Monosomy An abnormality of the 23rd chromosome in which one member of the pair is missing.

Monozygotic twins Twins formed by the splitting of the same zygote.

Motherese Changes in speech patterns involving exaggeration of pitch, higher pitch, use of rhythm and melody, slowing down, and simplification.

Multiparous A mother who has given birth more than once.

Myelin A protective coating over nerve cells that aids in the conduction of action potentials.

Myelination The development of a protective coating over nerve conduction pathways that improves transmission of information.

N

Natural family planning Limiting or enhancing the possibility of conception by using a method for determining the days of ovulation.

Natural selection The theory of the evolution of species, proposed by Charles Darwin, in which genetic changes are explained by different survival rates of offspring that have characteristics that are better or less well-suited to the environment.

Nature Refers to the belief that behavior and development are controlled primarily by hereditary influences.

Nausea and vomiting of early pregnancy (NVP) Normal feelings of nausea, disgust and digestive unrest during the first 2 – 3 months of pregnancy, occurring in about 80% of pregnancies.

Negative feedback Feedback that maintains a system's characteristics over time in spite of small deviations.

Negative pressure The first phase of sucking, in which the gums create a seal around the nipple and the jaw drops to create suction inside the mouth.

Negative reinforcer The absence of a consequence of an action that increases the frequency of that action.

Neonatal The period immediately following birth.

Neural plasticity is the ability of the brain and nervous system to seek novelty, learn, and remember by continuing to alter the patterns of connections between neurons.

Neuroception The nonconscious evaluation of safety or threat, meaning that the autonomic nervous system (both the sympathetic and parasympathetic branches) makes the decision about how to respond and not the conscious mind.

Neurogenesis The process of mitosis that creates new neurons and glial cells.

Neuroimaging The use of different types of radiation to detect electrical and chemical changes in specific regions of the brain; includes PET and fMRI methods.

Neurological assessment Testing of newborn reflexes and postures to determine the intactness of the brain and nervous system.

Neuron A cell in the nervous system.

Neuroscience The study of the brain and nervous system as it relates to psychological and behavioral functions such as moving, thinking, and feeling.

Neurotransmitters Neurochemicals, of which there a many varieties such as serotonin and dopamine, signal from one neuron to another processes such as voluntary reflex movements, state regulation, memory, emotion, and pain.

Nonnutritive sucking (NNS) Sucking in the absence of fluids, including spontaneous sucking and sucking on a pacifier.

Normal physiological jaundice A slight yellowing of the skin caused by immature functioning of the liver.

Nurture Refers to the belief that behavior and development are controlled primarily by environmental influences.

O

Object permanence The ability to remember the location of objects that are out of sight.

Observational research A research strategy in which the experimenter does not manipulate the subjects but takes advantage of natural variations in the environment.

Observed infant A view of infant experience that derives from scientific observations of infant behavior.

Obstetrician A physician who specializes in prenatal care, delivery, and reproductive health (see also gynecologist).

Oculomotor skills The movements of the eye, including lens focusing, convergence and divergence, scanning, and tracking.

Operant conditioning An increase in the likelihood that a particular response will occur following a reinforcement of that response.

Oral stage The period during the first eighteen months of life when the infant is particularly aware of sensations of pleasure and displeasure in the mouth region through activities such as sucking, chewing, biting, and swallowing.

Organic learning The use of all one's senses and every part of the body in the process of learning new movements.

Orienting response The direction of attention and action toward an attractive stimulus.

Outcome variable The presumed effect of a cause represented by a predictor variable in observational research; analogous to the dependent variable in experimental research.

Overextension Applying a single word to refer to more objects and situations than it normally refers to in adult speech.

Overregularization The extension of regular verb endings for the past tense to irregular verbs.

Ovum Female gamete; plural *ova*.

Oxytocin A pituitary hormone which gives a feeling of warmth, comfort and safety. Oxytocin is usually secreted when we are in close contact, with loving or supportive touch, to another person.

P

Paired-preference procedure A research technique that relies on differences in infant looking time to assess perceptual preference.

Parasympathetic nervous system Allows the body to relax, slow down, rest, process information, engage socially with others, learn and grow.

Parens patriae The legal concept that children are possessions of their parents.

Parental proactive behavior An approach to discipline in which the adult controls the child's environment by anticipating future problems.

Parental separation anxiety A parent's feelings of loss or distress when he or she is separated from the child.

Partial birth abortion An elective abortion procedure for larger fetuses in which labor is induced, the cervix dilated, and the fetus pulled out by the feet, leaving the head undelivered until the fetal brain has been extracted.

Participant observer A form of qualitative research in which the observer is explicitly part of the process of observation and takes account of his or her effect on the subjects.

Participatory memories Memories that are in the form of feeling or sensation rather than being conceptualized as a specific incident; composed of emotions, desires, and a sense of familiarity, but without any specific time or place.

Patterners Children who classify objects based on similarities in their forms or functions.

Pediatrician A physician who specializes in the care of infants and children.

Perinatal The period from about 1 month before to about 1 month after birth.

Phenotype The functioning organism; everything other than the DNA.

Phenylketonuria (PKU) A genetic disorder that causes central nervous system damage if not treated by dietary control.

Pituitary A hormone-producing endocrine gland. It is stimulated by the hypothalamus to produce hormones for stress regulation, maintenance of body state, sexual activity, milk production in nursing mothers, and growth.

Placenta A membrane surrounding the fetus that functions as a link between the bloodstreams of mother and fetus, which are not directly connected. The placenta passes nutrients and oxygen from the mother's blood to the fetus's through the umbilical cord and serves to eliminate the fetal wastes via the mother's bloodstream.

Polygenic inheritance When multiple genes are responsible for a single phenotypic characteristic.

Positive feedback Feedback that drastically alters a system as a result of a small deviation.

Positive reinforcer A consequence of an action that increases the probability of that action in the future.

Post traumatic stress syndrome (PTSD) The result of prolonged exposure to stress and threat resulting in a decreased ability of the individual to cope with stress (in the prefrontal cortex) in appropriate ways, creating people who are more likely to freeze, fight, or flee when they feel threatened.

Postpartum depression Sudden, transitory episodes of sadness or emotional lows; not related to pathological depression.

Prader-Willi syndrome A genetic disorder associated with low muscle tone, obesity, short stature, small hands and feet, and lowered intelligence.

Pragmatics The study of the functional uses of language, as opposed to the structural (grammatical) properties of language.

Predictor variable The presumed cause of an effect measured by an outcome variable in observational research; analogous to the independent variable in experimental research.

Prefrontal cortex Located roughly above the eyes, it forms a link between the limbic system and the cortex and therefore plays an important role in how the infant learns to regulate states and emotions.

Preimplantation genetic diagnosis (PGD) A method of testing cells from the zygote for genetic and chromosomal disorders before it they become implanted in the uterus.

Pretend role play A form of pretend play in which children act out the roles of their mother, their father, or other important figures in their lives.

Primary circular reactions Repetitive movements of the infant's body that are discovered by chance and repeated for fun.

Primiparous A woman who is giving birth for the first time.

Private speech An internalized dialogue with the self in which children describe their thoughts and actions out loud.

Probabilistic Refers to the nondeterministic influence of the genotype over the phenotype. A particular genotype will not lead to a specific phenotype for all individuals.

Procedural memories are automatic memories of "ways of doing things," like riding a bike.

Processor neurons analyze the stream of afferent information coming from the sensory receptors for the purpose of responding to these signals coming from outside and inside the body.

Productivity The ability of language to express multiple meanings using a small number of words simply by rearranging the word order in novel ways.

Prospective study A longitudinal research study in which data are gathered from subjects at periodic intervals, so that the subjects' current behavior and ideas are being observed.

Protoconversation An initial form of turn taking in adult-infant interaction in which the parent fills in the natural pauses in the infant's behavior, but the infant does not take any social initiatives.

Prototype The clearest example of a particular form or sound. Prototypes also represent the average of all exemplars across all relevant dimensions.

Proximodistal development Parts of the body closer to the trunk develop faster than the extremities.

Psychoanalysis The use of free association in psychotherapy leading to the interpretation of unconscious and participatory memories from the perspective of early childhood experiences.

Q

Qualitative research Research that focuses on the meaning of behavior for the participants.

Quantitative research Research that focuses on representing behavior using numerical variables.

R

Random assignment A procedure in which subjects are placed into experimental and control groups by the flip of a coin or some other nonbiased method.

Rapid eye movement (REM) sleep Sleep in which rapid vertical eye movements are accompanied by irregular body and respiration movements.

Reactive attachment disorder (RAD) Begins before age 5 and is marked by one of two types of patterns: (1) *Inhibitions*. The child is excessively inhibited, hypervigilant, or ambivalent and contradictory. (2) *Disinhibitions*. The child shows indiscriminate sociability with inability to form appropriate selective attachments.

Recovery An increase in infant looking time in response to a change in the stimulus during a habituation procedure.

Referential speech Speech that is object oriented and contains a few, but clearly articulated, words per utterance.

Reflective supervision A training method in the field of IPMH in which the clinician-supervisor dyad mirrors the clinician-caregiver and caregiver-child dyad in continuing the ethos of sustaining relationships based on mutual reflection and collaboration.

Reflex A semiautomatic response to a specific stimulus that, once elicited, must run its course.

Reinforcer An environmental stimulus that, when it appears following a specific individual response, increases the likelihood that the response will occur again.

Relational play The ability to combine two or more objects appropriately according to their function.

Relationship A lasting pattern of communication between two or more people in which past encounters provide a historical background for future encounters.

Reliability The extent to which multiple observers agree about the coding of ongoing behavior.

Representative research A study in which the results from the group of infants who are observed can be generalized to a wider range of infants from different cultures and socioeconomic groups.

Response-contingent procedure A research technique in which different stimuli are made contingent upon different infant actions. Display of one or the other action by the infant usually means a preference for the contingently related stimulus.

Retrospective study A research study in which the subject recollects his or her past or the experimenter traces the subject's records backward in time.

Right hemisphere The right half of the brain that controls movements on the left side of the body. It is also where the majority of social and emotional activity is processed. It undergoes major development during the first two years of life when infants are discovering how to regulate their emotions and form attachments to the primary people in their lives.

Roe v. Wade A 1973 ruling by the justices of the U.S. Supreme Court concluding that the decision to terminate a pregnancy is part of a woman's right to privacy guaranteed by the Constitution.

Role overload Refers to one person trying to fill too many roles or facing excessive demands from a single role.

Romanticism An eighteenth-century philosophical idea that children are inherently good and have the ability to develop successfully with minimal guidance.

Rosen method A somatic awareness approach that uses listening to the client's body with gentle touch and to the words they use to describe their experience, allowing the client to relax, relieve pain, and breathe more easily.

S

Schemes The currently available set of skills and knowledge that a person has.

Scientific theory A system of concepts that explains the observable world with structures, processes, or mechanisms that are presumed to exist but that cannot be observed directly.

Screening assessment Tests of newborn functioning used to predict the need for medical interventions.

Script A form of conceptual organization in which events are remembered according to the sequences in which they usually occur.

Secondary circular reaction Deliberate repetition of an association between an action and its effect. In this case, each repetition is a slight variation of the one before in which the infant is exploring different ways to create effects.

Secure attachment The infant returns to independent play following comfort seeking from the mother during the Strange Situation Test.

Self-affectivity People's sense of having inner emotional feelings that routinely go together with specific experiences.

Self-agency People's feeling that they are causal agents that can successfully affect their own bodies and the environment.

Self-coherence People's feeling that they and the objects around them are integrated wholes that have distinct boundaries.

Self-conscious emotion An emotion that requires an awareness of an existential self in relation to an existential other; examples are shame, embarrassment, guilt, and pride.

Self-history People's feeling that the past can be connected to the present by means of recreating one's own actions in similar situations; a sense of self-similarity.

Self-organization The emergence of organized patterns that create their own structure and maintain their own source of energy due to the mutual influences of each element of the system on the others.

Self-righting The ability of the infant organism to assimilate those aspects of the environment that serve to return development to a more typical pathway.

Semanticity The ability of language to carry meaning for both speaker and listener.

Sensorimotor stage According to Piaget, the first two years of life, in which the child "understands" the world through action and sensation rather than through concepts and ideas.

Separation anxiety disorder A child who refuses to be separated from the parent, even to go to bed, and has excessive distress when not at home with parents. The behavior must be intense, last at least 1 month, and be inappropriate for the child's age to meet the criteria for diagnosis.

Serotonin A neurochemical that alters mood by creating a state of quiet alertness and feelings of well-being, but too little of it can lead to feelings of depression. Most drugs for treating depression increase serotonin levels.

Sex-linked inheritance Refers to those characteristics that are carried in the genes of the sex chromosomes.

Shared environment That part of the family environment that contributes in the same way to the development of more than one sibling.

Sibling de-identification The process by which parents differentiate between siblings.

Sickle-cell anemia A genetic disorder that causes blood clots to form.

SIDS Sudden Infant Death Syndrome; a cause of death of unknown origins believed to be associated with errors in respiratory regulation, especially during sleep.

Situational constraints Elements of the context of a stimulus or event that determine a child's response to that event. In interactions with other children, for example, the peer's age, sex, and familiarity to the infant, the infant's experience interacting with other children, and the caregiver's location are all situational constraints that may determine the quality of the peer-infant interaction.

Social referencing A form of appraisal in which infants use the emotional expressions of others to regulate their own emotional reactions.

Somatic Individuals' conscious awareness of the experiences of their bodies.

Somatic awareness approaches Clinical approaches that use talk, body movement, and touch as a way to access the participatory memories of early childhood.

Somatic psychotherapy focuses on felt sensations in the body, breathing, and movement on the pathway to psychological well-being.

Sperm microinjection Injection of sperm directly into a ripe ovum.

Spermatozoon Male gamete; plural *spermatazoa*.

Stability Continuity with respect to group ranking, when individuals preserve their ranking with respect to the same reference group over age.

State An organized pattern of physical and physiological responding that is related to the infant's level of activation and arousal.

State of arousal An organized system of physical and physiological responding that is related to the internal level of arousal, from sleep to waking.

Stereopsis The ability to compare the different images coming from each eye.

Stress occurs when the body is unable to find a balance between sympathetic and parasympathetic activity.

Still-face An experimental manipulation in which mothers are asked to hold their faces in a neutral pose and cease talking to or otherwise interacting with their infants.

Subjective self A sense of self that involves an awareness of the feelings and experiences of others and also of the self's dependence upon and attachment to others, in addition to a nonverbal sense of "I."

Surrogate mother A woman who carries the fertilized embryo of another woman and brings the embryo through pregnancy to birth.

Symbol A representation of a thing or event that is conventionally shared among the members of a community.

Sympathetic nervous system Prepares the body for action by elevating heart rate, increasing metabolism, and temporarily suppressing growth functions such as digestion.

Synapse The connection between axons and dendrites by which action potentials are transmitted between neurons.

Synaptogenesis The process by which neurons become more complex, growing more dendrites and axon terminals and making an increasing number of synaptic connections between cells.

Syntax The structure or grammar of a language; the rules that determine word order.

System A relationship between of interdependent components that are governed by feedback processes and that exchange information and material between themselves and between the environment and themselves.

T

Tay-Sachs disease A genetic disorder that causes mental retardation, physical disabilities, and early death.

Telegraphic speech Speech having two or more words per utterance but with endings and connecting words left out.

Temperament A persistent pattern of emotion and emotion regulation in the infant's relationship to people and things in the environment.

Teratogen An agent that causes birth defects.

Teratology The study of birth defects.

Tertiary circular reactions Refers to the fact that new means are invented to achieve goals by trial-and-error experimentation.

Theory of mind The awareness that other people have independent beliefs and feelings.

Threat is the sense of being in danger from outside of ourselves (another person or a collision with an object) or inside (a physical pain or feeling of anxiety).

Transaction The process by which systems components affect each other.

Transitional object An object to which the infant develops an attachment; it may be used for comfort in the absence of the caregiver.

Transverse presentations A presentation in which the fetus is oriented on its side.

Trauma is the condition that results from prolonged sympathetic activation and the resulting depletion of the body's resources and lack of time for recovery. **Shock trauma** is the effect of a relatively brief and sudden event like an accidental injury or a sudden loss. **Developmental trauma** is when exposure to a threatening event occurs over a longer period of time, such as long-term parental neglect or abuse.

Trisomy A chromosome pair with an extra chromosome attached to it.

Turner's syndrome A chromosomal disorder that causes incomplete sexual determination and mental retardation.

U

Ultrasound Obtaining an outline of the fetus by means of high-frequency sound wave reflections.

Unconscious That part of the self that is not remembered during ordinary waking states.

Vacuum extraction The use of a suction device attached to the head to extract the infant from the birth canal.

V

Vagal tone, the availability of a functionally myelinated vagal PNS that can help us relax in the face of stress, is measured by the ability of the heart to adjust its beat-to-beat frequency in the face of stress.

Validity The extent to which an assessment procedure accurately measures the concept or goal of the experimenter.

Verbal self That part of the self that uses language to talk about inner states and to construct a coherent identity in the company of other people.

Vernix caseosa A white, cheesy coating that protects the fetal skin.

Vestibular-proprioceptive stimulation The movement of the infant's body, usually accomplished by carrying and rocking.

Viability The ability of the fetus to maintain its own life outside the uterus.

Visual cliff An experimental apparatus used to determine the nature of an infant's fear of heights.

Vital statistics Numerical estimates of events in a population related to birth, death, and the incidence of illnesses and accidents.

W

Wariness A quieting or sobering of an infant, usually in response to a novel situation. Wariness is believed to be a precursor to fear.

Watsu A somatic awareness technique in which the practitioner floats the client in a pool of warm water, using stretching and water resistance to create a state of relaxation.

Williams syndrome A genetic disorder in which individuals have short stature, heart defects, are indiscriminately social, and have intellectual deficits, especially in spatial abilities.

Y

Yolk sac A region of cells in the blastocyst that will eventually become the embryonic blood supply and internal organs.

Z

Zone of proximal development Those infant skills that are in the process of developing and are the most uncertain.

Zygote A fertilized ovum.

References

Abboud, L., & Liamputtong, P. (2005). When pregnancy fails: Coping strategies, support networks and experiences with health care of ethnic women and their partners. *Journal of Reproductive and Infant Psychology, 23*(1), 3–18.

Abbott, A., & Bartlett, D. J. (2001). Infant motor development and equipment use in the home. *Child: Care, Health and Development, 27*(3), 295–306.

Abel, E. L., Randall, C. L., & Riley, E. P. (1983). Alcohol consumption and prenatal development. In B. Tabakoff, P. B. Sutker, & C. L. Randall (Eds.), *Medical and social aspects of alcohol abuse*. New York: Plenum Press.

Aber, J. L., Belsky, J., Slade, A., & Crnic, K. (1999). Stability and change in mothers' representations of their relationship with their toddlers. *Developmental Psychology, 35*(4), 1038–1047.

Ablow, J. C., Marks, A. K., Shirley Feldman, S. S., & Huffman, L. C. (2013). Associations between first-time expectant women's representations of attachment and their physiological reactivity to infant cry. *Child Development, 84*(4), 1373-1391.

Abramovitch, R., Corter, C., & Landau, B. (1979). Sibling interaction in the home. *Child Development, 50,* 997–1003.

Abramovitch, R., Corter, C., Pepler, D. J., & Stanhope, L. (1986). Sibling and peer interaction: A final follow-up and a comparison. *Child Development, 57,* 217–229.

Abreu-Villaça, Y., Seidler, F. J., & Slotkin, T. A. (2004). Does prenatal nicotine exposure sensitize the brain to nicotine-induced neurotoxicity in adolescence? *Neuropsychopharmacology, 29,* 1440–1450.

Achenbach, T. M., Phares, V., Howell, C. T., Rauh, V. A., & Nurcombe, B. (1990). Seven-year outcome of the Vermont intervention program for low-birthweight infants. *Child Development, 61,* 1672–1681.

Acredolo, L., & Goodwyn, S. (1985). Symbolic gesturing in language development. *Human Development, 28,* 40–49.

Acredolo, L., & Goodwyn, S. (1988). Symbolic gesturing in normal infants. *Child Development, 59,* 450–466.

Adams, S. M., Jones, D. R., Esmail, A., & Mitchell, E. A. (2004). What affects the age of first sleeping through the night? *J Paediatr Child Health, 40*(3), 96–101.

Adamson, L. B. (1995). *Communication development during infancy.* Dubuque, IA: WCB Brown & Benchmark.

Adamson, L. B., & Bakeman, R. (1985). Affect and attention: Infants observed with mothers and peers. *Child Development, 56,* 582–593.

Adamson, L. B., Bakeman, R., Smith, C. B., & Walters, A. S. (1987). Adults' interpretation of infants' acts. *Developmental Psychology, 23,* 383–387.

Adinolfi, A. M. (1971). The postnatal development of synaptic contacts in the cerebral cortex. In M. B. Sterman, D. J. McGinty, & A. M. Adinolfi (Eds.), *Brain development and behavior* (pp. 182–196). New York: Academic Press.

Adolph, K. E. (1997). Learning in the development of infant locomotion. *Monographs of the Society for Research in Child Development, 62*(3), 1–140.

Adolph, K. E., Gibson, E. J., & Eppler, M. A. (1990). *Perceiving affordances of slopes: The ups and downs of toddler's locomotion.* Report of Emory Cognition Project. Atlanta, GA: Emory University.

Adolph, K. E., Tamis-LeMonda, C. S., Ishak, S., Karasik, L. B., & Lobo, S. A. (2008). Locomotor experience and use of social information are posture specific. *Developmental Psychology, 44*(6), 1705-1714. doi:10.1037/a0013852

Adolph, K. E., Vereijken, B., & Denny, M. A. (1998). Learning to crawl. *Child Development, 69*(5), 1299–1312.

Adolph, K. E., Vereijken, B., Denny, M. A., Gill, V. S., & Lucero, A. (1995, June). *Increased balance requirements constrain variability in infant crawling.* Poster presented at the American Psychological Society, New York.

Adolph, K. E., Vereijken, B., & Shrout, P. E. (2003). What changes in infant walking and why. *Child Development, 74*(2), 475–497.

465

Adrien, J. L., Lenoir, P., Martineau, J., Perrot, A., Hameury, L., Larmande, C., & Sauvage, D. (1993). Blind ratings of early symptoms of autism based upon family home movies. *Journal of the American Academy of Child Adolescent Psychiatry, 32,* 617–626.

Affonso, D. (1977). "Missing pieces": A study of postpartum feelings. *Birth and the Family Journal, 4,* 159–164.

Aggleton, J. P., & Wood, C. J. (1990). Is there a left-handed advantage in "ballistic" sports? *International Journal of Sport Psychology,* 21, 46–57.

Agiobu-Kemmer, I. (1986). Cognitive and affective aspects of infant development. In H. V. Curran (Ed.), *Nigerian children: Developmental perspectives* (pp. 42–67). London: Routledge & Kegan Paul.

Aguiar, A., & Baillargeon, R. (1998). Eight-and-a-half-month-old infants' reasoning about containment events. *Child Development, 69*(3), 636–653.

Ahl, R., Fausto-Sterling, A., García-Coll, C., & Seifer, R. (2013). Gender and discipline in 5-12-month-old infants: a longitudinal study. *Infant Behavior & Development, 36*(2), 199-209.

Ahnert, L., Gunnar, M. R., Lamb, M. E., & Barthel, M. (2004). Transition to Child Care: Associations With Infant-Mother Attachment, Infant Negative Emotion, and Cortisol Elevations. *Child Development, 75*(3), 639–650.

Ainsworth, M. (1979). Attachment as related to mother-infant interaction. In R. Hinde & J. Rosenblatt (Eds.), *Advances in the study of behavior* (pp. 115–148). New York: Academic Press.

Ainsworth, M., & Bell, S. (1970). Attachment, exploration, and separation: Illustrated by the behavior of one-year-olds in a strange situation. *Child Development, 41,* 49–67.

Ainsworth, M., Bell, S., & Stayton, D. (1971). Individual differences in strange situation behavior of one-year-olds. In H. R. Schaffer (Ed.), *The origins of human and social relations* (pp. 240–262). London: Academic Press.

Ainsworth, M., Blehar, M. C., Waters, E., & Wall, S. (1978). *Patterns of attachment.* Hillsdale, NJ: Erlbaum.

Akhtar, N. (2005). The robustness of learning through overhearing. *Developmental Science, 8*(2), 199–209.

Alan Guttmacher Institute. (1994). *Sex and America's teenagers.* New York, New York: Author.

Albers, E., Riksen-Walraven, J., & de Weerth, C. (2010). Developmental stimulation in child care centers contributes to young infants' cognitive development. *Infant Behavior & Development, 33*(4), 401-408.

Aldridge, V., Dovey, T. M., & Halford, J. G. (2009). The Role of Familiarity in Dietary Development. *Developmental Review, 29*(1), 32-44.

Alexander, G. R., & Korenbrot, C. C. (1995). The role of prenatal care in preventing low birth weight. *The Future of Children, 5,* 103–120.

Alexander, G., & Saenz, J. (2011). Postnatal testosterone levels and temperament in early infancy. *Archives Of Sexual Behavior, 40*(6), 1287-1292

Alkon, A, Ramler, M., and MacLennan, K. "Evaluation of Mental Health Consultation in Child Care Centers." *Early Childhood Education Journal* 31(2) (2003): 91–99.

Alink, L. R. A., Mesman, J., van Zeijl, J., Stolk, M. N., Juffer, F., Koot, H. M., et al. (2006). The Early Childhood Aggression Curve: Development of Physical Aggression in 10– to 50–Month-Old Children. *Child Development, 77*(4), 954–966.

Allen, D. A., Affleck, G., McGrade, B. J., & McQueeney, M. (1984). Effects of single-parent status on mothers and their high-risk infants. *Infant Behavior and Development, 7,* 347–359.

Allen, S. (1998). A qualitative analysis of the process, mediating variables and impact of traumatic childbirth. *Reproductive and Infant Psychology, 16,* 107–131.

Allman, J., Rosin, A., Kumar, R., & Hasenstaub, A. (1998). Parenting and survival in anthropoid primates: Caretakers live longer. *Proceedings of the National Academy of Sciences of the United States of America, 95,* 6866–6869.

Almeida, A., Merminod, G., & Schechter, D. S. (2009). Mothers with Severe Psychiatric Illness and Their Newborns: A Hospital-Based Model of Perinatal Consultation. *Zero to Three, 29*(5), 40-45.

Als, H., Duffy, F. H., & McAnulty, G. B. (1988). Behavioral differences between preterm and full-term newborns as measured with the APIB system scores: I. *Infant Behavior and Development, 11,* 305–318.

Alvarez, W. F. (1985). The meaning of maternal employment for mothers and their perceptions of their three-year-old children. *Child Development, 56,* 350–360.

Alwan, S., Reefhuis, J., Rasmussen, S., Olney, R., & Friedman, J. (2007). Use of selective serotonin-reuptake inhibitors in pregnancy and the risk of birth defects. *New England Journal of Medicine, 356*(26), 2684–2692.

Angulo-Kinzler, R. M., & Horn, C. L. (2001). Selection and memory of a lower limb motor-perceptual task in 3–month-old infants. *Infant Behavior & Development, 24*(3), 239–257.

Anzures, G., Pascalis, O., Quinn, P. C., Slater, A. M., & Lee, K. (2011). Minimizing skin color differences does not eliminate the own-race recognition advantage in infants. *Infancy, 16*(6), 640-654. doi:10.1111/j.1532-7078.2010.00066.x

Amabile, T. A., & Rovee-Collier, C. (1991). Contextual variation and memory retrieval at six months. *Child Development, 62,* 1155–1166.

American Academy of Pediatrics. (1997). Breastfeeding and the use of human milk: Policy statement. *Pediatrics, 100*(6), 1035–1039.

American Academy of Pediatrics. (2003). *Pediatric nutrition handbook, 5th Edition.* American Academy of Pediatrics

Ammerman, S. D., Perelli, E., Adler, N., & Irwin, C. E. (1992). Do adolescents understand what physicians say about sexuality and health? *Clinical Pediatrics, 31,* 590–595.

Anders, T. F., Goodlin-Jones, B. L., & Zelenko, M. (1998). Infant regulation and sleep-wake state development. *Zero to Three 19*(2), 5–8.

Andersen, S. L. (2003). Trajectories of brain development: Point of vulnerability or window of opportunity? (Special issue: Brain development, sex differences and stress: Implications for psychopathology). *Neuroscience and Biobehavioral Reviews, 27,* 3-18.

Anderson, D. R., & Lorch, E. P. (1983). Looking at television: Action or reaction? In J. Bryant & D. R. Anderson (Eds.), *Children's understanding of television: Research on attention and comprehension* (pp. 1–33). New York: Academic Press.

Anderson, G. C. (1999). Kangaroo care of the premature infant. In E. Goldstein & A. Sostek (Eds.), *Nurturing the premature infant: Developmental intervention in the neonatal intensive care nursery* (pp. 351–366). Oxford, England: Oxford University Press.

Anderson, G. C., Burroughs, A. K., & Measel, C. P. (1983). Non-nutritive sucking opportunities: A safe and effective treatment for preterm neonates. In T. Field & A. Sostek (Eds.), *Infants born at risk* (pp. 215–245). New York: Grune & Stratton.

Andersson, B. E. (1992). Effects of day-care on cognitive and socioemotional competence of thirteen-year-old Swedish schoolchildren. *Child Development, 63,* 20–36.

Anisfeld, M. (1979). Interpreting "imitative" responses in early infancy. *Science, 205,* 214–215.

Anzman-Frasca, S., Liu, S., Gates, K. M., Paul, I. M., Rovine, M. J., & Birch, L. L. (2013). Infants' transitions out of a fussing/crying state are modifiable and are related to weight status. *Infancy, 18*(5), 662-686. doi: 10.1111/infa.12002

Apgar, V. (1953). A proposal for a new method of evaluation in the newborn infant. *Current Research in Anesthesia and Analgesia, 32,* 260.

Arden, R., Gottfredson, L. S., Miller, G., & Pierce, A. (2009). Intelligence and semen quality are positively correlated. *Intelligence, 37,* 277-282.

Arehart-Treichel, J. (1979, December 1). Down's syndrome: The father's role. *Science News,* 381–382.

Areias, M. E., Kumar, R., Barros, H., & Figueiredo, E. (1996). Correlates of postnatal depression in mothers and fathers. *British Journal of Psychiatry, 169*(1), 36–41.

Arendt, R., Singer, L., Angelopoulos, J, Bass-Busdiecker, O., & Mascia, J. (1998). Sensorimotor development in cocaine-exposed infants. *Infant Behavior and Development, 21*(4), 627–640.

Arterberry, M., Yonas, A., & Bensen, A. S. (1989). Self-produced locomotion and the development of responsiveness to linear perspective and texture gradients. *Developmental Psychology, 25*(6), 976–982.

Aschersleben, G., Hofer, T., & Jovanovic, B. (2008). The link between infant attention to goal-directed action and later theory of mind abilities. *Developmental Science, 11*(6), 862-868. doi:10.1111/j.1467-7687.2008.00736.x

Asendorpf, J. B., & Baudonniere, P. M. (1993). Self-awareness and other-awareness: Mirror self-recognition and synchronic imitation among unfamiliar peers. *Developmental Psychology, 29,* 88–95.

Asendorpf, J. B., Denissen, J. A., & van Aken, M. G. (2008). Inhibited and aggressive preschool children at 23 years of age: Personality and social transitions into adulthood. *Developmental Psychology, 44*(4), 997-1011.

Asendorpf, J. B., Warkentin, V., & Baudonniere, P. (1996). Self-awareness and other-awareness II: Mirror self-recognition, social contingency awareness, and synchronic imitation. *Developmental Psychology, 32*(2), 313–321.

Aslin, R. N. (1981). Development of smooth pursuit in human infants. In D. F. Fisher, R. A. Monty, & J. W. Sanders (Eds.), *Eye movements: Cognition and visual perception* (pp. 540–557). Hillsdale, NJ: Erlbaum.

Atkinson, J. (1995). Through the eyes of an infant. In R. Gregory, J. Harris, P. Heard, & D. Rose (Eds.), *The artful eye* (pp. 141.-156). New York: Oxford University Press.

Augusti, E., Melinder, A., & Gredebäck, G. (2010). Look who's talking: Pre-verbal infants' perception of face-to-face and back-to-back social interactions. *Frontiers In Psychology, 1,* 161.

Aureli, T. (1994). Shared focus in mother-child joint activity in the second year of life. *Early Development & Parenting, 3,* 145–152.

Aureli, T. (1997). *L'osservazione del comportamento del bambino.* Bologna, Italy: Società editrice il Mulino.

Aureli, T., & Presaghi, F. (2010). Developmental trajectories for mother-infant coregulation in the second year of life. *Infancy, 15*(6), 557-585. doi:10.1111/j.1532-7078.2010.00034.x

Aviezer, O., Sagi, A., Joels, T., & Ziv, Y. (1999). Emotional availability and attachment representations in Kibbutz infants and their mothers. *Developmental Psychology, 35*(3), 811–821.

Avni, F., Cos, T., Cassart, M., Massez, A., Donner, C., Ismaili, K., et al. (2007). Evolution of fetal ultrasonography. *European Radiology, 17*(2), 419–431.

Axia, G., Bonichini, S., & Benini, F. (1999). Attention and reaction to distress in infancy: A longitudinal study. *Developmental Psychology, 35*(2), 500–504.

Aylward, G. P. (2004). Presidential Address. Prediction of Function from Infancy to Early Childhood: Implications for Pediatric Psychology. *Journal of Pediatric Psychology, 29*(7), 555–564.

Badaly, D., & Adolph, K. E. (2008). Beyond the average: Walking infants take steps longer than their leg length. *Infant Behavior & Development, 31*(3), 554-558.

Baddeley, A. (1994). The remembered self and the enacted self. In U. Neisser & R. Fivush (Eds.), *The remembering self: Construction and accuracy in the self-narrative* (pp. 236–242). Cambridge, England: Cambridge University Press.

Bahrick, L. E. (1987). Infants' intermodal perception of two levels of temporal structure in natural events. *Infant Behavior and Development, 10,* 387–416.

Bahrick, L. E. (1988). Intermodal learning in infancy: Learning on the basis of two kinds of invariant relations in audible and visible events. *Child Development, 59,* 197–209.

Bahrick, L. E., Gogate, L. J., & Ruiz, I. (2002). Attention and memory for faces and actions in infancy: The salience of actions over faces in dynamic events. *Child Development, 73*(6), 1629–1643.

Bahrick, L. E., Netto, D., & Hernandez-Reif, M. (1998). Intermodal perception of adult and child faces and voices by infants. *Child Development, 69*(5), 1263–1275.

Bahrick, L. E., & Newell, L. C. (2008). Infant discrimination of faces in naturalistic events: Actions are more salient than faces. *Developmental Psychology, 44*(4), 983-996

Bahrick, L. E., & Pickens, J. N. (1988). Classification of bimodal English and Spanish language passages by infants. *Infant Behavior and Development, 11,* 277–296.

Bai, D. L., & Bertenthal, B. I. (1992). Locomotor status and the development of spatial search skills. *Child Development, 63,* 215–226.

Baillargeon, R. (1987). Object permanence in 31/2– and 41/2–month-old infants. *Developmental Psychology, 23,* 655–664.

Baillargeon, R., & DeVos, J. (1991). Object permanence in young infants: Further evidence. *Child Development, 62,* 1227–1246.

Baillargeon, R., & Graber, M. (1988). Evidence of location memory in 8–month-old infants in a nonsearch AB task. *Developmental Psychology, 24,* 502–511.

Baillargeon, R., Needham, A., & DeVos, J. (1992). The development of young infants' intuitions about support. *Early Development & Parenting, 1,* 69–78.

Baillargeon, R. H., Sward, G. D., Keenan, K., & Cao, G. (2011). Opposition-defiance in the second year of life: A population-based cohort study. *Infancy, 16*(4), 418-434. doi:10.1111/j.1532-7078.2010.00043.x

Baird, P. A. (2002). Overseeing embryo research: what is needed? *Clin Invest Med, 25*(1–2), 19–20.

Baird, P. A., & Sadovnick, A. D. (1987). Life expectancy in Down's syndrome. *Journal of Pediatrics, 110,* 849–854.

Baird, P. A., Yee, I. M., & Sadovnick, A. D. (1994). Population-based study of long-term outcomes after amniocentesis. *Lancet, 344* (8930), 1134–1136.

Bakeman, R., & Adamson, L. B. (1984). Coordinating attention to people and objects in mother-infant and peer-infant interaction. *Child Development, 55,* 1278–1289.

Bakeman, R., & Brownlee, J. (1980). The strategic use of parallel play: A sequential analysis. *Child Development, 51,* 873–878.

Bakermans-Kranenburg, M. J., van Ijzendoorn, M. H., & Kroonenberg, P. M. (2004). Differences in attachment security between African-American and white children: Ethnicity or socio-economic status? *Infant Behavior & Development, 27*(3), 417–433.

Bakker, H., de Graaf-Peters, V. B., van Eykern, L. A. Otten, B., & Hadders-Algra, M. (2010). Development of proximal arm muscle control during reaching in young infants: From variation to selection. *Infant Behavior & Development, 33,* 30-38.

Balamore, U., & Wozniak, R. H. (1984). Speech-action coordination in young children. *Developmental Psychology, 20,* 850–858.

Baldwin, D. A. (1993). Early referential understanding: Infants' ability to recognize referential acts for what they are. *Developmental Psychology, 29,* 832–843.

Baldwin, D. A. (1995). Understanding the link between joint attention and language. In C. Moore & P. J. Dunham (Eds.), *Joint attention: Its origins and role in development* (pp. 131–158). Hillsdale, NJ: Erlbaum.

Baldwin, D. A., Markman, E. M., Bill, B., Desjardins, R. N., Irwin, J. M., & Tidball, G. (1996). Infants' reliance on a social criterion for establishing word-object relations. *Child Development, 67,* 3135–3153.

Baldwin, D. A., Markman, E. M., & Melartin, R. L. (1993). Infants' ability to draw inferences about nonobvious object properties: Evidence from exploratory play. *Child Development, 64,* 711–728.

Ball, H. L. (2002). Reasons to bed-share: Why parents sleep with their infants. *Journal of Reproductive and Infant Psychology, 20*(4), 207–221.

Ball, H. L., Hooker, E., & Kelly, P. J. (2000). Parent-infant co-sleeping: Fathers' roles and perspectives. *Infant and Child Development, 9*(2), 67–74.

Balog, J. (1976). A new look at our infant mortality. *Birth and the Family Journal, 3,* 15–23.

Bandura, A. (1977). *Social learning theory.* Englewood Cliffs, NJ: Prentice-Hall.

Bandura, A. (1989). Human agency in social cognitive theory. *American Psychologist, 44*(9), 1175–1184.

Bandura, A. (1996). *Social foundations of thought and action: A social cognitive theory.* Englewood Cliffs, NJ: Prentice-Hall.

Barber, J. S., & East, P. L. (2009). Home and parenting resources available to siblings depending on their birth intention status. *Child Development, 80*(3), 921-939. doi:10.1111/j.1467-8624.2009.01306.x

Barbu-Roth, M., Anderson, D. I., Desprès, A., Provasi, J., Cabrol, D., & Campos, J. J. (2009). Neonatal stepping in relation to terrestrial optic flow. *Child Development, 80*(1), 8-14. doi:10.1111/j.1467-8624.2008.01241.x

Bard, K. A. (1994). Evolutionary roots of intuitive parenting: Maternal competence in chimpanzees. *Early Development and Parenting, 3,* 19–28.

Bard, K. A., Platzman, K. A., Lester, B. M., & Suomi, S. J. (1992). Orientation to social and nonsocial stimuli in neonatal chimpanzees and humans. *Infant Behavior and Development, 15,* 43–56.

Barglow, P. (1987a). Effect of maternal absence due to employment on the quality of infant-mother attachment in a low-risk sample. *Child Development, 58,* 945–954.

Barglow, P. (1987b). Some further comments about infant day-care research. *Zero to Three, 8,* 26–28.

Bar-Haim, Y., Ziv, T., Lamy, D., & Hodes, R. M. (2006). Nature and Nurture in Own-Race Face Processing. *Psychological Science, 17*(2), 159–163.

Barnard, K. (1985) *Nursing Child Assessment Satellite Training (NCAST), Feeding and Teaching Scale.* Parent-Child Interaction (PCI) Program: University of Washington.

Barnard, K. E., Bee, H. L., & Hammond, M. A. (1984). Developmental changes in maternal interactions with term and preterm infants. *Infant Behavior and Development, 7,* 101–113.

Barnett, D., Ganiban, J., & Ciccheti, D. (1999). Maltreatment, negative expressivity, and the development of type D attachments from 12 to 24 months of age. *Monographs of the Society for Research in Child Development, 64*(3), 97–118.

Baron-Cohen, S., Allen, J., & Gillberg, C. (1992). Can autism be detected at 18 months? *British Journal of Psychiatry, 161,* 839–843.

Baron-Cohen, S., Cox, A., Baird, G., Sweettenham, J., & Nightingale, N. (1996). Psychological markers in the detection of autism in infancy in a large population. *British Journal of Psychiatry, 168*(2), 158–163.

Barr, R., & Hayne, H. (2003). It's not what you know, it's who you know: Older siblings facilitate imitation during infancy. *International Journal of Early Years Education, 11*(1), 7–21.

Barr, R., Muentener, P., & Garcia, A. (2007). Age-related changes in deferred imitation from television by 6- to 18-month-olds. *Developmental Science, 10*(6), 910-921. doi:10.1111/j.1467-7687.2007.00641.x

Barr, R., Shuck, L., Salerno, K., Atkinson, E., & Linebarger, D. L. (2010). Music interferes with learning from television during infancy. *Infant And Child Development, 19*(3), 313-331.

Barr, R. G. (1990). The early crying paradox: A modest proposal. *Human Nature, 1,* 355–389.

Barr, R. G., & Hayne, H. (1999). Developmental changes in imitation from television during infancy. *Child Development, 70*(5), 1067–1081.

Barr, R. G., Quek, V. S. H., Cousineau, D., Oberlander, T. F., Brian, J. A., & Young, S. N. (1994). Effects of intraoral sucrose on crying, mouthing, and hand-mouth contact in newborn and six-week-old infants. *Developmental Medicine Child Neurology, 36,* 608–618.

Barr, R. G., Rotman, A., Yaremko, J., Leduc, D., & Francoeur, T. E. (1992). The crying of infants with colic: A controlled empirical description. *Pediatrics, 90,* 14–21.

Barratt, M. S., & Roach, M. A. (1995). Early interactive processes: Parenting by adolescent and adult single mothers. *Infant Behavior and Development, 18,* 97–109.

Barratt, M. S., Roach, M. A., & Leavitt, L. A. (1996). The impact of low-risk prematurity on maternal behavior and toddler outcomes. *International Journal of Behavioral Development, 19*(3), 581–602.

Barrett, D. E., Radke-Yarrow, M., & Klein, R. E. (1982). Chronic malnutrition and child behavior: Effects of early caloric supplementation on social and emotional functioning at school age. *Developmental Psychology, 18,* 541–556.

Barrett, H., Broesch, T., Scott, R., He, Z., Baillargeon, R., Wu, D., & ... Laurence, S. (2013). Early false-belief understanding in traditional non-Western societies. *Proceedings. Biological Sciences / The Royal Society, 280*(1755), 20122654. doi:10.1098/rspb.2012.2654

Barrett, K. C. (1995). A functionalist approach to shame and guilt. In J. P. Tangney & K. W. Fischer (Eds.), *Self-conscious emotions: The psychology of shame, guilt, embarrassment, and pride* (pp. 25–63). New York: Guilford Press.

Barrett, K. C., & Campos, J. J. (1987). Perspectives on emotional development II: A functionalist approach to emotions. In J. D. Osofsky (Ed.), *Handbook of infant development* (2nd ed., pp. 555–578). New York: Wiley.

Barrett, K. C., & Nelson-Goens, G. C. (1997). Emotion communication and the development of the social emotions. In K. C. Barrett (Ed.), *New directions in child development: The communication of emotion: Current research from diverse perspectives, 77* (pp. 69–88). San Francisco: Jossey-Bass.

Barrett, T., Traupman, E., & Needham, A. (2008). Infants' visual anticipation of object structure in grasp planning. *Infant Behavior & Development, 31*(1), 1-9.

Barrile, M., Armstrong, E. S., & Bower, T. G. R. (1999). Novelty and frequency as determinants of newborn preference. *Developmental Science, 2*(1), 47–52.

Barss, V. A., Benacerraf, B. R., & Frigoletto, F. D. (1985). Ultrasonographic determination of chorion type in twin gestation. *Obstetrics and Gynecology, 66,* 779–783.

Barth, R. P., Fetro, J. V., Leland, N., & Volkan, K. (1992). Preventing adolescent pregnancy with social and cognitive skills. *Journal of Adolescent Research, 7,* 208–232.

Barton, M. E., & Tomasello, M. (1991). Joint attention and conversation in mother-infant-sibling triads. *Child Development, 62,* 517–529.

Bates, E., Camaioni, L., & Volterra, V. (1975). The acquisition of performatives prior to speech. *Merrill-Palmer Quarterly, 21,* 205–226.

Bates, E., O'Connell, B., & Shore, C. (1987). Language and communication in infancy. In J. D. Osofsky (Ed.), *Handbook of infant development* (2nd ed., pp. 149–203). New York: Wiley.

Bates, E., Thal, D., Whitesell, K., Fenson, L., & Oakes, L. (1989). Integrating language and gesture in infancy. *Developmental Psychology, 25,* 1104–1119.

Bates, J. E. (1980). The concept of difficult temperament. *Merrill-Palmer Quarterly, 26,* 299–319.

Bates, J. E. (1987). Temperament in infancy. In J. D. Osofsky (Ed.), *Handbook of infant development* (2nd ed., pp. 35–69). New York: Wiley.

Bates, J. E., & Bayles, K. (1984). Objective and subjective components in mothers' perceptions of their children from age 6 months to 3 years. *Merrill-Palmer Quarterly, 30,* 111–130.

Bates, E., Carlson-Luden, V., & Bretherton, I. (1980). Perceptual aspects of tool using in infancy. *Infant Behavior and Development, 3,* 127–140.

Bates, J. E., Freeland, C. A., & Lounsbury, M. L. (1979). Measurement of infant difficultness. *Child Development, 50,* 794–803.

Bates, J. E., Maslin, C. A., & Frankel, K. A. (1985). Attachment security, mother-child interaction, and temperament as predictors of behavior-problem ratings at age three years. *Monographs of the Society for Research in Child Development, 50* (Serial No. 209), 167–193.

Bates, E., O'Connell, B., & Shore, C. (1987). Language and communication in infancy. In J. D. Osofsky (Ed.), *Handbook of infant development* (2nd ed., pp. 149–203). New York: Wiley.

Bates, J. E., Wachs, T. D., & Emde, R. N. (1994). Toward practical uses for biological concepts of temperament. In J. E. Bates & T. D. Wachs (Eds.), *Temperament: Individual differences at the interface of biology and behavior* (pp. 275–306). Washington, DC: American Psychological Association.

Bateson, M. C. (1975). Mother-infant exchanges: The epigenesis of conversation interaction. *Annals of the New York Academy of Science, 263,* 101–113.

Bateson, P. P. G. (1966). The characteristics and context of imprinting. *Biological Review, 41,* 177–220.

Battin, M., Ling, E. W., Whitfield, M. F., Mackinnon, M., & Effer, S. B. (1998). Has the outcome for extremely low gestational age (ELGA) infants improved following recent advances in neonatal intensive care? *American Journal of Perinatology, 15*(8), 469–477.

Bauer, P. J. (1993). Memory for gender-consistent and gender-inconsistent event sequences by twenty-five-month-old children. *Child Development, 64,* 285–297.

Bauer, P. J. (1996). What do infants recall of their lives? Memory for specific events by one- to two-year-olds. *American Psychologist, 51*(1), 29–41.

Bauer, P. J., & Dow, G. A. (1994). Episodic memory in 16– and 20–month-old children: Specifics are generalized but not forgotten. *Developmental Psychology, 30,* 403–417.

Bauer, P. J., & Leventon, J. S. (2013). Memory for one-time experiences in the second year of life: Implications for the status of episodic memory. *Infancy, 18*(5), 755-781. doi: 10.1111/infa.12005

Bauer, P. J., Schwade, J. A., Wewerka, S. S., & Delaney, D. (1999). Planning ahead: Goal-directed problem solving by 2–year-olds. *Developmental Psychology, 35*(8), 1321–1337.

Baumrind, D. (1973). The development of instrumental competence through socialization. In A. Pick (Ed.), *Minnesota symposium on child development, 11,* 1112–1132. Minneapolis: University of Minnesota Press.

Baumrind, D. (1993). The average expectable environment is not good enough: A response to Scarr. *Child Development, 64,* 1299–1317.

Bayley, N. (1969). *The Bayley scale of infant development.* (Manual). Stanford, CA: Psychological Corporation.

Beatson, J., & Taryan, S. (2003). Predisposition to depression: the role of attachment. *Aust N Z J Psychiatry, 37*(2), 219–225.

Beauchamp, G., Cowart, B., Mennella, J., & Marsh, R. (1994). Infant salt taste: Developmental, methodological, and contextual factors. *Developmental Psychobiology; 27,* 353–365.

Beck, R. A., Kambiss, S., & Bass, J. W. (1993). The retreat of Hemophilus influenzae type B invasive disease: Analysis of and immunization program and implications for OTO-HNS. *Otolaryngological Head and Neck Surgery, 109,* 712–721.

Becker, J. (1977). A learning analysis of the development of peer oriented behavior in nine-month-old infants. *Developmental psychology, 13,* 481–491.

Beckwith, L., Cohen, S. E., & Hamilton, C. E. (1999). Maternal sensitivity during infancy and subsequent life events relate to attachment representation at early adulthood. *Developmental Psychology, 35*(3), 693–700.

Beebe, B. (2004). Co-constructing mother-infant distress in face-to-face interactions: Contributions of microanalysis. *Zero to Three, 24*(5), 40–48.

Beebe, B. & Jaffee, J. (2008). Dyadic microanalysis of mother-infant communication informs practice. In A. Fogel, B. J. King, & S. Shanker (Eds.). *Human development in the 21st century: Visionary policy ideas from systems scientists.* Cambridge, UK: Cambridge University Press.

Beebe, B., Jaffe, J., Buck, K., Chen, H., Cohen, P., Blatt, S., & ... Andrews, H. (2007). Six-week postpartum maternal self-criticism and dependency and 4-month mother-infant self- and interactive contingencies. *Developmental Psychology, 43*(6), 1360-1376.

Beebe, B., Jaffe, J., Markese, S., Buck, K., Chen, H., Cohen, P., & ... Feldstein, S. (2010). The origins of 12-month attachment: A microanalysis of 4-month mother-infant interaction. *Attachment & Human Development, 12*(1-2), 6-141. doi:10.1080/14616730903338985

Beebe, B., Steele, M., Jaffe, J., Buck, K. A., Chen, H., Cohen, P., & ... Feldstein, S. (2011). Maternal anxiety symptoms and mother-infant self- and interactive contingency. *Infant Mental Health Journal, 32*(2), 174-206. doi:10.1002/imhj.20274

Beier, J. S., & Spelke, E. S. (2012). Infants' Developing Understanding of Social Gaze. *Child Development, 83*(2), 486-496.

Beijersbergen, M. D., Juffer, F., Bakermans-Kranenburg, M. J., & van IJzendoorn, M. H. (2012). Remaining or becoming secure: Parental sensitive support predicts attachment continuity from infancy to adolescence in a longitudinal adoption study. *Developmental Psychology, 48*(5), 1277-1282.

Bell, R. Q., & Costello, N. S. (1964). Three tests for sex differences in tactile sensitivity in the newborn. *Biologia Neonatorum, 7,* 335–347.

Bellagamba, F., & Tomasello, M. (1999). Re-enacting intended acts: Comparing 12– and 18–month-olds. *Infant Behavior and Development, 22*(2), 277–282.

Belsky, J. (1980). Child maltreatment: An ecological integration. *American Psychologist, 35,* 320–335.

Belsky, J. (1981). Early human experience: A family perspective. *Developmental Psychology, 17,* 3–23.

Belsky, J. (1984). The determinants of parenting: A process model. *Child Development, 55,* 83–96.

Belsky, J. (1995). Expanding the ecology of human development: An evolutionary perspective. In P. Moen & G. H. Elder (Eds.), *Examining lives in context: Perspectives on the ecology of human development* (pp. 545–561). Washington, DC: American Psychological Association.

Belsky, J. (1996). Parent, infant, and social-contextual antecedents of father-son attachment security. *Developmental Psychology, 32*(5), 905–913.

Belsky, J., & Braungart, J. M. (1991). Are insecure-avoidant infants with extensive day-care experience less stressed by and more independent in the strange situation? *Child Development, 62,* 567–671.

Belsky, J., Goode, M. K., & Most, R. K. (1980). Maternal simulation and infant exploratory competence; Cross-sectional, correlational, and experimental analyses. *Child Development, 51,* 1168–1178.

Belsky, J., Houts, R. M., & Pasco Fearon, R. M. (2010). Infant Attachment Security and the Timing of Puberty: Testing an Evolutionary Hypothesis. *Psychological Science (Sage Publications Inc.), 21*(9), 1195-1201.

Belsky, J., & Isabella, R. A. (1985). Marital and parent-child relationships in family of origin and marital change following the birth of a baby: A retrospective analysis. *Child Development, 56,* 342–349.

Belsky, J., & Most, R. K. (1981). From exploration to play: A cross-sectional study of infant free play behavior. *Developmental Psychology, 17,* 630–639.

Belsky, J., & Rovine, M. J. (1988). Nonmaternal care in the first year of life and the security of infant-parent attachment. *Child Development, 59,* 157–167.

Belsky, J., Rovine, M. J., & Taylor, D. G. (1984). The Pennsylvania infant and family development project III: The origins of individual differences in infant-mother attachment: Maternal and infant contributions. *Child Development, 55,* 718–728.

Belsky, J., Ward, M. J., & Rovine, M. (1986). Prenatal expectations, postnatal experiences, and the transition to parenthood. In R. D. Ashmore & D. M. Brodzinsky (Eds.), *Thinking about the family: Views of parents and children* (pp. 15–38). Hillsdale, NJ: Erlbaum.

Belsky, J., Woodworth, S., & Crnic, K. (1996). Trouble in the second year: Three questions about family interaction. *Child Development, 67,* 556–578.

Bendersky, M., & Lewis, M. (1998). Arousal modulation in cocaine-exposed infants. *Developmental Psychology, 34*(3), 555–564.

Benn, R. K. (1986). Factors promoting secure attachment relationships between employed mothers and their sons. *Child Development, 57,* 1224–1231.

Bennett, W. J. (1987). The role of the family in the nurture and protection of the young. *American Psychologist, 42,* 246–250.

Benson, J. B. (1993). Season of birth and onset of locomotion: Theoretical and methodological implications. *Infant Behavior and Development, 16,* 69–81.

Berenbaum, S. A., & Bailey, J. M. (2003). Effects on gender identity of prenatal androgens and genital appearance: evidence from girls with congenital adrenal hyperplasia. *J Clin Endocrinol Metab, 88*(3), 1102–1106.

Berg, W. K., & Berg, K. M. (1979). Psychophysiological development in infancy: State, sensory function, and attention. In J. D. Osofsky (Ed.), *Handbook of infant development* (pp. 283–343). New York: Wiley.

Berg, W. K., & Berg, K. M. (1987). Psychophysiological development in infancy: State, startle, and attention. In J. D. Osofsky (Ed.), *Handbook of infant development* (2nd ed., pp. 121–145). New York: Wiley.

Bergelson, E., & Swingley, D. (2012). At 6–9 months, human infants know the meanings of many common nouns.

PNAS Proceedings Of The National Academy Of Sciences Of The United States Of America, 109(9), 3253-3258.

Berger, L. M. (2004). Income, family structure, and child maltreatment risk. *Children and Youth Services Review, 26*(8), 725–748.

Berger, S., Friedman, R., & Polis, M. (2011). The role of locomotor posture and experience on handedness and footedness in infancy. *Infant Behavior & Development, 34*(3), 472-480. doi:10.1016/j.infbeh.2011.05.003

Berger, S. E., & Adolph, K. E. (2003). Infants use handrails as tools in a locomotor task. *Developmental Psychology, 39*(3), 594–605.

Berger, S. E., Adolph, K. E., & Kavookjian, A. E. (2010). Bridging the gap: Solving spatial means-ends relations in a locomotor task. *Child Development, 81*(5), 1367-1375. doi:10.1111/j.1467-8624.2010.01478.x

Berk, L. E. (1986). Development of private speech among preschool children. *Early Child Development and Care, 24,* 113–136.

Berko, J. (1958). The child's learning of English morphology. *Word, 14,* 150–177.

Berlin, L. J., Appleyard, K., & Dodge, K. A. (2011). Intergenerational Continuity in Child Maltreatment: Mediating Mechanisms and Implications for Prevention. *Child Development, 82*(1), 162-176.

Berlin, L. J., Cassidy, J., & Belsky, J. (1995). Loneliness in young children and infant-mother attachment: A longitudinal study. *Merrill-Palmer Quarterly, 41,* 91–103.

Berlin, L. J., Ispa, J. M., Fine, M. A., Malone, P. S., Brooks-Gunn, J., Brady-Smith, C., & ... Bai, Y. (2009). Correlates and consequences of spanking and verbal punishment for low-income White, African American, and Mexican American toddlers. *Child Development, 80*(5), 1403-1420. doi:10.1111/j.1467-8624.2009.01341.x

Berlin, L. J., O'Neal, C., & Brooks-Gunn, J. (1998). What makes early intervention programs work? The program, its participants, and their interactions. *Zero to Three, 18*(4), 4–15.

Berman, P. W., Goodman, V., Sloan, V. L., & Fernandez, L. (1978). Preference for infants among black and white children: Sex and age differences. *Child Development, 49,* 917–919.

Berman, P. W., Monda, C. C., & Merscough, R. P. (1977). Sex differences in young children's responses to an infant: An observation within a day-care setting. *Child Development, 48,* 711–715.

Bernard, K. (2011). This is my baby: Foster parents' feelings of commitment and displays of delight. *Infant Mental Health Journal, 32*(2), 251-262.

Bernard, K., Dozier, M., Bick, J., Lewis-Morrarty, E., Lindhiem, O., & Carlson, E. (2012). Enhancing Attachment Organization among Maltreated Children: Results of a Randomized Clinical Trial. *Child Development, 83*(2), 623-636.

Bernier, A., Beauchamp, M., Bouvette-Turcot, A., Carlson, S., & Carrier, J. (2013). Sleep and cognition in preschool years: specific links to executive functioning. *Child Development, 84*(5), 1542-1553.

Bernier, A., Carlson, S. M., Bordeleau, S., & Carrier, J. (2010). Relations between physiological and cognitive regulatory systems: Infant sleep regulation and subsequent executive functioning. *Child Development, 81*(6), 1739-1752. doi:10.1111/j.1467-8624.2010.01507.x

Bernier, A., & Dozier, M. (2003). Bridging the attachment transmission gap: The role of maternal mind-mindedness. *International Journal of Behavioral Development, 27*(4), 355–365.

Bernier, A., Carlson, S. M., & Whipple, N. (2010) From external regulation to self-regulation: Early parenting precursors of young children's executive functioning.; *Child Development, 81,* 326-339.

Bernier, A., & Meins, E. (2008). A threshold approach to understanding the origins of attachment disorganization. *Developmental Psychology, 44*(4), 969-982.

Berrueta-Clement, J. R., Schweinhart, L. J., Barnett, W. S., Epstein, A. S., & Weikart, D. P. (1984). *Changed lives: The effects of the Perry Preschool Program on youths through age 19 (Monograph No. 8).* Ypsilanti, MI: High Scope/Educational Research Foundation.

Bertella, L., Girelli, L., Grugni, G., Marchi, S., Molinari, E., & Semenza, C. (2005). Mathematical skills in Prader-Willi Syndrome. *Journal of Intellectual Disability Research, 49*(2), 159–169.

Bertenthal, B. I., & Bai, D. L. (1989). Infants' sensitivity to optical flow for controlling posture. *Developmental Psychology, 25,* 936–945.

Bertenthal, B. I., Campos, J. J., & Barrett, K. C. (1984). Self-produced locomotion: An organizer of emotional, cognitive, and social development in infancy. In R. N. Emde & R. J. Harmon (Eds.), *Continuities and discontinuities in development* (pp. 175–210). New York: Plenum Press.

Bertenthal, B. I., & Pinto, J. (1993). Complementary processes in the perception and production of human movements. In L. B. Smith & E. Thelen (Eds.), *A dynamic systems approach to development: Applications* (pp. 209–239). Cambridge, MA: MIT Press.

Bertenthal, B. I., Proffitt, D. R., Kramer, S. J., & Spetner, N. B. (1987). Infants' encoding of kinetic displays varying in relative coherence. *Developmental Psychology, 23*(2), 171–178.

Berthiaume, M., David, J., Saucier, J. F., & Borgeat, F. (1998). Correlates of pre-partum depressive symptomatology: A multivariate analysis. *Reproductive and Infant Psychology, 16,* 45–56.

Best, J. R., & Miller, P. H. (2010). A developmental perspective on executive function. *Child Development, 81*(6), 1641-1660. doi:10.1111/j.1467-8624.2010.01499.x

Bever, T. G. (1970). The cognitive basis for linguistic structures. In J. R. Haynes (Ed.), *Cognition and the development of language* (pp. 40–72). New York: Wiley.

Bhat, A. N., & Galloway, J. C. (2006). Toy-oriented changes during early arm movements: Hand kinematics. *Infant Behavior & Development, 29*(3), 358–372.

Bhatt, R. S., Rovee-Collier, C., & Weiner, S. (1994). Developmental changes in the interface between perception and memory retrieval. *Developmental Psychology, 30,* 151–162.

Bick, J., Dozier, M., Bernard, K., Grasso, D., & Simons, R. (2013). Foster mother-infant bonding: associations between foster mothers' oxytocin production, electrophysiological brain activity, feelings of commitment, and caregiving quality. *Child Development, 84*(3), 826-840.

Bigelow, A., MacLean, J., Wood, C., & Smith, J. (1990). Infants' responses to child and adult strangers: An investigation of height and facial configuration variables. *Infant Behavior and Development, 13,* 21–32.

Bigelow, A., MacLean, K., Proctor, J., Myatt, T., Gillis, R., & Power, M. (2010). Maternal sensitivity throughout infancy: continuity and relation to attachment security. *Infant Behavior & Development, 33*(1), 50-60.

Bigelow, A. E. (1992). Locomotion and search behavior in blind infants. *Infant Behavior and Development, 15,* 179–189.

Bigelow, A. E. (1998). Infants' sensitivity to familiar imperfect contingencies in social interaction. *Infant Behavior and Development, 21*(1), 149–162.

Bigelow, A. E., MacDonald, D., & MacDonald, L. (1995). The development of infants' search for their mothers, unfamiliar people, and objects. *Merrill-Palmer Quarterly, 41,* 191–205.

Bigelow, A. E. Power, M. (2012). The effect of mother–infant skin-to-skin contact on infants' response to the Still Face Task from newborn to three months of age. *Infant Behavior & Development, Vol 35*(2), Apr, 2012. pp. 240-251

Bigelow, A. E., & Rochat, P. (2006). Two-Month-Old Infants' Sensitivity to Social Contingency in Mother-Infant and Stranger-Infant Interaction. *Infancy, 9*(3), 313–325.

Bigelow, A. E., & Walden, L. M. (2009). Infants' response to maternal mirroring in the still face and replay tasks. *Infancy, 14*(5), 526-549. doi:10.1080/15250000903144181

Bijeljac-Babic, R., Bertoncini, J., & Mehler, J. (1993). How do 4–day-old infants categorize multisyllabic utterances? *Developmental Psychology, 29,* 711–721.

Bijou, S. W., & Baer, D. M. (1965). *Child development: Vol. 2. Universal stage of infancy.* New York: Appleton-Century-Crofts.

Biringen, Z., Emde, R. N., Campos, J. J., & Appelbaum, M. I. (1995). Affective reorganization in the infant, the mother, and the dyad: The role of upright locomotion and its timing. *Child Development, 66,* 499–514.

Birth (June 1988). Report for American College of Obstetricians and Gynecologists. *Birth, 15,* 113.

Black, M. M., & Krishnakumar, A. (1998). Children in low-income, urban settings: Interventions to promote mental health and well-being. *American Psychologist, 53*(6), 635–646.

Black, R. E. (2001). Micronutrients in pregnancy. *Br J Nutr, 85 Suppl 2,* S193–197.

Blackford, J. U., & Walden, T. A. (1998). Individual differences in social referencing. *Infant Behavior and Development, 21*(1), 89–102.

Blackman, J. A., Lindgren, S. D., Hein, H. A., & Harper, D. C. (1987). Long-term surveillance of high-risk children. *American Journal of Diseases of Children, 141,* 1293–1299.

Blackwell, C. C., Weir, D. M., Busuttil, A., Saadi, A. T., Essery, S. D., Raza, M. W., James, V. S., & MacKenzie, D. A. (1994). The role of infectious agents in sudden infant death syndrome. *FEMS Immunological Medicine and Microbiology, 9,* 91–100.

Blair, C. (2010). Stress and the development of self-regulation in context. *Child Development Perspectives, 4*(3), 181-188. doi:10.1111/j.1750-8606.2010.00145.x

Blair, C., Granger, D., Kivlighan, K., Mills-Koonce, R., Willoughby, M., Greenberg, M., & ... Fortunato, C. (2008). Maternal and child contributions to cortisol response to emotional arousal in young children from low-income, rural communities. *Developmental Psychology, 44*(4), 1095-1109.

Blair, C., Granger, D. A., Willoughby, M., Mills-Koonce, R., Cox, M., Greenberg, M. T., & ... Fortunato, C. K. (2011). Salivary cortisol mediates effects of poverty and parenting on executive functions in early childhood. *Child Development, 82*(6), 1970-1984.

Blake, J., McConnell, S., Horton, G., & Benson, N. (1992). The gestural repertoire and its evolution over the second year. *Early Development and Parenting, 1,* 127–136.

Blank, A., Mofenson, L. M., Willoughby, A., & Yaffe, S. J. (1994). Maternal and pediatric AIDS in the United States: The current situation and future research directions. *Acta-Paediatrica-Supplement, 400,* 106–110.

Blank, M., & Klig, S. (1982). The child and the school experience. In C. B. Kopp & J. B. Krakow (Eds.), *The child: Development in social context* (pp. 456–513). Reading, MA: Addison-Wesley.

Blandon, A. Y., Calkins, S. D., Keane, S. P., & O'Brien, M. (2010). Contributions of child's physiology and maternal behavior to children's trajectories of temperamental reactivity. *Developmental Psychology, 46*(5), 1089-1102. doi:10.1037/a0020678

Blasi, A., Mercure, E., Lloyd-Fox, S., Thomson, A., Brammer, M., Sauter, D,. . .Murphy, D. G. (2011). Early specialization for voice and emotion processing in the infant brain. *Current Biology, 21,* 1220-1224.

Blass, E. M. (1997). Changing influences of sucrose and visual engagement in 2– to 12–week-old human infants: Implications for maternal face recognition. *Infant Behavior and Development, 20*(4), 423–434.

Blass, E. M., & Ciaramitaro, V. (1994). A new look at some old mechanisms in human newborns: Taste and tactile determinants of state, affect, and action. *Monographs of the Society for Research in Child Development, 59,* 1–102.

Blass, E. M., Fillion, T. J., Rochat, P., Hoffmeyer, L. B., & Metzger, M. A. (1989). Sensorimotor and motivational determinants of hand-mouth coordination in 1– to 3–day-old human infants. *Developmental Psychology, 25,* 963–975.

Blass, E. M., Ganchrow, J. R., & Steiner, J. E. (1984). Classical conditioning in newborn humans 2 to 48 hours of age. *Infant Behavior and Development, 7,* 223–235.

Blehar, M. C., Lieberman, A., & Ainsworth, M. (1977). Early face-to-face interaction and its relation to later mother-infant attachment. *Child Development, 48,* 182–194.

Bloch, H. (1990). Status and function of early sensory-motor coordination. In H. Bloch & B. I. Bertenthal (Eds.), *Sensory-motor organizations and development in infancy and early childhood* (pp. 163–178). The Netherlands: Kluwer Academic.

Block, J. A., & Block, J. (1980). The role of ego-control and ego-resiliency in the organization of behavior. In W. A. Collins (Ed.), *Minnesota symposia on child psychology* (Vol. 13, pp. 1550–1574). Hillsdale, NJ: Erlbaum.

Bloom, K., D'Odorico, L., & Beaumont, S. (1993). Adult preferences for syllabic vocalizations: Generalizations to parity and native language. *Infant Behavior and Development, 16,* 109–120.

Bloom, K., & Lo, E. (1990). Adult perceptions of vocalizing infants. *Infant Behavior and Development, 13,* 209–219.

Bloom, L., & Beckwith, R. (1989). Talking with feeling: Integrating affective and linguistic expression in early language development. *Cognition and Emotion, 3*(4), 313–342.

Bloom, L., Margulis, C., Tinker, E., & Fujita, N. (1996). Early conversations and word learning: Contributions from child and adult. *Child Development, 67,* 3154–3175.

Bloom, L., Merkin, S., & Wootten, J. (1982). Wh-questions: Linquistic factors that contribute to the sequence of acquisition. *Child Development, 53,* 1084–1092.

Bocci, V., von Brenmen, K., Corradeschi, F., Franchi, F., Luzzi, E., & Paulesu, L. (1993). Presence of interferon-gamma and interleukin-6 in colostrum of normal women. *Lymphokine-Cytokine Research, 12,* 21–24.

Boddy, J. M., & Skuse, D. H. (1994). The process of parenting in failure to thrive. *Journal of Child Psychology and Psychiatry and Allied Disciplines, 35,* 401–424.

Bodle, J. H., Zhou, L. Y., Shore, C. M., & Dixon, W. E. (1996). Transfer by responsibility in parent-child play during the second year. *Early Development and Parenting, 5*(4), 185–194.

Boehm, L. (1977). The development of independence: A comparative study. *Child Development, 28,* 85–92.

Bohannon, J. N., III, & Stanowicz, L. (1988). The issue of negative evidence: Adult responses to children's language errors. *Developmental Psychology, 24,* 684–689.

Bohlin, G., & Hagekull, B. (1993). Stranger wariness and sociability in the early years. *Infant Behavior and Development, 16,* 53–67.

Bohlin, G., Hagekull, B., Germer, M., Anderson, K., & Lindberg, L. (1989). Avoidant and resistant reunion behaviors as predicted by maternal interactive behavior and infant temperament. *Infant Behavior and Development, 12,* 105–117.

Bohlin, G., Hagekull, B., & Lindberg, L. (1994). Infantile colic and parental experiences. *Early Development and Parenting, 3,* 63–69.

Bojczyk, K. E., & Corbetta, D. (2004). Object Retrieval in the 1st Year of Life: Learning Effects of Task Exposure and Box Transparency. *Developmental Psychology, 40*(1), 54–66.

Bonichini, S., Axia, G., St. James-Roberts, I., & DeCian, S. (2008). Infant crying and maternal holding in the first 2 months of age: an Italian diary study. *Infant & Child Development, 17,* 581-592.

Bookstein, F. L., Sampson, P. D., Streissguth, A. P., & Barr, H. M. (1996). Exploiting redundant measurement of dose and developmental outcome: New methods from the behavioral teratology of alcohol. *Developmental Psychology, 32*(3), 404–415.

Boom, D. C. van den (1994). The influence of temperament and mothering on attachment and exploration: An experimental manipulation of sensitive responsiveness among lower-class mothers with irritable infants. *Child Development, 65,* 1457–1477.

Boom, D. C. van den, & Gravenhorst, J. B. (1995). Prenatal and perinatal correlates of neonatal irritability. *Infant Behavior and Development, 18,* 117–121.

Boom, D. C. van den, & Hoeksma, J. B. (1994a). The effect of infant irritability on mother-infant interaction: A growth-curve analysis. *Developmental Psychology, 30*(4), 581–590.

Boom, D. C. van den, & Hoeksma, J. B. (1994b). How is development conceptualized in mother-child interaction? In W. Koops, J. Hoeksma, & D. C. van den Boom (Eds.), *Early mother-child interaction and attachment: Old and new approaches.* Amsterdam: Elsevier.

Bor, W., Brennan, P. A., Williams, G. M., Najman, J. M., & O'Callaghan, M. (2003). A mother's attitude towards her infant and child behaviour five years later. *Aust N Z J Psychiatry, 37*(6), 748–755.

Bornstein, M. H. (1985). Habituation of attention as a measure of visual information processing in human infants: Summary, systematization, and synthesis. In G. Gottlieb & N. A. Krasnegor (Eds.), *Measurement of audition and vision in the first year of postnatal life: A methodological overview* (pp. 260–281). Norwood, NJ: Ablex.

Bornstein, M. H., & Arterberry, M. E. (2003). Recognition, discrimination and categorization of smiling by 5–month-old infants. *Developmental Science, 6*(5), 585–599.

Bornstein, M. H., Arterberry, M. E., & Mash, C. (2004). Long-Term Memory for an Emotional Interpersonal Interaction Occurring at 5 Months of Age. *Infancy, 6*(3), 407–416.

Bornstein, M. H., Arterberry, M. E., Mash, C., & Manian, N. (2011). Discrimination of facial expression by 5-month-old infants of nondepressed and clinically depressed mothers. *Infant Behavior & Development, 34*(1), 100-106. doi:10.1016/j.infbeh.2010.10.002

Bornstein, M. H., & Benasich, A. A. (1986). Infant habituation: Assessments of short-term reliability and individual differences at five months. *Child Development, 57,* 87–99.

Bornstein, M. H., Cote, L. R., Maital, S., Painter, K., Park, S.-Y., Pascual, L., et al. (2004). Cross-Linguistic Analysis of Vocabulary in Young Children: Spanish, Dutch, French, Hebrew, Italian, Korean, and American English. *Child Development, 75*(4), 1115–1139.

Bornstein, M. H., & Krinsky, S. J. (1985). Perception of symmetry in infancy: The salience of vertical symmetry and the perception of pattern wholes. *Journal of Experimental Child Psychology, 39,* 1–19.

Bornstein, M. H., Krinsky, S. J., & Benasich, A. A. (1986). Fine orientation discrimination and shape constancy in infants. *Journal of Experimental Child Psychology, 41,* 49–60.

Bornstein, M. H., & Mash, C. (2010). Experience-based and on-line categorization of objects in early infancy. *Child Development, 81*(3), 884-897. doi:10.1111/j.1467-8624.2010.01440.x

Bornstein, M., Mash, C., Arterberry, M., & Manian, N. (2012). Object perception in 5-month-old infants of clinically depressed and nondepressed mothers. *Infant Behavior & Development, 35*(1), 150-157. doi:10.1016/j.infbeh.2011.07.008

Bornstein, M. H., Putnick, D. L., Heslington, M., Gini, M., Suwalsky, J. D., Venuti, P., & … Zingman de Galperín, C. (2008). Mother-child emotional availability in ecological perspective: Three countries, two regions, two genders.*Developmental Psychology, 44*(3), 666-680. doi:10.1037/0012-1649.44.3.666

Bornstein, M. H., Tal, J., Rahn, C., Galperin, C. Z., Pecheux, M., Lamour, M., Toda, S., Azuma, H., Ogino, M., & Tamis-LeMonda, C. S. (1992). Functional analysis of the contents of maternal speech to infants of 5 and 13 months in four cultures: Argentina, France, Japan, and the United States. *Developmental Psychology, 28,* 593–603.

Bornstein, M. H., & Tamis-LeMonda, C. S. (1995). Parent-child symbolic play: Three theories in search of an effect. *Developmental Review, 15,* 382–400.

Bornstein, M. H., Tamis-LeMonda, C. S., Tal, J., Ludemann, P., Toda, S., Rahn, C. W., Pecheux, M. G., Azuma, H., & Vardi, D. (1992). Maternal responsiveness to infants in three societies: The United States, France, and Japan. *Child Development, 63,* 808–821.

Boss, J. A. (1994). First trimester prenatal diagnosis: Earlier is not necessarily better. *Journal of Medical Ethics, 20,* 146–151.

Botting, N., Powls, A., Cooke, R. W., & Marlow, N. (1998). Cognitive and educational outcome of very-low-birth-weight children in early adolescence. *Developmental Medicine and Child Neurology, 40*(10), 652–660.

Bouchard, K. E., Mesgarani, N., Johnson, K. & Chang, E. F. (2012) Functional organization of human sensorimotor cortex for speech articulation. *Nature, 495,* 327-332.

Bourgeois, K. S., Khawar, A. W., Neal, S. A., & Lockman, J. J. (2005). Infant manual exploration of objects, surfaces, and their interrelations. *Infancy, 8*(3), 233–252.

Bowerman, M. (1978). Systematizing semantic knowledge: Changes over time in the child's organization of word meaning. *Child Development, 49,* 977–987.

Bowlby, J. (1969). *Attachment and loss: Vol. 1. Attachment.* New York: Basic Books.

Bowlby, J. (1980). *Attachment and loss: Vol. 3. Loss, sadness and depression.* New York: Basic Books.

Bowman, M. C., & Saunders, D. M. (1994). Community attitudes to maternal age and pregnancy after assisted reproductive technology: Too old at 50 years? *Human Reproduction, 9,* 167–171.

Boyce, W. T., Schaefer, C., & Uitti, C. (1985). Permanence and change: Psychosocial factors in the outcome of adolescent pregnancy. *Social Science Medicine, 21*(11), 1279–1287.

Boyson-Bardies, B. (1994). Speech development: Contributions from cross-linguistic studies. In A. Vyt, H. Block, & M. Bornstein (Eds.), *Early child development in the French tradition: Contributions from current research* (pp. 191–206). Hillsdale, NJ: Erlbaum.

Bracewell, M., & Marlow, N. (2002). Patterns of motor disability in very preterm children. *Mental Retardation and Developmental Disabilities Research Reviews, 8*(4), 241–248.

Brackbill, Y. (1979). Obstetrical medication and infant behavior. In J. Osofsky (Ed.), *Handbook of infant development* (pp. 380–402). New York: Wiley.

Bradley, R. H., & Caldwell, B. M. (1976). The relation of infants' home environment to mental test performance at fifty-four months: A follow-up study. *Child Development, 47,* 1172–1173.

Bradley, R. H., & Caldwell, B. M. (1995). Caregiving and the regulation of childgrowth and development: Describing proximal aspects of caregiving systems. *Developmental Review, 15,* 38–85.

Bradley, R. H., Whiteside, L., Mundfrom, D. J., Casey, P. H., Kelleher, K. J., & Pope, S. K. (1994). Early indications of resilience and their relation to experiences in the home environments of low birthweight, premature children living in poverty. *Child Development,* 65, 346–360.

Braine, M. D. S. (1976). Children's first word combinations. *Monographs of the Society for Research in Child Development, 164* (Serial No. 164), pp. 1–104.

Brake, S. C., Fifer, W. P., Alfasi, G., & Fleischman, A. (1988). The first nutritive sucking response of premature newborns. *Infant Behavior and Development, 11,* 1–19.

Brand, R. J., Baldwin, D. A., & Ashburn, L. A. (2002). Evidence for 'motionese': Modifications in mothers' infant-directed action. *Developmental Science, 5*(1), 72–83.

Brand, R. J., & Shallcross, W. L. (2008). Infants prefer motionese to adult-directed action. *Developmental Science,11*(6), 853-861. doi:10.1111/j.1467-7687.2008.00734.x

Brand, R. J., Shallcross, W. L., Sabatos, M. G., & Massie, K. P. (2007). Fine-grained analysis of motionese: Eye gaze, object exchanges, and action units in infant-versus adult-directed action. *Infancy, 11*(2), 203–214.

Brannon, E. M., Lutz, D., & Cordes, S. (2006). The development of area discrimination and its implications for number representation in infancy. *Developmental Science, 9*(6), F59–F64.

Braun, J. (2009, October 6). Prenatal exposure to BPA might explain aggressive behavior in some 2-year-old girls. *ScienceDaily.* Retrieved April 24, 2012, from http://www.sciencedaily.com/releases/2009/10/091006114637.htm.

Bråten, S. (1998). Infant learning by altercentric participation: The reverse of egocentric observation in autism. In S. Br;araten (Ed.), *Intersubjective communication and emotion in early ontogeny. Studies in emotion and social interaction, 2nd series* (pp. 105–124). New York: Cambridge University Press.

Bråten, S. (2003). Participant Perception of Others' Acts: Virtual Otherness in Infants and Adults. *Culture & Psychology, 9*(3), 261–276.

Braun K. (2011) The prefrontal-limbic system: development, neuroanatomy, function, and implications for socioemotional development.*Clinics in Perinatology, 38,* 685-702.

Braungart-Rieker, J., Garwood, M. M., Powers, B. P., & Notaro, P. C. (1998). Infant affect and affect regulation during the still-face paradigm with mothers and fathers: The role of infant characteristics and parental sensitivity. *Developmental Psychology, 34*(6), 1428–1437.

Brauth, S. E., Hall, W. S., & Dooling, R. J. (Eds.) (1991). *Plasticity of development.* Cambridge, MA: MIT Press.

Brazelton, T. B. (1977). Implications of infant development among the Mayan Indians of Mexico. In P. H. Lieder-man, S. R. Tulkin, & A. Rosenfeld (Eds.), *Culture and infancy* (pp. 336–352). New York: Academic Press.

Brazelton, T. B., Koslowski, B., & Main, M. (1974). The origins of reciprocity. In M. Lewis & L. Rosenblum (Eds.), *The effect of the infant on its caregiver* (pp. 150–185). New York: Wiley.

Bremmer, J. (1978). Egocentric vs. allocentric spatial coding in nine-month-old infants: Factors influencing choice of code. *Developmental Psychology, 14,* 346–355.

Bremner, J. G., Johnson, S. P., Slater, A., Mason, U., Cheshire, A., & Spring, J. (2007). Conditions for young infants' failure to perceive trajectory continuity. *Developmental Science, 10*(5), 613–624.

Bremner, G., & Slater, A. (Eds.). (2004). *Theories of infant development.* Malden, MA: Blackwell Publishing, Ltd.

Brennan, P. A., Grekin, E. R., & Mednick, S. A. (1999). Maternal smoking during pregnancy and adult male criminal outcomes. *Archives of General Psychiatry, 56,* 215–219.

Bretherton, I. (1985). Attachment theory: Retrospect and prospect. *Monographs of the Society for Research in Child Development, 50* (Serial No. 209), 3–35.

Bretherton, I. (1987). New perspectives on attachment relations: Security, communication, and internal working models. In J. D. Osofsky (Ed.), *Handbook of infant development* (2nd ed., pp. 1061–1100). New York: Wiley.

Bretherton, I., Fritz, J., Zahn-Waxler, C., & Ridgeway, D. (1986). Learning to talk about emotions: A functionalist perspective. *Child Development, 57,* 529–548.

Bridges, L. J., & Connell, J. P. (1991). Consistency and inconsistency in infant emotional and social interactive behavior across contexts and caregivers. *Infant Behavior and Development, 14,* 471–487.

Bridges, L. J., Grolnick, W. S., & Connell, J. P. (1997). Infant emotion regulation with mothers and fathers. *Infant Behavior and Development, 20,* 47–57.

Brighi, A. (1997). Patterns of mother-infant interaction and contingency learning in full-term infants. *Early Development and Parenting, 6*(1), 37–45.

Bril, B., & Breniere, Y. (1993). Posture and independent locomotion in early childhood: Learning to walk or learning dynamic postural control? In G. J. P. Savelsbergh (Ed.), *The development of coordination in infancy* (pp. 337–358). Amsterdam: Elsevier.

Bril, B., & Sabatier, C. (1986). The cultural context of motor development: Postural manipulations in the daily life of Bambara babies (Mali). *International Journal of Behavioral Development, 9,* 439–453.

Broerse, J., & Elias, G. (1994). Changes in the content and timing of mothers' talk to infants. *British Journal of Developmental Psychology, 12,* 131–145.

Bronfenbrenner, U. (1979). *The ecology of human development: Experiments by nature and design.* Cambridge, MA: Harvard University Press.

Bronfenbrenner, U. (1986). Ecology of the family as a context for human development: Research perspectives. *Developmental Psychology, 22*(6), 723–742.

Bronfenbrenner, U. & Ceci, S. J. (1994). Nature-nurture reconceptualized in developmental perspective: a bioecological model. *Psychological Review, 101,* 568-86.

Bronson, G. W. (1972). Infants' reactions to unfamiliar persons and novel objects. *Monographs of the Society for Research in Child Development, 47* (Serial No. 148), 1–46.

Brook, A. (2001b). *From conception to crawling: Foundations for developmental movement.* www.anniebrook.com.

Brook, J. S., Zheng, L., Whiteman, M., & Brook, D. W. (2001). Aggression in toddlers: Associations with parenting and marital relations. *Journal of Genetic Psychology, 162*(2), 228–241.

Brooker, R. J., Neiderhiser, J. M., Kiel, E. J., Leve, L. D., Shaw, D. S., & Reiss, D. (2011). The association between infants' attention control and social inhibition is moderated by genetic and environmental risk for anxiety. *Infancy, 16*(5), 490-507. doi:10.1111/j.1532-7078.2011.00068.x

Brookhart, J., & Hock, E. (1976). The effects of experimental context and experiential background on infants' behavior toward their mothers and a stranger. *Child Development, 47,* 333–340.

Brooks, J., & Lewis, M. (1976). Infants' responses to strangers: Midget, adult, and child. *Child Development, 47,* 323–332.

Brooks-Gunn, J., & Furstenberg, F. (1986). Antecedents and consequences of parenting: The case of adolescent motherhood. In A. Fogel & G. F. Melson (Eds.), *Origins of nurturance: Developmental, biological, and cultural perspectives on caregiving* (pp. 166–185). Hillsdale, NJ: Erlbaum.

Brooks-Gunn, J., Han, W.-J., & Waldfogel, J. (2002). Maternal employment and child cognitive outcomes in the first three years of life: The NICHD study of early child care. *Child Development, 73*(4), 1052–1072.

Brooks-Gunn, J., Han, W., & Waldfogel, J. (2010). First-year maternal employment and child development in the first 7 years: Abstract. *Monographs Of The Society For Research In Child Development, 75*(2), vii-ix.

Brooks-Gunn, J., Klebanov, P. K., Liaw, F., & Spiker, D. (1993). Enhancing the development of low-birthweight, premature infants: Changes in cognition and behavior over the first three years. *Child Development, 64,* 736–753.

Brown, J. R., & Dunn, J. (1992). Talk with your mother or your sibling? Developmental changes in early family conversations about feelings. *Child Development, 63,* 336–349.

Brown, R. (1973). *A first language: The early stages.* Cambridge, MA: Harvard University Press.

Brown, R., Cazden, C., & Bellugi-Klima, V. (1969). The child's grammar from I to III. In J. P. Hill (Ed.), *Minnesota Symposium of Child Psychology* (Vol. 2). St. Paul: University of Minnesota Press.

Brownell, C. A. (1986). Convergent developments: Cognitive-developmental correlates of growth in infant/toddler peer skills. *Child Development, 57,* 275–286.

Brownell, C. A. (1988). Combinatorial skills: Converging developments over the second year. *Child Development, 59,* 675–685.

Brownell, C., Iesue, S., Nichols, S., & Svetlova, M. (2013). Mine or yours? Development of sharing in toddlers in relation to ownership understanding. *Child Development, 84*(3), 906-920.

Brownell, C. A., Nichols, S. R., Svetlova, M., Zerwas, S., & Ramani, G. (2010). The head bone's connected to the neck bone: When do toddlers represent their own body topography?. *Child Development, 81*(3), 797-810. doi:10.1111/j.1467-8624.2010.01434.x

Brownell, C. A., Ramani, G. B., & Zerwas, S. (2006). Becoming a Social Partner With Peers: Cooperation and Social Understanding in One- and Two-Year-Olds. *Child Development, 77*(4), 803–821.

Brownell, C. A., Svetlova, M., Anderson, R., Nichols, S. R., & Drummond, J. (2013). Socialization of early prosocial behavior: Parents' talk about emotions is associated with sharing and helping in toddlers. *Infancy, 18*(1), 91-119. doi:10.1111/j.1532-7078.2012.00125.x

Brownell, C. A., Svetlova, M., & Nichols, S. (2009). To share or not to share: When do toddlers respond to another's needs?. *Infancy, 14*(1), 117-130.

Brownell, C. A., Zerwas, S., & Ramani, G. B. (2007). 'So big': The development of body self-awareness in toddlers. *Child Development, 78*(5), 1426–1440.

Bruder, C. E., Piotrowski, A., Gijsbers, A. A., Andersson, R., Erickson, S., Diaz, de Ståhl, T.. . . Dumanski, J.P. (2008). Phenotypically concordant and discordant monozygotic twins display different DNA copy-number-variation profiles. *American Journal Of Human Genetics, 82,* 763-771

Bruner, J. (1983). *Child's talk: Learning to use language.* New York: Norton.

Brunner, D. P., Munch, M., Biedermann, K., Huch, R., Huch, A., & Borbely, A. A. (1994). Changes in sleep and sleep electroencephalogram during pregnancy. *Sleep, 17,* 576–582.

Bryne, J. M., & Horowitz, F. D. (1979). Rocking as a soothing intervention: The influence of direction and type of movement. *Infant Behavior and Development, 2,* 209–214.

Buehler, C., & O'Brien, M. (2011). Mothers' part-time employment: Associations with mother and family well-being. *Journal Of Family Psychology, 25*(6), 895-906.

Buehler, B. A., Rao, V., & Finnell, R. H. (1994). Biochemical and molecular teratology of fetal hydantoin syndrome. *Neurological Clinics, 12,* 741–748.

Bugental, D. B., & Happaney, K. (2004). Predicting Infant Maltreatment in Low-Income Families: The Interactive

Effects of Maternal Attributions and Child Status at Birth. *Developmental Psychology, 40*(2), 234–243.

Bugental, D. B., Martorell, G. A., & Barraza, V. (2003). The hormonal costs of subtle forms of infant maltreatment. *Horm Behav, 43*(1), 237–244.

Bugental, D., & Schwartz, A. (2009). A cognitive approach to child mistreatment prevention among medically at-risk infants. *Developmental Psychology, 45*(1), 284-288. doi:10.1037/a0014031

Bukatko, D., & Daehler, M. W. (1995). *Child development: A thematic approach* (2nd ed.). Boston: Houghton Mifflin.

Bullock, M., & Lutkenhaus, P. (1988). The development of volitional behavior in the toddler years. *Child Development, 59,* 664–674.

Burack, J. A., Shulman, C., Katzir, E., Schaap, T., Brennan, J. M., Iarocci, G., Wilansky, P., & Amir, N. (1999). Cognitive and behavioral development of Israeli males with fragile X and Down syndrome. *International Journal of Behavioral Development, 23*(2), 519–531.

Burchinal, M. R., Bryant, D. M., Lee, M. W., & Ramey, C. T. (1992). Early day care, infant-mother attachment, and maternal responsivenss in the infant's first year. *Early Childhood Research Quarterly, 7,* 383–396.

Burchinal, M. R., Campbell, F. A., Bryant, D. M., Wasik, B. H., & Ramey, C. T. (1997). Early intervention and mediating processes in cognitive performance children of low-income African American families. *Child Development, 68*(5), 935–954.

Burchinal, M. R., Roberts, J. E., Nabors, L. A., & Bryant, D. M. (1996). Quality of center child care and infant cognitive language development. *Child Development, 67,* 606–620.

Burney, R., & Leerkes, E. (2010). Links between mothers' and fathers' perceptions of infant temperament and coparenting. *Infant Behavior & Development, 33*(2), 125-135. doi:10.1016/j.infbeh.2009.12.002

Bushnell, E. W., & Boudreau, J. P. (1993). Motor development and the mind: The potential role of motor abilities as a determinant of aspects of perceptual development. *Child Development, 64,* 1005–1021.

Buss, A. H., & Plomin, R. (1984). *Temperament: Early developing personality traits.* Hillsdale, NJ: Erlbaum.

Buss, K. A. (2011). Which fearful toddlers should we worry about? Context, fear regulation, and anxiety risk. *Developmental Psychology, 47*(3), 804-819.

Buss, K. A., & Goldsmith, H. H. (1998). Fear and anger regulation in infancy: Effects on the temporal dynamics of affective expression. *Child Development, 69*(2), 359–374.

Buss, K. A., & Kiel, E. J. (2004). Comparison of Sadness, Anger, and Fear Facial Expressions When Toddlers Look at Their Mothers. *Child Development, 75*(6), 1761–1773.

Butler, J., Floccia, C., Goslin, J., & Panneton, R. (2011). Infants' discrimination of familiar and unfamiliar accents in speech. *Infancy, 16*(4), 392-417. doi:10.1111/j.1532-7078.2010.00050.x

Butler, J., & Rovee-Collier, C. (1989). Contextual gating of memory retrieval. *Developmental Psychobiology, 22,* 533–552.

Butterfield, J., & Covey, M. (1962). Letter to the Editor: Practical epigram of the Apgar Score. *Journal of the American Medical Association, 181,* 353.

Butterworth, G. (1977). Object disappearance and error in Piaget's stage IV task. *Journal of Experimental Child Psychology, 23,* 391–401.

Butterworth, G. (1990). Self-perception in infancy. In D. Cicchetti & M. Beeghly (Eds.), *The self in transition: Infancy to childhood* (pp. 119–137). Chicago: University of Chicago Press.

Butterworth, G. (1993). Dynamic approaches to infant perception and action: Old and new theories about the origins of knowledge. In L. B. Smith & E. Thelen (Eds.), *A dynamic systems approach to development: Applications. MIT Press/Bradford Books series in cognitive psychology* (pp. 171–187). Cambridge, MA: MIT Press.

Butterworth, G. (2000). Joint visual attention in infancy. In J. G. Bremner & A. Fogel (Eds.), *Handbook of infancy research* (pp. 221–239). Oxford, England: Blackwell.

Butterworth, G., & Cochran, E. (1980). Towards a mechanism of joint visual attention in human infancy. *International Journal of Behavioral Development, 3,* 253–272.

Butterworth, G. & Hopkins, B. (1993). Origins of handedness. *Developmental Medicine and Child Neurology, 35,* 177–184.

Bystrova, K., Ivanova, V., Edhborg, M., Matthiesen,A.S., Ransjö-Arvidson, A. B.,; Mukhamedrakhimov, R., Widström A-M.. (2009). Early contact versus separation: Effects on mother—Infant interaction one year later. *Birth: Issues in Perinatal Care, 36,* 97-109.

Cabrera, N. J., Shannon, J. D., West, J., & Brooks-Gunn, J. (2006). Parental Interactions With Latino Infants: Variation by Country of Origin and English Proficiency. *Child Development, 77*(5), 1190–1207.

Cairns, R. (1979). *Social development: The origins and plasticity of interchanges.* San Francisco: W. H. Freeman.

Caldera, Y. M., & Hart, S. (2004). Exposure to Child Care, Parenting Style and Attachment Security. *Infant and Child Development, 13*(1), 21–33.

Caldera, Y. M., Huston, A. C., & O'Brien, M. (1989). Social interactions and play patterns of parents and toddlers with feminine, masculine, and neutral toys. *Child Development, 60,* 70–76.

Calhoun, M. L., Rose, T. L., Hanft, B., & Sturkey, C. (1991). Social reciprocity interventions: Implications for developmental therapists. Physical and Occupational Therapy in *Pediatrics, 11,* 45–56.

Calkins, S., & Fox, N. A. (1994). Individual differences in the biological aspects of temperament. In J. E. Bates & T.

D. Wachs (Eds.), *Temperament: Individual differences at the interface of biology and behavior* (pp. 199–217). Washington, DC: American Psychological Association.

Calkins, S. D. (2002). Does aversive behavior during toddlerhood matter?: The effects of difficult temperament on maternal perceptions and behavior. *Infant Mental Health Journal, 23*(4), 381–402.

Calkins, S. D., Fox, N. A., & Marshall, T. R. (1996). Behavioral and physiological antecedents of inhibited and uninhibited behavior. *Child Development, 67,* 523–540.

Calkins, S. D., Gill, K. L., Johnson, M. C., & Smith, C. L. (1999). Emotional reactivity and emotional regulation strategies as predictors of social behavior with peers during toddlerhood. *Social Development, 8*(3), 310–334.

Calkins, S. D., & Johnson, M. C. (1998). Toddler regulation of distress to frustrating events: Temperamental and maternal correlates. *Infant Behavior and Development, 21*(3), 379–395.

Calkins, S. D., Smith, C. L., Gill, K. L., & Johnson, M. C. (1998). Maternal interactive style across contexts: Relations to emotional, behavioral, and physiological regulation during toddlerhood. *Social Development, 7*(3), 350–369.

Callaghan, J. W. (1981). A comparison of Anglo, Hopi, and Navajo mothers and infants. In T. M. Field, A. M. Sostek, P. Vietze, & P. H. Leiderman (Eds.), *Culture and early interactions* (pp. 503–536). Hillsdale, NJ: Erlbaum.

Callaghan, T. C. (1999). Early understanding and production of graphic symbols. *Child Development, 70*(6), 1314–1324.

Camaioni, L. (200). Early language. In J. G. Bremner & A. Fogel (Eds.), *Handbook of infant development* (pp. 605–635). Oxford, England: Blackwell.

Camaioni, L., Aureli, T., Bellagamba, F., & Fogel, A. (1999). *The transition from conventional to symbolic shared reference in mother-infant communication.* Paper presented at the 9th European Conference on Developmental Psychology.

Camaioni, L., Aureli, T., Bellagamba, F., & Fogel, A. (2003). A longitudinal examination of the transition to symbolic communication in the second year of life. *Infant and Child Development, 12*(1), 1–26.

Camaioni, L., Baumgartner, E., & Perucchini, P. (1991). Content and structure in toddlers' social competence with peers from 12 to 36 months of age. *Early Child Development and Care, 67,* 17–27.

Camaioni, L., Perucchini, P., Muratori, F. & Milone, A. (1997). A longitudinal examination of the communicative gestures deficit in young children with autism. *Journal of Autism and Developmental Disorders, 27,* 715–725.

Campbell, D. W., & Eaton, W. O. (1999). Sex differences in the activity level of infants. *Infant and Child Development, 8*(1), 1–17.

Campbell, M. K., & Mottola, M. F. (2001). Recreational exercise and occupational activity during pregnancy and birth weight: a case-control study. *Am J Obstet Gynecol, 184*(3), 403–408.

Campos, J. J. (1976). Heart rate: A sensitive tool for the study of emotional development in the infant. In L. P. Lipsitt (Ed.), *Developmental psychobiology: The significance of infancy* (pp. 405–426). Hillsdale, NJ: Erlbaum.

Campos, J. J., & Barrett, K. C. (1984). Toward a new understanding of emotions and their development. In C. E. Izard, J. Kagan, & R. B. Zajonc (Eds.), *Emotions, cognition, and behavior* (pp. 229–263). New York: Cambridge University Press.

Campos, J. J., Campos, R., & Barrett, K. (1989). Emergent themes in the study of emotional development and emotion regulation. *Developmental Psychology, 25*(3), 394–402.

Campos, J. J., Emde, R. N., Gaensbauer, T., & Henderson, C. (1975). Cardiac and behavioral interrelationships in the reactions of infants to strangers. *Developmental Psychology, 11,* 589–601.

Campos, J. J., Langer, A., & Krowitz, A. (1970). Cardiac responses on the visual cliff in prelocomotor human infants. *Science, 170,* 196–197.

Campos, R. G. (1989). Soothing pain-elicited distress in infants with swaddling and pacifiers. *Child Development, 60,* 781–792.

Camras, L. A. (1993). A dynamic systems perspective on expressive development. In K. Strongman (Ed.), *International review of studies on emotion* (pp. 210–224). New York: Wiley.

Canfield, R. L., & Haith, M. M. (1991). Young infants' visual expectations for symmetric and asymmetric stimulus sequences. *Developmental Psychology, 27,* 198–208.

Caplan, M., Vespo, J., Pedersen, J., & Hay, D. F. (1991). Conflict and its resolution in small groups of one- and two-year-olds. *Child Development, 62,* 1513–1524.

Capra, F. (1996). *The web of life.* New York: Anchor Books.

Cardinal, T. M., & Lumeng, J. C. (2007). Too much tube time? Television viewing and childhood obesity. *Zero to Three, 28*(1), 31–36.

Carlile, K. S., & Holstrum, W. J. (1989). Parental involvement behaviors: A comparison of Chamorro and Caucasian parents. *Infant Behavior and Development, 12,* 479–494.

Carlson, E. A. (1998). A prospective longitudinal study of attachment disorganization/disorientation. *Child Development, 69*(4), 1107–1128.

Carlson, S. M., Mandell, D. J., & Williams, L. (2004). Executive Function and Theory of Mind: Stability and Prediction From Ages 2 to 3. *Developmental Psychology, 40*(6), 1105–1122.

Carlson, V., Cicchetti, D., Barnett, D., & Braunwald, K. (1989). Disorganized/disoriented attachment relationships in maltreated infants. *Developmental Psychology, 25,* 525–531.

Carmen, R. del, Pedersen, F. A., Huffman, L. C., & Bryan, Y. E. (1993). Dyadic distress management predicts subsequent security of attachment. *Infant Behavior and Development, 16,* 131–147.

Caron, A. J., Caron, R. F., & Antell, S. E. (1988). Infant understanding of containment: An affordance perceived or a relationship conceived? *Developmental Psychology, 24,* 620–627.

Caron, A. J., Caron, R. F., & MacLean, D. J. (1988). Infant discrimination of naturalistic emotional expressions: The role of face and voice. *Child Development, 59,* 604–616.

Caron, R. F., Caron, A. J., & Myers, R. S. (1982). Abstraction of invariant face expressions in infancy. *Child Development, 53,* 1008–1015.

Carpenter, M., Akhtar, N., & Tomasello, M. (1998). Fourteen- through 18–month-old infants differentially imitate intentional and accidental actions. *Infant Behavior and Development, 21*(2), 315–330.

Carpenter, M., Call, J., & Tomasello, M. (2005). Twelve- and 18–month-olds copy actions in terms of goals. *Developmental Science, 8*(1), F13–F20.

Carpenter, M., Nagell, K., & Tomasello, M. (1998). Social cognition, joint attention, and communicative competence from 9 to 15 months of age. *Monographs of the Society for Research in Child Development, 63*(4), 1–176.

Carpenter, M., Tomasello, M., & Striano, T. (2005). Role reversal imitation and language in typically developing infants and children with autism. *Infancy, 8*(3), 253–278.

Carrico, R., & Berthier, N. (2008). Vision and precision reaching in 15-month-old infants. *Infant Behavior & Development, 31*(1), 62-70.

Carson, C. P., Klee, T., Carson, D. K., & Hime, L. K. (2003). Phonological profiles of 2–year-olds with delayed language development: predicting clinical outcomes at age 3. *Am J Speech Lang Pathol, 12*(1), 28–39.

Caruso, D. A. (1993). Dimensions of quality in infants' exploratory behavior: Relationships to problem-solving ability. *Infant Behavior and Development, 16,* 441–454.

Caselli, M., Rinaldi, P., Stefanini, S., & Volterra, V. (2012). Early action and gesture "Vocabulary" and its relation with word comprehension and production. *Child Development, 83*(2), 526-542.

Caspi, A., & Silva, P. A. (1995). Temperamental qualities at age three predict personality traits in young adulthood: Longitudinal evidence from birth cohort. *Child Development, 66,* 486–498.

Cassidy, J. (1994). Emotion regulation: Influences of attachment relationships. *Monographs of the Society for Research in Child Development, 59,* 228–249.

Cassidy, J., & Berlin, L. J. (1994). The insecure/ambivalent pattern of attachment: Theory and research. *Child Development, 65,* 971–991.

Cassidy, J. W., & Standley, J. M. (1995). The effect of music listening on physiological responses of premature infants in the NICU. *Journal of Music Therapy, 32*(4), 208–227.

Catherwood, D. (1993). The robustness of infant haptic memory: Testing its capacity to withstand delay and haptic interference. *Child Development, 64,* 702–710.

Catling-Paull, C., Johnston, R., Ryan, C., Foureur, M. J. & Homer, C. S. (2011). Clinical interventions that increase the uptake and success of vaginal birth after caesarean section: a systematic review. *Journal Of Advanced Nursing, 67,*1646-1661.

Caudill, W., & Weinstein, H. (1969). Maternal care and infant behavior in Japan and America. *Psychiatry, 32,* 12–43.

Caughy, M. O., DiPietro, J. A., & Strobino, D. M. (1994). Daycare participation as a protective factor in the cognitive development of low-income children. *Child Development, 65,* 457–471.

Cecchini, M., Baroni, El., Di Vito, C., & Lai, C. (2011). Smiling in newborns during communicative wake and active sleep. *Infant Behavior & Development, 34,* 417-423.

Centers for Disease Control (1995, June). Recommended childhood immunization schedule—United States, 1995. *Morbidity and Mortality Weekly Report, 44, no. RR-5,* 1–8.

Centers for Disease Control and Prevention (CDC), (2001, January 12). Recommended childhood immunization schedule–United States, 2001. *Morbidity and Mortality Weekly Report, 50*(01). 7–10, 19.

Cernoch, J. M., & Porter, R. H. (1985). Recognition of maternal axillary odors by infants. *Child Development, 56,* 1593–1598.

Cervantes, C. A., & Callanan, M. A. (1998). Labels and explanations in mother-child emotion talk: Age and gender differentiation. *Developmental Psychology, 34*(1), 88–98.

Chabrol, H., Walburg, V., Teissedre, F., Armitage, J., & Santrisse, K. (2004). Influence of mother's perceptions on the choice to breastfeed or bottle-feed: Perceptions and feeding choice. *Journal of Reproductive and Infant Psychology, 22*(3), 189–198.

Chandler, M., Fritz, A. S., & Hala, S. (1989). Small-scale deceit: Deception as a marker of two-, three-, and four-year-olds' early theories of mind. *Child Development, 60,* 1263–1277.

Chang, L., Smith, L. M., LoPresti, C., Yonekura, M. L., Kuo, J., Walot, I., et al. (2004). Smaller subcortical volumes and cognitive deficits in children with prenatal methamphetamine exposure. *Psychiatry Research: Neuroimaging, 132*(2), 95–106.

Chaplin, T., & Aldao, A. (2013). Gender differences in emotion expression in children: a meta-analytic review. *Psychological Bulletin, 139*(4), 735-765.

Charman, T., Swettenham, J., Baron-Cohen, S., Cox, A., Baird, G., & Drew, A. (1997). Infants with autism: An investigation of empathy, pretend play, joint attention, and imitation. *Developmental Psychology, 33*(5), 781–789.

Chase-Lansdale, P. L., & Owen, M. T. (1987). Maternal employment in a family context: Effects on infant-mother and infant-father attachments. *Child Development, 58,* 1505–1512.

Chasiotis, A., Kiessling, F., Winter, V., & Hofer, J. (2006). Sensory motor inhibition as a prerequisite for theory-of-mind: A comparison of clinical and normal preschoolers differing in sensory motor abilities. *International Journal of Behavioral Development, 30*(2), 178–190.

Chatoor, I., Ganiban, J., Colin, V., Plummer, N., & Harmon, R. J. (1998). Attachment and feeding problems: a reexamination of nonorganic failure to thrive and attachment insecurity. *J Am Acad Child Adolesc Psychiatry, 37*(11), 1217–1224.

Chen, L., Metcalfe, J., Jeka, J., & Clark, J. (2007). Two steps forward and one back: Learning to walk affects infants' sitting posture. *Infant Behavior & Development, 30*(1), 16-25.

Chen, X., Chen, H., Li, D., & Wang, L. (2009). Early childhood behavioral inhibition and social and school adjustment in chinese children: a 5-year longitudinal study. *Child Development, 80*(6), 1692-1704

Chen, Y., Keen, R., Rosander, K., & von Hofsten, C. (2010). Movement planning reflects skill level and age changes in toddlers. *Child Development, 81*(6), 1846-1858. doi:10.1111/j.1467-8624.2010.01514.x

Chen, Z., & Sanchez, R. P., & Campbell, T. (1997). From beyond to within their grasp: The rudiments of analogical problem solving in 10– to 13–month-olds. *Developmental Psychology, 33*(5), 790–801.

Cherlin, A. J., & Furstenberg, F. F., Jr. (1986). *The new American grandparent.* New York: Basic Books.

Cherney, I. D. (2003). Young children's spontaneous utterances of mental terms and the accuracy of their memory behaviors: A different methodological approach. *Infant and Child Development, 12*(1), 89–105.

Chin-Quee, D. S., & Scarr, S. (1994). Lack of early child care effects on school-age children's social competence and academic achievement. *Early Development and Parenting, 3,* 103–112.

Chisholm, J. S. (1983). *Navajo infancy: An ethological study of child development.* New York: Aldine.

Chisholm, K. (1998). A three year follow-up of attachment and indiscriminate friendliness in children adopted from Romanian orphanages. *Child Development, 69*(4), 1092–1106.

Chomitz, V. R., Cheung, L. W. Y., & Liebermann, E. (1995). The role of lifestyle in preventing low birth weight. *The Future of Children, 5,* 121–138.

Chomsky, N. (1975). *Reflections on language.* New York: Pantheon.

Chouinard, M. M. (2007). Children's questions: A mechanism for cognitive development. *Monographs of the Society for Research in Child Development, 72*(1, Serial No. 286).

Christakis, D. A., Zimmerman, F. J., DiGiuseppe, D. L., & McCarty, C. A. (2004). Early television exposure and subsequent attentional problems in children. *Pediatrics, 113*(4), 708–713.

Christensen, H., Poyser, C., Pollitt, P., & Cubis, J. (1999). Pregnancy may confer a selective cognitive advantage. *Journal of Reproductive and Infant Psychology, 17*(1), 7–25.

Chubet, C. T. (1988). *Feeding your baby: Breast, bottle, and baby foods.* Stamford, CT: Longmeadow Press.

Cicchetti, D., & Mans, L. (1976, September). *Down's syndrome and normal infants' responses to impending collision.* Paper presented at the meeting of the American Psychological Association, Washington, DC.

Cicchetti, D., Rogosch, F. A., Gunnar, M. R., & Toth, S. L. (2010). The dfferential impacts of early physical and sexual abuse and internalizing problems on daytime cortisol rhythm in school-aged children. *Child Development, 81*(1), 252-269.

Cicchetti, D., Rogosch, F. A., Howe, M. L., & Toth, S. L. (2010). The effects of maltreatment and neuroendocrine regulation on memory performance. *Child Development, 81*(5), 1504-1519. doi:10.1111/j.1467-8624.2010.01488.x

Clapp, J. F., 3rd, Kim, H., Burciu, B., Schmidt, S., Petry, K., & Lopez, B. (2002). Continuing regular exercise during pregnancy: effect of exercise volume on fetoplacental growth. *Am J Obstet Gynecol, 186*(1), 142–147.

Clarici, A., Clarici, A., Travan, L., Accardo, A., De Vonderweid, U., & Bava, A. (2002). Crying of a newborn child: Alarm signal or protocommunication? *Perceptual and Motor Skills, 95*(3, Pt 1), 752–754.

Clark, E. V. (1978). Strategies for communicating. *Child Development, 49,* 953–959.

Clark, H. H., & Clark, E. V. (1977). *Psychology and language: An introduction to psycholinguistics.* New York: Harcourt Brace Jovanovich.

Clark, J. E., Truly, T. L., & Phillips, S. J. (1993). On the development of walking as a limit-cycle system. In L. B. Smith & E. Thelen (Eds.), *A dynamic systems approach to development: Applications* (pp. 71–93). Cambridge, MA: MIT Press.

Clark, J. E., Whitall, J., & Phillips, S. J. (1988). Human interlimb coordination: The first 6 months of independent walking. *Developmental Psychobiology, 21,* 445–456.

Clark, R., Hyde, J. S., Essex, M. J., & Klein, M. H. (1997). Length of maternity leave and quality of mother-infant interactions. *Child Development, 68*(2), 364–383.

Clarke, S. & Taffel, S. (1995). Changes in cesarean delivery in the United States, 1988 and 1993. *Birth, 22,* 63–67.

Clarke-Stewart, A. (1978). And daddy makes three: The father's impact on mother and young child. *Child Development, 44,* 466–478.

Clarke-Stewart, A. (1984). Day care: A new context for research and development. In M. Perlmutter (Ed.), *Minnesota symposia on child psychology* (Vol. 17, pp. 1015–1034). Hillsdale, NJ: Erlbaum.

Clarke-Stewart, K. A. (1998). Historical shifts and underlying themes in ideas about rearing young children in the United States: Where have we been? Where are we going? *Early Development and Parenting, 7,* 101–117.

Claxton, L., McCarty, M., & Keen, R. (2009). Self-directed action affects planning in tool-use tasks with toddlers. *Infant Behavior & Development, 32*(2), 230-233.

Clearfield, M. W. (2004). The role of crawling and walking experience in infant spatial memory. *Journal of Experimental Child Psychology, 89*(3), 214–241.

Clearfield, M. (2011). Learning to walk changes infants' social interactions. *Infant Behavior & Development, 34*(1), 15-25.

Clements, M., & Barnett, D. (2002). Parenting and attachment among toddlers with congenital anomalies: Examining the strange situation and attachment Q-sort. *Infant Mental Health Journal, 23*(6), 625–642.

Clifton, R. K., Perris, E., & Bullinger, A. (1991). Infants' perception of auditory space. *Developmental Psychology, 27,* 187–197.

Clifton, R. K., Rochat, P., Litovsky, R. Y., & Perris, E. E. (1991). Object representation guides infants' reaching in the dark. *Journal of Experimental Psychology: Human Perception and Performance, 17,* 323–329.

Clifton, R. K., Rochat, P., Robin, D. J., & Berthier, N. E. (1994). Multimodal perception in the control of infant reaching. *Journal of Experimental Psychology: Human Perception and Performance, 20,* 876–886.

Cnattingius, S. (2004). The epidemiology of smoking during pregnancy: Smoking prevalence, maternal characteristics, and pregnancy outcomes. *Nicotine & Tobacco Research, 6*(2) S125–S140.

Coale, A. J., & Banister, J. (1994). Five decades of missing females in China. *Demography, 31,* 459–479.

Cofer, L. F. (2008). Dynamic views of education. In A. Fogel, B. J. King, & S. Shanker (Eds.). *Human development in the 21st century: Visionary policy ideas from systems scientists.* Cambridge, UK: Cambridge University Press.

Cofer, L. F., Grice, J. W., Sethre-Hofstad, L., Radi, C. J., Zimmerman, L. K., Palmer-Seal, D., & Santa-Maria, G. (1999). Developmental perspectives on morningness-eveningness and social interactions. *Human Development, 42,* 169–198.

Cogswell, M. E., Serdula, M. K., Hungerford, D. W., & Yip, R. (1995). Gestational weight gain among average-weight and overweight women: What is excessive? *American Journal of Obstetrics and Gynecology, 172,* 705–712.

Cohen, L., Zilkha, S., Middleton, J., & O'Donnohue, N. (1978). Perinatal mortality: Assisting parental affirmation. *American Journal of Orthopsychiatry, 48,* 727–731.

Cohen, L. B., DeLoache, J. S., & Strauss, M. S. (1979). Infant visual perception. In J. Osofsky (Ed.), *Handbook of infant development* (pp. 419–435). New York: Wiley.

Cohen, L. B., & Oakes, L. M. (1993). How infants perceive a simple causal event. *Developmental Psychology, 29,* 421–433.

Cohen, L. B., & Strauss, M. S. (1979). Concept acquisition in the human infant. *Child Development, 50,* 419–424.

Cohen, M., Brown, D. R., & Myers, M. M. (2001). Cardiovascular responses to pacifier experience and feeding in newborn infants. *Developmental Psychobiology, 39*(1), 34–39.

Cohen, N. L., & Tomlinson-Keasey, C. (1980). The effects of peers and mothers on toddlers' play. *Child Development, 51,* 921–924.

Cohen, P., Kasen, S., Brook, J. S., & Hartmark, C. (1998). Behavior patterns of young children and their offspring: A two-generation study. *Developmental Psychology, 34*(6), 1202–1208.

Cohen, R. (1981). Factors influencing maternal choice of childbirth alternatives. *Journal of the American Academy of Child Psychiatry, 20,* 1–15.

Cohn, J. F., Campbell, S. B., Matias, R., & Hopkins, J. (1990). Face-to-face interactions of postpartum depressed and nondepressed mother-infant pairs at 2 months. *Developmental Psychology, 26*(1), 15–23.

Cohn, J. F., Matias, R., Tronick, E. Z., Lyons-Ruth, K., & Connell, D. (1986). Face-to-face interactions, spontaneous and structured, of mothers with depressive symptoms. In T. Field & E. Z. Tronick (Eds.), *Maternal depression and child development, New directions for child development* (pp. 31–46). San Francisco: Jossey-Bass.

Cohn, J. F., & Tronick, E. Z. (1983). Three-month-old infants' reaction to simulated maternal depression. *Child Development, 54,* 185–193.

Cohn, J. F., & Tronick, E. Z. (1988). Mother-infant face-to-face interaction: Influence in bidirectional and unrelated to periodic cycles in either partner's behavior. *Developmental Psychology, 24*(3), 386–392.

Coldren, J. T., & Colombo, J. (1994). The nature and processes of preverbal learning: Implications from nine-month-old infants' discrimination problem solving. *Monographs of the Society for Research in Child Development, 59,* 1–94.

Cole, P. M., Barrett, K. C., & Zahn-Waxler, C. (1992). Emotion displays in two-year-olds during mishaps. *Child Development, 63,* 314–324.

Cole, P. M., Luby, J., & Sullivan, M. W. (2008). Emotions and the development of childhood depression: Bridging the gap. *Child Development Perspectives, 2*(3), 141-148. doi:10.1111/j.1750-8606.2008.00056.x

Cole, P. M., Tan, P. Z., Hall, S. E., Zhang, Y., Crnic, K. A., Blair, C. B., & Li, R. (2011). Developmental Changes in Anger Expression and Attention Focus: Learning to Wait. *Developmental Psychology, 47*(4), 1078-1089.

Coleman, J. M., Pratt, R. R., Stoddard, R. A., Gerstmann, D. R., & Abel, H. H. (1997). The effects of the male and female singing and speaking voices on selected physiological and behavioral measures of premature infants in the intensive care unit. *International Journal of Arts Medicine, 5*(2), 4–11.

Coleman-Phox, K., Odouli, R., ; Li, D., (2008). Use of a Fan During Sleep and the Risk of Sudden Infant Death Syndrome, *Arch Pediatr Adolesc Med., 162(*10):963–968. doi:10.1001/archpedi.162.10.963.

Colman, R. A., & Widom, C. S. (2004). Childhood abuse and neglect and adult intimate relationships: A prospective study. *Child Abuse & Neglect, 28*(11), 1133–1151.

Coley, R. L., & Chase-Lansdale, P. L. (1998). Adolescent pregnancy and parenthood: Recent evidence and future directions. *American Psychologist, 53*(2), 152–166.

Coley, R., & Lombardi, C. (2013). Does maternal employment following childbirth support or inhibit low-income children's long-term development?. *Child Development, 84*(1), 178-197.

Coll, C. T. G., Halpern, L. F., Vohr, B. R., Seifer, R., & Oh, W. (1992). Stability and correlates of change of early temperament in preterm and full-term infants. *Infant Behavior and Development, 15,* 137–153.

Colletta, N. D., & Lee, D. (1983). The impact of support for black adolescent mothers. *Journal of Family Issues, 4,* 127–143.

Collins, J. E. (1994). Fetal surgery: Changing the outcome before birth. *Journal of Obstetrics, Gynecology & Neonatal Nursing, 23,* 166–169.

Colombo, J., Frick, J. E., Ryther, J. S., Coldren, J. T., & Mitchell, D. W. (1995). *Merrill-Palmer Quarterly, 41,* 104–113.

Colombo, J., Mitchell, D. W., O'Brien, M., & Horowitz, F. D. (1987). The stability of visual habituation during the first year of life. *Child Development, 58,* 474–487.

Colonnesi, C., Bögels, S. M., de Vente, W., & Majdandžić, M. (2013). What coy smiles say about positive shyness in early infancy. *Infancy, 18*(2), 202-220. doi:10.1111/j.1532-7078.2012.00117.x

Committee on Nutrition, American Academy of Pediatrics. (1998). *Pediatric nutrition handbook* (4th ed.). Elk Grove Village, IL: American Academy of Pediatrics.

Connell, J. P. (1985). A component process approach to the study of individual differences and developmental change in attachment system functioning. In M. E. Lamb, R. A. Thompson, W. Gardner, & E. L. Charnov, (Eds.), *Infant-mother attachment* (pp. 223–247). Hillsdale, NJ: Erlbaum.

Conner, J. M., & Nelson, E. C. (1999). Neonatal intensive care: Satisfaction measured from a parent's perspective. *Pediatrics, 103,* 336–349.

Connolly, K., & Dalgleish, M. (1989). The emergence of a tool-using skill in infancy. *Developmental Psychology, 25,* 894–912.

Connolly, M. E. & Tracewell, R.(2012). Breastfeeding and obesity.*Bariatric Nursing and Surgical Patient Care, 7, 132-135.* doi:10.1089/bar.2012.9967.

Conrad, R. (1998). Darwin's baby and baby's Darwin: Mutual recognition in observational research. *Human Development, 41*(1), 47–64.

Conrad, R. (2004). '[A]s if she defied the world in her joyousness': Rereading Darwin on emotion and emotional development. *Human Development, 47*(1), 40–65.

Conradt, E., & Ablow, J. (2010). Infant physiological response to the still-face paradigm: contributions of maternal sensitivity and infants' early regulatory behavior. *Infant Behavior & Development, 33*(3), 251-265. doi:10.1016/j.infbeh.2010.01.001

Cooper, R. P., Abraham, J., Berman, S., & Staska, M. (1997). The development of infants' preference for motherese. *Infant Behavior and Development, 20*(4), 477–488.

Cooper, R. P., & Aslin, R. N. (1994). Developmental differences in infant attention to the spectral properties of infant-directed speech. *Child Development, 65,* 1663–1677.

Coplan, R., Findlay, L. C., & Schneider, B. H. (2010). Where do anxious children "fit" best? Childcare and the emergence of anxiety in early childhood. *Canadian Journal Of Behavioural Science/Revue Canadienne Des Sciences Du Comportement, 42*(3), 185-193.

Copstick, S., Taylor, K., Hayes, R., & Morris, N. (1986). The relation of time of day to childbirth. *Journal of Reproductive and Infant Psychology, 4*(1–2), 13–22.

Corbetta, D., & Snapp-Childs, W. (2009). Seeing and touching: the role of sensory-motor experience on the development of infant reaching. *Infant Behavior & Development, 32*(1), 44-58. doi:10.1016/j.infbeh.2008.10.004

Corkum, V., & Moore, C. (1995). Development of joint visual attention in infants. In C. Moore & P. J. Dunham (Eds.), *Joint attention: Its origins and role in development* (pp. 61–83). Hillsdale, NJ: Erlbaum.

Corter, C. (1977). Brief separation and communication between infant and mother. In T. Alloway, P. Pliner, & L. Krames (Eds.), *Attachment behavior* (pp. 143–168). New York: Plenum Press.

Corter, C., Abramovitch, R., & Pepler, D. J. (1983). The role of the mother in sibling interaction. *Child Development, 54,* 1599–1605.

Cossette, L., Malcuit, G., & Pomerleau, A. (1991). Sex differences in motor activity during early infancy. *Infant Behavior and Development, 14,* 175–186.

Costa, R., & Figueiredo, B. (2011). Infant's psychophysiological profile and temperament at 3 and 12 months. *Infant Behavior & Development, 34*(2), 270-279

Coster, W. J., Gersten, M. S., Beeghly, M., & Cicchetti, D. (1989). Communicative functioning in maltreated toddlers. *Developmental Psychology, 25*(6), 1020–1029.

Cottrell, B. H., & Shannahan, M. K. (1987). A comparison of fetal outcome in birth chair and delivery table births. *Research in Nursing and Health, 10,* 239–243.

Countermine, M. S., & Teti, D. M. (2010). Sleep arrangements and maternal adaptation in infancy. *Infant Mental Health Journal, 31,* 647-663.

Courage, M. L., Edison, S. C., & Howe, M. L. (2004). Variability in the early development of visual self-recognition. *Infant Behavior & Development, 27*(4), 509–532.

Courage, M. L., & Howe, M. L. (2010). To watch or not to watch: Infants and toddlers in a brave new electronic world. *Developmental Review, 30*(2), 101-115.

Courage, M. L., & Setliff, A. E. (2009). Debating the impact of television and video material on very young children: Attention, learning, and the developing brain. *Child Development Perspectives, 3*(1), 72-78. doi:10.1111/j.1750-8606.2008.00080.x

Courchesne, E. (2004). Brain development in autism: Early overgrowth followed by premature arrest of growth. *Mental Retardation and Developmental Disabilities Research Reviews, 10*(2), 106–111.

Cowan, C. P., & Cowan, P. A. (1981). *Couple role arrangements and satisfaction during family formation.* Boston: Society for Research in Child Development.

Cox, M. C., Owen, M. T., Henderson, V. K., & Margand, N. A. (1992). Prediction of infant-father and infant-mother attachment. *Developmental Psychology, 28,* 474–483.

Crain-Thoreson, C., & Dale, P. (1992). Do early talkers become early readers? Linguistic precocity, preschool language, and emergent literacy. *Developmental Psychology, 28,* 421–429.

Crais, E., Douglas, D. D., & Campbell, C. C. (2004). The intersection of the development of gestures and intentionality. *J Speech Lang Hear Res, 47*(3), 678–694.

Craton, L. G. (1996). The development of perceptual completion abilities: Infants' perception of stationary, partially occluded objects. *Child Development, 67*(3), 890–904.

Crockenberg, S. B. (1981). Infant irritability, mother responsiveness, and social support influences on the security of infant-mother attachment. *Child Development, 52,* 857–865.

Crockenberg, S. B., & Acredolo, C. (1983). Infant temperament ratings: A function of infants, of mothers, or both? *Infant Behavior and Development, 6,* 61–72.

Crockenberg, S. B., & Smith, P. (1982). Antecedents of mother-infant interaction and infant irritability in the first three months of life. *Infant Behavior and Development, 6,* 61–72.

Crockenberg, S. C., & Leerkes, E. M. (2004). Infant and Maternal Behaviors Regulate Infant Reactivity to Novelty at 6 Months. *Developmental Psychology, 40*(6), 1123–1132.

Crockenberg, S., Leerkes, E., & Lekka, S. (2007). Pathways from marital aggression to infant emotion regulation: the development of withdrawal in infancy. *Infant Behavior & Development, 30*(1), 97-113.

Cronin, C. M. G., Shapiro, C. R., Casiro, O. G., & Cheang, M. S. (1995). The impact of very low-birth-weight infants on the family is long lasting. *Archives of the Pediatric and Adolescent Medicine, 149,* 151–158.

Crook, C. K. (1978). Taste perception in the newborn infant. *Infant Behavior and Development, 1,* 52–69.

Crosnoe, R., Leventhal, T., Wirth, R. J., Pierce, K. M., & Pianta, R. C. (2010). Family socioeconomic status and consistent environmental stimulation in early childhood. *Child Development, 81*(3), 972-987. doi:10.1111/j.1467-8624.2010.01446.x

Crowley, P. H., Gulati, D. K., Hayden, T. L., Lopez, P., & Dyer, R. A. (1979). A chiasma-hormonal hypothesis relating Down's syndrome and maternal age. *Nature, 280,* 417–419.

Cruz-Sanchez, F. F., Lucena, J., Ascaso, C., Tolosa, E., Quinto, L., & Rossi, M. L. (1997). Cerebellar cortex delayed maturation in sudden infant death syndrome. *Journal of Neuropathology and Experimental Neurology, 56*(4), 340–346.

Cuisinier, M., Janssen, H., de Graauw, D., & Hoogduin, K. (1998). Predictors of maternal reactions to excessive crying of newborns. Findings from a prospective study in a naturalistic situation. *Early Development and Parenting, 7,* 41–49.

Cummings, J. S., Pellegrini, D. S., Notarius, C. I., & Cummings, E. M. (1989). Children's responses to angry adult behavior as a function of marital distress and history of interparent hostility. *Child Development, 60,* 1035–1043.

Curley, J. P., Jensen, C. L., Mashoodh, R., & Champagne, F. A. (2011). Social influences on neurobiology and behavior *Epigenetic effects during development. Psychoneuroendocrinology, 36,* 352-371.

Cutillo, D. M., Hammond, E. A., Reeser, S. L., Kershner, M. A., Lukin, B., Godmilow, L., & Donnenfeld, A. E. (1994). Chorionic villus sampling utilization following reports of a possible association with fetal limb defects. *Prenatal Diagnosis, 14,* 327–332.

da Costa, S. P., van der Schans, C. P., Boelema, S. R. van der Meij, E., Boerman, M. A., & Bos, A. F. (2010). Sucking patterns in fullterm infants between birth and 10 weeks of age. *Infant Behavior & Development, 33,* 61-67.

Dahl, R. E., Scher, M. S., Williamson, D. E., Robles, N., & Day, N. (1995). A longitudinal study of prenatal marijuana use: Effects of sleep and arousal at age 3 years. *Archives of Pediatric and Adolescent Medicine, 149,* 145–150.

Dale, P. S. (1976). *Language development: Structure and function* (2nd ed.). New York: Holt, Rinehart and Winston.

D'Alton (1994). Prenatal diagnostic procedures. *Seminars in Perinatology, 18,* 140–162.

Damast, A. M., Tamis-LeMonda, C. S., & Bornstein, M. H. (1996). Mother-child play: Sequential interactions and the relation between maternal beliefs and behaviors. *Child Development, 67*(4), 1752–1766.

Danforth, D. N. (Ed.) (1977). *Obstetrics and gynecology* (3rd ed.). New York: Harper & Row.

Daniels, D., Plomin, R., & Greenhalgh, J. (1984). Correlates of difficult temperament in infancy. *Child Development, 55,* 1184–1194.

Dannemiller, J. L., & Stephens, B. R. (1988). A critical test of infant pattern preference models. *Child Development, 59,* 210–216.

Darj, E., & Nordstrom, M. L. (1999). The Misgav Ladach method for ceasarean section compared to the Pfanenstiel method. *Acta Obstetrica et Gynecologica Scandinavica, 78,* 37–41.

Darwin, C. R. (1859). *The origin of species.* New York: Modern Library.

Davenport-Slack, B., & Boylan, C. H. (1974). Psychological correlates of childbirth pain. *Psychosomatic Medicine, 36,* 215–223.

Daum, M. M., Prinz, W., & Aschersleben, G. (2009). Means-end behavior in young infants: The interplay of action perception and action production. *Infancy, 14*(6), 613-640. doi:10.1080/15250000903263965

Davies, P. T., Manning, L. G., & Cicchetti, D. (2013). Tracing the cascade of children's insecurity in the interparental relationship: The role of stage-salient tasks. *Child Development, 84*(1), 297-312

Davis, C. G., & Mantler, J. (2004). *The consequences of financial stress for individuals, families, and society.* Ottawa, ON, Canada: Carleton University, Centre for Research on Stress, Coping, and Well-being, Department of Psychology.

Davis, D. (1985). Infant car safety: The role of perinatal caregivers. *Birth, 12*(Supplement), 21–27.

Davis, E. P., & Sandman, C. A. (2010).The timing of prenatal exposure to maternal cortisol and psychosocial stress is associated with human infant cognitive development. *Child Development, 81,* 131-148.

Davis, H. (1978). A description of aspects of mother-infant vocal interaction. *Journal of Child Psychology and Psychiatry, 19,* 379–386.

Dawson, G., Frey, K., Panagiotides, H., Yamada, E., Hessl, D., & Osterling, J. (1999). Infants of depressed mothers exhibit atypical frontal electrical brain activity during interactions with mother and with a familiar, nondepressed adult. *Child Development, 70*(5), 1058–1066.

Dawson, G., Rogers, S., Munson, J., Smith, M., Winter, J., Greenson, J., & ... Varley, J. (2010). Randomized, controlled trial of an intervention for toddlers with autism: the Early Start Denver Model. *Pediatrics, 125*(1), e17-23. doi:10.1542/peds.2009-0958

Dawson, G., Webb, S. J., Carver, L., Panagiotides, H., & McPartland, J. (2004). Young children with autism show atypical brain responses to fearful versus neutral facial expressions of emotion. *Developmental Science, 7*(3), 340–359.

DC: 0–3R. (2005). *Diagnostic Classification of Mental Health and Developmental Disorders Of Infancy and Early Childhood.* NY: Zero to Three Press.

de l'Etoile, S., & Leider, C. (2011). Acoustic parameters of infant-directed singing in mothers with depressive symptoms. *Infant Behavior & Development, 34*(2), 248-256. doi:10.1016/j.infbeh.2010.12.013

Deák, G., Walden, T., Kaiser, M., & Lewis, A. (2008). Driven from distraction: how infants respond to parents' attempts to elicit and re-direct their attention. *Infant Behavior & Development, 31*(1), 34-50.

Dearing, E., McCartney, K., & Taylor, B. A. (2009). Does higher quality early child care promote low-income children's math and reading achievement in middle childhood?. *Child Development,80*(5), 1329-1349. doi:10.1111/cdev.2009.80.issue-510.1111/j.1467-8624.2009.01336.x

DeBoysson-Bardies, B. (1990). Some reflexions on sensory-motor organization of speech during the first year of life. In H. Bloch & B. I. Bertenthal (Eds.), *Sensory-motor organizations and development in infancy and early childhood* (pp. 457–466). The Netherlands: Kluwer Academic.

DeBoysson-Bardies, B., Sagant, L., & Durand, C. (1984). Discernible differences in the babbling of infants according to target language. *Journal of Child Language, 11,* 1–15.

DeCasper, A. J., & Fifer, W. P. (1980). Of human bonding: Newborns prefer their mothers' voices. *Science, 208,* 1174–1176.

DeCasper, A. J., & Sigafoos, A. D. (1983). The intrauterine heartbeat: A potent reinforcer for newborns. *Infant Behavior and Development, 6,* 19–26.

DeCasper, A. J., & Spence, M. J. (1986). Prenatal maternal speech influences newborns' perception of speech sounds. *Infant Behavior and Development, 9,* 133–150.

DeChateau, P. (1987). Parent-infant socialization in several western European countries. In J. D. Osofsky (Ed.), *Handbook of infant development* (2nd ed., pp. 642–668). New York: Wiley.

de Haan, M., Belsky, J., Reid, V., Volein, A., & Johnson, M. H. (2004). Maternal personality and infants' neural and visual responsivity to facial expressions of emotion. *Journal of Child Psychology and Psychiatry, 45*(7), 1209–1218.

Degangi, G. A., Breinbauer, C., Doussard Roosevelt, J., Porges, S., & Greenspan, S. (2000). Prediction of childhood problems at three years in children experiencing disorders of regulation during infancy. *Infant Mental Health Journal, 21*(3), 156–175.

DeGangi, G. A., Sickel, R. Z., Wiener, A. S., & Kaplan, E. P. (1996). Fussy babies: To treat or not to treat? *British Journal of Occupational Therapy, 59*(10), 457–464.

DeHart, G., Sroufe, L., & Cooper, R. (2000). *Child Development: Its nature and course* (4th ed.). Boston: McGraw-Hill.

De Jonge, A., Teunissen, T. A., & Lagro-Janssen, A. L. (2004). Supine position compared to other positions during the second stage of labor: a meta-analytic review. *J Psychosom Obstet Gynaecol, 25*(1), 35–45.

De Jonge, A., van der Goes, B., Ravelli, A., Amelink-Verburg, M., Mol, B., Nijhuis, J., Gravenhorst, J., Buitendijk, S. 2009). *BJOG–An International Journal of Obstetrics and Gynaecology, 116*, 9: 1177–1184.

Delavenne, A., Gratier, M., & Devouche, E. (2013). Expressive timing in infant-directed singing between 3 and 6 months. *Infant Behavior & Development, 36*(1), 1-13. doi:10.1016/j.infbeh.2012.10.004

DeLeon, C., & Karraker, K. (2007). Intrinsic and extrinsic factors associated with night waking in 9-month-old infants. *Infant Behavior & Development, 30*(4), 596-605.

Delevati, N. M., & Bergamasco, N. H. P. (1999). Pain in the neonate: An analysis of facial movements and crying in response to nociceptive stimuli. *Infant Behavior and Development, 22*(1), 137–143.

DeLoache, J. S., & LoBue, V. (2009). The narrow fellow in the grass: Human infants associate snakes and fear. *Developmental Science, 12*(1), 201-207. doi:10.1111/j.1467-7687.2008.00753.x

DeLoache, J. S., & Plaetzer, B. (1985, April). *Tea for two: Joint mother-child symbolic play.* Presented at the meeting of the Society for Research in Child Development, Toronto, Canada.

DeLoache, J. S., Simcock, G., & Macari, S. (2007). Planes, trains, automobiles--and tea sets: Extremely intense interests in very young children. *Developmental Psychology, 43*(6), 1579-1586

DeLoache, J. S., Sugarman, S., & Brown, A. L. (1985). The development of error correction strategies in young children's manipulative play. *Child Development, 56*, 928–939.

DeMeis, D. K., Hock, E., & McBride, S. L. (1986). The balance of employment and motherhood: Longitudinal study of mothers' feelings about separation from their first-born infants. *Developmental Psychology, 22*, 627–632.

Demetriou, H., & Hay, D. F. (2004). Toddlers' reactions to the distress of familiar peers: The importance of context. *Infancy, 6*(2), 299–318.

Demos, V. E. (1982). Facial expressions of infants and toddlers: A descriptive analysis. In T. Field & A. Fogel (Eds.), *Emotion and early interaction* (pp. 188–209). Hillsdale, NJ: Erlbaum.

den Bak, I. M., & Ross, H. S. (1996). I'm telling: The content, context, and consequences of children's tattling on their siblings. *Social Development, 5*(3), 292–309.

Denham, S. (1986). Social cognition, prosocial behavior and emotion in preschoolers: Contextual validation. *Child Development, 57*, 194–201.

Denzin, N. K. & Lincoln, Y. S. (1994). *Handbook of qualitative research.* Thousand Oaks, CA: Sage Publications.

DePaolis, R., Vihman, M., & Keren-Portnoy, T. (2011). Do production patterns influence the processing of speech in prelinguistic infants?. *Infant Behavior & Development, 34*(4), 590-601.

de Schipper, E. J., Riksen-Walraven, J. M., & Geurts, S. A. E. (2006). Effects of Child-Caregiver Ratio on the Interactions Between Caregivers and Children in Child-Care Centers: An Experimental Study. *Child Development, 77*(4), 861–874.

Desor, J. A., Miller, O., & Turner, R. (1973). Taste in acceptance of sugars by human infants. *Journal of Comparative and Physiological Psychology, 85,* 496–501.

Desrochers, S., Morissette, P., & Ricard, M. (1995). Two perspectives on pointing in infancy. In C. Moore & P. J. Dunham (Eds.), *Joint attention: Its origins and role in development* (pp. 85–101). Hillsdale, NJ: Erlbaum.

DeStefano, C. T., & Mueller, E. (1982). Environmental determinants of peer social activity in 18–month-old males. *Infant Behavior and Development, 5,* 175–183.

deVilliers, J. C., & deVilliers, P. A. (1973). A cross-sectional study of the acquisition of grammatical morphemes in child speech. *Journal of Pyscholinguistic Research, 2,* 267–278.

De Wolff, M. S., & van Ijzendoorn, M. H. (1997). Sensitivity and attachment: A meta-analysis on parental antecedents of infant attachment. *Child Development, 68*(4), 571–591.

Diamond, A. (1988). Abilities and neural mechanisms underlying AB performance. *Child Development, 59,* 523–527.

Diamond, A., & Doar, B. (1989). The performance of human infants on a measure of frontal cortex function, the delayed response task. *Developmental Psychobiology, 22*(3), 271–294.

Diamond, A., Prevor, M. B., Callender, G., & Druin, D. P. (1997). Prefrontal cortex cognitive deficits in children treated early and continuously for PKU. *Monographs of the Society for Research in Child Development, 62*(4), 1–205.

Dick-Read, G. (1972). *Childbirth without fear: The original approach to natural childbirth* (Rev. ed.). H. Wessel & H. Ellis (Eds.). New York: Harper & Row. (Original work published 1933)

Dickson, K. L., Fogel, A., & Messinger, D. (1997). The social context of smiling and laughter in infants. In M. Mascolo & S. Griffen (Eds.), *The development of emotion* (pp. 253–273). New York: Plenum Press.

Dickson, K. L., Walker, H., & Fogel, A. (1997). The relationship between smile-type and play-type during parent-infant play. *Developmental Psychology, 33,* 925–933.

Dickstein, S., & Parke, R. D. (1988). Social referencing in infancy: A glance at fathers and marriage. *Child Development, 59,* 506–511.

DiLalla, L. F., & Watson, M. W. (1988). Differentiation of fantasy and reality: Preschoolers' reactions to interruptions in their play. *Developmental Psychology, 24,* 286–291.

Dinehart, L. H. B., Kaiser, M. Y., & Hughes, C. R. (2009). Language delay and the effect of milieu teaching on children born cocaine exposed: A pilot study, *Journal of Developmental and Physical Disabilities, 21*. 9-22.

DiPietro, J. A. (2010). Psychological and psychophysiological considerations regarding the maternal-fetal relationship. *Infant and Child Development,19*, 27-38.

DiPietro, J. A., Hilton, S. C., Hawkins, M., Costigan, K. A., & Pressman, E. K. (2002). Maternal stress and affect influence fetal neurobehavioral development. *Developmental Psychology, 38*(5), 659–668.

DiPietro, J., Bornstein, M., Hahn, C., Costigan, K., & Achy-Brou, A. (2007). Fetal heart rate and variability: stability and prediction to developmental outcomes in early childhood. *Child Development, 78*(6), 1788-1798.

DiPietro, J. A., Hodgson, D. M., Costigan, K. A., & Johnson, T. R. B. (1996). Fetal neurobehavioral development. *Child Development, 67* (5), 2553–2567.

DiPietro, J. A., Larson, S. K., & Porges, S. W. (1987). Behavioral and heart rate pattern differences between breast-fed and bottle-fed neonates. *Developmental Psychology, 23*(4), 467–474.

Dirix, C. H., Nijhuis, J. G., Jongsma, H. W., & Hornstra, G. (2009). Aspects of fetal learning and memory. *Child Development, 80*(4), 1251-1258. doi:10.1111/j.1467-8624.2009.01329.x

Dittrichová, J., Brichacek, V., Mandys, F., Paul, K., Sobotkova, D., Tautermannova, M., Vondracek, J., & Zezulakova, J. (1996). Relationship of early behavior to later developmental outcome for preterm children. *International Journal of Behavioral Development, 19*(3), 517–532.

Dix, T., Stewart, A. D., Gershoff, E. T., & Day, W. H. (2007). Autonomy and children's reactions to being controlled: Evidence that both compliance and defiance may be positive markers in early development. *Child Development, 78*(4), 1204–1221.

Dixon, L., Hamilton-Giachritsis, C., & Browne, K. (2005). Attributions and behaviours of parents abused as children: a mediational analysis of the intergenerational continuity of child maltreatment (Part II). *Journal of Child Psychology and Psychiatry, 46*(1), 58–68.

Dixon, S. D., LeVine, R. A., Richman, A., & Brazelton, T. B. (1984). Mother-child interaction around a teaching task: An African-American comparison. *Child Development, 55,* 1252–1264.

Doan, S. N., & Wang, Q. (2010). Maternal discussions of mental states and behaviors: Relations to emotion situation knowledge in European American and immigrant Chinese children. *Child Development*, *81*(5), 1490-1503. doi:10.1111/j.1467-8624.2010.01487.x

Dobrova-Krol, N. A., van IJzendoorn, M. H., Bakermans-Kranenburg, M. J., & Juffer, F. (2010). Effects of Perinatal HIV Infection and Early Institutional Rearing on Physical and Cognitive Development of Children in Ukraine. *Child Development, 81*(1), 237-251.

Doheny, L., Hurwitz, S., Insoft, R., Ringer, S., & Lahav, A, (2012). Exposure to biological maternal sounds improves cardiorespiratory regulation in extremely preterm infants.*The Journal Of Maternal-Fetal & Neonatal Medicine*, *25*,1591-4;

Dolinoy, D. C., Weidman, J. R., & Jirtle, R. L. (2007). Epigenetic gene regulation: linking early developmental environment to adult disease. *Reprod Toxicol, 23*(3), 297–307.

Domar, A. D., Rooney, K. L.,Wiegand, B., Orav, E. J., Alper, M. M., Berger, B. M., & Nikolovski, J. (2011). Impact of a group mind/body intervention on pregnancy rates in IVF patients. *Fertility And Sterility, 95,* 2269-2273.

Dondi, M. (1999). Maturità e specificità del comportamento facciale nelle più precoci fasi dello sviluppo. *Giornale Italiano di Psicologia, 26*(1), 23–53.

Dondi, M., Messinger, M., Colle, M., Tabasso, A., Simeon, F., Barba, B., Fogel, A. (2007). A new perspective on neonatal smiling: Differences between expert coders and naive observers. *Infancy.*

Dondi, M., Simion, F., & Caltran, G. (1999). Can newborns discriminate between their own cry and the cry of another newborn infant? *Developmental Psychology, 35*(2), 418–426.

D'Onofrio, B. M., Singh, A. L., Iliadou, A., Lambe, M., Hultman, C. M., Neiderhiser, J. M., . . . Lichtenstein, P. (2010). A quasi-experimental study of maternal smoking during pregnancy and offspring academic achievement. *Child Development, 81,* 80-100.

Donovan, W. L., & Leavitt, L. A. (1989). Maternal self-efficacy and infant attachment: Integrating physiology, perceptions, and behavior. *Child Development, 60,* 460–472.

Donovan, W. L., Leavitt, L. A., & Walsh, R. O. (1998). Conflict and depression predict maternal sensitivity to infant cries. *Infant Behavior and Development, 21*(3), 505–517.

Dougherty, T. M., & Haith, M. M. (1997). Infant expectations and reaction time as predictors of childhood speed of processing and IQ. *Developmental Psychology, 33*(1), 146–155.

Dow, K. E., & Reopelli, R. J. (1985). Ethanol neurotoxicity: Effects on neurite formation and neutrotrophic factor production in vitro. *Science, 228,* 591–593.

Downing, G. (2005). Emotion, body, and parent-infant interaction. In J. Nadel and D. Muir (Eds.), *Emotional Development*, pp. 429–450. Oxford, UK: Oxford University Press.

Downing, G. (2008). A different way to help. . In A. Fogel, B. J. King, & S. Shanker (Eds.). *Human development in the 21st century: Visionary policy ideas from systems scientists.* Cambridge, UK: Cambridge University Press.

Downing, G., Bürgin, D., Reck, C., & Ziegenhain, U. (2008). Interfaces between intersubjectivity and attachment: Three perspectives on a mother–infant inpatient case. *Infant Mental Health Journal, 29*(3), 278-295.

Drachman, D. B., & Coulombre, A. J. (1962). Experimental clubfoot and arthrogryposis multiplex congenita. *Lancet, 2*, 523–536.

Dragonas, R., Petrogiannis, K., & Adam, H. (1997). Working women, their emotional well-being and pregnancy in Greece. *Journal of Reproductive and Infant Psychology, 15*, 239–256.

Draper, J. (2002). It's the first scientific evidence': Men's experience of pregnancy confirmation. *Journal of Advanced Nursing, 39*(6), 563–570.

Drotar, D., & Irvin, N. (1979). Disturbed maternal bereavement following infant death. *Child Care, Health and Development, 5*, 239–247.

Dubowitz, L. M. S., Dubowitz, V., & Goldberg, C. (1970). Clinical assessment of gestational age in the newborn infant. *Journal of Pediatrics, 77*, 1–10.

Duncan, G. J. (2003). Modeling the Impacts of Child Care Quality on Children's Preschool Cognitive Development. *Child Development, 74*(5), 1454–1475.

Duncan, G. J., Ziol-Guest, K. M., & Kalil, A. (2010). Early-childhood poverty and adult attainment, behavior, and health. *Child Development, 81*(1), 306-325.

Dunfield, K., Kuhlmeier, V. A., O'Connell, L., & Kelley, E. (2011). Examining the diversity of prosocial behavior: Helping, sharing, and comforting in infancy. *Infancy,16*(3), 227-247. doi:10.1111/j.1532-7078.2010.00041.x

Dunham, P. J., & Dunham, F. (1995). Developmental antecedents of taxonomic and thematic strategies. *Developmental Psychology, 31*, 483–493.

Dunham, P. J., & Dunham, F. (1996). The semantically reciprocating robot: Adult influences on children's early conversational skills. *Social Development, 5*(3), 261–274.

Dunham, P. J., Dunham, F., & Curwin, A. (1993). Joint-attentional states and lexical acquisition at 18 months. *Developmental Psychology, 29*, 827–831.

Dunham, P. J., Dunham, F., Tran, S., & Akhtar, N. (1991). The nonreciprocating robot: Effects on verbal discourse, social play, and social referencing at two years of age. *Child Development, 62*, 1489–1502.

Dunn, D. T., Newell, M. L., Ades, A. E., & Peckham, C. S. (1992). Risk of human immunodeficiency virus type 1 transmission through breastfeeding. *Lancet, 340*, 585–588.

Dunn, J. (1998). Siblings, emotion, and the development of understanding. In S. Br;araten (Ed.), *Intersubjective communication and emotion in early ontogeny. Studies in emotion and social interaction, 2nd series* (pp. 158–168). Cambridge, England: Cambridge University Press.

Dunn, J., Bretherton, I., & Munn, P. (1987). Conversations about feeling states between mothers and their young children. *Developmental Psychology, 23*, 132–139.

Dunn, J., & Kendrick, C. (1980). Interactions between young siblings in the context of family relationships. In M. Lewis & L. Rosenblum (Eds.), *The child and its family* (pp. 334–369). New York: Plenum Press.

Dunn, J., & Kendrick, C. (1981). Social behavior of young siblings in the family context: Differences between same-sex and different-sex dyads. *Child Development, 52*, 1265–1273.

Dunn, J., & Kendrick, C. (1982). *Siblings: love, envy, and understanding*. Cambridge, MA: Harvard University Press.

Dunn, J., Kreps, C., & Brown, J. (1996). Children's family relationships between two and five: Developmental changes and individual differences. *Social Development, 5*(3), 230–250.

Dunn, J., & Munn, P. (1985). Becoming a family member: Family conflict and the development of social understanding in the second year. *Child Development, 56*, 480–492.

Dunn, J., & Munn, P. (1987). Development of justification in disputes with mother and sibling. *Developmental Psychology, 23*, 791–798.

Dunn, J., Plomin, R., & Daniels, D. (1986). Consistency and change in mothers' behavior toward young siblings. *Child Development, 57*, 348–356.

Dunn, J., & Shatz, M. (1989). Becoming a conversationalist despite (or because of) having an older sibling. *Child Development, 60*, 399–410.

Dunsmore, J. C., & Halberstadt, A. G. (1997). How does family emotional expressiveness affect children's schemas? In K. C. Barrett (Ed.), *New directions in child development: The communication of emotion: Current research from diverse perspectives, 77* (pp. 45–68). San Francisco: Jossey-Bass.

Dupont, F. (1989). *Daily life in ancient Rome* (C. Woodall, Trans.). Oxford, England: Blackwell.

Dworetzky, J. P., & Davis, N. J. (1989). *Human development: A life span approach*. St. Paul, MN: West.

Dyer, A. B., Lickliter, R., & Gottlieb, G. (1989). Maternal and peer imprinting in mallard ducklings under experimentally simulated natural social conditions. *Developmental Psychobiology, 22*, 463–475.

Dyregrov, A., & Matthiesen, S. B. (1987). Stillbirth, neonatal death, and sudden infant death (SIDS): Parental reactions. *Scandinavian Journal of Psychology, 28*, 104–114.

Eakins, P. S. (Ed.). (1986). *The American way of birth*. Philadelphia: Temple University Press.

Easterbrooks, M. A. (1989). Quality of attachment to mother and to father: Effects of perinatal risk status. *Child Development, 60*, 825–830.

Easterbrooks, M. A., & Goldberg, W. (1984). Toddler development in the family: Impact of father involvement and parenting characteristics. *Child Development, 55*, 740–752.

Easterbrooks, M. A., & Goldberg, W. (1985). Effects of early maternal employment on toddlers, mothers, and fathers. *Developmental Psychology, 21*, 774–783.

Ebert, J. D., & Sussex, I. M. (1970). *Interacting systems in development* (2nd ed.). New York: Holt, Rinehart and Winston.

ECCO-The European CanCer Organisation (2011, September 26). Chemotherapy during pregnancy does not seem to cause developmental problems in children. *Science Daily*. Retrieved April 24, 2012, from http://www.sciencedaily.com/releases/2011/09/110926183421.htm.

Eckerman, C. O. (1993). Toddler's achievement of coordinated action with conspecifics: A dynamic systems perspective. In L. B. Smith & E. Thelen (Eds.), *A dynamic systems approach to development: Applications* (pp. 333–357). Cambridge, MA: MIT Press.

Eckerman, C. O., & Whatley, J. L. (1977). Toys and social interaction between infant peers. *Child Development, 48,* 1645–1656.

Eckerman, C. O., & Didow, S. M. (1989). Toddlers' social coordinations: Changing responses to another's invitation to play. *Developmental Psychology, 25,* 794–804.

Eckerman, C. O., Hsu, H., Molitor, A., Leung, E. H. L., & Goldstein, R. F. (1999). Infant arousal in an en-face exchange with a new partner: Effects of prematurity and perinatal biological risk. *Developmental Psychology, 35*(1), 282–293.

Eckerman, C. O., Oehler, J. M., Medvin, M. B., & Hannan, T. E. (1994). Premature newborns as social partners before term age. *Infant Behavior and Development, 17,* 55–70.

Eckerman, C. O., & Stein, M. R. (1990). How imitation begets imitation and toddlers' generation of games. *Developmental Psychology, 26,* 370–378.

Eckerman, C. O., & Whatley, J. L. (1975). Infants' reactions to unfamiliar adults varying in novelty. *Developmental Psychology, 11,* 562–566.

Eckerman, C. O., Whatley, J. L., & Kutz, S. (1975). Growth of social play with peers during the second year of life. *Developmental Psychology, 11,* 42–49.

Eckerman, C. O., Whatley, J. L., & McGehee, L. J. (1979). Approaching and contacting the object another manipulates: A social skill of the one-year-old. *Developmental Psychology, 15,* 585–593.

The Economist (2008). Measles and MMR make their encore. http://www.economist.com/world/britain/displaystory.cfm?story_id=12725316

The effects of early social-emotional and relationship experience on the development of young orphanage children (2008). *Monographs of the Society for Research in Child Development*, *73*(3), 1-297

Egeland, B., & Hiester, M. (1995). The long-term consequences of infant day-care and mother-infant attachment. *Child Development, 66,* 474–485.

Eichenbaum, H. & Cohen, N. (2001). *Memory systems of the brain.* Oxford University Press

Eiden, R. D.,Veira, Y., & Granger, D. A. (2009). Prenatal Cocaine Exposure and Infant Cortisol Reactivity. *Child Development,80,* 528-543.

Eilers, R. E., & Gavin, W. J. (1981). The evaluation of infant speech perception skills: Statistical techniques and theory development. In R. Stark (Ed.), *Language behavior in infancy and early childhood* (pp. 219–243). New York: Elsevier.

Eimas, P. D., & Quinn, P. C. (1994). Studies on the formation of perceptually based basic-level categories in young infants. *Child Development, 65,* 903–917.

Eimas, P. D., Siqueland, E. R., Jusczyk, P., & Vigorito, J. (1971). Speech perception in infants. *Science, 171,* 303–306.

Einarson, A., Selby, P., & Koren, G. (2001). Abrupt discontinuation of psychotropic drugs during pregnancy: Fear of teratogenic risk and impact of counselling. *Journal of Psychiatry & Neuroscience, 26*(1), 44–48.

Einfeld, S. L. (2005). Behaviour Problems in Children with Genetic Disorders Causing Intellectual Disability. *Educational Psychology, 25*(2–3), 341–346.

Eisenberg, M., Park, Y., Hollenbeck, A., Lipshultz, L., Schatzkin, A., & Pletcher, M. (2011). Fatherhood and the risk of cardiovascular mortality in the NIH-AARP Diet and Health Study. *Human Reproduction (Oxford, England)*, *26*(12), 3479-3485. doi:10.1093/humrep/der305

Einspieler, C., Widder, J., Holzer, A., & Kenner, T. (1988). The predictive value of behavioral risk factors for sudden infant death. *Early Human Development, 18,* 101–109.

Eisenberg, N., Qing, Z., Spinrad, T. L., Valiente, C., Fabes, R. A., & Liew, J. (2005). Relations among positive parenting, children's effortful control, and externalizing problems: A three-wave longitudinal study. *Child Development*, *76*(5), 1055-1071.

Eisenberg, R. B. (1976). *Auditory competence in early life*. Baltimore: University Park Press.

Eizirik, L. S., Bohlin, G., & Hagekull, B. (1994). Interaction between mother and pre-term infant at 34 weeks post-conceptional age. *Early Development and Parenting, 3,* 171–180.

Ekas, N. V., Braungart-Rieker, J. M., Lickenbrock, D. M., Zentall, S. R., & Maxwell, S. M. (2011). Toddler emotion regulation with mothers and fathers: Temporal associations between negative affect and behavioral strategies. *Infancy*, *16*(3), 266-294. doi:10.1111/j.1532-7078.2010.00042.x

Ekas, N. V., Lickenbrock, D. M., & Braungart-Rieker, J. M. (2013). Developmental trajectories of emotion regulation across infancy: Do age and the social partner influence temporal patterns. *Infancy*, *18*(5), 729-754. doi:10.1111/infa.12003

Ellis, B. J., Bates, J. E., Dodge, K. A., Fergusson, D. M., Horwood, L. J., Pettit, G. S., et al. (2003). Does father absence place daughters at special risk for early sexual activity and teenage pregnancy? *Child Development, 74*(3), 801–821.

Ellis, S., & Rogoff, B. (1982). The strategies and efficacy of child versus adult teachers. *Child Development, 53,* 730–735.

Ellison, P. T. (2010). Fetal programming and fetal psychology. *Infant and Child Development,19,* 6-20.

Ellsworth, C. P., Muir, D. W., & Hains, S. M. J. (1993). Social competence and person-object differentiation: An analysis of the still-face effect. *Developmental Psychology, 29*(1), 63–73.

Emde, R. N., Gaensbauer, T. J., & Harmon, R. J. (1976). Emotional expression in infancy. *Psychological Issues, 10*(1).

Emde, R. N., & Hewitt, J. K. (2001). Infancy to early childhood: Genetic and environmental influences on developmental change. New York: Oxford University Press.

Emde, R. N., Plomin, R., Robinson, J., Corley, R., DeFries, J., Fulker, D. W., Reznick, J. S., Campos, J., Kagan, J., & Zahn-Waxler, C. (1992). Temperament, emotion, and cognition at fourteen months: The MacArthur longitudinal twin study. *Child Development, 63,* 1437–1455.

Engle, S. (2010, January 28). Prenatal exposure to phthalates affects childhood neurodevelopment. *ScienceDaily,* Retrieved April 24, 2012, from http://www.sciencedaily.com./releases/2010/01/100128091746.htm.

Enlow, M. B., Kitts, R. L., Blood, E., Bizarro,A., Hofmeister, M., & Wright, R. J. (2011). Maternal posttraumatic stress symptoms and infant emotional reactivity and emotion regulation. *Infant Behavior & Development, 34,* 487-503.

Entwisle, D. R., & Alexander, K. L. (1987). Long-term effects of cesarean delivery on parents' beliefs and children's schooling. *Developmental Psychology, 23,* 676–682.

Ereky-Stevens, K. (2008). Associations between mothers' sensitivity to their infants' internal states and children's later understanding of mind and emotion. *Infant And Child Development, 17*(5), 527-543. doi:10.1002/icd.572

Erickson, M. F., Sroufe, L. A., & Egeland, B. (1985). Relationship between quality of attachment and behavior problems in preschool in a high-risk sample. In I. Bretherton & E. Waters (Eds.), *Growing points of attachment theory and research. Monographs of the Society for Research in Child Development, 50* (Serial No. 209), 147–166.

Erikson, E. (1950). *Childhood and society.* New York: Norton.

Ershoff, D. H., Ashford, T. H., & Goldenberg, R. L. (2004). Helping pregnant women quit smoking: An overview. *Nicotine & Tobacco Research, 6,*(2) S101–S105.

Escalona, S. K., & Corman, H. H. (1968). *Albert Einstein scales of sensorimotor development.* Unpublished manuscript.

Escobar, G. J., Yanover, M., Gardner, M. N., Goembeski, D., Armstrong, M. A., Shum, F., & Kipnis P. (1998). Structured review of neonatal deaths in a managed care organization. *Pediatric Perinatal Epidemiology, 12*(4), 422–436.

Espy, K. A., Fang, H., Johnson, C., Stopp, C., Wiebe, S. A., & Respass, J. (2011). Prenatal tobacco exposure. Developmental outcomes in the neonatal period. *Developmental Psychology, 47,*153-169.

Espy, K. A., Riese, M. L., & Francis, D. J. (1997). Neurobehavior in preterm neonates exposed to cocaine, alcohol, and tobacco. *Infant Behavior and Development, 20*(3), 297–309.

Essex, M. J., Boyce, W. T., Hertzman, C., Lam, L. L., Armstrong, J. M., Neumann, S. M. A., & Kobor, M. S. (2013). Epigenetic vestiges of early developmental adversity: Childhood stress exposure and DNA methylation in adolescence. [Special issue: genomics]. *Child Development, 84,* 58-75.

Essex, M. J., Klein, M. H., Cho, E., & Kalin, N. H. (2002). Maternal stress beginning in infancy may sensitize children to later stress exposure: effects on cortisol and behavior. *Biol Psychiatry, 52*(8), 776–784.

Éthier, L. S., Lemelin, J.-P., & Lacharité, C. (2004). A longitudinal study of the effects of chronic maltreatment on children's behavioral and emotional problems. *Child Abuse & Neglect, 28*(12), 1265–1278.

Evans, E., Hawton, K., & Rodham, K. (2005). Suicidal phenomena and abuse in adolescents: A review of epidemiological studies. *Child Abuse & Neglect, 29*(1), 45–58.

Evans, C., & Porter, C. (2009). The emergence of mother-infant co-regulation during the first year: links to infants' developmental status and attachment. *Infant Behavior & Development, 32*(2), 147-158. doi:10.1016/j.infbeh.2008.12.005

Evans, T., Whittingham, K., & Boyd, R. (2012). What helps the mother of a preterm infant become securely attached, responsive and well-adjusted? *Infant Behavior & Development, 35,* 1-11.

Eyer, D. (1996). *Motherguilt: How our culture blames mothers for what's wrong with society.* New York: Random House.

Fabrena, H., Jr., & Nutini, H. (1994). Sudden infant and child death as a cultural phenomenon: A Tlaxcalan case study. *Psychiatry, 57,* 225–243.

Fabrizi L., Slater, R., Worley, A., Meek, J., Boyd, S., Olhede, S. & Fitzgerald, M. (2011). A shift in sensory processing that enables the developing human brain to discriminate touch from pain. *Current Biology, 21,* 1552-1558.

Fagard, J., & Jacquet, A. (1989). Onset of bimanual coordination and symmetry versus asymmetry of movement. *Infant Behavior and Development, 12,* 229–235.

Fagen, J. W., Ohr, P. S., Singer, J. M., & Klein, S. J. (1989). Crying and retrograde amnesia in young infants. *Infant Behavior and Development, 12,* 13–24.

Fagen, J. W., Prigot, J., Carroll, M., Pioli, L., Stein, A., & Franco, A. (1997). Auditory context and memory retrieval in young infants. *Child Development, 68*(6), 1057–1066.

Fagot, B. I. (1997). Attachment, parenting, and peer interactions of toddler children. *Developmental Psychology, 33*(3), 489–499.

Fagot, B. I., & Hagan, R. (1991). Observations of parent reactions to sex-stereotyped behaviors: Age and sex effects. *Child Development, 62,* 617–628.

Fagot, B. I., & Kavanagh, K. (1993). Parenting during the second year: Effects of children's age, sex, and attachment classification. *Child Development, 64,* 258–271.

Fagot, B. I., & Leinbach, M. D. (1989). The young child's gender schema: Environmental input, internal organization, *Child Development, 60,* 663–672.

Fagot, B. I., & Leinbach, M. D., & Hagan, R. (1990). Gender labeling and the adoption of sex-typed behaviors. *Developmental Psychology, 22,* 440–443.

Fagot, B. I., Leinbach, M. D., & O'Boyle, C. (1992). Gender labeling, gender stereotyping, and parenting behaviors. *Developmental Psychology, 28,* 225–230.

Fantz, R. L., Fagan, J. F., & Miranda, S. B. (1975). Early visual selection. In L. B. Cohen & P. Salapatek (Eds.), *Infant perception: From sensation to cognition* (Vol. 1, pp. 130–155). New York: Academic Press.

Fares, S. L., & Adler, N. E. (1998). "Top-of-the-head" descriptions of baby and self: Links to reported health behaviors and social context in early pregnancy. *Journal of Social and Personal Relationships, 15*(4), 555–564.

Farran, D. C., & Haskins, R. (1980). Reciprocal influence in the social interactions of mothers and three-month-old children from different socioeconomic backgrounds. *Child Development, 51,* 780–791.

Farver, J. M., & Howes, C. (1993). Cultural differences in American and Mexican mother-child pretend play. *Merrill-Palmer Quarterly, 39,* 344–358.

Farver, J. M., & Wimbarti, S. (1995). Paternal participation in toddlers' pretend play. *Social Development, 4,* 17–29.

Fausto-Sterling, A. (2012). *Sex/Gender: Biology in a Social World.* New York: Routledge.

Fausto-Sterling, A., Coll, C., & Lamarre, M. (2012). Sexing the baby: Part 1 – What do we really know about sex differentiation in the first three years of life?. *Social Science & Medicine, 74*(11), 1684-1692.

Fearon, R., Bakermans-Kranenburg, M. J., van IJzendoorn, M. H., Lapsley, A., & Roisman, G. I. (2010). The significance of insecure attachment and disorganization in the development of children s externalizing behavior: A meta-analytic study. *Child Development, 81*(2), 435-456.

Feeney, G. (1994). Fertility decline in East Asia. *Science, 266,* 1518–1523.

Feinberg, A. P. (2007). Phenotypic plasticity and the epigenetics of human disease. *Nature, 447*(7143), 433–440.

Feiring, C. Lewis, M., & Starr, M. D. (1984). Indirect effects and infants' reactions to strangers. *Developmental Psychology, 20,* 485–491.

Feldenkrais, M. (1981). *The elusive obvious.* Cupertino, CA: Meta Publications.

Feldman, R. (2006). From biological rhythms to social rhythms: Physiological precursors of mother-infant synchrony. *Developmental Psychology, 42*(1), 175–188.

Feldman, R., Dollberg, D., & Nadam, R. (2011). The expression and regulation of anger in toddlers: relations to maternal behavior and mental representations. *Infant Behavior & Development, 34*(2), 310-320.

Feldman, R., & Eidelman, A. I. (2003). Direct and indirect effects of breast milk on neurobehavioral and cognitive development of premature infants. *Developmental Psychobiology, 43*(2), 109–119.

Feldman, R., & Eidelman, A. I. (2009). Biological and environmental initial conditions shape the trajectories of cognitive and social-emotional development across the first years of life. *Developmental Science, 12*(1), 194-200. doi:10.1111/j.1467-7687.2008.00761.x

Feldman, R., Greenbaum, C. W., & Yirmiya, N. (1999). Mother-infant affect synchrony as an antecedent of the emergence of self-control. *Developmental Psychology, 35*(1), 223–231.

Feldman, R., Sussman, A. L., & Zigler, E. (2004). Parental leave and work adaptation at the transition to parenthood: Individual, marital, and social correlates. *Journal of Applied Developmental Psychology, 25*(4), 459–479.

Feldman, R., & Vengrober, A. (2011). Posttraumatic stress disorder in infants and young children exposed to war-related trauma. *Journal of the American Academy of Child & Adolescent Psychiatry, 50,* 645-658.

Feldman, R. (2007). Evidence for a neuroendocrinological foundation of human affiliation: Plasma oxytocin levels across pregnancy and the postpartum period predict mother-infant bonding. *Psychological Science (Wiley-Blackwell), 18*(11), 965-970.

Feldman, R., Magori-Cohen, R., Galili, G., Singer, M., & Louzoun, Y. (2011). Mother and infant coordinate heart rhythms through episodes of interaction synchrony. *Infant Behavior & Development, 34*(4), 569-577. doi:10.1016/j.infbeh.2011.06.008

Feldman, S. S., & Nash, S. C. (1978). Interest in babies during young adulthood. *Child Development, 49,* 617–622.

Feldman, S. S., & Nash, S. C. (1979a). Changes in responsiveness to babies during adolescence. *Child Development, 50,* 942–949.

Feldman, S. S., & Nash, S. C. (1979b). Sex differences in responsiveness to babies among mature adults. *Developmental Psychology, 15,* 430–436.

Fender, J., Richert, R., Robb, M., & Wartella, E. (2010). Parent teaching focus and toddlers' learning from an infant DVD. *Infant & Child Development, 19*(6), 613-627.

Fennell, C. T. (2012). Object familiarity enhances infants' use of phonetic detail in novel words.*Infancy, 17*(3), 339-353. doi:10.1111/j.1532-7078.2011.00080.x

Fenson, L., Dale, P., Reznick, S., Bates, E., Thal, D., & Pethick, S. (1994). Variability in early communicative development. *Monographs of the Society for Research in Child Development, 59* (5, Serial No. 242).

Fenson, C., Kagan, J., Kearsley, R. B., & Zelazo, P. R. (1976). The developmental progression of manipulative play in the first two years. *Child Development, 47,* 232–236.

Fenson, L., Sapper, V., & Minner, D. G. (1974). Attention and manipulative play in the one-year-old child. *Child Development, 45,* 757–764.

Ferber, S. G. (2004). The nature of touch in mothers experiencing maternity blues: The contribution of parity. *Early Human Development, 79*(1), 65–75.

Ferber, S. G., Laudon, M., Kuint, J., Weller, A., & Zisapel, N. (2002). Massage therapy by mothers enhances the adjustment of circadian rhythms to the nocturnal period in full-term infants. *J Dev Behav Pediatr, 23*(6), 410–415.

Ferland, M. B., & Mendelson, M. J. (1989). Infants' categorization of melodic contour. *Infant Behavior and Development, 12,* 341–355.

Fernald, A. (1985). Four-month-old infants prefer to listen to motherese. *Infant Behavior and Development, 8,* 181–195.

Fernald, A. (1989). Intonation and communicative intent in mothers' speech to infants: Is the melody the message? *Child Development, 60,* 1497–1510.

Fernald, A. (1993). Approval and disapproval: Infant responsiveness to vocal affect in familiar and unfamiliar languages. *Child Development, 64,* 657–674.

Fernald, A., & Kuhl, P. (1987). Acoustic determinants of infant preference for motherese speech. *Infant Behavior and Development, 10,* 279–293.

Fernald, A., & Marchman, V. A. (2012). Individual Differences in Lexical Processing at 18 Months Predict Vocabulary Growth in Typically Developing and Late-Talking Toddlers. *Child Development, 83*(1), 203-222.

Fernald, A., & Morikawa, H. (1993). Common themes and cultural variations in Japanese and American mothers' speech to infants. *Child Development, 64,* 637–656.

Fernald, A., Perfors, A., & Marchman, V. A. (2006). Picking up speed in understanding: Speech processing efficiency and vocabulary growth across the 2nd year. *Developmental Psychology, 42*(1), 98–116.

Fernald, A., & Simon, T. (1984). Expanded intonation contours in mothers' speech to newborns. *Developmental Psychology, 20,* 104–113.

Fernald, A., Taeschner, T., Dunn, J., Papousek, M., DeBoysson-Bardies, B., & Fukui, I. (1989). A cross-language study of prosodic modifications in mothers' and fathers' speech to preverbal infants, *Journal of Child Language, 16,* 477–501.

Fessler, D. M. T., Eng, S. J., & Navarrete, C. D. (2005). Elevated disgust sensitivity in the first trimester of pregnancy: Evidence supporting the compensatory prophylaxis hypothesis. *Evolution and Human Behavior, 26,*344–351.

Fidler, A. E., Zack, E., & Barr, R. (2010). Television viewing patterns in 6- to 18-month-olds: The role of caregiver–infant interactional quality. *Infancy, 15*(2), 176-196. doi:10.1111/j.1532-7078.2009.00013.x

Field, T. (1979). Differential behavioral and cardiac responses of 3–month-old infants to mirror and peer. *Infant Behavior and Development, 2,* 179–84.

Field, T. (1991). Young children's adaptations to repeated separations from their mothers. *Child Development, 61,* 539–547.

Field, T. (1994). The effects of mother's physical and emotional unavailability on emotion regulation. *Monographs of the Society for Research in Child Development, 59,* 208–227.

Field, T. (1998). Maternal depression effects on infants and early interventions. *Preventive Medicine, 27,* 200–203.

Field, T. (1998). Touch therapy effects on development. *International Journal of Behavioral Development, 22*(4), 779–797.

Field, T. (2011) Prenatal depression effects on early development: A review. *Infant Behavior & Development, 34,* 1-14.

Field, T., Dempsey, J. R., Hatch, J., Ting, G., & Clifton, R. K. (1979). Cardiac and behavioral responses to repeated tactile and auditory stimulation by preterm and term neonates. *Developmental Psychology, 15,* 406–416.

Field, T. & Diego, M. (2008). Vagal activity, early growth and emotional development. *Infant Behavior & Development, 31,* 361-373.

Field, T., Diego, M., & Hernandez-Reif, M. (2006). Prenatal depression effects on the fetus and newborn: A review. *Infant Behavior & Development, 29*(3), 445–455.

Field, T., Diego, M., & Hernandez-Reif, M. (2011). Potential underlying mechanisms for greater weight gain in massaged preterm infants. *Infant Behavior & Development, 34,* 383-389.

Field, T., Diego, M., Hernandez-Reif, M., Figueiredo, B., Ezell, S., & Siblalingappa, V. (2010). Depressed mothers and infants are more relaxed during breastfeeding versus bottlefeeding interactions; *Infant Behavior & Development, 33,* 241-244.

Field, T., Grizzle, N., Scafidi, F., Abrams, S., Richardson, S., Kuhn, C., & Schanberg, S. (1996). Massage therapy for infants of depressed mothers. *Infant Behavior and Development, 19,* 107–112.

Field, T., Grizzle, N., Scafidi, F., & Schanberg, S. (1996). Massage and relaxation therapies' effects on depressed adolescent mothers. *Adolescence, 31,* 903–911.

Field, T., Healy, B., Goldstein, S., Perry, S., Bendell, D., Schanberg, S., Zimmerman, E. A., & Kuhn, C. (1988). Infants of depressed mothers show "depressed" behavior even with nondepressed adults. *Child Development, 59,* 1569–1579.

Field, T., Healy, B., & LeBlanc, W. G. (1989). Sharing and synchrony of behavior states and heart rate in nondepressed versus depressed mother-infant interactions. *Infant Behavior and Development, 12,* 357–376.

Field, T., Hernandez-Reif, M., Diego, M., Feijo, L., Vera, Y., & Gil, K. (2004). Massage therapy by parents improves early growth and development. *Infant Behavior & Development, 27,* 435–442.

Field, T., Hernandez-Reif, M., Feijo, L., & Freedman, J. (2006). Prenatal, perinatal and neonatal stimulation: A survey of neonatal nurseries. *Infant Behavior & Development, 29*(1), 24–31.

Field, T., Morrow, C., & Adlestein, D. (1993). Depressed mothers' perceptions of infant behavior. *Infant Behavior and Development, 16,* 99–108.

Field, T., Sandberg, D., Garcia, R., Vega-Lahr, N., Goldstein, S., & Guy, L. (1985). Pregnancy problems, postpartum depression, and early mother-infant interactions. *Developmental Psychology, 21,* 1152–1156.

Field, T. & Sostek, A. (1983). *Infants born at risk: Physiological, perceptual and cognitive processes.* New York: Grune & Stratton.

Field, T., Vega-Lahr, N., & Jagadish, S. (1984). Separation stress of nursery school infants and toddlers graduating to new classes. *Infant Behavior and Development, 7,* 277–284.

Field, T., Vega-Lahr, N., Scafidi, F., & Goldstein, S. (1986). Effects of maternal unavailability on mother-infant interactions. *Infant Behavior and Development, 9,* 473–478.

Field, T., Widmayer, S. M., Stringer, S., & Ignatoff, E. (1980). Teenage, lower class, black mothers and their preterm infants: An intervention and developmental follow-up. *Child Development, 51,* 426–436.

Field, T., Woodson, R., Greenberg, R., & Cohen, D. (1982). *Discrimination and imitation of facial expressions by neonates.* Paper presented at the International Conference on Infant Studies, Austin, TX.

Fifth Special Report to the U.S. Congress on Alcohol and Health (1984). *Alcohol Health and Research World, 9,* 1–72.

Finkelstein, N., Dent, C., Gallacher, K., & Ramey, C. (1978). Social behavior of infants and toddlers in a day-care environment. *Developmental Psychology, 14,* 257–262.

Fischer, J., & Rozenberg, C. (1999). The maternity care coalition: Strategy for survival in the context of managed care and welfare reform. *Zero to Three, 19*(4), 14–19.

Fischer, K. W. (1987). Relations between brain and cognitive development. *Child Development, 58,* 623–632.

Fish, M., Stifter, C. A., & Belsky, J. (1991). Conditions of continuity and discontinuity in infant negative emotionality: Newborn to five months. *Child Development, 62,* 1525–1537.

Fiscus, S., Adimora, A., Schoenbach, V., Lim. W., McKinney, R., Rupar, D., Kenny, J., Woods, C., & Wilfert, C. (1996). Perinatal HIV infection and the effect of Zidovudine therapy on transmission in rural and urban counties. *Journal of the American Medical Association, 275,* 1483–1488.

Fivaz-Depeursinge, E., & Corboz-Warnery, A. (1999). *The primary triangle: A developmental systems view of mother, fathers, and infants.* New York: Basic Books.

Fivush, R. (1994). Constructing narrative, emotion, and self in parent-child conversations about the past. In U. Neisser & R. Fivush (Eds.), *The remembering self: Construction and accuracy in the self-narrative* (pp. 205–232). Cambridge, England: Cambridge University Press.

Flaherman, V. J. & Newman, T. B, (2011). Regulatory monitoring of feeding during the birth hospitalization. *Pediatrics, 127,* 1177-1179.

Fleming, A. S., & Orpen, G. (1986). Psychobiology of maternal behavior in rats, selected other species and humans. In A. Fogel & G. F. Melson (Eds.), *Origins of nurturance: Developmental, biological, and cultural perspectives on caregiving* (pp. 184–208). Hillsdale, NJ: Erlbaum.

Fleming, A. S., Ruble, D. N., Flett, G. L., & Van Wagner, V. (1990). Adjustment in first-time mothers: Changes in mood and mood content during the early postpartum months. *Developmental Psychology, 26,* 137–143.

Fleming, N., Newton, E. R., & Roberts, J. (2003). Changes in postpartum perineal muscle function in women with and without episiotomies. *J Midwifery Womens Health, 48*(1), 53–59.

Fleury, V. (2011) A change in boundary conditions induces a discontinuity of tissue flow in chicken embryos and the formation of the cephalic. *The European Physical Journal. E, Soft Matter, 34,* 73.

Flom, R., Gentile, D., & Pick, A. (2008). Infants' discrimination of happy and sad music. *Infant Behavior & Development, 31*(4), 716-728. doi:10.1016/j.infbeh.2008.04.004

Flom, R., & Pick, A. D. (2003). Verbal encouragement and joint attention in 18–month-old infants. *Infant Behavior & Development, 26*(2), 121–134.

Flom, R., Whipple, H., & Hyde, D. (2009). Infants' Intermodal Perception of Canine ("Canis Familairis") Facial Expressions and Vocalizations. *Developmental Psychology, 45*(4), 1143-1151.

Floor, P., & Akhtar, N. (2006). Can 18–Month-Old Infants Learn Words by Listening In on Conversations? *Infancy, 9*(3), 327–339.

Flykt, M., Kanninen, K., Sinkkonen, J., & Punamäki, R. (2010). Maternal depression and dyadic interaction: The role of maternal attachment style:. *Infant And Child Development, 19*(5), 530-550.

Fogel, A. (1977). Temporal organization in mother-infant face-to-face interaction. In H. R. Schaffer (Ed.), *Studies in mother-infant interaction* (pp. 119–152). New York: Academic Press.

Fogel, A. (1979). Peer vs. mother directed behavior in 1– to 3–month-old infants. *Infant Behavior and Development, 2,* 215–226.

Fogel, A. (1981). The ontogeny of gestural communication: The first six months. In R. Stark (Ed.), *Language behavior in infancy and early childhood* (pp. 17–44). New York: Elsevier.

Fogel, A. (1982a). Affect dynamics in early infancy: Affective tolerance. In T. Field & A. Fogel (Eds.), *Emotion and early interaction* (pp. 15–56). Hillsdale, NJ: Erlbaum.

Fogel, A. (1982b). Early adult-infant face-to-face interaction: Expectable sequences of behavior. *Journal of Pediatric Psychology, 7,* 1–22.

Fogel, A. (1985). Coordinative structures in the development of expressive behavior in early infancy. In G. Zivin (Ed.), *The development of expressive behavior: Biology-environment interactions* (pp. 249–267). New York: Academic Press.

Fogel, A. (1990a). The process of developmental change in infant communicative action: Using dynamic systems theory to study individual ontogenies. In J. Colombo & J. Fagen (Eds.), *Individual differences in infancy: Reliability, stability, and prediction* (pp. 177–201). Hillsdale, NJ: Erlbaum.

Fogel, A. (1990b). Sensorimotor factors in communicative development. In H. Bloch & B. Bertenthal (Eds.), *Sensorimotor organization and development in infancy and early childhood. NATO ASI Series* (pp. 54–80). The Netherlands: Kluwer Academic.

Fogel, A. (1993). *Developing through relationships.* Chicago: University of Chicago Press.

Fogel, A. (2000). A relational perspective on the development of self and emotion. In J. A. Bosma & E. S. Kunnen (Eds.), *Identity and emotions: A self-organizational perspective.* Cambridge, England: Cambridge University Press.

Fogel, A. (2004). Remembering infancy: Accessing our earliest experiences. In G. Bremner & A. Slater (Eds.), *Theories of infant development.* Blackwell Publishers.

Fogel, A. (2008). Relationships that support human development. . In A. Fogel, B. J. King, & S. Shanker (Eds.). *Human development in the 21st century: Visionary policy ideas from systems scientists.* Cambridge, UK: Cambridge University Press.

Fogel, A. (2010) Historical reflections on infancy. In J. G. Bremmer, T. D. Wachs (Eds.). *The Wiley-Blackwell handbook of infant development volume 1: Basic research* (2nd edition, pp. 3-31). West Sussex, UK: Wiley-Blackwell, Ltd.

Fogel, A. (2013). *Body Sense: The Science and Practice of Embodied Self-Awareness.* NY: W. W. Norton.

Fogel, A., & Branco, A. U. (1997). Meta-communication as a source of indeterminism in relationship development. In A. Fogel, M. Lyra, & J. Valsiner (Eds.), *Dynamics and indeterminism in developmental and social processes* (pp. 138–155). Hillsdale, NJ: Erlbaum.

Fogel, A., Dedo, J. Y., & McEwen, I. (1992). Effect of postural position and reaching on gaze during mother-infant face-to-face interaction. *Infant Behavior and Development, 15,* 231–244.

Fogel, A., Dickson, K. L., Hsu, H., Messinger, D., Nelson-Goens, G. C., & Nwokah, E. (1997). Communicative dynamics of emotion. In K. C. Barrett (Ed.), *New directions in child development: The communication of emotion: Current research from diverse perspectives, 77* (pp. 5–24). San Francisco: Jossey-Bass.

Fogel, A. & Garvey, A. (2007). Alive communication. *Infant Behavior and Development, 30,* 251–257.

Fogel, A., Garvey, A., Hsu, H., & West-Stroming, D. (2006). *Change processes in relationships: A relational – historical research approach.* Cambridge, UK: Cambridge University Press.

Fogel, A., & Hannan, T. E. (1985). Manual actions of 2– to 3–month-old human infants during social interaction. *Child Development, 56,* 1271–1279.

Fogel, A., Hsu, H., Shapiro, A. F., Nelson-Goens, G. C., & Secrist, C. (2006). Effects of normal and perturbed social play on the duration and amplitude of different types of infant smiles. <u>Developmental Psychology, 42,</u> 459–473.

Fogel, A., & Lyra, M. (1997). Dynamics of development in relationships. In F. Masterpasqua & P. Perna (Eds.), *The psychological meaning of chaos: Self-organization in human development and psychotherapy* (pp. 75–94). Washington, DC: American Psychological Association.

Fogel, A., Lyra, M. C., & Valsiner, J. (Eds.). (1997). *Dynamics and indeterminism in developmental and social processes.* Hillsdale, NJ: Erlbaum.

Fogel, A., Melson, G. F., Toda, S., & Mistry, J. (1987). Young children's responses to unfamiliar infants: The effects of adult involvement. *International Journal of Behavioral Development, 10,* 37–50.

Fogel, A., & Melson, G. F. (1988). *Child development.* St. Paul, MN: West.

Fogel, A., Nelson-Goens, G. C., Hsu, H. C., & Shapiro, A. F. (2000). Do different infant smiles reflect different positive emotions? <u>Social Development, 9</u> (4), 497–520.

Fogel, A., Nwokah, E., Dedo, J., Messinger, D., Dickson, K. L., Matusov, E., & Holt, S. A. (1992). Social process theory of emotion: A dynamic systems perspective. *Social Development, 1,* 122–142.

Fogel, A., Nwokah, E., Hsu, H. C., Dedo, J. Y., & Walker, H. (1993). Posture and communication in mother-infant interaction. In G. J. P. Savelsbergh (Ed.), *The development of coordination in infancy* (pp. 395–422). Amsterdam: Elsevier.

Fogel, A., Nwokah, E., & Karns, J. (1993). Parent-infant games as dynamic social systems. In K. B. MacDonald (Ed.), *Parents and children playing* (pp. 391–417). Albany, NY: SUNY Press.

Fogel, A., Stevenson, M. B., & Messinger, D. (1992). A comparison of the parent-child relationship in Japan and the United States. In J. L. Roopnarine & D. B. Carter (Eds.), *Parent-child relations in diverse cultural settings* (pp. 205–230). Norwood, NJ: Ablex.

Fogel, A., & Thelen, E. (1987). Development of early expressive and communicative action: Reinterpreting the evidence from a dynamic systems perspective. *Developmental Psychology, 23,* 747–761.

Fogel, A., Toda, S., & Kawai, M. (1988). Mother-infant face-to-face interaction in Japan and the United States: A laboratory comparison using 3–month-old infants. *Developmental Psychology, 24,* 398–406.

Foli, K. J. (2010). Depression in adoptive parents: A model of understanding through grounded theory. *Western Journal of Nursing Research, 32,* 379-400.

Fonagy, P., Gergely G., Jurist, E. & Target, M. (2004). *Affect Regulation, Mentalization, and the Development of the Self.* London: Karnac Books.

Fonagy, P., & Target, M. (2005). Commentary: Bridging the transmission gap: An end to an important mystery of attachment research? *Attachment & Human Development, 7*(3), 333–343.

Fonagy, P., Target, M., Steele, H., & Steele, M. (1998). Reflective-functioning manual, version 5.0, for application to adult attachment interviews. *London: University College London.*

Forbes, L. M., Evans, E. M., Moran, G., & Pederson, D. R. (2007). Change in Atypical Maternal Behavior Predicts Change in Attachment Disorganization From 12 to 24 Months in a High-Risk Sample. *Child Development, 78*(3), 955–971.

Ford, J. H., MacCormac, L., & Hiller, J. (1994). Pregnancy and lifestyle study: Association between occupational and environmental exposure to chemicals and reproductive outcome. *Mutation Research, 313,* 153–164.

Forestier, D. F., Kaplan, C., & Cox, W. (1988). Prenatal diagnosis and management of bleeding disorders with fetal blood sampling. *American Journal of Obstetrics and Gynecology, 158,* 939–946.

Forget-Dubois, N., Dionne, G., Lemelin, J., Pérusse, D., Tremblay, R. E., & Boivin, M. (2009). Early child language mediates the relation between home environment and school readiness. *Child Development*, 80(3), 736-749. doi:10.1111/j.1467-8624.2009.01294.x

Forkert, P.G., Lash, L., Tardif, R., Tanphaichitr, N., Vandevoort, C., & Moussa, M, (2003). Identification of trichloroethylene and its metabolites in human seminal fluid of workers exposed to trichloroethylene. *Drug Metabolism And Disposition: The Biological Fate Of Chemicals, 31,*306-311.

Forrest, J. D., & Fordyce, R. R. (1993). Women's contraceptive attitudes and use in 1992. *Family Planning Perspectives, 25,* 175–179.

Forrest, J. D., & Fordyce, R. R. (1993b). Locomotor coordination in infancy: The transition from walking to running. In G. J. P. Savelsbergh (Ed.), *The development of coordination in infancy* (pp. 359–393). Amsterdam: Elsevier.

Forrester, L. W., Phillips, S. J., & Clark, J. E. (1993). Locomotor coordination in infancy: The transition from walking to running. In G. J. P. Savelsbergh (Ed.), *The development of coordination in infancy* (pp. 359–393). Amsterdam: Elsevier.

Foster, E., & Watkins, S. (2010). The value of reanalysis: TV viewing and attention problems. *Child Development, 81*(1), 368-375. doi:10.1111/j.1467-8624.2009.01400.x

Fox, C. R., & Gelfand, D. M. (1994). Maternal depressed mood and stress as related to vigilance, self-efficacy, and mother-child interactions. *Early Development and Parenting, 3,* 233–243.

Fox, N. A. (1977). Attachment of kibbutz infants to mother and metapelet. *Child Development, 48,* 1228–1239.

Fox, N. A. (1989). Psychophysiological correlates of emotional reactivity during the first year of life. *Developmental Psychology, 25,* 364–372.

Fox, N. A., & Davidson, R. J. (1988). Patterns of brain electrical activity during the expression of discrete emotions in ten-month-old infants. *Developmental Psychology, 24,* 230–236.

Fox, N. A., Kimmerly, N. L., & Schafer, W. D. (1991). Attachment to mother/attachment to father: A meta-analysis. *Child Development, 62,* 210–225.

Fox, R., & McDaniels, C. (1982). The perception of biological motion by human infants. *Science, 218,* 486–487.

Fox, S. E., Levitt, P., & Nelson, C. A. 3rd. (2010). How the timing and quality of early experiences influence the development of brain architecture. *Child Development, 81,* 28-40.

Fraiberg, S., Adelson,E., & Shapiro,V., (1975). Ghosts in the nursery: A psychoanalytic approach to the problem of impaired mother-infant relationships. *Journal of the American Academy of Child Psychiatry, 14,* 387–421.

Fraley, R. C. (2002). Attachment stability from infancy to adulthood: Meta-analysis and dynamic modeling of developmental mechanisms. *Personality and Social Psychology Review, 6*(2), 123–151.

Franco, F., Fogel, A., Messinger, D., & Frazier, C. (1996). Cultural differences in physical contact between Hispanic and Anglo mother-infant dyads living in the United States. *Early Development and Parenting, 5,* 119–127.

Frank, R. (2001). Body of awareness: A somatic and developmental approach to psychotherapy. New Jersey: The Analytic Press.

Frankenburg, W. K., Dodd, J. B., Fandal, A. W., Kuzuk, E., & Cohrs, M. (1975). *DDST: Reference manual* (Rev. ed.). Denver: Ladoka Project and Publication Foundation.

Frazier, P. A., Byer, A. L., Fischer, A. R., Wright, D. M., & DeBord, K. A. (1996). Adult attachment style and partner choice: Correlational and experimental findings. *Personal Relationships, 3*(2), 117–136.

Frazier, B. M., Gelman, S. A., Wellman, H. M. (2009). Preschoolers' Search for Explanatory Information Within Adult–Child Conversation. *Child Development, 80*(6), 1592-1611.

Freeman, N. H. (1980). *Strategies of representation in young children: Analysis of spatial skill and drawing processes.* London: Academic Press.

Freeman, R. (1990). Intrapartum fetal monitoring—A disappointing story (editorial; comment). *New England Journal of Medicine, 322*(9), 624–626.

Freides, David (2001). *Developmental disorders: A neuropsychological approach.* Malden: Blackwell Publishing.

French, V. (2002). *History of parenting: The ancient Mediterranean world.* Mahwah, NJ, US: Lawrence Erlbaum Associates Publishers.

Freud, A. (1965). *Normality and pathology in childhood.* New York: International Universities Press.

Freud, S. (1900/1953). [*The interpretation of dreams.*] In J. Strachey (Ed. and Trans.), *The standard edition of the complete works of Sigmund Freud* (Vol. 3, pp. 485–699). London: Hogarth Press. (Original work published 1900)

Friedman, N. P., Miyake, A., Robinson, J. L., & Hewitt, J. K. (2011). Developmental trajectories in toddlers' self-restraint predict individual differences in executive functions 14 years later: A behavioral genetic analysis. *Developmental Psychology, 47*(5), 1410-1430.

Fries, A. B., Ziegler, T. E., Kurian, J. R., Jacoris, S., & Pollak, S. D. (2005). Early experience in humans is associated with changes in neuropeptides critical for regulating social behavior. *Proc Natl Acad Sci U S A, 102*(47), 17237–17240.

Frymer-Kensky, T. (1995). Motherprayer: The pregnant woman's spiritual companion. New York: Riverhead Books.

Frick, J. E., Colombo, J., & Saxon, T. F. (1999). Individual and developmental differences in disengagement of fixation in early infancy. *Child Development, 70*(3), 537–548.

Fried, P. A. (2002). Conceptual issues in behavioral teratology and their application in determining long-term sequelae of prenatal marihuana exposure. *Journal of Child Psychology and Psychiatry, 43*(1), 81–102.

Friedman, S. L., & Jacobs, B. S. (1981). Sex differences in neonates' behavioral responsiveness to repeated auditory stimulation. *Infant Behavior and Development, 4,* 175–183.

Friedman, S. L., Randolph, S., & Kochanoff, A. (2000). Child care research at the dawn of a new millennium: Taking stock of what we know. In J. G. Bremner & A. Fogel (Eds.), *Handbook of infancy research* (pp. 415–437). Oxford, England: Blackwell.

Friedrich-Cofer, L. K. (1986). Body, mind, and morals in the framing of social policy. In L. K. Friedrich-Cofer (Ed.), *Human nature of public policy: Scientific views of women, children and families* (pp. 97–173). New York: Praeger.

Friend, K. B., Goodwin, M. S., & Lipsitt, L. P. (2004). Alcohol use and sudden infant death syndrome. *Developmental Review, 24*(3), 235–251.

Frigoletto, F. D., Greene, M. F., Benacerraf, B. R., Barss, V. A., & Saltzman, D. H. (1986). Ultrasonographic fetal surveillance in the management of the isoimmunized pregnancy. *New England Journal of Medicine, 315,* 430–432.

Frith, U., & Frith, C. (2001). The biological basis of social interaction. *Current Directions in Psychological Science, 10*(5), 151–155.

Frodi, A. M., & Lamb, M. E. (1978). Sex differences in responsiveness to infants: A developmental study of psychophysiological and behavioral responses. *Child Development, 49,* 1182–1188.

Frodi, A. M., & Lamb, M. E. (1980). Child abuser's response to infant smiles and cries. *Child Development, 51,* 238–241.

Frodi, A. M., Lamb, M. E., Leavitt, L. A., & Donovan, W. L. (1978). Father's and mother's responses to infant smiles and cries. *Infant Behavior and Development, 1,* 187–198.

Frosch, C. A., Mangelsdorf, S. C., & McHale, J. L. (1998). Correlates of marital behavior at 6 months postpartum. *Developmental Psychology, 34*(6), 1438–1449.

Furdon, S. A., Pfeil, V. C., & Snow, K. (1998). Operationalizing Donna Wong's principle of atraumatic care: Pain management in the NICU. *Pediatric Nursing, 24*(4), 336–342.

Furman, W., Rahe, D. F., & Hartup, W. W. (1979). Rehabilitation of socially withdrawn preschool children through mixed-age and same-age socialization. *Child Development, 50,* 915–922.

Furrow, D. (1984). Social and private speech at two years. *Child Development, 55,* 355–362.

Furstenberg, F. F., Jr., Brooks-Gunn, J., & Morgan, P. (1987). *Adolescent mothers in later life.* New York: Cambridge University Press.

Gaddini, R. (1970). Transitional objects and the process of individuation. *Journal of the American Academy of Child Psychiatry, 9,* 347–365.

Gaensbauer, T. J. (2004). Telling their stories: Representation and reenactment of traumatic experiences occurring in the first year of life. *Zero to Three, 24*(5), 25–31.

Gallese, V., Rochat, M., Cossu, G., & Sinigaglia, C. (2009). Motor cognition and its role in the phylogeny and ontogeny of action understanding. *Developmental Psychology, 45*(1), 103-113. doi:10.1037/a0014436

Galtry, J., & Callister, P. (2005). Assessing the Optimal Length of Parental Leave for Child and Parental Well-Being: How Can Research Inform Policy? *Journal of Family Issues, 26*(2), 219–246.

Galvin, E. S. (1989). Children and child care in China: Some observations. *Children Today,* 19–23.

Gandelman, R. (1992). *The psychobiology of behavioral development.* New York: Oxford University Press.

Gandour, M. J. (1989). Activity level as a dimension of temperament in toddlers: Its relevance for the organismic specificity hypothesis. *Child Development, 60,* 1092–1098.

Garbarino, J. A. (1982). Sociocultural risk: Dangers to competence. In C. Kopp & J. B. Krakow (Eds.), *The child: Development in a social context* (pp. 246–268). Reading, MA: Addison-Wesley.

Garbarino, J. A. (1992). The meaning of poverty in the world of children. *American Behavioral Scientist, 35,* 220–237.

Garcia-Coll, C., Kagan, J., & Reznick, J. S. (1984). Behavioral inhibition in young children. *Child Development, 55,* 1005–1019.

Garciaguirre, J. S., Adolph, K. E., & Shrout, P. E. (2007). Baby carriage: Infants walking with loads. *Child Development, 78*(2), 664–680.

Gardner, C. A. (1989). Is an embryo a person? *Nation,* 557–559.

Gardosi, J., Hutson, N., & Lynch, C. (1989). Randomized, controlled trial of squatting in the second stage of labor. *Lancet, 2,* 74–77.

Garner, P. W. (2003). Child and Family Correlates of Toddlers' Emotional and Behavioral Responses to a Mishap. *Infant Mental Health Journal, 24*(6), 580–596.

Garner, P. W., Jones, D. C., & Palmer, D. J. (1994). Social cognitive correlates of preschool children's sibling caregiving behavior. *Developmental Psychology, 30,* 905–911.

Gartner, L. M., Morton, J., Lawrence, R. A., Naylor, A. J., O'Hare, D., Schanler, R. J., et al. (2005). Breastfeeding and the use of human milk. *Pediatrics, 115*(2), 496–506.

Gartstein, M. A., & Bateman, A. E. (2008). Early manifestations of childhood depression: Influences of infant temperament and parental depressive symptoms. *Infant And Child Development, 17*(3), 223-248.

Garvey, C. (1974). Some properties of social play. *Merrill-Palmer Quarterly, 20,* 163–180.

Gatts, J. D., Wallace, D. H., Glasscock, G. F., McKee, E., & Cohen, R. S. (1994). A modified newborn intensive care unit environment may shorten hospital stay. *Journal of Perinatology, 14,* 422–427.

Gavidia-Payne, S., & Stoneman, Z. (1997). Family predictors of maternal and paternal involvement in programs for young children with disabilities. *Child Development, 68*(4), 701–717.

Gelfand, D. M. (2000). Infant mental health in a changing society. In J. G. Bremner & A. Fogel (Eds.), *Handbook of infancy research* (pp. 362–385). Oxford, England: Blackwell.

Gelfand, D. M., Teti, D. M., & Fox, C. E. R. (1992). Sources of parenting stress for depressed and nondepressed mothers of infants. *Journal of Clinical Child Psychology, 21,* 262–272.

Geller, G., Tambor, E. S., Chase, G. A., Hofman, K. J., Faden, R. R., & Holtzman, N. A. (1993). Incorporation of genetic counselling in primary care practice. *Archives of Family Medicine, 2,* 1119–1125.

Gelles, R. (1978). Violence toward children in the United States. *American Journal of Orthopsychiatry, 48,* 580–592.

Gelman, S. A., Collman, P., & Maccoby, E. E. (1986). Inferring properties from categories vs. inferring categories from properties: The case of gender. *Child Development, 57,* 396–404.

Gelman, S. A., Taylor, M. G., & Nguyen, S. P. (2004). Mother-child conversations about gender. *Monographs of the Society for Research in Child Development, 69*(1, Serial No. 275).

Gentile, S. (2011). Selective serotonin reuptake inhibitor exposure during early pregnancy and the risk of birth defects. *Acta Psychiatrica Scandinavica, 123,* 266-275.

Gerken, L., Landau, B., & Remez, R. E. (1990). Function morphemes in young children's speech perception and production. *Developmental Psychology, 26,* 204–216.

Germo, G. R., Chang, E. S., Keller, M. A., & Goldberg, W. A. (2007). Child sleep arrangements and family life: perspectives from mothers and fathers. *Infant and Child Development, 16*(4), 433–456.

Gershoff, E. T. (2002). Corporal punishment by parents and associated child behaviors and experiences: A meta-analytic and theoretical review. *Psychological Bulletin, 128*(4), 539–579.

Gervain, J., Macagno, F., Cogoi, S., Peña, M., & Mehler, J. (2008). The neonate brain detects speech structure. *Proceedings Of The National Academy Of Sciences Of The United States Of America, 105*(37), 14222-14227. doi:10.1073/pnas.0806530105

Gesell, A. (1925). *The mental growth of the preschool child.* New York: Macmillan.

Gesell, A. (1928). *Infancy and human growth.* New York: Macmillan.

Gettler, L., McDade, T., Feranil, A., & Kuzawa, C. (2011). Longitudinal evidence that fatherhood decreases testosterone in human males. *Proceedings Of The National Academy Of Sciences Of The United States Of America, 108*(39), 16194-16199. doi:10.1073/pnas.1105403108

Gewirtz, J. L. (1972). *Attachment and dependency.* New York: Halsted Press.

Gianino, A., & Tronick, E. Z. (1988). The mutual regulation model: The infant's self and interactive regulation and coping and defensive capacities. In T. M. Field, P. M. McCabe, & N. Schneiderman (Eds.), *Stress and coping across development* (pp. 300–323). Hillsdale, NJ: Erlbaum.

Gibson, E. J., Riccio, G., Schmuckler, M. A., Stoffregen, T. A., Rosenberg, D., & Taormina, J. (1987). Detection of the traversability of surfaces by crawling and walking infants. *Journal of Experimental Psychology: Human Perception and Performance, 13,* 533–544.

Gibson, E. J., & Walk, R. D. (1960). The "visual cliff." *Scientific American, 202,* 64–71.

Gibson, J. J. (1966). *The senses considered as perceptual systems.* Boston, MA: Houghton Mifflin.

Gielen, A. C., O'Campo, P. J., Faden, R. R., Kass, N. E., & Xue, X. (1994). Interpersonal conflict and physical violence during the childbearing years. *Social Science and Medicine, 39,* 781–787.

Gies, F., & Gies, J. (1987). *Marriage and the family in the Middle Ages.* New York: Harper & Row.

Giesbrecht, G. F., Miller, M. R., & Müller, U. (2010). The anger-distress model of temper tantrums: Associations with emotional reactivity and emotional competence. *Infant And Child Development, 19*(5), 478-497.

Gliga, T., Elsabbagh, M., Andravizou, A., & Johnson, M. (2009). Faces attract infants' attention in complex displays. *Infancy, 14*(5), 550-562. doi:10.1080/15250000903144199

Gilliland, F. D., Li, Y. F., & Peters, J. M. (2001). Effects of maternal smoking during pregnancy and environmental tobacco smoke on asthma and wheezing in children. *Am J Respir Crit Care Med, 163*(2), 429–436.

Gingras, J., Mitchell, E., & Grattan, K. (2005). Fetal homologue of infant crying. *Archives of Disease in Childhood -- Fetal & Neonatal Edition, 90*(5), F415–F418.

Ginsburg, C. (1999). Body-image, movement, and consciousness: Examples from a somatic practice in the Feldenkrais method. *Journal of Consciousness Studies, 6*(2–3), 79–91.

Ginsburg, G. P., & Kilbourne, B. K. (1988). Emergence of vocal alternation in mother-infant interchanges. *Journal of Child Language, 15,* 221–235.

Glazer, S. (1993). Outlook, testing theories. *C. Q. Researcher, 3,* 304–306.

Glicksman, E (2012). Catching autism earlier, *Monitor on Psychology, 43,* 57-60.

Glink, P. (1998). A collaborative effort in perinatal support for birthing teens. *Zero to Three, 18*(5), 44–50.

Gloger-Tippelt, G., Gomille, B., Koenig, L., & Vetter, J. (2002). Attachment representations in 6–year-olds: Related longitudinally to the quality of attachment in infancy and mothers' attachment representations. *Attachment & Human Development, 4*(3), 318–339.

Gloger-Tippelt, G. S., & Huerkamp, M. (1998). Relationship change at the transition to parenthood and security of infant-mother attachment. *International Journal of Behavioral Development, 22*(3), 633–655.

Godfrey, A. B., & Kilgore, A. (1998). An approach to help very young infants sleep through the night. *Zero to Three, 19*(2), 15–21.

Gogate, L., Maganti, M., & Laing, K. (2013). Maternal naming of object wholes versus parts to preverbal infants: a fine-grained analysis of scaffolding at 6-8 months. *Infant Behavior & Development, 36*(3), 470-479.

Goldfarb, J. (1993). Breastfeeding, AIDS, and other infectious diseases. *Clinical Perinatology,* 20, 225–243.

Goldfield, E. C. (1989). Transition from rocking to crawling: Postural constraints on infant movement. *Developmental Psychology, 25,* 913–919.

Goldfield, E. C. (1993). Dynamic systems in development: Action systems. In L. B. Smith & E. Thelen (Eds.), *A dynamic systems approach to development: Applications* (pp. 51–70). Cambridge, MA: MIT Press.

Goldin-Meadow, S., Goodrich, W., Sauer, E., & Iverson, J. (2007). Young children use their hands to tell their mothers what to say. *Developmental Science, 10*(6), 778-785. doi:10.1111/j.1467-7687.2007.00636.x

Golding, J., & Peters, T. J. (1985). What else do SIDS risk prediction scores predict? *Early Human Development, 12,* 247–260.

Goldman, M. B. (1994). Sudden infant death syndrome: Back to sleep campaign. *Caring, 13,* 52–55.

Goldman-Rakic, P. S. (1987). Development of cortical circuitry and cognitive function. *Child Development, 58,* 601–622.

Goldsmith, D. F., & Rogoff, B. (1997). Mothers' and toddlers' coordinated joint focus of attention: Variations with maternal dysphoric symptoms. *Developmental Psychology, 33*(1), 113–119.

Goldsmith, H. H., & Alansky, J. (1987). Maternal and infant temperamental predictors of attachment: A meta-analytic review. *Journal of Consulting and Clinical Psychology, 55,* 805–816.

Goldsmith, H. H., Buss, K. A., & Lemery, K. S. (1997). Toddler and childhood temperament: Expanded content, stronger genetic evidence, new evidence for the importance of environment. *Developmental Psychology, 33*(6), 891–905.

Goldsmith, H. H., Buss, A. H., Plomin, R., Rothbart, M. K., Thoman, A., Chess, S., Hinde, R. A., & McCall, R. B. (1987). Roundtable: What is temperament? Four approaches. *Child Development, 58,* 505–529.

Goldsmith, H. H., & Campos, J. J. (1990). The structure of temperamental fear and pleasure in infants: A psychometric perspective. *Child Development, 61,* 1944–1964.

Goldsmith, H. H., Lemery, K. S., Buss, K. A., & Campos, J. J. (1999). Genetic analyses of focal aspects of infant temperament. *Developmental Psychology, 35*(4), 972–985.

Goldsmith, H. H., Pollak, S. D., & Davidson, R. J. (2008). Developmental neuroscience perspectives on emotion regulation. *Child Development Perspectives, 2*(3), 132-140. doi:10.1111/j.1750-8606.2008.00055.

Goldstein, M. H., King, A. P., & West, M. J. (2003). Social interaction shapes babbling: testing parallels between birdsong and speech. *Proc Natl Acad Sci U S A, 100*(13), 8030–8035.

Goldstein, M. H., Schwade, J. A., & Bornstein, M. H. (2009). The value of vocalizing: Five-month-old infants associate their own noncry vocalizations with responses from caregivers. *Child Development, 80*(3), 336-644. doi:10.1111/j.1467-8624.2009.01287.x

Goldstein, M. H., Schwade, J., Briesch, J., & Syal, S. (2010). Learning while babbling: Prelinguistic object-directed vocalizations indicate a readiness to learn. *Infancy, 15*(4), 362-391. doi:10.1111/j.1532-7078.2009.00020.x

Goldstein, S. R., & Young, C. A. (1996). "Evolutionary" stable strategy of handedness in major league baseball. *Journal of Comparative Psychology,* **110**, 164–169.

Golinkoff, R. M., & Ames, G. J. (1979). A comparison of fathers' and mothers' speech with their young children. *Child Development, 50,* 28–32.

Golombok S, Rust J, Zervoulis K, Croudace T, Golding J, Hines M. Developmental trajectories of sex-typed behavior in boys and girls: A longitudinal general population study of children aged 2.5-8 years. *Child Development* [serial online]. September 2008;79(5):1583-1593. Available from: PsycINFO, Ipswich, MA. Accessed December 4, 2013.

Golub, M. S. (1996). Labor analgesia and infant brain development. *Pharmacology of Biochemical Behavior, 55*(4), 619–628.

Golub, M. S., Macintosh, M. S., & Baumrind, N. (1998). Developmental and reproductive toxicity of inorganic arsenic: Animal studies and human concerns. *Journal of Toxicology and Environmental Health, 1*(3), 199–241.

Goodman, J. C., McDonough, L., & Brown, N. B. (1998). The role of semantic context and memory in the acquisition of novel nouns. *Child Development, 69*(5), 1330–1344.

Goodnow, J. (1977). *Children drawing.* Cambridge, MA: Harvard University Press.

Goodwin, R. D., Fergusson, D. M., & Horwood, L. J. (2005). Childhood abuse and familial violence and the risk of panic attacks and panic disorder in young adulthood. *Psychol Med, 35*(6), 881–890.

Goodwyn, S. W., & Acredolo, L. P. (1993). Symbolic gesture versus word: Is there a modality advantage for onset of symbol use? *Child Development, 64,* 688–701.

Goossens, F. A., & van Ijzendoorn, M. H. (1990). Quality of infants' attachments to professional caregivers: Relation to infant-parent attachment and day-care characteristics. *Child Development, 61,* 832–837.

Gordon, T. (1988). The case against disciplining children at home or in school. *Person-Centered Review, 3,* 59–85.

Gorman, K. S., & Pollitt, E. (1992). Relationship between weight and body proportionality at birth, growth during the first year of life, and cognitive development at 36, 48, and 60 months. *Infant Behavior and Development, 15,* 279–296.

Gornick, J. C., & Meyers, M. K. (2003). *Families that work: Policies for reconciling parenthood and employment.* New York: Russell Sage Foundation.

Gottfried, A. W., Rose, S. A., & Bridger, W. H. (1977). Cross-modal transfer in human infants. *Child Development, 48,* 118–123.

Gottlieb, G. (1991a). Experiential canalization of behavioral development: Theory. *Developmental Psychology, 27,* 4–13.

Gottlieb, G. (1991b). Experiential canalization of behavioral development: Results. *Developmental Psychology, 27,* 35–39.

Gottlieb, G. (1995). Some conceptual deficiencies in "developmental" behavior genetics. *Human Development, 38*(3), 131–141.

Goubet, N., & Clifton, R. K. (1998). Object and event representation in 6 1/2–month-old infants. *Developmental Psychology, 34*(1), 63–76.

Grace, D. M., David, B. J., & Ryan, M. K. (2008). Investigating preschoolers' categorical thinking about gender through imitation, attention, and the use of self-categories. *Child Development, 79*(6), 1928-1941. doi:10.1111/j.1467-8624.2008.01234.x

Graf Estes, K., & Hurley, K. (2013). Infant-directed prosody helps infants map sounds to meanings. *Infancy, 18*(5), 797-824. doi: 10.1111/infa.12006

Graham, A., Ablow, J., & Measelle, J. (2010). Interparental relationship dynamics and cardiac vagal functioning in infancy. *Infant Behavior & Development, 33*(4), 530-544. doi:10.1016/j.infbeh.2010.07.005

Graham, F. K., Leavitt, L., Strock, B., & Brown, H. (1978). Precocious cardiac orienting in a human anencephalic infant. *Science, 199,* 322–324.

Grandin, T. (2005). *Animals in translation: Using the mysteries of autism to decode animal behavior.* New York: Simon & Shuster.

Grandin, T., & Scariano, M. (1986). *Emergence: Labeled autistic.* Novato, CA: Arena Press.

Granrud, C. E., & Yonas, A. (1984). Infants' perception of pictorially specified interposition. *Journal of Experimental Child Psychology, 37,* 500–511.

Granrud, C. E., Yonas, A., & Opland, E. A. (1985). Infants' sensitivity to the depth cue of shading. *Perception and Psychophysics, 37,* 415–419.

Grant, V. J. (1994). Sex of infant differences in mother-infant interaction: A reinterpretation of past findings. *Developmental Review, 14,* 1–26.

Grant-Beuttler, M., Glynn, L. M., Salisbury, A. L., Davis, E. P., Holliday, C., & Sandman, C. A. (2011). Development of Fetal Movement between 26 and 36-Weeks' Gestation in Response to Vibro-Acoustic Stimulation. *Frontiers In Psychology, 2,* art 350.

Gratier, M. (2003). Expressive timing and interactional synchrony between mothers and infants: cultural similarities, cultural differences, and the immigration experience. *Cognitive Development, 18*(4), 533. doi:10.1016/j.cogdev.2003.09.009

Gray, V., Karmiloff-Smith, A., Funnell, E., & Tassabehji, M. (2006). In-depth analysis of spatial cognition in Williams syndrome: A critical assessment of the role of the LIMK1 gene. *Neuropsychologia, 44*(5), 679–685.

Gredebäck, G., Stasiewicz, D., Falck-Ytter, T., Rosander, K., & von Hofsten, C. (2009). Action type and goal type modulate goal-directed gaze shifts in 14-month-old infants. *Developmental Psychology, 45*(4), 1190-1194. doi:10.1037/a0015667

Green, J. A., Gustafson, G. E., Irwin, J. R., Kalinowski, L. L., & Wood, R. M. (1995). Infant crying: Acoustics, perception, and communication. *Early Development and Parenting, 4*(4), 161–175.

Green, J. A., Gustafson, G. E., & McGhie, A. C. (1998). Changes in infants' cries as a function of time in a cry bout. *Child Development, 69*(2), 271–279.

Green, J. E., Dorfman, A., Jones, S. L., Bender, S., Patton, L., & Schulman, J. D. (1988). Chorionic villus sampling: Experience with an initial 940 cases. *Obstetrics and Gynecology, 71,* 208–212.

Green, J. M. (1998). Postnatal depression or perinatal dysphoria? Findings from a longitudinal community-based study using the Edinburgh Postnatal Depression Scale. *Journal of Reproductive and Infant Psychology, 16*(2–3), 143–155.

Greenberger, E., O'Neil, R., & Nagel, S. K. (1994). Linking workplace and homeplace: Relations between the nature of adults' work and their parenting behaviors. *Developmental Psychology, 30,* 990–1002.

Greenfield, P. M. (2009). Linking social change and developmental change: Shifting pathways of human development. *Developmental Psychology, 45,* 401-418.

Greenfield, P., & Smith, J. H. (1976). *The structure of communication in early language development.* New York: Academic Press.

Greenleaf, P. (1978). *Children throughout the ages: A history of childhood.* New York: Barnes & Noble.

Greenough, W. T., Black, J. E., & Wallace, C. S. (1987). Experience and brain development. *Child Development, 58,* 539–559.

Greenspan, S. I. (2008). A dynamic developmental model of mental health and mental illness. . In A. Fogel, B. J. King, & S. Shanker (Eds.). *Human development in the 21st century: Visionary policy ideas from systems scientists.* Cambridge, UK: Cambridge University Press.

Greenspan, S. I. & Wieder, S. (1997). An integrated approach to interventions for young children with severe difficulties in relating and communicating. *Zero to Three, 17*(5), 5–17.

Grieser, D. L., & Kuhl, P. K. (1988). Maternal speech to infants in a tonal language: Support for universal prosodic features in motherese. *Developmental Psychology, 24*(1), 14–20.

Grieser, D. L., & Kuhl, P. K. (1989). Categorization of speech by infants: Support for speech-sound prototypes. *Developmental Psychology, 25,* 577–588.

Grimes, D. A. (1994). The morbidity and mortality of pregnancy: Still risky business. *American Journal of Obstetrics and Gynecology, 170,* 1489–1494.

Grimm, E. (1967). Psychological and social factors in pregnancy, delivery and outcome. In S. Richardson & A. Guttmacher (Eds.), *Childbearing: Its social and psychological aspects* (pp. 305–348). Baltimore: Williams & Wilkins.

Grobstein, C. (1988). *Science and the unborn.* New York: Basic Books.

Grodstein, F., Goldman, M. B., & Cramer, D. W. (1994). Infertility in women and moderate alcohol use. *American Journal of Public Health, 84,* 1429–1432.

Groh, A. M. & Roisman, G. I. (2009). Adults' autonomic and subjective emotional responses to infant vocalizations: The role of secure base script knowledge. *Developmental Psychology, 45,* 889-893.

Grolnick, W. S., Bridges, L. J., & Connel, J. P. (1996). Emotion regulation in two-year-olds: Strategies and emotional expression in four contexts. *Child Development, 67,* 928–941.

Grolnick, W. S., Cosgrove, T. J., & Bridges, L. J. (1996). Age-graded change in the initiation of positive affect. *Infant Behavior and Development, 19,* 153–157.

Gross, J., & Hayne, H. (1999). Young children's recognition and description of their own and others' drawings. *Developmental Science, 2*(4), 476–489.

Grosse, S. D. (2010). Late-treated phenylketonuria and partial reversibility of intellectual impairment. *Child Development, 81*(1), 200-211. doi:10.1111/j.1467-8624.2009.01389.x

Grossman, K., Grossman, K. E., Spangler, G., Suess, G., & Unzner, L. (1985). Maternal sensitivity and newborns' orientation responses as related to quality of attachment in northern Germany. *Monographs of the Society for Research in Child Development, 50* (Serial No. 209), 233–256.

Grossmann, T., Oberecker, R., Koch, S., & Friederici, A. (2010). The developmental origins of voice processing in the human brain. *Neuron, 65*(6), 852-858. doi:10.1016/j.neuron.2010.03.001

Grossmann, T., Parise, E., & Friederici, A. D. (2010). The detection of communicative signals directed at the self in infant prefrontal cortex. *Frontiers In Human Neuroscience, 4*doi:10.3389/fnhum.2010.00201

Grossmann, T., Striano, T., & Friederici, A. D. (2006). Cross-modal integration of emotional information from face and voice in the infant brain. *Developmental Science, 9*(3), 309–315.

Grover, S., & Permezel, M. (1994). What's new?: Gynaecology. *Medical Journal of Australia, 161,* 330–331.

Gruen, A. (1987). The relationship of sudden infant death and parental unconscious conflicts. *Pre- and Perinatal Psychology Journal, 2,* 50–56.

Gruendel, J. M. (1977). Referential extension in early language development. *Child Development, 48,* 1567–1576.

Grunwaldt, E., Bates, T., & Guthrie, D. (1960). The onset of sleeping through the night in infancy. *Pediatrics, 26,* 667–668.

Grych, J. H., & Clark, R. (1999). Maternal employment and development of the father-infant relationship in the first year. *Developmental Psychology, 35*(4), 893–903.

Gudmundson, J., & Leerkes, E. (2012). Links between mothers' coping styles, toddler reactivity, and sensitivity to toddler's negative emotions. *Infant Behavior & Development, 35*(1), 158-166.

Guerin, D. W., Gottfried, A. W., & Thomas, C. W. (1997). Difficult temperament and behaviour problems: A longitudinal study from 1.5 to 12 years. *International Journal of Behavioral Development, 21*(1), 71–90.

Guffanti, S., Grancini, F., Scalfaro, C., & Podesta, A. F. (2004). [Sudden infant death syndrome (SIDS)]. *Pediatr Med Chir, 26*(2), 96–104.

Guillain, A., Foxonet, C., Petersen, A., & Ramos, M. (1997). Socialization and cognition in children between the age of 18 and 24 months. *Early Development and Parenting, 6*(2), 59–71.

Gunnar, M. (1994). Psychoendocrine studies of temperament and stress in early childhood: Expanding current models. In J. E. Bates & T. D. Wachs (Eds.), *Temperament: Individual differences at the interface of biology and behavior* (pp. 175–198). Washington, DC: American Psychological Association.

Gunnar, M. R., & Barr, R.G. (1998). Stress, early brain development, and behavior. *Infants and Young Children, 11*(1), 1–14.

Gunnar, M. & Cheatham, C. L. (2003). Brain and behavior interface: Stress and the developing brain. *Infant Mental Health Journal, 24,* 195–211.

Gunnar, M. R., Kryzer, E., Van Ryzin, M. J., & Phillips, D. A. (2010). The rise in cortisol in family day care: Associations with aspects of care quality, child behavior, and child sex. *Child Development, 81*(3), 851-869. doi:10.1111/j.1467-8624.2010.01438.x

Gunnar, M., Leighton, K., & Peleaux, R. (1984). Effects of temporal predictability on the reactions of 1–year-olds to potentially frightening toys. *Developmental Psychology, 20,* 449–458.

Gunnar, M., Mangelsdorf, S., Larson, M., & Hertsgaard, L. (1989). Attachment, temperament, and adrenocortical activity in infancy: A study of psychoendocrine regulation. *Developmental Psychology, 25,* 355–363.

Gunnar, M. R., & Stone, C. (1984). The effects of positive maternal affect on infant responses to pleasant, ambiguous, and fear-provoking toys. *Child Development, 55,* 1231–1236.

Gurevich, R. (2009) How much does IVF cost? http://infertility.about/od/ivf/f/-ivf_cost.htm

Guse, T., Wissing, M., & Hartman, W. (2006). The effect of a prenatal hypnotherapeutic programme on postnatal maternal psychological well-being. *Journal of Reproductive and Infant Psychology, 24*(2), 163–177.

Gusella, J. L., Muir, D., & Tronick, E. Z. (1988). The effect of manipulating maternal behavior during an interaction on three- and six-month-olds' affect and attention. *Child Development, 59,* 1111–1124.

Gustafson, G. E. (1984). The effects of the ability to locomote on infants' social and exploratory behaviors: An experimental study. *Developmental Psychology, 20,* 397–405.

Gustafson, G. E., & Green, J. A. (1991). Developmental coordination of cry sounds with visual regard and gestures. *Infant Behavior and Development, 14,* 51–57.

Gustafson, G. E., Green, J. A., & Kalinowski, L. L. (1995, March). *Crying and vocalizing: A nascent system for communicating different meanings?* Poster presented at the meeting of the Society for Research in Child Development, Indianapolis, IN.

Gustafson, G. E., Green, J. A., & West, M. J. (1979). The infant's changing role in mother-infant games: The growth of social skills. *Infant Behavior and Development, 2,* 301–308.

Guttmacher, A. (1973). *Pregnancy, birth and family planning: A guide for expectant parents in the 1970s.* New York: Viking Press.

Hack, M., Klein, N. K., & Taylor, H. G. (1995). Long-term developmental outcomes of low birth weight infants. *The Future of Children, 5,* 176–196.

Haden, C. A., Ornstein, P. A., Eckerman, C. O., & Didow, S. M. (2001). Mother-child conversational interactions as events unfold: Linkages to subsequent remembering. *Child Development, 72*(4), 1016–1031.

Hagekull, B. (2003). Early temperament and attachment as predictors of the Five Factor Model of personality. *Attachment & Human Development, 5*(1), 2–18.

Hagekull, B., & Bohlin, G. (2004). Predictors of Middle Childhood Psychosomatic Problems: An Emotion Regulation Approach. *Infant and Child Development, 13*(5), 389–405.

Hagekull, B., Stenberg, G., & Bohlin, G. (1993). Infant-mother social referencing interactions: Description and antecedents in maternal sensitivity and infant irritability. *Early Development and Parenting, 2,* 183–191.

Hagerman, R. J. (1996). Biomedical advances in developmental psychology: The case of fragile X syndrome. *Developmental Psychology, 32*(3), 416–424.

Haight, W., Masiello, T., Dickson, K. L., Huckeby, E., & Black, J. E. (1994). The everyday contexts and social functions of spontaneous mother-child pretend play in the home. *Merrill-Palmer Quarterly, 40,* 509–522.

Haight, W., & Miller, P. J. (1992). The development of everyday pretend play: A longitudinal study of mothers' participation. *Merrill-Palmer Quarterly, 38,* 331–349.

Haight, W. L., Wang, X., Fung, H. H., Williams, K., & Mintz, J. (1999). Universal, developmental, and variable aspects of young children's play: A cross-cultural comparison of pretending at home. *Child Development, 70*(6), 1477–1488.

Hains, S. M. J., & Muir, D. W. (1996). Effects of stimulus contingency in infant-adult interactions. *Infant Behavior and Development, 19,* 49–61.

Haith, M. M. (1980). *Rules that babies look by: The organization of newborn visual activity.* Hillsdale, NJ: Erlbaum.

Hakman, M., & Sullivan, M. (2009). The effect of task and maternal verbosity on compliance in toddlers. *Infant & Child Development, 18*(2), 195-205

Hala, S., Chandler, M., & Fritz, A. S. (1991). Fledgling theories of mind: Deception as a marker of three-year-olds' understanding of false belief. *Child Development, 62,* 83–97.

Haley, D. W., & Stansbury, K. (2003). Infant Stress and Parent Responsiveness: Regulation of Physiology and Behavior During Still-Face and Reunion. *Child Development, 74*(5), 1534–1546.

Hallock, M. B., Worobey, J., & Self, P. A. (1989). Behavioral development in chimpanzee *(Pan troglodytes)* and human newborns across the first month of life. *International Journal of Behavioral Development, 12,* 527–540.

Halonen, J. S., & Passman, R. (1978). Pacifier's effects upon play and separations from the mother for the one-year-old in a novel environment. *Infant Behavior and Development, 1,* 70–78.

Hamela-Olkowska, A., Marcyniak, M., Sienko, J., Czajkowski, K., Brandt, M., Jalinik, K., et al. (2003). [Sexuality in pregnant women]. *Med Wieku Rozwoj, 7*(3 Suppl 1), 175–180.

Hamlin, J., Hallinan, E. V., & Woodward, A. L. (2008). Do as I do: 7-month-old infants selectively reproduce others' goals. *Developmental Science, 11*(4), 487-494. doi:10.1111/j.1467-7687.2008.00694.x

Hamlin, J., Wynn, K., Bloom, P., & Mahajan, N. (2011). How infants and toddlers react to antisocial others. *Proceedings Of The National Academy Of Sciences Of The United States Of America, 108,* 19931-19936

Hanawalt, B. A. (1993). *Growing up in medieval London: The experience of childhood in history.* New York: Oxford University Press.

Hane, A., Fox, N. A., Henderson, H. A., & Marshall, P. J. (2008). Behavioral reactivity and approach-withdrawal bias in infancy. *Developmental Psychology, 44*(5), 1491-1496. doi:10.1037/a0012855

Hanna, E., & Meltzoff, A. N. (1993). Peer imitation by toddlers in laboratory, home and day-care contexts: Implications for social learning and memory. *Developmental Psychology, 29,* 701–710.

Hannan, T. E. (1987). A cross-sequential assessment of the occurrences of pointing in three- to twelve-month-old infants. *Infant Behavior and Development, 10,* 11–22.

Hannon, E. E., & Trehub, S. E. (2005). Tuning in to musical rhythms: infants learn more readily than adults. *Proc Natl Acad Sci U S A, 102*(35), 12639–12643.

Hansen, M. (1993). Surrogacy contract upheld; California Supreme Courts says such agreements don't violate public policy. *American Psychological Association, 79,* 34.

Harbourne, R., Lobo, M., Karst, G., & Galloway, J. (2013). Sit happens: Does sitting development perturb reaching development, or vice versa?. *Infant Behavior & Development, 36*(3), 438-450. doi:10.1016/j.infbeh.2013.03.011.

Hardy, J. B., Aston, N. M., Brooks-Gunn, J., Shapiro, S., & Miller, T. L. (1998). Like mother, like child: Intergenerational patterns of age at first birth and associations with childhood and adolescent characteristics and adult outcomes in the second generation. *Developmental Psychology, 34*(6), 1220–1232.

Hardyck, C., & Petrinovich, L. F. (1977). Left-handedness. *Psychological Bulletin, 84,* 385–404.

Hareven, T. K. (1982). *Family time and industrial time.* New York: Cambridge University Press.

Hareven, T. K. (1985). Historical changes in the family and the life course: Implications for child development. *Monographs of the Society for Research in Child Development, 50* (Serial No. 211), 8–23.

Harkness, S., Super, C. M., Moscardino, U., Rha, J., Blom, M., Huitrón, B., et. al. (2007). Cultural models and developmental agendas: Implications for arousal and self-regulation in early infancy. *The Journal of Developmental Processes, 2*(1), 5–39.

Harley, K., & Reese, E. (1999). Origins of autobiographical memory. *Developmental Psychology, 35*(8), 1338–1348.

Harlow, H., & Harlow, M. (1965). The affectional systems. In A. Schrier, H. Harlow, & F. Stollnitz (Eds.), *Behavior of non-human primates* (Vol. 2). New York: Academic Press.

Harris, L. J., Spradlin, M. P., & Almerigi, J. B. (2007) Mothers and fathers' lateral biases for holding their newborn infants: A study of images from the World Wide Web, *Laterality, 12*:1, 64–86

Harris, M., Jones, D., & Grant, J. (1985). The social-interactional context of maternal speech to infants: An explanation for the event-bound nature of early word use? *First Language, 5,* 89–100.

Harris, P. L. (1989). *Children and emotion: The development of psychological understanding.* New York: Basil Blackwell.

Harris, P. L. (1998). Fictional absorption: Emotional responses to make-believe. In S. Br;araten (Ed.), *Intersubjective communication and emotion in early ontogeny. Studies in emotion and social interaction, 2nd series* (pp. 336–353). Cambridge, England: Cambridge University Press.

Harris, P. L., & Kavanaugh, R. D. (1993). Young children's understanding of pretense. *Monographs of the Society for Research in Child Development, 58,* 1–92.

Hart, B., & Risley, T. R. (1992). American parenting of language-learning children: Persisting differences in family-child interactions observed in natural home environments. *Developmental Psychology, 28,* 1096–1105.

Hart, H., & Rubia, K. (2012). Neuroimaging of child abuse: A critical review. *Frontiers In Human Neuroscience, 6*doi:10.3389/fnhum.2012.00052

Hart, S., Boylan, L. M., Carroll, S., Musick, Y., & Lampe, R. M. (2003). Brief report: Breast-fed one-week-olds demonstrate superior neurobehavioral organization. *Journal of Pediatric Psychology, 28*(8), 529–534.

Hart, S., Field, T., Del Valle, C., & Letourneau, M. (1998). Infants protest their mothers' attending to an infant-size doll. *Social Development, 7*(1), 54–61.

Hart, S., Field, T., Letourneau, M., & Del Valle, C. (1998). Jealousy protests in infants of depressed mothers. *Infant Behavior and Development, 21*(1), 137–148.

Hart, S. L., & Behrens, K. Y. (2013). Affective and behavioral features of jealousy protest: Associations with child temperament, maternal interaction style, and attachment. *Infancy, 18*(3), 369-399. doi:10.1111/j.1532-7078.2012.00123.x

Harter, S. (1983). Developmental perspectives on the self-system. In P. H. Mussen (Series Ed.) & E. M. Hetherington (Vol. Ed.), *Handbook of child psychology: Vol. 4. Socialization, personality, and social development* (pp. 176–194). New York: Wiley.

Hartley, L. (1995). *Wisdom of the body moving.* Berkeley, CA: North Atlantic Books.

Hartmann, A. F., Radin, M. B., & McConnell, B. (1992). Parent-to-parent support: A critical component of health care services for families. *Issues in Comprehensive Pediatric Nursing, 15,* 55–67.

Hartmann, H., & Molz, G. (1979). Unexpected death in infancy. In J. Howells (Ed.), *Modern perspectives in the psychiatry of infancy* (pp. 360–395). New York: Brunner-Mazel.

Hartmann, K., Viswanathan, M., Palmieri, R., Gartlehner, G., Thorp, J., Jr., & Lohr, K. N. (2005). Outcomes of routine episiotomy: a systematic review. *Jama, 293*(17), 2141–2148.

Harty, J. R. (1990). Pharmacotherapy in infantile autism. *Focus on Autistic Behavior, 5,* 1–15.

Harwood, R. L., Schölmerich, A., Schulze, P. A., & Gonzalez, Z. (1999). Cultural differences in maternal beliefs and behaviors: A study of middle-class Anglo and Puerto Rican mother-infant pairs in four everyday situations. *Child Development, 70*(4), 1005–1016.

Hass, J. K., & Walter, T. (2006–2007). Parental grief in three societies: Networks and religion as social supports in mourning. *Omega, 54*(3), 179–198.

Hassett, J., Siebert, E., & Wallen, K. (2008). Sex differences in rhesus monkey toy preferences parallel those of children. *Hormones And Behavior, 54*(3), 359-364.

Hastings, P. D., Sullivan, C., McShane, K. E., Coplan, R. J. Utendale, W. T., & Vyncke, J. D. (2008). Parental socialization, vagal regulation, and preschoolers' anxious difficulties: Direct mothers and moderated fathers. *Child Development, 79,* 45-64.

Hata, T., Shu-Yan D., & Marumo, G. (2010). Ultrasound for evaluation of fetal neurobehavioural development: from 2-D to 4-D ultrasound. *Infant & Child Development, 19,* 99-118.

Hatton, D. D., Bailey, D. B., Burchinal, M. R., & Ferrell, K. A. (1997). Developmental growth curves of preschool children with vision impairments. *Child Development, 68*(5), 788–806.

Hauf, P. (2012). Infants use compression information to infer objects' weights: Examining cognition, exploration, and prospective action in a preferential-reaching task. *Child Development, 83*(6), 1978-1995.

Hauser-Cram, P., Warfield, M. E., Shonkoff, J. P., Krauss, M. W., Upshur, C. C., & Sayer, A. (1999). Family influences on adaptive development in young children with Down syndrome. *Child Development, 70*(4), 979–989.

Hawley, P. H., & Little, T. D. (1999). On winning some and losing some: A social relations approach to social dominance in toddlers. *Merrill-Palmer Quarterly, 45*(2), 185–214.

Hay, D. F., Caplan, M., Castle, J., & Stimson, C. A. (1991). Does sharing become increasingly "rational" in the second year of life? *Developmental Psychology, 27,* 987–993.

Hay, D. F., Hurst, S., Waters, C. S., & Chadwick, A. (2011). Infants' use of force to defend toys: The origins of instrumental aggression. *Infancy, 16*(5), 471-489. doi:10.1111/j.1532-7078.2011.00069.x

Hay, D. F., Murray, P., Cecire, S., & Nash, A. (1985). Social learning of social behavior in early life. *Child Development, 56,* 43–57.

Hay, D. F., Pawlby, S., Sharp, D., Asten, P., Mills, A., & Kumar, R. (2001). Intellectual problems shown by 11–year-old children whose mothers had postnatal depression. *Journal of Child Psychology and Psychiatry, 42*(7), 871–889.

Hay, D. F., Pawlby, S., Waters, C. S., Perra, O., & Sharp, D. (2010). Mothers' antenatal depression and their children's antisocial outcomes. *Child Development,81*(1), 149-165. doi:10.1111/j.1467-8624.2009.01386.x

Hayden, A., Bhatt, R. S., Kangas, A., Zieber, N., & Joseph, J. E. (2012). Race-based perceptual asymmetry in face processing is evident early in life. *Infancy, 17*(5), 578-590. doi:10.1111/j.1532-7078.2011.00098.x

Hayne, H., Barr, R., & Herbert, J. (2003). The effect of prior practice on memory reactivation and generalization. *Child Development, 74*(6), 1615–1627.

Hayne, H., & Findlay, N. (1995). Contextual control of memory retrieval in infancy: Evidence for associative priming. *Infant Behavior and Development, 18*(2), 195–207.

Hayne, H., & Rovee-Collier, C. (1995). The organization of reactivated memory in infancy. *Child Development, 66,* 893–906.

Hazell, L. (1975). A study of 300 elective home births. *Birth and the Family Journal, 2,* 11–18.

Hazen, N. (1982). Spatial exploration and spatial knowledge: Individual and developmental differences in very young children. *Child Development, 53,* 826–833.

Hazlewood, V. (1977). The role of auditory stimuli in crying inhibition in the neonate. *Journal of Audiology Research, 17,* 225–240.

He, J., Hane, A., Degnan, K., Henderson, H. A., Xu, Q., & Fox, N. A. (2013). Anger and positive reactivity in infancy: Effects on maternal report of surgency and attention focusing in early childhood. *Infancy, 18*(2), 184-201. doi:10.1111/j.1532-7078.2012.00113.x

Health Watch (1997, January 7). *NBC Nightly News.* New York: NBC.

Healy, B. T. (1989). Autonomic nervous system correlates of temperament. *Infant Behavior and Development, 12,* 289–304.

Hebb, D. O. (1949). *The organization of behavior.* New York: Oxford University Press.

Heckhausen, J. (1988). Becoming aware of one's competence in the second year: Developmental progression within the mother-child dyad. *International Journal of Behavioral Development, 11,* 305–326.

Heffron, M. C., & Murch, T. (2010). *Reflective Supervision and Leadership for Infant and Early Childhood Programs.* Zero To Three Press.

Heiman, T. (2002). Parents of children with disabilities: Resilience, coping, and future expectations. *Journal of Developmental and Physical Disabilities, 14*(2), 159–171.

Heimann, M. (1989). Neonatal imitation, gaze aversion, and mother-infant interaction. *Infant Behavior and Development, 12,* 495–505.

Heimann, M., Ullstadius, E., Dahlgren, S. O., & Gillberg, C. (1992). Imitation in autism: A preliminary research note. *Behavioral Neurology, 5,* 219–227.

Heineman, T. & Ehrensaft, D., (Eds) (2006). *Building A Home Within: Meeting the Emotional Needs of Children and Youth in Foster Care.* Baltimore, MD: Brooks Publishing.

Heinicke, C. M., & Guthrie, D. (1992). Stability and change in husband-wife adaptation and the development of the positive parent-child relationship. *Infant Behavior and Development, 15,* 109–127.

Heinicke, C. M., & Westheimer, I. (1966). *Brief separations.* New York: Academic Press.

Henderson, A. E., Wang, Y., Matz, L. E., & Woodward, A. L. (2013). Active experience shapes 10-month-old infants' understanding of collaborative goals. *Infancy,18*(1), 10-39. doi:10.1111/j.1532-7078.2012.00126.x

Henrichs, J. Schenk, J. J., Schmidt, H. G., Velders, F. P., Hofman, A., Jaddoe, V. W. V., & . . . Verhulst, F. C.(2009). Maternal pre- and postnatal anxiety and infant temperament. The generation R study. *Infant & Child Development, 18*(6), 556-572.

Heinze, S. D., & Sleigh, M. J. (2003). Epidural or no epidural anaesthesia: relationships between beliefs about childbirth and pain control choices. *Journal of Reproductive and Infant Psychology, 21*(4), 323–333.

Helmrath, T., & Steinitz, E. (1978). Death of an infant: Parental grieving and the failure of social support. *Journal of Family Practice, 6,* 785–790.

Helweg, L. A., Lundemose, J. B., & Bille, H. (1994). Overheating and sudden infant death: Temperature regulation in relation to the prone position, the possible pathogenesis of sudden infant death. *Ugeskrift For Laeger, 156,* 7193–7196.

Hemminki, E. & Meriläinen, J. (1996) Long-term effects of cesarean sections: Ectopic pregnancies and placental problems, *American Journal of Obstetrics and Gynecology,* 174:1569–1574.

Henderson, L., Yoder, P., Yale, M., & McDuffie, A. (2002). Getting the point: electrophysiological correlates of protodeclarative pointing. *International Journal Of Developmental Neuroscience: The Official Journal Of The International Society For Developmental Neuroscience, 20*(3-5), 449-458.

Henriksson, K. M., & McNeil, T. F. (2004). Health and development in the first 4 years of life in offspring of women with schizophrenia and affective psychoses: Well-Baby Clinic information. *Schizophr Res, 70*(1), 39–48.

Henshaw, S. K. (1994). Recent trends in the legal status of induced abortion. *Journal of Public Health Policy, 15,* 165–172.

Hepach, R., Vaish, A., & Tomasello, M. (2013). A new look at children's prosocial motivation. *Infancy, 18*(1), 67-90. doi:10.1111/j.1532-7078.2012.00130.x

Hepper, P., Wells, D., & Lynch, C. (2005). Prenatal thumb sucking is related to postnatal handedness. *Neuropsychologia, 43*(3), 313–315.

Herault, J., Matineau, J., Petit, E., & Perrot, A. (1994). Genetic markers in autism: Association study on short arm of chromosome 11. *Journal of Autism and Developmental Disorders, 24,* 233–236.

Herbert, J., Gross, J., & Hayne, H. (2007). Crawling is associated with more flexible memory retrieval by 9–month-old infants. *Developmental Science, 10*(2), 183–189.

Hernandez, D. J. (1997). Child development and the social demography of childhood. *Child Development, 68*(1), 149–169.

Hernandez Blasi, C., & Bjorklund, D. F. (2003). Evolutionary developmental psychology: A new tool for better understanding human ontogeny. *Human Development, 46*(5), 259–281.

Herrick, K., Phillips, D. I., Haselden, S., Shiell, A. W., Campbell-Brown, M., & Godfrey, K. M. (2003). Maternal consumption of a high-meat, low-carbohydrate diet in late pregnancy: relation to adult cortisol concentrations in the offspring. *J Clin Endocrinol Metab, 88*(8), 3554–3560.

Herring, A., Donath, A., Yarmolenko, M., Uslar, E., Conzen, C., Kanakis, D. . . . Keyvani K, (2012). Exercise during pregnancy mitigates Alzheimer-like pathology in mouse offspring. *FASEB Journal: Official Publication Of The Federation Of American Societies For Experimental Biology, 26,* 117-28.

Hertenstein, M. J. (2002). Touch: Its communicative functions in infancy. *Human Development, 45*(2), 70–94.

Heshusius, L. (1994). Freeing ourselves from objectivity: Managing subjectivity or turning toward a participatory mode of consciousness? *Educational Researcher, 23*(3), 15–22.

Hess, E. H. (1959). Imprinting. *Science, 130,* 133–141.

Hesse, E., & van Ijzendoorn, M. H. (1998). Parental loss of close family members and propensities towards absorption in offspring. *Developmental Science, 1*(2), 299–305.

Hetherington, E. M., & Parke, R. D. (1993). *Child psychology: A contemporary viewpoint* (4th ed.). New York: McGraw-Hill.

Hewlett, B. S., Lamb, M. E., Shannon, D., Leyendecker, B., & Schölmerich, A. (1998). Culture and early infancy among central African foragers and farmers. *Developmental Psychology, 34*(4), 653–661.

Higgins, C. I., Campos, J. J., & Kermoian, R. (1996). Effect of self-produced locomotion on infant postural compensation to optic flow. *Developmental Psychology, 32*(5), 836–841.

Hildebrandt, K. H., Lake, M. A., & Parry, T. B. (1994). Infant coping with everyday stressful events. *Merrill-Palmer Quarterly, 40* (2), 171–189.

Hilder, A. S. (1994). Ethnic differences in the sudden infant death syndrome: What we can learn from immigrants to the UK. *Early Human Development, 38,* 143–149.

Hilliard, L. J., & Liben, L. S. (2010). Differing levels of gender salience in preschool classrooms: Effects on children's gender attitudes and intergroup bias. *Child Development, 81*(6), 1787-1798. doi:10.1111/j.1467-8624.2010.01510.x

Hildyard, K. L., & Wolfe, D. A. (2002). Child neglect: Developmental issues and outcomes. *Child Abuse & Neglect, 26*(6–7), 679–695.

Hill, W. L., Borovsky, D., & Rovee-Collier, C. (1988). Continuities in infant memory development. *Developmental Psychobiology, 21,* 43–62.

Hines, M., Golombok, S., Rust, J., Johnston, K. J., Golding, J., Avon Longitudinal Study of, P., et al. (2002). Testosterone during pregnancy and gender role behavior of preschool children: A longitudinal, population study. *Child Development, 73*(6), 1678–1687.

Hirst, W. (1994). The remembered self in amnesics. In U. Neisser & R. Fivush (Eds.), *The remembering self: Construction and accuracy in the self-narrative* (pp. 253–276). Cambridge, England: Cambridge University Press.

Hobara, M. (2003). Prevalence of transitional objects in young children in Tokyo and New York. *Infant Mental Health Journal, 24*(2), 174–191.

Hobson, R. P. (1991). Against the theory of "theory of mind." *British Journal of Developmental Psychology, 9*(1), 33–51.

Hobson, R. P. (1993). The emotional origins of social understanding. *Philosophical Psychology, 6,* 227–249.

Hobson, R. P., Chdambi, G., Lee, A., & Meyer, J. (2006). Foundations for self-awareness: An exploration through autism. *Monographs of the Society for Research in Child Development, 71*(2, Serial No. 284).

Hobson, R. P., & Meyer, J. A. (2005). Foundations for self and other: A study in autism. *Developmental Science, 8*(6), 481–491.

Hock, E., & DeMeis, D. K. (1990). Depression in mothers of infants: The role of maternal employment. *Developmental Psychology, 26,* 285–291.

Hodapp, R. M., Goldfield, E. C., & Boyatzis, C. J. (1984). The use and effectiveness of maternal scaffolding in mother-infant games. *Child Development, 55,* 772–781.

Hodnett, E. D., Downe, S., Edwards, N., & Walsh, D. (2005). Home-like versus conventional institutional settings for birth. *Birth, 32*(2), 151.

Hodnett, E. D., & Osborn, R. W. (1989). Effects of continuous intrapartum professional support on childbirth outcomes. *Research in Nursing and Health, 12*(5), 289–297.

Hoehl, S., Reid, V. M., Parise, E., Handl, A., Palumbo, L., & Striano, T. (2009). Looking at eye gaze processing and its neural correlates in infancy—Implications for social development and autism spectrum disorder. *Child Development, 80*(4), 968-985. doi:10.1111/j.1467-8624.2009.01311.x

Hofer, M. A. (1981). *The roots of human behavior: An introduction to the psychobiology of early development.* New York: Freeman.

Hoff, E. (2003). The Specificity of Environmental Influence: Socioeconomic Status Affects Early Vocabulary Development Via Maternal Speech. *Child Development, 74*(5), 1368–1378.

Hoff-Ginsberg, E. (1986). Function and structure in maternal speech: Their relation to the child's development of syntax. *Developmental Psychology, 22,* 155–163.

Hoicka, E., & Gattis, M. (2008). Do the wrong thing: How toddlers tell a joke from a mistake. *Cognitive Development, 23*(1), 180-190.

Holden, C. (1988). Family planning: A growing gap. *Science, 242,* 370–371.

Holden, G. W. (1983). Avoiding conflict: Mothers as tacticians in the supermarket. *Child Development, 54,* 233–240.

Holden, G. W. (1985). How parents create a social environment via proactive behavior. In T. Garling & J. Valsiner (Eds.), *Children within environments: Towards a psychology of accident prevention* (pp. 160–186). New York: Plenum Press.

Holland, R. L., & Smith, D. A. (1989). Management of the second stage of labor. A review (Part II). *South Dakota Journal of Medicine, 42,* 5–8.

Holowka, S., & Petitto, L. A. (2002). Left hemisphere cerebral specialization for babies while babbling. *Science, 297,*1515.

Holsti, L., Oberlander, T. F., & Brant, R. (2011). Does breastfeeding reduce acute procedural pain in preterm infants in the neonatal intensive care unit? A randomized clinical trial. *Pain, 152,* 2575-2581.

Holt, S. A., Fogel, A., & Wood, R. W. (1998). Innovation in social games. In M. D. P. de Lyra & J. Valsiner (Eds.), *Construction of psychological processes in interpersonal communication: Vol. 4. Child development in culturally structured environments* (pp. 787–823). Norwood, NJ: Ablex.

Homae, F., Watanabe, H., Nakano, T., & Taga, G. (2011). Large-scale brain networks underlying language acquisition in early infancy. *Frontiers In Psychology 2,* article 93.

Hong, K., & Townes, B. (1976). Infant's attachment to inanimate objects: A cross-cultural study. *Journal of the American Academy of Child Psychiatry, 15,* 49–61.

Honig, A. S. (2004). Longitudinal outcomes from the Family Development Research Program. *Early Child Development and Care, 174*(2), 125–130.

Honig, A. S., & Deters, K. (1996). Grandmothers and mothers: An intergenerational comparison of child-rearing practices with pre-schoolers. *Early Development and Parenting, 5*(1), 47–55.

Hooker, D. (1952). *The prenatal origin of behavior.* Lawrence: University of Kansas Press.

Hopkins, B., & Butterworth, G. (1997). Dynamical systems approaches to the development of action. In J. G.7 Bremner & A. Slater (Eds.), *Infant development: Recent advances* (pp. 75–100). Hove, England: Psychology Press/Erlbaum.

Hopkins, B., Janssen, B., Kardaun, O., & van der Schoot, T. (1988). Quieting during early infancy: Evidence for a developmental change? *Early Human Development, 18,* 111–124.

Hopkins, B., & von Wulfften Palthe, T. (1987). The development of state during early infancy. *Developmental Psychobiology, 20*(2), 165–175.

Hormann, E. (1977). Breast feeding the adopted baby. *Birth and the Family Journal, 4,* 165–173.

Hornik, R., & Gunnar, M. R. (1988). A descriptive analysis of infant social referencing. *Child Development, 59,* 626–634.

Hornik, R., Risenhoover, N., & Gunnar, M. R. (1987). The effects of maternal positive, neutral and negative affective communications on infant responses to new toys. *Child Development, 58,* 937–944.

Hoshi, N., & Chen, S. J. (1998). Emotion communication of Japanese mothers and their infants. *Research and clinical center for child development: Annual report 1997–1998, 21,* 27–34.

Hossain, Z., Field, T., Pickens, J., Malphurs, J., & Del Valle, C. (1997). Fathers' caregiving in low-income African-American and Hispanic-American families. *Early Development and Parenting, 6*(2), 73–82.

Howard, S. S. (1995). Treatment of male infertility. *New England Journal of Medicine, 332,* 312–317.

Howe, N. (1991). Sibling-directed internal state language, perspective taking, and affective behavior. *Child Development, 62,* 1503–1512.

Howe, N., & Rinaldi, C. M. (2004). 'You be the big sister': Maternal-Preschooler Internal State Discourse, Perspective-taking, and Sibling Caretaking. *Infant and Child Development, 13*(3), 217–234.

Howes, C. (1988). Relations between early child care and schooling. *Developmental Psychology, 24,* 53–57.

Howes, C. (1997). Children's experiences in center-based child care as a function of teacher background and adult:child ratio. *Merrill-Palmer Quarterly, 43*(3), 404–425.

Howes, C., Galinsky, E., & Kontos, S. (1998). Child care caregiver sensitivity and attachment. *Social Development, 7*(1), 23–36.

Howes, C., & Matheson, C. C. (1992). Sequences in the development of competent play with peers: Social and social pretend play. *Developmental Psychology, 28,* 961–974.

Howes, C., Phillips, D. A., & Whitebook, M. (1992). Thresholds of quality: Implications for the social development of children in center-based child care. *Child Development, 63,* 449–460.

Howes, C., & Smith, E. W. (1995). Children and their child care caregivers: Profiles of relationships. *Social Development, 4,* 45–59.

Howes, C., & Stewart, P. (1987). Child's play with adults, toys, and peers: An examination of family and child-care influences. *Developmental Psychology, 23,* 423–430.

Hrdy, S. B. (1999). *Mother nature: A history of mothers, infants, and natural selection.* Pantheon.

Hsieh, F. J., Shyu, M. K., Sheu, B. C., Lin, S. P., Chen, C. P., & Huang, F. Y. (1995). Limb defects after chorionic villus sampling. *Obstetrics and Gynecology, 85,* 84–88.

Hsu, H. C., Fogel, A., & Cooper, R. B. (2000). Infant vocal development during the first 6 months: Speech quality and melodic complexity. Infant and Child Development, 9, 1–6.

Hsu, H. C., & Fogel, A. (2001). Infant vocal development in a dynamic mother-infant communication system. Infancy, 2 (1), 87–109.

Hsu, H., & Fogel, A. (2003) Social regulatory effects of infant nondistress vocalization on maternal behavior. Developmental Psychology, 39(6), 976–991.

Hsu, H., Fogel, A., & Messinger, D. (2001). Infant non-distress vocalization during mother-infant face-to-face interaction: Factors associated with quantitative and qualitative differences. Infant Behavior and Development, 24, 107–128.

Hudson, D. B., Campbell-Grossman, C., Fleck, M. O., Elek, S. M., & Shipman, A. (2003). Effects of the New Fathers Network on first-time fathers' parenting self-efficacy and parenting satisfaction during the transition to parenthood. *Issues Compr Pediatr Nurs, 26*(4), 217–229.

Hudson, J. A., & Sheffield, E. G. (1998). Déjà vu all over again: Effects of reenactment on toddlers' event memory. *Child Development, 69*(1), 51–67.

Hudson, V., & den Boer, A. (2004). *Bare branches: The security implications of Asia's surplus mail population.* Cambridge, MA: MIT Press.

Huebner, C. E. (2002). Evaluation of a clinic-based parent education program to reduce the risk of infant and toddler maltreatment. *Public Health Nurs, 19*(5), 377–389.

Huffman, L. C., Bryan, Y. E., Carmen, R. del, Pedersen, F. A., Doussard-Roosevelt, J. A., & Porges, S. W. (1998). Infant temperament and cardiac vagal tone: Assessments at twelve weeks of age. *Child Development, 69*(3), 624–635.

Huffman, L. C., Bryan, Y. E., Pedersen, F. A., Lester, B. M., Newman, J. D., & Carmen, R. del. (1994). Infant cry acoustics and maternal ratings of temperament. *Infant Behavior and Development, 17,* 45–53.

Hughes, C., & Ensor, R. (2007). Executive function and theory of mind: Predictive relations from ages 2 to 4. *Developmental Psychology, 43*(6), 1447-1459.

Hughes, M. A., McCollum, J., Sheftel, D., & Sanchez, G. (1994). How parents cope with the experience of neonatal intensive care. *Children's Health Care, 23*(1), 1–14.

Hughes, P., Turton, P., Hopper, E., & Evans, C.D. (2002). Assessment of guidelines for good practice in psychoso-cial care of mothers after stillbirth: a cohort study. *Lancet, 360 (9327),*114-118.

Huizink, A., Mulder, E., & Buitelaar, J. (2004). Prenatal stress and risk for psychopathology: Specific effects or induction of general susceptibility?. *Psychological Bulletin, 130*(1), 115–142.

Humphrey, M., & Kirkwood, R. (1982). Marital relationship among adopters. *Adoption and Fostering, 6,* 44–48.

Hunter, F. T., McCarthy, M. E., MacTurk, R. H., & Vietze, P. M. (1987). Infants' social-constructive interactions with mothers and fathers. *Developmental Psychology, 23,* 249–254.

Hunter, R. S., Kilstrom, N., Kraybill, E. N., & Loda, F. (1978). Antecedents of child abuse and neglect in premature infants: A prospective study in a newborn intensive care unit. *Pediatrics, 61,* 629–635.

Hunziker, U. A., & Barr, R. G. (1986). Increased carrying reduces infant crying: A randomized controlled trial. *Pediatrics, 77,* 641–648.

Hurd, Y. L., Wang, X., Anderson, V., Beck, O., Minkoff, H., & Dow-Edwards, D. (2005). Marijuana impairs growth in mid-gestation fetuses. *Neurotoxicol Teratol, 27*(2), 221–229.

Huston, A. C., Anderson, D. R., Wright, J. C., Linebarger, D. L., & Schmitt, K. L. (2001). Sesame Street viewers as adolescents: The recontact study. In S. M. Fisch & R. T. Truglio (Eds.), *"G" is for growing: Thirty years of research on children and Sesame Street Muppets* (pp. 131–143). Mahwah, NJ: Lawrence Erlbaum Associates, Inc.

Huth-Bocks, A. C., Levendosky, A. A., Bogat, G. A., & von Eye, A. (2004). The Impact of Maternal Characteristics and Contextual Variables on Infant-Mother Attachment. *Child Development, 75*(2), 480–496.

Huth-Bocks, A. C., Levendosky, A. A., Theran, S. A., & Bogat, G. A. (2004). The Impact of Domestic Violence on Mothers' Prenatal Representations of Their Infants. *Infant Mental Health Journal, 25*(2), 79–98.

Hutt, R. L., Buss, K. A., & Kiel, E. J. (2013). Caregiver protective behavior, toddler fear and sadness, and toddler Cortisol reactivity in novel contexts. *Infancy, 18*(5), 708-728. doi: 10.1111/j.1532-7078.2012.00141.x

Huttenlocher, P., & Dabholkar, A. (1997). Regional differences in synaptogenesis in human cerebral cortex. *Journal of Comparative Neurology* (4), 387.

Huttenlocher, J., Haight, W., Bryk, A., Seltzer, M., & Lyons, T. (1991). Early vocabulary growth: Relation to language input and gender. *Developmental Psychology, 27,* 236–248.

Hyde, J. S., Else-Quest, N. M., Goldsmith, H. H., & Biesanz, J. C. (2004). Children's Temperament and Behavior Problems Predict Their Employed Mothers' Work Functioning. *Child Development, 75*(2), 580–594.

Hyman, C. A., & Mitchell, R. (1977). A psychological study of child battering. *Health Visitor, 48,* 294–296.

Hyslop L; Prathalingam N; Nowak L; Fenwick J; Harbottle S; Byerley S; Rhodes J; Watson B; Henderson R; Murdoch A; Herbert M, (2012). A novel isolator-based system promotes viability of human embryos during laboratory processing. *Plos One, 7,* e31010.

Hyssala, L., Hyttinen, M., Tautava, P., & Sillanpaa, M. (1993). The Finnish family competence study: The transition to fatherhood. *Journal of Genetic Psychology, 154,* 199–208.

Ibañez, L. V., Grantz, C. J., & Messinger, D. S. (2013). The development of referential communication and autism symptomatology in high-risk infants. *Infancy, 18*(5), 687-707. doi: 10.1111/j.1532-7078.2012.00142.x

Illingworth, R. (1991). *Normal child: Some problems of the early years and their treatment* (10th ed.). London: Churchill Livingstone.

Imaizumi, Y. (2003). A comparative study of zygotic twinning and triplet rates in eight countries, 1972-1999. *Journal of Biosocial Science, 35,* 287-302.

Imbens-Bailey, A., & Pan, B. A. (1998). The pragmatics of self- and other-reference in young children. *Social Development, 7*(2), 217–233.

Imhoff-Kunsch, B., Stein, A. D., Martorell, R., Parra-Cabrera, S., Romieu, I., & Ramakrishnan, U. (2011). Prenatal docosahexaenoic acid supplementation and infant morbidity: randomized controlled trial. *Pediatrics, 128,* e505-12

Ingersoll, E. W., & Thoman, E. B. (1994). The breathing bear: Effects on respiration in premature infants. *Physiology and Behavior,* 56, 855–895.

Ingudomnukul, E., Baron-Cohen, S., Wheelwright, S., & Knickmeyer, R. (2007). Elevated rates of testosterone-related disorders in women with autism spectrum conditions. *Hormones & Behavior, 51*(5), 597–604.

Innocenti, P., Morrow, E. H., & Dowling, D. K. (2011). Experimental evidence supports a sex-specific selective sieve in mitochondrial genome evolution. *Science, 332,* 845-848.

Isabella, R. A. (1993). Origins of attachment: Maternal interactive behavior across the first year. *Child Development, 64,* 605–621.

Isabella, R. A. (1998). Origins of attachment: The role of context, duration, frequency of observation, and infant age in measuring maternal behavior. *Journal of Social and Personal Relationships, 15*(4), 538–554.

Isabella, R. A., & Belsky, J. (1991). Interactional synchrony and the origins of infant-mother attachment: A replication study. *Child Development, 62,* 373–384.

Isabella, R. A., Belsky, J., & von Eye, A. (1989). Origins of infant-mother attachment: An examination of interactional synchrony during the infant's first year. *Developmental Psychology, 25*(1), 12–21.

Ispa, J. (1981). Peer support among Soviet day care toddlers. *International Journal of Behavioral Development, 4,* 255–270.

Ispa, J. M., Fine, M. A., Halgunseth, L. C., Harper, S., Robinson, J., Boyce, L., et al. (2004). Maternal Intrusiveness, Maternal Warmth, and Mother-Toddler Relationship Outcomes: Variations Across Low-Income Ethnic and Acculturation Groups. *Child Development, 75*(6), 1613–1631.

Iverson, J. M., & Fagan, M. K. (2004). Infant Vocal-Motor Coordination: Precursor to the Gesture-Speech System? *Child Development, 75*(4), 1053–1066.

Iverson, J. M., & Goldin-Meadow, S. (2005). Gesture Paves the Way for Language Development. *Psychological Science, 16*(5), 367–371.

Izard, C., Stark, K., Trentacosta, C., & Schultz, D. (2008). Beyond emotion regulation: Emotion utilization and adaptive functioning. *Child Development Perspectives, 2*(3), 156-163. doi:10.1111/j.1750-8606.2008.00058.x

Izard, C. E. (1981, April). *The primacy of emotion in human development.* Paper presented at the meeting of the Society for Research in Child Development, Boston, MA.

Izard, C. E., & Abe, J. A. A. (2004). Developmental Changes in Facial Expressions of Emotions in the Strange Situation During the Second Year of Life. *Emotion, 4*(3), 251–265.

Izard, C. E., Haynes, M. O., Chisholm, G., & Baak, K. (1991). Emotional determinants of infant-mother attachment. *Child Development, 62,* 906–917.

Izard, C. E., Hembree, E. A., & Huebner, R. R. (1987). Infants' emotion expressions to acute pain: Developmental change and stability of individual differences. *Developmental Psychology, 23,* 105–113.

Izard, C. E., & Malatesta, C. Z. (1987). Perspectives on emotional development I: Differential emotions theory of early emotional development. In J. D. Osofsky (Ed.), *Handbook of infant development* (2nd ed., pp. 494–554). New York: Wiley.

Jack, F., Simcock, G., & Hayne, H. (2012). Magic memories: Young children's verbal recall after a 6-year delay. *Child Development, 83*(1), 159-172. doi:10.1111/j.1467-8624.2011.01699.x

Jack, K. E., & Chao, C. R. (1992). Female voluntary surgical contraception via minilaparotomy under local anesthesia. *International Journal of Gynecological Obstetrics, 39,* 111–116.

Jackson, J. F. (1993). Human behavioral genetics, Scarr's theory, and her views on interventions: A critical review and commentary on their implications for African American children. *Child Development, 64,* 1318–1332.

Jacobson, J. L. (1981). The role of inanimate objects in early peer interaction. *Child Development, 52,* 618–626.

Jacobson, J. L., Boersma, D. C., Fields, R. B., & Olson, K. L. (1983). Paralinguistic features of adult speech to infants and small children. *Child Development, 54,* 436–442.

Jacobson, S. W. (1979). Matching behavior in the young infant. *Child Development, 50,* 425–430.

Jacobson, S. W., Fein, G. G., Jacobson, J. L., Schwartz, P. M., & Dowler, J. K. (1985). The effect of intrauterine PCB exposure on visual recognition memory. *Child Development, 56,* 853–860.

Jacobson, S. W., & Frye, K. F. (1991). Effect of maternal social support on attachment: Experimental evidence. *Child Development, 62,* 572–582.

Jacobson, S. W., & Jacobson, J. L. (2001). Alcohol and drug-related effects on development: A new emphasis on contextual factors. *Infant Mental Health Journal, 22*(3), 416–430.

Jacobson, S. W., Jacobson, J. L., O'Neill, J. M., Padgett, R. J., Frankowski, J. J., & Bihun, J. T. (1992). *Child Development, 63,* 711–724.

Jahromi, L. B., Putnam, S. P., & Stifter, C. A. (2004). Maternal Regulation of Infant Reactivity From 2 to 6 Months. *Developmental Psychology, 40*(4), 477–487.

Jahromi, L. B., & Stifter, C. A. (2007). Individual differences in the contribution of maternal soothing to infant distress reduction. *Infancy, 11*(3), 255–269.

James, D. K. (2010). Fetal learning: A critical review. *Infant and Child Development, 19,* 45-54.

James, J. (2011). Can consuming caffeine while breatfeeding harm your baby? An interview with Ruth Lawrence, PhD. *Journal of Caffeine Research,* 1(4), 192-194. doi: 10.1089/jcr.2011.1212.

Jansen, J., de Weerth, C., & Riksen-Walraven, J. M. (2008). Breastfeeding and the mother-infant relationship--A review. *Developmental Review, 28,* 503-521.

Jaroszewicz, A. M., & Boyd, I. H. (1973). Clinical assessment of gestational age in the newborn. *South African Medical Journal, 47,* 2123–2124. Järvinen-Pasley, A., Wallace, G. L., Ramus, F., Happé, F., & Heaton, P. (2008). Enhanced perceptual processing of speech in autism. *Developmental Science,11,*109-21.

Jarvis, P. A., & Creasey, G. L. (1991). Parental stress, coping, and attachment in families with an 18–month-old infant. *Infant Behavior and Development, 14,* 383–395.

Jean, A., & Stack, D. (2009). Functions of maternal touch and infants' affect during face-to-face interactions: new directions for the still-face. *Infant Behavior & Development, 32*(1), 123-128. doi:10.1016/j.infbeh.2008.09.008

Jean, A. D. L., Stack, D. M. & Fogel, A. (2009). A longitudinal investigation of maternal touching across the first 6 months of life: Age and context effects. *Infant Behavior & Development, 32,* 344-349.

Jennings, K. D. (2004). Development of goal-directed behaviour and related self-processes in toddlers. *International Journal of Behavioral Development, 28*(4), 319–327.

Jennings, K. D., Sandberg, I., Kelley, S. A., Valdes, L., Yaggi, K., Abrew, A., & Macey-Kalcevic, M. (2008). Understanding of self and maternal warmth predict later self-regulation in toddlers. *International Journal Of Behavioral Development, 32,* 108-118.

Jensen, M. (2005). Lower sperm counts following prenatal tobacco exposure. *Human Reproduction, 20*(9), 2559–2566.

Jessee, A., Mangelsdorf, S. C., Brown, G. L., Schoppe-Sullivan, S. J., Shigeto, A., & Wong, M. S. (2010). Parents' differential susceptibility to the effects of marital quality on sensitivity across the first year. *Infant Behavior & Development, 33,* 442-452.

Johnson, D. J., Jaeger, E., Randolph, S. M., Cauce, A. M., & Ward, J. (2003). Studying the effects of early child care experiences on the development of children of color in the United States: Toward a more inclusive research agenda. *Child Development, 74*(5), 1227–1244.

Johnson, E. K., & Seidl, A. H. (2009). At 11 months, prosody still outranks statistics. *Developmental Science, 12*(1), 131-141. doi:10.1111/j.1467-7687.2008.00740.x

Johnson, J. L., McAndrew, F. T., & Harris, P. B. (1991). Sociobiology and the naming of adopted and natural children. *Ethology and Sociobiology, 12,* 365–375.

Johnson, M. H. (2000). Functional brain development during infancy. In J. G. Bremner & A. Fogel (Eds.), *Handbook of infancy research* (pp. 130–154). Oxford, England: Blackwell.

Johnson, M. H. (2010) Funtional brain development during infancy. In J. G. Bremmer & T. D. Wachs (Eds.). *The Wiley-Blackwell handbook of infant development volume 1: Basic research.* (2nd edition, pp.295-313), West Sussex, UK: Wiley-Blackwell.

Johnson, M. H., Dziurawiee, S., Ellis, H., & Morton, J. (1991). Newborns' preferential tracking of face-like stimuli and its subsequent decline. *Cognition, 40,* 1–19.

Johnson, M. H., Grossmann, T., & Kadosh, K. (2009). Mapping functional brain development: Building a social brain through interactive specialization.*Developmental Psychology, 45*(1), 151-159. doi:10.1037/a0014548

Johnson, S. (1997). Young infants' perception of object unity: Implications for development of attentional and cognitive skills *Current Directions in Psychological Science, 6,* 5–11.

Johnson, S., Slaughter, V., & Carey, S. (1998). Whose gaze will infants follow? The elicitation of gaze-following in 12–month-olds. *Developmental Science, 1*(2), 233–238.

Johnson, S. C., Ok, S.-J., & Luo, Y. (2007). The attribution of attention: 9–month-olds' interpretation of gaze as goal-directed action. *Developmental Science, 10*(5), 530–537.

Johnson, S. P., Bremner, J. G., Slater, A., Mason, U., Foster, K., & Cheshire, A. (2003). Infants' perception of object trajectories. *Child Development, 74*(1), 94–108.

Johnson, T. R. B., Besinger, R. E., & Thomas, R. L. (1989). The latest clues to fetal behavior and well-being. *Contemporary Pediatrics,* 66–84.

Jones, C. (1987). *Mind over labor.* New York: Viking.

Jones, C. P., & Adamson, L. B. (1987). Language use in mother-child and mother-child-sibling interactions. *Child Development, 58,* 356–366.

Jones, L. C., & Hermann, J. A. (1992). Parental division of infant care: Contextual influences and infant characteristics. *Nursing Research, 41,* 228–234.

Jones, N. A., Field, T., Fox, N. A., Davalos, M., Malphurs, J., Carraway, K., Schanberg, S., & Kuhn, C. (1997). Infants of intrusive and withdrawn mothers. *Infant Behavior and Development, 20,* 175–186.

Jones, R. K., Fennell, J., Higgins, J. A., & Blanchard, K. (2009). Better than nothing or savvy risk-reduction practice? The importance of withdrawal. *Contraception, 79,* 407-10.

Jones, S. S. (1996). Imitation or exploration? Young infants' matching of adults' oral gestures. *Child Development, 67*(5), 1952–1969.

Jones, S. S., Collins, K., & Hong, H. W. (1991). An audience effect on smile production in 10–month-old infants. *Psychological Science, 2,* 45–49.

Jones, S. S., Raag, T., & Collins, K. L. (1990). Smiling in older infants: Form and maternal response. *Infant Behavior and Development, 13,* 147–165.

Jones, S. S., Smith, L. B., & Landau, B. (1991). Object properties and knowledge in early lexical learning. *Child Development, 62,* 499–516.

Jones, W., & Klin, A. (2013). Attention to eyes is present but in decline in 2-6-month-old infants later diagnosed with autism. *Nature,* Advance online publication. doi.10.1038/nature 12715.

Joosen, K. J., Mesman, J., Bakermans-Kranenburg, M. J., Pieper, S., Zeskind, P. S., & van IJzendoorn, M. H. (2013). Physiological reactivity to infant crying and observed maternal sensitivity. *Infancy, 18*(3), 414-431. doi:10.1111/j.1532-7078.2012.00122.x

Josefsson, A., Berg, G., Nordin, C., & Sydsjo, G. (2001). Prevalence of depressive symptoms in late pregnancy and postpartum. *Acta Obstet Gynecol Scand, 80*(3), 251–255.

Judd, J. M. (1985). Assessing the newborn from head to toe. *Nursing '85, 15,* 34–41.

Juffer, F., & Rosenboom, L. G. (1997). Infant-mother attachment of internationally adopted children in the Netherlands. *International Journal of Behavioral Development, 20*(1), 93–107.

Juffer, F., Rosenboom, L. G., Hoksbergen, R. A. C., Riksen-Walraven, J. M. A., & Kohnstamm, G. A. (1997). Attachment and intervention in adoptive families with and without biological children. In W. Koops, J. B. Hoeksma, & D. C. van den Boom (Eds.), *Development of interaction and attachment: Traditional and non-traditional approaches* (pp. 93–108). Amsterdam: Royal Netherlands Academy of Arts and Sciences.

Jusczyk, P. W. (1985). The high-amplitude sucking technique as a methodological tool in speech perception research. In G. Gottlieb & N. A. Krasnegor (Eds.), *Measurement of audition and vision during the first year of postnatal life: A methodological overview* (pp. 414–438). Norwood, NJ: Ablex.

Jusczyk, P. W., Cutler, A., & Redanz, N. J. (1993). Infants' preference for the predominant stress patterns of English words. *Child Development, 64,* 675–687.

Jusczyk, P. W., Kennedy, L. J., & Jusczyk, A. (1995). Young infants' retention of information about syllables. *Infant Behavior and Development, 18*(1), 27–41.

Kagan, J. (1987). Perspectives on infancy. In J. D. Osofsky (Ed.), *Handbook of infant development* (2nd ed., pp. 1150–1198). New York: Wiley.

Kagan, J. (1989). *Unstable ideas.* Cambridge, MA: Harvard University Press.

Kagan, J., Arcus, D., Snidman, N., Feng, W. Y., Hendler, J., & Greene, S. (1994). *Reactivity in infants: A cross-national comparison.* Developmental Psychology, 30, 342–345.

Kagan, J., Kearsley, R., & Zelazo, P. (1978). *Infancy: Its place in human development.* Cambridge, MA: Harvard University Press.

Kagan, J., & Reznick, J. S. (1984). Cardiac reaction as an index of task involvement. *Australian Journal of Psychology, 36,* 135–147.

Kagan, J., Reznick, J. S., & Snidman, N. (1987). The physiology and psychology of behavioral inhibition in children. *Child Development, 58,* 1459–1473.

Kagan, J., Reznick, J. S., Snidman, N., Gibbons, J., & Johnson, M. O. (1988). Childhood derivatives of inhibition and lack of inhibition to the unfamiliar. *Child Development, 59,* 1580–1589.

Kagan, J., Snidman, N., & Arcus, D. (1998). Childhood derivatives of high and low reactivity in infancy. *Child Development, 69*(6), 1483–1493.

Kagan, J., Snidman, N., Kahn, V., & Towsley, S. (2007). The preservation of two infant temperaments into adolescence. *Monographs of the Society for Research in Child Development, 72*(2), 1–95.

Kahrs, B., Jung, W., & Lockman, J. (2013). Motor origins of tool use. *Child Development, 84*(3), 810-816.

Kaiser, M., Kearney, G., Scott, K., DuClos, C., & Kurlfink, J. (2008). Tracking childhood exposure to lead and developmental disabilities: examining the relationship in a population-based sample. *Journal Of Public Health Management And Practice: JPHMP, 14*(6), 577-580.

Kaitz, M., Maytal, H., Devor, N., Bergman, L., & Mankuta, D. (2010). Maternal anxiety, mother-infant interactions, and infants' response to challenge. *Infant Behavior & Development, 33*(2), 136-148. doi:10.1016/j.infbeh.2009.12.003

Kaitz, M., Meirov, H., & Landman, I. (1993). Infant recognition by tactile cues. *Infant Behavior and Development, 16,* 333–341.

Kaler, S. R., & Kopp, C. B. (1990). Compliance and comprehension in very young toddlers. *Child Development, 61,* 1997–2003.

Kaley, F., Reid, V., & Flynn, E. (2011). The psychology of infant colic: A review of current research. *Infant Mental Health Journal, 32,* 526-541.

Kalmar, M. (1996). The course of intellectual development in preterm and fullterm children: An 8–year longitudinal study. *International Journal of Behavioral Development, 19*(3), 491–516.

Kanazawa, T., Shimizu, S., Kamada, J., Tanabe, H., & Itoigawa, N. (1997). Intelligence and learning disabilities in 6– to 8-year-old children weighing under 1,000 grams at birth. *International Journal of Behavioral Development, 20*(1), 179–188.

Kaplan, P. S., Bachorowski, J., & Zarlengo-Strouse, P. (1999). Child-directed speech produced by mothers with symptoms of depression fails to promote associative learning in 4–month-old infants. *Child Development, 70*(3), 560–570.

Kaplan, P. S., Danko, C. M., & Diaz, A. (2010). A privileged status for male infant-directed speech in infants of depressed mothers? Role of father involvement. *Infancy, 15*(2), 151-175. doi:10.1111/j.1532-7078.2009.00010.x

Kaplan, P. S., Dungan, J. K., & Zinser, M. C. (2004). Infants of Chronically Depressed Mothers Learn in Response to Male, But Not Female, Infant-Directed Speech. *Developmental Psychology, 40*(2), 140–148.

Kapoor, S. K., Amand, K., & Kumar, G. (1994). Risk factors for stillbirths in a secondary level hospital at Ballabgarh, Haryana: A case control study. *Indian Journal of Pediatrics, 61,* 161–166.

Karasik, L. B., Adolph, K. E., Tamis-LeMonda, C. S., & Zuckerman, A. L. (2012). Carry on: Spontaneous object carrying in 13-month-old crawling and walking infants. *Developmental Psychology, 48*(2), 389-397. doi:10.1037/a0026040

Karasik, L. B., Tamis-LeMonda, C. S., & Adolph, K. E. (2011). Transition from crawling to walking and infants' actions with objects and people. *Child Development, 82*(4), 1199-1209.

Karcew, S. (1994). Fetal consequences and risks attributed to the use of prescribed and over-the-counter (OTC) preparations during pregnancy. *International Journal of Clinical Pharmacological Therapy, 32,* 335–343.

Karlson, E. W., Mandl, L. A., Hankinson, S. E., & Grodstein, F. (2004). Do breast-feeding and other reproductive factors influence future risk of rheumatoid arthritis? Results from the Nurses' Health Study. *Arthritis Rheum, 50*(11), 3458–3467.

Karmel, M. (1959). *Thank you, Doctor Lamaze: A mother's experiences in painless childbirth.* Philadelphia: Lippincott.

Karmiloff-Smith, A. (2007). Atypical epigenesis. *Developmental Science, 10*(1), 84–88.

Karns, J. T. (2001). Health, nutrition, and safety. In J. G. Bremner & A. Fogel (Eds.), *Handbook of infant development* (pp. 438–460). Oxford, England: Blackwell.

Karr-Morse, R., & Wiley, M. S. (1997). *Ghosts from the nursery: Tracing the roots of violence.* New York: Atlantic Monthly Press.

Karrer, R., Monti, L., & Ackles, P. K. (1989, October). *Late ERP's of one-month-old infants in a visual oddball task.* Presented at the Society for Psychophysiological Research, New Orleans.

Kärtner, J., Keller, H., & Yovsi, R. D. (2010). Mother infant interaction during the first 3 months: The emergence of culture-specific contingency patterns. *Child Development, 81*(2), 540-554.

Karzon, R. G. (1985). Discrimination of polysyllabic sequences by one- to four-month-old infants. *Journal of Experimental Child Psychology, 39,* 326–342.

Kasari, C., Gulsrud, A. C., Wong, C., Kwon, S., & Locke, J. (2010). Randomized controlled caregiver mediated joint engagement intervention for toddlers with autism. *Journal Of Autism And Developmental Disorders, 40*(9), 1045-1056.

Kataria, S., Frutiger, A. D., Lanford, B., & Swanson, M. S. (1988). Anterior fontanel closure in healthy term infants. *Infant Behavior and Development, 11,* 229–233.

Katz, V. L., & Kuller, J. A. (1994). Recurrent miscarriage. *American Journal of Perinatology, 11,* 386–387.

Kaufman, R., & Adam, E. (2002). Findings in female offspring of women exposed in utero to diethylstilbestrol. *Obstetrics And Gynecology, 99*(2), 197–200.

Kavšek, M. (2004). Predicting later IQ from infant visual habituation and dishabituation: A meta-analysis. *Journal of Applied Developmental Psychology, 25*(3), 369–393.

Kawakami, K., Takai-Kawakami, K., Kurihara, H., Shimizu, Y., & Yanaihara, T. (1996). The effect of sounds on newborn infants under stress. *Infant Behavior and Development, 19,* 375–379.

Kaye, K. (1977). Toward the origin of dialogue. In H. R. Schaffer (Ed.), *Studies in mother-infant interaction* (pp. 75–120). New York: Academic Press.

Kaye, K. (1982). *The mental and social life of babies.* Chicago: University of Chicago Press.

Kaye, K., & Fogel, A. (1980). The temporal structure of face-to-face communication between mothers and infants. *Developmental Psychology, 16,* 454–464.

Kaye, K., & Marcus, J. (1978). Imitation over a series of trials without feedback. *Infant Behavior and Development, 1,* 141–155.

Kaye, K., & Wells, A. J. (1980). Mother's jiggling and the burst-pause pattern of neonatal feeding. *Infant Behavior and Development, 3,* 29–46.

Kedar, Y., Casasola, M., & Lust, B. (2006). Getting There Faster: 18– and 24–Month-Old Infants' Use of Function Words to Determine Reference. *Child Development, 77*(2), 325–338.

Keith-Speigel, P. (1983). *Children and consent to participate in research*. In G. B. Melton & M. J. Saks (Eds.), *Children's competence to consent* (pp. 179–211). New York: Plenum Press.

Keller, H., Chasiotis, A., Risau-Peters, J., Volker, S., Zach, U., & Restemeier, R. (1996). Psychobiological aspects of infant crying. *Early Development and Parenting, 5*(1), 1–13.

Keller, H., Lohaus, A., Kuensemueller, P., Abels, M., Yovsi, R., Voelker, S., et al. (2004). The Bio-Culture of Parenting: Evidence From Five Cultural Communities. *Parenting: Science and Practice, 4*(1), 25–50

Keller, H., Otto, H., Lamm, B., Yovsi, R., & Kärtner, J. (2008). The timing of verbal/vocal communications between mothers and their infants: a longitudinal cross-cultural comparison. *Infant Behavior & Development, 31*(2), 217-226.

Keller, H., Yovsi, R., Borke, J., Kartner, J., Jensen, H., & Papaligoura, Z. (2004). Developmental Consequences of Early Parenting Experiences: Self-Recognition and Self-Regulation in Three Cultural Communities. *Child Development, 75*(6), 1745–1760.

Keller, M. A., & Goldberg, W. A. (2004). Co-Sleeping: Help or Hindrance for Young Children's Independence? *Infant and Child Development, 13*(5), 369–388.

Kelley, M. L., Smith, T. S., Green, A. P., Berndt, A. E., & Rogers, M. C. (1998). Importance of fathers' parenting to African-American toddler's social and cognitive development. *Infant Behavior and Development, 21*(4), 733–744.

Kelly, D. J., Quinn, P. C., Slater, A. M., Lee, K., Gibson, A., Smith, M., et al. (2005). Three-month-olds, but not newborns, prefer own-race faces. *Developmental Science, 8*(6), F31–F36.

Kelly, J. F., & Booth, C. L. (2002). The early child care study of children with special needs. In L. M. Glidden (Ed.), *International review of research in mental retardation, Vol 25* (pp. 71–106). San Diego, CA: Academic Press.

Kelly, Y. J., Sacker, A., Gray, R. Kelly, J., Wolke, D., Head, J., & Quigley,M. A. (2012). Light drinking during pregnancy: Still no increased risk for socioemotional difficulties or cognitive deficits at 5 years of age? *Journal of Epidemiology and Community Health, 66,* 41-48.

Kellman, P., & Spelke, E. (1983). Perception of partly occluded objects in infancy. *Cognitive Psychology, 15,* 483–494.

Kemper, T. L., & Bauman, M. L. (1993). The contribution of neuropathologic studies to the understanding of autism. *Neurological Clinics, 11,* 175–187.

Kendrick, C., & Dunn, J. (1980). Caring for a second baby: Effects on interaction between mother and firstborn. *Developmental Psychology, 16,* 303–311.

Kennedy, D., & Koren, G. (1998). Valproic acid use in psychiatry: Issues in treating women of reproductive age. *Journal of Psychiatry and Neuroscience, 23*(4), 223–228.

Kennedy, K. I., Fortney, J. A., Bonhomme, M. G., Potts, M., Lamptey, P., & Carswell, W. (1990). Do the benefits of breastfeeding outweigh the risk of postnatal transmission of HIV via breastmilk? *Tropical Doctor, 20,* 25–29.

Kent, R. D. (1981). Articulatory-acoustic perspectives on speech development. In R. Stark (Ed.), *Language development in infancy and early childhood* (pp. 105–106). New York: Elsevier.

Kermoian, R., & Campos, J. J. (1988). Locomotor experience: A facilitator of spatial cognitive development. *Child Development, 59,* 908–917.

Kerr, M. E. (2008). Why do siblings often turn out very differently? In A. Fogel, B. J. King, & S. Shanker (Eds.). *Human development in the 21st century: Visionary policy ideas from systems scientists.* Cambridge, UK: Cambridge University Press.

Kesmodel, U., Wisborg, K., Olsen, S. F., Henriksen, T. B., & Secher, N. J. (2002). Moderate alcohol intake in pregnancy and the risk of spontaneous abortion. *Alcohol and Alcoholism, 37*(1), 87–92.

Kessen, W., Haith, M., & Salapatek, P. (1970). Human infancy: A bibliography and guide. In P. H. Mussen (Ed.), *Carmichael's manual of child psychology* (3rd ed., pp. 808–856). New York: Wiley.

Kestenberg-Amighi, J. (2004). Contact and connection: A cross-cultural look at parenting styles in Bali and the United States. *Zero to Three, 24,* 32–40.

Ketting, E., & Visser, A. P. (1994). Contraception in the Netherlands: The low abortion rate explained. *Patient and Educational Counseling, 23,* 161–171.

Khalsa, S. S., Rudrauf, D., Feinstein, J. S., & Tranel, D. (2009). The pathways of interoceptive awareness. *Nature Neuroscience,12,* 1494-1496.

Kiely, M., Drum, M. A., & Kessel, W. (1998). Early discharge: Risks, benefits, and who decides. *Clinical Perinatology, 25,* 539–553.

Kier, C. A., & Lewis, C. N. (1993). Sibling attachment: The development of a new infant-based measure (SPPIR). *Early Development and Parenting, 2,* 243–246.

Kirkorian, H. L., Pempek, T. A., Murphy, L. A., Schmidt, M. E., & Anderson, D. R. (2009). The impact of background television on parent-child interaction. *Child Development, 80*(5), 1350-1359. doi:10.1111/cdev.2009.80.issue-510.1111/j.1467-8624.2009.01337.x

Killen, M., & Wainryb, C. (2000). Independence and interdependence in diverse cultural contexts. In S. Harkness & C. Raeff (Eds.), *Variability in the social construction of the child. New directions for child and adolescent development* (No. 87, pp. 5–21). San Francisco: Jossey-Bass, Inc.

Kim, P., Leckman, J. F., Mayes, L. C. Feldman, R., Wang, X., Swain, J. E. (2010)The plasticity of human maternal brain: Longitudinal changes in brain anatomy during the early postpartum period. *Behavioral Neuroscience, 124,* 695-700.

Kisilevsky, B. S., & Hains, S. M. J. (2010). Exploring the relationship between fetal heart rate and cognition. *Infant and Child Development, 19,* 60-75.

Kisilevsky, B. S., Hains, S. M. J., Brown, C. A., Lee, C. T., Cowperthwaite, B., Stutzman, S. S. . . .Wang, Z. (2009). Fetal sensitivity to properties of maternal speech and language. *Infant Behavior & Development, 32,* 59-71.

Kisilevsky, B., Hains, S., Jacquet, A., Granier-Deferre, C., & Lecanuet, J. (2004). Maturation of fetal responses to music. *Developmental Science, 7*(5), 550–559.

Kisilevsky, B. S., Hains, S. M. J., Lee, K., Muir, D. W., Xu, F., Fu, G., Zhao, Z. Y., & Yang, R. L. (1998). The still-face effect in Chinese and Canadian 3– to 6–month-old infants. *Developmental Psychology, 34*(4), 629–639.

Kisilevsky, B., Hains, S., Lee, K., Xie, X., Huang, H., Ye, H., et al. (2003). Effects of experience on fetal voice recognition. *Psychological Science, 14*(3), 220–224.

Kisilevsky, B. S., & Muir, D. W. (1984). Neonatal habituation and dishabituation to tactile stimulation during sleep. *Developmental Psychology, 20,* 367–373.

Klaus, M. H., Kennell, J. H., Plumb, N., & Zeuhlke, S. (1970). Human maternal behavior at the first contact with her young. *Pediatrics, 46,* 187–192.

Klein, P. S., Feldman, R., & Zarur, S. (2002). Mediation in a sibling context: The relations of older siblings' mediating behavior and younger siblings' task performance. *Infant and Child Development, 11*(4), 321–333.

Klein, R. P., & Durfee, J. T. (1976). Effects of stress on attachment behavior in infants. *Journal of Genetic Psychology, 132,* 321–322.

Klerman, L. V., & Goldenberg, R. L. (1999). Prenatal care: A new perspective. *Zero to Three, 19*(4), 3–8.

Klimes-Dougan, B., & Kopp, C. B. (1999). Children conflict tactics with mothers: A longitudinal investigation of the toddler and preschool years. *Merrill-Palmer Quarterly, 45*(2), 226–241.

Klin, A., & Jones, W (2008). Altered face scanning and impaired recognition of biological motion in a 15-month-old infant with autism. *Developmental Science. 11,* 40-46.

Klinnert, M. D. (1984). The regulation of infant behavior by maternal facial expression. *Infant Behavior and Development, 7,* 447–465.

Klinnert, M. D., Emde, R. N., Butterfield, P., & Campos, J. J. (1986). Social referencing: The infant's use of emotional signals from a friendly adult with mother present. *Developmental Psychology, 22,* 427–432.

Klinnert, M. D., Gavin, L. A., Wamboldt, F. S., & Mrazek, D. A. (1992). Marriages with children at medical risk: The transition to parenthood. *Journal of the American Academy of Child and Adolescent Psychiatry, 31*(2), 334–342.

Kloeblen-Tarver, A., Thompson, N., & Miner, K. (2002). Intent to breast-feed: The impact of attitudes, norms, parity, and experience. *American Journal of Health Behavior, 26*(3), 182.

Klopfer, P. (1988). Metaphors for development: How important are experiences early in life? *Developmental Psychobiology, 21,* 671–678.

Knickmeyer, R., Baron-Cohen, S., Raggatt, P., Taylor, K., & Hackett, G. (2006). Fetal testosterone and empathy. *Hormones & Behavior, 49*(3), 282–292.

Knickmeyer, R., Baron-Cohen, S., Raggatt, P., & Taylor, K. (2005). Foetal testosterone, social relationships, and restricted interests in children. *Journal of Child Psychology and Psychiatry, 46*(2), 198–210.

Knowles, J. K, & Penn, A. A. (2011) Perinatal brain development, malformation, and injury. *Colloquium series on the developing brain 2*(2), 1-84.

Kochanska, G., Barry, R. A., Stellern, S. A., & O'Bleness, J. J. (2009). Early attachment organization moderates the parent–child mutually coercive pathway to children's antisocial conduct. *Child Development, 80*(4), 1288-1300. doi:10.1111/j.1467-8624.2009.01332.x

Kochanska, G., Coy, K. C., Tjebkes, T. L., & Husarek, S. J. (1998). Individual differences in emotionality in infancy. *Child Development, 69*(2), 375–390.

Kochanska, G., Forman, D. R., & Coy, K. C. (1999). Implications of the mother-child relationship in infancy for socialization in the second year of life. *Infant Behavior and Development, 22*(2), 249–265.

Kochanska, G., Friesenborg, A. E., Lange, L. A., & Martel, M. M. (2004). Parents' Personality and Infants' Temperament as Contributors to Their Emerging Relationship. *Journal of Personality and Social Psychology, 86*(5), 744–759.

Kochukhova, O., & Gredebäck, G. (2010). Preverbal infants anticipate that food will be brought to the mouth: An eye tracking study of manual feeding and flying spoons. *Child Development, 81*(6), 1729-1738. doi:10.1111/j.1467-8624.2010.01506.x

Kochanska, G., & Kim, S. (2013). Early attachment organization with both parents and future behavior problems: from infancy to middle childhood. *Child Development, 84*(1), 283-296.

Kochanska, G., Koenig, J. L., Barry, R. A., Kim, S., & Yoon, J. (2010). Children's conscience during toddler and preschool years, moral self, and a competent, adaptive developmental trajectory. *Developmental Psychology, 46*(5), 1320-1332. doi:10.1037/a0020381

Kochanska, G., Murray, K. T., & Harlan, E. T. (2000). Effortful control in early childhood: Continuity and change, antecedents, and implications for social development. *Developmental Psychology, 36*(2), 220-232.

Kochanska, G., Tjebkes, T. L., & Forman, D. R. (1998). Children's emerging regulation of conduct: Restraint, compliance, and internalization from infancy to the second year. *Child Development, 69*(5), 1378–1389.

Koepke, J. E., Hamm, M., Legerstee, J., & Russell, M. (1983). Neonatal imitation: Two failures to replicate. *Infant Behavior and Development, 6,* 97–102.

Koester, L. S., Brooks, L., & Traci, M. A. (2000). Tactile contact by deaf and hearing mothers during face-to-face interactions with their infants. *Journal of Deaf Studies and Deaf Education, 5*(2), 127–139.

Kogan, N., & Carter, A. S. (1996). Mother-infant reengagement following the still-face: The role of maternal emotion availability in infant affect regulation. *Infant Behavior and Development, 19,* 359–370.

Kojima, H. (1986). Becoming nurturant in Japan: Past and present. In A. Fogel & G. F. Melson (Eds.), *Origins of nurturance: Developmental, biological, and cultural perspectives on caregiving* (pp. 359–376). Hillsdale, NJ: Erlbaum.

Kokkinaki, T. (2008). Interactive silences within spontaneous early infant-father 'dialogues.'. *Infant And Child Development, 17*(5), 509-525. doi:10.1002/icd.568

Kolak, A., & Vernon-Feagans, L. (2008). Family-level coparenting processes and child gender as moderators of family stress and toddler adjustment. *Infant & Child Development, 17*(6), 617-638.

Kolak, A. M., & Volling, B. L. (2011). Sibling jealousy in early childhood: Longitudinal links to sibling relationship quality. *Infant And Child Development, 20*(2), 213-226.

Kolbert, K., & Miller, A. (1994). Government in the examining room: Restrictions on the provision of abortion. *Journal of Medical Women's Association, 49,* 153–155.

Kolling, T., Goertz, C., Stefanie, F., & Knopf, M. (2010). Memory development

Kolers, P. A., & Roediger, H. L. (1984). Procedures of mind. *Journal of Verbal Learning & Verbal Behavior, 23*(4), 425-449.

throughout the second year: overall developmental pattern, individual differences, and developmental trajectories. *Infant Behavior & Development, 33*(2), 159-167

Kong, A., Frigge, M.L., Masson, G., Besenbacher, S., Sulem, P., Magnusson, G.. . . Stefansson, K. (2012). Rate of de novo mutations and the importance of father's age to disease risk. *Nature,488,* 471-475.

Konner, M. (1975). Relations among infants and juveniles in comparative perspective. In M. Lewis & L. A. Rosenblum (Eds.), *Friendship and peer relations* (pp. 108–140). New York: Wiley.

Konner, M. (1977). Infancy among the Kalahari Desert San. In P. H. Leiderman, S. R. Tulkin, & A. Rosenfeld (Eds.), *Culture and infancy* (pp. 680–699). New York: Academic Press.

Kontos, S., Howes, C., Shinn, M., & Galinsky, E. (1997). Children's experience in family child care and relative care as a function of family income and ethnicity. *Merrill-Palmer Quarterly, 43*(3), 386–403.

Koomen, H. M. Y., & Hoeksma, J. B. (1992). Maternal interactive behavior towards children with and children without cleft lip and palate. *Early Development and Parenting, 1,* 169–181.

Koops, W. (1996). Historical developmental psychology: The sample case of paintings. *International Journal of Behavioral Development, 19*(2), 393–413.

Kopp, C. B. (1982). Antecedents of self-regulation: A developmental perspective. *Developmental Psychology, 18,* 199–214.

Kopp, C. B. (1989). Regulation of distress and negative emotions: A developmental view. *Developmental Psychology, 25,* 343–354.

Kopp, C. B., & Vaughn, B. E. (1982). Sustained attention during exploratory manipulation as a predictor of cognitive competence in preterm infants. *Child Development, 53,* 174–182.

Korner, A. (1987). Preventive intervention with high-risk newborns: Theoretical, conceptual, and methodological perspectives. In J. D. Osofsky (Ed.), *Handbook of infant development* (2nd ed. pp. 503–534). New York: Wiley.

Korner, A., Brown, B. W., Reade, E. P., Stevenson, D. K., Fernbach, S. A., & Thom, V. A. (1988). State behavior of preterm infants as a function of development, individual and sex differences. *Infant Behavior and Development, 11,* 111–124.

Kornfeld, J. R. (1971). Theoretical issues in child phonology. *Proceedings of the Seventh Annual Meeting of the Chicago Linguistics Society* (pp. 454–468). Chicago: University of Chicago Press.

Kornhaber, A., & Woodward, K. L. (1981). *Grandparent/grandchild: The vital connection.* Garden City, NY: Anchor Press.

Korte, D., & Scaer, R. (1990). *A good birth, a safe birth.* New York: Bantam.

Kotch, J. B., & Cohen, S. R. (1986). SIDS counselors' reports of own and parents' reactions to reviewing the autopsy report. *Omega Journal of Death and Dying, 16,* 129–139.

Koterba, E. A., & Iverson, J. M. (2009). Investigating motionese: The effect of infant-directed action on infants' attention and object exploration. *Infant Behavior & Development, 32*(4), 437-444.

Kovack-Lesh, K. A., Oakes, L. M., & McMurray, B. (2012). Contributions of attentional style and previous experience to 4-month-old infants' categorization. *Infancy, 17*(3), 324-338. doi:10.1111/j.1532-7078.2011.00073.x

Kovács, Á. (2009). Early bilingualism enhances mechanisms of false-belief reasoning. *Developmental Science, 12*(1), 48-54. doi:10.1111/j.1467-7687.2008.00742.x

Kozer, E., Nikfar, S., Costei, A., Boskovic, R., Nulman, I., & Koren, G. (2002). Aspirin consumption during the first trimester of pregnancy and congenital anomalies: a meta-analysis. *Am J Obstet Gynecol, 187*(6), 1623–1630.

Kramer, L. (2010). The essential ingredients of successful sibling relationships: An emerging framework for advancing theory and practice. *Child Development Perspectives, 4*(2), 80-86. doi:10.1111/j.1750-8606.2010.00122.x

Kramer, L., & Gottman, J. M. (1992). Becoming a sibling: "With a little help from my friends." *Developmental Psychology, 28,* 685–699.

Kramer, L., Perozynski, L. A., & Chung, T. Y. (1999). Parental responses to sibling conflict: The effects of development and parent gender. *Child Development, 70*(6), 1401–1414.

Kravitz, H., Goldenberg, D., & Neyhus, A. (1978). Tactual exploration by normal infants. *Developmental Medicine and Child-Neurology, 20*(6), 720–726.

Kremenitzer, J. P., Vaughan, H. G., Jr., Kurtzberg, D., & Dowling, K. (1979). Smooth-pursuit eye movements in the newborn infant. *Child Development, 50,* 442–448.

Kreppner, J. M., Rutter, M., Beckett, C., Castle, J., Colvert, E., Groothues, C., et al. (2007). Normality and impairment following profound early institutional deprivation: A longitudinal follow-up into early adolescence. *Developmental Psychology, 43*(4), 931–946.

Kretch, K. S., & Adolph, K. E. (2013). Cliff or step? Posture-specific learning at the edge of a drop-off. *Child Development, 84*(1), 226-240. doi:10.1111/j.1467-8624.2012.01842.x

Kretchmar, M. D., & Jacobvitz, D. B. (2002). Observing mother-child relationships across generations: Boundary patterns, attachment and the transmission of caregiving. *Family Process, 41*(3), 351–374.

Kristen, S., Sodian, B., Thoermer, C., & Perst, H. (2011). Infants' Joint Attention Skills Predict Toddlers' Emerging Mental State Language. *Developmental Psychology, 47*(5), 1207-1219.

Kristensen, D. M., Hass, U., Lesné, L., Lottrup, G., Jacobsen, P. R., Desdoits-Lethimonier, C. . . . Leffers H, (2011). Intrauterine exposure to mild analgesics is a risk factor for development of male reproductive disorders in human and rat. *Human Reproduction, 26,* 235-244.

Kropp, J. P., & Haynes, O. M. (1987). To identify general and specific emotion signals of infants. *Child Development, 58,* 187–190.

Kuchuk, A., Vibbert, M., & Bornstein, M. H. (1986). The perception of smiling and its experiential correlates in three-month-old infants. *Child Development, 57,* 1054–1061.

Kuczaj, S. A., & Maratsos, M. P. (1983). Initial verbs of yes-no questions: A different kind of general grammatical category. *Developmental Psychology, 19,* 440–444.

Kuczynski, L., & Kochanska, G. (1995). Function and content of maternal demands: Developmental significance of early demands for competent action. *Child Development, 66,* 616–628.

Kuczynski, L., Zahn-Waxler, C., & Radke-Yarrow, M. (1987). Development and content of imitation in the second and third years of life: A socialization perspective. *Developmental Psychology, 23,* 276–282.

Kuehn, D., Aros, S. C., Fernando A., Maria U., Nancy Henriquez, C/, Kleinsteuber, K. C. . . . Mills, J. L. (2012). A prospective cohort study of the prevalence of growth, facial, and central nervous system abnormalities in children with heavy prenatal alcohol exposure. *Alcoholism: Clinical and Experimental Research, 36,* 1811-1819.

Kuhl, P. K. (1981). Auditory category formation and developmental speech perception. In R. Stark (Ed.), *Language behavior in infancy and early childhood* (pp. 155–170). New York: Elsevier.

Kuhl, P. K. (1998). Language, culture, and intersubjectivity: The creation of shared perception. In S. Br;araten (Ed.), *Intersubjective communication and emotion in early ontogeny. Studies in emotion and social interaction, 2nd series* (pp. 297–315). Cambridge, England: Cambridge University Press.

Kulin, N. A., Pastuszk, A., Sage, S. R., Schick-Boschetto, B., Spivey, G., Feldkamp, M., Ormond, K., Matsui, D., Stein-Schechman, A. K., Cook, L., Brochu, J., Rieder, M., & Koren, G. (1998). Pregnancy outcome following maternal use of the new selective serotonin reuptake inhibitors. *Journal of the American Medical Association, 279,* 609–610.

Kuller, J. A., & Katz, V. L. (1994). Miscarriage: A historical perspective. *Birth, 21,* 227–228.

Kumar, T. C. (1994). The value and use of different contraceptive methods. *Human Reproduction, 9,* 578–585.

Kumari, A. S. (2001). Pregnancy outcome in women with morbid obesity. *Int J Gynaecol Obstet, 73*(2), 101–107.

Kurzweil, S. R. (1988). Recognition of mother from multisensory interactions in early infancy. *Infant Behavior and Development, 11,* 235–243.

Laakso, M. L., Poikkeus, A. M., & Lyytinen, P. (1999). Shared reading interaction in families with and without genetic risk for dyslexia: Implications for toddlers' language development. *Infant and Child Development, 8,* 179–195.

Labrell, F. (1994). A typical interaction behavior between fathers and toddlers: Teasing. *Early Development and Parenting, 3,* 125–130.

Laible, D., Panfile, T., & Makariev, D. (2008). The quality and frequency of mother-toddler conflict: Links with attachment and temperament. *Child Development, 79*(2), 426-443. doi:10.1111/j.1467-8624.2007.01134.x

Laible, D. J., & Thompson, R. A. (2002). Mother-child conflict in the toddler years: Lessons in emotion, morality, and relationships. *Child Development, 73*(4), 1187–1203.

Lamb, M. E. (1978). Influences of the child on marital quality and family interaction during the prenatal, perinatal and infancy periods. In R. M. Lerner & G. B. Spanier (Eds.), *Child influences on marital and family interaction* (pp. 259–289). New York: Academic Press.

Lamb, M. E., & Bornstein, M. H. (1987). *Development in infancy* (2nd ed.). New York: Random House.

Lamb, M. E., Frodi, A. M., Frodj, M., & Hwang, C. P. (1982). Characteristics of maternal and paternal behavior in traditional and nontraditional Swedish families. *International Journal of Behavior and Development, 5,* 131–141.

Lamb, M. E., Gaensbauer, T. J., Malkin, C. M., & Schultz, L. A. (1985). The effects of child maltreatment on security of infant-adult attachment. *Infant Behavior and Development, 8,* 35–45.

Lamb, M. E., Pleck, J. H., Charnov, E. L., & Levine, J. A. (1987). A biosocial perspective on paternal behavior and involvement. In J. B. Lancaster, A. Rossi, J. Altmann, & L. R. Sherrod (Eds.), *Parenting across the lifespan: Biosocial perspectives* (pp. 66–87). Chicago: Aldine.

Lamb, M. E., Sternberg, K. J., & Prodromidis, M. (1992). Nonmaternal care and the security of infant-mother attachment: A reanalysis of the data. *Infant Behavior and Development, 15,* 71–83.

Lamb, M. E., Thompson, R., Gardner, W., Charnov, E., & Estes, D. (1984). Security of infantile attachment as assessed in the strange situation: Its study and biological interpretation. *Behavioral and Brain Sciences, 7,* 127–147.

Lambie, G. W. (2005). Child Abuse and Neglect: A Practical Guide for Professional School Counselors. *Professional School Counseling, 8*(3), 249–258.

Lampert, R. W., & Schochet, S. S. (1968). Demyelination and remyelination in lead neuropathy. *Journal of Neuropathology and Experimental Neurology, 27,* 527–545.

Landa, R. J., Holman, K. C., O'Neill, A. H., & Stuart, E. A. (2011). Intervention targeting development of socially synchronous engagement in toddlers with autism spectrum disorder: A randomized controlled trial. *Journal Of Child Psychology And Psychiatry, 52*(1), 13-21.

Landau, B., & Spelke, E. (1988). Geometric complexity and object search in infancy. *Developmental Psychology, 24,* 512–521.

Landesman-Dwyer, S. (1981). Maternal drinking and pregnancy outcome. *Applied Research in Mental Retardation, 3,* 241–263.

Landry, S. H. (1995). The development of joint attention in premature low birth weight infants: Effects of early medical complications and maternal attention-directing behaviors. In C. Moore & P. J. Dunham (Eds.), *Joint atten-*

tion: Its origins and role in development (pp. 223–250). Hillsdale, NJ: Erlbaum.

Landry, S. H., & Chapieski, M. L. (1989). Joint attention and infant toy exploration: Effects of Down's syndrome and prematurity. *Child Development, 60,* 103–118.

Landry, S. H., Garner, P. W., Swank, P. R., & Baldwin, C. D. (1996). Effects of maternal scaffolding during joint toy play with preterm and full-term infants. *Merrill-Palmer Quarterly, 42*(2), 177–199.

Landry, S. H., Smith, K. E., & Swank, P. R. (2006). Responsive Parenting: Establishing Early Foundations for Social, Communication, and Independent Problem-Solving Skills. *Developmental Psychology, 42*(4), 627–642.

Langlois, J. H., Ritter, J. M., Casey, R. J., & Sawin, D. B. (1995). Infant attractiveness predicts maternal behaviors and attitudes. *Developmental Psychology, 31,* 464–472.

Langlois, J. H., Ritter, J. M., Roggman, L. A., & Vaughn, L. S. (1991). Facial diversity and infant preferences for attractive faces. *Developmental Psychology, 27,* 79–84.

Langlois, J. H., Roggman, L. A., Casey, R. J., Ritter, J. M., Rieser-Danner, L. S., & Jenkins, V. Y. (1987). Infant preferences for attractive faces: Rudiments of a stereotype? *Developmental Psychology, 23,* 363–369.

Laranjo, J., Bernier, A., Meins, E., & Carlson, S. M. (2010). Early manifestations of children's theory of mind: The roles of maternal mind-mindedness and infant security of attachment. *Infancy, 15*(3), 300-323. doi:10.1111/j.1532-7078.2009.00014.x

Largo, R. H. (1993). Early motor development in preterm children. In G. J. P. Savelsbergh (Ed.), *The development of coordination in infancy* (pp. 425–444). Amsterdam: Elsevier.

Larsson, I., & Svedin, C. G. (2002). Teachers' and parents' report on 3– to 6–year-old children's sexual behavior--a comparison. *Child Abuse & Neglect, 26*(3), 247–266.

Laughlin, C. D. (1991). Pre- and perinatal brain development and enculturation: A biogenetic structural approach. *Human Nature, 2,* 171–213.

Laughon, S. K., Zhang, J., Grewal, J., Sundaram, R., Beaver, J., & Reddy, U. M. (2012). Induction of labor in a contemporary obstetric cohort. *American Journal Of Obstetrics And Gynecology, 206 ,* 486.e1-9.

Lavelli, M. & Fogel, A. (2002). Developmental changes in mother-infant face-to-face communication: Birth to 3 months. <u>Developmental Psychology, 38</u>, 288–305.

Lavelli, M. & Fogel, A. (2005). Developmental changes in the relationship between infant's attention and emotion during early face-to-face communication: The 2–month transition. <u>Developmental Psychology, 41,</u> 265–280.

Lavelli, M., & Poli, M. (1998). Early mother-infant interaction during breast- and bottle-feeding. *Infant Behavior and Development, 21*(4), 667–684.

Law, K. L., Stroud, L. R., LaGasse, L. L., Niaura, R., Liu, J., & Lester, B. M. (2003). Smoking during pregnancy and newborn neurobehavior. *Pediatrics, 111*(6 Pt 1), 1318–1323.

Lawrence, A., Lewis, L., Hofmeyr, G. J., Dowswell, T., & Styles, C. (2009). Maternal positions and mobility during first stage labour, *Cochrane Database of Systematic Reviews,* CD003934; 2

Lawson, K. R., Parrinello, R., & Ruff, H. A. (1992). Maternal behavior and infant attention. *Infant Behavior and Development, 15,* 209–229.

Lawson, K. R., & Ruff, H. A. (1984). Infants' visual following: The effects of size and sound. *Developmental Psychology, 20,* 427–434.

Leach, P. (1997). Infant care from infants' viewpoint: The views of some professionals. *Early Development and Parenting, 6*(2), 47–58.

Leadbeater, B. J., Bishop, S. J., & Raver, C. C. (1996). Quality of mother-toddler interactions, maternal depressive symptoms, and behavior problems in preschoolers of adolescent mothers. *Developmental Psychology, 32*(2), 280–288.

Lebedeva, G., & Kuhl, P. (2010). Sing that tune: infants' perception of melody and lyrics and the facilitation of phonetic recognition in songs. *Infant Behavior & Development, 33*(4), 419-430.

Leboyer, F. (1975). *Birth without violence.* New York: Knopf.

Lecanuet, J.-P., Granier-Deferre, C., Jacquet, A.-Y., Capponi, I., & Ledru, L. (1993). Prenatal discrimination of a male and a female voice uttering the same sentence. *Early Development and Parenting, 2,* 217–228.

Lee, C., & Bates, J. (1985). Mother-child interaction at age two years and perceived difficult temperament. *Child Development, 56,* 1314–1325.

Lee, H. M., Bhat, A., Scholz, J. P., & Galloway, J. C. (2008). Toy-oriented changes during early arm movements: IV: Shoulder-elbow coordination. *Infant Behavior & Development, 31,* 447-469.

Lee, K. T., Mattson, S. N., & Riley, E. P. (2004). Classifying children with heavy prenatal alcohol exposure using measures of attention. *Journal of the International Neuropsychological Society, 10*(2), 271–277.

Lee, M., Vernon-Feagans, L., Vazquez, A., & Kolak, A. (2003). The Influence of Family Environment and Child Temperament on Work/Family Role Strain for Mothers and Fathers. *Infant and Child Development, 12*(5), 421–439.

Lee, S., Ralston, H., Drey, E., Partridge, J., & Rosen, M. (2005). Fetal pain: a systematic multidisciplinary review of the evidence. *JAMA: The Journal Of The American Medical Association, 294*(8), 947–954.

Lee, V. E., Brooks-Gunn, J., Schnur, E., & Liaw, F. R. (1990). Are Head Start effects sustained? A longitudinal follow-up comparison of disadvantaged children attending Head Start, no preschool, and other preschool programs. *Child Development, 61,* 495–507.

Leerkes, E. (2011). Maternal sensitivity during distressing tasks: A unique predictor of attachment security. *Infant Behavior & Development, 34*(3), 443-446.

Leerkes, E. M., & Wong, M. S. (2012). Infant distress and regulatory behaviors vary as a function of attachment security regardless of emotion context and maternal involvement.*Infancy, 17*(5), 455-478. doi:10.1111/j.1532-7078.2011.00099.x

Lefebvre, F., Bard, H., Veilleux, A., & Martel, C. (1988). Outcome at school age of children with birth weights of 1,000 grams or less. *Developmental Medicine and Child Neurology, 30*(2), 170–180.

Legendre, A., & Munchenbach, D. (2011). Two-to-three-year-old children's interactions with peers in child-care centres: Effects of spatial distance to caregivers. *Infant Behavior & Development, 34*(1), 111-125

Leger, D. W., Thompson, R. A., Merritt, J. A., & Benz, J. J. (1996). Adult perception of emotion intensity in human infant cries: Effects of infant age and cry acoustics. *Child Development, 67,* 3238–3249.

Legerstee, M. (1991). Changes in the quality of infant sounds as a function of social and nonsocial stimulation. *First Language, 11,* 327–343.

Legerstee, M. (1992). A review of the animate-inanimate distinction in infancy: Implications for models of social and cognitive knowing. *Early Development and Parenting, 1,* 59–67.

Legerstee, M., Pomerleau, A., Malcuit, G., & Feider, H. (1987). The development of infants' responses to people and a doll: Implications for research in communication. *Infant Behavior and Development, 10,* 81–95.

Legerstee, M., & Varghese, J. (2001). The role of maternal affect mirroring on social expectancies in three-month-old infants. *Child Development, 72*(5), 1301–1313.

Le Goff, J. (1987). *The medieval world.* (L. G. Cochrane, Trans.). London, England: Collins and Brown.

Leifer, G. (1999). *Thompson's introduction to maternity and pediatric nursing (3rd ed.)* Philadelphia: Saunders.

Leifer, M. (1980). *Psychological effects of motherhood: A study of first pregnancy.* New York: Praeger.

Leitch, D. B. (1999). Mother-infant interaction: Achieving synchrony. *Nursing Research, 48*(1), 55–58.

Lelorde, G., Barthelemy, C., Martineau, J., & Bruneau, N. (1991). Free acquisition, free imitation, physiological curiosity and exchange and development therapies in autistic children. *Brain Dysfunction, 4,* 335–347.

Lemche, E., Kreppner, J. M., Joraschky, P., & Klann-Delius, G. (2007). Attachment organization and the early development of internal state language: A longitudinal perspective. *International Journal of Behavioral Development, 31*(3), 252–262.

Lemery, K. S., & Goldsmith, H. H. (1999). Genetically informative designs for the study of behavioral development.

International Journal of Behavioral Development, 23(2), 293–317.

Lemery, K. S., Goldsmith, H. H., Klinnert, M. D., & Mrazek, D. A. (1999). Developmental models of infant and childhood temperament. *Developmental Psychology, 35*(1), 189–204.

Lemmer, C. M. (1987). Early discharge: Outcomes in primiparas and their infants. *Journal of Obstetric and Gynecological Nursing,* 230–236.

Lempers, J. D., Flavell, E. R., & Flavell, J. H. (1977). The development in very young children of tacit knowledge concerning visual perception. *Genetic Psychology Monographs, 95,* 3–53.

Lenneberg, E. H. (1969). On explaining language. *Science, 164,* 635–643.

Leo, I., & Simion, F. (2009). Newborns' Mooney-face perception. *Infancy, 14*(6), 641-653. doi:10.1080/15250000903264047

Lesko, W., & Leski, M. (1984). *The maternity sourcebook.* New York: Warner Books.

Leslie, G. I., Gibson, F. L., McMahon, C., Tennant, C., & Saunders, D. M. (1998). Infants conceived using in-vitro fertilization do not over-utilize health care resources after the neonatal period. *Human Reproduction, 13*(8), 2055–2059.

Lester, B. M. (2005). *Why is my baby crying: The parents' survival guide for coping with crying problems and colic.* NY: Harper.

Lester, B. M., Boukydis, Z. C. F., Garcia-Coll, C. T., Hole, W., & Peucker, M. (1992). Infantile colic: Acoustic cry characteristics, maternal perception of cry, and temperament. *Infant Behavior and Development, 15,* 15–26.

Lester, B. M., & Dreher, M. (1989). Effects of marijuana use during pregnancy on newborn cry. *Child Development, 60,* 765–771.

Lester, B. M., & Sparrow, J. D. (Eds.). (2011). Nurturing Children and Families: Building on the Legacy of T. Berry Brazelton. John Wiley & Sons.

Leung, E., & Rheingold, H. L. (1981). Development of pointing as a social gesture. *Developmental Psychology, 17,* 215–220.

Levitt, P., Reinoso, B., & Jones, L. (1998). The critical impact of early cellular environment on neuronal development. *Preventive Medicine, 27*(2), 180–183.

Levy, G., & Haaf, R. A. (1994). Detection of gender-related categories by 10–month-old infants. *Infant Behavior and Development, 17,* 457–459.

Levy, H. L., Karolkewicz, V., Houghton, S. A., & MacCready, R. A. (1970). Screening the "normal" population in Massachusetts for phenylketonuria. *New England Journal of Medicine, 282,* 1455–1458.

Leve, L. D., Kerr, D. R., Shaw, D., Ge, X., Neiderhiser, J. M., Scaramella, L. V., & ... Reiss, D. (2010). Infant pathways to externalizing behavior: Evidence of genotype environment interaction. *Child Development, 81*(1), 340-356. doi:10.1111/j.1467-8624.2009.01398.x

Levy, T. M. (Ed). (2000). *Handbook of attachment interventions.* San Diego, CA: Academic Press.

Levy, Y. (1999). Early metalinguistic competence: Speech monitoring and repair behavior. *Developmental Psychology, 35*(3), 822–834.

Levy-Shiff, R. (1994). Individual and contextual correlates of marital change across the transition to parenthood. *Developmental Psychology, 30,* 591–601.

Levy-Shiff, R., Dimitrovsky, L., Shulman, S., & Har-Even, D. (1998). Cognitive appraisals, coping strategies, and support resources as correlates of parenting and infant development. *Developmental Psychology, 34*(6), 1417–1427.

Levy-Shiff, R., Goldschmidt, I., & Har-Even, D. (1991). Transition to parenthood in adoptive families. *Developmental Psychology, 27,* 131–140.

Levy-Shiff, R., Sharir, H., & Mogilner, M. B. (1989). Mother- and father–preterm infant relationship in the hospital preterm nursery. *Child Development, 60,* 93–102.

Lewis, B. A., Singer, L. T., Short, E. J., Minnes, S., Arendt, R., Weishampel, P., et al. (2004). Four-year language outcomes of children exposed to cocaine in utero. *Neurotoxicol Teratol, 26*(5), 617–627.

Lewis, C., Kier, C., Hyder, C., Prenderville, N., Pullen, J., & Stephens, A. (1996). Observer influences on fathers and mothers: An experimental manipulation of the structure and function of parent-infant conversation. *Early Development and Parenting, 5*(1), 57–68.

Lewis, J. D., & Elman, J. L.(2008). Growth-related neural reorganization and the autism phenotype: a test of the hypothesis that altered brain growth leads to altered connectivity. *Developmental Science, 11,* 135-55.

Lewis, M. (1995). Embarrassment: The emotion of self-exposure and evaluation. In J. P. Tangney & K. W. Fischer (Eds.) *Self-conscious emotions: The psychology of shame, guilt, embarrassment, and pride* (pp. 198–218). New York: Guilford Press.

Lewis, M. (2005). The Child and Its Family: The Social Network Model. *Human Development, 48*(1–2), 8–27.

Lewis, M., Alessandri, S. M., & Sullivan, M. W. (1992). Differences in shame and pride as a function of children's gender and task difficulty. *Child Development, 63,* 630–638.

Lewis, M., & Brooks-Gunn, J. (1979). *Social cognition and the acquisition of self.* New York: Plenum Press.

Lewis, M., & Carmody, D. P. (2008). Self-representation and brain development. *Developmental Psychology, 44*(5), 1329-1334. doi:10.1037/a0012681

Lewis, M., & Feiring, C. (1978). The child's social world. In R. M. Lerner & G. B. Spanier (Eds.), *Child influences on marital and family interaction* (pp. 119–150). New York: Academic Press.

Lewis, M., & Feiring, C. (1989). Infant, mother, and mother-infant interaction behavior and subsequent attachment. *Child Development, 60,* 831–837.

Lewis, M., & Michalson, L. (1983). *Children's emotions and moods.* New York: Plenum Press.

Lewis, M., & Ramsay, D. S. (1995). Developmental change in infants' responses to stress. *Child Development, 66,* 657–670.

Lewis, M., & Ramsay, D. (2004). Development of self-recognition, personal pronoun use, and pretend play during the 2nd year. *Child Development, 75*(6), 1821–1831.

Lewis, M., Stanger, C., & Sullivan, M. W. (1989). Deception in 3–year-olds. *Developmental Psychology, 25,* 439–443.

Lewis, M., Sullivan, M. W., Ramsay, D. S., & Alessandri, S. M. (1992). Individual differences in anger and sad expressions during extinction: Antecedents and consequences. *Infant Behavior and Development, 15,* 443–452.

Lewis, M., Sullivan, M. W., Stanger, C., & Weiss, M. (1989). Self development and self-conscious emotions. *Child Development, 60,* 146–156.

Lewis, M., Young, G., Brooks, J., & Michalson, L. (1975). The beginning of friendship. In M. Lewis & L. Rosenblum (Eds.), *Friendship and peer relations* (pp. 305–341). New York: Wiley.

Lewis, M. D. (1993). Emotion-cognition interactions in early infant development. *Cognition and Emotion, 7,* 145–170.

Lewis, M. D. (1995). Cognition-emotion feedback and the self-organization of developmental paths. *Human Development, 38* (2), 71–102.

Lewis, M. D. (1993). Early socioemotional predictors of cognitive competency at 4 years. *Developmental Psychology, 29,* 1036–1045.

Lewis, M. D. (2008). Emotional habits of brain and behavior: A window on personality development. In A. Fogel, B. J. King, & S. Shanker (Eds.). *Human development in the 21st century: Visionary policy ideas from systems scientists.* Cambridge, UK: Cambridge University Press.

Lewis, M. D., Koroshegyi, C., Douglas, L., & Kampe, K. (1997). Age-specific associations between emotional responses to separation and cognitive performance in infancy. *Developmental Psychology, 33*(1), 32–42.

Lewis, M. D., Lamey, A. V., & Douglas, L. (1999). A new dynamic systems method for the analysis of early socioemotional development. *Developmental Science, 2*(4), 457–475.

Lewis, M. D., & Ramsay, D. S. (1997). Stress reactivity and self-recognition. *Child Development, 68*(4), 621–629.

Lewis, S. E., & Nicolson, P. (1998). Talking about early motherhood: Recognizing loss and reconstructing depression. *Reproductive and Infant Psychology, 16,* 177–197.

Lewit, E. M., & Baker, L. S. (1995). Unintentional injuries. *Future of Children, 5,* 214–231.

Lewit, E. M., Baker, L. S., Corman, H., & Shiono, P. H. (1995). The direct cost of low birth weight. *Future of Children, 5,* 35–56.

Lewkowicz, D. J. (1988). Sensory dominance in infants: 1. Six-month-old infants' response to auditory-visual compounds. *Developmental Psychology, 24,* 155–171.

Lewkowicz, D. J. (1994). Limitations on infants' response to rate-based auditory-visual relations. *Development Psychology, 30,* 880–892.

Lewkowicz, D. J. (1996). Infants' response to the audible and visible properties of the human face: 1. Role of the lexical-syntactic content, temporal synchrony, gender, and manner of speech. *Developmental Psychology, 32*(2), 347–366.

Lewkowicz, D. J. (2008). Perception of dynamic and static audiovisual sequences in 3- and 4-month-old infants. *Child Development, 79*(5), 1538-1554. doi:10.1111/j.1467-8624.2008.01204.x

Lewkowicz, D. J. (2011). The biological implausibility of the nature–nurture dichotomy and what it means for the study of infancy. *Infancy, 16*(4), 331-367. doi:10.1111/j.1532-7078.2011.00079.x

Lewkowicz, D. J., & Hansen-Tift, A. M. (2012). Infants deploy selective attention to the mouth of a talking face when learning speech. *PNAS Proceedings Of The National Academy Of Sciences Of The United States Of America, 109*(5), 1431–1436.

Ley, R. G., & Koepke, J. E. (1982). Attachment behavior out of doors: Naturalistic observations of sex and age differences in the separation behavior of young children. *Infant Behavior and Development, 5,* 195–201.

L'Hoir, M., Westers, P., Konig, P., Visser, A., Guedeke, M., & Wolters, W. (1994). Parental management of infants born following a cot-death victim who were monitored compared to infants who, despite similar histories, were not monitored: A controlled study. *European Journal of Pediatrics, 153,* 694–699.

Li, D. K., Yang, C., Andrade, S., Tavares, V. & Ferber, J. R. (2011). Maternal exposure to angiotensin converting enzyme inhibitors in the first trimester and risk of malformations in offspring: a retrospective cohort study. *BMJ (Clinical Research Ed.), 343,* d5931.

Li, R., Zhao, Z., Mokdad, A., Barker, L., & Grummer-Strawn, L. (2003). Prevalence of breastfeeding in the United States: the 2001 National Immunization Survey. *Pediatrics, 111*(5 Part 2), 1198–1201.

Liaw, F., & Brooks-Gunn, J. (1993). Patterns of low-birth-weight children's cognitive development. *Developmental Psychology, 29,* 1024–1035.

Lickliter, R. (2008). Developmental dynamics: The new view from the life sciences. In A. Fogel, B. J. King, & S. Shanker (Eds.). *Human development in the 21st century:*

Visionary policy ideas from systems scientists. Cambridge, UK: Cambridge University Press.

Lickliter, R., & Hellewell, T. B. (1992). Contextual determinants of auditory learning in Bobwhite quail embryos and hatchlings. *Developmental Psychobiology, 25,* 017–031.

Liebal, K., Carpenter, M., & Tomasello, M. (2010). Infants' use of shared experience in declarative pointing. *Infancy, 15*(5), 545-556. doi:10.1111/j.1532-7078.2009.00028.x

Lieberman, A. B. (1992). *Easing Labor Pain: The Complete Guide to a More Comfortable and Rewarding Birth.* Harvard Common Press: Boston.

Lieberman, A. F. (1995). *Emotional Life of the Toddler.* NY: Free Press.

Lieberman, A. F., Padrón, E., van Horn, P., & Harris, W. W. (2005). Angels in the nursery: The intergenerational transmission of benevolent parental influence. *Infant Mental Health Journal, 26,* 504–520.

Lieberman, A. F., Weston, D. R., & Pawl, J. H. (1991). Preventive intervention and outcome with anxiously attached dyads. *Child Development, 62,* 199–209.

Lieberman, E., Lang, J. M., Frigoletto, F., Richardson, D. K., Ringer, S. A., & Cohen, A. (1997). Epidural analgesia, intrapartum fever, and neonatal sepsis evaluation. *Pediatrics, 99*(3), 415–419.

Lillard, A. S., & Witherington, D. C. (2004). Mothers' Behavior Modifications During Pretense and Their Possible Signal Value for Toddlers. *Developmental Psychology, 40*(1), 95–113.

Lindahl, L. B., & Heimann, M. (1997). Research report: Social proximity in early mother-infant interactions: Implications for gender differences? *Early Development and Parenting, 6*(2), 83–88.

Lindsay, J. A., Johnson, H. M., Wallace, F. M., & Soos, J. M. (1994). Can superantigens trigger sudden infant death? *Medical Hypotheses, 43,* 81–85.

Lindsey, E. W., & Mize, J. (2001). Contextual differences in parent-child play: Implications for children's gender role development. *Sex Roles, 44*(3–4), 155–176.

Linebarger, D. L., & Vaala, S. E. (2010). Screen media and language development in infants and toddlers: An ecological perspective. *Developmental Review, 30*(2), 176-202.

Lippit, JA. (2001, June/July) Policy and policy making for infants, toddlers, and their families: A primer for practitioners. *Zero to Three,* 4–8

Lipscomb, S., Leve, L. D., Harold, G. T., Neiderhiser, J. M., Shaw, D. S., Ge, X., & Reiss, D. (2011). Trajectories of Parenting and Child Negative Emotionality during Infancy and Toddlerhood: A Longitudinal Analysis. *Child Development, 82*(5), 1661-1675.

Lipsitt, L. P. (1979). The pleasures and annoyances of infants: Approach and avoidance behavior. In E. Thoman (Ed.),

The origins of the infant's social responsiveness (pp. 105–119). Hillsdale, NJ: Erlbaum.

Lipsitt, L. P., Engen, T., & Kaye, H. (1963). Developmental changes in the olfactory threshold of the neonate. *Child Development, 34,* 371–376.

Lipsitt, L. P., Sturges, W. Q., & Burke, P. (1979). Perinatal indicators and subsequent crib death. *Infant Behavior and Development, 2,* 325–328.

Liszkowski, U., Albrecht, K., Carpenter, M., & Tomasello, M. (2008). Infants' visual and auditory communication when a partner is or is not visually attending. *Infant Behavior & Development, 31*(2), 157-167.

Little, A. B. (1988). There's many a slip 'twixt implantation and the crib (editorial). *New England Journal of Medicine, 319*(4), 241–242.

Little, J., & Vainio, H. (1994). Mutagenic lifestyles? A review of evidence of associations between germ-cell mutations in humans and smoking, alcohol consumption and use of "recreational" drugs. *Mutation Research, 313,* 131–151.

Lobo, M. A., Galloway, J. C., & Savelsbergh, G. J. P. (2004). General and Task-Related Experiences Affect Early Object Interaction. *Child Development, 75*(4), 1268–1281.

Lobo, M. A., & Galloway, J. C. (2008). Postural and object-oriented experiences advance early reaching, object exploration, and means-end behavior. *Child Development, 79*(6), 1869-1890. doi:10.1111/j.1467-8624.2008.01231.x

Lock, A. (1980). *The guided reinvention of language.* New York: Academic Press.

Lock, A. (2000). Preverbal communication. In J. G. Bremner & A. Fogel (Eds.), *Handbook of infancy research* (pp. 504–521). Oxford, England: Blackwell.

Locke, J. L. (1979). The child's processing of phonology. In W. A. Collins (Ed.), *Minnesota symposia on child psychology: Vol. 12. Children's language and communication* (pp. 1261–1289). Hillsdale, NJ: Erlbaum.

Locke, J. L. (1993). *The child's path to spoken language.* Cambridge, MA: Harvard University Press.

Lodish, H. F. (1995). Through the glass lightly. *Science, 267,* 1609–1611.

Loehlin, J. C. (1989). Partitioning environmental and genetic contributions to behavioral development. *American Psychologist, 44*(10), 1285–1292.

Loh, C.-C., & Vostanis, P. (2004). Perceived mother-infant relationship difficulties in postnatal depression. *Infant and Child Development, 13*(2), 159–171.

Lollis, S. P. (1990). Effects of maternal behavior on toddler behavior during separation. *Child Development, 61,* 99–103.

Loomans, E. M., Hofland, L., van der Stelt, O., van der Wal, M. F., Koot, H. M., Van den Bergh, B. R., & Vrijkotte, T.G. (2012). Caffeine intake during pregnancy and risk of problem behavior in 5- to 6-year-old children. *Pediatrics, 130,* e305-313.

Lorber, M. F., & Egeland, B. (2011). Parenting and infant difficulty: Testing a mutual exacerbation hypothesis to predict early onset conduct problems. *Child Development, 82*(6-), 2006-2020.

Lord, C., Bishop, S. L., & Society for Research in Child, D. (2010). Autism Spectrum Disorders: Diagnosis, Prevalence, and Services for Children and Families. Social Policy Report. Volume 24, Number 2. *Society For Research In Child Development.*

Lorenz, K. Z. (1952). The comparative method in studying innate behavior. *Symposium of the Society for Experimental Biology,* 41, 221–268.

Lorenz, K. Z. (1965). *Evolution and modification of behavior.* Chicago: University of Chicago Press.

Losoya, S. H., Callor, S., Rowe, D. C., & Goldsmith, H. H. (1997). Origins of familial similarity in parenting: A study of twins and adoptive siblings. *Developmental Psychology, 33*(6), 1012–1023.

Louik, C., Lin, A., Werler, M., Hernández-Díaz, S., & Mitchell, A. (2007). First-trimester use of selective serotonin-reuptake inhibitors and the risk of birth defects. *New England Journal of Medicine, 356*(26), 2675–2683.

Love, J. M., Harrison, L., Sagi-Schwartz, A., Van Ijzendoorn, M. H., Ross, C., Ungerer, J. A., et al. (2003). Child Care Quality Matters: How Conclusions May Vary With Context. *Child Development, 74*(4), 1021–1033.

Lowe, J., MacLean, P., Duncan, A., Aragón, C., Schrader, R., Caprihan, A., & Phillips, J. (2012). Association of maternal interaction with emotional regulation in 4- and 9-month infants during the Still Face Paradigm. *Infant Behavior & Development, 35*(2), 295-302. doi:10.1016/j.infbeh.2011.12.002

Lowinger, S. (1999). Infant irritability and early mother-infant reciprocity patterns. *Infant and Child Development, 8*(2), 71–84.

Lozoff, B., Klein, N. K., Nelson, E. C., McClish, D. K., Manual, M., & Chacon, M. E. (1998). Behavior of infants with iron-deficiency anemia. *Child Development, 69*(1), 24–36.

Lu, M. C. & Lu, J. S. (2007). *Maternal nutrition and infant mortality in the context of relationality.* Washington, DC: The joint center for political and economic studies health policy institute, www.jointcenter.org.

Lubic, R. W. (1999). Giving birth is powerful! *Zero to Three, 19*(4), 20–24.

Luby, J. L. (2010). The neonatal intensive care unit: Attending to mental health outcomes. *Journal of the American Academy of Child & Adolescent Psychiatry, 49,* 439-440.

Luby, J. L., Heffelfinger, A. K., Mrakotsky, C., Brown, K. M., Hessler, M. J., Wallis, J. M., et al. (2003). The clinical picture of depression in preschool children. *J Am Acad Child Adolesc Psychiatry, 42*(3), 340–348.

Lucas-Thompson, R., Goldberg, W., Germo, G., Keller, M., Davis, E., & Sandman, C. (2009). Sleep arrangements and night waking at 6 and 12 months in relation to infants' stress-induced cortisol responses. *Infant & Child Development, 18*(6), 521-544.

Ludemann, P. M. (1991). Generalized discrimination of positive facial expressions by seven- and ten-month-old infants. *Child Development, 62,* 55–67.

Ludemann, P. M., & Nelson, C. A. (1988). Categorical representation of facial expressions by 7–month-old infants. *Developmental Psychology, 24,* 492–501.

Ludington-Hoe, S. M., & Swinth, J. (1996). Developmental aspects of kangaroo care. *Journal of Obstetric, Gynecologic, and Neonatal Nursing, 25*(8), 691–703.

Ludwig, J., & Phillips, D. (2007). The benefits and costs of Head Start. *Social Policy Report, 21*(3), 3–19.

Lugo-Gil, J., & Tamis-LeMonda, C. S. (2008). Family resources and parenting quality: Links to children's cognitive development across the first 3 years. *Child Development, 79*(4), 1065-1085. doi:10.1111/j.1467-8624.2008.01176.x

Lundy, B. L., Jones, N. A., Field, T., Nearing, G., Davalos, M., Pietro, P. A., Schanberg, S., & Kuhn, C. (1999). Prenatal depression effects on neonates. *Infant Behavior and Development, 22*(1), 119–129.

Lunt, R., & Law, D. (1974). A review of the chronology of eruption of deciduous teeth. *Journal of the American Dental Association, 89,* 872–879.

Luo, Y., & Johnson, S. C. (2009). Recognizing the role of perception in action at 6 months. *Developmental Science, 12*(1), 142-149. doi:10.1111/j.1467-7687.2008.00741.x

Lupe, P. J., & Gross, T. L. (1986). Maternal upright posture and mobility in labor: A review. *Obstetrics and Gynecology, 67* (5), 727–734.

Lupien, S. J., Parent, S., Evans, A. C., Tremblay, R. E., Zelazo, P., Corbo, V., & … Séguin, J. R. (2011). Larger amygdala but no change in hippocampal volume in 10-year-old children exposed to maternal depressive symptomatology since birth. *PNAS Proceedings Of The National Academy Of Sciences Of The United States Of America, 108*(34), 14324-14329. doi:10.1073/pnas.1105371108

Lyons, S. (1998). A prospective study of post traumatic stress symptoms 1 month following childbirth in a group of 42 first-time mothers. *Reproductive and Infant Psychology, 16,* 91–105.

Lyons, S. J., Henly, J. R., & Schuerman, J. R. (2005). Informal support in maltreating families: Its effect on parenting practices. *Children and Youth Services Review, 27*(1), 21–38.

Lyons-Ruth, K. (2000). 'I sense that you sense that I sense…': Sander's recognition process and the specificity of relational moves in the psychotherapeutic setting. *Infant Mental Health Journal, 21*(1-2), 85-98.

Lyons-Ruth, K., Alpern, L., & Repacholi, B. (1993). Disorganized infant attachment classification and maternal psychosocial problems as predictors of hostile-aggressive behavior in the preschool classroom. *Child Development, 64,* 572–585.

Lyons-Ruth, K., Bronfman, E., & Parsons, E. (1999). Maternal frightened, frightening, or atypical behavior and disorganized infant attachment patterns. *Monographs of the Society for Research in Child Development, 64*(3), 67–96.

Lyons-Ruth, K., Connell, D. B., Grunebaum, H. U., & Botein, S. (1990). Infants at social risk: Maternal depression and family support services as mediators of infant development and security of attachment. *Child Development, 61,* 85–98.

Lyons-Ruth, K., Easterbrooks, M. A., & Cibelli, C. D. (1997). Infant attachment strategies, infant mental lag, and maternal depressive symptoms: Predictors of internalizing and externalizing problems at age 7. *Developmental Psychology, 33*(4), 681–692.

Lyra, M., & Ferreira, M. (1987, August). *Dialogue and the construction of the mother-infant dyad.* Paper presented at the International Society for Behavioral Development Conference, Tokyo, Japan.

Lyra, M. C., & Rossetti-Ferreira, M. C. (1995). Transformation and construction in social interaction: A new perspective on analysis of the mother-infant dyad. In J. Valsiner (Ed.), *Child development within culturally structured environments (Vol. 3). Comparative-cultural and co-constructionist perspectives* (pp. 316–351). Norwood, NJ: Ablex.

MacCallum, F., Golombok, S., & Brinsden, P. (2007). Parenting and child development in families with a child conceived through embryo donation. *Journal of Family Psychology, 21*(2), 278–287.

MacFarlane, A. (1975). Olfaction in the development of social preferences in the human neonate. In Ciba Foundation Symposium (Ed.), *Parent-infant interaction* (pp. 605–617). New York: Elsevier.

MacKenzie, M. J., Nicklas, E., Waldfogel, J., & Brooks-Gunn, J. (2012). Corporal punishment and child behavioural and cognitive outcomes through 5 years of age: Evidence from a contemporary urban birth cohort study. *Infant And Child Development, 21*(1), 3-33.

Mackner, L. M., Black, M. M., & Starr, R. H., Jr. (2003). Cognitive development of children in poverty with failure to thrive: A prospective study through age 6. *Journal of Child Psychology and Psychiatry, 44*(5), 743–751.

Madden, M. E. (1994). The variety of emotional reactions to miscarriage. *Journal of Women's Health, 21,* 85–104.

Madigan, S., Goldberg, S., Moran, G., & Pederson, D. R. (2004). Naive observers' perceptions of family drawings by 7–year-olds with disorganized attachment histories. *Attachment & Human Development, 6*(3), 223–239.

Madigan, S., Moran, G., & Pederson, D. R. (2006). Unresolved states of mind, disorganized attachment relationships, and disrupted interactions of adolescent mothers and their infants. *Developmental Psychology, 42*(2), 293–304.

Madsen, M. C., & Shapira, A. (1970). Cooperative and competitive behavior of urban Afro-American, Anglo-American, Mexican-American, and Mexican village children. *Developmental Psychology, 3,* 16–20.

Maguire-Jack, K., Gromoske, A. N., & Berger, L. M. (2012). Spanking and Child Development During the First 5 Years of Life. *Child Development, 83*(6), 1960-1977.

Maguire, M. J., Hirsh-Pasek, K., Golinkoff, R., & Brandone, A. C. (2008). Focusing on the relation: Fewer exemplars facilitate children's initial verb learning and extension. *Developmental Science, 11*(4), 628-634. doi:10.1111/j.1467-7687.2008.00707.x

Mahajan, N., & Woodward, A. L. (2009). Seven-month-old infants selectively reproduce the goals of animate but not inanimate agents. *Infancy, 14*(6), 667-679. doi:10.1080/15250000903265184

Mahler, M., Pine, F., & Bergman, A. (1975). *The psychological birth of the human infant.* New York: Basic Books.

Main, M., & Cassidy, J. (1988). Categories of response to reunion with the parent at age 6: Predictable from infant attachment classifications and stable over a 1–month period. *Developmental Psychology, 24,* 415–426.

Main, M., & George, C. (1985). Responses of abused and disadvantaged toddlers to distress in agemates: A study in the day care setting. *Developmental Psychology, 21,* 407–412.

Main, M., Kaplan, N., & Cassidy, J. (1985). Security in infancy, childhood, and adulthood: A move to the level of representation. In I. Bretherton & E. Waters (Eds.), Growing points of attachment theory and research. *Monographs of the Society for Research in Child Development, 50* (Serial No. 209), 66–104.

Main, M., & Solomon, J. (1986). Discovery of an insecure disorganized/disoriented attachment pattern: Procedures, findings, and implications for the classification of behavior. In M. Yogman & T. B. Brazelton (Eds.), *Affective development in infancy* (pp. 95–124). Norwood, NJ: Ablex.

Main, M., & Weston, D. R. (1981). The quality of the toddler's relationship to mother and father: Related to conflict behavior and the readiness to establish new relationships. *Child Development, 52,* 932–940.

Major, B., Appelbaum, M., Beckman, L., Dutton, M. A., Russo, N. F., & West, C. (2009). Abortion and mental health: Evaluating the evidence. *American Psychologist, 64,* 863-890.

Malatesta, C. Z., Culver, C., Tesman, J. R., & Shepard, B. (1989). The development of emotion expression during the first two years of life. *Monographs of the Society for Research in Child Development, 54* (Serial No. 219), 1–104.

Malatesta, C. Z., & Haviland, J. M. (1982). Learning display rules: The socialization of emotion expression in infancy. *Child Development, 53,* 991–1003.

Malatesta-Magai, C., Leak, S., Tesman, J., Shepard, B., Culver, C., & Smaggia, B. (1994). Profiles of emotional development: Individual differences in facial and vocal expression of emotion during the second and third years of life. *International Journal of Behavioral Development, 17,* 239–269.

Malphurs, J. E., Raag, T., Field, T., Pickens, J., & Nogueras-Pelaez, M. (1996). Touch by intrusive and withdrawn mothers with depressive symptoms. *Early Development and Parenting, 5*(2), 111–115.

Mandler, J. M., & McDonough, L. (1998). On developing a knowledge base in infancy. *Developmental Psychology, 34*(6), 1274–1288.

Mandy, A., Gard, P. R., Ross, K., & Valentine, B. H. (1998). Psychological sequelae in women following either parturition or non-gynecological surgery. *Reproductive and Infant Psychology, 16,* 133–141.

Mangelsdorf, S. C. (1992). Developmental changes in infant-stranger interaction. *Infant Behavior and Development,* 15, 191–208.

Mangelsdorf, S. C., Plunkett, J. W., Dedrick, C. F., Berlin, M., Meisels, S. J., McHale, J. L., & Dichtellmiller, M. (1996). Attachment security in very low birth weight infants. *Developmental Psychology, 32*(5), 914–920.

Mannering, A. M., Harold, G. T., Leve, L. D., Shelton, K. H., Shaw, D. S., Conger, R. D., & ... Reiss, D. (2011). Longitudinal Associations between Marital Instability and Child Sleep Problems across Infancy and Toddlerhood in Adoptive Families. *Child Development*, 82(4), 1252-1266.

Maratsos, M., Kuczaj, S., Fox, D., & Chalkley, M. (1979). Some empirical studies in the acquisition of transformational relations: Passives, negatives, and the past tense. In W. A. Collins (Ed.), *Minnesota symposia on child psychology: Vol. 12. Children's language and communication* (pp. 1242–1260). Hillsdale, NJ: Erlbaum.

March of Dimes (2009). Medical Costs for One Premature Baby Could Cover A Dozen Healthy Births. http://www.marchofdimes.com/aboutus/49267_55250.asp (retrieved January 3, 2010).

Marchman, V. A., & Fernald, A. (2008). Speed of word recognition and vocabulary knowledge in infancy predict cognitive and language outcomes in later childhood. *Developmental Science, 11*(3), F9-F16. doi:10.1111/j.1467-7687.2008.00671.x

Marcos, H. (1995). Mother-child and father-child communication in the second year: A functional approach. *Early Development and Parenting, 4,* 49–61.

Marcos, H., & Chanu, M. K. (1992). Learning how to insist and clarify in the second year: Reformulation of requests

in different contexts. *International Journal of Behavioral Development, 15,* 359–376.

Marcos, H., & Verba, M. (1990, April). *Referential communication with adults and infants in the second year.* Paper presented at the International Conference on Infant Studies, Montreal, Canada.

Marcovitch, S., Goldberg, S., Gold, A., & Washington, J. (1997). Determinants of behavioural problems in Romanian children adopted in Ontario. *International Journal of Behavioral Development, 20*(1), 17–31.

Marcovitch, S., & Zelazo, P. D. (1999). The a-not-b error: Results from a logistic meta-analysis. *Child Development, 70*(6), 1297–1313.

Marcovitch, S., Zelazo, P. D., & Schmuckler, M. A. (2002). The effect of the number of A trials on performance on the A-not-B task. *Infancy, 3*(4), 519–529.

Marcus, G. F., Pinker, S., Ullman, M., & Hollander, M. (1992). Overregularization in language acquisition. *Monographs of the Society for Research in Child Development, 57*(4), 1–182.

Markman, H. J., & Kadushin, F. S. (1986). Preventive effects of Lamaze training for first-time parents: A short-term longitudinal study. *Journal of Consulting Clinical Psychology, 54*(6), 872–874.

Marlier, L., Schaal, B., & Soussignan, R. (1998a). Bottle-fed neonates prefer an odor experienced in utero to an odor experienced postnatally in the feeding context. *Developmental Psychobiology, 33*(2), 133–145.

Marlier, L., Schaal, B., & Soussignan, R. (1998b). Neonatal responsiveness to the odor of amniotic and lacteal fluids: A test of perinatal chemosensory continuity. *Child Development, 69*(3), 611–623.

Marsh, H. L., Stavropoulos, J., Nienhuis, T., & Legerstee, M. (2010). Six- and 9-month-old infants discriminate between goals despite similar action patterns.*Infancy, 15*(1), 94-106. doi:10.1111/j.1532-7078.2009.00002.x

Martin, R. P., Noyes, J., Wisenbaker, J., & Huttunen, M. O. (1999). Prediction of early childhood negative emotionality and inhibition from maternal distress during pregnancy. *Merrill-Palmer Quarterly, 45*(3), 370–391.

Martin, S. L., Harris-Britt, A., Li, Y., Moracco, K. E., Kupper, L. L., & Campbell, J. C. (2004). Changes in Intimate Partner Violence During Pregnancy. *Journal of Family Violence, 19*(4), 201–210.

Martinez-Frias, M. L., Rodriguez-Pinilla, E., Bermejo, E., & Prieto, L. (1998). Prenatal exposure to sex hormones: A case-control study. *Teratology, 57*(1), 8–12.

Martini, M., & Kirkpatrick, J. (1981). Early interactions in Marquesas islands. In T. M. Field, A. M. Sostek, P. Vietze, & P. H. Leiderman (Eds.), *Culture and early interactions.* Hillsdale, NJ: Erlbaum.

Martone, R. (2012) Scientists discover children's cells living in mothers' brains. *Scientific American,* Retrieved from http://

www.scientificamerican.com/article.cfm?id=scientists-discover-childrens-cells-living-in-mothers-brain

Marvin, R., Cooper, G., Hoffman, K. & Powell, B. (2002). The Circle of Security project: Attachment-based intervention with caregiver–pre-school child dyads. *Attachment & Human Development, 4,* 107–124.

Masataka, N. (1992). Motherese in a signed language. *Infant Behavior and Development, 15,* 453–460.

Masataka, N. (1999). Preference for infant-directed singing in 2–day-old hearing infants of deaf parents. *Developmental Psychology, 35*(4), 1001–1005.

Maschinot, B. (2008). *The changing face of the United States: The influence of culture on early child development.* Zero to Three.

Mascolo, M. F., & Fischer, K. W. (1995). Development transformations in appraisals for pride, shame, and guilt. In J. P. Tangney & K. W. Fischer (Eds.), *Self-conscious emotions: The psychology of shame, guilt, embarrassment, and pride* (pp. 64–113). New York: Guilford Press.

Mash, C., & Bornstein, M. H. (2012). 5-month-olds' categorization of novel objects: Task and measure dependence. *Infancy, 17*(2), 179-197. doi:10.1111/j.1532-7078.2011.00076.x

Mason, C., (2009). The development of developmental neuroscience. *Journal of Neuroscience, 29,* 12735-12735.

Masur, E. F. (1993). Transitions in representational ability: Infants' verbal, vocal, and action imitation during the second year. *Merrill-Palmer Quarterly, 39,* 437–456.

Masur, E. F., & Rodemaker, J. E. (1999). Mothers' and infants' spontaneous vocal, verbal, and action imitation during the second year. *Merrill-Palmer Quarterly, 45*(3), 392–412.

Matas, L., Arend, R. A., & Sroufe, L. A. (1978). Continuity of adaptation in the second year: The relationship between quality of attachment and later competence. *Child Development, 49,* 547–556.

Matatyaho, D. J., & Gogate, L. J. (2008). Type of maternal object motion during synchronous naming predicts preverbal infants' learning of word-object relations. *Infancy, 13*(2), 172-184.

Matheny, A. P., Jr., Wilson, R. S., & Thoben, A. S. (1987). Home and mother: Relations with infant temperament. *Developmental Psychology, 23,* 323–331.

Mathews, T. J., Menacker, F., & MacDorman, M. F. (2002). Infant mortality statistics from the 2000 period linked birth/infant death data set. *Natl Vital Stat Rep, 50*(12), 1–28.

Matias, R., & Cohn, J. E. (1993). Are max-specified infant facial expressions during face-to-face interaction consistent with differential emotions theory? *Developmental Psychology, 29,* 524–531.

Maton, K., & Bishop-Josef, S. (2006). Psychological Research, Practice, and Social Policy: Potential Pathways of Influence. *Professional Psychology: Research & Practice, 37*(2), 140–145.

Matthiesen, A-S., Ransjö-Arvidson, A-B., Nissen, E., & Uvnäs-Moberg, K. (2001). Postpartum maternal oxytocin release by newborns: Effects of infant hand massage and sucking. *Birth: Issues in Perinatal Care, 28,* 13-19.

Maughan, B., Taylor, A., Caspi, A., & Moffitt, T. E. (2004). Prenatal Smoking and Early Childhood Conduct Problems: Testing Genetic and Environmental Explanations of the Association. *Archives of General Psychiatry, 61*(8), 836–843.

Maun, A. R., Williams, R. S., Graber, B., & Myers, W. G. (1994). The passage of Florida's statute on assisted reproductive technology. *Obstetrics and Gynecology, 84,* 889–893.

Maurer, D. (1985). Infants' perception of facedness. In T. M. Field & N. A. Fox (Eds.), *Social perception in infants* (pp. 73–100). Norwood, NJ: Ablex.

Maurer, D., & Salapatek, P. (1976). Developmental changes in the scanning of faces by young infants. *Child Development, 47,* 523–527.

Mauthner, N. S. (1998). Re-assessing the importance and role of the marital relationship in postnatal depression: Methodological and theoretical implications. *Reproductive and Infant Psychology, 16,* 157–175.

Mayberry, R. I., Lock, E., & Kazmi, H. (2002). Linguistic ability and early language exposure. *Nature, 417*(6884), 38.

Mayer, S., & Musatti, T. (1992). Towards the use of symbol: Play with objects and communication with adults and peers in the second year. *Infant Behavior and Development, 15,* 1–13.

Mayes, L. C., Carter, A. S., & Stubbe, D. (1993). Individual differences in exploratory behavior in the second year of life. *Infant Behavior and Development, 16,* 269–284.

Mayes, L. C., Feldman, R., Granger, R. H., Haynes, O. M., Bornstein, M. H., & Schottenfeld, R. (1997). The effects of polydrug use with and without cocaine on mother-infant interaction at 3 and 6 months. *Infant Behavior and Development, 20*(4), 489–502.

Maziade, M., Boudreault, M., Cote, R., & Thivierge, J. (1986). Influence of gentle birth delivery procedures an other perinatal circumstances on infant temperament: Developmental and social implications. *The Journal of Pediatrics, 108,* 134–136.

McBride-Chang, C., & Kail, R. V. (2002). Cross-cultural similarities in the predictors of reading acquisition. *Child Development, 73*(5), 1392–1407.

McCalin, M., & Mandell, F. (1994). Sudden infant death syndrome: The nurse counselor's response to bereavement counseling. *Journal of Community Health Nursing, 11,* 177–186.

McCall, R. B. (2009). Evidence-based programming in the context of practice and policy. *Social Policy Report, 23(3),* 3-18.

McCall, R. B., & Carriger, M. S. (1993). A meta-analysis of infant habituation and recognition memory performance as predictors of later IQ. *Child Development, 64,* 57–79.

McCarty, M. E., Clifton, R. K., & Collard, R. R. (1999). Problem solving in infancy: The emergence of an action plan. *Developmental Psychology, 35*(4), 1091–1101.

McCarty, M. E., Clifton, R. K., & Collard, R. R. (2001). The beginnings of tool use by infants and toddlers. *Infancy, 2*(2), 233–256.

McClearn, G. E. (1970). Genetic influences on behavior and development. In P. H. Mussen (Ed.), *Child psychology* (3rd ed., Vol. 1). New York: Wiley.

McClure, V. S. (1989). *Infant massage: A handbook for loving parents.* New York: Bantam Books.

McConkie, R. A., & Iafolla, A. K. (1993). Medium-chain acyl CoA dehydrogenase deficiency: Its relationship to SIDS and the impact on genetic counseling. *Journal of Genetic Counseling, 2,* 17–27.

McCormick, C. M., & Maurer, D. M. (1988). Unimanual hand preferences in 6–month-olds: Consistency and relation familial-handedness. *Infant Behavior and Development, 11,* 21–29.

McCune, L. (1989, April). *Toward an integrative theory of early language acquisition: Evidence from longitudinal trends in vocal behavior.* Paper presented at the biennial meeting of the Society for Research in Child Development, Kansas City, MO.

McCune, L. (1995). A normative study of representational play at the transition to language. *Developmental Psychology, 31,* 198–206.

McCune-Nicholich, L. (1981). Toward symbolic functioning: Structure of early pretend games and potential parallels with language. *Child Development, 52,* 785–797.

McDonald, D. (1978). Paternal behavior at first contact with the newborn in a birth environment without intrusions. *Birth and the Family Journal, 5,* 123–132.

McDonald, M. A., Sigman, M., Espinosa, M. P., & Neumann, C. G. (1994). Impact of temporary food shortage on children and their mothers. *Child Development, 65*(2), 404–415.

McDonald, R., & Avery, D. (1983). *Dentistry for the child and adolescent* (4th ed.). St. Louis, MO: Mosby.

McDonnell, P. M., Anderson, V. E. S., & Abraham, W. C. (1983). Asymmetry and orientation of arm movements in three- to eight-week-old infants. *Infant Behavior and Development, 6,* 287–298.

McDonough, L., & Mandler, J. M. (1998). Inductive generalization in 9– and 11–month-olds. *Developmental Science, 1*(2), 227–232.

McElwain, N. L., Cox, M. J., Burchinal, M. R., & Macfie, J. (2003). Differentiating among insecure mother-infant attachment classifications: A focus on child-friend interaction and exploration during solitary play at 36 months. *Attachment & Human Development, 5*(2), 136–164.

McElwain, N. L., & Volling, B. L. (2004). Attachment security and parental sensitivity during infancy: Associations with friendship quality and false-belief understanding at age 4. *Journal of Social and Personal Relationships, 21*(5), 639–667.

McElwain, N. L., Wu, X., & Booth-LaForce, C. (2011). Infant-Mother Attachment and Children's Friendship Quality: Maternal Mental-State Talk as an Intervening Mechanism. *Developmental Psychology, 47*(5), 1295-1311.

McFarlane (2004*).* Elective cesarean birth: Issues and ethics of an informed decision. *Journal of Midwifery & Women's Health, 49*(5), 421–429.

McGlaughlin, A., & Grayson, A. (1999). A prospective study of crying during the first year of infancy. *Journal of Reproductive and Infant Psychology, 17*(1), 41–52.

McGraw, M. B. (1935). *Growth: A study of Johnny and Jimmy.* New York: Appleton.

McGuire, J. (1988). Gender stereotypes of parents with two-year-olds and beliefs about gender differences in behavior. *Sex Roles, 19,* 233–240.

McIntosh, J. R., & Koonce, M. P. (1989). Mitosis. *Science, 246,* 622–628.

McKay, J., Shaver-Hast, L., Sharnoff, W., Warren, M. E., & Wright, H. (2009). A Family Approach to Treatment of Postpartum Depression. *Zero to Three, 29*(5), 35-39.

McKenna, J. J. (1988). An anthropological perspective on the sudden infant death syndrome: The neurological and structural bases of speech breathing and why SIDS appears to be a species-specific malady: II. *Pre- and Perinatal Psychology Journal, 2,* 149–178.

McKenna, J. J., & Volpe, L. E. (2007). Sleeping with baby: an internet-based sampling of parental experiences, choices, perceptions, and interpretations in a western industrialized context. *Infant and Child Development, 16*(4), 359–385.

McKenzie, B., & Over, R. (1983). Young infants fail to imitate facial and manual gestures. *Infant Behavior and Development, 6,* 85–95.

McKenzie, B. E., Skouteris, H., Day, R. H., Hartman, B., & Yonas, A. (1993). Effective action by infants to contact objects by reaching and leaning. *Child Development, 64,* 415–429.

McKim, M. K. (1987). Transition to what? New parents' problems in the first year. *Family Relations Journal of Applied Family and Child Studies, 36,* 22–25.

McLoyd, V. C. (1998). Socioeconomic disadvantage and child development. *American Psychologist, 53*(2), 185–204.

McMahon, C. A., Tennant, C., Ungerer, J., & Saunders, D. (1999). Don't count your chickens: A comparative study of the experience of pregnancy after IVF conception. *Journal of Reproductive and Infant Psychology, 17*(4), 345–356.

McNeill, D. (1970). *The acquisition of language.* New York: Harper & Row.

McPherson, M. G. (1983). Improving services to infants and young children with handicapping conditions and their families: The Division of Maternal and Child Health as collaborator. *Zero to Three, 4,* 1–6.

McShane, J. (1980). *Learning to talk.* Cambridge, England: Cambridge University Press.

McWilliams, L., & Bailey, S. (2010). Associations between adult attachment ratings and health conditions: evidence from the National Comorbidity Survey Replication. *Health Psychology, 29*(4), 446-453.

Mead, M., & Newton, N. (1967). Cultural patterning of perinatal behavior. In S. Richardson & A. Guttmacher (Eds.), *Childbearing: Its social and psychological aspects* (pp. 76–104). Baltimore: Williams & Wilkins.

Mead, R. (1999, August 9). Annals of reproduction: Eggs for sale. *The New Yorker, 75,* 56–65.

Meade, C. S., & Ickovics, J. R. (2005). Systematic review of sexual risk among pregnant and mothering teens in the USA: Pregnancy as an opportunity for integrated prevention of STD and repeat pregnancy. *Social Science & Medicine, 60*(4), 661–678.

Meadow-Orlans, K. P., & Spencer, P. E. (1996). Maternal sensitivity and the visual attentiveness of children who are deaf. *Early Development and Parenting, 5*(4), 213–223.

Meaney, M. J. (2010). Epigenetics and the biological definition of gene x environment interactions. *Development, 81,* 41-79.

Meares, R., Grimwalde, J., & Wood, C. (1976). A possible relationship between anxiety in pregnancy and puerperal depression. *Journal of Psychosomatic Research, 20,* 605–610.

Meder, A. (1989). Effects of hand-rearing on the behavioral development of infant and juvenile gorillas. *Developmental Psychobiology, 22,* 357–376.

Meer, A. L. H. van der, Weel, F. R. van der, & Lee, D. N. (1995). The functional significance of arm movements in neonates. *Science, 267,* 693–696.

Mehl, L., Peterson, G., Sokolsky, W., & Whitt, M. (1976). Outcomes of early discharge after normal birth. *Birth and the Family Journal, 3,* 101–107.

Meijer, A. M., & van den Wittenboer, G. L. H. (2007). Contribution of Infants' Sleep and Crying to Marital Relationship of First-Time Parent Couples in the 1st Year After Childbirth. *Journal of Family Psychology, 21*(1), 49–57.

Meins, E., Centifanti, L. C. M., Fernyhough, C., & Fishburn, S. (2013). Maternal Mind-Mindedness and Children's Behavioral Difficulties: Mitigating the Impact of Low Socioeconomic Status. *Journal of Abnormal Child Psychology,41,* 543-553.

Meins, E., Fernyhough, C., de Rosnay, M., Arnott, B., Leekam, S. R., & Turner, M. (2012). Mind-mindedness as a multidimensional construct: Appropriate and nonattuned mind-related comments independently predict infant–mother attachment in a socially diverse sample.*Infancy, 17*(4), 393-415. doi:10.1111/j.1532-7078.2011.00087.x

Meins, E., Fernyhough, C., Russell, J., & Clark-Carter, D. (1998). Security of attachment as a predictor of symbolic and mentalising abilities: A longitudinal study. *Social Development, 7*(1), 1–24.

Melson, G. (1980). *The family as an ecosystem.* New York: Burgess.

Melson, G., & Cohen, A. (1981). Contextual influences on children's activity: Sex differences in effects of peer presence and interpersonal attraction. *Genetic Psychology Monographs, 103,* 243–260.

Melson, G., & Fogel, A. (1982). Young children's interest in unfamiliar infants. *Child Development, 53,* 693–700.

Melson, G., & Fogel, A. (1988, March). The development of nurturance in young children. *Young Children,* 57–65.

Melson, G., Fogel, A., & Toda, S. (1986). Children's ideas about infants and their care. *Child Development, 57,* 1519–1527.

Meltzoff, A. (1988). Infant imitation and memory: Nine-month-olds in immediate and deferred tests. *Child Development, 59,* 217–225.

Meltzoff, A. N., & Brooks, R. (2008). Self-experience as a mechanism for learning about others: A training study in social cognition. *Developmental Psychology, 44*(5), 1257-1265. doi:10.1037/a0012888

Meltzoff, A., & Moore, M. K. (1989). Imitation in newborn infants: Exploring the range of gestures imitated and the underlying mechanisms. *Developmental Psychology, 25,* 954–962.

Meltzoff, A., & Moore, M. K. (1994). Imitation, memory, and the representation of persons. *Infant Behavior and Development, 17,* 83–99.

Meltzoff, A., & Moore, M. K. (1997). Explaining facial imitation: A theoretical model. *Early Development and Parenting, 6*(1), 179–192.

Meltzoff, A., & Moore, W. (1977). Imitation of facial and manual gestures by human neonates. *Science, 198,* 75–78.

Mendelsohn, A., Brockmeyer, C., Dreyer, B., Fierman, A., Berkule-Silberman, S., & Tomopoulos, S. (2010). Do verbal interactions with infants during electronic media exposure mitigate adverse impacts on their language development as toddlers?. *Infant & Child Development, 19*(6), 577-593.

Mendes, D. M. L. F., Seidl-de-Moura, M. L. & Siqueira, J. d. O. (2009).The ontogenesis of smiling and its association with mothers' affective behaviors: A longitudinal study. *Infant Behavior & Development, 32,* 445-453.

Mennella, J. A. (1997). A cross-cultural perspective. *Nutrition Today, 32*(4), 144–151.

Mennella, J. & Beauchamp, G. (1993). Early flavor experiences: When do they start? *Zero to Three, 14*(2), 1–7.

Mennella, J., Jagnow, C., & Beauchamp, G. (2001). Prenatal and postnatal flavor learning by human infants. *Pediatrics, 107*(6), E88–E88.

Mercer, R. T., Ferketich, S., May, K., DeJoseph, J., & Sollid, D. (1988). Further exploration of maternal and paternal fetal attachment. *Research in Nursing and Health, 11,* 83–95.

Meredith, H. (1975). Somatic changes during human pre-natal life. *Child Development, 46,* 603–610.

Messinger, D. S., Dolcourt, J., King, J., Bodnar, A., & Beck, D. (1996). The survival and developmental outcome of extremely low birthweight infants. *Infant Mental Health Journal, 17*(4), 375–385.

Messinger, D. S., & Fogel, A. (1998). Give and take: The development of conventional infant gestures. *Merrill-Palmer Quarterly, 44*(4), 566–590.

Messinger, D. S., Fogel, A., & Dickson, K. L. (1998). What's in a smile? *Developmental Psychology, 35*(3), 701–708.

Messinger, D., Fogel, A., & Dickson, K.L. (2001). All smiles are positive, but some smiles are more positive than others. *Developmental Psychology, 37,* 642–653.

Messinger, D. S. & Lester, B. M. (2008) Prenatal substance exposure and human development. . In A. Fogel, B. J. King, & S. Shanker (Eds.). *Human development in the 21st century: Visionary policy ideas from systems scientists.* Cambridge, UK: Cambridge University Press.

Messmer, P. R., Rodriguez, S., Adams, J., Wells-Gentry, J., Washburn, K., Zabaleta, I., & Abreu, S. (1999). Effect of kangaroo care on sleep time for neonates. *Pediatric Nursing, 23*(4), 408–414.

Metosky, P., & Vondra, J. (1995). Prenatal drug exposure and play and coping in toddlers: A comparison study. *Infant Behavior and Development, 18,* 15–25.

Meyer, L., Mailloux, J., Marcoux, S., Blanchett, P., & Meyer, F. (1987). Maternal and neonatal morbidity in instrumental deliveries with the Kobayashi vacuum extractor and low forceps. *Acta Obstetrica et Gynecologica Scandinavica, 66*(7), 643–647.

Meyers, B. J., & Kaltenbach, K. (1992). Cocaine-exposed infants: Myths and misunderstandings. *Zero to Three, 12,* 1–5. Arlington, VA: National Center for Clinical Infant Programs.

Mezulis, A. H., Hyde, J. S., & Clark, R. (2004). Father Involvement Moderates the Effect of Maternal Depression During a Child's Infancy on Child Behavior Problems in Kindergarten. *Journal of Family Psychology, 18*(4), 575–588.

Michaelson, K. L., et al. (1988). *Childbirth in America: Anthropological perspectives.* South Hadley, MA: Bergin & Garvey.

Mick, E., Biederman, J., Faraone, S. V., Sayer, J., & Kleinman, S. (2002). Case-control study of attention-deficit hyperactivity disorder and maternal smoking, alcohol use and drug use during pregnancy. *Journal of the American Academy of Child & Adolescent Psychiatry, 41*(4), 378–385.

Middlemiss, W. (2003). Brief report: Poverty, stress and support: Patterns of parenting behaviour among lower income black and lower income white mothers. *Infant and Child Development, 12*(3), 293–300.

Miebert, C. J. (1991). Dimensions of subjectivity in parents' ratings of infant temperament. *Child Development, 62,* 352–361.

Miller, M., Bowen, J. R., Gibson, F. L., Hand, P. J., & Ungerer, J. A. (2001). Behaviour problems in extremely low birthweight children at 5 and 8 years of age. *Child: Care, Health and Development, 27*(6), 569–581.

Miller, P. J., Mintz, J., Hoogstra, L., Fung, H., & Potts, R. (1992). The narrated self: Young children's construction of self in relation to others in conversational stories of personal experience. *Merrill-Palmer Quarterly, 38,* 45–67.

Miller, W. R. (1964). The acquisition of formal features of language. *American Journal of Orthopsychiatry, 34,* 862–867.

Mills-Koonce, W., Gariépy, J., Propper, C., Sutton, K., Calkins, S., Moore, G., & Cox, M. (2007). Infant and parent factors associated with early maternal sensitivity: A caregiver-attachment systems approach. *Infant Behavior & Development, 30*(1), 114-126.

Mills-Koonce, W. R., Garrett-Peters, P., Barnett, M., Granger, D. A., Blair, C., & Cox, M. J., (2011). Father contributions to cortisol responses in infancy and toddlerhood. *Developmental Psychology, 47,* 388-395.

Mills-Koonce, W., Propper, C., & Barnett, M. (2012). Poor infant soothability and later insecure-ambivalent attachment: developmental change in phenotypic markers of risk or two measures of the same construct?. *Infant Behavior & Development, 35*(2), 215-225.

Miner, J. L., & Clarke-Stewart, K. (2008). Trajectories of externalizing behavior from age 2 to age 9: Relations with gender, temperament, ethnicity, parenting, and rater. *Developmental Psychology, 44*(3), 771-786. doi:10.1037/0012-1649.44.3.771.

Mintzer, D., Als, H., Tronick, E. A., & Brazelton, T. B. (1985). Parenting an infant with a birth defect: The regulation of self-esteem. *Zero to Three, 5,* 1–7.

Mistry, R. S., Biesanz, J. C., Taylor, L. C., Burchinal, M., & Cox, M. J. (2004). Family Income and Its Relation to Preschool Children's Adjustment for Families in the NICHD Study of Early Child Care. *Developmental Psychology, 40*(5), 727–745.

Mitra, S. C., Ganesh, V., & Apuzzio, J. J. (1994). Effect of maternal cocaine abuse on renal arterial flow and urine output of the fetus. *American Journal of Obstetrics and Gynecology, 171,* 1556–1559.

Mix, K. S., Levine, S. C., & Huttenlocher, J. (1997). Numerical abstraction in infants: Another look. *Developmental Psychology, 33*(3), 423–428.

Miyake, K., Chen, S., & Campos, J. J. (1985). Infant temperament, mother's mode of interaction, and attachment in

Japan: An interim report. In I. Bretherton & E. Waters (Eds.). *Growing points of attachment theory and research. Monographs of the Society for Research in Child Development,* 50 (Serial No. 209), 276–297.

Mock, S. E. & Arai, S. M (2011). Childhood trauma and chronic illness in adulthood socioeconomic status as explanatory factors and buffers. *Frontiers in Developmental Psychology.* Retrieved from http://www.frontiersin.org/developmental_psychology/10.3389/fpsyg.2010.00246/abstract.

Moffitt, T. E., Arseneault, L., Belsky,D., Dickson, N., Hancox, R. J. Harrington, H., … Caspi, A. (2011). A gradient of childhood self-control predicts health, wealth, and public safety. *Proceedings of the National Academy of Sciences of the United States of America,108,* 2693-2698.

Molfese, V. J., DiLalla, L. F., & Bunce, D. (1997). Prediction of the intelligence test scores of 3– to 8–year-old children by home environment, socioeconomic status, and biomedical risks. *Merill-Palmer Quarterly, 43*(2), 219–234.

Molina, M., & Jouen, F. (1998). Modulation of the palmar grasp behavior in neonates according to texture property. *Infant Behavior and Development, 21*(4), 659–667.

Molnar, G. E. (1978). Analysis of motor disorder in retarded infants and young children. *American Journal of Mental Deficiency, 83,* 213–222.

Molteno, C. D., Jacobson, S. W., Carter, R., & Jacobson, J. L. (2010). Infant symbolic play as an early indicator of fetal alcohol-related deficit. *Infancy, 15*(6), 586-607. doi:10.1111/j.1532-7078.2010.00031.x

Moon, C., Cooper, R. P., & Fifer, W. P. (1993). Two-day-olds prefer their native language. *Infant Behavior and Development, 16,* 495–500.

Moon., C, Lagercrantz, H., & Kuhl, P. K. (2012). Language experienced in utero effects vowel perception after birth: A two-country study. *Acta Paediatrica,* 156-160.

Moore, C., Angelopoulos, M., & Bennett, P. (1997). The role of movement in the development of joint visual attention. *Infant Behavior and Development, 20,* 83–92.

Moore, C., Mealiea, J., Garon, N., & Povinelli, D. J. (2007). The development of body self-awareness. *Infancy, 11*(2), 157–174.

Moore, G. A., Hill-Soderlund, A. L., Propper, C. B., Calkins, S. D., Mills-Koonce, W., & Cox, M. J. (2009). Mother—infant vagal regulation in the face-to-face still-face paradigm is moderated by maternal sensitivity. *Child Development,* 80(1), 209-223. doi:10.1111/j.1467-8624.2008.01255.x

Moore, G. A., Moore, G. A., & Calkins, S. D. (2004). Infants' Vagal Regulation in the Still-Face Paradigm Is Related to Dyadic Coordination of Mother-Infant Interaction. *Developmental Psychology, 40*(6), 1068–1080.

Moore, M., & Meltzoff, A. (2008). Factors affecting infants' manual search for occluded objects and the genesis of object permanence. *Infant Behavior & Development, 31*(2), 168-180.

Moore, M. K., & Meltzoff, A. N. (2004). Object Permanence After a 24–Hr Delay and Leaving the Locale of Disappearance: The Role of Memory, Space, and Identity. *Developmental Psychology, 40*(4), 606–620.

Morales, M., Mundy, P., Crowson, M. M., Neal, A. R., & Delgado, C. E. F. (2005). Individual differences in infant attention skills, joint attention, and emotion regulation behaviour. *International Journal of Behavioral Development, 29*(3), 259–263.

Morales, M., Mundy, P., & Rojas, J. (1998). Following the direction of gaze and language development in 6–month-olds. *Infant Behavior and Development, 21*(2), 373–377.

Moran, G., Krupka, A., Tutton, A., & Symons, D. (1987). Patterns of maternal and infant imitation during play. *Infant Behavior and Development, 10,* 477–491.

Morange-Majoux, F., Cougnot, P., & Bloch, H. (1997). Hand tactual exploration of textures in infants from 4 to 6 months. *Early Development and Parenting, 6,* 127–135.

Moreno, A., Posada, G., & Goldyn, D. (2006). Presence and quality of touch influence coregulation in mother-infant dyads. *Infancy, 9*(1), 1–20.

Moreno, A. J., Posada, G. E., & Goldyn, D. T. (2006). Presence and quality of touch influence coregulation in mother-infant dyads. *Infancy, 9*(1), 1–20.

Moreno, C., Ardanaz, E., Olivera, J. E., Castilla, J., & de Pedro, C. J. (1994). A temporal-spatial cluster of sudden infant death syndrome in Navarre, Spain. *European Journal of Epidemiology, 10,* 129–134.

Morgan, B., Finan, A., Yarnold, R., Petersen, S., Horsfield, M., Rickett, A., et al. (2002). Assessment of infant physiology and neuronal development using magnetic resonance imaging. *Child Care Health Dev, 28 Suppl 1,* 7–10.

Morokuma, S., Doria, V., Ierullo, A., Kinukawa, N., Fukushima, K., … Papageorghiou A. T. (2008). Developmental change in fetal response to repeated low-intensity sound. *Developmental Science, 11,* 47-52.

Morrissey, T. W. (2009). Multiple child-care arrangements and young children's behavioral outcomes. *Child Development,80*(1), 59-76. doi:10.1111/j.1467-8624.2008.01246.x

Morrow, C. E., Bandstra, E. S., Anthony, J. C., Ofir, A. Y., Xue, L., & Reyes, M. B. (2003). Influence of prenatal cocaine exposure on early language development: Longitudinal findings from four months to three years of age. *Developmental and Behavioral Pediatrics, 24*(1). pp. 39–50.

Morrongiello, B. A., Fenwick, K. D., & Chance, G. (1990). Sound localization acuity in very young infants: An observer-based testing procedure. *Developmental Psychology, 26,* 75–84.

Morrongiello, B. A., & Rocca, P. T. (1987). Infants' localization of sounds in the horizontal plane: Effects of auditory and visual cues. *Child Development, 58,* 918–927.

Moscardino, U., & Axia, G. (2006). Infants' responses to arm restraint at 2 and 6 months: A longitudinal study. *Infant Behavior & Development, 29*(1), 59–69.

Moscucci, O. (2003). Holistic obstetrics: the origins of "natural childbirth" in Britain. *Postgrad Med J, 79*(929), 168–173.

Mosier, C. E., & Rogoff, B. (1994). Infants' instrumental use of their mothers to achieve their goals. *Child Development, 65,* 70–79.

Moszkowski, R., Stack, D., & Chiarella, S. (2009). Infant touch with gaze and affective behaviors during mother-infant still-face interactions: Co-occurrence and functions of touch. *Infant Behavior & Development, 32*(4), 392-403. doi:10.1016/j.infbeh.2009.06.006

Moszkowski, R., Stack, D., Girouard, N., Field, T., Hernandez-Reif, M., & Diego, M. (2009). Touching behaviors of infants of depressed mothers during normal and perturbed interactions. *Infant Behavior & Development, 32*(2), 183-194. doi:10.1016/j.infbeh.2008.12.009

Moulson, M. C., Fox, N. A., Zeanah, C. H., & Nelson, C. A. (2009). Early adverse experiences and the neurobiology of facial emotion processing. *Developmental Psychology, 45*(1), 17-30. doi:10.1037/a0014035

Moulson, M. C., Westerlund, A., Fox, N. A., Zeanah, C. H., & Nelson, C. A. (2009). The effects of early experience on face recognition: An event-related potential study of institutionalized children in Romania. *Child Development, 80*(4), 1039-1056. doi:10.1111/j.1467-8624.2009.01315.x

Mount, K. S., Crockenberg, S. C., Jó, P., & Wagar, J. (2010). Maternal and child correlates of anxiety in 2½-year-old children. *Infant Behavior & Development, 33*(4), 567-578. doi:10.1016/j.infbeh.2010.07.008

Moustakas, C. (1994). *Phenomenological research methods.* Thousand Oaks, CA: Sage Publications.

Mueller, E., Bleier, M., Krakow, J., Hegedus, K., & Cournoyer, P. (1977). The development of peer verbal interaction among two-year-old boys. *Child Development, 48,* 284–287.

Mueller, E., & Brenner, J. (1977). The growth of social interaction in a toddler play group: The role of peer experience. *Child Development, 48,* 854–861.

Mueller, E., & Lucas, T. (1975). A developmental analysis of peer interaction among toddlers. In M. Lewis & L. Rosenblum (Eds.), *Friendship and peer relations* (pp. 65–90). New York: Wiley.

Mullally, A., Cleary, B. J., Barry. J., Fahey, T. P., & Murphy, D.J., (2011). Prevalence, predictors and perinatal outcomes of peri-conceptional alcohol exposure--retrospective cohort study in an urban obstetric population in Ireland. *BMC Pregnancy And Childbirth, 11,* 27.

Mullen, M., Snidman, N., & Kagan, J. (1993). Free-play behavior in inhibited and uninhibited children. *Infant Behavior and Development, 16,* 383–389.

Mumme, D. L., Fernald, A., & Herrera, C. (1996). Infants' responses to facial and vocal emotional signals in a social referencing paradigm. *Child Development, 67,* 3219–3237.

Munakata, Y. (1997). Perseverative reaching in infancy: The roles of hidden toys and motor history in the *AB* task. *Infant Behavior and Development, 20*(3), 405–416.

Mundy, P., & Gomes, A. (1998). Individual differences in joint attention skill development in the second year. *Infant Behavior and Development, 21*(3), 469–482.

Mundy, P., Kasari, C., & Sigman, M. (1992). Nonverbal communication, affective sharing, and intersubjectivity. *Infant Behavior and Development, 15,* 377–381.

Munk-Olsen, T., Laursen, T. M., Pedersen, C. B., Mors, O., & Mortensen, P. B. (2006). New parents and mental disorders: a population-based register study. *Jama, 296*(21), 2582–2589.

Munn, P., & Dunn, J. (1989). Temperament and the developing relationship between siblings. *International Journal of Behavioral Development, 12,* 433–451.

Murai, N., Murai, N., & Takahashi, I. (1978). A study of moods in postpartum women. *Tohuku Psychologica Ioliak, 37,* 32–40.

Murgatroyd, C, Spengler, D.(2011). Epigenetic programming of the HPA axis: early life decides. *Stress.14,* 581-9.

Muris, P. (2006). The pathogenesis of childhood anxiety disorders: Considerations from a developmental psychopathology perspective. *International Journal of Behavioral Development, 30*(1), 5–11.

Murray, A. D. (1988). Newborn auditory brainstem evoked responses (ABRs): Longitudinal correlates in the first year. *Child Development, 59,* 1542–1554

Murray, L., de Rosnay, M., Pearson, J., Bergeron, C., Schofield, E., Royal-Lawson, M., & Cooper, P. J. (2008). Intergenerational transmission of social anxiety: The role of social referencing processes in infancy. *Child Development, 79*(4), 1049-1064. doi:10.1111/j.1467-8624.2008.01175.x.

Murray, L., Fiori-Cowley, A., Hooper, R., & Cooper, P. (1996). The impact of postnatal depression and associated adversity on early mother-infant interactions and later infant outcomes. *Child Development, 67*(5), 2512–2526.

Murray, L., & Trevarthen, C. (1985). Emotional regulation of interactions between two-month-olds and their mothers. In T. Field & N. Fox (Eds.), *Social perception in infants.* Norwood, NJ: Ablex.

Myers, M., Fifer, W., Grose-Fifer, J., Sahni, R., Stark, R., & Schulze, K. (1997). " A novel quantitative measure of Trace-alternat EEG activity and its association with sleep states of preterm infants." *Developmental Psychobiology, 31,* 167–174.

Myers, B. J., Jarvis, P. A., & Creasey, G. L. (1987). Infants' behavior and their mothers and grandmothers. *Infant Behavior and Development, 10,* 245–259.

Myowa-Yamakoshi, M., & Takeshita, H. (2006). Do Human Fetuses Anticipate Self-Oriented Actions? A Study by Four-Dimensional (4D) Ultrasonography. *Infancy, 10*(3), 289–301.

Nachmias, M., Gunnar, M., Mangelsdorf, S., Parritz, R. H., & Buss, K. (1996). Behavioral inhibition and stress reactivity: The moderating role of attachment security. *Child Development, 67,* 508–522.

Nadel, J., Carchon, I., Kervella, C., Marcelli, D., & Plantey-Reserbat, D. (1999). Expectancies for social contingency in 2–month-olds. *Developmental Science, 2*(2), 164–173.

Nadel, J., & Fontaine, A. (1989). Communication by imitation: A developmental and comparative approach to transitory social competence. In B. H. Schneider & G. Attili (Eds.), *Social competence in developmental perspective* (pp. 131–144). The Netherlands: Kluwer Academic.

Nadel, J., & Tremblay-Leveau, H. (1999). Early perception of social contingencies and interpersonal intentionality: Dyadic and triadic paradigms. In P. Rochat (Ed.), *Early social cognition* (pp. 391–415). Mahwah, NJ: Lawrence Erlbaum Associates.

Naeye, R. (1980). Sudden infant death. *Scientific American, 242,* 56–62.

Nagan, H. Y., Miu, P., Ko, L., & Ma, H. K. (1990). Long-term neurological sequelae following vacuum extractor delivery. *Australia and New Zealand Journal of Obstetrical Gynaecology, 30*(2), 111–114.

Nagasawa, M., Okabe, S., Mogi, K. & Kikusui, T. (2012). Oxytocin and mutual communication in mother-infant bonding. *Frontiers in Human Neuroscience, 6,* ArtID 31.

Nagata, M., Nagai, Y., Sobajima, H., Ando, T., & Honjo, S. (2004). Depression in the early postpartum period and attachment to children--in mothers of NICU infants. *Infant and Child Development, 13*(2), 93–110.

Naigles, L. G., & Kako, E. T. (1993). First contact in verb acquisition: Defining a role for syntax. *Child Development, 64,* 1665–1687.

Naigles, L. R., Hoff, E., Vear, D., Tomasello, M., Brandt, S., Waxman, S. R., & Childers, J. B. (2009). Flexibility in early verb use: Evidence from a multiple-N dairy study: V. Productivity and grammatical flexibility in early verb use. *Monographs Of The Society For Research In Child Development, 74*(2), 49-67. doi:10.1111/j.1540-5834.2009.00518.x

Nakano, S. (1995). Let your toddler journey to separation: Child separation and reconstruction of playful interactions in the Japanese mother and child. *Research and Clinical Center for Child Development, 17,* 23–44.

Nakata, T., & Trehub, S. E. (2004). Infants' responsiveness to maternal speech and singing. *Infant Behavior & Development, 27*(4), 455–464.

Nakazima, S. (1972). Phonemicization and symbolization in language development. In E. H. Lenneberg & E. Lenneberg (Eds.), *Foundations of language development: A multidisciplinary approach* (Vol. 1, pp. 306–332). New York: Academic Press.

Nakhai-Pour, H. R., Broy, P., Sheehy, O., & Bérard, A. (2011). Use of nonaspirin nonsteroidal anti-inflammatory drugs during pregnancy and the risk of spontaneous abortion. *Canadian Medical Association Journal, 183,* 1713-1720.

National AIA Resource Center, (2005). Boarder Babies, Abandoned Infants, and Discarded Infants, http://aia.berkeley.edu/media/pdf/abandoned_infant_fact_sheet_2005.pdf (retrieved Jan. 4, 2010).

National Safety Council. (1987). *Accident facts.* Chicago: Author. *National Vital Statistics Reports,* vol. 54, no. 8, Dec. 29, 2005.

Nehlig, A., & Debry, G. (1994). Potential teratogenic and neurodevelopmental consequences of coffee and caffeine exposure: A review of human and animal data. *Neurotoxicology and Teratology, 16,* 531–543.

Neisser, U. (1991). Two perceptually given aspects of the self and their development. Special Issue: The development of self: The first three years. *Developmental Review, 11* (3), 197–209.

Nelson, C. A. (1985). The perception and recognition of facial expressions in infancy. In T. M. Field & N. A. Fox (Eds.), *Social perception in infants* (pp. 101–125). Norwood, NJ: Ablex.

Nelson, C. A. (1987). The recognition of facial expressions in the first two years of life: Mechanisms of development. *Child Development, 58,* 889–909.

Nelson, C. A. (1994). Neural bases of infant temperament. In J. E. Bates & T. D. Wachs (Eds.), *Temperament: Individual differences at the interface of biology and behavior* (pp. 47–82). Washington, DC: American Psychological Association.

Nelson, C. A. (2007). A neurobiological perspective on early human deprivation. *Child Development Perspectives, 1*(1), 13–18.

Nelson, D. C. K., Egan, L. C., & Holt, M. B. (2004). When children ask, 'what is it?' What do they want to know about artifacts? *Psychological Science, 15*(6), 384–389.

Nelson, D. G. K., & O'Neil, K. (2005). How do parents respond to children's questions about the identity of artifacts? *Developmental Science, 8*(6), 519–524.

Nelson, E., Campbell, J., & Michel, G. (2013). Unimanual to bimanual: tracking the development of handedness from 6 to 24 months. *Infant Behavior & Development, 36*(2), 181-188. doi:10.1016/j.infbeh.2013.01.009

Nelson, K. (1973). Structure and strategy in learning to talk. *Monographs of the Society for Research in Child Development, 38* (Serial No. 149), 1–136.

Nelson, K. (1978). How children represent knowledge of their world in and out of language: A preliminary report. In R. S. Siegler (Ed.), *Children's thinking: What develops?* (pp. 213–240). Hillsdale, NJ: Erlbaum.

Nelson, K. (2010). Developmental narratives of the experiencing child. *Child Development Perspectives*, *4*(1), 42-47. doi:10.1111/j.1750-8606.2009.00116.x

Nelson, K., Rescorla, L., Gruendel, J., & Benedict, H. (1978). Early lexicons: What do they mean? *Child Development, 49,* 960–968.

Nelson, N. M., Enkin, M. W., Saigel, S., Bennett, K. J., Milner, R., & Sackett, D. L. (1980). A randomized clinical trial of the Leboyer approach to childbirth. *New England Journal of Medicine, 299,* 655–660.

Nettlebladt, P., Fagerstrom, C., & Udderberg, N. (1976). The significance of reported childbirth pain. *Journal of Psychosomatic Research, 20,* 215–221.

Nelson, P., Adamson, L. B., & Bakeman, R. (2008). Toddlers' joint engagement experience facilitates preschoolers' acquisition of theory of mind. *Developmental Science*, *11*(6), 847-852. doi:10.1111/j.1467-7687.2008.00733.x

Network, N. E. C. C. R. (2002). Child-care structure - process - outcome: Direct and indirect effects of child-care quality on young children's development. *Psychological Science, 13*(3), 199–206.

Neumann, P. J., Gharib, S. D., & Weinstein, M. C. (1994). The cost of a successful delivery with in vitro fertilization. *New England Journal of Medicine, 331,* 239–243.

New England Center for Children (NECC) http://www.necc.org/autism_resources/fact_sheets.asp (retrieved Jan. 4, 2010).

Newman, D. L., Caspi, A., Moffitt, T. E., & Silva, P. A. (1997). Antecedents of adult interpersonal functioning: Effects of individual differences in age 3 temperament. *Developmental Psychology, 33*(2), 206–217.

Newman, R. S. (2011). 2-year-olds' speech understanding in multitalker environments. *Infancy*, *16*(5), 447-470. doi:10.1111/j.1532-7078.2010.00062.x

Nguyen, S. P. (2012). The role of external sources of information in children's evaluative food categories. *Infant And Child Development, 21*(2), 216-234. doi:10.1002/icd.745

NICHD Early Child Care Research Network (1996). Characteristics of infant child care: Factors contributing to positive caregiving. *Early Childhood Research Quarterly, 11,* 269–306.

NICHD Early Child Care Research Network (1997a). Child care in the first year of life. *Merrill-Palmer Quarterly, 43*(3), 340–360.

NICHD Early Child Care Research Network (1997b). Familial factors associated with characteristics of nonmaternal care for infants. *Journal of Marriage and the Family, 59,* 389–408.

NICHD Early Child Care Research Network (1997c). Poverty and patterns of child care. In G. J. Duncan & J. Brooks-Gunn (Eds.), *Consequences of growing up poor* (pp. 100–130). New York: Russell Sage.

NICHD Early Child Care Research Network (1998a). Early child care and self-control, compliance, and problem behavior in 24 and 36 months. *Child Development, 69*(4), 1145–1170.

NICHD Early Child Care Research Network (1998b). Relations between family predictors and child outcomes: Are they weaker for children in child care? *Developmental Psychology, 34*(5), 1119–1128.

NICHD Early Child Care Research Network (1999). Chronicity of maternal depressive symptoms, maternal sensitivity, and child functioning at 36 months. *Developmental Psychology, 35*(8), 1297–1310.

NICHD-Early Child Care Research Network. (2004). Type of child care and children's development at 54 months. *Early Childhood Research Quarterly, 19*(2), 203–230.

Nichols, F. H., & Humenick, S. S. (1988). *Childbirth education: Practice, research, and theory.* Philadelphia: W. B. Saunders.

Nickel, L. R., Thatcher, A. R., Keller, F., Wozniak, R. H. and Iverson, J. M. (2013), Posture development in infants at heightened versus low risk for autism spectrum disorders. infancy, 18: 639–661. doi: 10.1111/infa.12025

Niebyl, J. R., & Goodwin, T. M. (2002). Overview of nausea and vomiting of pregnancy with an emphasis on vitamins and ginger. *Am J Obstet Gynecol, 186*(5 Suppl Understanding), S253–255.

Niedenthal, P. M., Augustinova, M., Rychlowska, M., Droit-Volet, S., Zinner, L., Knafo, A., & Brauer, M. (2012). Negative relations between pacifier use and emotional competence. *Basic and Applied Social Psychology,34,* 387-394.

Nielsen, M., Simcock, G., & Jenkins, L. (2008). The effect of social engagement on 24-month-olds' imitation from live and televised models. *Developmental Science*, *11*(5), 722-731. doi:10.1111/j.1467-7687.2008.00722.x

Ninio, A. (1980). Picture-book reading in mother-infant dyads belonging to two subgroups in Israel. *Child Development, 51,* 587–590.

Ninio, A. (1983). Joint book reading as a multiple vocabulary acquisition device. *Developmental Psychology, 19,* 445–451.

Nishida, T. K., & Lillard, A. S. (2007). The informative value of emotional expressions: 'Social referencing' in mother-child pretense. *Developmental Science, 10*(2), 205–212.

Nitschke, J. B., Nelson, E. E., Rusch, B. D., Fox, A. S., Oakes, T. R., & Davidson, R. J. (2004). Orbitofrontal cortex tracks positive mood in mothers viewing pictures of their newborn infants. *Neuroimage, 21*(2), 583–592.

Nwokah, E., Davies, P., Islam, A., Hsu, H., & Fogel, A. (1993). Vocal affect in three-year-olds: A quantitative acoustic analysis of child laughter. *Acoustical Society of America, 94,* 3076–3090.

Nwokah, E., & Fogel, A. (1993). Laughter in mother-infant emotional communication. *Humor, 6–2,* 137–161.

Nwokah, E., Hsu, H., Dobrowolska, O., & Fogel, A. (1994). The development of laughter in mother-infant communication: Timing parameters and temporal sequences. *Infant Behavior and Development, 16,* 23–25.

Nyaradi, A., Li, J., Hickling, S., Foster, J., & Oddy, W. H. (2013). The role of nutrition in children's neurocognitive development, from pregnancy through childhood. *Frontiers In Human Neuroscience, 7*doi:10.3389/fnhum.2013.00097

Oakes, L. M., Coppage, D. J., & Dingel, A. (1997). By land or by sea: The role of perceptual similarity in infants' categorization of animals. *Developmental Psychology, 33*(3), 396–407.

Oakes, L. M., Plumert, J. M., Lansink, J. M., & Merryman, J. D. (1996). Evidence for task-dependent categorization in infancy. *Infant Behavior and Development, 19,* 425–440.

Oakes, L. M., & Tellinghuisen, D. J. (1994). Examining in infancy: Does it reflect active processing? *Developmental Psychology, 30,* 748–756.

Obradovi, J., Bush, N. R., Stamperdahl, J., Adler, N. E., & Boyce, W. (2010). Biological sensitivity to context: The interactive effects of stress reactivity and family adversity on socioemotional behavior and school readiness. *Child Development, 81*(1), 270-289.

O'Brien, M., Asay, J. H., & McCluskey-Fawcett, K. (1999). Family functioning and maternal depression following premature birth. *Reproductive and Infant Psychology, 17*(2), 175–188.

O'Connell, B., & Bretherton, I. (1984). Toddler's play, alone and with mother: The role of maternal guidance. In I. Bretherton (Ed.), *Symbolic play* (pp. 337–366). Orlando, FL: Academic Press.

O'Conner, M. J., Sigman, M., & Brill, N. (1987). Disorganization of attachment in relation to maternal alcohol consumption. *Journal of Consulting and Clinical Psychology, 55,* 831–836.

O'Connor, T., Ben-Shlomo, Y., Heron, J., Golding, J., Adams, D., & Glover, V. (2005). Prenatal anxiety predicts individual differences in cortisol in pre-adolescent children. *Biological Psychiatry, 58*(3), 211–217.

O'Connor, T. G., Caspi, A., Defries, J. C., & Plomin, R. (2003). Genotype-environment interaction in children's adjustment to parental separation. *J Child Psychol Psychiatry, 44*(6), 849–856.

Oehler, J. M., & Eckerman, C. O. (1988, April). *Regulatory effects of human speech and touch in premature infants prior to term age.* Presentation at the International Conference on Infant Studies, Washington, DC.

Ogunyemi, D., Hullett, S., Leeper, J., & Risk, A. (1998). Prepregnancy body mass index, weight gain during pregnancy, and perinatal outcome in a rural black population. *Journal of Maternal and Fetal Medicine, 7*(4), 190–193.

O'Hara, M. W. (1997). The nature of postpartum depressive disorders. In L. Murray & P. J. Cooper (Eds.), *Postpartum depression and child development* (pp. 3–31). New York: Guilford Press.

O'Hara, M. W., Schlechte, J. A., Lewis, D. A., & Varner, M. W. (1991). Controlled prospective study of postpartum mood disorders: Psychological, environmental, and hormonal variables. *Journal of Abnormal Psychology, 100*(1), 63–73.

Oken, E., Kleinman, K. P., Olsen, S. F., Rich-Edwards, J. W., & Gillman, M. W. (2004). Associations of seafood and elongated n-3 fatty acid intake with fetal growth and length of gestation: results from a US pregnancy cohort. *Am J Epidemiol, 160*(8), 774–783.

Oken, E., Taveras, E. M., Kleinman, K. P., Rich-Edwards, J. W., & Gillman, M. @. (2007) Gestational weight gain and child adiposity at age 3 years. *American Journal of Obstetrics & Gynecology, 196*(4), 322 e1–322.e8

Okuma, K., & Tanimura, M. (2009). A preliminary study on the relationship between characteristics of TV content and delayed speech development in young children. *Infant Behavior & Development, 32*(3), 312-321.

Olausson, H., Lamarre, Y., Backlund, H., Morin, C., Wallin, B. G., Starck,. . . Bushnell, M. C. (2002). Unmyelinated tactile afferents signal touch and project to insular cortex. *Nature Neuroscience, 5,* 900-4.

Olds, S. B., London, M. L., & Ladewig, P. A. (1984). Nursing assessment of the newborn. *Maternal-newborn nursing: A family-centered approach* (pp. 660–707). Menlo Park, CA: Addison-Wesley.

O'Leary, J. (2007). Pregnancy and infant loss: supporting parents and their children. *Zero to Three, 27*(6) 42–49.

Oller, D. K. & Eilers, R. E. (1988). The role of audition in infant babbling. *Child Development, 59,* 441–449.

O'Neal, C. R., Brotman, L., Miller Huang, K-Y., Gouley, K. K., Kamboukos, D., Calzada, E. J., & Pine, D. S. (2010). Understanding relations among early family environment, cortisol response, and child aggression via a prevention experiment. *Child Development, 81.*290-305.

O'Neill, D. K. (1996). Seven-year-old children's sensitivity to a parent's knowledge state when making requests. *Child Development, 67,* 659–677.

Onzawa, K., Glover, V., Adams, D., Modi, N., & Kumar, R. C. (2001). Infant massage improves mother-infant interaction for mothers with postnatal depression. *Journal of Affective Disorders, 63*(1–3), 201–207.

Oppenheim, D., Sagi, A., & Lamb, M. E. (1988). Infant-adult attachments on the kibbutz and their relation to socioemotional development 4 years later. *Developmental Psychology, 24,* 427–433.

O'Reilly-Green, C., & Cohen, W. R. (1993). Pregnancy in women aged 40 and older. *Obstetrics and Gynecology, 20,* 313–331.

Örnkloo, H., & von Hofsten, C. (2007). Fitting Objects Into Holes: On the Development of Spatial Cognition Skills. *Developmental Psychology, 43*(2), 404–416.

Orton, F., Rosivatz, E., Scholze M., & Kortenkamp, A. (2011). Widely used pesticides with previously unknown endocrine activity revealed as in vitro antiandrogens. *Environmental Health Perspectives, 119,* 794-800.

Osofsky, J. (2007). *Young Children and Trauma: Intervention and Treatment.* NY: The Guilford Press.

Osofsky, H., Rosenthal, M., & Butterbaugh, G. (1999). Addressing infertility: Opportunities for the mental health professional to support families. *Zero to Three, 19*(4), 25–31.

Oster, H. (1978). Facial expression and affect development. In M. Lewis & L. A. Rosenblum (Eds.), *The development of affect* (pp. 43–75). New York: Plenum Press.

Oster, H., Hegley, D., & Nagel, L. (1992). Adult judgments and fine-grained analysis of infant facial expressions: Testing the validity of a priori coding formulas. *Developmental Psychology, 28,* 1115–1131.

Ostler, T. (2009). Mental illness in the peripartum period. *Zero to Three, 29*(5), 4.

Osterling, J., & Dawson, G. (1994). Early recognition of children and autism: A study of first birthday home videotapes. *Journal of Autism and Developmental Disorders, 24,* 247–257.

Osterling, J., Dawson, G., & Munson, J. (2002). Early recognition of 1-year-old infants with autism spectrum disorder versus mental retardation. *Development And Psychopathology, 14*(2), 239-251.

Ostrov, J. M., Gentile, D. A., & Crick, N. R. (2006). Media exposure, aggression and prosocial behavior during early childhood: A longitudinal study. *Social Development, 15*(4), 612–627.

Otaki, M., Durrett, M., Richards, P., Nyquist, L., & Pennebaker, J. (1986). Maternal and infant behavior in Japan and America: A partial replication. *Journal of Cross-Cultural Psychology, 17,* 251–268.

Otsuka, Y., Konishi, Y., Kanazawa, S., Yamaguchi, M. K., Abdi, H., & O'Toole, A. J. (2009). Recognition of moving and static faces by young infants. *Child Development, 80*(4), 1259-1271. doi:10.1111/j.1467-8624.2009.01330.x

Ouellet-Morin, I., Boivin, M., Dionne, G., Lupien, S. J., Arsenault, L., Barr, R. G., . . . Tremblay, R. E. (2008). Variations in heritability of cortisol reactivity to stress as a function of early familial adversity among 19-month-old twins. *Archives of General Psychiatry, 65,* 211-218.

Ozonoff, S., Iosif, A., Baguio, F., Cook, I. C., Hill, M., Hutman, T., & ... Young, G. S. (2010). A prospective study of the emergence of early behavioral signs of autism. *Journal Of The American Academy Of Child & Adolescent Psychiatry, 49*(3), 256-266.e2.

Ozonoff, S., & South, M. (2001). Early social development in young children with autism: Theoretical and clinical implications. In J. G. Bremner & A. Fogel (Eds.), *Handbook of Infant Development* (pp. 72–96). Oxford, England: Blackwell.

Ozonoff, S., Young, G., Carter, A., Messinger, D., Yirmiya, N., Zwaigenbaum, L., & ... Stone, W. (2011). Recurrence risk for autism spectrum disorders: a Baby Siblings Research Consortium study. *Pediatrics, 128*(3), e488-e495.

Paiva, J. V., Hutto, C., Antunes, C., & Scott, G. (1994). Correlation between timing of rupture of amniotic membranes and risk of HIV-1 perinatal transmission. *International Conference on AIDS, 10,* 307–308.

Palacios, J., & Sánchez-Sandoval, Y. (2006). Stress in parents of adopted children. *International Journal of Behavioral Development, 30*(6), 481–487.

Palmer, C. F. (1989). The discriminating nature of infants' exploratory actions. *Developmental Psychology, 25,* 885–893.

Palmer, S., Fais, L., Golinkoff, R., & Werker, J. (2012). Perceptual narrowing of linguistic sign occurs in the 1st year of life. *Child Development, 83*(2), 543-553.

Palo, P., Piiroinen, O., Honkonen, E., Lakkala, T., & Aula, P. (1994). Transabdominal chorionic villus sampling and amniocentesis for prenatal diagnosis: 5 years' experience at a university centre. *Prenatal Diagnosis, 14,* 157–162.

Panneton, R. K., & DeCasper, A. J. (1986, April). *Newborns' postnatal preference for a prenatally experienced melody.* Paper presented at the International Conference on Infant Studies, Los Angeles, CA.

Papousek, H. (1967). Conditioning during early postnatal development. In Y. Brackbill & G. G. Thompson (Eds.), *Behavior in infancy and early childhood* (pp. 268–284). New York: Free Press.

Papousek, H., & Papousek, M. (1977). Mothering and the cognitive headstart: Psychobiological considerations. In H. R. Schaffer (Ed.), *Studies in mother-infant interaction* (pp. 63–88). London: Academic Press.

Papousek, H., & Papousek, M. (1987). Intuitive parenting: A dialectic counterpart of the infant's integrative competence. In J. D. Osofsky (Ed.), *Handbook of infant development* (2nd ed., pp. 302–331). New York: Wiley.

Papousek, M. (1989). Determinants of responsiveness to infant vocal expression of emotional state. *Infant Behavior and Development, 12,* 507–524.

Papousek, M. (1994). Melodies in caregivers' speech: A species-specific guidance towards language. *Early Development and Parenting, 3,* 5–17.

Papousek, M., & Papousek, H. (1981). Musical elements in the infant's vocalization: Their significance for communication, cognition, and creativity. In. L. P. Lipsitt & C. K. Rovee-Collier (Eds.), *Advances in infancy research* (Vol. 1, pp. 64–86). Norwood, NJ: Ablex.

Papousek, M., Papousek, H., & Bornstein, M. H. (1985). The naturalistic vocal environment of young infants: On the significance of homogeneity and variability in parental speech. In T. M. Field & N. A. Fox (Eds.), *Social perception in infants* (pp. 171–186). Norwood, NJ: Ablex.

Papousek, M., Papousek, H., & Symmes, D. (1991). The meanings of melodies in motherese in tone and stress languages. *Infant Behavior and Development, 14*, 415–440.

Papousek, M., & von Hofacker, N. (1995). Persistent crying and parenting: Search for a butterfly in a dynamic system. *Early Development and Parenting, 4*(4), 209–224.

Parade, S., & Leerkes, E. (2011). Marital aggression predicts infant orienting toward mother at six months. *Infant Behavior & Development, 34*(2), 235-238. doi:10.1016/j.infbeh.2010.12.005

Parade, S. H., McGeary, J., Seifer, R., & Knopik, V. (2012). Infant development in family context: call for a genetically informed approach. *Frontiers in genetics, 3*.

Paradis, A. D., Fitzmaurice, G. M., Koenen, K. C. & Buka, S. L. (2011). Maternal smoking during pregnancy and criminal offending among adult offspring. *Journal of Epidemiology and Community Health, 65,* 1145-1150.

Parfitt, R. R. (1977). *The birth primer*. Philadelphia: Running Press.

Park, K. A., & Waters, E. (1989). Security of attachment and preschool friendship. *Child Development, 60,* 1076–1081.

Park, S., Belsky, J., Putnam, S., & Crnic, K. (1997). Infant emotionality, parenting, and 3–year inhibition: Exploring stability and lawful discontinuity in a male sample. *Developmental Psychology, 33*(2), 218–227.

Parke, R. (1995). Fathers and families. In M. Bornstein (Ed.) *Handbook of Parenting* (Vol. 3, pp. 27–63). Mahwah, NJ, Erlbaum.

Parker, B., McFarlane, J., & Soeken, K. (1994). Abuse during pregnancy: Effects on maternal complications and birth weight in adult and teenage women. *Obstetrics and Gynecology, 84,* 323–328.

Parks, W. (1996). Human immunodeficiency virus. In W. Nelson, R. Behrman, R. Kliegman, & A. Arving (Eds.), *Nelson's textbook of pediatrics (*15th ed., pp. 916–919). Philadelphia: Saunders.

Parlade, M., Messinger, D. S., Delgado, C. F., Kaiser, M., Van Hecke, A., & Mundy, P. C. (2009). Anticipatory smiling: Linking early affective communication and social outcome. *Infant Behavior & Development, 32*(1), 33-43. doi:10.1016/j.infbeh.2008.09.007

Parmelee, A. H., Jr., Schulz, H. R., & Disbrow, M. W. (1961). Sleep patterns of the newborn. *Journal of Pediatrics, 58,* 241–250.

Parrinello, R. M., & Ruff, H. A. (1988). The influence of adult intervention on infants' level of attention. *Child Development, 59,* 1125–1135.

Parritz, R. H. (1996). A descriptive analysis of toddler coping in challenging circumstances. *Infant Behavior and Development, 19,* 171–180.

Parten, M. B. (1932). Social participation among preschool children. *Journal of Abnormal and Social Psychology, 27,* 243–269.

Pascalis, O., de Schonen, S., Morton, J., Deruelle, C., & Fabre-Grenet, M. (1995). Mother's face recognition by neonates: A replication and extension. *Infant Behavior and Development, 18,* 79–85.

Passman, R. H. (1977). Providing attachment objects to facilitate learning and reduce distress: Effects of mothers and security blankets. *Developmental Psychology, 13,* 25–28.

Passman, R. H., & Weisberg, P. (1975). Mothers and blankets as agents for promoting play and exploration by young children in a novel environment: The effects of social and non-social attachment objects. *Developmental Psychology, 11,* 170–177.

Patterson, M. L., & Werker, J. F. (1999). Matching phonetic information in lips and voice is robust in 4.5–month-old infants. *Infant Behavior and Development, 22*(2), 237–247.

Patton, M. Q. (1990). *Qualitative evaluation and research methods* (2nd ed.). London: Sage.

Paul, R., Fuerst, Y., Ramsay, G., Chawarska, K., & Klin, A. (2011). Out of the mouths of babes: Vocal production in infant siblings of children with ASD. *Journal Of Child Psychology And Psychiatry, 52*(5), 588-598

Pauli-Pott, U., Mertesacker, B., & Beckmann, D. (2004). Predicting the development of infant emotionality from maternal characteristics. *Development and Psychopathology, 16*(1), 19–42.

Paulson, G., & Gottlieb, G. (1968). Developmental reflexes: The reappearance of foetal and neonatal reflexes in aged patients. *Brain, 91,* 37–52.

Paulson, J. F., & Bazemore, S. D. (2010). Prenatal and postpartum depression in fathers and its association with maternal depression: A meta-analysis. *JAMA: Journal Of The American Medical Association, 303*(19), 1961-1969. doi:10.1001/jama.2010.605

Paulson, R., Boostanfar, R., Saadat, P., Mor, E., Tourgeman, D., Slater, C., et al. (2002). Pregnancy in the Sixth Decade of Life: Obstetric outcomes in women of advanced reproductive age. *Journal of the American Medical Association, 288*(18), 2320.

Pawl, J. H. (1992). Interventions to strengthen relationships between infants and drug-abusing or recovering parents. *Zero to Three, 13,* 6–10.

Pearson, J. L., Hunter, A. G., Ensminger, M. E., & Kellam, S. G. (1990). Black grandmothers in multigenerational households: Diversity in family structure and parenting involvement in Woodlawn community. *Child Development, 61,* 434–442.

Pecheux, M. G., Labrell, F., & Pistorio, M. (1993). What do parents talk about to infants? *Early Development and Parenting, 2,* 89–97.

Peckham, C. S. (1993). Mother-to-child transmission of HIV: Risk factors and timing. *International Conference on AIDS, 9,* abstract no. PS-04–2.

Pedersen, D. R., & Moran, G. (1996). Expressions of the attachment relationship outside of the strange situation. *Child Development, 67*(3), 915–927.

Pedersen, F., Suwalsky, J. T., Cain, R. L., & Zaslow, M. J. (1987). Paternal care of infants during maternal separations: Associations with father-infant interaction at one year. *Psychiatry, 50,* 193–205.

Pedlow, R., Sanson, A., Prior, M., & Oberklaid, F. (1993). Stability of maternally reported temperament from infancy to 8 years. *Developmental Psychology, 29,* 998–1007.

Peduto, V. A., Musu, M., Gatto, G., & Ghilli, L. (1994). Sudden infant death syndrome (SIDS): Risk conditions and intervention strategies. *Minerva-Anesthesiology, 60,* 393–402.

Peiper, A. (1963). *Cerebral function in infancy and childhood.* New York: Consultants Bureau.

Peipert, J. F. Madden, T., Allsworth, J. E. & Secura, G. M., (2012). Preventing unintended pregnancies by providing no-cost contraception. *Obstetrics And Gynecology, 120,* 1291-1297.

Pelaez, M., Field, T., Pickens, J., & Hart, S. (2008). Disengaged and authoritarian parenting behavior of depressed mothers with their toddlers. *Infant Behavior & Development, 31*(1), 145-148.

Pelaez-Nogueras, M., Field, T., Cigales, M., Gonzalez, A., & Clasky, S. (1994). Infants of depressed mothers show less "depressed" behavior with their nursery teachers. *Infant Mental Health Journal, 15,* 358–367.

Pelaez-Nogueras, M., Field, T. M., Hossain, Z., & Pickens, J. (1996). Depressed mothers' touching increases infants' positive affect and attention in still-face interactions. *Child Development, 67*(4), 1780–1792.

Pellegrini, A. D., & Smith, P. K. (1998). Physical activity play: The nature and function of a neglected aspect of play. *Child Development, 69*(3), 577–598.

Peltola, M. J., Leppänen, J. M., Palokangas, T. & Hietanen, J. K. (2008). Fearful faces modulate looking duration and attention disengagement in 7-month-old infants. *Developmental Science,11* 60-68.

Peña, I. C., Teberg, A. J., & Hoppenbrouwers, T. (1987). The Gesell developmental schedule in Hispanic low-birth weight infants during the first year of life. *Infant Behavior and Development, 10,* 199–216.

Penela, E. C., Henderson, H. A., Hane, A. A., Ghera, M. M., & Fox, N. A. (2012). Maternal caregiving moderates the relation between temperamental fear and social behavior with peers. *Infancy, 17*(6), 715-730. doi:10.1111/j.1532-7078.2012.00114.x

Perone, S., Madole, K. L., Ross-Sheehy, S., Carey, M., & Oakes, L. M. (2008). The relation between infants' activity with objects and attention to object appearance. *Developmental Psychology, 44*(5), 1242-1248. doi:10.1037/0012-1649.44.5.1242

Ronald, A., Pennell, C. E., & Whitehouse, A. J. (2010). Prenatal maternal stress associated with ADHD and autistic traits in early childhood. *Frontiers In Psychology, 1,* 223.

Quinn, P. C., & Tanaka, J. W. (2009). Infants' processing of featural and configural information in the upper and lower halves of the face. *Infancy, 14*(4), 474-487. doi:10.1080/15250000902994248

Perera, F., Rauh, V., Whyatt, R., Tang, D., Tsai, W., Bernert, J., et al. (2005). A summary of recent findings on birth outcomes and developmental effects of prenatal ETS, PAH, and pesticide exposures. *NeuroToxicology, 26*(4), 573–587.

Perlman, M., & Ross, H. S. (1997). The benefits of parent intervention in children's disputes: An examination of concurrent changes in children's fighting styles. *Child Development, 68*(4), 690–700.

Perris, E. E., & Clifton, R. K. (1988). Reaching in the dark toward sound as a measure of auditory localization in infants. *Infant Behavior and Development, 11,* 473–491.

Perris, E. E., Myers, N. A., & Clifton, R. K. (1990). Long-term memory for a single infancy experience. *Child Development, 61,* 1796–1807.

Perry, B. (2005). Applying principles of neurodevelopment to clinical work with maltreated and traumatized children: The neurosequential model of therapeutics. In N. B. Webb (Ed.) *Working with traumatized youth in child welfare.* NY: The Guilford Press.

Peterson, C. (1999). Children's memory for medical emergencies: 2 years later. *Developmental Psychology, 35*(6), 1493–1506.

Peterson, C., & Bell, M. (1996). Children's memory for traumatic injury. *Child Development, 67,* 3045–3070.

Peterson, C., Grant, V. V., & Boland, L. D. (2005). Childhood amnesia in children and adolescents: Their earliest memories. *Memory, 13*(6), 622-637. doi:10.1080/09658210444000278

Peterson, C., Grant, V. V., & Boland, L. D. (2005). Childhood amnesia in children and adolescents: Their earliest memories. *Memory, 13*(6), 622-637. doi:10.1080/09658210444000278

Peterson, C., & Rideout, R. (1998). Memory for medical emergencies experienced by 1– and 2–year-olds. *Developmental Psychology, 34*(5), 1059–1072.

Petitto, L. (1985, October). *On the use of prelinguistic gestures in hearing and deaf children: Implications for theories of language acquisition.* Paper presented at the Tenth Annual Boston

University Conference on Language Acquisition, Boston, MA.

Pettit, G. S., & Bates, J. E. (1984). Continuity of individual differences in the mother-infant relationship from 6 to 13 months. *Child Development, 55,* 729–739.

Phillips, D., & McCartney, K. (2005). *The Disconnect between Research and Policy on Child Care.* New York, NY, US: Cambridge University Press.

Phillips, D., McCartney, K., & Scarr, S. (1987). Child-care quality and children's social development. *Developmental Psychology, 23,* 537–543.

Phillips, R. D., Wagner, S. H., Fells, C. A., & Lynch, M. (1990). Do infants recognize emotion in facial expressions?: Categorical and "metaphorical" evidence. *Infant Behavior and Development, 13,* 71–84.

Phipps, M. G., Blume, J. D., & DeMonner, S. M. (2002). Young maternal age associated with increased risk of postneonatal death. *Obstet Gynecol, 100*(3), 481–486.

Piaget, J. (1952). *The origins of intelligence in children.* New York: International Universities Press.

Piaget, J. (1954). *The construction of reality in the child.* New York: Ballantine Books.

Piaget, J. (1962). *Play, dreams and imitation in childhood.* New York: Norton.

Piaget, J., & Inhelder, B. (1969). *The psychology of the child.* New York: Basic Books.

Pickens, J. N., & Field, T. (1995). Facial expressions and vagal tone of infants of depressed and non-depressed mothers. *Early Development and parenting, 4,* 83–89.

Pierce, T., Boivin, M., Frenette, E., Forget-Dubois, N., Dionne, G., & Tremblay, R. (2010). Maternal self-efficacy and hostile-reactive parenting from infancy to toddlerhood. *Infant Behavior & Development, 33*(2), 149-158.

Pike, A., Iervolino, A. C., Eley, T. C., Price, T. S., & Plomin, R. (2006). Environmental risk and young children's cognitive and behavioral development. *International Journal of Behavioral Development, 30*(1), 55–66.

Pine, J. M., Lieven, E. V. M., & Rowland, C. F. (1997). Stylistic variation at the "single-word" stage: Relations between maternal speech characteristics and children's vocabulary composition and usage. *Child Development, 68*(5), 807–819.

Pipes, P. L. (1985). *Nutrition in infancy and early childhood* (2nd ed.). St. Louis: Mosby.

Pipp, S., Easterbrooks, M. A., & Brown, S. R. (1993). Attachment status and complexity of infants' self- and other-knowledge when tested with mother and father. *Social Development, 2,* 4–12.

Pipp, S., Easterbrooks, M. A., & Harmon, R. J. (1992). The relation between attachment and knowledge of self and mother in one- to three-year-old infants. *Child Development, 63* (3), 738–750.

Pipp, S., Fischer, K. W., & Jennings, S. (1987). Acquisition of self- and mother knowledge in infancy. *Developmental Psychology, 23,* 86–96.

Pipp-Siegel, S., Siegel, C. H., & Dean, J. (1999). Neurological aspects of the disorganized/disoriented attachment classification system: Differentiating quality of the attachment relationship from neurological impairment. *Monographs of the Society for Research in Child Development, 64*(3), 25–44.

Pistrang, N. (1984). Women's work involvement and experience of new motherhood. *Journal of Marriage and Family,* 433–446.

Placek, P. J. (1986). Commentary: Cesarean rates still rising. *Statistical Bulletin, 67,* 9.

Plomin, R. (1990). The role of inheritance in behavior. *Science, 248,* 183–188.

Plomin, R. (1994). Nature, nurture, and social development. *Social Development, 3,* 37–53.

Plomin, R., DeFries, J. C. Craig, I. W., & McGuffin, P. (2003). *Behavioral genetics in the postgenomic era.* Washington, DC: American Psychological Association

Plomin, R., & Rutter, M. (1998). Child development, molecular genetics, and what to do with genes once they are found. *Child Development, 69*(4), 1223–1242.

Plomin, R., & Saudino, K. J. (1994). Quantitative genetics and molecular genetics. In J. E. Bates & T. D. Wachs (Eds.) *Temperament: Individual differences at the interface of biology and behavior* (pp. 143–171). Washington, DC: American Psychological Association.

Plowman, L., Stirling, U., & Stirling, S. (2004). "Hey, Hey, Hey! It's Time to Play": Children's interactions with smart toys. In J. Goldstein (Ed.), *Toys, games, and media* (pp. 207–223). Mahwah, NJ: Lawrence Erlbaum Associates, Inc.

Poehlmann, J., Schwichtenberg, A. J. M., Bolt, D. M., Hane, A., Burnson, C. & Winters, J (2011). Infant physiological regulation and maternal risks as predictors of dyadic interaction trajectories in families with a preterm infant. *Developmental Psychology, 47,* 91-105

Pogarsky, G., Lizotte, A. J., & Thornberry, T. P. (2003). The delinquency of children born to young mothers: Results from the Rochester Youth Development Study. *Criminology, 41*(4), 1249–1286

Pollak, S. D., Nelson, C. A., Schlaak, M. F., Roeber, B. J., Wewerka, S. S., Wiik, K. L., & ... Gunnar, M. R. (2010). Neurodevelopmental effects of early deprivation in postinstitutionalized children. *Child Development, 81*(1), 224-236. doi:10.1111/j.1467-8624.2009.01391.x

Pollak, S. D., Vardi, S., Bechner, A. M. P., & Curtin, J. J. (2005). Physically Abused Children's Regulation of Attention in Response to Hostility. *Child Development, 76*(5), 968–977.

Pollitt, E., Garza, C., & Leibel, R. L. (1984). Nutrition and public policy. In H. W. Stevenson & A. E. Siegel (Eds.),

Child development research and social policy (pp. 421–470). Chicago: University of Chicago Press.

Pollitt, E., Golub, M., Gorman, K., Grantham-McGregor, S., Levitsky, D., Schurch, B., Strupp, B., & Wachs, T. (1996). A reconceptualization of the effects of undernutrition on children's biological, psychosocial, and behavioral development. *Social Policy Report: Society for Research in Child Development, 10*(5).

Porcher, F. K. (1992). HIV infected pregnant women and their infants: Primary health care implications. *Nurse Practitioner, 17,* 46–54.

Porges, S. W. (2004). Neuroception: A subconscious system for detecting threats and safety. *Zero to Three, 24*(5), 19–24.

Porges, S. W., Doussard-Roosevelt, J., Shifter, C., McClenny, B., & Riniolo, T. (1999) Sleep state and vagal regulation of heart period patterns in the human newborn: An extension of the polyvagal theory. Psychophysiology, *36,* 14–2.

Porges, S. W., Furman, S. A. (2011).The early development of the autonomic nervous system provides a neural platform for social behaviour: A polyvagal perspective *Infant and Child Development, 20,* 106-118.

Porreco, R. P., Harden, L., Gambotto, M., & Shapiro, H. (2005). Expectation of pregnancy outcome among mature women. *Am J Obstet Gynecol, 192*(1), 38–41.

Porter, C. L., & Jones, B. L. (2011). Does brief bradycardia at the onset of arm–restraint predict infants' emotional reactivity during restraint?. *Infancy, 16*(2), 166-179. doi:10.1111/j.1532-7078.2010.00035.x

Porter, R. H., Cernoch, J. M., & Perry, S. (1983). The importance of odors in mother-infant interactions. *Maternal Child Nursing Journal, 12*(3), 147–154.

Porter, R. H., Makin, J. W., Davis, L. B., & Christensen, K. M. (1992). Breast-fed infants respond to olfactory cues from their own mother and unfamiliar lactating females. *Infant Behavior and Development, 15,* 85–93.

Posada, G., Carbonell, O. A., Alzate, G., & Plata, S. J. (2004). Through Colombian Lenses: Ethnographic and Conventional Analyses of Maternal Care and Their Associations With Secure Base Behavior. *Developmental Psychology, 40*(4), 508–518.

Posada, G., Gao, Y., Wu, F., Posada, R., Tascon, M., Schölmerich, A., Sagi, A., Kondo-Ikemura, K., Haaland, W., & Synnevaag, B. (1995). The secure-base phenomenon across cultures: Children's behavior, mothers' preferences, and experts' concepts. *Monographs of the Society for Research in Child Development, 244*(60), 27–48.

Posner, M. I., Rothbart, M K., Sheese, B. E., & Voelker, P. (2012). Control networks and neuromodulators of early development. (Special Section: Neuromodulation of Behavioral and Cognitive Development Across the Life Span) *Developmental Psychology, 48* 827-835.

Post, S., Neimark, J, & Moss, O. (2007). *Why good things happen to good people: The Exciting New Research that Proves the Link Between Doing Good and Living a Longer, Healthier, Happier Life.* NY: Random House.

Poulin-Dubois, D., Serbin, L. A., & Derbyshire, A. (1998). Toddlers' intermodal and verbal knowledge about gender. *Merrill-Palmer Quarterly, 44*(3), 338–354.

Poulin-Dubois, D., Serbin, L. A., Kenyon, B., & Derbyshire, A. (1994). Infants' intermodal knowledge about gender. *Developmental Psychology, 30,* 436–442.

Powell, D. R. (2001). Early intervention and risk. In J. G. Bremner & A. Fogel (Eds.), *Handbook of infant development.* Oxford, England: Blackwell.

Powell, M. (1991). The psychosocial impact of Sudden Infant Death Syndrome on siblings. Committee of the Health Psychology Interest Group of the Psychological Society of Ireland: Having babies: Issues in reproductive and infant psychology. *Irish Journal of Psychology, 12,* 235–247.

Power, T. G., Chapieski, M. L., & McGrath, M. P. (1985). Assessment of individual differences in infant exploration and play. *Developmental Psychology, 21,* 974–981.

Power, T. G., & Parke, R. D. (1986). Patterns of early socialization: Mother- and father-infant interaction in the home. *International Journal of Behavioral Development, 9,* 331–341.

Prange, M. T., Coats, B., Duhaime, A. C., & Margulies, S. S. (2003). Anthropomorphic simulations of falls, shakes, and inflicted impacts in infants. *J Neurosurg, 99*(1), 143–150.

Prechtl, H. F. R. (1977). *The neurological examination of the full term newborn infant* (2nd ed.). London: Heinemann.

Pressman, E. K., DiPietro, J. A., Costigan, K. A., Shupe, A. K., & Johnson, T. R. B. (1998). Fetal neurobehavioral development: Associations with socioeconomic class and fetal sex. *Developmental Psychobiology, 33*(1), 79–91.

Price, T. S., Grosser, T., Plomin, R., & Jaffee, S. R. (2010). Fetal genotype for the xenobiotic metabolizing enzyme NQO1 influences intrauterine growth among infants whose mothers smoked during pregnancy. *Child Development*, *81*(1), 101-114. doi:10.1111/j.1467-8624.2009.01383.x

Pridham, K. F. (1998). Guided participation and development of care-giving competencies for families of low birth-weight infants. *Journal of Advanced Nursing, 28*(5), 948–958.

Propper, C., Moore, G., Mills-Koonce, W., Halpern, C., Hill-Soderlund, A. L., Calkins, S. D., & ... Cox, M. (2008). Gene-environment contributions to the development of infant vagal reactivity: The interaction of dopamine and maternal sensitivity. *Child Development, 79*(5), 1377-1394. doi:10.1111/j.1467-8624.2008.01194.x

Provence, S. (1982). Infant day care: Relationships between theory and practice. In E. F. Zigler & E. W. Gordon

(Eds.), *Day care: Scientific and social policy issues* (pp. 33–35). Boston: Auburn House.

Provence, S., & Naylor, A. (1983). *Working with disadvantaged parents and children: Scientific issues and practice.* New Haven, CT: Yale University Press.

Prysak, M., Lorenz, R. P., & Kisly, A. (1995). Pregnancy outcome in nulliparous women 35 years and older. *Obstetrics and Gynecology, 85,* 65–70.

Puddifoot, J. E., & Johnson, M. P. (1999). Active grief, despair, and difficulty coping: Some measured characteristics of male response following their partner's miscarriage. *Journal of Reproductive and Infant Psychology, 17*(1), 89–93.

Pungello, E. P., Kainz, K., Burchinal, M., Wasik, B. H., Sparling, J. J., Ramey, C. T., & Campbell, F. A. (2010). Early educational intervention, early cumulative risk, and the early home environment as predictors of young adult outcomes within a high-risk sample. *Child Development, 81*(1), 410-426. doi:10.1111/j.1467-8624.2009.01403.x

Pye, C. (1986). Quiche Mayan speech to children. *Journal of Child Language, 13*(1), 85–100.

Qouta, S., Punamäki, R-L., & El Sarraj, E. (2008). Child development and family mental health in war and military violence: The Palestinian experience. [Special issue: Chronic exposure to catastrophic war experiences and political violence: Links to the well-being of children and their families]. *International Journal of Behavioral Development, 32,* 310-321.

Quinn, P. C., Cummins, M., Kase, J., Martin, E., & Weissman, S. (1996). Development of categorical representations for *above* and *below* spatial relations in 3– to 7–month-old infants. *Developmental Psychology, 32*(5), 942–950.

Quinn, T. C. (1995). The epidemiology of the acquired immunodeficiency syndrome in the 1990s. *Emergency Medical Clinics of North America, 13,* 1–25.

Rabain-Jamin, J., & Wornham, W. L. (1993). Practices and representations of child care and motor development among West Africans in Paris. *Early Development and Parenting, 2,* 107–119.

Rader, N., & Zukow-Goldring, P. (2012). Caregivers' gestures direct infant attention during early word learning: The importance of dynamic synchrony. *Language Sciences, 34*(5), 559-568.

Radke-Yarrow, M., & Zahn-Waxler, C. (1984). Roots, motives, and patterns in children's pro-social behavior. In E. Staub, D. Bartal, J. Karylowski, & J. Reykowski (Eds.), *The development and maintenance of pro-social behaviors* (pp. 68–89). New York: Plenum Press.

Radke-Yarrow, M., Zahn-Waxler, C., Richardson, D. T., Susman, A., & Martinez, P. (1994). Caring behavior in children of clinically depressed and well mothers. *Child Development, 65,* 1405–1414.

Raiha, H., Lehtonen, L., Huhtala, V., Saleva, K., & Korvenranta, H. (2002). Excessively crying infant in the family:

Mother-infant, father-infant and mother-father interaction. *Child: Care, Health and Development, 28*(5), 419–429.

Raikes, H., Luze, G., Brooks-Gunn, J., Raikes, H. A., Pan, B. A., Tamis-LeMonda, C. S., et al. (2006). Mother-Child Bookreading in Low-Income Families: Correlates and Outcomes During the First Three Years of Life. *Child Development, 77*(4), 924–953.

Räikkönen, K., Pesonen, A. K., Heinonen, K., Lahti, J., Komsi, N., Eriksson, J. G….Strandberg, T. E. (2009). Maternal licorice consumption and detrimental cognitive and psychiatric outcomes in children. *American Journal Of Epidemiology, 170,* 1137-1146.

Räikkönen, K., Pesonen, A., Järvenpää, A., & Strandberg, T. E. (2004). Sweet babies: Chocolate consumption during pregnancy and infant temperament at six months. *Early Human Development, 76*(2), 139–145.

Rakoczy, H., Tomasello, M., & Striano, T. (2004). Young children know that trying is not pretending: A test of the 'Behaving-As-If' construal of children's early concept of pretense. *Developmental Psychology, 40*(3), 388–399.

Ramey, C. T., & Ramey, S. L. (1998). Early intervention and early experience. *American Psychologist, 53*(2), 109–120.

Ramey, S. L. (1999). Head Start and preschool education: Toward continued improvement. *American Psychologist, 54*(5), 344–346.

Ramig, P. R. (1993). High reported spontaneous stuttering recovery rates: Fact or fiction? *Language, Speech, and Hearing Services in Schools, 24,* 156–160.

Ramlau-Hansen, C., Thulstrup, A., Bonde, J., & Olsen, J. (2007). Parental infertility and semen quality in male offspring: A follow-up study. *American Journal of Epidemiology, 166*(5), 568–570.

Ramsay, D. S. (1980). Onset of unimanual handedness in infants. *Infant Behavior and Development, 3,* 377–386.

Ramsey, C. N., Abell, T. N., & Baker, L. C. (1986). The relationship between family functioning, life events, family structure, and the outcome of pregnancy. *Journal of Family Practice, 22,* 521–527.

Ransjo-Arvidson, A. B., Matthiesen, A. S., Lilja, G., Nissen, E., Widstrom, A. M., & Uvnas-Moberg, K. (2001). Maternal analgesia during labor disturbs newborn behavior: effects on breastfeeding, temperature, and crying. *Birth, 28*(1), 5–12.

Rapoport, R., Rapoport, R. N., & Strelitz, A. (1977). *Fathers, mothers and society: Toward new alliances.* New York: Basic Books.

Rappoport, D. (1976). Pour une naissance sans violence: Résultats d'une première enquête. *Bulletin de Psychologie, 29,* 552–560.

Rautava, P., Koski, M. L., Sillanpaa, M., & Tuominen, J. (1992). The Finnish family competence study: Childbearing attitudes in pregnant nulliparae. *Acta Paedopsychiatrica, 55,* 3–8.

Raver, C. C. (1996). Relations between social contingency in mother-child interaction and 2–year-olds' social competence. *Developmental Psychology, 32*(5), 850–859.

Raver, C. C. (1996). Success at catching and keeping toddler's attention: An examination of joint attention among low-income mothers and their 2–year-olds. *Early Development and Parenting, 5*(4), 225–236.

Ravn, I. H., Smith, L., Lindemann, R.. Smeby, N. A., Kyno, N. M., Bunch, E. H., & Sandvik, L. (2011) Effect of early intervention on social interaction between mothers and preterm infants at 12 months of age: A randomized controlled trial. *Infant Behavior & Development, 34,* 215-225

Reardon, P., & Bushnell, E. W. (1988). Infants' sensitivity to arbitrary pairings of color and taste. *Infant Behavior and Development, 11,* 245–250.

Rebuffat, E., Groswasser, J., Kelmanson, I., Sottiaux, M., & Kahn, A. (1994). Polygraphic evaluation of night-to-night variability in sleep characteristics and apneas in infants. *Sleep, 17,* 329–332.

Redcay, E., Haist, F., & Courchesne, E. (2008). Functional neuroimaging of speech perception during a pivotal period in language acquisition. *Developmental Science, 11*, 237-252.

Reddy, V. (1991). Playing with others' expectations: Teasing and mucking about in the first year. In A. Whiten (Ed.), *Natural theories of mind: Evolution, development, and simulation of everyday mindreading* (pp. 143–158). Cambridge, MA: Basil Blackwell.

Reddy, V. (2000). Coyness in early infancy. *Developmental Science, 3*(2), 186–192.

Reddy, V. (2000). Mind knowledge in the first year: Understanding attention and intention. In J. G. Bremner & A. Fogel (Eds.), *Handbook of infancy research* (pp. 155–181). Oxford, England: Blackwell.

Reddy, V., Chisholm, V., Forrester, D., Conforti, M., & Maniatopoulou, D. (2007). Facing the perfect contingency: interactions with the self at 2 and 3 months. *Infant Behavior & Development, 30*(2), 195-212.

Reeb, K. G., Graham, A. V., Zyzanski, S. J., & Kitson, G. C. (1987). Predicting low birthweight and complicated labor in urban black women: A biopsychosocial perspective. *Social Science and Medicine, 25,* 1321–1327.

Reed, G., & Leiderman, P. H. (1981). Age-related changes in attachment behavior in polymatrically reared infants: The Kenyan Gusii. In T. Field, T. M. Sostek, P. Vietze, & P. Leiderman, (Eds.), *Culture and early interactions* (pp. 85–101). Hillsdale, NJ: Erlbaum.

Reefhuis, J., Honein, M. A., Schieve, L. A., Correa, A., Hobbs, C. A., Rasmussen, S. A., & National Birth Defects Prevention Study, (2009). Assisted reproductive technology and major structural birth defects in the United States. *Human Reproduction, 24,* 360-366.

Reese, M. (1985). Moshe Feldenkrais's work with movement: A parallel approach to Milton Erickson's hypnotherapy. In J. K. Zeig (Ed.), *Ericksonian psychotherapy: Vol. 1: Structures* (pp. 213–229). New York: Brunner-Mazel.

Reilly, J., McIntire, M., & Bellugi, U. (1985, October). *Faces: The relationship between language and affect.* Paper presented at the 10th Annual Boston University Conference on Language Development, Boston, MA.

Reinecke, M. A., & Fogel, A. (1994). The development of referential offering in the first year. *Early Development and Parenting, 3,* 181–186.

Reiner, W. G., & Gearhart, J. P. (2004). Discordant sexual identity in some genetic males with cloacal exstrophy assigned to female sex at birth. *N Engl J Med, 350*(4), 333–341.

Reissland, N. (1988). Neonatal imitation in the first hour of life: Observations in rural Nepal. *Developmental Psychology, 24,* 464–469.

Reissland, N., & Harris, P. (1991). Children's use of display rules in pride-eliciting situations. *British Journal of Developmental Psychology, 9,* 431–435.

Reite, M., Kaemingk, K., & Boccia, M. L. (1989). Maternal separation in bonnent monkey infants: Altered attachment and social support. *Child Development, 60,* 473–480.

Remez, L. (1996). Few married women use a method in Côte d'Ivoire, but fertility is decreasing. *International Family Planning Perspectives, 22*(3), 130–132.

Rempel, L. A., & Rempel, J. K. (2004). Partner influence on health behavior decision-making: Increasing breastfeeding duration. *Journal of Social and Personal Relationships, 21*(1), 92–111.

Rennels, J., & Davis, R. (2008). Facial experience during the first year. *Infant Behavior & Development, 31*(4), 665-678. doi:10.1016/j.infbeh.2008.04.009

Repacholi, B. M., & Gopnik, A. (1997). Early reasoning about desires: Evidence from 14– and 18–month olds. *Developmental Psychology, 33*(1), 12–21.

Repacholi, B. M., Meltzoff, A. N., & Olsen, B. (2008). Infants' understanding of the link between visual perception and emotion: 'If she can't see me doing it, she won't get angry.'. *Developmental Psychology, 44*(2), 561-574.

Reynolds, A. J. (1998). Developing early childhood programs for children and families at risk: Research-based principles to promote long-term effectiveness. *Children and Youth Services Review, 20*(6), 503–523.

Reznick, J. S., Kagan, J., Snidman, N., Gersten, M., Baak, K., & Rosenberg, A. (1986). Inhibited and uninhibited children: A follow-up study. *Child Development, 57,* 660–680.

Rheingold, H. L., Cook, K. V., & Kolowitz, V. (1987). Commands activate the behavior and pleasure of 2–year-old children. *Developmental Psychology, 23,* 146–151.

Rheingold, H. L., Hay, D. F., & West, M. J. (1976). Sharing in the second year of life. *Child Development, 47,* 1148–1158.

Rhodes, J. E. (1993). Easing postpartum school transitions through parent mentoring programs. *Prevention in Human Services, 10,* 169–178.

Ricard, M., & Decarie, T. G. (1993). Distance-maintaining in infants' reaction to an adult stranger. *Social Development, 2,* 154–161.

Ricciuti, H. N. (1974). Fear and the development of social attachments in the first year of life. In M. Lewis & L. Rosenblum (Eds.), *The origins of fear* (pp. 39–58). New York: Wiley.

Ricciuti, H. N., & Poresky, R. H. (1972). Emotional behavior and development in the first year of life: An analysis of arousal, approach-withdrawal, and affective responses. In A. Pick (Ed.), *Minnesota symposia on child psychology* (Vol. 6, pp. 200–221). Minneapolis: University of Minnesota Press.

Richardson, D. K., Gray, J. E., Gortmaker, S. L., Goldman, D. A., Pursley, D. M., & McCormick, M. C. (1998). Declining severity adjusted mortality: Evidence of improving neonatal intensive care. *Pediatrics, 102*(4), 893–899.

Richardson, K. (2008). How dynamic systems have changed our minds. In A. Fogel, B. J. King, & S. Shanker (Eds.). *Human development in the 21st century: Visionary policy ideas from systems scientists.* Cambridge, UK: Cambridge University Press.

Richert, R. A., Robb, M. B., & Smith, E. I. (2011). Media as Social Partners: The Social Nature of Young Children's Learning from Screen Media. *Child Development, 82*(1), 82-95.

Rickman, M. D., & Davidson, R. J. (1994). Personality and behavior in parents of temperamentally inhibited and uninhibited children. *Developmental Psychology, 30,* 346–354.

Ricks, S. S. (1985). Father-infant interactions: a review of empirical research. *Family Relations, 34,* 505–511.

Ridgeway, D., Waters, E., & Kuczaj, S. A., II. (1985). Acquisition of emotion-descriptive language: Receptive and productive vocabulary norms for ages 18 months to 6 years. *Developmental Psychology, 21,* 901–908.

Rieck, M., Arad, I., & Netzer, D. (1996). Developmental evaluation of very-low-birthweight infants: Longitudinal and cross-sectional studies. *International Journal of Behavioral Development, 19*(3), 549–562.

Rieger, M., Pirke, K., Buske-Kirschbaum, A., Wurmser, H., Papousek, M., & Hellhammer, D. (2004). Influence of stress during pregnancy on HPA activity and neonatal behavior. *Annals Of The New York Academy Of Sciences, 1032,* 228–230.

Riese, M. L. (1987). Longitudinal assessment of temperament from birth to 2 years: A comparison of full-term and preterm infants. *Infant Behavior and Development, 10,* 347–363.

Ritter, J. M., Casey, R. J., & Langlois, J. H. (1991). Adults' responses to infants varying in appearance of age and attractiveness. *Child Development, 62,* 68–82.

Ritz, B., Yu, F., Fruin, S., Chapa, G., Shaw, G., & Harris, J. (2002). Ambient air pollution and risk of birth defects in Southern California. *American Journal Of Epidemiology, 155*(1), 17–25.

Rizzo, T. A., Metzger, B. E., Dooley, S. L., & Cho, N. H. (1997). Early malnutrition and child neurobehavioral development: Insights from the study of children of diabetic mothers. *Child Development, 68*(1), 26–38.

Robboy, S., & Jaubert, F. (2007). Neoplasms and pathology of sexual developmental disorders (intersex). *Pathology, 39*(1), 147–163.

Roben, C., Bass, A. J., Moore, G. A., Murray-Kolb, L., Tan, P. Z., Gilmore, R. O., & ... Teti, L. O. (2012). Let me go: The influences of crawling experience and temperament on the development of anger expression. *Infancy, 17*(5), 558-577. doi:10.1111/j.1532-7078.2011.00092.x

Roben, C., Cole, P., & Armstrong, L. (2013). Longitudinal relations among language skills, anger expression, and regulatory strategies in early childhood. *Child Development, 84*(3), 891-905.

Roberts, K., & Cuff, M. D. (1989). Categorization studies of 9– to 15–month-old infants: Evidence for superordinate categorization? *Infant Behavior and Development, 12,* 265–288.

Robertson, S. S. (1987). Human cyclic motility: Fetal-newborn continuities and newborn state differences. *Developmental Psychobiology, 20,* 425–442.

Robertson, S. S. (1990). Temporal organization in fetal and newborn movement. In H. Bloch & B. I. Bertenthal (Eds.), *Sensory-motor organizations and development in infancy and early childhood* (pp. 105–122). The Netherlands: Kluwer Academic.

Robertson, S. S., Bacher, L. F., & Huntington, N. L. (2001). The integration of body movement and attention in young infants. *Psychological Science, 12*(6), 523–526.

Robinson, C. H. (1978). *Fundamentals of normal nutrition* (3rd ed.). New York: Macmillian.

Robinson, J., Little, C., & Biringen, Z. (1993). Emotional communication in mother-toddler relationship: Evidence for early gender differentiation. *Merrill-Palmer Quarterly, 39,* 496–515.

Robinson, J. L., Kagan, J., Reznick, J. S., & Corley, R. (1992). The heritability of inhibited and uninhibited behavior: A twin study. *Developmental Psychology, 28* (6), 1030–1037.

Robinson, M., Mattes, E., Oddy, W. H., Pennell, C. E., Van Eekelen, A., Mclean, N., J. Jacoby, P. L. . .. Newnham, J. P. (2011). Prenatal stress and risk of behavioral morbidity from age 2 to 14 years: The influence of the number, type, and timing of stressful life events. *Development and Psychopathology, 23,* 507-520.

Robson, A., & Cline, B. (1998). Developmental consequences of intrauterine growth retardation. *Infant Behavior and Development, 21*(2), 331344.

Rocha, N. A. C. F., dos Santos Silva, F. P., & Tudella, E. (2006). The impact of object size and rigidity on infant reaching. *Infant Behavior & Development, 29*(2), 251–261.

Rochat, P. (1987). Mouthing and grasping in neonates: Evidence for early detection of what hard or soft substances afford for action. *Infant Behavior and Development, 10,* 435–449.

Rochat, P. (2010). Emerging self-concept. In J. G. Bremmer & T. D. Wachs (Eds.). *The Wiley-Blackwell handbook of infant development volume 1: Basic research.*(2nd edtion, pp. 320-344). West Sussex, UK: Wiley-Blackwell.

Rochat, P. (1989). Object manipulation and exploration in 2– to 5–month-old infants. *Developmental Psychology, 25,* 871–884.

Rochat, P., Blass, E. M., & Hoffmeyer, L. B. (1988). Oropharyngeal control of hand-mouth coordination in newborn infants. *Developmental Psychology, 24,* 459–463.

Rochat, P., & Goubet, N. (1995). Development of sitting and reaching in 5– to 6–month-old infants. *Infant Behavior and Development, 18,* 53–68.

Rochat, P., Goubet, N., & Senders, S. J. (1999). To reach or not to reach? Perception of body effectivities by young infants. *Infant and Child Development, 8,* 129–148.

Rochat, P., & Hespos, S. J. (1997). Differential rooting response by neonates: Evidence for an early sense of self. *Early Development and Parenting, 6*(3–4), 105–112.

Rochat, P., & Morgan, R. (1995). Spatial determinants in the perception of self-produced leg movements by 3– to 5–month-old infants. *Developmental Psychology, 31,* 626–636.

Rochat, P., Querido, J. G., & Striano, T. (1999). Emerging sensitivity to the timing and structure of protoconversation in early infancy. *Developmental Psychology, 35*(4), 950–957.

Rochat, P., & Senders, S. J. (1990, April). *Sitting and reaching in infancy.* Paper presented at the Seventh International Conference on Infant Studies, Montreal, Canada.

Rochat, T., & Richter, L. (2007). International adoption: Benefits, risks, and vulnerabilities. *Zero to Three, 27*(5), 23–29.

Rocissano, L., Slade, A., & Lynch, V. (1987). Dyadic synchrony and toddler compliance. *Developmental Psychology, 23,* 698–704.

Rock, A. M. L., Trainor, L. J., & Addison, T. L. (1999). Distinctive messages in infant-directed lullabies and play songs. *Developmental Psychology, 35*(2), 527–534.

Rodholm, M., & Larsson, K. (1979). Father-infant interaction at the first contact after delivery. *Early Human Development, 3,* 21–27.

Rodriguez, A., & Bohlin, G. (2005). Are maternal smoking and stress during pregnancy related to ADHD symptoms in children? *Journal of Child Psychology and Psychiatry, 46,* 246-254.

Rodriguez, E. T., & Tamis-LeMonda, C. S. (2011). Trajectories of the Home Learning Environment across the First 5 Years: Associations with Children's Vocabulary and Literacy Skills at Prekindergarten. *Child Development, 82*(4), 1058-1075.

Roebuck-Spencer, T. M., Mattson, S. N., Marion, S. D., Brown, W. S., & Riley, E. P. (2004). Bimanual coordination in alcohol-exposed children: Role of the corpus callosum. *Journal of the International Neuropsychological Society, 10*(4), 536–548.

Rogers, S. J., & DiLalla, D. L. (1990). Age of symptom onset in young children with pervasive developmental disorders. *Journal of American Academy of Child and Adolescent Psychiatry, 29,* 863–872.

Roggman, L. A., Boyce, L. K., Cook, G. A., Christiansen, K., & Jones, D. (2004). Playing With Daddy: Social Toy Play, Early Head Start, and Developmental Outcomes. *Fathering, 2*(1), 83–108.

Roggman, L. A., Langlois, J. H., Hubbs-Tait, L., & Rieser-Danner, L. A. (1994). Infant day-care, attachment, and the "file drawer problem." *Child Development, 65,* 1429–1443.

Rogoff, B. (1990). *Apprenticeship in thinking: Cognitive development in social context.* New York: Oxford University Press.

Rogoff, B., Mistry, J., Goncu, A., & Mosier, C. (1993). Guided participation in cultural activity by toddlers and caregivers. *Monographs of the Society for Research in Child Development, 58* (8 Serial No. 236), 1–179.

Rogowski, J. (1998). Cost-effectiveness of care for very low birth weight infants. *Pediatrics, 102*(1), 35–43.

Rogowski, J. (1999). Measuring the cost of neonatal and perinatal care. *Pediatrics, 103*(5), 329–335.

Ronald, A., Pennell, C. E. & Whitehouse, A. J. O. (2010) Prenatal maternal stress associated with ADHD and autistic traits. *Frontiers in Developmental Psychology,* Retrieved from http://www.frontiersin.org/developmental psychology /10.3389/fpsyg.2010.00223/abstract

Ronnqvist, L., & Hofsten, C. von. (1994). Neonatal finger and arm movements as determined by a social and an object context. *Early Development and Parenting, 3,* 81–94.

Rooks, J. P., Weatherby, N. L., Ernst, E. K. M., Stapleton, S., Rosen, D., & Rosenfeld, A. (1989). Outcome of care in birth centers. *New England Journal of Medicine, 321,* 1804–1811.

Roopnarine, J. L., Fouts, H. N., Lamb, M. E., & Lewis-Elligan, T. Y. (2005). Mothers' and Fathers' Behaviors Toward Their 3– to 4–Month-Old Infants in Lower, Middle, and Upper Socioeconomic African American Families. *Developmental Psychology, 41*(5), 723–732.

Rose, S. A., & Feldman, J. F. (1997). Memory and speed: Their role in the relation of infant information processing to later IQ. *Child Development, 68*(4), 630–641.

Rose, S. A., Feldman, J. F., & Jankowski, J. J. (2009). A cognitive approach to the development of early language. *Child Development, 80*(1), 134-150. doi:10.1111/j.1467-8624.2008.01250.x

Rose, S. A., Futterweit, L. R., & Jankowski, J. J. (1999). The relation of affect to attention and learning in infancy. *Child Development, 70*(3), 549–559.

Rose, S. A., Schmidt, K., & Bridget, W. H. (1976). Cardiac and behavioral responsivity to tactile stimulation in premature and full-term infants. *Developmental Psychology, 12,* 311–320.

Rosen, K. S., & Burke, P. B. (1999). Multiple attachment relationships within families: Mothers and fathers with two young children. *Developmental Psychology, 35*(2), 436–444.

Rosen, K. S., & Rothbaum, F. (1993). Quality of parental caregiving and security of attachment. *Developmental Psychology, 29,* 358–367.

Rosen, W. D., Adamson, L. B., & Bakeman, R. (1992). An experimental investigation of infant social referencing: Mothers' messages and gender differences. *Developmental Psychology, 28,* 1172–1178.

Rosenberg, M. (2009). China's One Child Policy, http://geography.about.com/odpopulationgeography/a/onechild.htm,, Nov. 4, 2009.

Roseberry, S., Hirsh-Pasek, K., Parish-Morris, J., & Golinkoff, R. M. (2009). Live action: Can young children learn verbs from video?. *Child Development, 80*(5), 1360-1375. doi:10.1111/j.1467-8624.2009.01338.x

Rosenblatt, J. S. (1972). Learning in newborn kittens. *Scientific American, 277,* 18–25.

Rosenblith, J. F., & Sims-Knight, J. E. (1985). *In the beginning: Development in the first two years.* Belmont, CA: Brooks/Cole.

Rosenfield, J. A., Zahorik, P. M., Saint, W., & Murphy, G. (1993). Women's satisfaction with birth control. *Journal of Family Practice, 36,* 169–173.

Rosenstein, D., & Oster, H. (1988). Differential facial responses to four basic tastes in newborns. *Child Development, 59,* 1555–1568.

Rosenthal, N. K. (1991). The relation of peer interaction among infants and toddlers in family day care to characteristics of the child care environment. *Journal of Reproductive and Infant Psychology, Special Issues: International Perspective on Day Care for Young Children, 9,* 151–167.

Rosenthal, N. K. (1999). Out-of-home child care research: A cultural perspective. *International Journal of Behavioral Development, 23*(2), 477–518.

Rosett, H. L. (1980). The effects of alcohol on the fetus and offspring. In O. J. Kalant (Ed.), *Alcohol and drug problems in women. Neurobehavioral Toxicology and Teratology, 6,* 379–385.

Ross, H. S. (1996). Negotiating principles of entitlement in sibling property disputes. *Developmental Psychology, 32*(1), 90–101.

Ross, H. S. (2013). Effects of ownership rights on conflicts between toddler peers. *Infancy,18*(2), 256-275. doi:10.1111/j.1532-7078.2012.00121.x

Ross, H. S., Conant, C. L., Cheyne, J. A., & Alevizos, E. (1992). Relationships and alliances in the social interaction of kibbutz toddlers. *Social Development, 1,* 1–17.

Ross, H. S., & Goldman, B. D. (1977a). Establishing new social relations in infancy. In T. Alloway, P. Pliner, & L. Krames (Eds.), *Attachment behavior* (pp. 225–239). New York: Plenum Press.

Ross, H. S., & Goldman, B. D. (1977b). Infant's sociability toward strangers. *Child Development, 48,* 638–642.

Ross, H. S., & Lollis, S. P. (1987). Communication within infant social games. *Developmental Psychology, 23,* 241–248.

Ross, J., Anderson, J. R., & Campbell, R. N. (2011). I Remember Me: Mnemonic Self-Reference Effects in Preschool Children. *Monographs Of The Society For Research In Child Development, 76*(3), 1-102.

Rossi, A. (1968). Transition to parenthood. *Journal of Marriage and the Family, 30,* 26–39.

Ross-Sheehy, S., Oakes, L. M., & Luck, S. J. (2003). The development of visual short-term memory capacity in infants. *Child Development, 74*(6), 1807–1822.

Roth, G., & Assor, A. (2010). Parental conditional regard as a predictor of deficiencies in young children's capacities to respond to sad feelings. *Infant & Child Development, 19*(5), 465-477. doi:10.1002/icd.676

Rothbart, M. K. (1986). Longitudinal observation of infant temperament. *Developmental Psychology, 22,* 356–365.

Rothbart, M. K., & Derryberry, D. (1981). Development of individual differences in temperament. In M. E. Lamb (Ed.), *Advances in developmental psychology* (Vol. 1, pp. 191–230). Hillsdale, NJ: Erlbaum.

Rothbart, M. K., Derryberry, D., & Posner, M. I. (1994). A psychobiological approach to the development of temperament. In J. E. Bates & T. D. Wachs (Eds.), *Temperament: Individual differences at the interface of biology and behavior* (pp. 83–116). Washington, DC: American Psychological Association.

Rothbart, M. K., & Posner, M. I. (1985). Temperament and the development of self-regulation. In L. C. Hartlage & C. F. Telzrow (Eds.), *The neuropsychology of individual differences: A developmental perspective* (pp. 93–123). New York: Plenum Press.

Rothbart, M. K., Sheese, B. E., & Posner, M. I. (2007). Executive attention and effortful control: Linking temperament, brain networks, and genes. *Child Development Perspectives, 1*(1), 2–7.

Roth-Hanania, R., Davidov, M., & Zahn-Waxler, C. (2011). Empathy development from 8 to 16 months: early signs of concern for others. *Infant Behavior & Development*, *34*(3), 447-458.

Rounds, K. A. (1991). Early intervention services for very young children and their families under P.L. 99–457. *Special issues: Learning disabilities. Child and Adolescent Social Work Journal, 8,* 489–499.

Rovee-Collier, C., & Barr, R. (2000). Infant learning and memory. In J. G. Bremner & A. Fogel (Eds.), *Handbook of infancy research.* Oxford, England: Blackwell.

Rovee-Collier, C., & Cuevas, K. (2009). Multiple memory systems are unnecessary to account for infant memory development: An ecological model. *Developmental Psychology*, *45*(1), 160-174. doi:10.1037/a0014538

Rovee-Collier, C. K., Enright, M., Lucas, D., Fagan, J., & Gekoski, M. J. (1981). The forgetting of newly acquired and reactivated memories of 3–month-old infants. *Infant Behavior and Development, 4,* 317–331.

Rowe, M. L., & Goldin-Meadow, S. (2009). Early gesture selectively predicts later language learning. *Developmental Science*, *12*(1), 182-187. doi:10.1111/j.1467-7687.2008.00764.x

Roy, T. S., Andrews, J. E., Seidler, F. J., & Slotkin, T. A. (1998). Nicotine evokes cell death in embryonic rat brain during neurulation. *Journal of Pharmacology and Experimental Therapy, 287*(3), 1136–1144.

Rubenstein, J., & Howes, C. (1976). The effects of peers on toddler interaction with mother and toys. *Child Development, 47,* 597–605.

Rubenstein, J., Howes, C., & Pedersen, F. A. (1982). Second order effects of peers on mother-toddler interaction. *Infant Behavior and Development, 5,* 185–194.

Rubin, G. B., Fagen, J. W., & Carroll, M. H. (1998). Olfactory context and memory retrieval in 3–month-old infants. *Infant Behavior and Development, 21*(4), 641–658.

Rubin, K. H., Hastings, P., Chen, X., Stewart, S., & McNichol, K. (1998). Intrapersonal and maternal correlates of aggression, conflict, and externalizing problems in toddlers. *Child Development, 69*(6), 1614–1629.

Rubinstein, A. J., Kalakanis, L., & Langlois, J. H. (1999). Infant preferences for attractive faces: A cognitive explanation. *Developmental Psychology, 35*(3), 848–855.

Ruda, M. A., Ling, Q.-D., Hohmann, R. G., Peng, Y. B., & Tachibana, T. (2000). Altered nocireceptive neuronal circuits after neonatal peripheral inflammation. *Science, 289*(5479), 628–630.

Ruff, H. A. (1978). Infant recognition of invariant forms of objects. *Child Development, 49,* 293–306.

Ruff, H. A. (1984). Infant's manipulative exploration of objects: Effects of age and object characteristics. *Developmental Psychology, 20,* 9–20.

Ruff, H. A. (1985). Detection of information specifying the motion of objects by 3– and 5–month-old infants. *Developmental Psychology, 21,* 295–305.

Ruff, H. A. (1986). Components of attention during infants' manipulative exploration. *Child Development, 57,* 105–114.

Ruff, H. A., & Kohler, C. J. (1978). Tactual-visual transfer in six-month-old infants. *Infant Behavior and Development, 1,* 259–264.

Ruff, H. A., & Lawson, K. R. (1990). Development of sustained, focused attention in young children during free play. *Developmental Psychology, 26,* 85–93.

Ruff, H. A., Saltarelli, L. M., Capozzoli, M., & Dubiner, K. (1992). The differentiation of activity in infants' exploration of objects. *Developmental Psychology, 28* (5), 851–861.

Ruffman, T., Slade, L., & Crowe, E. (2002). The relation between children's and mothers' mental state language and theory-of-mind understanding. *Child Development, 73*(3), 734–751.

Ruffwarg, H. P., Muzio, J. N., & Dement, W. C. (1966). Ontogenetic development of the human sleep-dream cycle. *Science, 153,* 604–619.

Russell, M. J., Mendelson, T., & Peeke, H. V. (1983). Mothers' identification of their infant's odors. *Ethology and Sociobiology, 4*(1), 29–31.

Rutter, M. (1979). Maternal deprivation, 1972–1978: New findings, new concepts, new approaches. *Child Development, 50,* 283–305.

Rutter, M. (1987). Continuities and discontinuities from infancy. In J. D. Osofsky (Ed.), *Handbook of infant development* (2nd ed.). New York: Wiley.

Rutter, M., & O'Connor, T. G. (2004). Are There Biological Programming Effects for Psychological Development? Findings From a Study of Romanian Adoptees. *Developmental Psychology, 40*(1), 81–94.

Rutter. M, Sunuga-Barke, E. J., Beckett, C, Castle, J., Kreppner, J. V., Kumsta, R. . . . Bell, C. A. (2010). Deprivation-specific psychological patterns: Effects of institutional deprivation. *Monographs Of The Society For Research In Child Development, 75*(1), 1-252.

Sagi, A. (1981). Mothers' and non-mothers' identification of infant cries. *Infant Behavior and Development, 4,* 37–40.

Sagi, A., Donnell, F., van Ijzendoorn, M. H., Mayseless, O. & Aviezer, O. (1994). Sleeping out of home in a kibbutz communal arrangement: It makes a difference for infant-mother attachment. *Child Development, 65,* 992–1004.

Sagi, A., van Ijzendoorn, M. H., Scharf, M., Joels, T., Koren-Karie, N., Mayseless, O., & Aviezer, O. (1997). Ecological constraints for intergenerational transmission of attachment. *International Journal of Behavioral Development, 20*(2), 287–299.

Sagi, A., Lamb, M. E., Lewkowicz, K. S., Shoham, R., Dvir, R., & Estes, D. (1985). Security of infant-mother, -father, and -metapelet attachments among kibbutz-reared Israeli children. In I. Bretherton & E. Waters (Eds.), *Growing points of attachment theory and research. Monographs of the Society for Research in Child Development, 50* (Serial No. 209), 257–275.

Sagi-Schwartz, A. (2008). The well being of children living in chronic war zones: The Palestinian-Israeli case. [Special issue: Chronic exposure to catastrophic war experiences and political violence: Links to the well-being of children and their families]. *International Journal of Behavioral Development, 32,* 322-336.

Saha, S., Barnett, A., Foldi, C., Burne, T., Eyles, D., Buka, S., & McGrath, J. (2009). Advanced paternal age is associated with impaired neurocognitive outcomes during infancy and childhood. *Plos Medicine, 6*(3), e40.

Salapatek, P., & Banks, M. S. (1978). Infant sensory assessment: Vision. In F. D. Minifie & L. L. Lloyd (Eds.), *Communicative and cognitive abilities: Early behavioral assessment* (pp. 86–107). Baltimore: University Park Press.

Saldeen, P., & Saldeen, T. (2004). Women and omega-3 Fatty acids. *Obstet Gynecol Surv, 59*(10), 722–730; quiz 745–726.

Salk, L. (1973). The role of the heartbeat in relations between mother and infant. *Scientific American, 228,* 24–29.

Saltaris, C., Serbin, L. A., Stack, D. M., Karp, J. A., Schwartzman, A. E., & Ledingham, J. E. (2004). Nurturing cognitive competence in preschoolers: A longitudinal study of intergenerational continuity and risk. *International Journal of Behavioral Development, 28*(2), 105–115.

Sameroff A, (2010). A unified theory of development: a dialectic integration of nature and nurture. *Child Development, 81,* 6-22.

Sameroff, A. J. (1984). Developmental systems: Contexts and evolution. In P. H. Mussen (Ed.), *Handbook of child psychology: Vol. I. History, theory, and methods* (4th ed., pp. 237–294). New York: Wiley.

Sameroff, A. J., & Emde, R. N. (1989). *Relationship disturbances in early childhood: A developmental approach.* New York: Basic Books.

Sameroff, A., & MacKenzie, M. (2003). Research strategies for capturing transactional models of development: The limits of the possible. *Development and Psychopathology, 15*(3), 613–640.

Sameroff, A. J., & Seifer, R. (1983). Familial risk and child competence. *Child Development, 54,* 1254–1268.

Sameroff, A. J., Seifer, R., & Elias, P. K. (1982). Sociocultural variability in infant temperament ratings. *Child Development, 53,* 164–173.

Samuels, C. A. (1985). Attention to eye contact opportunity and facial motion by three-month-old infants. *Journal of Experimental Child Psychology, 40,* 105–114.

Samuels, C. A., Scholz, K., & Edmundson, S. (1992). The effects of baby bath and massage by fathers on the family system: The Sunraysia Australia intervention project. *Early Development and Parenting, 1,* 39–49.

Samuels, H. R. (1980). The effect of an older sibling on infant locomotor exploration of a new environment. *Child Development, 51,* 606–609.

Sancier, B., & Mapp, P. (1992). Who helps working women care for the young and old? *Affiliate Journal of Women and Social Work, 7,* 61–62.

Sander, L. W. (1962). Issues in early mother-child interaction. *Journal of the American Academy of Child Psychiatry, 1,* 141–166.

Sander, L. W., Stechler, G., Burns, P., & Lee, A. (1979). Change in infant and caregiver variables over the first two months of life: Integration of action in early development. In E. B. Thoman (Ed.), *Origins of the infant's social responsiveness* (pp. 349–407). Hillsdale, NJ: Lawrence Erlbaum Associates.

Sandman, C. A., Wadhwa, P., Hetrick, W. H., Porto, M., & Peeke, H. V. S. (1997). Human fetal heart rate dishabituation between thirty and thirty-two weeks' gestation. *Child Development, 68*(6), 1031–1040.

Sansavini, A., Bertoncini, J., & Giovanelli, G. (1997). Newborns discriminate the rhythm of multisyllabic stressed words. *Developmental Psychology, 33*(1), 3–11.

Sansavini, A., Rizzardi, M., Alessandroni, R., & Giovanelli, G. (1996). The development of Italian low- and very-low-birthweight infants from birth to 5 years: The role of biological and social risks. *International Journal of Behavioral Development, 19*(3), 533–547.

Sardana, R. (1985). Examining for defects. *Nursing Mirror, 160,* 38–42.

Saudino, K. (2012). Sources of continuity and change in activity level in early childhood. *Child Development, 83*(1), 266-281

Savage-Rumbaugh, S., Murphy, J., Sevcik, R. A., Brakke, K. E., Williams, S. L., & Rumbaugh, D. M. (1993). Language comprehension in ape and child. *Monographs of the Society for Research in Child Development, 58* (3–4, Serial No. 233), 1–221.

Savelsbergh, G. J. P., & van der Kamp, J. (1993). The coordination of infant's reaching, grasping, catching and posture: A natural physical approach. In G. J. P. Savelsbergh (Ed.), *The development of coordination in infancy* (pp. 289–317). Amsterdam: Elsevier.

Saylor, C. F., Boyce, G. C., & Price, C. (2003). Early predictors of school-age behavior problems and social skills in children with intraventricular hemorrhage (IVH) and/or extremely low birthweight (ELBW). *Child Psychiatry & Human Development, 33*(3), 175–192.

Scaife, M., & Bruner, J. S. (1975). The capacity for joint visual attention in the infant. *Nature, 253,* 265–266.

Scaramella, L. V., Conger, R. D., Simons, R. L., & Whitbeck, L. B. (1998). Predicting risk for pregnancy by late adolescence: A social contextual perspective. *Developmental Psychology, 34*(6), 1233–1245.

Scaramella, L. V., & Leve, L. D. (2004). Clarifying Parent-Child Reciprocities During Early Childhood: The Early Childhood Coercion Model. *Clinical Child and Family Psychology Review, 7*(2), 89–107.

Scarr, S. (1992). Developmental theories for the 1990s: Development and individual differences. *Child Development, 63*(1), 1–19.

Scarr, S., & Eisenberg, M. (1993). Child care research: Issues, perspectives, and results. *Annual Review of Psychology, 44,* 613–632.

Scarr, S., & McCartney, K. (1983). How people make their own environments: A theory of genotype-environment effects. *Child Development, 21,* 391–402.

Schachner, A., & Hannon, E. E. (2011). Infant-directed speech drives social preferences in 5-month-old infants. *Developmental Psychology, 47,* 19-25.

Schachter, F. S., & Stone, R. K. (1985). Difficult sibling, easy sibling: Temperament and the within-family environment. *Child Development, 56,* 1335–1344.

Schafer, G., Plunkett, K., & Harris, P. L. (1999). What's in a name? Lexical knowledge drives infant preferences in the absence of referential input. *Developmental Science, 2*(2), 187–194.

Schaffer, H. R., & Crook, C. K. (1979). Maternal control techniques in a directed play situation. *Child Development, 50,* 989–996.

Schaffer, H. R., & Crook, C. K. (1980). Child compliance and maternal control techniques. *Developmental Psychology, 16,* 54–56.

Schaffer, H. R., & Emerson, P. (1964). Patterns of response to physical contact in early human development. *Journal of Child Psychiatry and Psychology, 5,* 1–13.

Schanberg, S., Bartolome, J., & Kuhn, C. (1987, January). *Touching and the brain.* Paper presented at the American College of Neuropsychopharmacology, San Juan, Puerto Rico.

Schetter, S. D., (2011). Psychological science on pregnancy: stress processes, biopsychosocial models, and emerging research issues. *Annual Review Of Psychology, 62,* 531-58.

Schiffman, P. C., Westlake, R. E., Santiago, T. V., & Edelman, N. H. (1980). Ventilatory control in parents of victims of sudden-infant-death syndrome. *New England Journal of Medicine, 302,* 486–491.

Schindler, P. J., Moely, B. E., & Frank, A. L. (1987). Time in day care and social participation of young children. *Developmental Psychology, 23,* 255–261.

Schleidt, M., & Genzel, C. (1990). The significance of mother's perfume for infants in the first weeks of their life. *Ethology and Sociobiology, 11,* 145–155.

Schlesinger, M., & Langer, J. (1999). Infants' developing expectations of possible and impossible tool-use events between ages 8 and 12 months. *Developmental Science, 2*(2), 195–205.

Schmale, R., Cristià, A., Seidl, A., & Johnson, E. K. (2010). Developmental changes in infants' ability to cope with dialect variation in word recognition. *Infancy, 15*(6), 650-662. doi:10.1111/j.1532-7078.2010.00032.x

Schmidt, L. A., Miskovic, V., Boyle, M., & Saigal, S.,(2010) Frontal electroencephalogram asymmetry, salivary cortisol, and internalizing behavior problems in young adults who were born at extremely low birth weight. *Child Development, 81,*183-99.

Schmidt, M., Pempek, T. A., Kirkorian, H. L., Lund, A., & Anderson, D. R. (2008). The effects of background television on the toy play behavior of very young children. *Child Development, 79*(4), 1137-1151. doi:10.1111/j.1467-8624.2008.01180.x

Schmitt, K. L., & Anderson, D. R. (2002). Television and reality: Toddlers' use of visual information from video to guide behavior. *Media Psychology, 4*(1), 51–76.

Schmitow, C., & Kochukhova, O. (2013). How infants look at others' manual interactions: the role of experience. *Infant Behavior & Development, 36*(2), 223-227.

Schmitz, S., Fulker, D. W., Plomin, R., Zahn-Waxler, C., Emde, R. N., & DeFries, J. C. (1999). Temperament and problem behavior during early childhood. *International Journal of Behavioral Development, 23*(2), 333–355.

Schmuckler, M. A. (1996). Visual-proprioceptive intermodal perception in infancy. *Infant Behavior and Development, 19,* 221–232.

Schneider, K. J. (1998). Toward a science of the heart: Romanticism and the revival of psychology. *American Psychologist, 53*(3), 277–289.

Schneider, M. L., Roughton, E. C., Koehler, A. J., & Lubach, G. R. (1999). Growth and development following prenatal stress exposure in primates: An examination of ontogenetic vulnerability. *Child Development, 70*(2), 263–274.

Schneider-Rosen, K., & Wenz-Gross, M. (1990). Patterns of compliance from eighteen to thirty months of age. *Child Development, 61,* 104–112.

Schölmerich, A., Fracasso, M. P., Lamb, M. E., & Broberg, A. G. (1995). Interactional harmony at 7 and 10 months of age predicts security of attachment as measured by Q-sort ratings. *Social Development, 4,* 64–68.

Schölmerich, A., Lamb, M. E., Leyendecker, B., & Fracasso, M. P. (1997). Mother-infant teaching interactions and attachment security in Euro-American and Central-American immigrant families. *Infant Behavior and Development, 20,* 165–174.

Scholz, K., & Samuels, C. A. (1992). Neonatal bathing and massage intervention with fathers, behavioral effects 12 weeks after birth of the first baby: The Sunraysia Australia Intervention Project. *International Journal of Behavioral Development, 15,* 67–81.

Schön, R. A. & Silvén, M. (2007). Natural parenting--Back to basics in infant care. *Evolutionary Psychology, 5,* 102-183.

Schore, A. (2003). *Affect dysregulation and disorders of the self.* Norton.

Schore, A. N. (2012). *The Science of the Art of Psychotherapy (Norton Series on Interpersonal Neurobiology)*: WW Norton & Company.

Schreiber, J. (1977). Birth, the family and the community: A southern Italian example. *Birth and the Family Journal, 4,* 153–157.

Schuetze, P., & Eiden, R. D. (2006). The association between maternal smoking and secondhand exposure and autonomic functioning at 2–4 weeks of age. *Infant Behavior & Development, 29*(1), 32–43.

Schuetze, P., Lewis, A., & DiMartino, D. (1999). Relation between time spent in daycare and exploratory behaviors in 9–month-old infants. *Infant Behavior and Development, 22*(2), 267–276.

Schuetze, P., & Zeskind, P. S. (1997). Relation between reported maternal caffeine consumption during pregnancy and neonatal state and heart rate. *Infant Behavior and Development, 20*(4), 559–562.

Schulman-Galambos, C., & Galambos, R. (1979). Brain stem evoked response audiometry in newborn hearing screening. *Archives of Otolaryngology, 105,* 86–90.

Schum, T. R., Kolb, T. M., McAuliffe, T. L., Simms, M. D., Underhill, R. L., & Lewis, M. (2002). Sequential acquisition of toilet-training skills: a descriptive study of gender and age differences in normal children. *Pediatrics, 109*(3), E48.

Schum, T. R., McAuliffe, T. L., Simms, M. D., Walter, J. A., Lewis, M., & Pupp, R. (2001). Factors associated with toilet training in the 1990s. *Ambul Pediatr, 1*(2), 79–86.

Schwartz, A., Campos, J., & Baisel, E. (1973). The visual cliff: Cardiac and behavioral correlates on the deep and shallow sides at 5 and 9 months of age. *Journal of Experimental Child Psychology, 15,* 85–99.

Schwartz, C. E., Wright, C. I., Shin, L. M., Kagan, J., & Rauch, S. L. (2003). Inhibited and uninhibited infants "grown up": Adult Amygdalar response to novelty. *Science, 300,* 1952–1953.

Schwartz, P. (1983). Length of daycare attendance and attachment behavior in eighteen-month-old infants. *Child Development, 54,* 1073–1078.

Schwarzer, G., Freitag, C., Buckel, R., & Lofruthe, A. (2013). Crawling is associated with mental rotation ability by 9-month-old infants. *Infancy, 18*(3), 432-441. doi:10.1111/j.1532-7078.2012.00132.x

Sebire, N. J., Jolly, M., Harris, J. P., Wadsworth, J., Joffe, M., Beard, R. W., et al. (2001). Maternal obesity and pregnancy outcome: a study of 287,213 pregnancies in London. *Int J Obes Relat Metab Disord, 25*(8), 1175–1182.

Secret, M., & Sprang, G. (2001). The effects of family-friendly workplace environments on work-family stress of employed parents. *Journal of Social Service Research, 28*(2), 21–45.

Seidl, A., & Cristià, A. (2008). Developmental changes in the weighting of prosodic cues. *Developmental Science, 11*(4), 596-606. doi:10.1111/j.1467-7687.2008.00704.x

Seifer, R., LaGasse, L. L., Lester, B., Bauer, C. R., Shankaran, S., Bada, H. S., et al. (2004). Attachment Status in Children Prenatally Exposed to Cocaine and Other Substances. *Child Development, 75*(3), 850–868.

Seifer, R., Sameroff, A. J., Anagnostopolou, R., & Elias, P. K. (1992). Mother-infant interaction during the first year: Effects of situation, maternal mental illness, and demographic factors. *Infant Behavior and Development, 15,* 405–426.

Seifer, R., Sameroff, A. J., Barrett, L. C., & Krafchuk, E. (1994). Infant temperament measured by multiple observations and mother report. *Child Development, 65,* 1478–1490.

Seifer, R., & Schiller, M., Sameroff, A. J., Resnick, S., & Riordan, K. (1996). Attachment, maternal sensitivity, and infant temperament during the first year of life. *Developmental Psychology, 32*(1), 12–25.

Seimyr, L., Edhborg, M., Lundh, W., & Sjogren, B. (2004). In the shadow of maternal depressed mood: experiences of parenthood during the first year after childbirth. *J Psychosom Obstet Gynaecol, 25*(1), 23–34.

Selby, J. M., & Bradley, B. S. (2003). Infants in Groups: A Paradigm for the Study of Early Social Experience. *Human Development, 46*(4), 197–221.

Self, P., & Horowitz, F. D. (1979). The assessment of the newborn infant. In J. Osofsky (Ed.), *Handbook of infant development* (pp. 240–268). New York: Wiley.

Seligman, M. E. P., & Maier, S. (1967). Failure to escape traumatic shock. *Journal of Experimental Psychology, 74,* 1–9.

Sell, E. J., Hill-Mangan, S., & Holberg, C. J. (1992). Natural course of behavioral organization in premature infants. *Infant Behavior and Development, 15*(4), 461–478.

Selman, R. L. (1980). *The growth of interpersonal understanding: Developmental and clinical analyses.* New York: Academic Press.

Serbin, L. A., Poulin-Dubois, D., & Eichstedt, J. A. (2002). Infants' response to gender-inconsistent events. *Infancy, 3*(4), 531–542.

Serifica, F. C. (1978). The development of attachment behaviors: An organismic-developmental perspective. *Human Development, 21,* 119–140.

Service, R. F. (1994). Barriers hold back new contraception strategies. *Science, 266,* 1489.

Service V., Lock, A., & Chandler, P. (1989). Individual differences in early communicative development: A social constructivist perspective. In S. Tetzchner, L. Siegel & L. Smith (Eds.), *The social cognitive aspects of normal atypical language development* (pp. 23–49). New York: Springer-Verlag.

Seto, A., Einarson, T., & Koren, G. (1997). Pregnancy outcome following first trimester exposure to antihistamines: Meta-analysis. *American Journal of Perinatology, 14*(3), 199–124.

Sewall, M. (1930). Some causes of jealousy in young children. *Smith College Studies in Social Work, 1,* 6–22.

Sgandurra, G., Cecchi, F., Serio, S. M., Del Maestro, M., Laschi, C., Dario, P., & Cioni, G. (2012). Longitudinal study of unimanual actions and grasping forces during infancy. *Infant Behavior & Development, 35,* 205-214.

Shachar-Dadon, A., Schulkin, J., & Leshem, M. (2009). Adversity before conception will affect adult progeny in rats. *Developmental Psychology, 45*(1), 9-16. doi:10.1037/a0014030

Shah, D., & Sachdev, H. P. (2004). Maternal micronutrients and fetal outcome. *Indian J Pediatr, 71*(11), 985–990.

Shahmoon-Shanok, R. (1999). Adopting parenthood: An enduring transformation marking identity and intimacy capacities. *Zero to Three, 19*(4), 32–36.

Shand, N., & Kosawa, Y. (1985). Japanese and American behavior types at three months: Infants and infant-mother dyads. *Infant Behavior and Development, 8,* 225–240.

Shapira, A., & Madsen, M. C. (1969). Cooperative and competitive behavior of kibbutz and urban children in Israel. *Child Development, 40,* 609–617.

Sharan, P. (1988). One view of the cultural context for the study of childrearing in India. *Newsletter of the International Society for the Study of Behavioral Development, 13,* 1–3.

Sharon, N., Mor, I., Golan-lev, T., Fainsod, A., & Benvenisty, N. (2011). Molecular and functional characterizations of gastrula organizer cells derived from human embryonic stem cells. *Stem Cells, 29,* 600-608.

Shatz, M. (1978). The relationship between cognitive processes and the development of communication skills. In C. B. Keasey (Ed.), *Nebraska symposium on motivation.* Lincoln: University of Nebraska Press.

Shea, A., Walsh, C., MacMillan, H., & Steiner, M. (2004). Child maltreatment and HPA axis dysregulation: Relationship to major depressive disorder and past traumatic stress disorder in females. *Journal of Psychoneuroendocrinology,* 24–36.

Sheppard, J. J., & Mysak, E. D. (1984). Ontogeny of infantile oral reflexes and emerging chewing. *Child Development, 55,* 831–843.

Sheridan, C. J., Matuz, T., Draganova, R., Eswaran, H., & Preissl, H. (2010) Fetal magnetoencephalography—Achievements and challenges in the study of prenatal and early postnatal brain responses: A review. *Infant and Child Development,19,* 80-93.

Sherrod, K. B., Crawley, S., Petersen, G., & Bennett, P. (1978). Maternal language to prelinguistic infants: Semantic aspects. *Infant Behavior and Development, 1,* 335–346.

Shirley, M. M. (1931). *The first two years: A study of twenty-five babies: Vol. 1. Postural and locomotor development.* Minneapolis: University of Minnesota Press.

Shnider, S. (1981). Choice of anesthesia for labor and delivery. *Journal of Obstetrics and Gynecology, 58* (5 Suppl.), 24S-34S.

Shonkoff, J. P. (2010). Building a New Biodevelopmental Framework to Guide the Future of Early Childhood Policy. *Child Development, 81*(1), 357-367.

Shonkoff, J. P., Garner, A. S., Siegel, B. S., Dobbins, M. I., Earls, M. F. Garner,. . . Committee on psychosocial aspects of child and family health, Committee on early childhood, adoption, and dependent care, Section on developmental and behavioral pediatrics (2012). The lifelong effects of early childhood adversity and toxic stress. *Pediatrics,129,*e232-e246.

Shonkoff, J. P., Hauser-Cram, P., Krauss, M. W., & Upshur, C. C. (1992). Development of infants with disabilities and their families. *Monographs of the Society for Research in Child Development, 57,* 1–163.

Shulman, S., Becker, A., & Sroufe, L. A. (1999). Adult-child interactions as related to adult's family history and child's attachment. *International Journal of Behavioral Development, 23*(4), 959–976.

Shwalb, B. J., Shwalb, D., & Shoji, J. (1994). Structure and dimensions of maternal perceptions of Japanese infant temperament. *Developmental Psychology, 30,* 131–141.

Shy, K. K., Luthy, D. A., Bennett, F. C., Whitfield, M., Larson, E. B., Belle, G. van, Hughes, J. P., Wilson, J. A., & Stenchever, M. A. (1990). Effects of electronic fetal-heart-rate monitoring, as compared with periodic ausculation, on the neurological development of premature infants. *New England Journal of Medicine, 322*(9), 588–593.

Sidebotham, P., & Heron, J. (2003). Child maltreatment in the 'children of the nineties:' The role of the child. *Child Abuse & Neglect, 27*(3), 337–352.

Siegel, D. (2001). *The developing mind: How relationships and the brain interact to shape who we are.* NY: The Guilford Press.

Sigman, M., & Kasari, C. (1995). Joint attention across contexts in normal and autistic children. In C. Moore & P. J. Dunham (Eds.), *Joint attention: Its origins and role in development* (pp. 189–203). Hillsdale, NJ: Erlbaum.

Sigman, M., Neumann, C., Carter, E., Cattle, D. J., D'Souza, S., & Bwibo, N. (1988). Home interactions and the development of Embu toddlers in Kenya. *Child Development, 59,* 1251–1261.

Sigman, M., & Ruskin, E. (1999). Continuity and change in the social competence of children with autism, Down syndrome, and developmental delays. *Monographs of the Society for Research in Child Development, 64*(1), 1–139.

Silberner, J. (1986). Survival of the fetus. *Science News, 130,* 234–235.

Silver, M. (1985). Life after Tay-Sachs. *Jewish Monthly, 99,* 14–23.

Silverman, I., Dickens, S. E., Eals, M., & Fine, J. (1993). Perceptions of maternal and paternal solicitude by birth children and adoptees: Relevance for maternal bonding theory. *Early Development and Parenting, 2,* 135–144.

Simcock, G., & DeLoache, J. S. (2008). The effect of repetition on infants' imitation from picture books varying in iconicity. *Infancy, 13*(6), 687-697. doi:10.1080/15250000802459102

Simcock, G., & Hayne, H. (2003). Age-related changes in verbal and nonverbal memory during early childhood. *Developmental Psychology, 39*(5), 805–814.

Simons, R. L., Lorenz, F. O., Wu, C. I., & Conger, R. D. (1993). Social network and marital support as mediators and moderators of the impact of stress and depression on parental behavior. *Developmental Psychology, 29,* 368–381.

Singer, L. M., Brodzinsky, D. M., Ramsay, D., Steir, M., & Waters, E. (1985). Mother-infant attachment in adoptive families. *Child Development, 56,* 1543–1551.

Singer, L. M., Salvator, A., Guo, S., Collin, M., Lilien, L., & Baley, J. (1999). Maternal psychological distress and parenting stress after the birth of a very low-birth-weight infant. *Journal of the American Medical Association, 281*(9), 799–805.

Singer, L. T., Minnes, S., Short, E., Arendt, R., Farkas, K., Lewis, B., Klein, N., Russ, S., Min, M. O., & Kirchner, H. L. (2004). Cognitive outcomes of preschool children with prenatal cocaine exposure. *JAMA, 291*(20), 2448–2456.

Singh, L., Nestor, S., Parikh, C., & Yull, A. (2009). Influences of infant-directed speech on early word recognition. *Infancy, 14*(6), 654-666. doi:10.1080/15250000903263973

Singh, V. K., Warren, R. P., Odell, J. D., Warren, W. L., & Cole, P. (1993). Antibodies to myelin basic protein in children with autistic behavior. *Brain Behavior and Immunization, 7,* 97–103.

Siskind, V., Schofield, F., Rice, D., & Bain, C. (1989). Breast cancer and breastfeeding: Results from an Australian case-control study. *American Journal of Epidemiology, 130,* 229–236.

Sitskoorn, M. M., & Smitsman, A. W. (1995). Infants' perception of dynamic relations between objects: Passing through or support? *Developmental Psychology, 31,* 437–447.

Sitskoorn, M. M., & Smitsman, A. W. (1997). Perception of dynamic object relations in infancy. *Infant Behavior and Development, 20,* 141–150.

Sjogren, B., Edman, G., Widstrom, A. M., Mathiesen, A. S., & Uvnas-Moberg, K. (2004). Maternal foetal attachment and personality during first pregnancy. *Journal of Reproductive and Infant Psychology, 22*(2), 57–69.

Skarin, K. (1977). Cognitive and contextual determinants of stranger fear in six- and eleven-month-old infants. *Child Development, 48,* 537–544.

Skinner, B. F. (1938). *The behavior of organisms.* Englewood Cliffs, NJ: Prentice-Hall.

Skotheim, S., Braarud, H., Høie, K., Markhus, M., Malde, M., Graff, I., & ... Stormark, K. (2013). Subclinical levels of maternal depression and infant sensitivity to social contingency. *Infant Behavior & Development, 36*(3), 419-426. doi:10.1016/j.infbeh.2013.03.009

Slade, A. (1986). Symbolic play and separation-individuation: A naturalistic study. *Bulletin of the Menninger Clinic, 50,* 541–563.

Slade, A. (1987a). A longitudinal study of maternal involvement and symbolic play during the toddler period. *Child Development, 58,* 367–375.

Slade, A. (1987b). Quality of attachment and early symbolic play. *Developmental Psychology, 23,* 78–85.

Slade, A. (2005). Parental reflective functioning: An introduction. *Attachment and Human Development, 7,* 269–281.

Slade, A. (2007). Reflective parenting programs: Theory and development. *Psychoanalytic Inquiry, 26*(4), 640-657.

Slade, E. P., & Wissow, L. S. (2004). Spanking in early childhood and later behavior problems: a prospective study of infants and young toddlers. *Pediatrics, 113*(5), 1321–1330.

Slama, R., Bouyer, J., Windham, G., Fenster, L., Werwatz, A., & Swan, S. (2005). Influence of paternal age on the risk of spontaneous abortion. *American Journal of Epidemiology, 161*(9), 816–823.

Slater, A., Morison, V., & Rose, D. (1984). Habituation in the newborn. *Infant Behavior and Development, 7,* 183–200.

Slater, A., Quinn, P. C., Kelly, D. J., Lee, K., Longmore, C. A., McDonald, P. R., & Pascalis, O. (2010). The shaping of the face space in early infancy: Becoming a native face processor. *Child Development Perspectives, 4*(3), 205-211. doi:10.1111/j.1750-8606.2010.00147.x

Slater, A., von der Schulenburg, C., Brown, E., Badenoch, M., Butterworth, G., Parsons, S., & Samuels, C. (1998). Newborn infants prefer attractive faces. *Infant Behavior and Development, 21*(2), 345–354.

Slater, R., Cantarella, A., Gallella, S., Worley, A., Boyd, S., Meek, J., et al. (2006). Cortical Pain Responses in Human Infants. *Journal of Neuroscience, 26*(14), 3662–3666.

Slaughter, D. T. (1980). Social policy issues affecting infants. In B. Weissbourd & J. Musick (Eds.), *Infants: Their social environments* (pp. 150–178). Chicago: National Association for the Education of Young Children.

Slaughter, V., Peterson, C. C., & Carpenter, M. (2008). Maternal talk about mental states and the emergence of joint visual attention. *Infancy, 13*(6), 640-659. doi:10.1080/15250000802458807

Slobin, D. (1970). Universals of grammatical development in children. In G. B. Flores d'Arcais & W. J. M. Levelt (Eds.), *Advances in psycholinguistics* (pp. 12–38). Amsterdam: North-Holland.

Smidt-Jensen, S., & Hahnemann, N. (1988). Transabdominal chorionic villus sampling for fetal genetic diagnosis: Technical and obstetrical evaluation of 100 cases. *Prenatal Diagnosis, 8,* 7–17.

Smigel, K. L. (1988). Breast-feeding linked to decreased cancer risk for mother, child. *Journal of the National Cancer Institute, 80,* 1362–1363.

Smith, P. B., & Pederson, D. R. (1988). Maternal sensitivity and patterns of infant-mother attachment. *Child Development, 59,* 1097–1101.

Smith, R. (1999, March). The timing of birth. *Scientific American, 280*(3), 68–75.

Smith, S. L., Gerhardt, K. J., Griffiths, S. K., Huang, X., & Abrams, R. M. (2003). Intelligibility of Sentences Recorded from the Uterus of a Pregnant Ewe and from the Fetal Inner Ear. *Audiology & Neurotology, 8*(6), 347–353.

Smitsman, A. W., Dejonckheere, P. N., & De Wit, T. J. (2009). The significance of event information for 6- to 16-month-old infants' perception of containment. *Developmental Psychology, 45*(1), 207-223. doi:10.1037/a0014034

Smotherman, W. P., & Robinson, S. R. (1987). Prenatal expression of species-typical action patterns in the rat fetus. *Journal of Comparative Psychology, 101*(2), 190–196.

Smyke, A. T., Zeanah, C. H., Fox, N. A., Nelson, C. A., & Guthrie, D. (2010). Placement in foster care enhances quality of attachment among young institutionalized children. *Child Development, 81*(1), 212-223.

Snow, M. E., Jacklin, C. N., & Maccoby, E. E. (1981). Birth-order differences in peer sociability at thirty-three months. *Child Development, 52,* 589–595.

Soderstrom, M., & Morgan, J. L. (2007). Twenty-two-month-olds discriminate fluent from disfluent adult-directed speech. *Developmental Science, 10*(5), 641–653.

Sodian, B., Thoermer, C., & Metz, U. (2007). Now I see it but you don't: 14–month-olds can represent another person's visual perspective. *Developmental Science, 10*(2), 199–204.

Sogaard, A. J., Kritz-Silverstein, D., & Wingard, D. L. (1994). Finnmark heart study: Employment status and parenthood as predictors of psychological health in women, 20–49 years. *International Journal of Epidemiology, 23,* 82–90.

Soken, N. H., & Pick, A. D. (1992). Intermodal perception of happy and angry expressive behaviors by seven-month-old infants. *Child Development, 63,* 787–795.

Soken, N. H., & Pick, A. D. (1999). Infants' perception of dynamic affective expressions: Do infants distinguish specific expressions? *Child Development, 70*(6), 1275–1282.

Sokolov, J. L. (1993). A local contingency analysis of the fine-tuning hypothesis. *Developmental Psychology, 29,* 1008–1023.

Solarz, A. (2001). Investing in Children, Families, and Communities: Challenges for an Interdivisional Public Policy. *American Journal of Community Psychology, 29*(1), 1.

Soley, G., & Hannon, E. E. (2010). Infants prefer the musical meter of their own culture: A cross-cultural comparison. *Developmental Psychology, 46*(1), 286-292

Soliday, E. (2007). Infant feeding and cognition: Integrating a developmental perspective. *Child Development Perspectives, 1*(1), 19–25.

Sollie, D., & Miller, B. (1980). The transition to parenthood as a critical time for building family strengths. In N. Stinnet & P. Knaub (Eds.), *Family strengths: Positive models of family life* (pp. 19–36). Lincoln: University of Nebraska Press.

Solmeyer, A., & Feinberg, M. (2011). Mother and father adjustment during early parenthood: the roles of infant temperament and coparenting relationship quality. *Infant Behavior & Development, 34*(4), 504-514. doi:10.1016/j.infbeh.2011.07.006

Solter, A. (2008). A 2-year-old child's memory of hospitalization during early infancy. *Infant and Child Development, 17,* 593-605.

Sommerville, J. A., Hildebrand, E. A., & Crane, C. C. (2008). Experience matters: The impact of doing versus watching on infants' subsequent perception of tool-use events. *Developmental Psychology, 44*(5), 1249-1256. doi:10.1037/a0012296

Søndergaard, C., Henriksen, T. B., Obel, C., & Wisborg, K. (2001). Smoking during pregnancy and infantile colic. *Pediatrics, 108,* 342–346.

Sorce, J., Emde, R., Campos, J., & Klinnert, M. (1985). Maternal emotional signaling: Its effect on the visual cliff behavior of 1–year-olds. *Developmental Psychology, 21,* 195–200.

Sorenson, E. R. (1979). Early tactile communication and the patterning of human organization: A New Guinea case study. In M. Bullowa (Ed.), *Before speech* (pp. 217–229). New York: Cambridge University Press.

Soska, K. C., & Johnson, S. P. (2013). Development of three-dimensional completion of complex objects. *Infancy, 18*(3), 325-344. doi:10.1111/j.1532-7078.2012.00127.x

Sostek, A. M., Smith, Y. F., Katz, K. S., & Grant, E. G. (1987). Developmental outcome of preterm infants with intraventricular hemorrhage at one and two years of age. *Child Development, 58,* 779–786.

Southgate, V., & Csibra, G. (2009). Inferring the outcome of an ongoing novel action at 13 months. *Developmental Psychology, 45*(6), 1794-1798.

Spangler, G., & Grossmann, K. E. (1993). Biobehavioral organization in securely and insecurely attached infants. *Child Development, 64,* 1439–1450.

Spanier, A. (2011, May 1). Chemical in plastic, BPA, exposure may be associated with wheezing in children. *ScienceDaily,*

Retrieved April 24, 2012, from http://www.sciencedaily.com/releases/2011/05/110501183817.htm.

Spemann, H. (1938). *Embryonic development and induction.* New Haven, CT: Yale University Press.

Spence, M. J., & Freeman, M. S. (1996). Newborn infants prefer the maternal low-pass filtered voice, but not the maternal whispered voice. *Infant Behavior and Development, 19,* 199–212.

Spence, S. H., Najman, J. M., Bor, W., O'Callaghan, M., & Williams, G. M. (2002). Maternal anxiety and depression, poverty and marital relationship factors during early childhood as predictors of anxiety and depressive symptoms in adolescence. *Journal of Child Psychology and Psychiatry, 43*(4), 457–470.

Speraw, S. R. (1994). The experience of miscarriage: How couples define quality in health care delivery. *Journal of Perinatology, 14,* 208–215.

Spieker, S. J., & Bensley L. (1994). Roles of living arrangements and grandmother social support in adolescent mothering and infant attachment. *Developmental Psychology, 30,* 102–111.

Spiker, D., Ferguson, J., & Brooks-Gunn, J. (1993). Enhancing maternal interactive behavior and child social competence in low birth weight, premature infants. *Child Development, 64,* 754–768.

Spinelli, M. (2012). Antidepressant treatment during pregnancy. *The American Journal of Psychiatry,169,* 121-124.

Spinillo, A., Iasci, A., Dal-Maso, J., Di-Lenardo, L., Grella, P., & Guaschino, S. (1994). The effect of fetal infection with human immunodeficiency virus type 1 on birthweight and length of gestation. *European Journal of Obstetrics and Gynecology, 57,* 13–17.

Spinrad, T. L., Eisenberg, N., Gaertner, B., Popp, T., Smith, C. L., Kupfer, A., et al. (2007). Relations of maternal socialization and toddlers' effortful control to children's adjustment and social competence. *Developmental Psychology, 43*(5), 1170–1186.

Spinrad, T. L., Stifter, C. A., Donelan-McCall, N., & Turner, L. (2004). Mothers' regulation strategies in response to toddlers' affect: Links to later emotion self-regulation. *Social Development, 13*(1), 40–55.

Spitz, H. H. (1992). Does the Carolina Abecedarian early intervention project prevent sociocultural mental retardation? *Intelligence, 16,* 225.

Spitz, R. (1965). *The first year of life.* New York: International Universities Press.

Sprengelmeyer, R. R., Perrett, D. I., Fagan, E. C., Cornwell, R. E., Lobmaier, J. S., Sprengelmeyer, A. A., & ... Young, A. W. (2009). The cutest little baby face: A hormonal link to sensitivity to cuteness in infant faces. *Psychological Science, 20*(2), 149-154.

Sroufe, L. A. (1979). Socioemotional development. In J. Osofsky (Ed.), *Handbook of infant development* (pp. 462–516). New York: Wiley.

Sroufe, L. A. (1983). Individual patterns of adaptation from infancy to preschool. In M. Perlmutter (Ed.), *Minnesota symposia on child psychology* (Vol. 16, pp. 165–182). Hillsdale, NJ: Lawrence Erlbaum.

Sroufe, L. A. (1989). Relationships, self, and individual adaptation. In A. J. Sameroff and R. N. Emde (Eds.), *Relationships disturbances in early childhood: A developmental approach* (pp. 70–94). New York: Basic Books.

Sroufe, L. A. (1995). *Emotional development: The organization of emotional life in the early years.* Cambridge, England: Cambridge University Press.

Sroufe, L. A., Coffino, B., & Carlson, E. A. (2010). Conceptualizing the role of early experience: Lessons from the Minnesota Longitudinal Study. *Developmental Review, 30*(1), 36-51.

Sroufe, L. A., & Waters, E. (1976). The ontogenesis of smiling and laughter: A perspective on the organization of development in infancy. *Psychological Review, 83,* 173–186.

Sroufe, L. A., & Wunsch, J. P. (1977). The development of laughter in the first year of life. *Child Development, 43,* 1326–1344.

Stack, D. M. (2000). The salience of touch and physical contact during infancy: Unravelling some of the mysteries of the somaesthetic sense. In J. G. Bremner & A. Fogel (Eds.), *Handbook of infancy research* (pp. 268–292). Oxford, England: Blackwell.

Stack, D. M., & Arnold, S. L. (1998). Changes in mothers' touch and hand gestures influence infant behavior during face-to-face interchanges. *Infant Behavior and Development, 21*(3), 451–468.

Stack, D. M., & LePage, D. E. (1996). Infants' sensitivity to manipulations of maternal touch during face-to-face interactions. *Social Development, 5*(1), 41–55.

Stack, D. M., & Muir, D. W. (1992). Adult tactile stimulation during face-to-face interactions modulates five-month-olds' affect and attention. *Child Development, 63,* 1509–1525.

Stacks, A., Oshio, T., Gerard, J., & Roe, J. (2009). The moderating effect of parental warmth on the association between spanking and child aggression: A longitudinal approach. *Infant And Child Development, 18*(2), 178-194

Stanton, A. N., Scott, D. J., & Downhan, M. A. (1980). Is overheating a factor in some unexpected infant deaths? *Lancet, 78*(5), 1054–1057.

Stark, R. E. (1978). Features of infant sounds: The emergence of cooing. Journal of *Child Language, 3,* 379–390.

Stark, R. E., Rose, S. N., & McLagen, M. (1975). Features of infant sounds: The first eight weeks of life. *Journal of Child Language, 2,* 205–222.

Starkey, D. (1981). The origins of concept formation: Object sorting and object preference in early infancy. *Child Development, 52,* 489–497.

Stattin, H., & Klackenberg-Larsson, I. (1991). The short- and long-term implications for parent-child relations of parents' prenatal preferences for their child's gender. *Developmental Psychology, 27*(1), 141–147.

Stayton, D. J., Ainsworth, M. D. S., & Main, M. B. (1973). The development of separation behavior in the first year of life: Protest, following, greeting. *Developmental Psychology, 9,* 213–225.

Steele, H., & Siever, L. (2010). An attachment perspective on borderline personality disorder: Advances in gene–environment considerations. Current psychiatry reports, 12(1), 61-67.

Steele, H., & Steele, M. (2008). On the origins of reflective functioning. *Mentalization: Theoretical considerations, research findings, and clinical implications*, 133-156.

Steele, H., Steele, M., Croft, C., & Fonagy, P. (1999). Infant-mother attachment at one year predicts children's understanding of mixed emotions at six years. *Social Development, 8*(2), 161–178.

Steele, H., Steele, M., & Fonagy, P. (1996). Associations among attachment classifications of mothers, fathers, and their infants. *Child Development, 67,* 523–540.

Steele, M., Murphy, A., & Steele, H. (2010). Identifying therapeutic action in an attachment-centered intervention with high risk families. *Clinical Social Work Journal, 38*(1), 61-72.

Stein, A., Cambell, E. A., Day, A., McPherson, K., & Cooper, P. J. (1987). Social adversity, low birth weight, and preterm delivery. *British Medical Journal, 295,* 291–293.

Steiner, J. E. (1973). The gustofacial response: Observation on normal and anencephalic newborn infants. In J. F. Bosma (Ed.), *Fourth symposium on oral sensation and perception.* (DHEW Publication No. NIH 73–546) (pp. 15–28). Bethesda, MD: Department of Health, Education, and Welfare.

Steiner, J. E. (1977). Facial expressions of the neonate infant indicating the hedonics of food-related chemical stimuli. In J. M. Weiffenbach (Ed.), *Taste and development* (pp. 204–219). Bethesda, MD: Department of Health, Education, and Welfare.

Stella-Prorok, E. M. (1983). Mother-child language in the natural environment. In K. E. Nelson (Ed.), *Children's language* (pp. 389–407). Hillsdale, NJ: Erlbaum.

Stenberg, C., Campos, J. J., & Emde, R. N. (1983). The facial expression of anger in seven-month-old infants. *Child Development, 54,* 178–184.

Stenberg, G. (2013). Do 12-month-old infants trust a competent adult? *Infancy, 18*(5), 873-904. doi: 10.1111/infa.12011

Stenberg, G., & Hagekull, B. (1997). Social referencing and mood modification in 1–year-olds. *Infant Behavior and Development, 20,* 209–217.

Sterman, M. B., & Hoppenbrouwers, T. (1971). The development of sleep-waking and rest-activity patterns from fetus to adult in man. In M. B. Sterman, D. J. McGinty, & A. M. Adinolfi (Eds.), *Brain development and behavior* (pp. 203–228). New York: Academic Press.

Stern, D. N. (1985). *The interpersonal world of the infant: A view from psychoanalysis and developmental psychology.* New York: Basic Books.

Stern, D. N. (1995). *The motherhood constellation.* New York: Basic Books.

Stern, D. N., Jaffe, J., Beebe, B., & Bennett, S. J. (1975). Vocalizing in unison and in alternation: Two modes of communication within the mother-infant dyad. *Annals of the New York Academy of Science, 263,* 89–100.

Stern, D. N., Spieker, S., Barnett, R. K., & MacKain, K. (1983). The prosody of maternal speech: Infant age and context related changes. *Journal of Child Language, 10,* 1–15.

Sternberg, R. J., & Davidson, J. E. (1985). Cognitive development in the gifted and talented. In F. D. Horowitz & M. O'Brien (Eds.), *The gifted and talented: Developmental perspectives* (pp. 37–74). Washington, DC: American Psychological Association.

Stettler, N., Stallings, V. A., Troxel, A. B., Zhao, J., Schinnar, R., Nelson, S. E., et al. (2005). Weight gain in the first week of life and overweight in adulthood: a cohort study of European American subjects fed infant formula. *Circulation, 111*(15), 1897–1903.

Stevens, B., Johnston, C., Franck, L., Petryshen, P., Jack, A., & Foster, G. (1999). The efficacy of developmentally sensitive interventions and sucrose for relieving procedural pain in very low birth weight neonates. *Nursing Research, 48,* 35–43.

Stevens, J. H. (1984). Black grandmothers' & black adolescent mothers' knowledge about parenting. *Developmental Psychology, 20,* 1017–1025.

Stevenson, M. R., & Black, K. N. (1988). Paternal absence and sex-role development: A meta-analysis. *Child Development, 59,* 793–814.

Stewart, A. (1983). Severe perinatal hazards. In M. Rutter (Ed.), *Developmental neuropsychiatry* (pp. 117–132). New York: Churchill Livingstone.

Stewart, D. E. (1994). Incidence of postpartum abuse in women with a history of abuse during pregnancy. *Canadian Medical Association Journal, 151,* 1601–1604.

Stewart, R. A. (1981). Supplementary foods: Their nutritional role in infant feedings. In J. Bond, L. Filer, G. LeVeille, A. Thomson, & W. Weil (Eds.), *Infant and child feeding* (pp. 101–128). New York: Academic Press.

Stewart, R. A. (1983). Sibling interaction: The role of the older child as teacher for the younger. *Merrill-Palmer Quarterly, 29,* 47–68.

Stewart, R. A., Mobley, L. A., Van Tuyl, S. S., & Salvador, M. A. (1987). The firstborn's adjustment to the birth of a sibling: A longitudinal assessment. *Child Development, 58,* 341–355.

Stiefel, G. S., Plunkett, J. W., & Meisels, S. J. (1987). Affective expression among preterm infants of varying levels of biological risk. *Infant Behavior and Development, 10,* 151–164.

Stifter, C. A., Bono, M., & Spinrad, T. (2003). Parent characteristics and conceptualizations associated with the emergence of infant colic. *Journal of Reproductive and Infant Psychology, 21*(4), 309–322.

Stifter, C. A., Coulehan, C. M., & Fish, M. (1993). Linking employment to attachment: The mediating effects of maternal separation anxiety and interactive behavior. *Child Development, 64,* 1451–1460.

Stifter, C. A., Fox, N. A., & Porges, S. W. (1989). Facial expressivity and vagal tone in 5– and 10–month-old infants. *Infant Behavior and Development, 12,* 127–137.

Stifter, C. A., & Moyer, D. (1991). The regulation of positive affect: Gaze aversion activity during mother-infant interaction. *Infant Behavior and Development, 14,* 111–123.

Stiles, J. (1995). The early use and development of graphic formulas: Two case study reports of graphic formula production by 2–to-3-year-old children. *International Journal of Behavioral Development, 18*(1), 127–149.

Stiles, J., & Jernigan, T. L. (2010) The basics of brain development. *Neuropsychology Review,20,* 327-348.

Stillbirth Collaborative Research Network Writing Group (2011). Causes of death among stillbirths. *The Journal Of The American Medical Association, 306,* 2459-2468.

Stipek, D. (1995). The development of pride and shame in toddlers. In J. P. Tangney & K. W. Fischer (Eds.), *Self-conscious emotions: The psychology of shame, guilt, embarrassment, and pride* (pp. 237–252). New York: Guilford Press.

St. James-Roberts, I., Conroy, S., & Wilsher, K. (1998). Links between maternal care and persistent infant crying in the early months. *Child Care, Health, and Development, 24*(5), 353–376.

St James-Roberts, I., Goodwin, J., Peter, B., Adams, D., & Hunt, S. (2003). Individual differences in responsivity to a neurobehavioural examination predict crying patterns of 1–week-old infants at home. *Dev Med Child Neurol, 45*(6), 400–407.

St. James-Roberts, I., & Plewis, I. (1996). Individual differences, daily fluctuations, and developmental changes in amounts of infant waking, fussing, crying, feeding, and sleeping. Child Development, 67(5), 2527–2540.

St James-Roberts, I., Sleep, J., Morris, S., Owen, C., & Gillham, P. (2001). Use of a behavioural programme in the first 3 months to prevent infant crying and sleeping problems. *J Paediatr Child Health, 37*(3), 289–297.

Stockman, I. J., & Vaughn-Cooke, F. (1992). Lexical elaboration in children's locative action expressions. *Child Development, 63,* 1104–1125.

Stone, L. J., Smith, H., & Murphy, L. (1973). *The competent infant.* New York: Basic Books.

Stone, S., & Porter, C. (2013). "Be still my beating heart": linkages between mother-infant co-regulation and brief bradycardia at the onset of arm-restraint in 6-month-old infants. *Infant Behavior & Development, 36*(2), 228-237

Stone, W. L., Lemanek, K. L., Fishel, P. T., Fernandez, M. C., & Altemeier, W. A. (1990). Play and imitation skills in the diagnosis of autism in young children. *Pediatrics, 86,* 267–272.

Stoneman, Z., Brody, G. H., & MacKinnon, C. (1984). Naturalistic observations of children's activities and roles while playing with their siblings and friends. *Child Development, 55,* 617–627.

Strain, P. S., & Bovey, E. H. (2011). Randomized, Controlled Trial of the LEAP Model of Early Intervention for Young Children with Autism Spectrum Disorders. *Topics In Early Childhood Special Education, 31*(3), 133-154.

Strassberg, Z., & Treboux, D. (2000). Interpretations of child emotion expressions and coercive parenting practices among adolescent mothers. *Social Development, 9*(1), 80–95.

Strathearn, L., Li, J., Fonagy, P., & Montague, P. (2008). What's in a smile? Maternal brain responses to infant facial cues [corrected] [published erratum appears in Pediatrics 2008 Sep;122(3):689]. *Pediatrics, 122*(1), 40-51.

Straus, M. A. (1995). *Beating the devil out of them: Corporal punishment in American families.* New York: Lexington Books.

Straus, M. A., & Kantor, G. K. (2005). Definition and measurement of neglectful behavior: Some principles and guidelines. *Child Abuse & Neglect, 29*(1), 19–29.

Strauss, A., & Corbin, J. (1990). *Basics of qualitative research: Grounded theory procedures and techniques.* Newbury Park, CA: Sage.

Strauss, M. S., & Curtis, L. E. (1981). Infant's perception of numerosity. *Child Development, 52,* 1146–1152.

Street, S. Y., James, K. H., Jones, S. S., & Smith, L. B. (2011). Vision for Action in Toddlers: The Posting Task. *Child Development, 82*(6-), 2083-2094.

Streissguth, A. P., Barr, H. M., Sampson, P. D., & Bookstein, F. L. (1994). Prenatal alcohol and offspring development: The first fourteen years. *Drug and Alcohol Dependency, 36,* 89–99.

Striano, T. (2004). Direction of Regard and the Still-Face Effect in the First Year: Does Intention Matter? *Child Development, 75*(2), 468–479.

Striano, T., Henning, A., & Stahl, D. (2005). Sensitivity to social contingencies between 1 and 3 months of age. *Developmental Science, 8*(6), 509–518.

Striano, T., & Rochat, P. (1999). Developmental link between dyadic and triadic social competence in infancy. *British Journal of Developmental Psychology, 17,* 1–12.

Striano, T., & Rochat, P. (in press). Emergence of selective social referencing in infancy. *Infancy.*

Stright, A., Gallagher, K. C., & Kelley, K. (2008). Infant temperament moderates relations between maternal parenting in early childhood and children's adjustment in first grade. *Child Development, 79,* 186-200.

Strobino, B. A., & Pantel-Silverman, J. (1987). First-trimester vaginal bleeding and the loss of chromosomally normal and abnormal conceptions. *American Journal of Obstetrics and Gynecology, 157,* 1150–1154.

Stroufe, L. A., Egeland, B., Carlson, E. A., & Collins, W. A. (2005). *The development of the person: The Minnesota study of risk and adaptation from birth to adulthood.* New York: The Guilford Press.

Stuchbery, M., Matthey, S., & Barnett, B. (1998). Postnatal depression and social supports in Vietnamese, Arabic, and Anglo-Celtic mothers. *Social Psychiatry and Psychiatric Epidemiology, 33*(10), 483–490.

Stupica, B., Sherman, L. J., & Cassidy, J. (2011). Newborn Irritability Moderates the Association Between Infant Attachment Security and Toddler Exploration and Sociability. *Child Development, 82*(5), 1381-1389

Suanda, S. H., & Namy, L. L. (2013). The organization of words and symbolic gestures in 18-month-olds' lexicons: Evidence from a disambiguation task. *Infancy, 18*(2), 276-288. doi:10.1111/j.1532-7078.2012.00131.x

Sullivan, M. W., Rovee-Collier, C. K., & Tynes, D. M. (1979). A conditioning analysis of infant longterm memory. *Child Development, 50,* 152–162.

Sun, L. C., & Roopnarine, J. L. (1996). Mother-infant, father-infant and involvement in childcare and household labor among Taiwanese families. *Infant Behavior and Development, 19,* 121–129.

Suomi, S. J. (1987). Genetic and maternal contributions to individual differences in rhesus monkey biobehavioral development. In N. A. Krasnegor, E. M. Blass, M. A. Hofer, & W. P. Smotherman (Eds.), *Perinatal development: A psychobiological perspective* (pp. 397–420). New York: Academic Press.

Suomi, S. J., & Harlow, H. F. (1972). Social rehabilitation of isolate reared monkeys. *Developmental Psychology, 6,* 487–496.

Super, C. (1976). Environmental effects on motor development: The case of "African infant precocity." *Developmental Medicine and Child Neurology, 18,* 561–567.

Super, C. (1981). Behavioral development in infancy. In R. Munroe & B. Whiting (Eds.), *Handbook of cross-cultural human development* (pp. 95–128). New York: Garland.

Super, C., Herrera, M. G., & Mora, J. O. (1990). Long-term effects of food supplementation and psychosocial intervention on the physical growth of Colombian infants at risk of malnutrition. *Child Development, 61,* 29–49.

Surkan, P. J., Hsieh, C. C., Johansson, A. L., Dickman, P. W., & Cnattingius, S. (2004). Reasons for increasing trends in large for gestational age births. *Obstet Gynecol, 104*(4), 720–726.

Surkan, P., Kennedy, C., Hurley, K., & Black, M. (2011). Maternal depression and early childhood growth in developing countries: systematic review and meta-analysis. *Bulletin Of The World Health Organization, 89*(8), 608-615. doi:10.2471/BLT.11.088187

Susman-Stillman, A., Kalkoske, M., Egeland, B., & Waldman, I. (1996). Infant temperament and maternal sensitivity as predictors of attachment security. *Infant Behavior and Development, 19,* 33–47.

Suwalsky, J. T., & Klein, R. P. (1980). Effects of naturally occurring nontraumatic separations from mother. *Infant Mental Health Journal, 1,* 196–201.

Svetlova, M., Nichols, S. R., & Brownell, C. A. (2010). Toddlers prosocial behavior: From instrumental to empathic to altruistic helping. *Child Development, 81*(6), 1814-1827. doi:10.1111/j.1467-8624.2010.01512.x

Swain, I. U., Zelazo, P. R., & Clifton, R. K. (1993). Newborn infants' memory for speech sounds retained over 24 hours. *Developmental Psychology, 29,* 312–323.

Swan, A. M. (1993). Helping children who stutter: What teachers need to know. *Childhood Education, 69,* 138–141.

Swingley, D. (2007). Lexical Exposure and Word-Form Encoding in 1.5–Year-Olds. *Developmental Psychology, 43*(2), 454–464.

Swoboda, P. J., Kass, J., Morse, P. A., & Leavitt, L. A. (1978). Memory factors in vowel discrimination of normal and at-risk infants. *Child Development, 49,* 332–339.

Sydsjö, G., Sydsjö, A., Gunnervik, C., Bladh, M., & Josefsson, A. (2012). Obstetric outcome for women who received individualized treatment for fear of childbirth during pregnancy. *Acta Obstetricia Et Gynecologica Scandinavica, 91,* 44-49.

Symons, D. K., & McLeod, P. J. (1994). Maternal, infant, and occupational characteristics that predict postpartum employment patterns. *Infant Behavior and Development, 17,* 71–82.

Szyf, M. (2007). The dynamic epigenome and its implications in toxicology. *Toxicol Sci, 100*(1), 7–23.

Szyf, M. & Bick, J. (2013). DNA methylation: A mechanism for embedding early life experiences in the genome. [Special issue: genomics]. Child Development, *84,*49-57.

Takahashi, K. (1986). Examining the strange-situation procedure with Japanese mothers and 12–month-old infants. *Developmental Psychology, 22,* 265–270.

Tallandini, M. A., & Scalembra, C. (2006). Kangaroo Mother Care and Mother-Premature Infant Dyadic Interaction. *Infant Mental Health Journal, 27*(3), 251–275.

Tamis-LeMonda, C. S., Adolph, K. E., Lobo, S. A., Karasik, L. B., Ishak, S., & Dimitropoulou, K. A. (2008). When infants take mothers' advice: 18-month-olds integrate perceptual and social information to guide motor action. *Developmental Psychology, 44*(3), 734-746. doi:10.1037/0012-1649.44.3.734

Tamis-LeMonda, C. S., & Bornstein, M. H. (1989). Habituation and maternal encouragement of attention in infancy as predictors of toddler language, play, and representational competence. *Child Development, 60,* 738–751.

Tamis-LeMonda, C. S., & Bornstein, M. H. (1990). Language, play, and attention at one year. *Infant Behavior and Development, 13,* 85–98.

Tamis-LeMonda, C. S., Bornstein, M. H., Baumwell, L., & Damast, A. M. (1996). Responsive parenting in the second year: Specific influences on children's language and play. *Early Development and Parenting, 5*(4), 173–183.

Tamis-LeMonda, C. S., Bornstein, M. H., Cyphers, L., Toda, S., & Ogino, M. (1992). Language and play at one year: A comparison of toddlers and mothers in the United States and Japan. *International Journal of Behavioral Development, 15,* 19–42.

Tan, L. E. (1985). Laterality and motor-skills in four-year-olds. *Child Development, 56,* 119–124.

Tanner, J. M. (1970). Physical growth. In P. H. Mussen (Ed.), *Manual of child psychology* (3rd ed., pp. 77–156). New York: Wiley.

Tardif, T. (1996). Nouns are not always learned before verbs: Evidence from Mandarin speakers' early vocabularies. *Developmental Psychology, 32*(3), 492–504.

Tardif, T., Gelman, S. A., & Xu, F. (1999). Putting the "noun bias" in context: A comparison of English and Mandarin. *Child Development, 70*(3), 620–635.

Tardif, T., & Wellman, H. M. (2000). Acquisition of mental state language in Mandarin- and Cantonese-speaking children. *Developmental Psychology, 36*(1), 25–43.

Tardif, T., Fletcher, P., Liang, W., Zhang, Z., Kaciroti, N., & Marchman, V. A. (2008). Baby's first 10 words. *Developmental Psychology, 44*(4), 929-938.

Taumoepeau, M., & Ruffman, T. (2006). Mother and Infant Talk About Mental States Relates to Desire Language and Emotion Understanding. *Child Development, 77*(2), 465–481.

Taumoepeau, M., & Ruffman, T. (2008). Stepping stones to others' minds: Maternal talk relates to child mental state language and emotion understanding at 15, 24, and 33

months. *Child Development, 79*(2), 284-302. doi:10.1111/j.1467-8624.2007.01126.x

Taylor, H., Baker, D., ALSPAC and the Study Team. (1997). Employment, parity, and single parenthood: Their impact on health in pregnancy. *Journal of Reproductive and Infant Psychology, 15,* 221–237.

Taylor, S. D. (1994). Demand for predictive genetic testing for Huntington's disease in Australia, 1987 to 1993. *Medical Journal of Australia, 161,* 351–355.

Technical Bulletin Number 189 (1994). Exercise during pregnancy and the postpartum period. *International Journal Gynecology and Obstetrics, 45,* 65–70.

Teitelbaum, P., Teitelbaum, O., Nye, J., Fryman, J., & Maurer, R. G. (1998). Movement analysis in infancy may be useful for early diagnosis of autism. *Proceedings of the National Academy of Sciences of the United States of America, 95,* 13982–13987.

Teitler, J. O. (2001). Father involvement, child health and maternal health behavior. *Children and Youth Services Review, 23*(4–5), 403–425.

Termine, N. T., & Izard, C. E. (1988). Infants' responses to their mothers' expressions of joy and sadness. *Developmental Psychology, 24,* 223–229.

Terr, L. (1994). *Unchained memories.* New York: Basic Books.

Tessier, R., Nadeau, L., Boivin, M., & Tremblay, R. E. (1997). The social behavior of 11– to 12–year-old children born as low birthweight and/or premature infants. *International Journal of Behavioral Development, 21*(4), 795–811.

Tessier, R., Tarabulsy, G. M., Larin, S., Josee, L., Gagon, M.-F., & Johanne, T. (2002). A home-based description of attachment in physically disabled infants. *Social Development, 11*(2), 147–165.

Teti, D. M., & Ablard, K. E. (1989). Security of attachment and infant-sibling relationships: A laboratory study. *Child Development, 60,* 1519–1528.

Teti, D. M., Bond, L. A., & Gibbs, E. D. (1988). Mothers, fathers, and siblings: A comparison of play styles and influence upon infant cognitive level. *International Journal of Behavioral Development, 11,* 415–432.

Teti, D. M., & Gelfand, D. M. (1991). Behavioral competence among mothers of infants in the first year: The mediational role of maternal self-efficacy. *Child Development, 62,* 918–929.

Teti, D. M., Gelfand, D. M., Messinger, D. S., & Isabella, R. (1995). Maternal depression and the quality of early attachment: An examination of infants, preschoolers, and their mothers. *Developmental Psychology, 31,* 364–376.

Teti, D. M., & Lamb, M. E. (1989). Socioeconomic and marital outcomes of adolescent marriage, adolescent childbirth, and their co-occurrence. *Journal of Marriage and the Family, 51,* 203–212.

Teti, D. M., Nakagawa, R. D., & Wirth, O. (1991). Security of attachment between preschoolers and their mothers:

Relations among social interaction, parenting stress, and mothers' sorts of the attachment Q-set. *Developmental Psychology, 27,* 440–447.

Teti, D. M., O'Connell, M. A., & Reiner, C. D. (1996). Parenting sensitivity, parental depression and child health: The mediational role of parental self-efficacy. *Early Development and Parenting, 5*(4), 237–250.

Tharapel, A. T., Tharapel, S. A., & Bannerman, R. M. (1985). Recurrent pregnancy losses and parental chromosome abnormalities: A review. *British Journal of Obstetrics and Gynecology, 92,* 899–914.

Thelen, E. (1989). The (re)discovery of motor development: Learning new things from an old field. *Developmental Psychology, 25,* 946–949.

Thelen, E. (1990). Dynamical systems and the generation of individual differences. In J. Colombo & J. Fagen (Eds.), *Individual differences in infancy: Reliability, stability, prediction* (pp. 19–43). Hillsdale, NJ: Erlbaum.

Thelen, E., Bradshaw, G., & Ward, J. A. (1981). Spontaneous kicking in month-old infants: Manifestation of a human central locomotor program. *Behavioral and Neural Biology, 32,* 45–53.

Thelen, E., & Fogel, A. (1989). Toward an action-based theory of infant development. In J. Lockman & N. Hazen (Eds.), *Action in social context: Perspectives on early development* (pp. 23–64). New York: Plenum Press.

Thelen, E., Skala, K. D., & Kelso, J. A. (1987). The dynamic nature of early coordination: Evidence from bilateral leg movements in young infants. *Developmental Psychology, 23,* 179–186.

Thelen, E., & Smith, L. B. (Eds.) (1994). *A dynamic systems approach to the development of cognition and action.* Cambridge, MA: MIT Press.

Thelen, E., & Ulrich, B. D. (1991). Hidden skills. *Monographs of the Society for Research in Child Development, 56,* 1–106.

Thérien, J-P. (2012). The United Nations and human development: From ideology to global policies. *Global Policy, 3*(1), 1-12.

The Urban Institute. (2000, March). *Child care arrangements for children under five: Variation across states* (Series B, No. B-7, New Federalism: National Survey of America's Families). Washington, DC: J. Capizzano, G. Adams, & R. Sonenstein.

Thiessen, E. D., & Yee, M. N. (2010). Dogs, bogs, labs, and lads: What phonemic generalizations indicate about the nature of children's early word-form representations. *Child Development, 81*(4), 1287-1303. doi:10.1111/j.1467-8624.2010.01468.x

Thigpen, B. (2007). Outdoor play: Combating sedentary lifestyles. *Zero to Three, 28*(1), 19–23.

Thike, K. B., Wai, K. T., Oo, N., & Yi, K. H. (1993). Contraceptive practice before female sterilization. *Asia Oceania Journal of Obstetrics and Gynecology, 19,* 241–248.

Thoman, E. B. (1993). Obligation and option in the premature nursery. *Developmental Review, 13,* 1–30.

Thoman, E. B., Acebo, C., Dreyer, C. A., Becker, P. T., & Freese, M. P. (1979). Individuality in the interactive process. In E. B. Thomas (Ed.), *Origins of the infant's social responsiveness* (pp. 305–338). Hillsdale, NJ: Erlbaum.

Thoman, E. B., Leiderman, P. H., & Olson, J. P. (1972). Neonate-mother interactions during breast feeding. *Developmental Psychology, 6,* 110–118.

Thomas, A., & Chess, S. (1977). *Temperament and development.* New York: Brunner/Mazel.

Thomas, R., & Zimmer-Gembeck, M. J. (2011). Accumulating evidence for parent-child interaction therapy in the prevention of child maltreatment. *Child Development, 82*(1), 177-192.

Thompson, C. (1995). Umbilical cords: Turning garbage into clinical gold. *Science, 268,* 805–806.

Thompson, L. M., Murphy, P., O'Hara, J., & Wallymahmed, A. (1997). Levels of daily hassles and uplifts in employed and non-employed pregnant women. *Journal of Reproductive and Infant Psychology, 15,* 271–280.

Thompson, R. A. (1998). Empathy and its origins in early development. In S. Br;araten (Ed.), *Intersubjective communication and emotion in early ontogeny. Studies in emotion and social interaction, 2nd series* (pp. 144–157). Cambridge, England: Cambridge University Press.

Thompson, R. A., Connell, J. P., & Bridges, L. J. (1988). Temperament, emotion, and social interactive behavior in the strange situation: A component process analysis of attachment system functioning. *Child Development, 59,* 1102–1110.

Thompson, R. A., & Lamb, M. E. (1982). Stranger sociability and its relationships to temperament and social experiences during the second year. *Infant Behavior and Development, 5,* 277–287.

Thompson, R. A., Lewis, M. D., & Calkins, S. D. (2008). Reassessing emotion regulation. *Child Development Perspectives, 2*(3), 124-131. doi:10.1111/j.1750-8606.2008.00054.x

Thompson, R. A., & Newton, E. K. (2013). Baby altruists? Examining the complexity of prosocial motivation in young children. *Infancy, 18*(1), 120-133. doi:10.1111/j.1532-7078.2012.00139.x

Thorpe, K. J., Dragonas, T., & Golding, J. (1992). The effects of psychosocial factors on the mother's emotional well-being during early parenthood: A cross-cultural study of Britain and Greece. *Journal of Reproductive and Infant Psychology, 10,* 205–217.

Thorpe, L. A. & Trehub, S. E. (1989). Duration illusion and auditory grouping in infancy. *Developmental Psychology, 25,* 122–127.

Thurin, A., Hausken, J., Hillensji, T., Jablonowska, B., Pinborg, A., Strandell, A., et al. (2004). Elective single-embryo transfer versus double-embryo transfer in in vitro fertilization. *New England Journal of Medicine, 351*(23), 2392–2402.

Tian, Y., & Kanade, T. (2001, February). Recognizing Action Units for Facial Expression Analysis. *IEEE Transactions on Pattern Analysis & Machine Intelligence, 23*(2), 97.

Tiedemann, D. (1927). Tiedemann's observations on the development of the mental faculties of children (S. Langer, Trans.). *Pedagogical Seminary and Journal of Genetic Psychology, 34,* 205–230.

Tincoff, R., & Jusczyk, P. W. (2012). Six-month-olds comprehend words that refer to parts of the body. *Infancy, 17*(4), 432-444. doi:10.1111/j.1532-7078.2011.00084.x

Tinsley, B. R., & Parke, R. D. (1984). Grandparents as support and socialization agents. In M. Lewis (Ed.), *Beyond the dyad* (pp. 89–102). New York: Plenum Press.

Tita A. et al. (2009). Timing of elective repeat cesarean delivery at term and neonatal outcomes. *New England Journal of Medicine, 360*, 111-120.

Titus, S. L. (1976). Family photographs and transition to parenthood. *Journal of Marriage and the Family, 38,* 525–530.

Titus-Ernstoff, L., Troisi, R., Hatch, E., Wise, L., Palmer, J., Hyer, M., et al. (2006). Menstrual and reproductive characteristics of women whose mothers were exposed in utero to diethylstilbestrol (DES). *International Journal of Epidemiology, 35*(4), 862–868.

Toda, S., & Fogel, A. (1989, April). *Infant behavior in the still-face situation at 3 and 6 months.* Paper presented at the Society for Research in Child Development, Kansas City, MO.

Toda, S., & Fogel, A. (1993). Infant response to the still-face situation at 3 and 6 months. *Developmental Psychology, 29,* 532–538.

Toda, S., Fogel, A., & Kawai, M. (1990). Maternal speech to three-month-old infants in the United States and Japan. *Journal of Child Language, 17,* 279–294.

Tomasello, M. (1995). Joint attention as social cognition. In C. Moore & P. J. Dunham (Eds.), *Joint attention: Its origins and role in development* (pp. 103–130). Hillsdale, NJ: Erlbaum.

Tomasello, M., Call, J., & Gluckman, A. (1997). Comprehension of novel communicative signs by apes and human children. *Child Development, 68*(6), 1067–1080.

Tomasello, M., & Farrar, M. J. (1986). Joint attention and early language. *Child Development, 57,* 1454–1463.

Tomasello, M., Mannle, S., & Kruger, A. C. (1986). Linguistic environment of 1– to 2–year-old twins. *Developmental Psychology, 22,* 169–176.

Tomasello, M., Savage-Rumbaugh, S., & Kruger, A. C. (1993). Imitative learning of actions on objects by children, chimpanzees, and enculturated chimpanzees. *Child Development, 64,* 1688–1705.

Tomlinson, M., Cooper, P., & Murray, L. (2005). The Mother-Infant Relationship and Infant Attachment in a South African Peri-Urban Settlement. *Child Development, 76*(5), 1044–1054.

Tortora, S. (2006). The dancing dialogue: Using the communicative power of movement with young children. NY: Brookes Publishing.

Toselli, M., Farneti, P., & Grossi, E. (2001). Role of motor imitation in traversability of surfaces by walking infants. *Percept Mot Skills, 93*(2), 523–530.

Toselli, M., Farneti, P., & Salzarulo, P. (1998). Maternal representation and care of infant sleep. *Early Development and Parenting, 7,* 73–78.

Touraine, J. L., Sanhadji, K., & Firouzi, R. (1994). Susceptibility of human fetal cells to HIV infection, in vitro and in viol in the SICD-HU Model. *International Conference on AIDS, 10,* 307 (abstract no. PC0157).

Towers, C. V., Deveikis, A., Asrat, T., Nageotte, M. P., & Freeman, R. K. (1993). Role of "bloodless C section" to decrease maternal child HIV transmission: A pilot study. *International Conference on AIDS, 9,* 712 (abstract no. P0–C16–2978).

Trainor, L. J. (1996). Infant preferences for infant-directed versus noninfant-directed playsongs and lullabies. *Infant Behavior and Development, 19,* 83–92.

Trainor, L. J., Clark, E. D., Huntley, A., & Adams, B. A. (1997). The acoustic basis of preferences for infant-directed singing. *Infant Behavior and Development, 20*(3), 383–396.

Trainor, L. J., Wu, L., & Tsang, C. D. (2004). Long-term memory for music: infants remember tempo and timbre. *Dev Sci, 7*(3), 289–296.

Trainor, L. J., & Zacharias, C. A. (1998). Infants prefer higher-pitched singing. *Infant Behavior and Development, 21*(4), 799–806.

Trause, M. A., Boslett, M., Voos, D., Rudd, C., Klaus, M., & Kennell, J. (1978). A birth in the hospital: The effect on the sibling. *Birth and the Family Journal, 5,* 207–210.

Trehub, S. E., Bull, D., & Thorpe, L. A. (1984). Infants' perception of melodies: The role of melodic contour. *Child Development, 55,* 821–830.

Trehub, S. E., Thorpe, L. A., & Morrongiello, B. A. (1987). Organizational processes in infants' perception of auditory patterns. *Child Development, 58,* 741–749.

Trehub, S. E., Unyk, A. M., & Trainor, L. J. (1993). Adults identify infant-directed music across cultures. *Infant Behavior and Development, 16,* 193–211.

Trevarthen, C. (1973). Behavioral embryology. In E. C. Carterette & M. P. Friedman (Eds.), *Handbook of perception: Vol. 3. Biology of perceptual systems* (pp. 61–78). New York: Academic Press.

Trevarthen, C. (1977). Descriptive analysis of infant communicative behavior. In H. R. Schaffer (Ed.), *Studies of mother-infant interaction* (pp. 227–270). London: Academic Press.

Trevarthen, C. (1980). Neurological development and the growth of psychological functions. In J. Sants (Ed.), *Developmental psychology and society* (pp. 46–95). New York: St. Martin's Press.

Trevarthen, C. (1998). The concept and foundations of infant intersubjectivity. In S. Br;araten (Ed.), *Intersubjective communication and emotion in early ontogeny. Studies in emotion and social interaction, 2nd series* (pp. 15–46). New York: Cambridge University Press.

Trevarthen, C., & Aitken, K. J. (2001). Infant intersubjectivity: research, theory, and clinical applications. *J Child Psychol Psychiatry, 42*(1), 3–48.

Trevarthen, C., Aitken, K., Papoudi, D., & Robarts, J. (1998). *Children with autism: Diagnosis and interventions to meet their needs* (2nd ed.). Philadelphia: Jessica Kingsley.

Trevarthen, C., & Hubley, P. (1978). Secondary intersubjectivity: Confidence, confiding and acts of meaning in the first year. In A. Lock (Ed.) *Action, gesture, and symbol: The emergence of language* (pp. 183–227). New York: Academic Press.

Tronick, E. (2007) *The neurobehavioral and social-emotional development of infants and children.* NY: W.W. Norton and Co.

Tronick, E., Als, H., Adamson, L., Weise, S., & Brazelton, T. B. (1978). The infant's response to entrapment between contradictory messages in face-to-face interaction. *Journal of Child Psychiatry, 17,* 1–13.

Tronick, E. Z., Thomas, R. B., & Daltabuit, M. (1994). The Quechua Manta pouch: A caretaking practice for buffering the Peruvian infant against the multiple stressors of high altitude. *Child Development, 65,* 1005–1013.

Tsang, C., & Conrad, N. (2010). Does the message matter? The effect of song type on infants' pitch preferences for lullabies and playsongs. *Infant Behavior & Development, 33*(1), 96-100. doi:10.1016/j.infbeh.2009.11.006

Turati, C., Montirosso, R., Brenna, V., Ferrara, V., & Borgatti, R. (2011). A smile enhances 3-month-olds' recognition of an individual face. *Infancy, 16*(3), 306-317. doi:10.1111/j.1532-7078.2010.00047.x

Turkheimer, M., Bakeman, R., & Adamson, L. B. (1989). Do mothers support and peers inhibit skilled object play in infancy? *Infant Behavior and Development, 12,* 37–44.

Turkheimer, E., Haley, A., Waldron, M., D'Onofrio, B., & Gottesman, I. (2003). Socioeconomic status modifies heritability of IQ in young children. *Psychological Science, 14*(6), 623–628.

Uchiyama, I., Anderson, D. I., Campos, J. J., Witherington, D., Frankel, C. B., Lejeune, L., & Barbu-Roth, M. (2008). Locomotor experience affects self and emotion. *Developmental Psychology, 44*(5), 1225-1231. doi:10.1037/a0013224

Ueno, M., Uchiyama, I., Campos, J. J., Dahl, A., & Anderson, D. I. (2012). The organization of wariness of heights in experienced crawlers. *Infancy, 17*(4), 376-392. doi:10.1111/j.1532-7078.2011.00083.x

Umemura, T., Jacobvitz, D., Messina, S., & Hazen, N. (2013). Do toddlers prefer the primary caregiver or the parent with whom they feel more secure? The role of toddler emotion. *Infant Behavior & Development, 36*(1), 102-114

Ungerer, J., Brody, L., & Zelazo, P. (1978). Long-term memory for speech in 2– to 4–week-old infants. *Infant Behavior and Development, 1,* 177–186.

United Nations Department of Economic and Social Affairs (1986). *Demographic yearbook.* New York: United Nations.

United States Bureau of the Census. (1988). *Current Population Reports,* Series P-70, No. 20. Washington, DC: U.S. Government Printing Office.

United States Bureau of the Census (2009). http://www.census.gov/main/www/-popclock.html.

University of Rochester Medical Center (2010, February 26). Good parenting triumphs over prenatal stress. *ScienceDaily.* Retrieved June 26, 2013, from http://www.sciencedaily.com /releases/2010/02/100225140906.htm

U.S Department of Transportation, National Highway Traffic Safety Administration (2007). http://www-nrd.nhtsa.dot.gov/pdf/nrd-30/NCSA/RNOTES/2007/809845.pdf. (retrieved Jan. 4, 2010).

Uzgiris, I. C. (1983). Imitation in infancy: Its interpersonal aspects. In M. Perlmutter (Ed.), *Minnesota symposia on child psychology* (Vol. 17, pp. 1–32). Hillsdale, NJ: Erlbaum.

Uzgiris, I. C., & Hunt, J. M. (1975). *Toward ordinal scales of psychological development in infancy.* Champaign: University of Illinois Press.

Vahratian, A., Siega-Riz, A. M., Savitz, D. A., & Thorp, J. M., Jr. (2004). Multivitamin use and the risk of preterm birth. *Am J Epidemiol, 160*(9), 886–892.

Vaish, A., Carpenter, M., & Tomasello, M. (2010). Young children selectively avoid helping people with harmful intentions. *Child Development, 81*(6), 1661-1669. doi:10.1111/j.1467-8624.2010.01500.x

Vaish, A., & Woodward, A. (2010). Infants use attention but not emotions to predict others' actions. *Infant Behavior & Development, 33*(1), 79-87.

Valentino, K., Cicchetti, D., Toth, S. L., & Rogosch, F. A. (2011). Mother–child play and maltreatment: A longitudinal analysis of emerging social behavior from infancy to toddlerhood. *Developmental Psychology, 47*(5), 1280-1294. doi:10.1037/a0024459

Valenzuela, M. (1997). Maternal sensitivity in a developing society: The context of urban poverty and infant chronic undernutrition. *Developmental Psychology, 33*(5), 845–855.

Valkenburg, P. M., & Vroone, M. (2004). Developmental changes in infants' and toddlers' attention to television entertainment. *Communication Research, 31*(3), 288–311.

Vallotton, C. (2009). Do infants influence their quality of care? Infants' communicative gestures predict caregivers' responsiveness. *Infant Behavior & Development, 32*(4), 351-365.

Vallotton, C. (2011). Babies open our minds to their minds: How 'listening' to infant signs complements and extends our knowledge of infants and their development. *Infant Mental Health Journal, 32*(1), 115-133.

van Aken, C., Junger, M., Verhoeven, M., van Aken, M., & Deković, M. (2008). The longitudinal relations between parenting and toddlers' attention problems and aggressive behaviors. *Infant Behavior & Development, 31*(3), 432-446

van Beek, Y., & Samson, J. F. (1994). Communication in preterm infants: Why is it different? *Early Development and Parenting, 3,* 37–50.

van der Bruggen, C. O., Stams, G. M., Bögels, S. M., & Paulussen-Hoogeboom, M. C. (2010). Parenting behaviour as a mediator between young children's negative emotionality and their anxiety/depression. *Infant And Child Development, 19*(4), 354-365.

Vandell, D. L. (1979). Effects of a playgroup experience on mother-son and father-son interaction. *Developmental Psychology, 15,* 379–385.

Vandell, D., Belsky, J., Burchinal, M., Steinberg, L., & Vandergrift, N. (2010). Do effects of early child care extend to age 15 years? Results from the NICHD study of early child care and youth development. *Child Development, 81*(3), 737-756. doi:10.1111/j.1467-8624.2010.01431.x

Vandell, D. L., Hyde, J. S., Plant, E. A., & Essex, M. J. (1997). Fathers and "others" as infant-care providers: Predictors of parents' emotional well-being and marital satisfaction. *Merrill-Palmer Quarterly, 43*(3), 361–385.

Vandell, D. L., Owen, M. T., Wilson, K. S., & Henderson, V. K. (1988). Social development in infant twins: Peer and mother-child relationships. *Child Development, 59,* 168–177.

Vandell, D. L., & Ramanan, J. (1992). Effects of early and recent maternal employment on children from low-income families. *Child Development, 63,* 938–949.

Vandell, D. L., & Wilson, K. S. (1987). Infants' interactions with mother, sibling, and peer: Contrasts and relations between interaction systems. *Child Development, 58,* 176–186.

Vandell, D. L., Wilson, K. S., & Buchanan, N. R. (1980). Peer interaction in the first year of life: An examination of its structure, content, and sensitivity to toys. *Child Development, 51,* 481–488.

Van den Bergh, B. R., Mulder, E. J., Mennes, M., & Glover, V. (2005). Antenatal maternal anxiety and stress and the neurobehavioural development of the fetus and child: links and possible mechanisms. A review. *Neurosci Biobehav Rev, 29*(2), 237–258.

Van de Perre, P., Simonon, A., Hitimana, D. G., Dabis, F., Msellati, P., Mukamabano, B., Butera, J. B., Van-Goe-

them, C., Karita, E., & Lepage, P. (1993). Infective and anti-infective properties of breastmilk from HIV-1–infected women. *Lancet, 341,* 914–918.

Van de Walle, G. A., & Spelke, E. (1996). Spatiotemporal integration and object perception in infancy: Perceiving unity versus form. *Child Development, 67,* 2621–2640.

van Doesum, K. M., Riksen-Walraven, J., Hosman, C. H., & Hoefnagels, C. (2008). A randomized controlled trial of a home-visiting intervention aimed at preventing relationship problems in depressed mothers and their infants. *Child Development, 79*(3), 547-561.

VanDoorninck, W. J., Caldwell, B. M., Wright, C., & Frankenburg, W. K. (1981). The relationship between twelve-month home stimulation and school achievement. *Child Development, 52,* 1080–1083.

van Geert, P. (1991). A dynamic systems model of cognitive and language growth. *Journal of Psychological Review, 98* (1), 3–53.

van Geert, P. (1993). A dynamic systems model of cognitive growth: Competition and support under limited resource conditions. In L. B. Smith & E. Thelen (Eds.), *A dynamic systems approach to development: Applications. MIT Press/Bradford Books series in cognitive psychology* (pp. 265–331). Cambridge, MA: MIT Press.

van Geert, P. (1998). We almost had a great future behind us: The contribution of non-linear dynamics to developmental-science-in-the-making. *Developmental Science, 1*(1), 143–159.

Van Giffen, K., & Haith, M. H. (1984). Infant visual response to Gestalt geometric forms. *Infant Behavior and Development, 7,* 335–346.

Van Hecke, A. V., Mundy, P. C., Acra, C. F., Block, J. J., Delgado, C. E. F., Parlade, M. V., et al. (2007). Infant Joint Attention, Temperament, and Social Competence in Preschool Children. *Child Development, 78*(1), 53–69.

Van Hecke, A., Mundy, P., Block, J. J., Delgado, C. F., Parlade, M. V., Pomares, Y. B., & Hobson, J. A. (2012). Infant responding to joint attention, executive processes, and self-regulation in preschool children. *Infant Behavior & Development, 35*(2), 303-311.

van Hof, P., van der Kamp, J., & Savelsbergh, G. J. P. (2002). The relation of unimanual and bimanual reaching to crossing the midline. *Child Development, 73*(5), 1353–1362.

van Hof, P., van der Kamp, J., & Savelsbergh, G. P. (2008). The relation between infants' perception of catchableness and the control of catching. *Developmental Psychology, 44*(1), 182-194. doi:10.1037/0012-1649.44.1.182

van IJzendoorn, M. H., Bakermans-Kranenburg, M. J. & Ebstein, R. P. (2011). Methylation matters in child development: Toward developmental behavioral epigenetics. *Child Development Perspectives, 5,* 305-310.

van Ijzendoorn, M. H., Goldberg, S., Kroonenberg, P. M., & Frenkel, O. J. (1992). The relative effects of maternal and child problems on the quality of attachment: A meta-analysis of attachment in clinical samples. *Child Development, 63,* 840–858.

van Ijzendoorn, M. H., & Kroonenberg, P. M. (1988). Cross-cultural patterns of attachment: A meta-analysis of the strange situation. *Child Development, 59,* 147–156.

van Ijzendoorn, M. H., Rutgers, A. H., Bakermans-Kranenburg, M. J., van Daalen, E., Dietz, C., Buitelaar, J. K., et al. (2007). Parental sensitivity and attachment in children with autism spectrum disorder: Comparison with children with mental retardation, with language delays, and with typical development. *Child Development, 78*(2), 597–608.

Varendi, H., Porter, R., and Winberg, J. (1997). Natural odour preferences of newborn infants change over time. *Acta Paediatrica, 86,* 985–990.

Vaughn, B. E., Bradley, C. F., Joffe, L. S., Seifer, R., & Barglow, P. (1987). Maternal characteristics measured prenatally are predictive of ratings of temperamental "difficulty" on the Carey Infant Temperament Questionnaire. *Developmental Psychology, 23,* 152–161.

Vaughn, B. E., Deane, K. E., & Waters, E. (1985). The impact of out-of-home care on child-mother attachment quality: Another look at some enduring questions. In I. Bretherton & E. Waters (Eds.), Growing points of attachment theory and research. *Monographs of the Society for Research in Child Development, 50* (1–2, Whole No. 209), 110–135.

Vaughn, B. E., Egeland, B., Sroufe, L. A., & Waters, E. (1979). Individual differences in infant-mother attachment at twelve and eighteen months: Stability and change in families under stress. *Child Development, 50,* 971–975.

Vaughn, B. E., Kopp, C. B., & Krakow, J. B. (1984). The emergence and consolidation of self-control from 18 to 30 months of age: Normative trends and individual differences. *Child Development, 55,* 990–1004.

Vaughn, B. E., Kopp, C. B., Krakow, J. B., Johnson, K., & Schwartz, S. S. (1986). Process analyses of the behavior of very young children in delay tasks. *Developmental Psychology, 22,* 752–759.

Vaughn, B. E., Stevenson-Hinde, J., Waters, E., Kotsaftis, A., Lefever, G. B., Shouldice, A., Trudel, M., & Belsky, J. (1992). Attachment security and temperament in infancy and early childhood: Some conceptual clarifications. *Developmental Psychology, 28,* 463–473.

Vaughn, B. E., Taraldson, B. J., Crichton, L., & Egeland, B. (1981). The assessment of infant temperament: A critique of the Carey Infant Temperament Questionnaire. *Infant Behavior and Development, 4,* 1–18.

Velde, E. R., & Cohlen, B. J. (1999). The management of infertility. *New England Journal of Medicine, 340*(3), 224–226.

Venezia, M., Messinger, D. S., Thorp, D., & Mundy, P. (2004). The Development of Anticipatory Smiling. *Infancy, 6*(3), 397–406.

Ventura, S. J., & Hamilton, B. E. (2011). U.S. teenage birth rate resumes decline. *NCHS Data Brief, number 58,* 1-8.

Vereijken, C. M. J. L., Riksen-Walraven, J. M., & Kondo-Ikemura, K. (1997). Maternal sensitivity and infant attachment security in Japan: A longitudinal study. *International Journal of Behavioral Development, 21*(1), 35–49.

Verlinsky, Y., & Kuliev, A. (1994). Human preimplantation diagnosis: Needs, efficiency and efficacy of genetic and chromosomal analysis. *Baillieres Clinical Obstetrics and Gynacology, 8,* 177–196.

Vertes, R. P. (1986). A life-sustaining function for REM sleep: A theory. *Neuroscience and Behavioral Reviews, 10*(4), 371–376.

Vibbert, M., & Bornstein, M. H. (1989). Specific associations between domains of mother-child interaction and toddler referential language and pretense play. *Infant Behavior and Development, 12,* 163–184.

Volbrecht, M. M., & Goldsmith, H. (2010). Early Temperamental and Family Predictors of Shyness and Anxiety. *Developmental Psychology, 46*(5), 1192-1205.

Völker, S. (2007). Infants' vocal engagement oriented towards mother versus stranger at 3 months and avoidant attachment behavior at 12 months. *International Journal of Behavioral Development, 31*(1), 88–95.

Volling, B. L., & Belsky, J. (1992). Infant, father, and marital antecedents of infant-father attachment security in dual-earner and single-earner families. *International Journal of Behavioral Development, 15,* 83–100.

Volling, B. L., & Elins, J. L. (1998). Family relationships and children's emotional adjustment as correlates of maternal and paternal differential treatment: A replication with toddler and preschool siblings. *Child Development, 69*(6), 1640–1656.

Volling, B. L., & Feagans, L. V. (1995). Infant day care and children's social competence. *Infant Behavior and Development, 18*(2), 177–188.

Von Hemel, J. O., Majoor-Krakauer, D. F., Jahoda, M. G. J., & Sachs, E. S. (1986). First trimester diagnosis from chorionic villi of a der(15), t(9;15), (q33;Q14)mat identified by DA/DAPI staining. *Journal of Medical Genetics, 23,* 89–90.

von Hofsten, C., Kochukhova, O., & Rosander, K. (2007). Predictive tracking over occlusions by 4–month-old infants. *Developmental Science, 10*(5), 625–640.

Von Kries, R., Toschke, A. M., Koletzko, B., & Slikker, W., Jr. (2002). Maternal smoking during pregnancy and childhood obesity. *Am J Epidemiol, 156*(10), 954–961.

Vorhees, C. V., & Mollnow, E. (1987). Behavioral teratogenesis: Long-term influences on behavior from early exposure to environmental agents. In J. D. Osofsky (Ed.), *Handbook of infant development* (pp. 599–616). New York: Wiley.

Votruba-Drzal, E., Coley, R., Maldonado-Carreño, C., Li-Grining, C. P., & Chase-Lansdale, P. (2010). Child care and the development of behavior problems among economically disadvantaged children in middle childhood. *Child Development, 81*(5), 1460-1474. doi:10.1111/j.1467-8624.2010.01485.x

Vouloumanos, A., Hauser, M. D., Werker, J. F. & Martin, A. (2010). The tuning of human neonates preference for speech. *Child Development, 81,* 517-527.

Vreugdenhil, H., Slijper, F., Mulder, P., & Weisglas-Kuperus, N. (2002). Effects of perinatal exposure to PCBs and dioxins on play behavior in Dutch children at school age. *Environmental Health Perspectives, 110*(10), A593.

Vrtička, P., & Vuilleumier, P. (2012). Neuroscience of human social interactions and adult attachment style. *Frontiers In Human Neuroscience, 6*doi:10.3389/fnhum.2012.00212

Vutyavanich, T., Kraisarin, T., & Ruangsri, R. (2001). Ginger for nausea and vomiting in pregnancy: randomized, double-masked, placebo-controlled trial. *Obstet Gynecol, 97*(4), 577–582.

Vygotsky, L. S. (1978). Mind in society. Cambridge, MA: Harvard University Press.

Wachs, T. D. (1982). Early experience and early cognitive development: The search for specificity. In I. Uzgiris & J. Hunt (Eds.), *Research with scales of psychological development in infancy* (pp. 371–400). Champaign: University of Illinois Press.

Wachs, T. D. (1988). Relevance of physical environment influences for toddler temperament. *Infant Behavior and Development, 11,* 431–445.

Wachs, T. D. (1993). Nature of relations between the physical and social microenvironment of the two-year-old child. *Early Development and Parenting, 2,* 81–87.

Wachs, T. D. (2000). *Necessary but not sufficient: The respective roles of single and multiple influences on individual development.* Washington, DC: American Psychological Association.

Wachs, T. D., & Bates, J. E. (2000). Temperament. In J. G. Bremner & A. Fogel (Eds.), *Handbook of infancy research* (pp. 28–45). Oxford, England: Blackwell.

Wachs, T. D., Bishry, Z., Sobhy, A., McCabe, G., Galal, O., & Shaheen, F. (1993). Relation of rearing environment to adaptive behavior of Egyptian toddlers. *Child Development, 64,* 586–604.

Wachs, T. D., Black, M. M., & Engle, P. L. (2009). Maternal depression: A global threat to children's health, development, and behavior and to human rights. *Child Development Perspectives, 3*(1), 51-59. doi:10.1111/j.1750-8606.2008.00077.x

Wachs, T. D., & Gruen, G. E. (1982). *Early experience and human development.* New York: Plenum Press.

Waddington, C. H. (1966). *Principles of development and differentiation.* New York: Macmillan.

Wade, J. (1996). *Changes of mind: A holonomic theory of the evolution of consciousness.* New York: State University of New York Press.

Wakefield, A., Murch, S., Anthony, A., Linnell, J., Casson, D., Malik, M., Berelowitz, A., Dhillon, M., Thomson, P., Valentine, A., Davies, S., Walker-Smith, J. (1998). Ileal-lymphoid-nodular hyperplasia, non-specific colitis, and pervasive developmental disorder in children. *The Lancet, 35,* 637–641.

Wakschlag, L. S., Chase-Lansdale, P. L., & Brooks-Gunn, J. (1996). Not just "Ghosts from the nursery": Contemporaneous intergenerational relationships and parenting in young African-American families. *Child Development, 67*(5), 2131–2147

Wakschlag, L. S., Leventhal, B. L., Pine, D. S., Pickett, K. E., & Carter, A. S. (2006). Elucidating Early Mechanisms of Developmental Psychopathology: The Case of Prenatal Smoking and Disruptive Behavior. *Child Development, 77*(4), 893–906.

Wakschlag, L. S., Pickett, K. E., Cook, E., Jr., Benowitz, N. L., & Leventhal, B. L. (2002). Maternal smoking during pregnancy and severe antisocial behavior in offspring: A review. *American Journal of Public Health, 92*(6), 966–974.

Walden, T., Kim, G., McCoy, C., & Karrass, J. (2007). Do you believe in magic? Infants' social looking during violations of expectations. *Developmental Science, 10*(5), 654–663.

Walden, T. A., & Ogan, T. A. (1988). The development of social referencing. *Child Development, 59,* 1230–1240.

Waldenstrom, U. (1999). Effects of birth center care on fathers' satisfaction with care, experience of the birth and adaption to fatherhood. *Journal of Reproductive and Infant Psychology, 17*(4), 357–368.

Walker, B. E., & Quarles, J. (1976). Palate development in mouse foetuses after tongue removal. *Archives of Oral Biology, 21,* 405–412.

Walker-Andrews, A. S., & Lennon, E. (1991). Infants' discrimination of vocal expressions: Contributions of auditory and visual information. *Infant Behavior and Development, 14,* 131–142.

Wallach, M. A. (1985). Creativity testing and giftedness. In F. D. Horowitz & M. O'Brien (Eds.), *The gifted and talented: Developmental perspectives* (pp. 99–123). Washington, DC: American Psychological Association.

Wang, Q. (2006). Relations of Maternal Style and Child Self-Concept to Autobiographical Memories in Chinese, Chinese Immigrant, and European American 3–Year-Olds. *Child Development, 77*(6), 1794–1809.

Wang, X., Dow-Edwards, D., Anderson, V., Minkoff, H., & Hurd, Y. L. (2004). In Utero Marijuana Exposure Associated with Abnormal Amygdala Dopamine D-sub-2 Gene Expression in the Human Fetus. *Biological Psychiatry, 56*(12), 909–915.

Ward, M. J., Vaughn, B. E., & Robb, M. D. (1988). Social-emotional adaptation and infant-mother attachment in siblings: Role of the mother in cross-sibling consistency. *Child Development, 59,* 643–651.

Warneken, F., & Tomasello, M. (2007). Helping and cooperation at 14 months of age. *Infancy, 11*(3), 271–294.

Warneken, F., & Tomasello, M. (2013). Parental presence and encouragement do not influence helping in young children. *Infancy, 18*(3), 345-368.

Wartner, U. G., Grossmann, K., Fremmer-Bombik, E., & Suess, G. (1994). Attachment patterns at age six in south Germany: Predictability from infancy and implications for preschool behavior. *Child Development, 65*(4), 1014–1027.

Wasik, B. H., Ramey, C. T., Bryant, D. M., & Sparling, J. J. (1990). A longitudinal study of two early intervention strategies: Project CARE. *Child Development, 61,* 1682–1696.

Waters, E. (1983). The stability of individual differences in infant attachment: Comments on the Thompson, Lamb, and Estes contributions. *Child Development, 54,* 516–520.

Watson, A. C., Painter, K. M., & Bornstein, M. H. (2001). Longitudinal relations between 2–year-olds' language and 4–year-olds' theory of mind. *Journal of Cognition and Development, 2*(4), 449–457.

Watson, J. S. (1973). Smiling, cooing, and "the game." *Merrill-Palmer Quarterly, 18,* 323–339.

Waxman, S. R., & Senghas, A. (1992). Relations among word meanings in early lexical development. *Developmental Psychology, 28,* 862–873.

Weatherill, R. P., Almerigi, J. B., Levendosky, A. A., Bogat, G. A., von Eye, A., & Harris, L. J. (2004). Is maternal depression related to side of infant holding? *International Journal of Behavioral Development, 28*(5), 421–427.

Weatherston, D. J. (2000, October/November). The infant mental health specialist. *Zero to Three,* 3–10.

Weaver, I. C., Cervoni, N., Champagne, F. A., D'Alessio, A. C., Sharma, S., Seckl, J. R., et al. (2004). Epigenetic programming by maternal behavior. *Nat Neurosci, 7*(8), 847–854.

Webb, S., Jones, E., Merkle, K., Venema, K., Greenson, J., Murias, M., & Dawson, G. (2011). Developmental change in the ERP responses to familiar faces in toddlers with autism spectrum disorders versus typical development. *Child Development, 82*(6), 1868-1886.

Webster, J., Sweett, S., & Stolz, T. A. (1994). Domestic violence in pregnancy: A prevalence study. *Medical Journal of Australia, 161,* 466–470.

Wedenberg, E. (1956). Auditory tests on newborn infants. *Acta Oto-laryngologica, 46,* 446–461.

Weed, S., & Jensen, L. (1993). A second year evaluation of three abstinence sex education programs. *Journal of Research and Development in Education, 26,* 92–96.

Weikum, W. M., Oberlander, T. F., Hensch, T. K., & Werker, J. F. (2012). Prenatal exposure to antidepressants and depressed maternal mood alter trajectory of infant speech perception. *PNAS Proceedings Of The National Academy Of Sciences Of The United States Of America, 109*(Suppl 2), 17221-17227. doi:10.1073/pnas.1121263109

Weinberg, M. K., & Tronick, E. Z. (1994). Beyond the face: An empirical study of infant affective configurations of facial, vocal, gestural, and regulatory behaviors. *Child Development, 65,* 1503–1515.

Weinberg, M. K., Tronick, E. Z., Cohn, J. F., & Olson, K. L. (1999). Gender differences in emotional expressivity and self-regulation during early infancy. *Developmental Psychology, 35*(1), 175–188.

Weinfield, N. S., Whaley, G. J. L., & Egeland, B. (2004). Continuity, discontinuity, and coherence in attachment from infancy to late adolescence: Sequelae of organization and disorganization. *Attachment & Human Development, 6*(1), 73–97.

Weinraub, M., & Lewis, M. (1977). The determinants of children's responses to separation. *Monographs of the Society for Research in Child Development, 42* (Serial No. 172), 1–127.

Weinraub, M., & Putney, E. (1978). The effects of heights on infant's social responses to unfamiliar persons. *Child Development, 49,* 598–603.

Weintraub, K. S., & Furman, L. N. (1987). Child care: Quality, regulation, and research. *Social Policy Report: Society for Research in Child Development, 2,* 27–68.

Weir, R., & Feldman, W. (1975). A study of infant feeding practices. *Birth and the Family Journal, 2,* 63–64.

Weir, R. H. (1966). Questions on the learning of phonology. In F. Smith & G. A. Miller (Eds.), *The genesis of language: A psycholinguistic approach* (pp. 112–140). Cambridge, MA: MIT Press.

Wellman, H. M., Cross, D., & Bartsch, K. (1986). Infant search and object permanence: A meta-analysis of the A-not-B error. *Monographs of the Society for Research in Child Development, 51* (3, Serial No. 214), 1–51.

Wellman, H. M., & Lempers, J. D. (1977). The naturalistic communicative abilities of two-year-olds. *Child Development, 48,* 1052–1057.

Wellman, H. M., Lopez-Duran, S., LaBounty, J., & Hamilton, B. (2008). Infant attention to intentional action predicts preschool theory of mind. *Developmental Psychology, 44*(2), 618-623.

Welsh, M. C., Pennington, B. F., Ozonoff, S., Rouse, B., & McCabe, E. R. B. (1990). Neurospsychology of early-treated phenylketonuria: Specific executive function deficits. *Child Development, 61,* 1697–1713.

Wendland-Carro, J., Piccinini, C. A., & Millar, W. S. (1999). The role of an early intervention on enhancing the quality of mother-infant interaction. *Child Development, 70*(3), 713–721.

Wente, A., & Crockenberg, S. (1976). Transition to fatherhood: Pre-natal Lamaze preparation, adjustment difficulty and the adult husband-wife relationship. *Family Coordinator, 25,* 351–357.

Wentworth, N., & Haith, M. M. (1992). Event-specific expectations of 2– and 3–month-old infants. *Developmental Psychology, 28,* 842–850.

Were, E. O., & Karanja, J. K. (1994). Attitudes of males to contraception in a Kenyan rural population. *East African Medical Journal, 71,* 106–109.

Werker, J. F., & Lalonde, C. E. (1988). Cross-language speech perception: Initial capabilities and developmental change. *Developmental Psychology, 24,* 674–683.

Werker, J. F., & Tees, R. C. (1984). Cross-language speech perception: Evidence for perceptual reorganization during the first year of life. *Infant Behavior and Development, 7,* 49–63.

Werner, E. (1979). *Cross-cultural child development.* Monterey, CA: Brooks-Cole.

Werner, E. (1986, April). *The infant's view of planet Earth.* Paper presented at the International Conference on Infant Studies, Los Angeles, CA.

Werner, E., Bierman, J., & French, F. (1971). *The children of Kauai.* Honolulu: University of Hawaii Press.

Werntoft, E., & Dykes, A. K. (2001). Effect of acupressure on nausea and vomiting during pregnancy. A randomized, placebo-controlled, pilot study. *J Reprod Med, 46*(9), 835–839.

Wertsch, J. V., & Tulviste, P. (1992). L. S. Vygotsky and contemporary development psychology. *Developmental Psychology, 28,* 548–557.

West, M. J., & Rheingold, H. L. (1978). Infant stimulation of maternal instruction. *Infant Behavior and Development, 1,* 205–215.

Westbrook, M. (1978). Analyzing affective responses to past events: Women's reactions to a childbearing year. *Journal of Clinical Psychology, 34,* 967–971.

Wheeler, S. R. (1994). Psychosocial needs of women during miscarriage or ectopic pregnancy. *American Obstetrical and Gynecological Nursing Journal, 68,* 221–231.

Whiffen, V. E. (1988). Vulnerability to postpartum depression: A prospective multivariate study. *Journal of Abnormal Psychology, 97*(4), 467–474.

White D, Gros-Louis J, King A, Papakhian M, West M. (2007) Constructing culture in cowbirds (Molothrus ater). *Journal of Comparative Psychology. 121,* 113–122.

White, E. (1992). Foster parenting the drug affected baby. *Zero to Three, 13,* 13–16.

White, T., Matthey, S., Boyd, K., & Barnett, B. (2006). Postnatal depression and post-traumatic stress after childbirth: Prevalence, course and co-occurrence. *Journal of Reproductive and Infant Psychology, 24*(2), 107–120.

Whitehurst, G. J., Falco, F. L., Lonigan, C. J., Fischel, J. E., DeBaryshe, B. D., Valdez-Menchaca, M. C., & Caulfield, M. (1988). Accelerating language development through picture book reading. *Developmental Psychology, 24,* 552–559.

Whitelaw, N. C., & Whitelaw, E. (2006). How lifetimes shape epigenotype within and across generations. *Hum Mol Genet, 15 Spec No 2,* R131–137.

Whiten, A., & Milner, P. (1986). The educational experiences of Nigerian infants. In H. V. Curran (Ed.), *Nigerian children: Developmental perspectives* (pp. 260–280). London: Routledge & Kegan Paul.

Whitham, J. C., Gerald, M. S., Maestripieri, D. (2007). Intended receivers and functional significance of grunt and girney vocalizations in free-ranging femal rhesus monkeys. *Ethology, 113,* 862–874.

Whiting, B. (1974). Folk wisdom and child-rearing. *Merrill-Palmer Quarterly, 20,* 9–19.

Whiting, B., & Whiting, J. W. (1975). *Children of six cultures: A psychocultural analysis.* Cambridge, MA: Harvard University Press.

Whiting, J. (1981). Environmental constraints on infant care practices. In R. Monroe, R. Monroe, & B. Whiting (Eds.), *Handbook of cross-cultural development* (pp. 67–89). New York: Garland Publishing.

Whyatt, R. M., Rauh, V., Barr, D. B., Camann, D. E., Andrews, H. F., Garfinkel, R., et al. (2004). Prenatal insecticide exposures and birth weight and length among an urban minority cohort. *Environ Health Perspect, 112*(10), 1125–1132.

Whyte, H., Hannah, M. E., Saigal, S., Hannah, W. J., Hewson, S., Amankwah, K., et al. (2004). Outcomes of children at 2 years after planned cesarean birth versus planned vaginal birth for breech presentation at term: the International Randomized Term Breech Trial. *Am J Obstet Gynecol, 191*(3), 864–871.

Wicki, W. (1999). The impact of family resources and satisfaction with division of labor on coping and worries after the birth of the first child. *International Journal of Behavioral Development, 23*(2), 431–456.

Wideman, M. V., & Singer, J. E. (1984). The role of psychological mechanisms in preparation for childbirth. *American Psychologist, 39,* 1357–1371.

Widmayer, S. M., Peterson, L. M., Lerner, M., Carnahan, S., Calderon, A., Wingerd, J., & Marshall, R. (1990). Predictors of Haitian-American infant development at twelve months. *Child Development, 61,* 410–415.

Wiebe, S. A., Espy, K., Stopp, C., Respass, J., Stewart, P., Jameson, T. R., & ... Huggenvik, J. I. (2009). Gene-environment interactions across development: Exploring DRD2 genotype and prenatal smoking effects on self-regulation. *Developmental Psychology, 45*(1), 31-44. doi:10.1037/a0014550

Wiesenfeld, A. R., Malatesta, C. Z., & DeLoache, L. (1981). Differential parental response to familiar and unfamiliar infant distress signals. *Infant Behavior and Development, 4,* 281–295.

Wigfield, R., Gilbert, R., & Fleming, P. J. (1994). SIDS: Risk reduction measures. *Early Human Development, 38,* 161–164.

Wijnroks, L. (1998). Early maternal stimulation and the development of cognitive competence and attention of preterm infants. *Early Development and Parenting, 7,* 19–30.

Wilcox, A. J., Weinberg, C. R., & Baird, D. D. (1995). Timing of sexual intercourse in relation to ovulation. Effects on the probability of conception, survival of the pregnancy, and sex of the baby. *New England Journal of Medicine, 333*(7), 1517–1521.

Wilcox, T., & Baillargeon, R. (1998). Object individuation in young infants: Further evidence with an event-monitoring paradigm. *Developmental Science, 1*(1), 127–142.

Wilkie, C. F., & Ames, E. W. (1986). The relationship of infant crying to parental stress in the transition to parenthood. *Journal of Marriage and the Family, 48,* 545–550.

Williams, D. (1999). *Like colour to the blind: Soul searching and soul finding.* London: Jessica Kingsley.

Wilson, M. N. (1986). The black extended family: An analytical consideration. *Developmental Psychology, 22,* 246–258.

Wilson, S. L. (2003). Post-Institutionalization: The Effects of Early Deprivation on Development of Romanian Adoptees. *Child & Adolescent Social Work Journal, 20*(6), 473–483.

Winnicott, D. (1971). *Playing and reality.* New York: Basic Books.

Winslow, M., & Guitar, B. (1994). The effects of structured turn-taking on disfluencies: A case study. *Language, Speech, and Hearing Services in Schools, 25,* 251–257.

Winston, R. M. L., & Handyside, A. H. (1993). New challenges in human in vitro fertilization. *Science, 260,* 932–936.

Wolf, D., & Gardner, H. (1979). Style and sequence in early symbolic play. In N. Smith & M. Franklin (Eds.), *Symbolic function in childhood* (pp. 64–92). Hillsdale, NJ: Erlbaum.

Wolff, J., Gu, H., Gerig, G., Elison, J., Styner, M., Gouttard, S., & ... Piven, J. (2012). Differences in white matter fiber tract development present from 6 to 24 months in infants with autism. *American Journal Of Psychiatry, 169*(6), 589–600.

Wolff, P. H. (1966). The causes, controls, and organization of behavior in the neonate. *Psychological Issues, 5,* (Monograph No. 17).

Wolff, P. H. (1987). *The development of behavioral states and the expression of emotions in early infancy: New proposals for investigation.* Chicago: University of Chicago Press.

Wolff, P. H. (1993). Behavioral and emotional states in infancy: A dynamic perspective. In L. B. Smith & E. Thelen (Eds.), *A dynamic systems approach to development: Applications* (pp. 189–208). Cambridge, MA: MIT Press.

Wong, V., & Wong, S. N. (1991). Brainstem suditory evoked potential study in children with autistic disorder. *Journal of Autism and Developmental Disorders, 21,* 329–340.

Wood, J. J., Emmerson, N. A., & Cowan, P. A. (2004). Is early attachment security carried forward into relationships with preschool peers? *British Journal of Developmental Psychology, 22*(2), 245–253.

Wood, J. N., & Spelke, E. S. (2005). Infants' enumeration of actions: Numerical discrimination and its signature limits. *Developmental Science, 8*(2), 173–181.

Wood, R. M. (2009). Changes in cry acoustics and distress ratings while the infant is crying. *Infant and Child Development, 18,* 163-177.

Woodson, R., Drinkwin, J., & Hamilton, C. (1985). Effects of nonnutritive sucking on state and activity: Term-preterm comparisons. *Infant Behavior and Development, 8,* 435–441.

Woodson, R., & Hamilton, C. (1988). The effect of nonnutritive sucking on heart rate in preterm infants. *Developmental Psychobiology, 21* (3), 207–213.

Woodward, A. L. (1999). Infants' ability to distinguish between purposeful and non-purposeful behaviors. *Infant Behavior and Development, 22*(2), 145–160.

Woodward, A. L., & Hoyne, K. L. (1999). Infants' learning about words and sounds in relation to objects. *Child Development, 70*(1), 65–77.

Woodward, A. L., & Sommerville, J. A. (2000). Twelve-month-old infants interpret action in context. *Psychological Sciences, 11*(1), 73–77.

Woodward, A. L., Markman, E. M., & Fitzsimmons, C. M. (1994). Rapid word learning in 13– and 18–month-olds. *Developmental Psychology, 30*(4), 553–556.

Woolley, J. D., & Cox, V. (2007). Development of beliefs about storybook reality. *Developmental Science, 10*(5), 681–693.

Worobey, J., & Blajda, V. M. (1989). Temperament ratings at 2 weeks, 2 months, and 1 year: Differential stability of activity and emotionality. *Developmental Psychology, 25,* 257–262.

Worobey, J., & Lewis, M. (1989). Individual differences in the reactivity of young infants. *Developmental Psychology, 25,* 663–667.

Wortley, P., Lindegren, M., & Fleming, P. (2001, May 11). Successful implementation of perinatal HIV prevention guidelines. *MMWR, 50*(RR06), 15–28.

Wright, L. (1994). Prenatal diagnosis in the 1990s. *Journal of Obstetrical and Gynecological Neonatal Nursing, 23,* 506–515.

Wu, G., Bazer, F. W., Cudd, T. A., Meininger, C. J., & Spencer, T. E. (2004). Maternal Nutrition and fetal development. *J. Nutr. 134,* 2169–2172.

Wu, S. S., Ma, C.-X., Carter, R. L., Ariet, M., Feaver, E. A., Resnick, M. B., et al. (2004). Risk factors for infant maltreatment: A population-based study. *Child Abuse & Neglect, 28*(12), 1253–1264.

Wurmser, H., Rieger, M., Domogalla, C., Kahnt, A., Buchwald, J., Kowatsch, M., et al. (2006). Association between life stress during pregnancy and infant crying in the first six months postpartum: A prospective longitudinal study. *Early Human Development, 82*(5), 341–349.

Wyndham, N., Marin Figueira, P. G., & Patrizio, P. (2012). A persistent misperception: assisted reproductive technology can reverse the "aged biological clock". *Fertility And Sterility, 97,* 1044-1047.

Wynn, K. (1998). Numerical competence in infants. In C. Donlan (Ed.), *The development of mathematical skills. Studies in developmental psychology* (pp. 3–25). Hove, England: Psychology Press/Taylor & Francis.

Wyss, N. M., Kannass, K. N., & Haden, C. A. (2013). The effects of distraction on cognitive task performance during toddlerhood. *Infancy, 18*(4), 604-628. doi:10.1111/j.1532-7078.2012.00128.x

Xie, H., Cairns, B. D., & Cairns, R. B. (2001). Predicting teen motherhood and teen fatherhood: Individual characteristics and peer affiliations. *Social Development, 10*(4), 488–511.

Xu, F., Spelke, E. S., & Goddard, S. (2005). Number sense in human infants. *Developmental Science, 8*(1), 88–101.

Yale Bush Center Infant Care Leave Project (1985). *Facts on parents in the workforce and infant care.* New Haven, CT: Author.

Yale, M. E., Messinger, D. S., Cobo-Lewis, A. B., & Delgado, C. F. (2003). The temporal coordination of early infant communication. *Developmental Psychology, 39*(5), 815–824.

Yale, M. E., Messinger, D. S., Cobo-Lewis, A. B., Oller, D. K., & Eilers, R. E. (1999). An event-based analysis of the coordination of early infant vocalization and facial actions. *Developmental Psychology, 35*(2), 505–513.

Yalom, I. D. (1968). Postpartum blues syndrome. *Archives of General Psychiatry, 28,* 16–27.

Yampolskaya, S., Greenbaum, P., & Berson, I. (2009). Profiles of child maltreatment perpetrators and risk for fatal assault: a latent class analysis, *Journal of Family Violence. 24*(5), Jul 2009, pp. 337–348.

Yates, D. J., & Bremner, J. G. (1988). Conditions for Piagetian stage IV search errors in a task using transparent occluders. *Infant Behavior and Development, 11,* 411–417.

Yates, M., Kolmakova, A., Zhao, Y. & Rodriguez, A. (2011). Clinical impact of scavenger receptor class B type I gene polymorphisms on human female fertility. *Human Reproduction, 26,* 1910-1916.

Yato, Y., Kawai, M., Negayama, K., Sogon, S., Tomiwa, K., & Yamamoto, H. (2008). Infant responses to maternal still-face at 4 and 9 months. *Infant Behavior & Development, 31*(4), 570-577. doi:10.1016/j.infbeh.2008.07.008

Yonas, A., Pettersen, L., & Granrud, C. E. (1982). Infants' sensitivity to familiar size as information for distance. *Child Development, 53,* 1285–1290.

Yoon, J. D., & Johnson, S. C. (2009). Biological motion displays elicit social behavior in 12-month-olds. *Child Development, 80*(4), 1069-1075. doi:10.1111/j.1467-8624.2009.01317.x

Yoshikawa, H. (1999). Welfare dynamics, support services, mothers' earnings, and child cognitive development: Implications for contemporary welfare reform. *Child Development, 70*(3), 779–801.

Yoshikawa, H., Aber, J., & Beardslee, W. R. (2012). The effects of poverty on the mental, emotional, and behavioral health of children and youth: Implications for prevention. *American Psychologist, 67*(4), 272-284. doi:10.1037/a0028015

Yoshikawa, H., & Hsueh, J. (2001). Child Development and Public Policy: Toward a Dynamic Systems Perspective. *Child Development, 72*(6), 1887.

Young, G., & Lewis, M. (1979). Effects of familiarity and maternal attention on infant peer relations. *Merrill-Palmer Quarterly, 25,* 105–120.

Young, G., Segalowitz, S. J., Misek, P., Alp, I. E., & Boulet, R. (1983). Is early reaching left handed? Review of manual specialization research. In G. Young, S. J. Segalowitz, C. M. Corter, & S. Trehub (Eds.), *Manual specialization and the developing brain* (pp. 337–353). New York: Academic Press.

Young, I. D., Rickett, A. B., & Clarke, M. (1986). Genetic analysis of malformations causing perinatal mortality. *Journal of Medical Genetics, 23,* 58–63.

Young, T., Turner, J., Denny, G., & Young, M. (2004). Examining external and internal poverty as antecedents of teen pregnancy. *Am J Health Behav, 28*(4), 361–373.

Youngblut, J. M., Loveland-Cherry, C. J., & Horan, M. (1993). Maternal employment, family functioning, and preterm infant development at 9 and 12 months. *Research in Nursing and Health, 16,* 33–43.

Younger, B., & Gotlieb, S. (1988). Development of categorization skills: Changes in the nature or structure of infant form categories? *Developmental Psychology, 24,* 611–619.

Younger, B. A., & Fearing, D. D. (1999). Parsing items into separate categories: Developmental changes in infant categorization. *Child Development, 70*(2), 291–303.

Younger, B. A., & Johnson, K. E. (2004). Infants' comprehension of toy replicas as symbols for real objects. *Cognitive Psychology, 48*(2), 207–242.

Yu, C., & Smith, L. B. (2012). Embodied Attention and Word Learning by Toddlers. *Cognition, 125*(2), 244-262.

Yumoto, C., Jacobson, S. W., & Jacobson, J. L. (2008). Fetal substance exposure and cumulative environmental risk in an African American cohort. *Child Development, 79*(6), 1761-1776. doi:10.1111/j.1467-8624.2008.01224.x

Zahn-Waxler, C., Radke-Yarrow, M., Wagner, E., & Chapman, M. (1992). Development of concern for others. *Developmental Psychology, 28,* 126–136.

Zahn-Waxler, C., & Robinson, J. (1995). Empathy and guilt: Early origins of feelings of responsibility. In J. P. Tangney & K. W. Fischer (Eds.) *Self-conscious emotions: The psychology of shame, guilt, embarrassment, and pride* (pp. 143–173). New York: Guilford Press.

Zahn-Waxler, C., Robinson, J. L., & Emde, R. N. (1992). The development of empathy in twins. *Developmental Psychology, 28,* 1038–1047.

Zaradic, P. A., & Pergams, O. R. W. (2007). JDP Forum: Videophilia: Implications for childhood development and conservation. *The Journal of Developmental Processes, 2*(1), 130–144.

Zarbatany, L., & Lamb, M. E. (1985). Social referencing as a function of information source: Mothers versus strangers. *Infant Behavior and Development, 8,* 25–33.

Zaslow, M. J., & Eldred, C. A. (Eds.) (1997). The promise and limitations of parenting education for teen mothers on welfare: Lessons from the New Chance Observational Study. *Parenting behavior in a sample of young mothers in poverty: Results of the New Chance Observational Study.* Washington, D.C.: Child Trends.

Zeanah, C. H., Larrieu, J., Heller, S., & Valliere, J. (2005) Infant-parent relationship assessment. In C. H. Zeanah (Ed.) *Handbook of Infant Mental Health, 2nd Edition* (pp. 222–235). NY: The Guilford Press.

Zeanah, C. H., Smyke, A. T., Koga, S. F., & Carlson, E. (2005). Attachment in Institutionalized and Community Children in Romania. *Child Development, 76*(5), 1015–1028.

Zeanah P. D., Stafford B., Nagle G., Rice T. (2005, January). *Addressing Social-Emotional Development and Infant Mental Health in Early Childhood Systems.* Los Angeles, CA: National Center for Infant and Early Childhood Health Policy; Building State Early Childhood Comprehensive Systems Series, No. 12, 4–5.

Zebrowitz, L. A., & Montepare, J. M. (1992). Impressions of babyfaced individuals across the life span. *Developmental Psychology, 28,* 1143–1152.

Zeifman, D. M. (2004). Acoustic features of infant crying related to intended caregiving intervention. *Infant and Child Development, 13*(2), 111–122.

Zeitz, D. (1969). *Child welfare: Services and perspectives.* New York: Wiley.

Zelazo, N. A., Zelazo, P. R., Cohen, K. M., & Zelazo, P. D. (1993). Specificity of practice effects on elementary neuromotor patterns. *Developmental Psychology, 29,* 686–691.

Zelazo, P. R. (1976). From reflexive to instrumental behavior. In L. P. Lipsitt (Ed.), *Developmental psychobiology: The significance of infancy* (pp. 232–267). Hillsdale, NJ: Erlbaum.

Zelazo, P. R., Brody, L. R., & Chaikan, H. (1984). Neonatal habituation and dishabituation of head turning to rattle sounds. *Infant Behavior and Development, 7,* 311–321.

Zentner, M. R., & Kagan, J. (1998). Infants' perception of consonance and dissonance in music. *Infant Behavior and Development, 21*(3), 483–492.

Zeskind, P. S. (1980). Adult responses to cries of low and high risk infants. *Infant Behavior and Development, 3,* 167–178.

Zeskind, P. S., & Barr, R. G. (1997). Acoustic characteristics of naturally occurring cries of infants with "colic." *Child Development, 68*(3), 394–403.

Zeskind, P. S., & Iacino, R. (1984). Effects of maternal visitation to preterm infants in the neonatal intensive care unit. *Child Development, 55,* 1887–1893.

Zeskind, P. S., & Iacino, R. (1987). The relation between length of hospitalization and the mental and physical development of preterm infants. *Infant Behavior and Development, 10,* 217–221.

Zeskind, P. S., Klein, L., & Marshall, T. R. (1992). Adults' perceptions of experimental modifications of durations of pauses and expiratory sounds in infant crying. *Developmental Psychology, 28,* 1153–1162.

Zeskind, P. S., & Marshall, T. R. (1991). Temporal organization in neonatal arousal: Systems, oscillations, and development. In M. Weiss & P. Zelazo (Eds.), *Newborn attention: Biological constraints and the influence of experiences* (pp. 22–62). Norwood, NJ: Ablex.

Zeskind, P. S., Marshall, T. R., & Goff, D. M. (1992). Rhythmic organization of heart rate in breast-fed and bottle-fed newborn infants. *Early Development and Parenting, 1,* 79–87.

Zeskind, P. S., & Stephens, L. E. (2004). Maternal selective serotonin reuptake inhibitor use during pregnancy and newborn neurobehavior. *Pediatrics, 113*(2), 368–375.

Zeskind, P. S., Wilhite, A., & Marshall, T. R. (1993). Infant cry as a graded signal: Expiratory sounds alter mothers' perceptions. *Early Development and Parenting, 2,* 99–105.

Zevalkink, J., Riksen-Walraven, J. M., & Van Lieshout, C. F. M. (1999). Attachment in the Indonesian caregiving context. *Social Development, 8*(1), 21–40.

Zhang, Y., Lin, L., Cao, Y., Chen, B., Zheng, L. & Ge, R. S. (2009). Phthalate levels and low birth weight: a nested case-control study of Chinese newborns. *The Journal Of Pediatrics, 155,* 500-504.

Zhu, J., Madsen, K., Vestergaard, M., Olesen, A., Basso, O., & Olsen, J. (2005). Paternal age and congenital malformations. *Human Reproduction, 20*(11), 3173–3177.

Zieber, N., Bhatt, R. S., Hayden, A., Kangas, A., Collins, R., & Bada, H. (2010). Body representation in the first year of life. *Infancy, 15*(5), 534-544. doi:10.1111/j.1532-7078.2009.00026.x

Ziemer, C. J., Plumert, J. M., & Pick, A. D. (2012). To grasp or not to grasp: Infants' actions toward objects and pictures. *Infancy, 17*(5), 479-497. doi:10.1111/j.1532-7078.2011.00100.x

Zimmerman, F. J., Christakis, D. A., & Meltzoff, A. N. (2007). Associations between media viewing and language development in children under age 2 years. *J Pediatr, 151*(4), 364–368.

Zimmerman, F. J., Christakis, D. A., & Meltzoff, A. N. (2007). Television and DVD/video viewing in children younger than 2 years. *Arch Pediatr Adolesc Med, 161*(5), 473–479.

Zimmermann, P., Fremmer-Bombik, E., Spangler, G., & Grossmann, K. E. (1995, March). *Attachment in adolescence: A longitudinal perspective.* Poster presented at the Biennial Meeting of the Society for Research in Child Development, Indianapolis, IN.

Zimmerman, R. K., & Grebink, G. S. (1992). Childhood immunizations: A practical approach for clinicians. *American Family Physician, 45,* 1759–1772.

Zlatin, M. A. (1973). *Explorative mapping of the vocal tract and primitive syllabification in infancy: The first six months.* Purdue University Contributed Papers, Fall.

Zlochower, A. J., & Cohn, J. F. (1996). Vocal timing in face-to-face interaction of clinically depressed and nondepressed mothers and their 4–month-old infants. *Infant Behavior and Development, 19,* 371–374.

Zosuls, K. M., Ruble, D. N., Tamis-LeMonda, C. S., Shrout, P. E., Bornstein, M. H., & Greulich, F. K. (2009). The acquisition of gender labels in infancy: Implications for gender-typed play. *Developmental Psychology, 45*(3), 688-701.

Zucker, K. J. (1999). Intersexuality and gender identity differentiation. *Annu Rev Sex Res, 10,* 1–69.

Zukow, P. G. (1980). A microanalytic study of the role of the caregiver in the relationship between and language acquisition during the one word period (Doctoral dissertation, University of California, 1980). *Dissertation Abstracts International, 42,* 18.

Zukow, P. G. (1986). The relationship between interaction with the caregiver and the emergence of play activities during the one-word period. *British Journal of Developmental Psychology, 4,* 223–234.

Zukow, P. G. (1990). Socio-perceptual bases for the emergence of language: An alternative to innatist approaches. *Developmental Psychobiology, 23,* 705–726.

Zukow-Goldring, P. (1996). Sensitive caregiving fosters the comprehension of speech: When gestures speak louder than words. *Early Development and Parenting, 5*(4), 195–211.

Zukow-Goldring, P. (1997). A social ecological realist approach to the emergence of the lexicon: Educating attention to amodal invariants in gesture and speech. In C. Dent-Read & P. Zukow-Goldring (Eds.), *Evolving explanations of development: Ecological approaches to organism-environment systems* (pp. 199–250). Washington, DC: American Psychological Association.

Zmyj, N., Daum, M. M., & Aschersleben, G. (2009). The development of rational imitation in 9- and 12-month-old infants. *Infancy, 14*(1), 131-141.

Name Index

Subject Index